# PEARSON EDUCATION
# SECONDARY GROUP

1 Lake Street
Upper Saddle River, NJ 07458
201-236-5401...781-455-1309
Fax: 201-236-5553...781-433-8425
E-Mail: marty.smith@phschool.com

**Martha G. Smith**
President
Pearson Education
Secondary Group

To the Teacher:

As a former social studies teacher, I cannot imagine a more important time to be a social studies educator.

Since the terrorist attacks on New York City and Washington, D.C., on September 11, 2001, you have served at the front line of efforts to understand the causes and effects of those momentous events. In the social studies classroom, you have helped your students understand our nation's heritage of unity and determination in times of crisis. You have had the opportunity to instill in your students the core values of democracy, free enterprise, and the rule of law. Your students have probably explored concepts of freedom and justice, through primary sources from the Declaration of Independence to the "I Have a Dream" speech, and the rights and responsibilities of citizenship, through the Constitution of the United States. They may be learning and applying critical thinking skills as well—debating, for example, the benefits and challenges of living in an open and tolerant society.

As a social studies educator, you can help your students master the fundamentals of history, geography, civics, and economics, providing a context within which to analyze current events. With your guidance, this knowledge can inform and encourage young people's participation in the democratic process.

Today more than ever, you play a crucial role in the maturing of responsible citizens. You help create tomorrow's leaders—the future defenders of America's freedoms, as defined by one President during another time of great crisis:

> "In the future days which we seek to make secure, we look forward to a world founded upon four essential human freedoms. The first is freedom of speech and expression—everywhere in the world. The second is freedom of every person to worship God in his own way—everywhere in the world. The third is freedom from want . . . everywhere in the world. The fourth is freedom from fear . . . anywhere in the world."

> —President Franklin Delano Roosevelt
> State of the Union Address, January 6, 1941

Sincerely,

Martha G. Smith

# TEACHER'S EDITION

PRENTICE HALL

2003

TEXAS EDITION

MAGRUDER'S

# AMERICAN GOVERNMENT

PEARSON
Prentice Hall

Needham, Massachusetts
Upper Saddle River, New Jersey
Glenview, Illinois

IBSN 0-13-063711-4

2 3 4 5 6 7 8 9 10   06 05 04 03

PRENTICE HALL

2003

MAGRUDER'S

# AMERICAN GOVERNMENT

TEXAS EDITION

## Constitution Consultant

Dr. Christine Compston
University of Massachusetts
Boston, Massachusetts

## Reading Consultant

Dr. Bonnie Armbruster
University of Illinois at
Urbana-Champaign
Champaign, Illinois

## Internet Consultant

Dr. Larry Elowitz
Professor of Political Science
Georgia College and State University
Milledgeville, Georgia

## Curriculum and Assessment Specialist

Jan Moberley
Dallas, Texas

## Block Scheduling Consultant

Gwen L. Patterson
Marcus High School
Flower Mound, Texas

## Program Advisors

Pat Easterbrook
Social Studies Consultant
Cary, North Carolina

Michal Howden
Social Studies Consultant
Zionsville, Indiana

Kathy Lewis
Social Studies Consultant
Fort Worth, Texas

Rick Moulden
Social Studies Consultant
Federal Way, Washington

Sharon Pope
Social Studies Consultant
Houston, Texas

Joe Wieczorek
Social Studies Consultant
Baltimore, Maryland

# TABLE OF CONTENTS

# The trusted authority, setting a new standard for the future.

**Texas Edition**
*Magruder's American Government*

Student Edition
Teacher's Edition

## Classroom Resources

Teaching Resources with ExamView® Test Bank CD-ROM
  Program Overview with Pacing Guide
  Block Scheduling with Lesson Suggestions
  Unit Books
    Guided Reading and Review
    Section Quizzes
    Skills Applications
    Answer Keys
  Close Up on The Supreme Court
  Close Up on Primary Sources
  Close Up on Participation
  Close Up Election Kit
  The Living Constitution
  Political Cartoons
  Constitution Study Guide
  Constitution Study Guide Teacher's Manual
  Government Resource Handbook
  Basic Principles of the Constitution Posters
  Chapter Tests with ExamView® Test Bank CD-ROM

Simulations and Debates
  Guide to the Essentials (English)
  Guide to the Essentials (Spanish)
  Guide to the Essentials (Teacher's Manual)
Guided Reading and Review Workbook (English)
Guided Reading and Review Workbook (Spanish)
Guided Reading and Review Workbook Teacher's
  Edition (English)
Guided Reading and Review Workbook Teacher's
  Edition (Spanish)
Section Support Transparencies
Section Reading Support Transparency System
Basic Principles of the Constitution Transparencies
Magruder's Instruction Plus!
  Section Support Transparencies
  Prentice Hall Presentation Pro CD-ROM
  Keep it Current Web-based Activities
  American Government Video Collection
  Guide to the Essentials (English)
  Close Up Current Issues

## Program Highlights:

- Comprehensive and up-to-date content
- Content that is accessible and relevant for all students
- Quality technology resources that engage and challenge students
- Outstanding instructional support that saves teachers time
- Partnership with Close Up Foundation provides in-depth resources

## Assessment

Prentice Hall Assessment System
  <u>Program Assessment</u>
    Chapter Tests with ExamView® Test Bank CD-ROM
      Government Assessment Rubrics
  <u>Test Prep</u>
    *Diagnose and Prescribe*
      Diagnostic Tests for High School Social Studies Skills
    *Review and Reteach*
      Review Book for American Government
    *Practice and Assess*
      Test Prep Book for American Government
      Test-Taking Strategies with Transparencies for High School
      Test-Taking Strategies Posters
ExamView® Test Bank CD-ROM

## Technology

Prentice Hall Presentation Pro CD-ROM
Resource Pro® CD-ROM
Simulations and Data Graphing CD-ROM
Social Studies Skills Tutor CD-ROM
Interactive Constitution CD-ROM
Keep it Current Web-based Activities with CD-ROM
ABC News Civics and Government Videotape Library
American Government Video Collection
Close Up Foundation Bill of Rights Videotape Series
    *To Keep and Bear Arms*
    *For Which it Stands*
    *One Nation Under God?*
    *Sentenced to Die*
Companion Web site

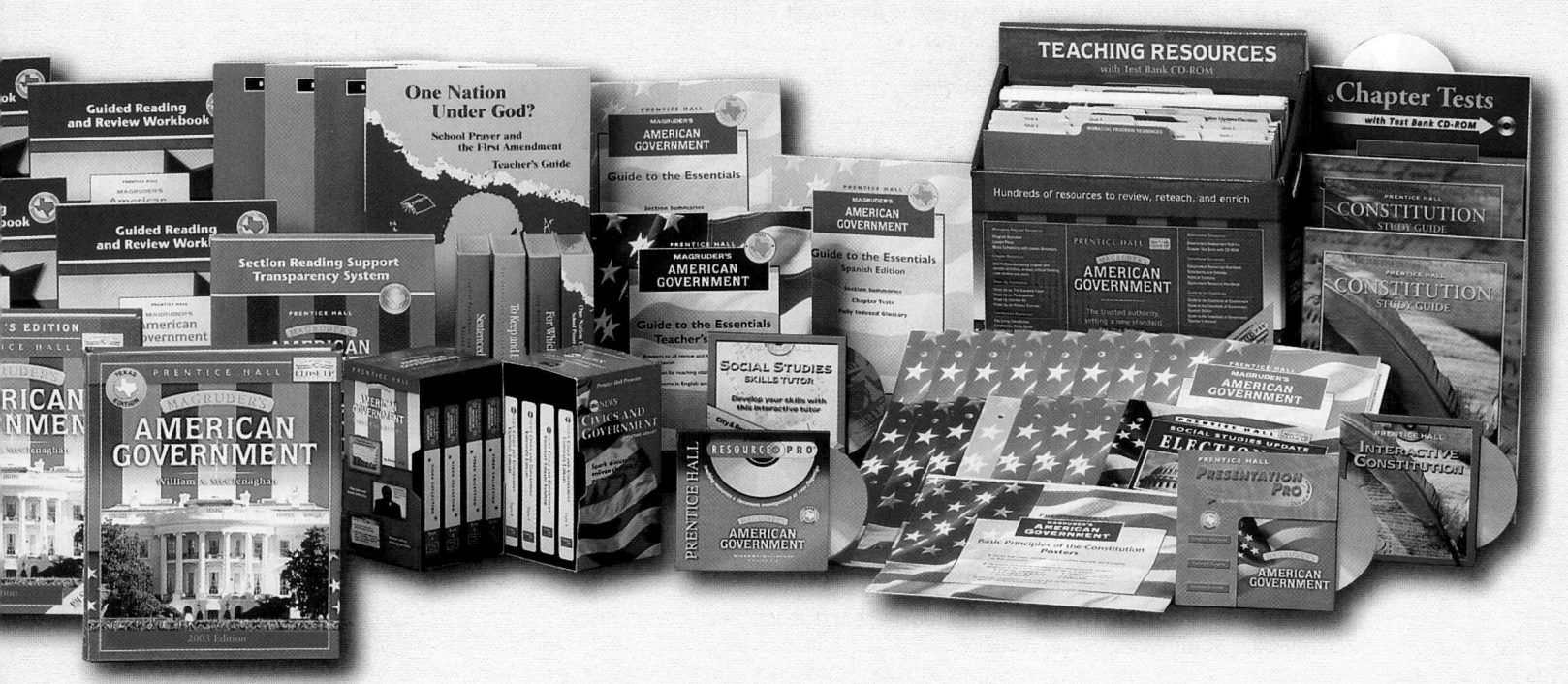

# NATIONAL STANDARDS CHART

## National Standards for Civics and Government

Published in 1994 by the Center for Civic Education, the *National Standards for Civics and Government* present a detailed composite of what students in grades K–4, 5–8, and 9–12 should know and be able to do in the areas of civics and government. The chart on these two pages lists the Standards for grades 9–12 and shows which chapters in *Magruder's American Government* focus on each standard.

### I.  What are civic life, politics, and government?

| | |
|---|---|
| **A.  What is civic life? What is politics? What is government? Why are government and politics necessary? What purposes should government serve?** | |
| 1. Defining civic life, politics, and government | Chapter 1 |
| 2. Necessity of politics and government | Chapter 1 |
| 3. The purposes of politics and government | Chapter 1 |
| **B.  What are the essential characteristics of limited and unlimited government?** | |
| 1. Limited and unlimited governments | Chapters 2, 11, 12, 23 |
| 2. The rule of law | Chapter 3 |
| 3. Civil society and government | Chapter 3 |
| 4. The relationship of limited government to political and economic freedom | Chapter 3, Chapter 23 |
| **C.  What are the nature and purposes of constitutions?** | |
| 1. Concepts of "constitution" | Chapter 2 |
| 2. Purposes and uses of constitutions | Chapter 3 |
| 3. Conditions under which constitutional government flourishes | Chapter 2 |
| **D.  What are alternative ways of organizing constitutional governments?** | |
| 1. Shared powers and parliamentary systems | Chapter 22 |
| 2. Confederal, federal, and unitary systems | Chapter 1 |
| 3. Nature of representation | Chapter 1, Chapter 10 |

### II.  What are the foundations of the American political system?

| | |
|---|---|
| **A.  What is the American idea of constitutional government?** | |
| 1. The American idea of constitutional government | Chapter 2 |
| 2. How American constitutional government has shaped the character of American society | Chapter 6 |
| **B.  What are the distinctive characteristics of American society?** | |
| 1. Distinctive characteristics of American society | Chapters 2, 11, 12, 13, 14 |
| 2. The role of voluntarism in American life | Chapter 19 |
| 3. The role of organized groups in political life | Chapter 5, Chapter 9 |
| 4. Diversity in American society | Chapter 9, Chapter 21 |
| **C.  What is American political culture?** | |
| 1. American national identity and political culture | Chapters 2, 11, 12, 13, 14 |
| 2. Character of American political conflict | Chapter 7 |
| **D.  What values and principles are basic to American constitutional democracy?** | |
| 1. Liberalism and American constitutional democracy | Chapter 1 |
| 2. Republicanism and American democracy | Chapter 2, Chapter 4 |
| 3. Fundamental values and principles | Chapter 1 |
| 4. Conflicts among values and principles in American political and social life | Chapter 6 |
| 5. Disparities between ideals and reality in American political and social life | Chapter 21 |

### III.  How does the government established by the Constitution embody the purposes, values, and principles of American democracy?

| | |
|---|---|
| **A.  How are power and responsibility distributed, shared, and limited in the government established by the United States Constitution?** | |
| 1. Distributing governmental power and preventing its abuse | Chapters 3, 4, 11–15, 18 |
| 2. The American federal system | Chapter 4 |
| **B.  How is the national government organized and what does it do?** | |
| 1. The institutions of the national government | Chapters 4, 15, 18 |
| 2. Major responsibilities of the national government in domestic and foreign policy | Chapter 4, Chapter 17 |
| 3. Financing government through taxation | Chapter 16 |

| | |
|---|---|
| **C. How are state and local governments organized, and what do they do?** | |
| 1. The constitutional status of state and local governments | **Chapter 4** |
| 2. Organization of state and local governments | **Chapter 24** |
| 3. Major responsibilities of state and local governments | **Chapter 4, Chapter 25** |
| **D. What is the place of law in the American constitutional system?** | |
| 1. The place of law in American society | **Chapter 3, Chapter 18** |
| 2. Judicial protection of the rights of individuals | **Chapter 20** |
| **E. How does the American political system provide for choice and opportunities for participation?** | |
| 1. The public agenda | **Chapter 7** |
| 2. Public opinion and behavior of the electorate | **Chapter 6, Chapter 8** |
| 3. Political communication: television, radio, the press, and political persuasion | **Chapter 8** |
| 4. Political parties, campaigns, and elections | **Chapters 5, 7, 13** |
| 5. Associations and groups | **Chapter 9** |
| 6. Forming and carrying out public policy | **Chapter 5** |

## IV. What is the relationship of the United States to other nations and to world affairs?

| | |
|---|---|
| **A. How is the world organized politically?** | |
| 1. Nation-states | **Chapter 22** |
| 2. Interactions among nation-states | **Chapter 17** |
| 3. International organizations | **Chapter 17** |
| **B. How do the domestic politics and constitutional principles of the United States affect its relations with the world?** | |
| 1. The historical context of United States foreign policy | **Chapter 17** |
| 2. Making and implementing Unites States foreign policy | **Chapter 17** |
| 3. The ends and means of United States foreign policy | **Chapter 17** |
| **C. How has the United States influenced other nations, and how have other nations influenced American politics and society?** | |
| 1. Impact of the American concept of democracy and individual rights on the world | **Chapter 22** |
| 2. Political developments | **Chapter 22** |
| 3. Economic, technological, and cultural developments | **Chapter 23** |
| 4. Demographic and environmental developments | **Chapter 17** |
| 5. United States and international organizations | **Chapter 17** |

## V. What are the roles of the citizen in American democracy?

| | |
|---|---|
| **A. What is citizenship?** | |
| 1. The meaning of citizenship in the United States | **Chapter 21** |
| 2. Becoming a citizen | **Chapter 21** |
| **B. What are the rights of citizens?** | |
| 1. Personal rights | **Chapter 19, Chapter 20** |
| 2. Political rights | **Chapter 20, Chapter 21** |
| 3. Economic rights | **Chapter 23** |
| 4. Relationship among personal, political, and economic rights | **Chapter 2** |
| 5. Scope and limits of rights | **Chapter 19, Chapter 20** |
| **C. What are the responsibilities of citizens?** | |
| 1. Personal responsibilities | **Chapter 1** |
| 2. Civic responsibilities | **Chapters 6, 16, 24** |
| **D. What civic dispositions or traits of private and public character are important to the preservation and improvement of American constitutional democracy?** | |
| 1. Dispositions that lead the citizen to be an independent member of society | **Chapter 1** |
| 2. Dispositions that foster respect for individual worth and human dignity | **Chapter 1** |
| 3. Dispositions that incline the citizen to public affairs | **Chapter 6, Chapter 9** |
| 4. Dispositions that facilitate thoughtful and effective participation in public affairs | **Chapter 1** |
| **E. How can citizens take part in civic life?** | |
| 1. The relationship between politics and the attainment of individual and public goals | **Chapter 2, Chapter 9** |
| 2. The difference between political and social participation | **Chapter 19** |
| 3. Forms of political participation | **Chapter 6, Chapter 9** |
| 4. Political leadership and careers in public service | **Chapter 15** |
| 5. Knowledge and participation | **Chapter 6** |

*D*emocracy is not a spectator sport—civic responsibility demands active participation. The enthusiastic participation of young people in our political process is critical to strengthening our democracy in the future. Yet, a 1999 Close Up Foundation/Prentice Hall national survey found that almost 70 percent of high school students have little or no interest in a future job related to government and politics. And an Education Department study that same year found that three-quarters of high school seniors are not "proficient" in civics. That's why the Close Up Foundation has partnered with Prentice Hall—to bring your students an engaging, current, and relevant look at their government. As the nation's largest nonprofit, nonpartisan civic education organization, Close Up has developed new, imaginative ways for young people, educators, and others to gain a practical understanding of how government influences their lives, and how they can become involved, active citizens. For more than 30 years, in programs that have reached millions of people, Close Up has been a leader in the social studies field.

It's only natural that the leader in experiential education and civic participation should join the most popular American government text to help make democracy come alive in your classroom. To meet your needs, we offer a wide range of materials designed to help your classroom become a training ground for active citizens. Together, Close Up and Prentice Hall can provide you with the resources to help you put civic responsibility back where it belongs—in the hands of your students.

*Stephen A. Janger*

Stephen A. Janger
President and Chief Executive Officer
Close Up Foundation

# ★ *Close Up*

## *Close Up Washington—Not Just Another Class Trip*

*O*ur flagship program is an exciting weeklong study visit of the nation's capital, providing high school students and their teachers a firsthand look at the people and the places that make this city unique. Through seminars with Washington policymakers and visits to government offices and historical sites, participants witness democracy in action. Our interactive curriculum and hands-on approach to learning

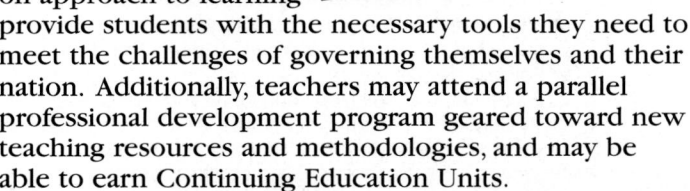

provide students with the necessary tools they need to meet the challenges of governing themselves and their nation. Additionally, teachers may attend a parallel professional development program geared toward new teaching resources and methodologies, and may be able to earn Continuing Education Units.

## Close Up on C-SPAN—*Talk Television That Doesn't Insult Your Intelligence*

*O*ur nationally televised discussions of news and current events features elected officials, journalists, and a variety of public policy experts engaged in a dialogue with Close Up students and teachers. Producing more than 1,300 hours of interactive telecasts since 1979, *Close Up on C-SPAN* is one of the longest-running public affairs programs on television. The program airs Fridays on C-SPAN from October through June at 7:00 p.m. ET.

# Foundation

## Close Up Publications

Our award-winning materials on U.S. government, history, current events, and international relations continue to be essential resources for educators and students. Close Up Publications will help bring a variety of issues to life in your classroom, encouraging further research, sparking lively discussions, and challenging students to formulate their own opinions.

★ *Current Issues: Critical Policy Choices Facing the Nation and the World* features timely information on the top domestic and foreign policy issues on the American agenda.

★ *Words of Ages* is an interdisciplinary text that blends American literature, history, and art. More than 125 excerpts reveal to your students how America's greatest authors, poets, and artists interpreted some of the greatest events in U.S. history.

★ *The Bill of Rights: A User's Guide* analyzes the Bill of Rights amendment by amendment, examining the history of each right and explaining how the Supreme Court has interpreted that right. An ABA Silver Gavel Award winner.

★ *Ordinary Americans: U.S. History Through the Eyes of Everyday People* collects nearly 200 primary source readings, many of which are multicultural, that retell 500 years of U.S. history from the perspectives of ordinary Americans.

★ *Ordinary Americans: The Red Scare* is a video that brings to life this time of propaganda, blacklists, and rising political tension. Firsthand accounts and dramatic file footage reveal the paranoia, uncertainty, and fear that gripped the nation and affected the lives of ordinary citizens.

★ *Profiles of Freedom: A Living Bill of Rights* focuses on four landmark Supreme Court cases that will help your students discover how one person can affect the rights of every U.S. citizen. This 28-minute video is an American Bar Association Silver Gavel Award winner.

www.closeup.org

800-CLOSE UP (256-7387)

# But I'm Not a Reading Teacher!

*F*ew people choose to be social studies teachers in order to focus on reading. Yet a significant number of today's students lack reading proficiency. Without it, they cannot access the wealth of social studies content they need to absorb from textbooks, primary sources, literature, and more. When students can't read well, they don't read and won't read.

## Best Practices in Reading

Instead of plunging in and plodding through a section, students need a plan of action, a strategy. Best practices for teaching reading in social studies focus on **comprehension strategies**—teaching students what to do *before reading, during reading,* and *after reading.*

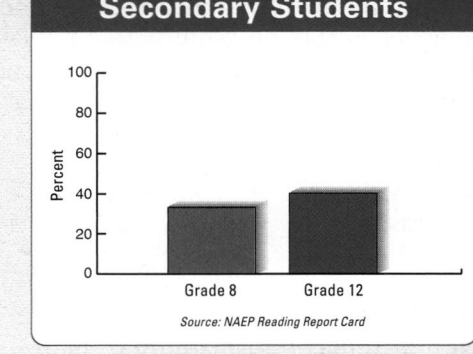

**Reading Proficiency in Secondary Students**

Source: NAEP Reading Report Card

Here are some ways to implement these strategies with struggling readers:

**Before Reading**  Both teacher and student preparations precede reading.

- Use an anecdote, photo, artifact, or audio to set the scene.
- Display a map or other visual aid to encourage students to identify what they already know and to make predictions by applying this knowledge to a new situation.
- Model for students how to look at pictures, captions, and headings in order to predict what they will be learning.

**During Reading**  Student-directed, individual activities take place during reading. Providing guided practice will help students develop these habits.

- Show students how to take notes, using graphic organizers that match the type of information they are reading. For example, use a Venn diagram for comparing and contrasting, a flowchart for sequencing, and a concept web for finding main ideas and supporting details.
- Teach students to ask themselves questions as they read.
- Demonstrate for students how to make connections between what they read and what they already know.

**After Reading**  Both student-directed and teacher-directed activities can follow reading.

- Conduct a sample self-check for students—"What have I learned?"
- Teach students to ask themselves, "How does this relate to what I already know?"
- Demonstrate both formal and informal assessments that students will encounter.

## Comprehension Strategies

### Before Reading
- Activate prior knowledge
- Build needed prior knowledge
- Focus attention
- Set purpose for reading
- Make predictions

### During Reading
- Confirm predictions
- Read and self-monitor
- Take notes and ask questions

### After Reading
- Recall information
- Respond to new learning
- Extend and transfer new learning
- Assess reading success

**Reading success happens when students can construct meaning from information.**

# Prentice Hall Support Throughout the Program

The structure of each Prentice Hall program embeds the development of solid reading skills in the Student Edition. Each section of *Magruder's American Government* starts with a section preview containing Objectives, Why It Matters, and a Political Dictionary.

At the end of each section, students will find opportunities to recall and apply information and construct meaning from it.

**Notice that the *Objectives* align with the subheadings in the section.**

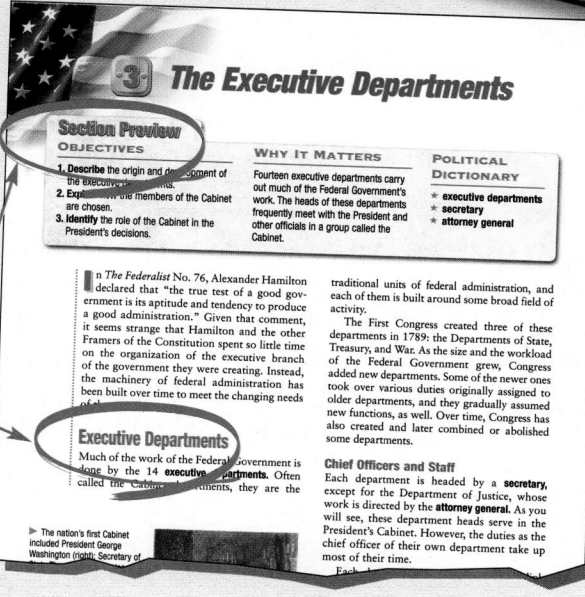

## Teacher's Edition

Additional reading strategies as well as ways to customize instruction for English language learners and nontraditional students give you focused strategies to improve students' comprehension.

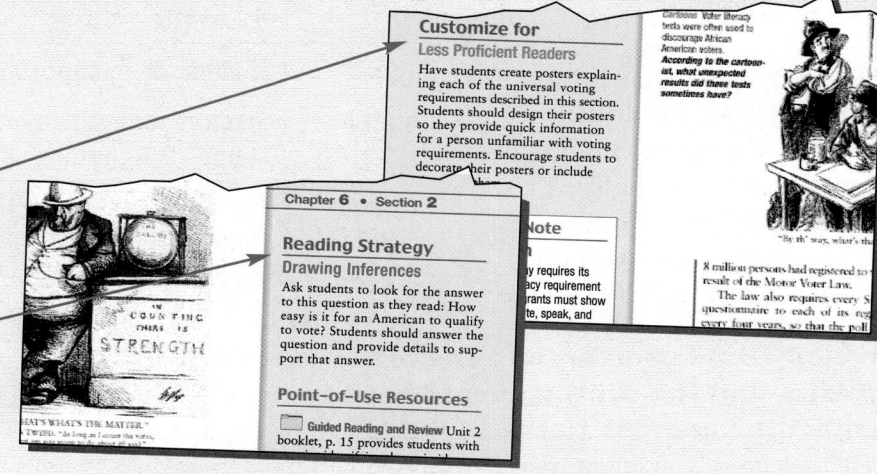

## 📖 Section Reading Support Transparency System

Every section of the text has a companion reading support transparency that answers the Questions to Explore and delivers the main points through a graphic organizer.

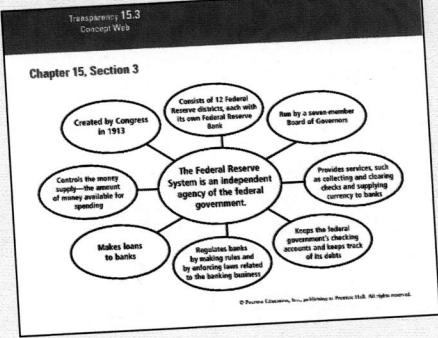

## 📕 Guide to the Essentials

Look in the Teaching Resources box for the Guide to the Essentials in both English and Spanish. Students use this book to review and master new content through summaries written below grade level.

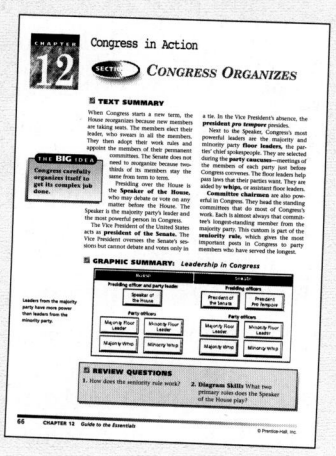

# Why Should I Teach Skills?

> **"Give a man a fish, and he eats for a day. Teach a man to fish and he eats for a lifetime."**
>
> — Anonymous

*F*ollowing this advice, if we present our students with only content, we are, in essence, giving them the fish. If we are to prepare students for life, we need to teach the skills needed to make sense out of the increasing volume of information in the world. To help students become lifelong learners, we need to develop their abilities to question, read, analyze, interpret, and evaluate information, as well as to communicate their ideas to others.

## Best Practices in Skills Integration

These guidelines will help you to embed skills development within content instruction.

1. **Plan each unit around an enduring understanding or big idea.** For example, if the unit you are about to teach is The Early Republic, 1789–1825, the big idea might be "new institutions face many challenges to their existence."

| Topic: The Electoral College | | |
|---|---|---|
| | **Example** | **Skill** |
| **Facts** | Number of electoral votes per State | Map reading |
| **Concepts** | Electors today are expected to "rubber stamp" their parties' choices. | Drawing inferences |
| **Big Ideas** | The electoral college has three major defects. | Problem solving |

2. **Develop each lesson around the facts, concepts, the big idea, and the skills students need to be able to connect the content to the big idea.** For part of a lesson on foreign relations, you might want to focus on the Embargo Act and its impact.

3. **Teach skills that are new or that add another level of complexity to a previously mastered skill.** Follow the elements of good skill instruction:

   • Set a purpose for using the skill.
   • Present the steps to follow.
   • Model the process for using the skill.
   • Guide practice and provide feedback.
   • Apply to a prompt such as a picture, map, or reading passage.

4. **Reinforce skills whenever possible.** Ask critical thinking questions about maps, photos, graphs, charts, and primary sources.

5. **Assess both content and skills mastery regularly.** It is important to determine whether students are remembering important information, but equally important to determine whether they are internalizing skills as lifelong learners.

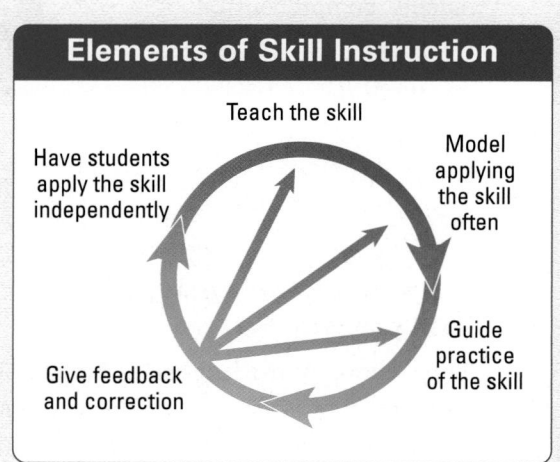

**Elements of Skill Instruction**

Teach the skill

Model applying the skill often

Guide practice of the skill

Give feedback and correction

Have students apply the skill independently

# Prentice Hall Support for Skills

Skills mastery means developing habits of mind that enable us to turn information into meaning. Every Prentice Hall social studies program contains a wealth of resources to build skills for life.

Learn   Assess   Apply

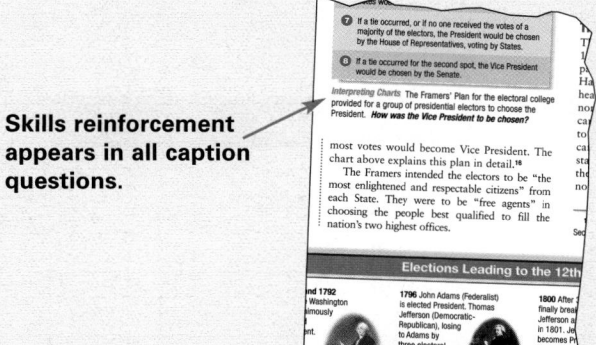

Skills reinforcement appears in all caption questions.

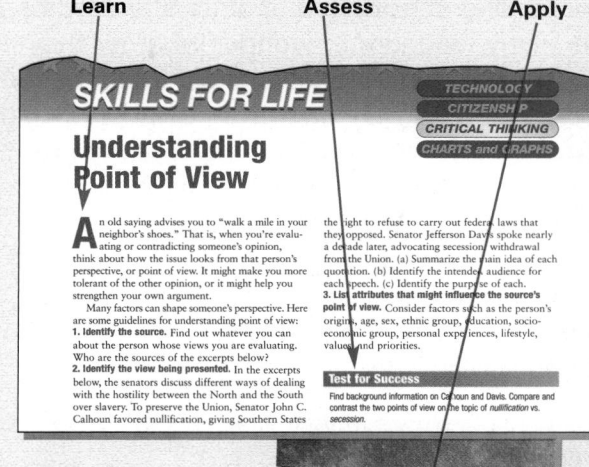

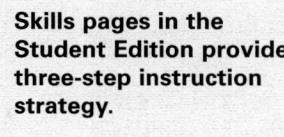

Skills pages in the Student Edition provide three-step instruction strategy.

Social Studies Skills Tutor CD-ROM provides two levels of interactive instruction and practice in 20 core social studies skills.

# Prentice Hall Vertical Alignment System

Mastery also requires that students learn skills at increasing levels of complexity as they progress through school. Prentice Hall programs take the guesswork out of aligning skills instruction by developing 20 core social studies skills with increasing difficulty from grade to grade.

| The 20 Core Social Studies Skills | |
|---|---|
| 1. Using the Cartographer's Tools | 11. Comparing and Contrasting |
| 2. Using Special Purpose Maps | 12. Analyzing Primary Sources |
| 3. Analyzing Graphic Data | 13. Recognizing Bias and Propaganda |
| 4. Analyzing Images | 14. Identifying Frame of Reference and Point of View |
| 5. Identifying Main Ideas/Summarizing | 15. Decision-making |
| 6. Sequencing | 16. Problem-solving |
| 7. Identifying Cause & Effect/ Making Predictions | 17. Using Reliable Information |
| 8. Drawing Inferences and Conclusions | 18. Transferring Information from One Medium to Another |
| 9. Making Valid Generalizations | 19. Synthesizing Information |
| 10. Distinguishing Fact & Opinion | 20. Supporting a Position |

# Should I Teach To The Test?

*T*he increasing importance of state standards and student accountability leads many teachers to wonder whether they must limit their classes to the content of high-stakes exams. While based on state standards and student needs, a truly effective social studies program requires **alignment of curriculum, instruction, and assessment.** When each of these elements dovetails with the others, *all* instruction prepares students for assessment based on curriculum objectives.

In an aligned system, both teacher and student know what is expected. There are no secrets or surprises. To ensure alignment:

- Teach the objectives in your standards to the specified level of understanding.
- Make sure that students know what they should learn before you teach.
- Test those same objectives as precisely as possible to the same depth of understanding that the standards require.

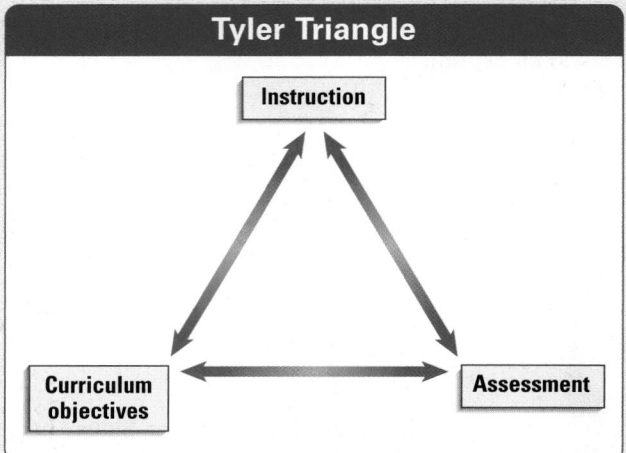

**Tyler Triangle**

Instruction

Curriculum objectives

Assessment

## Constructing Aligned Assessments

The principle of aligning assessment questions to curriculum objectives and instruction needs to be applied for both standardized tests and teacher-created exams.

### At the state level

To create assessments based on state standards, test writers dissect the objectives for the pieces of appropriate content and the thinking level required of the student. Test questions are written, reviewed, piloted, reviewed once again, and placed in testing banks.

### At the classroom level

While state tests occur perhaps once a year, teachers must use an ongoing system of testing to measure student learning throughout the year. Teachers need to plan instruction and assessment simultaneously, with both of them based on the state curriculum objectives.

# Best Practices in Assessment

Good assessment is part of an integrated cycle that is repeated throughout the school year. Following the principle of alignment, good assessment grows out of preparation that begins long before any test is administered and leads to improvements in teaching and learning long after the test. Here are some ways to integrate ongoing assessment into instruction:

| Assessment Techniques | |
|---|---|
| **Diagnose and Prescribe**<br>Evaluate student abilities at the beginning of the year. | The best way to know if students are ready for the difficulty level you intend to use is to give a diagnostic test when school opens. Students will not know the content you are about to teach them, but they should bring with them a number of social studies skills that they will apply to new content. Evaluate student facility in these areas:<br><br>• Map and globe skills<br>• Critical thinking and reading<br>• Graph and chart skills<br>• Communications |
| **Plan and Align**<br>Plan instruction to align with assessment. | • Examine objectives carefully.<br>• Choose learning activities making sure that more than a knowledge level (or memorized level) is expected of students.<br>• Test students on all of the objectives, omitting none.  Do not test information not contained in an objective.<br>• Test skill development at the same time you assess content.<br>• Integrate skill and content questions so that students must use what they know and combine it with new information that they gather.<br>• Test students' understanding of the objectives on many levels of thinking. |
| **Review and Reteach**<br>Weave ongoing review into aligned instruction and assessment. | One quick and easy way to check how much students remember from one unit to the next is to include some review questions on each of your tests.<br><br>• Find ways to connect new learning to previous learning as you put your lessons together.  This previous learning could come from units previously studied during the same year or from content studied in other courses.<br>• Choose review questions that are aligned to your current lessons. |
| **Practice and Assess**<br>Apply assessment results to improve teaching and learning. | • Use individual student information for tutoring and devising individualized plans for improvement.<br>• Use whole-class data to determine if your teaching was aligned to the assessment. If many students missed an item, it was probably not aligned to your instruction and intent. Make changes when you teach this unit again.<br>• Use review data on both individuals and the whole class to make a list of those objectives with which students may have difficulty on an end-of-year test. |

# Prentice Hall Assessment System

The Prentice Hall Assessment System provides comprehensive support for both program content assessment and preparation for high-stakes standardized tests.

## Program Assessment

Use the Chapter Tests to assess core content for every chapter.

Develop your own customized tests and practice worksheets with the ExamView® Test Bank® CD-ROM, selecting from hundreds of test questions and using the word-processing and editing capabilities. Create online tests and study guides and receive instant feedback on student progress.

Use a variety of assessment options to evaluate students' performance, such as activity-based assessment or portfolio assessment.

Give students clear expectations and a means of self-assessment through a variety of rubrics, which include criteria, indicators, and standards.

# Standardized Test Preparation

Prentice Hall Assessment System gives you the tools to help your students succeed on standardized tests, from the beginning of the year to the culminating high-stakes exam.

## Diagnose and Prescribe

📖 Profile student skills with Diagnostic Tests A & B.

📖 Address student needs with program resources correlated to diagnostic test questions.

## Review and Reteach

📖 Provide cumulative content review with unit-level questions and study sheets.

## Practice and Assess

📖 Build assessment skills using Test-Taking Strategies with Transparencies.

Reinforce assessment skills with Test-Taking Posters.

📖 Practice taking tests and improve scores on standardized tests with the Test Preparation Workbook.

# How Am I Doing?

*P*aired with the demand for high student achievement has come the drive for greater teacher accountability. More and more states and districts are establishing standards for teaching and new systems of teacher evaluation.

In the past, professional appraisals focused on teacher behaviors. Nationwide, the focus of teacher evaluation is now shifting to what students will be able to do. Student success emerges as the most critical measure of teaching—the teacher has not taught if students have not learned. The goal is becoming the learner-centered class, alive with critical thinking, problem-solving activities, collaborative learning, projects, and investigations. Evaluation criteria now measure how well teachers promote this kind of learning.

Prentice Hall social studies programs provide a variety of ways to support learner-centered instruction. Below you will find a guide to program resources to help you address criteria commonly found in teacher evaluations.

| Common Criteria | Where to Look for Support |
| --- | --- |
| **Active, successful student participation in the learning process** | • Structured reading support<br>• Activities at section and chapter levels<br>• Group and individual activities |
| **Learner-centered instruction** | • Critical thinking questions in captions<br>• Technology for students: Social Studies Skills Tutor CD-ROM, Interactive Constitution CD-ROM, Simulations and Data Graphing CD-ROM<br>• Customize For... in TE |
| **Evaluation and feedback on student progress** | • Section and chapter assessments in student edition<br>• Diagnostic tests and correlations to program resources in Prentice Hall Assessment System<br>• ExamView® Test Bank CD-ROM |
| **Management of student discipline, instructional strategies, time, and materials** | • TE lesson plans<br>• Chapter interleaf<br>• Resource Pro® |
| **Professional communications** | • Letters to families<br>• Resource Pro® |
| **Professional development** | • eTeach<br>• PHSuccessNet<br>• www.phschool.com/sales_support/texas/index.html<br>• Skylight Professional Development services at www.skylightedu.com |
| **Compliance with policies, operating procedures, and requirements** | • Resource Pro® |
| **Improvement of academic performance of all students** | • Prentice Hall Assessment System |

Prentice Hall offers professional development opportunities that are not only standards-driven and results-based, but also available in a variety of formats. From quality instructional materials to online support, Prentice Hall is committed to help you meet your immediate and long-term professional development goals.

## Annotated Teacher's Edition

Management of student discipline, instructional strategies, time, and materials are made easy with point-of-use notes and planning tools. Throughout each chapter, inset notes support customized lesson plans right where you need them—so it's simple to meet the needs of all your students.

## eTeach

This exclusive online teacher-to-teacher exchange lets you participate in an online seminar and discussion about the teaching of social studies. Each month, a new Master Teacher hosts a different topic.

## Prentice Hall Presentation Pro CD-ROM

This in-class presentation tool brings concepts to life!

- Ready-to-use "talking points" for each section of *Magruder's American Government*
- Lively graphics, handy charts, maps with overlays, and more
- Tools for reviewing key concepts

## Resource Pro® CD-ROM

Unmatched classroom management tool!

- Planning lessons—Create customized lesson plans with a few clicks of a mouse.
- Meeting local standards—Import your own local or state objectives into lesson plans.
- Making planning easier—Transport hundreds of pages of resources in electronic format—no more carrying resource books back and forth from school to home.

## Prentice Hall Professional Development and Training

Professional development starts with the resources you use every day. The combination of print, onsite, and online teacher resources offers a variety of ongoing, accessible support available anytime, anywhere.

Through our partnership with Skylight Professional Development, Prentice Hall now offers customized in-service programs based on individual educational goals, grade levels, and state standards and curriculum.

eTeach

*Meet This Month's Master Teacher*

**MARSHA K. RUSSELL**, a lifelong Texan, earned a Bachelor of Music degree in Vocal Performance from Southwestern University, and a Master of Arts in English Literature at the University of Texas at Austin, where she has also done post-graduate work. During the first seven of her sixteen years as a public school teacher in Austin, she taught seventh and eighth grade English and American History, and during the past nine years she has been on the faculty of the Liberal Arts Academy, a magnet school for gifted students housed at A. S. Johnston High School. Here she has created programs in Humanities - World History examined through the lens of art, literature, music, architecture, city

Prentice Hall is committed to being your partner in education.

T19

# Unchanging Principles in a Changing World

## by Bruce Wright

Bruce Wright has taught government for sixteen years. He currently teaches at Liberty High School, Liberty, Texas.

As I react to the new world that technology and recent events now present to me, I find some solace in my father's words, "Some things don't change." However, in my life, things have definitely changed. I have been an American government teacher for sixteen years and a city councilman for my small town for the past five. In fulfilling these roles, I have a unique vantage point from which to observe trends in both education and local community service, and I am amazed at the changes I've seen.

## Then and Now

I began my career teaching fifth grade. My students were eager to learn, intensely involved in our classroom adventures, and always trusted me to do the right thing. Today, my high school American government students are considerably less enthusiastic and are sure that I, their teacher, can't be trusted.

Decades ago, before the advent of the vast machinery of instant communication, Americans tended to trust those in government and looked to them as models for good citizenship. I certainly did. It was a teacher, in fact, who convinced me that being a community leader was the expected role of a good citizen. Today, as a councilman, I operate in a media fishbowl and must work to prove to ordinary citizens that I'm not a cheat or a criminal—not unlike my effort to convince my students that I can be trusted. Yes, I'd say that things have changed.

On the other hand, there are important things that have remained constant, and the idea that some basic principles are common to all generations is central to the way I teach American government. Those principles so eloquently expressed in the Declaration of Independence and fleshed out in the United States Constitution are just as sound today as ever. It turns out that the same ideas that motivated my father's generation, and subsequently my generation, are the key to motivating today's students to become informed and active participants in democracy.

## The Enduring Principles of American Government

The threads that bind the fabric of America together are the broad enduring principles found in our defining document. These Six Basic Principles of the Constitution—as they are introduced and developed in *Magruder's* today, and have been in succeeding editions of *Magruder's* for over 50 years—inform students not only about America's past but also about our current challenges as a nation.

**Popular Sovereignty**  People are the ultimate source of governmental power in the American system. This means that we must be the fixers of the majority of our problems. We—you and I—must work to help our neighbors. We should make the rules, and that is a notion that really rings true with students. How can students experience this principle? Through public service. This is precisely what led me to participate in local government. My serving as a councilman in a small town validates the idea of civic duty and encourages students to do the same.

**Limited Government**  Citizens must zealously guard against the accumulation of power in government. Limiting government not only safeguards individual rights, it also requires that ordinary citizens assume a viable role in their democracy. Any student can tell you that a teacher without any limits or constraints is "the very definition of tyranny."[1]

**Separation of Powers**  Are individuals protected by this division of power among the branches of government? Yes. None of us would want a law enforcement agent to give us a speeding ticket, proclaim our guilt, and collect the payment right on the side of the road. We have a better chance for fair treatment when one person or agency doesn't act as judge, jury, and executioner.

**Checks and Balances**  Do the parts of government need a watchguard to ensure that they play within their set boundaries? You bet! When one branch performs oversight over one of the others, we are the beneficiaries. Checks and balances are like second opinions in medicine. They provide accountability, and prevent not only tyranny but error.

**Judicial Review**  The ability of the federal courts to ensure that all parts of the government play by the rules is crucial. The sad reality is that government doesn't always act according to constitutional principles. All of the protections embedded in the other principles—as well as the guarantees in the Bill of Rights—would be in jeopardy without a referee to call "Out of bounds!"

**Federalism**  So what is the need for two overlapping and sometimes redundant levels of government? Why not have just one? Students can easily grasp that garbage collection in their town and speed limits on local dirt roads can scarcely be considered matters of national concern, while dependence on foreign oil and combating international terrorism cannot be adequately addressed by their city council.

## Idealism in Action

Young people have an idealistic world view. If teachers can somehow bring these six constitutional principles to them to be examined in the light of their twenty-first century idealism, we would have it made. *Magruder's* allows—even encourages—this process. For example, students espouse the principle of fairness. I'm certain that every teacher has heard those oft-repeated words, "but that's not fair."

What's "fair" has been a central issue for *Magruder's* for over 50 years. In the chapter "Civil Rights and Liberties," the 1952 edition of *Magruder's* uses individual

[1] *The Federalist* No.47: James Madison

Supreme Court cases to explore how judicial review has shaped the nation's concept of what students would call "fairness." This exploration is continued and expanded in the 2002 edition.

Another way the edition that you are reading focuses on how the basic constitutional principles have been reexamined and reinterpreted over time is through "The Living Constitution" features. One such time line highlights *Plessy* v. *Ferguson* (1896), in which the Supreme Court declared "separate but equal" facilities acceptable; *Brown* v. *Board of Education of Topeka* (1954), which struck down "separate but equal;" and *Regents of University of California* v. *Bakke* (1978), in which the Court ruled that affirmative action is acceptable but strict quotas are not. Plenty of material for a discussion of fairness there! And for the question of how enduring principles can be brought to bear on current issues.

You can approach that last question from a different angle in light of the aftermath of September 11, 2001: Questions about the rights of citizens and aliens during a national emergency have historical resonance as well as immediacy, and clearly impact students' sense of fairness and idealism.

Idealism is not limited to students, however. Most teachers entered their profession out of a sense of idealism. I know I did. And idealism is our common ground with students. We can show them how to put their idealism to work. Students must realize that their actions as citizens of their communities are not optional—they are vital.

# The *Living* Constitution

## The Supreme Court and Civil Rights                    1900

The Constitution describes Americans' civil rights only in general terms. The courts, especially the Supreme Court, have had to decide how these constitutional guarantees apply to specific situations. As the time line entries show, some Court decisions have supported and broadened civil liberties, while other decisions have restricted them.

**1883** In the *Civil Rights Cases,* the Court rules that the 14th Amendment does not ban racial discrimination by private individuals or businesses.

**1896** In *Plessy* v. *Ferguson,* the Court rules that "separate but equal" facilities for different races are acceptable.

Age is irrelevant to participation. Whether citizens are voting, volunteering, or just being neighborly, a town cannot survive without its citizens acting out their beliefs in a way that supports and builds community. Ask your city council for ways that students can get involved. Involved students are unlikely to tolerate others tearing up a city that they are actively building.

## The Big Questions

We can also use student involvement in community service and their interest in community fairness to lead them to an exploration of the ideas—the basic principles—on which their communities are based. The critical part of our children's education is in the area of social studies. Ours are the classrooms in which the big questions are asked and where they are likely to be answered. If we want students to be able to think, speak, reason, and solve, then we must begin to re-address the ideas that we hold important. This is something that has not changed—not since my school days or my Dad's or even the first edition of *Magruder's* in 1917. It goes back beyond the Founders themselves, and their discussion of the issues in the newspapers of the 1780s. If we can create a framework for our students to re-examine the basic founding principles, then this generation will decide, on their own, that these ideas were not only worth embracing then, but are now worth embracing and defending again.

**1944** In *Korematsu* v. *United States*, the Court upholds the internment of Japanese Americans during World War II.

**1954** In *Brown* v. *Board of Education*, the Court rules that "separate but equal" public schools are unconstitutional.

**1988** In *New York State Club Association* v. *City of New York*, the Court upholds a law that stops most private clubs from denying membership to women.

**1925**  **1950**  **1975**  **2000**

**1978** In *Regents of University of California* v. *Bakke*, the Court rules that affirmative action is acceptable but strict quotas are not.

**2001** In *Hunt* v. *Cromartie*, the Court holds that, while race cannot be the controlling factor in drawing electoral district lines, it can be one of the several factors that shape that process.

### Analyzing Time Lines

1. Which Supreme Court decision endorsed the principle of "separate but equal" facilities? Which decision rejected this idea?
2. Besides African Americans, what groups of people could be affected by the Supreme Court's recent civil liberties rulings?

# Texas Essential Knowledge and Skills Correlation

Correlated to *Magruder's American Government*

| **(1) History. The student understands major political ideas and forms of government in history. The student is expected to:** | |
|---|---|
| (A) Explain major political ideas in history such as<br>natural law<br>natural rights,<br>divine right of kings,<br>and social contract theory; and | <br>4, 7, 10<br>4, 38, 40–43<br>4, 7–8<br>4, 8, 10, 25, 40–43 |
| (B) Identify the characteristics of classic forms of government such as<br>absolute monarchy,<br>authoritarianism,<br>classical republic,<br>despotism,<br>feudalism,<br>liberal democracy,<br>and totalitarianism. | <br><br>10, 12, 32<br>12–14<br>12<br>12–14<br>12<br>12–13, 18–22, 25<br>12–14 |

| **(2) History. The student understands how constitutional government, as developed in the United States, has been influenced by people, ideas, and historical documents. The student is expected to:** | |
|---|---|
| (A) Analyze the principles and ideas that underlie the Declaration of Independence and the U.S. Constitution, including those of<br>Thomas Hobbes,<br>John Locke,<br>and Charles de Montesquieu; | <br><br>7–8, 10<br>8, 10–11, 53, 66<br>10, 53, 66 |
| (B) Analyze the contributions of the political philosophies of the Founding Fathers, including<br>John Adams,<br>Alexander Hamilton,<br>Thomas Jefferson,<br><br>and James Madison, on the development of the U.S. government; | <br><br>38, 57, 365–367, 401, 547<br>51, 56, 58, 69, 119, 126, 291–292, 306, 356, 365, 391, 468, 506, 787–790<br>8–10, 19, 38, 40–43, 76–78, 119, 126–127, 263, 291, 306, 366–367, 391, 393, 538, 547<br>9, 50–51, 54, 56–58, 69–70, 78, 127, 238, 262–3, 275, 391, 405, 415, 781–787 |
| (C) Analyze debates and compromises necessary to reach political decisions using historical documents; and | 33, 51–53, 56–58, 75–78, 760–761, 771–773, 781–792 |
| (D) Identify significant individuals in the field of government and politics, including<br>Abraham Lincoln,<br>George Washington,<br><br>and selected contemporary leaders. | <br><br>12, 18, 21, 128, 380, 401, 429, 576, 754–5, 797–798<br>36, 46, 49, 50, 57–58, 62, 82, 120, 263, 357, 360, 366, 401, 424, 426, 438, 481, 754–755<br>Voices on Government: 9, 91, 246, 281, 291, 339, 355, 402, 431, 455, 470, 519, 572, 602, 648, 662, 696, 743<br>See also: 161–163, 355, 390–392, 399, 400, 402–403, 407–408, 428–429, 485–489, 216, 262, 323, 364, 388, 469, 476, 608–609 |

| **(3) History. The student understands the roles played by individuals, political parties, interest groups, and the media in the U.S. political system, past and present. The student is expected to:** | |
|---|---|
| (A) Give examples of the processes used by<br>individuals,<br>political parties,<br>interest groups,<br>or the media to affect public policy; and | <br>176–195, 555–558, 584, 603–612, 613–614<br>114–18, 120–121, 125, 132–135, 142, 178–186, 368–374<br>196–197, 198–203, 216, 234–254<br>211–212, 216, 223–230 |

| | |
|---|---|
| (B) Analyze the impact of political changes brought about by individuals, political parties, interest groups, or the media, past and present. | 161, 555–558<br>114–118, 132–136<br>236–240, 243–247, 250–251, 558<br>196, 202, 215–216, 233, 223–230, 250, 391–392 |

**(4) Geography. The student understands why certain places and regions are important to the United States. The student is expected to:**

| | |
|---|---|
| (A) Analyze the political significance to the United States of the location and geographic characteristics of selected places such as<br>Cuba and,<br>Taiwan, and | 481–498<br><br>483, 486<br>650–652 |
| (B) Analyze the economic significance to the United States of the location and geographic characteristics of selected places and regions such as oil fields in the Middle East. | 489, 492–494, 501 |

**(5) Geography. The student understands how government policies can affect the physical can affect the physical and human characteristics of places and regions. The student is expected to:**

| | |
|---|---|
| (A) Analyze and evaluate the consequences of a government policy that affects the physical characteristics of a place or region and | 304, 418, 422, 434–435, 493, 662, 652, 805 |
| (B) Analyze and evaluate the consequences of a government policy that affects the human characteristics of a place or region. | 404, 409, 434, 481–489, 493, 534–535, 594–621, 652 |

**(6) Economics. The student understands the roles played by local, state, and national governments in both the public and private sectors of the U.S. free enterprise system. The student is expected to:**

| | |
|---|---|
| (A) Analyze government policies that influence the economy at the local, state, and national levels. | 21, 294–300, 454–463, 658–664, 733–737 |
| (B) Identify the sources of revenue and expenditures of the U.S. government and analyze their impact on the U.S. economy; and | 294–300, 446–452, 454–456, 458–462 |
| (C) Compare the role of government in the U.S. free enterprise system and other economic systems. | 21, 294–300, 656–679 |

**(7) Economics. The student understands the relationship between U.S. government policies and international trade. The student is expected to:**

| | |
|---|---|
| (A) Explain the effects of international trade on U.S. economic and political policies; and | 489, 492–494, 641–643 |
| (B) Explain the government's role in setting international trade policies. | 422, 469, 641–643 |

**(8) Government. The student understands the American beliefs and principles reflected in the U.S. Constitution. The student is expected to:**

| | |
|---|---|
| (A) Explain the importance of a written constitution; | 38–39, 64–70, 85, 684–688 |
| (B) Evaluate how the federal government serves the purposes set forth in the Preamble to the U.S. Constitution; | The Purpose of Government: 4, 8–10<br>The Defense Department: 472–473<br>The Military Departments: 473–475<br>Freedom of Religion: 537–545<br>Freedom of Speech and Press: 546–553<br>Freedom of Assembly and Petition: 555–559<br>Due Process of Law: 564–568<br>Freedom of Security and the Person: 569–574<br>Equality Before the Law: 564–568<br>Diversity and Discrimination in American Society: 594–599<br>Free Enterprise System: 659–661<br>Federal Civil Rights Laws: 608–612<br>American Citizenship: 613–618 |

| | |
|---|---|
| (C) Analyze how the Federalist Papers explain the principles of the American constitutional system of government; | 9, 56, 58, 61, 67, 69, 263, 468, 506, 783–790 |
| (D) Evaluate constitutional provisions for limiting the role of government, including | |
| republicanism, | 13, 64, 97 |
| checks and balances, | 39, 53, 64, 67–70, 259, 262–265, 290, 301, 304, 309, 310–314, 346, 351, 405, 503, 685 |
| federalism, | 1, 64, 70, 73–74, 88–95, 101–103, 113, 138, 506, 534–536 |
| separation of powers, | 1, 39, 53, 64, 66–67, 259, 351, 623, 685, 806 |
| popular sovereignty, | 1, 39, 53, 64, 65, 73–74, 113, 623, 685 |
| and individual rights; | Federalism and Individual Rights: 534–536<br>Freedom of Religion: 537–545<br>Freedom of Speech and Press: 546–553<br>Freedom of Assembly and Petition: 555–559<br>Due Process of Law: 564–568<br>Freedom of Security and the Person: 569–574<br>Rights of the Accused: 576–583, 584<br>Punishment: 585–588<br>Equality Before the Law: 601–607<br>Federal Civil Rights Laws: 608–612 |
| (E) Analyze the processes by which the U.S. Constitution can be changed and evaluate their effectiveness; and | 72–77, 79–82, 85 |
| (F) Analyze how the American beliefs and principles reflected in the U.S. Constitution contribute to our national identity. | Basic Concepts of Democracy: 18–22, 25<br>Creating the Constitution: 48–54<br>The Basic Principles: 65–70<br>A Commitment to Freedom: 532<br>Freedom of Religion: 537–545<br>Freedom of Speech and Press: 546–553<br>Freedom of Assembly and Petition: 555–559<br>Due Process of Law: 564–568<br>Freedom of Security and the Person: 569–574<br>Rights of the Accused: 576–583, 584<br>Punishment: 585–589<br>Equality Before the Law: 601–606<br>Federal Civil Rights Laws: 608–612<br>American Citizenship: 613–618<br>American Free Enterprise System: 659–661 |

**(9) Government. The student understands the structure and functions of the government created by the U.S. Constitution. The student is expected to:**

| | |
|---|---|
| (A) Analyze the structure and functions of the legislative branch of government, including | |
| the bicameral structure of Congress, | 51–52, 262–263, 685, 689 |
| the role of committees, | 325–333, 336–338, 344–346 |
| and the procedure for enacting laws; | 334–340, 342–346 |
| (B) Analyze the structure and functions of the executive branch of government, including | |
| the constitutional powers of the President, | 342, 346, 354–358, 393–397, 399–403, 405–408, 424 |
| the growth of presidential power, | 390–392 |
| and the role of the Cabinet and executive departments; | 81–82, 395, 414–435, 437–440, 458–462, 468–475 |
| (C) Analyze the structure and functions of the judicial branch of government, including the federal court system and types of jurisdiction; | 506–529, 534–588, 601–606, 702–705, 707–712 |
| (D) Analyze the functions of selected independent executive agencies and regulatory commissions such as | 412–480 |
| the National Aeronautics and Space Administration and, | 430–431, 460, 479–480 |
| the Federal Communications Commission; | 431–433, 435, 551 |
| (E) Explain how certain provisions of the U.S. Constitution provide for checks and balances among the three branches of government; | 39, 53, 67–69, 259, 262–265, 290, 301, 304, 309, 310–314, 346, 351, 399, 405, 510, 685 |

| | |
|---|---|
| (F) Analyze selected issues raised by judicial activism and judicial restraint; | 509–510, 517–522, 535–536, 539–542, 566, 567–568, 573–574 |
| (G) Explain the major responsibilities of the federal government for domestic and foreign policy; | 8–10, 97–99, 101–103, 301–304, 399–403, 419–423, 430–435, 446–452, 458–462, 468–475, 477–480, 481–489, 491– 498, 564–568, 569–574, 576–588, 601–606, 608–618, 658–664 |
| (H) Compare the structure and functions of the Texas state government to the federal system; and | 684–700, 702–705, 707–712, 733–737, 739–744 |
| (I) Analyze the structure and functions of local government. | 718–723, 725–737, 739–744 |

**(10) Government. The student understands the concept of federalism. The student is expected to:**

| | |
|---|---|
| (A) Explain why the Founding Fathers created a distinctly new form of federalism and adopted a federal system of government instead of a unitary system; | 53, 88–95, 733–737 |
| (B) Categorize government powers as national, state, or shared; | 88–95, 97–103 |
| (C) Analyze historical conflicts over the respective roles of national and state governments; and | 88–95, 524–526 |
| (D) Evaluate the limits on the national and state governments in the U.S. federal system of government. | 39, 65–66, 88–95, 259, 290, 351, 503, 533–534, 681, 733, 739–740 |

**(11) Government. The student understands the processes for filling public offices in the U.S. system of government. The student is expected to:**

| | |
|---|---|
| (A) Compare different methods of filling public offices, including elected and appointed offices at the local, state, and national levels; and | 178–186, 188–194, 196–202, 375, 377–384, 393–397, 427–428, 437–440, 509–510, 689–700, 707–712 |
| (B) Analyze and evaluate the process of electing the President of the United States. | 178–180, 365–367, 368–375, 377–384 |

**(12) Government. The student understands the role of political parties in the U.S. system of government. The student is expected to:**

| | |
|---|---|
| (A) Identify the functions of political parties; | 116–124, 132–135, 186, 366–367, 368–375 |
| (B) Analyze the two–party system and evaluate the role of third parties in the United States; | 119–135 |
| (C) Analyze the role of political parties in the electoral process at local, state, and national levels; and | 116–18, 132–135, 145, 366–367, 368–375 |
| (D) Identify opportunities for citizens to participate in political party activities at local, state, and national levels. | 137–142, 368–379 |

**(13) Government. The student understands the similarities and differences that exist among the U.S. system of government and other political systems. The student is expected to:**

| | |
|---|---|
| (A) Compare the U.S. systems of government with other political systems; | 12–16, 119, 122–123, 624–655 |
| (B) Analyze advantages and disadvantages of federal, confederate, and unitary systems of government; and | 12, 14–15, 16, 626–632, 634–638 |
| (C) Analyze advantages and disadvantages of presidential and parliamentary systems of government. | 12, 15–16, 626–632, 634–638 |

**(14) Citizenship. The student understands rights guaranteed by the U.S. Constitution. The student is expected to:**

| | |
|---|---|
| (A) Understand the roles of limited government and the rule of law to the protection of individual rights; | 65–66, 259, 503, 530–621 |
| (B) Analyze the rights guaranteed by the Bill of Rights, including first amendment freedoms; | 76, 78, 89, 463, 530–588 |
| (C) Analyze issues addressed in selected cases such as *Engel* v. *Vitale,* *Miranda* v. *Arizona,* and *Schenck* v. *U.S.* that involve Supreme Court interpretations of rights guaranteed by the U.S. Constitution; | 537, 539, 800<br>582–583, 803<br>547–548, 804 |
| (D) Analyze the role of each branch of government in protecting the rights of individuals; | 70, 532–621, 591 |
| (E) Explain the importance of due process rights to the protection of individual rights and to the limits on the powers of government; and | 537, 564–568, 740, 801, 802, 805 |

*(continued)*

| | |
|---|---|
| (F) Analyze the impact of the incorporation doctrine involving due process and the Bill of Rights on individual rights, federalism, and majority rule. | 534–536 |

**(15) Citizenship. The student understands the difference between personal and civic responsibilities. The student is expected to:**

| | |
|---|---|
| (A) Explain the difference between personal and civic responsibilities; | 25<br>Examples: Military Service: 479–480, 637<br>Casting Your Vote: 195<br>Serving on a Jury: 706 |
| (B) Evaluate whether and/or when the obligation of citizenship requires that personal desires and interests be subordinated to the public good; | 18–20, 533–534, 546–553, 555–559 |
| (C) Evaluate whether and/or when the rights of individuals are inviolable even against claims for the public good; and | 22, 533, 534, 537–544, 546–553, 555–559, 564–568, 569–574, 576–584, 585–589 |
| (D) Analyze the consequences of political decisions and actions on society. | Examples:<br>Segregation: 602<br>Breaking Down Barriers: 607<br>Federal Civil Rights Laws: 608–611<br>The Right to Vote: 148–150 |

**(16) Citizenship. The student understands the importance of voluntary individual participation in the U.S. democratic society. The student is expected to:**

| | |
|---|---|
| (A) Analyze the effectiveness of various methods of participation in the political process at local, state, national levels; | 137–142, 145, 159–163, 205, 236–240, 249–254, 601–606, 608–612, 613–618 |
| (B) Analyze historical and contemporary examples of citizen movements to bring about political change or to maintain continuity; | 159–163, 236–240, 242–247, 601–606, 608–612 |
| (C) Analyze the factors that influence an individual's political attitudes and actions; and | 123–125, 164–172, 196–202, 208–213, 223–230 |
| (D) Compare and evaluate characteristics, style, and effectiveness of state and national leaders, past and present. | 374–375, 401–403, 481–489, 694–700 |

**(17) Citizenship. The student understands the importance of the expression of different points of view in a democratic society. The student is expected to:**

| | |
|---|---|
| (A) Analyze different points of view of political parties and interest groups on important contemporary issues; | 123–124, 209, 242–247 |
| (B) Analyze the importance of free speech and press in a democratic society; and | 74–75, 91, 159–163, 546–554 |
| (C) Express and defend a point of view on an issue of contemporary interest in the United States. | 59, 83, 85, 109, 124, 143, 145, 173, 175, 203, 204, 231, 255, 257, 274, 285, 287, 292, 300, 304, 315, 384, 385, 392, 397, 409, 441, 452, 463, 465, 470, 475, 479, 480, 496, 498, 499, 527, 529, 559, 561, 568, 574, 589, 591, 612, 618, 619, 621, 653, 670, 677, 693, 703, 705, 711, 712, 713, 715, 745 |

**(18) Culture. The student understands the relationship between government policies and the culture of the United States. The student is expected to:**

| | |
|---|---|
| (A) Evaluate a political policy or decision in the United States that was a result of changes in American culture; and | 159–163, 602–607, 608–612 |
| (B) Analyze changes in American culture brought about by government policies such as | |
| voting rights, | 150, 159–163 |
| the GI Bill, | 731–732 |
| and racial integration; and | 603, 608–610, 621 |
| (C) Describe an example of a government policy that has affected a particular racial, ethnic, or religious group. | 159–163, 409, 534–535, 537–544, 592–620 |

**(19) Science, technology, and society. The student understands the role government plays in developing policies and establishing conditions that influence scientific discoveries and technological innovations. The student is expected to:**

| | |
|---|---|
| (A) Identify examples of government assisted research that, when shared with the private sector, have resulted in improved consumer products such as computer and communication technologies; and | 22, 101–103 |
| (B) Analyze how U.S. government policies fostering competition and entrepreneurship have resulted in scientific discoveries and technological innovations. | 101–103, 297–298, 664 |

**(20) Science, technology, and society. The student understands the impact of advances in science and technology on government and society. The student is expected to:**

| | |
|---|---|
| (A) Analyze the potential impact on society of recent scientific discoveries and technological innovations; and | 22, 71, 151, 192–194, 211–212, 217, 222–223, 253, 436, 531, 701 |
| (B) Analyze the reaction of government to scientific discoveries and technological innovations. | 75, 192–194, 300, 303, 370, 422, 653, 741 |

**(21) Social Studies skills. The student applies critical–thinking skills to organize and use information acquired from a variety of sources including electronic technology. The student is expected to:**

| | |
|---|---|
| (A) Analyze information by sequencing, | 25, 61, 85, 110, 111, 145, 161, 175, 233, 340, 344, 345, 387, 398, 411, 443, 453, 461, 465, 501, 511, 520, 529, 558, 591, 621, 655, 693, 732 |
| categorizing, | 16, 25, 39, 61, 70, 95, 103, 108, 109, 111, 133, 143, 172, 173, 203, 231, 255, 256, 257, 285, 315, 317, 317, 347, 349, 384, 385, 387, 397, 409, 441, 463, 475, 499, 511, 527, 559, 589, 591, 619, 653, 677, 679, 713, 737, 745 |
| identifying cause–and–effect relationships, | 22, 43, 77, 82, 145, 163, 205, 265, 278, 284, 292, 298, 308, 316, 333, 361, 363, 367, 386, 411, 422, 429, 440, 442, 490, 500, 501, 518, 522, 544, 561, 612, 638, 726, 732, 747 |
| comparing, | 10, 25, 32, 54, 55, 65, 70, 103, 109, 118, 131, 143, 173, 203, 209, 214, 221, 231, 237, 246, 247, 254, 255, 265, 285, 292, 293, 296, 314, 315, 327, 341, 346, 347, 384, 385, 392, 397, 409, 418, 441, 443, 456, 462, 463, 475, 480, 493, 499, 501, 507, 527, 529, 536, 559, 571, 588, 589, 606, 619, 621, 632, 635, 637, 638, 643, 653, 654, 655, 669, 677, 679, 688, 693, 713, 730, 735, 740, 744, 745 |
| contrasting, | 10, 32, 47, 54, 55, 65, 70, 75, 103, 109, 118, 130, 131, 143, 173, 203, 209, 214, 221, 231, 233, 247, 255, 265, 285, 292, 293, 296, 314, 315, 316, 317, 323, 327, 335, 341, 345, 346, 347, 384, 385, 392, 397, 409, 410, 411, 440, 441, 442, 463, 475, 480, 499, 501, 507, 511, 527, 536, 559, 588, 589, 606, 619, 629, 632, 638, 641, 651, 653, 655, 664, 669, 670, 677, 679, 688, 693, 713, 727, 732, 744, 745 |
| finding the main idea, | 10, 11, 16, 24, 32, 33, 39, 43, 47, 54, 58, 60, 70, 75, 77, 78, 82, 84, 95, 96, 103, 108, 109, 110, 118, 124, 131, 135, 136, 142, 143, 144, 150, 157, 158, 163, 172, 173, 174, 187, 191, 202, 203, 204, 213, 214, 221, 230, 231, 232, 240, 247, 249, 254, 255, 265, 273, 274, 278, 284, 285, 286, 292, 300, 304, 308, 309, 314, 315, 316, 327, 328, 333, 340, 346, 347, 348, 358, 363, 364, 367, 375, 384, 385, 392, 397, 403, 404, 408, 409, 410, 418, 422, 423, 429, 435, 440, 441, 442, 452, 456, 457, 462, 463, 464, 475, 476, 480, 489, 498, 499, 500, 511, 516, 522, 526, 527, 528, 536, 544, 545, 553, 558, 559, 560, 568, 574, 583, 584, 588, 589, 590, 599, 606, 607, 612, 618, 619, 620, 632, 638, 643, 644, 649, 652, 653, 654, 664, 670, 671, 676, 677, 678, 688, 693, 700, 701, 705, 712, 713, 714, 723, 732, 737, 744, 745, 746 |
| summarizing, | 54, 55, 77, 104, 118, 125, 233, 265, 293, 308, 317, 341, 397, 408, 411, 418, 511, 515, 558, 561, 568, 583, 588, 591, 620, 643, 652, 744, 747 |
| making generalizations and predictions, | 22, 23, 59, 83, 108, 109, 111, 135, 142, 151, 172, 173, 175, 194, 202, 203, 221, 226, 247, 273, 287, 297, 308, 315, 327, 340, 346, 347, 363, 408, 409, 411, 418, 441, 462, 463, 465, 475, 499, 527, 536, 544, 549, 558, 559, 583, 589, 604, 619, 653, 677, 688, 700, 713, 737, 745, 747 |
| and drawing inferences and conclusions; | 7, 8, 10, 16, 17, 20, 22, 25, 29, 32, 33, 36, 37, 39, 47, 50, 54, 69, 70, 77, 80, 82, 85, 89, 95, 101, 103, 107, 108, 109, 111, 118, 121, 123, 124, 127, 131, 134, 142, 143, 145, 150, 154, 155, 157, 163, 173, 175, 176, 184, 191, 197, 199, 201, 203, 205, 209, 212, 213, 224, 225, 227, 229, 230, 231, 233, 237, 238, 240, 243, 250, 251, 253, 255, 257, 264, 265, 268, 270, 272, 273, 276, 278, 282, 283, 284, 285, 287, 291, 292, 295, 299, 300, 302, 303, 304, 305, 307, 308, 310, 312, 314, 315, 317, 321, 322, 323, 324, 328, 330, 331, 332, 333, 337, 338, 343, 344, 346, 347, 349, 356, 357, 358, 359, 367, 369, 374, 375, 378, 380, 384, 385, 391, 392, 394, 395, 397, 399, 401, 403, 406, 408, 409, 411, 416, 418, 420, 421, 422, 423, 425, 426, 429, 431, 432, 433, 434, 435, 439, 443, 447, 451, 452, 456, 459, 462, 463, 465, 470, 472, 473, 475, 480, 485, 487, 499, 501, 508, 509, 510, 512, 513, 514, 515, 519, 520, 522, 523, 524, 525, 526, 527, 529, 535, 536, 541, 542, 543, 544, 547, 548, 550, 552, 558, 559, 561, 565, 566, 567, 568, 573, 579, 581, 583, 588, 589, 591, 595, 596, 597, 598, 599, 600, 602, 610, 612, 614, 618, 619, 621, 632, 633, 642, 643, 648, 649, 652, 653, 655, 661, 663, 664, 665, 668, 669, 670, 673, 674, 675, 676, 677, 687, 691, 695, 696, 700, 701, 704, 706, 707, 712, 713, 719, 720, 722, 723, 724, 727, 728, 729, 731, 732, 734, 735, 737, 740, 743, 745, 747 |

*(continued)*

| | |
|---|---|
| (B) Create a product on a contemporary government issue or topic using critical methods of inquiry; | 85, 175, 221, 222, 233, 349, 387, 403, 443, 465, 501, 561, 575, 591, 679 |
| (C) Explain a point of view on a government issue; | 23, 59, 109, 124, 143, 149, 173, 175, 202, 203, 204, 231, 247, 255, 257, 274, 285, 287, 292, 300, 304, 315, 317, 333, 347, 349, 356, 358, 384, 385, 387, 392, 397, 409, 423, 441, 443, 452, 463, 465, 470, 475, 479, 480, 496, 498, 499, 527, 529, 536, 549, 559, 561, 568, 574, 583, 588, 589, 612, 618, 619, 621, 653, 662, 670, 677, 693, 700, 703, 705, 711, 712, 713, 715, 745, 747 |
| (D) Analyze and evaluate the validity of information from primary and secondary sources for bias, | 7, 25, 56, 61, 71, 85, 91, 96, 99, 109, 120, 125, 127, 131, 136, 141, 143, 145, 150, 153, 154, 156, 157, 165, 166, 173, 175, 182, 185, 187, 195, 203, 205, 214, 218, 219, 221, 231, 232, 240, 241, 255, 257, 274, 278, 283, 285, 287, 291, 292, 305, 314, 315, 317, 341, 347, 349, 385, 397, 407, 409, 436, 438, 441, 443, 447, 462, 463, 476, 483, 499, 515, 516, 527, 559, 561, 572, 584, 589, 591, 600, 619, 621, 644, 652, 653, 677, 713, 724, 745 |
| propaganda, | 17, 25, 61, 254, 679 |
| point of view, | 10, 11, 23, 25, 35, 55, 56, 58, 59, 61, 67, 70, 78, 81, 83, 85, 91, 96, 99, 103, 109, 111, 120, 121, 125, 127, 131, 136, 141, 143, 145, 149, 150, 153, 154, 156, 158, 165, 166, 171, 173, 175, 182, 185, 186, 187, 201, 203, 205, 209, 214, 218, 219, 221, 229, 231, 233, 240, 246, 247, 249, 254, 255, 257, 274, 278, 281, 283, 285, 287, 291, 292, 305, 309, 315, 317, 322, 328, 338, 339, 340, 341, 347, 349, 355, 362, 363, 364, 372, 383, 385, 387, 391, 392, 397, 402, 404, 407, 409, 411, 422, 423, 429, 431, 438, 440, 441, 443, 447, 455, 457, 462, 463, 465, 470, 474, 476, 480, 483, 499, 501, 515, 516, 519, 527, 529, 535, 545, 549, 553, 558, 559, 561, 572, 576, 579, 583, 584, 589, 591, 599, 602, 607, 618, 619, 621, 644, 648, 649, 652, 653, 655, 662, 671, 675, 677, 679, 685, 693, 696, 700, 701, 703, 704, 705, 709, 713, 715, 724, 732, 742, 743, 745, 747 |
| and frame of reference; | 25, 35, 59, 71, 78, 83, 85, 91, 96, 103, 109, 120, 125, 136, 143, 150, 172, 173, 186, 203, 221, 231, 241, 247, 249, 255, 257, 285, 287, 292, 300, 302, 304, 305, 310, 315, 341, 347, 349, 363, 384, 385, 391, 395, 397, 401, 404, 409, 410, 411, 417, 440, 441, 443, 463, 465, 499, 501, 516, 527, 529, 544, 545, 558, 559, 561, 572, 584, 589, 591, 618, 619, 644, 652, 653, 671, 675, 677, 679, 693, 713, 724, 745 |
| (E) Evaluate government data using charts, | 6, 29, 68, 73, 75, 94, 128, 133, 140, 161, 179, 180, 191, 193, 205, 219, 269, 276, 299, 303, 308, 324, 335, 345, 359, 366, 391, 395, 417, 420, 461, 472, 507, 509, 514, 518, 520, 541, 578, 595, 614, 615, 719 |
| tables, | 15, 39, 45, 52, 57, 65, 76, 93, 96, 108, 124, 135, 165, 167, 197, 226, 227, 264, 272, 302, 312, 330, 331, 332, 357, 362, 374, 381, 406, 449, 432, 448, 460, 526, 536, 573, 600, 710, 720 |
| graphs, | 22, 134, 138, 142, 155, 162, 168, 182, 199, 212, 225, 244, 251, 277, 280, 295, 296, 300, 325, 333, 439, 449, 456, 473, 485, 497, 510, 571, 587, 588, 598, 609, 616, 637, 665, 670, 679, 708, 734, 741 |
| and maps, and | 31, 57, 100, 183, 251, 277, 280, 295, 296, 300, 325, 333, 487, 492, 697 |
| (F) Use appropriate mathematical skills to interpret social studies information such as maps and graphs. | 142, 162, 168, 287, 295, 448, 449, 493, 621, 679 |

**(22) Social Studies skills. The student communicates in written, oral, and visual forms. The student is expected to:**

| | |
|---|---|
| (A) Use social studies terminology correctly; | Examples: 287, 349, 501, 536 |
| (B) Use standard grammar, spelling, sentence structure, and punctuation; | 61, 85, 205, 287, 349, 443, 465 |
| (C) Transfer information from one medium to another, including written to visual and statistical to written or visual, using computer software as appropriate; and | 10, 16, 25, 58, 61, 82, 85, 111, 118, 124, 131, 145, 157, 172, 175, 194, 202, 205, 287, 317, 327, 346, 349, 367, 403, 408, 411, 418, 422, 443, 465, 489, 498, 501, 529, 558, 591, 621, 715, 732 |
| (D) Create written, oral, and visual presentations of social studies information. | 10, 16, 17, 25, 32, 58, 61, 82, 83, 85, 108, 109, 111, 118, 124, 131, 135, 142, 145, 150, 157, 163, 172, 175, 194, 202, 205, 221, 230, 233, 247, 254, 257, 273, 284, 287, 292, 300, 308, 317, 327, 346, 349, 358, 363, 367, 375, 376, 384, 387, 392, 398, 403, 408, 411, 418, 429, 435, 440, 443, 456, 465, 489, 498, 501, 515, 527, 529, 536, 554, 558, 559, 561, 568, 574, 575, 583, 589, 591, 599, 618, 619, 621, 632, 638, 643, 649, 652, 653, 655, 677, 679, 688, 693, 712, 713, 715, 723, 732, 737, 738, 744, 747 |

**(23) Social Studies skills. The student uses problem–solving and decision making skills, working independently and with others, in a variety of settings. The student is expected to:**

| | |
|---|---|
| (A) Use a problem–solving process to identify a problem, gather information, list and consider options, consider advantages and disadvantages, choose and implement a solution, and evaluate the effectiveness of the solution; and | 61, 104, 111, 172, 175, 186, 194, 257, 287, 375, 376, 384, 387, 435, 480, 529, 554, 599, 715, 732, 744 |
| (B) Use a decision–making process to identify a situation that requires a decision, gather information, identify options, predict consequences, and take action to implement a decision. | 61, 95, 104, 111, 135, 145, 172, 175, 186, 194, 230, 240, 293, 376, 387, 435, 440, 465, 529 |

PRENTICE HALL

2003

·MAGRUDER'S·

# AMERICAN GOVERNMENT

Revised by

## William A. McClenaghan

Department of Political Science
Oregon State University

PEARSON

Prentice
Hall

Needham, Massachusetts
Upper Saddle River, New Jersey
Glenview, Illinois

# Magruder's American Government,

first published in 1917 and revised annually, is an enduring symbol of the author's faith in American ideals and American institutions. The life of Frank Abbott Magruder (1882–1949) was an outstanding example of Americanism at its very best. His career as a teacher, author, and tireless worker in civic and religious undertakings remains an inspiring memory to all who knew him.

The Close Up Foundation is the nation's largest civic education organization. Since 1971, Close Up has been a leader in the social studies field, reaching millions of students, educators, and other adults. The Foundation's mission of informed participation in government and democracy drives its experiential civic education programs in Washington, D.C., for students and teachers, as well as its television programs on C-SPAN, and its award-winning publications and videos. Close Up's work represents a multidimensional approach to citizenship education by increasing community involvement and civic literacy—one student, one citizen, at a time.

## Program Consultants

### Special Texas Consultants

**Dr. Robert L. Lineberry**
University of Houston
Houston, Texas

**T.R. Fehrenbach**
Commissioner Emeritus,
Texas Historical Commission
San Antonio, Texas

**Chief Justice Richard Barajas**
8th Circuit Court of Appeals *and*
Cathedral High School
El Paso, Texas

### Constitution Consultant

**Dr. Christine L. Compston**
University of Massachusetts
Boston, Massachusetts

### Reading Consultant

**Dr. Bonnie Armbruster**
University of Illinois at Urbana-Champaign
Champaign, Illinois

### Curriculum and Assessment Specialist

**Jan Moberley**
Dallas, Texas

### Internet Consultant

**Dr. Larry Elowitz**
Professor of Political Science
Georgia College and State University
Milledgeville, Georgia

### Block Scheduling Consultant

**Gwen L. Patterson**
Marcus High School
Flower Mound, Texas

## Texas Program Consultant

Sharon Pope has devoted her career to advancing social studies education in the state of Texas. A graduate of Rice University, with a master's degree from the University of St. Thomas, Sharon taught in both Spring Branch and Cypress Fairbanks districts, was a social studies supervisor in Spring Branch ISD, and served as president of TSSSA. She has worked with the authors, as well as with the members of the Texas Advisory Board (listed on facing page), to ensure that this book meeets the needs of Texas educators.

PEARSON
Prentice
Hall

ISBN 0-13-063700-9
2 3 4 5 6 7 8 9 10  07 06 05 04 03

# Table of Contents

# UNIT 2

v ★★★★

vii ★★★

# Special Features

## CLOSE UP Features

## Close Up on the Supreme Court

**Background information and key arguments on landmark Supreme Court Cases**

## Close Up on Primary Sources

**Excerpted documents highlight key issues**

Franklin D.
Roosevelt

## *Spotlight* on Texas Government

**Background information on Texas government and politics**

## SKILLS FOR LIFE

**Step-by-step lessons to learn and practice important skills**

### Technology

### Citizenship

### Critical Thinking

### *Charts and Graphs*

## *Voices* on Government

**Opinions, views, and comments on the American political system**

*Kay Bailey Hutchison*

## Comparative Government

Charts and graphs that compare government around the world

## The *Living* Constitution

Time lines that show how the Constitution is a living document

## You Can Make a Difference

Examples of student activism and participation in government

## The *Living* Constitution

### Redefining Federalism | 1800 | 1850

The Framers of the Constitution sought to balance the rights of individual States and the powers of the new Federal Government. Their solution was a federal system, which divides powers between the two levels of government. Although the Constitution is the "supreme law of the land," questions about States' rights and national power have arisen throughout American history, as the Supreme Court cases on this time line show.

**1819**
In *McCulloch* v. *Maryland*, the Court rules that a State cannot tax the Federal Government.

**1824**
In *Gibbons* v. *Ogden*, the Court affirms the Federal Government's right to regulate interstate trade.

**1886**
In *Wabash, St. Louis & Pacific Railway Co.* v. *Illinois*, the Court rules that States cannot regulate railroad rates on the parts of interstate journeys that fall within their borders.

## Political Cartoons

# Maps, Graphs, Charts, Diagrams, Time Lines, and Tables

## Maps

## Graphs, Charts, Diagrams

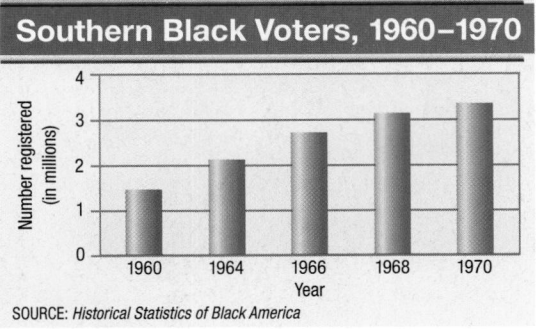

**Southern Black Voters, 1960–1970**

SOURCE: *Historical Statistics of Black America*

# The Six Basic Principles of the Constitution

*The Constitution of the United States is built on six basic principles of government. The Framers of the Constitution drew on their knowledge and experience to craft a document that serves as "the supreme law of the land." The descriptions at the beginning of each unit will help you see how these six principles—and the Constitution itself—have proved an enduring yet flexible guide for governing the nation for over 200 years.*

## Popular Sovereignty

The Preamble to the Constitution begins with this bold phrase: "We the people…" These words announce that in the United States, the people establish government and give it its power. The people are sovereign. Since the government receives its power from the people, it can govern only with their consent.

## Limited Government

Because the people are the source of government power, the government has only as much authority as the people give it. Much of the Constitution, in fact, consists of specific limitations on government power. Limited government means that neither the government itself nor any government official is "above the law" and can overstep these constitutional bounds.

## Separation of Powers

Government power is not only limited; it is also divided. The Constitution assigns specific powers to each of the three branches: the legislative (Congress), the executive (President), and the judicial (federal courts). This separation of powers is intended to prevent misuse of power by one branch of government.

## Checks and Balances

The system of checks and balances extends the restrictions established by the separation of powers. Each branch of government has the built-in authority and responsibility to restrain the power of the other two branches. This system is time-consuming, but also prevents tyranny by one branch of government.

## Judicial Review

Who decides whether an act of government oversteps the limits placed on it by the Constitution? Historically, the judges in the federal courts have made the decisions. The principle of judicial review was established early in the history of the nation. It means that federal courts have the power to review government acts and to nullify, or cancel, any that are unconstitutional, or violate a provision of the Constitution.

## Federalism

A federal system divides power between a central government and smaller, local governments. This sharing of power is intended to ensure that the central government is powerful enough to be effective, yet not so powerful as to overwhelm States or citizens. It also allows individual States to deal with local problems at the local level—so long as their actions are constitutional.

## What are the keys to social studies success?

In every social studies course, you will need to know how to use the following 20 core skills. Building these skills year by year will make you a stronger student.

Read through this list of skills and their definitions. Which ones do you know well? Which ones do you need to strengthen? Beside each definition, the page where you can find help in developing that skill is listed.

| Skill | Definition | Example |
|---|---|---|
| **GEOGRAPHIC LITERACY** | | |
| **1. Using the Cartographer's Tools** | The ability to use the <br>• compass rose to find directions and relative location. <br>• scale to estimate distance. <br>• latitude and longitude grid to determine exact location. <br>• key, or legend, to understand map symbols and colors. | p. 753–754 |
| **2. Using Special-Purpose Maps** | The ability to analyze and interpret maps of <br>• natural features, such as elevation and climate. <br>• features made by people, such as land use, roads, countries, population density, and battles. | p. 266 |
| **VISUAL ANALYZING** | | |
| **3. Analyzing Graphic Data** | The ability to read and interpret numeric information represented in <br>• bar graphs. <br>• line graphs. <br>• circle graphs. | p. 665 |
| **4. Analyzing Images** | The ability to identify and interpret symbols, tone, and message in <br>• paintings and drawings. <br>• photos. <br>• posters and political cartoons. | p. 185 |
| **CRITICAL THINKING AND READING** | | |
| **5. Identifying Main Ideas/ Summarizing** | Identifying the main idea is the ability to distinguish the general idea of a passage from its supporting details. <br>Summarizing is the ability to combine main ideas into an overview. | p. 104 |
| **6. Sequencing** | The ability to organize items in order according to time, size, or priority. | p. 398 |
| **7. Identifying Cause and Effect/ Making Predictions** | Identifying cause and effect is the ability to understand how an action or event leads to a result. <br>Making predictions is the ability to use cause-and-effect understanding to determine the likely outcome of subsequent events or actions. | p. 409 |

| Skill | Definition | Example |
|---|---|---|
| 8. Drawing Inferences and Conclusions | Drawing inferences is the ability to determine the necessary consequences of an assumption: if this is true, that must be true. Drawing conclusions is the ability to analyze several inferences to make a reasoned judgment. | p. 633 |
| 9. Making Valid Generalizations | The ability to apply conclusions from specific circumstances to larger circumstances while maintaining accuracy. | p. 523 |
| 10. Distinguishing Fact and Opinion | The ability to separate those statements that can be proven to be true from those that reflect a personal viewpoint. | p. 125 |
| 11. Comparing and Contrasting | The ability to identify how different ideas, objects, historical figures, or situations are alike and/or different. | p. 55 |
| 12. Analyzing Primary Sources | The ability to evaluate a firsthand account for accuracy, tone, viewpoint, and frame of reference. | p. 11 |
| 13. Recognizing Bias and Propaganda | The ability to identify a stated or unstated viewpoint or slant that is designed to promote one set of beliefs over another. | p. 17 |
| 14. Identifying Frame of Reference and Point of View | The ability to identify an opinion expressed in writing or visual art and to understand the influences that shaped the writer's or artist's position. | p. 341 |
| 15. Decision Making | The ability to state a question clearly, identify and evaluate possible choices, and select the option that seems to produce the best outcome. | p. 376 |
| 16. Problem Solving | The ability to state a problem clearly, identify possible solutions, determine the likely outcome of each, select an option, and then evaluate its effectiveness. | p. 104 |
| COMMUNICATIONS | | |
| 17. Using Reliable Information | The ability to locate and apply information for a variety of purposes that has been evaluated for its accuracy, age, authority, and bias. | p. 436 |
| 18. Transferring Information From One Medium to Another | The ability to translate numerical or visual information into text and to translate written information into graphs, tables, or diagrams. | p. 575 |
| 19. Synthesizing Information | The ability to analyze and combine information from several sources to draw conclusions and/or to create a new presentation of information. | p. 523 |
| 20. Supporting a Position | The ability to present evidence or reasoning that defends a given opinion or statement. | p. 527 |

# UNIT 1

## Foundations of American Government

### Introducing the Unit

Unit 1 introduces students to both the origins of American government and the government as it exists today. Chapter 1 analyzes the purposes and major forms of government and the concepts behind American democracy. Chapter 2 explores the origins of the American governmental system from its early development to the creation and adoption of the Constitution. Chapter 3 describes the six basic principles on which the Constitution is built and the formal and informal procedures for interpreting the Constitution. Chapter 4 shows the division of power between the National Government and the States, and how constitutional provisions encourage cooperation between and among the States.

### Focus Activity

Concentrate students' attention on the purpose of government by writing the following quotation on the board:

> "Why has government been instituted at all? Because the passions of men will not conform to the dictates of reason and justice, without constraint."
> —American statesman Alexander Hamilton (1787)

Have students consider the following after they have read the quotation.

◆ How does Hamilton view the role of the government?
◆ Do you agree with this statement? Why or why not?
◆ Use these questions as springboards to a general class discussion about students' views on the purposes for which government exists.

## IN THIS UNIT

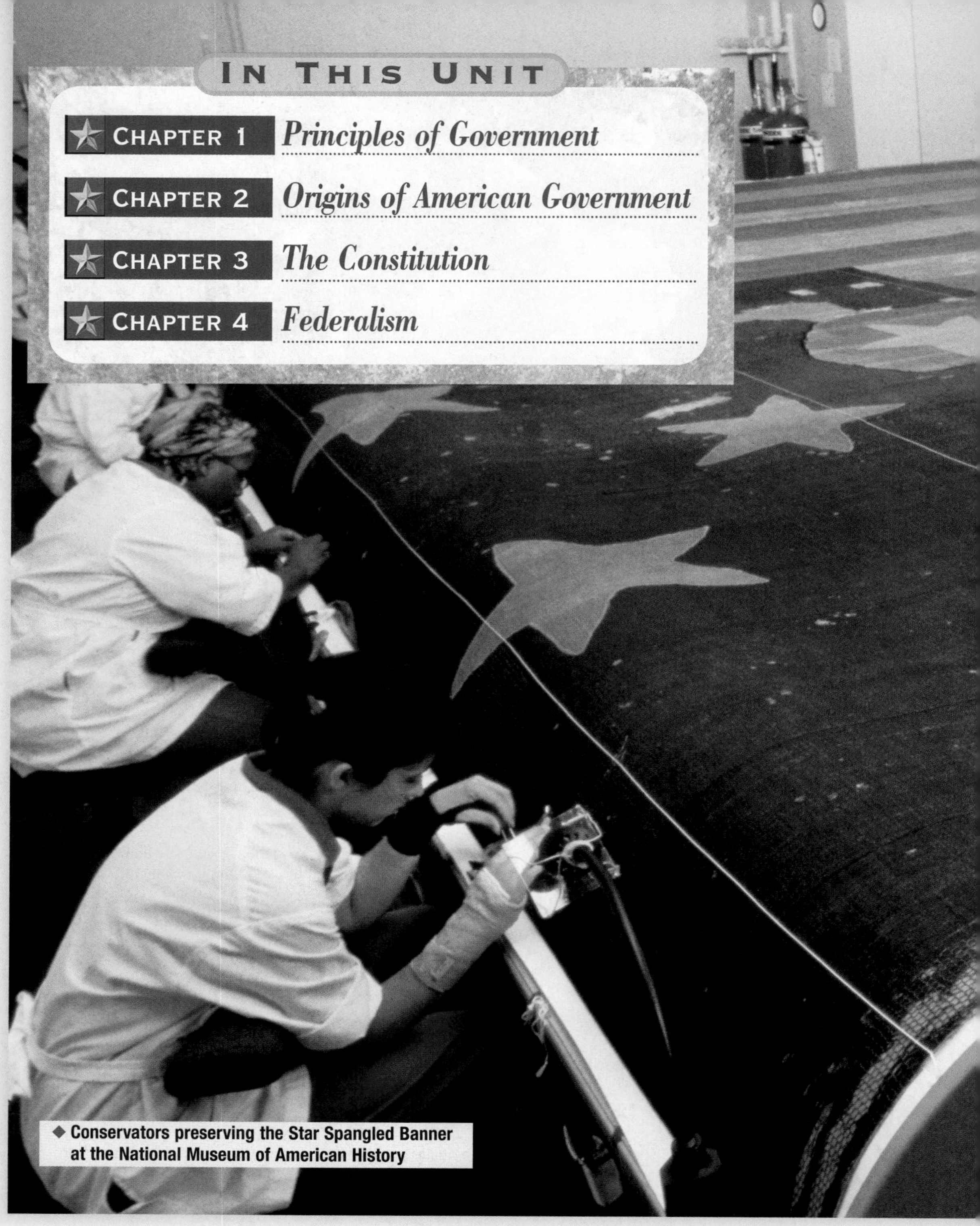

◆ **Conservators preserving the Star Spangled Banner at the National Museum of American History**

 *Corner*

The following Close Up features appear in this unit.
*Close Up on the Supreme Court* may be found on the following pages of this unit: 23, 59, 83, 109
*Close Up on Primary Sources* may be found on the following pages of this unit: 11, 33, 78, 96

To keep up-to-date on Close Up news and activities, visit Close Up Online at

**www.closeup.org**

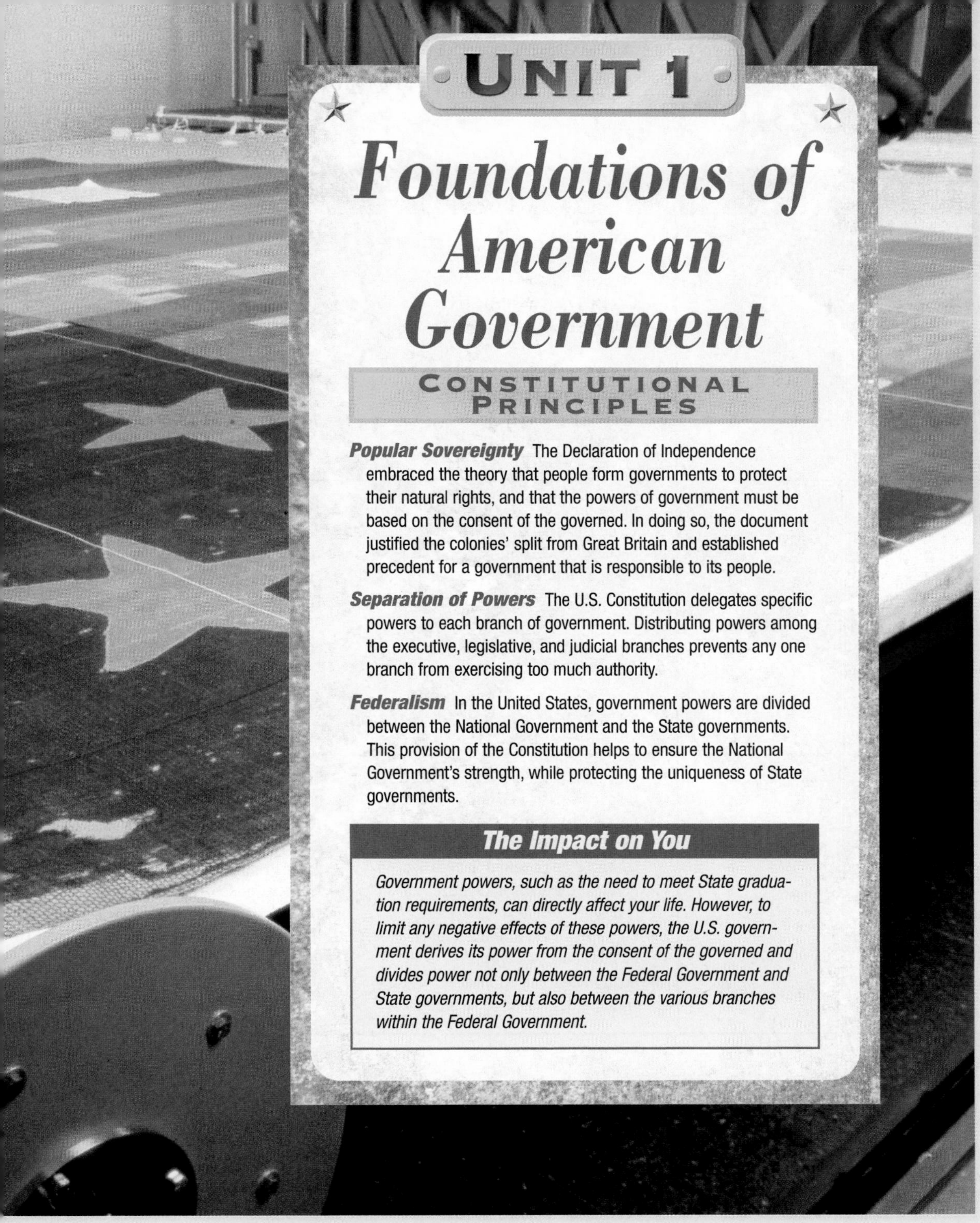

# UNIT 1

# *Foundations of American Government*

## CONSTITUTIONAL PRINCIPLES

***Popular Sovereignty*** The Declaration of Independence embraced the theory that people form governments to protect their natural rights, and that the powers of government must be based on the consent of the governed. In doing so, the document justified the colonies' split from Great Britain and established precedent for a government that is responsible to its people.

***Separation of Powers*** The U.S. Constitution delegates specific powers to each branch of government. Distributing powers among the executive, legislative, and judicial branches prevents any one branch from exercising too much authority.

***Federalism*** In the United States, government powers are divided between the National Government and the State governments. This provision of the Constitution helps to ensure the National Government's strength, while protecting the uniqueness of State governments.

### *The Impact on You*

*Government powers, such as the need to meet State graduation requirements, can directly affect your life. However, to limit any negative effects of these powers, the U.S. government derives its power from the consent of the governed and divides power not only between the Federal Government and State governments, but also between the various branches within the Federal Government.*

## Pressed for Time?

### Instruction Plus!

The resources you need to support your instruction of this chapter are conveniently located in a single box. This innovative package provides an instructional advantage in the classroom with its ready-to-use tools in a variety of formats.

- **Magruder's American Government Video Collection**
- **Keep It Current Web-based Activities Presentation Pro CD-ROM**
- **Section Support Transparencies**
- **Guide to the Essentials Current Issues**

## Spotlight on Technology

**Take it to the Net**
Offers student-appropriate Internet activities and links that extend core content. Visit us at the Social Studies area. **www.phschool.com**
Be sure to check out this month's **eTeach** online discussion with a Master Government Teacher.

**Keep It Current CD-ROM**
Includes government-related projects by unit. Use it to link to the Prentice Hall School Web site where you will find daily updates.

**Magruder's American Government Video Collection**
Chapter-by-chapter video selections bring key government concepts to life.

**ABC News Civics and Government Videotape Library**
These high-interest stories from ABC News relate to core content.

**Simulations and Data Graphing CD-ROM** Provides interactive federal budget and stock market simulations, and skills practice with statistical data.

**Prentice Hall Presentation Pro CD-ROM** Provides multimedia lecture notes for each chapter.

**ExamView® Test Bank CD-ROM**
Allows you to create, edit, and print out chapter level tests.

**Resource Pro® CD-ROM**
Teaching Resources that offer lesson planning flexibility, test-generation capability, and resource manageability.

**Social Studies Skills Tutor CD-ROM** Provides interactive practice in geographic literacy, critical thinking and reading, visual analysis, and communications.

**Section Support Transparencies**
Illustrates key government concepts through graphs, charts, photos, and cartoons.

**Basic Principles of the Constitution Transparencies**
Illustrates key principles of the Constitution.

**Section Reading Support Transparency System**
Delivers the main idea of each section in the student text through graphic organizers.

# Principles of Government

| Section Objectives | Print and Technology Resources | |
|---|---|---|
| **1 Government and the State** *(pp. 4–10)* <br><br> **1.** Define government and the basic powers every government holds. <br> **2.** Describe the defining characteristics of the state. <br> **3.** Explain major political ideas in history, such as the divine right of kings. <br> **4.** Evaluate how the Federal Government serves the purposes set forth in the Preamble to the Constitution. <br><br> TEKS 1A, 2A, 2D, 8B, 8C, 21A, 21D, 21E, 22A, 22B, 22C, 22D | • **Unit 1 booklet** <br> Guided Reading and Review, p. 2 <br> Section 1 Quiz, p. 3 <br> • **Lesson Plans booklet** Section 1, p. 12 <br> • **Political Cartoons booklet** Section 1, p. 4 <br> • **Block Scheduling with Lesson Strategies booklet** p. 19 <br> • **Section Reading Support Transparencies** | • **Close Up on Primary Sources booklet** John Locke and Thomas Jefferson, p. 3; *The Social Contract,* p. 54 <br> • **Close Up on Participation booklet** Protecting the Environment, pp. 10–11 <br> • **Government Assessment Rubrics booklet** p. 20 <br> • **Section Support Transparencies** 7, 106 <br> • **Presentation Pro CD-ROM** Section 1 |
| **2 Forms of Government** *(pp. 12–16)* <br><br> **1.** Identify the characteristics of classic forms of government. <br> **2.** Define systems of government based on who can participate. <br> **3.** Analyze advantages and disadvantages of federal, confederate, and unitary systems of government. <br> **4.** Analyze advantages and disadvantages of presidential and parliamentary systems. <br><br> TEKS 1B, 2D, 13A, 13B, 13C, 21A, 21D, 21E, 22A, 22B, 22C, 22D | • **Unit 1 booklet** <br> Guided Reading and Review, p. 4 <br> Section 2 Quiz, p. 5 <br> • **Lesson Plans booklet** Section 2, p. 13 <br> • **Political Cartoons booklet** Section 2, p. 5 <br> • **Section Reading Support Transparencies** | • **The Living Constitution booklet** p. 8 <br> • **Section Support Transparencies** 8, 107 <br> • **Presentation Pro CD-ROM** Section 2 <br> • **Simulations and Data Graphing CD-ROM** <br> • **Social Studies Skills Tutor CD-ROM** |
| **3 Basic Concepts of Democracy** *(pp. 18–22)* <br><br> **1.** Evaluate whether and/or when the obligation of citizenship requires that personal interests be subordinated to the public good. <br> **2.** Analyze the connections between democracy and the free enterprise system. <br> **3.** Analyze the potential impact of the Internet on democracy. <br><br> TEKS 6A, 6C, 8F, 20A, 20B, 21A, 21E, 21F, 22A, 22B, 22C, 22D | • **Unit 1 booklet** <br> Guided Reading and Review, p. 6 <br> Section 3 Quiz, p. 7 <br> Skills for Life Activity, p. 8 <br> • **Lesson Plans booklet** Section 3, p. 14 <br> • **Political Cartoons booklet** Section 3, p. 6 <br> • **Close Up on the Supreme Court booklet** *Baker* v. *Carr,* p. 2 <br> • **Section Reading Support Transparencies** | • **Simulations and Debates booklet** pp. 46–47 <br> • **The Basic Principles of the Constitution Posters** <br> • **Basic Principles of the Constitution Transparencies** 9 <br> • **Section Support Transparencies** 9, 108 <br> • **Presentation Pro CD-ROM** Section 3 |

# Block Scheduling Strategies

The *Magruder's American Government* program addresses block-scheduling strategies in a variety of ways. For easy reference, side-column activities that fit a block format are marked  **Block Strategy.** Each section also contains a **Block Scheduling Strategies** box describing at least two block-format activities that address and extend core content from the section. The **Block Scheduling with Lesson Strategies booklet** found in the Teaching Resources contains additional block-scheduling activities for each chapter.

## Take It to the Net

Visit the Social Studies area at the Prentice Hall School Web site. Once there, you can find additional links, current events connections, and activities to enrich chapter content for *Magruder's American Government,* as well as a Self-Test for students. Be sure to check out this month's **eTeach** online discussion with a Master Teacher.

### www.phschool.com

## Pressed for Time?

If you are running short on time to cover this chapter, consider one of the following options:
- Use the **Presentation Pro CD-ROM** to create an outline for this chapter.
- Use one of the **Pressed for Time** activities found on p. 3.
- Use the Section Summaries for Chapter 1, from **Guide to the Essentials of American Government (English and Spanish).**

## Video Connections

Prentice Hall offers two video programs to reinforce and extend chapter content. Show students *The Blessings of Liberty* from the **ABC News Civics and Government Videotape Library** and *Prayer in Schools: A Nationwide Debate* from the **Magruder's American Government Video Collection.**

## Assessment Options
- Section Quizzes, **Unit 1 booklet,** pp. 3, 5, 7
- Chapter 1 Assessment, pp. 24–25
- **Guide to the Essentials of American Government,** Chapter 1 Test, p. 17

PRENTICE HALL
ASSESSMENT
SYSTEM

### Core Assessment
Chapter 1, Chapter Tests booklet
ExamView® Test Bank CD-ROM Chapter 1
Government Assessment Rubrics

### Standardized Test Preparation
#### Diagnose and Prescribe
Diagnostic Tests for High School
Social Studies Skills
#### Review and Reteach
Review Book for Government
#### Practice and Assess
Test-Taking Strategies With
   Transparencies for High School
Test Prep Book for Government

# Chapter 1 Teacher's Edition Index

# CHAPTER 1

## Principles of Government

### Introducing the Chapter

In this chapter, students will learn about the different forms of government, how governments came about and what they do, and how government functions in the United States.

### Make It Relevant

**You Can Make a Difference**

Discuss with students Danny Seo's statement that teenagers working together "can change the world." Guide the class in brainstorming a list of possible school-year-long projects that attempt to do just that. Encourage students to identify projects that go beyond the school and improve the community, are feasible, and raise public awareness about an important issue. Choose a project from the list by majority vote, and organize groups of students to tackle individual tasks.

**Service Learning**

### CONSTITUTIONAL PRINCIPLES

Emphasize the following basic principles as students read Chapter 1. Have the class respond to the questions, and then ask volunteers to explain which they consider the most important principle of government.

**Popular Sovereignty** How can democracies and dictatorships be described as opposites in terms of popular sovereignty?

**Separation of Powers** Why can a parliamentary government never achieve the separation of powers that a presidential government can?

**Federalism** In what ways is the American Constitution set above both levels of government?

CHAPTER 1

# Principles of Government

*"The way of democracy is both frustrating and invigorating. It lacks the orderly directives of dictatorship, and instead relies on millions to demonstrate self-discipline and enlightened concern for the common good."*

—Nancy Landon Kassebaum (1996)

Governments hold power in every society, but they exercise that power in different ways. Governments have various structures and forms, from dictatorships to democracies. American democracy rests on such basic concepts as individual rights and majority rule.

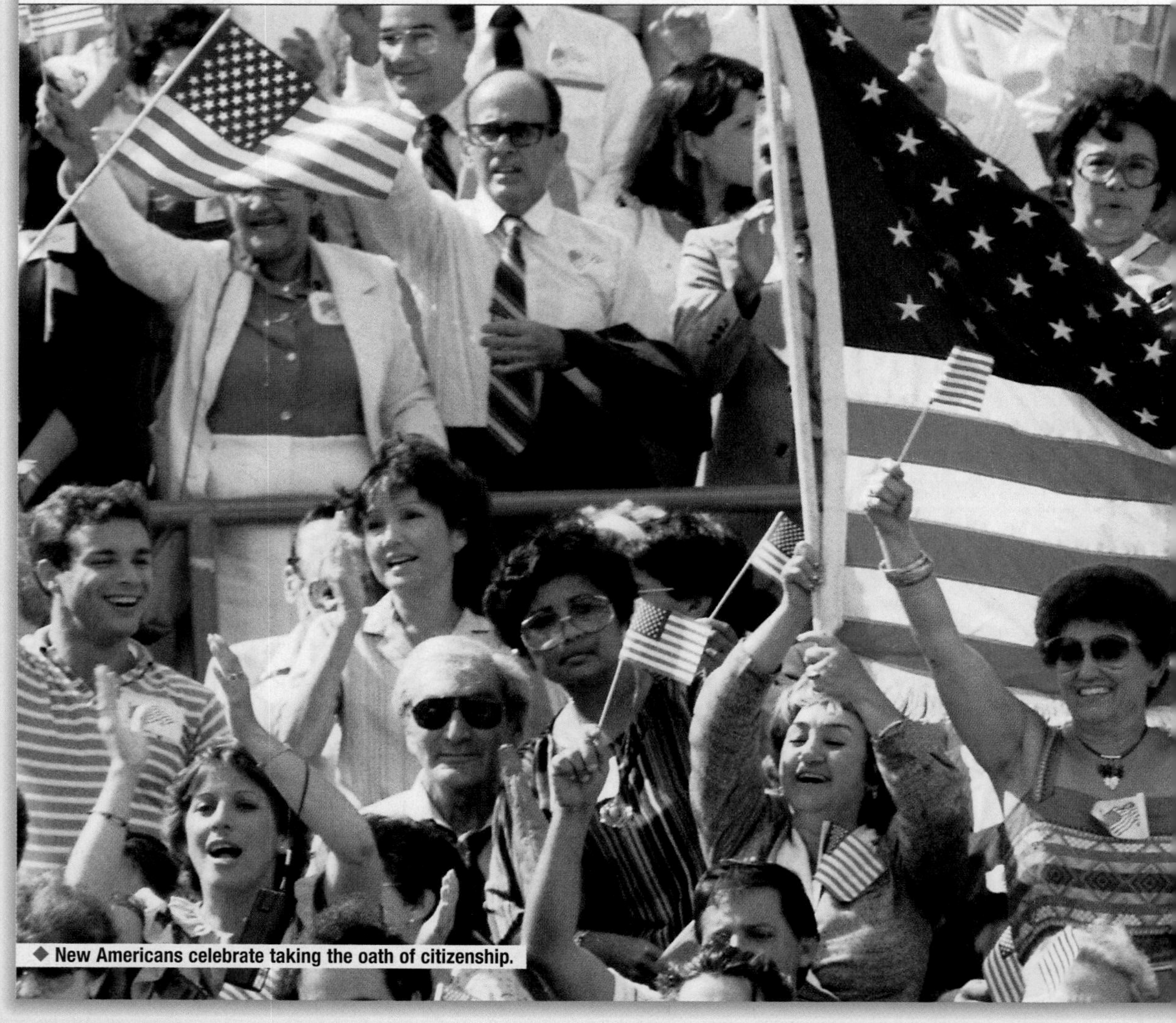

◆ New Americans celebrate taking the oath of citizenship.

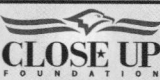

### CLOSE UP FOUNDATION Corner

The following resources are available only from the Close Up Foundation to support the concepts discussed in Chapter 1 "Principles of Government":

- *The Bill of Rights: A User's Guide*
- *Perspectives: Readings on Contemporary American Government*
- *Active Citizenship Today Field Guide for Students*

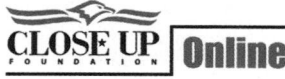

**CLOSE UP FOUNDATION Online**

To keep up-to-date on Close Up news and activities, visit Close Up Online at

**www.closeup.org**

Close Up Foundation
44 Canal Center Plaza
Alexandria, VA 22314-1592
800-765-3131

## ★ You Can Make a Difference

**AS SENATOR KASSEBAUM** knew, democracy relies on all of its citizens. Activists of any age can work for causes they believe in. Danny Seo, once called the "Green Teen," says, "If all of us start taking action, we can change the world." Danny first took up a cause—animal rights and the environment—on Earth Day 1989, his twelfth birthday. With other kids in Shillington, Pennsylvania, he started Earth 2000. In a few years, the grassroots group became a national movement. Danny has won many awards for his activism. He wrote a guide for young activists and became a popular advocate for an eco-friendly lifestyle.

### Keep It Current

Items marked with this logo are periodically updated on the Internet. Keep up-to-date with what's in the news. To get current information on forms of government, go to **www.phschool.com**

### SECTION 1

## Government and the State (pp. 4–10)

★ Government enables a society to protect the peace and carry out its policies.
★ A state, not to be confused with one of the fifty States of the United States, is a land with people, a defined territory, and a sovereign government.
★ Several theories attempt to explain the origin of the state.
★ Among these theories, the political philosophy of John Locke had the most profound impact on the Declaration of Independence and the United States Constitution.
★ The goals of the Federal Government are described in the Preamble to the Constitution.

### SECTION 2

## Forms of Government (pp. 12–16)

★ Each government is unique, but governments can be grouped into categories according to three sets of characteristics.
★ Democratic governments rely on the participation of the people, while dictatorships concentrate power in the hands of a few.
★ The distribution of power between local governments and a central government determines whether a government is unitary, federal, or confederate.
★ Presidential governments divide power among several branches of government, while parliamentary governments focus power in one dominant branch.

### SECTION 3

## Basic Concepts of Democracy (pp. 18–22)

★ Democracy is built upon five principles: respect for the individual, equality of all persons, acceptance of majority rule and minority rights, compromise, and protection of individual freedoms.
★ The free enterprise system of the United States, like democracy, relies on individual freedoms.
★ In a mixed economy, the government plays a role in the economy.
★ The Internet has opened up new opportunities for democracy, but users must carefully evaluate the information that they find.

## Pressed for Time?

### To Omit the Chapter
If you wish to skip Chapter 1, ask students to read the Chapter in Brief and assign the Guide to the Essentials before continuing to another chapter. You may also want to assign the Chapter 1 Test in the Chapter Test booklet. Then specific portions of Chapter 1 may be assigned to students needing reinforcement of key terms and concepts.

### To Preview the Chapter
To introduce students to key terms and concepts in each section, have them read the Chapter in Brief. You may also assign the Reading Strategy activities on pp. 5, 13, and 19 of this book.

### To Review the Chapter
When students have completed Chapter 1, you might want to assign the Guide to the Essentials or the Guided Reading and Review worksheets on pp. 2, 4, and 6 of the Unit 1 booklet.

### To Cover the Chapter Quickly
To cover the material in Chapter 1 quickly, use the following activity.

**Focus** Begin by having students list any kinds of government that they can think of. You might prompt them by suggesting countries that have the type of government students are having trouble remembering. List all types on the board.

**Instruct** Work with students to define and describe each type of government listed, and provide more examples. Assign small groups a type, and have them develop, on a large piece of paper or poster board, a graphic organizer describing it. Post the organizers around the class as a study guide.

**Close/Reteach** Turn the discussion to democracy, and elicit ideas from students for how democracy functions in the United States. Then contrast democracy in the United States with that in other countries.

■ **Block Strategy (Average)**

## Keep It Current

## Internet Update

Use the Prentice Hall School Web site and the Keep It Current CD-ROM to find quick content updates.

Visit **www.phschool.com** for current events articles that are linked to Chapter 1. Critical thinking questions are included.

**Keep It Current CD-ROM** includes government-related projects by unit. Students complete each project using current information that they obtain by linking to the Prentice Hall School Web site from the CD-ROM.

**1** ***Government and the State***

### Section Preview

#### OBJECTIVES

1. **Define** government and the basic powers every government holds.
2. **Describe** the four defining characteristics of the state.
3. **Explain** major political ideas in history such as the divine right of kings.
4. **Evaluate** how the Federal Government serves the purposes set forth in the Preamble to the Constitution.

#### WHY IT MATTERS

Government is essential to the existence of human beings in a civilized society. What any particular government is like and what that government does have an extraordinary impact on the lives of all people who live within its reach.

#### POLITICAL DICTIONARY

★ **government**
★ **public policy**
★ **legislative power**
★ **executive power**
★ **judicial power**
★ **constitution**
★ **dictatorship**
★ **democracy**
★ **state**
★ **sovereign**

Today, the United States is at war. That war—the war against terrorism—is a new and a different kind of war, against a new and a different kind of enemy. The conflict began with sudden and shocking violence on September 11, 2001, when terrorists hijacked four airliners. They crashed two of them into the twin towers of the World Trade Center in New York City and another into the Pentagon. The heroic actions of the passengers on the fourth plane forced it to crash in western Pennsylvania, short of its intended target, which was probably in Washington D.C. The government, acting with the full support of the American people, began to respond to that monstrous assault immediately. President Bush vowed that the nation will "answer these attacks and rid the world of [the] evil" of terrorism. Congress quickly authorized the President to use "all necessary and appropriate force" against those who brought on this war.

Government in this country is now focused on the fight against terrorism at home and abroad. Still, government has many other tasks to perform. It punishes criminals, protects civil rights, and regulates trade. Although Americans disagree on government's role in providing services, today's government also provides for education, guards the public's health, cares for the elderly, and does much, much more.

## What Is Government?

**Government** is the institution through which a society makes and enforces its public policies. Government is made up of those people who exercise its powers, those who have authority and control over a country's people.

The **public policies** of a government are, in short, all of those things a government decides to do. Public policies cover matters ranging from taxation, defense, education, crime, and health care to transportation, the environment, civil rights, and working conditions. The list of public policy issues is nearly endless.

Governments must have power in order to make and carry out public policies. Power is the ability to command or prevent action, the ability to achieve a desired end.

Every government has and exercises three basic kinds of power: (1) **legislative power**—the power to make law and to frame public policies; (2) **executive power**—the power to execute, enforce, and administer law; and (3) **judicial power**—the power to interpret laws, to determine their meaning, and to settle disputes that arise within the society. These powers of government are often outlined in a country's constitution. A **constitution** is the body of fundamental laws setting out the principles, structures, and processes of a government.

The ultimate responsibility for the exercise of these powers may be held by a single person or by a small group, as in a **dictatorship.** In this form of government, those who rule cannot be held responsible to the will of the people. When the responsibility for the exercise of these powers rests with a majority of the people, that form of government is known as a **democracy.** In a democracy, supreme authority rests with the people.

Government is among the oldest of all human inventions. Its origins are lost in the mists of time. But, clearly, government first appeared when human beings realized that they could not survive without some way to regulate both their own and their neighbors' behavior.

The earliest known evidences of government date from ancient Egypt. More than 2,300 years ago, the Greek philosopher Aristotle observed that "man is by nature a political animal."[1] As he wrote those words, Aristotle was only recording a fact that, even then, had been obvious for thousands of years.

What did Aristotle mean by "political"? That is to say, what is "politics"? Although people often equate the two, politics and government are very different things. Politics is a process, while government is an institution.

More specifically, politics is the process by which a society decides how power and resources will be distributed within that society. Politics enables a society to decide who will reap the benefits, and who will pay the costs, of its public policies.

The word *politics* is sometimes used in a way that suggests that it is immoral or something to be avoided. But, again, politics is a *process,* the means by which government is conducted. It is neither "good" nor "bad," but it is necessary. Indeed, it is impossible to conceive of government without politics.

## The State

Over the course of human history, the state has emerged as the dominant political unit in the world. The **state** can be defined as a body of people, living in a defined territory, organized politically (that is, with a government), and with the power to make and enforce law without the consent of any higher authority.

▲ ***Patriotism in a Time of Crisis*** Americans showed their pride in their country and support for their government in the wake of the terrorist attacks on the World Trade Center and the Pentagon.

There are more than 190 states in the world today. They vary greatly in size, military power, natural resources, and economic importance. Still, each of them possesses all four characteristics of a state: population, territory, sovereignty, and government.

Note that the state is a legal entity. In popular usage, a state is often called a "nation" or a "country." In a strict sense, however, the word *nation* is an ethnic term, referring to races or other large groups of people. The word *country* is a geographic term, referring to a particular place, region, or area of land.

### Population

Clearly, a state must have people—a population. The size of that population, however, has nothing directly to do with the existence of a state. One of the world's smallest states, in population terms, is San Marino. Bounded on all sides by Italy, it has only some 25,000

---

[1]In most of the world's written political record, the words *man* and *men* have been widely used to refer to all of humankind. This text follows that form when presenting excerpts from historical writings or documents and in references to them.

## The Four Characteristics of the State

| Population | Territory | Sovereignty | Government |
| --- | --- | --- | --- |
|  | 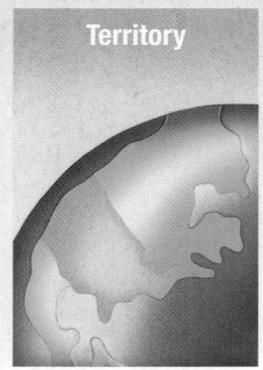 |  |  |

*Interpreting Charts* To be considered a state, a group of people must have a defined body of land and an independent, sovereign government. ***Does your school qualify as a state? If not, which requirements does it lack?***

people. The People's Republic of China is the world's most populous state with more than 1.25 *billion* people—just about one fifth of the world's population. The more than 285 million who live in the United States make it the world's third most populous, after China and India.

The people who make up a state may or may not be *homogeneous*. The adjective homogeneous describes members of a group who share customs, a common language, and ethnic background. Today, the population of the United States includes people from a wide variety of backgrounds. Still, most Americans think of themselves as exactly that: Americans.

### Territory
Just as a state cannot exist without people, so it must have land—territory, with known and recognized boundaries. The states in today's world vary as widely in terms of territory as they do in population. Here, too, San Marino ranks as one of the world's smallest states. It covers less than 24 square miles—smaller than thousands of cities and towns in the United States.[2]

Russia, the world's largest state, stretches across some 6.6 million square miles. The total area of the United States is 3,787,425 square miles.

### Sovereignty
Every state is **sovereign**—it has supreme and absolute power within its own territory and can decide its own foreign and domestic policies. It is neither subordinate nor responsible to any other authority.

Thus, as a sovereign state, the United States can determine its form of government. Like any other state in the world, it can frame its economic system and shape its own foreign policies. Sovereignty is the one characteristic that distinguishes the state from all other, lesser political units.

The States within the United States are not sovereign and so are not states in the international, legal sense. Each State is subordinate to the Constitution of the United States.[3]

### Government
Every state is politically organized. That is, every state has a government. Recall, a government is the institution through which society makes and

---

[2]The United States also recognizes the State of Vatican City, with a permanent population of some 850 persons and a roughly triangular area of only 109 acres. The Vatican is wholly surrounded by the City of Rome. American recognition of the Vatican, which had been withdrawn in 1867, was renewed in 1984.

[3]In this book, state printed with a small "s" denotes a state in the family of nations, such as the United States, Great Britain, and Mexico. State printed with a capital "S" refers to a State in the American union.

enforces its public policies. A government is the agency through which the state exerts its will and works to accomplish its goals. Government includes the machinery and the personnel by which the state is ruled.

Natural law is the law that would govern humans living in a state of nature, if government or laws imposed by humans did not exist. Natural law includes standards of justice that transcend laws made by humans. Some thinkers argue that any human-made law that conflicts with the universal justice of natural law is not really a law. Others argue that government is necessary to avoid what the English philosopher Thomas Hobbes (1588–1679) called "the war of every man against every man." Without government, said Hobbes, there would be "continual fear and danger of violent death and life [would be] solitary, poor, nasty, brutish, and short."

## Major Political Ideas

For centuries, historians, philosophers, and others have pondered the question of the origin of the state. Over time, many different answers have been offered, but history provides no conclusive evidence to support any of them. However, four theories have emerged as the most widely accepted explanations for the origin of the state.

*The Force Theory* Many scholars have long believed that the state was born of force. They hold that one person or a small group claimed control over an area and forced all within it to submit to that person's or group's rule. When that rule was established, all the basic elements of the state—population, territory, sovereignty, and government—were present.

*The Evolutionary Theory* Others claim that the state developed naturally out of the early family. They hold that the primitive family, of which one person was the head and thus the "government," was the first stage in political development. Over countless years the original family became a network of related families, a clan. In time the clan became a tribe. When the tribe first gave up its nomadic ways and first tied itself to the land, the state was born.

*The Divine Right Theory* The theory of divine right was widely accepted in much of the Western world from the fifteenth through the eighteenth centuries. It held that God created the state and had given those of royal birth a "divine right" to rule. The people were bound to obey their ruler as they would God; opposition to "the divine right of kings" was both treason and mortal sin. During the seventeenth century, philosophers began to question this theory. Much of the thought upon which present-day democracies rest began as a challenge to the theory of divine right.

### Background Note
#### Global Awareness
The ancient Chinese felt that a single ruler should govern all of humanity with a universal code of principles. The Chinese emperor, called the "Son of Heaven," was believed by the Chinese people to be able to communicate with both Heaven and Earth. The emperor ruled through a complex bureaucracy of educated professionals. But although the government was based on a "mandate of heaven," if the emperor's rule was found to be unjust, the people were justified in rebelling against him. It was believed, too, that Heaven could show its displeasure by sending famine and other natural disasters.

### Point-of-Use Resources

📁 **Close Up on Primary Sources**
Jean-Jacques Rousseau, *The Social Contract* (1762), p. 54

Force

Evolutionary

Divine Right

Social Contract

◀ Different explanations have been offered for the origin of the state. Pharoah Akhenaton of Egypt (middle) believed that power flowed from Aton, the god of the sun disk. *Critical Thinking Can more than one of these theories accurately explain the origin of the state? Explain why or why not.*

## Preparing for Standardized Tests

Have students read the passages under *Origins of the State* on pp. 7–8 and then answer the question below.

Which two theories might be used to explain the origins of Japan, which has an emperor typically chosen from the same familial lines?

**A** the force theory and the divine right theory

**B** the evolutionary theory and the force theory

**C** the social contract theory and the divine right theory

**D** the evolutionary theory and the divine right theory

*Answer to . . .*
**Critical Thinking** Answers will vary. Students may suggest that as each of the four theories is widely accepted and equally plausible, any one of them could explain the origin of the state; however, the origin can never be known with complete "accuracy."

## Extended Class Periods

**Time** 90 minutes.
**Purpose** To carry out a panel discussion about the origin of the state.
**Grouping** Four groups.
**Activity** Assign each group one of the different theories of the origin of the state. Each group should develop arguments that favor their theory over others. Groups will designate two members as "experts" in the field to present the group's case.
**Roles** Discussion leader, recorder, experts.
**Close** Hold a panel discussion in which "experts" make their case as to why their theory is the best explanation for the origin of the state. Allow other students to ask questions of the panel members.

■ **Block Strategy**
**(Average)**

## Point-of-Use Resources

🗀 **Government Assessment Rubrics** Cooperative Learning Project: Process, p. 20

🗀 **Block Scheduling with Lesson Strategies** Additional activities for Chapter 1 appear on p. 19.

The notion of divine right was not unique to European history. The rulers of many ancient civilizations, including the Chinese, Egyptian, Aztec, and Mayan civilizations, were held to be gods or to have been chosen by the gods. The Japanese emperor, the *mikado,* governed by divine right until 1945.

*The Social Contract Theory* In terms of the American political system, the most significant of the theories of the origin of the state is that of the "social contract." Philosophers such as Thomas Hobbes, James Harrington (1611–1677), and John Locke (1632–1704) in England and Jean Jacques Rousseau (1712–1778) in France developed this theory in the seventeenth and eighteenth centuries.

Hobbes wrote that in earliest history humans lived in a state of unbridled freedom, in which no government existed and no person was subject to any superior power. That which people could take by force belonged to them. All people were similarly free in this state of nature. No authority existed to protect one person from the aggression of another. Thus, individuals were only as safe as their own physical strength and intelligence could make them.

Human beings overcame their unpleasant condition, says the social contract theory, by agreeing with one another to create a state. By contract, people within a given area agreed to give up to the state as much power as was needed to promote the safety and well-being of all. In the contract (that is, through a constitution), the members of the state created a government to exercise the powers they had voluntarily given to the state.

In short, the social contract theory argues that the state arose out of a voluntary act of free people. It holds that the state exists only to serve the will of the people, that they are the sole source of political power, and that they are free to give or to withhold that power as they choose. The great concepts that this theory promoted—popular sovereignty, limited government, and individual rights—were immensely important to the shaping of the American governmental system.

The Declaration of Independence (see pages 40–43) justified revolution through the social contract theory, arguing that King George III and his ministers had violated the contract. Thomas Jefferson called the document "pure Locke."

## The Purpose of Government

What does government do? You can find a very meaningful answer to that question in the Preamble to the United States Constitution. The American system of government was created to serve the purposes set out there.

FROM THE
*Constitution* ❝We the People of the United States, in Order to form a more perfect Union, establish Justice, insure domestic Tranquility, provide for the common defence, promote the general Welfare, and secure the Blessings of Liberty to ourselves and our Posterity, do ordain and establish this Constitution for the United States of America.❞
—Preamble to the Constitution

Reproduced by permission of Johnny Hart and Field Enterprises

*Interpreting Political Cartoons* American government was influenced strongly by the social contract theory. **How does this cartoon poke fun at that theory?**

*Answer to . . .*

**Interpreting Political Cartoons** By implying that government does not improve conditions, but makes them worse.

## Form a More Perfect Union

The United States, which had just won its independence from Great Britain, faced an altogether uncertain future in the postwar 1780s. In 1781, the Articles of Confederation, the nation's first constitution, created "a firm league of friendship" among the 13 States. That league soon proved to be neither firm nor friendly. The government that the Articles established was powerless to overcome the intense rivalries and jealousies among the States that marked the time.

The Constitution of today was written in 1787. The original States adopted it in order to link them, and the American people, more closely together. That Constitution was built in the belief that in union there is strength.

## Establish Justice

To provide justice, said Thomas Jefferson, is "the most sacred of the duties of government." No purpose, no goal of public policy, can be of greater importance in a democracy.

But what, precisely, is justice? The term is difficult to define, for justice is a concept—an idea, an invention of the human mind. Like other concepts such as truth, liberty, and fairness, justice means what people make it mean.

As the concept of justice has developed over time in American thought and practice, it has come to mean this: The law, in both its content and its administration, must be reasonable, fair, and impartial. Those standards of justice have not always been met in this country. We have not attained our professed goal of "equal justice for all." However, this, too, must be said: The history of this country can be told largely in terms of our continuing attempts to reach that goal.

"Injustice anywhere," said Martin Luther King, Jr., "is a threat to justice everywhere." You will encounter this idea again and again in this book.

## Insure Domestic Tranquility

Order is essential to the well-being of any society, and keeping the peace at home has always been a prime function of government. Most people can only imagine what it would be like to live in a state of anarchy—without government, law, or order. In fact, people do live that way in some parts of the world today. For

years now, Somalia, which is located on the eastern tip of Africa, has not had a functioning government; rival warlords control different parts of the country.

In *The Federalist* No. 51, James Madison observed: "If men were angels, no government would be necessary." Madison, who was perhaps the most thoughtful of the Framers of the Constitution, knew that most human beings fall far short of this standard.

## Provide for the Common Defense

Defending the nation against foreign enemies has always been one of government's major responsibilities. You can see its importance in the fact that defense is mentioned far more often in the Constitution than any of the other functions of the government. The nation's defense and its foreign policies are but two sides of the same coin: the security of the United States.

---

## Voices on Government

Barbara Jordan was the first African American woman ever elected to the Texas legislature. She went on to represent her State in the U.S. House of Representatives (1973–1979). Famous for her eloquent speeches, Barbara Jordan often seemed to serve as the conscience of the government. In her keynote speech at the 1976 Democratic National Convention, she noted:

❝ *A nation is formed by the willingness of each of us to share in the responsibility for upholding the common good.*
*A government is invigorated when each of us is willing to participate in shaping the future of this nation. . . .*
*Let each person do his or her part. If one citizen is unwilling to participate, all of us are going to suffer. For the American idea, though it is shared by all of us, is realized in each one of us.* ❞

### Evaluating the Quotation

*How do Jordan's expectations for Americans relate to the basic ideas that underlie our democracy?*

---

### ACTIVITY

## Heterogeneous Groups

**Enrichment** Divide the class into small groups. Assign each group one of the five government functions documented in the Constitution (and also in this section). Using newspapers, magazines, and various art supplies, ask groups to create a collage that illustrates how government carries out each particular function on a daily basis. Allow students to use both current and historical examples as they depict the government's ability to fulfill the obligations established in the Preamble to the Constitution. **(Basic)**

### Background Note

#### Economics

A portion of each year's federal budget is allocated to federal departments that seek in some way to promote "the general welfare." For example, in 2001, the Department of Education had a budget of about $42 billion to spend in areas of education not covered by State and local funds. The Environmental Protection Agency requested $7.3 billion in its fiscal year 2002 budget to restore and preserve the quality of the environment. The Food and Drug Administration, which tests various foods and medicines to ensure their safety for public use, asked for $1.4 billion when submitting their budget request for fiscal year 2002.

### Point-of-Use Resources

**Close Up on Participation** Protecting the Environment, pp. 10–11, uses the topic of environmental awareness to help students plan and carry out service learning projects.

---

## Spotlight on Technology

### Magruder's American Government Video Collection

The Magruder's Video Collection explores key issues and debates in American government. Each segment examines an issue central to chapter content through use of historical and contemporary footage. Commentary from civic leaders in academics, government, and the media follow each segment. Critical-thinking questions focus students' attention on key issues, and may be used to stimulate discussion.

Use the Chapter 1 video segment to explore the roots of American constitutional government. (time: about 5 minutes) This segment examines the ideas of the Enlightenment thinkers from whom the Framers drew inspiration. It concludes with an examination of the Iroquois League, whose system of government in part parallels that of the American States.

### *Answer to . . .*

**Evaluating the Quotation** Democracy is most effective when individuals work together for the common good; Jordan encourages Americans to participate in government and uphold the common good.

## Point-of-Use Resources

**Guide to the Essentials** Chapter 1, Section 1, p. 14 provides support for students who need additional review of section content. Spanish support is available in the Spanish edition of the Guide on p. 7.

**Quiz** Unit 1 booklet, p. 3 includes matching and multiple-choice questions to check students' understanding of Section 1 content.

**Presentation Pro CD-ROM** Quizzes and multiple-choice questions check students' understanding of Section 1 content.

## Answers to . . .

### Section 1 Assessment

**1.** A state is a body of people living in a defined territory with a government and the power to make laws without the consent of a higher authority; a government is the institution through which states make and enforce their policies.
**2.** Dictatorships are ruled by a single person or a small group of people.
**3.** Constitutions set out the principles, structures, and processes of governments.
**4.** Examples include interpreting laws, determining the meanings of laws, and settling societal disputes.
**5.** Answers should demonstrate an understanding of the tension between the need for order and the need to follow natural law. Students might also point out that when those in power overstep their bounds and violate natural law, it is the responsibility of the governed to rise up and defend those standards of justice.
**6.** Possible answers: They believed in the divine right theory; they did not believe the people were capable of governing themselves; no other method of government was widely known or practiced; control over the military was necessary for maintaining control over the people.
**7.** The Preamble says that the people agreed to join together to create a state with a constitution.

The United States has become the world's most powerful nation, but the world remains a dangerous place. The United States must maintain its vigilance and its armed strength. Just a glance at today's newspaper or at one of this evening's television news programs will furnish abundant proof of that fact.

### Promote the General Welfare

Few people realize the extent to which government acts as the servant of its citizens, yet you can see examples everywhere. Public schools are one illustration of government's work to promote the general welfare. So, too, are government's efforts to protect the quality of the air you breathe, the water you drink, and the food you eat. The list of tasks government performs for your benefit goes on and on.

Some governmental functions that are common in other countries—operating steel mills, airlines, and coal mines, for example—are not carried out by government in this country. In general, the services that government provides in the United States are those that benefit all or most people. These are the services that are not very likely to be provided by the voluntary acts of private individuals or groups.

### Secure the Blessings of Liberty

This nation was founded by those who loved liberty and prized it above all earthly possessions. They believed with Thomas Jefferson that "the God who gave us life gave us liberty at the same time." They subscribed to Benjamin Franklin's maxim: "They that can give up essential liberty to obtain a little temporary safety deserve neither liberty nor safety."

The American dedication to freedom for the individual recognizes that liberty cannot be absolute. It is, instead, a relative matter. No one can be free to do whatever he or she pleases, for that behavior would interfere with the freedoms of others. As Clarence Darrow, the great defense lawyer, once said: "You can only be free if I am free."

Both the Federal Constitution and the State constitutions set out many guarantees of rights and liberties for the individual in this country. That does not mean that those guarantees are so firmly established that they exist forever, however. To preserve and protect them, each generation must learn and understand them anew, and be willing to stand up for them when necessary.

For many people, the inspiration to protect our rights and liberties arises from deep feelings of patriotism. Patriotism is the love of one's country; the passion which aims to serve one's country, either in defending it from invasion, or by protecting its rights and maintaining its laws and institutions in vigor and purity. Patriotism is the characteristic of a good citizen, the noblest passion that animates a man or woman in the character of a citizen. As a citizen, you, too, must agree with Jefferson: "Eternal vigilance is the price of liberty."

## Section 1 Assessment

**Key Terms and Main Ideas**
1. What is the difference between a **government** and a **state**?
2. Who holds power in a **dictatorship**?
3. What is the purpose of a **constitution**?
4. Give an example of a use of **judicial power**.

**Critical Thinking**
5. **Drawing Inferences** You have read that some thinkers argue that a human-made law that conflicts with natural law is not a law—that an unjust law is not a law. Do you agree? Explain.
6. **Understanding Point of View** In the past, most European kings and queens were strong believers in absolute monarchy. What are two possible explanations for why they held this belief?
7. **Drawing Conclusions** Explain how the language of the Preamble reflects the idea of the social contract.

 **Take It to the Net**

8. Read about Hobbes, Locke, and the French thinker Charles de Montesquieu and create a chart that describes the main ideas of each. Keep in mind that the ideas of these philosophers underlie the Declaration of Independence and the Constitution. Use the links provided in the Social Studies area at the following Web site for help in completing this activity. **www.phschool.com**

**Take It to the Net**

8. Direct students to the Social Studies area at the Prentice Hall School Web site. The *Magruder's American Government* companion Web site includes the directions and links needed to complete the activity. It also provides a printable Internet activity worksheet with scoring rubrics for assessment. Charts should be clearly organized and accurately describe the philosophers' main ideas.

# on Primary Sources

## Second Treatise of Government

*In 1690, English philosopher John Locke produced two treatises (essays) on government. In his second treatise, he discussed the responsibilities of a government and claimed that the people have the right to overthrow an unjust government. Locke's ideas greatly influenced Thomas Jefferson and other supporters of the American Revolution. In this selection, Locke explains why people form governments.*

John Locke
1632–1704

To understand political power aright . . . we must consider what estate all men are naturally in, and that is, a state of perfect freedom to order their actions, and dispose of their possessions and persons as they think fit, within the bounds of the law of nature, without asking leave or depending upon the will of any other man. . . .

Men being . . . by nature, all free, equal and independent, no one can be put out of this estate and subjected to the political power of another without his own consent, which is done by agreeing with other men, to join and unite into a community for their comfortable, safe and peaceable living, one amongst another, in a secure enjoyment of their properties, and a greater security against any that are not of it. . . .

When any number of men have, by the consent of every individual, made a community, they have thereby made that community one body, with a power to act as one body, which is only by the will and determination of the majority. . . . And thus every man, by consenting with others to make one body politic under one government, puts himself under an obligation to every one in that society to submit to the determination [decision] of the majority, and to be concluded by it. . . .

If man in the state of nature . . . be absolute lord of his own person and possessions, equal to the greatest and subject to nobody, why will he part with his freedom, this empire, and subject himself to

the dominion [authority] and control of any other power? . . . It is obvious to answer that though in the state of nature he hath such a right, yet the enjoyment of it is very uncertain and constantly exposed to the invasion of others; for all being kings as much as he, every man his equal, . . . the enjoyment of the property he has in this state is very unsafe, very insecure. This makes him willing to quit this condition which, however free, is full of fears and continual dangers; and it is not without reason that he seeks out and is willing to join in society with others . . . for the mutual preservation of their lives, liberties and estates, which I call by the general name—property.

The great and chief end, therefore, of men uniting into commonwealths, and putting themselves under government, is the preservation of their property. . . .

### Analyzing Primary Sources

1. According to Locke, what freedoms did people have before the founding of governments?
2. What are the potential dangers of a person living in what Locke called "perfect freedom"?
3. According to Locke, how are governments formed?
4. What trade-off does Locke say occurs when people live under governments?

## Corner

📁 **Close Up on Primary Sources** John Locke and Thomas Jefferson, p. 3, extends this feature with a primary source activity.

**Online**

To keep up-to-date on Close Up news and activities, visit Close Up Online at

**www.closeup.org**

---

## Second Treatise on Government

**Focus** Before students read the selection, ask them to suggest ways that governments benefit people. Then ask them to suggest ways in which governments impose dangers or inconveniences on people's lives. Write all ideas on the chalkboard. Then ask students how society might be different without a government.

**Instruct** Explain that while we take government for granted today, throughout history there has been great debate over the usefulness and necessity of governments. Have students read the selection, summarizing Locke's reasons for why people form governments. Point out that one of Locke's premises—that governments are entered into by the consent of free and equal men—was controversial in 1690 when this piece was written. Ask volunteers to read their summaries, and discuss. Ask: Do any of these reasons sound controversial today?

**Close/Reteach** Remind students that John Locke's ideas had an enormous impact on American colonists who were dissatisfied with English rule. Have students, as they read the selection, write down any phrases or ideas that sound familiar to them in terms of American history and government.

💿 **Keep It Current CD-ROM** includes government-related projects by unit. The CD-ROM links to the Prentice Hall School Web site and may be used for daily updates.

### Answers to . . .
**Analyzing Primary Sources**
1. People had the freedom to choose their own actions and control themselves and their possessions without the consent of others.
2. One free person's life, liberty, or estate (property) will be threatened by another free person's actions.
3. By people voluntarily coming together and agreeing to live in a group according to the will of the majority.
4. People trade perfect freedom for increased security. They do so by mutually agreeing to abide by the will of the majority.

**11**

**2** **Forms of Government**

**Objectives** You may wish to call students' attention to the objectives in the Section Preview. The objectives are reflected in the main headings of the section.

**Bellringer** Ask students if they have ever referred to someone as a *dictator*, in anger or as a joke. Then ask if they have ever taken an informal vote on something—which movie to see, or activity to pursue—in order to make the decision *democratically*. Tell students that when they used these terms, they were referring to two types of government that are common throughout the world.

**Vocabulary Builder** Ask students to find base words or roots in the first five terms in the Political Dictionary. Have them use these word parts to try to determine the meaning of each term. They should check their suggested meanings against the definitions given in the section.

## Pressed for Time?

### Quick Lesson Plan

**1. Focus** Tell students that governments can be classified according to their characteristics. Ask students to discuss what they know about different forms of government.

**2. Instruct** Ask students to name the three ways of classifying forms of government. Lead a discussion of each classification, using comparison and contrast to bring out the main differences between the forms of government discussed within each category.

**3. Close/Reteach** Remind students that the form of American government differs from that of many other governments in the world. Have students make a chart showing the three classifications, the forms of government discussed in each classification, and a brief description of each form.

## Section Preview

### OBJECTIVES

1. **Identify** the characteristics of classic forms of government.
2. **Define** systems of government based on who can participate.
3. **Analyze** advantages and disadvantages of federal, confederate, and unitary systems of government.
4. **Analyze** advantages and disadvantages of presidential and parliamentary systems.

### WHY IT MATTERS

You can group most of the world's governments into categories by asking three specific questions about each government. For example, the United States is a democracy with a federal and presidential system of government.

### POLITICAL DICTIONARY

★ autocracy
★ oligarchy
★ unitary government
★ federal government
★ division of powers
★ confederation
★ presidential government
★ parliamentary government

oes the form a government takes, the way in which it is structured, have any importance? Political scientists, historians, and other social commentators have long argued that question. The English poet Alexander Pope weighed in with this couplet in 1733:

 **PRIMARY Sources** *"For Forms of Government let fools contest; Whate'er is best adminster'd is best. . . . "*
—*Essay on Man*

Was Pope right? Does it matter what form a government takes? Pope thought not, but you can form your own opinion as you read this section.

## Classic Forms of Government

Classic forms of government are those forms that have appeared throughout human history. They include the following:

• *Feudalism*, the dominant political system in medieval Europe, is based on the rule of local lords bound to a king by ties of loyalty.

• A *classical republic* is a representative democracy in which a small group of elected leaders represent the concerns of the electorate. During the classical era, Greek city-states experimented with this form of government. Rome later followed the Greek example.

• An *absolute monarchy* is a form of government in which a king or queen holds total control

of the military and the government.

• *Authoritarianism* is a form of government in which an individual or group has unlimited authority. No effective restraint on the power of government exists.

• *Despotism* is rule by a despot, a ruler with absolute power who uses his rule tyrannically.

• *Liberal democracy* is based on the protection of individual rights and freedoms and on the consent of the governed. A liberal democracy focuses on protecting individual rights from the tyranny of the majority. [4]

• *Totalitarianism* is a type of government that attempts to control all facets of citizens' lives.

## Who Can Participate

All governments can be classified according to (1) who can participate in the governing process, (2) the geographic distribution of governmental power within the state, and (3) the relationship between the legislative (lawmaking) and the executive (law-executing) branches of the government.[5] To many people, the most meaningful of these classifications is the one that depends on the

---
[4]The word *democracy* is derived from the Greek words *dēmos* meaning "the people" and *kratia* meaning "rule" or "authority." The Greek word *dēmokratia* means "rule by the people." The term *liberal* derives from "liberty."

[5]Note that these classifications are not mutually exclusive. A government can be defined using two or three of these classifications.

## 🔲 Block Scheduling Strategies

Consider these suggestions to manage extended class time:

■ Present small groups of students with the following scenario: The class has been transported to an island or other isolated area, and must decide on a new government. Have each group list the type of government it wants, the functions it will perform, how it will benefit the people, and how leaders will be selected. When they have finished, have each group share its plan, and then have the

class vote on which one is best. Point out to students that no two governments are exactly alike.

■ Assign small groups of students a region of the world. Groups should choose several countries from their region and research the kind of government, geographic distribution, relationship between branches, and other government-related information for each country. Then have the class create a global map of government around the world.

number of persons who can take part in the governing process. Here there are two basic forms to consider: democracies and dictatorships.

## Democracy

In a democracy, supreme political authority rests with the people. The people hold the sovereign power, and government is conducted only by and with the consent of the people.[5]

Abraham Lincoln gave immortality to this definition of democracy in his Gettysburg Address in 1863: "government of the people, by the people, for the people." Nowhere is there a better, more concise statement of the American understanding of democracy.

A democracy can be either direct or indirect in form. A direct democracy, also called a pure democracy, exists where the will of the people is translated into public policy (law) directly by the people themselves, in mass meetings. This can work only in very small communities, where it is possible for the citizenry to meet in a central place, and where the problems of government are few and relatively simple.

Direct democracy does not exist at the national level anywhere in the world today. However, the New England town meeting, which you will read about in Chapter 25, and the *Landsgemeinde* in a few of the smaller Swiss cantons are excellent examples of direct democracy in action.[6]

Americans are more familiar with the indirect form of democracy—that is, with representative democracy. In a representative democracy, a small group of persons, chosen by the people to act as their representatives, expresses the popular will. These agents of the people are responsible for carrying out the day-to-day conduct of government—the making and executing of laws and so on. They are held accountable to the people for that conduct, especially at periodic elections.

At these elections, the people have an opportunity to express their approval or disapproval of their representatives by casting ballots for or against them. To put it another way, representative

▲ **Direct Democracy Today** At this town meeting in New Hampshire, every citizen in the town enjoys the right to speak out and vote on issues. *Critical Thinking* **Why are town meetings impractical in large cities?**

democracy is government by popular consent—government with the consent of the governed.

Some people insist that the United States is more properly called a republic rather than a democracy. They hold that in a republic the sovereign power is held by those eligible to vote, while the political power is exercised by representatives chosen by and held responsible to those citizens. For them, democracy can be defined only in terms of direct democracy.

Many Americans use the terms *democracy, republic, representative democracy,* and *republican* form of government interchangeably, although they are not the same things. Whatever the terms used, remember that in a democracy the people are sovereign. They are the only source for any and all of government's power. In other words, the people rule.

## Dictatorship

Dictatorship is probably the oldest, and it is certainly the most common, form of government known to history.[7] A dictatorship exists where those who rule cannot be held responsible to the will of the people. The government is not

---

[6]The *Landsgemeinde*, like the original New England town meeting, is an assembly open to all local citizens qualified to vote. In a more limited sense, lawmaking by initiative petition is also an example of direct democracy; see Chapter 24.

[7]The word *dictatorship* comes from the Latin *dictare*, meaning to dictate, issue orders, give authoritative commands. *Dictator* was the ancient Roman republic's title for the leader who was given extraordinary powers in times of crisis. Julius Caesar (100–44 B.C.) was the last of the Roman dictators, in 49 B.C.

---

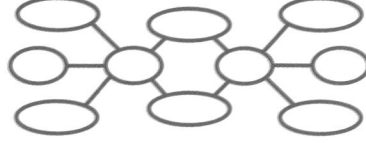
**13**

---

Federal Government to protect us in the face of terrorism. The debate over the nature of

a metaphor for how federalism worked at that time.

## 3 Basic Concepts of Democracy

**Objectives** You may wish to call students' attention to the objectives in the Section Preview. The objectives are reflected in the main headings of the section.

**Bellringer** Have students suppose that tomorrow they will vote in a national election, in which they will freely choose among the candidates of several parties. Then they will stand in line for hours waiting to buy food at the government-run market. Ask them what is wrong with this picture. Explain that in this section, they will learn about how democracy and free enterprise go hand in hand.

**Vocabulary Builder** Write the headings *Government* and *Economics* on the board. Ask students to put the terms from the Political Dictionary in one category or the other (or both). Have students explain their reasoning.

### Pressed for Time?

#### Quick Lesson Plan

**1. Focus** Tell students that several basic concepts form the foundation of American democracy. Ask students to discuss what they know about any of these concepts.

**2. Instruct** Ask students what rights the minority has in a democracy. Discuss the concept of "majority rule, minority rights" and the other basic concepts of democracy. Then focus on the concept of individual freedom and how it links democracy with the free enterprise system.

**3. Close/Reteach** Remind students that individual freedom is at the core of our democracy. Have students draw a double web diagram to organize the information in the section. The topics in the two main circles should be "Democracy" and "Free Enterprise System." Diagrams should show that individual freedom is a concept shared by both main topics.

*Answer to . . .*

**Critical Thinking** Worth of the individual and equality for all people.

---

## 3 Basic Concepts of Democracy

### Section Preview

#### OBJECTIVES

1. **Evaluate** whether and/or when the obligation of citizenship requires that personal interests be subordinated to the public good.
2. **Analyze** the connections between democracy and the free enterprise system.
3. **Analyze** the potential impact of the Internet on democracy.

#### WHY IT MATTERS

Democracy rests on your rights and freedoms as an individual and a member of society. The free enterprise system is a natural counterpart to democracy because it relies on the freedom of the individual to succeed.

#### POLITICAL DICTIONARY

★ compromise
★ free enterprise system
★ law of supply and demand
★ mixed economy

---

What do you make of James Bryce's assessment of democracy? "No government demands so much from the citizen as Democracy, and none gives so much back." What does democratic government demand from you? What does it give you in return?

### Citizenship in a Democracy

Democracy is not inevitable. It does not exist in the United States simply because Americans regard it as the best of all possible political systems. Rather, democracy exists in this country

▲ At Gettysburg, Pennsylvania, Abraham Lincoln declared that the United States was "conceived in liberty, and dedicated to the proposition that all men are created equal." *Critical Thinking Which of the five foundations of democracy are best described by this quote?*

because the American people believe in its basic concepts. It will continue to exist only for as long as we, the people, continue to subscribe to and practice those concepts.

Winston Churchill (1874–1965) once argued for democracy this way: "No one pretends that democracy is perfect or all-wise. Indeed, it has been said that democracy is the worst form of government except all those other forms that have been tried from time to time."

The American concept of democracy rests on these basic notions:

(1) A recognition of the fundamental worth and dignity of every person;

(2) A respect for the equality of all persons;

(3) A faith in majority rule and an insistence upon minority rights;

(4) An acceptance of the necessity of compromise; and

(5) An insistence upon the widest possible degree of individual freedom.

These ideas form the very minimum that anyone who believes in democracy must agree to.

#### Worth of the Individual

Democracy is firmly based upon a belief in the fundamental importance of the individual. Each individual, no matter what his or her station in life, is a separate and distinct being.

This concept of the dignity and worth of the individual is of overriding importance in democratic thought. At various times, of course, the welfare of one or a few individuals

---

*accountable for its policies, nor for how they are ... the government. After crushing all effective*

---

### 📖 Block Scheduling Strategies

Consider these suggestions to manage extended class time:

■ Have students, before they have read the section, list what they consider to be the basic rights of individuals. After they have finished, organize them into small groups and ask them to read the section. Then have each group revise their lists based on what they have read. Ask: What factors limit an individual's rights in a democracy, and why?

■ Ask students to list ways that the government is involved in the economy. Now have them consider how life would be different if the American economy was a pure free market economy rather than mixed. Have students write editorials that either urge the removal of government regulations in a specific industry or urge more government regulation of a specific industry.

is subordinated to the interests of the many in a democracy. People can be forced to do certain things whether they want to or not. Examples range from paying taxes to registering for the draft to stopping at a stop sign.

When a democratic society forces people to pay a tax or obey traffic signals, it is serving the interests of the many. However, it is *not* simply serving the interests of a mass of people who happen to outnumber the few. Rather, it is serving the many who, as individuals, together make up that society.

### Equality of All Persons

Hand-in-hand with the belief in the worth of the individual, democracy stresses the equality of all individuals. It holds, with Jefferson, that "all men are created equal."

Certainly, democracy does *not* insist on an equality of condition for all persons. Thus, it does not claim that all are born with the same mental or physical abilities. Nor does it argue that all persons have a right to an equal share of worldly goods.

Rather, the democratic concept of equality insists that all are entitled to (1) equality of opportunity and (2) equality before the law. That is, the democratic concept of equality holds that no person should be held back for any such arbitrary reasons as those based on race, color, religion, or gender. The concept holds that each person must be free to develop himself or herself as fully as he or she can (or cares to), and that each person should be treated as the equal of all other persons by the law.

We have come a great distance toward the goal of equality for all in this country. It is clear, however, that the journey is far from over.

### Majority Rule, Minority Rights

In a democracy, the will of the people and not the dictate of the ruling few determines public policy. But what is the popular will, and how is it determined? Some device must exist by which these crucial questions can be answered. The only satisfactory device democracy knows is that of majority rule. Democracy argues that a majority of the people will be right more often than they will be wrong, and that the majority will also be right more often than will any one person or small group.

▲ *Equality of Opportunity* The democratic ideal states that people should have equal opportunity to reach their fullest potential as individuals.

Democracy can be described as an experiment or a trial-and-error process designed to find satisfactory ways to order human relations. Democracy does *not* say that the majority will always arrive at the best decisions on public matters. In fact, the democratic process does not intend to come up with "right" or "best" answers. Rather, the democratic process searches for *satisfactory* solutions to public problems.

Of course, democracy insists that the majority's decisions will usually be more, rather than less, satisfactory. Democracy does admit the possibility of mistakes; it acknowledges the possibility that "wrong" or less satisfactory answers will sometimes be found. Democracy also recognizes that seldom is any solution to a public problem so satisfactory that it cannot be improved upon, and that circumstances can change over time. So, the process of experimentation, of seeking answers to public questions, is never-ending.

Certainly, a democracy cannot work without the principle of majority rule. Unchecked, however, a majority could destroy its opposition and, in the process, destroy democracy as well. Thus, democracy insists upon majority rule restrained by minority rights. The majority must always recognize the right of any minority to become, by fair and lawful means, the majority. The majority must always be willing to listen to a minority's argument, to hear its objections, to bear its criticisms, and to welcome its suggestions.

## Reading Strategy
### Predicting
Have students read the first page of the section, stopping after the list of the five basic concepts underlying American democracy. Then have them predict which of these concepts links democracy with the free enterprise system. Have them read the rest of the section to verify their predictions.

### Background Note
#### Recent Scholarship
"The Warren Court," Morton J. Horwitz observes, "recognized not only that representation of minorities was an integral part of democracy but also that truly effective representation required that all people be guaranteed dignity and worth." In *The Warren Court and the Pursuit of Justice,* Horwitz uses the decisions on civil rights and civil liberties cases to show how the concept of democracy was expanded during the reign of the Warren Court. Unlike the idea of democratic government outlined by the Framers, Horwitz asserts, this new, expanded understanding of democratic government included cultural as well as political components.

### Point-of-Use Resources

 Guided Reading and Review Unit 1 booklet, p. 6 provides students with practice identifying the main ideas and key terms of this section.

 Lesson Plans For lesson planning suggestions, see p. 14 of the Lesson Plans booklet.

 Political Cartoons See p. 6 of the Political Cartoons booklet for a cartoon relevant to this section.

 Section Support Transparencies Transparency 9, *Visual Learning;* Transparency 108, *Political Cartoon*

## Organizing Information

To make sure students understand the main points of this section, you may wish to use the tree map graphic organizer to the right.

Tell students that a tree map outlines a main topic, its main ideas, and its supporting details. Have students use a tree map to outline the basic principles on which American democracy rests.

**Teaching Tip** A template for this graphic organizer can be found in the Section Support Transparencies, Transparency 3.

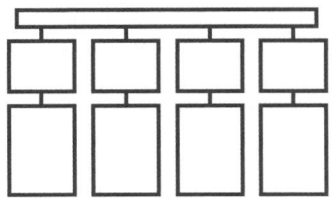

## Point-of-Use Resources

**Guide to the Essentials** Chapter 1, Section 3, p. 16 provides support for students who need additional review of section content. Spanish support is available in the Spanish edition of the Guide on p. 9.

**Quiz** Unit 1 booklet, p. 7 includes matching and multiple-choice questions to check students' understanding of Section 3 content.

**Presentation Pro CD-ROM** Quizzes and multiple-choice questions check students' understanding of Section 3 content.

## Answers to . . .

### Section 3 Assessment

**1.** Compromise is vital in a democracy as it ensures that public decisions are acceptable to all individuals and that all points of view have been considered.

**2.** Characteristics include private or corporate ownership of capital goods, investments that are determined by private decision rather than state control, and free markets.

**3.** When supplies of goods and services become plentiful, prices drop; when supplies become scarce, prices rise.

**4.** Citizens can find a wealth of information about government issues online and can thus be better informed; some States are using online voting.

**5.** Promote free market: encourage private ownership, individual initiative, profit motive, competition. Conflicting: Regulating companies, food production, and pollution; establishing zoning ordinances.

**6.** Answers will vary, but should suggest that while most decisions are made by the majority, the minority still retain their fundamental rights.

## Answers to . . .

**Analyzing Texas Government** Possible answers: Bilingual education, difficulty assimilating, minority rights, job opportunities.

---

## Spotlight on Texas Government

**The Growth of the Hispanic Population** Texas's population has grown dramatically during the last 50 years, exceeding the national average, and Hispanics have been the most rapidly growing segment of the Texan population. Between 1990 and 2000, the Hispanic population was up 54%, compared with 11% for non-Hispanic whites and 19% for blacks.

Hispanics, about 90 percent of whom are Mexican Americans, make up nearly one third of Texas residents. Not surprisingly, Texas has many Hispanic elected officials: Over 2,000 Hispanic citizens hold office in Texas, out of about 5,000 Hispanic officials nationwide. The Texas delegation to Congress recently included five Mexican Americans, all members of the House of Representatives.

### Analyzing Texas Government

*What particular concerns might Hispanic voters bring to Texas politics?*

---

individual initiative, private enterprise—is the best guarantee of a better life for everyone.

## Democracy and the Internet

The Internet provides a prime example of how the U.S. government fosters technological innovations. The Net was born in 1969, in the Defense Department, when its Advanced Research Projects Agency built a four-computer network to enable its scientists to communicate more effectively with one another. Further developed by the private sector, the Internet enables more than 50 million Americans to send and receive e-mail, to buy or sell practically anything, and to entertain and inform themselves.

Democracy demands that the people be widely informed about their government. Thus, democracy and the Internet would seem to be made for one another. Once online, anyone can access a huge amount of information about public affairs. Internet users can check out the Web sites of political candidates, find out what's happening on the floor of Congress, and read about recent Supreme Court decisions. Theoretically, this makes knowledgeable participation in the democratic process easier than ever before.

However, the speed with which and the quantity in which information can be found on the World Wide Web does *not* guarantee the reliability of that data. Experience shows that there is a vast amount of unverified, often unverifiable, and frequently false information in cyberspace. Citizens must take responsibility for checking the reliability of the sources they use. Every fact or quote found online should be checked against a second, independent source whenever possible.

What effect is this easy access to information likely to have on democracy? Many people believe that voters will soon be able to cast their ballots online, or even to vote directly on issues. Arizona first experimented with online voting in the 2000 Democratic presidential primary, and other States are exploring the possibilities. A leap to online elections appears unlikely to us today, particularly since it could entail moving from representative to direct democracy. It seems clear, however, that those who choose to can now be better informed on the issues they care about.

## Section 3 Assessment

### Key Terms and Main Ideas

1. Why is **compromise** an important part of democracy?
2. List three characteristics of the **free enterprise system.**
3. How does the **law of supply and demand** help determine the price of an item?
4. What has been the impact of the Internet on the democratic process?

### Critical Thinking

5. **Recognizing Cause and Effect** List three examples of government actions that promote the free market and three examples of government actions that might conflict with the free market.

6. **Drawing Inferences** Should the rights of individuals ever be subordinated to claims for the public good? Explain.
7. **Predicting Consequences** How might the growth of the Internet affect the relationship between government and the people?

 **Take It to the Net**

8. Read about the origins of the American economy. Then review the different types of economic systems. Select a few aspects of the American economic system that you have seen first-hand and explain how they benefit you. Use the links provided in the Social Studies area at the following Web site for help in completing this activity. **www.phschool.com**

---

**7.** Possible answers: It could encourage citizens to participate more in government because of access to information and online voting. People can communicate with each other and organize more easily around an issue.

**Take It to the Net**

**8.** Direct students to the Social Studies area at the Prentice Hall Web site. The *Magruder's American Government* companion Web site includes the directions and links needed to complete the activity. It also provides a printable Internet activity worksheet with scoring rubrics for assessment. Students should make relevant connections between aspects of the American economic system and their own experiences.

# *on the Supreme Court*

## Must Voting Districts Be Equal in Population?

*If two voting districts have the same number of representatives in the State legislature but contain unequal numbers of voters, each voter in the more populous district has less influence than each voter in the less populous district. Does the Constitution require States to ensure that all voting districts are roughly equal in population?*

### Baker v. Carr (1962)

Tennessee's constitution required that the seats in that State's legislature be distributed among the State's 95 counties on the basis of the number of qualified voters in each county. A 1901 law directed that those seats be redistributed, in line with new census figures, every ten years. No reapportionments were made over the next sixty years, however.

Charles W. Baker, the mayor of Nashville, and several others went to the federal courts with a suit against Tennessee's chief election officer, Secretary of State Joe C. Carr. They claimed that the apportionment made in 1901 had been faulty, and they insisted that population changes over the years since had made it even more unfair. They argued that the inequalities produced by that unfair distribution of seats amounted to a violation of the equal protection of the laws guaranteed by the 14th Amendment to the federal Constitution.

The federal district court dismissed the suit, ruling that State apportionment was an issue for the elected branches and could not be reviewed by the courts. The plaintiffs appealed to the Supreme Court.

### Arguments for Baker

1. The federal courts have the authority to consider this case because they have the power to prevent States from depriving people of their constitutional rights (in this case, the right to equal protection of the laws).
2. Although the States are responsible for electing their own officials and structuring their

own governments, they must do so in ways that do not deprive their citizens of their constitutional rights.
3. The Tennessee apportionment harms voters in more-populous districts and thus violates the Equal Protection Clause of the 14th Amendment.

### Arguments for Carr

1. The Constitution does not authorize the Federal Government to interfere in the States' election of their own officials.
2. The States have great flexibility to structure their own governments, and the Federal Government may not override the States' choices in this matter.
3. The Tennessee apportionment was created by the Tennessee legislature. The manner of electing officials is a political question, one not subject to review by the federal courts.

---

### Decide for Yourself

1. Review the constitutional grounds on which each side based its arguments and the specific arguments each side presented.
2. Debate the opposing viewpoints presented in this case. Which viewpoint do you favor?
3. Predict the impact of the Court's decision on State elections and on the composition of State legislatures. (To read a summary of the Court's decision, turn to the Supreme Court Glossary on page 799.)

---

 *Corner*

📁 **Close Up on the Supreme Court** *Baker* v. *Carr*, p. 2 provides an activity to extend coverage of this case.

 **Online**

To keep up-to-date on Close Up news and activities, visit Close Up Online at

**www.closeup.org**

---

## Must Voting Districts Be Equal in Population?

**Focus** Review the three ways of classifying governments. Then have students classify the structure of the U.S. government. *(Federal, Presidential, Representative Democracy)* Ask students to think about how the issues in the case relate to the preservation of representative democracy and a federal system of government.

**Instruct** Ask students to explain how keeping voting districts equal in population furthers the democratic principle of majority rule. *(It ensures that a district with a smaller population cannot defeat the will of the majority in the district with the larger population.)*

**Close/Reteach** Ask students to write a statement to the Supreme Court explaining why it is important that Nashville be fully represented in the State legislature. Students should mention at least one important urban project, such as highway improvements, that an over-represented rural minority might defeat if voting districts are not kept equal in population.

💿 **Keep It Current CD-ROM** includes government-related projects by unit. The CD-ROM links to the Prentice Hall School Web site and may be used for daily updates.

---

### Answers to . . .

**Decide for Yourself**

**1.** Baker argued that citizens denied the full value of their vote were being deprived of their constitutional rights, and that this was a violation of the equal protection of the laws guaranteed by the 14th Amendment. Hence, the federal court should step in. Carr argued that the States have rights to make certain determinations without interference from the federal courts.
**2.** Answers will vary, but should be supported with valid reasoning.
**3.** The Court held that the case should be tried in federal court; this led to the *Wesberry* decision, which upheld the "one man, one vote" representation concept.

## Assessment

### Practicing the Vocabulary

1. sovereign
2. government
3. public policy
4. confederation
5. dictatorship
6. parliamentary government
7. unitary government
8. constitution
9. legislative power
10. mixed economy

### Reviewing Main Ideas

#### Section 1

**11.** A state is a body of people living in a defined territory, organized with a government and the power to make laws without the consent of a higher authority.
**12.** The force theory says that one person or group forced others to submit to its rule; the evolutionary theory says that the state evolved from an original family; the divine right theory says that God created the state and gave its rulers the right to rule; the social contract theory says that people joined together to form the state.
**13.** The social contract theory.
**14.** To form strong unions, to establish justice, to secure peace and avoid anarchy, to provide defense against foreign enemies, to promote the general welfare, and to ensure personal liberty.
**15.** Answers will vary, but should allude to the reasons for forming a state given above.

#### Section 2

**16.** Who may participate in governing? Where is the geographic distribution of power in the state? What is the relationship between the legislative and executive branches?
**17. (a)** The people. **(b)** No one; in a dictatorship, the person(s) in power has the final authority.
**18.** In an autocracy a single person holds power, while in an oligarchy a small group holds power.
**19.** Unitary: A centralized government with the central agency controlling all government powers; Federal: The powers of government are divided between a central government and local governments; Confederate: An alliance of independent states with a central organization carrying out powers the states give it.

### Political Dictionary

government (p. 4)
public policy (p. 4)
legislative power (p. 4)
executive power (p. 4)
judicial power (p. 4)
constitution (p. 5)
dictatorship (p. 5)
democracy (p. 5)

state (p. 5)
sovereign (p. 6)
autocracy (p. 13)
oligarchy (p. 13)
unitary government (p. 14)
federal government (p. 14)
division of powers (p. 14)
confederation (p. 15)

presidential government (p. 15)
parliamentary government (p. 16)
compromise (p. 20)
free enterprise system (p. 20)
law of supply and demand (p. 21)
mixed economy (p. 21)

### Practicing the Vocabulary

**Matching** *Choose a term from the list above that best matches each description.*

1. Describes a state that has supreme power within its territory
2. The institution through which society makes and enforces its policies
3. That which a government decides to do
4. An alliance of independent states that expressly delegates limited powers to a central government
5. A form of government that is often totalitarian and authoritarian; can be led by one person or many people

**Fill in the Blank** *Choose a term from the list above that best completes the sentence.*

6. In a _____, the executive branch of government is led by members of the legislative branch.
7. A _____ is also known as a centralized government.
8. The basic structure and principles of a government may be found in its _____.
9. _____ is the power to write new laws.
10. Government regulates and promotes businesses in a _____.

### Reviewing Main Ideas

#### Section 1

**11.** What characteristics define a state?
**12.** Briefly describe the four most widely held theories that attempt to explain the origin of the state.
**13.** What theory on the origin of the state was most influential in the founding of the United States?
**14.** For what reasons do people form governments?
**15.** Describe briefly the purposes of government set out in the Preamble to the Constitution.

#### Section 2

**16.** List the three questions that can be used to classify governments.
**17. (a)** In a democracy, to whom is the government responsible? **(b)** In a dictatorship, to whom is the government responsible?
**18.** What is the difference between an autocracy and an oligarchy?

**19.** Name and briefly describe the three forms of government that can result depending on how governmental power is distributed geographically.
**20.** Explain how power is distributed in a presidential government.

#### Section 3

**21.** Briefly describe the five basic concepts of democracy.
**22.** What is the difference between equality of opportunity and equality of condition?
**23.** Describe the relationship between the rights of the individual and the rights of the overall society.
**24. (a)** What is the free enterprise system? **(b)** How does it differ from a mixed economy?
**25.** List one benefit and one drawback of using the Internet for research.

**20.** The two branches, executive and legislative, are separate and serve to check and balance each other.

#### Section 3

**21.** Concepts include worth of the individual, equality of all people, a rule by the majority but with equal rights for the minority; the necessity of compromise, and the protection of individual freedom.

**22.** Equality of condition means that no person may be discriminated against on the basis of race, religion, gender, or color; equality of opportunity means that each person is free to develop as he or she can or wants to.
**23.** Individuals are free to do as they please as long as the rights of society as a whole are not abridged; a balance must be struck between the two.

**24. (a)** An economic system characterized by private ownership of goods and private investment, with profit and competition determined by a free market. **(b)** In a mixed economy, private enterprise is combined with government regulation and participation.
**25.** Benefits include a wealth of information and ease of use; drawbacks include lack of regulation and difficulty determining accuracy.

## Critical Thinking Skills

**26.** *Applying the Chapter Skill* Using a library or the Internet, find an American propaganda poster from World War I or World War II. **(a)** Who was this poster attempting to influence? **(b)** What was the poster encouraging the reader to do? **(c)** Do you believe students today would react positively to this poster? Explain your answer.

**27.** *Recognizing Point of View* Consider Martin Luther King, Jr.'s statement that "injustice anywhere is a threat to justice everywhere." **(a)** What is your understanding of that statement? **(b)** Why is such a belief necessary to maintain a democratic society?

**28.** *Drawing Inferences* Review the chapter and list the American beliefs and principles that are reflected in the United States Constitution. Then explain how those beliefs and principles contribute to our national identity.

**29.** *Making Comparisons* One of the five basic concepts of democracy is equality of all persons. **(a)** Which do you feel is more important to a democracy, equality of opportunity, described in the chapter, or equality of income, housing, and property? **(b)** Can these two forms of equality co-exist in pure form? Explain your answer.

## Analyzing Political Cartoons

Using your knowledge of government and this cartoon, answer the questions below.

*"The Athenians are here, Sire, with an offer to back us with ships, money, arms, and men—and of course, their usual lectures about democracy."*

**30.** What form of government is represented by the King in this cartoon?
**31.** What does this cartoon imply about the origins of democracy?

### Take It to the Net

Additional support materials and activities for Chapter 1 of *Magruder's American Government* can be found in the Social Studies area at the Prentice Hall School Web site. www.phschool.com

### ★ You Can Make a Difference

Do certain issues—pollution, poverty, recycling—interest you? Perhaps you're not ready to start your own grassroots organization. You can still make a difference by joining an existing group working on that issue. First, take time to examine and define the causes you care about. Which of these can be classified as personal and which as civic responsibilities? Watch the news. Read newspapers and news magazines. Take notes of the issues that you feel strongly about. What do you want to do about them? Your answer can help you define your role as an activist.

## Participation Activities

**32.** *Current Events Watch* In several countries around the world, groups are working to form new states. Examples include Quebec, in Canada, and the Basque region of Spain. Read through news reports to learn more about an independence movement active today. **(a)** Describe how the proposed country would meet the four criteria of a state. **(b)** What steps would be necessary to win independence? **(c)** In your opinion, how likely is it that this independence movement will succeed?

**33.** *Time Line Activity* Scan world news reports for an example of a country that is currently moving toward, or away from, democracy. Research political events there over the last fifty years, including revolutions, new constitutions, and free elections. Assemble at least five events into a time line. How long did the transition from one form of government to the other take?

**34.** *It's Your Turn* Write your own "social contract" in which you express your feelings about what should be required of members of a political society, and what government should provide the people. Start by creating a chart with two columns. In one column, list the responsibilities of the citizens in your proposed social contract. In the other column, list what you feel government should provide its citizens. Then detail your ideas for the contract. Proofread and revise for corrections. Then, prepare a final copy. **(Creating a Chart)**

### Take It to the Net

**Chapter 1 Self-Test** As a final review activity, take the Chapter 1 Self-Test in the Social Studies area at the Web site listed below, and receive immediate feedback on your answers.

**www.phschool.com**

## Critical Thinking Skills

**26.** Answers will vary, but should answer each question and demonstrate an understanding of propaganda techniques.
**27.** Answers will vary, but should demonstrate an understanding that injustice invalidates the very rights that are central to a democratic society.
**28.** Strength through union; justice for all; maintaining order; defending against foreign enemies; promoting the general welfare; securing the blessings of liberty. Answers will vary; students may observe that Americans as a group agree on the importance of these beliefs and principles.
**29.** Answers will vary; for **(a)** students might suggest that even if people's housing, income, and property are unequal, all people still have the *opportunity* to achieve equality in those areas; for **(b),** students should demonstrate understanding that the ideals cannot really co-exist in a democracy based on a free enterprise system.

## Analyzing Political Cartoons

**30.** Autocracy.
**31.** Possible answer: That its originators thought that monarchy should give way to democracy.

## You Can Make a Difference

Refer students to the Close Up on Participation booklet in the *Teaching Resources* for ideas on planning and implementing service learning projects.

## Participation Activities

**32.** Reports should address all of the questions asked, and should allude to the characteristics of states described in the chapter.
**33.** Time lines should include all relevant political and historical events, and be clearly organized and easy to read.
**34.** "Social contracts" should clearly outline the rights and responsibilities of citizens and governments.

## Point-of-Use Resources

**Guide to the Essentials of American Government** Chapter 1 Test, page 17 provides multiple-choice questions to test students' knowledge of the chapter.

**Test Bank CD-ROM** Chapter 1 Test

**Chapter Test** Chapter Tests booklet

# Origins of American Government

| Section Objectives | Print and Technology Resources |
|---|---|

### 1 Our Political Beginnings (pp. 28–32)

1. Identify the three basic concepts of government that influenced government in America.
2. Explain the significance of the following landmark documents: the Magna Carta, the Petition of Right, the English Bill of Rights.
3. Describe the three types of colonies that the English established in North America.

**TEKS 1A, 14A, 21A, 21D, 21E, 22A, 22B, 22D**

- **Unit 1 booklet**
  Guided Reading and Review, p. 9
  Section 1 Quiz, p. 10
- **Lesson Plans booklet** Section 1, p. 15
- **Political Cartoons booklet** Section 1, p. 7
- **Block Scheduling with Lesson Strategies booklet** p. 20
- **Section Reading Support Transparencies**

- **Close Up on Primary Sources booklet** Maryland Toleration Act, p. 28; English Petition of Right, p. 55; English Bill of Rights, p. 56
- **Basic Principles of the Constitution Transparencies** 10
- **Section Support Transparencies** 10, 109
- **Presentation Pro CD-ROM** Section 1

### 2 The Coming of Independence (pp. 34–39)

1. Explain how Britain's colonial policies contributed to the growth of self-government in the colonies.
2. Identify some of the steps that led to growing feelings of colonial unity.
3. Compare the outcome of the First Continental Congress to that of the Second Continental Congress.
4. Analyze the ideas of the Declaration of Independence.
5. Describe the drafting of first State constitutions and summarize the constitutions' common features.

**TEKS 2A, 2B, 8D, 21A, 21D, 21E, 22A, 22B, 22C, 22D**

- **Unit 1 booklet**
  Guided Reading and Review, p. 11
  Section 2 Quiz, p. 12
- **Lesson Plans booklet** Section 2, p. 16
- **Political Cartoons booklet** Section 2, p. 8
- **Block Scheduling with Lesson Strategies booklet** p. 20
- **Section Reading Support Transparencies**

- **Close Up on Primary Sources booklet** Magna Carta and the Founding of the United States, p. 4; Speech to the Virginia Provincial Convention, p. 29; *The Wealth of Nations*, p. 30; *Common Sense*, p. 31; Virginia Declaration of Rights, p. 57
- **The Living Constitution booklet** p. 3
- **Government Assessment Rubrics booklet** p. 14
- **Section Support Transparencies** 11, 110
- **Presentation Pro CD-ROM** Section 2

### 3 The Critical Period (pp. 44–47)

1. Describe the structure of the government set up under the Articles of Confederation.
2. Explain why the weaknesses of the Articles led to a critical period for the government in the 1780s.
3. Describe how the need for a stronger National Government led to plans for a Constitutional Convention.

**TEKS 10A, 21A, 22A, 22B, 22C, 22D**

- **Unit 1 booklet**
  Guided Reading and Review, p. 13
  Section 3 Quiz, p. 14
- **Lesson Plans booklet** Section 3, p. 17
- **Section Reading Support Transparencies**

- **Political Cartoons booklet** Section 3, p. 9
- **Section Support Transparencies** 12, 111
- **Presentation Pro CD-ROM** Section 3

### 4 Creating the Constitution (pp. 48–54)

1. Identify the Framers of the Constitution and discuss how the delegates organized the proceedings at the Philadelphia Convention.
2. Compare and contrast the Virginia Plan and the New Jersey Plan for a new constitution.
3. Summarize the major compromises that the delegates agreed to make and the effects of those compromises.
4. Identify some of the sources from which the Framers of the Constitution drew inspiration.
5. Describe the delegates' reactions to the Constitution as they completed their work in Philadelphia.

**TEKS 2A, 2B, 2C, 2D, 8F, 21A, 21E, 22A, 22B, 22D**

- **Unit 1 booklet**
  Guided Reading and Review, p. 15
  Section 4 Quiz, p. 16
- **Lesson Plans booklet** Section 4, p. 18
- **Political Cartoons booklet** Section 4, p. 10
- **The Living Constitution booklet** p. 5
- **Section Reading Support Transparencies**

- **Basic Principles of the Constitution Transparencies** 15
- **Section Support Transparencies** 13, 112
- **Presentation Pro CD-ROM** Section 4
- **Simulations and Data Graphing CD-ROM**
- **Social Studies Skills Tutor CD-ROM**

### 5 Ratifying the Constitution (pp. 56–58)

1. Analyze the debates and compromises necessary for ratifying the Constitution.
2. Analyze how *The Federalist Papers* explain the principles of the American constitutional system of government.
3. Describe the inauguration of the new government of the United States of America.

**TEKS 2B, 2C, 2D, 8C, 21A, 21D, 21E, 22A, 22B, 22C, 22D**

- **Unit 1 booklet**
  Guided Reading and Review, p. 17
  Section 5 Quiz, p. 18
  Skills for Life Activity, p. 19
- **Lesson Plans booklet** Section 5, p. 19
- **Political Cartoons booklet** Section 5, p. 11
- **Section Reading Support Transparencies**

- **Close Up on the Supreme Court booklet** *U.S.* v. *Eichman*, p. 3
- **The Basic Principles of the Constitution Posters**
- **Section Support Transparencies** 14, 113
- **Presentation Pro CD-ROM** Section 5

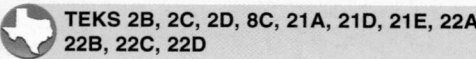

## Block Scheduling Strategies

The *Magruder's American Government* program addresses block-scheduling strategies in a variety of ways. For easy reference, side-column activities that fit a block format are marked ■ **Block Strategy.** Each section also contains a **Block Scheduling Strategies** box describing at least two block-format activities that address and extend core content from the section. The **Block Scheduling with Lesson Strategies booklet** found in the Teaching Resources contains additional block-scheduling activities for each chapter.

### Take It to the Net

Visit the Social Studies area at the Prentice Hall School Web site. Once there, you can find additional links, current events connections, and activities to enrich chapter content for *Magruder's American Government,* as well as a Self-Test for students. Be sure to check out this month's **eTeach** online discussion with a Master Teacher.

### www.phschool.com

### Pressed for Time?

If you are running short on time to cover this chapter, consider one of the following options:
● Use the **Presentation Pro CD-ROM** to create an outline for this chapter.
● Use one of the **Pressed for Time** activities found on p. 27.
● Use the Section Summaries for Chapter 2, from **Guide to the Essentials of American Government (English and Spanish).**

### Video Connections

Prentice Hall offers two video programs to reinforce and extend chapter content. Show students *The Blessings of Liberty* from the **ABC News Civics and Government Videotape Library** and *Prayer in Schools: A Nationwide Debate* from the **Magruder's American Government Video Collection.**

## Assessment Options

● Section Quizzes, **Unit 1 booklet,** pp. 10, 12, 14, 16, 18
● Chapter 2 Assessment, pp. 60–61
● **Guide to the Essentials of American Government,** Chapter 2 Test, p. 23

### Core Assessment
Chapter 2 Test, Chapter Tests booklet
ExamView® Test Bank CD-ROM Chapter 2
Government Assessment Rubrics

### Standardized Test Preparation
#### Diagnose and Prescribe
Diagnostic Tests for High School
Social Studies Skills

#### Review and Reteach
Review Book for Government

#### Practice and Assess
Test-Taking Strategies With
    Transparencies for High School
Test Prep Book for Government

## Chapter 2 Teacher's Edition Index

# Origins of American Government

## Introducing the Chapter

In this chapter students will learn about the ideas and events that shaped American government, beginning with its English roots and leading to the writing and ratification of the Constitution.

## CONSTITUTIONAL PRINCIPLES

Emphasize the following basic principles as students read Chapter 2. Have the class respond to the questions, and then ask volunteers to describe events in English and American history that helped shape these principles.

**Popular Sovereignty** In what ways did the principle of popular sovereignty guide the Framers as they developed the Constitution? Why might some people see a strong central government as an enemy to popular sovereignty?

**Separation of Powers** How did the different plans for revising the Articles of Confederation address the idea of separation of powers? In what ways does the principle of separation of powers relate to that of popular sovereignty?

# Origins of American Government

*"It is, Sir, the people's Constitution, the people's government, made for the people, made by the people, and answerable to the people."*

—Daniel Webster (1830)

The Constitution grew out of a long heritage of law and politics. Before Americans could create their new government, they endured years of turmoil and revolution. In writing the Constitution, the Framers had to consider the rights and interests of many factions. Two hundred years later, Americans still seek and debate their rights.

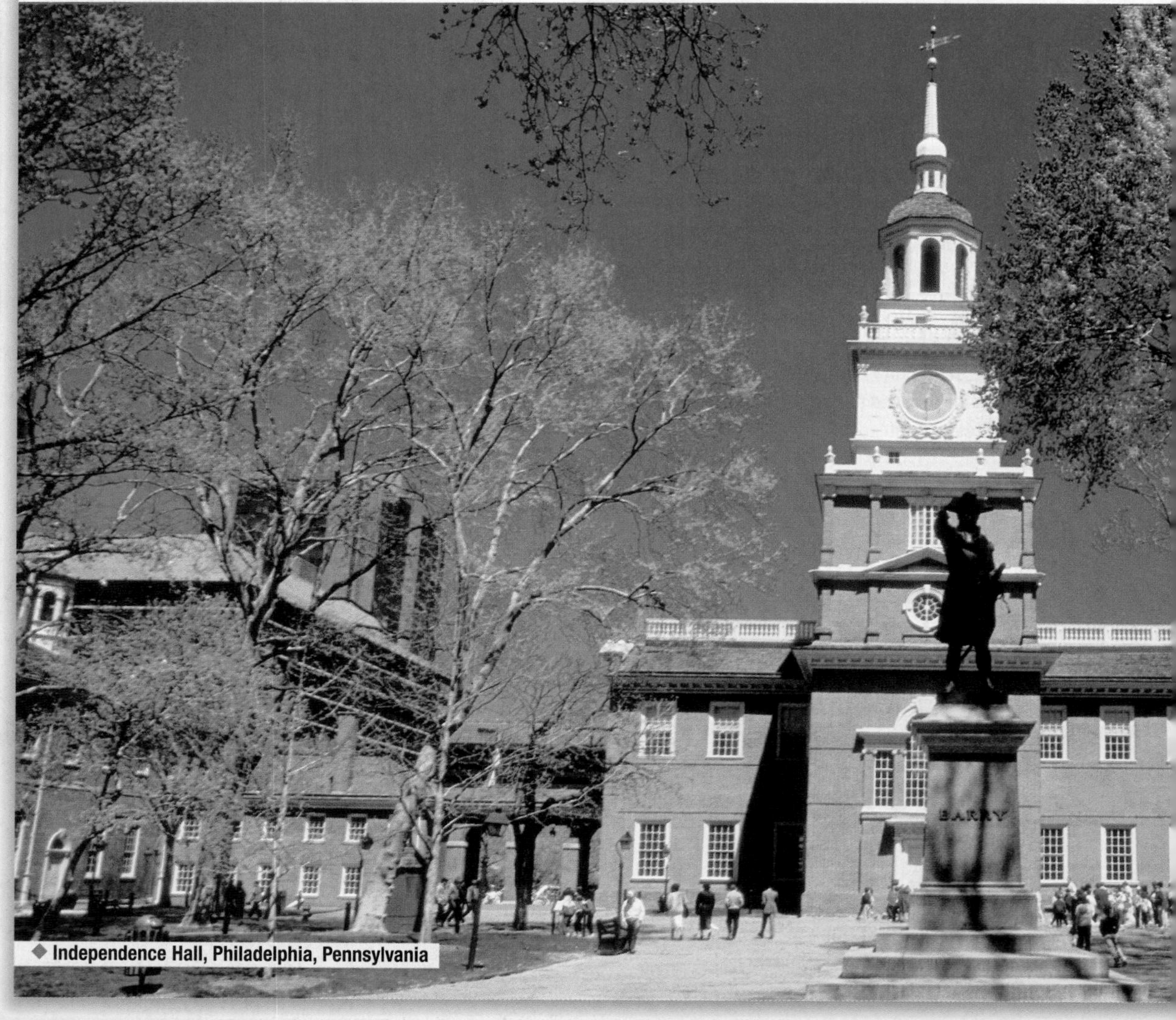

◆ Independence Hall, Philadelphia, Pennsylvania

**Corner**

The following resources are available only from the Close Up Foundation to support the concepts discussed in Chapter 2 "Origins of American Government":

◆ *The Bill of Rights: A User's Guide*
◆ *Bill of Rights Video Series*
◆ *The First Amendment: America's Blueprint for Tolerance*
◆ *Words of Ages: Witnessing U.S. History Through Literature*

To keep up-to-date on Close Up news and activities, visit Close Up Online at

**www.closeup.org**

Close Up Foundation
44 Canal Center Plaza
Alexandria, VA 22314-1592
800-765-3131

## You Can Make a Difference

**WHO IS ENTITLED** to the basic rights promised in the Constitution? Everyone? Or just adults who can vote? In 1996, Ben Smilowitz decided that high school students needed an organization to stand up for their constitutional rights. "You can't just sit back and watch," he said. The 17-year-old from West Hartford, Connecticut, became a co-founder of the International Student Activism Alliance. Members throughout the country alert each other about issues of students' rights, such as censorship and privacy. Ben also worked to get two student representatives appointed to the Connecticut State board of education. By staying informed, you can protect your constitutional rights.

### Keep It Current

Items marked with this logo are periodically updated on the Internet. Keep up-to-date with what's in the news. To get current information on issues related to the Constitution, go to **www.phschool.com**

### SECTION 1

#### Our Political Beginnings (pp. 28–32)

★ American colonists benefited from a developing English tradition of ordered, limited, and representative government.
★ This tradition was based on landmark documents, including the Magna Carta, the Petition of Right, and the English Bill of Rights.
★ The English established three types of colonial governments, all of which provided training for the colonists in the art of government.

### SECTION 2

#### The Coming of Independence (pp. 34–39)

★ Great Britain became more involved with the colonies in the 1760s.
★ The colonists reacted to the changes in British policies by taking small steps toward unity.
★ Twelve of the 13 colonies joined in the First Continental Congress to plan opposition to the British policies.
★ In May of 1775, the Second Continental Congress began. It became the government of the new United States and produced the Declaration of Independence.
★ The newly formed States wrote constitutions that would later influence the U.S. Constitution.

### SECTION 3

#### The Critical Period (pp. 44–47)

★ To provide a more lasting plan of government, the Second Continental Congress created the Articles of Confederation.
★ The Articles contained many weaknesses and led to bickering among the States.
★ The chaos of this critical period led to a movement for change toward a more powerful central government at the Constitutional Convention in May 1787.

### SECTION 4

#### Creating the Constitution (pp. 48–54)

★ The Constitutional Convention in Philadelphia involved delegates from every State but Rhode Island.
★ The Virginia and New Jersey Plans each offered ways to organize the new government.
★ The delegates agreed to compromises that allowed them to agree on the configuration of Congress and other issues.

### SECTION 5

#### Ratifying the Constitution (pp. 56–58)

★ The Federalists promoted the Constitution.
★ The Anti-Federalists attacked the document out of fear of the plan's strong central government and because it lacked a bill of rights.
★ The new Congress convened in March 1789 in what was then the capital, New York City. On April 30, 1789, George Washington was inaugurated as the nation's first President.

## Keep It Current

### Internet Update

Use the Prentice Hall School Web site and the Keep It Current CD-ROM to find quick content updates.

 Visit **www.phschool.com** for current events articles that are linked to Chapter 2. Critical Thinking questions are included.

**Keep It Current CD-ROM** includes government-related projects by unit. Students complete each project using current information that they obtain by linking to the Prentice Hall School Web site from the CD-ROM.

### To Omit the Chapter

If you wish to skip Chapter 2, ask students to read the Chapter in Brief and assign the Guide to the Essentials before continuing to another chapter. You may also want to assign the Chapter 2 Test in the Chapter Test booklet. Then specific portions of Chapter 2 may be assigned to students needing reinforcement of key terms and concepts.

### To Preview the Chapter

To introduce students to key terms and concepts in each section, have them read the Chapter in Brief. You may also assign the Reading Strategy activities on pp. 29, 35, 45, 49, and 57 of this book.

### To Review the Chapter

When students have completed Chapter 2, you might want to assign the Guide to the Essentials or the Guided Reading and Review worksheets on pp. 9, 11, 13, 15, and 17 of the Unit 1 booklet.

### To Cover the Chapter Quickly

To cover the material in Chapter 2 quickly, use the following activity.

**Focus** Ask students to consider the political conditions that colonists lived under during British rule. Have them identify government practices enacted by the British government that colonists wished to stop.

**Instruct** Point out to students that many actions taken by the colonists were meant to address the problems they were having with the British government. Have students create a time line identifying steps that colonists took to establish their independence and their own government.

**Close/Reteach** Ask students to consider the structure of the government outlined by the U.S. Constitution. Have students identify the sources that influenced the Constitution and ways that it addressed problems colonists experienced under British rule.

**Block Strategy (Average)**

**1** *Our Political Beginnings*

**Objectives** You may wish to call students' attention to the objectives in the Section Preview. The objectives are reflected in the main headings of the section.

**Bellringer** Have students name some basic human rights and freedoms. Then ask them where they got their ideas about what their rights and freedoms are. Explain that in this section, they will learn where colonial Americans got their ideas about people's political rights and freedoms.

**Vocabulary Builder** Have students examine each term in the Political Dictionary for any word parts that might be helpful in remembering the term's meaning. Ask them to write a possible meaning and then check their results in a dictionary.

## Pressed for Time?

### Quick Lesson Plan

**1. Focus** Tell students that every nation's government can trace its roots to influential political ideas and documents. Ask students to discuss what they know about the roots of American government.

**2. Instruct** Ask students to name the historical English documents that embody the basic concepts of American government. Then lead a discussion on those documents and how well the ideas they contained were applied in the three types of American colonies.

**3. Close/Reteach** Remind students of the three basic ideas of government and the three types of colonies. Then have them list the types and describe how well each one exemplified the three basic ideas of government.

## Point-of-Use Resources

📁 **Block Scheduling with Lesson Strategies** Activities for Chapter 2 are presented on p. 20.

# *Our Political Beginnings*

## Section Preview

### OBJECTIVES

1. **Identify** the three basic concepts of government that influenced government in the English colonies.
2. **Explain** the significance of the following landmark English documents: the Magna Carta, the Petition of Right, the English Bill of Rights.
3. **Describe** the three types of colonies that the English established in North America.

### WHY IT MATTERS

Our system of government has its origins in the concepts and political ideas that English colonists brought with them when they settled North America. The colonies served as a school for learning about government.

### POLITICAL DICTIONARY

★ limited government
★ representative government
★ Magna Carta
★ Petition of Right
★ English Bill of Rights
★ charter
★ bicameral
★ proprietary
★ unicameral

The American system of government did not suddenly spring into being with the signing of the Declaration of Independence in 1776. Nor was it suddenly created by the Framers of the Constitution in 1787.

The beginnings of what was to become the United States can be found in the mid-sixteenth century when explorers, traders, and settlers first made their way to North America. The French, Dutch, Spanish, Swedes, and others contributed to the European domination of this continent—and to the domination of those Native Americans who were here for centuries before the first Europeans arrived. It was the English, however, who came in the largest numbers. And it was the English who soon controlled the 13 colonies that stretched for some 1,300 miles along the Atlantic coast.

◀ English settlers brought to North America a political system as well as the skills needed to create household items, such as this carved Hadley chest.

## Basic Concepts of Government

The earliest English settlers brought with them knowledge of a political system—established laws, customs, practices, and institutions—that had been developing for centuries.

The political system they knew was that of England, of course. But some aspects of that structure had come to England from other times and places. For example, the concept of the rule of law that influenced English political ideas had roots in the early river civilizations of Africa and Asia.[1] More directly, the ancient Romans who occupied much of England from A.D. 43 to 410 left behind a legacy of law, religion, and custom to the people. From this rich political history, the English colonists brought to North America three ideas that were to loom large in the shaping of government in the United States.

---

[1]For example, King Hammurabi of Babylonia developed a codified system of laws known as Hammurabi's Code around 1750 B.C. Its 282 laws covered real estate, trade, and business transactions, as well as criminal law. The code distinguished between major and minor offenses, established the state as the authority that would enforce the law, and tried to guarantee social justice. Many of the laws of the Old Testament of the Bible are similar to concepts in Hammurabi's Code—for example, "an eye for an eye." The English and the English colonists were familiar with and devoutly attracted to this Biblical concept of the rule of law.

## 🖥 Block Scheduling Strategies

Consider these suggestions to manage extended class time:

■ Organize the class into three groups, assigning each group one of the following documents: the Magna Carta, the Petition of Right, or the English Bill of Rights. Have each group research its assigned document to determine how it helped shape the ideas of ordered government, limited government, and representative govern-ment. Finally, have groups present their information to the class.

■ Have students create maps of colonial America identifying each colony as royal, proprietary, or charter. Then ask students to create summaries of the types of colonies, identifying the similarities and differences between them. Have volunteers share their summaries with the class. Afterwards, lead a discussion on the three types of colonies.

## Foundations of American Rights

| 1215 **Magna Carta** ❶❷❸ | | 1689 **English Bill of Rights** ❶❷❹❺❻❼ | | 1776 **Virginia Bill of Rights** ❺❽❾❿⓫ |

| 1200 | 1400 | 1600 | 1800 |

1791
**Bill of Rights**
❶❷❸❹❺❻❼
❽❾❿⓫

**RIGHTS**

❶ Trial by jury
❷ Due process
❸ Private property
❹ No cruel punishment
❺ No excessive bail or fines
❻ Right to bear arms
❼ Right to petition
❽ No unreasonable searches and seizures
❾ Freedom of speech
❿ Freedom of the press
⓫ Freedom of religion

*Interpreting Charts* The rights established in these landmark documents were revolutionary in their day. They did not, however, extend to all people when first granted. Over the years, these rights have influenced systems of government in many countries. *How might the right to petition, first granted in the English Bill of Rights, prevent abuse of power by a monarch?*

### Ordered Government

Those first English colonists saw the need for an orderly regulation of their relationships with one another—that is, for government. They created local governments, based on those they had known in England. Many of the offices and units of government they established are still with us today: the offices of sheriff, coroner, assessor, and justice of the peace, the grand jury, counties, townships, and several others.

### Limited Government

The colonists also brought with them the idea that government is not all-powerful. That is, government is restricted in what it may do, and each individual has certain rights that government cannot take away.

This concept is called **limited government,** and it was deeply rooted in English belief and practice by the time the first English ships reached the Americas. It had been planted in England centuries earlier, and it had been developing there for nearly 400 years before Jamestown was settled in 1607.

### Representative Government

The early English settlers also carried another important concept to America: **representative government.** This idea that government should

serve the will of the people had also been developing in England for centuries. With it had come a growing insistence that the people should have a voice in deciding what government should and should not do. As with the concept of limited government, this notion of "government of, by, and for the people" found fertile soil in America, and it flourished here.

## Landmark English Documents

These basic notions of ordered government, of limited government, and of representative government can be traced to several landmark documents in English history.

### The Magna Carta

A group of determined barons forced King John to sign the **Magna Carta**— the Great Charter—at Runnymede in 1215. Weary of John's military campaigns and heavy taxes, the

▶ King John's conflicts with English nobles led to the signing of the Magna Carta.
*Critical Thinking* **Could the basic notions of ordered, limited, and representative government have developed without the signing of the Magna Carta? Explain your answer.**

## Organizing Information

To make sure students understand the main points of this section, you may wish to use the flowchart graphic organizer to the right.

Tell students that a flowchart shows a sequence of events. Ask students to use the flowchart to record the sequence of English and colonial political ideas that shaped early American government.

**Teaching Tip** A template for this graphic organizer can be found in the Section Support Transparencies, Transparency 4.

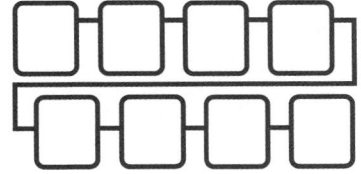

## Make It Relevant

### Students Make a Difference

Stanford Pugsley discovered that it pays to know the way your government works. The 16-year-old student from Salt Lake City, Utah, found a little known 1986 law and used it to become a member of his local board of education.

Stan wanted to get involved. He thought that "once kids start getting interested and not just worrying about their own lives, they'll get the whole view and make a difference in the world."

To get *his* start on making a difference, Stan collected 500 signatures of his peers, and requested appointment to the board as a nonvoting member. That's what the law required—and that's how Stanford Pugsley became the first student on the Salt Lake City Board of Education.

## Customize for

### English Language Learners

Have students create crossword puzzles using the vocabulary terms of this section. Using definitions from the text, students will create a puzzle that they can exchange with a classmate. Students should complete a puzzle and return it to the original creator for grading.

## Point-of-Use Resources

📁 **Close Up on Primary Sources**
English Petition of Right (1628), p. 55

barons who developed the Magna Carta were seeking protection against heavy-handed and arbitrary acts by the king.

The Magna Carta included such fundamental rights as trial by jury and due process of law—protection against the arbitrary taking of life, liberty, or property. These protections against the absolute power of the king were originally intended only for the privileged classes. Over time, they became the rights of all English people and were incorporated into other documents. The Magna Carta established the principle that the power of the monarchy was not absolute.

### The Petition of Right

The Magna Carta was respected by some monarchs and ignored by others for 400 years. During this time, England's Parliament, a representative body with the power to make laws, slowly grew in influence. In 1628, when Charles I asked Parliament for more money in taxes, Parliament refused until he signed the **Petition of Right.**

The Petition of Right limited the king's power in several ways. Most importantly, the document demanded that the king no longer imprison or otherwise punish any person but by the lawful judgment of his peers, or by the law of the land. It also insisted that the king not impose martial law (rule by the military) in time of peace, or require homeowners to shelter the king's troops without their consent. In addition, the Petition stated that no man should be:

 *compelled to make or yield any gift, loan, benevolence, tax, or such like charge, without common consent by act of parliament.* **🙷**
—X, Petition of Right

The Petition challenged the idea of the divine right of kings, declaring that even a monarch must obey the law of the land.

### The Bill of Rights

In 1688, after years of revolt and turmoil, Parliament offered the crown to William and Mary of Orange. The events surrounding their ascent to the throne are known in English history as the Glorious Revolution. To prevent abuse of power by William and Mary and all future monarchs, Parliament, in 1689, drew up

a list of provisions to which William and Mary had to agree.

This document, the **English Bill of Rights,** prohibited a standing army in peacetime, except with the consent of Parliament, and required that all parliamentary elections be free. In addition, the document declared

**PRIMARY Sources** *that the pretended power of suspending the laws, or the execution of laws, by regal authority, without consent of Parliament is illegal . . . .*

*that levying money for or to the use of the Crown . . . without grant of Parliament . . . is illegal . . .*

*that it is the right of the subjects to petition the king . . . and that prosecutions for such petitioning are illegal . . .* **🙷**
—English Bill of Rights

The English Bill of Rights also included such guarantees as the right to a fair trial, and freedom from excessive bail and from cruel and unusual punishment.

Our nation has built on, changed, and added to those ideas and institutions that settlers brought here from England. Still, much in American government and politics today is based on these early English ideas.

## The English Colonies

England's colonies in North America have been described as "13 schools of government." The colonies were the settings in which Americans first began to learn the difficult art of government.[2]

The 13 colonies were established separately, over a span of some 125 years. During that long period, outlying trading posts and isolated farm settlements developed into organized

---

[2]The Europeans who came to the Americas brought with them their own views of government, but this does not mean that they brought the idea of government to the Americas. Native Americans had governments. They had political institutions that worked to accomplish the goals of the state; they had political leaders; and they had policies toward other states.

Some Native American political organizations were very complex. For example, five Native American tribes in present-day New York State—the Seneca, Cayuga, Oneida, Onondaga, and Mohawk—formed a confederation known as the Iroquois League. The League was set up to end conflicts among the tribes, but it was so successful as a form of government that it lasted for over 200 years.

---

## Preparing for Standardized Tests

Have students read the Primary Sources passages from the English Bill of Rights on this page and then answer the question below.

What was Parliament's primary concern in writing the English Bill of Rights?

**A** To limit the power of the monarchy.

**B** To keep the king from pretending things.

**C** To transfer all power from the monarchy to Parliament.

**D** To make petitioning illegal.

communities. The first colony, Virginia, was founded with the first permanent English settlement in North America at Jamestown in 1607.[3] Georgia was the last to be formed, with the settlement of Savannah in 1733.

Each of the colonies was born out of a particular set of circumstances, and so each had its own character. Virginia was originally organized as a commercial venture. Its first colonists were employees of the Virginia Company, a private trading corporation. Massachusetts was first settled by people who came to North America in search of greater personal and religious freedom. Georgia was founded largely as a haven for debtors, a refuge for the victims of England's harsh poor laws.

But the differences between and among the colonies are really of little importance. Of much greater significance is the fact that all of them were shaped by their English origins. The many similarities among all 13 colonies far outweighed the differences.

Each colony was established on the basis of a **charter,** a written grant of authority from the king. Over time, these instruments of government led to the development of three different kinds of colonies: royal, proprietary, and charter.

## Royal Colonies

The royal colonies were subject to the direct control of the Crown. On the eve of the American Revolution in 1775, there were eight: New Hampshire, Massachusetts, New York, New Jersey, Virginia, North Carolina, South Carolina, and Georgia.

The Virginia colony did not enjoy the quick success its sponsors had promised. So, in 1624, the king revoked the London Company's charter, and Virginia became the first royal colony. Later, as the original charters of other colonies

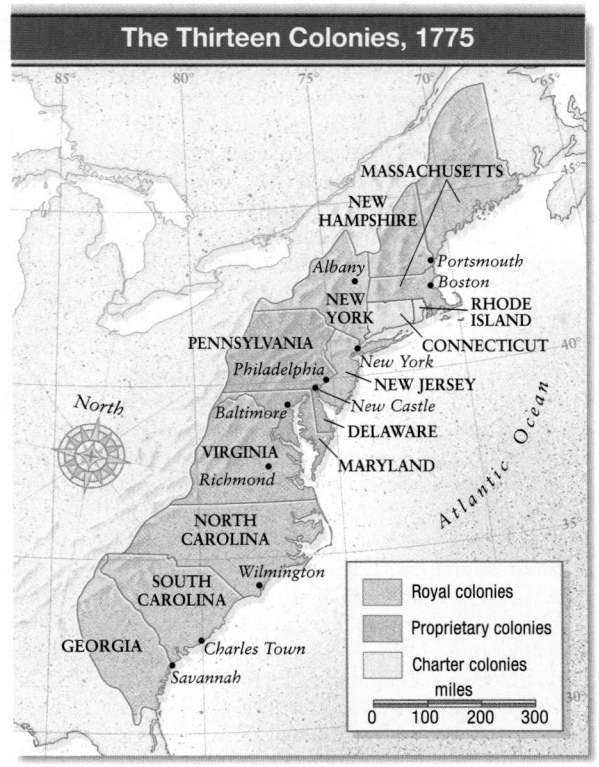

## The Thirteen Colonies, 1775

MASSACHUSETTS
NEW HAMPSHIRE
Albany • •Portsmouth
•Boston
NEW YORK RHODE ISLAND
PENNSYLVANIA CONNECTICUT
Philadelphia • •New York
NEW JERSEY
North Baltimore• •New Castle
DELAWARE
VIRGINIA MARYLAND
Richmond•
NORTH CAROLINA
SOUTH CAROLINA •Wilmington
GEORGIA •Charles Town
Savannah

Atlantic Ocean

| | Royal colonies |
| | Proprietary colonies |
| | Charter colonies |

miles
0   100   200   300

**Interpreting Maps** Despite the different circumstances surrounding the settlement of each colony, they all shared a common English background. ***How were royal colonies governed?***

were canceled or withdrawn for a variety of reasons, they became royal colonies.

A pattern of government gradually emerged for each of the royal colonies. The king named a governor to serve as the colony's chief executive. A council, also named by the king, served as an advisory body to the royal governor. In time, the governor's council became the upper house of the colonial legislature. It also became the highest court in the colony. The lower house of a **bicameral** (two-house) legislature was elected by those property owners qualified to vote.[4] It

---

[3]St. Augustine, Florida, is the oldest continuously populated European settlement in what is now the United States. St. Augustine was founded by Pedro Menéndez in 1565 to establish Spanish authority in the region.

[4]The Virginia legislature held its first meeting in the church at Jamestown on July 30, 1619, and was the first representative body to meet in the North American English colonies. It was made up of burgesses—that is, representatives—elected from each settlement in the colony. Virginia called the lower house of its colonial legislature the House of Burgesses; South Carolina, the House of Commons; Massachusetts, the House of Representatives.

### Background Note
#### A Diverse Nation

In 1619, a year before the *Mayflower* reached Plymouth, the first Africans in English North America reached Jamestown. They were indentured servants, not slaves, and they numbered about twenty. At the time, African slavery was common in the American colonies settled by Portugal and Spain, but the practice did not become widespread in the English colonies until after the establishment of the Royal African Company in 1672. After that, the number of Africans who were brought to the colonies—now as slaves, not indentured servants—rose sharply.

### Point-of-Use Resources

📁 **Close Up on Primary Sources**
Maryland Toleration Act (1649), p. 28; English Bill of Rights (1689), p. 56

🖥 **Section Support Transparencies**
Transparency 10, *Visual Learning;* Transparency 109, *Political Cartoon*

*Answer to . . .*
**Interpreting Maps** By a governor appointed by the king; a bicameral legislature made the laws, but the governor and Crown had to approve them.

## Point-of-Use Resources

 **Guide to the Essentials** Chapter 2, Section 1, p. 18 provides support for students who need additional review of section content. Spanish support is available in the Spanish edition of the Guide on p. 11.

**Quiz** Unit 1 booklet, p. 10 includes matching and multiple-choice questions to check students' understanding of Section 1 content.

**Presentation Pro CD-ROM** Quizzes and multiple-choice questions check students' understanding of Section 1 content.

### Answers to . . .

## Section 1 Assessment

**1.** Refer to the explanations of ordered government, limited government, and representative government on p. 29.

**2.** The Magna Carta introduced the rights of trial by jury and due process of law—protection against the arbitrary taking of life, liberty, or property. The Petition of Right limited the king's powers and declared that monarchs must obey laws. The English Bill of Rights prohibited standing armies in peacetime, required that parliamentary elections be free, and guaranteed fair trials and freedom from excessive punishment.

**3.** Royal colonies: under direct control of Crown; Proprietary colonies: governed by the owner; Charter colonies: enjoyed large degree of self-government.

**4.** A bicameral legislative body has two houses, while a unicameral legislative body has just one.

**5.** Answers should reflect an understanding that these documents created limited government in England; this prevented an absolute monarchy by putting restrictions on the government and granting inalienable rights to the people.

**6.** Similar: all started with charters and were based on English government. Different: all had varying degrees of self-government.

---

owed much of its influence to the fact that it shared with the governor and his council the power of the purse—that is, the power to tax and spend. The governor, advised by the council, appointed the judges for the colony's courts.

The laws passed by the legislature had to be approved by the governor and the Crown. Royal governors often ruled with a stern hand, following instructions from London. Much of the resentment that finally flared into revolution was fanned by their actions.

### The Proprietary Colonies

By 1775, there were three **proprietary** colonies: Maryland, Pennsylvania, and Delaware.[5] These colonies were organized by a proprietor, a person to whom the king had made a grant of land. By charter, that land could be settled and governed much as the proprietor (owner) chose. In 1632 the king had granted Maryland to Lord Baltimore and in 1681, Pennsylvania to William Penn. In 1682 Penn also acquired Delaware.

The governments of these three colonies were much like those in the royal colonies. The governor, however, was appointed by the proprietor. In Maryland and Delaware, the legislatures were bicameral. In Pennsylvania, the legislature was a **unicameral** (one-house) body. There, the governor's council did not act as one house of the

---

[5]New York, New Jersey, North Carolina, South Carolina, and Georgia also began as proprietary colonies. Each later became a royal colony.

---

legislature. As in the royal colonies, appeals from the decisions of the proprietary colonies could be carried to the king in London.

### The Charter Colonies

Connecticut and Rhode Island were charter colonies. They were based on charters granted in 1662 and 1663, respectively, to the colonists themselves.[6] They were largely self-governing.

The governors of Connecticut and Rhode Island were elected each year by the white, male property owners in each colony. Although the king's approval was required before the governor could take office, it was not often asked. Laws made by their bicameral legislatures were not subject to the governor's veto nor was the Crown's approval needed. Judges in charter colonies were appointed by the legislature, but appeals could be taken from the colonial courts to the king.

The Connecticut and the Rhode Island charters were so liberal for their time that, with independence, they were kept with only minor changes as State constitutions—until 1818 and 1843, respectively. In fact, many historians say that had Britain allowed the other colonies the same freedoms and self-government, the Revolution might never have occurred.

---

[6]The Massachusetts Bay Colony was established as the first charter colony in 1629. Its charter was later revoked and Massachusetts became a royal colony in 1691. Religious dissidents from Massachusetts founded Connecticut in 1633 and Rhode Island in 1636.

---

## Section -1- Assessment

**Key Terms and Main Ideas**

1. Explain the concepts of ordered government, **limited government**, and **representative government.**
2. What were some of the fundamental rights and principles established in the **Magna Carta,** the **Petition of Right,** and the **English Bill of Rights?**
3. Identify and describe the three types of government in the English colonies.
4. Explain the difference between a **bicameral** and a **unicameral** legislative body.

**Critical Thinking**

5. **Testing Conclusions** Documents such as the Magna Carta and the Petition of Right prevented the development of an absolute monarchy in England. To what degree is this an accurate statement?
6. **Making Comparisons** In what ways were the colonial governments similar? How did they differ?

### Take It to the Net

7. Find out more about colonial charters. What rights and privileges did charters grant to colonists? Pick one charter and write a paragraph explaining why it was important for the development of that colony. Use the links provided in the Social Studies area at the following Web site for help in completing this activity. **www.phschool.com**

---

### Take It to the Net

**7.** Direct students to the Social Studies area at the Prentice Hall School Web site. The *Magruder's American Government* companion Web site includes the directions and links needed to complete the activity. It also provides a printable Internet activity worksheet with scoring rubrics for assessment. Students' paragraphs should be supported with relevant facts and quotes from the charters.

# The Magna Carta

*Signed by England's King John in 1215, the Magna Carta (Great Charter) was the first document to limit the power of England's monarchs. The result of tough negotiations between the king and rebellious nobles, the Magna Carta established the principle that rulers are subject to law—a major step toward constitutional government.*

We . . . by this our present Charter, have confirmed, for us and our heirs forever: —

1. That the English Church shall be free and shall have her whole rights and her liberties inviolable [secure from harm]. . . .

9. Neither we nor our bailiffs shall seize any land or rent for any debt while the chattels [possessions] of the debtor are sufficient for the payment of the debt. . . .

12. No scutage [tax] or aid [subsidy] shall be imposed in our kingdom, unless by the common counsel of our kingdom. . . .

14. And also to have the common council of the kingdom to assess and aid, . . . and for the assessing of scutages, we will cause to be summoned the archbishops, bishops, abbots, earls, and great barons, . . . And besides, we will cause to be summoned . . . all those who hold of us in chief, at a certain day . . . and to a certain place; and in all the letters of summons, we will express the cause of the summons; and the summons being thus made, the business shall proceed on the day appointed, according to the counsel of those who shall be present, although all who have been summoned have not come. . . .

39. No free-man shall be seized, or imprisoned, or dispossessed, or outlawed, or in any way destroyed; nor will we condemn him, nor will we commit him to prison, excepting by the legal judgment of his peers, or by the laws of the land.

40. To none will we sell, to none will we deny, to none will we delay right or justice.

*King John signs the Magna Carta.*

41. All merchants shall have safety and security in coming into England, and going out of England, and in staying and in traveling through England . . . to buy and sell, . . . excepting in the time of war, and if they be of a country at war against us. . . .

42. It shall be lawful to any person . . . to go out of our kingdom, and to return safely and securely, by land or by water, saving his allegiance to us, unless it be in time of war, for some short space, for the common good of the kingdom. . . .

52. If any have been disseised [deprived] or dispossessed by us, without a legal verdict of their peers, of their lands, castles, liberties, or rights, we will immediately restore these things to them. . . .

63. Wherefore our will is . . . that the men in our kingdom have and hold the aforesaid liberties, rights, and concessions . . . fully and entirely, to them and their heirs, . . . in all things and places forever.

## Analyzing Primary Sources

1. What basic American right has its origins in Article 39 of the Magna Carta?
2. Which article provides the basis for the Fifth Amendment to the Constitution, which states that no person can "be deprived of life, liberty, or property, without due process of law"?
3. What limits does Article 12 place on the king's power to tax?

---

**Close Up on Primary Sources** The Magna Carta and the Founding of the United States, p. 4, extends this feature with a primary source activity.

*Corner*

Online

To keep up-to-date on Close Up news and activities, visit Close Up Online at

**www.closeup.org**

---

## The Magna Carta

**Focus** Ask students to identify reasons why people would want to limit the power of their ruler or government. Then ask them how they might go about limiting this power. Explain that written agreements such as the Magna Carta are one way to limit a government's power.

**Instruct** Ask students to read the excerpts from the Magna Carta. For each article, have students identify the practice(s) it was intended to stop. Encourage them to supply the historical background of the articles wherever possible. Once students have finished, lead a discussion covering each article.

**Close/Reteach** Have students write magazine articles about the Magna Carta. Articles should address these questions: Is this document the most important in the history of English and American government? Why or why not?

**Keep It Current CD-ROM** includes government-related projects by unit. The CD-ROM links to the Prentice Hall School Web site and may be used for daily updates.

---

*Answers to . . .*
**Analyzing Primary Sources**
1. The right to a trial by jury has its origins in Article 39 of the Magna Carta.
2. Article 52 provides the basis for the Fifth Amendment.
3. The king may not impose taxes without the general consent of the people.

# 2 The Coming of Independence

**Objectives** You may wish to call students' attention to the objectives in the Section Preview. The objectives are reflected in the main headings of the section.

**Bellringer** Ask students what problems a basketball team with five star players might have. Elicit that individual brilliance without teamwork does not win championships. Explain that in this section, they will learn how 13 individual colonies learned to work together.

**Vocabulary Builder** Have students study the terms in the Political Dictionary to find three terms that are directly related to the idea of colonies working together. As students read the section, have them use the text to tie all of the terms to the development of a unified American government.

## Pressed for Time?

### Quick Lesson Plan

**1. Focus** Tell students that a spirit of cooperation developed slowly among the American colonies as they responded to increasingly harsh British actions. Ask students to discuss what they know about early attempts at cooperation.

**2. Instruct** Tell students that the unity reflected in the Declaration of Independence did not come easily. Lead a discussion of how unity developed over time and what pushed the colonies to join together. Conclude by asking whether State constitutions added to that unity.

**3. Close/Reteach** Remind students that colonial unity developed over time in response to specific events. Have students make a chart showing each colonial attempt at promoting cooperation and the reason behind it.

## Section Preview

### OBJECTIVES

1. **Explain** how Britain's colonial policies contributed to the growth of self-government in the colonies.
2. **Identify** some of the steps that led to growing feelings of colonial unity.
3. **Compare** the outcomes of the First and Second Continental Congresses.
4. **Analyze** the ideas in the Declaration of Independence.
5. **Describe** the drafting of the first State constitutions and summarize the constitutions' common features.

### WHY IT MATTERS

Changes in British colonial policies led to resentment in the colonies and eventually to the American Revolution. Ideas expressed in the early State constitutions influenced the development of the governmental system under which we live today.

### POLITICAL DICTIONARY

★ confederation
★ Albany Plan of Union
★ delegate
★ boycott
★ repeal
★ popular sovereignty

"**W**e must all hang together, or assuredly we shall all hang separately." Benjamin Franklin spoke these words on July 4, 1776, as he and the other members of the Second Continental Congress approved the Declaration of Independence. Those who heard him may well have chuckled. But they also may have felt a shiver, for the good doctor's humor carried a deadly serious message.

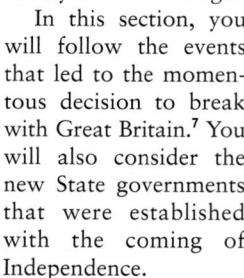

In this section, you will follow the events that led to the momentous decision to break with Great Britain.[7] You will also consider the new State governments that were established with the coming of Independence.

▲ Colonists who made their tea in this pot voiced their opposition to the Stamp Act.

## Britain's Colonial Policies

The 13 colonies, which had been separately established, were separately controlled under the king, largely through the Privy Council and the Board of Trade in London. Parliament took little part in the management of the colonies. Although it did become more and more interested in matters of trade, it left matters of colonial administration almost entirely to the Crown.[8]

Over the century and a half that followed the first settlement at Jamestown, the colonies developed within that framework of royal control. In theory, they were governed in all important matters from London. But London was more than 3,000 miles away, and it took nearly two months to sail that distance across a peril-filled Atlantic. So, in practice, the colonists became used to a large measure of self-government.

Each colonial legislature began to assume broad lawmaking powers. Many found the power of the purse to be very effective. They often bent a royal governor to their will by not voting the money for his salary until he came to terms with them. As one member of New Jersey's Assembly put it: "Let us keep the dogges poore, and we'll make them do as we please."

---

[7]England became Great Britain by the Act of Union with Scotland in 1707.

[8]Much of English political history can be told in terms of the centuries-long struggle for supremacy between monarch and Parliament. That conflict was largely settled by England's Glorious Revolution of 1688, but it did continue through the American colonial period and into the nineteenth century. However, Parliament paid little attention to the American colonies until very late in the colonial period.

## 🗖 Block Scheduling Strategies

Consider these suggestions to manage extended class time:

■ Ask students to assume the roles of members of the Second Continental Congress who are writing their memoirs. Have each student write a description based on how Britain's colonial policies contributed to self-government in the colonies as well as what caused feelings of colonial unity to grow. Have students read their memoirs to a partner or share with the class.

■ To extend the Constitutional Principles activity on page 38, ask students to continue examining the Declaration of Independence to determine if violations of any other constitutional principles were used as justification for independence. Have students identify any references to these principles and explain how they were used to justify independence.

By the mid-1700s, the relationship between Britain and the colonies had become, in fact if not in form, federal. This meant that the central government in London was responsible for colonial defense and for foreign affairs. It also provided a uniform system of money and credit and a common market for colonial trade. Beyond that, the colonies were allowed a fairly wide amount of self-rule. Little was taken from them in direct taxes to pay for the central government. The few regulations set by Parliament, mostly about trade, were largely ignored.

This was soon to change. Shortly after George III came to the throne in 1760, Britain began to deal more firmly with the colonies. Restrictive trading acts were expanded and enforced. New taxes were imposed, mostly to support British troops in North America.

Many colonists took strong exception to these moves. They objected to taxes imposed on them from afar. This arrangement, they claimed, was "taxation without representation." They saw little need for the costly presence of British troops on North American soil, since the French had been defeated and their power broken in the French and Indian War (1754–1763).

The colonists considered themselves British subjects loyal to the Crown. They refused, however, to accept Parliament's claim that it had a right to control their local affairs.

The king's ministers were poorly informed and stubborn. They pushed ahead with their policies, despite the resentments they stirred in America. Within a few years, the colonists faced a fateful choice: to submit or to revolt.

## Growing Colonial Unity

A decision to revolt was not one to be taken lightly—or alone. The colonies would need to learn to work together if they wanted to succeed. Indeed long before the 1770s, several attempts had been made to promote cooperation among the colonies.

### Early Attempts

In 1643 the Massachusetts Bay, Plymouth, New Haven, and Connecticut settlements formed the New England Confederation. A **confederation** is a joining of several groups for a common purpose. In the New England Confederation, the settlements formed a "league of friendship" for defense against the Native Americans. As the danger from Native Americans passed and friction among the settlements grew, the confederation lost importance and finally dissolved in 1684.

In 1696 William Penn offered an elaborate plan for intercolonial cooperation, largely in trade, defense, and criminal matters. It received little attention and was soon forgotten.

### The Albany Plan

In 1754 the British Board of Trade called a meeting of seven of the northern colonies at Albany: Connecticut, Maryland, Massachusetts, New Hampshire, New York, Pennsylvania, and Rhode Island. The main purpose of the meeting was to discuss the problems of colonial trade and the danger of attacks by the French and their Native American allies. Here, Benjamin Franklin offered what came to be known as the **Albany Plan of Union.**

## *Voices* on Government

**Benjamin Franklin** dedicated years to public service, including time as a delegate to the Second Continental Congress, a commissioner to France during the War for Independence, and a member of the Constitutional Convention. Franklin proposed the Albany Plan of Union to provide for the defense of the American colonies. In his autobiography, he spoke of its defeat and defended his plan:

❝ *The different and contrary Reasons of dislike to my Plan, makes me suspect that it was really the true Medium; and I am still of Opinion it would have been happy for both Sides the Water if it had been adopted. The Colonies so united would have been sufficiently strong to have defended themselves; there would then have been no need of Troops from England; of course the subsequent Pretence for Taxing America, and the bloody Contest it occasioned, would have been avoided.* ❞

### Evaluating the Quotation

*What did Franklin see as the ultimate result of the failure to adopt the Albany Plan of Union? Do you think this was a reasonable conclusion?*

## Reading Strategy
### Predicting Content
Before they read the section, have students read all the headings. Ask them to use those headings to write a prediction about the content of the section in one or two sentences. Tell students to read the section to test their predictions.

## Point-of-Use Resources

**Guided Reading and Review** Unit 1 booklet, p. 11 provides students with practice identifying the main ideas and key terms of this section.

**Lesson Plans** For lesson planning suggestions, see p. 16 of the Lesson Plans booklet.

**Political Cartoons** See p. 8 of the Political Cartoons booklet for a cartoon relevant to this section.

**Section Support Transparencies** Transparency 11, *Visual Learning;* Transparency 110, *Political Cartoon*

## Organizing Information

To make sure students understand the main points of this section, you may wish to use the flowchart graphic organizer to the right.

Tell students that a flowchart shows a sequence of events. Ask students to use the flowchart to record the sequence of events that led to the forming of the first State constitutions.

**Teaching Tip** A template for this graphic organizer can be found in the Section Support Transparencies, Transparency 4.

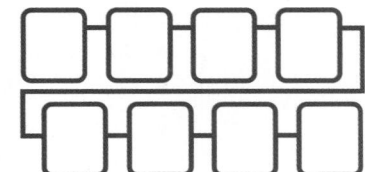

## Answer to . . .

**Evaluating the Quotation** Franklin thought the ultimate result was the War for Independence. Students' answers will vary on the reasonableness of that conclusion; some may suggest that since the differences between the colonies and England were so great, war was inevitable.

## Learning Styles

**Linguistic** Remind students of key historical events that led to the colonies' decision to break away from Britain. Based on this discussion and what they have learned in class, have students write their own Declaration of Rights and Grievances to the king. Encourage them to include in the letter of protest those acts and policies the colonists strongly denounced.

**(Average)**

## Background Note

### Political Talk

While angry colonists did indeed boycott British goods in the 1760s and '70s, that is not what they would have called it—the word *boycott* had not been invented yet. The term comes from the name of Captain C. C. Boycott, an unfortunate English landlord. Boycott was the first among a number of absentee landlords against whom the Irish Land League protested in the 1870s. The word *boycott*, originally written with a capital "B," gained wide popularity in the United Kingdom in the 1880s, and was subsequently adopted into American usage.

In his plan, Franklin proposed the formation of an annual congress of **delegates** (representatives) from each of the 13 colonies. That body would have the power to raise military and naval forces, make war and peace with the Native Americans, regulate trade with them, tax, and collect customs duties.

Franklin's plan was ahead of its time. It was agreed to by the representatives attending the Albany meeting, but it was turned down by the colonies and by the Crown. Franklin's plan was to be remembered later.

### The Stamp Act Congress

Britain's harsh tax and trade policies of the 1760s fanned resentment in the colonies. Parliament had passed a number of new laws, among them the Stamp Act of 1765. That law required the use of tax stamps on all legal documents, on certain business agreements, and on newspapers.

The new taxes were widely denounced, in part because the rates were perceived as severe, but largely because they amounted to "taxation without representation." In October of 1765, nine colonies—all except Georgia, New Hampshire, North Carolina, and Virginia—sent delegates to the Stamp Act Congress in New York. They prepared a strong protest, called the Declaration of Rights and Grievances, against the new British policies and sent it to the king. These actions marked the first time a significant number of the colonies had joined to oppose the British government.

▲ This colored engraving, printed in 1793, is the earliest known American depiction of the Boston Tea Party. *Critical Thinking **What did the colonists hope to accomplish by destroying the cargo of tea?***

Parliament repealed the Stamp Act, but frictions mounted. New laws were passed and new policies were made to tie the colonies more closely to London. Colonists showed their resentment and anger in wholesale evasion of the laws. Mob violence erupted at several ports, and many colonists supported a **boycott** of English goods. A boycott is a refusal to buy or sell certain products or services. On March 5, 1770, British troops in Boston fired on a jeering crowd, killing five, in what came to be known as the Boston Massacre.

Organized resistance was carried on through Committees of Correspondence, which had grown out of a group formed by Samuel Adams in Boston in 1772. These committees soon spread throughout the colonies, providing a network for cooperation and the exchange of information among the patriots.

Protests multiplied. The famous Boston Tea Party took place on December 16, 1773. A group of colonists, disguised as Native Americans, boarded three tea ships in Boston harbor and dumped the cargo into the sea to protest British control of the tea trade.

## The First Continental Congress

In the spring of 1774, Parliament passed yet another set of laws, this time to punish the colonists for the troubles in Boston and elsewhere. These new laws, denounced in America as the Intolerable Acts, prompted widespread calls for a meeting of all the colonies.

Delegates from every colony except Georgia met in Philadelphia on September 5, 1774. Many of the ablest men of the day were there: Samuel Adams and John Adams of Massachusetts; Roger Sherman of Connecticut; Stephen Hopkins of Rhode Island; John Dickinson and Joseph Galloway of Pennsylvania; John Jay and Philip Livingston of New York; George Washington, Richard Henry Lee, and Patrick Henry of Virginia; and John Rutledge of South Carolina.

For nearly two months the members of that First Continental

## Answer to . . .

**Critical Thinking** They wanted to demonstrate their resolve to not let British goods be sold in the colonies.

## Preparing for Standardized Tests

Have students read the passages under *Growing Colonial Unity* on pp. 35–36 and then answer the following question.

What is the best explanation for why early attempts at colonial cooperation failed?

**A** No one put forth a formal plan.

**B** The British Board of Trade prevented colonists from proposing plans.

**C** Colonists were content with the government as it was.

**(D)** Colonists still considered themselves British subjects, and did not feel particular loyalty to the other colonies.

▲ Washington once complained that his soldiers were forced to "eat every kind of horse food but hay." He won the respect of the men who served under his command when he demanded that Congress provide better treatment for the army. *Critical Thinking **How does this nineteenth-century engraving of Washington and his troops welcoming a provision train of supplies reinforce Washington's image as a strong leader?***

### Background Note
#### Economics

The Second Continental Congress had not only to invent a new system of government during a war, but it also had to cope with the worst period of inflation in U.S. history. Between 1775 and 1779, the value of the $191 million in Continental bills the Congress printed to finance the war sank dramatically. In 1777, it took $3 in bills to purchase goods worth $1 in gold or silver. By 1779, the ratio had shot up to 42 to 1, skyrocketed to 100 to 1 in 1780, and then to 146 to 1 in 1781. In 1781, the Congress offered to buy back the bills at a rate of 40 to 1—an inglorious end for the first national currency.

### Point-of-Use Resources

📁 **Close Up on Primary Sources**
Patrick Henry, Speech to the Virginia Provincial Convention (1775), p. 29; Virginia Declaration of Rights (1776), p. 57

Congress discussed the colonies' difficult situation and debated plans for action. They sent a Declaration of Rights, protesting Britain's colonial policies, to King George III. The delegates urged each of the colonies to refuse all trade with England until the hated taxes and trade regulations were **repealed**, or recalled. The delegates also called for the creation of local committees to enforce that boycott.

The meeting adjourned on October 26, with a call for a second congress to be convened the following May. Over the next several months, all the colonial legislatures, including Georgia's, gave their support to the actions of the First Continental Congress.

## The Second Continental Congress

During the fall and winter of 1774–1775, the British government continued to refuse to compromise, let alone reverse, its colonial policies. It reacted to the Declaration of Rights as it had to other expressions of colonial discontent—with even stricter and more repressive measures.

The Second Continental Congress met in Philadelphia on May 10, 1775. By then, the Revolution had begun. The "shot heard 'round the world" had been fired. The battles of Lexington and Concord had been fought three weeks earlier, on April 19.

### Representatives

Each of the 13 colonies sent representatives to the Congress. Most of those who had attended the First Continental Congress were again present. Most notable among the newcomers were Benjamin Franklin of Pennsylvania and John Hancock of Massachusetts.

Hancock was chosen president of the Congress.[9] Almost at once, a continental army was created, and George Washington was appointed its commander in chief. Thomas Jefferson then took Washington's place in the Virginia delegation.

### Our First National Government

The Second Continental Congress became, by force of circumstance, the nation's first national government. However, it rested on no constitutional base. It was condemned by the British as an unlawful assembly and a den of traitors. But it was supported by the force of public opinion and practical necessity.

From July 1776 to March 1781, when the Articles of Confederation went into effect, it did everything any government would do in the circumstances.

---

[9]Peyton Randolph, who had also served as president of the First Continental Congress, was originally chosen for the office. He resigned on May 24, however, because the Virginia House of Burgesses, of which he was the speaker, had been called into session. Hancock was then elected to succeed him.

*Answer to . . .*

**Critical Thinking** Sample answer: Washington is at the center of the engraving, and the other people are clearly paying deference to him.

A C T I V I T Y

## Extended Class Periods

**Time** 90 minutes.
**Purpose** Paraphrase the first paragraph of the Declaration of Independence.
**Grouping** Three to four students.
**Activity** Have group members discuss the meaning of the opening paragraph of the Declaration. Then have students work together to rewrite the paragraph to express their understanding of its meaning.
**Roles** Discussion leader, recorder, and spokesperson.
**Close** When the recorder has prepared the final draft, ask the spokesperson to read the group's paragraph to the class. Then have the class discuss the group's interpretation.

🖥 **Block Strategy
(Basic)**

## Point–of–Use Resources

📁 **Government Assessment Rubrics** Analyzing a Primary Source, p. 14

📁 **Block Scheduling with Lesson Strategies** Additional activities for Chapter 2 appear on p. 20.

📁 **The Living Constitution** Popular Sovereignty, p. 3

📁 **Close Up on Primary Sources** Adam Smith, *The Wealth of Nations* (1776), p. 30; Thomas Paine, *Common Sense* (1776), p. 31

📠 **Basic Principles of the Constitution Transparencies** Transparencies 9–15, *Popular Sovereignty*

# The Declaration of Independence

Slightly more than a year after the Revolution began, John Adams of Massachusetts and Richard Henry Lee of Virginia proposed to Congress:

**PRIMARY Sources** "Resolved, *That these United Colonies are, and of right ought to be, free and independent States, that they are absolved from all allegiance to the British Crown, and that all political connection between them and the State of Great Britain is, and ought to be, totally dissolved.*"

—Resolution of June 7, 1776

Congress named Benjamin Franklin, John Adams, Roger Sherman, Robert Livingston, and Thomas Jefferson to prepare a proclamation of independence. Their momentous product, the Declaration of Independence, was almost wholly the work of Jefferson.

Jefferson relied heavily on the works of John Locke, who argued that the legitimacy of government sprang from the individual, or, as Jefferson wrote, from "the consent of the governed." Locke argued that the individual was born free and was entitled to the Natural Rights of "life, liberty, and estate"—a phrase Jefferson refashioned as "certain inalienable rights" among which were "life, liberty and the pursuit of happiness." If governments failed to protect these rights, subjects were entitled to withdraw their support and resort to armed conflict if all other means of protest failed.

Many of the delegates had serious doubts about the wisdom of a complete separation from England. Only after spirited debate led by the tireless Adams did the delegates finally agree to Adams's and Lee's resolution on July 2. Two days later, on July 4, 1776, they adopted the Declaration of Independence, proclaiming the existence of the new nation.

The Declaration announces the independence of the United States in its first paragraph, which focuses on the concept of natural rights—those basic rights that all humans should enjoy and that are endowed naturally instead of by law. The Declaration equates natural rights with several famous truths:

**PRIMARY Sources** "We hold these truths to be self-evident, that all men are created equal, that they are endowed by their Creator with certain unalienable Rights, that among these are Life, Liberty and the pursuit of Happiness. That to secure these rights, Governments are instituted among Men, deriving their just powers from the consent of the governed; That whenever any Form of Government becomes destructive of these ends it is the Right of the People to alter or to abolish it, and to institute new Government, laying its foundations on such principles and organizing its powers in such form, as to them shall seem most likely to effect their Safety and Happiness."

—The Unanimous Declaration of the Thirteen United States of America

With these brave words, the United States of America was born. The 13 colonies became free and independent States. The 56 men who signed the Declaration sealed it with this final sentence:

"*And for the support of this Declaration, with a firm reliance on the protection of Divine Providence, we mutually pledge to each other, our lives, our Fortunes, and our sacred Honor.*"

## The First State Constitutions

In January 1776, New Hampshire adopted a constitution to replace its royal charter. Less than three months later, South Carolina followed suit. Then, on May 10, nearly two months before the adoption of the Declaration of Independence, the Congress urged each of the colonies to adopt: "such governments as shall, in the opinion of the representatives of the people, best conduce to the happiness and safety of their constituents."

### Drafting State Constitutions

In 1776 and 1777, most of the States adopted written constitutions—bodies of fundamental laws setting out the principles, structures, and processes of their governments. Assemblies or conventions were commonly used to draft and then adopt these new documents.

Massachusetts set a lasting example in the constitution-making process. There, a convention

# CONSTITUTIONAL PRINCIPLES

**Popular Sovereignty**
The Declaration of Independence clearly points to Great Britain's failure to honor the popular sovereignty of the colonies as a reason for their declaring independence. Much of the declaration is spent listing specific grievances that highlight ways that King George III failed to honor the colonies' popular sovereignty.

**Activity**
Have students view excerpts from the Declaration of Independence on this page or the entire document found on pages 40–43 to find specific examples of how it uses popular sovereignty as a basis for declaring independence. Have students share their examples with the class, then lead a discussion on the significance of popular sovereignty to the Declaration of Independence.

submitted its work to the voters for ratification. The Massachusetts constitution of 1780 is the oldest of the present-day State constitutions. In fact, it is the oldest written constitution in force anywhere in the world today.[10]

## Common Features

The first State constitutions differed, sometimes widely, in detail. Yet they shared many similar features. The most common features were the principles of **popular sovereignty** (government can exist only with the consent of the governed), limited government, civil rights and liberties, and separation of powers and checks and balances. These principles are outlined in detail in the table at right.

The new State constitutions were rather brief documents. For the most part, they were declarations of principle and statements of limitation on governmental power. Memories of the royal governors were fresh, and the new State governors were given little real power. Most of the authority that was granted to State government was placed in the legislature. Elective terms of office were made purposely short, seldom more than one or two years. The right to vote was limited to those adult males who could meet rigid qualifications, including property ownership.

***

[10]From independence until that constitution became effective in 1780, Massachusetts relied on its colonial charter, in force prior to 1691, as its fundamental law.

### Common Features of State Constitutions

| | |
|---|---|
| **POPULAR SOVEREIGNTY** | The principle of popular sovereignty was the basis for every new State constitution. That principle says that government can exist and function only with the consent of the governed. The people hold power and the people are sovereign. |
| **LIMITED GOVERNMENT** | The concept of limited government was a major feature of each State constitution. The powers delegated to government were granted reluctantly and hedged with many restrictions. |
| **CIVIL RIGHTS AND LIBERTIES** | In every State it was made clear that the sovereign people held certain rights that the government must respect at all times. Seven of the new constitutions contained a bill of rights, setting out the "unalienable rights" held by the people. |
| **SEPARATION OF POWERS AND CHECKS AND BALANCES** | The powers granted to the new State governments were purposely divided among three branches: executive, legislative, and judicial. Each branch was given powers with which to check (restrain the actions of) the other branches of the government. |

*Interpreting Tables* Most of the newly created States adopted written constitutions in the two years following the Declaration of Independence. ***Why did the first State constitutions share several common features?***

We shall return to the subject of State constitutions later, in Chapter 24. For now, note this very important point: The earliest of these documents were, within a very few years, to have a marked impact on the drafting of the Constitution of the United States.

## Section **2** Assessment

**Key Terms and Main Ideas**

1. Why did some colonists support a **boycott** of English goods?
2. What was the **Albany Plan of Union** and how was it received by the colonies and by the Crown?
3. Explain the concept of **popular sovereignty.**
4. What was the outcome of the First Continental Congress?
5. In what ways did the Second Continental Congress serve as the first national government?

**Critical Thinking**

6. **Distinguishing Fact from Opinion** The Declaration of Independence states that all men are endowed "with certain unalienable Rights, that among these are Life, Liberty and the pursuit of Happiness." Is this statement a fact or opinion? Explain your answer.
7. **Expressing Problems Clearly** What problems arose from changes in British policy toward the colonies in the 1760s?

### Take It to the Net

8. Read the Albany Plan as proposed by Benjamin Franklin. Create a list of three ways that this plan could help the colonies. Next, create a list of three ways the Albany Plan could hurt the colonies. Use the links provided in the Social Studies area at the following Web site for help in completing this activity. **www.phschool.com**

### Take It to the Net

**8.** Direct students to the Social Studies area at the Prentice Hall School Web site. The *Magruder's American Government* companion Web site includes the directions and links needed to complete the activity. It also provides a printable Internet activity worksheet with scoring rubrics for assessment. Students' lists should be supported with specific examples from the text.

**6.** Some students might suggest that as the Framers' wrote the document, it was an opinion; others may say that as our government is based on this statement, it is now commonly held to be fact.
**7.** Answers will vary, but should reflect an understanding that the new policies made colonists re-evaluate their relationship to Britain and eventually led to war.

## Point-of-Use Resources

**Guide to the Essentials** Chapter 2, Section 2, p. 19 provides support for students who need additional review of section content. Spanish support is available in the Spanish edition of the Guide on p. 12.

**Quiz** Unit 1 booklet, p. 12 includes matching and multiple-choice questions to check students' understanding of Section 2 content.

**Presentation Pro CD-ROM** Quizzes and multiple-choice questions check students' understanding of Section 2 content.

## Answers to . . .

### Section 2 Assessment

**1.** Many colonists supported a boycott of English goods as an act of protest against Britain's taxes.
**2.** The Albany Plan of Union was a plan for the 13 colonies to form a congress which would have the power to raise armies, make war and peace, establish trade, and impose taxes. The colonies and the Crown rejected the plan.
**3.** Popular sovereignty is the idea that a government can only exist if it has the consent of those it governs.
**4.** The First Continental Congress resulted in all colonial legislatures giving their support to several plans of action, including formalized boycotts. The Congress also produced a document of protest—the Declaration of Rights—which was sent to the king.
**5.** The Second Continental Congress directed the war effort, borrowed money to finance the war, coined money, bought supplies, and made treaties with other governments.

## Answer to . . .

**Interpreting Tables** They were all based on the ideals that had united the States in their fight for independence.

# *The* Declaration *of* Independence

**In Congress, July 4, 1776**

*The Unanimous Declaration of the Thirteen United States of America*

▲ The Declaration of Independence was largely the work of Thomas Jefferson, who chaired the five-person committee assigned to the task.

When in the Course of human events, it becomes necessary for one people to dissolve the political bands which have connected them with another, and to assume among the powers of the earth, the separate and equal station to which the Laws of nature and of Nature's God entitle them, a decent respect to the opinions of mankind requires that they should declare the causes which impel them to the separation.

We hold these truths to be self-evident, that all men are created equal, that they are endowed by their Creator with certain unalienable Rights, that among these are Life, Liberty and the pursuit of Happiness. That to secure these rights, Governments are instituted among Men, deriving their just powers from the consent of the governed; That whenever any Form of Government becomes destructive of these ends it is the Right of the People to alter or to abolish it, and to institute new Government, laying its foundation on such principles and organizing its powers in such form, as to them shall seem most likely to effect their Safety and Happiness. Prudence, indeed, will dictate that Governments long established should not be changed for light and transient causes; and accordingly all experience hath shown, that mankind are more disposed to suffer, while evils are sufferable, than to right themselves by abolishing the forms to which they are accustomed. But when a long train of abuses and usurpations, pursuing invariably the same Object evinces a design to reduce them under absolute Despotism, it is their right, it is their duty, to throw off such Government, and to provide new Guards for their future security.

Such has been the patient sufferance of these Colonies; and such is now the necessity which constrains them to alter their former Systems of Government. The history of the present King of Great Britain is a history of repeated injuries and usurpations, all having in direct object the establishment of an absolute Tyranny over these States. To prove this, let Facts be submitted to a candid world.

He has refused his Assent to Laws, the most wholesome and necessary for the public good.

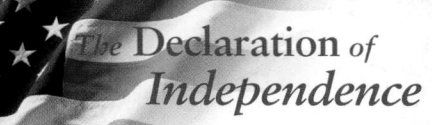
He has forbidden his Governors to pass Laws of immediate and pressing importance, unless suspended in their operation till his Assent should be obtained; and when so suspended, he has utterly neglected to attend to them.

He has refused to pass other Laws for the accommodation of large districts of people, unless those people would relinquish the right of Representation in the Legislature, a right inestimable to them and formidable to tyrants only.

He has called together legislative bodies at places unusual, uncomfortable, and distant from the depository of their Public Records, for the sole purpose of fatiguing them into compliance with his measures.

He has dissolved Representative Houses repeatedly, for opposing with manly firmness his invasions on the rights of the people.

He has refused for a long time, after such dissolutions, to cause others to be elected; whereby the Legislative powers, incapable of Annihilation, have returned to the People at large for their exercise; the State remaining in the mean time exposed to all the dangers of invasions from without, and convulsions within.

He has endeavored to prevent the population of these States; for that purpose obstructing the Laws for Naturalization of Foreigners; refusing to pass others to encourage their migration hither, and raising the conditions of new Appropriations of Lands.

He has obstructed the Administration of Justice, by refusing his Assent to Laws for establishing Judiciary powers.

He has made Judges dependent on his Will alone for the tenure of their offices, and the amount and payment of their salaries.

He has erected a multitude of New Offices, and sent hither swarms of Officers to harass our people and eat out their substance.

He has kept among us in time of peace, Standing Armies, without the Consent of our legislatures.

He has affected to render the Military independent of, and superior to, the Civil Power.

He has combined with others to subject us to a jurisdiction foreign to our constitutions, and unacknowledged by our laws; giving his Assent to their Acts of pretended Legislation:

For quartering large bodies of armed troops among us;

For protecting them, by a mock Trial, from punishment for any Murders which they should commit on the Inhabitants of these States;

For cutting off our Trade with all parts of the world;

For imposing Taxes on us without our Consent;

For depriving us, in many cases, of the benefits of Trial by Jury;

For transporting us beyond Seas to be tried for pretended offenses;

For abolishing the free System of English Laws in a neighboring Province, establishing therein an Arbitrary government, and enlarging

▲ In his painting *Drafting the Declaration of Independence,* artist Jean Leon Gerome Ferris (1888–1930) shows members of the committee reviewing Jefferson's proposed Declaration.

## Customize for

### More Advanced Students

Have students research the ideas of John Locke and the English tradition of government. *(Locke's* Second Treatise on Government *appears on p. 11 of this text; several primary source pieces are included in the* Close Up on Primary Sources *booklet in the* Teaching Resources*).* Then ask students to correlate these ideas with specific ideas in the Declaration. They may present the results of their project in essay or chart form.

## Customize for

### English Language Learners

Ask students to make a list of sentences from the Declaration that they find challenging. Have them work in pairs or small groups to restate the sentences in their own words. Students may create visuals to help explain particularly difficult sentences.

## Customize for

### Less Proficient Readers

Have students create three-column charts with the headings *Basic Rights, Wrongs Committed by Great Britain,* and *Colonists' Intentions.* As they read the Declaration, students should record words, phrases, or ideas in the appropriate columns. Encourage students to use their charts as a study guide for Chapter 4.

## Point-of-Use Resources

📁 **Close Up on Primary Sources**
English Petition of Right (1620), p. 52;
English Bill of Rights (1689), p. 56

▲ This hand-colored woodcut shows the scene at the signing of the Declaration of Independence.

▼ John Hancock was the first to sign the Declaration of Independence.

its Boundaries so as to render it at once an example and fit instrument for introducing the same absolute rule into these Colonies;

For taking away our Charters, abolishing our most valuable Laws, and altering fundamentally the Forms of our Governments;

For suspending our own Legislatures, and declaring themselves invested with Power to legislate for us in all cases whatsoever.

He has abdicated Government here, by declaring us out of his Protection, and waging War against us.

He has plundered our seas, ravaged our Coasts, burned our towns, and destroyed the lives of our people.

He is at this time transporting large Armies of foreign mercenaries to complete the works of death, desolation and tyranny, already begun with circumstances of Cruelty and perfidy scarcely paralleled in the most barbarous ages, and totally unworthy the Head of a civilized nation.

He has constrained our fellow Citizens taken Captive on the high Seas to bear Arms against their Country, to become the executioners of their friends and Brethren, or to fall themselves by their Hands.

He has excited domestic insurrections amongst us, and has endeavored to bring on the inhabitants of our frontiers the merciless Indian Savages whose known rule of warfare, is an undistinguished destruction of all ages, sexes, and conditions.

In every stage of these Oppressions We have Petitioned for Redress in the most humble terms. Our repeated Petitions have been answered only by repeated injury. A Prince, whose character is thus marked by every act which may define a Tyrant, is unfit to be the ruler of a free People.

Nor have We been wanting in attentions to our British brethren. We have warned them from time to time of attempts by their legislature to extend an unwarrantable jurisdiction over us. We have reminded them of the circumstances of our emigration and settlement here. We have appealed to their native justice and magnanimity, and we have conjured them by the ties of our common kindred to disavow these usurpations, which, would inevitably interrupt our connections and correspondence. They too have been deaf to the voice of justice and of consanguinity. We must, therefore, acquiesce in the necessity, which denounces our Separation, and hold them, as we hold the rest of mankind, Enemies in War, in Peace Friends.

We, therefore, the Representatives of the United States of America, in General Congress, Assembled, appealing to the Supreme Judge of the world for the rectitude of our intentions, do, in the Name, and by the Authority of the good People of these Colonies, solemnly publish and declare, That these United Colonies are, and of right ought to be Free and Independent States; that they are Absolved from all Allegiance to the British Crown, and that all political connection between them and the State of Great Britain, is and ought to be totally dissolved, and that as Free and Independent States, they have full Power to levy

War, conclude Peace, contract Alliances, establish Commerce, and to do all other Acts and Things which Independent States may of right do. And for the support of this Declaration, with a firm reliance on the protection of Divine Providence, we mutually pledge to each other our Lives, our Fortunes and our sacred Honor.

## *John Hancock*
President of the Continental Congress 1775–1777

**New Hampshire**
Josiah Bartlett
William Whipple
Mathew Thornton

**Massachusetts Bay**
Samuel Adams
John Adams
Robert Treat Paine
Elbridge Gerry

**Rhode Island**
Stephan Hopkins
William Ellery

**Connecticut**
Roger Sherman
Samuel Huntington
William Williams
Oliver Wolcott

**New York**
William Floyd
Philip Livingston
Francis Lewis
Lewis Morris

**New Jersey**
Richard Stockton
John Witherspoon
Francis Hopkinson
John Hart
Abraham Clark

**Delaware**
Caesar Rodney
George Read
Thomas M'Kean

**Maryland**
Samuel Chase
William Paca
Thomas Stone
Charles Carroll of
   Carrollton

**Virginia**
George Wythe
Richard Henry Lee
Thomas Jefferson
Benjamin Harrison
Thomas Nelson, Jr.
Francis Lightfoot Lee
Carter Braxton

**Pennsylvania**
Robert Morris
Benjamin Rush
Benjamin Franklin
John Morton
George Clymer
James Smith
George Taylor
James Wilson
George Ross

**North Carolina**
William Hooper
Joseph Hewes
John Penn

**South Carolina**
Edward Rutledge
Thomas Heyward, Jr.
Thomas Lynch, Jr.
Arthur Middleton

**Georgia**
Button Gwinnett
Lyman Hall
George Walton

---

## Reviewing the Declaration

### Vocabulary
Choose ten words in the Declaration with which you are unfamiliar. Look them up in the dictionary. Then, on a piece of paper, copy the sentence or phrase in the Declaration in which each unfamiliar word is used. After the sentence, write the definition of the unfamiliar word.

### Comprehension
1. Which truths in the second paragraph are "self-evident"?
2. Name the three unalienable rights listed in the Declaration.
3. From what source do governments derive their "just powers"?
4. In the series of paragraphs beginning, "He has refused his Assent," to whom does the word "He" refer?
5. According to the Declaration, what powers does the United States have "as Free and Independent States"?

### Critical Thinking
6. **Recognizing Cause and Effect** Why do you think the colonists were unhappy with the fact that their judges' salaries were paid by the king?
7. **Identifying Assumptions** Do you think that the statement "All men are created equal" was intended to apply to all human beings? Explain your reasoning.
8. **Making Comparisons** (a) What natural rights are cited in the Declaration? (b) Read the first ten amendments to the Constitution (the Bill of Rights) on pages 771–773. What additional natural rights are cited?

**Objectives** You may wish to call students' attention to the objectives in the Section Preview. The objectives are reflected in the main headings of the section.

**Bellringer** Ask students whether they would expect a revolutionary new computer software program to run free of glitches. Lead them to see that the first version of nearly anything is likely to have problems. Explain that in this section, they will learn about problems within the first government of the United States.

**Vocabulary Builder** Have students create a sentence that uses all three terms in the Political Dictionary. As students read the section, have them determine how sensible their sentences are, based on the actual definition of each term.

## Section Preview

### OBJECTIVES

1. **Describe** the structure of the government set up under the Articles of Confederation.
2. **Explain** why the weaknesses of the Articles led to a critical period for the government in the 1780s.
3. **Describe** how a growing need for a stronger national government led to plans for a Constitutional Convention.

### WHY IT MATTERS

The Articles of Confederation established a fairly weak central government, which led to conflicts among the States. The turmoil during this critical period for the young nation caused some States to take steps toward creating a stronger government.

### POLITICAL DICTIONARY

★ **Articles of Confederation**
★ **ratification**
★ **presiding officer**

---

**Pressed for Time?**

### Quick Lesson Plan

**1. Focus** Tell students that for a national government to work properly, it must have certain powers. Ask students to discuss the kinds of powers that make a national government strong.

**2. Instruct** Ask students to list the main weaknesses of the Articles of Confederation, focusing on the distribution of power between Congress and the States. Then lead a discussion on how the States undermined the limited powers given to Congress.

**3. Close/Reteach** Remind students that the weakness of the Articles led to a critical period in which States began to recognize the need for a stronger central government. Have students, as they read, list events that particularly pointed out this need.

---

The First and Second Continental Congresses rested on no legal base. They were called in haste to meet an emergency, and they were intended to be temporary. Something more regular and permanent was clearly needed. In this section, you will look at the first attempt to establish a lasting government for the new nation.

## The Articles of Confederation

Richard Henry Lee's resolution leading to the Declaration of Independence also had called on the Second Continental Congress to propose

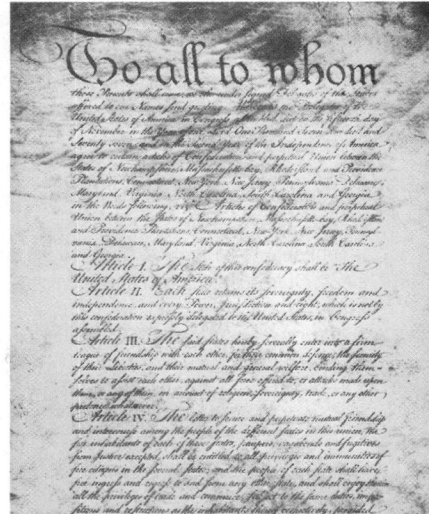

► Articles of Confederation

"a plan of confederation." Off and on, for 17 months, they considered the problem of uniting the former colonies. Finally, on November 15, 1777, the delegates approved a plan of government called the **Articles of Confederation.**

The Articles of Confederation established "a firm league of friendship" among the States. Under this plan, each State kept "its sovereignty, freedom, and independence, and every Power, Jurisdiction, and right . . . not . . . expressly delegated to the United States, in Congress assembled." The States came together "for their common defense, the security of their Liberties, and their mutual and general welfare. . . ."

The Articles did not go into effect immediately, however. The **ratification,** or formal approval, of each of the 13 States was needed first. Eleven States agreed to the document within a year. Delaware added its approval in February 1779. But Maryland did not ratify until March 1, 1781, and the Second Continental Congress declared the Articles effective on that date.

### Governmental Structure

The government set up by the Articles was simple indeed. A Congress was the sole body created. It was unicameral, made up of delegates chosen yearly by the States in whatever way their legislatures might direct. Each State had one vote in the Congress, whatever its population or wealth.

The Articles established no executive or judicial branch. These functions were to be handled by committees of the Congress. Each year the

---

## ▣ Block Scheduling Strategies

Consider these suggestions to manage extended class time:

■ Ask students to suppose that they are living during the critical period of the 1780s. They have realized that the weaknesses of the Articles of Confederation are creating difficult times for the government. Have each student write an editorial to a local newspaper identifying the problems of the Articles, explaining how these problems are affecting the nation's government, and offering suggestions for change.

■ Explain to students that Shays' Rebellion was an event that sharply divided American opinions on government. Have students research the rebellion to answer these questions: Which group supported the rebels? Did this group embrace or fear a strong national government? What were the long-term effects of the rebellion? How did it shape the Framers' debate on revising the Articles? Students may present their findings in graphic organizers or time lines.

Congress would choose one of its members as its president. That person would be its **presiding officer** (chair), but not the president of the United States. Civil officers such as postmasters were to be appointed by the Congress.

## Powers of Congress

Several important powers were given to the Congress. It could make war and peace; send and receive ambassadors; make treaties; borrow money; set up a money system; establish post offices; build a navy; raise an army by asking the States for troops; fix uniform standards of weights and measures; and settle disputes among the States.

## State Obligations

By agreeing to the Articles, the States pledged to obey the Articles and acts of the Congress. They would provide the funds and troops requested by the Congress; treat citizens of other States fairly and equally with their own; and give full faith and credit to the public acts, records, and judicial proceedings of every other State. In addition, the States agreed to surrender fugitives from justice to one another; submit their disputes to Congress for settlement; and allow open travel and trade between and among the States.

Beyond these few obligations, the States retained those powers not explicitly given to the Congress. They, not the Congress, were primarily responsible for protecting life and property. States were also accountable for promoting the general welfare of the people.

## Weaknesses

The powers of the Congress appear, at first glance, to have been considerable. Several important powers were missing, however. Their omission, together with other weaknesses, soon proved the Articles inadequate to the needs of the time.

The Congress did not have the power to tax. It could raise money only by borrowing and by asking the States for funds. Borrowing was, at best, a poor source. The Second Continental Congress had borrowed heavily to support the costs of fighting the Revolution, and many of those debts had not been paid. And, while the Articles remained in force, not one State came close to meeting the financial requests made by the Congress.

### Weaknesses of the Articles of Confederation

◆ One vote for each State, regardless of size.

◆ Congress powerless to lay and collect taxes or duties.

◆ Congress powerless to regulate foreign and interstate commerce.

◆ No executive to enforce acts of Congress.

◆ No national court system.

◆ Amendment only with consent of all States.

◆ A 9/13 majority required to pass laws.

◆ Articles only a "firm league of friendship."

*Interpreting Tables* The thirst for independence made the new States wary of strong central government. ***How is this caution reflected in the weaknesses built into the Articles of Confederation?***

Nor did the Congress have the power to regulate trade between the States. This lack of a central mechanism to regulate the young nation's commerce was one of the major factors that led to the adoption of the Constitution.

The Congress was further limited by a lack of power to make the States obey the Articles of Confederation or the laws it made. Congress could exercise the powers it did have only with the consent of 9 of the 13 State delegations. Finally, the Articles themselves could be changed only with the consent of all 13 of the State legislatures. This procedure proved an impossible task; not one amendment was ever added to the Articles of Confederation.

## The Critical Period, the 1780s

The long Revolutionary War finally ended on October 19, 1781. America's victory was confirmed by the signing of the Treaty of Paris in 1783. Peace, however, brought the new nation's economic and political problems into sharp focus. Problems, caused by the weaknesses of the Articles of Confederation, soon surfaced.

With a central government unable to act, the States bickered among themselves and grew increasingly jealous and suspicious of one another. They often refused to support the new central government, financially and in almost every other way. Several of them made agreements with foreign governments without the approval of the

## Reading Strategy
### Questioning

Ask students to read the section's main headings and subheadings and write a question about each. Have them look for answers to their questions as they read.

## Customize for
### English Language Learners

Have students create a time line of the events discussed in Section 3 that led to the Constitutional Convention in 1787. If you wish, you may distribute cards on which each event is written, and have students put them in order.

## Point-of-Use Resources

**Guided Reading and Review** Unit 1 booklet, p. 13 provides students with practice identifying the key terms and main ideas of this section.

**Lesson Plans** For lesson planning suggestions, see p. 17 of the Lesson Plans booklet.

**Political Cartoons** See p. 9 of the Political Cartoons booklet for a cartoon relevant to this section.

**Section Support Transparencies** Transparency 12, *Visual Learning;* Transparency 111, *Political Cartoon*

## Organizing Information

To make sure students understand the main points of this section, you may wish to use the tree map graphic organizer to the right.

Tell students that a tree map shows a topic, its main ideas and its supporting details. Ask students to use the tree map to outline the strengths, weaknesses, and consequences of the Articles of Confederation.

**Teaching Tip** A template for this graphic organizer can be found in the Section Support Transparencies, Transparency 3.

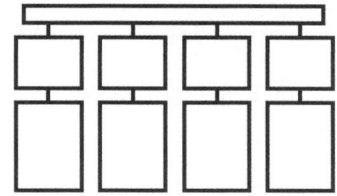

*Answer to ...*

**Interpreting Tables** The Articles do not provide for any elements of a strong central government, including an executive, a national court system, or the power to tax or regulate commerce.

**45**

A C T I V I T Y

## Heterogeneous Groups

**Reteaching** Have students create a graphic organizer of the information they have received about American government in the late 1770s and 1780s. Ask them to use the following as subject headings or categories: *Articles of Confederation, Critical Period,* and *Calls for a Stronger Government.* Encourage students to list provisions in the Articles of Confederation, problems that arose during the Critical Period, and related reasons why States took the first steps toward change.

**(Basic)**

National Government, even though that was forbidden by the Articles. Most even organized their own military forces. George Washington complained, "We are one nation today and 13 tomorrow. Who will treat with us on such terms?"

The States taxed one another's goods and even banned some trade. They printed their own money, often with little backing. Economic chaos spread throughout the colonies as prices soared and sound credit vanished. Debts, public and private, went unpaid. Violence broke out in a number of places as a result of the economic chaos.

The most spectacular of these events played out in western Massachusetts in a series of incidents that came to be known as Shays' Rebellion. As economic conditions worsened, property holders, many of them small farmers, began to lose their land and possessions for lack of payment on taxes and other debts. In the fall of 1786, Daniel Shays, a former American officer in the War for Independence, and other local leaders led an uprising that forced the Supreme Court in Springfield, Massachusetts, to close. Early

▲ **Shays' Rebellion** Following the series of incidents known as Shays' Rebellion, the Supreme Court of Massachusetts condemned to death Daniel Shays and about a dozen others. Shays petitioned for and received a pardon in 1788.

the next year they unsuccessfully attacked a federal arsenal. State forces moved in to quiet the rebellion and Shays fled to Vermont. In response to the rebellion, the Massachusetts legislature eventually passed laws to ease the burden of debtors.

## A Need for Stronger Government

The Articles had created a government unable to deal with the nation's troubles. Inevitably, demand grew for a stronger, more effective national government. Those who were most threatened by economic and political instability —large property owners, merchants, traders, and other creditors—soon took the lead in efforts to that end. The movement for change began to take concrete form in 1785.

### Mount Vernon

Maryland and Virginia, plagued by bitter trade disputes, took the first step in the movement for change. Ignoring the Congress, the two States agreed to a conference on their trade problems. Representatives from the two States met at Alexandria, Virginia, in March 1785. At George Washington's invitation, they moved their sessions to his home at nearby Mount Vernon.

Their negotiations proved so successful that on January 21, 1786, the Virginia General Assembly called for "a joint meeting of [all of] the States to recommend a federal plan for regulating commerce."

### Annapolis

That joint meeting opened at Annapolis, Maryland, on September 11, 1786. Turnout was poor, with representatives from only 5 of the 13 States attending.[11] Disappointed, but still hopeful, the convention called for yet another meeting of the States

> **PRIMARY Sources** *at Philadelphia on the second Monday in May next, to take into consideration the situation of the United States, to devise such further provisions as*

---

[11]New York, New Jersey, Pennsylvania, Delaware, and Virginia. Although New Hampshire, Massachusetts, Rhode Island, and North Carolina had appointed delegates, none attended the Annapolis meeting.

**Resource Pro® CD-ROM** contains an electronic version of each activity found in the Teaching Resources as well as additional resources such as Supreme Court cases. The Planning Express® feature allows you to customize and create daily lesson plans within minutes.

▲ **Mount Vernon** George Washington's graceful home overlooking the Potomac River served as the location for trade talks between Maryland and Virginia. The success of this meeting caused some to move for further steps toward a stronger federal government.

*shall appear to them necessary to render the constitution of the Federal Government adequate to the exigencies of the Union.* "
—Call of the Annapolis Convention

By mid-February of 1787, seven of the States had named delegates to the Philadelphia meeting. These were Delaware, Georgia, New Hampshire, New Jersey, North Carolina, Pennsylvania, and Virginia. Then on February 21, the Congress, which had been hesitating, also called upon the States to send delegates to Philadelphia

 **PRIMARY Sources** " *for the sole and express purpose of revising the Articles of Confederation and reporting to Congress and the several legislatures such alterations and provisions therein as shall when agreed to in Congress and confirmed by the States render the [Articles] adequate to the exigencies of Government and the preservation of the Union.* "
—The United States in Congress Assembled, February 21, 1787

That Philadelphia meeting became the Constitutional Convention.

## Section 3 Assessment

### Key Terms and Main Ideas

1. What were the **Articles of Confederation** and what powers did they grant to Congress?
2. Before the Articles of Confederation could go into effect, how many States were needed for **ratification?**
3. Identify at least three weaknesses of the government under the Articles of Confederation.
4. What was the result of the meetings at Mount Vernon and Annapolis in 1785 and 1786?

### Critical Thinking

5. **Identifying Central Issues** The Articles of Confederation contained several weaknesses. Why would the States purposefully create a weak government under the Articles?

6. **Drawing Conclusions** For what reasons is the period during which the Articles were in force called the Critical Period in American history?

 **Take It to the Net**

7. Read the text of the Articles of Confederation and compare it to the Declaration of Independence. Write a paragraph describing how the Articles of Confederation built upon the ideas expressed in the Declaration of Independence, and in what ways it went further. Use the links provided in the Social Studies area at the following Web site for help in completing this activity. **www.phschool.com**

**Take It to the Net**

7. Direct students to the Social Studies area at the Prentice Hall School Web site. The *Magruder's American Government* companion Web site includes the directions and links needed to complete the activity. It also provides a printable Internet activity worksheet with scoring rubrics for assessment. Students' paragraphs should reflect a close reading of both documents and an understanding of the idea that the Articles of Confederation, unlike the Declaration of Independence, provided a plan for a government.

## Answers to . . .

### Section 3 Assessment

1. The Articles of Confederation were plans for government developed by the delegates to the Second Continental Congress. They gave Congress the power to: make war and peace; send and receive ambassadors; make treaties; borrow money; set up a money system; establish post offices; build a navy and raise armies; fix standards of weights and measures; and settle disputes among the States.
2. All thirteen States were needed for ratification.
3. Congress could not tax or regulate trade; had no power to make the States cooperate; near-unanimous consent was required to pass laws; unanimous consent was required to amend Articles.
4. As a result of the Mount Vernon and Annapolis meetings, a movement for change began which led to the Constitutional Convention.
5. Possible answer: Having just fought a war against a central government that Americans saw as tyrannical, the States were reluctant to give too much power to their own central government.
6. After the Revolution the new nation had to focus on its problems, but the existing government was not up to the task. The new nation seemed to be on the verge of breaking apart.

4 **Creating the Constitution**

**Objectives** You may wish to call students' attention to the objectives in the Section Preview. The objectives are reflected in the main headings of the section.

**Bellringer** Ask students to think of a conflict that they have read about recently involving local or National Government. Have them brainstorm possible compromise solutions to the conflict. Explain that in this section, they will learn how compromises saved the Constitution.

**Vocabulary Builder** Have students read the terms in the Political Dictionary. Tell them that in 1787 the Constitution was like a house under construction. Ask students to describe the roles that a Framer, a Plan, and a Compromise might have today in the building of a house. Encourage them to recall those images as they read the text.

---

### Pressed for Time?

#### Quick Lesson Plan

**1. Focus** Tell students that the remarkable character of the delegates had much to do with their success in framing a Constitution. Ask them to discuss what they know about the Framers and their accomplishments at the Constitutional Convention.

**2. Instruct** Ask students why the Connecticut Compromise is often called the Great Compromise. Lead a discussion of the two competing plans and how the Framers combined their basic features.

**3. Close/Reteach** Remind students of the hard work that went into framing the Constitution. Have them create a flowchart of the process, beginning with the Framers' sources and ending with the completed Constitution.

---

## Section Preview

### OBJECTIVES

1. **Identify** the Framers of the Constitution and discuss how the delegates organized the proceedings at the Philadelphia Convention.
2. **Compare** and contrast the Virginia Plan and the New Jersey Plan for a new constitution.
3. **Summarize** the major compromises that the delegates agreed to make and the effects of those compromises.
4. **Identify** some of the sources from which the Framers of the Constitution drew inspiration.
5. **Describe** the delegates' reactions to the Constitution as they completed their work.

### WHY IT MATTERS

The Framers of the Constitution created a document that addressed the major concerns of the States attending the Philadelphia Convention. By reaching compromise on items about which they disagreed, the Framers created a new National Government capable of handling the nation's problems.

### POLITICAL DICTIONARY

★ **Framers**
★ **Virginia Plan**
★ **New Jersey Plan**
★ **Connecticut Compromise**
★ **Three-Fifths Compromise**
★ **Commerce and Slave Trade Compromise**

---

**P**icture this scene. It's hot—sweltering, in fact. Yet the windows are all closed to discourage eavesdroppers. Outside, soldiers keep interested onlookers at a distance. Inside, the atmosphere is tense as men exchange their views. Indeed, some become so angry that they threaten to leave the hall. A few carry out their threats.

This was the scene throughout much of the Philadelphia meeting that began on Friday, May 25, 1787.[12] Over the long summer months, the participants labored to build a new government that would best meet the needs of the nation. In this section, you will consider that meeting and its work.

▶ Delegates to the Constitutional Convention gathered in Independence Hall.

## The Framers

Twelve of the 13 States, all but Rhode Island, sent delegates to Philadelphia.[13] In total, 74 delegates were chosen by the legislatures in those 12 states. For a number of reasons, however, only 55 of them actually attended the convention.

Of that 55, this much can be said: Never, before or since, has so remarkable a group been brought together in this country. Thomas Jefferson, who was not among them, called the delegates "an assembly of demi-gods."

The group of delegates who attended the Philadelphia Convention, known as the **Framers** of the Constitution, included many outstanding individuals. These were men of wide knowledge and public experience, of wealth and prestige. Their collective record of public service was truly impressive. Many of them had fought in the Revolution; 39 had been members of the Continental Congress or the Congress of the

---

[12]Not enough States were represented on the date Congress had set, Monday, May 14, to begin the meeting. The delegates who were present met and adjourned each day until Friday the 25th, when a quorum (in this case, a majority) of the States was on hand.

[13]The Rhode Island legislature was controlled by the soft-money forces, mostly debtors and small farmers who were helped by inflation and so were against a stronger central government. The New Hampshire delegation, delayed mostly by lack of funds, did not reach Philadelphia until late July.

---

### Block Scheduling Strategies

Consider these suggestions to manage extended class time:

■ To extend the Learning Styles Activity from p. 49, have students use the materials they created to simulate the debate over the Virginia and New Jersey Plans. Have students conclude the debate by identifying and discussing the actual compromises that delegates made at the Convention.

■ Ask students to compare the chart of the Framers on p. 49 with the charts of the members of Congress in Chapter 10 (p. 280). Ask students to identify similarities as well as differences between the two groups. Have students explain how congressional leadership has changed, and whether they feel these changes have been beneficial or detrimental to the United States.

## Selected Framers of the Constitution

| Name | State | Background |
|---|---|---|
| George Washington | Virginia | Planter, commander of the Continental Army |
| James Madison | Virginia | Legislator, major figure in movement to replace Articles |
| Edmund Randolph | Virginia | Lawyer, governor of Virginia |
| George Mason | Virginia | Planter, author of Virginia's Declaration of Rights |
| Benjamin Franklin | Pennsylvania | Writer, printer, inventor, legislator, diplomat |
| Gouverneur Morris | Pennsylvania | Lawyer, merchant, legislator |
| Robert Morris | Pennsylvania | Merchant, major financier of the Revolution |
| James Wilson | Pennsylvania | Lawyer, legislator, close student of politics, history |
| Alexander Hamilton | New York | Lawyer, legislator, champion of stronger central government |
| William Paterson | New Jersey | Lawyer, legislator, attorney general of New Jersey |
| Elbridge Gerry | Massachusetts | Merchant, legislator, major investor in land, government securities |
| Rufus King | Massachusetts | Legislator, opponent of extensive changes to Articles |
| Luther Martin | Maryland | Lawyer, legislator, attorney general of Maryland |
| Oliver Ellsworth | Connecticut | Lawyer, legislator, judge, theologian |
| Roger Sherman | Connecticut | Merchant, mayor of New Haven, legislator, judge |
| John Dickinson | Delaware | Lawyer, historian, major advocate of independence |
| John Rutledge | South Carolina | Lawyer, legislator, principal author of South Carolina's constitution |
| Charles Pinckney | South Carolina | Lawyer, legislator, leader in move to replace Articles |

*Interpreting Tables* In reference to creating the Constitution, James Madison noted that considering "the natural diversity of human opinions on all new and complicated subjects, it is impossible to consider the degree of concord which ultimately prevailed as less than a miracle." *What similarities and differences can you see in the Framers' backgrounds? Do you think their personal experiences helped or hurt their ability to draft the Constitution?*

Confederation, or both. Eight had served in constitutional conventions in their own States, and seven had been State governors. Eight had signed the Declaration of Independence. Thirty-one of the delegates had attended college in a day when there were but a few colleges in the land, and their number also included two college presidents and three professors. Two were to become Presidents of the United States, and one a Vice President. Seventeen later served in the Senate and eleven in the House of Representatives.

Is it any wonder that the product of such a gathering was described by the English statesman William E. Gladstone, nearly a century later, as "the most wonderful work ever struck off at a given time by the brain and purpose of man"?

Remarkably, the average age of the delegates was only 42, and nearly half were only in their 30s. Indeed, most of the real leaders were in that age group—James Madison was 36, Gouverneur Morris 35, Edmund Randolph 34, and Alexander Hamilton 32. At 81, Benjamin Franklin was the oldest. His health was failing, however, and he was not able to attend many of the meetings. George Washington, at 55, was one of the few older members who played a key role in the making of the Constitution.

By and large, the Framers of the Constitution were of a new generation in American politics. Several of the better-known leaders of the Revolutionary period were not in Philadelphia. Patrick Henry said he "smelt a rat" and refused to attend. Samuel Adams, John Hancock, and Richard Henry Lee were not selected as delegates by their States. Thomas Paine was in Paris. So, too, was Thomas Jefferson, as American minister to France. John Adams was our envoy to England and Holland at the time.

## Organization and Procedure

The Framers met that summer in Philadelphia's Independence Hall, probably in the same room in which the Declaration of Independence had been signed 11 years earlier.

▶ This nineteenth-century engraving shows George Washington presiding over the Constitutional Convention in 1787. *Critical Thinking* **What impressions did the artist try to convey about this historic gathering?**

They organized immediately on May 25, unanimously electing George Washington president of the convention.[14] Then, and at the second session on Monday, May 28, they adopted several rules of procedure. A majority of the States would be needed to conduct business. Each State delegation was to have one vote on all matters, and a majority of the votes cast would carry any proposal.

### Working in Secrecy

The delegates also decided to keep their deliberations secret. The convention had drawn much public attention and speculation. So, to protect themselves from outside pressures, the delegates adopted a rule of secrecy. On the whole, the rule was well kept.

A secretary, William Jackson, and other minor, nonmember officials were appointed. Jackson kept the convention's *Journal.* That official record, however, was quite sketchy. It was mostly a listing of members present, motions put forth, and votes taken; and it was not always accurate at that.

Fortunately, several delegates kept their own accounts of the proceedings. Most of what is known of the work of the convention comes from James Madison's voluminous *Notes.* His brilliance and depth of knowledge led his colleagues to hold him in great respect. Quickly, he became the convention's floor leader. Madison contributed more to the Constitution than did any of the others, and still he was able to keep a close record of its work. Certainly, he deserves the title "Father of the Constitution."

The Framers met on 89 of the 116 days from May 25 through their final meeting on September 17. They did most of their work on the floor of the convention. They handled some matters in committees, but the full body ultimately settled all questions.

### A Momentous Decision

The Philadelphia Convention was called to recommend revisions in the Articles of Confederation. However, almost at once the delegates agreed that they were, in fact, meeting to create a *new* government for the United States. On May 30 they adopted this proposal:

**PRIMARY Sources** ❝*Resolved, . . . that a national Government ought to be established consisting of a supreme Legislative, Executive and Judiciary.* ❞
—Edmund Randolph, Delegate from Virginia

With this momentous decision, the Framers redefined the purpose of the convention. From that point on, they set about the writing of a new constitution. This new constitution was intended to replace the Articles of Confederation. Their debates were spirited, even bitter. At times the convention seemed near collapse. Once they had passed Randolph's resolution, however, the goal of a majority of the convention never changed.

---

[14]Twenty-nine delegates from seven States were present on that first day. The full number of 55 was not reached until August 6, when John Francis Mercer of Maryland arrived. In the meantime, some delegates had departed, and others were absent from time to time. Some 40 members attended most of the daily sessions of the convention.

## CONSTITUTIONAL PRINCIPLES

### Separation of Powers

Although the Virginia and New Jersey Plans were very different from each other, both plans proposed a government that separated powers among various government branches. Each plan included legislative, judicial, and executive elements for the National Government, yet had different ideas about how each of these elements would function.

### Activity

Have students review material about the Virginia and New Jersey Plans found in this section. Then ask each student to create a Venn diagram highlighting similarities of and differences between each plan's proposed role for its legislative, judicial, and executive elements. Have students include differences in the outer circles and similarities in the overlapping circle.

# The Virginia Plan

No State had more to do with the calling of the convention than Virginia did. It was not surprising, then, that its delegates should offer the first plan for a new constitution. On May 29 the **Virginia Plan,** largely the work of Madison, was presented by Randolph.

The Virginia Plan called for a new government with three separate branches: legislative, executive, and judicial. The legislature—Congress—would be bicameral. Representation in each house was to be based either upon each State's population or upon the amount of money it gave for the support of the central government. The members of the lower house, the House of Representatives, were to be popularly elected in each State. Those of the upper house, the Senate, were to be chosen by the House from lists of persons nominated by the State legislatures.

Congress was to be given all of the powers it held under the Articles. In addition, it was to have the power "to legislate in all cases to which the separate States are incompetent" to act, to veto any State law in conflict with national law, and to use force if necessary to make a State obey national law.

Under the proposed Virginia Plan, Congress would choose a "National Executive" and a "National Judiciary." Together, these two branches would form a "Council of revision." They could veto acts passed by Congress, but a veto could be overridden by the two houses. The executive would have "a general authority to execute the National laws." The judiciary would "consist of one or more supreme tribunals [courts], and of inferior tribunals."

The Virginia Plan also provided that all State officers should take an oath to support the Union, and that each State be guaranteed a republican form of government. Under the plan, Congress would have the exclusive power to admit new States to the Union.

The Virginia Plan, then, would create a new constitution by thoroughly revising the Articles. Its goal was the creation of a truly national government with greatly expanded powers and, importantly, the power to enforce its decisions.

The Virginia Plan set the agenda for much of the convention's work. But some delegates—especially those from the smaller States of Delaware, Maryland, and New Jersey, and from New York—found it too radical.[15] Soon they developed their counterproposals. On June 15 William Paterson of New Jersey presented the position of the small States.

# The New Jersey Plan

Paterson and his colleagues offered several amendments to the Articles, but not nearly so thorough a revision as that proposed by the Virginia Plan. The **New Jersey Plan** retained the unicameral Congress of the Confederation, with each of the States equally represented. To those powers Congress already had, would be added closely limited powers to tax and to regulate trade between the States.

The New Jersey Plan also called for a federal executive of more than one person. This plural executive would be chosen by Congress and could be removed by it at the request of a majority of the States' governors. The "federal judiciary" would be composed of a single "supreme Tribunal," appointed by the executive.

Among their several differences, the major point of disagreement between the two plans centered on this question: How should the States be represented in Congress? Would it be on the basis of their populations or financial contributions, as in the Virginia Plan? Or would it be on the basis of State equality, as in the Articles and the New Jersey Plan?

For weeks the delegates returned to this conflict, debating the matter again and again. The lines were sharply drawn. Several delegates, on both sides of the issue, threatened to withdraw. Finally, the dispute was settled by one of the key compromises the Framers were to make as they built the Constitution.

# Compromises

The disagreement over representation in Congress was critical. The large States expected to dominate the new government. The small

---

[15]The Virginia Plan's major support came from the three largest States: Virginia, Pennsylvania, and Massachusetts. New York was then only the fifth largest State. Alexander Hamilton, the convention's most outspoken champion of a stronger central government, was regularly outvoted by his fellow delegates from New York.

---

## Preparing for Standardized Tests

Have students read the passages under *The Virginia Plan* and then answer the question below.

From the passages, you can infer that smaller States might have found the Virginia Plan unfair because

**A** it thoroughly rejected the Articles.

**B** by basing representation in the houses on population or monetary support, it favored the larger States.

**C** it did not call for an executive branch.

**D** it did not provide for a national judiciary.

A C T I V I T Y

## American Government, American Humor

Share the following quotation with students:

*You see, the men that laid out our Constitution in the first place looked far enough ahead to see, in fact they must have had a premonition that at some time in the distant future there would be a bunch of men in there that didn't know any more about Government than I know about Einstein's theory.*

*Well, those old fellows in those days almost made it foolproof, so due to their farsightedness no one we put in can do us a whole lot of damage.*

*The old founders of the Constitution made it so it didn't matter who was in office, things would drag along about the same.*

—Will Rogers

**Discussion** Ask students to describe Rogers's attitude toward the Framers, toward the Constitution, and toward modern politicians.

**(Average)**

## Point–of–Use Resources

**Simulations and Data Graphing CD-ROM** offers data graphing tools that give students practice with creating and interpreting graphs.

### Slavery in the United States, 1790

| State | Total Population | Slave Population | Percent Slave Population |
|---|---|---|---|
| Connecticut | 238,000 | 2,648 | 1.11 |
| Delaware | 59,000 | 8,887 | 15.06 |
| Georgia | 83,000 | 29,264 | 35.26 |
| Maryland | 320,000 | 103,036 | 32.20 |
| Massachusetts | 476,000 | 0 | 0.0 |
| New Hampshire | 142,000 | 157 | 0.11 |
| New Jersey | 184,000 | 11,423 | 6.21 |
| New York | 340,000 | 21,193 | 6.23 |
| North Carolina | 394,000 | 100,783 | 25.58 |
| Pennsylvania | 434,000 | 3,707 | 0.85 |
| Rhode Island | 69,000 | 958 | 1.39 |
| South Carolina | 249,000 | 107,094 | 43.01 |
| Virginia | 692,000 | 292,627 | 42.29 |

SOURCES: *Historical Statistics of Black America;*
*Historical Statistics of the United States, Colonial Times to 1970*

*Interpreting Tables* The agricultural economy of the southern States relied on slave labor to produce cotton and other crops. ***Why did the southern States want slaves counted in their States' total population?***

States feared that they would not be able to protect their interests. Tempers flared on both sides. The debate became so intense that Benjamin Franklin suggested that "henceforth prayers imploring the assistance of Heaven . . . be held in this Assembly every morning before we proceed to business."

### The Connecticut Compromise

The conflict was finally settled by a compromise suggested by the Connecticut delegation. Under the **Connecticut Compromise,** it was agreed that Congress should be composed of two houses. In the smaller Senate, the States would be represented equally. In the House, the representation of each State would be based upon its population.

Thus, by combining basic features of the rival Virginia and New Jersey Plans, the convention's most serious dispute was resolved. The agreement satisfied the smaller States in particular, and it made it possible for them to support the creation of a strong central government.

The Connecticut Compromise was so pivotal to the writing of the Constitution that it has often been called the Great Compromise.

### The Three-Fifths Compromise

Once it had been agreed to base the seats in the House on each State's population, this question arose: Should slaves be counted in the populations of the southern States?

Again debate was fierce. Most delegates from the slave-holding States argued that slaves should be counted. Most of the northerners took the opposing view. The table above shows the significant percentage of slaves among the populations of the southern States.

Finally, the Framers agreed to the **Three-Fifths Compromise.** It provided that all "free persons" should be counted, and so, too, should "three-fifths of all other persons." (Article I, Section 2, Clause 3. For "all other persons" read "slaves.") For the three-fifths won by the southerners, the northerners exacted a price. That formula was also to be used in fixing the amount of money to be raised in each State by any direct tax levied by Congress. In short, the southerners could count their slaves, but they would have to pay for them.

This odd compromise disappeared from the Constitution with the adoption of the 13th Amendment, which abolished slavery, in 1865. For nearly 140 years now, there have been no "all other persons" in this country.

### The Commerce and Slave Trade Compromise

The convention agreed that Congress had to have the power to regulate foreign and interstate

## Make It Relevant

### Careers in Government—Preservationist

The original Constitution is displayed in the National Archives Building in Washington, D.C., where thousands of people from around the world view it each year. Its excellent condition is owed to the work of *preservationists,* so-named because they preserve historical documents. Many preservationists work in American government, at such places as the National Archives and Records Administration, the Library of Congress, and the Smithsonian Institution.

**Skills Activity** Direct pairs of students to conduct research on how an old book could be repaired. Then have individual students write paragraphs explaining why they would or would not be interested in a career as a preservationist.

**(Average)**

**Answer to . . .**

**Interpreting Tables** If representation were based on population, then counting slaves would give the southern States greater political power.

trade. To many southerners that power carried a real danger, however. They worried that Congress, likely to be controlled by northern commercial interests, would act against the interests of the agricultural South.

They were particularly fearful that Congress would try to pay for the new government out of export duties, and southern tobacco was the major American export of the time. They also feared that Congress would interfere with the slave trade.

Before they would agree to the commerce power, the southerners insisted on certain protections. So, according to the **Commerce and Slave Trade Compromise,** Congress was forbidden the power to tax the export of goods from any State. It was also forbidden the power to act on the slave trade for a period of at least 20 years. It could not interfere with "the migration or importation of such persons as any State now existing shall think proper to admit," except for a small head tax, at least until the year 1808.[16]

### A "Bundle of Compromises"

The convention spent much of its time, said Franklin, "sawing boards to make them fit." The Constitution drafted at Philadelphia has often been called a "bundle of compromises." These descriptions are apt, if they are properly understood.

There were differences of opinion among the delegates, certainly. After all, the delegates came from 12 different States that were widely separated in geographic and economic terms. The delegates often reflected the interests of their States. Bringing these interests together did require compromise. Indeed, final decisions on issues such as selection of the President, the treaty-making process, the structure of the national court system, and the amendment process were reached as a result of compromise.

But by no means did all, or even most, of what shaped the document come from compromises. The Framers agreed on many of the basic issues they faced. Thus, nearly all the delegates were convinced that a new *national* government, a federal government, had to be created, and had to

have the powers necessary to deal with the nation's grave social and economic problems. The Framers were also dedicated to the concepts of popular sovereignty and of limited government. None questioned for a moment the wisdom of representative government. The principles of separation of powers and of checks and balances were accepted almost as a matter of course.

Many disputes did occur, and the compromises by which they were resolved came only after hours and days and even weeks of heated debate. The point here, however, is that the differences were not over the most fundamental of questions. They involved, instead, such vital but lesser points as these: the details of the structure of Congress, the method by which the President was to be chosen, and the practical limits that should be put on the several powers to be given to the new central government.

## Sources of the Constitution

The Framers were well educated and widely read. They were familiar with the governments of ancient Greece and Rome and those of contemporary Great Britain and Europe. They knew the political writings of their time, of such works as William Blackstone's *Commentaries on the Laws of England,* Charles de Montesquieu's *The Spirit of the Laws,* Jean Jacques Rousseau's *Social Contract,* John Locke's *Two Treatises of Government,* and many others.

More immediately, the Framers drew on their own experiences. Remember, they were familiar with the Second Continental Congress, the Articles of Confederation, and their own State governments. Much that went into the Constitution came directly, sometimes word for word, from the Articles. A number of provisions were drawn from the several State constitutions, as well.

## The Convention Completes Its Work

For several weeks, through the hot Philadelphia summer, the delegates took up resolution after resolution. Finally, on September 8, a committee was named "to revise the stile of and arrange the articles which had been agreed to" by the

---

[16]Article I, Section 9, Clause 1. Congress promptly banned the importation of slaves in 1808, and in 1820 it declared the slave trade to be piracy. The smuggling of the enslaved into this country continued until the outbreak of the Civil War, however.

## Spotlight on Technology

### Magruder's American Government Video Collection

The Magruder's Video Collection explores key issues and debates in American government. Each segment examines an issue central to chapter content through use of historical and contemporary footage. Commentary from civic leaders in academics, government, and the media follow each segment. Critical-thinking questions focus students' attention on key issues, and may be used to stimulate discussion.

Use the Chapter 2 video segment to explore the issue of school prayer with your class. (time: about 5 minutes) This segment sets the scene with the 1962 *Engel* v. *Vitale* Supreme Court case on school prayer, then examines current debate on the issue: specifically, student-led prayer at school-sponsored events.

## Point-of-Use Resources

**Guide to the Essentials** Chapter 2, Section 4, p. 21 provides support for students who need additional review of section content. Spanish support is available in the Spanish edition of the Guide on p. 14.

**Quiz** Unit 1 booklet, p. 16 includes matching and multiple-choice questions to check students' understanding of Section 4 content.

**Presentation Pro CD-ROM** Quizzes and multiple-choice questions check students' understanding of Section 4 content.

## Answers to . . .

### Section 4 Assessment

**1.** The Framers were the delegates to the Philadelphia Convention; most came from wealthy backgrounds, were well educated, and had public experience.
**2.** To create an entirely new constitution.
**3.** The Virginia Plan called for representation to be based on a State's population or the amount of money it gave to support the central government. Smaller States would not be given as much representation as larger States in this plan and thus opposed it.
**4.** That Congress would be composed of two houses—including a Senate with equal representation and a House with representation based on population.
**5.** Writings by European thinkers, the Framers' own experiences, ideas from the Articles, and State constitutions.
**6.** The Virginia Plan called for representation based on a State's population or monetary contributions. It also called for one federal executive. The New Jersey Plan called for equal representation, and provided for plural federal executives.
**7.** Possible answer: Southern States felt that these items were vital to the protection of their commercial interests. In exchange for these concessions, the southern States had to pay extra taxes on slaves.

▲ Detail from Washington's chair at the Constitutional Convention.

convention. That group, the Committee of Stile and Arrangement headed by Gouverneur Morris, put the Constitution in its final form.

Then, on September 17, the convention approved its work and 39 names were placed on the finished document.[17] Perhaps none of the Framers was completely satisfied with his work. Nevertheless, wise old Benjamin Franklin put into words what many of the Framers must have thought on that final day:

**PRIMARY Sources** "Sir, I agree with this Constitution to all its faults, if they are such; because I think a general Government necessary for us . . . I doubt . . . whether any other Convention we can obtain, may be able to make a better Constitution. For when you assemble a number of men to have the advantage of their joint wisdom, you inevitably assemble with those men, all their prejudices, their passions, their errors of opinion, their local interests, and their selfish views. From such an assembly can a perfect production be

expected? It therefore astonishes me, Sir, to find this system approaching so near to perfection as it does . . . "
—Notes of Debates in the Federal Convention of 1787, James Madison

On Franklin's motion, the Constitution was signed. Madison tells us that

**PRIMARY Sources** ". . . Doctor Franklin, looking toward the President's chair, at the back of which a rising sun happened to be painted, observed to a few members near him, that Painters had found it difficult to distinguish in their art a rising from a setting sun. I have, said he, often and often in the course of the Session . . . looked at that behind the President without being able to tell whether it was rising or setting. But now at length I have the happiness to know that it is a rising and not a setting sun. "
—Notes of Debates in the Federal Convention of 1787, James Madison

---

[17]Three of the 41 delegates present on that last day refused to sign the proposed Constitution: Edmund Randolph of Virginia, who later did support ratification and served as Attorney General and then Secretary of State under President Washington; Elbridge Gerry of Massachusetts, who later became Vice President under Madison; and George Mason of Virginia, who continued to oppose the Constitution until his death in 1792. George Read of Delaware signed both for himself and for his absent colleague John Dickinson.

## Section 4 Assessment

### Key Terms and Main Ideas

1. Identify the **Framers** of the Constitution and describe, in general, their backgrounds and experiences.
2. What momentous decision did the Framers make at the beginning of the Philadelphia Convention?
3. Why did the delegates from the smaller States object to the **Virginia Plan?**
4. What was agreed to under the **Connecticut Compromise?**
5. What sources influenced the Framers in writing the Constitution?

### Critical Thinking

6. **Making Comparisons** Compare and contrast the Virginia Plan and the New Jersey Plan.
7. **Determining Relevance** The Three-Fifths Compromise and the Commerce and Slave Trade Compromise were included

in the Constitution at the insistence of the southern States. Why did States in the South think these items were important and what price, if any, did southern States pay for their inclusion?
8. **Drawing Conclusions** The Constitution has been called a "bundle of compromises." Is this an accurate description of the document? Explain your answer.

### Take It to the Net

9. Select two of the delegates to the Constitutional Convention and learn more about their backgrounds. Summarize your findings and explain why your selected delegates were important to the creation of a new government. Use the links provided in the Social Studies area at the following Web site for help in completing this activity. **www.phschool.com**

**8.** Possible answer: Yes; it represents a consensus of opinion, which was achieved through numerous compromises.

### Take It to the Net

**9.** Direct students to the Social Studies area at the Prentice Hall School Web site. The *Magruder's American Government* companion Web site includes the directions and links needed to complete the activity. It also provides a printable Internet activity worksheet with scoring rubrics for assessment. Students' summaries should include relevant biographical facts about the delegates.

# SKILLS FOR LIFE

## Making Comparisons

You've probably been making comparisons ever since you first tasted food. Making comparisons means examining two or more ideas, objects, events, or people to find out how they are either similar or different. In the study of government, you will often use this skill to evaluate differing proposals on public issues. To make valid comparisons, use these steps:

**1. Identify the basis of comparison.** Comparing two or more items works only when the items have some attribute in common. Consider the Virginia Plan and the New Jersey Plan, discussed on page 51. Both plans put forth models for creating a new government. What else did they have in common?

**2. Identify the attributes of each item to be compared.** An easy way to compare complex items is to create a list or chart of their key attributes. The charts at right summarize the main features of the Virginia and New Jersey Plans.

**3. Find ways in which the items are similar.** Once you put the attributes in a chart, it becomes easy to identify similarities. Study the charts. Then list the similarities of the Virginia Plan and the New Jersey Plan.

**4. Find ways in which the items are different.** The two Constitution plans differ not only in what they offer, but also in what they do not offer. List the differences.

**5. Summarize and evaluate your comparison.** Decide whether the two items you are comparing are mostly similar or mostly different, and analyze why. Write a sentence or two summarizing the main differences between the Virginia Plan and the New Jersey Plan.

### Test for Success

Controversy over the size and powers of the Federal Government is as lively today as ever. Find two sources of opinion on this issue and write a brief comparison of them.

### Virginia Plan

- Branches of government: legislative, executive, judicial
- Structure of legislative branch: bicameral, with a lower house, the House of Representatives, and an upper house, the Senate
- How representation is apportioned: by population or by amount of money contributed to the National Government
- Congress retains powers given to it under the Articles of Confederation: Yes.
- National powers vs. State powers: strong
- Structure of executive branch: single executive who executes national laws
- How executive is chosen: by Congress
- Structure of judicial branch: one or more supreme courts with lower courts
- How judiciary is chosen: by Congress

### New Jersey Plan

- Branches of government: legislative, executive, judicial
- Structure of legislative branch: unicameral Congress of the Confederation
- How representation is apportioned: equal number of votes for every State
- Congress retains powers given to it under the Articles of Confederation: Yes.
- National powers vs. State powers: weak
- Structure of executive branch: plural executive (more than one person)
- How executive is chosen: by Congress
- Structure of judicial branch: single supreme court
- How judiciary is chosen: by the executive

## Point-of-Use Resources

📁 **Skills for Life Activity** Unit 1 booklet, p. 19 provides an additional skill activity for this chapter.

💿 **Social Studies Skills Tutor CD-ROM** Provides interactive practice in geographic literacy, critical thinking and reading, visual analysis, and communications.

### Test for Success

Answers should accurately assess the sources, following Steps 1–5.

### Making Comparisons

**Focus** Have students compare the Virginia and New Jersey Plans by role-playing members of the Constitutional Convention.

**Instruct** Lead a class discussion in which students, acting as delegates to the Constitutional Convention, compare the two constitutional plans. Select leaders to guide the discussion of the similarities and differences of the plans, making lists of the attributes on the chalkboard.

**Close/Reteach** Ask why the plans agreed on certain issues and differed greatly on others. Hold a brief debate on the advantages and disadvantages of each plan. Ask students whether their comparison has yielded enough information to make an informed choice between the two plans.

### Answers . . .

**1.** Both plans attempted to allocate power between the State and Federal Governments and to allocate power among various branches of government.
**2.** Have students study the two lists, and make certain they understand the meaning of each attribute.
**3.** Similarities include identical branches of government; Congress retains powers given to it under the Articles of Confederation; executive chosen by Congress.
**4.** Differences include unicameral vs. bicameral legislature; proportional representation vs. equal representation; weak vs. strong national/State powers; one supreme court vs. one or more; judiciary chosen by Congress vs. by the executive.
**5.** Summaries should include the points made in the above answers.

**5** **Ratifying the Constitution**

**Objectives** You may wish to call students' attention to the objectives in the Section Preview. The objectives are reflected in the main headings of the section.

**Bellringer** Ask students to think of a time when they have had a heated debate with others over an issue important to both sides. Encourage students to discuss the emotions that can arise in such a situation. Explain that in this section, they will read about a clash of ideas over ratifying the Constitution.

**Vocabulary Builder** Have students find the two terms in the Political Dictionary that are opposites. Ask them to propose the meanings of both terms, based on their understanding of the word *federal*.

## Pressed for Time?

### Quick Lesson Plan

**1. Focus** Tell students that even though the Framers had eliminated the weaknesses of the Articles of Confederation, many people opposed the new Constitution. Ask students to discuss what they know about that opposition.

**2. Instruct** Ask students whether they think the Anti-Federalists would have preferred the Articles of Confederation to the proposed Constitution. Have them identify the Anti-Federalists' main criticisms. Then lead a discussion of the fight for ratification.

**3. Close/Reteach** Remind students that the fight for ratification of the Constitution was long and hard. Have them summarize that fight by answering three questions: Who were the combatants? What did each side want? How did the fight end?

**Answer to . . .**

**Interpreting Political Cartoons** That the future of the nation depends on the ratification of the Constitution.

## Section Preview

### OBJECTIVES

1. **Analyze** debates and compromises necessary for ratifying the Constitution.
2. **Analyze** how *The Federalist Papers* explain the principles of the American constitutional system of government .
3. **Describe** the inauguration of the new government of the United States of America.

### WHY IT MATTERS

The Constitution could not take effect until it had been ratified by nine States. The battle between those who supported and those who opposed the Constitution was hard fought in all the States.

### POLITICAL DICTIONARY

★ **Federalists**
★ **Anti-Federalists**
★ **quorum**

Today, the Constitution of the United States is the object of extraordinary respect and admiration, both here and abroad. But in 1787 and 1788, it was widely criticized, and in every State many people opposed its adoption. The battle over ratification of the Constitution was decided only after much debate and compromise.

## Debates and Compromises

Remember, the Articles of Confederation provided that changes could be made to them only if all of the State legislatures agreed. But the Framers had seen how crippling the unanimity requirement could be. So, the new Constitution provided that

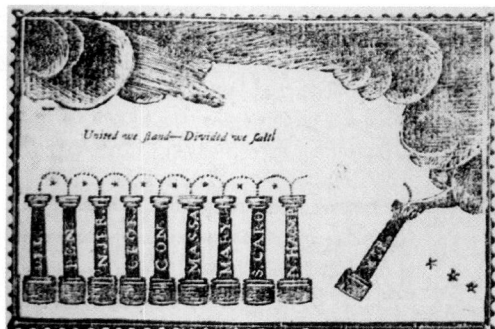

▲ *Interpreting Political Cartoons* This cartoon, printed in the New Hampshire *Gazette* on June 26, 1788, shows the States as pillars, with nine upright and a tenth being raised. **What is the message of the words in the cartoon?**

FROM THE *Constitution* **"** *The ratification of the conventions of nine States shall be sufficient for the establishment of this Constitution between the States so ratifying the same.* **"**
—Article VII

The Congress of the Confederation agreed to this irregular procedure. After a short debate, it sent copies of the new document to the States on September 28, 1787.

### Federalists and Anti-Federalists

The Constitution was printed, circulated, and debated vigorously. Two groups emerged in each of the States: the **Federalists,** who favored ratification, and the **Anti-Federalists,** who opposed it.

The Federalists were led by many of those who had attended the Philadelphia Convention. Among them, the most active and the most effective were James Madison and Alexander Hamilton. Their opposition was headed by such well-known Revolutionary War figures as Patrick Henry, Richard Henry Lee, John Hancock, and Samuel Adams.

The Federalists stressed the weaknesses of the Articles. They argued that the Republic's difficulties could be overcome only by a new government based on the new Constitution.

The Anti-Federalists attacked nearly every part of the new document. Many objected to the ratification process, to the absence of any mention of God, to the denial to the States of

## Block Scheduling Strategies

Consider these suggestions to manage extended class time:

■ Have students review the Revolutions Around the World map on p. 57 of the Student Edition. Assign one or two of the revolutions to small groups of students. For each, have students research the causes, ideals, and outcomes of the revolution. Use students' research results to conduct a discussion comparing the American Revolution to other revolutions around the world.

■ Using the graphic organizers students have made for the Organizing Information activity as well as the materials prepared for the Extended Class Periods activity on p. 57, organize a debate in which half the class supports the Federalist position and half the Anti-Federalist position.

a power to print money, and to many other features of the Framers' proposals.

Two major features of the proposed Constitution drew the heaviest fire: (1) the greatly increased powers of the central government and (2) the lack of a bill of rights. Both of these features were of particular concern to Jefferson. John Adams, however, viewed the Constitution "with great satisfaction" as the best means to unite the new nation. Adams would have preferred more power for the presidency than the Constitution provided. But like Jefferson, his greater concern was the absence of a bill of rights.

### Nine States Ratify

The contest for ratification was close in several States, but the Federalists finally won in all of them. Delaware was the first State to ratify. On June 21, 1788, New Hampshire brought the number of ratifying States to nine.

Under Article VII, New Hampshire's ratification should have brought the Constitution into effect, but it did not. Neither Virginia nor New York had yet ratified, and without either of these key States the new government could not hope to succeed.

### Virginia's Ratification

Virginia's vote for ratification followed New Hampshire's by just four days. The brilliant debates in its convention were followed closely throughout the State. The Federalists were led by Madison, the young John Marshall, and Governor Edmund Randolph (even though he had refused to sign the Constitution at Philadelphia). Patrick Henry, leading the opposition, was joined by such outstanding Virginians as James Monroe, Richard Henry Lee, and George Mason (another of the non-signers).

Although George Washington was not one of the delegates to Virginia's convention, his strong support for ratification proved vital. With Madison, he was able to get a reluctant Jefferson to support the document. Had Jefferson fought as did other Anti-Federalists, Virginia might never have ratified the Constitution.

### An Era of Revolutions

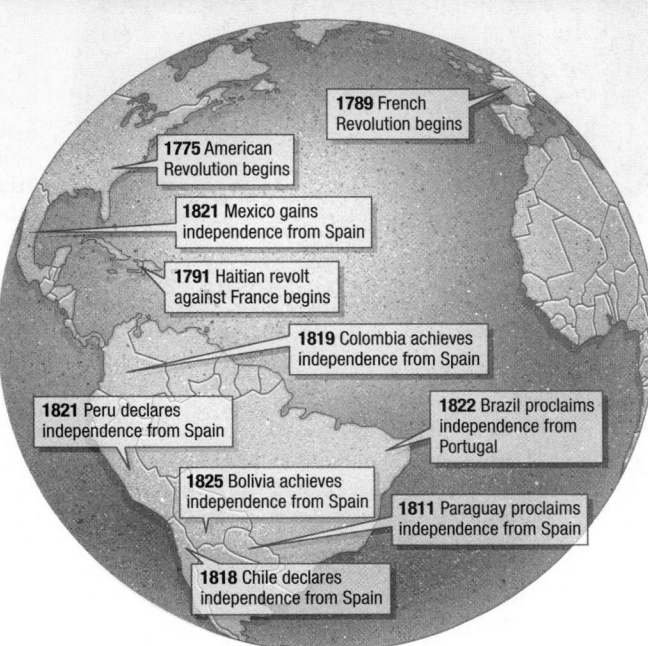

1789 French Revolution begins

1775 American Revolution begins

1821 Mexico gains independence from Spain

1791 Haitian revolt against France begins

1819 Colombia achieves independence from Spain

1821 Peru declares independence from Spain

1822 Brazil proclaims independence from Portugal

1825 Bolivia achieves independence from Spain

1811 Paraguay proclaims independence from Spain

1818 Chile declares independence from Spain

*Interpreting Maps* The American Revolution was one of many struggles for independence that took place around the world between 1775 and 1825. ***Do you think this global turmoil was coincidence, or were the events in various countries somehow connected?***

### Ratification of the Constitution

| State | Date | Vote |
|---|---|---|
| Delaware | December 7, 1787 | 30–0 |
| Pennsylvania | December 12, 1787 | 46–23 |
| New Jersey | December 18, 1787 | 38–0 |
| Georgia | January 2, 1788 | 26–0 |
| Connecticut | January 9, 1788 | 128–40 |
| Massachusetts | February 6, 1788 | 187–168 |
| Maryland | April 28, 1788 | 63–11 |
| South Carolina | May 23, 1788 | 149–73 |
| New Hampshire | June 21, 1788 | 57–46 |
| Virginia | June 25, 1788 | 89–79 |
| New York | July 26, 1788 | 30–27 |
| North Carolina | November 21, 1789* | 195–77 |
| Rhode Island | May 29, 1790 | 34–32 |

*Second vote; ratification was originally defeated on August 4, 1788, by a vote of 184–84.

*Interpreting Tables* Virginia's ratification came only after a long struggle. ***In what other States was ratification won by only a narrow margin?***

### Organizing Information

To make sure students understand the main points of this section, you may wish to use the double web graphic organizer to the right.

Tell students that a double web compares and contrasts information about two ideas. Ask students to use the double web to compare the Federalists and the Anti-Federalists.

**Teaching Tip** A template for this graphic organizer can be found in the Section Support Transparencies, Transparency 2.

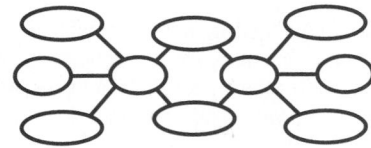

## Reading Strategy

### Organizing Information/ Outline

Ask students to copy down the main headings and subheadings in outline form, leaving space for details. Have them fill in the details as they read the section.

### A C T I V I T Y

### Extended Class Periods

**Time** 90 minutes.

**Purpose** Interpret historical writings.

**Grouping** Groups of three to four students.

**Activity** Using copies of several essays from *The Federalist* brought in by the teacher, groups will summarize and interpret the essay they have been assigned and present their work to the class.

**Roles** Discussion leader, recorder, timekeeper, spokesperson.

**Close** The teacher will place a copy of each essay on an overhead transparency for the class to view. After groups have recorded their interpretation of the essay, have the spokespersons read the summary to the class, highlighting the most important points of the documents.

🖥 **Block Strategy (Average)**

## Point–of–Use Resources

📁 **Guided Reading and Review** Unit 1 booklet, p. 17 provides students with practice identifying the main ideas and key terms of this section.

📁 **Lesson Plans** For lesson planning suggestions, see p. 19 of the Lesson Plans booklet.

📁 **Political Cartoons** See p. 11 of the Political Cartoons booklet for a cartoon relevant to this section.

### *Answers to . . .*

**Interpreting Maps** Answers will vary, but should be supported with relevant examples.

**Interpreting Tables** New Hampshire, New York, and Rhode Island.

## Point-of-Use Resources

**Guide to the Essentials** Chapter 2, Section 5, p. 22 provides support for students who need additional review of section content. Spanish support is available in the Spanish edition of the Guide on p. 15.

**Quiz** Unit 1 booklet, p. 19 includes matching and multiple-choice questions to check students' understanding of Section 5 content.

**Presentation Pro CD-ROM** Quizzes and multiple-choice questions check students' understanding of Section 5 content.

**Section Support Transparencies** Transparency 14, *Visual Learning;* Transparency 113, *Political Cartoon*

**ABC News Civics and Government Videotape Library** *The Blessings of Liberty,* Introduction and the 1789–1803 segment (time: about 40 minutes)

## Answers to . . .

### Section 5 Assessment

**1.** The Federalists believed that the Constitution should be ratified, because the many problems facing the new Republic could not be solved within the framework of the weak Articles.
**2.** The Anti-Federalists were well-known Revolutionary War figures who opposed the Constitution. They were particularly opposed to the increased power of the central government and the lack of a bill of rights.
**3.** The ratification process was unusual because unanimity was not required to ratify. However, the government needed more than nine states to ratify to ensure its survival.
**4.** They were among the leading States in terms of economics and political leadership.
**5.** Possible answer: The Anti-Federalists wanted in particular to ensure that the government could not be tyrannical. With a strong central government and no outline of basic rights, they felt individual freedom was threatened.

▲ *Defending the Constitution* All the essays in *The Federalist* were signed with the pen name Publius. Modern scholars attribute fifty-one to Hamilton (right), five to Jay (left), and twenty-nine to Madison.

### The Federalist Papers

A narrow vote in the New York convention brought the number of States to 11. New York ratified only after a long battle. The Anti-Federalists were led by Governor George Clinton and by two of the State's three delegates to the Philadelphia Convention.[18]

The contest in New York gave rise to a remarkable campaign document: *The Federalist.* It was a collection of 85 essays supporting the Constitution written by Alexander Hamilton, James Madison, and John Jay. Those essays were first published as letters to the people in various newspapers of the State and soon were collected in book form. Though written in haste, they remain an excellent commentary on the Constitution, and are among the best political writings in the English language.

## Inaugurating the Government

On September 13, 1788, with 11 of the 13 States "under the federal roof," the Congress of the Confederation paved the way for its successor.[19] It chose New York as the temporary capital.[20] It set the first Wednesday in January as the date on which the States would choose presidential electors. The first Wednesday in February was set as the date on which those electors would vote, and the first Wednesday in March as the date for the inauguration of the new government.

The new Congress convened on March 4, 1789. It met in Federal Hall, on Wall Street in New York City. But because it lacked a **quorum** (majority), it could not count the electoral votes until April 6. Finally, on that day, it found that George Washington had been elected President by a unanimous vote. John Adams was elected Vice President with a substantial majority.

On April 30, after his historic trip from Mount Vernon to New York, Washington took the oath of office as the first President of the United States.

[18]Robert Yates and John Lansing had quit Philadelphia in July, arguing that the convention had gone beyond its authority. Like many other Anti-Federalist leaders, Governor Clinton later supported the Constitution.
[19]Neither North Carolina nor Rhode Island had ratified the new Constitution before it became effective. As you can see in the table on p. 57, the Constitution failed in a first convention in North Carolina and was finally approved by a second one in late November of 1789. Rhode Island did not hold a ratifying convention until May of 1790, more than a year after Washington's inauguration.
[20]The District of Columbia did not become the nation's capital until 1800. Congress moved its sessions from New York to Philadelphia in December 1790. It held its first meeting in the new "federal city," Washington, D.C., on November 17, 1800.

## Section **5** Assessment

**Key Terms and Main Ideas**
**1.** What was the **Federalist** position on the Constitution? Why did they feel that way?
**2.** Who were the **Anti-Federalists?**
**3.** What was "irregular" about the ratification of the Constitution?

**Critical Thinking**
**4. Expressing Problems Clearly** Why might the failure of New York and Virginia to ratify have doomed the Constitution?
**5. Understanding Point of View** The Anti-Federalists were greatly concerned that the proposed Constitution increased the powers of the central government and lacked a bill of rights. Why would these specific issues have been important to them?

 **Take It to the Net**

**6.** Read an analysis of *The Federalist Papers.* Then create a graphic organizer showing how these articles exemplified the Federalists' beliefs. Include at least four beliefs and cite examples. Use the links provided in the Social Studies area at the following Web site for help in completing this activity. **www.phschool.com**

 **Take It to the Net**

**6.** Direct students to the Social Studies area at the Prentice Hall School Web site. The *Magruder's American Government* companion Web site includes the directions and links needed to complete the activity. It also provides a printable Internet activity worksheet with scoring rubrics for assessment. Students' graphic organizers should accurately reflect the beliefs of the Federalists and be supported with specific examples.

# Is Flag-Burning "Free Speech"?

*Free speech, one of Americans' most cherished freedoms, is commonly thought of in terms of spoken or printed words. Yet speech also can take the form of a symbolic action, like the burning of the American flag. Can the government restrict such forms of symbolic speech? In other words, can it restrict the ways in which national symbols such as the flag can be used in protests?*

## United States v. Eichman (1990)

In the 1989 case *Texas* v. *Johnson*, the Supreme Court struck down a State law that forbade the destruction of the United States flag. That law, ruled the Court, violated the First Amendment guarantee of free expression. Congress reacted to the decision by passing the Flag Protection Act of 1989, which stated that anyone who "knowingly mutilates, defaces, physically defiles, burns, maintains on the floor or ground, or tramples upon" a United States flag can be prosecuted. (Disposing of worn or soiled flags was permitted under the law.) Violators could be fined or imprisoned for up to one year.

The United States prosecuted Eichman and others for knowingly setting fire to several American flags. These flag-burnings took place both on the steps of the Capitol (to protest certain government policies) and in Seattle (to protest the passage of the Flag Protection Act itself).

The defendants asked the courts to dismiss the charges on the grounds that the Act violated the First Amendment. They cited *Texas* v. *Johnson* as giving First Amendment protection to flag-burning as a means of expression. Federal courts in Washington State and the District of Columbia both ruled that the Act was unconstitutional. The Federal Government then appealed these decisions to the Supreme Court.

## Arguments for the United States

1. The Flag Protection Act does not outlaw flag-burning in order to prevent the expression of a particular point of view. Rather, it prohibits mistreatment of the flag for any reason in order to protect the flag's identity as a national symbol.

2. Desecration (abuse) of the flag is deeply offensive to many Americans. The government should have the right to protect its national symbols against mistreatment.

3. Protection of the flag would not interfere with protesters' ability to express their opinions by other means.

## Arguments for Eichman

1. The government's effort to protect the flag limits the free expression of opposition to government policies.

2. The destruction of a flag does not diminish the flag's importance as a symbol of this country.

3. Although many people are offended by flag desecration, the government cannot prohibit expression of ideas simply because the ideas may be offensive or disagreeable to many people.

### Decide for Yourself

1. Review the constitutional grounds on which each side based its arguments and the specific arguments each side presented.

2. Debate the opposing viewpoints presented in this case. Which viewpoint do you favor?

3. Predict the impact of the Court's decision on ways in which people may choose to protest government policies. (To read a summary of the Court's decision, turn to the Supreme Court Glossary on page 799.)

 **CLOSE UP** FOUNDATION *Corner*

📁 Close Up on the Supreme Court *U.S.* v. *Eichman*, p. 3 provides an activity to extend coverage of this case.

 **CLOSE UP** FOUNDATION **Online**

To keep up-to-date on Close Up news and activities, visit Close Up Online at

**www.closeup.org**

---

 **CLOSE UP** FOUNDATION

## Is Flag-Burning "Free Speech"?

**Focus** Remind students that many Anti-Federalists opposed the ratification of the Constitution until a promise was made to add a Bill of Rights protecting basic civil rights and liberties. Discuss why many of those who participated in the American Revolution might oppose the Constitution unless it protected the right to freely criticize the government.

**Instruct** Explain that an earlier Supreme Court case upheld the right of a student to display an American flag with a peace sign taped to it. Ask students whether they agree with that ruling. Then have them compare and contrast flag burning and taping a peace sign on the flag as forms of symbolic protest. Should it matter that flag burning is a more offensive form of symbolic protest than taping a peace sign to the flag?

**Close/Reteach** One of the arguments in support of Eichman's position is that destroying the flag does not diminish its importance as a national symbol. Have students write a newspaper editorial expressing whether they agree or disagree with that argument.

💿 **Keep It Current CD-ROM** includes government-related projects by unit. The CD-ROM links to the Prentice Hall School Web site and may be used for daily updates.

### Answers to . . .
**Decide for Yourself**

**1.** The U.S. used the grounds of the Federal Government having the authority to protect national symbols to argue that the Flag Protection Act was constitutional. Eichman used the grounds of First Amendment liberties, as well as the precedent set in *Texas* v. *Johnson*, to argue that he was using free speech.
**2.** Answers will vary, but should be supported with valid reasoning.
**3.** The Court ruled in favor of Eichman, holding that flag burning was a valid expression of First Amendment protected speech.

## Practicing the Vocabulary

**1–10:** Sentences should accurately reflect the meaning of each term in the context of chapter content.

**11.** *b* does not belong; *a*, *c*, and *d* all refer to documents of the English political tradition that influenced the colonists in America.

**12.** *a* does not belong; *b*, *c*, and *d* all relate to plans for the legislature put forth at the Constitutional Convention.

**13.** *c* does not belong; *a*, *b*, and *d* each refer to principles of government with which the colonists were familiar.

**14.** *d* does not belong; *a*, *b*, and *c* refer to people or groups that played a part in shaping the Constitution.

## Reviewing Main Ideas
### Section 1

**15.** Ordered government, limited government, representative government.

**16. (a)** It introduced key individual rights which were protections against the absolute power of the monarchy. **(b)** It limited the king's power in several ways. **(c)** It extended key individual rights as protection against abuse of power.

**17.** Some started as commercial ventures; others as havens for those seeking religious freedom.

### Section 2

**18. (a)** The British did not bother to exert too much direct control over the colonies. **(b)** Britain began to take a more active role in the colonies.

**19.** They were angered and began to come together to plan a response.

**20. (a)** A committee of five men, led by Thomas Jefferson. **(b)** Equality, life, liberty, and happiness for all men, and the right for people to alter or abolish the government they live under. **(c)** They indicate a relationship of equality.

**21.** Each was based on the principles of popular sovereignty, limited government, civil liberties, separation of powers, and checks and balances.

### Section 3

**22.** Called for a unicameral Congress that chose a president, who presided only over the Congress itself. The powers of Congress included the

## Political Dictionary

limited government **(p. 29)**
representative government **(p. 29)**
Magna Carta **(p. 29)**
Petition of Right **(p. 30)**
English Bill of Rights **(p. 30)**
charter **(p. 31)**
bicameral **(p. 31)**
proprietary **(p. 32)**
unicameral **(p. 32)**
confederation **(p. 35)**

Albany Plan of Union **(p. 35)**
delegate **(p. 36)**
boycott **(p. 36)**
repeal **(p. 37)**
popular sovereignty **(p. 39)**
Articles of Confederation **(p. 44)**
ratification **(p. 44)**
presiding officer **(p. 45)**
Framers **(p. 48)**

Virginia Plan **(p. 51)**
New Jersey Plan **(p. 51)**
Connecticut Compromise **(p. 52)**
Three-Fifths Compromise **(p. 52)**
Commerce and Slave Trade
    Compromise **(p. 53)**
Federalists **(p. 56)**
Anti-Federalists **(p. 56)**
quorum **(p. 58)**

## Practicing the Vocabulary

***Using Words in Context*** *For each of the terms below, write a sentence that shows how it relates to this chapter.*

1. Articles of Confederation
2. Three-Fifths Compromise
3. charter
4. boycott
5. bicameral
6. ratification
7. quorum
8. proprietary
9. Commerce and Slave Trade Compromise
10. delegate

***Word Relationships*** *Three of the terms in each of the following sets of terms are related. Choose the term that does not belong and explain why it does not belong.*

11. **(a)** Magna Carta **(b)** Albany Plan of Union **(c)** English Bill of Rights **(d)** Petition of Right
12. **(a)** Articles of Confederation **(b)** Virginia Plan **(c)** New Jersey Plan **(d)** Connecticut Compromise
13. **(a)** limited government **(b)** popular sovereignty **(c)** ratification **(d)** representative government
14. **(a)** Framers **(b)** Federalists **(c)** Anti-Federalists **(d)** boycott

## Reviewing Main Ideas

**Section 1**

15. What three ideas about government did the colonists bring with them from England?
16. How was the development of English government affected by **(a)** the Magna Carta? **(b)** The Petition of Right? **(c)** The English Bill of Rights?
17. Explain the development of colonial government.

**Section 2**

18. Describe how the British governed the colonies **(a)** before the 1760s. **(b)** After the 1760s.
19. What was the colonists' response to the change in British policies in the 1760s?
20. **(a)** Who wrote the Declaration of Independence? **(b)** What rights are outlined in the document? **(c)** How do they signify the colonists' relationship to Britain?
21. Describe the common features of the first State constitutions.

**Section 3**

22. What were the major characteristics of the Articles of Confederation?
23. How did the States respond to the weaknesses of the Articles of Confederation?

**Section 4**

24. Who were the Framers of the Constitution?
25. Explain the New Jersey Plan. Why was it introduced at the Constitutional Convention?
26. What major issues did the Framers disagree upon and what, if any, compromises did they reach?

**Section 5**

27. Why did the Federalists want to replace the Articles?
28. What were the main arguments used by the Anti-Federalists?
29. Why was ratification by Virginia and New York essential for the success of the Constitution?

power to make war, borrow money, build a navy and raise an army. Congress could not tax or regulate trade. It also had no real power to force the States to obey its laws or the Articles.

**23.** Several leaders, recognizing the need for a change in the Articles, called meetings for the purpose of discussing plans to revise and improve the Articles.

### Section 4
**24.** The Framers were well-educated men experienced in government and public service.
**25.** It called for equal State representation; it was introduced to protect the position of the smaller States.
**26.** How States would be represented; the Connecticut and Three-Fifths compromises.

### Section 5
**27.** They felt the Articles were too weak to govern the new nation.
**28.** That the proposed Constitution, with its call for a strong central government and no bill of rights, did not provide people with basic liberties.
**29.** They were among the leading States in terms of economics and political leadership.

## Critical Thinking

**30.** ***Applying the Chapter Skill*** The proposed Constitution sent to the States in 1787 drew heated reactions. Review the discussion of the fight for ratification on pages 56–58. Then create a table summarizing the positions of the Federalists and Anti-Federalists. Compare the arguments of the two groups and write a sentence or two explaining how their views on the Constitution differed.

**31.** ***Drawing Conclusions*** Turn to the essays from *The Federalist* on pages 783–790. Choose one of the essays and analyze how it explains at least one of the principles of the American constitutional system of government.

**32.** ***Formulating Questions*** Weaknesses in the Articles of Confederation surfaced during the Critical Period in American history. Write three questions that will help you understand why many leaders of the day urged a stronger national government, and how they could achieve this.

**33.** ***Checking Consistency*** How does the history of America from the 1600s to 1789 demonstrate that "questions of politics and economics are, in fact, inseparable"?

## Analyzing Political Cartoons

Using your knowledge of American government and this cartoon, answer the questions below.

JOIN, or DIE.

**34.** This cartoon, originally published by Benjamin Franklin in 1754, appeared in several versions during the American Revolution. **(a)** What do the segments of the snake represent? **(b)** How do you know?

**35.** **(a)** What is the message of the cartoon? **(b)** In your opinion, is this cartoon an effective means of persuasion? Why or why not?

 **Take It to the Net**

Additional support materials and activities for Chapter 2 of *Magruder's American Government* can be found in the Social Studies area at the Prentice Hall School Web site. **www.phschool.com**

 **You Can Make a Difference**

What issues and rights are important to students in your school? What about disputes between different student groups? Is there a council that mediates when the interests of different students come into conflict? Write an editorial for your school newspaper in which you point out some issues in your school. Suggest methods that could be used to find compromises for these conflicts.

## Participation Activities

**36.** ***Current Events Watch*** The Framers drew on their skills, knowledge, and experience in creating the Constitution. What kinds of experience and training do political leaders draw on today? Select a current political leader—a member of Congress or the governor of your State, for example—and write a brief biography of this person. Your biographical sketch should identify the skills, knowledge, and experience that person draws upon in his or her current position.

**37.** ***Time Line Activity*** Using information from the chapter, create a time line showing the steps that led to the ratification of the Constitution. Include at least eight entries in your time line. You might begin with the First Continental Congress of 1774. What, in your opinion, was the most important step in the process? Why?

**38.** ***It's Your Turn*** It is 1788. Write a letter to the editor of your local paper in which you express your opinion on whether or not the Constitution should be ratified. First, create a list of what you see as the positive aspects of the document. Then, list the negative features. Note any suggestions you have for improvements. Next, write a draft of the letter in which you politely offer your ideas. Revise your letter, making certain that each idea is clearly explained. Proofread your letter and draft a final copy. **(Writing a Letter)**

 **Take It to the Net**

**Chapter 2 Self-Test** As a final review activity, take the Chapter 2 Self-Test in the Social Studies area at the Web site listed below, and receive immediate feedback on your answers.

**www.phschool.com**

## Point-of-Use Resources

**Guide to the Essentials of American Government** Chapter 2 Test, page 23 provides multiple-choice questions to test students' knowledge of the chapter.

**Test Bank CD-ROM** Chapter 2 Test

**Chapter Test** Chapter Tests booklet

## Critical Thinking Skills

**30.** Tables will vary, but positions of both groups should be complete and include specific points from the text. Sentences should reflect an understanding that Federalists supported a strong central government while Anti-Federalists did not.

**31.** Answers will vary. Generally speaking, *The Federalist* No. 10 explains the advantages of a representative form of government; *The Federalist* No. 51 discusses separation of powers and the federal system of government; *The Federalist* No. 78 addresses the system of checks and balances.

**32.** Questions will vary. Sample questions: If the new country went to war, how could taxes be raised to support it? If one State had a trade dispute with another, who settles that dispute? If an Article was found to be insufficient, how could it be changed?

**33.** Answers will vary. Students might observe that the growing colonial dissatisfaction that ultimately led to revolution grew out of increased involvement by the British in the colonial economies. Much of the conflict during the Critical Period that led to the Constitutional Convention grew out of the economic competition between the States.

## Analyzing Political Cartoons

**34. (a)** The thirteen colonies. **(b)** Each segment is labeled with the initials of a colony or region.

**35. (a)** That the colonies must unite in order to survive. **(b)** Answers will vary, but should be persuasive.

## You Can Make a Difference

Editorials should be persuasive and clearly present the issues.

## Participation Activities

**36.** Students' biographies will vary, but should demonstrate a clear connection between the person's particular skills and his or her work in politics.

**37.** Time lines will vary, but should include all events relevant to the ratification of the Constitution.

**38.** Students' letters should reveal at least an elementary understanding of the strengths and weaknesses of the Constitution, and should be supported with facts and quotes from the chapter.

# The Constitution

| Section Objectives | Print and Technology Resources |
|---|---|
| **1 The Six Basic Principles**<br>*(pp. 64–70)*<br><br>**1.** Outline the important elements of the Constitution.<br>**2.** List the six basic principles of the Constitution and evaluate constitutional principles for limiting the role of government.<br><br>TEKS 2A, 2B, 8A, 8C, 8D, 8F, 9E, 10A, 21A, 21D, 21E, 22A, 22B, 22C, 22D | • **Unit 1 booklet**<br>Guided Reading and Review, p. 20<br>Section 1 Quiz, p. 21<br>• **Lesson Plans booklet** Section 1, p. 20<br>• **Political Cartoons booklet** Section 1, p. 12<br>• **Block Scheduling with Lesson Strategies booklet** p. 20<br>• **Section Reading Support Transparencies**<br>• **Close Up on Primary Sources booklet** The Mayflower Compact, p. 52; Fundamental Orders of Connecticut, p. 53; *Marbury* v. *Madison,* p. 64; William Rehnquist: On Judicial Activism, p. 66<br>• **The Living Constitution booklet** p. 7<br>• **Basic Principles of the Constitution Transparencies** 8, 16<br>• **Section Support Transparencies** 15, 114<br>• **Presentation Pro CD-ROM** Section 1<br>• **Social Studies Skills Tutor CD-ROM** |
| **2 Formal Amendment**<br>*(pp. 72–77)*<br><br>**1.** Analyze the processes by which the United States Constitution can be changed and evaluate their effectiveness.<br>**2.** Understand the history of the 27 amendments to the Constitution.<br><br>TEKS 2B, 2C, 8D, 8E, 21A, 21D, 21E, 22A, 22B | • **Unit 1 booklet**<br>Guided Reading and Review, p. 22<br>Section 2 Quiz, p. 23<br>• **Lesson Plans booklet** Section 2, p. 21<br>• **Political Cartoons booklet** Section 2, p. 13<br>• **Block Scheduling with Lesson Strategies booklet** p. 20<br>• **Close Up on Primary Sources booklet** Jefferson's Letters from France, p. 5<br>• **Section Reading Support Transparencies**<br>• **The Living Constitution booklet** p. 9<br>• **Government Assessment Rubrics booklet** p. 12<br>• **Basic Principles of the Constitution Transparencies** 1<br>• **Section Support Transparencies** 16, 115<br>• **Presentation Pro CD-ROM** Section 2<br>• **Simulations and Data Graphing CD-ROM** |
| **3 Informal Procedures**<br>*(pp. 79–82)*<br><br>**1.** Identify how basic legislation has changed the Constitution over time.<br>**2.** Explain the powers of the executive branch and the courts to amend the Constitution.<br>**3.** Analyze the role of party practices and custom in shaping the Federal Government.<br><br>TEKS 8E, 21A, 21C, 21D, 22A, 22B, 22C, 22D | • **Unit 1 booklet**<br>Guided Reading and Review, p. 24<br>Section 3 Quiz, p. 25<br>Skills for Life Activity, p. 26<br>• **Lesson Plans booklet** Section 3, p. 22<br>• **Political Cartoons booklet** Section 3, p. 14<br>• **Section Reading Support Transparencies**<br>• **Close Up on the Supreme Court booklet** *Ingraham* v. *Wright,* p. 4<br>• **The Living Constitution booklet** p. 5<br>• **The Basic Principles of the Constitution Posters**<br>• **Section Support Transparencies** 17, 116<br>• **Presentation Pro CD-ROM** Section 3 |

# Block Scheduling Strategies

The *Magruder's American Government* program addresses block-scheduling strategies in a variety of ways. For easy reference, side-column activities that fit a block format are marked ▣ **Block Strategy.** Each section also contains a **Block Scheduling Strategies** box describing at least two block-format activities that address and extend core content from the section. The **Block Scheduling with Lesson Strategies booklet** found in the Teaching Resources contains additional block-scheduling activities for each chapter.

## Take It to the Net

Visit the Social Studies area at the Prentice Hall School Web site. Once there, you can find additional links, current events connections, and activities to enrich chapter content for *Magruder's American Government,* as well as a Self-Test for students. Be sure to check out this month's **eTeach** online discussion with a Master Teacher.

### www.phschool.com

## Assessment Options

- Section Quizzes, **Unit 1 booklet,** pp. 21, 23, 25
- Chapter 3 Assessment, pp. 84–85
- **Guide to the Essentials of American Government,** Chapter 3 Test, p. 27

### Core Assessment

Chapter 3 Test, Chapter Tests booklet
ExamView® Test Bank CD-ROM Chapter 3
Government Assessment Rubrics

### Standardized Test Preparation

#### Diagnose and Prescribe

Diagnostic Tests for High School
Social Studies Skills

#### Review and Reteach

Review Book for Government

#### Practice and Assess

Test-Taking Strategies With
    Transparencies for High School
Test Prep Book for Government

## Pressed for Time?

If you are running short on time to cover this chapter, consider one of the following options:

- Use the **Presentation Pro CD-ROM** to create an outline for this chapter.
- Use one of the **Pressed for Time** activities found on p. 27.
- Use the Section Summaries for Chapter 2, from **Guide to the Essentials of American Government (English and Spanish).**

## Video Connections

Prentice Hall offers two video programs to reinforce and extend chapter content. Show students *The Blessings of Liberty* from the **ABC News Civics and Government Videotape Library** and *Prayer in Schools: A Nationwide Debate* from the **Magruder's American Government Video Collection.**

# Chapter 3 Teacher's Edition Index

# The Constitution

## Introducing the Chapter

In this chapter, students will learn about the basic principles on which the Constitution was founded, and how amendments to the Constitution can be made.

### Make It Relevant

★ *You Can Make a Difference*

The 26th Amendment enabled 18-year-olds to vote, but those who have not yet turned 18 can still participate in government. Have small groups of students contact the League of Women Voters, the Young Democrats of America, the Young Republicans National Federation, or other groups of their choice to learn how teenagers below voting age can participate in the political process. Groups should report what they learn to the class. Then have individual students develop personal goals and plans for playing a role in American government.

**Service Learning**

## CONSTITUTIONAL PRINCIPLES

Emphasize the following basic principles as students read Chapter 3. Have the class respond to the questions, and then ask volunteers to choose a single basic principle and explain why it is vital to the function of American government.

**Separation of Powers** What powers does the Constitution grant to the National Government? How does the Constitution delegate powers to the States?

**Limited Government** What are some of the powers denied the National Government? What powers are denied the States?

**Federalism** What guarantees does the National Government make to the States? What services do the States provide to the National Government?

# The Constitution

*"These principles form the bright constellation which has gone before us and guided our steps through an age of revolution and reformation."*
—Thomas Jefferson (1801)

The Constitution rests on basic principles that have made the United States government unique in world history. Those principles have not gone out of date, yet the Constitution has been changed in various ways to adapt to a growing nation. Some provisions have been modified by laws and custom, while formal amendments have revised the original words.

◆ George Washington presiding over the Constitutional Convention

**CLOSE UP**
FOUNDATION

*Corner*

The following resources are available only from the Close Up Foundation to support the concepts discussed in Chapter 3 "The Constitution":

◆ *The Bill of Rights: A User's Guide*
◆ *Bill of Rights Video Series*
◆ *We the People: The President and the Constitution*

**CLOSE UP** | **Online**
FOUNDATION

To keep up-to-date on Close Up news and activities, visit Close Up Online at

**www.closeup.org**

Close Up Foundation
44 Canal Center Plaza
Alexandria, VA 22314-1592
800-765-3131

# Chapter 3 in Brief

## You Can Make a Difference

**WHEN THE 26TH AMENDMENT** was ratified in 1971, it created 11 million new voters from 18 to 20 years old. Campaigns urged teenagers to register to vote and get involved. Young people's votes made the difference in many recent elections. Some teenagers even ran for local offices and won. In Detroit, students at Cass Technical High School got first-hand experience working as interns in government and community agencies. Robyn Ray's time with the Equal Justice Council changed her attitude about voting. "When certain judges are up for election, I'll know how to vote. And if there is a chance to work and vote for judicial reform, I'll be there."

### SECTION 1

#### The Six Basic Principles (pp. 64–70)

★ The Constitution lays the framework for our Federal Government.
★ The Federal Government is based on the rule of law and the idea that all power resides in the people.
★ The Constitution divides power among the executive, legislative, and judicial branches of government.
★ A system of checks and balances prevents any one branch from gaining too much power.

### SECTION 2

#### Formal Amendment (pp. 72–77)

★ Since 1789, 27 amendments have been added to the Constitution.
★ The first ten amendments, known as the Bill of Rights, guarantee several basic freedoms.
★ Formal amendments may be added through four different methods.
★ The formal amendment process reflects both federalism and popular sovereignty.

### SECTION 3

#### Informal Procedures (pp. 79–82)

★ Informal procedures are actions by government that are not written in the Constitution.
★ The Constitution left many aspects of government open to new ideas and innovations.
★ All three branches of the Federal Government have contributed to the informal procedures process.
★ Political parties, not mentioned in the Constitution, have become an important part of the system of government.

 **Keep It Current**

Items marked with this logo are periodically updated on the Internet. Keep up-to-date with what's in the news. To get current information on the Constitution, go to **www.phschool.com**

## Keep It Current

### Internet Update

Use the Prentice Hall School Web site and the Keep It Current CD-ROM to find quick content updates.

 Visit **www.phschool.com** for current events articles that are linked to Chapter 3. Critical Thinking questions are included.

**Keep It Current CD-ROM** includes government projects by unit. Students complete each project using current information that they obtain by linking to the Prentice Hall School Web site from the CD-ROM.

## Pressed for Time?

### To Omit the Chapter

If you wish to skip Chapter 3, ask students to read the Chapter in Brief and assign the Guide to the Essentials before continuing to another chapter. You may also want to assign the Chapter 3 Test in the Chapter Test booklet. Then specific portions of Chapter 3 may be assigned to students needing reinforcement of key terms and concepts.

### To Preview the Chapter

To introduce students to key terms and concepts in each section, have them read the Chapter in Brief. You may also assign the Reading Strategy activities on pp. 65, 73, and 80 of this book.

### To Review the Chapter

When students have completed Chapter 3, you might want to assign the Guide to the Essentials or the Guided Reading and Review worksheets on pp. 20, 22, and 24 of the Unit 1 booklet.

### To Cover the Chapter Quickly

To cover the material in Chapter 3 quickly, use the following activity.

**Focus** Have students examine the amendments to the Constitution. Ask them whether these are the only ways that the U.S. government has changed since the Constitution's ratification. Once they've identified other changes, inform students that in this chapter they will learn about the principles that the Constitution is based on and the methods of amending it.

**Instruct** Discuss the principles that the Constitution is based on with the class. Have students write a brief explanation of each principle. Then ask students to explain why the Framers of the Constitution would have wanted to base the document on these principles.

**Close/Reteach** Discuss the formal and informal methods to amend and interpret the Constitution with the class. For each method, have students write an explanation of it and describe whether it follows or violates the principles of the Constitution.

◼ **Block Strategy (Average)**

# 1 The Six Basic Principles

**Objectives** You may wish to call students' attention to the objectives in the Section Preview. The objectives are reflected in the main headings of the section.

**Bellringer** Ask who has belonged to organizations such as Boy Scouts, Girl Scouts, or 4H. Have students explain the basic principles, or rules, of these organizations. Then discuss the value of such principles. Explain that in this section, students will learn about the basic principles of the Constitution.

**Vocabulary Builder** Ask students to pick out the terms from the Political Dictionary that they think might be basic principles of the Constitution. Have them suggest a meaning for each. As students read the section, have them revise their meanings.

## Pressed for Time?

### Quick Lesson Plan

**1. Focus** Explain that the Constitution is based on six principles. Ask students to discuss the value of basing such a document on a set of principles rather than on detailed provisions.

**2. Instruct** List the six basic principles on the chalkboard, and circle *Limited Government.* Lead a discussion in which students try to link the principle of limited government with the other principles.

**3. Close/Reteach** Remind students that the Constitution is fairly brief, because it deals with matters of basic principle. Next to the six principles listed on the board, write their definitions in mixed-up order. Have students match each principle with its correct definition.

## Point-of-Use Resources

📁 **Block Scheduling with Lesson Strategies** Activities for Chapter 3 are presented on p. 20.

---

## Section Preview

### OBJECTIVES

1. **Outline** the important elements of the Constitution.
2. **List** the six basic principles of the Constitution and evaluate constitutional principles for limiting the role of government.

### WHY IT MATTERS

The Constitution is a brief, straightforward document that has guided American government for over 200 years. Its authors wrote the Constitution based on the principle of republicanism—that political power rests in the body of citizens entitled to vote and is exercised by representatives chosen by them.

### POLITICAL DICTIONARY

★ **Preamble**
★ **articles**
★ **constitutionalism**
★ **rule of law**
★ **separation of powers**
★ **checks and balances**
★ **veto**
★ **judicial review**
★ **unconstitutional**
★ **federalism**

---

The Constitution of the United States dates from the latter part of the eighteenth century. It was written in 1787, and took effect in 1789. The fact that the Constitution is more than 200 years old does *not* mean, however, that now, in the twenty-first century, it is only an interesting historical artifact, fit for museums and dusty shelves. It is, instead, a vitally important and vibrant document.

The Constitution is this nation's fundamental law. It is, by its own terms, "the supreme Law of the Land"—the highest form of law in the United States.

## An Outline of the Constitution

The Constitution sets out the basic principles upon which government in the United States was built and operates today. The document lays out the basic framework and procedures of our government, and sets out the limits within which that government must conduct itself.

The Constitution is a fairly brief document. Its little more than 7,000 words can be read in half an hour. You will find the text of the Constitution beginning on page 758. As you read it, think about the surprising fact that this brief document has successfully guided this nation through two centuries of tremendous growth and change. One of the Constitution's greatest strengths is that its words deal largely with matters of basic principle. Unlike most other constitutions—those of the 50 States and those of most other nations—the document is not weighted down with detailed and cumbersome provisions.

As you read the Constitution, you will also see that it is organized in a simple and straightforward way. It begins with a short, noteworthy

▶ Although the members of the Federal Government are continually changing, from leaders of the past like Senator Henry Cabot Lodge (R., Massachusetts) to new lawmakers such as first-term Senator Michael Crapo (R., Idaho), the Constitution provides a lasting link between the past and present.

---

## 🔲 Block Scheduling Strategies

Consider these suggestions to manage extended class time:

■ Present students with the following scenario: They are Framers and are in the process of writing the Constitution. Elicit from the class the differences between themselves and the real Framers; for example, the real Framers did not include women or minorities. Have small groups of students write an additional section of the Constitution from their own perspectives.

■ After students complete the Learning Styles Activity on p. 69, have them review Chapter 2 to determine historic precedents that may have inspired the Framers of the Constitution to follow the six basic principles. For example, students could point out that the failure of the British to respect the political wishes of the colonists might have encouraged the Framers to follow the principle of popular sovereignty.

introduction, the **Preamble,** and the balance of the original document is divided into seven numbered sections called **articles.** The first three articles deal with the three branches of the National Government: Congress, the presidency, and the federal court system. These articles outline the basic organization and powers of each branch and the methods by which the members of Congress, the President and Vice President, and federal judges are chosen. Article IV deals mostly with the place of the States in the American Union and with their relationship with the National Government and with one another. Article V explains how formal amendments may be added to the document. Article VI declares that the Constitution is the nation's supreme law. Finally, Article VII states the requirements for ratification.

The seven articles of the original document are followed by 27 amendments, printed in the order in which they were adopted.

## The Basic Principles

The Constitution is built around six basic principles: popular sovereignty, limited government, separation of powers, checks and balances, judicial review, and federalism.

### Popular Sovereignty

In the United States, all political power resides in the people. The people are sovereign. They are the *only* source for any and all governmental power. Government can govern only with the consent of the governed.

The principle of popular sovereignty, so boldly proclaimed by the Declaration of Independence, is

### Articles of the Constitution

| Section | Subject |
| --- | --- |
| Preamble | States the purpose of the Constitution |
| Article I | Legislative branch |
| Article II | Executive branch |
| Article III | Judicial branch |
| Article IV | Relations among the States |
| Article V | Amending the Constitution |
| Article VI | National debts, supremacy of national law, and oaths of office |
| Article VII | Ratifying the Constitution |

*Interpreting Tables* The Constitution sets up the basic structure of our Federal Government. ***How do the first three articles differ from those that follow?***

woven throughout the Constitution. In its very opening words, in the Preamble, the Constitution declares: "We the People of the United States . . . do ordain and establish this Constitution for the United States of America."

In essence, the National Government draws its power from the people of the United States, and the people have given their government the power that it has through the Constitution. Similarly, each one of the State governments draws its authority from the people of that State, through that State's constitution.

### Limited Government

The principle of limited government holds that no government is all-powerful, that a government may do *only* those things that the people have given it the power to do.

In effect, the principle of limited government is the other side of the coin of popular sovereignty. It is that principle stated the other way around: The people are the only source of any and all of government's authority; and government has only that authority the people have given to it.

The concept of limited government can be expressed another way: Government must obey the law. Stated this way, the principle is often called **constitutionalism**—that is, that government must be conducted according to constitutional

## Reading Strategy

### Self-Questioning

Ask students to write seven comprehension questions as they read—one about how the Constitution is organized and one about each of the six principles. When they finish the section, have them answer the questions they wrote.

### Background Note

#### Common Misconceptions

The great principle of popular sovereignty set forth in the Constitution was hardly embraced by all of the Framers. In fact, the idea of granting the people as a whole too much say in government frightened many of them. Alexander Hamilton, for example, wrote that the "turbulent and changing" opinions of the masses "seldom judge or determine right," and referred to the "imprudence of democracy." George Washington, presiding at the Constitutional Convention, admonished the delegates not to produce a document that would simply "please the people."

### Point–of–Use Resources

📁 **Guided Reading and Review** Unit 1 booklet, p. 20 provides students with practice identifying the main ideas and key terms of this section.

📁 **Lesson Plans** For lesson planning suggestions, see p. 20 of the Lesson Plans booklet.

📁 **Political Cartoons** See p. 12 of the Political Cartoons booklet for a cartoon relevant to this section.

📖 **Section Support Transparencies** Transparency 15, *Visual Learning;* Transparency 114, *Political Cartoon*

### *Answer to . . .*

**Interpreting Tables** The first three outline the three-part federal structure, while the ones that follow address other aspects of the federal system.

## Organizing Information

To make sure students understand the main points of this section, you may wish to use the web graphic organizer to the right.

Tell students that a web shows a main idea and its supporting details. Ask students to use the web to outline the basic principles of the Constitution.

**Teaching Tip** A template for this graphic organizer can be found in the Section Support Transparencies, Transparency 1.

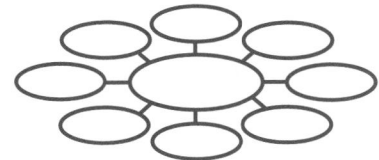

## Customize for
### More Advanced Students

Remind students that two Presidents have been impeached: Andrew Johnson in 1868 and Bill Clinton in 1998. Ask students to create a report that illustrates the similarities and differences between these two cases. Encourage students to include in their reports information about the specific charges that were filed, the outcomes of the Senate votes to acquit in each case, and how these proceedings affected each President's remaining time in office. Ask volunteers to present their findings to the class.

### ACTIVITY
### American Government, American Humor

Share the following quotation with students:

*"The single most exciting thing you encounter in government is competence, because it is so rare."*

—Daniel Patrick Moynihan

**Discussion** Ask students what Moynihan, a former Senator of New York, meant by his remark. Then have students explain whether and why the Framers of the Constitution might have agreed with it. How do each of the six principles guard against the incompetence Moynihan humorously refers to? What other bad traits do the principles guard against?

**(Average)**

### Answer to . . .

**Interpreting Diagrams** The President appoints Supreme Court justices and federal judges; Congress creates lower courts, may impeach judges, and approves or rejects appointment of judges (Senate).

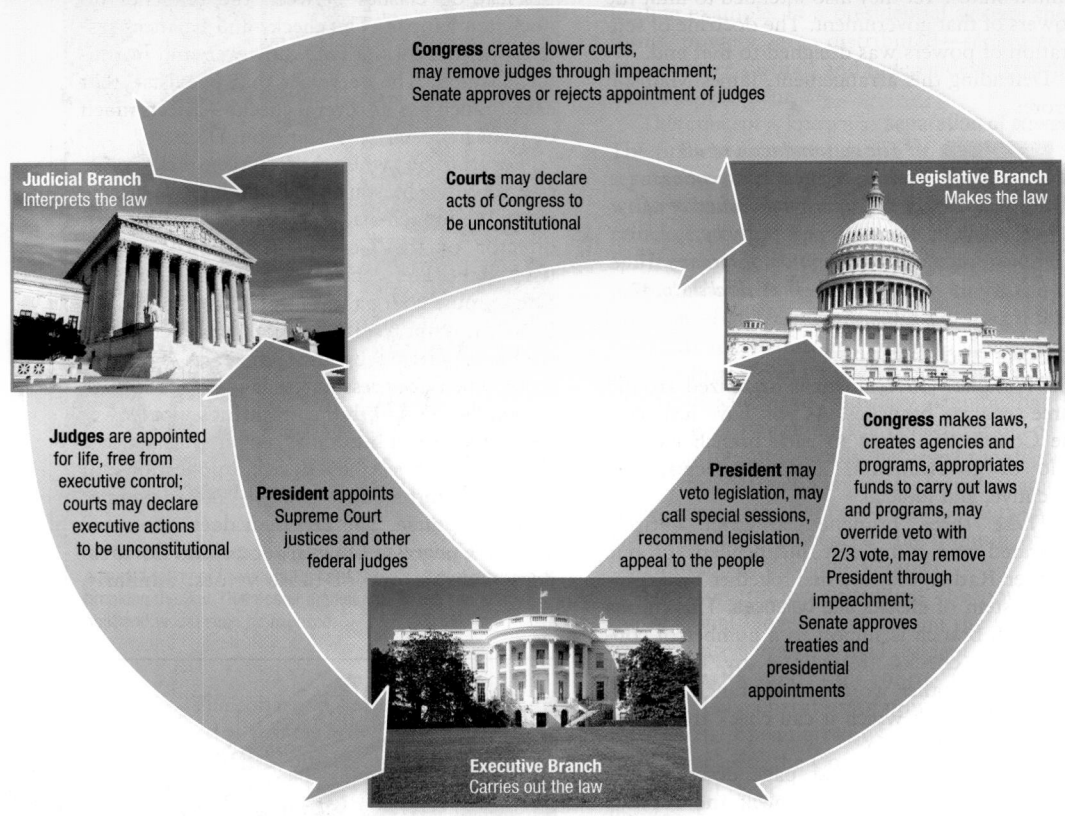

**Checks and Balances**

Congress creates lower courts, may remove judges through impeachment; Senate approves or rejects appointment of judges

**Judicial Branch** Interprets the law

Courts may declare acts of Congress to be unconstitutional

**Legislative Branch** Makes the law

Judges are appointed for life, free from executive control; courts may declare executive actions to be unconstitutional

President appoints Supreme Court justices and other federal judges

President may veto legislation, may call special sessions, recommend legislation, appeal to the people

Congress makes laws, creates agencies and programs, appropriates funds to carry out laws and programs, may override veto with 2/3 vote, may remove President through impeachment; Senate approves treaties and presidential appointments

**Executive Branch** Carries out the law

*Interpreting Diagrams* Under the system of checks and balances, each branch of government can check the actions of the others. *In what way can the power of the judiciary be checked by the other branches?*

the Senate can reject one of the President's appointees. And twice in our history, the House of Representatives has impeached, or brought charges against, a President—Andrew Johnson in 1868 and Bill Clinton in 1998—although on both occasions the President was acquitted by the Senate.

But, again, these and other direct confrontations are not common. Congress, the President, and even the courts try to avoid them. The check-and-balance system makes compromise necessary—and compromise is a vital part of democratic government.

Over time, the check-and-balance system has worked quite well. It has done what the Framers

intended it to do. It has prevented "an unjust combination of the majority." At the same time, it has not very often forestalled a close working relationship between the executive and legislative branches.

Note, however, that that working relationship runs more smoothly when the President and a majority in both houses of Congress have been of the same political party. When the other party controls one or both houses, conflicts play a larger than usual part in that relationship.

In fact, the American people have lately become accustomed to divided government, to a political environment in which one of the major parties holds the presidency and the other party controls Congress. Since the Eisenhower era in the 1950s, one of the two major parties (most often the Republican party) has usually occupied the White House, while the other party (regularly the Democratic party) has had a firm grip on Capitol Hill.

That now-familiar pattern of divided government has had a marked effect on the conduct of business between the President and Congress. Much of the executive-legislative relationship has been rooted in partisanship in recent years. It has been much more difficult and much more confrontational over those years than it has been through most of the nation's history.

### Judicial Review

One aspect of the principle of checks and balances is of such overriding importance in the American constitutional system that it stands, by itself, as one of that system's basic principles: judicial review.

The power of **judicial review** is the power of courts to determine whether what government does is in accord with what the Constitution provides. More precisely, judicial review may be defined this way: It is the power of a court to determine the constitutionality of a governmental action.

In part, then, judicial review is the power to declare **unconstitutional**—to declare illegal, null and void, of no force and effect—a governmental action found to violate some provision in the Constitution. The power of judicial review is held by all federal courts and by most State courts, as well.[2]

The Constitution does not provide for judicial review in so many words. Yet it seems clear that the Framers intended that the federal courts, and in particular the Supreme Court, should have that power. In *The Federalist* No. 78 Alexander Hamilton wrote that "independent judges" would prove to be "an essential safeguard against the effects of occasional ill humors in society." In *The Federalist* No. 51 James Madison called the judicial power one of the "auxiliary precautions" against the possible dominance of one branch of government over another.

In practice, the Supreme Court established the power of judicial review in the landmark case of *Marbury* v. *Madison* in 1803. (We shall take a close look at that case and the doctrine of judicial review in Chapter 18.) Since *Marbury*, the Supreme Court and other federal and State courts have used the power in thousands of cases. For the most part, the courts have

---

[2]Generally, the power is held by all courts of record. These are courts that keep a record of their proceedings and have the power to punish for contempt. Usually, only the lowest courts in a State—justice of the peace courts, for example—are not courts of record.

▲ The Supreme Court has struck down federal laws that regulated child labor and outlawed the burning of the United States flag. *Critical Thinking* **What characteristic of a law can lead the Supreme Court to overturn it?**

## CONSTITUTIONAL PRINCIPLES

### Judicial Review
In the case of *Marbury* v. *Madison,* the Supreme Court chose not to exercise the power to force Secretary of State James Madison to follow through on President Adams's appointment of William Marbury as justice of the peace. Ironically, by not choosing to use that power, the Court established the process of judicial review—by which the Court dramatically expanded its power.

### Activity
Have students review Supreme Court cases that deal with judicial review in the Close Up on Supreme Court Cases booklet. Then have them consider the rulings from these cases and write a brief essay on the importance of the power of judicial review. Ask students to consider what might happen if the courts did not have the power of judicial review.

## Point-of-Use Resources

**Guide to the Essentials** Chapter 3, Section 1, p. 24 provides support for students who need additional review of section content. Spanish support is available in the Spanish edition of the Guide on p. 17.

**Quiz** Unit 1 booklet, p. 21 includes matching and multiple-choice questions to check students' understanding of Section 1 content.

**Close Up on Primary Sources** *Marbury* v. *Madison* (1803), p. 64; William Rehnquist, On Judicial Activism (1998), p. 66

**Presentation Pro CD-ROM** Quizzes and multiple-choice questions check students' understanding of Section 1 content.

## Answers to . . .

### Section 1 Assessment

**1.** To state the broad purposes of the Constitution, and introduce the concepts of popular sovereignty and representative government that it will explain in detail.
**2.** Each branch—executive, legislative, judicial—is subject to a number of constitutional restraints by the other branches. For example, the courts may declare acts of Congress unconstitutional; Congress may remove judges through impeachment.
**3.** The law is considered null and void.
**4.** Definitions will vary, but should be based on the text.
**5.** The legislative branch protects individual rights by passing laws, but only those laws allowable under the Constitution; the executive branch must follow the law as it executes the law; the judicial branch is the guardian that ensures the other two branches do not usurp individual rights.

upheld challenged governmental actions. That is, in most cases in which the power of judicial review is exercised, the actions of government are found to be constitutional.

That is not always the case. To date, the Supreme Court has decided some 150 cases in which it has found an act or some part of an act of Congress to be unconstitutional. It has struck down several presidential and other executive branch actions as well. The Court has also voided hundreds of actions of the States and their local governments, including more than 1,000 State laws.

### Federalism

As you know, the American governmental system is federal in form. The powers held by government are distributed on a territorial basis. The National Government holds some of those powers, and others belong to the 50 States.

The principle of **federalism**—the division of power among a central government and several regional governments—came to the Constitution out of both experience and

▲ This statue in Concord, Massachusetts, pays tribute to the Minutemen who fought British troops to protect self-government.

necessity. In Philadelphia, the Framers faced a number of difficult problems, not the least of them: How to build a new, stronger, more effective National Government while preserving the existing States and the concept of local self-government.

The colonists had rebelled against the harsh rule of a powerful and distant central government. They had fought for the right to manage their local affairs without the meddling and dictation of the king and his ministers in far-off London. Surely, they would not now agree to another such government.

The Framers found their solution in federalism. In short, they constructed the federal arrangement, with its division of powers, as a compromise. It was an alternative to the system of nearly independent States, loosely tied to one another in the weak Articles of Confederation, and a much feared, too powerful central government. We shall explore the federal system at length in the next chapter.

## Section 1 Assessment

### Key Terms and Main Ideas

**1.** What is the purpose of the **Preamble** to the Constitution?
**2.** Explain how certain provisions of the Constitution provide for **checks and balances** among the branches of government.
**3.** What is the immediate effect if a law is declared **unconstitutional?**
**4.** Explain **federalism** in your own words.

### Critical Thinking

**5.** **Drawing Inferences** Analyze the role of each branch of government in protecting the rights of individuals.
**6.** **Understanding Point of View** Why were the Framers of the Constitution careful to limit the powers of the Federal Government?

**7.** **Drawing Conclusions** Some people consider the judicial branch the least democratic of the three branches of the government because federal judges are not elected and cannot be easily removed. How can voters and their elected representatives check the power of the judicial branch?

 **Take It to the Net**

**8.** Read about the division of power in the United States, Britain, and France and write a paragraph explaining how this element of the Constitution differentiates our Federal Government from the French and British systems. Use the links provided in the Social Studies area at the following Web site for help in completing this activity. **www.phschool.com**

**6.** Answers should reflect an understanding that they wanted to respect self-government at the State level and prevent tyranny.
**7.** Judges may be removed by Congress, and Congress is directly accountable to the people who elect them.

 **Take It to the Net**

**8.** Direct students to the Social Studies area at the Prentice Hall School Web site. The *Magruder's American Government* companion Web site includes the directions and links needed to complete the activity. It also provides a printable Internet activity worksheet with scoring rubrics for assessment. Paragraphs should be supported with relevant examples.

# Using the Internet for Research

The Internet is a network of computers that links governments, organizations, and individuals around the world. The World Wide Web is one part of the Internet. Since the Internet has no central organization, finding the information you need can be difficult. To focus your search you can use search engines, the databases that track thousands of Web pages by subject.

Congress uses the Internet to communicate with the public. Congressional Web sites provide general information about legislators, committees, and hearings. These sites also provide information on proposed legislation. Use the steps below to locate and track the progress of a bill in Congress.

**1. Plan the scope of your search.** Choose a research topic that is not too vague. Searching for a broad subject can yield thousands of results that would be impossible to sift through. Try to state your research topic as a specific question. Then think of search terms that might return answers to your question. For example, rather than searching for broad terms such as *Congress* or *legislation*, identify a public issue that Congress is working on, such as *funding for disaster relief*. Then do a search on that topic.

**2. Refine your search.** Your first set of results usually includes Web sites that do not contain the information you need. Many search engines offer an advanced search option that allows you to narrow your search. You might decide to make your search terms more specific; for instance, *disaster relief AND earthquakes*. Or you might exclude unwanted information, as in *disaster relief NOT hurricanes*.

**3. Navigate the sites.** Once you find a site that meets your needs, explore its home page to determine how to find the information you need. Does the information in the site fully answer your question? Does the site have its own search tool to explore information contained in the site? Does it provide links to other Web sites that might better aid your research? To whom does the site belong, and is it a reliable source? (The Social Studies area at the following Web site has many useful research links: **www.phschool.com**)

For example, if your search led you to the Web site of the Federal Emergency Management Agency (FEMA), you might search within the site for *budget AND earthquakes* to find out how much funding FEMA has requested to cover damage from a particular earthquake. Then you might go to a congressional site to find out the status of the budget request for FEMA.

## Test for Success

Conduct Internet research on an important public issue that is currently being debated in Congress. Find out what legislation is being proposed on this topic. Check the status of the legislation. Has it been proposed in both houses of Congress? At what stage is the bill in each house?

▶ Aftermath of the October 1989 earthquake in Oakland, California

## Point-of-Use Resources

📁 **Skills for Life Activity** Unit 1 booklet, p. 26 provides an additional skill activity for this chapter.

💿 **Social Studies Skills Tutor CD-ROM** Provides interactive practice in geographic literacy, critical thinking and reading, visual analysis, and communications.

## Test for Success

The congressional Web site is the best place to track the status of current legislation. It is administered by the Library of Congress (LOC). See the *Magruder's* companion Web site for links. **www.phschool.com**

## SKILLS FOR LIFE

TECHNOLOGY

## Using the Internet for Research

**Focus** Use an Internet search engine to locate Web sites that provide information on some aspect of disaster management. Possible topics include: public health advice about potential health threats; disaster readiness in homes and cities; evacuation procedures; drills and other pre-planning; early warning systems for hurricanes, tornadoes, and earthquakes; research into the behavior of storms and into the movement of Earth's tectonic plates; funding for disaster relief; logistical issues in post-disaster cleanup and rebuilding.

**Instruct** Direct pairs of students to keep a "search log" that identifies the key words used, the number of sites identified in each search, the number and names of sites reviewed, and the names of the most useful site(s). When students have completed their searches, have each pair share their experiences with the class.

**Close/Reteach** Lead a class discussion in which you guide students to compile a list of do's and don'ts in Web searching.

### Answers . . .

**1.** Explain to students that search engines vary in the way they search, the places they search, and in how the search terms must be stated. Encourage student teams to try a variety of search engines.

**2.** Most search engines require specific terms in a specific format. Directions on how to format and refine your searches are available at each site. Have students read about "Boolean operators" and how they work. Some sites let you search by means of a question.

**3.** Explain to students that because anyone can post information on the Internet, and many individuals and groups do so anonymously, they must find the source of a Web site before they can rely on the information it gives. Government Web sites and those of major news media are generally reliable.

**·2· Formal Amendment**

**Objectives** You may wish to call students' attention to the objectives in the Section Preview. The objectives are reflected in the main headings of the section.

**Bellringer** Ask students to consider what might happen if a group of baseball owners sought to move the pitcher's mound back five feet. Discuss the formal process that would precede such a major change. Explain that in this section, they will learn about the formal process of changing the Constitution.

**Vocabulary Builder** Have students look at the terms in the Political Dictionary. Write the word *amendment* on the board. Ask students to find a shorter word, related to sewing, in the larger word. *(mend)* Ask how this word might apply to the Constitution.

## Pressed for Time?

### Quick Lesson Plan

**1. Focus** Tell students that the Constitution has survived for more than 200 years because it contains timeless principles yet can be amended. Ask students to discuss what they know about the formal amendment process.

**2. Instruct** Ask students to name the four ways the Constitution can be formally amended. Then discuss why one of the four methods has dominated and which method best reflects the principle of popular sovereignty.

**3. Close/Reteach** Remind students that the formal amendment process has yielded 27 amendments, including the ten contained in the Bill of Rights. Have groups of students prepare to orally explain all four methods of amendment.

## Section Preview

### OBJECTIVES

1. **Analyze** the processes by which the United States Constitution can be changed and evaluate their effectiveness.
2. **Understand** the history of the 27 amendments to the Constitution.

### WHY IT MATTERS

The Constitution has grown and changed with the United States through the addition of 27 amendments. The first ten amendments guarantee many of our basic freedoms and are known as the Bill of Rights.

### POLITICAL DICTIONARY

★ amendment
★ formal amendment
★ Bill of Rights

The Constitution of the United States has now been in force for more than 200 years—longer, by far, than the written constitution of any other nation in the world.[3]

When the Constitution became effective in 1789, the United States was a small agricultural nation of fewer than four million people. That population was scattered for some 1,300 miles along the eastern edge of the continent. Travel and communications among the 13 States were limited to horseback and sailing ships. The new States struggled to stay alive in a generally hostile world.

Today, more than 285 million people live in the United States. The now 50 States stretch across the continent and beyond, and the country also has many far-flung commitments. The United States is today the most powerful nation on Earth, and its modern, highly industrialized and technological society has produced a standard of living that has long been the envy of the rest of the world.

How has the Constitution, written in 1787, endured despite that astounding change and

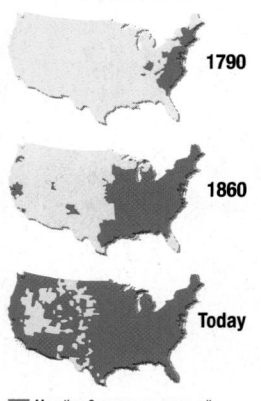

**Population Growth**

1790

1860

Today

■ More than 2 persons per square mile
SOURCE: MapQuest.com, Inc.

◄ The United States population has grown and expanded across the continent since the Constitution was adopted. The Constitution has been amended to meet the changing needs of the country.

growth? Strict constructionists point out that the Constitution is based on timeless principles. These principles should not be tampered with lest the words of the Constitution become meaningless. We must thus look to the Framers' original intent for guidance when grappling with today's issues. Liberal constructionists, on the other hand, believe that the answer to this question lies with the concept of a "Living Constitution." That is, that the Constitution has endured because it can change and grow with the times.

This process of constitutional change can occur in two basic ways: (1) by formal amendment and (2) by informal procedures. In this section, you will look at the first of them: the addition of formal amendments to the Constitution.

## Changing the Constitution

The Framers knew that even the wisest of constitution makers cannot build for all time. Thus, the Constitution provides for its own **amendment**—that is, for changes in its written words.

Article V sets out two methods for the proposal and two methods for the ratification of constitutional amendments. So, there are four

---

[3]The British constitution dates from well before the Norman Conquest of 1066, but it is not a single, written document. Rather, it is an "unwritten constitution," a collection of principles, customs, traditions, and significant parliamentary acts that guide British government and practice. Israel, which has existed only since 1948, is the only other state in the world without a written constitution.

## ▣ Block Scheduling Strategies

Consider these suggestions to manage extended class time:

■ Have students draw numbers from 1 to 27, each number corresponding to one of the 27 amendments. Have each student create a visual that depicts the amendment they have selected. After students have finished, they present their visuals to the class and have their classmates identify which amendment is being shown.

■ Organize the class into several small groups, assigning each group several amendments so that all 27 amendments are covered. Have students use the text and outside resources to study the historical debate surrounding each amendment's passage. Have students consider arguments for and against the amendment. Finally, have each group present information about their amendments to the class.

## Formal Amendment Process

### Step 1
### Amendment Is Proposed

Proposed by Congress by a $\frac{2}{3}$ vote in both houses — $\frac{2}{3}$

Proposed at a national convention called by Congress when requested by $\frac{2}{3}$ (34) of the State legislatures — $\frac{2}{3}$

### Step 2
### Amendment Is Ratified

Ratified by the State legislatures of $\frac{3}{4}$ (38) of the States — $\frac{3}{4}$

Ratified by conventions held in $\frac{3}{4}$ (38) of the States — $\frac{3}{4}$

*Interpreting Diagrams* The four different ways in which amendments may be added to the Constitution are shown here. Conventions are rarely used. All but one of the 27 amendments were proposed in Congress and then ratified by the State legislatures. ***How does the formal amendment process illustrate federalism?***

possible methods of **formal amendment**—changes or additions that become part of the written language of the Constitution itself. The diagram above sets out these four methods.

**First Method** An amendment may be proposed by a two-thirds vote in each house of Congress and be ratified by three fourths of the State legislatures. Today, 38 State legislatures must approve an amendment for it to become a part of the Constitution. Twenty-six of the Constitution's 27 amendments were adopted in this manner.

**Second Method** An amendment may be proposed by Congress and then ratified by conventions, called for that purpose, in three fourths of the States. Only the 21st Amendment, added in 1933, was adopted in this way. Conventions were used to ratify the 21st Amendment largely because Congress felt that the conventions' popularly elected delegates would be more likely to reflect public opinion on the question of repeal than would State legislators.

**Third Method** An amendment may be proposed by a national convention, called by Congress at the request of two thirds of the State legislatures—today, 34. As you can see in the diagram, it must then be ratified by three fourths

of the State legislatures. To this point, Congress has not called such a convention.[4]

**Fourth Method** An amendment may be proposed by a national convention and ratified by conventions in three fourths of the States. Remember that the Constitution itself was adopted in much this same way.

### Federalism and Popular Sovereignty

Note that the formal amendment process emphasizes the federal character of the governmental system. Proposal takes place at the national level and ratification is a State-by-State matter. Also note that when the Constitution is amended, that action represents the expression of the people's sovereign will. The people have spoken.

Some criticize the practice of sending proposed amendments to the State legislatures rather than to ratifying conventions, especially

---

[4]The calling of a convention has been a near thing twice in recent years. Between 1963 and 1969, 33 State legislatures, one short of the necessary two thirds, sought an amendment to erase the Supreme Court's "one-person, one-vote" decisions; see Chapter 24. Also, between 1975 and 1983, 32 States asked for a convention to propose an amendment that would require that the federal budget be balanced each year, except in time of war or other national emergency.

**RESOURCE PRO**

**Resource Pro® CD-ROM** contains an electronic version of each activity found in the Teaching Resources as well as additional resources such as Supreme Court cases. The Planning Express® feature allows you to customize and create daily lesson plans within minutes.

## Reading Strategy
### Finding Evidence
The Framers purposely made the process of amending the Constitution difficult. Have students look for evidence to support this conclusion as they read.

### Background Note
### Recent Scholarship
"…Orderly constitutional revision…was the 'original intent' of the Founders" writes David E. Kyvig in *Explicit and Authentic Acts: Amending the U.S. Constitution, 1776–1995.* Kyvig also asserts that this intent was as radical as the Revolution itself. Analyzing major attempts—both successful and unsuccessful—to change the federal Constitution, he argues that there is a major distinction between formal amendments and informal procedures such as judicial interpretation, legislative actions, and presidential assumptions of power. The radical formal amendment process, he concludes, in practice "as well as by design…has no equal in the American constitutional order."

## Point-of-Use Resources

**Guided Reading and Review** Unit 1 booklet, p. 22 provides students with practice identifying the main ideas and key terms of this section.

**Lesson Plans** For lesson planning suggestions, see p. 21 of the Lesson Plans booklet.

**Political Cartoons** See p. 13 of the Political Cartoons booklet for a cartoon relevant to this section.

### Answer to...
**Interpreting Diagrams** It involves both the Federal Government and the States.

amended frivolously.

## Reading Strategy

### Previewing and Predicting

Ask students to read the section's title, main headings, and subheadings and write a sentence predicting the content of each section. When they have finished reading Section 3, have them compare their predictions to the actual text.

---

### Background Note

#### Behind the Scenes

When Washington warned of the "baneful effects of parties," he knew what he was talking about! While history correctly records his unanimous election to the presidency in 1789, the victory came without electoral votes from New York. Federalists controlling the State Senate and Anti-Federalists controlling the Assembly (House) could not reach an agreement on whom to elect to the State's electoral college delegation. Therefore, New York didn't send a delegate—and ultimately didn't participate in Washington's election.

---

### Point-of-Use Resources

📁 **Guided Reading and Review** Unit 1 booklet, p. 24 provides students with practice identifying the main ideas and key terms of this section.

📁 **Lesson Plans** For lesson planning suggestions, see p. 22 of the Lesson Plans booklet.

📁 **Political Cartoons** See p. 14 of the Political Cartoons booklet for a cartoon relevant to this section.

📰 **Section Support Transparencies** Transparency 17, *Visual Learning;* Transparency 116, *Political Cartoon*

---

### Answer to . . .

**Critical Thinking** Answers should consider whether a President abuses his power as commander in chief when he commits troops abroad.

---

have *not* been a major part of the process by which the Constitution has kept pace with more than two centuries of far-reaching change.

▲ **Across the Border** Congress can pass laws under its constitutional right to regulate interstate commerce, or trade that crosses State boundaries.

and offices in the now huge executive branch have been created by acts of Congress.

As another example, the Constitution deals with the matter of presidential succession, but only up to a point. The 25th Amendment says that if the presidency becomes vacant, the Vice President automatically succeeds to the office. Who becomes President if both the presidency and the vice presidency are vacant? The Constitution leaves the answer to that question to Congress and its lawmaking power.

Second, Congress has added to the Constitution by the way in which it has used many of its powers. The Constitution gives to Congress the expressed power to regulate foreign and interstate commerce.[6] But what is

▲ President Bush used his power as commander in chief to commit armed forces to Afghanistan in 2001. *Critical Thinking* **Should the President be able to make war without a declaration of war by Congress?**

the law. We shall consider these guarantees at some length in Chapters 19 and 20. The 10th Amendment does not deal with civil rights as such. Rather, it spells out the concept of reserved

"foreign commerce"? What is "interstate commerce"? What, exactly, does Congress have the power to regulate? The Constitution does not say, and at the time of ratification, "commerce" was understood as only "trade in tangible commodities." Congress has done much to define those words, however, by exercising its commerce power with the passage of literally thousands of laws. As it has done so, Congress has informally amended—added much to—the Constitution.

### Executive Action

The manner in which various Presidents have used their powers has also produced changes in the way the Constitution is interpreted. For example, the Constitution states that only Congress can declare war.[7] But the Constitution also makes the President the commander in chief of the nation's armed forces.[8] Acting under that authority, several Presidents have made war without a declaration of war by Congress. In fact, Presidents have used the armed forces abroad in combat without such a declaration on no fewer than 200 separate occasions in our history.

Among many examples of expanded executive powers is the use of executive agreements in the conduct of foreign affairs. An **executive agreement** is a pact made by the President directly with the head of a foreign state. A **treaty**, on the other hand, is a formal agreement between two or more sovereign states. The principal difference between these agreements and treaties is that executive agreements need not be approved by the Senate. They are as legally binding as treaties, however. Recent Presidents have often used them in our dealings with other countries, instead of the much more cumbersome treaty-making process outlined in Article II, Section 2 of the Constitution.

### Court Decisions

The nation's courts, most tellingly the United States Supreme Court, interpret and apply the Constitution in many

---

[6]Article I, Section 8, Clause 3.
[7]Article I, Section 8, Clause 11.
[8]Article II, Section 2, Clause 1.

---

## Organizing Information

To make sure students understand the main points of this section, you may wish to use the tree map graphic organizer to the right.

Tell students that a tree map shows an outline of a topic, its main ideas, and its supporting details. Ask students to use the tree map to outline the informal processes for interpreting the Constitution.

**Teaching Tip** A template for this graphic organizer can be found in the Section Support Transparencies, Transparency 3.

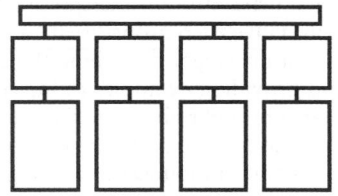

cases they hear. You have already read about several of these instances of constitutional interpretation by the Court, such as in *Marbury v. Madison,* 1803. You will encounter more of these landmark cases throughout this book, for the Supreme Court is, as Woodrow Wilson once put it, "a constitutional convention in continuous session."

## Party Practices

The nation's political parties have also been a major source of Constitutional interpretation over the course of American political history, despite the fact that the Constitution makes no mention of political parties. In fact, most of the Framers were opposed to their growth. In his Farewell Address in 1796, George Washington warned the people against what he called "the baneful effects of the spirit of party." Washington feared the divisive effect of party politics. Yet, even as he spoke, parties were developing in this country. They have played a major role in the shaping of government and its processes ever since. There are numerous examples of that point.

Neither the Constitution nor any law provides for the nomination of candidates for the presidency. From the 1830s on, however, the major parties have held national conventions to do just that. The parties have converted the **electoral college,** the group that makes the formal selection of the nation's President, from what the Framers intended into a "rubber stamp" for each State's popular vote in presidential elections. Both houses of Congress are organized and conduct much of their business on the basis of party. The President makes appointments to office with an eye to party politics. In short, government in the United States is in many ways government through party.

## Custom

Unwritten customs may be as strong as written laws, and many customs have developed in our governmental system. Again, there are many examples. By custom, not because the Constitution says so, the heads of the 14 executive departments make up the **Cabinet,** an advisory body to the President traditionally made up of the heads of the executive departments and other officers.[9]

## Voices on Government

**John Marshall** (Chief Justice of the United States) set precedents that established important powers of the federal courts. Marshall served as Chief Justice of the United States from 1801 until 1835. As a Federalist, he established the independence of the judicial branch. In *Marbury v. Madison,* Marshall claimed for the Supreme Court the power to declare a law unconstitutional, and he affirmed the superiority of federal authority under the Constitution in *McCulloch v. Maryland* and *Gibbons v. Ogden.* In *McCulloch v. Maryland,* he wrote:

❝ *This provision is made in a constitution, intended to endure for ages to come, and consequently, to be adapted to the various crises of human affairs.* ❞

### Evaluating the Quotation

*(a) Write a paragraph explaining your understanding of Marshall's statement. (b) How might Jefferson and Madison have responded to Marshall's statement?*

On each of the eight occasions when a President died in office, the Vice President succeeded to that office—most recently in 1963. Yet, the written words of the Constitution did not provide for this practice until the adoption of the 25th Amendment in 1967. Until then, the Constitution said only that the powers and duties of the presidency—but *not* the office itself—should be transferred to the Vice President.[10]

It is a long-established custom that the Senate will only approve those presidential appointees that are acceptable to the senator or senators of the President's party from the State involved, for example, a federal judge or a United States marshal. This practice is known as **senatorial courtesy,** and it is closely followed in the Senate. Notice that its practical effect is to shift a portion of the appointing power from the

---

[9]The Constitution provides for the Cabinet (the heads of departments who are in the line of presidential succession) only indirectly, in Article 2, Section 2.

[10]Read, carefully, Article II, Section 1, Clause 6, and then Section 1 of the 25th Amendment.

## Customize for
### Less Proficient Readers

Distribute five index cards to each student. Ask students to list each of the five basic informal procedures for interpreting the Constitution, one on each card. On the back of each card, students should write specific examples of each of these ways. (for example, political parties—national conventions.) When completed, students can use these index cards to quiz each other on the procedures.

## Point–of–Use Resources

📁 **The Living Constitution** Separation of Powers, p. 5

📖 **Basic Principles of the Constitution Transparencies** Transparencies 23-29, *Separation of Powers*

## CONSTITUTIONAL PRINCIPLES

### Separation of Powers
The five methods of informally interpreting the Constitution have altered the separation of powers that were laid out in the document. For instance, although the Constitution only allows Congress to declare war, Presidents have used their powers as commander in chief of the armed forces to make war.

### Activity
Have each student consider one of the informal procedures for interpreting the Constitution and identify how it has altered the separation of powers as laid out by the Constitution. Then ask students to write brief papers either supporting or opposing the change made by the informal procedures.

*Answer to . . .*
**Evaluating the Quotation**
(a) Paragraphs will vary but should show an understanding that, according to Marshall, the process of judicial review will allow the Constitution to endure over time. (b) Jefferson and Madison might have responded that the Constitution will endure because it contains timeless principles, not because the judiciary can or should interpret it.

## Answers to . . .
## Section 3 Assessment

**1.** Informal procedures are the day-to-day process of making small changes to the Constitution based on changes in society. It does not require a lengthy proposal and ratification process or written changes to the Constitution as does formal amendment.

**2.** The Cabinet serves as an advisory body to the President, and is traditionally made up of the heads of the executive departments and other officers.

**3.** The electoral college formally selects the nation's President.

**4.** It is a pact made by the President with the head of a foreign state.

**5.** Answers will vary, but should suggest that informal procedures allowed Congress to add substance to the Constitution, which began as a very basic document.

**6.** Answers will vary, but might suggest a President would lose support of the Senate were he or she to abandon long-held customs, even though the Constitution gives the President that power.

## Answer to . . .

**Critical Thinking** Possible answer: They no longer believed that Presidents would follow custom alone.

▲ The tradition of limiting Presidents to two terms became a major issue in the presidential campaign of 1940 and again in 1944. *Critical Thinking* **Why did Roosevelt's reelection lead supporters of the "no-third-term" tradition to push for a constitutional amendment?**

President, where the formal wording of the Constitution puts it, to certain members of the Senate.

Both the strength and the importance of unwritten customs can be seen in the reaction to the rare circumstances in which one of them has not been observed. For nearly 150 years, the "no-third-term tradition" was a closely followed rule in presidential politics. The tradition began in 1796, when George Washington refused to seek a third term as President, and several later Presidents followed that lead. In 1940, and again in 1944, however, Franklin Roosevelt broke the no-third-term custom. He sought and won a third and then a fourth term in the White House. As a direct result, the 22nd Amendment was added to the Constitution in 1951. What had been an unwritten custom became a written part of the Constitution itself.

## Section 3 Assessment

### Key Terms and Main Ideas

1. How do informal procedures for interpreting the Constitution differ from formal amendment?
2. What role does the **Cabinet** play in government?
3. What is the current role of the **electoral college?**
4. What is an **executive agreement?**

### Critical Thinking

5. **Drawing Conclusions** Explain, in your own words, why informal procedures are such an important part of constitutional change.
6. **Determining Cause and Effect** What do you think would happen if the President appointed federal officials without concern for senatorial courtesy? How does the Constitution provide for a solution?

 **Take It to the Net**

7. Read about the ways in which the Constitution can be amended. Then write a "constitution" for your classroom that consists of 10 rules for good classroom behavior. Debate whether these rules should remain fixed or be flexible. If fixed, will they become outdated? If flexible will they eventually become meaningless, as students interpret them to get away with whatever behavior they want? Use the links provided in the Social Studies area at the following Web site for help in completing this activity. **www.phschool.com**

## Take It to the Net

**7.** Direct students to the Social Studies area at the Prentice Hall School Web site. The *Magruder's American Government* companion Web site includes the directions and links needed to complete the activity. It also provides a printable Internet activity worksheet with scoring rubrics for assessment. Charts should include specific facts and examples.

# CLOSE UP FOUNDATION *on the Supreme Court*

## May Schools Use Corporal Punishment?

*The 8th Amendment declares, in part, that "cruel and unusual punishment" may not be inflicted. It does not, however, state on whom such punishment may not be inflicted. The amendment is commonly applied to convicted criminals. Does it also protect others, such as students, from physical punishments?*

### Ingraham v. Wright (1977)

James Ingraham and Roosevelt Andrews, students in the eighth and ninth grades in a Dade County, Florida, junior high school, were paddled in 1970 for violating school rules. Florida law allowed corporal punishment of students as a means of maintaining discipline, so long as it was not "degrading or unduly severe" and was administered only after the principal or teacher in charge of the school had been consulted.

Ingraham and Andrews filed suit in federal court against Willie J. Wright (their school's principal) and other school officials. They said that the paddlings had violated their 8th Amendment protection against cruel and unusual punishment. They presented evidence showing the seriousness of the discipline they had received, which caused both students physical injuries. The trial court ruled against them, finding that the punishment was not sufficiently arbitrary, severe, or unacceptable under contemporary standards to violate the 8th Amendment.

The students then appealed to the court of appeals. A panel of the court concluded that the punishment was too severe, and that the students should have been given an opportunity to be heard before being punished. The entire court of appeals then heard the case. It concluded that the punishment did *not* violate the Constitution and that students did *not* have a right to a hearing before being punished. The students then appealed to the Supreme Court.

### Arguments for Ingraham

1. The 5th Amendment gives students the right to receive proper notice and to have an opportunity to be heard before the government can punish them. These rights help ensure that the government does not punish people improperly.
2. Severe paddlings are unacceptable in a civilized society and should not be permitted under the 8th Amendment.
3. Convicted criminals cannot be paddled. Criminals should not have greater constitutional protection against cruel and unusual punishment than school children do.

### Arguments for Wright

1. Corporal punishment has long been accepted as a means of maintaining discipline in public schools. When this case arose, only two States prohibited corporal punishment in schools.
2. Because teachers may be sued for damages if they use excessive or unreasonable force, there is no need to create a special constitutional rule governing the use of corporal punishment in school.
3. The 8th Amendment protects criminals, and should not be applied to schoolchildren.

### Decide for Yourself

1. Review the constitutional grounds on which each side based its arguments and the specific arguments each side presented.
2. Debate the opposing viewpoints presented in this case. Which viewpoint do you favor?
3. Predict the impact of the Court's decision on the rights of public school students. (To read a summary of the Court's decision, turn to the Supreme Court Glossary on page 799.)

---

## CLOSE UP FOUNDATION *Corner*

📁 **Close Up on the Supreme Court** *Ingraham* v. *Wright,* p. 4 provides an activity to extend coverage of this case.

### CLOSE UP FOUNDATION Online

To keep up-to-date on Close Up news and activities, visit Close Up Online at

**www.closeup.org**

---

## May Schools Use Corporal Punishment?

**Focus** Have the class read the Eighth Amendment and then discuss whether it ought to apply to school discipline. Ask: What types of punishment are appropriate for students with disciplinary problems?

**Instruct** After students have read the feature, explain that law students often learn cases by creating an outline that summarizes the facts, issues, and holding of a case in separate short paragraphs. Have students read the Court's decision and then help the class create an outline, or brief, on the chalkboard. Encourage students to create and use briefs as a study aid for the rest of the court cases in the textbook.

**Close/Reteach** Explain the concept of due process. Among other things, due process requires that the government follow fair and just procedures whenever it threatens to deprive an individual of life, liberty, or property. Discuss the reasons why the Supreme Court determined in *Ingraham* that students were not entitled to notice and a hearing under the due process clause.

💿 **Keep It Current CD-ROM** includes government-related projects by unit. The CD-ROM links to the Prentice Hall School Web site and may be used for daily updates.

---

### *Answers to . . .*
#### Decide for Yourself

**1.** Ingraham used the grounds of the Fifth Amendment (proper notice) and the Eighth Amendment (cruel and unusual punishment) to argue that the students were unfairly punished. Wright argued that the Eighth Amendment did not apply to students, and that corporal punishment is both traditional and fair.
**2.** Answers will vary, but should be supported with valid reasoning.
**3.** The Court decided in favor of Wright, holding that the Eighth Amendment did not apply to school discipline.

## Practicing the Vocabulary

1. Cabinet
2. electoral college
3. constitutionalism
4. judicial review
5. checks and balances
6. federalism
7. amendment
8. Bill of Rights
9. formal amendment
10. rule of law

## Reviewing Main Ideas
### Section 1

**11.** It begins with a short introduction called the Preamble. The rest of the document is divided into seven numbered sections, called articles, that outline the organization and powers of each branch of government, the role of the States, and the amendment and ratification processes.
**12.** Popular sovereignty, limited government, checks and balances, separation of powers, judicial review, and federalism.
**13. (a)** Popular sovereignty holds that the people are the source of all government power, and limited government implies that the government can do only those things that the people have given it the power to do. **(b)** Because the Framers wanted to create a government that, by limiting its powers, could not become tyrannical.
**14.** The purpose of checks and balances is to prevent one branch of government from having too much power over the other branches.
**15. (a)** Judges may overturn a law when they decide that it is unconstitutional. **(b)** Presidents may veto legislation and call special sessions.

### Section 2

**16.** Twenty-seven amendments have been added to the Constitution.
**17. (a)** The most common method has been for the amendment to be proposed by a two-thirds vote in each house of Congress and ratified by three fourths of the State legislatures. **(b)** Proposal by Congress with ratification by three fourths of State legislatures.
**18.** It emphasizes the federal character of the governmental system, as proposal takes place at the national level and ratification at the State level.

## Political Dictionary

Preamble (p. 65)
articles (p. 65)
constitutionalism (p. 65)
rule of law (p. 66)
separation of powers (p. 66)
checks and balances (p. 67)

veto (p. 67)
judicial review (p. 69)
unconstitutional (p. 69)
federalism (p. 70)
amendment (p. 72)
formal amendment (p. 73)

Bill of Rights (p. 76)
executive agreement (p. 80)
treaty (p. 80)
electoral college (p. 81)
Cabinet (p. 81)
senatorial courtesy (p. 81)

## Practicing the Vocabulary

*Matching* Choose a term from the list above that best matches each description.

1. The President's advisory board
2. A group that makes the formal selection of the nation's President
3. The idea that government must work in accordance with the principles of the Constitution
4. The power of courts to determine if a law or government action is constitutional
5. A system by which any one branch of government can be restrained by one or both of the other branches

*Fill in the Blank* Choose a term from the list above that best completes each sentence below.

6. Under the principle of _____ , the Federal Government has three equal branches.
7. _____ is the process by which the Constitution has been changed and added to during the course of United States history.
8. The first ten amendments to the United States Constitution are known as the _____.
9. _____ results in changes to the written words of the Constitution.
10. The principle of _____ states that government must be bound by a fundamental law.

## Reviewing Main Ideas

**Section 1**
11. How is the text of the Constitution organized?
12. What are the six basic principles of the Constitution?
13. **(a)** How are popular sovereignty and limited government related? **(b)** Why were these principles important to the Framers of the Constitution?
14. What is the purpose of checks and balances?
15. **(a)** How can the judicial branch check the legislative branch? **(b)** How can the executive branch check the legislative branch?

**Section 2**
16. How many amendments have been formally added to the Constitution?
17. **(a)** What has been the most common method for adding an amendment to the Constitution? **(b)** Which method has only been used once?
18. How does the formal amendment process show the importance of federalism?

19. **(a)** Which amendment required the longest amount of time to ratify? **(b)** How long did it take?
20. What event led to the 13th, 14th, and 15th amendments?

**Section 3**
21. What are five informal procedures for changing the interpretation of the Constitution?
22. How can Congress change the interpretation of the Constitution?
23. Identify two examples of presidential powers that illustrate informal procedures for interpreting the Constitution.
24. What is the role of custom in government?

**19. (a)** the 27th amendment **(b)** nearly 203 years
**20.** The Civil War.

### Section 3
**21.** Passage of basic legislation by Congress, actions taken by the President, key decisions of the Supreme Court, activities of political parties, and custom.
**22.** By passing laws that elaborate on the brief provisions of the Constitution and by passing laws that expand congressional power.
**23.** Informal procedures have given Presidents the authority to use the armed forces without congressional declaration of war and to use executive agreement in place of formal treaties.
**24.** Customs have served as important guidelines in areas in which the Constitution is not explicit.

## Critical Thinking Skills

25. **Applying the Chapter Skill** Use the Internet to find three recent proposed amendments to the Constitution. Who is promoting these amendments, and why?

26. **Drawing Conclusions** The Preamble to the Constitution begins with the words "We the People." **(a)** Was every person living in the United States in 1789 included in that collective "We"? **(b)** Which, if any, of the 27 amendments to the Constitution corrected that situation?

27. **Demonstrating Reasoned Judgment** James Madison defended the concepts of separation of powers and checks and balances in *The Federalist* No. 51. What did he mean when he wrote that, to guard against a concentration of power in one of the branches of government, "ambition must be made to counteract ambition"?

28. **Testing Conclusions** Find evidence from the text to support the following conclusion: It is important for the beliefs and principles of the American people to be set out in a written constitution.

## Analyzing Political Cartoons

Using your knowledge of American government and this cartoon, answer the questions below.

29. What point is the cartoonist trying to make about the ease or difficulty of proposing constitutional amendments?
30. Based on your reading, do you agree or disagree with the cartoonist's opinion? Explain your answer.

 **Take It to the Net**

Additional support materials and activities for Chapter 3 of *Magruder's American Government* can be found in the Social Studies area at the Prentice Hall School Web site.
**www.phschool.com**

---

 **You Can Make a Difference**

The passage of the 26th Amendment brought a spurt of interest in voting and political action by young people. Do you think many teenagers today are still as interested in politics and voting? Prepare a 10-question survey of student attitudes. Ask, for instance, whether the person is registered to vote, knows where to vote, and plans to vote in an upcoming election. Does he or she think that giving 18-year-olds the vote was a good idea? Then use your survey to interview people between the ages of 16 and 21. Record your answers in a table.

## Participation Activities

31. **Current Events Watch** The Constitution gives the President the power to appoint all federal judges. However, it also gives the Senate the power to confirm or reject those appointments by majority vote. Research the recent appointment of a federal judge and write a brief report on his or her background and how senators from the opposing party responded to the President's nomination.

32. **Time Line Activity** Create a time line of the Equal Rights Amendment, beginning with its proposal in 1972 and ending with its failure to be ratified ten years later. List the number of States that voted to ratify it each year and include the three-year extension to the time limit passed in 1979. Compare this time line to the table on page 76. What does your time line tell you about the ratification process? Do you think the ten-year time limit was fair? Explain your answer.

33. **It's Your Turn** You are a newspaper editor in the late 1700s. Alexander Hamilton has just referred to democracy as "mobocracy." Write an editorial in response to Hamilton's view. Define the position that you want to take in the editorial. Next, list your arguments. As you revise your editorial, make certain that your arguments are persuasive. Finally, proofread and make a final copy.

 **Take It to the Net**

**Chapter 3 Self-Test** As a final review activity, take the Chapter 3 Self-Test in the Social Studies area at the Web site listed below, and receive immediate feedback on your answers.

**www.phschool.com**

## Point–of–Use Resources

**Guide to the Essentials of American Government** Chapter 3 Test, page 27 provides multiple-choice questions to test students' knowledge of the chapter.

**Test Bank CD-ROM** Chapter 3 Test

**Chapter Test** Chapter Tests booklet

---

## Critical Thinking Skills

**25.** Answers will vary, but should be supported with specific facts and draw valid conclusions.

**26. (a)** The collective "We" did not include African Americans, women, and Native Americans as full and equal citizens. **(b)** The 13th, 14th, 15th, 19th, and 24th amendments applied expressly to either women or minorities.

**27.** Students' responses should include the concept that the three branches of government, each in pursuit of its own advantage, would prevent excess of the other; i.e., the strength of the federal system is in keeping any one branch from getting the upper hand for long.

**28.** Answers will vary, but should discuss the importance of having a basic framework for government and an outline of the procedures that is written and therefore less likely to be abused; around these basics, changes and additions may be made.

## Analyzing Political Cartoons

**29.** Possible answer: The cartoonist is suggesting that it is as simple as posting a letter.

**30.** Answers will vary, but should suggest that the amendment process is quite complex.

## You Can Make a Difference

Surveys should be thoughtful and ask relevant questions.

## Participation Activities

**31.** Reports should be supported with specific facts and quotes where applicable.

**32.** Time lines should include all relevant events surrounding the Equal Rights Amendment. Answers will vary but should be supported with factual information.

**33.** Editorials will vary, but should address issues relevant to the Anti-Federalist position, and should be persuasive.

# Federalism

| Section Objectives | Print and Technology Resources |
|---|---|
| **1 Federalism: The Division of Power** *(pp. 88–95)*<br><br>1. Define federalism and explain why the Framers chose this system of government rather than a unitary system.<br>2. Categorize government powers as national, State, or shared.<br>3. Explain the place of local governments in the federal system.<br>4. Analyze how conflicts are resolved over the respective roles of national and State governments.<br><br>**TEKS** 2B, 8A, 8B, 8D, 8F, 10A, 10B, 10C, 10D, 21A, 21D, 21E, 22A, 22B | • **Unit 1 booklet** Guided Reading and Review, p. 27 Section 1 Quiz, p. 28<br>• **Lesson Plans booklet** Section 1, p. 23<br>• **Political Cartoons booklet** Section 1, p. 15<br>• **Block Scheduling with Lesson Strategies booklet** p. 21<br>• **Section Reading Support Transparencies**<br>• **Close Up on Primary Sources booklet** Baron de Montesquieu: *The Spirit of the Laws,* p. 58; American Presidents on Federalism, p. 6<br>• **Close Up on the Supreme Court booklet** *McCulloch* v. *Maryland,* pp. 28–29<br>• **The Living Constitution booklet** p. 4<br>• **Basic Principles of the Constitution Transparencies** 23, 43<br>• **Section Support Transparencies** 18, 117<br>• **Presentation Pro CD-ROM** Section 1 |
| **2 The National Government and the 50 States** *(pp. 97–103)*<br><br>1. Summarize the nation's obligations to the States.<br>2. Examine the process for admitting new States to the Union.<br>3. Explore the benefits of cooperative federalism.<br><br>**TEKS** 6A, 8D, 9G, 10D, 17C, 19B, 21A, 21C, 21D, 21E, 22A, 22B, 22D, 23A, 23B | • **Unit 1 booklet** Guided Reading and Review, p. 29 Section 2 Quiz, p. 30<br>• **Lesson Plans booklet** Section 2, p. 24<br>• **Political Cartoons booklet** Section 2, p. 16<br>• **Block Scheduling with Lesson Strategies booklet** p. 21<br>• **Section Reading Support Transparencies**<br>• **Government Assessment Rubrics booklet** p. 26<br>• **Section Support Transparencies** 19, 118<br>• **Presentation Pro CD-ROM** Section 2<br>• **Simulations and Data Graphing CD-ROM**<br>• **Social Studies Skills Tutor CD-ROM** |
| **3 Interstate Relations** *(pp. 105–108)*<br><br>1. Examine why States form interstate compacts.<br>2. Understand the purpose of the Full Faith and Credit Clause.<br>3. Define extradition and explain its purpose.<br>4. Discuss the purpose of the Privileges and Immunities Clause.<br><br>**TEKS** 6A, 8D, 9G, 10D, 21A, 21B, 21C, 21D, 21E, 22A, 22B, 22C, 22D, 23A, 23B | • **Unit 1 booklet** Guided Reading and Review, p. 31 Section 3 Quiz, p. 32 Skills for Life Activity, p. 33<br>• **Lesson Plans booklet** Section 3, p. 25<br>• **Political Cartoons booklet** Section 3, p. 17<br>• **Close Up on the Supreme Court booklet** *Printz* v. *U.S.,* p. 109<br>• **Section Reading Support Transparencies**<br>• **Government Assessment Rubrics booklet** p. 20<br>• **The Basic Principles of the Constitution Posters**<br>• **Section Support Transparencies** 20, 119<br>• **Presentation Pro CD-ROM** Section 3 |

# Block Scheduling Strategies

The *Magruder's American Government* program addresses block-scheduling strategies in a variety of ways. For easy reference, side-column activities that fit a block format are marked ⊞ **Block Strategy.** Each section also contains a **Block Scheduling Strategies** box describing at least two block-format activities that address and extend core content from the section. The **Block Scheduling with Lesson Strategies booklet** found in the Teaching Resources contains additional block-scheduling activities for each chapter.

## Take It to the Net

Visit the Social Studies area at the Prentice Hall School Web site. Once there, you can find additional links, current events connections, and activities to enrich chapter content for *Magruder's American Government,* as well as a Self-Test for students. Be sure to check out this month's **eTeach** online discussion with a Master Teacher.

### www.phschool.com

## Pressed for Time?

If you are running short on time to cover this chapter, consider one of the following options:

- Use the **Presentation Pro CD-ROM** to create an outline for this chapter.
- Use one of the **Pressed for Time** activities found on p. 27.
- Use the Section Summaries for Chapter 2, from **Guide to the Essentials of American Government (English and Spanish).**

##  Video Connections

Prentice Hall offers two video programs to reinforce and extend chapter content. Show students *The Blessings of Liberty* from the **ABC News Civics and Government Videotape Library** and *Prayer in Schools: A Nationwide Debate* from the **Magruder's American Government Video Collection.**

## Assessment Options

- Section Quizzes, **Unit 1 booklet,** pp. 28, 30, 32
- Chapter 4 Assessment, pp. 110–111
- **Guide to the Essentials of American Government,** Chapter 4 Test, p. 31

## Core Assessment

Chapter 4 Test, Chapter Tests booklet
ExamView® Test Bank CD-ROM Chapter 4
Government Assessment Rubrics

## Standardized Test Preparation

### Diagnose and Prescribe

Diagnostic Tests for High School
Social Studies Skills

### Review and Reteach

Review Book for Government

### Practice and Assess

Test-Taking Strategies With
    Transparencies for High School
Test Prep Book for Government

# Chapter 4 Teacher's Edition Index

# Federalism

## Introducing the Chapter

In this chapter, students will learn about the political system called federalism—why the United States chose this system, how it operates, and how it distributes power between the National and State Governments.

## CONSTITUTIONAL PRINCIPLES

Emphasize the following basic principles as students read Chapter 4. Have the class respond to the questions, and then ask volunteers to explain how these three principles are related.

**Separation of Powers** What powers does the Constitution grant to the National Government? How does the Constitution delegate powers to the States?

**Limited Government** What are some of the powers denied to the National Government? What powers are denied to the States?

**Federalism** What guarantees does the National Government make to the States? What services do the States provide to the National Government?

# Federalism

*"The true 'essence' of federalism is that the States as States have legitimate interests which the National Government is bound to respect even though its laws are supreme."*

—Justice Sandra Day O'Connor (1985)

The federal system divides power between the National Government and the States. In this way, federalism ensures that the National Government is strong enough to meet the nation's needs. At the same time, federalism preserves the strength and uniqueness of the individual States.

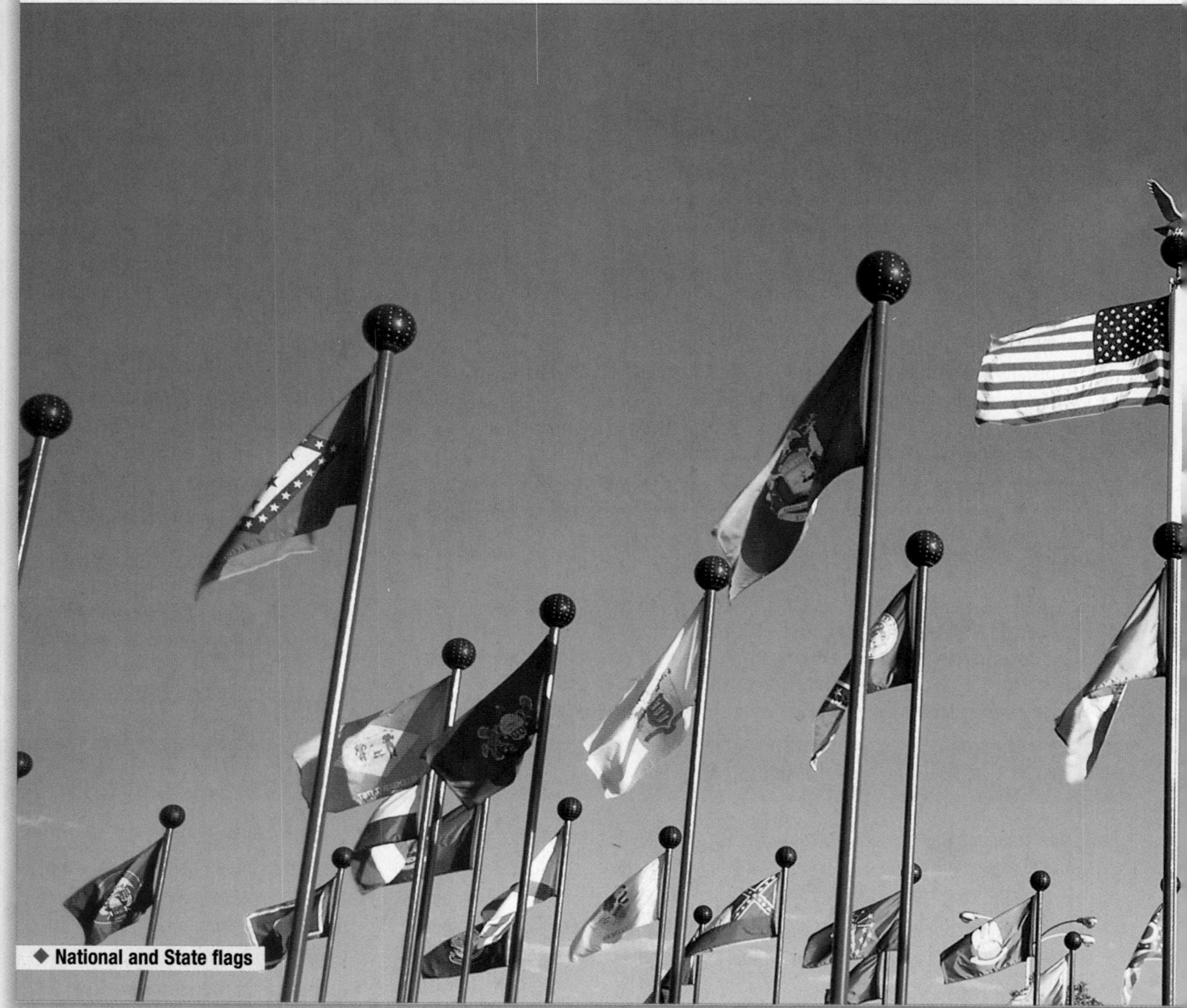

◆ National and State flags

CLOSE UP
FOUNDATION

*Corner*

The following resources are available only from the Close Up Foundation to support the concepts discussed in Chapter 4 "Federalism":

◆ *Perspectives: Readings on Contemporary American Government*

◆ *We the People: The President and the Constitution*

CLOSE UP
FOUNDATION
Online

To keep up-to-date on Close Up news and activities, visit Close Up Online at

**www.closeup.org**

Close Up Foundation
44 Canal Center Plaza
Alexandria, VA 22314-1592
800-765-3131

## ★ You Can Make a Difference

**UNDER FEDERALISM,** National and State government agencies cooperate in a variety of ways. One way is by sponsoring programs for high school and college students. In Colorado, for example, young men and women in the Youth in Natural Resources (YNR) program help protect parks and natural resources by building trails and mapping the State's resources. At the same time, they study environmental science, earn money, and develop career skills. One team leader, college student Brian Roman, said, "When I think of the YNR program, I think of hope—hope for the wildlife in Colorado . . . hope in tomorrow's leaders."

### Keep It Current

Items marked with this logo are periodically updated on the Internet. Keep up-to-date with what's in the news. To get current information on issues involving federalism, go to **www.phschool.com**

---

### SECTION 1

#### Federalism: The Division of Power (pp. 88–95)

★ The Framers sought to create a central government strong enough to meet the nation's needs and still preserve the strength of the States.
★ The National Government has only those powers delegated to it by the Constitution.
★ The States are governments of reserved powers, or powers that the Constitution does not grant to the National Government or deny to the States.
★ Most of the powers of the National Government are exercised by the National Government alone.
★ The concurrent powers are possessed by both the National Government and the States.
★ Local governments exist only as part of their parent State.
★ The Constitution stands above all other forms of law in the United States.

### SECTION 2

#### The National Government and the 50 States (pp. 97–103)

★ The National Government guarantees the States a representative government, protection against invasion and internal disorder, and respect for territorial integrity.
★ Congress has the power to admit new States.
★ The American federal system involves a broad range of shared powers between the National Government and the States.

### SECTION 3

#### Interstate Relations (pp. 105–108)

★ The States can make interstate compacts that enable them to cooperate on matters of mutual concern.
★ The Constitution requires each State to respect the laws, official records, and court actions of other States.
★ The Constitution requires each State to return fugitives to the State from which they fled.
★ No State can draw unreasonable distinctions between its own residents and residents of other States.

---

### Keep It Current

## Internet Update

Use the Prentice Hall School Web site and the Keep It Current CD-ROM to find quick content updates.

Visit **www.phschool.com** for current events articles that are linked to Chapter 4. Critical Thinking questions are included.

**Keep It Current CD-ROM** includes government-related projects by unit. Students complete each project using current information that they obtain by linking to the Prentice Hall School Web site from the CD-ROM.

---

## Pressed for Time?

### To Omit the Chapter

If you wish to skip Chapter 4, ask students to read the Chapter in Brief and assign the Guide to the Essentials before continuing to another chapter. You may also want to assign the Chapter 4 Test in the Chapter Test booklet. Then specific portions of Chapter 4 may be assigned to students needing reinforcement of key terms and concepts.

### To Preview the Chapter

To introduce students to key terms and concepts in each section, have them read the Chapter in Brief. You may also assign the Reading Strategy activities on pp. 89, 98, and 106 of this book.

### To Review the Chapter

When students have completed Chapter 4, you might want to assign the Guide to the Essentials or the Guided Reading and Review worksheets on pp. 27, 29, and 31 of the Unit 1 booklet.

### To Cover the Chapter Quickly

To cover the material in Chapter 4 quickly, use the following activity.

**Focus** Ask students whether they are supposed to follow local, State, or national laws. Once students have had time to answer, explain to them that in this chapter they will learn that they are legally bound to follow all of these laws.

**Instruct** Discuss the various aspects of federalism in the United States with the class. Then organize the class into three groups, assigning each group one of the chapter's sections. Ask each group to create a fact sheet and brief presentation detailing significant information from its section, and then present its information to the class.

**Close/Reteach** Use the three Constitutional Principles presented on page 86 to prompt a discussion on federalism in the United States. As a class, review any topics that students are having difficulty understanding.

■ **Block Strategy (Average)**

**1** # Federalism: The Division of Power

**Objectives** You may wish to call students' attention to the objectives in the Section Preview. The objectives are reflected in the main headings of the section.

**Bellringer** Have students discuss whether they get to make decisions about their lives or whether their parents make all the decisions. Tell them that they are really discussing how power is divided in their families. Explain that in this section, they will learn about the division of power between the National Government and the States.

**Vocabulary Builder** Tell students that the Political Dictionary terms all relate to a problem the Framers of the Constitution faced. Have students draw a conclusion about what that problem was. Then ask them, as they read, to relate each term to how power is distributed.

## Section Preview

### OBJECTIVES

1. **Define** federalism and explain why the Framers chose this system of government rather than a unitary system.
2. **Categorize** government powers as national, State, or shared.
3. **Explain** the place of local governments in the federal system.
4. **Analyze** how conflicts are resolved over the respective roles of national and State governments.

### WHY IT MATTERS

The federal system divides government power in order to prevent its abuse. There are two basic levels of government in the federal system—National and State. The Supreme Court settles disputes between the two.

### POLITICAL DICTIONARY

★ federalism
★ division of powers
★ delegated powers
★ expressed powers
★ implied powers
★ inherent powers
★ reserved powers
★ exclusive powers
★ concurrent powers

## Pressed for Time?

### Quick Lesson Plan

1. **Focus** Tell students that government power is divided between the National Government and the States. Ask students to discuss what they know about how power is divided.
2. **Instruct** Ask students why they cannot read the Constitution to determine all the specific powers assigned to the National Government and to the States. Then lead a discussion of the various types of powers and how local governments fit into the dual nature of federalism.
3. **Close/Reteach** Remind students of the types of powers assigned to and denied to the National Government and the States. Have students list those types and provide one or two examples of each.

## Point-of-Use Resources

📁 **Block Scheduling with Lesson Strategies** Activities for Chapter 4 are presented on p. 21.

**Y**ou know that federal law requires young men to register for military service at age 18; that most employers must pay their workers at least $5.15 an hour and time-and-a-half for overtime; and that no person can be denied a job on the basis of his or her race or ethnicity.

You also know that State law says that you must have a driver's license in order to drive a car; that it is illegal for anyone under 21 to buy alcoholic beverages, or for anyone under 18 to buy cigarettes or other tobacco products; and that only those persons who can satisfy certain requirements can buy or own firearms.

These examples illustrate a very complex system: the division of governmental power in the United States between National and State governments. This section will help you better understand that complicated arrangement.

▲ State laws forbid the sale of cigarettes to minors.

### Why Federalism?

When the Framers of the Constitution met at Philadelphia in 1787, they faced a number of difficult issues. Not the least of them: How

could they possibly create a new central government that would be strong enough to meet the nation's needs and, at the same time, preserve the strength of the existing States?

Few of the Framers favored a strong central government based on the British model; and all of them knew that the Revolution had been fought in the name of self-government. Yet they also knew that the government under the Articles of Confederation had proved too weak to deal with the nation's many problems.

Remember, most of the Framers were dedicated to the concept of limited government. They were convinced (1) that governmental power poses a threat to individual liberty, (2) that therefore the exercise of governmental power must be restrained, and (3) that to divide governmental power, as federalism does, is to curb it and so prevent its abuse.

### Federalism Defined

**Federalism** is a system of government in which a written constitution divides the powers of government on a territorial basis between a central, or national, government and several regional governments, usually called states or provinces. Each of these levels of government has its own

## 🔲 Block Scheduling Strategies

Consider these suggestions to manage extended class time:

■ Refer students to the quotation by Justice Oliver Wendell Holmes on p. 95 of their textbooks. Have students respond to the quote in a class discussion, and work together to restate the quotation in their own words. Then have them write paragraphs that describe what government would be like today without the Supremacy Clause.

■ Divide the class into two groups. One group should create a graphic organizer showing the powers granted to the government (one column identifying the powers, second column identifying which level of government has them, third column explaining why). The other group should create a similar graphic organizer showing the powers denied to the government. Have students refer to the text and to Article 1, Section 8 of the Constitution for details.

substantial set of powers. Neither level, acting alone, can change the basic division of powers the constitution has created. In addition, each level of government operates through its own agencies and acts directly through its own officials and laws.

The American system of government stands as a prime example of federalism. The basic design of this system is set out in the Constitution. This document provides for a **division of powers** between the National Government and the States. That is, it assigns certain powers to the National Government and certain powers to the States. This division of powers was implied in the original Constitution and then spelled out in the Bill of Rights:

FROM THE *Constitution* **"***The powers not delegated to the United States by the Constitution, nor prohibited by it to the States, are reserved to the States respectively, or to the people.***"**

—10th Amendment

In effect, federalism produces a dual system of government. That is, it provides for two basic levels of government, each with its own area of authority. Each operates over the same people and the same territory at the same time.

Federalism's major strength is that it allows local action in matters of local concern, and national action in matters of wider concern. Local traditions, needs, and desires vary from one State to another, and federalism allows for this very significant fact.

Illustrations of this point are nearly endless. For example, a third of the States are directly involved in the liquor business, operating it as a public monopoly; elsewhere private enterprise is the rule. In 48 States many gas stations are self-service; in New Jersey and Oregon, the law forbids motorists to pump their own gas. Only one State—North Dakota—does not require voters to register in order to cast their ballots. Only Nebraska has a unicameral (one-house) legislature. Oregon is the only State that has legalized physician-assisted suicide. Only five States—Alaska, Delaware, New Hampshire, Montana, and Oregon—do not impose a general sales tax.

While federalism allows individual States to handle State and local matters, it also provides for the strength that comes from union.

▲ The National Government provides protection from harm for the entire country. State governments provide protection from harm within State borders. *Critical Thinking* **How do these photos illustrate the federal system?**

National defense and foreign affairs offer useful illustrations of this point. So, too, do domestic affairs. Take, for example, a natural disaster. When a flood, drought, winter storm, or other catastrophe hits a particular State, the resources of the National Government and all of the other States may be mobilized to aid the stricken area.

## Powers of the National Government

The National Government is a government of **delegated powers.** That is, it has only those powers delegated (granted) to it in the Constitution. There are three distinct types of delegated powers: expressed, implied, and inherent.

### The Expressed Powers

The **expressed powers** are delegated to the National Government in so many words—spelled out, expressly, in the Constitution. These powers are also sometimes called the "enumerated powers."

You can find most of the expressed powers in Article I, Section 8. There, in 18 clauses, the Constitution expressly gives 27 powers to Congress. They include the power to lay and collect taxes, to coin money, to regulate foreign

## Reading Strategy

### Organizing Information/Outline

Ask students to copy down the section's main headings and subheadings in outline form, leaving space for details. Have them fill in the details as they read the section.

### Background Note

#### Roots of Democracy

The roots of the federal system can be traced back over 3,000 years to the ancient Israelites, who combined their tribes to maintain national unity in the 13th century B.C. Ten centuries later, the Greeks applied federal principles in forming leagues of city-states, primarily for defensive purposes. The Achaean League (280–146 B.C.) was foremost among these. Taxes were collected, an army was raised from Achaea's eleven member states, and the federal government—headed by a general who was elected president and served also as commander in chief—established uniform weights and measures and a federal judiciary.

### Point–of–Use Resources

📁 **Guided Reading and Review** Unit 1 booklet, p. 27 provides students with practice identifying the main ideas and key terms of this section.

📁 **Lesson Plans** For lesson planning suggestions, see p. 23 of the Lesson Plans booklet.

📁 **Political Cartoons** See p. 15 of the Political Cartoons booklet for a cartoon relevant to this section.

## Organizing Information

To make sure students understand the main points of this section, you may wish to use the Venn diagram to the right.

Tell students that a Venn diagram compares two groups by showing characteristics they have alone and those they share. Ask students to use the Venn diagram to list powers that the National Government has and those that the States have. Powers that both groups share should be put in the space where the circles overlap.

**Teaching Tip** A template for this graphic organizer can be found in the Section Support Transparencies, Transparency 6.

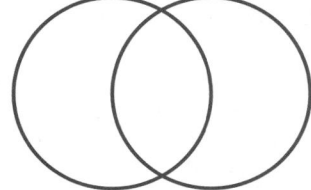

*Answer to . . .*

**Critical Thinking** They show that while local matters can be handled by a single State's resources, for large national concerns huge amounts of resources from the National Government and the States may be pooled.

**89**

## American Government, American Humor

Share the following quotation with students:

*"Were we directed from Washington when to sow and when to reap, we should soon want for bread."*

—Thomas Jefferson

**Discussion** Ask students what Jefferson meant by his remark. Then ask how Jefferson's perspective is still relevant to the "tug-of-war" power struggle that is a regular part of American federalism.

**(Average)**

## Background Note

### Constitutionalism

For Constitutionalists—those who believe in a strict interpretation of the Constitution—the exercise of the implied powers goes much too far, and the Necessary and Proper Clause has been stretched to cover many more situations than the Framers ever intended. The ratification of the 16th Amendment is also open to debate. In this view, research of state legislative records shows that this amendment was not ratified, and that the declaration that it had been by then Secretary of State Philander Knox may well have been fraudulent.

## Answer to . . .

**Critical Thinking** Establishing diplomatic relations is a power traditionally held by sovereign states, and is thus an inherent power.

Expered Power    Implied Power    Inherent Power

▲ The powers delegated to the National Government include the power to coin money, to prohibit race-based discrimination, and to conduct foreign relations. In 1971, Richard Nixon (right) became the first American President to visit China; his historic trip led to United States recognition of the government of the People's Republic of China. *Critical Thinking Why is establishing diplomatic relations considered an inherent power?*

and interstate commerce, to raise and maintain armed forces, to declare war, to fix standards of weights and measures, to grant patents and copyrights, and to do many other things.

Several other expressed powers are set out elsewhere in the Constitution. Article II, Section 2 gives several powers to the President. They include the power to act as commander in chief of the armed forces, to grant reprieves and pardons, to make treaties, and to appoint major federal officials. Article III grants "the judicial Power of the United States" to the Supreme Court and other courts in the federal judiciary. Finally, several expressed powers are found in various amendments to the Constitution; thus, the 16th Amendment gives Congress the power to levy an income tax.

### The Implied Powers

The **implied powers** are not expressly stated in the Constitution but are reasonably suggested—implied—by the expressed powers. The constitutional basis for the implied powers is found in one of the expressed powers. Article I, Section 8, Clause 18 gives Congress the "necessary and proper power." The Necessary and Proper Clause says that Congress has the power

**FROM THE Constitution** *"to make all Laws which shall be necessary and proper for carrying into Execution the foregoing Powers and all other Powers vested by this Constitution in the Government of the United States, or in any Department or Officer thereof."*

—Article I, Section 8, Clause 18

Through congressional and court interpretation, the words *necessary and proper* have been interpreted to mean, in effect, "convenient and useful." Indeed, the Necessary and Proper Clause is sometimes called the Elastic Clause, because, over time, it has been stretched to cover so many situations.

Here are but a few examples of the exercise of implied powers. Congress has provided for the regulation of labor-management relations, the building of hydroelectric power dams, and the building of the 42,000-mile interstate highway system. It has made federal crimes of such acts as moving stolen goods, gambling devices, and kidnapped persons across State lines. It has prohibited racial discrimination in granting access to such places as restaurants, theaters, hotels, and motels.

## Preparing for Standardized Tests

Have students read the passages under *Powers of the National Government* on pp. 89–91 and then answer the question below.

Which of the following is *not* a power of the National Government?

**A** raising and maintaining armed forces

**B** granting patents and copyrights

**C** enacting uniform marriage and divorce laws

**D** prohibiting racial discrimination in access to such places as restaurants and hotels

Congress has taken these actions, and many more, because the power to do so is reasonably implied by just one of the expressed powers: the power to regulate interstate commerce.[1]

## The Inherent Powers

The **inherent powers** belong to the National Government because it is the government of a sovereign state within the world community. Although the Constitution does not expressly provide for them, they are powers that national governments have historically possessed. It stands to reason that the Framers intended that the National Government they created would hold a limited number of powers as necessary to any national government.

The inherent powers are few in number. The major ones include the power to regulate immigration, to deport undocumented aliens, to acquire territory, to grant diplomatic recognition to other states, and to protect the nation against rebellion or other attempts to overthrow the government.

One can argue that most of the inherent powers are implied by one or more of the expressed powers. For example, the power to regulate immigration is suggested by the expressed power to regulate foreign trade. The power to acquire territory can be drawn from the treaty-making power and the several war powers. But the doctrine of inherent powers holds that it is not necessary to go to these lengths to find these powers in the Constitution. In short, these powers exist because the United States exists.

## Powers Denied to the National Government

Although the Constitution delegates certain powers to the National Government, it also denies the National Government certain powers. It does so in three distinct ways.

First, the Constitution denies some powers to the National Government in so many words—expressly.[2] Among them are the powers to levy

---

[1]Article I, Section 8, Clause 3. The doctrine of implied powers is treated in greater detail in Chapter 11.

[2]Most of the expressed denials of power are found in Article I, Section 9 and in the 1st through the 8th amendments.

## *Voices* on Government

**Senator Fred Thompson** (R., Tennessee) was first elected to the United States Senate in 1994 and won his first full term in 1996. Senator Thompson ardently supports the protection of State and local governments from unnecessary Federal intrusion. He has this to say on the subject of federalism:

*"The Founding Fathers divided power between the federal government and the states. The constitutional principle of federalism—embodied in the Tenth Amendment—raises two fundamental questions that policy makers should answer: What should government be doing? And what level of government should do it? Everything flows from them. That's why federalism is at the heart of our democracy. "*

### Evaluating the Quotation

*(a) How would Senator Thompson respond to the statement that State and local governments are often in the best position to respond to the people's concerns? (b) What types of constitutional issues arise for Federal and State governments when they respond to the people's concerns?*

duties on exports; prohibit the free exercise of religion, speech, press, or assembly; conduct illegal searches or seizures; nor deny to any person accused of a crime a speedy and public trial or a trial by jury.

Second, several powers are denied to the National Government because of the silence of the Constitution. Recall that the National Government is a government of delegated powers; it has only those powers the Constitution gives to it expressly, implicitly, or inherently.

Among the powers not granted to the National Government are creating a national school system, enacting uniform marriage and divorce laws, and setting up units of local government within any of the States. The Constitution says nothing that would give the National Government the power to do any of these things—expressly, implicitly, or inherently.

Third, some powers are denied to the National Government because of the federal system itself.

## CONSTITUTIONAL PRINCIPLES

**Limited Government**
Although the Necessary and Proper Clause of the Constitution seems to give Congress an almost unlimited power to make laws on any topic that it wishes, there are some limitations. The process of judicial review allows the nation's courts to determine which laws are unconstitutional, thereby limiting the types of laws that Congress creates to those that are necessary and proper.

**Activity**
Have students consider the powers given to Congress by the Necessary and Proper Clause and the court's practice of judicial review. Ask students to consider whether both of these powers are necessary to U.S. government. Allow time for students to create arguments to support their positions, then hold a debate on the topic.

Clearly the Constitution does not intend that the National Government should have any power to take action that would threaten the existence of that system. For example, in the exercise of its power to tax, Congress cannot tax any of the States or their local units in the carrying out of their governmental functions. If it could, it would have the power to tax out of existence one or more, or all, of the States.[3]

## The States

The 50 States are the other half of the very complicated equation we call federalism. Their role in the American federal system is no less important than the role of the National Government.

### Powers Reserved to the States

As you recall, the 10th Amendment declares that the States are governments of reserved powers. (See page 89.) The **reserved powers** are those powers that the Constitution does not grant to the National Government and does not, at the same time, deny to the States.

Thus, any State can forbid persons under 18 to marry without parental consent, or those under 21 to buy liquor. It can ban the sale of pornography, outlaw prostitution, and permit some forms of gambling and prohibit others. A State can require that doctors, lawyers, hairdressers, and plumbers be licensed in order to

▲ *Land Use* Enacting land use laws in order to preserve open spaces is one of many powers reserved to the States.

practice in the State. It can confiscate automobiles and other property used in connection with such illicit activities as illegal drug trafficking or prostitution. It can establish public schools, enact land use laws, regulate the services and restrict the profits of such public utilities as natural gas, oil, electric power, and telephone companies, and do much, much more.

In short, the sphere of powers held by each State—the scope of the reserved powers—is huge. The States can do all of those things just mentioned, and much more, because (1) the Constitution does not give the National Government the power to take these actions and (2) it does not deny the States the power to take them.

How broad the reserved powers really are can be understood from this fact: Most of what government does in this country today is done by the States (and their local governments), not by the National Government. The point can also be seen from this fact: The reserved powers include the vitally important police power—the power of a State to protect and promote the public health, the public morals, the public safety, and the general welfare.

The Constitution does not grant expressed powers to the States, with one exception. Section 2 of the 21st Amendment gives the States a virtually unlimited power to regulate the manufacture, sale, and consumption of alcoholic beverages.

### Powers Denied to the States

Just as the Constitution denies many powers to the National Government, it also denies many powers to the States. Some of these powers are denied to the States in so many words.[4] For example, no State can enter into any treaty, alliance, or confederation. Nor can a State print or coin money or deprive any person of life, liberty, or property without due process of law.

Some powers are denied to the States inherently—that is, by the existence of the federal system. Thus, no State (and no local government)

---

[3]But note that when a State, or one of its local units, performs a so-called nongovernmental function—for example, maintains liquor stores, runs a bus system, or operates a farmers market—it is liable to federal taxation. We shall come back to this point later, in Chapter 25.

[4]Most of these expressed prohibitions of power to the States (and so, too, to their local governments) are found in Article I, Section 10 and in the 13th, 14th, 15th, 19th, 24th, and 26th Amendments.

can tax any of the agencies or functions of the National Government. Remember, too, each State has its own constitution. That document also denies many powers to the State.[5] We shall look at State constitutions later, and in more detail, in Chapter 24.

## Shared Powers

Most of the powers that the Constitution delegates to the National Government are **exclusive powers.** These are the powers that can be exercised by the National Government alone. These powers cannot be exercised by the States under any circumstances.

Some of these powers are expressly denied to the States. Examples include the power to coin money, to make treaties with foreign states, and to lay duties (taxes) on imports. Some powers are not expressly denied to the States but are, nonetheless, among the exclusive powers of the Federal Government because of the nature of the particular power involved. The power to regulate interstate commerce is a leading example of this point. If the States could exercise that power, trade between and among the States would be at best chaotic and at worst impossible.[6]

Some of the powers delegated to the National Government are **concurrent powers.** The concurrent powers are those powers that both the National Government and the States possess and exercise. They include, for example, the power to levy and collect taxes, to define crimes and set punishments for them, and to condemn (take) private property for public use.

Under this system of dual, or cooperative, federalism the concurrent powers are held and exercised separately and simultaneously by the two basic levels of government. That is, the concurrent powers are those powers that the Constitution does not grant exclusively to the National Government and that, at the same

---

[5]Study your own State's constitution on the powers denied to the States. As you do, note the significance of the words "or to the people" in the 10th Amendment in the Federal Constitution.

[6]The States cannot regulate interstate commerce as such, but they can and do affect it. For example, in regulating highway speeds, the States regulate vehicles not only operating wholly within the State, but also those operating from State to State. Generally, the States can affect interstate commerce, but they may not impose an unreasonable burden on it.

**The Division of Powers**

| National Powers | Concurrent Powers | State Powers |
|---|---|---|
| • Coin money | • Levy and collect taxes | • Regulate trade and business within the State |
| • Regulate interstate and foreign trade | • Borrow money | • Establish public schools |
| • Raise and maintain armed forces | • Establish courts | • Pass license requirements for professionals |
| • Declare war | • Define crimes and set punishments | • Regulate alcoholic beverages |
| • Govern U.S. territories and admit new States | • Claim private property for public use | • Conduct elections |
| • Conduct foreign relations | | • Establish local governments |

*Interpreting Tables* The federal system determines the way that powers are divided and shared between the National and the State governments. *Name one national, one State, and one concurrent power.*

time, does not deny to the States. The concurrent powers, in short, are those powers that make it possible for a federal system of government to function.

## The Federal System and Local Governments

Government in the United States is often discussed in terms of three levels: national, State, and local. However convenient this view may be, it is at best misleading. Recall that there are only two basic levels in the federal system: the National Government and the State governments.

Governments do exist at the local level all across the country, of course. In fact, there are more than 87,000 units of local government in the United States today. You will take a look at them later in this book. For now, keep this important point in mind: All of these thousands of local governments are parts—subunits—of the various State governments.

Each of these local units is located within one of the 50 States. In its constitution and in its laws,

**93**

A C T I V I T Y

## Learning Styles

**Linguistic** Review with students the Supremacy Clause. Have students write a position paper on the following topic: *What would happen if the courts could not declare acts of State governments unconstitutional?* Encourage students to include information on past court decisions to support their argument.

**(Challenging)**

## Background Note

### Recent Scholarship

Were the Framers on the right track when they drafted the Constitution? Editors Alan Brinkley, Nelson W. Polsby, and Kathleen M. Sullivan present a collection of informative and provocative essays written by leading scholars to answer this question in their book *New Federalist Papers: Essays in Defense of the Constitution.* The essays explore broad themes relating to the Constitution: the idea of community, differences between the American system and parliamentary forms of government, and the balance of power between States and the Federal Government. They also deal with topics of current interest, including term limits, campaign finance reform, line item veto, federal budget, and the role of the media. The authors provide perspectives on key issues and raise questions appropriate for class discussions. Though their perspectives differ, they ultimately agree that the Framers "got it right."

## Point-of-Use Resources

📁 **Close Up on the Supreme Court**
*McCulloch* v. *Maryland* (1819), pp. 28–29

## Answer to . . .

**Interpreting Charts** When laws governing oil tanker safety were passed at both the State and national levels, the Supreme Court ruled on which would take precedence.

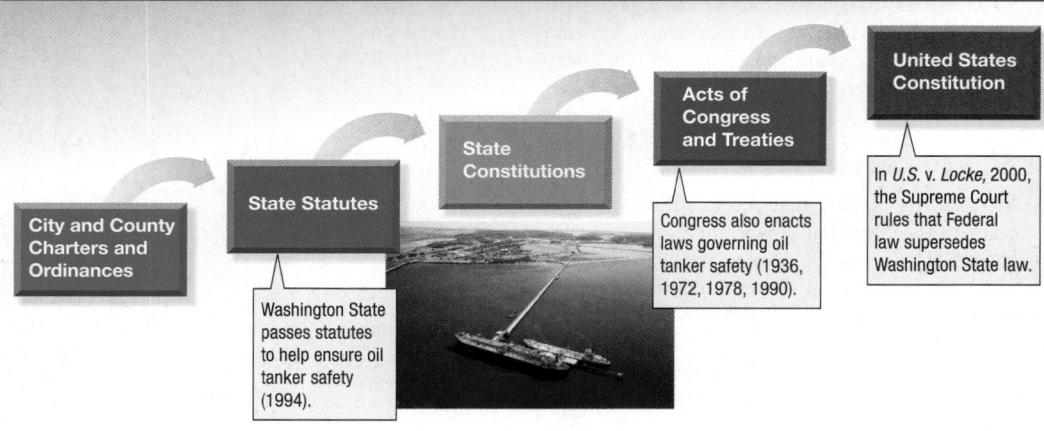

**The Supremacy Clause**

United States Constitution

In *U.S.* v. *Locke,* 2000, the Supreme Court rules that Federal law supersedes Washington State law.

Acts of Congress and Treaties

Congress also enacts laws governing oil tanker safety (1936, 1972, 1978, 1990).

State Constitutions

State Statutes

Washington State passes statutes to help ensure oil tanker safety (1994).

City and County Charters and Ordinances

*Interpreting Charts* The Supremacy Clause creates a hierarchy of laws. Local law (city and county charters and ordinances) must yield to State law. State law must yield to federal law. At the top of the hierarchy is the United States Constitution, which stands above all other forms of law in the United States. *How does the case of* **United States** *v.* **Locke** *illustrate this hierarchy of laws?*

each State has created these units. None exists apart from its parent State. Local government can provide services, regulate activities, collect taxes, and do many other things. It can do these things, however, only because the State has established and given it the power to do so. In short, when local governments exercise their powers, they are actually exercising State powers.

Another way of putting all of this is to remind you of a point that was first made in Chapter 1. Each of the 50 States has a unitary form of government—a central government that creates local units of government for its own convenience.

## Resolving Conflicts

As you have just seen, the division of powers in the American federal system produces a dual system of government, one in which two basic levels of government operate over the same territory and the same people at the same time.

---

[7]Acts of Congress and treaties stand on equal planes with one another. Neither can conflict with any provision in the Constitution. In the rare case of conflict between the provisions of an act and those of a treaty, the one more recently adopted takes precedence—as the latest expression of the sovereign people's will. The Supreme Court has regularly held to that position from the first cases it decided on the point, *The Head Money Cases,* 1884.

Such an arrangement is bound to result in conflicts between national law and State law.

### The Supremacy Clause

The Framers anticipated these conflicts—and so they wrote the Supremacy Clause into the Constitution. That provision declares that

**FROM THE** *Constitution* **"** *This Constitution, and the Laws of the United States which shall be made in Pursuance thereof; and all Treaties made, or which shall be made, under the Authority of the United States, shall be the supreme Law of the Land; and the Judges in every State shall be bound thereby, any Thing in the Constitution or Laws of any state to the Contrary notwithstanding.* **"**

—Article VI, Section 2

As you can see from the chart above, the U.S. Constitution and the laws and treaties of the United States are "the supreme Law of the Land." This means that the Constitution stands above all other forms of law in the United States. Acts of Congress and treaties stand immediately beneath the Constitution.[7]

The Supremacy Clause has been called the "linchpin of the Constitution" because it joins the National Government and the States into a

**RESOURCE PRO®**

**Resource Pro® CD-ROM** contains an electronic version of each activity found in the Teaching Resources as well as additional resources such as Supreme Court cases. The Planning Express® feature allows you to customize and create daily lesson plans within minutes.

single governmental unit, a federal government. In other words, the Supremacy Clause holds together the complex structure that is the American federal system.

## The Supreme Court and Federalism

The Supreme Court is the umpire in the federal system. One of its chief duties is to apply the Supremacy Clause to the conflicts that the dual system of government inevitably produces.

The Court was first called to settle a clash between a national and a State law in 1819. The case, *McCulloch* v. *Maryland*, involved the controversial Second Bank of the United States. The bank had been chartered by Congress in 1816. In 1818, the Maryland legislature, hoping to cripple the bank, placed a tax on all notes issued by its Baltimore branch. James McCulloch, the branch cashier, refused to pay the tax, and the Maryland courts convicted him for that refusal.

The Supreme Court unanimously reversed the Maryland courts. Speaking for the Court, Chief Justice John Marshall based the decision squarely on the Constitution's Supremacy Clause:

 *❝ [If] any one proposition could command the universal assent of mankind, we might expect it would be this—that the government of the Union, though limited in its powers, is supreme within its sphere of action . . . . [T]he states have no power . . . to retard, impede,*

*burden, or in any manner control, the operations of the constitutional laws enacted by Congress. . . . ❞ [8]*
—*McCulloch* v. *Maryland*, Opinion of the Court

Since this landmark case, it has been impossible to overstate the significance of the Court's function as the umpire of the federal system. Had the Court not taken this role, the federal system and probably the United States itself could not have survived its early years. Justice Oliver Wendell Holmes once made the point in these words:

 *❝ I do not think the United States would come to an end if we [the Court] lost our power to declare an Act of Congress void. I do think the Union would be imperiled if we could not make that declaration as to the laws of the several States. ❞*

—Collected Legal Papers[9]

---

[8]The case is also critically important in the development of the constitutional system because in deciding it, the Court for the first time upheld the doctrine of implied powers. It also held the National Government to be immune from any form of State taxation.

[9]The Supreme Court first held a State law unconstitutional in a case from Georgia, *Fletcher* v. *Peck*, 1810. The Court found that a Georgia law of 1795 making a grant of land to John Peck amounted to a contract between the State and Peck. It ruled that the legislature's later repeal of that law violated the Constitution's Contract Clause (Article I, Section 10, Clause 1). Since then, the Court has found more than 1,000 State laws unconstitutional (and has upheld the constitutionality of thousands of others).

## Section **1** Assessment

**Key Terms and Main Ideas**

1. Why did the Framers settle on **federalism** as the system of government for the new nation?
2. Explain each of the following: **expressed powers, implied powers,** and **inherent powers.**
3. Do local governments have powers other than those granted to them by the States? Explain your answer.
4. What is the significance of *McCulloch* v. *Maryland* in the development of the federal system?

**Critical Thinking**

5. **Making Decisions** Suppose you are creating a student government. Would you base your government on the federal system? Explain your answer.

6. **Drawing Conclusions** How did the Framer's make provisions for addressing issues that they could not foresee?
7. **Determining Relevance** Name several issues in your community that are best addressed by local government.
8. Thomas Jefferson considered the 10th Amendment as the "foundation of the Constitution." Explain Jefferson's reasoning.

 **Take It to the Net**

9. There are many different perspectives on the ways federalism works in the United States. Read several of these perspectives. Then choose one, and outline it in detail. Use the links provided in the Social Studies area at the following Web site for help in this activity. **www.phschool.com**

 **Take It to the Net**

9. Direct students to the Social Studies area at the Prentice Hall Web site. The *Magruder's American Government* companion Web site includes the directions and links needed to complete the activity. It also provides a printable Internet activity worksheet with scoring rubrics for assessment. Outlines should be clearly constructed and include relevant details.

## Answers to . . .

### Section 1 Assessment

**1.** The Framers believed that without restraint, a strong central government posed a threat to individual liberty. They chose federalism because it would restrain the central government's power.

**2.** Expressed powers are those that are explicitly stated in the Constitution, while implied powers are those that are not stated, but can be reasonably assumed. Inherent powers are those that are not explicitly stated, but are powers that national governments have historically had.

**3.** No; local governments exist because States create them and grant them specific powers.

**4.** This case was the first time the Court settled a clash between State and federal law.

**5.** Answers should reflect an understanding that federalism provides a system of government in which national authority is balanced by local authority.

**6.** Possible answer: They instituted the Supremacy Clause. By declaring the Constitution as the final authority on all points of law, this clause ensures that the National and State Governments can settle disputes no matter what conflict arises.

**7.** Answers will vary, but should reflect an understanding of local and federal powers.

**8.** Answers should show an understanding of the underlying philosophy of the 10th Amendment.

 **on Primary Sources**

# More Power to the States

*Linda Chavez is the president of the Center for Equal Opportunity in Washington, D.C. She served as White House Director of Public Liaison in the Reagan administration. Here, Ms. Chavez argues that shifting responsibility for many social programs back to the States keeps power closer to the people.*

*The United States flag and the Wisconsin State flag fly at Wisconsin's State capitol in Madison.*

One of the things the Founders of our nation most feared was centralized government power. Indeed, our Constitution and our Bill of Rights were written explicitly to ensure that power rested with the people and that no single branch of government—whether the executive, legislative, or judicial—gains a monopoly of power.

The Tenth Amendment to the Constitution also guaranteed that powers not specifically delegated to the federal government or prohibited to the states by the Constitution be retained by the states or the people.

Despite the intent of the founders, the history of our government, particularly in the last half of the twentieth century, has been one of growing federal power. Some of this has been accomplished directly by the government taking over certain functions; some has come indirectly, especially by the "power of the purse strings."

Whenever the federal government gives money to the states or to local governments or agencies, certain obligations or rules follow. . . . [T]he federal government gives billions of dollars a year to support public elementary and secondary schools, and along with the money comes federal dictates about exactly how the money can be spent. . . .

For a limited number of functions—national defense being the most obvious—the federal government is clearly the only institution that can properly manage and fund the necessary programs. . . . But many other functions that the federal government performs, and taxes citizens to pay for, would be better decided on and funded at the local or state level, where people can keep track of what is being done and how much it costs. . . .

Efficiency and accountability are two reasons why state and local governments are better equipped to undertake certain tasks, but another . . . is flexibility. Some social problems are particularly difficult to solve, and what may work in one community may not be appropriate for another. . . .

Unfortunately, the federal government's involvement sometimes makes matters worse. It takes the decision making out of the hands of elected officials closest to the people and puts it in the hands of unelected bureaucrats in Washington. The founders of our nation anticipated the problems of centralized power and established constitutional guarantees to safeguard against it, but the people must make sure those guarantees are enforced.

### Analyzing Primary Sources

1. According to Chavez, how has the Federal Government extended its power over the States?
2. Why is Chavez concerned about the growing power of the Federal Government?
3. Why does Chavez believe States are better able to handle local problems?

 **Corner**

**Close Up on Primary Sources** American Presidents on Federalism, p. 6, extends this feature with a primary source activity.

To keep up-to-date on Close Up news and activities, visit Close Up Online at
**www.closeup.org**

# The National Government and the 50 States

The National
Government and
the 50 States

2

## Section Preview

### OBJECTIVES

1. **Summarize** the obligations that the Constitution places on the nation for the welfare of the States.
2. **Explain** the process for admitting new States to the Union.
3. **Examine** the many and growing areas of cooperative federalism.

### WHY IT MATTERS

Cooperation between the National and State governments affects us all. We benefit from federal protection against invasion, from natural disaster relief, and from monies granted to State and local governments, to name just a few examples.

### POLITICAL DICTIONARY

★ enabling act
★ act of admission
★ grants-in-aid program
★ revenue sharing
★ categorical grant
★ block grant
★ project grant

---

Have you ever really focused on the words *United States?* The United States is a union of States, the several States joined together, the States united.

The Constitution created and is intended to preserve that union. To that end, the Constitution (1) requires the National Government to guarantee certain things to the States and (2) makes it possible for the National Government to do certain things for the States.

## The Nation's Obligations to the States

The Constitution places several obligations on the National Government for the benefit of the States. Most of them are found in Article IV.

### Republican Form of Government

The Constitution requires the National Government to "guarantee to every State in this

---

[10] Article IV, Section 4.
[11] The leading case here is *Luther* v. *Borden,* 1849. This case grew out of Dorr's Rebellion, a revolt led by Thomas W. Dorr against the State of Rhode Island in 1841–1842. Dorr and his followers had written and proclaimed a new constitution for the State. When they tried to put the new document into operation, however, the governor in office under the original constitution declared martial law, or temporary rule by military authorities. The governor also called on the Federal Government for help. President John Tyler took steps to put down the revolt, and it quickly collapsed. Although the question of which of the competing governments was the legitimate one was a major issue in *Luther* v. *Borden,* the Supreme Court refused to decide the matter.

---

Union a Republican Form of Government."[10] The Constitution does not define "Republican Form of Government," and the Supreme Court has regularly refused to do so. The term is generally understood to mean a "representative government."

The Supreme Court has held that the question of whether a State has a republican form of government is a political question. That is, it is one to be decided by the political branches of the government—the President and Congress—and not by the courts.[11]

▲ After the Civil War, the "Republican Form of Government" figured prominently as laws were broadened to help recognize African American voting rights.

---

---

## Reading Strategy

### Drawing Inferences

Tell students that the relationship between the National Government and the States involves cooperation. Have them find evidence, as they read, to support that statement.

### Background Note

#### Political Talk

The way that ordinary Americans have used the term *United States* shows how popular attitudes toward the concept of federalism have changed over time. From the birth of the nation until the Civil War, for example, people generally used the name as a plural noun—saying "The United States are. . ." This usage emphasized the individuality of the States at a time when people thought of themselves primarily as citizens of their particular State. Since then, people have referred to the nation in the singular—saying "The United States is . . ."—a usage stressing the singularity of the Union rather than the separateness of the States.

## Point-of-Use Resources

📁 **Guided Reading and Review** Unit 1 booklet, p. 29 provides students with practice identifying the main ideas and key terms of this section.

📁 **Lesson Plans** For lesson planning suggestions, see p. 24 of the Lesson Plans booklet.

📁 **Political Cartoons** See p. 16 of the Political Cartoons booklet for a cartoon relevant to this section.

### *Answer to . . .*

**Interpreting Tables** The community appeals to local government; if it cannot respond, it appeals to first State and then federal organizations. This process demonstrates that while States have particular responsibilities, if they cannot meet them the National Government has the responsibility to help.

| The Major Disaster Process | |
|---|---|
| **STEP 1** | **Local Government Responds**. If overwhelmed, turns to the State for assistance. |
| **STEP 2** | **The State Responds** with State resources, such as the National Guard and State agencies. |
| **STEP 3** | **Damage Assessment** by local, State, Federal, and volunteer organizations. |
| **STEP 4** | **A Major Disaster Declaration** is requested by the governor, based on damage assessment. |
| **STEP 5** | **FEMA Evaluates** the request and recommends action to the White House. |
| **STEP 6** | **The President Approves** the request or FEMA informs the governor it has been denied. |

*Interpreting Tables* The Federal Emergency Management Agency (FEMA) helps State and local governments in the case of a natural disaster such as a hurricane. *Explain the steps that lead to a community receiving federal disaster aid. How does this process illustrate federalism?*

SOURCE: Federal Emergency Management Agency

The only extensive use ever made of the republican-form guarantee came in the years immediately following the Civil War. Congress declared that several southern States did not have governments of a republican form. It refused to admit senators and representatives from those States until the States had ratified the 13th, 14th, and 15th amendments and broadened their laws to recognize the voting and other rights of African Americans.

### Invasion and Internal Disorder

The Constitution states that the National Government must also

FROM THE *Constitution* **"**protect each of them [States] against Invasion; and on Application of the Legislature, or of the Executive (when the Legislature cannot be convened) against domestic Violence. **"**
—Article IV, Section 4

Today it is clear that an invasion of any one of the 50 States would be met as an attack on the United States itself. This constitutional guarantee is therefore now of little, if any, significance.

That was not the case in the late 1780s. During that time, it was not at all certain that all 13 States would stand together if a foreign power attacked one of them. So, before the 13 States agreed to give up their war-making powers, each demanded an ironclad pledge that an attack on any single State would be met as an attack on all States.

The federal system assumes that each of the 50 States will keep the peace within its own borders. Thus, the primary responsibility for curbing insurrection, riot, or other internal disorder rests with the individual States. However, the Constitution does accept that a State might not be able to control some situations. It therefore guarantees protection against internal disorder, or what the Constitution calls "domestic Violence," in each of them.

The use of federal force to restore order within a State has historically been a rare event. Several instances did occur in the 1960s, however. When racial unrest exploded into violence in Detroit during the "long, hot summer" of 1967, President Lyndon Johnson ordered units of the United States Army into the city. He acted at the request of the governor of Michigan, George Romney, and only after Detroit's police and firefighters, supported by State Police and National Guard units, could not control riots, arson, and looting

## Organizing Information

To make sure students understand the main points of this section, you may wish to use the double web graphic organizer to the right.

Tell students that a double web compares and contrasts information. Ask students to use the double web to outline the roles of the National Government and those of the State governments, and to show how these governments affect each other.

**Teaching Tip** A template for this graphic organizer can be found in the Section Support Transparencies, Transparency 2.

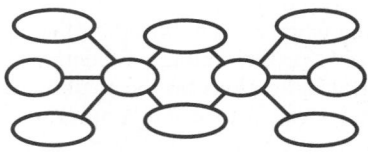

in the city. In 1968, again at the request of the governors involved, federal troops were sent into Chicago and Baltimore to help put down the violence that erupted following the assassination of Martin Luther King, Jr.

Normally, a President has sent troops into a State only in answer to a request from its governor or legislature. If national laws are being broken, national functions interfered with, or national property endangered, however, a President does not need to wait for such a plea.[12]

The ravages of nature—storms, floods, drought, forest fires, and such—can be more destructive than human violence. Here, too, acting to protect the States against "domestic Violence," the Federal Government stands ready to aid stricken areas.

### Respect for Territorial Integrity

The National Government is constitutionally bound to respect the territorial integrity of each of the States. That is, the National Government must recognize the legal existence and the physical boundaries of each State.

The basic scheme of the Constitution imposes this obligation. Several of its provisions do so, as well. For example, Congress must include, in both of its houses, members chosen in each one of the States.[13] Recall, too, that Article V of the Constitution declares that no State can be deprived of its equal representation in the United States Senate without its own consent.

## Admitting New States

Only Congress has the power to admit new States to the Union. As part of the National Government's guarantee of respect for each State's territorial integrity, the Constitution places only

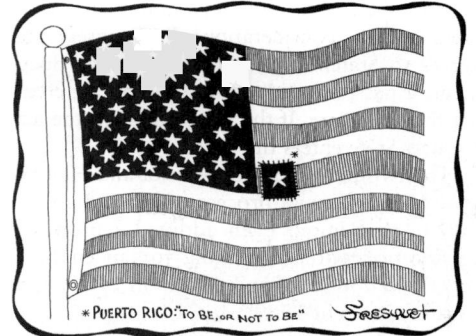

*Interpreting Political Cartoons* Whether or not Puerto Rico should become the 51st State has been the subject of continuing debate. **What does the cartoon suggest about the issue?**

*PUERTO RICO: "TO BE, OR NOT TO BE"*

one restriction on that power. A new State cannot be created by taking territory from one or more of the existing States without the consent of the legislature(s) of the State(s) involved.[14]

Congress has admitted 37 States since the original 13 formed the Union, as the map on the next page shows. Five States (Vermont, Kentucky, Tennessee, Maine, and West Virginia) were created from parts of already existing States. Texas was an independent republic before admission. California was admitted shortly after being ceded to the United States by Mexico. Each of the other 30 States entered the Union only after a longer period of time, frequently more than 15 years, as an organized territory.

### Admission Procedure

The process of admission to the Union is usually fairly simple. The area desiring Statehood first asks Congress for admission. If and when Congress chooses, it passes an **enabling act,** an act directing the people of the territory to frame a proposed State constitution. A convention prepares the constitution, which is then put to a popular vote in the proposed State. If the voters

---

[12]President Grover Cleveland ordered federal troops to put an end to rioting in the Chicago rail yard during the Pullman Strike in 1894 despite the objections of Governor William Altgeld of Illinois. The Supreme Court upheld his actions in *In re Debs,* 1895. The Court found that rioters had threatened federal property and impeded the flow of the mails and interstate commerce. Thus, more than a single State was involved. Since then, several Presidents have acted without a request from the State involved. More recently, President Dwight Eisenhower did so at Little Rock, Arkansas, in 1957, and President John Kennedy did so at the University of Mississippi in 1962 and at the University of Alabama in 1963. In each of those instances, the President acted to halt the unlawful obstruction of school integration orders issued by the federal courts.

[13]In the House, Article I, Section 2, Clause 1; in the Senate, Article I, Section 3, Clause 1 and the 17th Amendment.
[14]Article IV, Section 3, Clause 1. Some argue that this provision was violated with West Virginia's admission in 1863. That State was formed from the 40 western counties that had broken away from Virginia over the issue of secession from the Union. The consent required by the Constitution was given by a minority of the members of the Virginia legislature—those who represented the 40 western counties. Congress accepted their action, holding that they were the only group legally capable of acting as the Virginia legislature at the time.

---

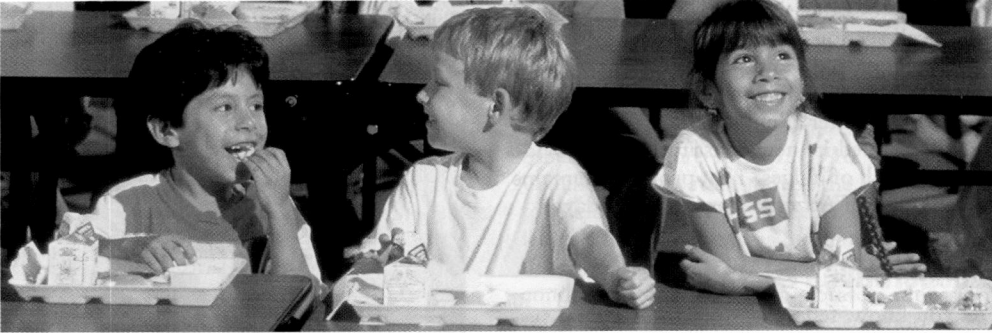

▲ Federal monies help fund school lunch programs in schools across the country.
*Critical Thinking* **What examples of cooperative federalism affect your own life?**

Grants-in-aid are based on the National Government's taxing power. The Constitution gives Congress that power in order

**FROM THE Constitution** *"to pay the Debts and provide for the common Defense and general Welfare of the United States. . . ."*

—Article I, Section 8, Clause 1

Today, these grants total more than $250 billion, and account for some 25 percent of all State and local government spending each year.

These grants make it possible for the Federal Government to operate in many policy areas in which it would otherwise have no constitutional authority—for example, in such fields as education, low-income housing, local law enforcement, and mental health. In this way, grants-in-aid blur the line of division of powers in the federal system.

Critics of grants-in-aid have long made this point. They also argue that the grants often give Washington a major—and they say an unwarranted—voice in making public policy at the State and local levels.

### Revenue Sharing

One form of federal monetary aid, known as **revenue sharing,** was in place from 1972 to 1987. Under this program, Congress gave an annual share of the huge federal tax revenue to the States and their cities, counties, and townships. Altogether, those "shared revenues" amounted to more than $83 billion over the years the program was in force.

Virtually no strings were attached to this money. In fact, Congress placed only one major restriction on the use of the funds. The money could not be spent for any program in which discrimination on the basis of race, sex, national origin, age, religious belief, or physical disability was evident. Otherwise, the "shared revenues" could be used very largely as the States and their local units chose to spend them.

Needless to say, revenue sharing was quite popular with and strongly supported by many governors, mayors, and other State and local officials. It was opposed by the Reagan Administration, however, and fell victim to the financial needs of the deficit-ridden National Government. Various efforts to revive revenue sharing in today's more prosperous climate have not won significant support in Congress, at least to this point in time.

### Types of Federal Grants

Today, Congress appropriates money for three types of grants-in-aid. These include categorical grants, block grants, and project grants.

Over time, most grants have been categorical. **Categorical grants** are made for some specific, closely defined purpose: for school lunches or for the construction of airports or wastewater treatment plants, for example. Categorical grants are usually made with conditions attached. These "strings" require the State to (1) use the federal monies only for the specific purpose involved, (2) make its own monetary contribution, often a matching amount but sometimes much less, (3) provide an agency to administer the grant,

## CONSTITUTIONAL PRINCIPLES

### Federalism

One example of the Federal Government using categorical grants to influence State law is the Transportation Equity Act for the Twenty-First Century (TEA-21), which was passed in 1998. It created the Seat Belt Incentive Grant Program. This program allows States a share of $500 million over a five-year period if they meet certain strict seat-belt requirements.

### Activity

Encourage students to consider why the Federal Government would pass such an act, and discuss these reasons as a class. Have students conduct research to find out the requirements for federal funding. Then ask them to find out whether your State has met at least four of the six requirements necessary to receive money from the grant.

and (4) obey a set of guidelines tailored to the particular purpose for which the monies are given.

**Block grants** have come into wide use over the last several years. They are made for much more broadly defined purposes than are categorical grants, such as health care, social services, or welfare. They are also made with fewer strings attached, so State and local governments have much greater freedom in deciding just how and on what to spend block grant dollars. Beginning in the Reagan years, from the 1980s on, many programs once supported by separate and fragmented categorical grants have been merged into broader block grants.

Congress also provides money for **project grants.** These are grants made to States, localities, and sometimes private agencies that apply for them. The Department of Health and Human Services makes many project grants—through its National Institutes of Health, for example, to support scientists engaged in research on cancer, diabetes, neurological disease, and other medical issues. Many State and local governments also apply for these grants to fund their job training and employment programs.

### Other Forms of Federal Aid

The National Government aids the States in several other important ways. For example, the FBI gives extensive help to State and local police.

The army and the air force equip and train each State's National Guard units. The Census Bureau's data are essential to State and local school, housing, and transportation officials as they plan for the future.

Many other forms of aid are not nearly so visible. "Lulu payments," for example, are federal monies that go to local governments in those areas in which there are large federal landholdings. These direct payments are made in lieu of—to take the place of—the property taxes that those local governments cannot collect from the National Government.

### State Aid to the National Government

Intergovernmental cooperation is a two-way street. That is, the States and their local units of government also aid the National Government in many ways.

Thus, State and local election officials conduct national elections in each State. These elections are financed with State and local funds, and they are regulated largely by State laws. The legal process by which aliens can become citizens, called naturalization, takes place most often in State, not federal, courts. Those who commit federal crimes and are sought by the FBI and other federal law enforcement agencies are often picked up by State and local police officers and then held in local jails. And the examples go on and on.

## Section **2** Assessment

### Key Terms and Main Ideas
1. What are three obligations that the Constitution places on the National Government for the benefit of the States?
2. Explain the difference between an **enabling act** and an **act of admission.**
3. (a) What is a **block grant?**
   (b) How do block grants reflect cooperative federalism?
4. In what ways do the States aid the National Government?

### Critical Thinking
5. **Recognizing Ideologies** If the Framers had been alive, how do you think they might have reacted when, only a few years ago, several States had to raise the legal drinking age to avoid losing a substantial portion of their federal grants for highway construction? Explain your answer.

6. **Making Comparisons** Suppose your State is to receive increased federal funding for a program to provide day care for some working parents. Is this funding likely to come as a categorical grant, a block grant, or a project grant? Why?
7. **Expressing Problems Clearly** In what type of situation would your State be most likely to need federal protection against "domestic Violence?" Explain your answer.

 **Take It to the Net**

8. Should Puerto Rico become the 51st State? Find out about the island's history, its status as a Commonwealth, and the arguments for and against Statehood. Then plan a debate on the following question: Should Puerto Rico become a State? Use the links provided in the Social Studies area at the following Web site for help in completing this activity. **www.phschool.com**

**Take It to the Net**

8. Direct students to the Social Studies area at the Prentice Hall Web site. The *Magruder's American Government* companion Web site includes the directions and links needed to complete the activity. It also provides a printable Internet activity worksheet with scoring rubrics for assessment. Debates should be well-organized and demonstrate an understanding of the admission processes for States.

## Point-of-Use Resources

**Guide to the Essentials** Chapter 4, Section 2, p. 29 provides support for students who need additional review of section content. Spanish support is available in the Spanish edition of the Guide on p. 22.

**Quiz** Unit 1 booklet, p. 30 includes matching and multiple-choice questions to check students' understanding of Section 2 content.

**Presentation Pro CD-ROM** Quizzes and multiple-choice questions check students' understanding of Section 2 content.

## Answers to . . .

### Section 2 Assessment

**1.** Obligations include a guarantee that each State will have a republican, or representative, form of government, protection against invasion or natural disaster, and respect for the territorial integrity of each State.
**2.** An enabling act is an act by Congress that directs the people of a territory to propose a State constitution; an act of admission is the congressional act which actually creates the new State.
**3. (a)** A grant that can be used for broad purposes by State and local governments, with few conditions attached. **(b)** They function at the State level but are funded by the National Government.
**4.** They regulate national elections, oversee naturalization procedures, and help capture federal criminal suspects.
**5.** Possible answer: They would disapprove, because the grant gives the Federal Government power within States.
**6.** Possible answer: Categorical grant, because providing daycare to poor working parents is a type of narrow purpose that is usually covered by categorical grants.
**7.** Possible answer: States are most likely to seek federal protection against domestic violence in cases of natural disaster.

## CRITICAL THINKING

### Expressing Problems Clearly

**Focus** Guide the class to analyze *McCulloch* v. *Maryland* in order to hold a mock Supreme Court deliberation on the case.

**Instruct** Divide the class in two, representing the two sides in the case. Have each group, one at a time, follow Steps 1–3, creating a list of the key issues on their side of the case and finding supporting arguments. Involve the whole class in Step 4, drafting a statement or question that summarizes the essential problem in the case.

**Close/Reteach** Choose one volunteer from each group to act as the lawyers for the plaintiff and the defense. Each side should confer to help prepare their "counsel" to argue the case. Guide both sides to prepare a case that carefully addresses the problem identified in Step 4.

### Answers . . .

**1.** Discuss the excerpt from Marshall's ruling to make sure students understand the language in the quotation.
**2.** The plaintiff, the second Bank of the United States, wants to avoid paying a tax levied on it by the State of Maryland. The defendant, Maryland, wants to be able to levy the tax in hopes of driving the national bank out of business.
**3.** The plaintiff (Second Bank) argues that the act to tax is not constitutional because it was passed by a State legislature. The defendant (Maryland) argues that the bank is unconstitutional and that States delegate power to the Federal Government.
**4.** Possible answer: In *McCulloch* v. *Maryland,* the Supreme Court addressed the question of whether States could exercise power over the Federal Government by taxing its operations.

# SKILLS FOR LIFE

# Expressing Problems Clearly

To express a problem clearly means to describe the nature of an issue that is difficult, puzzling, or open to debate. Expressing a problem clearly is the first step in solving it.

**1. Gather information.** When you are confronted with a problem, gather information on the topic. For example, in *McCulloch* v. *Maryland* (1819), Chief Justice John Marshall addressed questions about the relationship between the Federal Government and the States. Reread the passage about *McCulloch* v. *Maryland* on page 95. Then read the excerpt below.

**2. Identify the basic concepts involved.** Specific problems often relate to a general principle. For example, the Supreme Court often chooses to rule on a specific case that illustrates a broad principle that can be applied to similar cases. To identify the problem in *McCulloch* v. *Maryland*, state what each side wants to achieve.

**3. Identify supporting details or arguments.** In the *McCulloch* excerpt, find the arguments that support the plaintiffs' view and the defendants' view.

**4. Express the problem clearly.** Now that you have identified the main area of dispute and stripped away details, you're ready to express the problem clearly. In your own words, state the nature of the problem that the Supreme Court addressed in 1819.

### Test for Success

Find a newspaper editorial in print or on the Internet. Analyze the editorial using the steps listed above to express the problem or controversy in a clear and concise way.

How does each side make its case?

What are the arguments for and against the bank?

What's the main issue in this case?

How can I summarize the case?

"In the case now to be determined, the defendant, a sovereign State [Maryland], denies the obligation of a law enacted by [Congress], and the plaintiff [the National Bank] contests the validity of an act which has been passed by the legislature of that State. . . .

In discussing this question, the counsel for the State of Maryland have deemed it of some importance . . . to consider [the U.S. Constitution] not as emanating from the people, but as the act of sovereign and independent States. The powers of the [national] government, it has been said, are delegated by the States . . . and must be exercised in subordination to the States, who alone possess supreme dominion. . . .

It being the opinion of the Court, that the act incorporating the bank is constitutional . . . we proceed to inquire . . . [w]hether the State of Maryland may, without violating the constitution, tax that branch [the branch in Maryland]?

That the power of taxation is . . . retained by the States; that it is not [reduced] by the grant of a similar power to the government of the Union . . . are truths which have never been denied. But . . . States are expressly forbidden to lay any duties on imports or exports . . . . If [this limitation on States' power to tax] must be conceded, the same [principle] would seem to restrain . . . a State from such other exercise of this power. . . . On this ground the counsel for the bank place its claim to be exempted from the power of a State to tax its operations."

—*Chief Justice John Marshall,* McCulloch v. Maryland, *1819*

### Test for Success

Guide students to find the core controversy, or problem, by identifying opposing views on the topic and the details that support those views.

## Point-of-Use Resources

**Skills for Life Activity** Unit 1 booklet, p. 33 provides an additional skill activity for this chapter.

**Social Studies Skills Tutor CD-ROM** Provides interactive practice in geographic literacy, critical thinking and reading, visual analysis, and communications.

### 3 Interstate Relations

## Section Preview

### OBJECTIVES

1. **Explain** why States make interstate compacts.
2. **Understand** the purpose of the Full Faith and Credit Clause.
3. **Define** *extradition* and explain its purpose.
4. **Discuss** the purpose of the Privileges and Immunities Clause.

### WHY IT MATTERS

What if Texas citizens were not allowed to travel into Oklahoma, or needed a special passport to do so? What if your North Carolina driver's license were not valid when you drove through Ohio? Fortunately, several key provisions in the Constitution promote cooperation between and among the States.

### POLITICAL DICTIONARY

★ interstate compact
★ Full Faith and Credit Clause
★ extradition
★ Privileges and Immunities Clause

As you know, conflict among the States was a major reason for the adoption of the Constitution in 1789. The fact that the new document strengthened the hand of the National Government, especially regarding commerce, lessened many of those frictions. So, too, did several of the Constitution's provisions that deal directly with the States' relationships with one another. This section is concerned with those provisions.

## Interstate Compacts

No State can enter into any treaty, alliance, or confederation. However, the States may, with the consent of Congress, enter into **interstate compacts**—agreements among themselves and with foreign states.[15]

By 1920, the States had made only 26 compacts. Since then, the number of interstate compacts has been growing. New York and New Jersey led the way in 1921 with a compact creating the Port of New York Authority to manage and develop the harbor facilities bordering both States. More than 200 compacts are now in force, and many involve several States. In fact,

all 50 States have joined in two of them: the Compact for the Supervision of Parolees and Probationers and the Compact on Juveniles. These two compacts enable States to share important law-enforcement data. Other agreements cover a widening range of subjects. They include, for example, compacts designed to coordinate the development and conservation of such resources as water, oil, wildlife, and fish; prevent forest fires; prevent stream and harbor pollution; provide for tax collections; promote motor vehicle safety; facilitate the licensing of drivers; and encourage the cooperative use of public universities.

▲ Seven western States belong to the Colorado River Compact, which apportions the waters of the Colorado River Basin.

---

[15]Article I, Section 10, Clause 3. The Supreme Court has held that Congressional consent is not needed for compacts that do not tend to increase the political power of the States, *Virginia* v. *Tennessee*, 1893. But it is often difficult to decide whether an agreement is political or nonpolitical. So, most interstate agreements are submitted to Congress as a matter of course.

## Reading Strategy

### Predicting

Ask students to quickly skim the section, paying particular attention to headings, subheadings, boldfaced words, and graphics. Have them write down predictions about what they will learn concerning relations between States. Ask them to make any necessary corrections to their predictions after they have read the text.

### A C T I V I T Y

### Extended Class Periods

**Time** 90 minutes.
**Purpose** Explore interstate relations.
**Grouping** Three to five students.
**Activity** Have each group create a "new" State that lies within the current boundaries of the U.S., providing its location, population, and most abundant resources. Each group should make a list of 5–10 State laws that are most important to the State's people.
**Roles** Discussion leader, recorder, spokesperson.
**Close** Encourage spokespersons from the different groups to meet to discuss interstate compacts or other agreements that would benefit both parties. Lead a discussion about how the Constitution has eased tension among States by promoting cooperation among them.

■ **Block Strategy**
**(Average)**

## Point–of–Use Resources

**Guided Reading and Review** Unit 1 booklet, p. 31 provides students with practice identifying the main ideas and key terms of this section.

**Lesson Plans** For lesson planning suggestions, see p. 25 of the Lesson Plans booklet.

**Political Cartoons** See p. 17 of the Political Cartoons booklet for a cartoon relevant to this section.

**Government Assessment Rubrics** Cooperative Learning Project: Process, p. 20

# Full Faith and Credit

The Constitution states that

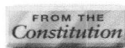 *"Full Faith and Credit shall be given in each State to the public Acts, Records, and judicial Proceedings of every other State."*
—Article IV, Section 1

The term *public acts* refers to the laws of a State. *Records* refers to such documents as birth certificates, marriage licenses, deeds to property, car registrations, and the like. The words *judicial proceedings* relate to the outcome of court actions: damage awards, the probating (proving) of wills, divorce decrees, and so forth.

The **Full Faith and Credit Clause** most often comes into play in court matters. Take this example: Allen sues Bill in Florida, and the Florida court awards Allen $50,000 in damages. Bill cannot escape payment of the damages by moving to Georgia, because Allen could simply ask the Georgia courts to enforce the damage award. Neither would the case have to be retried in Georgia. Instead, the Georgia courts would have to give full faith and credit to—recognize and respect the validity of—the judgment made by the Florida court.

▲ **Full Faith and Credit** The Full Faith and Credit Clause ensures that records such as birth certificates and marriage licenses are recognized in all 50 States.

In a similar vein, a person can prove age, place of birth, marital status, title to property, and similar facts by securing the necessary documents from the State where the record was made. The validity of these documents will be recognized in each of the 50 States.

### Exceptions

The Full Faith and Credit Clause is regularly observed and usually operates routinely between and among the States. This rule has two exceptions, however. First, it applies only to civil, not criminal, matters. One State cannot enforce another State's criminal law. Second, full faith and credit need not be given to certain divorces granted by one State to residents of another State.

On the second exception, the key question is always this: Was the person who obtained the divorce in fact a resident of the State that granted it? If so, the divorce will be accorded full faith and credit in other States. If not, then the State granting the divorce did not have the authority to do so, and another State can refuse to recognize it.

### *Williams v. North Carolina*

The matter of interstate "quickie" divorces has been troublesome for years, especially since the Supreme Court's decision in a 1945 case, *Williams v. North Carolina*. In that case, a man and a woman had traveled to Nevada, where each wanted to obtain a divorce so they could marry each other. They lived in Las Vegas for six weeks, the minimum period of State residence required by Nevada's divorce law. The couple received their divorces, were married, and soon after returned to North Carolina. Problems arose when that State's authorities refused to recognize their Nevada divorces. North Carolina brought the couple to trial and a jury convicted each of them of the crime of bigamous cohabitation (marrying and living together while a previous marriage is still legally in effect).

On appeal, the Supreme Court upheld North Carolina's denial of full faith and credit to the Nevada divorces. It ruled that the couple had not in fact established bona fide—good faith, valid—residence in Nevada. Rather, the Court held that

## Organizing Information

To make sure students understand the main points of this section, you may wish to use the web graphic organizer to the right.

Tell students that a web shows a main idea and its supporting details. Ask students to use the web to outline details about interstate relations, including compacts, Full Faith and Credit, extradition, and privileges and immunities.

**Teaching Tip** A template for this graphic organizer can be found in the Section Support Transparencies, Transparency 1.

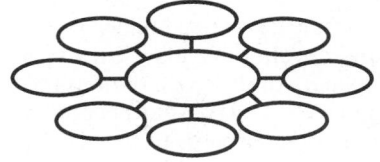

▲ Each State requires new residents to obtain a State-issued license. *Critical Thinking **Why are nonresident drivers allowed to drive from State to State without obtaining a new license?***

the couple had remained legal residents of North Carolina. The Court thus found that Nevada lacked the authority to grant their divorces.

A divorce granted by a State court to a bona fide resident of that State must be given full faith and credit in all other States. To become a legal resident of a State, a person must intend to reside there permanently, or at least indefinitely. Clearly, the Williamses had not intended to do so.

The *Williams* case, and later ones like it, cast dark clouds of doubt over the validity of thousands of other interstate divorces. The later marriages of people involved in these divorces, and the frequently tangled estate problems produced by their deaths, suggest the confused and serious nature of the matter.

## Extradition

According to the Constitution

> FROM THE *Constitution* **"** *A Person charged in any State with Treason, Felony, or other Crime, who shall flee from Justice, and be found in another State, shall on Demand of the executive Authority of the State from which he fled, be delivered up, to be removed to the State having Jurisdiction of the Crime.* **"**
>
> — Article IV, Section 2, Clause 2

This clause refers to **extradition,** the legal process by which a fugitive from justice in one State is returned to that State. Extradition is designed to prevent a person from escaping justice by fleeing a State.

The return of a fugitive from justice is usually a routine matter; governors regularly approve the extradition requests they receive from other States' chief executives. Some of those requests, however, are contested. This is especially true in cases with strong racial or political overtones, and in those increasingly frequent instances of parental kidnapping of children involved in custody disputes as a result of a divorce.

Until the 1980s, governors could, and on occasion did, refuse to return fugitives. In *Kentucky* v. *Dennison,* 1861, the Supreme Court held that the Constitution did not give the Federal Government any power with which to compel a governor to act in an extradition case. So, for more than a century, the Constitution's word *shall* in the Extradition Clause had to be read as "may."

The Supreme Court overturned this ruling in 1987. In *Puerto Rico* v. *Branstad,* a unanimous Court held that the federal courts can indeed order an unwilling governor to extradite a fugitive.

## Privileges and Immunities

The Constitution also provides that

> FROM THE *Constitution* **"** *The Citizens of each State shall be entitled to all Privileges and Immunities of Citizens in the several States.* **"**
>
> —Article IV, Section 2, Clause 1[16]

This clause, known as the **Privileges and Immunities Clause,** means that no State can draw unreasonable distinctions between its own residents and those persons who happen to live in other States.

Each State must recognize the right of any American to travel in or become a resident of that State. It must also allow any citizen, no matter where he or she lives, to use its courts and make contracts; buy, own, rent, or sell property; or marry within its borders.

---

[16]The provision is reinforced in the 14th Amendment.

## Background Note
### Constitutional Issues

When the Governor of Iowa refused Puerto Rico's request for extradition of an accused murderer in 1981, Puerto Rico filed suit in Federal District Court claiming violation of the Extradition Clause of the Constitution and the Extradition Act. The Court dismissed the case, citing *Kentucky* v. *Dennison.* In *Puerto Rico* v. *Branstad,* 1987, the Supreme Court reversed, holding that *Dennison* "can stand no longer." The Court noted that *Dennison* involved assisting escaped slaves, and had been heard in 1861 when "the practical power of the Federal Government was at its lowest ebb" and "secession was a fact, and civil war a threatening possibility." The Court concluded that "*Kentucky* v. *Dennison* is the product of another time" and that its conception of the relationship between the States and Federal Government "is fundamentally incompatible with more than a century of constitutional development." Additionally, the Court found "that the right given to 'demand' implies it is an absolute right; and it follows that there must be a correlative obligation to deliver."

## Point-of-Use Resources

📖 **Section Support Transparencies** Transparency 20, *Visual Learning;* Transparency 119, *Political Cartoon*

*Answer to . . .*

**Critical Thinking** The Privileges and Immunities Clause says that States may not draw unreasonable distinctions between its own residents and nonresidents.

## Point-of-Use Resources

Guide to the Essentials Chapter 4, Section 3, p. 30 provides support for students who need additional review of section content. Spanish support is available in the Spanish edition of the Guide on p. 23.

Quiz Unit 1 booklet, p. 32 includes matching and multiple-choice questions to check students' understanding of Section 3 content.

Presentation Pro CD-ROM Quizzes and multiple-choice questions check students' understanding of Section 3 content.

## Answers to . . .

### Section 3 Assessment

**1.** Treaties, alliances, and confederation.
**2.** It is a requirement that each State accept the public acts, records, and judicial proceedings of other States.
**3.** Extradition is meant to prevent a fugitive from being able to escape the law just by fleeing to another State.
**4. (a)** Traveling to or becoming a resident of another State; using a State's courts; buying, owning, renting, or selling property; marrying within State borders. **(b)** Giving hiring preferences to residents; lowering welfare benefits for nonresidents; setting higher fees for nonresidents using common property of the State.
**5.** Students might suggest that each State would try and respect each other's acts; others might say that States would not respect each other's acts as they got caught up in economic competition.
**6.** Answers will vary. Examples that are likely to affect students include interstate travel, marriage, purchase or rental of property, attendance at State universities, or obtaining professional or recreational licenses.

### Answer to . . .

**Interpreting Tables** Answers will vary, but should address the issue of whether colleges and universities should be considered a State's "common property."

| University | In-State | Out-of-State |
|---|---|---|
| Oklahoma State University | $2,412 | $6,492 |
| Tennessee State University | $2,308 | $7,132 |
| Indiana State University | $3,426 | $8,554 |
| University of North Carolina | $2,364 | $11,530 |
| University of Virginia | $4,130 | $16,603 |
| Idaho State University | $2,398 | $8,638 |
| Arkansas State University | $2,972 | $6,644 |
| University of Texas | $3,128 | $9,608 |
| Michigan State University | $5,079 | $11,820 |
| Florida State University | $2,195 | $9,184 |
| University of Massachusetts | $5,212 | $13,365 |

**Tuition at State Universities**

SOURCE: *Barron's Profiles of American Colleges*, 24th Edition, 2001

*Interpreting Tables* Under the Privileges and Immunities Clause, colleges and universities may charge different tuition rates for in-state and out-of-state residents. *Do you think that this practice is justified? Explain your answer.*

At the same time, a State cannot do such things as try to relieve its unemployment problems by requiring employers to give a hiring preference to in-State residents, *Hicklin* v. *Orbeck*, 1978. Nor can it set the welfare benefits it pays to newly arrived residents at a level below the benefits it provides to its long-term residents, *Saens* v. *Roe*, 1999.

However, the Privileges and Immunities Clause does allow States to draw *reasonable* distinctions between its own residents and those of other States. Thus, any State can require that a person live within the State for some time before he or she can vote or hold public office. It also can require some period of residence before one can be licensed to practice law, medicine, dentistry, and so on.

In another example, the wild fish and game in a State are considered to be the common property of the people of that State. So, a State can require nonresidents to pay higher fees for fishing or hunting licenses than those paid by residents—who pay taxes to provide fish hatcheries, enforce game laws, and so on. By the same token, a State university often charges higher tuition to students from other States than it does to residents.

## Section 3 Assessment

### Key Terms and Main Ideas

1. What agreements does the Constitution prohibit the States from making?
2. What is the meaning of the **Full Faith and Credit Clause?**
3. What is the purpose of **extradition?**
4. **(a)** Give at least two examples of actions protected under the **Privileges and Immunities Clause. (b)** What types of actions are not protected by this clause?

### Critical Thinking

5. **Predicting Consequences** What difficulties might result if each State were not required to give full faith and credit to the public acts, records, and judicial proceedings of other States? Provide at least two examples to support your conclusion.
6. **Drawing Inferences** Provide at least two examples of how the Privileges and Immunities Clause has affected your life or might do so in the future.

 **Take It to the Net**

7. Every State is a part of the Interstate Compact for the Placement of Children. Read this document and write a brief essay explaining its importance. Use the links provided in the Social Studies area at the following Web site for help in this activity. **www.phschool.com**

 **Take It to the Net**

7. Direct students to the Social Studies area at the Prentice Hall Web site. The *Magruder's American Government* companion Web site includes the directions and links needed to complete the activity. It also provides a printable Internet activity worksheet with scoring rubrics for assessment. Explanations should be supported with concrete examples.

# on the Supreme Court

## Should States Be Required to Enforce Federal Laws?

*States are required to obey the federal Constitution and federal laws and treaties. Can Congress require State officials to help enforce federal laws and regulations?*

### Printz v. United States (1997)

The Gun Control Act of 1968 outlined rules for the distribution of firearms. Dealers were prohibited from selling guns to persons under 21, out-of-state residents, and convicted felons and fugitives. The Brady Act, a 1993 amendment to that law, required the attorney general to establish by 1998 a national system for conducting instant background checks on prospective handgun buyers.

The Brady Act also created a temporary background check system. Before selling a handgun, a firearms dealer was required to obtain identification from the purchaser, and to forward that information to the "chief law enforcement officer" (CLEO) of the purchaser's residence. The Brady Act required CLEOs to make a reasonable effort to determine within the five business days whether the purchaser may lawfully possess a gun.

Jay Printz and Richard Mack, State officials serving as CLEOs in counties in Montana and Arizona, respectively, challenged the Brady Act in federal district court. They argued that the provisions requiring them to perform federal functions and execute federal laws were unconstitutional. The district court agreed with their argument, but the court of appeals found the entire Act constitutional, and the case went to the Supreme Court for review.

### Arguments for Printz

1. The balance of power between Federal and State governments would be disrupted if the Federal Government could force the States to implement federal laws, especially if the States had to pay the implementation costs.
2. Under the Constitution, executing the laws of the United States is the function of the President.

The Brady Act would transfer part of this function to State officials, over whom the President has no meaningful control.
3. The Framers of the Constitution rejected the idea of having the central government act through the States in favor of a federal system of government.

### Arguments for the United States

1. Congress has the expressed power to regulate commerce among the States. The Brady Act provisions are "necessary and proper" to carry out this power and thus are a lawful exercise of the power.
2. The burden imposed by the Brady Act on State officials is small, and therefore does not threaten the balance of power between States and the Federal Government.
3. Congress found that there is an "epidemic" of gun violence, and it can lawfully require State officials to help deal with emergency situations on a temporary basis.

---

### Decide for Yourself

1. Review the constitutional grounds on which each side based its arguments and the specific arguments each side presented.
2. Debate the opposing viewpoints presented in this case. Which viewpoint do you favor?
3. Predict the impact of the Court's decision on federal programs that require local enforcement. (To read a summary of the Court's decision, turn to the Supreme Court Glossary on page 799.)

---

 *Corner*

 **Online**

📁 **Close Up on the Supreme Court** *Printz* v. *United States,* p. 5 provides an activity to extend coverage of this case.

To keep up-to-date on Close Up news and activities, visit Close Up Online at

**www.closeup.org**

---

## Should States be Required to Enforce Federal Laws?

**Focus** Have students read the Supremacy Clause (Article VI, Section 2). Then review *McCulloch* v. *Maryland,* which holds that the Supremacy Clause makes the federal judiciary the "umpire" in disputes between the States and Federal Government. Ask students if the Supremacy Clause includes any safeguards against the federal judiciary abusing this power. *(Yes; its decisions may not violate the Constitution)*

**Instruct** Have students prepare an outline of the arguments for each side of the case. Next, have them use their outlines to determine which side favors a more limited Federal Government. *(Printz)* Then have students explain their answer to a classmate.

**Close/Reteach** According to Supreme Court Justice Holmes, the survival of the federal system depends on the national judiciary acting as an umpire. Divide the class into small groups to discuss whether they agree with Justice Holmes, and whether they can come up with any alternative ways of resolving such disputes.

💿 **Keep It Current CD-ROM** includes government-related projects by unit. The CD-ROM links to the Prentice Hall School Web site and may be used for daily updates.

---

### Answers to . . .
**Decide for Yourself**
**1.** Printz used the grounds of federalism and separation of powers to argue that State officials should not be required to perform federal duties. The U.S. used the commerce clause and the provision that States may help out in emergency situations to argue that the provision of the Act is "necessary and proper."
**2.** Answers will vary, but should be supported with valid reasoning.
**3.** The Court held that the Brady Act provision was unconstitutional, and that the Federal Government could not require CLEOs to enforce federal laws.

## Practicing the Vocabulary

1. expressed powers
2. act of admission
3. categorical grant
4. federalism
5. interstate compact
6. reserved powers
7. delegated powers
8. grants-in-aid program
9. enabling act
10. exclusive powers

## Reviewing Main Ideas

### Section 1

**11.** It enabled the Framers to create a strong central government while respecting the concerns of each of the existing States.
**12.** The National Government has delegated powers, which can be expressed, implied, or inherent.
**13. (a)** Expressly, by denying them in the Constitution; Silently, by *not* granting them expressly in the Constitution; As a result of federalism, because federalism checks the National Government's powers. **(b)** Expressly: prohibiting levy duties on exports; prohibiting freedom of religion, speech, or assembly; conducting illegal searches or seizures; denying trials by jury. Silently: by not creating a national education system; by not enacting uniform marriage and divorce laws; by setting up local governments. As a result of federalism: by not allowing the Federal Government to tax the States in their carrying out of governmental functions.
**14.** The States' powers are reserved powers—any and all powers that the Constitution does not give to the National Government or deny the States.
**15.** It is the final authority that interprets the Constitution in cases of conflict between the States and the National Government.

### Section 2

**16.** It must guarantee a republican form of government, protect each State from foreign invasion and domestic violence, and respect territorial integrity.
**17.** An area desiring Statehood petitions Congress to pass an enabling act to direct the framing of a proposed State constitution. After the voters

## Political Dictionary

federalism (p. 88)
division of powers (p. 89)
delegated powers (p. 89)
expressed powers (p. 89)
implied powers (p. 90)
inherent powers (p. 91)
reserved powers (p. 92)

exclusive powers (p. 93)
concurrent powers (p. 93)
enabling act (p. 99)
act of admission (p. 100)
grants-in-aid program (p. 101)
revenue sharing (p. 102)
categorical grant (p. 102)

block grant (p. 103)
project grant (p. 103)
interstate compact (p. 105)
Full Faith and Credit Clause (p. 106)
extradition (p. 107)
Privileges and Immunities Clause (p. 107)

## Practicing the Vocabulary

**Matching** *Choose a term from the list above that best matches each description.*

1. The powers that the Constitution grants to the National Government in so many words
2. Congressional measure admitting a United States territory into the Union as a State
3. A type of federal grant-in-aid that is used for a specific, narrowly defined purpose
4. A system of government in which a constitution divides the powers of government between a National Government and several regional governments
5. Agreements made by the States among themselves and with foreign powers

**Fill in the Blank** *Choose a term from the list above that best completes the sentence.*

6. _____ are those powers held by the States in the federal system.
7. _____ are those powers granted to the National Government in the Constitution.
8. Some people have questioned whether the _____ gives the National Government too much say in matters of State and local concern.
9. Congress directs a territory desiring Statehood to frame a proposed State constitution in a(n) _____ .
10. Those powers that can only be exercised by the National Government are called _____ .

## Reviewing Main Ideas

### Section 1

11. How did the principle of federalism enable the Framers to solve the problems they faced in 1787?
12. Briefly describe the powers the Constitution provides to the National Government.
13. **(a)** In what three ways does the Constitution deny powers to the National Government? **(b)** Give at least one example of each.
14. Briefly describe the powers of the States as stated in the Constitution.
15. What is the role of the Supreme Court in the federal system?

### Section 2

16. According to the Constitution, what are the National Government's obligations to the States?
17. Outline the steps Congress takes in admitting new States to the Union.

18. What is cooperative federalism?
19. Give at least three examples of cooperative federalism at work.
20. **(a)** What is a block grant? **(b)** Give an example of a program that a State might fund using block grant money.

### Section 3

21. List at least three examples of the kinds of interstate compacts that exist today.
22. Under what circumstances can a State deny full faith and credit to a law, a public record, or the outcome of a court case in another State?
23. Explain the purpose of the Privileges and Immunities Clause.
24. What is the significance of the Supreme Court's decision in *Williams* v. *North Carolina*?
25. Can governors refuse to return fugitives from justice to the State from which they fled? Explain your answer.

of the proposed State have approved this constitution, Congress can issue an act of admission.
**18.** The area of shared powers and cooperation between the Federal and State governments.
**19.** Federal grants-in-aid programs and other block grants; State aid in conducting, financing and regulating elections; State aid in helping handle Federal criminals.
**20. (a)** Federal grants to States given for broadly defined purposes with few restrictions. **(b)** Health care, social services, or welfare programs.

### Section 3

**21.** Examples include: sharing law-enforcement data; coordinating the development and conservation of natural resources; forest fire protection; control of water pollution; collection of taxes; motor vehicle safety and driver licensing; cooperative use of public universities.
**22.** One State cannot enforce another State's criminal law, and in certain cases of divorce full faith and credit need not be granted.
**23.** To prevent the unfair favoring of a State's residents over other residents.
**24.** It cast doubt over the validity of many interstate divorces.
**25.** No, as of the Supreme Court decision in 1987 which held that

## Critical Thinking Skills

**26.** *Applying the Chapter Skill* What problems might arise if the Federal Government did not have the power to regulate interstate commerce?

**27.** *Drawing Conclusions* Why might a governor be reluctant to call for federal troops in the event that violence breaks out in a city in his or her State?

**28.** *Expressing Problems Clearly* What are the advantages and disadvantages of the federal system? Support your answer with examples from the text.

**29.** *Drawing Conclusions* Teachers must obtain State certification in order to teach within a given State. Not all States recognize certification from other States, however. Explain how this can be so.

## Analyzing Political Cartoons

Using your knowledge of American government and this cartoon, answer the questions below.

LEVELS OF CONSCIOUSNESS

FEDERAL
STATE
LOCAL

**30.** What does the cartoon suggest about the relative importance of local government?

**31.** The cartoon portrays three levels of government—Federal, State, and local. From what you have read about the federal system, is this portrayal entirely accurate? Explain your answer.

## Take It to the Net

Additional support materials and activities for Chapter 4 of *Magruder's American Government* can be found in the Social Studies area at the Prentice Hall School Web site. **www.phschool.com**

## ★ You Can Make a Difference

Telephone or e-mail the offices of your representatives in Congress to find out the answers to the following questions: What local projects are supported by government block grants or by joint State/Federal funding in your community? How important are federal funds in your community or school? Is the money used for highways and parks? For school computers? For housing projects? Write a short report summarizing your findings. Include your opinion as to whether or not these funds are being used wisely.

## Participation Activities

**32.** *Current Events Watch* Find three to five examples in the news that illustrate a power of the National Government, such as sending troops abroad or regulating immigration. Do the same for powers reserved to the States, such as establishing and regulating public schools. Prepare an oral presentation explaining how the State and national powers that you have chosen affect you and your community.

**33.** *Time Line Activity* Research how your State (or another State of your choosing) became a State. Then create a time line in which you explain your findings. Illustrate main events in your time line with drawings or copies of photos. Be sure to point out anything unique about the process by which your selected State entered the Union.

**34.** *It's Your Turn* When you move to a new State, you have to change your driver's license, auto registration, and voter's registration. Find out how someone moving to your State would make these changes. Then create a newsletter for families moving to your State that explains the steps involved in obtaining the necessary new documents. **(Writing a Newsletter)**

## Take It to the Net

**Chapter 4 Self-Test** As a final review activity, take the Chapter 4 Self-Test in the Social Studies area at the Web site listed below, and receive immediate feedback on your answers.

**www.phschool.com**

## Point-of-Use Resources

 **Guide to the Essentials of American Government** Chapter 4 Test, page 31 provides multiple-choice questions to test students' knowledge of the chapter.

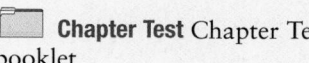 **Test Bank CD-ROM** Chapter 4 Test

**Chapter Test** Chapter Tests booklet

federal courts can order governors to extradite fugitives.

## Critical Thinking Skills

**26.** Possible answer: States might use unfair practices to compete economically or promote their own interests, which would weaken the nation as a whole.

**27.** Answers will vary. Students might suggest that a governor would want voters to think he or she was capable of handling the problems of the State.

**28.** Possible advantages: It checks the government's power and thus prevents its abuse; it allows local action when issues are of local concern and national action when issues are of national concern; it preserves the strength of each individual State. Possible disadvantages: It can produce conflict between national and State law; it can incite competition between States.

**29.** Teacher certification can be seen as a reasonable distinction between States. Each State may therefore be allowed to determine its own certification requirements.

## Analyzing Political Cartoons

**30.** The cartoon suggests that the character has less awareness of local government than of federal and State government.

**31.** No; local government derives its power from State government; it is not a separate government entity.

## You Can Make a Difference

Reports should address all of the questions posed, and be supported with specific facts or quotes.

## Participation Activities

**32.** Presentations should show an understanding of the various sides of the debate over the chosen issue; they should give evidence that the student has conducted research in current news media.

**33.** Time lines should be complete, accurately reflect chapter content, and be supported with relevant examples.

**34.** Newsletters should be well-organized and clearly written.

## Political Behavior: Government By the People

### Introducing the Unit

Unit 2 introduces students to the role American citizens play in their government. Chapter 5 examines the nature, function, and evolution of the American two-party political system, as well as the effect of minor parties on elections. Chapter 6 explores the history of voting rights in the United States, how States decide who can vote, the effects of civil rights laws, voter turnout, and the various factors that affect the way in which people vote. Chapter 7 analyzes how candidates are nominated to run for public office, how elections are conducted, and the role of money in the electoral process. Chapter 8 shows the role of public opinion in American politics, the means by which public opinions are expressed and measured, and the impact of the mass media on politics. Chapter 9 examines the various types of interest groups and the influence they have on public opinion and policy.

### Focus Activity

Concentrate students' attention on the American electorate by writing the following quotation on the board:

*"It is not the function of our Government to keep the citizen from falling into error; it is the function of the citizen to keep the Government from falling into error."*
—Justice Robert H. Jackson (1950)

Have students consider the following after they have read the quotation.

◆ How can American citizens "keep the Government from falling into error?"
◆ Do you agree with this statement? Why or why not?
◆ Use these questions as springboards to a general class discussion about students' views of the electorate.

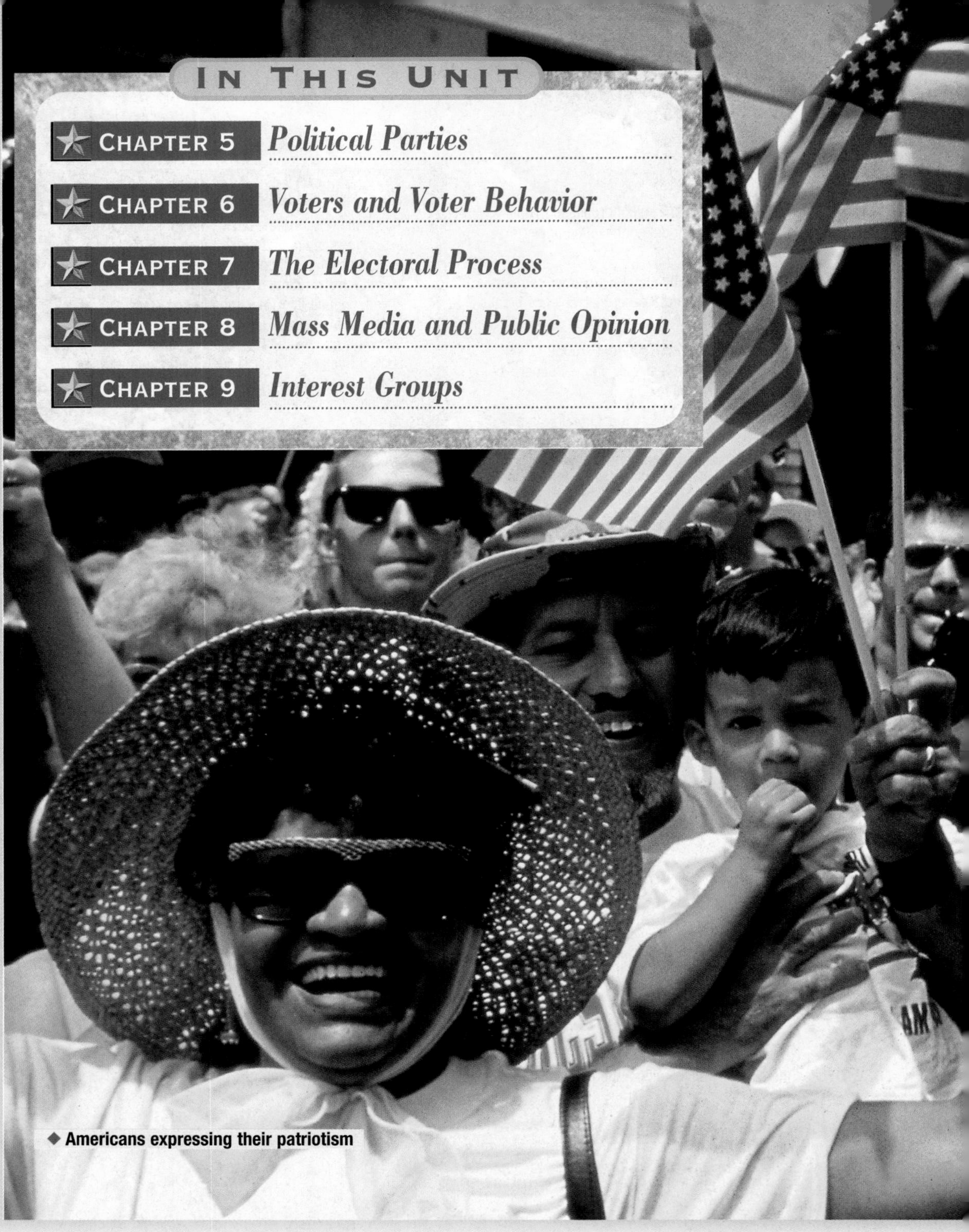

◆ Americans expressing their patriotism

### Corner

The following Close Up features appear in this unit.
*Close Up on the Supreme Court* may be found on the following pages: 143, 173, 203, 231, 255
*Close Up on Primary Sources* may be found on the following pages: 136, 158, 187, 214, 248

To keep up-to-date on Close Up news and activities, visit Close Up Online at

**www.closeup.org**

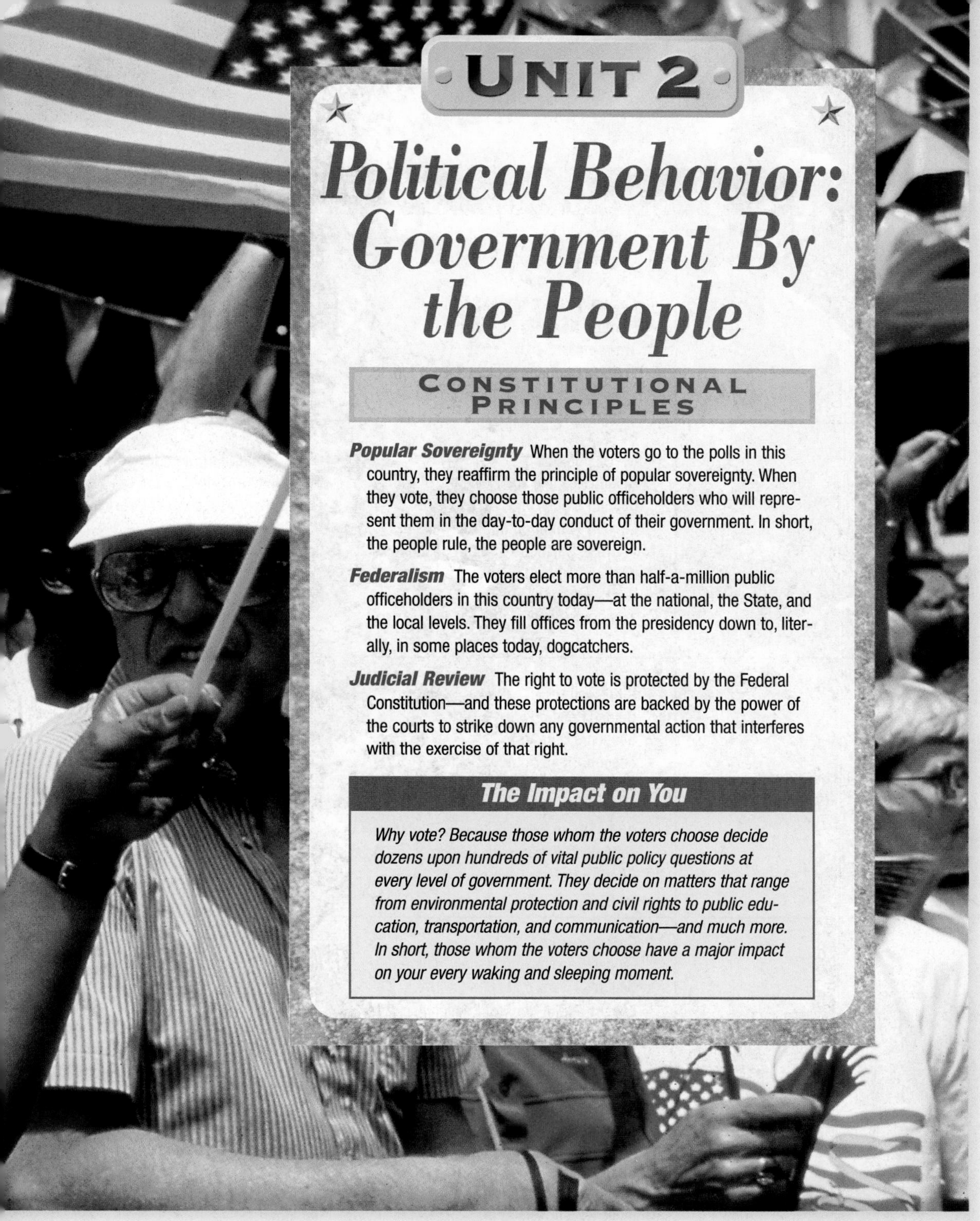

UNIT 2

# Political Behavior: Government By the People

## CONSTITUTIONAL PRINCIPLES

***Popular Sovereignty*** When the voters go to the polls in this country, they reaffirm the principle of popular sovereignty. When they vote, they choose those public officeholders who will represent them in the day-to-day conduct of their government. In short, the people rule, the people are sovereign.

***Federalism*** The voters elect more than half-a-million public officeholders in this country today—at the national, the State, and the local levels. They fill offices from the presidency down to, literally, in some places today, dogcatchers.

***Judicial Review*** The right to vote is protected by the Federal Constitution—and these protections are backed by the power of the courts to strike down any governmental action that interferes with the exercise of that right.

### The Impact on You

*Why vote? Because those whom the voters choose decide dozens upon hundreds of vital public policy questions at every level of government. They decide on matters that range from environmental protection and civil rights to public education, transportation, and communication—and much more. In short, those whom the voters choose have a major impact on your every waking and sleeping moment.*

## Pressed for Time?

### Instruction Plus!

The resources you need to support your instruction of this chapter are conveniently located in a single box. This innovative package provides an instructional advantage in the classroom with its ready-to-use tools in a variety of formats.

- **Magruder's American Government Video Collection**
- **Keep It Current Web-based Activities**
  **Presentation Pro CD-ROM**
- **Section Support Transparencies**
- **Guide to the Essentials**
  **Current Issues**

## Spotlight on Technology

**Take it to the Net**
Offers student-appropriate Internet activities and links that extend core content. Visit us at the Social Studies area. **www.phschool.com**
Be sure to check out this month's **eTeach** online discussion with a Master Government Teacher.

**Keep It Current CD-ROM**
Includes government-related projects by unit. Use it to link to the Prentice Hall School Web site where you will find daily updates.

**Magruder's American Government Video Collection**
Chapter-by-chapter video selections bring key government concepts to life.

**ABC News Civics and Government Videotape Library**
These high-interest stories from ABC News relate to core content.

**Simulations and Data Graphing CD-ROM** Provides interactive federal budget and stock market simulations, and skills practice with statistical data.

**Prentice Hall Presentation Pro CD-ROM** Provides multimedia lecture notes for each chapter.

**ExamView® Test Bank CD-ROM**
Allows you to create, edit, and print out chapter level tests.

**Resource Pro® CD-ROM**
Teaching Resources that offer lesson planning flexibility, test-generation capability, and resource manageability.

**Social Studies Skills Tutor CD-ROM** Provides interactive practice in geographic literacy, critical thinking and reading, visual analysis, and communications.

**Section Support Transparencies**
Illustrates key government concepts through graphs, charts, photos, and cartoons.

**Basic Principles of the Constitution Transparencies**
Illustrates key principles of the Constitution.

**Section Reading Support Transparency System**
Delivers the main idea of each section in the student text through graphic organizers.

# Political Parties

| Section Objectives | Print and Technology Resources |
|---|---|

### 1 Parties and What They Do
*(pp. 116–118)*

1. Define *political party.*
2. Identify the functions of political parties.

**TEKS 3A, 12A, 12C, 21A, 22A, 22B**

- **Unit 2 booklet**
  Guided Reading and Review, p. 2
  Section 1 Quiz, p. 3
- **Lesson Plans booklet** Section 1, p. 26
- **Section Reading Support Transparencies**
- **Political Cartoons booklet** Section 1, p. 18

- **Block Scheduling with Lesson Strategies booklet** p. 21
- **Section Support Transparencies** 21, 120
- **Presentation Pro CD-ROM** Section 1

---

### 2 The Two-Party System
*(pp. 119–124)*

1. Analyze the two-party system in the United States.
2. Compare the party system in the United States with that of other countries.
3. Describe party membership patterns in the United States.

**TEKS 13A, 16A, 17A, 21A, 21B, 21C, 21D, 21F, 22A, 22B, 22C, 22D**

- **Unit 2 booklet**
  Guided Reading and Review, p. 4
  Section 2 Quiz, p. 5
- **Lesson Plans booklet** Section 2, p. 27
- **Political Cartoons booklet** Section 2, p. 19
- **Section Reading Support Transparencies**

- **Block Scheduling with Lesson Strategies booklet** p. 21
- **Government Assessment Rubrics booklet** p. 24
- **Section Support Transparencies** 22, 121
- **Presentation Pro CD-ROM** Section 2

---

### 3 The Two-Party System in American History
*(pp. 126–131)*

1. Understand the origins of political parties in the United States.
2. Analyze the impact of political changes brought about by political parties during four major eras in American political history.

**TEKS 2B, 3B, 12B, 16B, 16C, 21A, 21D, 21E, 22A, 22B, 22C, 22D**

- **Unit 2 booklet**
  Guided Reading and Review, p. 6
  Section 3 Quiz, p. 7
- **Lesson Plans booklet** Section 3, p. 28
- **Political Cartoons booklet** Section 3, p. 20
- **Close Up on Primary Sources booklet**
  Jefferson's First Inaugural Address, p. 34
- **Section Reading Support Transparencies**

- **Close Up on the Supreme Court booklet**
  *Dred Scott* v. *Sandford,* pp. 32–33
- **The Living Constitution booklet** p. 5
- **Section Support Transparencies** 23, 122
- **Presentation Pro CD-ROM** Section 3
- **Social Studies Skills Tutor CD-ROM**

---

### 4 The Minor Parties
*(pp. 132–135)*

1. Identify the types of third parties that have been active in American politics.
2. Evaluate the role of third parties in the United States.

**TEKS 3B, 12A, 12B, 12C, 21A, 21E, 21F, 22A, 22B**

- **Unit 2 booklet**
  Guided Reading and Review, p. 8
  Section 4 Quiz, p. 9
- **Lesson Plans booklet** Section 4, p. 29
- **Political Cartoons booklet** Section 4, p. 21
- **Section Reading Support Transparencies**

- **Close Up on Primary Sources booklet**
  Reforming American Government, p. 7
- **Section Support Transparencies** 24, 123
- **Presentation Pro CD-ROM** Section 4
- **Simulations and Data Graphing CD-ROM**

---

### 5 Party Organization
*(pp. 137–142)*

1. Understand why the major parties have a decentralized structure.
2. Describe the national party machinery and how parties are organized at the State and local levels.
3. Identify the three components of the parties.
4. Examine the future of the major parties.

**TEKS 12D, 16A, 21A, 21C, 21D, 21E, 21F**

- **Unit 2 booklet**
  Guided Reading and Review, p. 10
  Section 5 Quiz, p. 11
  Skills for Life Activity, p. 12
- **Lesson Plans booklet** Section 5, p. 30
- **Political Cartoons booklet** Section 5, p. 22
- **Block Scheduling with Lesson Strategies booklet** p. 21
- **Close Up on the Supreme Court booklet**
  *Communist Party of Indiana* v. *Whitcomb,* p. 6

- **Section Reading Support Transparencies**
- **Government Assessment Rubrics booklet** p. 20
- **The Basic Principles of the Constitution Posters**
- **Basic Principles of the Constitution Transparencies** 44
- **Section Support Transparencies** 25, 124
- **Presentation Pro CD-ROM** Section 5

# Block Scheduling Strategies

The *Magruder's American Government* program addresses block-scheduling strategies in a variety of ways. For easy reference, side-column activities that fit a block format are marked ■ **Block Strategy.** Each section also contains a **Block Scheduling Strategies** box describing at least two block-format activities that address and extend core content from the section. The **Block Scheduling with Lesson Strategies booklet** found in the Teaching Resources contains additional block-scheduling activities for each chapter.

 *Take It to the Net*

Visit the Social Studies area at the Prentice Hall School Web site. Once there, you can find additional links, current events connections, and activities to enrich chapter content for *Magruder's American Government,* as well as a Self-Test for students. Be sure to check out this month's **eTeach** online discussion with a Master Teacher.

## www.phschool.com

## Pressed for Time?

If you are running short on time to cover this chapter, consider one of the following options:
- Use the **Presentation Pro CD-ROM** to create an outline for this chapter.
- Use one of the **Pressed for Time** activities found on p. 115.
- Use the Section Summaries for Chapter 5, from **Guide to the Essentials of American Government (English and Spanish).**

 **Video Connections**

Prentice Hall offers two video programs to reinforce and extend chapter content. Show students *The Blessings of Liberty* from the **ABC News Civics and Government Videotape Library** and *Prayer in Schools: A Nationwide Debate* from the **Magruder's American Government Video Collection.**

## Assessment Options
- Section Quizzes, **Unit 2 booklet,** pp. 3, 5, 7, 9, 11
- Chapter 5 Assessment, pp. 144–145
- **Guide to the Essentials of American Government,** Chapter 5 Test, p. 37

### Core Assessment
Chapter 5 Test, Chapter Tests booklet
ExamView® Test Bank CD-ROM Chapter 5
Government Assessment Rubrics

### Standardized Test Preparation

**Diagnose and Prescribe**
Diagnostic Tests for High School
Social Studies Skills

**Review and Reteach**
Review Book for Government

**Practice and Assess**
Test-Taking Strategies With
    Transparencies for High School
Test Prep Book for Government

# Chapter 5 Teacher's Edition Index

# Political Parties

### Introducing the Chapter

In this chapter students will learn about the political parties—the functions they perform, how they are structured, and how they have shaped the evolution of American government and politics.

## Make It Relevant

### ★ You Can Make a Difference

Both of the major political parties have various youth programs designed to introduce young people to the political process (and gain future members). Organize four small groups of students to investigate such programs. Have one group focus on the Republican Party, another group focus on the Democratic Party, a third group focus on a third party of their choice, and a fourth group contact a non-partisan group, such as the League of Women Voters. The groups should report what they learn about various youth-involvement programs to the class.

**Service Learning**

## CONSTITUTIONAL PRINCIPLES

Emphasize the following basic principles as students read Chapter 5. Have the class respond to the questions, and then ask volunteers to explain which single principle they think the Framers might have used to explain the rise of political parties.

**Separation of Powers** How do political parties provide a bridge between the executive and legislative branches of government?

**Federalism** In what ways do political parties function differently at the national and State levels?

# Political Parties

*"A party of order or stability, and a party of progress or reform, are both necessary elements of a healthy state of political life. "*
—John Stuart Mill (1859)

John Stuart Mill, a British philosopher, noted the benefits of two competing political parties. In this country, the balance of power has historically switched between two broad-based parties. Our major parties choose candidates and play important roles in government. Minor parties have challenged, but never really changed, this two-party system.

◆ A political party holds its national convention.

### CLOSE UP FOUNDATION *Corner*

The following resources are available only from the Close Up Foundation to support the concepts discussed in Chapter 5 "Political Parties":
◆ *Perspectives: Readings on Contemporary American Government*
◆ *We the People: The President and the Constitution*

To keep up-to-date on Close Up news and activities, visit Close Up Online at

**www.closeup.org**

Close Up Foundation
44 Canal Center Plaza
Alexandria, VA 22314-1592
800-765-3131

## You Can Make a Difference

**ONE GOOD WAY** to study party politics is to work in a campaign. Early in the 2000 presidential race, some college students learned about politics first hand in the New Hampshire primary. Political science majors from Quinnipiac College spent their winter break as volunteers in the Bush, Bradley, Gore, or McCain campaigns. They canvassed voters, helped with mailings, held up signs, and met candidates. "I like to have the hands-on kind of learning," said Jessica Cieslak about the Bradley campaign. Sally Roden, addressing postcards for Governor Bush, commented, "It seems like we're contributing small pieces to a greater puzzle."

### Keep It Current

Items marked with this logo are periodically updated on the Internet. Keep up-to-date with what's in the news. To get current information about the political parties, go to **www.phschool.com**

### SECTION 1

#### Parties and What They Do (pp. 116–118)

★ The primary purpose of the two major American political parties is to control government through winning election to public office.
★ Political parties nominate candidates, rally their supporters, participate in government, act as a "bonding agent" for their own officeholders, and act as a watchdog over the other party.

### SECTION 2

#### The Two-Party System (pp. 119–124)

★ The two-party system is a product of our history and tradition, the electoral system, and the American ideological consensus.
★ Multiparty systems provide more choice for the electorate but a less stable government. In one-party systems only the ruling party can participate in elections.
★ While the two major parties are broadly based, each party does tend to attract certain segments of the electorate.

### SECTION 3

#### The Two-Party System in American History (pp. 126–131)

★ The first American parties originated in the battle over ratifying the Constitution.
★ There have been three eras of single-party domination in U.S. history from 1800–1968.
★ An era of divided government—not dominated by either political party—began in 1968 and continues to this day.

### SECTION 4

#### The Minor Parties (pp. 132–135)

★ Minor parties in the United States include ideological parties, single-issue parties, economic protest parties, and splinter parties.
★ Even though they do not win national elections, minor parties play an important role as critics and innovators.
★ Strong third-party candidacies can influence elections.

### SECTION 5

#### Party Organization (pp. 137–142)

★ The major parties have a decentralized structure because of federalism and the sometimes divisive nominating process.
★ At the national level, the four basic elements of both major parties are the national convention, the national committee, the national chairperson, and the congressional campaign committee.
★ At the State level, the party is organized around a State central committee headed by a State chairperson, while local organizations vary widely.
★ Party structure can also be viewed as made up of the party organization, or machinery; the people who usually vote the party ticket; and the party's officeholders.
★ Parties are currently in decline: fewer people identify themselves as major party members, and many people vote a split ticket.

### Keep It Current

#### Internet Update

Use the Prentice Hall School Web site and the Keep It Current CD-ROM to find quick content updates.

 Visit **www.phschool.com** for current events articles that are linked to Chapter 5. Critical thinking questions are included.

**Keep It Current CD-ROM** includes government-related projects by unit. Students complete each project using current information that they obtain by linking to the Prentice Hall School Web site from the CD-ROM.

## Pressed for Time?

### To Omit the Chapter

If you wish to skip Chapter 5, ask students to read the Chapter in Brief and assign the Guide to the Essentials before continuing to another chapter. You may also want to assign the Chapter 5 Test in the Chapter Test booklet. Then specific portions of Chapter 5 may be assigned to students needing reinforcement of key terms and concepts.

### To Preview the Chapter

To introduce students to key terms and concepts in each section, have them read the Chapter in Brief. You may also assign the Reading Strategy activities on pp. 117, 120, 127, 133, and 138 of this book.

### To Review the Chapter

When students have completed Chapter 5, you might want to assign the Guide to the Essentials or the Guided Reading and Review worksheets on pp. 2, 4, 6, 8, and 10 of the Unit 2 booklet.

### To Cover the Chapter Quickly

To cover the material in Chapter 5 quickly, use the following activity.

**Focus** Begin by asking students for the names of the two major American political parties. Write them on the board, then ask for names of any minor parties students can think of. Add those names to the board.

**Instruct** Explain that almost from the nation's beginnings, the United States has had a two-party system. Ask students for historical precedents to that system, such as the debate over the ratification of the Constitution. Then discuss characteristics of two-party systems. Finally, describe the role of minor parties, encouraging students to explain how they impact the two-party system.

**Close/Reteach** Discuss how parties are structured at the national and State levels. Ask: How has the two-party system encouraged a "divided government?"

■ **Block Strategy (Average)**

# **·1·** **Parties and What They Do**

**Objectives** You may wish to call students' attention to the objectives in the Section Preview. The objectives are reflected in the main headings of the section.

**Bellringer** Ask students whether they have ever ridden in a car with someone who was such a bad driver that they wanted to stop the car and take over the driving. Explain that in this section, they will learn about how the political party that is out of office can't wait to take control of government from the party that is in.

**Vocabulary Builder** Ask students to determine what word or word part links all four terms in the Political Dictionary. Have a volunteer look up *party* and *partisan* in a dictionary to compare their government-related definitions.

## Section Preview

### OBJECTIVES

1. **Define** *political party*.
2. **Identify** the functions of political parties.

### WHY IT MATTERS

Political parties are essential to democratic government. In the United States, political parties have shaped the way the government works. Today, the major parties perform several important functions without which our government could not function.

### POLITICAL DICTIONARY

★ **political party**
★ **major parties**
★ **partisanship**
★ **party in power**

---

**"W**inning isn't everything; it's the only thing." So said legendary football coach Vince Lombardi. Lombardi was talking about teams in the National Football League. His words, however, could also be used to describe the Republican and Democratic parties. They, too, are in the business of competing and winning.

## What Is a Political Party?

A **political party** is a group of persons who seek to control government through the winning of elections and the holding of public office. This definition of a political party is broad enough to fit any political party. It certainly describes the two **major parties** in American politics, the Republican and the Democratic parties.

Another, more specific definition can be used to describe most political parties, both here and abroad. That is, a political party is a group of persons, joined together on the basis of common principles, who seek to control government in order to affect certain public policies and programs.

This definition, with its emphasis on principles and public policy positions, will not fit the two major American parties, however. The Republican and Democratic parties are not primarily principle- or issue-oriented. They are, instead, election-oriented.

## Political Party Functions

It is clear from American history, as well as from the histories of other peoples, that political parties are essential to democratic government. Parties are the major mechanisms behind the development of broad policy and leadership choices; they are the medium through which those options are presented to the people.

Political parties are a vital link between the people and their government; that is, between the governed and those who govern. Many observers argue that political parties are the principal means by which the will of the people is made known to government and by which government is held accountable to the people.

Parties serve the democratic ideal in another important way. They work to blunt conflict; they are "power brokers." Political parties bring conflicting groups together. They modify and encourage compromise among the contending views of different interests and groups, and so help to unify, rather than divide, the American people. They soften the impact of extremists at both ends of the political spectrum.

Again, political parties are indispensable to American government. This fact is underscored by the major functions they perform.

▲ Bumper stickers reveal party loyalty.

---

## Pressed for Time?

### Quick Lesson Plan

**1. Focus** Tell students that the main purpose of the major political parties is to control government by winning election to public office. Ask students to discuss why parties want to control government.

**2. Instruct** Have students name the main function of a political party. Ask why nominating candidates is so important, and then discuss the other functions of political parties. Have students consider whether these functions are the same for issues-oriented and election-oriented parties.

**3. Close/Reteach** Remind students that political parties serve the democratic ideal by linking people with government and by blunting conflict. Have students write a Help Wanted ad seeking to "hire" a political party. Ads should include what the functions of that party will be.

## Point–of–Use Resources

📁 **Block Scheduling with Lesson Strategies** Activities for Chapter 5 appear on p. 21.

---

## 🔲 Block Scheduling Strategies

Consider these suggestions to manage extended class time:

■ Have small groups of students work together to create posters that describe a political party. Posters should describe the five functions of political parties, a definition of the party, and at least two illustrations. Tell students that posters will be used in elementary school classrooms and should be age-appropriate.

■ Write this sentence from the text on the board: "...both parties want to win elections, and that consideration has much to do with the stands they take on most issues." Ask: Can a party that only wants to win an election be true to its ideals and philosophy? Why or why not? Have students write a 3–5 sentence response, taking a clear yes or no position. Then, conduct a class debate on this issue.

## Nominating Candidates

The major function of a political party is to nominate, or name, candidates for public office. That is, the parties select candidates and then present them to the voters. Then the parties work to help their candidates win elections.

To have a functioning democracy, there must be a procedure for finding (recruiting and choosing) candidates for office. There must also be a mechanism for gathering support (votes) for these candidates. Parties are the best device yet found to do those jobs.

The nominating function is almost exclusively a party function in the United States.[1] It is the one activity that most clearly sets political parties apart from other groups operating in politics.

## Informing and Activating Supporters

Parties inform the people, and inspire and activate their interest and participation in public affairs. Other groups also perform this function—in particular, the news media and interest groups.

Parties try to inform and inspire voters in several ways. Primarily, they campaign for their candidates, take stands on issues, and criticize the candidates and the positions of their opponents.

Each party tries to inform the people as it thinks they should be informed—to its own advantage. For example, a party selects information in order to present its own positions and candidates in the best possible light. It conducts this "educational" process through pamphlets, signs, buttons, and stickers; with advertisements in newspapers and magazines and on radio, television, and the Internet; in speeches, rallies, and conventions; and in many other ways.

Remember, both parties want to win elections, and that consideration has much to do with the stands they take on most issues. Both parties try to shape positions that will attract as many voters as possible—and that will, at the same time, offend as few voters as possible.

## The Bonding Agent Function

A bond is an insurance agreement protecting a person or a business against loss caused by a third party. In a sense, a political party acts as a

---

[1]The exceptions are in nonpartisan elections and in those rare instances in which an independent candidate enters a partisan contest. Nominations are covered at length in Chapter 7.

▲ *Campaign Fever* Without the support of thousands of enthusiastic campaign workers, political parties would fade away. Young volunteers represent the future of their parties.

"bonding agent," to ensure the good performance of its candidates and officeholders. In choosing its candidates, the party tries to make sure that they are men and women who are both qualified and of good character, or, at least, that their candidates are not unqualified and have no serious blemishes on their records.

The party also prompts its successful candidates to perform well in office. The democratic process imposes this bonding agent function on a party, whether the party really wants to perform it or not. If it fails to assume this responsibility, both the party and its candidates may suffer the consequences in future elections.

## Governing

In several respects, government in the United States is government by party. For example, public officeholders—those who govern—are regularly chosen on the basis of party. Congress and the State legislatures are organized on party lines, and they conduct much of their business based on **partisanship.** This means that firm allegiance to a political party is the basis for government action. In addition, most appointments to executive offices, at both the federal and State levels, are made with an eye to party considerations.

## Reading Strategy

### Organizing Information/ Graphic Organizer

Have students create a web diagram with *Political Parties* in the center circle. As they read, students should complete the web by defining political parties in the center circle and noting each function in an outer circle. They should use additional circles to add details.

### ACTIVITY

### Heterogeneous Groups

**Enrichment** Remind students that informing and activating supporters is one of the main functions of political parties. Discuss a current issue (i.e. local curfews for minors or mandatory State comprehension exams for high school seniors) that is of interest or concern for students. Divide the class into small groups. Have groups take different sides of the issue. Ask groups to create a slogan, bumper sticker, pamphlet, or other type of advertisement that presents their side of the issue most favorably. Each group should elect a spokesperson to present their ad to the class.

**(Basic)**

## Point-of-Use Resources

📁 **Guided Reading and Review** Unit 2 booklet, p. 2 provides students with practice identifying the main ideas and key terms of this section.

📁 **Lesson Plans** For lesson planning suggestions, see p. 26 of the Lesson Plans booklet.

📁 **Political Cartoons** See p. 18 of the Political Cartoons booklet for a cartoon relevant to this section.

📖 **Section Support Transparencies** Transparency 21, *Visual Learning;* Transparency 120, *Political Cartoon*

## Point-of-Use Resources

**Guide to the Essentials** Chapter 5, Section 1, p. 32 provides support for students who need additional review of section content. Spanish support is available in the Spanish edition of the Guide on p. 25.

**Quiz** Unit 2 booklet, p. 3 includes matching and multiple-choice questions to check students' understanding of Section 1 content.

**Presentation Pro CD-ROM** Quizzes and multiple-choice questions check students' understanding of Section 1 content.

## Answers to . . .

### Section 1 Assessment

**1.** A group of people who seek to control government by winning elections and holding political office.
**2.** Functions include nominating candidates, informing and activating supporters, acting as bonding agents, governing, and acting as watchdogs over the public's business.
**3.** Public officeholders and appointments are chosen based on party allegiance, and parties serve as channels for the legislative and executive branches to work together.
**4. (a)** Answers will vary. **(b)** Answers will vary.
**5.** They encourage compromise among different interests and groups.
**6.** Parties not in power serve as watchdogs over the party in power—they criticize and in so doing, attempt to gain public support.

## Answer to . . .

**Critical Thinking** The nominating candidates function, the informing and activating supporters function, and the governing function.

▲ From left to right: Al Gore accepts the Democratic nomination for President; Rick Lazio, Republican candidate for the Senate, discusses the issues with New York voters; the powerful House Ways and Means Committee holds a hearing. *Critical Thinking What party functions are represented by these three photos?*

In yet another sense, parties provide a basis for the conduct of government. In the complicated separation of powers arrangement, the executive and legislative branches must cooperate with one another if government is to accomplish anything. It is political parties that regularly provide the channels through which these two branches are able to work together.

Political parties have played a significant role in the process of constitutional change through informal procedures. Consider this important example: The Constitution's cumbersome system for electing the President works principally because political parties reshaped it in its early years and have made it work ever since.

### Acting as Watchdog

Parties act as watchdogs over the conduct of the public's business. This is particularly true of the party out of power. It plays this role as it criticizes the policies and behavior of the **party in power.**

In American politics the party in power is the party that controls the executive branch of government—the presidency at the national level or the governorship at the State level.

In effect, the party out of power attempts to convince the voters that they should "throw the rascals out," that the "outs" should become the "ins" and the "ins" the "outs." The scrutiny and criticism by the "out" party tends to make the "rascals" more careful of their public charge and more responsive to the wishes and concerns of the people. In short, the party out of power plays the important role of "the loyal opposition"—opposed to the party in power but loyal to the people and the nation.

## Section 1 Assessment

**Key Terms and Main Ideas**

1. What is a **political party?**
2. Explain two functions of political parties.
3. In what ways is American government conducted on the basis of **partisanship?**
4. **(a)** At this time, which is the **party in power** in your State? **(b)** In the nation?

**Critical Thinking**

5. **Analyzing Information** In what ways do political parties tend to unify, rather than divide, the American people?

6. **Drawing Conclusions** The party out of power serves an important function in American government. Explain that function.

 **Take It to the Net**

7. Locate both the Republican and Democratic party Web sites. Write a summary showing how the sites reflect the two parties' similarities and differences. Use the links provided in the Social Studies area at the following Web site for help in completing this activity. **www.phschool.com**

**Take It to the Net**

**7.** Direct students to the Social Studies area at the Prentice Hall School Web site. The *Magruder's American Government* companion Web site includes the directions and links needed to complete the activity. It also provides a printable Internet activity worksheet with scoring rubrics for assessment. Summaries should provide accurate comparisons.

# 2 The Two-Party System

## Section Preview

### OBJECTIVES

1. **Analyze** the two-party system in the United States.
2. **Compare** the party system in the United States with that of other countries.
3. **Describe** party membership patterns in the United States.

### WHY IT MATTERS

The two-party system in the United States is a product of historical forces, our electoral system, and the ideological consensus of the American people. It provides more political stability than a multiparty system and more choice than a one-party system.

### POLITICAL DICTIONARY

★ minor party
★ two-party system
★ single-member district
★ plurality
★ bipartisan
★ pluralistic society
★ consensus
★ multiparty
★ coalition
★ one-party system

**Objectives** You may wish to call students' attention to the objectives in the Section Preview. The objectives are reflected in the main headings of the section.

**Bellringer** Ask students to explain the saying "Two's company, three's a crowd." Tell them that in this section, they will learn about how that saying can be applied to the American party system.

**Vocabulary Builder** Ask students how most of the terms in the Political Dictionary are similar. (They contain words or word parts that suggest amounts.) Discuss how those words and word parts (*two, single, plural, bi-, multi-, one*) affect the meaning of these government terms. Note that even co- and con- suggest a number of people or groups getting together.

Does the name Earl Dodge mean anything to you? Probably not. Yet Mr. Dodge has run for President of the United States five times. He was the presidential candidate of the Prohibition Party in 1984, 1988, 1992, 1996, and again in 2000.

One of the reasons Mr. Dodge is not very well known is that he belongs to a **minor party,** one of the political parties without wide support. The two major parties dominate American politics. That is to say, this country has a **two-party system.** In a typical election, only the Republican or the Democratic Party's candidates have a reasonable chance of winning public office.

## Why a Two-Party System?

On the whole and through most of its history, the United States has been a two-party nation. Still, it is true that in some States, and in many local communities, one of the two major parties may be overwhelmingly dominant. And it is also true that this may remain the case for a long period of time; for example, the Democrats controlled politics in the South for decades. Nevertheless, for the most part, our government has been characterized by two strong major parties.

A number of factors help to explain why America has had and continues to have a two-party system. No one reason, taken alone, offers a wholly satisfactory explanation for the phenomenon. Taken together, however, several reasons do make quite a persuasive answer.

### The Historical Basis

The two-party system is rooted in the beginnings of the nation itself. The Framers of the Constitution were opposed to political parties. As you saw in Chapter 2, the ratification of the Constitution saw the birth of America's first two parties: the Federalists, led by Alexander Hamilton, and the Anti-Federalists, who followed Thomas Jefferson. In short, the American party system *began* as a two-party system.

The Framers hoped to create a unified country; they sought to bring order out of

▶ The symbols of the political parties turn up in many forms—especially in an election year.

### Pressed for Time?

#### Quick Lesson Plan

1. **Focus** Tell students that the two-party system is an established fact of American political life. Ask students to discuss what they know about why the United States has a two-party system.
2. **Instruct** Ask students how the two-party system developed in the United States. Discuss why the two-party system continues to be strong today. Extend the discussion to the advantages and disadvantages of multiparty and one-party systems.
3. **Close/Reteach** Remind students that they are free to join any political party. Ask: Are you likely to join one of the two major parties? Why or why not?

## ⊡ Block Scheduling Strategies

Consider these suggestions to manage extended class time:

■ Have students list details about each of the four reasons discussed in the section that the U.S. has a two-party system. Then have each student choose which reason they believe is the most compelling for keeping this system, and which is the least compelling for keeping it. Ask students to share their opinions with the class.

■ Point out to students that while the United States has a two-party system, many democracies around the world have multiparty systems. (Refer students to Chapter 22 for examples.) Ask student groups to consider how political life in the United States might be different with a multiparty system. Have each group create a profile of a multiparty system. What would be the benefits and drawbacks to such a system?

**119**

## Reading Strategy

### Self-Questioning

Ask students to stop at each heading as they read the section. Have them turn each heading into a question that begins with *What, How,* or *Why* and then read to answer that question.

## Point-of-Use Resources

**Guided Reading and Review** Unit 2 booklet, p. 4 provides students with practice identifying the main ideas and key terms of this section.

**Lesson Plans** For lesson planning suggestions, see p. 27 of the Lesson Plans booklet.

**Political Cartoons** See p. 19 of the Political Cartoons booklet for a cartoon relevant to this section.

**Section Support Transparencies** Transparency 22, *Visual Learning;* Transparency 121, *Political Cartoon*

## *Voices* on Government

**Mary Matalin** was a campaign advisor to George W. Bush and Dick Cheney in 2000. After the Bush administration took office, she was made assistant to the President and counselor on matters of politics and communication to Vice President Cheney. Here she comments on how political campaigns look from the inside:

❝ *Politics is about winning. . . . Participating in a presidential campaign full-time, as a professional, is very emotional and very draining. You don't want to put that much effort into a race unless you have a real chance. . . . In the culture of campaigns it's not ideological. Most of us have a philosophical grounding—we're working for Republicans only—but in terms of issues the differences between candidates are often pretty small.* ❞

### Evaluating the Quotation

*How does Matalin's view of political campaigns fit in with what you have read about the two major parties?*

the chaos of the Critical Period of the 1780s. To most of the Framers, parties were "factions," and therefore agents of divisiveness and disunity. George Washington reflected this view when, in his Farewell Address in 1796, he warned the new nation against "the baneful effects of the spirit of party."

In this light, it is hardly surprising that the Constitution made no provision for political parties. The Framers could not foresee the ways in which the governmental system they set up would develop. Thus, they could not possibly know that two major parties would emerge as prime instruments of government in the United States. Nor could they know that those two major parties would tend to be moderate, to choose middle-of-the-road positions, and so help to unify rather than divide the nation.

### The Force of Tradition

Once established, human institutions are likely to become self-perpetuating. So it has been with the two-party system. The very fact that the nation began with a two-party system has been a leading reason for the retention of a two-party system. Over time, it has become an increasingly important, self-reinforcing reason.

The point can be made this way: Most Americans accept the idea of a two-party system simply because there has always been one. This inbred support for the arrangement is a principal reason why challenges to the system—by minor parties, for example—have made so little headway. In other words, America has a two-party system *because* America has a two-party system.

### The Electoral System

Several features of the American electoral system tend to promote the existence of but two major parties. That is to say, the basic shape, and many of the details, of the election process work in that direction.

The prevalence of **single-member districts** is one of the most important of these features. Nearly all of the elections held in this country—from the presidential contest on down to those at the local levels—are single-member district elections. That is, they are contests in which only one candidate is elected to each office on the ballot. In these winner-take-all elections, the winning candidate is the one who receives a **plurality,** or the largest number of votes cast for the office. Note that a plurality need not be a majority, which is more than half of all votes cast.

The single-member district pattern works to discourage minor parties. Because only one winner can come out of each contest, voters usually face only two viable choices: They can vote for the candidate of the party holding the office, or they can vote for the candidate of the party with the best chance of replacing the current officeholder. In short, most voters think of a vote for a minor party candidate as a "wasted vote."

Another important aspect of the electoral system works to the same end. Much of American election law is purposely written to discourage non-major party candidates.[2] Republicans and Democrats regularly act in a **bipartisan** way in

---

[2]Nearly all election law in this country is State, not federal, law—a point discussed at length in the next two chapters. But, here, note this very important point: Nearly all of the more than 7,600 State legislators—nearly all of those persons who make State law—are either Democrats or Republicans. Only a handful of minor party members or independents now sit, or have ever sat, in State legislatures.

## Organizing Information

To make sure students understand the main points of this section, you may wish to use the double web graphic organizer to the right.

Tell students that a double web graphic organizer can be used to compare and contrast two topics. Have students use the double web to compare two-party systems with multiparty systems.

**Teaching Tip** A template for this graphic organizer can be found in the Section Support Transparencies, Transparency 2.

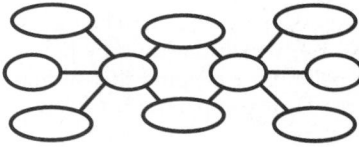

### Answer to . . .

**Evaluating the Quotation** She emphasizes that while the two major parties are not radically different, they take their competition seriously.

this matter. That is, the two major parties find common ground and work together here.

They deliberately shape election laws to preserve, protect, and defend the two major parties and the two-party system, and thus to frustrate the minor parties. In most States it is far more difficult for minor parties and independent groups to get their candidates listed on the ballot than for the major parties to do so.

The 2000 presidential election offered a striking illustration of the point. Both George W. Bush and Al Gore were on the ballots of all 50 States and the District of Columbia. None of the several other serious presidential hopefuls made the ballot everywhere in 2000.

To this point, non-major party candidates have made it to the ballot everywhere in only seven presidential elections. The Socialist Party's Eugene V. Debs was the first to do so, in 1912. The Socialist candidate in 1916, Allan L. Benson, also appeared on the ballots of all of the then 48 States. In 1980 Ed Clark, the Libertarian nominee, and independent John Anderson, and in 1988 Lenora Fulani of the New Alliance Party made the ballots of all 50 States and the District of Columbia. So, too, did Libertarian Andre Marrou and independent Ross Perot in 1992. Every ballot contained the names of Libertarian Harry Browne and the Reform Party's Ross Perot in 1996.

In 2000 Harry Browne of the Libertarian Party was on the ballot in 49 States and the District of Columbia. The Reform Party's Pat Buchanan made it in 49 States, Ralph Nader of the Green Party in 43 States and the District of Columbia, and the Constitution Party's Howard Phillips in 41 States. But most minor party candidates suffered their usual fate: they managed to gain the ballot in only a handful of States.

### The American Ideological Consensus

Americans are, on the whole, an ideologically homogeneous people. That is, over time, the American people have shared many of the same ideals, the same basic principles, and the same patterns of belief.

This is not to say that Americans are all alike. Clearly, this is not the case. The United States is a **pluralistic society**—one consisting of several distinct cultures and groups. Increasingly, the members of various ethnic, racial, religious, and other

"And I promise to always be loyal to my party, even if I have to change parties to do it!"

*Interpreting Political Cartoons* **What does the cartoon imply about what parties—and candidates—stand for?**

social groups compete for and share in the exercise of political power in this country. Still, there is a broad **consensus**—a general agreement among various groups—on fundamental matters.

Even given this overall consensus, it is certainly not true that Americans always agree with one another in all matters. Far from it. The nation has been deeply divided at times: during the Civil War and in the years of the Great Depression, for example, and over such critical issues as racial discrimination, the war in Vietnam, and abortion.

On the other hand, the nation has not been regularly plagued by sharp political divisions.

▲ Colorado Senator Ben Nighthorse Campbell was elected as a Democrat in 1992. He became a Republican in 1995, and was easily reelected in 1998. *Critical Thinking* **What might cause a politician to switch parties?**

## Extended Class Periods

**Time** 90 minutes.

**Purpose** Hold a classroom debate over the issue of having a two-party system of politics versus having a multiparty system.

**Grouping** Divide the class in half. Each half will take one side of the issue.

**Activity** Have teams consider topics such as voter turnout, public involvement in politics, tradition, stability, and diverse representation. Give each side a set amount of time to speak, as well as a set amount of time for rebuttal.

**Roles** Discussion leader, recorder, idea generators, spokesperson, timekeeper.

**Close** Appoint a group of students to act as a jury to decide which side made the best arguments for its case.

◼ **Block Strategy**
**(Average)**

## Point-of-Use Resources

▢ **Government Assessment Rubrics** Oral Presentation, p. 24

▢ **Block Scheduling with Lesson Strategies** Additional activities for Chapter 5 appear on p. 21.

▲ *Multiparty Government* German Chancellor Gerhard Schroeder (front row, center) was elected in 1998. With only 40.9 percent of the seats in the Assembly, Schroeder's Social Democratic Party (SPD) formed a coalition government with a smaller party, Alliance 90/The Greens.

The United States has been free of long-standing, bitter disputes based on such factors as economic class, social status, religious beliefs, or national origin.

Those conditions that could produce several strong rival parties simply do not exist in this country. In this way, the United States differs from most other democracies. In short, the realities of American society and politics simply do not permit more than two major parties.

This ideological consensus has had another very important impact on American parties. It has given the nation two major parties that look very much alike. Both tend to be moderate. Both are built on compromise and regularly try to occupy "the middle of the road." Both parties seek the same prize: the votes of a majority of the electorate. To do so, they must win over essentially the same people. Inevitably, each party takes policy positions that do not differ a great deal from those of the other major party.

This is not to say that there are no significant differences between the two major parties today. There are. For example, the Democratic Party, and those who usually vote for its candidates, are more likely to support such things as social welfare programs, government regulation of business practices, and efforts to improve the status of minorities. On the other hand, the Republican Party and its adherents are much more likely to favor the play of private market forces in the economy and to argue that the Federal Government should be less extensively involved in social welfare programs.

## Other Political Systems

The two-party system works for the United States, and most Americans accept it as the only viable system. Yet in Europe and elsewhere, the two-party system is not the rule. Some critics argue that the American two-party system should be replaced with a **multiparty** system in which several major and many lesser parties exist, seriously compete for, and actually win public offices. Multiparty systems have long been a feature of most European democracies, and they are now found in many other democratic societies elsewhere in the world.

In the typical multiparty system, each of the various parties is based on a particular interest, such as economic class, religious belief, sectional attachment, or political ideology. Those who favor such an arrangement for this country say that it would provide for a broader representation of the electorate and be more responsive to the will of the people. They claim that a multiparty system would give voters a much more meaningful choice among candidates and policy alternatives than the present two-party system does.

Clearly, multiparty systems do tend to produce a broader, more diverse representation of the electorate. At the same time, that strength is also a major weakness of a multiparty system because it often leads to instability in government. One party is often unable to win the support of a majority of the voters. As a result, the power to govern must be shared by a number of parties, in a **coalition.** A coalition is a temporary alliance of several groups who come together to form a working majority and so to control a government.

Several of the multiparty nations of Western Europe have long been plagued by governmental crises. They have experienced frequent changes in party control as coalitions shift and dissolve. Italy furnishes an almost nightmarish example: It has had a new government on the average of once every nine months ever since the end of World War II.

Historically, the American people have shunned a multiparty approach to politics. Two of the factors mentioned above—single-member districts and the American ideological consensus—seem to make the multiparty approach impossible in the United States.

## One-Party Systems

In nearly all dictatorships today, only one political party is allowed. That party is the party of the ruling clique. For all practical purposes, it is quite accurate to say that in those circumstances the resulting **one-party system** is really a "no-party" system.

In quite another sense, this country has had several States and many local areas that can be described in one-party terms. Until the late 1950s, the Democrats dominated the politics of the South. The Republican Party was almost always the winner in New England and in the upper Midwest.

Effective two-party competition has spread fairly rapidly in the past 30 years or so. Democrats have won many offices in every northern State. Republican candidates have become more and more successful throughout the once "Solid South." Nevertheless, about a third of the States can still be said to have a modified one-party system. That is, one of the major parties regularly wins most elections in those States. Also, while most States may have vigorous two-party competition at the Statewide level, within most of them are many areas dominated by a single party.

## Party Membership Patterns

Membership in a party is purely voluntary. A person is a Republican or a Democrat, or belongs to a minor party, or is an independent—belonging to no organized party—because that is what he or she chooses to be.[3]

Remember, the two major parties are broadly based. In order to gain more votes than their opponents, they must attract as much support as they possibly can. Each party has always been composed, in greater or lesser degree, of a cross section of the nation's population. Each is made up of Protestants, Catholics, and Jews; whites, African Americans, Latinos, and other minorities; professionals, farmers, and union members. Each party includes the young, the middle-aged,

▲ Dictator Joseph Stalin, who was both leader of the Communist Party and premier of the Soviet Union, ruthlessly crushed all political opposition. *Critical Thinking Why might silencing other political points of view be a disadvantage to a government?*

and the elderly; city-dwellers, suburbanites, and rural residents among its members.

It is true that the members of certain segments of the electorate tend to be aligned more solidly with one or the other of the major parties, at least for a time. Thus, in recent decades, African Americans, Catholics and Jews, and union members have voted more often for Democrats. In the same way, white males, Protestants, and the business community have been inclined to back the GOP.[4] Yet, never have all members of any group tied themselves permanently to either party.

Individuals identify themselves with a party for many reasons. Family is almost certainly the most important among them. Studies show that nearly two out of every three Americans follow the party allegiance of their parents.

---

[3]In most States a person must declare a preference for a particular party in order to vote in that party's primary election. That declaration is usually made as a part of the voter registration process, and it is often said to make one "a registered Republican (or Democrat)." The requirement is only a procedural one, however, and wholly a matter of individual choice.

[4]GOP is common shorthand for the Republican Party. The initials stand for Grand Old Party, a nickname acquired in the latter part of the 19th century. The nickname may owe its origins to British politics. Prime Minister William Gladstone was dubbed "the Grand Old Man," often abbreviated "GOM," by the English press in 1882. Soon after, "GOP" appeared in headlines in the *New York Tribune,* the *Boston Post,* and other American papers.

## Point-of-Use Resources

 **Guide to the Essentials** Chapter 5, Section 2, p. 33 provides support for students who need additional review of section content. Spanish support is available in the Spanish edition of the Guide on p. 26.

**Quiz** Unit 2 booklet, p. 5 includes matching and multiple-choice questions to check students' understanding of Section 2 content.

**Presentation Pro CD-ROM** Quizzes and multiple-choice questions check students' understanding of Section 2 content.

## Answers to . . .

### Section 2 Assessment

**1.** Historical precedents, tradition, an electoral system that promotes dominance by two major parties, and ideological consensus.
**2.** The U.S. is pluralistic because it has several distinct cultures and groups, but Americans have reached consensus on many matters, for example, having a two-party system.
**3. (a)** A multiparty system has several major and minor parties that all compete for public office. **(b)** Some people favor it because it provides a broader representation of the electorate and gives voters more choices.
**4.** Factors include family tradition, significant political or societal events, economic status, age, place of residence, level of education, and occupation.
**5.** That parties and the Americans supporting them have reached consensus on maintaining a strong two-party system.
**6.** Ads will vary, but should include the distinguishing factors discussed in the text.

## Answer to . . .

**Interpreting Tables** The Prohibition National Committee.

---

## Political Party Resources

### MAJOR POLITICAL PARTIES

**Republican Party**
310 First St. SE, Washington, DC 20003
http://www.rnc.org

**Democratic Party**
430 So. Capitol St. SE, Washington, DC 20003
http://www.democrats.org

### OTHER MAJOR POLITICAL ORGANIZATIONS

**The Libertarian Party** (Founded 1971)
2600 Virginia Ave., N.W., Washington, DC 20037  http://www.lp.org
Stresses individual liberty; opposes taxes, foreign involvements, government intrusion into private lives.

**The Communist Party USA** (Founded 1919)
235 West 23rd St., New York, NY 10011  http://www.cpusa.org
Terms itself "the Party of the American Working class."  Looks forward to the restructuring of American political and economic systems.

**Prohibition National Committee** (Founded 1869)
P.O. Box 2635, Denver, Colorado 80201  http://www.prohibitionists.org
Advocates a nationwide prohibition of the manufacture, distribution, and sale of alcoholic beverages.

**Green Party USA** (Founded 1972)
P.O. Box 1134, Lawrence, MA 01842  http://www.greens.org
Promotes environmental concerns with the slogan: "We do not inherit the Earth from our parents, we borrow it from our children."

**The Reform Party** (Founded 1995)
9129 E. Shonto Ln., Tucson, AZ 85749  http://www.reformparty.org
Founded by Ross Perot but now conservative party; promotes Christian beliefs, opposes immigration, free trade.

**The Socialist Labor Party** (Founded 1891)
(In Minnesota: Industrial Government Party)
P.O. Box 218, Mountain View, CA 94042  http://www.slp.org
Seeks the peaceful abolition of capitalism, and the social ownership of the means of production and distribution.

**The Constitution Party** (Founded 1992)
23 North Lime St., Lancaster, PA 17602  http://www.constitutionparty.org
Advocates "free pursuance of happiness, not the regulation of it."

**The Natural Law Party** (Founded 1992)
P.O. Box 1900, Fairfield, IA 52556  http://www.natural-law.org
Hopes "to bring national life into harmony with natural law."

*Interpreting Tables* **Which of the minor parties shown in the table has the most specific platform?**

Major events can also have a decided influence on the party affiliation of voters. Of these, the Civil War and the Depression of the 1930s have been the most significant in American political history.

Economic status also influences party choice, although generalizations are quite risky. Historically though, those in higher income groups are more likely to be Republicans, while those with lower incomes tend to be Democrats.

Several other factors also affect both party choice and voting behavior, including age, place of residence, level of education, and work environment. Some of those factors may conflict with one another in the case of a particular individual—and they often do. Therefore, predicting how a person or group will vote in any given election is a risky business, which keeps the pollsters and the analysts busy until the votes are counted.

## Section 2 Assessment

### Key Terms and Main Ideas

**1.** Briefly explain four reasons why the United States has a **two-party system.**
**2.** How do the terms **pluralistic** and **consensus** both apply to American society?
**3. (a)** What is a **multiparty system? (b)** Why do some people favor it for the United States?
**4.** Many factors tend to influence party choice. Name four.

### Critical Thinking

**5. Synthesizing Information** What does the fact that the major parties cooperate to discourage minor parties and yet compete vigorously against each other during elections tell you about party politics in the United States?

**6. Recognizing Ideologies** You are campaigning for one of the two major parties. Create a short political advertisement to appeal to large numbers of voters and to distinguish your party from the other major party.

 **Take It to the Net**

**7.** Survey the polling data on the Gallup Organization's Web site. Which issues do Americans seem to agree on? Which issues divide Americans? Graph the results of one poll that reflects a range of opinions. Then tell where you stand on that issue. Use the links provided in the Social Studies area at the following Web site for help in completing this activity. **www.phschool.com**

---

 **Take It to the Net**

**7.** Direct students to the Social Studies area at the Prentice Hall School Web site. The *Magruder's American Government* companion Web site includes the directions and links needed to complete the activity. It also provides a printable Internet activity worksheet with scoring rubrics for assessment. Graphs should be clearly constructed and accurately present poll data.

# Identifying Political Roots and Attitudes

As a voter, how will you evaluate political parties and candidates and make voting decisions? Will you vote the way your friends are voting? The better way of making voting decisions is to analyze the political traditions that have shaped the candidates' views, and then make a decision based on your own values.

Identifying political traditions will help you understand the shorthand that politicians often use. For instance, if a candidate says she's a "pro-labor Democrat" or a "religious conservative," these labels imply a whole set of beliefs with deep roots in American politics and culture. With no historical frame of reference, you would have difficulty interpreting what these labels really mean and what policies a candidate or party supports.

Whether you're examining your own political roots or someone else's, try these steps:

**1. Learn about political traditions.** You read in this section that American politics has long been dominated by two political parties, Republican and Democrat. A basic knowledge of the origins and history of these parties is necessary in order to understand most political dialogue in this country. (a) What specific policies or goals do many Republicans favor? (b) What do many Democrats favor?

**2. Identify major cultural influences.** Our beliefs can be influenced by several factors: education, occupation, location, ethnic and religious ties, and the types of activities we pursue.

While being careful not to stereotype people, we can often predict the political views of many people based on such cultural factors. For example, in areas where Christian groups are politically active, you might find strong support for prayer in public schools. What political views might you expect to be held by people who (a) like to hunt; (b) have a college degree; (c) are Native American; (d) work in a factory?

**3. Analyze the effects of personal experience.** People and events in our lives can have a powerful effect,

positive or negative, on our political views. During the 2000 presidential campaign, both Texas Governor George W. Bush and Vice President Albert Gore, Jr., said their political careers were inspired by their famous fathers. Arizona Senator John McCain, a former prisoner of war in Vietnam, favored a strong military. Some candidates base their political ideals on their religious beliefs. Have your political views been influenced by your personal experiences? Explain.

### Finding Your Political Roots

1. What is the first political event you can recall? How did you and others around you react to it?

2. If you have politically active family members or friends, to what political party do they belong?

3. If you discuss politics with family or friends, how have they influenced your thinking, if at all?

4. Where do you get information about politics—newspapers, television, the Internet? Are you influenced most by what you read or see or hear?

5. How would you describe your political attitudes? Do you lean toward a particular political party? Are your views mostly liberal, mostly conservative, or a mixture of both? Explain.

### Test for Success

(a) Use the questionnaire above and the steps outlined above to describe how political traditions influenced your political attitudes.
(b) Interview a friend or family member. Write a paragraph summarizing his or her political roots and attitudes.

## Point-of-Use Resources

**Skills for Life Activity** Unit 2 booklet, p. 12 provides an additional skill activity for this chapter.

**Social Studies Skills Tutor CD-ROM** Provides interactive practice in geographic literacy, critical thinking and reading, visual analysis, and communications.

### Identifying Political Roots and Attitudes

**Focus** Hold a discussion analyzing political roots and attitudes in your local area.

**Instruct** Ask students to do an initial brainstorm of some of the factors that influence the political opinions, preferences, and voting patterns in your local area. Then do Steps 1–3 as a class. (Keep in mind that some students may not wish to share information about family beliefs.) Now return to the initial brainstorming list and see if students can add items to the list.

**Close/Reteach** Lead a discussion on how the political roots and attitudes in your local area compare to those at the State and national levels.

### Answers . . .

**1.** Possible answers: **(a)** A shift of power to the State and local levels; reduction of federal taxes and spending; the elimination of some federal programs; opposition to gun control; pro-business policies; a foreign policy that opens overseas markets to U.S. companies; curbs on abortion; environmental policies that take more account of business interests. **(b)** Increased federal spending on social programs such as education; tax breaks and other programs to benefit low-income Americans; a foreign policy that protects U.S. jobs and wages; some limits on gun ownership; abortion rights; strong environmental protections.
**2.** Answers include: **(a)** Opposition to gun control. **(b)** Support for education programs. **(c)** Employment programs on reservations. **(d)** Pro-labor policies.
**3.** Influential factors might include income, ethnicity, health, parents' occupations, membership in clubs and organizations.

### Test for Success

(a) Have students analyze whether their political views generally agree or disagree with the prevailing local attitudes. (b) Encourage students to find an older person to interview, and analyze the effects of age and generation on political views.

**125**

### 3 The Two-Party System in American History

**Objectives** You may wish to call students' attention to the objectives in the Section Preview. The objectives are reflected in the main headings of the section.

**Bellringer** Ask students to name a team that has dominated its sport for a long period of time. Explain that in this section, they will learn about political parties that have dominated national politics for long periods of American history.

**Vocabulary Builder** Point out the terms in the Political Dictionary. Ask students which two terms suggest things that might have helped break up a dominant political party. Tell them that they will learn more about the destructive power of factions and sectionalism as they read the section.

### Pressed for Time?

#### Quick Lesson Plan

**1. Focus** Tell students that throughout much of American history, one of the two major parties has dominated national politics. Ask students to name as many of these political parties as they can and list them on the board in order by when they were founded.

**2. Instruct** Ask students to name the four major eras in the history of the American party system. Discuss which parties dominated the first three eras, how they came to power, why they lost power, and who led each party. Then have students explain why the fourth era has been marked by divided government.

**3. Close/Reteach** Remind students that no political party has dominated both Congress and the presidency in recent years. Have students draw a time line to show the dominant political party and other political parties throughout American history.

## Section Preview

### OBJECTIVES

1. **Understand** the origins of political parties in the United States.
2. **Analyze** the impact of political changes brought about by political parties during four major eras in American political history.

### WHY IT MATTERS

The origins and history of political parties in the United States help explain how the two major parties work today and how they affect American government.

### POLITICAL DICTIONARY

★ **incumbent**
★ **faction**
★ **electorate**
★ **sectionalism**

---

**H**enry Ford, the great auto maker, once said that all history is "bunk." Ford knew a great deal about automobiles and mass production, but he did not know much about history or its importance.

Listen, instead, to Shakespeare: "The past is prologue." Today is the product of yesterday. You are what you are today because of your history. Therefore, the more you know about your past, the better prepared you are for today, and for tomorrow.

Much the same can be said about the two-party system in American politics. The more you know about its past, the better you will understand its workings today.

### The Nation's First Parties

The beginnings of the American two-party system can be traced to the battle over the ratification of the Constitution. The conflicts of the time, centering on the proper form and role of government in the United States, were not stilled by the adoption of the Constitution. Rather, those conflicts were carried over into the early years of the Republic. They led directly to the formation of the nation's first full-blown political parties.

The Federalist Party was the first to appear. It formed around Alexander Hamilton, who served as secretary of the treasury in the new government organized by George Washington. The Federalists were, by and large, the party of "the rich and the well-born." Most of them had supported the Constitution.

Led by Hamilton, the Federalists worked to create a stronger national government. They favored vigorous executive leadership and a set of policies designed to correct the nation's economic ills. The Federalists' program appealed to financial, manufacturing, and commercial interests. To reach their goals, they urged a liberal interpretation of the Constitution.

Thomas Jefferson, the nation's first secretary of state, led the opposition to the Federalists.[5] Jefferson and his followers were more sympathetic to the "common man" than were the Federalists. They favored a very limited role for the new government created by the Constitution. In their view, Congress should dominate that new government, and its policies should help the nation's small shopkeepers, laborers, farmers, and planters. The Jeffersonians insisted on a strict construction of the provisions of the Constitution.

▲ This ticket provided admission to the convention that nominated President Roosevelt for a second term.

---

[5]As you recall, George Washington was opposed to political parties. As President, he named arch foes Hamilton and Jefferson to his new Cabinet to get them to work together—in an unsuccessful attempt to avoid the creation of formally organized and opposing groups.

---

### ⊞ Block Scheduling Strategies

Consider these suggestions to manage extended class time:

■ Write the following pairs of headings on the board: *Republicans in the 1990s, Democrats in the 1990s, Federalists in the 1790s, Anti-Federalists in the 1790s*. Have students compare and contrast the groups by providing details under each heading, using information from the textbook (have them review Chapters 2 and 3 in preparation).

■ Present students with the following two quotes: "I don't belong to an organized political party—I'm a Democrat" (Will Rogers); "There's not a dime's worth of difference about the two parties" (George Wallace). Ask students to infer how these two people felt about the two major parties. Then have them write a letter to either George Wallace or Will Rogers, supporting or refuting their quote.

Jefferson resigned from Washington's Cabinet in 1793 to concentrate on organizing his party. Originally, the new party took the name Anti-Federalist. Later it became known as the Jeffersonian Republicans or the Democratic-Republicans. Finally, by 1828, it became the Democratic Party.

These two parties first clashed in the election of 1796. John Adams, the Federalists' candidate to succeed Washington as President, defeated Jefferson by just three votes in the electoral college. Over the next four years, Jefferson and James Madison worked tirelessly to build the Democratic-Republican Party. Their efforts paid off in the election of 1800. Jefferson defeated the **incumbent,** or current officeholder, President Adams; Jefferson's party also won control of Congress. The Federalists never returned to power.

## American Parties: Four Major Eras

The history of the American party system since 1800 can be divided into four major periods. Through the first three of these periods, one or the other of the two major parties was dominant, regularly holding the presidency and usually both houses of Congress. The nation is now in a fourth period, much of it marked by divided government.

In the first of these periods, from 1800 to 1860, the Democrats won 13 of 15 presidential elections. They lost the office only in the elections of 1840 and 1848. In the second era, from 1860 to 1932, the Republicans won 14 of 18 elections, losing only in 1884, 1892, 1912, and 1916.

The third period, from 1932 to 1968, began with the Democrats' return to power and Franklin Roosevelt's first election to the presidency. The Democrats won seven of the nine presidential elections, losing only in 1952 and 1956. Through the fourth and current period, which began in 1968, the Republicans have won six of nine presidential elections, and they hold the White House today. But the Democrats have controlled both houses of Congress over much of the current period—although they do not do so today.

### The Era of the Democrats, 1800–1860

Thomas Jefferson's election in 1800 marked the beginning of a period of Democratic domination that was to last until the Civil War. As the time line on pages 128–129 shows, the Federalists, soundly defeated in 1800, had disappeared altogether by 1816.

For a time, through the Era of Good Feeling, the Democratic-Republicans were unopposed in national politics. However, by the mid-1820s, they had split into **factions,** or conflicting groups.

*Interpreting Political Cartoons* Political cartoonist Thomas Nast is credited with popularizing the party symbols in his 1874 cartoons for *Harper's Weekly*. At left, the Republican elephant trumpets Democratic Party defeats. At right, the Democratic donkey kicks Lincoln's Secretary of War. **What characteristics of the elephant and the donkey do you think Nast wanted to associate with each party?**

### Preparing for Standardized Tests

Have students read the passages under *The Era of the Democrats, 1800–1860* and then answer the question below.

From the passages, what can you infer was the main reason that Democrats had lost power by the end of this era?

**A** The Whigs were undefeatable.

**B** Because of so many factions, the Democratic Party had become fragmented.

**C** The Civil War caused disunity.

**D** President Jackson was not reelected.

## Reading Strategy
### Predicting

Tell students that historically, a single party has tended to dominate national politics for many years at a time, before a major historical event brings its domination to an abrupt end. Have students predict two major events that ended single-party domination and suggest why the events had this effect. Students should verify their predictions as they read the section.

## Point–of–Use Resources

**Guided Reading and Review** Unit 2 booklet, p. 6 provides students with practice identifying the main ideas and key terms of this section.

**Lesson Plans** For lesson planning suggestions, see p. 28 of the Lesson Plans booklet.

**Political Cartoons** See p. 20 of the Political Cartoons booklet for a cartoon relevant to this section.

**Close Up on Primary Sources** Jefferson's First Inaugural Address (1801), p. 34

**Section Support Transparencies** Transparency 23, *Visual Learning;* Transparency 122, *Political Cartoon*

*Answer to . . .*

**Interpreting Political Cartoons** Answers will vary; students should be able to explain why they chose certain characteristics.

## Heterogeneous Groups

**Enrichment** Separate the class into four groups. Assign each group one of the following time periods: *1800–1860, 1860–1932, 1932–1968,* and *1968–present.* Using historical resources, newspapers, magazines, and any necessary art supplies, have groups create a collage depicting the significant historical events and major contributions of the dominant party during this era. Encourage groups to include the names and years served of Presidents in the dominant political party. Ask for group volunteers to present their collage to the class.

■ **Block Strategy (Basic)**

## Point–of–Use Resources

☐ **Close Up on the Supreme Court** *Dred Scott* v. *Sandford* (1857), pp. 32–33

---

### Four Eras of Political Parties

**1800** Thomas Jefferson is elected President in 1800, ushering in an era of Democratic domination lasting until the Civil War.

**1860** The 1860 election of Abraham Lincoln and the start of the Civil War mark the beginning of 75 years of Republican Party control.

**Era of Democrats 1800–1860**

**Era of Republicans 1860–1932**

| ELECTION YEAR | 1800 1804 1808 1812 1816 1820 1824 1828 1832 1836 1840 1844 1848 1852 1856 1860 1864 1868 1872 1876 1880 1884 1888 |

PARTY WINNING THE PRESIDENCY

**1828** The Democratic-Republican Party is by now generally known as the Democratic Party.

**1854** The Republican Party is formed in 1854, attracting many former Whigs and antislavery Democrats. They elect their first President in 1860.

*Interpreting Time Lines* This time line shows the parties that have won each presidential election. **Since 1860, which party has controlled the presidency for the longest period of time?**

---

By the time of Andrew Jackson's administration (1829–1837), a potent National Republican (Whig) Party had arisen to challenge the Democrats. The major issues of the day—conflicts over public lands, the Second Bank of the United States, high tariffs, and slavery—all had made new party alignments inevitable.

The Democrats, led by Jackson, were a coalition of small farmers, debtors, frontier pioneers, and slaveholders. They drew much of their support from the South and West. The years of Jacksonian democracy produced three fundamental changes in the nation's political landscape: (1) voting rights for all white males, (2) a huge increase in the number of elected offices around the country, and (3) the practice of awarding public offices, contracts, and other governmental favors to those who supported the party in power.

The Whig Party was led by the widely popular Henry Clay and the great orator, Daniel Webster. The party consisted of a loose coalition of eastern bankers, merchants and industrialists, and many owners of large southern plantations. The Whigs were opposed to the tenets of Jacksonian democracy and strongly supported a high tariff. However, the Whigs' victories were few. Although they were the other major party from the mid-1830s to the 1850s, the Whigs were able to elect only two Presidents, both of

them war heroes: William Henry Harrison in 1840 and Zachary Taylor in 1848.

By the 1850s, the growing crisis over slavery split both major parties. Left leaderless by the deaths of Clay and Webster, the Whigs fell apart. Meanwhile, the Democrats split into two sharply divided camps, North and South. During this decade, the nation drifted toward civil war.

Of the several groupings that arose to compete for supporters among the former Whigs and the fragmented Democrats, the Republican Party was the most successful. Founded in 1854, it drew many Whigs and antislavery Democrats. The Republicans nominated their first presidential candidate, John C. Frémont, in 1856; they elected their first President, Abraham Lincoln, in 1860.

With Lincoln's election, the Republican Party became the only party in the history of American politics to make the jump from third-party to major-party status. As you will see, even greater things were in store for the Republicans.

### The Era of the Republicans, 1860–1932

The Civil War signaled the beginning of the second era of one-party domination. For nearly 75 years, the Republicans dominated the national scene. They were supported by business and financial interests, and by farmers, laborers, and newly freed African Americans.

---

*Answer to . . .*

**Interpreting Time Lines** The Republican Party.

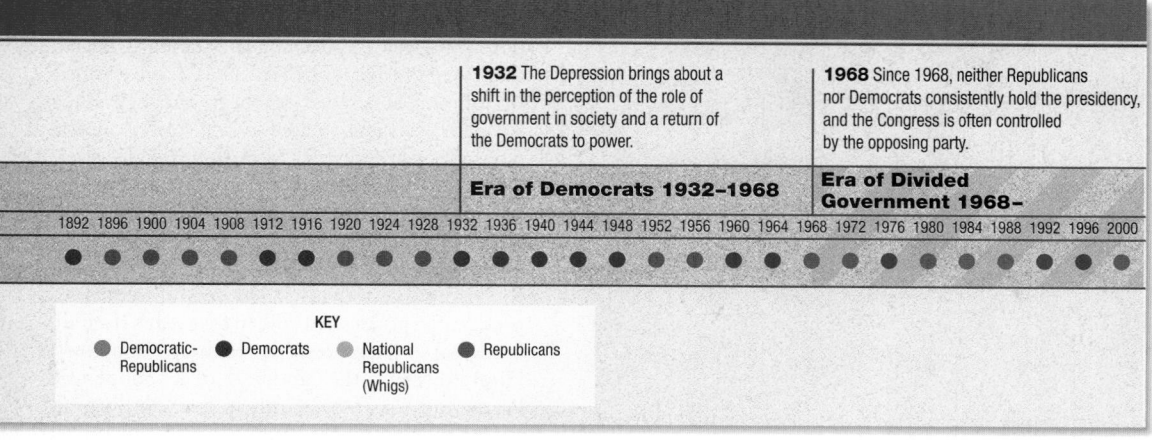

**1932** The Depression brings about a shift in the perception of the role of government in society and a return of the Democrats to power.

**1968** Since 1968, neither Republicans nor Democrats consistently hold the presidency, and the Congress is often controlled by the opposing party.

**Era of Democrats 1932–1968**

**Era of Divided Government 1968–**

1892 1896 1900 1904 1908 1912 1916 1920 1924 1928 1932 1936 1940 1944 1948 1952 1956 1960 1964 1968 1972 1976 1980 1984 1988 1992 1996 2000

KEY
● Democratic-Republicans   ● Democrats   ● National Republicans (Whigs)   ● Republicans

### ACTIVITY

## American Government, American Humor

Share the following quotation with students:

*"**Conservative**, n. A statesman who is enamored of existing evils, as distinguished from the Liberal, who wishes to replace them with others."*

—Ambrose Bierce, *The Devil's Dictionary*

**Discussion** Have students explain what Bierce meant by his definition. Ask: How might this definition apply to the two major political parties? **(Average)**

The Democrats, crippled by the war, were able to survive mainly through their hold on the "Solid South," after the era of Reconstruction came to a close in the mid-1870s. For the balance of the century, they slowly rebuilt their electoral base. In all that time, they were able to place only one candidate in the White House: Grover Cleveland in 1884 and again in 1892. Those elections marked only short breaks in Republican supremacy. Riding the crest of popular acceptance and unprecedented prosperity, the GOP remained the dominant party well into the twentieth century.

The election of 1896 was especially critical in the development of the two-party system. It climaxed years of protest by small business owners, farmers, and the emerging labor unions against big business, financial monopolies, and the railroads. The Republican Party nominated William McKinley and supported the gold standard. The Democratic candidate was William Jennings Bryan, a supporter of free silver, who was also endorsed by the Populist Party.

With McKinley's victory in 1896, the Republicans regained the presidency. In doing so, they drew a response from a broader range of the **electorate**—the people eligible to vote. This new strength allowed the Republicans to maintain their role as the dominant party in national politics for another three decades.

The Democratic Party lost the election of 1896, but it won on another score. Bryan, its young, dynamic presidential nominee, campaigned throughout the country as the champion of the "little man." He helped to push the nation's party politics back toward the economic arena, and away from the divisions of **sectionalism** that had plagued the nation for so many years. Sectionalism emphasizes a devotion to the interests of a particular region.

The Republicans suffered their worst setback of the era in 1912, when they renominated incumbent President William Howard Taft. Former President Theodore Roosevelt, denied the nomination of his party, left the Republicans to become the candidate of his "Bull Moose" Progressive Party. Traditional Republican support was divided between Taft and Roosevelt. As a result, the Democratic nominee, Woodrow Wilson, was able to capture the presidency. Four years later, Wilson was reelected by a narrow margin.

Again, however, the Democratic successes of 1912 and 1916 proved only a brief interlude. The GOP reasserted its control of the nation's politics by winning each of the next three presidential elections: Warren Harding won in 1920, Calvin Coolidge in 1924, and Herbert Hoover in 1928.

### The Return of the Democrats, 1932–1968

The Great Depression, which began in 1929, had a massive impact on nearly all aspects of American life. Its effect on the American political landscape was considerable indeed. The landmark election of 1932 brought Franklin Roosevelt to the presidency and the Democrats back to power at the

### Background Note

## Common Misconceptions

American political parties are an excellent example of what Abraham Lincoln (himself a good Republican) famously called "government of the people, by the people, for the people" in his 1863 Gettysburg Address. Interestingly, a clergyman and social reformer named Theodore Parker wrote of "government of all the people, by all the people, for all the people" 13 years earlier, in 1850. He used a similar phrase in a sermon in the Boston Music Hall in 1858. Lincoln's law partner, William Herndon, gave Lincoln a copy of the sermon. Herndon later wrote that Lincoln underlined this phrase in Hall's sermon: "Democracy is direct self-government, over all the people, by all the people, for all the people." Thus, historians have come to agree that Lincoln's famous phrase was in fact borrowed—although most Americans are unaware of it.

## CONSTITUTIONAL PRINCIPLES

### Separation of Powers

The issue of separation of powers took on a new urgency for the nation in 1937. The Supreme Court was in an era of conservative judicial activism, and had struck down many social laws, particularly those protecting workers' rights. In an attempt to balance the Court, FDR attempted to increase the number of sitting justices, in what became known as the "Court-packing scheme." Though his plan gained some support, it was quickly defeated by a large number of Americans who were horrified by what they saw as an overreach of power by the executive branch.

### Activity

Have students role-play FDR and his advisors who support the Court-packing scheme, and Americans who oppose it, including reporters, citizens, and Republicans. Encourage them to supply reasons and examples for their views.

## Point-of-Use Resources

📁 **The Living Constitution** Separation of Powers, p. 5

📖 **Basic Principles of the Constitution Transparencies** Transparencies 23-29, *Separation of Powers*

▲ This 1900 campaign poster uses powerful imagery to win Republican votes. *Critical Thinking* **How does the poster contrast Republican achievements since 1896 with earlier conditions when the Democrats were in power?**

national level. Also, and of fundamental importance, that election marked a basic shift in the public's attitude toward the proper role of government in the nation's social and economic life.

Franklin Roosevelt and the Democrats engineered their victory in 1932 with a new electoral base. It was built largely of southerners, small farmers, organized labor, and big-city political organizations. Roosevelt's revolutionary economic and social welfare programs, which formed the heart of the New Deal of the 1930s, further strengthened that coalition. It also brought increasing support from African Americans and other minorities to the Democrats.

President Roosevelt won reelection in 1936. He secured an unprecedented third term in 1940 and yet another term in 1944, each time by heavy majorities. Roosevelt's Vice President, Harry S Truman, completed the fourth term following FDR's death in 1945. Truman was elected to a full term of his own in 1948, when he turned back the GOP challenge led by Governor Thomas E. Dewey of New York.

The Republicans did manage to regain the White House in 1952, and they kept it in 1956. World War II hero Dwight Eisenhower led the Republicans to victory in these elections. Both times, Eisenhower defeated the Democratic nominee, Governor Adlai Stevenson of Illinois.

The Republicans' return to power was short-lived, however. Senator John F. Kennedy of Massachusetts recaptured the White House for the Democrats in 1960. He did so with a razor-thin win over the Republican standard bearer, then Vice President Richard M. Nixon. Lyndon B. Johnson succeeded to the presidency when Kennedy was assassinated in late 1963. Johnson won a full presidential term in 1964, by overwhelming his Republican opponent, Senator Barry Goldwater of Arizona.

### The Start of a New Era

Richard Nixon made a successful return to presidential politics in 1968. In that year's election, he defeated Vice President Hubert Humphrey. Humphrey was the candidate of a Democratic Party torn apart by conflicts over the war in Vietnam, civil rights, and a variety of social welfare issues. Nixon also faced a strong third-party effort by the American Independent Party nominee, Governor George Wallace of Alabama. The Republicans won with only a bare plurality over Humphrey and Wallace.

In 1972, President Nixon retained the White House when he routed the choice of the still-divided Democrats, Senator George McGovern of South Dakota. However, Nixon's role in the Watergate scandal forced him from office in 1974.

Vice President Gerald Ford then became President and filled out the balance of Nixon's second term. Beset by problems in the economy, by the continuing effects of Watergate, and by his pardon of former President Nixon, Ford lost the presidency in 1976. The former governor of Georgia, Jimmy Carter, and the resurgent Democrats gained the White House that year.

A steadily worsening economy, political fallout from the Iranian hostage crisis, and his own inability to establish himself as an effective President spelled defeat for Jimmy Carter in 1980. Led by Ronald Reagan, the former governor of California, the Republicans scored an impressive victory that year. Reagan won a second term by a landslide in 1984, overwhelming a Democratic ticket headed by former Vice President Walter Mondale.

The GOP kept the White House with a third straight win in 1988. Their candidate, George Bush, had served as Vice President throughout the Reagan years. Bush led a successful campaign against the Democrats and their nominee, Governor Michael Dukakis of Massachusetts.

The Reagan and Bush victories of the 1980s triggered wide-ranging efforts to alter many of the nation's foreign and domestic policies. These Republican successes also led many observers to conclude that most Americans now favored more conservative, rather than liberal, responses to most public-policy questions.

Republican successes did not continue, however. President Bush lost his bid for another term in 1992. Democrat Bill Clinton, then the governor of Arkansas, defeated Bush and turned back an independent challenge by Texas billionaire Ross Perot. Clinton won again in 1996, defeating the Republican candidate Bob Dole and, at the same time, thwarting a Perot third-party effort.

The GOP regained the presidency in a very close contest in 2000. Their candidate, George W. Bush, was then the governor of Texas and is the son of the former Republican President. Mr. Bush failed to win the popular vote but did capture a bare majority of the electoral votes—and so won the White House. His Democratic opponent, Vice President Al Gore, became the first presidential candidate since 1888 to win the popular vote and yet fail to win the presidency.

The years since 1968 have been marked by divided government. Throughout most of the period, the Republicans have held the White House while the Democrats have controlled Congress.[6] That situation was reversed in President Clinton's first term, however. In 1994,

*Interpreting Political Cartoons* **What does the cartoon suggest about voter preference? Do you agree?**

the Republicans captured control of both houses of Congress and maintained that hold through the elections of 2000.

In earlier periods, a newly elected President almost always swept many of his party's candidates into office with him. The victories of several recent Presidents—most recently George W. Bush's win in 2000—did not include that kind of coattail effect. The GOP lost seats in both houses of Congress in that election.

[6]The Democrats held almost uninterrupted control of Congress from 1933 to 1995. Over those years, the Republicans controlled both houses of Congress for only two two-year periods—first, after the congressional elections of 1946 and then after those of 1952. The GOP did win control of the Senate (but not the House) in 1980; the Democrats recaptured the upper chamber in 1986.

## Section 3 Assessment

### Key Terms and Main Ideas
1. Since political parties are not mentioned in the Constitution, why did they develop so quickly in the new nation?
2. Why would the development of **factions** within a political party hurt that party's chances for success?
3. Explain how **sectionalism** played an important role in party politics during at least one period of American history.
4. Describe one period of single-party domination.

### Critical Thinking
5. **Determining Relevance (a)** Does the present era of divided government mean that most voters favor split control of the White House and Congress? **(b)** Why might they favor this? **(c)** Why might they oppose it? **(d)** What else might it indicate?

6. **Drawing Conclusions** Identify three significant individuals in the field of government and politics who played a vital role in the development of the American party system. Explain why you chose each individual.

 **Take It to the Net**

7. Read more about either the Republican or the Democratic Party and one of the historical parties, the Whigs or the Federalists. Make a chart comparing the two parties on at least five topics, such as why they were formed, who tended to support them, and their stands on important issues. Use the links provided in the Social Studies area at the following Web site for help in completing this activity. www.phschool.com

 **Take It to the Net**

7. Direct students to the Social Studies area at the Prentice Hall School Web site. The *Magruder's American Government* companion Web site includes the directions and links needed to complete the activity. It also provides a printable Internet activity worksheet with scoring rubrics for assessment. Charts should be clearly organized and present all required data.

## Point-of-Use Resources

**Guide to the Essentials** Chapter 5, Section 3, p. 34 provides support for students who need additional review of section content. Spanish support is available in the Spanish edition of the Guide on p. 27.

**Quiz** Unit 2 booklet, p. 7 includes matching and multiple-choice questions to check students' understanding of Section 3 content.

**Presentation Pro CD-ROM** Quizzes and multiple-choice questions check students' understanding of Section 3 content.

## Answers to . . .

### Section 3 Assessment

1. The debate over the ratification of the Constitution created conflicts that led to the formation of parties.
2. If the people within the same party are divided, they are unlikely to present a united front as a party.
3. A move away from sectionalism by Democrats in 1896 helped the nation return to economic issues.
4. The period of 1932–1952 was dominated by the Democratic Party, with FDR being elected for four terms and then his Vice President, Truman, elected for another two.
5. Answers will vary; students might suggest that voters approve of divided government as it provides a check and balance; or that they oppose it, as it might hamper an administration's ability to enact change.
6. Possible answers include: Alexander Hamilton and Thomas Jefferson, who led the nation's first political parties; James Madison, who worked with Jefferson to build the Democratic-Republican Party; Abraham Lincoln, who led the Republican Party from third- to major-party status.

## Answer to . . .

**Interpreting Political Cartoons** That voters prefer people like themselves rather than leaders. Students should cite specific elections to support their opinions.

**Objectives** You may wish to call students' attention to the objectives in the Section Preview. The objectives are reflected in the main headings of the section.

**Bellringer** Ask students to explain why minor league teams are important to baseball. Explain that in this section, they will learn about minor political parties and why they are important to the American political system.

**Vocabulary Builder** Point out the four kinds of minor political parties listed in the Political Dictionary. Have students, using the descriptive words as clues, try to explain the origin of or give an example of a typical party in each of the four categories.

## Pressed for Time?

### Quick Lesson Plan

**1. Focus** Tell students that many minor parties have played a vital role in American politics. Ask students to discuss what they know about why minor parties are important to the political system.

**2. Instruct** Ask students to explain why the Communist Party is considered an ideological party. Have students describe the other three kinds of minor parties and offer examples of parties in each category. Then lead a discussion of how minor parties influence government.

**3. Close/Reteach** Remind students that minor parties arise for different reasons. Have them choose one of the minor parties named in the section and create a billboard advertisement touting the party's candidate for President.

---

# 4 · The Minor Parties

## Section Preview

### OBJECTIVES

1. **Identify** the types of third parties that have been active in American politics.
2. **Evaluate** the role of third parties in the United States.

### WHY IT MATTERS

Many minor parties have been active in American politics. They provide alternatives to the positions of the major parties, and sometimes have affected particular elections and shaped public policies.

### POLITICAL DICTIONARY

★ ideological parties
★ single-issue parties
★ economic protest parties
★ splinter parties

---

Libertarian, Reform, Socialist, Prohibition, Natural Law, Communist, American Independent, Green, Constitution—these are only some of the many parties that fielded presidential candidates for 2000. You know that none of these parties or their candidates had any real chance of winning. But this is not to say that minor (third) parties are unimportant. The bright light created by the two major parties too often blinds us to the vital role several minor parties have played in American politics.

## Types of Third Parties

Their number and variety make minor parties difficult to describe and classify. Some have limited their efforts to a particular locale, others to

▲ These are just two of the active minor parties in the United States.

a single State, and some to one region of the country. Still others have tried to woo the entire nation. Most have been short-lived, but a few have existed for decades. And, while most have lived mothlike around the flame of a single idea, some have had a broader, more practical base.

Still, four distinct types of minor parties can be identified:

1. The **ideological parties** are those based on a particular set of beliefs—a comprehensive view of social, economic, and political matters. Most of these minor parties have been built on some shade of Marxist thought; examples include the Socialist, Socialist Labor, Socialist Worker, and Communist parties.

Some ideological parties have had a quite different approach, however. One example is the Libertarian Party of today, which emphasizes individualism and calls for doing away with most of government's present functions and programs.

The ideological parties have seldom been able to win many votes. As a rule, however, they have been long-lived.

2. The **single-issue parties** concentrate on only one public-policy matter. Their names have usually indicated their primary concern. For example, the Free Soil Party opposed the spread of slavery in the 1840s and 1850s; the American Party, also called the "Know Nothings," opposed Irish-Catholic immigration in the 1850s; and the Right to Life Party opposes abortion today.

Most of the single-issue parties have faded into history. They died away as events have

---

## 🔲 Block Scheduling Strategies

Consider these suggestions to manage extended class time:

■ Review the four kinds of minor parties. Divide the class into four groups, assigning each one of the types of minor parties. Have them create party platforms for a new party that show the party's name, belief, issue, or economic concern; or for the splinter party, the issues over which the party has split. (Refer students to platforms on the Internet.) **www.phschool.com**

■ Remind students that, given the entrenched two-party system, it is unlikely that a minor party would ever win a major election. Have students debate the necessity of minor parties given that fact. Begin by eliciting any names of minor parties that students can recall. Ask them which issues these parties have publicized. Then ask them to consider whether these issues would be as well-known to the public were there only the two major parties.

## Four Types of Minor Parties

Ideological Party

Single Issue Party

Economic Protest Party

Splinter Party

*Interpreting Charts* **(a)** *According to the chart, which type of minor party is the most closely related to a major party?* **(b)** *Which type is likely to be the most cohesive and united?*

passed them by, as their themes have failed to attract voters, or as one or both of the major parties have taken their key issues as their own.

3. The **economic protest parties** have been rooted in periods of economic discontent. Unlike the socialist parties, these groups have not had any clear-cut ideological base. Rather, they have proclaimed their disgust with the major parties and demanded better times, and have focused their anger on such real or imagined enemies as the monetary system, "Wall Street bankers," the railroads, or foreign imports.

Most often, they have been sectional parties, drawing their strength from the agricultural South and West. The Greenback Party, for example, tried to take advantage of agrarian discontent from 1876 through 1884. It appealed to struggling farmers by calling for the free coinage of silver, federal regulation of the railroads, an income tax, and labor legislation. A descendant of the Greenbacks, the Populist Party of the 1890s also demanded public ownership of railroads, telephone and telegraph

companies, lower tariffs, and the adoption of the initiative and referendum.

Each of these economic protest parties has disappeared as the nation has climbed out of the difficult economic period in which that party arose.

4. **Splinter parties** are those that have split away from one of the major parties. Most of the more important minor parties in our politics have been splinter parties. Among the leading groups that have split away from the Republicans are Theodore Roosevelt's "Bull Moose" Progressive Party of 1912, and Robert La Follette's Progressive Party of 1924. From the Democrats have come Henry Wallace's Progressive Party and the States' Rights (Dixiecrat) Party, both of 1948, and George Wallace's American Independent Party of 1968.

Most splinter parties have formed around a strong personality—most often someone who has failed to win his major party's presidential nomination. These parties have faded or collapsed when that leader has stepped aside. Thus, the Bull Moose Progressive Party passed away

## Reading Strategy

### Finding Evidence

Tell students that minor political parties are important to the American political system. Have them find evidence that supports this statement, and also have them find evidence that contradicts this statement.

## Point-of-Use Resources

📁 **Guided Reading and Review** Unit 2 booklet, p. 8 provides students with practice identifying the main ideas and key terms of this section.

📁 **Lesson Plans** For lesson planning suggestions, see p. 29 of the Lesson Plans booklet.

📁 **Political Cartoons** See p. 21 of the Political Cartoons booklet for a cartoon relevant to this section.

📺 **ABC News Civics and Government Videotape Library** *Third-Party Candidates* (time: about 3 minutes)

💻 **Section Support Transparencies** Transparency 24, *Visual Learning;* Transparency 123, *Political Cartoon*

## Organizing Information

To make sure students understand the main points of this section, you may wish to use the Venn diagram to the right.

Tell students that a Venn diagram is useful for comparing two groups by showing characteristics that they have alone and those they share. Have students use a Venn diagram to compare major and minor parties. Characteristics that both parties share should appear in the space where the circles overlap.

**Teaching Tip** A template for this graphic organizer can be found in the Section Support Transparencies, Transparency 6.

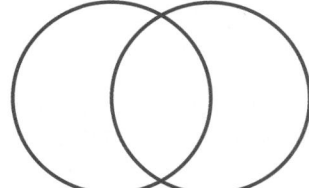

*Answer to . . .*

**Interpreting Charts (a)** Splinter parties. **(b)** Single-issue parties or ideological parties.

when Theodore Roosevelt returned to the Republican fold after the election of 1912. Similarly, the American Independent Party lost nearly all of its brief strength when Governor George Wallace rejoined the Democrats after his strong showing in the 1968 election.

The Green Party USA, founded in 1984, points up the difficulties of classifying minor parties in American politics. The Greens began as a classic single-issue party but, as the party has evolved, it simply will not fit into any of the categories set out here. The Green Party came to prominence in 2000, when it picked Ralph Nader as its presidential nominee. Nader's campaign was built around a smorgasbord of issues—environmental protection, of course, but also universal health care, gay and lesbian rights, restraints on corporate power, campaign finance reform, opposition to global free trade, and much more.

## The Role of Third Parties

Even though most Americans do not support them, minor parties have still had an impact on American politics and on the major parties.

For example, it was a minor party, the Anti-Masons, that first used a national convention to nominate a presidential candidate in 1831. The Whigs and then the Democrats followed suit in 1832. Ever since, national conventions have been used by both the Democrats and the Republicans to pick their presidential tickets.

Minor parties can have an impact in another way. A strong third-party candidacy can play a decisive role—often a "spoiler role"—in an election. Even if a minor party does not win any electoral votes, it can pull votes from one of the major parties, as the Green Party did in 2000. This spoiler effect can be felt in national, State, or local contests, especially where the two major parties compete on roughly equal terms.

The 1912 election dramatically illustrated this point. A split in the Republican Party and Roosevelt's resulting third-party candidacy produced the results shown below. Almost certainly, had Roosevelt not quit the Republican Party, Taft would have enjoyed a better showing, and Wilson would not have become President.

Historically, however, the minor parties have been most important in their roles of critic and innovator. Unlike the major parties, the minor

### The 1912 Presidential Election

**Woodrow Wilson — Democrat**
Popular Vote 6,296,547 41.87%
Electoral Vote 435

**Theodore Roosevelt — Progressive**
The nickname for the Progressives was the Bull Moose Party.
Popular Vote 4,118,571 27.39%
Electoral Vote 88

**William H. Taft — Republican**
Popular Vote 3,486,720 23.19%
Electoral Vote 8

**Eugene V. Debs — Socialist**
Popular Vote 900,672 5.9%
Electoral Vote 0

**Eugene Chafin — Prohibition**
Popular Vote 206,275 1.37%
Electoral Vote 0

*Interpreting Graphs* This bar graph shows the votes received by the major and the minor parties in 1912. *(a) Which party "came in second"? (b) Even though the Bull Moose Progressives were a minor party, how did they help determine which major party won the election?*

parties have been ready, willing, and able to take quite clear-cut stands on controversial issues. Minor-party stands have often drawn attention to some issue that the major parties have preferred to ignore or straddle.

Over the years, many of the more important issues of American politics were first brought to the public's attention by a minor party. Examples include the progressive income tax, woman suffrage, railroad and banking regulation, and old-age pensions.

Oddly enough, this very important innovator role of the minor parties has also been a major source of their frustration. When their proposals have gained any real degree of popular support, one and sometimes both of the major parties have taken over these ideas and then presented the policies as their own. The late Norman Thomas, who was the Socialist Party's candidate for President six times, complained that "the major parties are stealing from my platform."

Minor parties continue to be active today. The presidential nominees of more than 20 minor parties made it to the ballots of at least one State in 2000. At least that many will likely do so in the year 2004. In 2000 the most visible minor-party presidential campaigns were those of the Reform, Libertarian, Natural Law, Constitution, Socialist, Prohibition, and Green parties. More than a thousand candidates from a wide variety of minor parties also sought seats in Congress or ran for various State and local offices.

### Significant Minor Parties in Presidential Elections, 1880–2000*

| Year | Party | Candidate | % Popular Vote | Electoral Vote |
|------|-------|-----------|----------------|----------------|
| 1880 | Greenback | James B. Weaver | 3.36 | — |
| 1888 | Prohibition | Clinton B. Fisk | 2.19 | — |
| 1892 | Populist | James B. Weaver | 8.54 | 22 |
|      | Prohibition | John Bidwell | 2.19 | — |
| 1904 | Socialist | Eugene V. Debs | 2.98 | — |
| 1908 | Socialist | Eugene V. Debs | 2.82 | — |
| 1912 | Progressive (Bull Moose) | Theodore Roosevelt | 27.39 | 88 |
|      | Socialist | Eugene V. Debs | 5.99 | — |
| 1916 | Socialist | Allan L. Benson | 3.17 | — |
| 1920 | Socialist | Eugene V. Debs | 3.45 | — |
| 1924 | Progressive | Robert M. La Follette | 16.61 | 13 |
| 1932 | Socialist | Norman M. Thomas | 2.22 | — |
| 1948 | States' Rights (Dixiecrat) | Strom Thurmond | 2.41 | 39 |
|      | Progressive | Henry A. Wallace | 2.37 | — |
| 1968 | American Independent | George C. Wallace | 13.53 | 46 |
| 1996 | Reform | Ross Perot | 8.5 | — |
| 2000 | Green | Ralph Nader | 3.0 | — |

*Includes all minor parties that polled at least 2% of the popular vote
Source: *Historical Statistics of the United States, Colonial Times to 1970;* the Gallup Organization

*Interpreting Tables* **(a)** Which minor party received the most electoral votes in an election? **(b)** Which other parties received enough support to influence an election? Explain.

## Section 4 Assessment

### Key Terms and Main Ideas

1. Why do **single-issue parties** tend to be short-lived?
2. **(a)** What are **economic protest parties**? **(b)** Why are they formed in times of economic distress?
3. Most of the more important minor parties in our history have been of which type? Explain the effect of one such party.
4. Why is the innovator role a source of frustration to minor parties?

### Critical Thinking

5. **Expressing Problems Clearly** Suppose you are considering voting for a presidential candidate from a minor party. Explain the benefits and drawbacks of casting your vote that way.

6. **Predicting Consequences** Minor parties usually are willing to take definite stands on controversial issues. How might voters react to this tendency?

 **Take It to the Net**

7. Locate the Web site for one of the following minor parties: Reform, Libertarian, Natural Law, Constitution, Socialist, Prohibition, Green. Make an outline of the major issues on which the party ran in the most recent presidential election or in a previous election. Use the links provided in the Social Studies area at the following Web site for help in completing this activity. **www.phschool.com**

 **Take It to the Net**

7. Direct students to the Social Studies area at the Prentice Hall School Web site. The *Magruder's American Government* companion Web site includes the directions and links needed to complete the activity. It also provides a printable Internet activity worksheet with scoring rubrics for assessment. Outlines should include all major issues.

### Answers to . . .

### Section 4 Assessment

**1.** The issue around which such parties form might fail to attract voters or be addressed by one of the major parties.
**2. (a)** Economic protest parties form to express economic discontent with the major parties. **(b)** They tend to form in times of economic distress because if the country were thriving economically, they would have nothing to protest.
**3.** Most have been splinter parties. Effects will vary; some have been to divide support for the major parties.
**4.** Because usually when a minor party brings an issue to the forefront, it is taken over by the major parties and claimed for their own.
**5.** Answers will vary, but should draw on examples from the text.
**6.** Some students might suggest that voters are glad that someone is finally addressing important issues; others might say that voters tend to shy away from controversial issues and would be more likely to support the major parties.

### Answer to . . .

**Interpreting Tables (a)** The Progressive (Bull Moose) Party. **(b)** The Populist, Progressive, States' Rights, and American Independent parties.

 *on Primary Sources*

# Green Party Goals

*Ralph Nader accepted the presidential nomination of the Green Party on June 25, 2000. In his speech that day he laid out the goals of his party and encouraged all citizens who desire change to support his campaign.*

*Ralph Nader*

On behalf of all Americans who seek a new direction, who yearn for a new birth of freedom to build the just society, who see justice as the great work of human beings on Earth, who understand that community and human fulfillment are mutually reinforcing, who respect the urgent necessity to wage peace, to protect the environment, to end poverty and to preserve values of the spirit for future generations, who wish to build a deep democracy by working hard for a regenerative progressive politics, as if people mattered—to all these citizens and the Green vanguard, I welcome and am honored to accept the Green Party nomination for President of the United States.

The Green Party stands for a nation and a world that consciously advances the practice of deep democracy. A deep democracy facilitates people's best efforts to achieve social justice, a sustainable and bountiful environment and an end to systemic bigotry and discrimination against law-abiding people merely because they are different. Green goals place community and self-reliance over dependency on ever larger absentee corporations and their media, their technology, their capital, and their politicians. Green goals aim at preserving the commonwealth of assets that the people of the United States already own so that the people, not big business, control what they own, and using these vast resources of the public lands, the public airwaves, and trillions of worker pension dollars to achieve healthier environments, healthier communities, and healthier people. . . .

To the youth of America, I say, beware of being trivialized by the commercial culture that tempts you daily. I hear you saying often that you're not turned on to politics. The lessons of history are clear and portentous. If you do not turn on to politics, politics will turn on you. The fact that we have so many inequalities demonstrates this point. Democracy responds to hands-on participation. And to energized imagination. That's its essence. We need the young people of America to move into leadership positions to shape their future as part of this campaign for a just society. Let's prepare to take the politicians and the lobbyists on a tour of the People's America. . . .

With a new progressive movement, we the people have the ability to vastly improve our lives and to help shape the world's course to one of justice and peace for years to come.

### Analyzing Primary Sources
1. What are the goals of the Green Party?
2. Do you think that a third party like the Green Party could win the presidency? Why or why not?
3. Would you label this speech propaganda? Why or why not?

---

 *Corner*

**Close Up on Primary Sources** Reforming American Government, p. 7, extends this feature with a primary source activity.

 **Online**
To keep up-to-date on Close Up news and activities, visit Close Up Online at
**www.closeup.org**

## Section Preview

### OBJECTIVES

1. **Understand** why the major parties have a decentralized structure.
2. **Describe** the national party machinery and how parties are organized at the State and local levels.
3. **Identify** the three components of the parties.
4. **Examine** the future of the major parties.

### WHY IT MATTERS

The major parties of the United States have a decentralized structure, and the different parts and elements work together primarily during national elections. The parties themselves have been in decline, or losing influence, since the 1960s.

### POLITICAL DICTIONARY

★ ward
★ precinct
★ split-ticket voting

**H**ow strong, how active, and how well organized are the Republican and Democratic parties in your community? Contact the county chairperson or another official in one or both of the major parties. They are usually not very difficult to find. For starters, try the telephone directory.

## The Decentralized Nature of the Parties

The two major parties are often described as though they were highly organized, close-knit, well-disciplined groups. However, neither party is anything of the kind. Rather, both are highly decentralized, fragmented, disjointed, and often beset by factions and internal squabbling.

Neither party has a chain of command running from the national through the State to the local level. Each of the State party organizations is only loosely tied to the party's national structure. By the same token, local party organizations are often quite independent of their parent State organizations. These various party units usually cooperate with one another, of course—but that is not always the case.

---

[7]The party does have a temporary leader for a brief time every fourth year: its presidential candidate, from nomination to election day. A defeated presidential candidate is often called the party's "titular leader"—a leader in title, by custom, but not in fact. What's more, if he lost by a wide margin, the defeated candidate's leadership may be largely discredited.

### The Role of the Presidency

The President's party is usually more solidly united and more cohesively organized than the opposing party. The President is automatically the party leader. He asserts that leadership with such tools as his access to the media, his popularity, and his power to make appointments to federal office and to dispense other favors.

The other party has no one in an even faintly comparable position. Indeed, in the American party system, there is seldom any one person in the opposition party who can truly be called its leader. Rather, a number of personalities, frequently in competition with one another, form a loosely identifiable leadership group in the party out of power.[7]

▲ The parties have many local headquarters, such as this one in Bennington, Vermont.

## Block Scheduling Strategies

Consider these suggestions to manage extended class time:

■ As students read, have them take notes about what the text calls "the decentralized nature" of American political parties. Then have them consider the following question: If the two parties are in fact so decentralized, why don't they splinter into smaller parties more frequently? Have students poll family members, other adults, and other students on this question, and then present their polls as charts or graphs.

■ Have students reread the section of the text "The Future of the Major Parties." Ask small groups to write newspaper articles, set in 2050, about what has happened to the major parties. Articles should include historical precedents. Have groups read their articles to the class.

## Reading Strategy

### Organizing Information/Outline

Have students outline the structure of party organization as they read. Encourage them to use headings and subheads as outline entries.

---

### Background Note

#### Shifting Alliances

Although the nominating process involves intraparty contests, even the most bitter primary battles often end in renewed party unity. During the 1980 presidential primaries, for example, George Bush and Ronald Reagan fought each other for the Republican nomination. Bush criticized Reagan harshly, calling his proposals for tax cuts and increased defense spending "voodoo economics." But when Reagan won the nomination, he selected Bush as his running mate. Bush abandoned his criticisms of his former opponent, and the two went on to capture the White House together.

---

## Point–of–Use Resources

📋 **Guided Reading and Review** Unit 2 booklet, p. 10 provides students with practice identifying the main ideas and key terms of this section.

📋 **Lesson Plans** For lesson planning suggestions, see p. 30 of the Lesson Plans booklet.

📋 **Political Cartoons** See p. 22 of the Political Cartoons booklet for a cartoon relevant to this section.

📖 **Section Support Transparencies** Transparency 25, *Visual Learning;* Transparency 124, *Political Cartoon*

---

---

### *Spotlight* on Texas Government

**Political Parties** Although Democrats have a slight majority in the Texas House (78-72), the State is dominated by Republicans. This was not always the case. The Democratic Party was the leading political party in Texas during most of its history. Various other parties—the Whigs, American "Know-Nothing" Party, Greenback, and People's Party—offered voters an alternative at various times. The Republican Party briefly took control during the Reconstruction Era, but by the early 1900s there was no real opposition to the Democrats.

Then in 1961, John G. Tower became the first Republican U.S. Senator from Texas since Reconstruction. In 1978, William P. Clements became the first Republican Governor since Reconstruction. Republican Phil Gramm won Tower's seat when Tower retired in 1984, and Republican Kay Bailey Hutchinson won the second Senate seat in 1993. In 1994, George W. Bush, became Governor of Texas, giving Republicans control of the governor's mansion and both U.S. Senate seats. Today, the majority of State senators, the governor, the lieutenant governor, and most judges are Republicans.

#### Analyzing Texas Government

*What factors might account for the shift from Democratic to Republican dominance in Texas?*

---

### The Impact of Federalism

Federalism is one major reason for the decentralized nature of the two major political parties. Remember, the basic goal of the major parties is to gain control of government; they try to do this by winning elective offices.

Today there are more than half a million elective offices in the United States. In the American federal system, those offices are widely distributed at the national, the State, and the local levels. In short, because the governmental system is decentralized—giving many powers to States and localities—so, too, are the major parties that serve it.

### The Role of the Nominating Process

The nominating process is also a major cause of party decentralization. Recall, from page 117, that the nominating process has a central role in the life of political parties. You will consider the selection of candidates at some length in Chapter 7, but, for now, look at two related aspects of that process.

First, candidate selection is an intraparty process. That is, nominations are made within the party. Second, the nominating process can be, and often is, a divisive one. Where there is a fight over a nomination, that contest pits members of the same party against one another: Republicans fight Republicans; Democrats battle Democrats. In short, the prime function of the major parties—the making of nominations—is also a prime cause of their highly fragmented character.

## National Party Machinery

The structure of both major parties at the national level has four basic elements. These elements are the national convention, the national committee, the national chairperson, and the congressional campaign committees.

### The National Convention

The national convention is often described as the party's national voice. The convention meets in the summer of every presidential election year to nominate the party's presidential and vice-presidential candidates. It also performs some other functions, including the adoption of the party's rules and the writing of its platform.

Beyond that, the convention has little authority. It has no control over the selection of the party's candidates for other offices nor over the policy stands those nominees take. You will take a longer look at both parties' national nominating conventions in Chapter 13.

### The National Committee

Between conventions, the party's affairs are handled, at least in theory, by the national committee and by the national chairperson. For years, each party's national committee was composed of a committeeman and a committeewoman from each State and several of the territories. They were chosen by the State's party organization. However, in recent years, both parties have expanded the committee's membership.

Today, the Republican National Committee (RNC) also seats several of the party's chairpersons in each State, the District of Columbia, Guam, American Samoa, Puerto Rico, and the Virgin Islands. Representatives of such GOP-related groups as the National Federation of Republican Women also serve on the RNC.

▲ *Step Right Up* Volunteers of all ages help their parties in national, State, and local races.

▲ *Madam Chairperson* Mary Louise Smith was national chairperson of the Republican Party in the 1970s.

The Democratic National Committee (DNC) is an even larger body. In addition to the committeeman and -woman from each State, it now includes the party's chairperson and vice-chairperson from every State and the several territories. It also includes additional members from the party organizations of the larger States, and up to 75 at-large members chosen by the DNC itself. Several members of Congress, as well as governors, mayors, and Young Democrats, also have seats.

On paper, the national committee appears to be a powerful organization loaded with many of the party's leading figures. In fact, it does not have a great deal of clout. Most of its work centers on staging the party's national convention every four years.

### The National Chairperson

In each party, the national chairperson is the leader of the national committee. In form, he or she is chosen to a four-year term by the national committee, at a meeting held right after the national convention. In fact, the choice is made by the just-nominated presidential candidate and is then ratified by the national committee.

Only two women have ever held that top party post. Jean Westwood of Utah chaired the DNC from her party's 1972 convention until early 1973; and Mary Louise Smith of Iowa headed the RNC from 1974 until early 1977. Each lost her post soon after her party lost a presidential election. Ron Brown, the Democrats' National Chairman from 1989 to 1993, is the only African American ever to have held the office of national chairperson in either major party.

The national chairperson directs the work of the party's headquarters and its small staff in Washington. In presidential election years, the committee's attention is focused on the national convention and then the campaign. In between presidential elections, the chairperson and the committee work to strengthen the party and its fortunes. They do so by promoting party unity, raising money, recruiting new voters, and otherwise preparing for the next presidential season.

### The Congressional Campaign Committees

Each party also has a campaign committee in each house of Congress.[8] These committees work to reelect incumbents and to make sure that seats given up by retiring party members remain in the party. The committees also take a hand in selected campaigns to unseat incumbents in the other party, at least in those House or Senate races where the chances for success seem to justify such efforts.

In both parties and in both houses, the members of these campaign committees are chosen by their colleagues. They serve for two years—that is, for a term of Congress.

## State and Local Party Machinery

National party organization is largely the product of custom and of the rules adopted by the national conventions. At the State and

---

[8]They are the National Republican Campaign Committee and the Democratic Congressional Campaign Committee in the House; in the Senate, they are the National Republican Senatorial Campaign Committee and the Democratic Senatorial Campaign Committee.

**RESOURCE PRO®**

**Resource Pro® CD-ROM** contains an electronic version of each activity found in the Teaching Resources as well as additional resources such as Supreme Court cases. The Planning Express® feature allows you to customize and create daily lesson plans within minutes.

## Local Party Organization

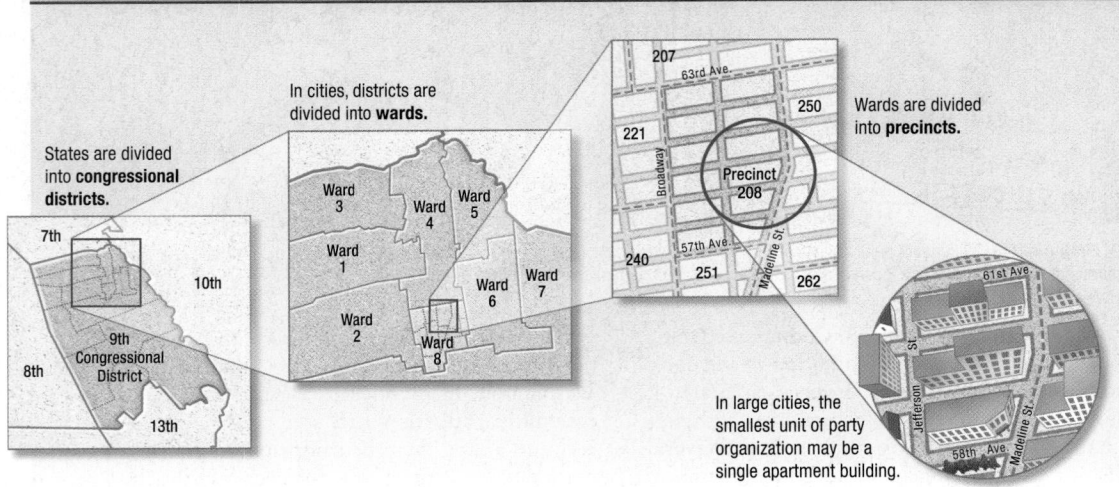

*Interpreting Diagrams (a) According to the diagram, which unit of local party organization is the largest in a State? (b) Which is the smallest?*

local levels, however, party structure is largely set by State law.

### The State Organization

At the State level, party machinery is built around a State central committee, headed by a State chairperson.

The chairperson may be an important political figure in his or her own right. More often than not, however, the chairperson fronts for the governor, a U.S. senator, or some other powerful leader or group in the politics of the State.

Together, the chairperson and the central committee work to further the party's interests in the State. Most of the time, they attempt to do this by building an effective organization and party unity, finding candidates and campaign funds, and so on. Remember, however, both major parties are highly decentralized, fragmented, and sometimes torn by struggles for power. This can complicate the chairperson's and the committee's job.

### Local Organization

Local party structures vary so widely that they nearly defy even a brief description. Generally, they follow the electoral map of the State, with a party unit for each district in which elective

offices are to be filled: congressional and legislative districts, counties, cities and towns, wards, and precincts. A **ward** is a unit into which cities are often divided for the election of city council members. A **precinct** is the smallest unit of election administration; the voters in each precinct report to one polling place.

In most larger cities, a party's organization is further broken down by residential blocks and sometimes even by apartment buildings. In some places, local party organizations are active year-round, but most often they are inactive except for those few hectic months before an election.

## The Three Components of the Party

There is another way to look at the structure of the two major parties: the roles of their members. From this perspective, the parties are made up of three basic and closely interrelated components:

1. *The party organization.* These are the leaders, the activists, and the hangers-on who control and run the party machinery.

2. *The party in the electorate.* This consists of the party's loyalists who vote the straight party ticket or usually vote for its candidates.

### Answers to . . .

**Interpreting Diagrams**
**(a)** Congressional districts.
**(b)** Precincts, except in large cities, where precincts may be further subdivided into units as small as an apartment building.

3. *The party in government.* These are the party's officeholders at all levels of government.

## The Future of the Major Parties

Political parties have never been very popular in this country. Rather, over time, most Americans have had very mixed feelings about them. Most of us have accepted parties as necessary institutions, but, at the same time, people feel that they should be closely watched and controlled. To many, political parties have seemed little better than necessary evils.

Political parties have been in a period of decline since at least the late 1960s. Their decline has led some analysts to conclude that the parties are not only in serious trouble, but that the party system itself may be on the point of collapse.

The present, weakened state of the parties can be traced to several factors. They include:

1. A sharp drop in the number of voters willing to identify themselves as Republicans or Democrats, and a growing number who regard themselves as independents.

▲ *Direct Access* Voters can see and hear the candidates for themselves by watching televised events such as this Republican debate during the 2000 presidential primary campaign. From left to right: Gary Bauer, Texas Governor George W. Bush, Alan Keyes, Arizona Senator John McCain, and Steve Forbes.

2. A big increase in **split-ticket voting,** or voting for candidates of different parties for different offices at the same election.

3. Various structural changes and reforms that have made the parties more "open," but have also led to greater internal conflict and disorganization. These changes range from the introduction of the direct primary in the early 1900s to recent and far-reaching changes in campaign finance laws.

4. Changes in the technology of campaigning, especially the heavy use of television and of

"YES, MR. VICE PRESIDENT, YOU GO ON RIGHT AFTER 'BUDDY'."

*Interpreting Political Cartoons* Both major parties use national conventions to adopt the party's platform, nominate the presidential ticket, and build party unity. *What do these cartoons suggest about the way in which the 2000 conventions were organized? (Buddy was President Clinton's dog.)*

## Make It Relevant

### Careers in Government—Accountant

The Federal Election Campaign Act requires political parties to report a great deal of financial information, especially campaign contributions and expenses, to the Federal Election Commission (FEC). This data is audited by accountants. In fact, accountants are at work in all levels of government, in most agencies and departments, keeping track of the multi-trillion dollar enterprise that is American government.

**Skills Activity** Distribute copies of blank tax returns to small groups of students. Give them sets of data, and have groups work together to fill out the form. Then have individual students write paragraphs explaining why they would or would not be interested in a career as a government accountant.

**(Challenging)**

## Point-of-Use Resources

 **Guide to the Essentials** Chapter 5, Section 5, p. 36 provides support for students who need additional review of section content. Spanish support is available in the Spanish edition of the Guide on p. 29.

**Quiz** Unit 2 booklet, p. 11 includes matching and multiple-choice questions to check students' understanding of Section 5 content.

**Presentation Pro CD-ROM** Quizzes and multiple-choice questions check students' understanding of Section 5 content.

## Answers to . . .

### Section 5 Assessment

**1.** The power not in party doesn't have a strong central leader (the President), federalism results in a division of power in parties, and the nominating process encourages competition and divisiveness.

**2.** Political parties use the national convention, during which delegates write the party's platform; and their national committees, which do the work of preparing for the convention.

**3.** Wards and precincts are party units created for the purposes of elections.

**4. (a)** Split-ticket voting is voting for candidates of different parties at the same election. **(b)** It weakens parties because it encourages lack of allegiance to a particular party.

**5.** Possible answer: With broad support of the American people for federalism and local and State autonomy, it is no surprise that local party organizations vary widely.

**6.** Questions will vary, but should refer to reasons why voters are disillusioned with the two major parties or the two-party system.

**7.** Answers will vary, but should reflect themes mentioned in the text.

## Answers to . . .

**Interpreting Graphs (a)** Independents. **(b)** Democrats.

---

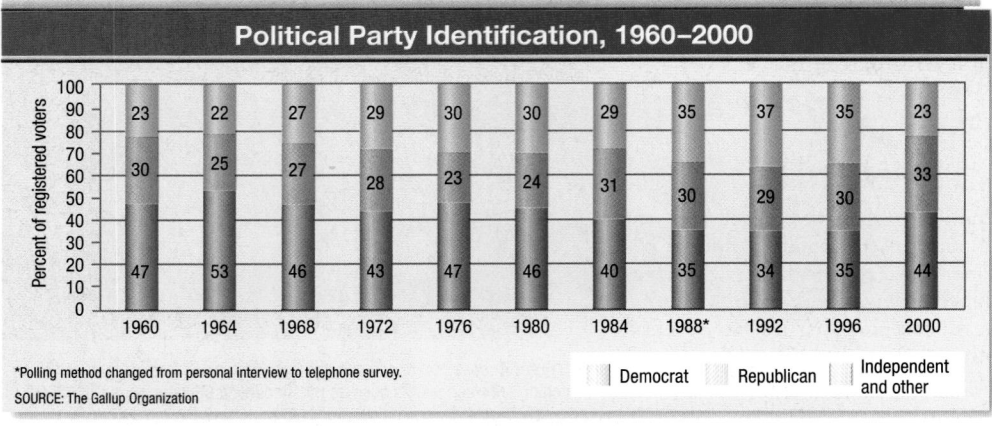

### Political Party Identification, 1960–2000

| | 1960 | 1964 | 1968 | 1972 | 1976 | 1980 | 1984 | 1988* | 1992 | 1996 | 2000 |
|---|---|---|---|---|---|---|---|---|---|---|---|
| Independent and other | 23 | 22 | 27 | 29 | 30 | 30 | 29 | 35 | 37 | 35 | 23 |
| Republican | 30 | 25 | 27 | 28 | 23 | 24 | 31 | 30 | 29 | 30 | 33 |
| Democrat | 47 | 53 | 46 | 43 | 47 | 46 | 40 | 35 | 34 | 35 | 44 |

Percent of registered voters

*Polling method changed from personal interview to telephone survey.
SOURCE: The Gallup Organization

■ Democrat  ■ Republican  ■ Independent and other

 *Interpreting Graphs* This graph shows the percentage of voters who identify with the two major parties and the percentage of independents. *(a) Which group shows the biggest gain in support between 1960 and 2000? (b) Which group lost the most support during that time?*

the Internet, professional campaign managers, and direct-mail advertising. These changes have made candidates much less dependent on party organizations since, in many cases, they can now "speak" directly to the electorate.

5. The growth, in both numbers and impact, of single-issue organizations in our politics. These groups support (or more often, oppose) candidates on the basis of the group's own closely defined views in some specific area of public policy—for example, the environment, gun control, or abortion—rather than on a candidate's stands on the full range of public policy questions.

You will look at these and several other matters affecting the condition of the parties over the next four chapters. As you do so, remember these points: Political parties are indispensable to democratic government—and so, then, to American government. Our two major parties have existed far longer than has any other party anywhere in the world. And, as you have seen, they perform a number of quite necessary functions. In short, the reports of their passing may not only be premature, they might in fact be quite farfetched.

## Section 5 Assessment

**Key Terms and Main Ideas**

1. What are the major causes of the decentralized nature of political parties?
2. What processes do political parties use to affect public policy?
3. Describe how **wards** and **precincts** are part of the local party organization.
4. **(a)** What is **split-ticket voting**? **(b)** How has its increase contributed to the weakened state of the two major parties?

**Critical Thinking**

5. **Drawing Conclusions** Based on what you know about parties, their goals, and the American people, why do you think local party organizations vary so widely?
6. **Formulating Questions** A growing number of voters consider themselves to be independents. Compose three questions that a pollster might ask in an attempt to learn why this is the case.
7. **Predicting Consequences** Do you think the major parties will survive and emerge from their current period of decline? Why or why not?

### Take It to the Net

8. Visit your State's Republican or Democratic Party Web site. What are its major elements and their contents? How easy is the site to navigate? How appealing is its design? Based on your evaluation of the existing site, design a State party site specifically for young voters. Use the links provided in the Social Studies area at the following Web site for help in completing this activity. **www.phschool.com**

---

 ### Take It to the Net

**8.** Direct students to the Social Studies area at the Prentice Hall School Web site. The *Magruder's American Government* companion Web site includes the directions and links needed to complete the activity. It also provides a printable Internet activity worksheet with scoring rubrics for assessment. Web sites should be appealing to young people and easy to navigate.

# Can Candidates Be Forced to Sign Oaths?

*Candidates must meet certain requirements in order to have their name placed on the ballot. For example, they must file a written application by a certain date. Can they be made to meet requirements regarding their personal beliefs as well?*

## Communist Party of Indiana v. Whitcomb (1974)

In 1972, the Communist Party of Indiana applied to place on the Indiana ballot candidates for President and Vice President of the United States. The Indiana State Election Board rejected their application because the Party did not submit a written statement, made under oath, that the Party did not "advocate the overthrow of local, State or National Government by violence." Indiana law required this statement from any political party that wanted to have the names of its candidates printed on the ballot.

The Communist Party filed suit against Indiana governor Edgar Whitcomb, arguing that the oath violated its First Amendment right of free speech. The court ruled that the oath did not violate the Constitution. The court ordered the State Election Board to list the Communist Party candidates if the Party submitted the required statement. The Party then submitted the statement, but added a sentence explaining that the word *advocate*, as the Party understood it, did not include the teaching of "principles divorced from action." The Election Board rejected this statement, and the parties returned to court. When the district court refused to change its order, the Communist Party of Indiana appealed to the Supreme Court.

## Arguments for the Communist Party

1. The constitutional right of free speech applies to a candidate's political beliefs, and a candidate or political party may not be prevented from running for elected office because of those beliefs.
2. Arguing that force is necessary in certain situations is not the same as actually preparing for violent action, and is protected speech under the First Amendment.
3. Even if the loyalty oath itself is constitutional, the Election Board discriminated against the Communist Party by requiring an oath from the Communists but not from the Democratic and Republican parties.

## Arguments for Whitcomb

1. Since States may lawfully ban acts of violence aimed at overthrowing the government, they may exclude from the ballot any candidates who do not renounce the use of violence.
2. States have broad power to administer the electoral process, set qualifications for voters, and supervise the conduct of elections. This broad power gives States the authority to regulate speech in the context of deciding which candidates will be on election ballots.
3. A group that seeks the violent overthrow of our democratic form of government should not be allowed to use the democratic process to gain public support for its destructive plans.

### Decide for Yourself

1. Review the constitutional grounds on which each side based its arguments and the specific arguments each side presented.
2. Debate the opposing viewpoints presented in this case. Which viewpoint do you favor?
3. Predict the impact of the Court's decision on States' ability to establish qualifications for public offices. (To read a summary of the Court's decision, turn to the Supreme Court Glossary on page 799.)

*Communist Party of Indiana* v. *Whitcomb*, p. 6 provides an activity to extend coverage of this case.

 *Corner*

**Close Up on the Supreme Court** *Communist Party of Indiana* v. *Whitcomb*, p. 6 provides an activity to extend coverage of this case.

 **Online**

To keep up-to-date on Close Up news and activities, visit Close Up Online at

**www.closeup.org**

---

## Can Candidates Be Forced to Sign Oaths?

**Focus** Have the class brainstorm a list of reasons why governments might need to regulate political parties *(such as, keeping voters informed of those who contribute money to a party.)* Then create a list of ways that the government might abuse that power. *(For instance, the party controlling the government might try to pass laws that favor their party.)*

**Instruct** Explain that many court cases involve reconciling a conflict between the legitimate rights or interests of both parties. Discuss and identify the rights claimed by each side. (*Communist Party: First Amendment freedom of speech; Indiana State Election Board: the power to administer elections and ban acts of violence*)

**Close/Reteach** Courts have long held that free speech is not absolute. Speech that directly leads to the violation of a law may be prohibited under the so-called "clear and present danger" test. Have students draw a political cartoon that expresses their opinion as to whether the Communist Party's refusal to take the oath meets the clear and present danger test.

**Keep It Current CD-ROM** includes government-related projects by unit. The CD-ROM links to the Prentice Hall School Web site and may be used for daily updates.

### *Answers to . . .*
**Decide for Yourself**

1. The Communist Party used the grounds of protected First Amendment speech to argue that requiring a loyalty oath violated members' rights. Whitcomb used the grounds of State rights to argue that States have the broad power to regulate speech in the context of elections.
2. Answers will vary, but should be supported with valid reasoning.
3. The Court ruled in favor of the Communist Party, holding that the loyalty oath violated the First and Fourteenth amendments.

# Assessment

## Practicing the Vocabulary

**1.–10.** Sentences should accurately describe each term in the context of chapter content.

**11.** False; a plurality is the largest number of votes cast.

**12.** True.

**13.** False; the correct term is economic protest party.

**14.** False; partisanship means firm allegiance to a party.

## Reviewing Main Ideas

### Section 1

**15.** To control government by winning elections and holding public office.

**16.** Unifying; they bring conflicting groups together and encourage compromise.

**17.** Public officeholders are elected on the basis of party; State legislatures are organized on party lines; parties serve as a liaison between the executive and legislative branches.

### Section 2

**18.** Single-member district systems discourage minor parties, and election laws have been deliberately written to discourage non-major party candidates.

**19.** It is a strength because it gives voters more choices and more broadly represents the electorate, and a weakness because it leads to instability in government.

**20.** Both major parties are moderate, built on compromise, and constructed to gain support from all Americans.

### Section 3

**21. (a)** The Federalist Party. **(b)** Led by Alexander Hamilton, it favored a strong central government.

**22. (a)** The Republican Party began in opposition to the Democratic Party. **(b)** It was unique because it was the only party to make the transition from third-party to major-party status.

**23.** It brought about a shift in the public's attitude toward the government's role, and in so doing ushered in a period of domination by the Democratic Party.

**24.** Divided government, whereby one party controls the White House and the other, Congress.

## Political Dictionary

| | | |
|---|---|---|
| political party (p. 116) | pluralistic society (p. 121) | ideological parties (p. 132) |
| major parties (p. 116) | consensus (p. 121) | single-issue parties (p. 132) |
| partisanship (p. 117) | multiparty (p. 122) | economic protest parties (p. 133) |
| party in power (p. 118) | coalition (p. 122) | splinter parties (p. 133) |
| minor party (p. 119) | one-party system (p. 123) | ward (p. 140) |
| two-party system (p. 119) | incumbent (p. 127) | precinct (p. 140) |
| single-member district (p. 120) | faction (p. 127) | split-ticket voting (p. 141) |
| plurality (p. 120) | electorate (p. 129) | |
| bipartisan (p. 120) | sectionalism (p. 129) | |

## Practicing the Vocabulary

***Using Words in Context*** *For each of the terms below, write a sentence that shows how it relates to this chapter.*

1. multiparty
2. pluralistic society
3. party in power
4. minor party
5. split-ticket voting
6. one-party system
7. consensus
8. splinter parties
9. single-member district
10. two-party system

***True/False*** *Determine whether each of the following statements is true or false. If it is true, write "true." If it is false, rewrite the sentence to make it true.*

11. A plurality is more than half the votes cast.
12. A ward is a unit into which cities are often divided for the election of city council members.
13. An ideological party arises over a particular issue or crisis and soon fades away.
14. Partisanship means membership in one of the major parties.

## Reviewing Main Ideas

### Section 1
15. What is the major function of a political party?
16. Which term better describes political parties in American politics: *divisive* or *unifying?* Why?
17. Cite two examples that show why American government may be described as government by party.

### Section 2
18. In what two ways does the American electoral system tend to promote a two-party system?
19. How can the diversity of views represented in a multiparty system be seen as both a strength and a weakness?
20. How is the ideological consensus of the American electorate reflected in the membership of the major parties?

### Section 3
21. **(a)** Which political party was the first to appear in the new United States? **(b)** Who was its leader and what type of government did it favor?

22. **(a)** How did the Republican Party begin? **(b)** How was its development unique in American politics?
23. What effect did the Great Depression have on American political parties?
24. What unusual feature characterizes the present era of American two-party history?

### Section 4
25. Briefly describe the four types of minor parties.
26. Historically, what have been the most important roles of minor parties? Briefly explain one of these roles.

### Section 5
27. Why is the party in power more cohesive than the opposition party?
28. Describe the role of the national chairperson.
29. List and explain four factors that have contributed to the present weakened state of the major parties.

### Section 4

**25.** Ideological parties are based on a particular set of beliefs; single-issue parties concentrate on one public policy matter; economic protest parties express general discontent with the ruling party; splinter parties have split from one of the major parties.

**26.** The roles of critic and innovator have been most important, as they have drawn attention to important issues that the major parties have not addressed.

### Section 5

**27.** It has a strong party leader (the President) with leadership tools that bring about cohesion.

**28.** The national chairperson directs the work of the party's headquarters and prepares for presidential elections.

**29.** Factors include: A drop in the number of voters who identify themselves with the major parties; an increase in split-ticket voting; structural changes that have brought conflict within parties; changes in campaigning due to technology; the growth of single-issue groups.

## Critical Thinking

**30.** *Applying the Chapter Skill* Choose an issue in the news. It might be a national issue such as gun control or a local issue such as allowing development of park land or mandatory school uniforms. State your position, and then tell where you got information about the issue, and who or what influenced your opinion. If you have not taken a stand on the issue, explain why you have no opinion.

**31.** *Determining Relevance* If there had not been a group opposed to the adoption of the Constitution in the 1780s, do you think a strong two-party system would have developed in the United States? Why or why not?

**32.** *Distinguishing Fact from Opinion* Explain why you agree or disagree with this statement: "A vote for a minor party candidate is a vote wasted."

**33.** *Drawing Conclusions* Create an outline for an essay in which you analyze the role of political parties in the electoral process at the local, State, and national levels. Include at least three conclusions about the party system in American politics.

## Analyzing Political Cartoons

Using your knowledge of American government and this cartoon, answer the questions below.

**34.** What does the cartoonist imply about the relationship between the two major parties? Explain how he conveys this idea.

**35.** Does the cartoonist regard the minor parties as a serious threat to the status quo? How do the major parties react to this threat?

 **You Can Make a Difference**

Even if you are not yet eligible to vote, you can still find a place in party politics. Local party organizations welcome volunteer help during a campaign. You may find yourself answering phones, tacking up posters, or stuffing envelopes—all part of grassroots politics. To begin, look up the local headquarters of the two major parties and any minor parties that are currently active in your area. Choose a candidate whose positions on issues are similar to your own. Then offer your help.

## Participation Activities

**36.** *Current Events Watch* Use newspapers or news magazines to analyze different points of view of political parties on important contemporary issues. First, find a local or national issue on which the major parties have taken opposing stands. Then prepare a report in which you explain the issue and identify the position that each party has taken on it. In your report, describe whether each party is united or divided in its response to the issue. Support your conclusions with examples.

**37.** *Time Line Activity* Using information from the chapter, create a time line showing the major political events of the current era of divided government. Include at least ten entries in your time line. You might begin with Richard Nixon's election to the presidency in 1968. So far, which party has held the White House more frequently during this era?

**38.** *It's Your Turn* Create a poster in which you identify opportunities for citizens to participate in political parties at the local, State, or national level. Display your class's posters around the school. **(Creating a Poster)**

 **Take It to the Net**

*Chapter 5 Self-Test* As a final review activity, take the Chapter 5 Self-Test in the Social Studies area at the Web site listed below, and receive immediate feedback on your answers.

**www.phschool.com**

 **Take It to the Net**

Additional support materials and activities for Chapter 5 of *Magruder's American Government* can be found in the Social Studies area at the Prentice Hall School Web site. **www.phschool.com**

 **Point-of-Use Resources**

**Guide to the Essentials of American Government** Chapter 5 Test, page 37 provides multiple-choice questions to test students' knowledge of the chapter.

**Test Bank CD-ROM** Chapter 5 Test

**Chapter Test** Chapter Tests booklet

### Critical Thinking Skills
**30.** Answers should include specific reasons and influences for students' positions.
**31.** Some students might suggest that without that historical event, debate would not have been polarized and the United States would have gone the multiparty route taken by most of Europe; others might say that the nature of American politics and the ideological consensus of the American people would have led to a two-party system eventually.
**32.** Answers will vary, but should either describe the important roles that minor parties play or point out that the two-party system is too entrenched for minor parties to really compete.
**33.** Outlines should demonstrate an understanding of the differences in the party system at various levels of government.

### Analyzing Political Cartoons
**34.** The cartoonist implies that they have a cordial relationship; he conveys this idea by showing them sitting together at a dining table.
**35.** No; their battering ram is much too small to break down the fortress, and the major parties seem barely able to hear their assault.

### You Can Make a Difference
Refer students to the Close Up on Participation booklet in the *Teaching Resources* for service learning-related projects.

### Participation Activities
**36.** Reports should include relevant examples and accurately state the party's position.
**37.** Time lines should include all relevant political events.
**38.** Posters should show an understanding of the structure of political parties at the level of government chosen.

# Voters and Voter Behavior

| Section Objectives | Print and Technology Resources |
|---|---|

**1 The Right to Vote**

*(pp. 148–150)*

1. Summarize the history of voting rights in the United States.
2. Identify and explain constitutional restrictions on the States' power to set voting qualifications.

**TEKS 3A, 10D, 17C, 21A, 21B, 21C, 22A, 22B**

- **Unit 2 booklet**
  Guided Reading and Review, p. 13
  Section 1 Quiz, p. 14
- **Lesson Plans booklet** Section 1, p. 31
- **Political Cartoons booklet** Section 1, p. 23
- **Section Reading Support Transparencies**

- **Block Scheduling with Lesson Strategies booklet** p. 22
- **Basic Principles of the Constitution Transparencies** 11
- **Section Support Transparencies** 26, 125
- **Presentation Pro CD-ROM** Section 1

**2 Voter Qualifications**

*(pp. 152–157)*

1. Identify the universal requirements for voting in the United States.
2. Explain the other requirements that States have used or still use as voting qualifications.

**TEKS 3A, 11A, 21A, 21D, 21E, 21F, 22A, 22B, 22C**

- **Unit 2 booklet**
  Guided Reading and Review, p. 15
  Section 2 Quiz, p. 16
- **Lesson Plans booklet** Section 2, p. 32
- **Political Cartoons booklet** Section 2, p. 24
- **Block Scheduling with Lesson Strategies booklet** p. 22
- **Section Reading Support Transparencies**

- **Close Up on Primary Sources booklet** Voter Registration Reform, p. 8
- **Government Assessment Rubrics booklet** p. 26
- **Section Support Transparencies** 27, 126
- **Presentation Pro CD-ROM** Section 2
- **Social Studies Skills Tutor CD-ROM**

**3 Suffrage and Civil Rights**

*(pp. 159–163)*

1. Describe the 15th Amendment and the tactics used to circumvent it in an effort to deny African Americans the vote.
2. Explain the significance of the early civil rights legislation passed in 1957, 1960, and 1964.
3. Analyze the provisions and effects of the Voting Rights Act of 1965.

**TEKS 3A, 3B, 16A, 16B, 18A, 18B, 18C, 21A, 21E, 21F, 22A, 22B**

- **Unit 2 booklet**
  Guided Reading and Review, p. 17
  Section 3 Quiz, p. 18
- **Lesson Plans booklet** Section 3, p. 33
- **Political Cartoons booklet** Section 3, p. 25
- **Section Reading Support Transparencies**
- **Close Up on Primary Sources booklet** Seneca Falls Declaration, p. 37; Lucy Stone's Letter to the New Jersey Tax

Collector, p. 38; Martin Luther King, Jr., *I Have a Dream Speech,* p. 45; Civil Rights Act, p. 46; Voting Rights Act, p. 47
- **The Living Constitution booklet** p. 11
- **Basic Principles of the Constitution Transparencies** 2
- **Section Support Transparencies** 28, 127
- **Presentation Pro CD-ROM** Section 3

**4 Voter Behavior**

*(pp. 164–172)*

1. Examine the problem of nonvoting in this country, and describe the size of the problem.
2. Identify why people do not vote.
3. Examine voting behavior of voters and nonvoters.
4. Understand the sociological and psychological factors that affect voting and how they work together to influence voter behavior.

**TEKS 16C, 17C, 21A, 21C, 21D, 21E, 22A, 22B, 22C**

- **Unit 2 booklet**
  Guided Reading and Review, p. 19
  Section 4 Quiz, p. 20
  Skills for Life Activity, p. 21
- **Lesson Plans booklet** Section 4, p. 34
- **Political Cartoons booklet** Section 4, p. 26
- **Close Up on the Supreme Court booklet** *Oregon* v. *Mitchell,* p. 7
- **Section Reading Support Transparencies**

- **Close Up on Participation booklet** Fighting for Teenagers' Rights, pp. 20–21
- **The Living Constitution booklet** p. 3
- **The Basic Principles of the Constitution Posters**
- **Section Support Transparencies** 29, 128
- **Presentation Pro CD-ROM** Section 4
- **Simulations and Data Graphing CD-ROM**

# Block Scheduling Strategies

The *Magruder's American Government* program addresses block-scheduling strategies in a variety of ways. For easy reference, side-column activities that fit a block format are marked ▣ **Block Strategy.** Each section also contains a **Block Scheduling Strategies** box describing at least two block-format activities that address and extend core content from the section. The **Block Scheduling with Lesson Strategies booklet** found in the Teaching Resources contains additional block-scheduling activities for each chapter.

## Take It to the Net

Visit the Social Studies area at the Prentice Hall School Web site. Once there, you can find additional links, current events connections, and activities to enrich chapter content for *Magruder's American Government,* as well as a Self-Test for students. Be sure to check out this month's **eTeach** online discussion with a Master Teacher.

### www.phschool.com

## Pressed for Time?

If you are running short on time to cover this chapter, consider one of the following options:
- Use the **Presentation Pro CD-ROM** to create an outline for this chapter.
- Use one of the **Pressed for Time** activities found on p. 27.
- Use the Section Summaries for Chapter 2, from **Guide to the Essentials of American Government (English and Spanish).**

## Video Connections

Prentice Hall offers two video programs to reinforce and extend chapter content. Show students *The Blessings of Liberty* from the **ABC News Civics and Government Videotape Library** and *Prayer in Schools: A Nationwide Debate* from the **Magruder's American Government Video Collection.**

## Assessment Options
- Section Quizzes, **Unit 2 booklet,** pp. 14, 16, 18, 20
- Chapter 6 Assessment, pp. 174–175
- **Guide to the Essentials of American Government,** Chapter 6 Test, p. 42

## Core Assessment
Chapter 6 Test, Chapter Tests booklet
ExamView® Test Bank CD-ROM Chapter 6
Government Assessment Rubrics

## Standardized Test Preparation
### Diagnose and Prescribe
Diagnostic Tests for High School
Social Studies Skills

### Review and Reteach
Review Book for Government

### Practice and Assess
Test-Taking Strategies With
    Transparencies for High School
Test Prep Book for Government

# Chapter 6 Teacher's Edition Index

## Voters and Voter Behavior

### Introducing the Chapter

In this chapter, students will learn about which Americans are qualified to vote, how they vote, and how this electorate has grown throughout U.S. history.

## CONSTITUTIONAL PRINCIPLES

Emphasize the following basic principles as students read Chapter 6. Have the class respond to the questions, and then ask if universal suffrage could exist in a nation without any of these principles.

**Popular Sovereignty** How does an expanded electorate contribute to popular sovereignty?

**Limited Government** In what ways can American citizens use their voting rights to limit the power of the National Government?

**Judicial Review** How have judicial actions concerning voting rights over the past few decades enacted change in government?

# Voters and Voter Behavior

> "It is not enough that people have the right to vote. . . . People must have the reason to vote as well."
>
> —Jesse Jackson (1988)

People who have struggled to win the right to vote know how important it is. Although, since 1789, suffrage has expanded to include many more people—notably African Americans and women—many Americans do not exercise this important right. A variety of factors influence whether and how people vote.

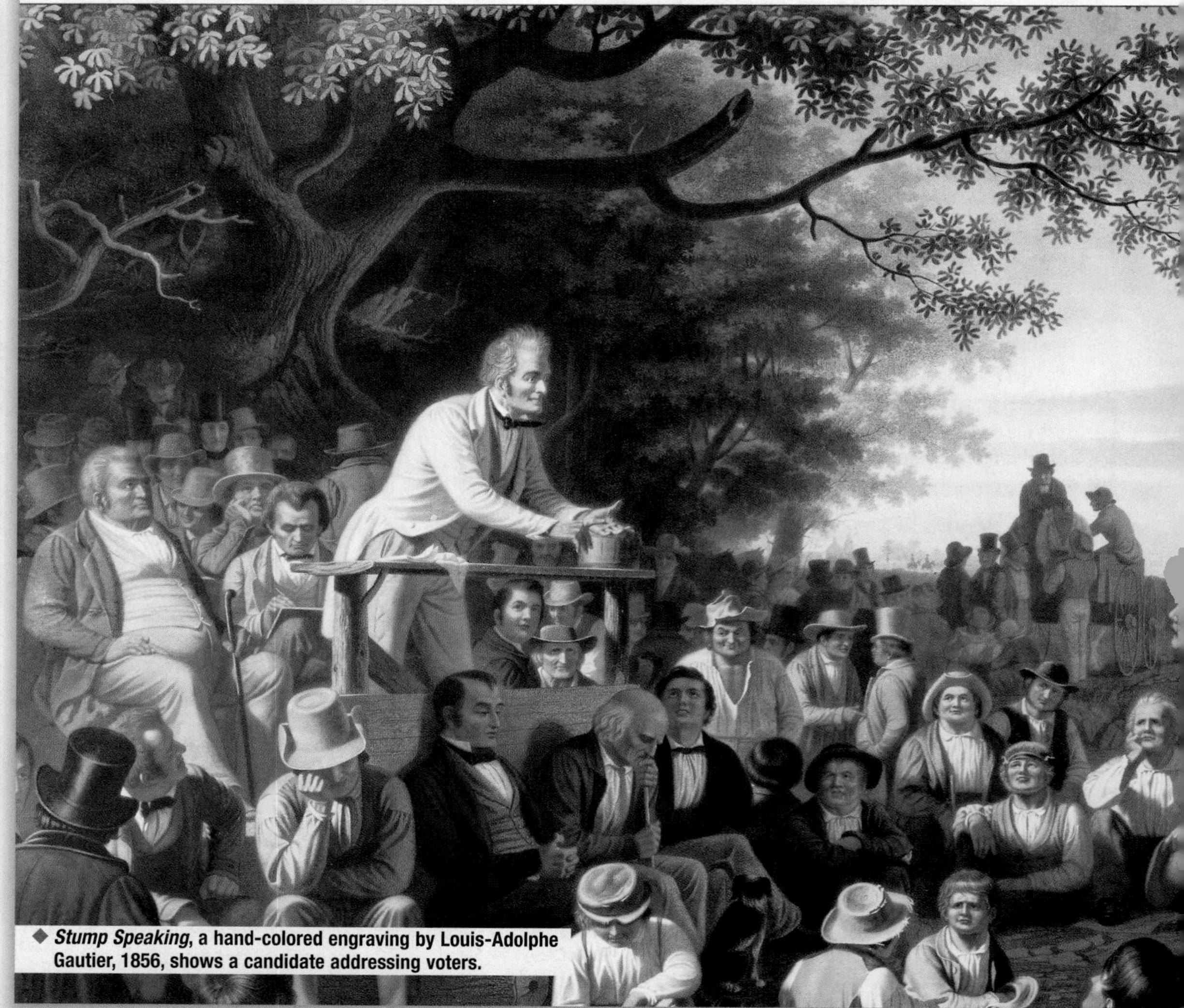

◆ *Stump Speaking*, a hand-colored engraving by Louis-Adolphe Gautier, 1856, shows a candidate addressing voters.

 ***Corner***

The following resources are available only from the Close Up Foundation to support the concepts discussed in Chapter 6 "Voters and Voter Rights":

◆ *Perspectives: Readings on Contemporary American Government*
◆ *The Bill of Rights Video Series*

To keep up-to-date on Close Up news and activities, visit Close Up Online at

**www.closeup.org**

Close Up Foundation
44 Canal Center Plaza
Alexandria, VA 22314-1592
800-765-3131

## ★ You Can Make a Difference

**IN MOST STATES** an important first step in exercising your right to vote is registration. In Roswell, Georgia, high school senior Tyler Mann discovered that less than half of 18- to 20-year-olds had registered for the 1996 presidential election. "I knew that people my age were concerned about public issues and the future of this country. . . . I thought about what I could do to increase participation in the voting process." Tyler started a project to encourage students to register as soon as they turned 18. With school approval, he made up a list of students' 18th birthdays. He sent them personal reminder letters and organized regular voter registration drives.

### Keep It Current

Items marked with this logo are periodically updated on the Internet. Keep up-to-date with what's in the news. To get current information on voters and voting trends, go to **www.phschool.com**

### SECTION 1

#### The Right to Vote (pp. 148–150)

★ The history of the United States has been marked by five stages in a steady expansion of suffrage, or the right to vote.
★ The Constitution places five restrictions on the States' power to set voting qualifications.

### SECTION 2

#### Voter Qualifications (pp.152–157)

★ All of the States have citizenship, residence, and age requirements for voting.
★ Other voting qualifications have been required by different States over time. Literacy tests and tax payment have been eliminated, but registration is still required by all but one State.

### SECTION 3

#### Suffrage and Civil Rights (pp. 159–163)

★ The 15th Amendment, ratified in 1870, declared that the right to vote cannot be denied to a citizen because of race.
★ Southern States used a variety of devices to circumvent the 15th Amendment and deny African Americans the vote. These tactics included literacy tests, white primaries, and gerrymandering.
★ Congress finally took action to protect minority voting rights in the Civil Rights Acts of 1957, 1960, and 1964.
★ The Voting Rights Act of 1965 and its later amendments finally ensured African American suffrage.

### SECTION 4

#### Voter Behavior (pp. 164–172)

★ Millions of Americans who are qualified to vote do not vote.
★ Those who choose not to vote often lack a feeling of political efficacy. Age, education, income, and geography also affect whether a person is likely to vote or not.
★ Sociological factors—such as occupation, gender, and ethnic background—influence a person's voting choices.
★ Psychological factors—including party identification and perception of the candidates and issues—also contribute to voter behavior.

## Keep It Current

### Internet Update

Use the Prentice Hall School Web site and the Keep It Current CD-ROM to find quick content updates.

Visit **www.phschool.com** for current events articles that are linked to Chapter 6. Critical thinking questions are included.

**Keep It Current CD-ROM** includes government-related projects by unit. Students complete each project using current information that they obtain by linking to the Prentice Hall School Web site from the CD-ROM.

## Pressed for Time?

### To Omit the Chapter
If you wish to skip Chapter 6, ask students to read the Chapter in Brief and assign the Guide to the Essentials before continuing to another chapter. You may also want to assign the Chapter 6 Test in the Chapter Test booklet. Then specific portions of Chapter 6 may be assigned to students needing reinforcement of key terms and concepts.

### To Preview the Chapter
To introduce students to key terms and concepts in each section, have them read the Chapter in Brief. You may also assign the Reading Strategy activities on pp. 149, 153, 160, and 165 of this book.

### To Review the Chapter
When students have completed Chapter 6, you might want to assign the Guide to the Essentials or the Guided Reading and Review worksheets on pp. 13, 15, 17, and 19 of the Unit 2 booklet.

### To Cover the Chapter Quickly
To cover the material in Chapter 6 quickly, use the following activity.

**Focus** Begin by asking students what the general eligibility requirements are for voters today. Write any responses on the chalkboard. Then ask how those requirements differed in the early years of the nation, and write down those responses. Compare the two sets of eligibility requirements.

**Instruct** Explain that the Constitution eliminates certain specific voting restrictions, such as race, but that voting requirements are actually determined by the States. Review the three universal State requirements—citizenship, residence, and age. Then discuss some of the other requirements States have instituted in the past.

**Close/Reteach** Emphasize the importance of the right to vote, and how it took many years for that right to be seen as a basic one. Then ask: Why do so many Americans choose not to vote? Elicit reasons from the class, and then discuss each.

■ **Block Strategy**
**(Average)**

## Objectives
Objectives You may wish to call students' attention to the objectives in the Section Preview. The objectives are reflected in the main headings of the section.

**Bellringer** Tell students that you have a thousand dollars to spend on the class and that they will vote on how to spend the money. However, only students who own a car will get to vote. Ask students what they think of this restriction. Explain that in this section, they will learn about restrictions on voting throughout American history.

**Vocabulary Builder** Ask students to pick out the two synonyms in the Political Dictionary. Then have them define or describe the terms.

## Pressed for Time?
### Quick Lesson Plan

**1. Focus** Tell students that the number of people with the right to vote has steadily risen throughout American history. Ask students to discuss what they know about laws that lifted restrictions on voting.

**2. Instruct** Ask students for the date by which all States had finally eliminated a religious test for voting. Discuss the other restrictions on voting rights that have been eliminated throughout American history. Conclude by talking about the Constitution's restrictions on States' power to set voting qualifications.

**3. Close/Reteach** Remind students that many restrictions on voting rights have been eliminated. Ask students to explain which of the five stages of suffrage expansion they think was the most important for American society.

## Point-of-Use Resources

Block Scheduling with Lesson Strategies Activities for Chapter 6 are presented on p. 22.

---

# 1 The Right to Vote

## Section Preview

### OBJECTIVES
1. **Summarize** the history of voting rights in the United States.
2. **Identify and explain** constitutional restrictions on the States' power to set voting qualifications.

### WHY IT MATTERS
Successful democratic government depends on the participation of its citizens through voting. The history of the United States has been marked by a steady expansion of the electorate through the elimination of restrictions on voting qualifications.

### POLITICAL DICTIONARY
★ suffrage
★ franchise
★ electorate

---

Soon, you will be eligible to vote—but will you exercise that right? The record suggests that while *you* may do so, many of your friends will not, at least not for some time. The record also suggests that some of your friends will never vote. Yet, clearly, the success of democratic government depends on popular participation, and, in particular, on the regular and informed exercise of the right to vote.

## The History of Voting Rights
The Framers of the Constitution purposely left the power to set suffrage qualifications to each State. **Suffrage** means the right to vote. **Franchise** is another term with the same meaning.[1]

▲ These historical flags (left to right: pre-1777, c. 1820, c. 1865) illustrate the expansion of the nation and growth of the electorate.

## Expansion of the Electorate
When the Constitution went into effect in 1789, the right to vote in the United States was restricted to white male property owners. In fact, probably not one in fifteen adult white males could vote in elections in the different States. Benjamin Franklin often lampooned this situation. He told of a man whose only property was a jackass and noted that the man would lose the right to vote if his jackass dies. "Now," asked Franklin, "in whom is the right of suffrage? In the man or the jackass?"

Today, the size of the American **electorate**—the potential voting population—is truly impressive. More than 205 million people, nearly all citizens who are at least 18 years of age, can qualify to vote. That huge number is a direct result of the legal definition of suffrage. In other words, it is the result of those laws that determine who can and cannot vote. It is also the result of some 200 years of continuing, often bitter, and sometimes violent struggle.

The history of American suffrage since 1789 has been marked by two long-term trends. First, the nation has experienced the gradual elimination of several restrictions on the right to vote. These restrictions were based on such factors as

---

[1]Originally, the Constitution had only two suffrage provisions. Article I, Section 2, Clause 1 requires each State to allow anyone qualified to vote for members of "the most numerous Branch" of its own legislature to vote as well for members of the national House of Representatives. Article II, Section 1, Clause 2 provides that presidential electors be chosen in each State "in such Manner as the Legislature thereof may direct."

---

## 🔲 Block Scheduling Strategies

Consider these suggestions to manage extended class time:

■ Have pairs or small groups of students create time lines that show the five stages in the growth of the American electorate. For each stage of the time line, students should estimate how much more of the population has become eligible to vote. (Have them look up population statistics in an almanac). Have students show the increases in a bar graph below the time line.

■ Have students discuss each of the restrictions the Constitution places on States' power to set voting requirements. Which do they feel is the most important, and which the least? Are there any restrictions not included in the Constitution that should be added? Have students write paragraphs of their opinions.

religious belief, property ownership, tax payment, race, and sex. Second, a significant share of what was originally the States' power over the right to vote has gradually been assumed by the Federal Government.

## Extending Suffrage: The Five Stages

The growth of the American electorate to its present size and shape has come in five fairly distinct stages. The two trends described above—elimination of voting restrictions and growing federal control over voting—are woven through those stages. You will see several illustrations of both of these trends over the course of this chapter.

1. The first stage of the struggle to extend voting rights came in the early 1800s. Religious qualifications, instituted in colonial days, quickly disappeared. No State has had a religious test for voting since 1810. Then, one by one, States began to eliminate property ownership and tax payment qualifications. By mid-century, almost all white adult males could vote in every State.

2. The second major effort to broaden the electorate followed the Civil War. The 15th Amendment, ratified in 1870, was intended to protect any citizen from being denied the right to vote because of race or color. Still, for nearly another century, African Americans were systematically prevented from voting, and they remained the largest group of disenfranchised citizens in the nation's population.

3. The 19th Amendment prohibited the denial of the right to vote because of sex. Its ratification in 1920 completed the third expansion

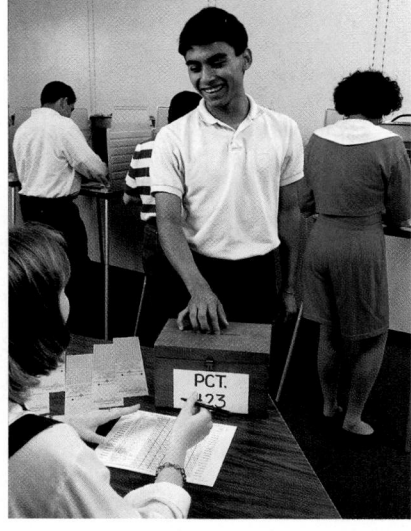

◀ This 18-year-old is casting a vote for the first time. *Critical Thinking* ***Do you think 18 is the right minimum age for voting? Why or why not?***

of suffrage. Wyoming, while still a territory, had given women the vote in 1869. By 1920 more than half of the States had followed that lead.

4. A fourth major extension took place during the 1960s. During that time, federal legislation and court decisions focused on securing African Americans a full role in the electoral process in all States. With the passage and vigorous enforcement of a number of civil rights acts, especially the Voting Rights Act of 1965 and its later extensions, racial equality finally became fact in polling booths throughout the country.

The 23rd Amendment, passed in 1961, added the voters of the District of Columbia to the presidential electorate. The 24th Amendment, ratified in 1964, eliminated the poll tax

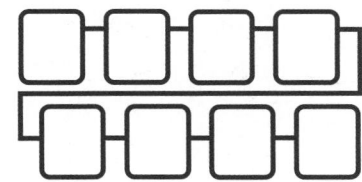

◀ **Suffragist Struggle** American suffragists first demanded the right to vote in 1848 at a meeting in Seneca Falls, New York. It took until 1920 to achieve ratification of the 19th Amendment.

---

## Organizing Information

To make sure students understand the main points of this section, you may wish to use the flowchart graphic organizer to the right.

Tell students that a flowchart can be used to record a sequence of events. Have students use a flowchart to record details about the five stages of the expansion of suffrage.

**Teaching Tip** A template for this graphic organizer can be found in the Section Support Transparencies, Transparency 4.

---

## Point-of-Use Resources

**Guide to the Essentials** Chapter 6, Section 1, p. 38 provides support for students who need additional review of section content. Spanish support is available in the Spanish edition of the Guide on p. 31.

**Quiz** Unit 2 booklet, p. 14 includes matching and multiple-choice questions to check students' understanding of Section 1 content.

**Section Support Transparencies** Transparency 26, *Visual Learning*; Transparency 125, *Political Cartoon*

**Basic Principles of the Constitution Transparencies** Transparency 11, *Popular Sovereignty*

**Presentation Pro CD-ROM** Quizzes and multiple-choice questions check students' understanding of Section 1 content.

## Answers to . . .

### Section 1 Assessment

**1.** The gradual elimination of voting restrictions and the expansion of the Federal Government's control over voting have greatly expanded suffrage.
**2.** Stages include: The early 1800s during which religious, property ownership and tax payment qualifications were eliminated; the post-Civil War era which saw the passage of the 15th Amendment; the passage of the 19th Amendment which expanded suffrage for women; the 1960s, which saw the passage of several civil rights acts; and the passage of the 23rd and 24th Amendments, eliminating poll taxes and adding the District of Columbia to the electorate.
**3.** Franchise is the right to vote.
**4.** Voters must be able to vote in all elections, cannot be deprived of the right to vote based on race, sex, or age (above 18), and States may not impose taxes as a condition to vote.
**5.** Answers will vary, but should present valid examples.
**6.** Outlines should indicate an understanding of the five stages in which suffrage has been expanded in the United States and reasonable inferences about what cultural changes

---

(as well as any other tax) as a condition for voting in any federal election.

5. The fifth and latest expansion of the electorate came with the adoption of the 26th Amendment in 1971. It provides that no State can set the minimum age for voting at more than 18 years of age. In other words, those 18 and over were given the right to vote by this amendment.

## The Power to Set Voting Qualifications

The Constitution does not give the Federal Government the power to set suffrage qualifications. Rather, that matter is reserved to the States. The Constitution does, however, place five restrictions on how the States use that power.

1. Any person whom a State allows to vote for members of the "most numerous branch" of its own legislature must also be allowed to vote for representatives and senators in Congress.[2] This restriction is of little real meaning today. With only minor exceptions, each of the States allows the same voters to vote in all elections within the State.

2. No State can deprive any person of the right to vote "on account of race, color, or previous condition of servitude" (15th Amendment).[3]

3. No State can deprive any person of the right to vote on account of sex (19th Amendment).[4]

4. No State can require the payment of any tax as a condition for taking part in the nomina-

tion or election of any federal officeholder. That is, no State can levy any tax in connection with the selection of the President, the Vice President, or members of Congress (24th Amendment).

5. No State can deprive any person who is at least 18 years of age of the right to vote because of age (26th Amendment).[5]

Beyond these five restrictions, remember that no State can violate any other provision in the Constitution in the setting of suffrage qualifications—or in anything else that it does. A case decided by the Supreme Court in 1975, *Hill* v. *Stone*, illustrates this point.

The Court struck down a section of the Texas constitution that declared that only those persons who owned taxable property could vote in city bond elections. The Court found the drawing of such a distinction for voting purposes—between those who do and those who do not own taxable property—to be an unreasonable classification, prohibited by the 14th Amendment's Equal Protection Clause.

---

[2]Article I, Section 2, Clause 1; the 17th Amendment extended the "most numerous branch" provision to the election of senators.

[3]The phrase "previous condition of servitude" refers to slavery. This amendment does not guarantee the right to vote to African Americans, or to anyone else. Instead, it forbids discrimination on these grounds when the States set suffrage qualifications.

[4]This amendment does not guarantee the right to vote to women as such. Technically, it forbids States the power to discriminate against males or females in establishing suffrage qualifications.

[5]This amendment does not prevent any State from allowing persons younger than age 18 to vote. It does prohibit a State from setting a maximum age for voting.

## Section **1** Assessment

**Key Terms and Main Ideas**

1. Describe two long-term trends that have characterized the history of **suffrage** in the United States.
2. Describe five distinct stages in the growth of the American **electorate.**
3. What is **franchise?**
4. What restrictions does the Constitution place on the States in setting suffrage qualifications?

**Critical Thinking**

5. **Demonstrating Reasoned Judgment** It is the year 1970. Suppose that you are a young adult testifying before Congress in favor of granting the vote to 18-year-olds. What arguments would you present in order to make your case?

6. **Drawing Inferences** What changes in American culture were brought about by the expansion of voting rights? Write an outline for an essay in which you analyze these changes.

 **Take It to the Net**

7. Read about the history of voting rights in the District of Columbia. In a paragraph, (a) explore why residents of the capital city have not had the same voting rights as the rest of the nation, and (b) describe the efforts to correct this problem. Use the links provided at the Social Studies area of the following Web site for help in completing this activity. **www.phschool.com**

---

might have been wrought as newly enfranchised voters participated in public policy-making.

 **Take It to the Net**

7. Direct students to the Social Studies area at the Prentice Hall School Web site. The *Magruder's American Government* companion Web site includes the directions and links needed to complete the activity. It also provides a printable Internet activity worksheet with scoring rubrics for assessment. Paragraphs should address the questions completely.

# SKILLS FOR LIFE

TECHNOLOGY
CITIZENSHIP
CRITICAL THINKING
CHARTS and GRAPHS

## Predicting Consequences

The Motor Voter Law requires States to allow people to register to vote when they apply for a driver's license. Several other of its provisions also make voter registration a more convenient process (see page 155).

The law became effective in 1995, and many predicted that it would reverse the downward trend in voter turnout. They were wrong. Voter registrations did reach record levels for the presidential elections of 1996 and 2000. But voter turnout in both elections fell well short of what it had been in 1992.

Consider another example. Many who fail to vote say that they are too busy—at work, at school, and so on—to take the time to go to the polls. Some suggest that this problem can be met by allowing both registration and voting via the Internet. To predict the consequences of Internet voting, follow these steps:

**1. Identify the problem, cause, or decision.** Begin by writing a question that summarizes and clarifies what you're trying to predict. What question might summarize issues involved in voting on the Internet?

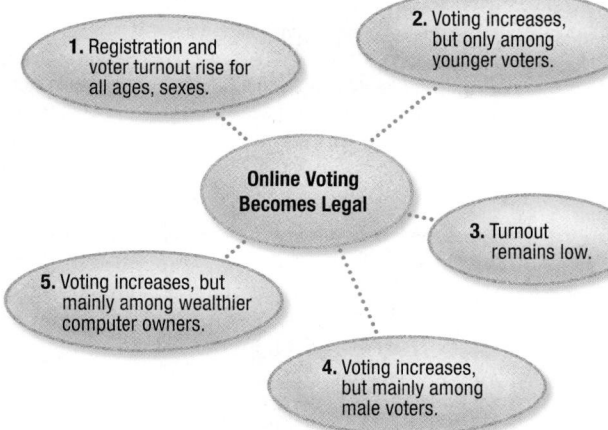

1. Registration and voter turnout rise for all ages, sexes.

2. Voting increases, but only among younger voters.

**Online Voting Becomes Legal**

3. Turnout remains low.

5. Voting increases, but mainly among wealthier computer owners.

4. Voting increases, but mainly among male voters.

**2. Brainstorm and chart possible outcomes.** Jot down all the possible consequences, good and bad, that you think could occur. At first, don't rule out any possibilities. Create a web diagram like the one above to display all the possibilities.

**3. Apply prior knowledge or new information.** To rule out some of the possible consequences, you probably need to apply existing or new knowledge about voting behavior. Policymakers often look for a historical *precedent*—a similar situation in the past. They also rely on their own intuition and experience. There is no precedent for Internet voting. But which prediction might you favor if you read about (a) a new study showing that most computer users are women, or (b) a new poll showing overwhelming voter disinterest in the election?

**4. Make a prediction.** State your prediction about the results of Internet voting in a way that makes your reasoning clear.

### Voting Booth

Information Voting Booth (IVB)

Home | Links | Search

| Photo | Candidate | Click To Vote | Attendance At Last Post | % Money From Companies & Organizations | Largest Single Contribution From A Company | % Money From Individuals | Largest Single Contribution From An Individual | Educational Qualifications | Stand On Issues | Champaign Web Site |
|---|---|---|---|---|---|---|---|---|---|---|
| | Wilson Henry | | 50% | 70% | 40,000 | 30% | $100 | | | |
| | Silvia Jones | | 75% | 65% | 25,000 | 35% | 5000 | | | |
| | Henry Oscar | | 98% | 20% | 400 | 80% | 150 | | | |
| | Fritz Hertz | | 20% | 79% | 5,000,000 | 21% | 50 | | | |

◄ Back | ▲ Up | ► Next

Efforts are underway in several States to allow voting on the Internet. Here is one mock-up of what an online ballot might look like.

### Test for Success

Use the steps above and the following facts to make a prediction about voting patterns: (1) Voter participation tends to be highest among older Americans. (2) The "baby boom" population is entering into its 50s and beyond.

## Point-of-Use Resources

📁 **Skills for Life Activity** Unit 2 booklet, p. 21 provides an additional skill activity for this chapter.

💿 **Social Studies Skills Tutor CD-ROM** Provides interactive practice in geographic literacy, critical thinking and reading, visual analysis, and communications.

### Test for Success

The likely prediction would be that voter participation will increase as the baby boom generation grows older.

---

## SKILLS FOR LIFE

*CRITICAL THINKING*

### Predicting Consequences

**Focus** Have the class work together to predict the consequences of the legalization of voting via the Internet.

**Instruct** Lead a brief class discussion to get students' initial reactions to the idea of online voting. Then have them complete Steps 1–3 by role playing a group of State election officials trying to decide whether to support a plan for Internet voting. Choose volunteers to lead the discussion and to create a tree diagram of possible good and bad consequences on the blackboard.

**Close/Reteach** At the end of the exercise, have the election "officials" draft a statement to the news media that predicts the consequences of online voting.

### Answers . . .

**1.** Possible answer: Would the legalization of online voting maintain fair, honest, and unbiased elections in this State?

**2.** Guide students to consider good and bad consequences that relate to the question they drafted in Step 1. For example, they might say that online voting could compromise honest elections because it could be open to fraud. It could make voting easier and more accessible, thereby increasing fairness; or it could be biased against lower income citizens without access to computers.

**3. (a)** option #1; **(b)** option #3.

**4.** The prediction can include both good and bad consequences.

**Objectives** You may wish to call students' attention to the objectives in the Section Preview. The objectives are reflected in the main headings of the section.

**Bellringer** Write the phrase *No Shirt, No Shoes—No Service!* on the board, and ask students where they have seen it and whether they think this restriction on who can enter a restaurant is fair. Explain that in this section, they will learn about the restrictions, or qualifications, on who can enter a voting booth.

**Vocabulary Builder** Point out the Political Dictionary. Have students try to link the first two terms and the last two terms to restrictions on voting. Ask students to verify their links as they read the section.

### Pressed for Time?

#### Quick Lesson Plan

**1. Focus** Tell students that to qualify for voting, people must meet the requirements set by their States. Ask students to discuss what they know about the requirements that every State has.

**2. Instruct** Ask students what prevents transients from voting in most States. Have students skim the section to identify this and other past and present voter qualifications required by States. List them on the board. Have students circle all requirements still held by at least one State. Discuss how the elimination of the uncircled requirements has expanded suffrage.

**3. Close/Reteach** Remind students that several requirements for voting have been eliminated because States used them to disfranchise certain groups. Ask students to write all of the subheadings from the section on a sheet of paper. Have them review the section and summarize the key points for each subheading.

## 2 Voter Qualifications

### Section Preview

**OBJECTIVES**

1. **Identify** the universal requirements for voting in the United States.
2. **Explain** the other requirements that States have used or still use as voting qualifications.

**WHY IT MATTERS**

All States have citizenship, residence, and age requirements for voting. Other voting qualifications differ from State to State. Some requirements—especially those that were used to disenfranchise certain groups—have been eliminated over time.

**POLITICAL DICTIONARY**

★ transient
★ registration
★ purge
★ poll books
★ literacy
★ poll tax

---

Are you qualified to vote? Probably not—at least not yet. Do you know why? In this section, you will see how the States, including yours, determine who is qualified to vote. You will also see that the various qualifications they set are not very difficult to meet.

### Universal Requirements

Today, every State requires that any person who wants to vote must be able to satisfy qualifications based on three factors: (1) citizenship, (2) residence, and (3) age. The States have some leeway in shaping the details of the first two of these factors; they have almost no discretion with regard to the third one.

### Citizenship

Aliens—foreign-born residents who have not become citizens—are generally denied the right

▲ These people are participating in a ceremony making them American citizens—one qualification for voting.

to vote in the United States. Still, nothing in the Constitution says that aliens cannot vote, and any State could allow them to do so if it chose. At one time about a fourth of the States permitted those aliens who had applied for naturalization to vote. Typically, the western States did so to help attract settlers.[6]

Only one State now draws any distinction between native-born and naturalized citizens with regard to suffrage. The Minnesota constitution requires a person to have been an American citizen for at least three months before he or she can vote in elections there.

In practice, a few aliens do vote, though in what number no one knows. They either wrongly believe that they are citizens or unlawfully claim to be citizens at their polling places.

### Residence

In order to vote in this country today, one must be a legal resident of the State in which he or she wishes to cast a ballot. In most States a person must have lived in the State for at least a certain period of time before he or she can vote.

The States adopted residence requirements for two reasons: (1) to keep a political machine from importing (bribing) enough outsiders to affect the outcome of local elections (a once common practice), and (2) to ensure that every

---

[6]Arkansas, the last State in which aliens could vote, adopted a citizenship requirement in 1926. In a few States, local governments can permit noncitizens to vote in local contests—e.g., city council elections—and a handful do.

---

### ⊞ Block Scheduling Strategies

Consider these suggestions to manage extended class time:

■ Divide the class into small groups, and assign each one of the universal voting requirements. Have each group debate the usefulness of their assigned requirement. When they have finished, ask them to present the pros and cons of their requirement to the rest of the class. Then ask each group if there should be any other universal voting requirements.

■ Tell students that in 1999, Congress passed the Civic Participation and Rehabilitation Act (H.R. 906), restoring federal voting rights to convicts who have been released from prison. Have students use the Internet to research the bill and the debate that surrounded its passage. (A link to the text of the bill can be found at **www.phschool.com**) Then have students reconstruct the debate over the bill in the classroom, incorporating their research and their own opinions.

voter has at least some time in which to become familiar with the candidates and issues in an election. For decades, all States imposed a comparatively lengthy residence requirement. They typically mandated at least a year in the State, 60 or 90 days in the county, and 30 days in the local ward or precinct.[7] Residence requirements for voting are not nearly so long today. The details vary, but only slightly, among the 50 States.

Nearly half of the States now require voters to have lived in the State for at least 30 days. In several States, the period is even shorter. For example, the requirement is only 20 days in Delaware and Oregon, 15 days in South Dakota, 14 days in Kansas, and 10 days in Alabama and Iowa. Arizona does have a 50-day rule, but it is the only State in which a new resident must wait for more than 30 days to become an eligible voter.[8] A growing number of States now require a voter to be a legal resident of the State but attach no time period to that requirement.

Today's much shorter requirements are a direct result of a 1970 law and a 1972 Supreme Court decision. In the Voting Rights Act Amendments of 1970, Congress banned any requirement of longer than 30 days for voting in presidential elections.[9] In *Dunn* v. *Blumstein,* 1972, the Supreme Court found Tennessee's requirement—at the time, a year in the State and 90 days in the county—unconstitutional. The Court held such a lengthy requirement to be an unsupportable discrimination against new residents and so in conflict with the 14th Amendment's Equal Protection Clause. The Supreme Court said that "30 days appears to be an ample period of time." Election law and practice among the States quickly accepted that standard.

Nearly every State does prohibit **transients,** or persons living in the State for only a short time, from gaining a legal residence there. Thus, a traveling sales agent, a member of the armed services, or a college student usually cannot vote in a State where he or she has only a temporary physical

---

[7]Recall, the precinct is the smallest unit of election administration; see page 140. The ward is a unit into which cities are often divided for the election of members of the city council.

[8]The Arizona requirement is 50 days for voting in State and local elections and 30 days for presidential elections. The Supreme Court upheld Arizona's residence law in *Marston* v. *Lewis* in 1973, but it also declared that that law "approaches the outer constitutional limits."

[9]The Supreme Court upheld this in *Oregon* v. *Mitchell* in 1970.

"THAT'S WHAT'S THE MATTER."
BOSS TWEED. "As long as I count the votes, what are you going to do about it? say?"

*Interpreting Political Cartoons* This 1870 cartoon depicts the "boss" of a corrupt New York City political "machine." ***According to this cartoon, what is the city boss's attitude toward democracy?***

residence. In several States, however, the courts have held that college students who claim the campus community as their legal residence can vote there.

## Age

The 26th Amendment, added to the Constitution in 1971, declares:

 **FROM THE Constitution** *❝The right of citizens of the United States, who are eighteen years of age or older, to vote shall not be denied or abridged by the United States or by any State on account of age.❞*
—26th Amendment

Thus, no State may set the minimum age for voting in any election at more than 18. In other words, the amendment extends suffrage to citizens who are at least 18 years of age. Notice, however, that any State could set the age at less than 18, if it chose to do so.

Until the 26th Amendment was adopted, the generally accepted age requirement for voting was 21. In fact, up to 1970, only four States had put the age under 21. Georgia was the first State to allow 18-year-olds to vote; it did so in 1943, in the midst of World War II. Kentucky followed suit in 1955. Alaska entered the Union in 1959 with the

**Reading Strategy**
**Drawing Inferences**
Ask students to look for the answer to this question as they read: How easy is it for an American to qualify to vote? Students should answer the question and provide details to support that answer.

**Point-of-Use Resources**

📁 **Guided Reading and Review** Unit 2 booklet, p. 15 provides students with practice identifying the main ideas and key terms of this section.

📁 **Lesson Plans** For lesson planning suggestions, see p. 32 of the Lesson Plans booklet.

📁 **Political Cartoons** See p. 24 of the Political Cartoons booklet for a cartoon relevant to this section.

📖 **Section Support Transparencies** Transparency 27, *Visual Learning;* Transparency 126, *Political Cartoon*

## Organizing Information

To make sure students understand the main points of this section, you may wish to use the web graphic organizer to the right.

Tell students that a web can be used to record a main idea and its supporting details. Have students use the web to record details about voting requirements for Americans.

**Teaching Tip** A template for this graphic organizer can be found in the Section Support Transparencies, Transparency 1.

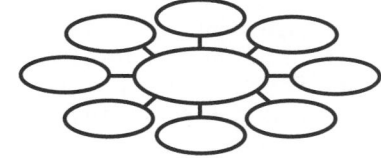

**Answer to . . .**
**Interpreting Political Cartoons** The boss depicted in the cartoon, Boss Tweed, shows no respect for democracy or the rights of voters, as evidenced by his use of intimidation and by employing voting officials who only "count" favorable votes.

*Interpreting Political Cartoons* **(a) What attitudes make this cartoon character a nonvoter? (b) What is the cartoonist's opinion of these attitudes?**

voting age set at 19, and Hawaii became a State later that same year with a voting age of 20.

Both Alaska and Hawaii set the age above 18 but below 21 to avoid potential problems caused by high school students voting in local school-district elections. Whatever the fears at the time, there have been no such problems in any State since the passage of the 26th Amendment.

Efforts to lower the voting age to 18 nation-wide began in the 1940s, during World War II. These efforts were capped by the adoption of the 26th Amendment in 1971, during the war in Vietnam. That amendment was ratified more quickly than any other amendment to the Constitution. This fact is testament to the emotional weight of the principal argument in its favor: "Old enough to fight, old enough to vote."

How have 18-to-20-year-olds responded to the 26th Amendment? In 1972, 58 percent of that age group registered to vote, and 48.4 percent of them reported that they did vote that year. By 1996, however, the registration figure had dropped to 45.6 percent, and only 31.2 percent said they actually went to the polls. Contrast the turnout of these young people with that of Americans 65 and older: In 1996, 77 percent of them were registered, and 67 percent voted. Indications are that the low-turnout behavior of 18-to-20-year-olds continued in 2000.

In a growing number of States, some 17-year-olds can now cast ballots in primary elections.

Those States allow anyone whose 18th birthday falls after the primary but before the g
in the primary

One State, Nebraska, has come very close to effectively lowering the voting age to 17 for all elections. There, any person who will be 18 by the Tuesday following the first Monday in November can qualify to vote in any election held during that calendar year.

## Other Qualifications

The States have imposed a number of other qualifications over time—notably, requirements based on literacy, tax payment, and registration. Only registration has survived as a significant requirement.

### Registration

Forty-nine States—all except North Dakota—require that most or all voters be registered to vote. **Registration** is a procedure of voter identification intended to prevent fraudulent voting. It gives election officials a list of those persons who are qualified to vote in an election. Several States also use voter registration to identify voters in terms of their party preference and, thus, their eligibility to take part in closed primaries.

Voter registration became a common feature of State election law in the early 1900s. Today, most States require all voters to register in order to vote in any election held within the State. A few do not impose the requirement for all elections, however. In Wisconsin, for example, only those in urban areas must register to vote.[10]

Typically, a prospective voter must register his or her name, age, place of birth, present address, length of residence, and similar facts. The information is logged by a local official, usually a registrar of elections or the county clerk. A voter typically remains registered unless or until he or she moves, dies, is convicted of a serious crime, or is committed to a mental institution.

State law directs local election officials to review the lists of registered voters and to remove the names of those who are no longer eligible to

[10]Wisconsin does not require registration by voters who live in rural areas or in cities with populations of less than 10,000.

vote. This process is known as **purging,** and it is usually supposed to be done every two or four years. Unfortunately, the requirement is often ignored. The **poll books** in those places are cluttered with a large number of persons who no longer meet voting requirements. Poll books are the lists of all registered voters in each precinct.

The registration requirement for voting has become controversial in recent years. Some people argue that it should be done away with. They view registration as a bar to voter turnout, especially among the poor and the less-educated.

Those critics buttress their case by noting that voter turnout began to decline in the early 1900s, just after most States adopted a registration requirement. They also point to the fact that voter turnout is much higher in most European democracies than in the United States. In those countries voter registration is not a matter of individual choice; by law, public officials must enter the names of all eligible citizens on registration lists. The United States is the only democratic country

in which each person decides whether or not he or she will register to vote.

Most people who have studied the problem favor keeping the registration requirement as a necessary defense against fraud. However, they also favor making the process a more convenient one. In short, they see the problem in these terms: Where is the line between making it so easy to vote that fraud is encouraged, and making it so difficult that legitimate voting is discouraged?

Most States have eased the registration process over the last several years, and in 1993 Congress passed a law that required every State (but North Dakota) to do so. That law, dubbed the "Motor Voter Law," became effective in 1995. It directs every State to (1) allow all eligible citizens to register to vote when they apply for or renew a driver's license; (2) provide for voter registration by mail; and (3) make registration forms available at the local offices of State employment, welfare, and other social service agencies. The Federal Election Commission reports that by 2000 some

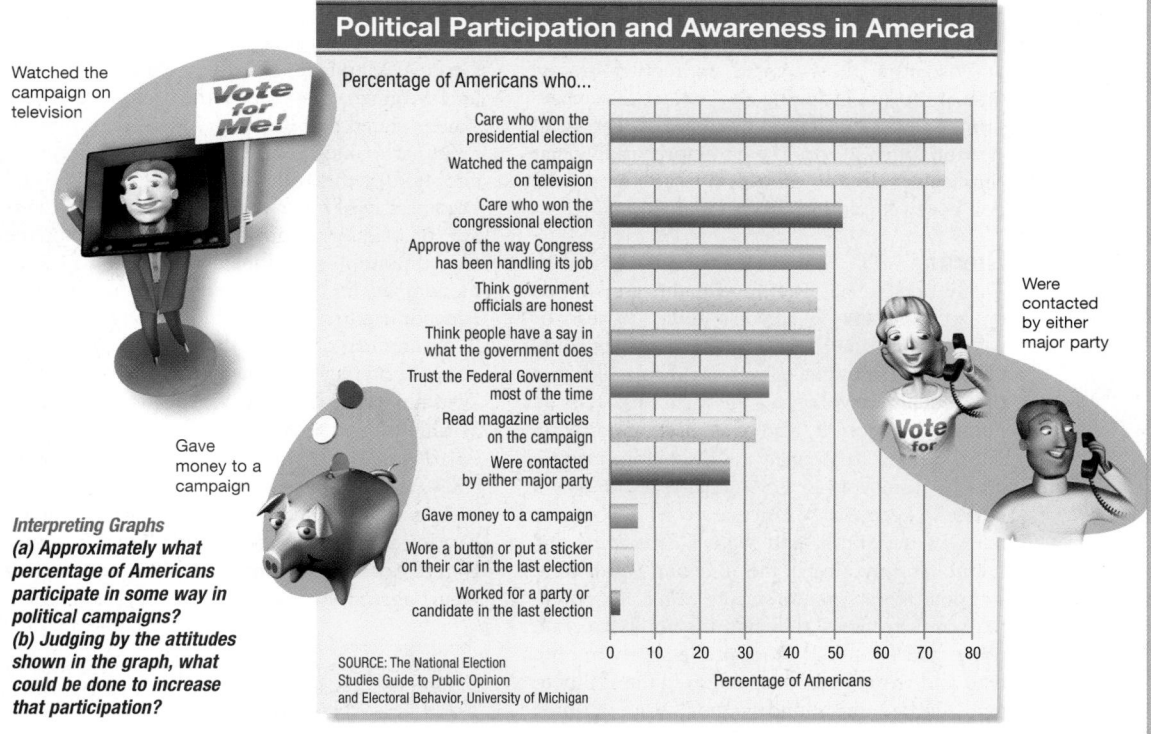

**Political Participation and Awareness in America**

Percentage of Americans who...

SOURCE: The National Election Studies Guide to Public Opinion and Electoral Behavior, University of Michigan

*Interpreting Graphs*
*(a) Approximately what percentage of Americans participate in some way in political campaigns?*
*(b) Judging by the attitudes shown in the graph, what could be done to increase that participation?*

## Preparing for Standardized Tests

Have students read the passages under *Other Qualifications* on pp. 154–156 and then answer the question below.

Which of the following is still a valid voting requirement in most States today?

**A** passing a literacy test
**B** registering
**C** paying a poll tax
**D** being a white male

---

**ACTIVITY**

### Extended Class Periods

**Time** 90 minutes.
**Purpose** Debate the issue of whether voter registration is a necessary requirement for voting.
**Grouping** Half the class will argue in favor of voter registration while the other half will argue against it. (A small group of students may also act as a jury.)
**Activity** As sides prepare their arguments, encourage them to consider issues such as voter turnout, election fraud, and the Motor Voter Law.
**Roles** Discussion leader, recorder, spokesperson, timekeeper.
**Close** Each side will be allotted an equal amount of time to present its arguments. In addition, each side will be granted time to make rebuttals to points made by the opposition. A jury may vote on which team presented its case most effectively.

     ■ **Block Strategy (Average)**

### Point–of–Use Resources

📁 **Government Assessment Rubrics** Class Discussion, p. 26

📁 **Block Scheduling with Lesson Strategies** Additional activities for Chapter 6 appear on p. 22.

*Answer to . . .*
**Interpreting Graphs (a)** About 16 percent. **(b)** Answers should be supported with specific reasons.

## Customize for
### Less Proficient Readers

Have students create posters explaining each of the universal voting requirements described in this section. Students should design their posters so they provide quick information for a person unfamiliar with voting requirements. Encourage students to decorate their posters or include visuals on them.

---

### Background Note
#### A Diverse Nation

Although no State today requires its citizens to fulfill a literacy requirement in order to vote, immigrants must show that they can read, write, speak, and understand English in order to become American citizens. This literacy test is one of several criteria—including possessing "good character" and demonstrating a knowledge of United States history and government—that aliens must meet as part of the naturalization process. Since only American citizens possess suffrage rights, then, there is a *de facto* literacy requirement which applies to those who must arrive at their citizenship through naturalization rather than birth.

---

### Point-of-Use Resources

**ABC News Civics and Government Videotape Library**
*The Blessings of Liberty, 1803–1861*
(time: about 15 minutes)

---

**Answer to . . .**

**Interpreting Political Cartoons** They disqualified white, male voters.

*Interpreting Political Cartoons* Voter literacy tests were often used to discourage African American voters. **According to the cartoonist, what unexpected results did these tests sometimes have?**

"By th' way, what's that big word?"

8 million persons had registered to vote as a direct result of the Motor Voter Law.

The law also requires every State to mail a questionnaire to each of its registered voters every four years, so that the poll books can be purged for deaths and changes of residence. It also forbids the States to purge for any other reason, including failure to vote.

Wisconsin allows voters to register at any time, up to and including election day. Elsewhere a voter must be registered by some date before an election, often 20 or 30 days beforehand.[11] That cutoff gives election officials time to prepare the poll books for an upcoming election.

### Literacy

Today, no State has a suffrage qualification based on voter **literacy**—a person's ability to read or write. At one time, the literacy requirement could be, and in many places was, used to make sure that a qualified voter had the capacity to cast an informed ballot. It also was used unfairly in many places to prevent or discourage certain groups from voting. For many years, it was a device to keep African Americans from voting in parts of the South, and Native Americans and Latinos from voting in the West and Southwest.

Some literacy requirements called for potential voters to prove they had the ability to read; other States required proof of the ability to both read and write. Still others required the ability to read, write, and "understand" some printed material, usually a passage taken from the State or Federal Constitution. Often, whites were asked simple questions; African Americans were asked questions so complex that they would stump even a judge who was familiar with the passage.

Connecticut adopted the first literacy qualifications in 1855. Massachusetts followed in 1857. Both of these States were trying to limit voting by Irish Catholic immigrants. Mississippi adopted a literacy requirement in 1890, and shortly, most of the other southern States followed suit. Southern literacy qualifications usually included an "understanding clause"—again, requiring potential voters to demonstrate comprehension of some printed material.

While those qualifications had been aimed at disenfranchising African Americans, they sometimes had unintended effects. Several States soon found that they needed to adjust their voting requirements by adding so-called "grandfather clauses" to their constitutions. These grandfather clauses were designed to enfranchise those white males who were unintentionally disqualified by their failure to meet the literacy or taxpaying requirements.

A grandfather clause was added to the Louisiana constitution in 1895; Alabama, Georgia, Maryland, North Carolina, Oklahoma, and Virginia soon added them as well. These clauses stated that any man, or his male descendants, who had voted in the State before the adoption of the 15th Amendment (1870) could become a legal voter without regard to any literacy or taxpaying qualifications. The Supreme Court found the Oklahoma provision, the last to be adopted (in 1910), in conflict with the 15th Amendment in *Guinn* v. *United States* in 1915.

A number of States outside the South also adopted literacy qualifications of various sorts. Wyoming did so in 1889, California in 1894, Washington in 1896, New Hampshire in 1902, Arizona in 1913, New York in 1921, Oregon in 1924, and Alaska in 1949.

Its unfair use finally led Congress to eliminate literacy as a suffrage qualification in the Voting Rights Act Amendments of 1970. The Supreme Court agreed in *Oregon* v. *Mitchell*, 1970:

---

[11]In Idaho, Maine, Minnesota, New Hampshire, and Wyoming, a person who is qualified to vote but misses the deadline can register (and then vote) on election day.

▲ This photo was taken in Mississippi, in 1978, when African American suffrage was supposed to be assured. *Critical Thinking What tactics does the sign use to intimidate African Americans who want to register to vote?*

> **" "** *In enacting the literacy test ban . . . Congress had before it a long history of the discriminatory use of literacy tests to disfranchise voters on account of their race.* **"**
>
> —Justice Hugo Black, Opinion of the Court

At the time Congress banned literacy tests, 18 States had some form of a literacy requirement for voting.

## Tax Payment

Property ownership, proved by the payment of property taxes, was once a very common suffrage qualification. For decades several States also demanded the payment of a special tax, called the **poll tax,** as a condition for voting. Those requirements and others that called for the payment of a tax in order to vote have disappeared.

The poll tax was once found throughout the South. Beginning with Florida in 1889, each of the 11 southern States adopted the poll tax as part of their effort to discourage voting by African Americans. The device proved to be of only limited effectiveness, however. That fact, and opposition to the use of the poll tax from within the South as well as elsewhere, led most of those States to abandon it. By 1966, the poll tax was still in use only in Alabama, Mississippi, Texas, and Virginia.[12]

The 24th Amendment, ratified in 1964, outlawed the poll tax, or any other tax, as a condition for voting in any federal election. The Supreme Court finally eliminated the poll tax as a qualification for voting in all elections in 1966. In *Harper* v. *Virginia Board of Elections,* the Court held the Virginia poll tax to be in conflict with the 14th Amendment's Equal Protection Clause. The Court could find no reasonable relationship between the act of voting on the one hand and the payment of a tax on the other.

## Persons Denied the Vote

Clearly, democratic government can exist only where the right to vote is very widely held. Still, every State does purposely deny the vote to certain persons. For example, none of the 50 States allows people in mental institutions, or any other persons who have been legally found to be mentally incompetent, to vote. Nearly all States also disqualify those who have been convicted of serious crimes. A few States also do not allow anyone dishonorably discharged from the armed forces to vote.

---

[12]By that time, the poll tax had been abolished in North Carolina (1924), Louisiana (1934), Florida (1937), Georgia (1945), South Carolina (1950), Tennessee (1951), and Arkansas (1964).

## Section 2 Assessment

**Key Terms and Main Ideas**

1. For what reasons do most States require voter **registration**?
2. What is the Motor Voter Law? What is its purpose?
3. **(a)** Why do election officials keep **poll books**? **(b)** Why is it a good idea to **purge** them every few years?
4. How was the **poll tax** used as a voting qualification?

**Critical Thinking**

5. **Drawing Conclusions (a)** Do you think that being able to read is necessary for being a well-informed voter? Why or why not? **(b)** Do you think literacy is more or less important now than it was 100 years ago?

6. **Recognizing Bias** What were grandfather clauses? How did they demonstrate a "double bias" against African Americans?

 **Take It to the Net**

7. Find your State's voting requirements. Do you qualify to vote? What if you move to another State? Make a chart comparing the voting requirements of your State with those of three other States. Use the links provided in the Social Studies area of the following Web site for help in completing this activity. **www.phschool.com**

### Take It to the Net

7. Direct students to the Social Studies area at the Prentice Hall School Web site. The *Magruder's American Government* companion Web site includes the directions and links needed to complete the activity. It also provides a printable Internet activity worksheet with scoring rubrics for assessment. Charts should be clearly organized and accurately compare the data.

otherwise would have been restricted by poll taxes or other requirements. They demonstrated a bias toward white males and against African Americans.

## Point-of-Use Resources

**Guide to the Essentials** Chapter 6, Section 2, p. 39 provides support for students who need additional review of section content. Spanish support is available in the Spanish edition of the Guide on p. 32.

**Quiz** Unit 2 booklet, p. 16 includes matching and multiple-choice questions to check students' understanding of Section 2 content.

**Presentation Pro CD-ROM** Quizzes and multiple-choice questions check students' understanding of Section 2 content.

## Answers to . . .

### Section 2 Assessment

**1.** Registration helps prevent fraudulent voting and determines eligibility for closed primaries.
**2.** The Motor Voter Law allows citizens to register to vote by mail or when they renew a driver's license, and provides that forms be available at local government offices. Its purpose is to encourage citizens to vote.
**3. (a)** Poll books are used to keep track of all registered voters in a district. **(b)** Purging is necessary to keep them current by eliminating people who moved away or died.
**4.** As only wealthier people could afford it, the poll tax served to discourage African Americans from voting. The Supreme Court found the poll tax to violate the 14th Amendment.
**5.** Answers will vary, but students should address issues discussed in the text and support their answers with examples.
**6.** Grandfather clauses were intended to allow white males to vote who

### Answer to . . .

**Critical Thinking** It discourages people who might think they won't be able to fill out the application correctly; it frightens people who might not want their names to appear in the newspaper.

**157**

## The Dangers of Voter Apathy

**Focus** Prior to reading the excerpt, ask students to identify reasons why voter participation has declined in recent years. As students provide answers, write them on the chalkboard.

**Instruct** Ask students to read the excerpt and analyze Gans's reasoning. Call on students to identify reasons that Gans suggests have contributed to voter apathy. Then have them write a reply to Gans stating whether they agree or disagree with his reasoning and explaining why. Encourage volunteers to share their replies with the class.

**Close/Reteach** Ask students to compare the reasons they gave for voter apathy to the reasons that Gans suggested. Then have students identify any additional causes of voter apathy that they can.

**Keep It Current CD-ROM** includes government-related projects by unit. The CD-ROM links to the Prentice Hall School Web site and may be used for daily updates.

### Answers to . . .

**Analyzing Primary Sources**

**1.** Voter participation declined by 20 percent.

**2.** People are either dropping out or failing to enter the political process because they hold negative attitudes toward government and politicians.

**3.** Improving civic education, making the two-party system more relevant to the needs of the electorate, and instilling values in young people that encourage a sense of community and concern for the future.

**4.** Answers will vary, but students should recognize that candidates elected by a small minority of eligible voters may not represent the will of the majority, which poses a threat to democratic government.

 *on Primary Sources*

# The Dangers of Voter Apathy

*Curtis Gans directs the Committee for the Study of the American Electorate, a non-partisan research organization that studies the causes of declining voter participation and looks for solutions. Here, Gans discusses low voter turnout and what can be done to reverse the trend.*

Over [recent decades], the percentage of eligible Americans who vote has declined by 20 percent in both presidential and off-year elections. More than 20 million Americans who used to vote frequently have ceased participating altogether. The United States—with voter turnouts of around 50 percent in presidential elections and 35 percent in off-year elections—now has the lowest rate of voter participation of any democracy in the world.

"Never mind what the voters are saying. What are the pollsters saying?"

What does the cartoon suggest about voter apathy?

More than half of America's nonparticipants are chronic nonvoters: people who have never voted or hardly ever vote, whose families have never voted, and who are poorer, less-educated, and less-involved participants in American society. But a growing number of Americans are simply dropping out of the political process—many of whom are educated, white-collar professionals. In addition, a growing number of younger Americans are failing to enter the political process. Both of these trends constitute a major national concern, for there is a very real danger that the habits of good citizenship will die and that government of the people, for the people, and by the people will become government of, for, and by the few. . . .

The scars of the Vietnam War and the Watergate scandal run deep. To many Americans, politics seem to be characterized by poor public leadership, increasingly complex issues, and ever-growing and inflexible government with few successes in meeting public needs. . . .

Sadly, for the average citizen, nonparticipation is becoming an increasingly rational act. Reversing this trend and instilling both hope and vigor among American voters will not be an easy task. But I think a few steps will improve participation in America. For example, we need to increase the amount and sophistication of civic education in our homes and schools. We must also develop policies that address the central concerns of the electorate, while realigning and strengthening the two-party system. . . . It is important for us to instill in our young people a sense of values that emphasizes something larger than the self.

In the end, voting is a religious act. Each citizen must come to believe that—despite the thousands of elections that are not decided by one vote—his or her vote *does* make a difference. It is that faith that needs to be restored.

### Analyzing Primary Sources

1. How much has voter participation declined in recent decades?
2. What reasons does Gans give to explain the decline in voter participation?
3. What suggestions does Gans give for increasing voter participation?
4. Why should we be concerned about the declining rate of voter participation in the United States?

 *Corner*

**Close Up on Primary Sources** Voter Registration Reform, p. 8, extends this feature with a primary source activity.

 **Online**

To keep up-to-date on Close Up news and activities, visit Close Up Online at

**www.closeup.org**

# ·3· Suffrage and Civil Rights

## Section Preview

### OBJECTIVES

1. **Describe** the 15th Amendment and the tactics used to circumvent it in an effort to deny African Americans the vote.
2. **Explain** the significance of the early civil rights legislation passed in 1957, 1960, and 1964.
3. **Analyze** the provisions and effects of the Voting Rights Act of 1965.

### WHY IT MATTERS

The 15th Amendment declared that the right to vote cannot be denied on account of race. Nevertheless, a variety of tactics were used in southern States to disenfranchise African Americans. The Supreme Court struck down a number of these efforts, and, beginning in the 1950s, Congress passed laws to protect minority voting rights.

### POLITICAL DICTIONARY

★ **gerrymandering**
★ **injunction**
★ **preclearance**

H ow important is the right to vote? For those who do not have it, that right can seem as important as life itself. Indeed, in the Deep South of the 1960s, civil rights workers suffered arrest, beatings, shocks with electric cattle prods, even death—all in the name of the right to vote. Their efforts inspired the nation and led to large-scale federal efforts to secure suffrage for African Americans and other minority groups in the United States.

## The Fifteenth Amendment

The effort to extend the franchise to African Americans began with the 15th Amendment, which was ratified in 1870. It declares that the right to vote cannot be denied to any citizen of the United States because of race, color, or previous condition of servitude. The amendment was plainly intended to ensure that African American men, nearly all of them former slaves and nearly all of them living in the South, could vote.

The 15th Amendment is not self-executing, however. In other words, simply stating a general principle without providing for a means to enforce implementation was not enough to carry out the intention of the amendment. To make it effective, Congress had to act. Yet for almost 90 years the Federal Government paid little attention to voting rights for African Americans.

During that period, African Americans were generally and systematically kept from the polls in much of the South. White supremacists employed a number of tactics to that end. Their major weapon was violence. Other tactics included more subtle threats and social pressures, such as firing an African American man who tried to register or vote, or denying his family credit at local stores.

More formal "legal" devices were used, as well. The most effective were literacy tests. White officials regularly manipulated these tests to disenfranchise African American citizens.

Registration laws served the same end. As written, they applied to all potential voters. In practice, however, they were often administered to keep African Americans from qualifying to vote. Poll taxes, "white primaries," gerrymandering, and several other devices were also regularly used to disenfranchise African Americans. **Gerrymandering** is the practice of drawing electoral district lines (the boundaries of the geographic area from which a candidate is elected to a public office) in order to limit the voting strength of a particular group or party.

The white primary arose out of the decades-long Democratic domination of politics in the South. It was almost a given that the Democratic candidate for an

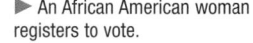

► An African American woman registers to vote.

**Objectives** You may wish to call students' attention to the objectives in the Section Preview. The objectives are reflected in the main headings of the section.

**Bellringer** Ask students whether they have ever crossed a city street against the light or outside of a crosswalk, and if they have ever been fined for doing so. Tell them that many cities and larger towns have jaywalking laws, but they are often not rigorously enforced. Explain that in this section, they will learn about a constitutional amendment that was not enforced for nearly a century.

**Vocabulary Builder** Draw an absurdly irregular shape on the board. Tell students that this shape shows the boundaries of a congressional district. Ask them which term in the Political Dictionary names a procedure that could result in a district with this shape.

### Pressed for Time?

#### Quick Lesson Plan

1. **Focus** Tell students that the 15th Amendment was ratified in 1870 but was not truly effective until 1965. Ask them to discuss what they know about the amendment and the laws that eventually gave it some force.
2. **Instruct** Ask students how some States used gerrymandering to get around the provisions of the 15th Amendment. Discuss this and other similar tactics and the laws that eventually arose to combat them.
3. **Close/Reteach** Remind students that the 15th Amendment gave African Americans the right to vote—in theory. Ask students how the Voting Rights Act helped turn that theory into practice.

## ⬚ Block Scheduling Strategies

Consider these suggestions to manage extended class time:
■ Have students write an editorial that could have appeared in the 1950s or early 1960s, condemning the 15th Amendment's lack of enforcement. Editorials should include specific examples of discrimination against African Americans, as described in the section. Have students share their editorials with the class.

■ Divide the class into small groups. Provide groups with several scenarios involving discrimination. Then have students determine whether each would be legal, using the civil rights or voting rights legislation described in this section. Ask each group to present its reasoning to the rest of the class.

## Reading Strategy

### Self-Monitoring

Tell students that they will be reading about a number of laws enacted to protect minority voting rights. Some of the laws are complex. Suggest that students ask themselves, as they read, whether the material makes sense to them. If not, they should reread the passage or read ahead a little to see if their confusion is cleared up.

## The *Living* Constitution

### Government by the People

The 26th Amendment, granting 18-year-olds the right to vote, was ratified on July 1, 1971. Much of the support for the amendment grew out of the civil rights and antiwar protest movements of the era. Many young people objected to the fact that they were old enough to fight and die in the Vietnam War, but not old enough to use the ballot box to voice their opinions on international and domestic issues.

### Using the Time Line

Historians argue that the spread of democracy has not been automatic, but has depended on the active demands of those excluded from participating in the political process. Review and discuss some of the civil rights struggles that brought about the voting reforms shown on the time line, such as woman suffrage. Then explore some of the ways young people can participate in the political process.

### Point-of-Use Resources

📁 **The Living Constitution** Two extension activities for this time line can be found on pp. 11–12.

📑 **Basic Principles of the Constitution Transparencies** Transparency 2, *The Living Constitution: Expanding Suffrage*

---

office would be elected. Therefore, almost always, it was only the Democrats who nominated candidates, generally in primaries. In several southern States, political parties were defined by law as "private associations." As such, they could exclude whomever they chose, and the Democrats regularly refused to admit African Americans. Because only party members could vote in the party's primary, African Americans were then excluded from a critical step in the public election process.

The Supreme Court finally outlawed the white primary in a case from Texas, *Smith* v. *Allwright,* 1944. The Court held that nominations are an integral part of the election process. Consequently, when a political party holds a primary it is performing a public function and it is, therefore, bound by the terms of the 15th Amendment.

The Supreme Court outlawed gerrymandering when used for purposes of racial discrimination in a case from Alabama, *Gomillion* v. *Lightfoot,* in 1960. In this case, the Alabama legislature had redrawn the electoral district boundaries of Tuskegee, effectively excluding all blacks from the city limits. The Court ruled that the legislature's act violated the 15th Amendment because the irregularly shaped district clearly was created to deprive blacks of political power.

Led by these decisions of the Supreme Court, the lower federal courts struck down many of the practices designed to disenfranchise African Americans in the 1940s and 1950s. Still, the courts could act only when those who claimed to be victims of discrimination sued. That case-by-case method was, at best, agonizingly slow.

Finally, and largely in response to the civil rights movement led by Dr. Martin Luther King, Jr., Congress was moved to act. It has passed several civil rights laws since the late 1950s. Those statutes contain a number of sections specifically intended to implement the 15th Amendment.

### Early Civil Rights Legislation

The first law passed by Congress to implement the 15th Amendment was the Civil Rights Act of 1957, which set up the United States Civil Rights Commission. One of the Commission's major duties is to inquire into claims of voter discrimination. The Commission reports its findings to Congress and the President and, through the media, to the public. The Act also gave the attorney general the power to seek federal court orders to prevent interference with any person's right to vote in any federal election.

---

## The *Living* Constitution

### Government by the People                                    1900

When the Constitution was written, only white male property owners (about 10 to 16 percent of the nation's population) had the right to vote. Over the past two centuries, though, the term "government by the people" has become a reality. During the first half of the 1800s, States gradually dropped property requirements for voting. Later, groups such as African Americans, women, and young adults gained the right to vote. Other reforms made the voting process fairer and easier. The time line lists some historic developments in the growing power of the people.

**1870**
Fifteenth Amendment—designed mainly to give former slaves the right to vote—protects the voting right of adult male citizens of every race.

**1913**
Seventeenth Amendment calls for members of the U.S. Senate to be elected directly by the people instead of by State legislatures.

---

### Preparing for Standardized Tests

Have students read the passages under *The Fifteenth Amendment* on pp. 159–160 and then answer the question below.

Why was the 15th Amendment ineffective for decades in ensuring the right of African Americans to vote?

Ⓐ Congress did nothing to implement it.

**B** Its wording was unclear and confusing.

**C** African Americans did not exercise their right to vote.

**D** Supreme Court decisions weakened the amendment.

The Civil Rights Act of 1960 added an additional safeguard. It provided for the appointment of federal voting referees. These officers were to serve anywhere a federal court found voter discrimination. They were given the power to help qualified persons to register and vote in federal elections.

## The Civil Rights Act of 1964

The Civil Rights Act of 1964 is much broader and much more effective than either of the two earlier measures. It outlaws discrimination in several areas, especially in job-related matters. With regard to voting rights, its most important section forbids the use of any voter registration or literacy requirement in an unfair or discriminatory manner.

The 1964 law continued a pattern set in the earlier laws. In major part, it relied on judicial action to overcome racial barriers and emphasized the use of federal court orders called injunctions. An **injunction** is a court order that either compels (forces) or restrains (limits) the performance of some act by a private individual or by a public official. The violation of an injunction amounts to contempt of court, a crime punishable by fine and/or imprisonment.

Dramatic events in Selma, Alabama, soon pointed up the shortcomings of this approach. Dr. King mounted a voter registration drive in that city in early 1965. He and his supporters hoped that they could focus national attention on the issue of African American voting rights—and they most certainly did.

Their registration efforts were met with insults and violence by local white civilians, by city and county police, and then by State troopers. Two civil rights workers were murdered, and many were beaten when they attempted a peaceful march to the State capitol. The nation saw much of the drama on television and was shocked. An outraged President Lyndon Johnson urged Congress to pass new and stronger legislation to ensure the voting rights of African Americans. Congress responded quickly.

## The Voting Rights Act of 1965

The Voting Rights Act of 1965 made the 15th Amendment, at long last, a truly effective part of the Constitution. Unlike its predecessors, this act applied to *all* elections held anywhere in this country—State and local, as well as federal.

Originally, the Voting Rights Act was to be in effect for a period of five years. Congress has

**1924**
General Citizenship Act grants all Native Americans the rights of citizenship, including the right to vote in federal elections.

**1995**
Federal "Motor Voter Law" takes effect, making it quicker and easier to register to vote.

**1925**     **1950**     **1975**     **2000**

**1920**
Nineteenth Amendment guarantees American women the right to vote in federal and State elections.

**1965**
Voting Rights Act protects the rights of minority voters and eliminates voting barriers such as the literacy test.

**1971**
Twenty-sixth Amendment sets the minimum voting age at 18.

### Analyzing Time Lines

1. Which amendments have granted voting rights to specific groups of people?
2. What has been the general trend of constitutional changes related to voting?

## Background Note
### Recent Scholarship

Taking a historical perspective, the essays in *Voting and the Spirit of American Democracy,* edited by Donald W. Rogers, demonstrate how changing social circumstances affected the workings of the political system—specifically the practice of voting and the meaning of the franchise in the American system of government. Written by historians and political scientists, the essays focus on three aspects of the history of voting: suffrage rights, voter turnout, and the voters' political efficacy. The articles, which begin with an overview of voting in the colonial and early national periods, trace major developments that resulted in broadening the franchise to include immigrants, African-Americans, and women. Each essay is followed by a short list of recommended readings.

## Point–of–Use Resources

📁 **Close Up on Primary Sources**
Seneca Falls Declaration (1848), p. 37; Lucy Stone's Letter to the New Jersey Tax Collector (1858), p. 38; Civil Rights Act (1964), p. 46; Voting Rights Act (1965), p. 47

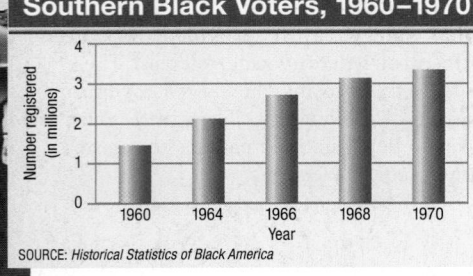

### Southern Black Voters, 1960–1970

SOURCE: *Historical Statistics of Black America*

*Interpreting Graphs* In the photo at left, civil rights demonstrators risk injury and even death in the 1965 Selma march for voting rights. **How many new African American voters registered in the South between 1960 and 1970?**

extended its life three times, in the Voting Rights Act Amendments of 1970, 1975, and most recently 1982. The present version of the law was made effective for 25 years; its provisions are scheduled to expire in 2007.

The 1965 law directed the attorney general to challenge the constitutionality of the remaining State poll-tax laws in the federal courts. That provision led directly to *Harper* v. *Virginia Board of Elections,* in 1966 (see page 157).

The law also suspended the use of any literacy test or similar device in any State or county where less than half of the electorate had been registered or had voted in the 1964 presidential election. The law authorized the attorney general to appoint voting examiners to serve in any of those States or counties. It also gave these federal officers the power to register voters and otherwise oversee the conduct of elections in those areas.

### Preclearance

The Voting Rights Act of 1965 created a further restriction on those States where a majority of the electorate had not voted in 1964. The act declared that no new election laws, and no changes in existing election laws, could go into effect in any of those States unless first approved —given **preclearance**—by the Department of Justice. Only those new or revised laws that do not "dilute" (weaken) the voting rights of minority groups can survive the preclearance process.

The preclearance hurdle has produced a large number of court cases since the passage of the law. Those cases show that the laws most likely to run afoul of the preclearance requirement are those that make these kinds of changes:

(1) the location of polling places;
(2) the boundaries of election districts;
(3) deadlines in the election process;
(4) from ward or district election to at-large elections;
(5) the qualifications candidates must meet in order to run for office.

Any State or county subject to the voter-examiner and preclearance provisions can be removed from the law's coverage through a "bail-out" process. That relief can come if the State can show the United States District Court in the District of Columbia that it has not applied any voting procedures in a discriminatory way for at least 10 years.

The voter-examiner and preclearance provisions of the 1965 Voting Rights Act originally applied to six entire States: Alabama, Georgia, Louisiana, Mississippi, South Carolina, and Virginia. The act also applied to 40 North Carolina counties.

The Supreme Court upheld the Voting Rights Act in 1966. In *South Carolina* v. *Katzenbach,* a unanimous Court declared:

**PRIMARY Sources** ❝ *The Voting Rights Act was designed by Congress to banish the blight of racial discrimination in voting, which has infected the electoral process in parts of our country for nearly a century. . . . Congress assumed the power to prescribe these remedies from Section 2 of the 15th Amendment, which authorizes the National Legislature to effectuate by "appropriate" measures the constitutional prohibition against racial discrimination in voting. We*

*Answer to . . .*

**Interpreting Graphs** About 1.7 million new African American voters registered.

**162**

hold that the sections of the Act which are properly before us are an appropriate means for carrying out Congress' constitutional responsibilities and are consonant with all other provisions of the Constitution. 🙶

—Chief Justice Earl Warren, Opinion of the Court

## Amendments to the Act

The 1970 amendments extended the law for another five years. The 1968 elections were added to the law's triggering formula; the result was that a number of counties in six more States (Alaska, Arizona, California, Idaho, New Mexico, and Oregon) were added to the law's coverage.

The 1970 law also provided that, for five years, no State could use literacy as the basis for any voting requirement. That temporary ban as well as residence provisions outlined in the law were upheld by the Supreme Court in *Oregon* v. *Mitchell* in 1970.

In 1975, the law was extended again, this time for seven years, and the five-year ban on literacy tests was made permanent. Since 1975, no State has been able to apply any sort of literacy qualification to any aspect of the election process.

The law's voter-examiner and preclearance provisions were also broadened in 1975. Since then they have also covered any State or county where more than 5 percent of the voting-age population belongs to certain "language minorities." These groups are defined to include all

▲ *I Have a Dream* This famous speech, delivered by civil rights leader Martin Luther King, Jr., was a highlight of the 1963 March on Washington, which drew more than 200,000 people.

persons of Spanish heritage, Native Americans, Asian Americans, and Alaskan Natives.

This addition expanded the law's coverage to all of Alaska and Texas and to several counties in 24 other States, as well. In these areas, all ballots and other official election materials must be printed both in English and in the language of the minority, or minorities, involved.

The 1982 amendments extended the basic features of the act for another 25 years. In 1992 the law's language-minority provisions were revised: they now apply to any community that has a minority-language population of 10,000 or more persons.

## Point-of-Use Resources

**Guide to the Essentials** Chapter 6, Section 3, p. 40 provides support for students who need additional review of section content. Spanish support is available in the Spanish edition of the Guide on p. 33.

**Close Up on Primary Sources** Martin Luther King, Jr., "I Have a Dream" Speech (1963), p. 45

**Quiz** Unit 2 booklet, p. 18 includes matching and multiple-choice questions to check students' understanding of Section 3 content.

**Presentation Pro CD-ROM** Quizzes and multiple-choice questions check students' understanding of Section 3 content.

## Answers to . . .

### Section 3 Assessment

**1.** Gerrymandering is the practice of drawing electoral district lines to favor a particular party; other devices included violence, social pressures, literacy tests, and poll taxes.

**2.** The 1964 law encouraged injunctions, court orders that force or restrain a particular action.

**3.** Preclearance is prior approval by the Department of Justice for a change to a law; States can bail out by showing that they have not applied discriminatory voting practices for at least 10 years.

**4. (a)** The Civil Rights Act of 1957; the Civil Rights Act of 1960; and the Civil Rights Act of 1964. **(b)** 1957: Set up the U.S. Civil Rights Commission; 1960: Provided for the appointment of federal voting referees; 1964: Outlawed discrimination in several areas and encouraged use of injunctions.

**5. (a)** That despite the 15th Amendment, most Americans still did not believe that African Americans deserved equality when it came to voting rights. **(b)** The civil rights movement as well as a growing public awareness of violence against African Americans brought about change.

## Section 3 Assessment

### Key Terms and Main Ideas

**1.** What is **gerrymandering**? What other devices were used to disenfranchise African Americans?

**2.** What part did **injunctions** play in the Civil Rights Act of 1964?

**3.** What is **preclearance**? How can a State "bail out" of the preclearance provisions of the Voting Rights Act of 1965?

**4. (a)** Identify the major civil rights laws enacted since 1950. **(b)** Describe voting rights provisions in these laws.

### Critical Thinking

**5. Drawing Conclusions** Even after the ratification of the 15th Amendment, African Americans in the South were denied the right to vote because the amendment was not implemented. **(a)** What does that tell you about American attitudes from 1870 until the 1950s? **(b)** Why did those attitudes change?

**6. Recognizing Cause and Effect (a)** How do you think the historical denial of voting rights to African Americans affected the makeup of Congress and many State legislatures? **(b)** How did that result, in turn, affect the likelihood that these legislatures would pass civil rights laws?

### Take It to the Net

**7.** Read about Dr. Martin Luther King, Jr.'s march from Selma to Montgomery, Alabama. Write a paragraph explaining how this march was instrumental in changing American opinion and spurring government action on voting rights. Use the links provided in the Social Studies area at the following Web site for help in completing this activity. **www.phschool.com**

### Take It to the Net

**7.** Direct students to the Social Studies area at the Prentice Hall School Web site. The *Magruder's American Government* companion Web site includes the directions and links needed to complete the activity. It also provides a printable Internet activity worksheet with scoring rubrics for assessment. Paragraphs should demonstrate an understanding of the event in the course of the civil rights movement.

**6.** Possible answers: **(a)** It meant that Congress was made up of people who did not represent all Americans and in many cases were not sympathetic to the plight of African Americans. **(b)** It reduced the likelihood of getting civil rights legislation passed.

**Objectives** You may wish to call students' attention to the objectives in the Section Preview. The objectives are reflected in the main headings of the section.

**Bellringer** Ask students whether they have ever tried to avoid going to a family event. Have two or three students explain why. Tell students that in this section, they will read about why many Americans refuse to attend one of the most important community and national events—elections.

**Vocabulary Builder** Tell students that most of the terms in the Political Dictionary contain words they recognize that can help them figure out the meaning of the whole phrase. Start with *off-year election*. Think the term through, aloud. ("I know the meaning of *election*. *Off-year* suggests that there's an *on-year*—what would that be?") Have students use the same approach with the other terms.

## Section Preview

### OBJECTIVES

1. **Examine** the problem of nonvoting in this country, and describe the size of the problem.
2. **Identify** why people do not vote.
3. **Examine** voting behavior of voters and nonvoters.
4. **Understand** the sociological and psychological factors that affect voting and how they work together to influence voter behavior.

### WHY IT MATTERS

Low voter turnout is a serious problem in this country. Among those who do vote, sociological and psychological factors work together to influence voter behavior over time and in particular elections.

### POLITICAL DICTIONARY

★ off-year election
★ political efficacy
★ political socialization
★ gender gap
★ party identification
★ straight-ticket voting
★ split-ticket voting
★ independent

---

**"Your** vote is your voice. Use it." That's the advice of Rock the Vote, an organization that encourages young voters ages 18–25 to participate in the election process. In the United States, and in other democratic countries, we believe in all voices being heard. That is, we believe in voting.

Over the next several pages you will look at voter behavior in this country—at who votes and who does not, and at why those people who do vote, vote as they do.

## Nonvoters

The word *idiot* came to our language from the Greek. In ancient Athens, idiots *(idiotes)* were those citizens who did not vote or otherwise take part in public life.

Tens of millions of Americans vote in presidential and congressional elections; in State elections; and in city, county, and other public elections. Still, there are many millions of other Americans who, for one reason or another, do not vote. There are some quite legitimate reasons for not voting, as you will see. But this troubling fact remains: Most of the millions of Americans who could—but do not—go to the polls cannot claim any of those justifications. Indeed, they would have been called idiots in the Greece of 2000 years ago.

## The Size of the Problem

The table on page 165 lays out the major facts of the nonvoter problem in American elections. Notice that on election day in 2000 there were an estimated 205.8 million persons of voting age in the United States. Yet only some 105.4 million of them—only 51.2 percent—actually voted in the presidential election. More than 100 million persons who might have voted did not.

In 2000 some 99 million votes were cast in the elections held across the country to fill the 435 seats in the House of Representatives. That means that only some 48 percent of the electorate voted in those congressional elections. (Notice the even lower rates of turnout in the **off-year elections**—that is, in the congressional elections held in the even-numbered years between presidential elections.)

Several facets of the nonvoter problem are not very widely known. Take, for example, this striking fact: There are millions of nonvoters *among those who vote*. Look again at the 2000 figures on page 165. More than six million persons who voted in the last presidential election could also have voted for a congressional candidate, but they did not choose to do so.

"Nonvoting voters" are not limited to federal elections. In fact, they are much more common in State and local elections. As a general rule, the farther down the ballot an office is, the fewer the

---

### Pressed for Time?

#### Quick Lesson Plan

**1. Focus** Tell students that there are millions of Americans who could vote but do not. Ask students to discuss what they know about why people do not vote.

**2. Instruct** Have students name three reasons that Americans who could vote do not vote. Briefly discuss how valid these reasons are, and then explore the various factors that influence voter behavior.

**3. Close/Reteach** Remind students that the problem of low voter turnout is serious. Ask them to create a form for analyzing voter behavior. The form should ask voters and nonvoters for information related to all the factors that affect voting.

---

## 🔲 Block Scheduling Strategies

Consider these suggestions to manage extended class time:

■ Divide the class into groups of four to six students. Assign groups the task of creating a public service announcement that encourages people to vote. Working together, students should write a one-minute television advertisement that could be aired to the national public during an election year. Encourage group members to discuss the various groups of people they wish to "target" with their ad. Each group should present their

work to the class. Students can vote on the most effective advertisement.

■ Have students create a fictional person (they might want to start with a magazine photo), for whom they identify the following factors: Age, sex, religion, race, region, income, education, occupation, and marital status. Have each student present his or her person to the class, and then have the class determine how the person would most likely vote.

Interpreting Political Cartoons *What reasons for nonvoting does this cartoon suggest?*

| Year | Population of Voting Age[1] | Votes Cast for President | | Votes Cast for U.S. Representatives | |
|---|---|---|---|---|---|
| | (in millions) | (in millions) | (percent) | (in millions) | (percent) |
| 1956 | 104.515 | 62.027 | 59.3 | 58.426 | 55.9 |
| 1958 | 106.447 | — | — | 45.818 | 43.0 |
| 1960 | 109.672 | 68.838 | 62.8 | 64.133 | 58.5 |
| 1962 | 112.952 | — | — | 51.267 | 45.4 |
| 1964 | 114.090 | 70.645 | 61.9 | 65.895 | 57.8 |
| 1966 | 116.638 | — | — | 52.908 | 45.4 |
| 1968 | 120.285 | 73.212 | 60.9 | 66.288 | 55.1 |
| 1970 | 124.498 | — | — | 54.173 | 43.5 |
| 1972 | 140.777 | 77.719 | 55.2 | 71.430 | 50.7 |
| 1974 | 146.388 | — | — | 52.495 | 35.9 |
| 1976 | 152.308 | 81.556 | 53.5 | 74.422 | 48.9 |
| 1978 | 158.369 | — | — | 55.332 | 34.9 |
| 1980 | 163.945 | 86.515 | 52.8 | 77.995 | 47.6 |
| 1982 | 169.643 | — | — | 64.514 | 38.0 |
| 1984 | 173.995 | 92.653 | 53.3 | 83.231 | 47.8 |
| 1986 | 177.922 | — | — | 59.619 | 33.5 |
| 1988 | 181.956 | 91.595 | 50.3 | 81.786 | 44.9 |
| 1990 | 185.812 | — | — | 61.513 | 33.1 |
| 1992 | 189.524 | 104.425 | 55.1 | 96.239 | 50.8 |
| 1994 | 193.650 | — | — | 70.781 | 36.6 |
| 1996 | 196.507 | 96.278 | 49.0 | 89.863 | 45.8 |
| 1998 | 200.929 | — | — | 66.033 | 33.9 |
| 2000 | 205.813 | 105.397 | 51.2 | 99.457 | 48.4 |

[1]As estimated by Census Bureau. Population 18 years of age and over since ratification of 26th Amendment in 1971; prior to 1971, 21 years and over in all States, except: 18 years and over in Georgia since 1943 and Kentucky since 1955, 19 years and over in Alaska and 20 and over in Hawaii since 1959.

SOURCE: *Statistical Abstract of the United States;* Federal Election Commission

**Interpreting Tables** This table shows voter turnout two ways: total numbers and percent of eligible voters. *(a) In what year shown did voting percentage peak for presidential races? (b) In what year did voting peak for congressional races?*

number of votes that will be cast for it. This phenomenon is sometimes called "ballot fatigue." The expression suggests that many voters exhaust their patience and/or their knowledge as they work their way down the ballot.

Some quick examples illustrate the phenomenon of ballot fatigue: In every State, more votes are regularly cast in the presidential election than in the gubernatorial election. More votes are generally cast for the governorship than for other Statewide offices, such as lieutenant governor or secretary of state. More voters in a county usually vote in the races for Statewide offices than vote in the contests for such county offices as sheriff, county clerk, or district attorney, and so on.

There are other little-recognized facets of the nonvoter problem, too. For example, the table on this page shows that turnout in congressional elections is consistently higher in presidential years than it is in off-year elections. That same pattern holds among the States in terms of the types of elections; more people vote in general elections than in either primary or special elections.

## Why People Do Not Vote

Why do we have so many nonvoters? Why, even in a presidential election, do as many as half of those who could vote stay away from the polls?

Clearly, the time that it takes to vote should not be a significant part of the answer. For most people, it takes more time to go to a video store and pick out a movie than it does to go to their neighborhood polling place and cast a ballot. So we must look elsewhere for answers.

### "Cannot-Voters"

To begin with, look at another of those little-recognized aspects of the nonvoter problem. Several million persons who are regularly identified as nonvoters can be more accurately described as "cannot-voters." That is, although it is true that they do not vote, the fact is that they cannot do so.

The 2000 data support the point. Included in that figure of more than 100 million who did not vote in the last presidential election are some 10 million who are resident aliens. Remember, they are barred from the polls in every State.

## Organizing Information

To make sure students understand the main points of this section, you may wish to use the Venn diagram to the right.

Tell students that a Venn diagram can be used to compare two groups by showing the characteristics they have alone and those they share. Have students use the Venn diagram to compare voters and nonvoters. Characteristics these groups share should appear in the space where the circles overlap.

**Teaching Tip** A template for this graphic organizer can be found in the Section Support Transparencies, Transparency 6.

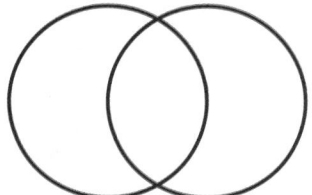

## Background Note
### Global Awareness

In recent years, leaders around the world have been searching for creative ways to combat voter apathy, using both "carrots" and "sticks". In the city of Vladivostock, Russia, local officials offered voters the chance to win lottery prizes such as televisions, cars, home appliances, and food as an incentive to cast their ballots in the local elections of June 2000. Meanwhile, the Parliament of the United Kingdom considered passing legislation which would punish citizens who fail to vote with a £5 (about $8) fine.

**Interpreting Political Cartoons** *What does the "weight" of the nonvoters tell you about the kind of difference they are making?*

Another 5 to 6 million citizens were so ill or otherwise physically disabled that they simply could not vote in an election. An additional 2 or 3 million persons were traveling suddenly and unexpectedly, and so could not vote.

Other groups of cannot-voters can be discovered in the nonvoting group. They include some 500,000 persons in mental health care facilities or under some other form of legal restraint because of their mental condition; nearly two million adults in jails and prisons; and perhaps as many as 100,000 who do not (cannot) vote because of their religious beliefs (for example, those who believe that acts such as voting amount to idolatry).

### Actual Nonvoters

Even so, there are millions of actual nonvoters in the United States. Thus, in 2000 more than 80 million Americans who could have voted in the presidential election did not.

There are any number of reasons for that behavior. For example, many people deliberately choose not go to the polls. They do not vote because they are convinced that it makes no real difference who wins a certain election. Others are satisfied with the political world as they see it. They believe that, no matter who wins elections, things will continue to go well.

However, a large number of those who deliberately stay away from the polls do so because they distrust politics and politicians.

They have no sense of **political efficacy.** That is, they lack any sense of their own influence or effectiveness in politics. Many of them believe that they have been squeezed out of the political process. They are convinced that "government by the people" has been taken over by entrenched politicians, powerful special interests, and the media.

### Factors Affecting Turnout

Other factors also affect whether voters show up at the polls. Cumbersome election procedures—for example, inconvenient registration requirements, long ballots, and long lines at polling places—discourage voters from turning out on election day. Bad weather also tends to discourage turnout.

Another possible, though hotly debated, factor is the so-called "time-zone fallout" problem. This refers to the fact that, in presidential elections, polls in States in the eastern and central time zones close before polls in States in the Mountain and Pacific time zones. Based on early returns from the East and Midwest, the news media often project the outcome of the presidential contest before all the voters in the West have gone to the polls. Some people fear that such reports have discouraged western voters from casting their ballots.

Of all the reasons that may be cited, however, the chief cause for nonvoting is, purely and simply, a lack of interest. Those who lack sufficient interest, who are indifferent and apathetic, and who just cannot be bothered are usually woefully uninformed. Most often, they do not know even the simplest facts about the candidates and issues involved in an election.

### Comparing Voters and Nonvoters

One useful way to get a handle on the problem of nonvoting is to contrast those persons who tend to go to the polls regularly with those who do not. There are many differences between them.

The people most likely to vote display such characteristics as higher levels of income, education, and occupational status. They are usually well integrated into community life. They tend to be long-time residents who are active in or at least comfortable with their surroundings. They are likely to have a strong sense of party identification and to believe

## Answer to . . .

**Interpreting Political Cartoons**
Nonvoters outweigh the voters, suggesting that their refusal to vote has a huge impact on elections.

## Preparing for Standardized Tests

Have students read the passages under *Factors Affecting Turnout* and then answer the question below.

Which of the following is described in the text as the main reason why people fail to vote?

**A** bad weather

**B** "time-zone fallout"

**C** lack of interest

**D** cumbersome election procedures

## Voting by Groups in Presidential Elections, 1968–2000 (By Percentage of Votes Reported Cast)

| | 1968 D | 1968 R | 1968 AIP | 1972 D | 1972 R | 1976 D | 1976 R | 1980 D | 1980 R | 1980 I | 1984 D | 1984 R | 1988 D | 1988 R | 1992 D | 1992 R | 1992 I | 1996 D | 1996 R | 1996 P | 2000 D | 2000 R | 2000 G |
|---|---|---|---|---|---|---|---|---|---|---|---|---|---|---|---|---|---|---|---|---|---|---|---|
| **National Vote** | 43.0 | 43.4 | 13.6 | 37.5 | 60.7 | 50 | 48 | 41 | 50.7 | 6.6 | 41 | 59 | 46 | 54 | 43.2 | 37.8 | 19 | 49.2 | 40.7 | 8.4 | 48.7 | 48.6 | 2.7 |
| **Sex** | | | | | | | | | | | | | | | | | | | | | | | |
| Men | 41 | 43 | 16 | 37 | 63 | 53 | 45 | 38 | 53 | 7 | 36 | 64 | 44 | 56 | 41 | 37 | 22 | 45 | 44 | 11 | 43 | 52 | 3 |
| Women | 45 | 43 | 12 | 38 | 62 | 48 | 51 | 44 | 49 | 6 | 45 | 55 | 48 | 52 | 46 | 38 | 16 | 54 | 39 | 7 | 53 | 45 | 2 |
| **Race** | | | | | | | | | | | | | | | | | | | | | | | |
| White | 38 | 47 | 15 | 32 | 68 | 46 | 52 | 36 | 56 | 7 | 34 | 66 | 41 | 59 | 39 | 41 | 20 | 46 | 45 | 9 | 43 | 55 | 3 |
| Nonwhite | 85 | 12 | 3 | 87 | 13 | 85 | 15 | 86 | 10 | 2 | 87 | 13 | 82 | 18 | 77 | 11 | 12 | 82 | 12 | 6 | 87 | 9 | 4 |
| **Education** | | | | | | | | | | | | | | | | | | | | | | | |
| College | 37 | 54 | 9 | 37 | 63 | 42 | 55 | 35 | 53 | 10 | 39 | 61 | 42 | 58 | 43 | 40 | 17 | 47 | 45 | 8 | 46 | 51 | 3 |
| High school | 42 | 43 | 15 | 34 | 66 | 54 | 46 | 43 | 51 | 5 | 43 | 57 | 46 | 54 | 40 | 38 | 22 | 52 | 34 | 14 | 52 | 46 | 2 |
| Grade school | 52 | 33 | 15 | 49 | 51 | 58 | 41 | 54 | 42 | 3 | 51 | 49 | 55 | 45 | 56 | 28 | 16 | 58 | 27 | 15 | 55 | 42 | 3 |
| **Age** | | | | | | | | | | | | | | | | | | | | | | | |
| Under 30 | 47 | 38 | 15 | 48 | 52 | 53 | 45 | 47 | 41 | 11 | 40 | 60 | 37 | 63 | 40 | 37 | 23 | 54 | 30 | 16 | 47 | 47 | 6 |
| 30–49 | 44 | 41 | 15 | 33 | 67 | 48 | 49 | 38 | 52 | 8 | 40 | 60 | 45 | 55 | 42 | 37 | 21 | 49 | 41 | 10 | 45 | 53 | 2 |
| 50 and older | 41 | 47 | 12 | 36 | 64 | 52 | 48 | 41 | 54 | 4 | 41 | 59 | 49 | 51 | 46 | 39 | 15 | 50 | 45 | 5 | 53 | 45 | 2 |
| **Religion** | | | | | | | | | | | | | | | | | | | | | | | |
| Protestant | 35 | 49 | 16 | 30 | 70 | 46 | 53 | 39 | 54 | 6 | 39 | 61 | 42 | 58 | 41 | 41 | 18 | 44 | 50 | 6 | 42 | 55 | 3 |
| Catholic | 59 | 33 | 8 | 48 | 52 | 57 | 41 | 46 | 47 | 6 | 39 | 61 | 51 | 49 | 47 | 35 | 18 | 55 | 35 | 10 | 52 | 46 | 2 |
| **Politics** | | | | | | | | | | | | | | | | | | | | | | | |
| Republican | 9 | 86 | 5 | 5 | 95 | 9 | 91 | 8 | 86 | 5 | 4 | 96 | 7 | 93 | 7 | 77 | 16 | 10 | 85 | 5 | 7 | 92 | 1 |
| Democrat | 74 | 12 | 14 | 67 | 33 | 82 | 18 | 69 | 26 | 4 | 79 | 21 | 85 | 15 | 82 | 8 | 10 | 90 | 6 | 4 | 89 | 10 | 2 |
| Independent | 31 | 44 | 25 | 31 | 69 | 38 | 57 | 29 | 55 | 14 | 33 | 67 | 43 | 57 | 39 | 30 | 31 | 48 | 33 | 19 | 44 | 49 | 7 |
| **Region** | | | | | | | | | | | | | | | | | | | | | | | |
| East | 50 | 43 | 7 | 42 | 58 | 51 | 47 | 43 | 47 | 9 | 46 | 54 | 51 | 49 | 47 | 35 | 18 | 60 | 31 | 9 | 55 | 42 | 3 |
| Midwest | 44 | 47 | 9 | 40 | 60 | 48 | 50 | 41 | 51 | 7 | 42 | 58 | 47 | 53 | 44 | 34 | 22 | 46 | 45 | 9 | 48 | 49 | 3 |
| South | 31 | 36 | 33 | 29 | 71 | 54 | 45 | 44 | 52 | 3 | 37 | 63 | 40 | 60 | 38 | 45 | 17 | 44 | 46 | 10 | 45 | 54 | 1 |
| West | 44 | 49 | 7 | 41 | 59 | 46 | 51 | 35 | 54 | 9 | 40 | 60 | 46 | 54 | 45 | 35 | 20 | 51 | 43 | 6 | 48 | 47 | 5 |

D = Democratic candidate; R = Republican candidate; AIP = American Independent Party candidate (George Wallace, 1968); I = Independent candidate (John B. Anderson, 1980; Ross Perot, 1992); P = Reform Party candidate (Ross Perot, 1996); G = Green Party candidate (Ralph Nader, 2000). Figures do not add to 100% in some groups because of rounding and/or minor party votes. SOURCE: The Gallup Organization.

**Interpreting Tables** Some groups of voters have favored one or the other major party over time. *In this table, which group most clearly demonstrates that point?*

that voting is an important act. They also are likely to live in those areas where laws, customs, and competition between the parties all promote turnout.

The opposite characteristics produce a profile of those less likely to vote. Nonvoters are likely to be younger than age 35, unmarried, and unskilled. More nonvoters live in the South and in rural, rather than urban or suburban, locales. Today, women are more likely to vote than men. This fact of political life has been apparent since the presidential election of 1988 and was reaffirmed in 2000.

A few of the factors that help determine whether or not a person will vote are so important that they influence turnout even when they are not supported by, or are in conflict with, other factors. Thus, those persons with a high sense of political efficacy are likely to vote—no matter what their income, education, age, race, and so on.

The degree of two-party competition has much the same kind of general, across-the-board effect. It, too, has an extraordinary impact on participation. Thus, the greater the competition between candidates, the more likely people will be to go to the polls, regardless of other factors.

# Spotlight on Technology

### Magruder's American Government Video Collection

The Magruder's Video Collection explores key issues and debates in American government. Each segment examines an issue central to chapter content through use of historical and contemporary footage. Commentary from civic leaders in academics, government, and the media follow each segment. Critical thinking questions focus students' attention on key issues, and may be used to stimulate discussion.

Use the Chapter 6 video segment to explore how Internet voting will affect politics and representative government. (time: 5 minutes) This segment highlights Internet voting in the presidential primaries in Arizona and Internet voting by overseas military personnel in the 2000 general primaries.

Despite the greater weight of some factors, however, note this point: It is the combined presence of several factors, not the of one of them alone, that usually determines whether a person will be a voter or a nonvoter.

## Voters and Voting Behavior

As you have just seen, tens of millions of potential voters do not go to the polls in this country. But many millions more do. How do those who do vote behave? What prompts many to vote most often for Republicans and many others to support the Democratic Party?

Answers to these questions are not as hard to find as you might think. Voting has been studied more closely than any other form of political participation in the United States. This is due partly to the importance of the topic and partly to the almost unlimited amount of data available. (There have been innumerable elections in which millions of voters have cast billions of votes over time.)[13] That research has produced a huge amount of information about why people tend to vote as they do.

### Studying Voting Behavior

Most of what is known about voter behavior comes from three sources.

*1. The results of particular elections.* Of course, how individuals vote in a given election is secret in the United States. However, careful study of the returns from areas populated largely by African Americans or Catholics or high-income families will indicate how those groups voted in a given election.

*2. The field of survey research.* The polling of scientifically determined cross sections of the population is the method by which public opinion is most often identified and measured. The Gallup Organization conducts perhaps the best known of these polls today.

*3. Studies of **political socialization**.* This is the process by which people gain their political attitudes and opinions. That complex process begins in early childhood and continues through each person's life. Political socialization involves all of the experiences and relationships that lead people to see the political process, and to act in it, as they do.

In the rest of this chapter, you will consider voter behavior—how and why people vote as they do. In Chapter 8, you will look at public opinion, at the techniques of survey research, and the process of political socialization.

### Factors That Influence Voters

Observers still have much to learn about voter behavior, but many sociological and psychological factors clearly influence the way people vote. Sociology is the study of groups and how people behave within groups. The sociological factors affecting voter behavior are really the many pieces of a voter's social and economic life. Those pieces are of two broad kinds: (1) a voter's personal characteristics—age, race, income, occupation, education, religion, and so

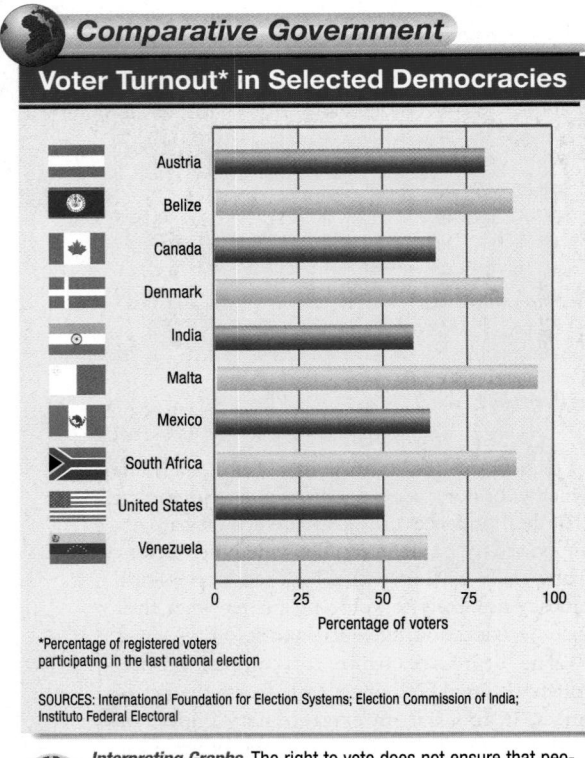

## Comparative Government

### Voter Turnout* in Selected Democracies

Austria
Belize
Canada
Denmark
India
Malta
Mexico
South Africa
United States
Venezuela

0    25    50    75    100
Percentage of voters

*Percentage of registered voters participating in the last national election

SOURCES: International Foundation for Election Systems; Election Commission of India; Instituto Federal Electoral

**Interpreting Graphs** The right to vote does not ensure that people will vote. Study the graph. *In which of these nations did more than three-quarters of eligible voters actually vote?*

[13]Much of the most useful research on voter behavior is done at academic institutions—most notably the Center for Political Studies at the University of Michigan.

on; and (2) a voter's group affiliations—family, co-workers, friends, and the like.

Psychology is the study of the mind and of individual behavior. The psychological factors that influence voter behavior are a voter's perceptions of politics, that is, how the voter sees the parties, the candidates, and the issues in an election.

The differences between these two kinds of influences are not so great as they might seem. In fact, they are closely related and constantly interact with one another. How voters look at parties, candidates, or issues is often shaped by their own social and economic backgrounds.

## Sociological Factors

From the table on page 167, you can draw a composite picture of the American voter in terms of a number of sociological factors. A word of caution here: Do not make too much of any one of these factors. As you examine the data, keep this point in mind: The table reports how voters, identified by a *single* characteristic, voted in each presidential election from 1968 through 2000. Remember, however, that each voter possesses *several* of the characteristics shown in the table.

The point can be illustrated this way: College graduates are more likely to vote Republican. So are persons over 50 years of age. Catholics are more likely to vote for Democrats. So are members of labor unions. How, then, would a 55-year-old, college-educated Catholic who belongs to the AFL-CIO vote?

### Income, Occupation

Voters in lower income brackets are more likely to be Democrats. Voters with higher incomes tend to be Republicans. This pattern has held up over time; in fact, it can be seen even in the exceedingly close presidential election of 2000. Voters with incomes below $15,000 a year backed Democrat Al Gore by a 3 to 2 margin; those making between $15,000 and $29,999 gave him a 4 to 3 edge. Those with incomes in the $30,000 to $49,999 range also supported Mr. Gore, but by only a very slight margin.

Voters with higher incomes backed Republican George W. Bush by telling margins. Thus, among voters making more than $100,000 a year, he held a 5 to 4 edge over his opponent.

▲ **Worth the Wait** Blacks in South Africa fought for many years to gain the right to vote. In the first multiracial elections, held in 1994, many people stood in long lines for hours in order to exercise this hard-won right.

Most often, how much one earns and what one does for a living are closely related. Professional and business people, and others with higher incomes, tend to vote for Republican candidates. Manual workers, and others in lower income groups, usually vote for Democrats. Thus, with the single exception of 1964, professional and business people have voted heavily Republican in every presidential election in the modern era, including 2000.

### Education

Studies on voter behavior reveal that there is also a close relationship between the level of a voter's education and how he or she votes. College graduates vote for Republicans in higher percentages than do high-school graduates; and high-school graduates vote Republican more often than do those who have only gone through grade school.

### Gender, Age

There are measurable differences between the partisan choices of men and women today. This phenomenon is known as the **gender gap,** and it first appeared in the presidential election of 1980. Women generally tend to favor the Democrats by a margin of five to ten percent, and men often give the GOP a similar edge.

A number of studies show that men and women are most likely to vote differently when such issues as abortion, health care or other social welfare matters, or military involvements

### ACTIVITY

### Heterogeneous Groups

**Enrichment** Divide the class into groups of four. Have students use the information provided in the text comparing voters and nonvoters to create representations of what the "typical" voter and nonvoter would look like. Encourage creativity while students use drawings, cutouts, or text to describe the various personal characteristics of their two individuals. Ask for a volunteer from each group to present their "characters" to the class.

🔲 **Block Strategy (Basic)**

## Customize for

### English Language Learners

Have students draw a simple two-column table. In the first column, have them list each of the factors that influence voting. (Have them use the section's headings and subheadings for clues to these). Then have them write descriptions of each factor, using simple phrases or single words.

### Point-of-Use Resources

🗀 **Close Up on Participation** Fighting for Teenagers' Rights, pp. 20–21 uses the topic of student membership on boards of education to help students plan and carry out service learning projects.

🗀 **The Living Constitution** Popular Sovereignty, p. 3

🗔 **Basic Principles of the Constitution Transparencies** Transparencies 9-15, *Popular Sovereignty*

## CONSTITUTIONAL PRINCIPLES

### Popular Sovereignty

The principle of popular sovereignty—that the people are the source of the government's power—is the very cornerstone of democracy, and voting is the main means by which the people express their political choices. Yet while more and more people around the globe are gaining the right to vote for the first time, Americans—who have had that right for over 200 years—are voting less and less often.

### Activity

Have the class list possible reasons for voter apathy. They should choose reasons from this chapter, and also brainstorm their own. Refer students to Chapter 13 for reasons relating to the electoral college and voting procedures. Have students use their list to generate poll questions about voter apathy. Students should administer the poll to adults or students over 18 years old, tabulate their results, and present them in the form of circle or bar graphs.

## Make It Relevant

### Students Make a Difference

Presidential candidate Senator John McCain (R.-Arizona) sat down with a group of South Carolina students in September, 1999, and answered their questions. McCain faced more student questions via the Internet, with topics ranging from school vouchers to social security. Both discussions—online and in person—were part of the Kids Voting USA program to educate young people about candidates and to encourage the habit of voting among children and adults. Through Kids Voting USA, students from elementary through high school visit polling places on election day and cast ballots, which are counted separately. Often, it is the insistence of their children that brings many adults to the polls. Crystal Lambert, a senior at the South Carolina meeting, had already registered to vote and was excited about her first presidential election.

abroad are prominent in an election. In 2000, 53 percent of all female voters cast their ballots for Democrat Al Gore for President.

Traditionally, younger voters have been more likely to be Democrats than Republicans. Older voters are likely to find the GOP and its candidates more attractive. Thus, in every presidential election from 1960 through 1980, the Democrats won a larger percentage of the votes of the under-30 age group than of the 50-and-over age bracket. That long-standing pattern was broken in 1984, when Ronald Reagan performed as well among young voters as with voters in other age groups. Bill Clinton restored the Democrats' advantage among young voters in 1996. Then in 2000, Al Gore and George W. Bush each won 47 percent of the under-30 vote. Older voters have increasingly voted Democratic. In 2000, Al Gore won 53 percent of the over-50 vote.

### Religious, Ethnic Background

In the North, a majority of Protestants prefer the GOP. Catholics and Jews are much more likely to be Democrats.

Historical factors account for much of this pattern. Most of those who first came from Europe to settle this country were of English stock and Protestant. The later tides of immigration, from southern and eastern Europe, brought many Catholics and Jews to the United States.

Those later immigrants were often greeted with hostility by the largely Protestant establishment. These minority groups settled most often in the larger cities, where local Democratic Party organizations helped them to become citizens and voters. From the New Deal period of the 1930s on, social welfare programs have strengthened the ties of most minority groups to the Democratic Party.[14]

In recent times, nonwhites have supported the Democratic Party consistently and massively. They form the only group that has given the Democratic candidate a clear majority in every presidential election since 1952. There are now more than 34 million African Americans, and they make up the second most important racial minority in the country.

---

[14]In 1960, John F. Kennedy became the first Roman Catholic President. His election marked a sharper split between Catholic and Protestant voters than that found in any of the elections covered by the table on page 167.

In the North, African Americans generally voted Republican until the 1930s, but then moved away from the party of Abraham Lincoln with the coming of the New Deal. The civil rights movement of the 1960s led to greater African American participation in the South. Today, African Americans vote overwhelmingly Democratic in that region, too.

The United States is now home to more than 35 million Latinos, people with Spanish-speaking backgrounds. Until now, Latinos have tended to favor Democratic candidates. Note, however, that the label "Latino" conceals differences among Cuban Americans, who most often vote Republican, and Mexican Americans and Puerto Ricans, who are strongly Democratic. The rate of turnout among Latinos is comparatively low—33 percent in 2000.

### Geography

Geography—the part of the country, the State, and/or the locale in which a person lives—also has an impact on voter behavior. After the Civil War, the States of the old Confederacy voted so consistently Democratic that the southeast quarter of the nation became known as the Solid South. For more than a century, most Southerners, regardless of any other factor, identified with the Democratic Party.

The Solid South is now a thing of the past. Republican candidates have been increasingly successful throughout the region over the past 30 years or so. This has been true in presidential elections and at the State and the local levels, as well. Historically, the States that have supported the Republicans most consistently are Maine and Vermont in the Northeast and Kansas, Nebraska, and the Dakotas in the Midwest.

Voters' attitudes also vary in terms of the size of the communities in which they live. Generally, the Democrats draw strength from the big cities of the North and East. Many white Democrats have moved from the central cities and taken their political preferences with them, but Republican voters still dominate much of suburban America. Voters in smaller cities and rural areas are also likely to be Republicans.

## Family and Other Groups

To this point, you have seen the American voter sketched in terms of several broad social and economic characteristics. The picture can also be drawn on the basis of much smaller and more personal groupings, especially family, friends, and co-workers.

Typically, the members of a family vote in strikingly similar ways. Nine out of ten married couples share the same partisan leanings. As many as two out of every three voters follow the political attachments of their parents. Those who work together and circles of friends also tend to vote very much alike.

This like-mindedness is hardly surprising. People of similar social and economic backgrounds tend to associate with one another. In short, a person's group associations usually reinforce the opinions he or she already holds.

## Psychological Factors

Although they are certainly important, it would be wrong to give too much weight to the sociological factors in the voting mix. For one thing, these factors are fairly static. That is, they tend to change only gradually and over time. To understand voter behavior, you must look beyond such factors as occupation, education, ethnic background, and place of residence. You must also take into account a number of psychological factors. That is, you must look at the voters' *perceptions* of politics: how they see and react to the parties, the candidates, and the issues in an election.

### Party Identification

A majority of Americans identify themselves with one or the other of the major parties early in life. Many never change. They support that party, election after election, with little or no regard for either the candidates or the issues.

The hefty impact of **party identification,** or the loyalty of people to a particular political party, is the single most significant and lasting predictor of how a person will vote. A person who is a Democrat or a Republican will, for that reason, very likely vote for all or most of that party's candidates in any given

## Voices on Government

**Ray Suarez** has been a news reporter and correspondent for about 25 years, most recently for *The News Hour with Jim Lehrer.* He has won numerous awards for his stories. In this excerpt, Suarez discusses how city populations and voting patterns are changing.

❝*One million Latinos in Chicago and its suburbs, and more than two million each in Los Angeles and New York, force you away from a binary black-white view of the struggles over the city. The new math means that standing between white and black is a new brown interest group waiting to be courted, often holding the balance of power in municipal elections. In Miami, San Antonio, and, increasingly, Dallas, you can't win without Latino support.*❞

### Evaluating the Quotation

*According to Suarez, how has the ethnic balance in cities been changing? How does this change affect politics?*

election. The practice of voting for candidates of only one party in an election is called **straight-ticket voting.**

Party identification is, therefore, a key factor in American politics. Among many other things, it means that each of the major parties can regularly count on the votes of millions of faithful supporters in every election.

Several signs suggest that, while it remains a major factor, party identification has lost some of its impact in recent years. One of those signs is the weakened condition of the parties themselves. Another is the marked increase in **split-ticket voting**—the practice of voting for the candidates of more than one party in an election. That behavior, which began to increase in the 1960s, is fairly common today.

Another telling sign is the large number of voters who now call themselves **independents.** This term is regularly used to identify those people who have no party affiliation. It includes voters who are independent of both the Republicans and the Democrats (and of any

*Answer to . . .*

**Evaluating the Quotation** Suarez says that there has been a huge increase in the number of Latinos in cities; he believes this is changing politics by creating a new electorate that has its own unique concerns and issues.

## Point-of-Use Resources

**Guide to the Essentials** Chapter 6, Section 4, p. 41 provides support for students who need additional review of section content. Spanish support is available in the Spanish edition of the Guide on p. 34.

**Quiz** Unit 2 booklet, p. 20 includes matching and multiple-choice questions to check students' understanding of Section 4 content.

**Presentation Pro CD-ROM** Quizzes and multiple-choice questions check students' understanding of Section 4 content.

## Answers to . . .

### Section 4 Assessment

**1.** People who have no political efficacy think they have no influence in politics, and thus are less likely to vote.
**2.** The gender gap is the set of measurable differences between the partisan choices of men and women.
**3.** If a person's party identification is strong, he or she will favor that party by voting a straight ticket.
**4.** Sociological factors include income, occupation, education, gender, age, religion, ethnic background, geography, family, and peer groups.
**5.** Possible answers: The composition of those who make up the government could change dramatically as more people are represented; or, there could be more competition among groups if people thought they had more political efficacy.
**6.** Questions will vary, but should touch on the themes described in this section.

---

minor party, as well). "Independent" is a tricky term, however.[15] Many who claim to be independents actually support one or the other of the major parties quite regularly.

The loose nature of party membership makes it difficult to determine just what proportion of the electorate is independent. The best guesses put the number of independents at somewhere between a fourth and a third of all voters today. The role that these independent voters play is especially critical in those elections where the opposing major party candidates are more or less evenly matched.

Until recently, the typical independent was less concerned, less well informed, and less active in politics than those voters who identified themselves as Republicans or Democrats. That description still fits many independents.

However, a new breed of independent voter appeared in the 1960s and 1970s, and their ranks have grown over the years. Largely because of the political events and personalities of that period, these "new" independents preferred not to join either major party. These independents are often young and above average in education, income, and job status.

---

[15]Note that the term "independent" is sometimes mistakenly used to suggest that independents form a more or less cohesive group that can be readily compared with Republicans and Democrats. (Although the Gallup Poll data on page 142 do not intend such comparisons, they can be misread to that effect.) In short, independents in American politics are not only independent of Republicans and Democrats; each of them is also independent of all other independents.

---

### Candidates and Issues

Party identification is a long-term factor. While most voters identify with one or the other of the major parties and most often support its candidates, they do not always vote that way. One or more short-term factors can cause them to switch sides in a particular election, or at least vote a split ticket. Thus, in 2000, exit polls indicate that 8 percent of those persons who usually vote Republican voted for Al Gore for President, and 11 percent of those who normally support Democratic candidates marked their ballots for George W. Bush.

The most important of these short-term factors are the candidates and the issues in an election. Clearly, the impression a candidate makes on the voters can have an impact on how they vote. What image does a candidate project? How is he or she seen in terms of personality, character, style, appearance, past record, abilities, and so on?

Just as clearly, issues can also have a large impact on voter behavior. The role of issues varies, however, depending on such things as the emotional content of the issues themselves, the voters' awareness of them, and the ways in which they are presented to the electorate.

Issues have become increasingly important to voters over the past 40 years or so. The tumultuous nature of politics over the period—highlighted by the civil rights movement, the Vietnam War, the feminist movement, the Watergate scandal, and economic problems—is likely responsible for this heightened concern.

---

## Section 4 Assessment

### Key Terms and Main Ideas
1. How does a person's sense of **political efficacy** affect his or her voting behavior?
2. What is the **gender gap?**
3. How are **party identification** and **straight-ticket voting** related?
4. List three sociological factors that affect voting behavior.

### Critical Thinking
5. **Predicting Consequences** What might be the results for the nation if all eligible voters were required to cast ballots? Why?

6. **Formulating Questions** Suppose you are a pollster. List three questions you would ask to determine if someone will vote in the next election, and three questions to find out what party he or she would be likely to support.

 **Take It to the Net**

7. Rock the Vote promotes participation in the political process among 18- to 24-year-olds. Visit their Web site, and make a chart showing which suggestions you think would be effective, which would not, and why. Add suggestions of your own, if you have any. Use the links provided in the Social Studies area at the following Web site for help in completing this activity. **www.phschool.com**

---

 **Take It to the Net**

**7.** Direct students to the Social Studies area at the Prentice Hall School Web site. The *Magruder's American Government* companion Web site includes the directions and links needed to complete the activity. It also provides a printable Internet activity worksheet with scoring rubrics for assessment. Charts should be cleary organized and include opinions backed with examples.

# CLOSE UP FOUNDATION on the Supreme Court

## Who Decides Who May Vote?

*The Constitution gives States authority to set voting qualifications. In the past, some States purposely used that power to exclude certain groups—most notably African Americans—from the electoral process. Does Congress have the authority to limit the power of States to set voter qualifications?*

### Oregon v. Mitchell (1970)

In 1970, the States of Oregon, Texas, and Idaho sued the Federal Government (specifically, Attorney General John Mitchell) to challenge four provisions of the Voting Rights Act Amendments passed by Congress that year. One provision lowered the minimum voting age to 18 in all elections in the United States—federal, State, and local. Another barred the use of any literacy test in any election in this country for a five-year period. A third provision prohibits the States from setting residence requirements for voting in presidential elections at more than 30 days. The final provision established national rules for absentee voting in presidential elections. (Absentee voting allows people unable to go to their polling places on election day to receive and mark their ballots, and return them—usually by mail—before or no later than election day.) These provisions were clearly intended to allow more people to participate in the electoral process.

The case was heard by the Supreme Court in its original jurisdiction. (In other words, the case was not appealed to the Court from a lower court.) Fifteen States, though not part of the suit, filed briefs (written arguments) with the Court in the case. The American Civil Liberties Union, the NAACP, the Democratic National Committee, and various other groups concerned with voting rights also filed briefs.

### Arguments for Oregon

1. Only the States have the power to set voting qualifications for State and local elections. Congress has no authority to require the States to allow persons between 18 and 21 to vote in State and local elections.

2. The Constitution does not give Congress the right to require the States to use different qualifications for voting in federal elections than those States adopt for their own elections.

3. States have the authority to set standards for voters, such as a minimum level of literacy or a minimum period of residence in the State.

### Arguments for Mitchell

1. Congress may set standards for voter qualifications in federal elections.

2. Congress may prevent the States from excluding certain groups of citizens from the voting rolls for State elections, if the exclusion tends to discriminate against people based on characteristics such as race or national origin. (Such discrimination by States violates the 14th Amendment's Equal Protection Clause.)

3. Congress may prevent States from imposing a residency requirement that makes it impossible for people who have recently moved to vote in presidential elections.

#### Decide for Yourself

1. Review the constitutional grounds on which each side based its arguments and the specific arguments each side presented.
2. Debate the opposing viewpoints presented in this case. Which viewpoint do you favor?
3. Predict the impact of the Court's decision on changes in voter eligibility and voter participation in the United States. (To read a summary of the Court's decision, turn to the Supreme Court Glossary on page 799.)

---

## CLOSE UP FOUNDATION Corner

📁 **Close Up on the Supreme Court** *Oregon* v. *Mitchell*, p. 7 provides an activity to extend coverage of this case.

## CLOSE UP FOUNDATION Online

To keep up-to-date on Close Up news and activities, visit Close Up Online at

**www.closeup.org**

---

## Who Decides Who May Vote?

**Focus** Remind students that under our federal system the Constitution gives the States the right to set voter qualifications, subject to five restrictions. Discuss and summarize those restrictions on the board. Then remind students that the Supremacy Clause also forbids the States from violating any provision of the Constitution.

**Instruct** Have students identify the constitutional provision the Federal Government's attorneys relied on. *(The Fourteenth Amendment's Equal Protection Clause)* Then discuss whether or not residency requirements and literacy tests pose a threat to democratic principles.

**Close/Reteach** Review the reasons for nonvoting discussed in Section 4. Then divide the class into five groups and have each group prepare a commercial encouraging people to vote. Each group should incorporate one of the five stages in the struggle to extend voting rights discussed in Section 1.

💿 **Keep It Current CD-ROM** includes government-related projects by unit. The CD-ROM links to the Prentice Hall School Web site and may be used for daily updates.

### Answers to . . .
#### Decide for Yourself

**1.** Oregon used the grounds that only States have the right to set voting requirements to argue that some provisions of the act were not constitutional. Mitchell rested on the Equal Protection Clause of the 14th Amendment to argue that Congress had the authority to challenge State provisions that denied basic voting rights to citizens.
**2.** Answers will vary, but should be supported with valid reasoning.
**3.** The Court struck down some of the provisions as they did not apply to State or local elections; however, it upheld the ban on literacy tests. This decision left some confusion in voting issues, which was later resolved by the 26th Amendment.

## Practicing the Vocabulary

**1.–10.** Sentences should define the vocabulary terms in the context of chapter content.

**11.** franchise
**12.** injunction
**13.** political efficacy
**14.** straight-ticket voting

## Reviewing Main Ideas
### Section 1

**15.** The gradual elimination of voting restrictions and the expansion of the Federal Government's control over voting.

**16.** Stages include: The early 1800s during which religious, property ownership and tax payment qualifications were eliminated; the post-Civil War era which saw the passage of the 15th Amendment; the passage of the 19th Amendment which expanded suffrage for women; the 1960s, which saw the passage of several civil rights acts; and the passage of the 23rd and 24th Amendments, eliminating poll taxes and adding the District of Columbia to the electorate.

**17.** Voters must be able to vote in all elections, cannot be deprived of the right to vote based on race, sex, or age (above 18), and States may not impose taxes as a condition to vote.

### Section 2

**18.** American citizenship, legal State residency, and age (minimum of 18 years old).

**19.** To keep political machines from bribing outsiders, and to ensure that all voters are familiar with the candidates and issues in an election.

**20.** Literacy requirements mean that a voter must be able to read and write; they were used to keep various ethnic groups from voting.

**21.** Intended to allow white males to vote who were unintentionally disqualified by requirements aimed at African Americans; in literacy tests, used to enfranchise white males who did not meet the literacy requirement.

**22.** It passed the Motor Voter Law.

### Section 3

**23. (a)** To ensure that voting rights cannot be denied to a citizen because of race, color, or previous condition of servitude. **(b)** By violence or social pressure, literacy tests and poll taxes, and gerrymandering.

**24.** It reports to Congress and the President and, through the media, to the public.

**25.** The drive met with violence by local whites, including police; when the nation saw this violence on television, Congress moved quickly to pass new legislation.

**26.** It challenged and overturned State poll taxes, and suspended the use of literacy tests or other discriminatory devices.

### Section 4

**27. (a)** A voter who votes in some elections, particularly national ones, but does not vote for local elections. **(b)** Voters often fail to vote for local elections because they have lost patience and/or because they do not feel they have the knowledge to participate.

**28.** Differences include income, education, occupation, community status, age, geography, and party affiliation.

**29.** Those who vote Democrat are typically younger, with lower incomes, and with less education than those who vote Republican.

**30.** It develops as result of social and psychological factors; it usually predicts how people will vote, though recently it has lost some impact.

## Political Dictionary

suffrage (p. 148)
franchise (p. 148)
electorate (p. 148)
transient (p. 153)
registration (p. 154)
purge (p. 155)
poll books (p. 155)

literacy (p. 156)
poll tax (p. 157)
gerrymandering (p. 159)
injunction (p. 161)
preclearance (p. 162)
off-year election (p. 164)
political efficacy (p. 166)

political socialization (p. 168)
gender gap (p. 169)
party identification (p. 171)
straight-ticket voting (p. 171)
split-ticket voting (p. 171)
independent (p. 171)

## Practicing the Vocabulary

**Using Words in Context** *For each of the terms below, write a sentence that shows how it relates to this chapter.*

1. suffrage
2. electorate
3. registration
4. poll tax
5. injunction
6. off-year election
7. political efficacy
8. political socialization
9. straight-ticket voting
10. independents

**Fill in the Blank** *Choose a term from the list above that best completes the sentence.*

**11.** Suffrage and _____ mean approximately the same thing.
**12.** A(n) _____ is a court order that can be used to compel a public official to carry out a law.
**13.** Some people do not have a sense of _____ and therefore do not bother to vote.
**14.** Voters with a strong allegiance to a party often engage in _____ when they go to the polls.

## Reviewing Main Ideas

### Section 1
**15.** What two long-term trends mark the expansion of the American electorate?
**16.** What are the five stages of the extension of suffrage?
**17.** What are the constitutional restrictions on the power of the States to set voting qualifications?

### Section 2
**18.** What are the universal requirements for voting in the United States?
**19.** For what two reasons did States adopt residence requirements for voting?
**20.** What is a literacy requirement for voting, and how was it used to deny suffrage to certain groups?
**21.** What is a grandfather clause, and what was its purpose in literacy tests?
**22.** How did Congress require States to ease their registration requirements in 1993?

### Section 3
**23. (a)** What was the purpose of the 15th Amendment? **(b)** List three ways that some southern States tried to circumvent the 15th Amendment.
**24.** To whom does the Civil Rights Commission report its findings?
**25.** How did Dr. Martin Luther King, Jr.'s voter registration drive affect the passage of national civil rights legislation?
**26.** Explain two key provisions of the Voting Rights Act of 1965.

### Section 4
**27. (a)** What is a nonvoting voter? **(b)** How is this phenomenon related to so-called "ballot fatigue"?
**28.** Describe three differences between voters and nonvoters.
**29.** Explain how income, education, and age usually affect party affiliation.
**30.** Explain how party identification develops, and how it affects the way individuals vote.

## Critical Thinking

**31. *Applying the Chapter Skill*** What do you think the consequences would be if voting requirements were eliminated and anyone who wished to could vote in federal, State, and local elections?

**32. *Identifying Central Issues*** What does the record of the expansion of suffrage tell you about trends in the United States from 1789 to the present?

**33. *Demonstrating Reasoned Judgment*** Do you think that resident aliens, those who have summer homes in a town, and other tax-paying transients should be allowed to vote in elections that determine how their taxes will be spent? Explain the reasons for your answer.

**34. *Testing Conclusions*** Some people suggest that we should not try to increase voter turnout in this country because that would only encourage uninformed voting and result in bad choices made for the wrong reasons. Do you agree or disagree? Why?

## Analyzing Political Cartoons

Use your knowledge of American history and government and this cartoon to answer the questions below.

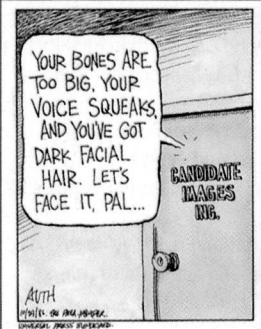

YOUR BONES ARE TOO BIG, YOUR VOICE SQUEAKS, AND YOU'VE GOT DARK FACIAL HAIR. LET'S FACE IT, PAL...

..YOU'RE A LOSER.

CANDIDATE IMAGES INC.

AUTH

**35.** Many factors affect voter behavior. At which factor is the cartoonist poking fun?

**36.** What do you think the cartoonist thinks of the way the American electorate chooses its leaders today versus 150 years ago?

## ★ You Can Make a Difference

Chances are that many of your 18-year-old friends and classmates have not registered to vote. You and your classmates can help other teens make a difference in the political process. Since laws vary from State to State, start by asking your local election officials how and where one registers to vote in your community. Take a poll of students to see how many have already registered. Then, working with school administrators, plan a voter registration drive, using posters and press releases to publicize your campaign.

## Participation Activities

**37. *Current Events Watch*** There are still places in the world where people are struggling to achieve the right to choose the leaders who govern them. Select one such country, and read about recent efforts to gain or expand suffrage there. Write a brief report on the struggle. Conclude by predicting whether and/or when the struggle for suffrage will succeed.

**38. *Time Line Activity*** Using information from the chapter, make a time line of the federal laws (including constitutional amendments) that were designed to ensure the suffrage of African Americans. Which, in your opinion, was the most important law? Why?

**39. *It's Your Turn*** You have been hired to increase voter turnout in local elections in your community. Review the causes for low voter turnout and determine how they might apply to various groups in your community. Prepare a proposal to the election committee. Describe three tactics you would use to increase local voter turnout and explain why they might work. **(Writing a Proposal)**

 **Take It to the Net**

***Chapter 6 Self-Test*** As a final review activity, take the Chapter 6 Self-Test in the Social Studies area at the Web site listed below, and receive immediate feedback on your answers.

**www.phschool.com**

 **Take It to the Net**

Additional support materials and activities for Chapter 6 of *Magruder's American Government* can be found in the Social Studies area at the Prentice Hall School Web site. **www.phschool.com**

---

## Critical Thinking Skills

**31.** Some students might suggest that more people would vote, and that as a result representation would be more diverse and better meet all citizens' needs; others might say that given voter apathy, even if there were fewer restrictions there would be little change.

**32.** That attitudes have greatly changed concerning equality for people of all races, ethnic background, and gender.

**33.** Answers will vary, but should show an understanding of the three universal requirements for voting.

**34.** Answers will vary, but should be supported with solid opinions and examples.

## Analyzing Political Cartoons

**35.** Physical appearance.

**36.** Possible answer: The cartoonist suggests that 150 years ago, people were concerned with issues and ideas, not media appeal.

## You Can Make a Difference

Have students refer to the Close Up on Participation booklet in the *Teaching Resources* for ideas on planning and carrying out service learning projects.

## Participation Activities

**37.** Reports should be accurate and include relevant historical facts; predictions should be based on those facts rather than on the student's opinion.

**38.** Time lines should include all relevant laws; opinions should be supported with reasons.

**39.** Proposals should indicate they are targeted to the various groups with low voter turnout; tactics should address issues discussed in the chapter.

---

## Point-of-Use Resources

 **Guide to the Essentials of American Government** Chapter 6 Test, page 42 provides multiple-choice questions to test students' knowledge of the chapter.

**Test Bank CD-ROM** Chapter 6 Test

**Chapter Test** Chapter Tests booklet

# The Electoral Process

| Section Objectives | Print and Technology Resources |
|---|---|
| **1 The Nominating Process**<br>*(pp. 178–186)*<br><br>1. Explain why the nominating process is a critical first step in the election process.<br>2. Describe self-announcement, the caucus, and the convention as nominating methods.<br>3. Discuss the direct primary as the principal nominating method used in the United States.<br>4. Understand why some candidates use the petition as a nominating device.<br><br>**TEKS 3A, 11A, 11B, 21A, 21D, 21E, 22A, I22B** | • **Unit 2 booklet**<br>Guided Reading and Review, p. 22<br>Section 1 Quiz, p. 23<br>• **Lesson Plans booklet** Section 1, p. 35<br>• **Political Cartoons booklet** Section 1, p. 27<br>• **Block Scheduling with Lesson Strategies booklet** p. 22<br>• **Section Reading Support Transparencies**<br><br>• **Close Up on Primary Sources booklet** Reforming the Electoral College, p. 9<br>• **The Living Constitution booklet** p. 3<br>• **Government Assessment Rubrics booklet** p. 10<br>• **Section Support Transparencies** 30, 129<br>• **Presentation Pro CD-ROM** Section 1 |
| **2 Elections**<br>*(pp. 188–194)*<br><br>1. Compare different methods of filling elected public offices.<br>2. Define the role of precincts and polling places in the election process.<br>3. Describe the various ways in which voters can cast their ballots.<br>4. Outline the role that voting machines and other innovations play in the election process.<br><br>**TEKS 11A, 20A, 20B, 21A, 21B, 21C, 21D, 21E, 22A, 22B, 22C, 22D, 23B** | • **Unit 2 booklet**<br>Guided Reading and Review, p. 24<br>Section 2 Quiz, p. 25<br>• **Lesson Plans booklet** Section 2, p. 36<br>• **Political Cartoons booklet** Section 2, p. 28<br>• **Section Reading Support Transparencies**<br><br>• **Block Scheduling with Lesson Strategies booklet** p. 22<br>• **Government Assessment Rubrics booklet** p. 20<br>• **Section Support Transparencies** 31, 130<br>• **Presentation Pro CD-ROM** Section 2<br>• **Social Studies Skills Tutor CD-ROM** |
| **3 Money and Elections**<br>*(pp. 196–202)*<br><br>1. Explain the issues raised by campaign spending.<br>2. Describe the various sources of funding for campaign spending.<br>3. Examine federal laws that regulate campaign finance.<br>4. Outline the role of the Federal Election Commission in enforcing campaign finance laws.<br>5. Describe loopholes in today's campaign finance laws.<br><br>**TEKS 3A, 3B, 16C, 17C, 21A, 21B, 21C, 21D, 21E, 22A, 22B, 22C, 22D** | • **Unit 2 booklet**<br>Guided Reading and Review, p. 26<br>Section 3 Quiz, p. 27<br>Skills for Life Activity, p. 28<br>• **Lesson Plans booklet** Section 3, p. 37<br>• **Political Cartoons booklet** Section 3, p. 29<br>• **Block Scheduling with Lesson Strategies booklet** p. 22<br>• **Close Up on the Supreme Court booklet** *Nixon* v. *Shrink Missouri Government PAC*, p. 8<br>• **Section Reading Support Transparencies**<br><br>• **The Living Constitution booklet** p. 4<br>• **Government Assessment Rubrics booklet** p. 20<br>• **The Basic Principles of the Constitution Posters**<br>• **Section Support Transparencies** 32, 131<br>• **Presentation Pro CD-ROM** Section 3<br>• **Simulations and Data Graphing CD-ROM** |

# Block Scheduling Strategies

The *Magruder's American Government* program addresses block-scheduling strategies in a variety of ways. For easy reference, side-column activities that fit a block format are marked ■ **Block Strategy.** Each section also contains a **Block Scheduling Strategies** box describing at least two block-format activities that address and extend core content from the section. The **Block Scheduling with Lesson Strategies booklet** found in the Teaching Resources contains additional block-scheduling activities for each chapter.

## Take It to the Net

Visit the Social Studies area at the Prentice Hall School Web site. Once there, you can find additional links, current events connections, and activities to enrich chapter content for *Magruder's American Government,* as well as a Self-Test for students. Be sure to check out this month's **eTeach** online discussion with a Master Teacher.

### www.phschool.com

## Pressed for Time?

If you are running short on time to cover this chapter, consider one of the following options:
- Use the **Presentation Pro CD-ROM** to create an outline for this chapter.
- Use one of the **Pressed for Time** activities found on p. 27.
- Use the Section Summaries for Chapter 2, from **Guide to the Essentials of American Government (English and Spanish).**

##  Video Connections

Prentice Hall offers two video programs to reinforce and extend chapter content. Show students *The Blessings of Liberty* from the **ABC News Civics and Government Videotape Library** and *Prayer in Schools: A Nationwide Debate* from the **Magruder's American Government Video Collection.**

## Assessment Options
- Section Quizzes, **Unit 2 booklet,** pp. 23, 25, 27
- Chapter 7 Assessment, pp. 204–205
- **Guide to the Essentials of American Government,** Chapter 7 Test, p. 46

### Core Assessment
Chapter 7 Test, Chapter Tests booklet
ExamView® Test Bank CD-ROM Chapter 7
Government Assessment Rubrics

### Standardized Test Preparation

#### Diagnose and Prescribe
Diagnostic Tests for High School
Social Studies Skills

#### Review and Reteach
Review Book for Government

#### Practice and Assess
Test-Taking Strategies With
    Transparencies for High School
Test Prep Book for Government

# Chapter 7 Teacher's Edition Index

## The Electoral Process

### Introducing the Chapter

In this chapter, students will learn about all aspects of the electoral process—nominations, the role of the States, how votes are tallied, and the role that money plays in political campaigns.

### Make It Relevant

**★ *You Can Make a Difference***

Project Vote Smart issues an acclaimed *Election Year Voter's Self-Defense Manual,* which, according to the organization, is "a compact sampling of voting records, campaign finance data, competing special interests' performance evaluations, contact information—and more." Have students conduct research and make a similar booklet for their community. Have students visit Project Vote Smart's Web site (www.vote-smart.org) for guidance on the specific type of information to include. Have students distribute copies of the booklet in their community.

**Service Learning**

### Constitutional Principles

Emphasize the following basic principles as students read Chapter 7. Have the class respond to the questions, and then ask volunteers to explain how the complicated rules of the electoral process serve to protect basic democratic principles.

**Popular Sovereignty** Which of the nominating procedures best supports the ideal of popular sovereignty?

**Limited Government** How do limits on campaign financing help ensure that the executive branch is not too powerful?

**Federalism** What roles do the States and National Government play in the electoral process?

CHAPTER 7

# The Electoral Process

*"Any American who cannot bother to vote and who thinks that a single vote does not matter is letting America down."*

—Marian Wright Edelman (1992)

Democracy can work only if Americans participate fully in the electoral process. This means making our voices heard through our votes at each stage of that process.

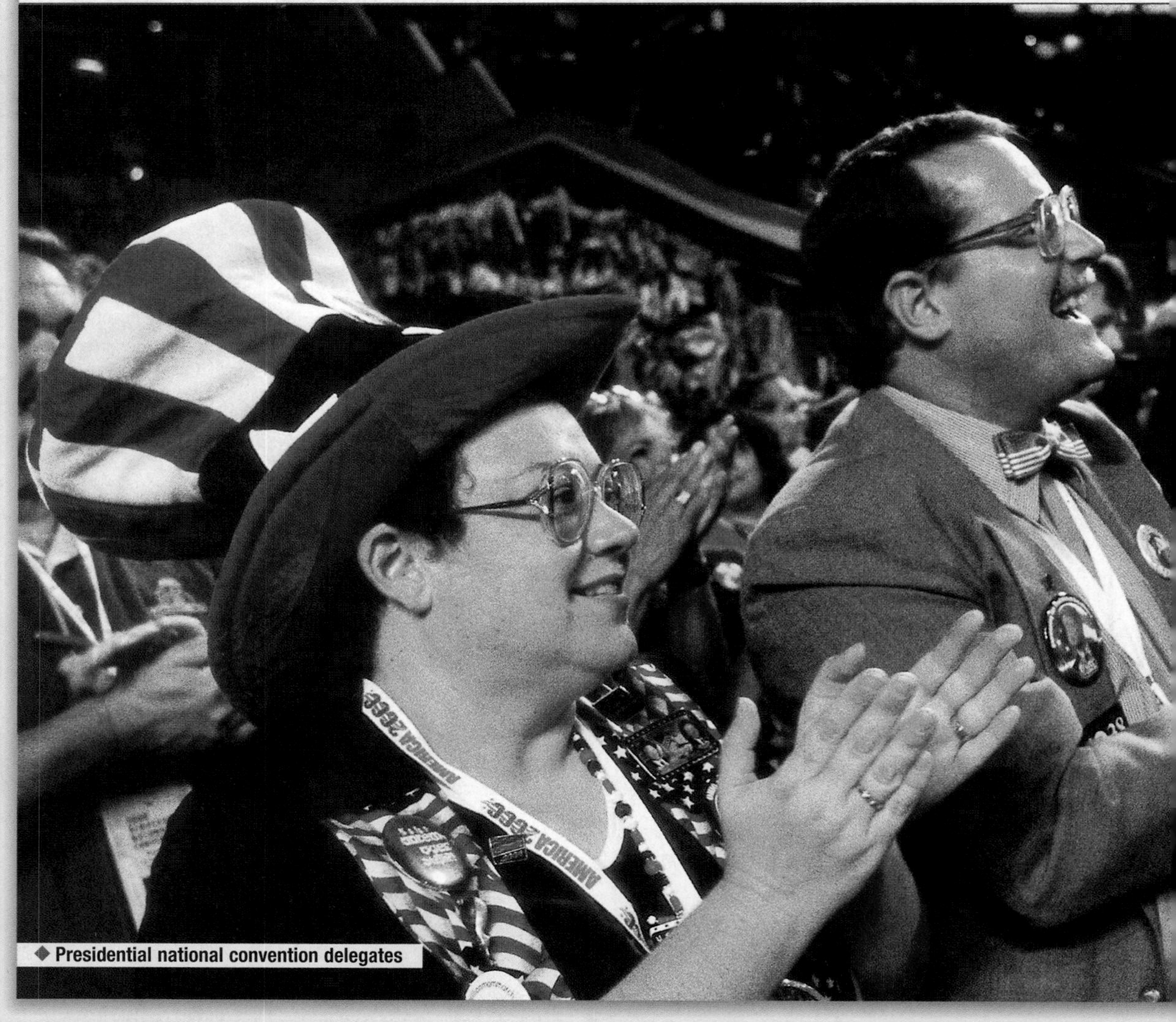

◆ Presidential national convention delegates

### CLOSE UP FOUNDATION Corner

The following resources are available only from the Close Up Foundation to support the concepts discussed in Chapter 7 "The Electoral Process":

- *Perspectives: Readings on Contemporary American Government*
- *We the People: The President and the Constitution*

**CLOSE UP FOUNDATION Online**

To keep up-to-date on Close Up news and activities, visit Close Up Online at

**www.closeup.org**

Close Up Foundation
44 Canal Center Plaza
Alexandria, VA 22314-1592
800-765-3131

## You Can Make a Difference

**ELECTION CAMPAIGNS TODAY** spend millions of dollars on advertising designed to sway voters. Groups such as Project Vote Smart try to offset this advertising by distributing unbiased, non-partisan information. Students in the National Internship Program of Project Vote Smart learn to research candidates and issues, write press releases, track legislation, and maintain the group's Web site. Interns also do the day-to-day work of political organizing, from answering phones to stuffing envelopes. They work at the project's headquarters in Montana or its office at Northeastern University in Boston, Massachusetts.

### SECTION 1

#### The Nominating Process (pp.178–186)

★ The nominating process is critically important to democratic government.
★ Five major nominating methods are used in American politics.
★ The most widely used nominating method today is the direct primary.

### SECTION 2

#### Elections (pp.188–194)

★ The election process is regulated mostly by State law.
★ Voting takes place in local precincts and polling places, although early voting is becoming increasingly common.
★ Every State now uses the Australian ballot, which is either the party-column or the office-group type.
★ Voting machines and electronic vote-counting systems are in wide use throughout the United States.

### SECTION 3

#### Money and Elections (pp.196–202)

★ Money plays a key role in politics but presents serious problems to democratic governments.
★ Most campaign money comes from private sources, including political action committees (PACs).
★ Federal campaign laws are administered by the Federal Election Commission (FEC).
★ Loopholes in campaign finance laws allow candidates and contributors to avoid some regulations.

### Keep It Current

Items marked with this logo are periodically updated on the Internet. Keep up-to-date with what's in the news. To get current information on the electoral process, go to **www.phschool.com**

## Keep It Current

### Internet Update

Use the Prentice Hall School Web site and the Keep It Current CD-ROM to find quick content updates.

Visit **www.phschool.com** for current events articles that are linked to Chapter 7. Critical thinking questions are included.

**Keep It Current CD-ROM** includes government-related projects by unit. Students complete each project using current information that they obtain by linking to the Prentice Hall School Web site from the CD-ROM.

## Pressed for Time?

### To Omit the Chapter

If you wish to skip Chapter 7, ask students to read the Chapter in Brief and assign the Guide to the Essentials before continuing to another chapter. You may also want to assign the Chapter 7 Test in the Chapter Test booklet. Then specific portions of Chapter 7 may be assigned to students needing reinforcement of key terms and concepts.

### To Preview the Chapter

To introduce students to key terms and concepts in each section, have them read the Chapter in Brief. You may also assign the Reading Strategy activities on pp. 179, 189, and 197 of this book.

### To Review the Chapter

When students have completed Chapter 7, you might want to assign the Guide to the Essentials or the Guided Reading and Review worksheets on pp. 22, 24, and 26 of the Unit 2 booklet.

### To Cover the Chapter Quickly

To cover the material in Chapter 7 quickly, use the following activity.

**Focus** Ask students to name any nominating methods they can. Prompt them by asking what the major parties hold each year, what States like New Hampshire are known for, and why people working for third-party candidates often ask for signatures.

**Instruct** Point out that nominations and elections occur all over the country all the time. Remind students of the many local elections that are held. Describe the mechanics of voting to students, including where elections are held, how they are organized, the kinds of ballots, and how they are cast.

**Close/Reteach** Ask students how campaigns are funded. Discuss the different kinds of contributors with students. Then lead a class debate on whether campaign funding encourages or restricts democratic society.

**Block Strategy (Average)**

# 1 The Nominating Process

## Section Preview

### OBJECTIVES

1. **Explain** why the nominating process is a critical first step in the election process.
2. **Describe** self-announcement, the caucus, and the convention as nominating methods.
3. **Discuss** the direct primary as the principal nominating method used in the United States today.
4. **Understand** why some candidates use the petition as a nominating device.

### WHY IT MATTERS

The nominating process narrows the field of possible candidates for office. It is thus an essential part of an election. The caucus and convention were important nominating methods in the past. The direct primary has largely replaced them. Self-announcement and petitions are also used today as nominating devices.

### POLITICAL DICTIONARY

★ nomination
★ general election
★ caucus
★ direct primary
★ closed primary
★ open primary
★ blanket primary
★ runoff primary
★ nonpartisan election

Suppose your teacher stood in front of the class and said: "Here's a $1,000 bill. Who'd like to have it?" You, and everyone else in the room, would promptly say, or at least think: "Me!" Suppose the teacher then said: "Okay, we'll hold an election. The person who wins the most votes gets the money."

What would happen? If the election were held immediately, it is likely that each member of the class would vote for himself or herself. A few might vote for a friend. Almost certainly, however, the election would end in a tie. No one would win the money.

But suppose the teacher said: "We'll hold the election tomorrow." What do you think

► Campaign signs urging voters to support particular candidates appear in towns and cities across the country before elections.

would happen then? As you think about the answer to that question, you begin to get a sense of the practical importance of the nominating process—the first step in the process of electing candidates to office.

## A Critical First Step

The nominating process is the process of candidate selection. **Nomination**—the naming of those who will seek office—is a critically important step in the election process.

You have already seen two major illustrations of the significance of the nomination process. In Chapter 5, you read about the making of nominations (1) as a prime function of political parties in the United States, and (2) as a leading reason for the decentralized character of the two major parties.

The nominating process also has a very real impact on the exercise of the right to vote. In the typical election in this country, voters can make only one of two choices for each office on the ballot. They can vote for the Republican or they can vote for the Democratic candidate.[1]

---

[1]Other choices are sometimes listed, of course—minor party or independent nominees. These are not often meaningful alternatives, however; most voters choose not to "waste" their votes on candidates who cannot win. Also, nonpartisan elections are an exception to this statement since candidates are not identified by party labels.

## Self-announced Candidates

**George Wallace**
Four-time Democratic governor of Alabama, Wallace won 13% of the popular vote in 1968 as the populist candidate of the newly formed American Independent Party.

**Eugene McCarthy**
A representative and senator from Minnesota (1949–1971), McCarthy sought the Democratic nomination for President in 1968 as a critic of the Vietnam War. He ran in 1976 as an independent, winning 0.9% of the popular vote.

**John Anderson**
A Republican representative from Illinois (1961–1981), Anderson ran for President as an independent in 1980, winning 6.7% of the popular vote.

**Ross Perot**
Business executive and billionaire Ross Perot ran as an independent for President in 1992, winning 19% of the popular vote. (In 1996, Perot received 8% of the popular vote as the Reform Party nominee.)

*Interpreting Charts* These presidential candidates made use of self-announcement as a nominating device. *(a) Why do some candidates choose self-announcement as a method for getting on the ballot? (b) How might a self-announced candidate affect the ultimate outcome of an election?*

This is another way of saying that we have a two-party system in the United States. It is also another way to say that the nominating stage is a critically important part of the electoral process. Those who make nominations place real, very practical limits on the choices that voters can make in an election.

In one-party constituencies (those areas where one party regularly wins elections), the nominating process is usually the only point at which there is any real contest for a public office. Once the dominant party has made its nomination, the general election is little more than a formality.

Dictatorial regimes point up the importance of the nominating process. Many of them hold **general elections**—regularly scheduled elections at which voters make the final selection of officeholders—much as democracies do. But typically, the ballots used in those elections list only one candidate for each office—the candidate of the ruling clique; and those candidates regularly win with majorities approaching 100 percent.

There are five ways in which nominations are made in the United States. They include (1) self-announcement, (2) caucus, (3) convention, (4) direct primary, and (5) petition.

## Self-Announcement

Self-announcement is the oldest form of the nominating process in American politics. First used in colonial times, it is still often found at the small-town and rural levels in many parts of the country.

The method is quite simple. A person who wants to run for office simply announces that fact. Modesty or local custom may dictate that someone else make the candidate's announcement, but, still, the process amounts to the same thing.

Self-announcement is sometimes used by someone who failed to win a regular party nomination or by someone unhappy with the party's choice. Note that whenever a write-in candidate appears in an election, the self-announcement process has been used. In recent history, four prominent presidential contenders have made

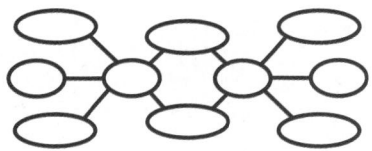

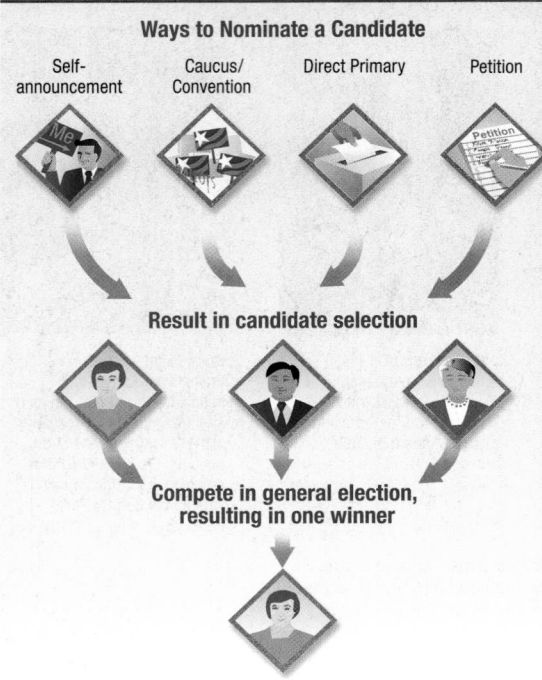

## Nominating and Electing a Candidate

**Ways to Nominate a Candidate**

Self-announcement     Caucus/Convention     Direct Primary     Petition

**Result in candidate selection**

**Compete in general election, resulting in one winner**

*Interpreting Diagrams* Nomination is a critical step in the election process because it narrows the field of candidates. In the general election, voters chose from this small field of candidates to select a single winner. **Why is it important for voters to participate in the nominating process?**

*"This day learned that the Caucus Club meets at certain Times in the Garret of Tom Dawes, the Adjutant of the Boston Regiment. He has a large House, and he has a moveable Partition in his Garret, which he takes down, and the whole Club meets in one Room. There they smoke tobacco till you cannot see from one End of the Garret to the other. There they drink flip I suppose, and they choose a Moderator, who puts Questions to the Vote regularly, and select Men, Assessors, Collectors, Wardens, Fire Wards, and Representatives are Regularly chosen before they are chosen in the Town."*
—The Works of John Adams (1856)

Originally the caucus was a private meeting consisting of a few influential figures in the community. As political parties appeared in the late 1700s, they soon took over the device and began to broaden the membership of the caucus.

The coming of independence brought the need to nominate candidates for State offices: governor, lieutenant governor, and others above the local level. The legislative caucus—a meeting of a party's members in the State legislature—took on the job. At the national level, both the Federalists and the Democratic-Republicans in Congress were, by 1800, choosing their presidential and vice-presidential candidates through the congressional caucus.

The legislative and congressional caucuses were quite practical in their day. Transportation and communication were difficult at best. Since legislators already gathered regularly in a central place, it made sense for them to take on the nominating responsibility.

The spread of democracy, especially in the newer States on the frontier, spurred opposition to caucuses, however. More and more, people condemned them for their closed, unrepresentative character.

Criticism of the caucus reached its peak in the early 1820s. The supporters of three of the

use of the process: George Wallace, who declared himself to be the American Independent Party's nominee in 1968; and independent candidates Eugene McCarthy in 1976; John Anderson in 1980; and Ross Perot in 1992.

## The Caucus

As a nominating device, a **caucus** is a group of like-minded people who meet to select the candidates they will support in an upcoming election. The first caucus nominations were made toward the end of the colonial period, probably in Boston in the mid-1720s.[2] One of the earliest descriptions of a caucus can be found in John Adams's diary, in an entry he made in February 1763:

---

[2]The origin of the term *caucus* is not clear. Most authorities suggest that it comes from the word *caulkers,* because the Boston Caucus Club met at times in a room formerly used as a meeting place by caulkers in Boston's shipyards. (Caulkers made ships watertight by filling seams or cracks in the hulls of sailing vessels with tar or oakum.)

leading contenders for the presidency in 1824—Andrew Jackson, Henry Clay, and John Quincy Adams—boycotted the DemocraticRepublicans' congressional caucus that year. In fact, Jackson and his supporters made "King Caucus" a leading campaign issue. The other major aspirant, William H. Crawford of Georgia, became the caucus nominee at a meeting attended by fewer than one third of the Democratic-Republican Party's members in Congress.

Crawford ran a poor third in the electoral college balloting in 1824, and the reign of King Caucus at the national level was ended. With its death in presidential politics, the caucus system soon withered at the State and local levels, as well.

The caucus is still used to make local nominations in some places, especially in New England. There, a caucus is open to all members of a party, and it only faintly resembles the original closed and private process.

## The Convention

As the caucus method collapsed, the convention system took its place. The first national convention to nominate a presidential candidate was held by a minor party, the Anti-Masons, in Baltimore in 1831. The newly formed National Republican (soon to become Whig) Party also held a convention later that same year. The Democrats picked up the practice in 1832. All major-party presidential nominees have been chosen by conventions ever since. By the 1840s, conventions had become the principal means for making nominations at every level in American politics.

On paper, the convention process seems perfectly suited to representative government. A party's members meet in a local caucus to pick candidates for local offices and, at the same time, to select delegates to represent them at a county convention.[3]

At the county convention, the delegates nominate candidates for county offices and select delegates to the next rung on the convention

ladder, usually the State convention. There, the delegates from the county conventions pick the party's nominees for governor and other State-wide offices. State conventions also send delegates to the party's national convention, where the party selects its presidential and vice-presidential candidates.

In theory, the will of the party's rank and file membership is passed up through each of its representative levels. Practice soon pointed up the weaknesses of the theory, however, as party bosses found ways to manipulate the process. By playing with the selection of delegates, usually at the local levels, they soon dominated the entire system.

As a result, the caliber of most conventions declined at all levels, especially during the late 1800s. How low some of them fell can be seen in this description of a Cook County, Illinois, convention in 1896:

**PRIMARY Sources** "Of [723] delegates, those who had been on trial for murder numbered 17; sentenced to the penitentiary for murder or manslaughter and served sentence, 7; served terms in the penitentiary for burglary, 36; served terms in the penitentiary for picking pockets, 2; served

◀ *Campaign Ribbons* These precursors of today's political buttons were widely used in the 1840s to 1890s.

[3]The meetings at which delegates to local conventions are chosen are still often called *caucuses*. Earlier, they were also known as primaries—that is, first meetings. The use of that name gave rise to the term *direct primary*, to distinguish that newer nominating method from the convention process.

## Spotlight on Technology

 **Magruder's American Government Video Collection**

The Magruder's Video Collection explores key issues and debates in American government. Each segment examines an issue central to chapter content through use of historical and contemporary footage. Commentary from civic leaders in academics, government, and the media follow each segment. Critical thinking questions focus students' attention on key issues, and may be used to stimulate discussion.

Use the Chapter 7 video segment to examine the importance of the Vice President to election politics. (time: about 5 minutes) This segment will explore how vice-presidential candidates are selected, how they help or hurt the presidential nominee, and how the vice presidency can serve as a stepping stone to the White House. A historical case study of the "Dump Nixon" campaign during the 1956 election is included.

## Customize for

### English Language Learners

Help students understand the different kinds of primaries by first giving them synonyms or descriptions for the names. Explain closed and open primaries by saying that all girls in the class may vote but not boys *(closed)*; and then that the entire class may vote *(open)*. Explain runoff primary by describing a foot race that ends in a tie. Finally, for nonpartisan primary, ask what other political term "partisan" sounds like *(party)*. Elicit that the "non" before "partisan" indicates that it does not have to do with a certain party.

*terms in the penitentiary for arson, 1; . . . jailbirds identified by detectives, 84; keepers of gambling houses, 7; keepers of houses of ill-fame, 2; convicted of mayhem, 3; ex-prize fighters, 11; poolroom proprietors, 2; saloon keepers, 265; . . . political employees, 148; no occupation, 71; . . .* "

—R.M. Easley, "The Sine qua Non of Caucus Reform," *Review of Reviews* (Sept. 1897)

Many people had hailed the change from caucus to convention as a major change for the better in American politics. The abuses of the new device soon dashed their hopes. By the 1870s, the convention system was itself under attack as a major source of evil in American politics. By the 1910s, the direct primary had replaced the convention in most States as the principal nominating method in American politics.[4]

## The Direct Primary

A **direct primary** is an intra-party election. It is held within a party to pick that party's candidates for the general election. Wisconsin adopted the first State-wide direct primary law in 1903; several other States soon followed its lead. Every State now makes at least some provision for its use.

[4]The few States that still use the convention include Connecticut, Michigan, Utah, and Virginia. In those States the convention system is closely regulated by State law. No adequate substitute has yet been found at the presidential level, however.

*Interpreting Political Cartoons* **What aspect of political primary campaigning does this cartoon suggest?**

"MY FORMER OPPONENT IS SUPPORTING ME IN THE GENERAL ELECTION. PLEASE DISREGARD ALL THE THINGS I HAVE SAID ABOUT HIM IN THE PRIMARY."

In most States, State law requires that the major parties use the primary to choose their candidates for the United States Senate and House of Representatives, for the governorship and all other State offices, and for most local offices as well. In a few States, however, different combinations of convention and primary are used to pick candidates for the top offices.

In Michigan, for example, the major parties choose their candidates for the U.S. Senate and House, the governorship, and the State legislature in primaries. Nominees for lieutenant governor, secretary of state, and attorney general are picked by conventions.[5]

Although the primaries are party-nominating elections, they are closely regulated by law in most States. The State usually sets the dates on which primaries are held, and it regularly conducts them, too. The State, not the parties, provides polling places and election officials, registration lists and ballots, and otherwise polices the process.

Two basic forms of the direct primary are in use today: (1) the closed primary and (2) the open primary. The major difference between the two lies in the answer to this question: Who can vote in a party's primary—only qualified voters who are party members, or *any* qualified voter?

### The Closed Primary

Twenty-six States and the District of Columbia use the **closed primary.** A closed primary is a party nominating election in which only declared party members can vote.[6]

In most of the closed primary States, party membership is established by registration. (See Chapter 6.) When voters appear at the polling places on primary election day, their names are

[5]In most States, minor parties are required to make their nominations by other, more difficult processes, usually in conventions or by petition. For the significance of this point, see Chapter 5.

[6]The Supreme Court has held that a State's closed primary law cannot forbid a party to allow independent voters to participate in its primary if the party itself chooses to do so. In *Tashjian* v. *Republican Party of Connecticut,* 1986, the Court struck down such a State law. Note that the Court did not outlaw the closed primary in this case, nor did it hold that a political party *must* allow Independents to vote in its primary. The Court found that the Connecticut law violated the 1st and 14th amendment guarantees of the right of association—here the right of Connecticut Republicans to associate with Independents (invite Independents to join with them in making of GOP nominations). The decision stated only that if the Republican Party of Connecticut wanted to include Independents, it may do so.

*Answer to . . .*

**Interpreting Political Cartoons** The cartoon refers to the practice of attacking the opposing candidate to win the primary, even though the candidate is from the same party.

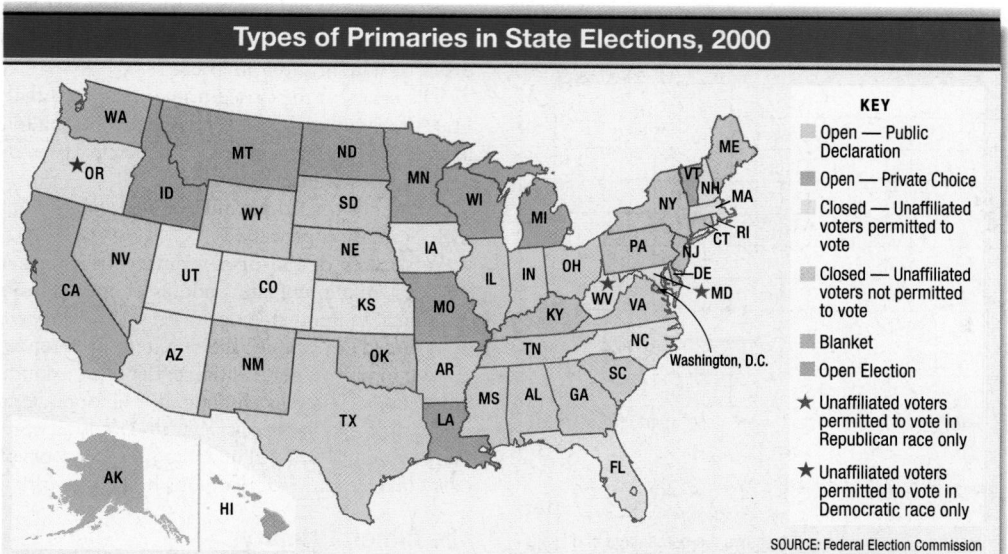

## Types of Primaries in State Elections, 2000

**KEY**
- Open — Public Declaration
- Open — Private Choice
- Closed — Unaffiliated voters permitted to vote
- Closed — Unaffiliated voters not permitted to vote
- Blanket
- Open Election
- ★ Unaffiliated voters permitted to vote in Republican race only
- ★ Unaffiliated voters permitted to vote in Democratic race only

SOURCE: Federal Election Commission

**Interpreting Maps** This map shows the types of primaries held in each State for State elections. In 2000, California, Alaska, and Washington used a blanket primary. As a result of the Court's decision in *California* v. *Jones,* these States will likely use a different form of the primary in future elections, however. **What type of primary is used in your State?**

checked against the poll books—the lists of registered voters for each precinct. Each voter is then handed the ballot of the party in which he or she is registered. That voter may mark *only* that party's ballot—that is, he or she may vote only in that party's primary.

### The Open Primary

The **open primary** is a party nominating election in which *any* qualified voter can take part. Although it is the form in which the direct primary first appeared, the open primary is now found in only 24 States, as you can see on the map above.

When voters go to their polling places in some open primary States, they are handed the ballots of each of the parties holding a primary election. Voters then pick the party primary in which they wish to participate in the privacy of the voting booth. In other open primary States, voters must ask for the ballot of the party in whose primary they want to participate. That is, voters must make a *public,* not a private, choice of party before they enter the voting booth.

Through 2000, three States used a different version of the open primary—the **blanket primary,**

sometimes called the "wide-open primary." Washington adopted the first blanket primary law in 1935. Alaska followed suit in 1970, and California did so in 1996. In those three States, every voter received the same primary ballot—a long one containing the names of all contenders, regardless of party, for each nomination to be made at the primary election. Voters could participate in the primary however they chose. They could confine themselves to one party's primary by voting to nominate only Democratic candidates or, instead, only Republican candidates. Or they could switch back and forth between the parties' primaries, voting to nominate a Democrat for one office, a Republican for another, and so on down the ballot.

The Supreme Court ruled against the blanket primary in 2000, however. In *Democratic Party of California* v. *Jones,* it found that the blanket primary process violated the 1st Amendment's guarantee of the right of association. The Court held that a State cannot force a political party to associate with outsiders—that is, with members of other parties or with independent voters—when it picks its candidates for public office. "In no area is the party's right to exclude

---

---

## CONSTITUTIONAL PRINCIPLES

### Popular Sovereignty

The direct primary was introduced to correct the abuses of the convention system, particularly the tendency for powerful leaders to manipulate nominations. The primary functions on the assumption that each voter's views should have an impact on the process. When States voted to choose the primary system in the early 1900s, popular sovereignty was often upheld as the guiding principle for that choice.

### Activity

Remind students that in a closed primary, only registered or declared party members may participate. Have students debate the closed vs. the open primary. Then ask students to consider the other kinds of primaries—blanket and nonpartisan. Ask: Which kind of primary seems to best uphold the principle of popular sovereignty?

---

**183**

## Make It Relevant

### Students Make a Difference

When Senator Bill Bradley's 1999 New Hampshire primary campaign called Catherine Laferriere's parents, they got a surprise. "I told them they could speak to my parents, but only after they spoke to me," explains Catherine. "I said I wanted to get involved." And she did—along with other teenage volunteers who stuffed envelopes, made phone calls, and went door-to-door.

"Although I may just be a drop in the bucket of the primary," says Matthew Paul, a volunteer for Senator John McCain, "every job counts." Anna Cole, who worked for Alan Keyes, agrees. "If teenagers are willing to show themselves to be responsible and maybe do the not-so-fun things first, the people who work on campaigns are more than willing to give them more responsibility." Anna Lyman got to canvass door-to-door with Vice President Al Gore. "Walking alongside him was really exciting," she says.

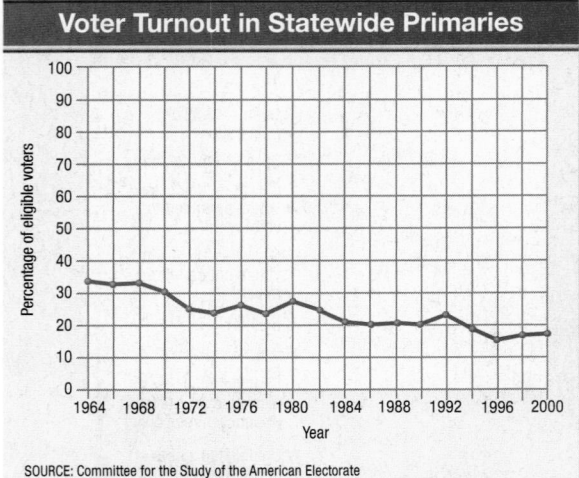

### Voter Turnout in Statewide Primaries

SOURCE: Committee for the Study of the American Electorate

*Interpreting Graphs* This graph shows the percentage of eligible voters who cast ballots in Statewide primaries from 1964 to 2000. **(a) What does this chart suggest about voter interest in these elections? (b) Why do you think primary turnout is greater in presidential years than it is in off-years?**

more important," said the Court, "than in the process of selecting its nominees."

Louisiana has yet another form of the open primary, which was not affected by the Court's decision in *Jones*. Its unique "open-election law" provides for what amounts to a combination primary and election. The names of all the people who seek nominations are listed by office on a single primary ballot. A contender who wins more than 50 percent of the primary votes wins the office. In these cases, the primary becomes the election. In contests where there is no majority winner, the two top vote-getters, regardless of party, face off in the general election.

### Closed vs. Open Primary

The two basic forms of the primary have caused arguments for decades. Those who favor the closed primary regularly make three arguments in support of it:

1. It prevents one party from "raiding" the other's primary in the hope of nominating weaker candidates in the other party.

2. It helps make candidates more responsive to the party, its platform, and its members.

3. It helps make voters more thoughtful, because they must choose between the parties in order to vote in the primaries.

The critics of the closed primary contend that:

1. It compromises the secrecy of the ballot, because it forces voters to make their party preferences known in public, and

2. It tends to exclude independent voters from the nomination process. [7]

Advocates of the open primary believe that their system of nominating addresses both of these criticisms. In many open primaries, (1) voters are not forced to make their party preferences known in public, and (2) the tendency to exclude independent voters is eliminated. The opponents of the open primary insist that it (1) permits primary "raiding" and (2) undercuts the concepts of party loyalty and party responsibility.

### The Runoff Primary

In most States, candidates need to win only a plurality of the votes cast in the primary to win their party's nomination. [8] (A plurality is the greatest number of votes won by any candidate, whether a majority or not.) In ten States, [9] however, an absolute majority is needed to carry a primary. If no one wins a majority in a race, a **runoff primary** is held a few weeks later. In the runoff primary, the two top vote-getters in the first party primary face one another, and the winner of that vote becomes the nominee.

### The Nonpartisan Primary

In most States all or nearly all of the elected school and municipal offices are filled in **nonpartisan elections.** These are elections in which candidates are not identified by party labels. About half of all State judges are chosen on nonpartisan

---

[7]See the discussion of *Tashjian* v. *Republican Party of Connecticut*, 1986, in footnote 6. The closed primary States have now amended their primary laws to comply with that decision.

[8]In Iowa, if no candidate wins at least 35 percent of the votes in a primary, the party must then nominate its candidate for that office by convention. In South Dakota, if no one who seeks a party's nomination for governor, U.S. senator, or U.S. representative wins at least 35 percent, the party's candidate for that office must be picked in a runoff primary two weeks later. In North Carolina a runoff is held when no candidate wins 40 percent of the primary vote.

[9]Alabama, Arizona, Arkansas, Florida, Georgia, Mississippi, Oklahoma, South Carolina, Texas—and Louisiana under its unique "open election" law.

ballots, as well. The nomination of candidates for these offices takes place on a nonpartisan basis, too, often in nonpartisan primaries.

Typically, a contender who wins a clear majority in a nonpartisan primary then runs unopposed in the general election, subject only to write-in opposition. In many States, however, a candidate who wins a majority in the primary is declared elected at that point. If there is no majority winner, the names of the two top contenders are placed on the general election ballot.

The direct primary first appeared as a partisan nominating device. Many people have long argued that it is not well suited for use in nonpartisan elections. Instead, they favor the petition method, which you will read about later in this section.

### Evaluation of the Primary

A number of criticisms have been leveled at the primary process. For example, in States that have a closed primary, many voters resent having to declare their party preferences. In those States where the typical open primary is used, many people are upset because they cannot express their choices for nominations in more than one party.[10] Many voters are also annoyed by the "bedsheet" ballot—that is, the long list of candidates that typically appears on the primary ballot. They fail to understand that the use of the primary almost automatically means a long ballot. These factors, combined with a lack of appreciation for the importance of primaries, results in this fact: Voter turnout in the primary elections in most States is usually less than half of that in general elections.

As a further criticism, when two or more candidates seek the same nomination, primary campaigns can be quite expensive. The fact that successful contenders for the nomination must mount—and find the money for—yet another campaign for the general election adds to the money problems that so many

[10]Remember that the direct primary came to American politics in the early 1900s as a reaction to the boss-dominated and often corrupt convention system of nominating candidates. The direct primary was intended to take the nominating function away from the party organization and put it in the hands of the party's membership. These conflicts and how they developed make it easier to understand the importance of how the nominating function is managed today.

candidates face. It is unfortunately true that the financial facts of political life in the United States mean that some well-qualified people do not seek public office simply because they cannot muster the necessary funds.

The nominating process, whatever its form, can also have a very divisive effect on a party. Remember, the process takes place *within* a party. Because primaries are so public in nature, the direct primary magnifies the potential for division within the party. A bitter contest in the primaries can so wound and divide a party that it cannot recover in time to present a united front for the general election. Many a primary fight has cost a party an election.

Finally, because many voters are uninformed, the primary places a premium on name familiarity. That is, it often gives an edge to a contender who has a well-known name or a name that sounds like that of a well-known person. This occurs even though name familiarity in and of itself has little or nothing to do with a candidate's qualifications.

Obviously, the primary is not without its problems, nor is any other nominating device. Still, it does give a party's members the opportunity to participate at the very core of the political process.

*Interpreting Political Cartoons* **What aspect of the primary process does this cartoon critique?**

**Resource Pro® CD-ROM** contains an electronic version of each activity found in the Teaching Resources as well as additional resources such as Supreme Court cases. The Planning Express® feature allows you to customize and create daily lesson plans within minutes.

## Point-of-Use Resources

**Guide to the Essentials** Chapter 7, Section 1, p. 43 provides support for students who need additional review of section content. Spanish support is available in the Spanish edition of the Guide on p. 36.

**Quiz** Unit 2 booklet, p. 23 includes matching and multiple-choice questions to check students' understanding of Section 1 content.

**Presentation Pro CD-ROM** Quizzes and multiple-choice questions check students' understanding of Section 1 content.

## Answers to ...

### Section 1 Assessment

**1.** In most States, it is the role of political parties to nominate candidates for office. This is usually done through the direct primary.

**2.** A closed primary is a party nominating election in which only declared party members may participate; an open primary is a party nominating election in which any qualified voter may participate.

**3.** A primary in which all voters receive the same ballot on which every contender for every nomination in both parties is listed.

**4.** A caucus is a group of like-minded people who meet to elect candidates they will support in an upcoming election. The election of 1824 as well as the general spread of democracy led to its decline.

**5.** Answers will vary, but should demonstrate an understanding of the criticisms of primaries, including the nature of closed primaries and the long ballots.

**6.** The nominating process narrows the field of candidates and offers voters the most choices.

**7.** Charts should include self-announcement, direct primary, and petition methods and should point out their similarities and differences.

▲ **Getting on the Ballot** Petitions are widely used as nominating devices, particularly in nonpartisan elections at the local level.

### The Presidential Primary

The presidential primary developed as an offshoot of the direct primary. It is not a nominating device, however. Rather, the presidential primary is an election that is held as one part of the process by which presidential candidates are chosen.

The presidential primary is a very complex process. It is one or both of two things, depending on the State involved. It is a process in which a party's voters elect some or all of a State party organization's delegates to that party's national convention; and/or it is a preference election in which voters can choose (vote their preference) among various contenders for a party's presidential nomination. Much of what happens in presidential politics in the early months of every fourth year centers on this very complicated process. (See Chapter 13 for an extended discussion of the presidential primary.)

### Petition

One other nominating method is used fairly widely at the local level in American politics today—nomination by petition. Where this process is used, candidates for public office are nominated by means of petitions signed by a certain required number of qualified voters in the election district.[11]

Nomination by petition is found most widely at the local level, chiefly for nonpartisan school posts and municipal offices in medium-sized and smaller communities. It is also the process usually required by State law for nominating minor party and independent candidates. (Remember, the States often purposely make the process of getting on the ballot difficult for those candidates.)

The details of the petition process vary widely from State to State, and even from one city to the next. Usually, however, the higher the office and/or the larger the constituency represented by the office, the greater the number of signatures needed for nomination.

---

[11] The petition device is also an important part of the recall and the initiative and referendum processes; see Chapter 24.

## Section 1 Assessment

**Key Terms and Main Ideas**

1. What is the role of political parties in the nomination process?
2. Explain the difference between a **closed primary** and an **open primary.**
3. What is a **nonpartisan election?**
4. What is a **caucus,** and what events led to its demise as a method for nominating candidates?

**Critical Thinking**

5. **Making Decisions** You read in this section that voter turnout in primaries is usually less than half of what it is in general elections. What steps could you take in your community to increase voter turnout in primary elections?
6. **Identifying Central Issues** Explain why the nominating process is a vital first step in the electoral process.

7. **Making Comparisons** Create a chart in which you compare the different methods of seeking public office described in this section.

 **Take It to the Net**

8. Read about the history of primaries and how they function. Then suppose you are a campaign manager, and create a list of the five most important considerations your candidate should keep in mind during the primaries. Use the links provided in the Social Studies area at the following Web site for help in completing this activity. **www.phschool.com**

 **Take It to the Net**

**8.** Direct students to the Social Studies area at the Prentice Hall School Web site. The *Magruder's American Government* companion Web site includes the directions and links needed to complete the activity. It also provides a printable Internet activity worksheet with scoring rubrics for assessment. Considerations listed should take into account the characteristics of primaries described in the text.

# Establishing Primary Elections

*In a 1901 speech to the Wisconsin legislature, Governor Robert La Follette called for ending the caucus and convention system and nominating each party's candidates directly by the voters. Shortly thereafter, Wisconsin became the first State to establish Statewide primary elections.*

Governor Robert La Follette
1855–1925

It is a fundamental principle of this republic that each citizen should have equal voice in government. This is recognized and guaranteed to him through the ballot. . . . Since government, with us, is conducted by the representatives of some political party, the citizen's voice in making and administering the laws is expressed through his party ballot. This privilege is vital. . . . It is here government begins. . . . Control lost at this point is never regained. . . .

For many years the evils of the caucus and convention system have multiplied. . . . The system in all its details is inherently bad. It not only favors, but . . . produces manipulation, scheming, trickery, fraud and corruption. The delegate elected in caucus is nominally [supposedly] the agent of the voter to act for him in convention. Too frequently . . . he acts not for the voter, but serves his own purpose instead. This fact in itself taints the trust from the outset, and poisons the system at its very source. No legitimate business could survive under a system where authority to transact its vital matters were delegated and re-delegated to agents and sub-agents, who controlled their own selection . . . and were responsible to nobody. . . .

The officials nominated by the [party] machine become its faithful servants and surrender judgment to its will. This they must do in self-preservation or they are retired to public life. Wielding a power substantially independent of the voter, it is quite unnecessary to regard him as an important factor in government . . . .

It is of primary importance that the public official should hold himself directly accountable to the citizen. This he will do only when he owes his nomination directly to the citizen. If between the citizen and the official there is a complicated system of caucuses and conventions, by the easy manipulation of which the selection of candidates is controlled by some other agency or power, then the official will so render his services as to have the approval of such agency or power. The overwhelming demand of the people of this state, whom you represent, is that such intervening power and authority, and the complicated system which sustains it, shall be torn down and cast aside. . . .

## Analyzing Primary Sources

1. Why does La Follette think that an elected official selected by caucus will be more loyal to party bosses than to the voters?
2. According to La Follette, how will primaries make officials more accountable to the people?
3. What argument does La Follette use to show that primary elections are the foundation of government in a republic?

---

 **Close Up on Primary Sources** Reforming the Electoral College, p. 9, extends this feature with a primary source activity.

 **Online**

To keep up-to-date on Close Up news and activities, visit Close Up Online at

**www.closeup.org**

---

## Establishing Primary Elections

**Focus** Before students read the article, point out to them that Robert La Follette, along with other so-called Progressives, saw the growing power and cooperation of big business and political machines as a threat to republican government. Have students look for clues of this philosophy as they read the article.

**Instruct** Have students, as they read, list the words and phrases La Follette uses to describe the caucus and convention system of nomination. How does he use language to support his arguments? Ask students to write a one or two-sentence summary of La Follette's opinion of the system, in their own words.

**Close/Reteach** Ask students to think of a political process or law that is the subject of controversy today, then write a short opinion piece on it in the style of La Follette's speech. Have them read their pieces to the class. If you wish, you might ask them not to reveal the subject of their pieces, and let other students guess what is being described.

**Keep It Current CD-ROM** includes government-related projects by unit. The CD-ROM links to the Prentice Hall School Web site and may be used for daily updates.

## Answers to . . .

**Analyzing Primary Sources**
**1.** Because the party bosses controlled the caucuses that allowed the candidates to get on the ballot.
**2.** By placing the power of nomination in the people (through primaries), La Follette believed that candidates would become more loyal to the people instead of the party bosses.
**3.** La Follette pointed out that in a republic, citizens express their choices through an elected representative. Thus, citizens should control every stage of the electoral process. By allowing caucuses and conventions to nominate candidates, citizen representation is lost at the beginning of the process.

**·2· Elections**

Objectives You may wish to call students' attention to the objectives in the Section Preview. The objectives are reflected in the main headings of the section.

**Bellringer** Have students suppose that they and a group of friends are trying to decide what to do on Saturday night. Some want to go to a party, but others want to see a movie. Ask them how they would resolve the issue. Explain that in this section, they will learn about how voting serves to resolve public issues and to fill elective offices.

**Vocabulary Builder** Have students suggest the meaning of each term in the Political Dictionary. *Ballot* may seem like the easiest to define, but tell students that the ballot exists in several forms today, as they will discover as they read the section.

---

## Section Preview

### OBJECTIVES

1. **Compare** different methods of filling elected public offices.
2. **Define** the role of precincts and polling places in the election process.
3. **Describe** the various ways in which voters can cast their ballots.
4. **Outline** the role that voting machines and other innovations play in the election process.

### WHY IT MATTERS

The election process lies at the very heart of the democratic concept. Indeed, it is impossible to picture a democratic government in which popular elections are not held.

### POLITICAL DICTIONARY

★ absentee voting
★ coattail effect
★ precinct
★ polling place
★ ballot

---

### Pressed for Time?

## Quick Lesson Plan

**1. Focus** Tell students that election law has changed over the years to try to eliminate corruption and make voting easier. Ask students to discuss what they know about voting procedures today.

**2. Instruct** Ask students whether most election law is federal or State, and why. Continue discussing the administration of elections and then turn to how the ballot and other aspects of elections have changed throughout American history.

**3. Close/Reteach** Remind students that most votes in national elections are cast on voting machines. Have students use this fact as the starting point for a paragraph on why voting procedures have changed over the years—and are still changing.

**M**any high school students are not old enough to vote. In some parts of the country, however, high school students can serve on local election boards. First in Hawaii and Oregon and now in several States, 16- and 17-year-olds can become full-fledged members of the panels that administer elections.

Americans hold more elections and vote more often than most people realize. Indeed, Sundays and holidays are about the only days of the year on which people do not go to the polls somewhere in the United States. Americans also elect far more officeholders than most people realize—in fact, more than 500,000 of them.

▲ *Election Observers* In many parts of the world, election observers are needed to ensure that elections are free and fair. Here former President Jimmy Carter observes an election in Haiti.

Obviously, the election of public officials is very serious business. In this section, you will read about the federal and State laws that seek to ensure the integrity of this vital process.

## Filling Public Offices

English novelist H. G. Wells once called elections democracy's "feast, its great function." Democratic government cannot succeed, however, unless elections are free, honest, and accurate. Many people look at the details of the election process as too complicated, too legalistic, too dry and boring to worry about. Those people miss the vital part such details play in making democracy work. Recall, you saw how important the details of election law can be when you looked at voter qualifications and voter registration in the last chapter and again just a few pages ago when you considered the complexities of the direct primary.

### Extent of Federal Control

Nearly all elections in the United States are held to choose people to fill offices at the State and local levels. Given this fact, it is quite understandable that most election law in the United States is State law.

Despite this fact, a body of federal election law does exist. The Constitution gives Congress the power to fix "[t]he Times, Places, and Manner of holding Elections" of members of

---

### ◻ Block Scheduling Strategies

Consider these suggestions to manage extended class time:

◼ Have small groups of students work to create a voting handbook for new citizens. Handbooks should describe how people can vote, the types of ballots they might encounter, and the voting machine. Handbooks should be clearly organized and easy to follow.

◼ Ask students to skim the section, and note the different methods the text describes for voting. Divide the class into small groups, and present them with this problem: Congress has charged them with the task of increasing voter turnout. They must evaluate the current voting methods, brainstorm ideas for new ones, and then make recommendations to Congress.

Congress.[12] Congress also has the power to set the time for choosing presidential electors, to set the date for casting electoral votes, and to regulate other aspects of the presidential election process.[13]

Congress has set the date for holding congressional elections as the first Tuesday following the first Monday in November of every even-numbered year. It has set the same date every fourth year for the presidential election.[14] Thus, the next (off-year) congressional elections will be held on November 5, 2002. The next presidential election will fall on November 2, 2004.

Congress has required the use of secret ballots and allowed the use of voting machines in federal elections. It has passed several laws to protect the right to vote in all elections. Congress has also prohibited various corrupt practices and regulated the financing of campaigns for federal office.

State law deals with all other matters relating to national elections. State law also covers all of the details involved in choosing the thousands of State and local officials.

## When Elections Are Held

Most States hold their elections to fill State offices on the same date Congress has set for national elections: in November of every even-numbered year. The "Tuesday-after-the-first-Monday" formula prevents election day from falling on Sundays (to maintain the principle of separation of church and state). This formula also prevents election day from falling on the first day of the month, which is often payday and therefore potentially subject to campaign pressures.

Some States do fix other dates for some offices, however. Louisiana, Mississippi, New Jersey, and Virginia elect the governor, other executive officers, and State legislators in November of the odd-numbered year. City, county, and other local election dates vary from State to State. When those elections are not held in November, they generally take place in the spring.

---

[12]Article I, Section 4, Clause 1; 17th Amendment; see pages 276 and 277.

[13]Article II, Section 1, Clause 4; 12th Amendment; see pages 378 and 379.

[14]Congress has made an exception for Alaska. Because of the possibility of severe weather in much of Alaska in early November, that State may, if it chooses, elect its congressional delegation and cast its presidential vote in October. So far, however, Alaska has used the November date.

## Voices on Government

Senator Maria Cantwell (D., Washington) was elected to the United States Senate in 2000 after a campaign in which she pledged to travel to every State in the Union and to forego money from special interests. During Senate debate over campaign finance reform legislation, Cantwell had this to say about the election process.

" The only way we have to truly level the playing field, both between candidates and parties of opposing ideologies, and more importantly, between new candidates and incumbents, is to commit the resources to the process of getting people elected. Not until we create a campaign system with a shorter and more intensive campaign period—something I think the public would truly applaud—funded with finite and equal resources available to all candidates, will we be able to really listen carefully to what the people want. "

### Evaluating the Quotation

*What advantages and disadvantages are there—for both voters and candidates—of "a shorter and more intensive campaign period . . . funded with finite and equal resources available to all candidates"?*

## Early Voting

Most States make provision for **absentee voting,** or voting by those unable to get to their regular polling places on election day. Absentee voting laws usually cover three groups of potential voters: (1) those too ill or disabled to make it to their polling places; (2) those who expect to be away from home on election day (on a business trip, away at college, or on vacation, for example); and (3) those serving in the armed forces. Voters can apply for an absentee ballot within a specified period before an election. They then mark that ballot, seal it, and return it to the proper local election official.

Another form of early voting has spread among the States in recent years. In an effort to make voting more convenient and increase voter turnout, a third of the States now allow voters to cast ballots over a period of several days before an election—not as absentee ballots, but as though

**189**

## Extended Class Periods

**Time** 90 minutes.
**Purpose** Administer an election.
**Grouping** Five groups.
**Activity** Students will hold an election for celebrity of the month. Generate a list of candidates by using the self-announcement form of nomination. Hold a primary to narrow the list of candidates. Have students "campaign" for their choices. Then have them choose a ballot method, and use it to cast votes.
**Roles** Candidates, election officials, ballot preparation/vote counters, and two groups to head candidates' campaigns.
**Close** Hold a general election. After the election, have students evaluate the process and discuss how honest, free, and accurate the election was.

**Block Strategy
(Average)**

## Point-of-Use Resources

**Government Assessment Rubrics** Cooperative Learning Project: Process, p. 20

**Block Scheduling with Lesson Strategies** Additional activities for Chapter 7 appear on p. 22.

they were voting on election day itself. Texas has the most liberal of these early voting laws. There, any registered voter can cast his or her ballot up to 17 days before any primary or general election.

### The Coattail Effect

The **coattail effect** occurs when a strong candidate running for an office at the top of the ballot helps attract voters to other candidates on the party's ticket. In effect, the lesser-known office seekers "ride the coattails" of the more prestigious personalities. In 1980 and 1984, for example, Ronald Reagan's coattails helped many Republican candidates win office. The coattail effect is usually most apparent in presidential elections. However, a popular candidate for senator or governor can have the same kind of pulling power.

A reverse coattail effect can occur, too. This happens when a candidate for high office is less than popular with many voters—for example, Barry Goldwater as the Republican presidential nominee in 1964, and George McGovern for the Democrats in 1972. President Carter's coattails were also of the reverse variety in 1980.

Some people argue that all State and local elections should be held on dates other than those set for federal elections. This, they say, would help voters pay more attention to State and local candidates and issues. At the same time, it would lessen the coattail effects of presidential contests.

## Precincts and Polling Places

A **precinct** is a voting district. Precincts are the smallest geographic units for conducting elections. State law regularly restricts their size, generally to an area with no more than 500 to 1,000 or so qualified voters. A **polling place**— the place where the voters who live in a precinct actually vote—is located somewhere in or near each precinct.

A precinct election board supervises the polling place and the voting process in each precinct. Typically, the county clerk or county board of elections draws precinct lines, fixes the location of each polling place, and picks the members of the precinct boards.

The precinct board opens and closes the polls at the times set by State law. In most States, the polls are open from 7:00 or 8:00 A.M. to 7:00 or 8:00 P.M. The precinct election board must also see that the ballots and the ballot boxes or voting machines are available. It must make certain that only qualified voters cast ballots in the precinct. Often the board also counts the votes cast in the precinct and then sends the results to the proper place, usually to the county clerk or county board of elections.

Poll watchers, one from each party, are allowed at each polling place. They may challenge any person they believe is not qualified to vote, check to be sure that their own party's supporters do vote, and monitor the whole process, including the counting of the ballots.

## Casting the Ballot

A **ballot** is the device by which a voter registers a choice in an election.[15] It can take a number of different forms. Whatever its form, however, it is clearly an important and sensitive part of the election process.

Each State now provides for a secret ballot. That is, State law requires that ballots be cast in such manner that others cannot know how a person has voted.

Voting was a public process through much of the nation's earlier history, however. Paper ballots were used in some colonial elections, but voting was more commonly *viva voce*—by voice. Voters simply stated their choices to an election board. With suffrage limited to the privileged few, many people defended oral voting as the only "manly" way in which to participate. Whatever the merits of that view, the expansion of the electorate brought with it a marked increase in intimidation, vote buying, and other corruptions of the voting process.

Paper ballots were in general use by the mid-1800s. The first ones were unofficial—slips of paper that voters prepared themselves and dropped in the ballot box. Soon candidates and parties began to prepare ballots and hand them to voters to cast, sometimes paying them to do so. Those party ballots were often printed on distinctively colored paper, and

---

[15]The word comes from the Italian *ballotta*, "little ball," and reflects the practice of dropping black or white balls into a box to indicate a choice. The term *blackball* comes from the same practice.

## Preparing for Standardized Tests

Have students read the passages under *Precincts and Polling Places* and then answer the question below.

Which of the following would NOT be a polling place?

**A** a school
**B** a county
**C** a church
**D** a recreation center

## Office-Group and Party-Column Ballots

### OFFICE-GROUP BALLOT

Voters select each candidate by marking an X in the square

**OFFICIAL BALLOT, GENERAL ELECTION**

Candidates are grouped by office

President and Vice President of the United States ☒
Four year term. Vote for one only.
- BUCHANAN, Pat/FOSTER, Ezola — Reform ☐
- GORE, Al/LIEBERMAN, Joe — Democratic ☐
- BUSH, George W./CHENEY, Dick — Republican ☐
- NADER, Ralph/LA DUKE, Winona — Green ☐

Names are listed in random order

Office of the United States Senate
Six year term. Vote for one only.
- HOLDEN, Bob — Democrat ☐
- MACY, Elgar — Republican ☐
- KLINE, Richard — Reform ☐

### PARTY-COLUMN BALLOT

Party symbol and name at the top of the column that lists all of the party's candidates running for office

**OFFICIAL BALLOT, GENERAL ELECTION**

| REPUBLICAN | DEMOCRATIC | REFORM | GREEN |

To vote for all the candidates of a party, voters mark an X in the circle

For President: GEORGE W. BUSH / AL GORE / PAT BUCHANAN / RALPH NADER
For Vice President: DICK CHENEY / JOE LIEBERMAN / EZOLA FOSTER / WINONA LA DUKE
For United States Senator: ELGAR MACY / BOB HOLDEN / RICHARD KLINE

To vote for candidates of different parties, voters mark an X in the square next to the chosen candidate or candidates

*Interpreting Diagrams* By highlighting the office, rather than the party, an office-group ballot encourages split-ticket voting. **How does a party-column ballot encourage voters to vote along party lines?**

**Background Note**
**The Mugwumps**
The reform effort that brought the Australian ballot to the U.S. was led by a group of elitist Republicans known as Mugwumps. The term has become a common description for party members who object to the party line. The first Mugwumps were a group that split from the Republican Party in 1884 to protest their party's nomination of James G. Blaine for President. Legend has it that the term derives from a little bird that sits on a fence "with his mug on one side and his wump on the other," but in fact the term comes from the Algonquin language, in which it means "chief or person of honor."

anyone watching could tell for whom voters were voting.

By the end of the 1800s, political machines—local political party organizations capable of mobilizing or "manufacturing" large numbers of votes on behalf of candidates for political office—were dominant in many places. They fought all attempts to make voting a more dependably fair and honest process. The political corruption of the post-Civil War years brought widespread demand for ballot reforms.

### The Australian Ballot

A new voting arrangement was devised in Australia, where it was first used in an election in Victoria in 1856. Its successes there led to its use in other countries. By 1900 nearly all of the States were using it. It remains the basic form of the ballot throughout the United States today.

The Australian Ballot has four essential features:
1. It is printed at public expense;
2. It lists the names of all candidates in an election;
3. It is given out only at the polls, one to each qualified voter;
4. It is marked in secret.

Two basic varieties of the Australian ballot have developed over the years. Most States now use the office-group ballot. Only a handful of States use the party-column ballot.

### The Office-Group Ballot

The office-group ballot is the original form of the Australian ballot. It is also sometimes called the Massachusetts ballot because of its early (1888) use there. On the office-group ballot, the candidates for an office are grouped together under the title of that office. Because the names of the candidates thus appear as a block, the form is also sometimes called the office-block ballot.

At first, the names of the candidates were listed in alphabetical order. Most States using the form now rotate the names. This is so that each candidate will have whatever psychological advantage there may be in having his or her name at the top of the list of candidates.

RESOURCE PRO

**Resource Pro® CD-ROM** contains an electronic version of each activity found in the Teaching Resources as well as additional resources such as Supreme Court cases. The Planning Express® feature allows you to customize and create daily lesson plans within minutes.

*Answer to . . .*
**Interpreting Diagrams** It lists candidates in a column by party, encouraging voters to choose all names associated with a party, particularly if the candidate at the top of the list is a strong one.

## Customize for
### Less Proficient Readers

Have students use cardboard boxes, newspapers, cloth or old curtains, and other art supplies to create a voting machine. Students may want to work in small groups and assign roles of architect, engineer, and laborers to divide up the work. Encourage students to use reference material to find pictures of actual voting machines. Find space in the classroom to display the machine. Students may "operate" their machines as part of the Extended Class Periods activity in Section 3.

---

### Background Note
### A Diverse Nation

Another innovation at many polls is the use of the bilingual ballot. The Voting Rights Act was amended in 1975 to require States to make bilingual ballots available in areas where 5 percent of the citizens of voting age are of a single-language minority, and either do not speak English proficiently enough to participate in the electoral process, or suffer low literacy rates. The law required alternative ballots in Spanish and several Asian languages; amended in 1982 and 1992, it now applies to any minority-language population of 10,000 or more persons.

---

### The Party-Column Ballot

The party-column ballot is also known as the Indiana ballot, from its early (1889) use in that State. It lists each party's candidates in a column under the party's name. Often there is a place at the top of each column where, with a single X, the voter can vote for all of that party's candidates.

Professional politicians tend to favor the party-column ballot. It encourages straight-ticket voting, especially if the party has a strong candidate at the head of the ticket. Most students of the political process favor the office-group form because it encourages voter judgment and split-ticket voting.

### Sample Ballots

Sample ballots, clearly marked as such, are available in most States before an election. In some States they are mailed to all voters, and they appear in most newspapers. They cannot be cast, but they can help voters prepare for an election.

First in Oregon (1907), and now in several States, an official voter's pamphlet is mailed to voters before every election. It lists all candidates and measures that will appear on the ballot. In Oregon, each candidate is allowed space to present his or her qualifications and position on the issues. Supporters and opponents of ballot measures are allowed space to present their arguments as well.

### Bedsheet Ballots

The ballot in a typical American election is lengthy, often and aptly called a "bedsheet" ballot. It frequently lists so many offices, candidates, and ballot measures that even the most well-informed voters have a difficult time marking it intelligently.

The long ballot came to American politics in the era of Jacksonian Democracy in the 1830s. Many held the view at the time that the greater the number of elective offices, the more democratic

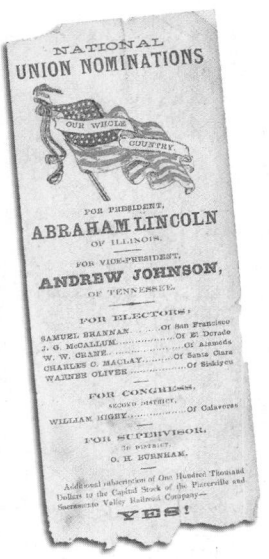

▲ *Campaign Ticket, 1864*
Sometimes tickets such as these were cast as ballots.

the governmental system. The idea remains widely accepted today.

Generally, the longest ballots are found at the local level, especially among the nation's 3,000-odd counties. The list of elected offices may include several commissioners, a clerk, a sheriff, one or more judges, a prosecutor, coroner, treasurer, assessor, surveyor, school superintendent, engineer, sanitarian, and even the proverbial dogcatcher.

Critics of the long ballot do not accept the argument that the more people you elect, the more democratic you are. They believe that quite the reverse is true: With a smaller number of elected offices to fill, the voter can better know the candidates and their qualifications. Critics also point to "ballot fatigue." This refers to the drop-off in voting that can run as high as 20 to 30 percent at or near the bottom of the typical bedsheet ballot.

There seems little, if any, good reason to elect such local officials as clerks, coroners, surveyors, and engineers. Their jobs do not carry policy-making responsibilities. Rather, they carry out policies made by others. Many people believe that in order to shorten the ballot (and save money), the rule should be: Elect those who make public policies, but appoint those whose job it is to administer those policies.

## Voting Machines and Innovations

Thomas Edison took out the first American patent for a voting machine. The community of Lockport, New York, first used his invention in 1892. The use of similar devices has long since spread to the polling places of every State.

Only a few States make the use of voting machines mandatory. Most often the machines are used only in some areas of a State, usually the more populous. All told, however, over half of all the votes in national elections today are cast on some form of voting machine.

The typical voting machine serves as its own booth. By pulling a lever, the voter encloses himself or herself within a three-sided curtain, and the machine itself becomes the fourth side of the voting booth. Pulling the lever also unlocks the voting machine. The ballot appears on the face of the machine, and the voter makes choices by pulling down the small levers over the names of the candidates he or she favors. The machine also has space for ballot measures, with *yes* and *no* levers for each of them.

In most States that use the party-column ballot, the voter can pull a master lever to vote a straight ticket. The machine is programmed so that a voter can cast only one vote per contest. Once all levers are in the desired positions, the voter opens the curtain. That action records the votes and, at the same time, clears the machine for the next voter.

Voting machines do away with the need for manual vote counting, reduce the number of people needed to administer elections, and speed the voting process. They also increase the number of voters who can be handled per precinct, make ballot mutilation impossible, and minimize fraud and counting errors.

## Electronic Vote Counting

Electronic data processing (EDP) techniques were first applied to the voting process in the 1960s. California and Oregon began the trend and since then, more than two thirds of the States have followed suit to some degree.

The most widely used adaptation of EDP in elections involves punch-card ballots, which are counted by computers. Many States and locales are now turning to two other EDP-based voting processes. One involves paper ballots that are counted by optical scanners. The other is a touch-screen system; see the illustration on this page for one version of this process.

## Vote-by-Mail Elections

A number of States conduct some elections by mail. Voters receive a ballot in the mail, make their choices, then mail the ballot back to election officials.

The first vote-by-mail election was held in Monterey County, California, in 1977; and the first large-scale use of mail-in ballots took place in San Diego in 1981. Vote-by-mail elections are now held in several other places.

Usually, vote-by-mail elections have been confined to the local level and to voting on city or county measures, not on candidates for local offices. A few States do choose local officials by mail-in ballots, however.

In fact, Oregon now holds all of its elections by mail and has done so since 1998. The State

held the first-ever all-mail primary election (including the presidential election) and the first-ever all-mail general election in 2000.

Vote-by-mail elections have stirred growing controversy. Critics fear that the process threatens the principle of the secret ballot. They worry about fraud, especially the possibility that some voters may be subjected to undue pressures when they mark their ballots at home or any place other than within the security of a voting booth.

Supporters, on the other hand, say that vote-by-mail elections can be as fraud-proof as any other method of voting. They also cite this fact:

## Electronic Voting Process

**Interpreting Diagrams** Electronic voting is becoming increasingly common, gradually replacing mechanical voting machines. Voters make their choices on a touchpad similar to that on an automated teller machine. *How are votes counted in an electronic voting system?*

## Point-of-Use Resources

**Guide to the Essentials** Chapter 7, Section 2, p. 44 provides support for students who need additional review of section content. Spanish support is available in the Spanish edition of the Guide on p. 37.

**Quiz** Unit 2 booklet, p. 25 includes matching and multiple-choice questions to check students' understanding of Section 2 content.

**Presentation Pro CD-ROM** Quizzes and multiple-choice questions check students' understanding of Section 2 content.

## Answers to . . .

### Section 2 Assessment

**1.** To allow ill or disabled persons, those who might be away from home on an election day, and those serving in the armed forces to vote.
**2.** It can ensure that lesser-known people on the ballot with a strong top candidate are elected; conversely, if the top candidate is not strong, it can lessen the chances of other people on the ballot.
**3.** Polling places are chosen by county clerks or county boards of electors.
**4. (a)** A ballot is the device by which a voter registers a choice in an election. **(b)** In the United States, ballots may be Australian, office-group, party-column, sample, or bedsheet.
**5.** Possible answer: Knowing how others vote might result in peer pressure or harassment.
**6. (a)** Advantages include higher voter turnout, lower costs, and convenience; disadvantages include possible fraud and, with online voting, computer problems such as viruses or jammed phone lines. **(b)** Answers will vary.

## Answer to . . .

**Critical Thinking** People might be more likely to vote if they can do so from home.

▲ This photo shows the mail-in ballot used by Oregon voters, who can vote by mail in all elections. *Critical Thinking* **How can voting by mail help increase the number of votes cast in an election?**

The mail-in process increases voter turnout in elections and, at the same time, reduces the costs of conducting them.

### Online Voting

Online voting—e-voting, or casting ballots on the Internet—will likely become widespread, perhaps even commonplace, in the next few years or so. Several States are now moving in that direction. Online voting has many of the same advantages and disadvantages as voting by mail.

Online voting is not an entirely new phenomenon. The first e-vote was cast in November 1997. In that year, election officials in Harris County, Texas, permitted astronaut David Wolf to vote in Houston's city election by e-mail from the space station *Mir*.

The nation's first public election in which voters cast their ballots online was held in Arizona in March 2000. The Arizona Democratic Party allowed voters to participate in the party's presidential primary by voting (1) in person at their precinct polling places, (2) by mail, or (3) via the Internet. The Defense Department also conducted a limited online voting project in November 2000. In that test program, some 250 members of the military who were stationed abroad cast votes in their home States by computer.

A number of public officials in several States and a number of dot.com companies promote online voting. These supporters claim that it will make participation much more convenient, increase voter turnout, and reduce the costs of conducting elections.

Many skeptics believe that the electronic infrastructure is not ready for e-voting. Some fear digital disaster: jammed phone lines, blocked access, hackers, viruses, denials of service attacks, fraudulent vote counts, and violations of voter secrecy. Critics also point out that because not everyone can afford home computers, online voting could undermine basic American principles of equality.

## Section **2** Assessment

**Key Terms and Main Ideas**

1. What is the purpose of **absentee voting**?
2. How can the **coattail effect** influence election results?
3. What factor determines the location of each voter's **polling place**?
4. **(a)** What is a **ballot**? **(b)** What different forms might it take in the United States?

**Critical Thinking**

5. **Predicting Consequences** Consider elections held in your school for class president and student council. How might the absence of secret ballots affect these elections?

6. **Expressing Problems Clearly (a)** What are the advantages and disadvantages of voting by mail and voting online? **(b)** Do you support these voting methods? Explain your answer.

 **Take It to the Net**

7. Find out more about voting in your State. Then create a brochure for newcomers to your State explaining registration requirements, State voting patterns, and any interesting information you discover about voting in your State. Use the links provided in the Social Studies area at the following Web site for help in completing this activity. **www.phschool.com**

 **Take It to the Net**

**7.** Direct students to the Social Studies area at the Prentice Hall School Web site. The *Magruder's American Government* companion Web site includes the directions and links needed to complete the activity. It also provides a printable Internet activity worksheet with scoring rubrics for assessment. Brochures should be clearly organized and easy to follow.

# SKILLS FOR LIFE

TECHNOLOGY
CITIZENSHIP
CRITICAL THINKING
CHARTS and GRAPHS

## Casting Your Vote

Why have people risked their lives to get and keep the right to vote? In the United States, we tend to take this right for granted. Yet if we were ever deprived of it, we would surely come to recognize its great value.

The voting process may vary slightly from place to place, but in general, these steps apply:

**1. Determine if you are eligible to vote.** To qualify to vote, you must be an American citizen at least 18 years of age and a resident of the State in which you vote.

**2. Register to vote.** In every State except North Dakota, you must register to vote. You can register locally, usually at city hall or the county courthouse. Registration tables are often set up in shopping malls, supermarkets, libraries, and fire stations before an election. You can register by mail, and in some places, via the Internet. To register you will need proof of your age, such as a birth certificate.

**3. Study the candidates and issues.** Identify the candidates for each office and the duties of the office. Then research the candidates' views on major issues. Besides voting for candidates for office, voters often have the opportunity to directly approve or reject proposed State and local

BALLOTS

laws. Don't wait until you are in the voting booth to become familiar with these issues.

**4. Go to your polling place.** In many States, voters receive a voter registration card identifying their precinct and polling place. Newspapers often publish lists of polling places prior to an election. Polls are usually open from 7:00 or 8:00 A.M. to 7:00 or 8:00 P.M. At the polling place, your name will be checked against a list of registered voters to make sure you are eligible to vote. You will be directed to a booth with a voting machine, or you will be given a paper ballot or punch card and directed to a voting booth.

**5. Cast your vote.** Follow the instructions on the voting machine or ballot, so your vote will be counted properly. Do not feel rushed. If you have a question, ask an attending official. Make sure you've made a selection in every contest in which you wish to vote.

### Test for Success

(a) Brainstorm at least three possible sources of voter information for voters in your area. (b) What sources would you consider most reliable?

## Point-of-Use Resources

**Skills for Life Activity** Unit 2 booklet, p. 28 provides an additional skill activity for this chapter.

**Social Studies Skills Tutor CD-ROM** Provides interactive practice in geographic literacy, critical thinking and reading, visual analysis, and communications.

### Test for Success

**(a)** Answers include city or town hall, a local election commission, news media, and interest groups. **(b)** Answers include government sources, major news sources, and nonpartisan civic groups, such as the League of Women Voters.

---

# SKILLS FOR LIFE

CITIZENSHIP

## Casting Your Vote

**Focus** Engage students in the voting process by conducting a voter information drive at school.

**Instruct** Divide the class into two groups. One will research how and where citizens can register to vote in your area. The other will get detailed directions on the locations of local polling places. If timing permits, have a third group research any upcoming ballot initiatives, compiling information on both sides of the issues. The groups should work together to create a voter information bulletin board. It should have pockets stuffed with cards providing the facts they gathered on registration and voting locations, so interested students can take a card from the pockets. The bulletin board can be created in the classroom or in a more visible location elsewhere in the school.

**Close/Reteach** Hold a brief class discussion on why voting is important. Explore why Americans tend to take the privilege for granted. Discuss obstacles to registering and voting, and brainstorm what communities can do to increase participation.

### Answers . . .

**1.** Poll students to find out how many will be eligible to vote in the next local, State, or national election.
**2.** If any students in the class are eligible to register, ask for volunteers to register and report to the class on how the process worked.
**3.** If an election is not occurring in the near future, students can still do research into when their elected representatives will come up for reelection and where they stand on key issues that would affect students' voting preferences.
**4.** Make sure students know their precinct number and polling place.
**5.** If possible, obtain sample ballots or mail-in ballots from a local source for students to become familiar with.

# ③ Money and Elections

**Money and Elections**

## Section Preview

### OBJECTIVES

1. **Explain** the issues raised by campaign spending.
2. **Describe** the various sources of funding for campaign spending.
3. **Examine** federal laws that regulate campaign finance.
4. **Outline** the role of the Federal Election Commission in enforcing campaign finance laws.
5. **Describe** loopholes in today's campaign finance laws.

### WHY IT MATTERS

Money is an indispensable campaign resource. Yet money also poses a variety of problems in the election process. That's why the use of money is regulated in today's elections.

### POLITICAL DICTIONARY

★ **political action committee (PAC)**
★ **subsidy**
★ **soft money**
★ **hard money**

▲ Seal of the Federal Election Commission, which administers federal law dealing with campaign finance.

**R**unning for public office costs money, and often a lot of it. That fact creates some difficult problems in American politics. It leaves open the possibility that candidates will try to buy their way into public office. It also makes it possible for special interests to try to buy favors from those who are in office.

Clearly, government by the people must be protected from these dangers. But how? Parties and candidates must have money. Without it, they cannot campaign or do any of the things they must do to win elections.

In short, money is an absolutely necessary campaign resource. Yet, the getting and spending of campaign funds can corrupt the entire political process.

## Campaign Spending

No one really knows how much money is spent on elections in the United States. Reliable estimates of total spending in recent presidential elections are shown in the table on page 197. These figures include nominations and general elections for offices at all levels.

The presidential election eats up by far the largest share of campaign dollars. For 2000, total spending for the major and minor parties—including primaries, conventions, and presidential campaigns—came to at least $1.5 billion.

The vast sums spent on congressional campaigns also continue to climb, election after election. Spending in all the Senate and House races in 1998 came to nearly $750 million. That figure passed the $1 billion mark in 2000.

Radio and television time, professional campaign managers and consultants, newspaper advertisements, pamphlets, buttons, posters and bumper stickers, office rent, polls, data processing, mass mailings, Web sites, travel—these and a host of other items make up the huge sums spent in campaigns. Television is by far the largest item in a typical campaign budget. A single half-hour of network TV time can run as much as $500,000, and a 30-second spot in prime time runs to at least $150,000. As Will Rogers put it years ago, "You have to be loaded just to get beat."

Of course the total amount spent in particular races varies widely. How much depends on the office involved, the opposition, the candidate, whether he or she is the incumbent, and the availability of campaign funds.

## Sources of Funding

Parties and their candidates draw their money from two basic sources—private contributors and the public treasury.

---

### ▣ Block Scheduling Strategies

Consider these suggestions to manage extended class time:

■ Have students develop a questionnaire based on campaign financing. Questions should probe people's feelings about whether too much is spent; how useful congressional regulations are; if contribution limits are fair; the role of the media; and whether campaigns should receive public funding. Have students poll family members, teachers and other adults, and then tabulate their results in the form of a summary and a pie chart.

■ Have students analyze the results of their polls to create a list of major problems with the current campaign finance system. Then have them brainstorm solutions to these problems. Have students share their solutions with the class, and use them as a springboard for discussion.

## Private and Public Sources

Private givers have always been the major source of campaign funds in American politics. Those givers include the following:

1. Small contributors—those who give $5 or $10 or so, and only occasionally. In fact only about 10 percent of people of voting age ever make campaign contributions; parties and candidates must thus look to other places for much of their funding.

2. Wealthy individuals and families—the so-called "fat cats," who can afford large donations and find it in their best interest to make them.

3. Candidates—both incumbents and challengers, their families, and, importantly, people who hold and want to keep appointive public offices. Ross Perot holds the all-time record in this category. He spent some $65 million of his own money on his independent bid for the presidency in 1992.

4. Various nonparty groups—especially **political action committees (PACs).** Political action committees are the political arms of special-interest groups, which have a major stake in public policy.

5. Temporary organizations—groups formed for the immediate purposes of a campaign, including fund-raising. Hundreds of these short-lived units spring up every two years, and at every level in American politics.

Then, too, parties and their candidates often hold fund-raisers of various sorts. The most common are $100-, $500-, and $1,000-a-plate luncheons, dinners, picnics, receptions, and similar gatherings. Some of these events reached the $100,000-or-more level during the 2000 presidential campaign. Direct mail requests, telethons, and Internet solicitations are also among the oft-used tools of those who raise campaign money.

Another source of funds has recently emerged: public subsidies from federal and/or State treasuries. A **subsidy** is a grant of money, usually from a government. Subsidies have so far been most important at the presidential level, as you will see shortly.[16]

### Why People Give

Campaign donations are a form of political participation. Those who make them do so for a number of reasons. Many contributors give simply because they believe in a party or a candidate. Many of those who give, however, want access to government, and they hope to get it by helping their "friends" win elections. Hence some contributors give to both sides in a contest: Heads they win and tails they still win.

Some big donors want appointments to public office, and others want to keep the ones they have. Some long for social recognition. For them, dinner at the White House, meeting with a Cabinet official, or knowing the governor on a first-name basis may be enough. Organized labor, business, professional, and various other groups have particular policy aims. They want certain laws passed, changed, or repealed, or certain administrative actions taken.

## Regulating Campaign Finance

Congress first began to regulate the use of money in federal elections in 1907. In that year, it became unlawful for any corporation or national bank to make "a money contribution in

---

[16]Public funds for presidential campaigns come from the federal treasury. Several States now also have some form of public financing for parties and/or candidates at the State and even the local level.

---

| Total Campaign Spending, 1960–2000 |||||
| Year | Estimated spending | Voter turnout* | Spending per voter |
| --- | --- | --- | --- |
| 1960 | $175 million | 68.8 million | $2.54 |
| 1964 | $200 million | 70.6 million | $2.83 |
| 1968 | $300 million | 73.2 million | $4.10 |
| 1972 | $425 million | 77.7 million | $5.47 |
| 1976 | $540 million | 81.6 million | $6.62 |
| 1980 | $1.2 billion | 86.6 million | $13.87 |
| 1984 | $1.8 billion | 92.7 million | $19.42 |
| 1988 | $2.7 billion | 91.6 million | $29.48 |
| 1992 | $3.2 billion | 104.4 million | $30.65 |
| 1996 | $4.0 billion | 96.5 million | $41.45 |
| 2000 | $5.1 billion | 105.4 million | $48.39 |

*Federal elections

SOURCES: Federal Election Commission; Herbert E. Alexander, *Financing Politics*

 **Interpreting Tables** Total campaign spending has risen dramatically in recent elections. ***What factors may account for this rise?***

---

---

## Organizing Information

To make sure students understand the main points of this section, you may wish to use the Venn diagram to the right.

Tell students that a Venn diagram can be used to compare two groups by showing attributes they have alone and those they share. Have students use a Venn diagram to compare PAC contributions with private contributions. Characteristics both groups have should appear in the space where the circles overlap.

**Teaching Tip** A template for this graphic organizer can be found in the Section Support Transparencies, Transparency 6.

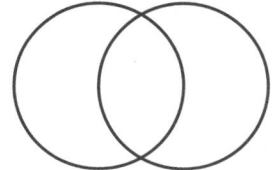

---

## American Government, American Humor

Share the following quotation with students:

*"Politicians [are] a set of men who have interests aside from the interests of the people, and who, to say the most of them, are, taken as a mass, at least one long step removed from honest men. I say this with the greater freedom, because, being a politician myself, none can regard it as personal."*

—Abraham Lincoln

**Discussion** Ask students what Lincoln meant by his remark. Ask: What might the "interests aside from the interests of the people" that Lincoln refers to have to do with money and elections?

**(Challenging)**

## Customize for

### More Advanced Students

Have students compare the campaign regulating system with the systems of other federal regulatory agencies. Using card catalogs, interviews, periodicals, and other resources, students should collect notes on federal regulation of the country's communications system, aviation system, securities industry, or some other target of federal regulation. Have them note both similarities and differences in the goals and practices of each regulatory system, presenting their findings in the form of a brief oral or written report, or a series of charts or graphs.

any election" to candidates for federal office. Since then, Congress has passed several laws to regulate the use of money in presidential and congressional campaigns. Today, these regulations are found in three detailed laws: the Federal Election Campaign Act (FECA) of 1971, the FECA Amendments of 1974, and the FECA Amendments of 1976.

The earliest federal laws were loosely drawn, not often obeyed, and almost never enforced. The 1971 law replaced them. The 1974 law was the major legislative response to the Watergate scandal of the Nixon years. The 1976 law was passed in response to a landmark Supreme Court decision, *Buckley* v. *Valeo*, in 1976. A few minor changes were made to these laws in 1979.

Congress does not have the power to regulate the use of money in State and local elections. Every State now regulates at least some aspects of campaign finance, however—some of them more effectively than others.[17]

## The Federal Election Commission

The Federal Election Commission (FEC) administers all federal law dealing with campaign finance. Set up by Congress in 1974, the FEC is

---

[17]A useful summary of State campaign finance laws can be found in *The Book of the States,* a biennial publication of the Council of State Governments.

an independent agency in the executive branch. Its six members are appointed by the President, with Senate confirmation.

The laws that the FEC enforces cover four broad areas. They (1) require the timely disclosure of campaign finance data, (2) place limits on campaign contributions, (3) place limits on campaign expenditures, and (4) provide public funding (subsidies) for several parts of the presidential election process.

### Disclosure Requirements

Congress first required the reporting of certain campaign finance information in 1910. Today, the disclosure requirements, which are intended to spotlight the place of money in federal campaigns, are very detailed. In fact, the reports that candidates must file with the FEC are so comprehensive that nearly all candidates for federal office find that their campaign organizations must include at least one and often several certified public accountants.

No individual or group can make a contribution in the name of another. Cash gifts of more than $100 are prohibited. So, too, are contributions from any foreign source.

All contributions to a candidate for federal office must be made through a single campaign committee. Only that committee can spend that candidate's campaign money. All contributions and spending must be closely accounted

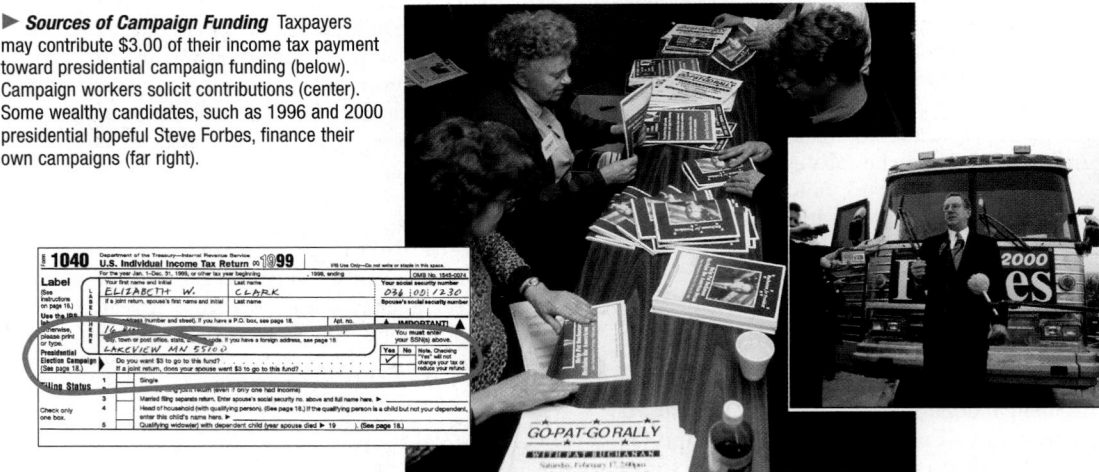

▶ *Sources of Campaign Funding* Taxpayers may contribute $3.00 of their income tax payment toward presidential campaign funding (below). Campaign workers solicit contributions (center). Some wealthy candidates, such as 1996 and 2000 presidential hopeful Steve Forbes, finance their own campaigns (far right).

for by that one committee. Any contribution or loan of more than $200 must be identified by source and by date. Any spending over $200 must also be identified by the name of the person or firm to whom payment was made, by date, and by purpose.

Any contribution of more than $5,000 must be reported to the FEC no later than 48 hours after it is received. So, too, must any sum of $1,000 or more that is received in the last 20 days of a campaign.

## Limits on Contributions

Congress first began to regulate campaign contributions in 1907, when it outlawed donations by corporations and national banks. A similar ban was first applied to labor unions in 1943. Individual contributions became subject to regulation in 1939.

Today, no person can give more than $1,000 to any federal candidate in a primary election. In addition, no person can give more than $1,000 to any federal candidate's general election campaign. Also, no person can give more than $5,000 in any year to a political action committee, or $20,000 to a national party committee. The total of any person's contributions to federal candidates and committees must be limited to no more than $25,000 in any one year.

Those limits may seem generous; in fact, they are very tight. Before those limits were imposed in 1974, many wealthy individuals gave far larger amounts. In 1972, for example, W. Clement Stone, a Chicago insurance executive, contributed more than $2 million to President Richard Nixon's reelection campaign. Richard Mellon Scaife, heir to oil, aluminum, and banking fortunes, gave more than $1 million to that campaign.

## PAC Contributions

Neither corporations nor labor unions can contribute to any candidate running for a federal office. Their political action committees, however, can and do.

Recall that PACs are the political arms of special-interest groups—business, labor, professional, cause, and other organizations that try to influence government policies. You will look at

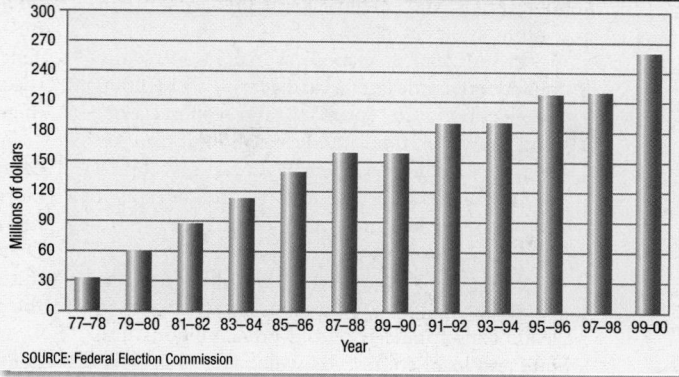

### PAC Contributions to Congressional Candidates

SOURCE: Federal Election Commission

***Interpreting Graphs*** Political action committees (PACs) have become a major source of campaign money. ***How do you think the growth of PACs has affected political campaigns since the 1970s?***

interest groups at length in Chapter 9, but their PACs deserve special attention here. While PACs operate in every part of the political scene, their clout comes mostly from their ability to raise campaign money and their willingness to give it to their "friends" who run for public office.

Some 4,000 PACs are registered with the Federal Election Commission today. Leading examples include: BIPAC (the Business-Industry Political Action Committee), COPE (the AFL-CIO's Committee on Political Education), AMPAC (the American Medical Association's Political Action Committee), and the National Education Association's NEAPAC.

Any list of the most powerful of these groups must also include the American Bankers Association's BANKPAC, the American Trial Lawyers PAC, and EMILY's List, which seeks to increase the number of women among the Democratic members of Congress. (EMILY's List takes its name from this political maxim: Early Money Is Like Yeast—it makes the dough rise.)

PACs fill their campaign war chests with contributions from their members. Members are found among the executives, employees, and stockholders of corporations, labor union members, doctors, dentists, teachers, and lawyers, those who favor or oppose gun control or abortion, and so on. These groups bundle all of their members' gifts of money, pooling them

## Background Note

### Leadership PACs

One large loophole in campaign financing concerns the leadership PACs, formed by politicians to help fund other politicians' candidacies. Sponsoring politicians can gain influence and enhance their status by raising large sums of money and donating it to colleagues. Leadership PACs must adhere to the same spending limits as other PACs. As the 2000 elections approached, by far the biggest fundraisers among the 126 leadership PACS were those sponsored by the top GOP leaders in the House; Americans for a Republican Majority, sponsored by House Majority Whip Tom DeLay, (R, Texas) was in the lead with $454,097.

## Point-of-Use Resources

The Living Constitution Limited Government, p. 4

Basic Principles of the Constitution Transparencies Transparencies 16-22, *Limited Government*

## CONSTITUTIONAL PRINCIPLES

### Limited Government

The concept of limited government means that government must obey the law. Fair, honest campaigns and elections are essential in nations that uphold the ideal of limited government. The Federal Election Commission is the body that ensures the fairness of campaigns and elections. The Commission has six members, and by law no more than three members may be of the same political party. Furthermore, four votes are required for all Commission actions. These

requirements ensure that the Commission is nonpartisan.

### Activity

Visit the Federal Election Commission Web site to learn more about what the FEC does (links are provided at **www.phschool.com**). Enter the Citizen's Guide area of the site, and choose one of the topics listed. Prepare a brief oral report, summary, or visual presentation of what you learn.

*Answer to . . .*

**Interpreting Charts** The growth of PACs has been a large factor in the overall increase in campaign funding.

ACTIVITY

## Heterogeneous Groups

**Enrichment** Use the "numbered heads" approach to discuss the four areas the FEC enforces. Divide the class into four groups. Then count off with the entire class, assigning each student a number from 1 to 4. Have all of the 1's meet and discuss the first area (disclosure of campaign finance data). Have the 2's, 3's, and 4's meet and discuss the other three areas (limits on campaign contributions, limits on campaign expenditures, and public funding for elections). Allow 10-15 minutes for groups to discuss each area. Then ask students to rejoin their original group to discuss all four of the areas enforced by the FEC.

**Block Strategy
(Average)**

together. Then they distribute money to those candidates who (1) are sympathetic to the PAC's policy goals, and (2) have a reasonable chance of winning their races.

No PAC can give more than $5,000 to any one federal candidate in an election, or $10,000 per election cycle (primary and general election). However, there is no overall limit on PAC giving to candidates. Each PAC can give up to $5,000 per election to as many candidates as it chooses. A PAC may also contribute up to $15,000 a year to a political party.

PACs put an estimated $400 million into the presidential and congressional campaigns in 2000. They funneled untold other millions into State and local contests as well.

### Limits on Expenditures

Congress first began to limit federal campaign spending in 1925. Most of the limits now on the books apply only to presidential (not congressional) elections. This fact is due mostly to the Supreme Court's decision in *Buckley* v. *Valeo*, 1976.

In *Buckley,* the High Court struck down several spending limits set by the FECA Amendments of 1974. It held each of those restrictions to be contrary to the First Amendment's guarantees of freedom of expression. In effect, said the Court, in politics "money is speech."

The most important of the provisions the Court threw out (1) limited campaign expenditures by candidates running for seats in the House or Senate, (2) limited how much of their own money candidates could put into their own campaigns, and (3) said that no person or group could spend more than $1,000 on behalf of any federal candidate without that candidate's permission.

The Court also held that several limits that the FEC law of 1974 placed on spending apply only to candidates who accept campaign subsidies from the FEC. Candidates who do not take FEC money are not bound by those limits.[18]

---

[18]As of the presidential election in 2000, only three major party aspirants have refused to accept federal funds—all three in the preconvention period, all three Republicans, and one of them twice: John Connally, who tried for the Republican nomination in 1980; Steve Forbes, who sought the GOP nod in 1996 and again in 2000; and George W. Bush in 2000. Mr. Bush did accept FEC funds for his general election campaign in 2000.

For 2000, major party contenders who used FEC money could spend no more than $40.5 million in the preconvention period. (George W. Bush, who did not accept FEC money until his general election campaign, spent approximately twice that much before the Republicans held their convention in Philadelphia in July.)

After the conventions, in the general election campaign, the two major party nominees (Al Gore and George W. Bush) could not spend more than $67.6 million. In addition, neither the Democratic nor the Republican national committee could lay out more than $13.7 million for the presidential campaign.

It is also possible for a minor party's presidential candidate to qualify for an FEC subsidy. In 2000, the Reform Party's Pat Buchanan received $12.7 million for his campaign.

### Public Funding of Presidential Campaigns

Congress first began to provide for the public funding of presidential campaigns in the Revenue Act of 1971. It broadened sections of that law in 1974 and again in 1976.

The 1971 law set up the Presidential Election Campaign Fund. Every person who files a federal income tax return can "check off" (assign) three dollars of his or her tax payment (six dollars on a joint return) to the fund. The monies in the fund are used every four years to finance (1) preconvention campaigns, (2) national conventions, and (3) presidential election campaigns. The FEC administers the public subsidy process.

1. *Preconvention Campaigns.* Presidential primary and caucus campaigns are supported by the private contributions a candidate raises plus the public money he or she receives from the FEC. To be eligible for public funds, a contender must raise at least $100,000 in contributions from individuals (not organizations). That amount must be gathered in $5,000 lots in each of at least 20 States, with each of those lots built from individual donations of not more than $250. This requirement is meant to discourage frivolous candidates.

For each presidential hopeful who passes this test, the FEC will match the first $250 of each individual's donation to that candidate, up to a total of half of the overall limit on primary spending. Thus, in 2000 the FEC could give some contenders nearly $20 million because the ceiling was close to $40 million for each candidate. The FEC does not match contributions from PACs or other political organizations.

For 2000, all the major party presidential hopefuls combined spent nearly $200 million on their preconvention campaigns. This figure included some $80 million in matching funds from the FEC.

2. *National Conventions.* If a major party applies for the money, it automatically receives a grant to pay for its national convention. The two parties each received $13.5 million from the FEC for that purpose in 2000. The Reform Party received $2.5 million for its convention, as well.

3. *Presidential Election Campaigns.* Every major party nominee automatically qualifies for a public subsidy to cover the costs of the general election campaign. For the 2000 election, that subsidy amounted to $67.6 million. A candidate can refuse that money, of course. Should that ever happen, the candidate would be free to raise however much he or she could from private sources.

So far (from 1976 through 2000), the nominees of both major parties have taken the public money each time. Because they did so, each automatically (1) could spend no more than the amount of the subsidy, and (2) could not accept campaign funds from any other source.

A minor party candidate can also qualify for public funding, but not automatically. To be eligible, the minor party must either (1) have won at least five percent of the popular vote in the last presidential election, or (2) win at least that much of the total vote in the current election.

In the latter case, the public money is received *after* the election and so could not possibly help the candidate in that election. (Remember, many provisions of both federal and State election law are purposely drawn to discourage minor party and independent efforts and thus help strengthen the two-party system.)

Except for Ross Perot in 1996, few minor party candidates have come even remotely close to winning five percent of the popular vote in any election since the subsidy arrangement was put in place. Over that period (1976 through 2000), however, two independent candidates did exceed the five-percent threshold.

John Anderson received 6.7 percent of the popular vote in 1980. He therefore received

*Interpreting Political Cartoons* **(a) Explain the difference between "hard" and "soft" money. (b) How does the cartoon help make that difference clear?**

$4.2 million from the FEC after that election. Ross Perot won 19 percent of the vote in 1992. Thus, the FEC ruled that he was eligible to receive $29.2 million from the Presidential Election Campaign Fund to finance his Reform Party candidacy in 1996. Perot won 8 percent of the popular vote in 1996, and so the Reform Party's candidate, Pat Buchanan, qualified for the federal subsidy in 2000.

## Loopholes in the Law

Nearly 40 years ago, President Lyndon Johnson described the then-current body of federal campaign finance law as "more loophole than law." We have come very close to the point at which that comment could be applied to today's federal election-money statutes. Three immense loopholes have appeared in those laws over the past 25 years, and huge torrents of cash have gushed through them. Those loopholes involve (1) soft money, (2) independent campaign spending, and (3) issue ads.

1. *Soft money.* Federal law neither limits nor requires the reporting of **soft money.** Soft money includes those contributions made to State and local party organizations for such "party-building activities" as voter registration and get-out-the-vote drives, party mailings and advertisements, and similar efforts.

## Point-of-Use Resources

**Guide to the Essentials** Chapter 7, Section 3, p. 45 provides support for students who need additional review of section content. Spanish support is available in the Spanish edition of the Guide on p. 38.

**Quiz** Unit 2 booklet, p. 27 includes matching and multiple-choice questions to check students' understanding of Section 3 content.

**Presentation Pro CD-ROM** Quizzes and multiple-choice questions check students' understanding of Section 3 content.

## Answers to . . .
### Section 3 Assessment

**1.** PACs are the political arms of special interest groups.
**2. (a)** A subsidy is a grant or gift of money, usually from a government.
**(b)** They are most important at the presidential level.
**3.** Because soft money is not limited and does not have to be reported, political organizations find it easy to filter it into political campaigns.
**4.** Soft money is given to political party organizations for "party-building activities" like voter registration drives and does not have to be regulated; hard money is given to campaigns directly, and must be regulated by the FEC.
**5.** Answers will vary; those who agree might suggest that "democracy" means the greater number of supporters; those who disagree might say that "democracy" means the ability for everyone to participate, not the participation itself.
**6.** Possible answer: Candidates would

## Answer to . . .
### Interpreting Political Cartoons
**(a)** Individuals, families, PACs, and temporary organizations.
**(b)** Each individual may only give him $1,000, and each PAC, only $5,000 in federal elections.

*"I may be awhile. I'm soliciting funds for my reëlection campaign."*

**Interpreting Political Cartoons (a)** From what sources might this candidate solicit funds? **(b)** What limitations will there be on these funds?

Soft money contributions come from wealthy individuals, many PACs, and elements of both major parties' national organizations. Those funds bypass the reporting requirements and the amount limits that apply to **hard money,** or campaign money that is subject to regulation by the FEC.

State and local organizations in both major parties have found it easy to filter this unregulated money into the parties' presidential and congressional campaigns. The soft money loophole ballooned from an estimated $19 million in 1980 to some $500 million in 2000.

2. *Independent campaign spending.* According to federal election law, an "independent person or group" is one that participates in a campaign entirely on its own, with no connection to a candidate or party involved in that election. Such a person or group can spend—not contribute to a candidate or a party, but *spend* as it chooses—an unlimited amount of money in that campaign. That spending can be made to help a candidate, of course; but it has much more often been directed *against* a candidate.

Congress tried to minimize such independent activity in 1974 by limiting that spending to no more than $1,000 per candidate in an election. In 1976, however, the Supreme Court struck down that limit in *Buckley* v. *Valeo,* again on the money-is-speech ground. Independent campaign spending has played an increasingly important part in both presidential and congressional elections ever since.

3. *Issue ads.* The congressional campaigns of 1998 and the presidential and congressional contests in 2000 saw a surge in a new form of political advertising: the so-called "issue ads." These pitches, found mostly on radio and television, deal with such controversial areas of public policy as social security, health care, and foreign trade.

Issue ads do not mention the names of those candidates the ads' sponsors support or hope to defeat. Since they do not say, in so many words, "Vote for Joe Smith" or "Vote Against Sue Sprat," they are not covered by the disclosure requirements or spending limits of federal law. Most voters have little trouble making the connections these ads intend, however.

## Section 3 Assessment

**Key Terms and Main Ideas**

1. What are **political action committees (PACs)?**
2. **(a)** What is a **subsidy? (b)** At what level in the election process are campaign subsidies most important?
3. How has **soft money** created a loophole in federal election-finance law?
4. How do soft money and **hard money** differ?

**Critical Thinking**

5. **Distinguishing Fact From Opinion** Explain why you agree or disagree with this statement: "Democracy would be best served if campaigns were entirely supported by the small contributions of millions of American voters."

6. **Drawing Conclusions** How might the electoral process change if campaign spending were more limited and current loopholes closed?

 **Take It to the Net**

7. Find the campaign finance information disclosed to the FEC by your representative and his or her opponent(s) during the last election. Make a chart showing how much money each candidate raised from various sources. How do the candidates' sources and amounts of funding compare? Use the links provided in the Social Studies area at the following Web site for help in completing this activity. **www.phschool.com**

have less to spend on campaigning, which could have the effect of downplaying advertising in the electoral process.

 **Take It to the Net**

7. Direct students to the Social Studies area at the Prentice Hall School Web site. The *Magruder's American Government* companion Web site includes the directions and links needed to complete the activity. It also provides a printable Internet activity worksheet with scoring rubrics for assessment. Charts should be clearly organized and accurately interpret the data.

# Can States Limit Campaign Contributions?

*Laws regulating campaign financing are designed to prevent wealthy persons and organizations from using large donations to gain influence over elected officials. In the 1976 case Buckley v. Valeo, however, the Supreme Court struck down several federal limits on campaign contributions as violating donors' right of free speech. Does that decision mean that States cannot limit campaign contributions?*

### Nixon v. Shrink Missouri Government PAC (2000)

In 1994, Missouri passed a law limiting the amount of money that individuals and organizations could give to political candidates. The specific limits depended on the particular office and were changed periodically to reflect changes in the cost of living. The Shrink Missouri Government Political Action Committee and Zev David Fredman, a candidate for State office, filed suit against Jeremiah J. Nixon, the Missouri attorney general, charging that the contribution limits violated their First Amendment rights. Shrink Missouri stated that it would have given more money to Fredman if the law had not prevented it, and Fredman argued that he could not campaign effectively without larger contributions.

The federal district court upheld the law. It held that the law supported the government's aim of increasing citizens' trust in government by reducing public fears that wealthy campaign donors had too much influence over government. The court of appeals reversed that decision, finding in part that the State legislature had not proven that large campaign contributions had caused actual corruption. Nixon then sought review by the Supreme Court.

### Arguments for Nixon

1. The State has a legitimate interest in preventing corruption and the appearance of corruption that large campaign contributions can create.
2. The contribution limits imposed by Missouri were not unreasonably low. They did not prevent candidates from raising enough money to run effective campaigns.

3. Money is property; it is not speech. The "right" to contribute money is not entitled to the same high level of protection as is freedom of speech.

### Arguments for Shrink Missouri

1. Missouri did not present actual evidence showing that large campaign contributions were creating corruption or even the appearance of corruption. Without such evidence, the abstract concern about the effect of large contributions does not justify restricting citizens' right to contribute.
2. Limits on campaign contributions make it more difficult for outside candidates who do not have the support of the media and of established political interests to conduct effective campaigns.
3. Campaign contributions are entitled to strong First Amendment protection, not because they themselves are speech but because they enable donors to promote the speech of candidates who share their views.

### Decide for Yourself

1. Review the constitutional grounds on which each side based its arguments and the specific arguments each side presented.
2. Debate the opposing viewpoints presented in this case. Which viewpoint do you favor?
3. Predict the impact of the Court's decision on ways in which States may seek to regulate campaign financing in the future. (To read a summary of the Court's decision, turn to the Supreme Court Glossary on page 799.)

---

CLOSE UP
FOUNDATION
*Corner*

📁 **Close Up on the Supreme Court** *Nixon* v. *Shrink Missouri Government PAC,* p. 8 provides an activity to extend coverage of this case.

CLOSE UP
FOUNDATION │ **Online**

To keep up-to-date on Close Up news and activities, visit Close Up Online at

**www.closeup.org**

---

CLOSE UP
FOUNDATION

## Can States Limit Campaign Contributions?

**Focus** Remind students that thus far this chapter has outlined spending regulations for federal elections. Ask: Does Congress have the power to regulate spending in State elections? *(No)* Explain that this case considers whether States, as opposed to the Federal Government, can regulate spending in State elections.

**Instruct** Call on a volunteer to explain why the *Buckley* case struck down a law regulating federal campaign contributions. *(The Court held that it violated the donors' right to free speech)* Then ask a volunteer to identify the conflicting interests in *Nixon.* *(Preventing corruption and protecting free speech)* Finally, ask a volunteer to identify which of those interests the *Nixon* case tends to favor. *(Preventing corruption)*

**Close/Reteach** Explain that persons or groups interested in the outcome of a court case involving the public interest are sometimes allowed to present their opinion to the court. Have the students write a so-called "friend of the court" brief expressing their opinion as to how the case should be decided.

💿 **Keep It Current CD-ROM** includes government-related projects by unit. The CD-ROM links to the Prentice Hall School Web site and may be used for daily updates.

### Answers to . . .
**Decide for Yourself**
1. Nixon argued that money is property and not speech, and that States have a role in preventing corruption. *Shrink Missouri* cited 1st Amendment protection of speech and lack of corruption evidence in arguing that campaign contributions were protected.
2. Answers will vary, but should be supported with valid reasoning.
3. The Court upheld the Missouri law, citing the precedent of the *Buckley* case with regard to limits on contributions to candidates for federal office.

## Practicing the Vocabulary

1. caucus
2. political action committee (PAC)
3. direct primary
4. polling place
5. ballot
6. runoff primary
7. coattail effect
8. soft money
9. open primary
10. precinct

## Reviewing Main Ideas
### Section 1

**11.** Statements will vary, but should demonstrate an understanding that nomination involves many choices.
**12.** Self-announcement, petition, caucus, convention, and primary.
**13.** At first self-announcement, and then the caucus were the major means of nomination. To make the process more democratic, conventions, primaries, and petition emerged as dominant nominating methods.
**14.** In closed primaries only party members may vote; in open primaries any qualified voter may vote; in blanket primaries, voters choose candidates from both parties on one ballot.
**15.** For: It prevents "raiding," helps make candidates more responsive to the party, and encourages voters to make informed choices. Against: It compromises ballot secrecy and excludes independent voters.

### Section 2

**16.** To ensure fair elections, which are the foundation of democracy.
**17.** Most elections take place at the State level, therefore most election law is State law.
**18. (a)** It sets some of the basic rules governing elections. **(b)** Congress fixes the "time, place, and manner" of congressional elections and the dates for choosing presidential electors and electoral balloting.
**19. (a)** In the office-group ballot, candidates for an office are grouped together by office; in a party-column ballot, candidates are listed by party. **(b)** Office-ballots encourage voter judgment and split-ticket voting; party-column ballots encourage straight-ticket voting.
**20.** Voting machines are fast and accurate; online voting is convenient.

## Political Dictionary

nomination (p. 178)
general election (p. 179)
caucus (p. 180)
direct primary (p. 182)
closed primary (p. 182)
open primary (p. 183)

blanket primary (p. 183)
runoff primary (p. 184)
nonpartisan election (p. 184)
absentee voting (p. 189)
coattail effect (p. 190)
precinct (p. 190)

polling place (p. 190)
ballot (p. 190)
political action committee (PAC) (p. 197)
subsidy (p. 197)
soft money (p. 201)
hard money (p. 202)

## Practicing the Vocabulary

**Matching** *Choose a term from the list above that best matches each description.*

1. A group of like-minded people who meet to choose candidates for office
2. The political arm of a special-interest group
3. An election held within a political party at which the voters choose candidates who will appear on the ballot in an upcoming general election
4. The place where voters go to cast their ballots
5. The device by which voters register their choices in an election

**Fill in the Blank** *Choose a term from the list above that best completes the sentence.*

6. In a _____, voters must choose between the two top finishers in an earlier primary election.
7. Because of the _____, candidates can benefit from the popularity of another candidate on the ballot from their party.
8. _____ is given to State and local party organizations for "party-building activities."
9. One commonly heard criticism of the _____ is that it encourages "raiding."
10. Each _____ has one polling place.

## Reviewing Main Ideas

### Section 1

**11.** You have read that the nominating process has "a very real impact on the exercise of the right to vote." Explain this statement in your own words.
**12.** What are the five broad categories that describe the way most nominations are made?
**13.** How has the nominating process in American politics changed over the course of American history?
**14.** Describe the different types of direct primaries that have been used in American politics.
**15.** Explain the arguments for and against the closed primary.

### Section 2

**16.** What is the overall purpose and importance of election law in the American political process?
**17.** To what extent are the States involved in governing elections?
**18. (a)** To what extent is the Federal Government involved in governing elections? **(b)** Give at least three examples of federal laws governing elections.

**19. (a)** Describe the basic difference between the office-group ballot and the party-column ballot. **(b)** What are the advantages of each?
**20.** Describe recent technological advances and changes that make it easier for Americans to vote.

### Section 3

**21.** Briefly describe the role and importance of money in the election process.
**22. (a)** Identify five types of private donors to political campaigns. **(b)** Why might these individuals and groups wish to contribute money to political candidates?
**23.** Outline the limitations placed on individual and PAC contributions to federal candidates and political parties.
**24. (a)** How does a candidate for President qualify for public funding? **(b)** What rules must candidates follow if they accept public funds?
**25.** Identify and explain the three major loopholes in today's federal election-money statutes.

### Section 3

**21.** Candidates require money to manage their campaigns and pay for advertising and other ways to get their messages to the public.
**22. (a)** Small contributors, individuals and families, candidates, nonparty groups and PACs, and temporary campaign organizations. **(b)** Because they believe in a party or candidate, or want to take part in the political process.

**23.** Individuals are limited to set amounts, not to exceed $25,000 per year. PACs have similar kinds of limitations and may not contribute over $15,000 a year to any one political party.
**24. (a)** They must raise at least $100,000 from individuals, in at least 20 States, in donations of not more than $250. **(b)** They cannot spend more than the amount of the subsidy, and can-

not accept campaign funds from any other source.
**25.** Independent campaign spending holds that a person not connected to a candidate or party can spend an unlimited amount of money; soft money allows organizations to get unregulated money; issue ads allow candidates to use unregulated ads as long as their names are not mentioned.

## Critical Thinking Skills

**26. *Applying the Chapter Skill*** Voting is an important way to participate in government, but is it the most effective? Analyze the effectiveness of various methods of participation in the political process at local, State, and national levels by writing an article comparing voting with joining a campaign, supporting a cause, and taking part in public debates.

**27. *Drawing Conclusions*** Use what you have read in this chapter to make an argument for or against the following statement: *In the American political system, the nomination of candidates is more important than the general election.*

**28. *Expressing Problems Clearly*** Should federal law prohibit candidates from accepting soft money? Write a well-reasoned paragraph explaining your answer.

## Analyzing Political Cartoons

Using your knowledge of American government and this cartoon, answer the questions below.

**29. (a)** Who are the characters in the cartoon? **(b)** Why are two of them covered in mud?

**30.** What can be the effect of a divisive primary on a political party?

---

### Take It to the Net

Additional support materials and activities for Chapter 7 of *Magruder's American Government* can be found in the Social Studies area at the Prentice Hall School Web site. **www.phschool.com**

---

### ★ You Can Make a Difference

Create an unbiased information sheet on political candidates. Obtain a list of candidates in a forthcoming local or State election—for example, people running for the State legislature. Start with a brief biography of each candidate. Include the person's personal and political history, stands he or she has taken on issues, and other relevant information. Use the back files of local newspapers as well as the Internet, the library, and other sources. Write your findings as a voters' guide.

## Participation Activities

**31. *Current Events Watch*** Keep track of stories in the news about money spent on election campaigns and about campaign finance reform. Then use what you have learned to write an essay explaining why you would favor or oppose legislation that limits the amount of money candidates can spend on campaigns.

**32. *Chart Activity*** Create a chart or calendar for the current election cycle in your State. The calendar should list the date of the next primary and general election, candidate filing deadlines, voter registration deadlines, and any other important dates. (Since in most States the secretary of state oversees election laws, that office is a good source for election information.)

**33. *It's Your Turn*** Write a letter to the governor of your State in which you express your opinion about public financing for the election of State and local officials. Begin your letter by stating your purpose. Then, write one paragraph for each of the reasons for your opinion. Conclude the letter by thanking the governor for considering your ideas. Proofread and correct errors. Then prepare a final copy. **(Writing a Letter)**

### Take It to the Net

***Chapter 7 Self-Test*** As a final review activity, take the Chapter 7 Self-Test in the Social Studies area at the Web site listed below, and receive immediate feedback on your answers.

**www.phschool.com**

---

## Critical Thinking Skills

**26.** Answers will vary; they should demonstrate an understanding of the potential impact of the ways to participate in government that are listed.

**27.** For: The nominating process is often the only time during which there is a real contest involving multiple choices. Against: It is during the general election that the officeholder is chosen.

**28.** Yes: Candidates who use soft money for political campaigns are exploiting a loophole in campaign finance laws and have an unfair advantage. No: soft money is a means of participating in the democratic process and of supporting candidates and causes in which one believes.

## Analyzing Political Cartoons

**29. (a)** The Republican and Democratic candidates. **(b)** They have just finished fighting in the presidential primary.

**30.** It can keep the party from staying strong and united in the general election.

## You Can Make a Difference

Voter guides should be easy to follow and include all relevant information in an informative, objective manner.

## Participation Activities

**31.** Essays should use specific examples and quotes from the news stories tracked, and should express a definite stance on the issue.

**32.** Charts or calendars should be clearly organized and include all required information.

**33.** Letters should include a clear purpose for writing, all relevant reasons for the student's opinion, and a respectful closing paragraph.

---

## Point-of-Use Resources

**Guide to the Essentials of American Government** Chapter 7 Test, page 46 provides multiple-choice questions to test students' knowledge of the chapter.

**Test Bank CD-ROM** Chapter 7 Test

**Chapter Test** Chapter Tests booklet

# Mass Media and Public Opinion

| Section Objectives | Print and Technology Resources |
|---|---|
| **1 The Formation of Public Opinion** (pp. 208–213) <br><br> 1. Examine the term *public opinion* and understand why it is difficult to define. <br> 2. Analyze the factors that influence an individual's political attitudes and actions, including family and education. <br><br> TEKS 3A, 3B, 16C, 21A, 21B, 21C, 21D, 21E, 22A, 22B, 22C, 22D | • **Unit 2 booklet** Guided Reading and Review, p. 29 Section 1 Quiz, p. 30 <br> • **Lesson Plans booklet** Section 1, p. 38 <br> • **Political Cartoons booklet** Section 1, p. 30 <br> • **Block Scheduling with Lesson Strategies booklet** p. 23 <br> • **Section Reading Support** <br><br> **Transparencies** <br> • **Close Up on Primary Sources booklet** African Americans and Television, p. 10; The Star Spangled Banner, p. 35; Pledge of Allegiance, American's Creed, Oath of Citizenship, p. 40 <br> • **Section Support Transparencies** 33, 132 <br> • **Presentation Pro CD-ROM** Section 1 |
| **2 Measuring Public Opinion** (pp. 215–221) <br><br> 1. Describe the challenges involved in measuring public opinion. <br> 2. Explain why opinion polls are the best measure of public opinion. <br> 3. Identify five steps in the polling process. <br> 4. Understand the challenges of evaluating polls. <br> 5. Recognize the limits on the impact of public opinion in a democracy. <br><br> TEKS 3A, 21A, 21B, 21D, 22A, 22B, 22C, 22D | • **Unit 2 booklet** Guided Reading and Review, p. 31 Section 2 Quiz, p. 32 <br> • **Lesson Plans booklet** Section 2, p. 39 <br> • **Political Cartoons booklet** Section 2, p. 31 <br> • **Section Reading Support Transparencies** <br><br> • **Block Scheduling with Lesson Strategies booklet** p. 23 <br> • **Government Assessment Rubrics booklet** p. 10 <br> • **Section Support Transparencies** 34, 133 <br> • **Presentation Pro CD-ROM** Section 2 <br> • **Social Studies Skills Tutor CD-ROM** |
| **3 The Mass Media** (pp. 223–230) <br><br> 1. Examine the role of the mass media in providing the public with political information. <br> 2. Give examples of the processes used by the media to affect public policy. <br> 3. Understand the factors that limit the influence of the media. <br><br> TEKS 3A, 16C, 16D, 17C, 20A, 21A, 21B, 21C, 21E, 22A, 22B, 22D | • **Unit 2 booklet** Guided Reading and Review, p. 33 Section 3 Quiz, p. 34 Skills for Life Activity, p. 35 <br> • **Lesson Plans booklet** Section 3, p. 40 <br> • **Political Cartoons booklet** Section 3, p. 32 <br> • **Section Reading Support Transparencies** <br> • **Close Up on the Supreme Court booklet** *Miami Herald Publishing Co.* v. <br><br> *Tornillo,* p. 9; *New York Times* v. *United States,* p. 50 <br> • **The Living Constitution booklet** p. 7 <br> • **The Basic Principles of the Constitution Posters** <br> • **Section Support Transparencies** 35, 134 <br> • **Presentation Pro CD-ROM** Section 3 |

# Block Scheduling Strategies

The *Magruder's American Government* program addresses block-scheduling strategies in a variety of ways. For easy reference, side-column activities that fit a block format are marked ■ **Block Strategy.** Each section also contains a **Block Scheduling Strategies** box describing at least two block-format activities that address and extend core content from the section. The **Block Scheduling with Lesson Strategies booklet** found in the Teaching Resources contains additional block-scheduling activities for each chapter.

## Take It to the Net

Visit the Social Studies area at the Prentice Hall School Web site. Once there, you can find additional links, current events connections, and activities to enrich chapter content for *Magruder's American Government,* as well as a Self-Test for students. Be sure to check out this month's **eTeach** online discussion with a Master Teacher.

### www.phschool.com

## Pressed for Time?

If you are running short on time to cover this chapter, consider one of the following options:
- Use the **Presentation Pro CD-ROM** to create an outline for this chapter.
- Use one of the **Pressed for Time** activities found on p. 27.
- Use the Section Summaries for Chapter 2, from **Guide to the Essentials of American Government (English and Spanish).**

 ## Video Connections

Prentice Hall offers two video programs to reinforce and extend chapter content. Show students *The Blessings of Liberty* from the **ABC News Civics and Government Videotape Library** and *Prayer in Schools: A Nationwide Debate* from the **Magruder's American Government Video Collection.**

## Assessment Options

- Section Quizzes, **Unit 2 booklet,** pp. 30, 32, 34
- Chapter 8 Assessment, pp. 232–233
- **Guide to the Essentials of American Government,** Chapter 8 Test, p. 50

### Core Assessment
Chapter 8 Test, Chapter Tests booklet
ExamView® Test Bank CD-ROM Chapter 8
Government Assessment Rubrics

### Standardized Test Preparation
#### Diagnose and Prescribe
Diagnostic Tests for High School
Social Studies Skills

#### Review and Reteach
Review Book for Government

#### Practice and Assess
Test-Taking Strategies With
    Transparencies for High School
Test Prep Book for Government

# Chapter 8 Teacher's Edition Index

# CHAPTER 8

## Mass Media and Public Opinion

### Introducing the Chapter

In this chapter, students will learn about how American public opinion is formed, how it is measured, and the influence that the mass media has on public opinion.

### Make It Relevant

**You Can Make a Difference**

Have the class develop, produce, and distribute a newsletter about a current issue of national importance. The newsletter should aspire to the standards of good journalism—being informative and objective, and presenting all sides of the issue. Assign groups specific tasks, such as researching, editing, designing, and producing the newsletter. Have the class distribute copies of their newsletter at appropriate community locations and events.

**Service Learning**

### Constitutional Principles

Emphasize the following basic principles as students read Chapter 8. Have the class respond to the questions, and then ask volunteers to explain why the sharing of public opinion is a vital part of a democracy.

**Popular Sovereignty** Why is public opinion important to the National Government and those who run it?

**Limited Government** How does the mass media serve as a check on the National Government?

**Judicial Review** Why is it critical that the court system review government policies on mass media and the dissemination of public opinion?

CHAPTER 8

# Mass Media and Public Opinion

*"The hand that rules the press, the radio, the screen, and the far-spread magazine rules the country."*

—Judge Learned Hand (1942)

Since Judge Hand made this observation, new types of media have emerged, but the power of the media remains strong. The media, along with influences such as family and education, help shape our opinions about politics and many other aspects of our lives.

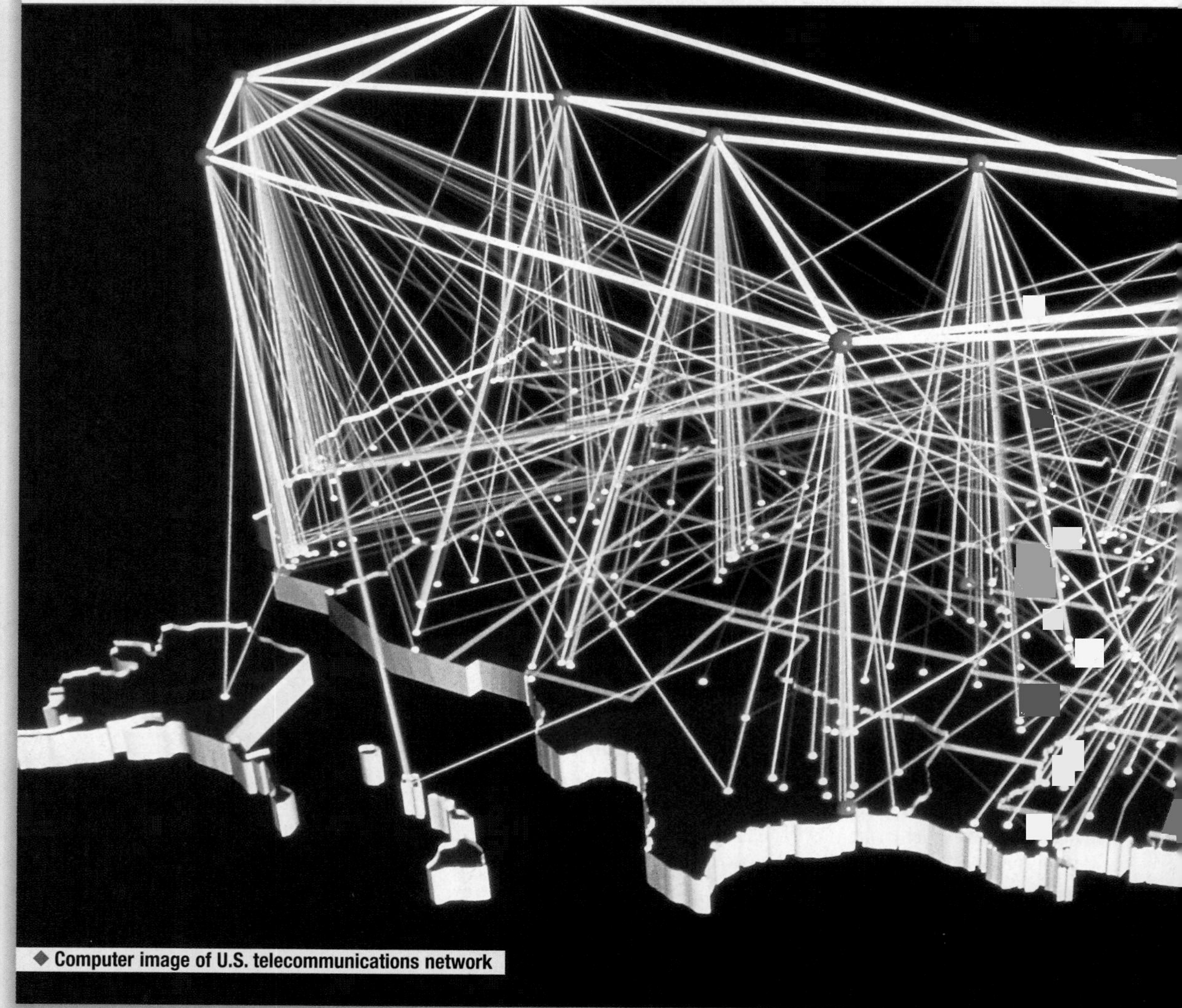

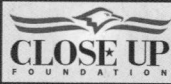

◆ Computer image of U.S. telecommunications network

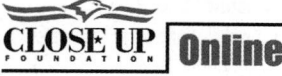

### CLOSE UP FOUNDATION Corner

The following resources are available only from the Close Up Foundation to support the concepts discussed in Chapter 8 "Mass Media and Public Opinion":

- *Perspectives: Readings on Contemporary American Government*
- *Words of Ages: Witnessing U.S. History Through Literature*
- *Profiles of Freedom: A Living Bill of Rights*

**CLOSE UP FOUNDATION Online**

To keep up-to-date on Close Up news and activities, visit Close Up Online at

**www.closeup.org**

Close Up Foundation
44 Canal Center Plaza
Alexandria, VA 22314-1592
800-765-3131

## ★ You Can Make a Difference

**ONE TEENAGER WHO** has already made a place for herself in the media world is Jessica Johnson. In 1997, she began to host a weekly radio show on station WFKX in Jackson, Tennessee. The show gave local young people a chance to talk about issues and to highlight community activists. In late 1999, Jessica became one of the "Point of View Journalists" (POV-J), a network of young writers working as reporters for the new Oxygen cable network and Web site. After graduating, Jessica plans to attend Howard University.

### SECTION 1

### The Formation of Public Opinion (pp. 208–213)

★ Public opinion refers to the attitudes of a significant number of people on matters of government and politics.
★ Family and education are two of the most important factors in shaping public opinion.
★ Additional factors that shape public opinion include peer groups, opinion leaders, historic events, and mass media.

### SECTION 2

### Measuring Public Opinion
(pp. 215–221)

★ Public opinion can be determined to some extent through elections, interest groups, the media, and personal contacts.
★ The best way to measure public opinion is through opinion polls.
★ The complex process of scientific polling results in the most reliable poll data.
★ Although it is important to measure public opinion, public opinion is only one of many factors that shape public policy.

### SECTION 3

### The Mass Media (pp. 223–230)

★ The American public gets information on public issues through several forms of mass media, especially through television.
★ The media influence American politics by helping to set the public agenda and by playing a central role in electoral politics.
★ The influence of the media is limited, in part because many people use mass media as sources of entertainment rather than information.

 **Keep It Current**

Items marked with this logo are periodically updated on the Internet. Keep up-to-date with what's in the news. To get current information on mass media and public opinion, go to **www.phschool.com**

### Keep It Current

## Internet Update

Use the Prentice Hall School Web site and the Keep It Current CD-ROM to find quick content updates.

 Visit **www.phschool.com** for current events articles that are linked to Chapter 8. Critical thinking questions are included.

**Keep It Current CD-ROM** includes government-related projects by unit. Students complete each project using current information that they obtain by linking to the Prentice Hall School Web site from the CD-ROM.

## Pressed for Time?

### To Omit the Chapter
If you wish to skip Chapter 8, ask students to read the Chapter in Brief and assign the Guide to the Essentials before continuing to another chapter. You may also want to assign the Chapter 8 Test in the Chapter Test booklet. Then specific portions of Chapter 8 may be assigned to students needing reinforcement of key terms and concepts.

### To Preview the Chapter
To introduce students to key terms and concepts in each section, have them read the Chapter in Brief. You may also assign the Reading Strategy activities on pp. 209, 216, and 224 of this book.

### To Review the Chapter
When students have completed Chapter 8, you might want to assign the Guide to the Essentials or the Guided Reading and Review worksheets on pp. 29, 31, and 33 of the Unit 2 booklet.

### To Cover the Chapter Quickly
To cover the material in Chapter 8 quickly, use the following activity.
**Focus** Choose a topic of current debate, and elicit students' opinions on it. Write down all differing opinions on the chalkboard. Then explain to students that all these opinions taken together constitute a public opinion.
**Instruct** Ask: In the months before a presidential election, how do you know which candidate is leading? Discuss the function of opinion polls with the class, including how they might influence a candidate's actions. Then discuss the functions of the mass media in providing information to the public and carrying politicians' messages.
**Close/Reteach** Have students suggest which medium might be seen as the most important tool for political candidates, and which might be the most important for informing the public about politics. Ask students to share their opinions with the class.

■ **Block Strategy (Average)**

# 1 The Formation of Public Opinion

**Objectives** You may wish to call students' attention to the objectives in the Section Preview. The objectives are reflected in the main headings of the section.

**Bellringer** Ask students for their "personal opinion" of who is the best singer or musical group. Then ask what factors shaped that opinion. Explain that in this section, they will learn about the factors that shape not personal or private opinion, but public opinion.

**Vocabulary Builder** Point out the Political Dictionary, and tell students that three of the terms describe factors that affect public opinion. Have students name the terms and suggest how they might affect public opinion.

## Pressed for Time?

### Quick Lesson Plan

**1. Focus** Tell students that many factors shape public opinion. Ask them to discuss what they know about the role of the family in forming a person's political opinions.

**2. Instruct** Have students describe public opinion, including how it differs from private opinion. Then lead a discussion of the several factors that shape public opinion.

**3. Close/Reteach** Remind students that family and education are powerful factors in shaping public opinion. Then ask students to suppose that they are about to vote in a presidential election. Ask them to list all the factors affecting public opinion and describe how each one might play a role in the election.

## Point-of-Use Resources

**Block Scheduling with Lesson Strategies** Activities for Chapter 8 are presented on p. 23.

## Section Preview

### OBJECTIVES

1. **Examine** the term *public opinion* and understand why it is difficult to define.
2. **Analyze** the factors that influence an individual's political attitudes and actions, including family and education.

### WHY IT MATTERS

You no doubt have opinions on a variety of issues, from school prayer to which political party should be in power. Several factors help shape your opinions. The two most important factors are family and education.

### POLITICAL DICTIONARY

★ public affairs
★ public opinion
★ mass media
★ peer group
★ opinion leader

---

Do you like broccoli? Blue fingernail polish? Hard rock? What about sports? Old cars? Country music?

You almost certainly have an opinion on each of those things. On some of them, you may hold strong opinions, and those opinions may be very important to you. Still, each of those opinions is your own view, your *private* opinion. *Public* opinion works a little differently.

## What Is Public Opinion?

Few terms in American politics are more widely used, and less well understood, than the term *public opinion*. It appears regularly in newspapers and magazines, and you hear it frequently on radio and television.

Quite often, the phrase is used to suggest that all or most of the American people hold the same view on some public issue, such as arms control or environmental protection. Thus, time and again, politicians say that "the people" want such and such, television commentators tell us that "the public" favors this or opposes that, and so on.

In fact, there are very few matters about which all or nearly all of "the people" think alike. "The public" holds many different and often conflicting views on nearly every public issue.

To understand what public opinion is, you must recognize this important point: Public opinion is a complex collection of the opinions of many different people. It is the sum of all of their views. It is *not* the single and undivided view of some mass mind.

### Different Publics

Many publics exist in the United States—in fact, too many to be counted. Each public is made up of all those individuals who hold the same view on some particular public issue. Each group of people with a differing point of view is a separate public with regard to that issue.

For example, the people who think that Congress should establish a national health insurance program belong to the public that holds that view. People who believe that the President is doing an excellent job as chief executive, or that capital punishment should be abolished, or that prayers should be permitted in the public schools are members of separate publics with those particular opinions. Clearly, many people belong to more than one of those publics; but almost certainly only a very few belong to all four of them.

Notice this important point: Not many issues capture the attention of all—or even nearly all—Americans. In fact, those that do are few and far between. Instead, most public issues attract the interest of *some* people (and sometimes millions of them), but those same issues are of little or no interest to many (and sometimes millions of) other people.

This point is crucial, too: In its proper sense, public opinion includes only those views that relate to **public affairs**. Public affairs include politics, public issues, and the making of public policies—those events and issues that concern the people at large. To be a public opinion, a view must involve something of general concern

---

## 🔲 Block Scheduling Strategies

Consider these suggestions to manage extended class time:

■ Have the class as a whole create a list of issues that interests it. Then ask students to write a sentence about each issue, explaining their stance on it. Finally, have them decide which factor—family, school, peer group, opinion leader, event, or mass media—had the most influence on that stance.

■ Divide the class into small groups, assigning each an issue of current debate. Tell each group to form a philosophy statement about their issue. Then, explain that their goal is to attract public support for their view on that issue. Have them decide how they could best do so—by convincing family or peer groups, providing strong leadership, or getting their message across through the media.

## The Political Spectrum

| LEFT ← | | CENTER | | → RIGHT |
|---|---|---|---|---|
| **Radical** Favors extreme change to create an altered or entirely new social system. | **Liberal** Believes that government must take action to change economic, political, and ideological policies thought to be unfair. | **Moderate** Holds beliefs that fall between liberal and conservative views, usually including some of both. | **Conservative** Seeks to keep in place the economic, political, and social structures of society. | **Reactionary** Favors extreme change to restore society to an earlier, more conservative state. |

*Interpreting Diagrams* People who have similar opinions on political issues are generally grouped according to whether they are "left," "right," or "center" on the political spectrum. The general range, or spectrum, of political opinions is shown here. *(a) How might a liberal and a conservative differ on an issue such as raising taxes? (b) Where do your views fall on the political spectrum?*

and of interest to a significant portion of the people as a whole.

Of course, the American people as a whole are interested in many things—rock groups and symphony orchestras, the New York Yankees and the Dallas Cowboys, candy bars and green vegetables, and a great deal more. Many people have opinions on each of these things, views that are sometimes loosely called "public opinion." But, again, in its proper sense, public opinion involves only those views that people hold on such things as parties and candidates, taxes, unemployment, welfare programs, national defense, foreign policy, and so on.

### Definition

Clearly, public opinion is so complex that it cannot be readily defined. From what has been said about it to this point, however, **public opinion** can be described this way: those attitudes held by a significant number of people on matters of government and politics.

As we have suggested, you can better understand the term in the plural—that is, as public opinions, the opinions of different publics. In addition, a view must be expressed in order to be a public opinion. Otherwise, it cannot be identified with any public. Public opinion is thus also made up of expressed group attitudes.

The expression of an opinion need not be oral (spoken). The expression can be written, of course—on paper or in an e-mail, for example. It can also take any number of other forms, as well: a protest demonstration, a film, a billboard, a vote for or against a candidate, and so on. The essential point is that a person's private thoughts on an issue enter the stream

of public opinion only when those thoughts are expressed publicly.

## Family and Education

No one is born with a set of attitudes about government and politics. Instead, each of us learns our political opinions, and we do so in a lifelong "classroom" and from many different "teachers." In other words, public opinion is formed out of a very complex process. The factors involved in it are almost infinite.

You have already considered much of this in Chapter 6 with regard to voting behavior. In effect, that detailed look at why people vote as they do amounted to an extensive look at how public opinion is formed.

"Harold, would you say you are left of center, right of center, center, left of left, right of left, left of right, or right of right, or what?"

*Interpreting Political Cartoons* **What does the cartoon suggest about the political spectrum?**

## Background Note
### Roots of Democracy

Jacques Necker, French king Louis XVI's finance minister, first popularized the term "public opinion" in the 18th century. Necker defined public opinion as an entity shaped by the collective views of the French bourgeoisie. According to the minister, public opinion was a formidable force, which "strengthens or weakens all human institutions" and should be taken into account by any savvy politician.

## Point-of-Use Resources

📁 **Close Up on Primary Sources**
The Star-Spangled Banner (1814), p. 35; Pledge of Allegiance (1892), American's Creed (1917), and Oath of Citizenship, p. 40

In Chapter 6, remember, we described the process by which each person acquires political opinions—the process of political socialization. That complex process begins in early childhood and continues through a person's lifetime. It involves all of the experiences and relationships that lead us to see the political world and to act in it as we do.[1]

There are many different agents of political socialization at work in the opinion-shaping process. Again, you looked at these agents in Chapter 6: age, race, income, occupation, residence, group affiliations, and many others. Here, look again at two of them, the family and education. These have such a vital impact that they deserve another and slightly different discussion here.

### The Family
Most parents do not think of themselves as agents of political socialization, nor do the other members of most families. Parents and other family members are, nonetheless, very important factors in this process.

Children first see the political world from within the family and through the family's eyes. They begin to learn about politics much as they begin to learn about most other things. Children learn from what their parents have to say, from the stories that their older brothers and sisters bring home from school, from watching television with the family, and so on.

Most of what smaller children learn in the family setting are not really political opinions. Clearly, toddlers are not concerned with the wisdom of spending billions of dollars on an anti-missile defense system or the pros and cons of the monetary policies of the Federal Reserve Board.

Young children do pick up some fundamental attitudes, however. With those attitudes, they acquire a basic slant toward such things as authority and rules of behavior, property, neighbors, people of other racial or religious groups, and the like. In short, children lay some important foundations on which they will later build their political opinions.

[1] The concept of socialization comes from the fields of sociology and psychology. There, it is used to describe all of the ways in which a society transforms individuals into members of that society. To put this another way: Socialization is the multi-sided, lifelong process in which people come to know, accept, and follow the beliefs and practices of their society. *Political socialization* is a part of that much broader process.

▲ Family and education are the primary factors that shape one's values and opinions. These photos show a preschooler, whose opinions are largely shaped by family (left); school-age children practicing American values by reciting the Pledge of Allegiance (center); and a young adult putting her values to work through community service (right). *Critical Thinking How have your family and education shaped your own opinions and values?*

*Answer to . . .*
**Critical Thinking** Answers will vary, but should mention the influence of family members' opinions and citizenship values learned in school.

A large number of scholarly studies report what common sense also suggests. The strong influence the family has on the development of political opinions is largely a result of the near monopoly the family has on the child in his or her earliest, most impressionable years. Those studies also show that

**PRIMARY Sources** *"Children tend to absorb the political views of parents and other caregivers, perhaps without realizing it. . . . Children raised in households in which the primary caregivers are Democrats tend to become Democrats themselves, whereas children raised in homes where their caregivers are Republican tend to favor the GOP."*
—Benjamin Ginsberg, Theodore Lowi, and Margaret Weir, *We the People*

## The Schools

The start of formal schooling marks the initial break in the influence of the family. For the first time, children become regularly involved in activities outside the home.

From the first day, schools teach children the values of the American political system. They work to indoctrinate the young, to instill in them loyalty to a particular cause or idea. In fact, training students to become good citizens is an important part of our educational system.

Schoolchildren salute the flag, recite the Pledge of Allegiance, and sing patriotic songs. They learn about George Washington, Abraham Lincoln, Susan B. Anthony, Martin Luther King, Jr., and other great Americans. From the early grades on, they pick up growing amounts of specific political knowledge, and they begin to form political opinions. In high school, they are often required to take a course in American government and even to read books such as this one.

School involves much more than books and classes, of course. It is a complex bundle of experiences and a place where a good deal of informal learning occurs—about the similarities and differences among individuals and groups, about the various ways in which decisions can be made, and about the process of compromise that must often occur in order for ideas to move forward.

Once again, the family and education are *not* the only forces at work in the process by which opinions are formed. A number of other influences are part of the mix. These two factors are singled out here to underscore their leading roles in that process.

## Other Factors

No factor, by itself, shapes a person's opinion on any single issue. Some factors do play a larger role than others, however. Thus, in addition to family and education, occupation and race are usually much more significant than, say, gender or place of residence.

For example, on the question of national health insurance, the particular job a person has—how well-paying it is, whether its benefits include coverage by a private health-insurance plan, and so on—will almost certainly have a greater impact on that person's views than his or her gender or place of residence. On the other hand, the relative weight of each factor that influences public opinion also depends on the issue in question. If the issue involves, say, equal pay for women or the restoration of Lake Michigan, then gender or where one lives will almost certainly loom larger in the opinion-making mix.

Besides family, education, and such factors as occupation and race, four other factors have a major place in the opinion-making process. They are the mass media, peer groups, opinion leaders, and historic events.

## Mass Media

The **mass media** include those means of communication that reach large, widely dispersed audiences (masses of people) simultaneously. No one needs to be told that the mass media, including newspapers, magazines, radio, the Internet, and in particular television, have a huge effect on the formation of public opinion.

Take this as but one indication of that fact: The Census Bureau reports that there is at least one television set in 98 percent of the nation's 120 million households. There are two or more sets in more than 91 million homes and millions more in many other places. Most of those sets are turned on for at least seven hours a day, for a mind-boggling total of more than a billion hours a day.

## Learning Styles

**Verbal/Auditory** Tell students that they will respond to views of a recognized opinion leader. Provide them with several choices. (These may include a local radio broadcaster, a national political figure, or a newspaper columnist.) Have students choose one of the opinion leaders and ask them to watch or read that person's views on a particular topic. As they reflect upon these views, ask students to list both supporting and opposing arguments. Finally, have them prepare a written or oral summary of their reactions to the opinion leader's views that can be shared with the class.

**Block Strategy (Average)**

## Point-of-Use Resources

**Simulations and Data Graphing CD-ROM** offers data graphing tools that give students practice with creating and interpreting graphs.

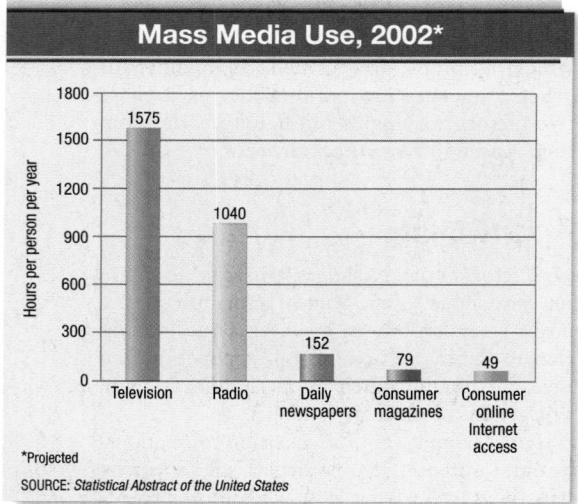

**Mass Media Use, 2002\***

Hours per person per year

- Television: 1575
- Radio: 1040
- Daily newspapers: 152
- Consumer magazines: 79
- Consumer online Internet access: 49

*Projected

SOURCE: Statistical Abstract of the United States

*Interpreting Graphs* This graph shows the hours that Americans spend each year on various forms of media. **Why do Americans spend more time watching television than on other forms of media?**

The chart above shows how much time Americans spend on various types of mass media. You will read more about the influence of mass media in Section 3.

## Peer Groups

**Peer groups** are made up of the people with whom one regularly associates, including friends, classmates, neighbors, and co-workers. When a child enters school, friends and classmates become an important factor in shaping his or her attitudes and behavior. The influence of peer groups continues throughout adulthood.

Belonging to a peer group usually reinforces what a person has already come to believe. One obvious reason for this is that most people trust the views of their friends. Another is that the members of a peer group have shared many of the same socializing experiences, and so tend to think along the same lines.

To put this observation another way, contradictory or other unsettling opinions are not often heard within a peer group. Most people want to be liked by their friends and associates. As a result, they are usually reluctant to stray too far from what their peers think and how their peers behave.

## Opinion Leaders

The views expressed by **opinion leaders** also bear heavily on public opinion. An opinion leader is any person who, for any reason, has an unusually strong influence on the views of others. These opinion shapers are a distinct minority in the total population, of course, but they are found everywhere.

Many opinion leaders hold public office. Some write for newspapers or magazines, or broadcast their opinions on radio or television. Others are prominent in business, labor, agriculture, and civic organizations. Many are professionals—doctors, lawyers, teachers, ministers, and rabbis—and have contact with large numbers of people on a regular basis. Many others are active members of their neighborhood or church, or have leadership roles in their local communities.

Whoever they may be—the President of the United States, a network television commentator, the governor, the head of a local citizens committee, or even a local talk-show host—these opinion leaders are people to whom others listen and from whom others draw ideas and convictions. Whatever their political, economic, or social standing or outlook may be, opinion leaders play a significant role in the formation of public opinion.

## Historic Events

Historic events can have a major impact on the views of large numbers of people—and so have a major impact on the content and direction of public policy. Our history affords many examples of this point, not the least of them the Great Depression. This period began in 1929 and lasted for the better part of a decade.

The Depression was a shattering national experience. Almost overnight, need and poverty became massive national problems. Millions of Americans—one out of every four in the labor force—lost their jobs. Millions more were impoverished. Hunger and despair stalked the land. In 1929, some two million people were unemployed in the United States. Just four years later, that number climbed to 13.5 million. In 1935, some 18 million men, women, and children were wholly dependent on public emergency relief programs. Some 10 million workers had no employment other than that provided by temporary public projects.

## Answer to . . .

**Interpreting Graphs** Possible answer: 98 percent of American households have television sets.

All of this changed the way millions of people viewed the proper place of government in the United States. The Depression persuaded a large majority of Americans to support a much larger role for government—and, in particular, for the National Government—in the nation's economic and social life.

As a result, the Great Depression also prompted a majority of Americans to shift their political loyalties from the Republican to the Democratic Party. The Republicans had dominated politics from Abraham Lincoln's election in 1860 to the onset of the Depression. Franklin D. Roosevelt's landslide victory in 1932 began nearly 40 years of Democratic domination.

The turbulent politics of the 1960s and early 1970s furnish another example of the way in which significant occurrences can impact and shape opinions. The American people had emerged from World War II and the prosperity of the 1950s with a largely optimistic view of the future and of the United States' place in the world. That rose-colored outlook was reflected in a

▲ During the Great Depression, millions of Americans were out of work.

generally favorable, even respectful, attitude toward government in this country.

The 1960s and early 1970s changed all that. Those years were highlighted by a number of traumatic events. Of special note were the assassinations of President John Kennedy in 1963 and of the Reverend Martin Luther King, Jr., and Senator Robert Kennedy in 1968. This period also included the civil rights movement and the Vietnam War, with all of the protests, violence, and strong emotions that accompanied both of those chapters in this nation's life. The era ended with the Watergate Scandal and the near-impeachment and subsequent resignation of President Richard Nixon in 1974.

Those years of turmoil and divisiveness produced a dramatic decline in the American people's estimate of their government—and most especially their evaluation of its trustworthiness. More recently, however, the September 11, 2001, terrorist attacks resulted in increased support for the President and for a strong United States foreign policy.

## Section 1 Assessment

### Key Terms and Main Ideas

1. What is **public opinion,** and what factors shape it?
2. Give three examples of an **opinion leader.**
3. Describe the political socialization of a young child.
4. **(a)** What are the **mass media? (b)** What evidence can you give that the mass media influence public opinion?

### Critical Thinking

5. **Drawing Conclusions** Is it likely that interaction with one's peer group would result in one switching membership

from the Democratic to the Republican Party? Explain your answer.
6. **Synthesizing Information** Why is it so difficult to define public opinion?

 **Take It to the Net**

7. Look at data for at least three issues on which Americans have expressed their opinions. Then take a poll of your class to find out whether your classmates agree with public opinion on these issues. Use the links provided in the Social Studies area at the following Web site for help in completing this activity. **www.phschool.com**

**Take It to the Net**

7. Direct students to the Social Studies area at the Prentice Hall School Web site. The *Magruder's American Government* companion Web site includes the directions and links needed to complete the activity. It also provides a printable Internet activity worksheet with scoring rubrics for assessment. Polls should ask relevant questions and include as large a sample of people as possible.

## Point-of-Use Resources

**Guide to the Essentials** Chapter 8, Section 1, p. 47 provides support for students who need additional review of section content. Spanish support is available in the Spanish edition of the Guide on p. 40.

**Quiz** Unit 2 booklet, p. 30 includes matching and multiple-choice questions to check students' understanding of Section 1 content.

**Presentation Pro CD-ROM** Quizzes and multiple-choice questions check students' understanding of Section 1 content.

## Answers to . . .

### Section 1 Assessment

**1.** Public opinion is the attitudes toward government and politics held by a significant number of people. It is shaped by family, education, peers, leaders, and mass media.
**2.** Examples include holders of public office, writers or broadcasters, professionals, business leaders, and active community members.
**3.** Children are politically socialized first by their families, then by their experiences in school.
**4. (a)** Those means of communication that can reach large, widely dispersed audiences simultaneously. **(b)** There is at least one television set in 98 percent of the nation's households.
**5.** No; most likely the members of that peer group already agree politically, and debate would not come up.
**6.** Possible answer: Public opinion is hard to define because there is no single "public," nor are all people interested in the same topics.

## The Latino Media Story

**Focus** Ask students what difficulties or problems they might have building a career in the American media if their primary language is not English. Then have them suggest ways that some of these problems might be solved or avoided.

**Instruct** Have students read the article and answer the corresponding questions. Then ask students to identify ways in which people are shaped by the media. What are some examples of how people are shaping the media rather than being shaped by it?

**Close/Reteach** Change means opportunity—for individuals who might wish careers in Hispanic media and for those who are alert to the public's interest in new kinds of stories and articles and formats. As the nation's population changes, the culture changes and so do its institutions.

**Keep It Current CD-ROM** includes government-related projects by unit. The CD-ROM links to the Prentice Hall School Web site and may be used for daily updates.

### Answers to . . .

**Analyzing Primary Sources**
**1.** Hispanics have a purchasing power of $490 billion a year.
**2.** Answers will vary. Issues of importance to Hispanics are likely to receive more attention, more publicity. Public opinion is likely to be shaped by the extended coverage.
**3.** Student responses will vary. Those with Hispanic backgrounds might think about looking for work in a part of the country where there is a large Hispanic population. Others may speak of new opportunities for bilingual journalists.

---

# on Primary Sources

## The Latino Media Story

*With the rise in the Latino population of the United States, the demand for Spanish-language newspapers, radio, and other media has grown. In this article from* **The Christian Science Monitor,** *staff writer Kim Campbell reports on how Latino media are scrambling to meet the new demand.*

Rural Georgia is not the place you'd expect to find a boom in Spanish-language media. But Dalton, a small town in the north, is now home to three Spanish-language newspapers and a Spanish-language pop radio station.

Hispanic media have grown in the past decade—newspapers alone have increased 55 percent—and with the news . . . from the [2000] census that Hispanics are the largest U.S. minority, more attention is being paid to how to reach this group that has a purchasing power of more than $490 billion a year. . . .

With the demand for more media has come a need for bilingual journalists. Some are being wooed away from mainstream media by Spanish-language publications and networks. Those who do the hiring say it can be tough to find staff who can speak and write well in both languages. Some Latinos, for example, don't speak Spanish; others have strong Spanish skills but can't do interviews in English or translate written reports.

Those who do cross over say there are advantages to working in Spanish-language media, including the opportunity to advance into management, to work with colleagues who understand the needs of the Hispanic community, and to practice advocacy-based journalism in which the target audience is clear. "There is this sense that you are really doing something to help the community," says Angelo Figueroa, editor of the monthly *People*

*Martin Berlanga, of Spanish-language network Univisión, prepares for a live shot in Austin, Texas.*

*en Español. . . .*

Spanish-language media often take a different approach from mainstream outlets—focusing, not surprisingly, on issues of importance to their audience. . . . In Miami, *The Miami Herald* and its Spanish-language sister paper, *El Nuevo Herald,* often take different approaches to the same issue. . . . "People pick up *El Nuevo Herald* not only because it's in Spanish, but because it speaks to them," says Barbara Gutiérrez, a reader representative for both papers, who points out that *El Nuevo Herald* has shorter articles and is more opinionated. "It's just a different kind of style, and closer, I think, to what many Hispanics are used to."

The census took some people by surprise, but Ms. Gutiérrez says she and her colleagues could see what was coming. She looks forward to what happens next: "The next 10 years are going to be very exciting."

### Analyzing Primary Sources

1. Why is the growth of the U.S. Latino population an important consideration to the media?
2. How might the rise in the Latino population affect the formation of public opinion?
3. If you were planning on a career in the media, how might the information in this article affect you?

---

## Corner

**Close Up on Primary Sources** African Americans and Television, p. 10, extends this feature with a primary source activity.

To keep up-to-date on Close Up news and activities, visit Close Up Online at
**www.closeup.org**

# 2 Measuring Public Opinion

## Section Preview

### OBJECTIVES

1. **Describe** the challenges involved in measuring public opinion.
2. **Explain** why opinion polls are the best measure of public opinion.
3. **Identify** five steps in the polling process.
4. **Understand** the challenges of evaluating polls.
5. **Recognize** the limits on the impact of public opinion in a democracy.

### WHY IT MATTERS

Have you ever responded to a poll? Taken a poll yourself? Polls are the most effective means for measuring public opinion. Other measures include election returns, the activities of interest groups, and direct personal contact.

### POLITICAL DICTIONARY

* **mandate**
* **interest group**
* **public opinion poll**
* **straw vote**
* **sample**
* **random sample**
* **quota sample**

How many times have you heard this phrase: "According to a recent poll . . ."? Probably more than you can count, especially in the months leading up to an important election. Polls are one of the most common means of gauging public opinion.

If public policy is to reflect public opinion, one needs to be able to find the answers to these questions: What are people's opinions on a particular issue? How many people share a given view on that issues? How firmly do they hold that view? In other words there must be a way to "measure" public opinion.

## Measuring Public Opinion

The general shape of public opinion on an issue can be found through a variety of means. These include voting; lobbying; books; pamphlets; magazine and newspaper articles; editorial comments in the press and on radio and television; paid advertisements; and letters to editors and public officials.

These and other means of expression are the devices through which the general direction of public opinion becomes known. Usually though, the means by which a view is expressed tells little—and often nothing reliable—about the size of the group that holds that opinion or how strongly it is held. In the American political system, this information is vital. To find this information, some effort must be made to measure public opinion. Elections, interest groups, the media, and personal contacts with the public all—at least to some degree—provide the means of measurement.

### Elections

In a democracy, the voice of the people is supposed to express itself through the ballot box. Election results are thus very often said to be indicators of public opinion. The votes cast for the various candidates are regularly taken as evidence of the people's approval or rejection of the stands taken by those candidates and their parties.

▲ The AIDS Memorial Quilt is a unique expression of public opinion. Here the quilt is laid out in front of the Washington Monument.

**215**

## Reading Strategy
### Problem Solving

Tell students that a local politician has come to them with a problem. She has to make a decision soon about a vital public-policy issue, but she has no idea how her constituents feel about it. Have students determine, as they read, what would be the best approach to measuring public opinion on the issue.

## Point-of-Use Resources

📁 **Guided Reading and Review** Unit 2 booklet, p. 31 provides students with practice identifying the main ideas and key terms of this section.

📁 **Lesson Plans** For lesson planning suggestions, see p. 39 of the Lesson Plans booklet.

📁 **Political Cartoons** See p. 31 of the Political Cartoons booklet for a cartoon relevant to this section.

📰 **Section Support Transparencies** Transparency 34, *Visual Learning;* Transparency 133, *Political Cartoon*

*Answer to . . .*
**Critical Thinking** They can gauge people's reactions to proposed programs, and learn about people's main concerns.

▶ Richard Gephardt (D., Missouri) meets a constituent.
*Critical Thinking*
**What kinds of information can officials learn from meeting directly with the public?**

As a result, a party and its victorious candidates regularly claim to have received a **mandate** to carry out their campaign promises. In American politics a mandate refers to the instructions or commands a constituency gives to its elected officials.[2]

In reality, however, election results are seldom an accurate measure of public opinion. Voters make choices in elections for any of several reasons, as you have seen. Very often, those choices have little or nothing to do with the candidates' stands on public questions. Then, too, candidates often disagree with some of the planks of their party's platform. In addition, candidates and parties often express their positions in broad, vague terms.

In short, much of what you have read about voting behavior, and about the nature of parties, adds up to this: Elections are, at best, only useful indicators of public opinion. To call the typical election a mandate for much of anything other than a general direction in public policy is to be on very shaky ground.

### Interest Groups

**Interest groups** are private organizations whose members share certain views and work to shape public policy. These organizations are also very aptly known as pressure groups and special-interest groups.

[2]The term *mandate* comes from the Latin *mandatum*, meaning a command.

Interest groups are a chief means by which public opinion is made known. They present their views (exert their pressures) through their lobbyists, by letters and telephone calls, in political campaigns, and by a number of other methods. In dealing with them, however, public officials often have difficulty determining two things: How many people does an interest group really represent? And just how strongly do those people hold the views that an organization says they hold?

### The Media

Earlier you read some very impressive numbers about television. Those huge numbers help describe the place of the media in the opinion process; you will read more of those numbers later. Here, recognize this point: The media are also a gauge for assessing public opinion.

The media are frequently described as "mirrors" as well as "molders" of opinion. It is often said that the views expressed in newspaper editorials, syndicated columns, news magazines, television commentaries, and so on, are fairly good indicators of public opinion. In fact, however, the media are not very accurate mirrors of public opinion, often reflecting only the views of a vocal minority.

### Personal Contacts

Most public officials have frequent and wide-ranging contacts in many different forms with large numbers of people. In each of these contacts, they try to read the public's mind. Indeed, their jobs demand that they do so.

Members of Congress receive bags of mail and hundreds of phone calls and e-mails everyday. Many of them make frequent trips "to keep in touch with the folks back home." Top administration figures are often on the road, too, selling the President's programs and gauging the people's reactions. Even the President does some of this, with speaking trips to different parts of the country.

Governors, State legislators, mayors, and other officials also have any number of contacts with the public. These officials encounter the public in their offices, in public meetings, at social gatherings, and even at ball games.

Can public officials find "the voice of the people" in all of those contacts? Many can and

## Organizing Information

To make sure students understand the main points of this section, you may wish to use the flowchart to the right.

Tell students that a flowchart can be used to show a sequence of events. Have students use the flowchart to show the steps taken in conducting a scientific poll.

**Teaching Tip** A template for this graphic organizer can be found in the Section Support Transparencies, Transparency 4.

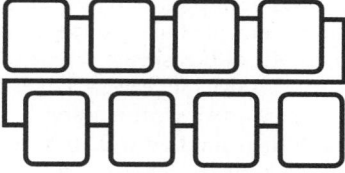

do, and often with surprising accuracy. But some public officials cannot. They fall into an ever-present trap: They find only what they want to find, only those views that support and agree with their own.

## Polls—The Best Measure

Public opinion is best measured by **public opinion polls,** devices that attempt to collect information by asking people questions.[3] The more accurate polls are based on scientific polling techniques.

### Straw Votes

Public opinion polls have existed in this country for more than a century. Until the 1930s, however, they were far from scientific. Most earlier polling efforts were of the **straw vote** variety. That is, they were polls that sought to read the public's mind simply by asking the same question of a large number of people. Straw votes are still fairly common. Newspapers often run "clip-out and mail-in" ballots, radio talk shows ask listeners to respond to questions with phone calls, and so on.

The straw-vote technique is highly unreliable, however. It rests on the false assumption that a relatively large number of responses will provide a fairly accurate picture of the public's views on a given question. The problem is this: Nothing in the process ensures that those who respond will represent a reasonably accurate cross section of the total population. The straw vote emphasizes the quantity rather than the quality of the sample to which its question is posed.

The most famous of all straw-polling mishaps took place in 1936. A periodical called the *Literary Digest* mailed postcard ballots to more than 10 million people and received answers from more than 2,376,000 of them. Based on that huge return, the magazine confidently predicted the outcome of the presidential election that year. It said that Governor Alfred Landon, the Republican nominee, would easily defeat incumbent Franklin Roosevelt. Instead, Roosevelt won in a landslide. He captured more than 60 percent of the popular vote and carried every State but Maine and Vermont.

---

[3]*Poll* comes from the old Teutonic word *polle,* meaning the top or crown of the head, the part that shows when heads are counted.

The *Digest* had drawn its sample on an altogether faulty basis: from automobile registration lists and telephone directories. The *Digest* had failed to consider that in the mid-Depression year of 1936, millions of people could not afford to own cars or have private telephones.

The *Digest* poll failed to reach most of the vast pool of the poor and unemployed, millions of blue-collar workers, and most of the ethnic minorities in the country. Those were the very segments of the population from which Roosevelt and the Democrats drew their greatest support. The magazine had predicted the winner of each of the three previous presidential elections, but its failure to do so in 1936 was so colossal that it ceased publication not long thereafter.

### Scientific Polling

Serious efforts to take the public's pulse on a scientific basis date from the mid-1930s. Attempts began with the work of such early pollsters as George Gallup and Elmo Roper. The techniques that they and others have developed since then have reached a highly sophisticated level.

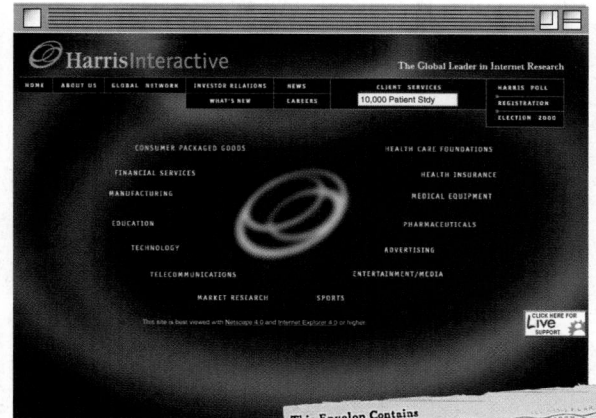

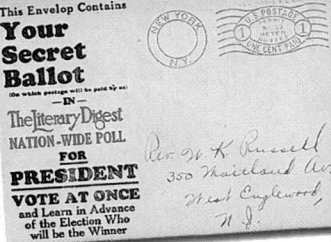

▲ *Polls Then and Now* The 1936 *Literary Digest* survey (right) drew a faulty conclusion about the winner of that year's presidential race because its sample was flawed. Today's scientific polls, such as the Harris Survey (above) are designed to avoid such errors.

## Make It Relevant

### Careers in Government—Pollster

Many government agencies employ pollsters for a wide variety of reasons. A common task of these pollsters is to help determine how the public will react to minor policy modifications, such as changing the hours that a park is open. Policymakers can then adjust their decisions accordingly. Thus, the work of pollsters is vital in ensuring that

government agencies offer the best possible services to the public they are charged to serve. **Skills Activity** Have a small group of students conduct a scientific poll. Then have individual students write paragraphs explaining why they would or would not be interested in a career as a government pollster. **(Challenging)**

## Background Note

### Political Talk

Politicians often consider polls when planning their campaign strategies and actions in office. However, no politician wants voters to think that his or her moves are dictated by poll results. George W. Bush's speech accepting his party's nomination for President at the 2000 Republican National Convention provides a good example of a politician's attempt to demonstrate his independence from polls—and, by implication, to criticize his opponent's reliance on them. "I believe great decisions are made with care, made with conviction, not made with polls," the candidate stated, "I do not need to take your pulse before I know my own mind."

*Interpreting Political Cartoons* **(a)** *According to the cartoon, how seriously should we view the answers to opinion polls?* **(b)** *Does the text agree or disagree with this assessment?*

There are now more than 1,000 national and regional polling organizations in this country. Many of them do mostly commercial work. That is, they tap the public's preferences on everything from toothpastes and headache remedies to television shows and thousands of other things. However, at least 200 of these polling organizations also poll the political preferences of the American people. Among the best known of the national pollsters today are the Gallup Organization (the Gallup Poll) and Louis Harris and Associates (the Harris Survey).

## The Polling Process

Scientific poll-taking is an extremely complex process that can best be described in five basic steps. In their efforts to discover and report public opinion, pollsters must (1) define the universe to be surveyed; (2) construct a sample; (3) prepare valid questions; (4) select and control how the poll will be taken; and (5) analyze and report their findings to the public.

### Defining the Universe

The *universe* is a term that means the whole population that the poll aims to measure. It is the group whose opinions the poll will seek to discover. That universe can be all voters in Chicago, or every high school student in Texas, or all Republicans in New England, or all Democrats in Georgia, or all Catholic women over age 35 in the United States, and so on.

### Constructing a Sample

If a poll's universe is very small—say, the 25 members of a high school class—the best way to find out what that universe thinks about some issue would be to poll every one of them. In most cases, however, it is not possible to interview a complete universe. This is certainly true in matters of public policy that affect all the people in the nation. There are simply too many people in that universe to talk to. So the pollster must select a **sample,** a representative slice of the total universe.

Most professional pollsters draw a **random sample,** also called a probability sample. In a random sample, the pollster interviews a certain number of randomly selected people who live in a certain number of randomly selected places. A random sample is thus a sample in

*Answer to . . .*

**Interpreting Political Cartoons**
**(a)** Not very seriously. **(b)** It largely disagrees; the text says that when polls are conducted properly, they are a very useful tool for assessing public opinion.

## Effect of Poll Wording on Reliability

**1**

The Federal Government should see to it that all people have adequate housing.

| Agree | Disagree |
|-------|----------|
| 55.1% | 44.9% |

**2**

Some people feel the Federal Government should see to it that all people have adequate housing, while others feel each person should provide his or her own housing. Which comes closest to how you feel about this?

| Government responsible | Government not responsible |
|------------------------|----------------------------|
| 44.6% | 55.4% |

**3**

Some people feel each person should provide his or her own housing, while others feel the Federal Government should see to it that all people have adequate housing. Which comes closest to how you feel about this?

| Government responsible | Government not responsible |
|------------------------|----------------------------|
| 29.5% | 70.5% |

SOURCE: *Questions and Answers in Attitude Surveys,* 1981

*Interpreting Charts* This chart demonstrates the importance of carefully wording each question in a poll. *(a) Which question is worded in the least biased manner? (b) How do you know?*

which each member of the universe and each geographic area within it have a mathematically equal chance of being included.

Each major national poll usually interviews just over 1,500 people to represent the universe of the nation's entire adult population (just over 200 million people today). How can the views of so few people represent the opinions of so many?

The answer to that question lies in the mathematical law of probability. Flip a coin 1,000 times. The law of probability says that, given an honest coin and an honest flip, heads will come up 500 times. Furthermore, the law states that the results of this test will be the same no matter how often you perform it, and no matter what kind of coin you use.

The law of probability is regularly applied in a great many situations. It is used by insurance companies to compute life expectancies, by food inspectors to check the quality of a farmer's truckload of beans, and by others who "play the odds," including pollsters who draw random samples.

In short, if the sample is of sufficient size and is properly selected at random from the entire universe, the law of probability says that the result will be accurate to within a small and predictable margin of error. Mathematicians tell us that a properly drawn random sample of some 1,500 people will reflect the opinions of the nation's entire adult population and will be accurate to within a margin of plus or minus (±) 3 percent.

Pollsters acknowledge that it is impossible to construct a sample that would be an absolutely accurate reflection of a large universe. Hence, the allowance for error. A margin of ±3 percent means a spread of 6 percentage points, of course. To reduce the sampling error from ±3 percent to ±1 percent, the size of the sample would have to be 9,500 people. The time and money needed to interview so big a sample make that a practical impossibility.

Some pollsters use a less complicated, but less reliable, sampling method. They draw a **quota sample,** a sample deliberately constructed to reflect several of the major characteristics of a given universe.

For example, if 51.3 percent of a universe is female, 17.5 percent of it is African American, and so on, then the quota sample will be made up of 51.3 percent females, 17.5 percent African Americans, and so on. Of course, most of the people in the sample will belong to more than one category. This fact is a major reason why such a sample is less reliable than random samples.

### Preparing Valid Questions

The way in which questions are worded is very important. Wording can affect the reliability of any poll. For example, most people will probably say "yes" to this question put this way: "Should local taxes be reduced?" Many of those same people will also answer "yes" to this question: "Should the city's police force be increased to

## Customize for

### More Advanced Students

Have students locate a public opinion poll in a newspaper, including the questions that were asked and the responses given. Then have them critique the questions as to their validity, based on the information given in the passages under *Preparing Valid Questions* on page 219. Finally, have students look at the results of the poll in light of their critique of the questions. They should consider whether they think the wording of the questions may have influenced the poll. Each individual should write one page in which he or she presents the critique. Ask for volunteers to share their critique with the class.

## Background Note

### Digital Polling

For polling organizations, obtaining a truly random sample of the American population is a complicated task. For example, when conducting a national telephone survey, pollsters cannot simply select random numbers from the phone book, as the owners of the 30 percent of American residential phones that are unlisted would have no chance of being included in the survey—thus introducing possible bias. Instead, most pollsters use a method called Random Digit Dialing (RDD). In RDD a computer generates a list of all the possible phone numbers for each exchange in the country. The pollsters then place phone calls to a subset of numbers randomly selected by the computer for each exchange.

▲ *A Famous Polling Failure* An elated Harry S Truman holds up a newspaper headline wrongly announcing his defeat in 1948. Pollsters and others had predicted an easy victory for Thomas E. Dewey in that election.

fight the rising tide of crime in our community?" Yet, expanding the police force almost certainly would require more local tax dollars.

Responsible pollsters acknowledge these issues and thus phrase their questions very carefully. They purposely try not to use "loaded," emotionally charged words, or terms that are difficult to understand. They also try to avoid questions that are worded in a way that will tend to shape the answers that are given to them.

### Interviewing

How the pollsters communicate with the sample respondents can also affect accuracy. Most polls are taken face-to-face. That is, the interviewers question the respondents in person. However, pollsters conduct an increasing number of surveys by telephone and by mail.

Professional pollsters see both advantages and drawbacks to each of these approaches. They all agree, however, that whichever technique they use to gather information, they must employ the same technique in questioning all the respondents in a sample.

The interview itself is a very sensitive point in the process. The pollster's appearance, dress, attitude, and tone of voice in asking questions can influence the replies he or she receives, and thus alter the validity of the poll's results.

If the questions are not carefully worded, some of the respondent's replies may be snap judgments or emotional reactions. Others may be answers that the person being interviewed thinks "ought" to be given; or they may be replies that the respondent thinks will please—or offend—the interviewer. Thus, polling organizations try to hire and train their interviewing staffs very carefully.

### Analyze and Report Findings

Polls, whether scientific or not, try to measure people's attitudes. To be of any real value, however, someone must analyze and report the results. Scientific polling organizations today collect huge amounts of raw data. In order to handle these data, computers and other electronic hardware have become routine parts of the process. Pollsters use these technologies to tabulate and interpret their data, draw their conclusions, and then publish their findings.

## Evaluating Polls

How good are polls? On balance, the major national polls are fairly reliable. So, too, are most of the regional surveys around the country. Still, they are far from perfect. Fortunately, most responsible pollsters themselves are quite aware of that fact and readily acknowledge the limits of their polls. Many of them are involved in continuing efforts to refine every aspect of the polling process.

Pollsters know that they have difficulty measuring the intensity, stability, and relevance of the opinions they report. *Intensity* is the strength of feeling with which an opinion is held. *Stability* (or fluidity) is the relative permanence or changeableness of an opinion. *Relevance* (or salience) is how important a particular opinion is to the person who holds it.

Another potential problem is that polls and pollsters are sometimes said to shape the opinions they are supposed to measure. Some critics of polls say that in an election, for example, pollsters often create a "bandwagon effect." That is, some voters, wanting to be with the winner, jump on the bandwagon of the candidate who is ahead in the polls. This charge is most often leveled against those polls that appear as syndicated columns in many newspapers.

In spite of these criticisms, it is clear that scientific polls are the most useful tools there are for the difficult task of measuring public opinion. Although they may not be always or precisely accurate, they do offer reasonably reliable guides to public thought. Moreover, they help to focus attention on public questions and to stimulate discussion of them.

## Limits on the Impact of Public Opinion

More than a century ago, the Englishman Lord Bryce described government in the United States as "government by public opinion." Clearly, the energy devoted to measuring public opinion in this country suggests something of its powerful role in American politics. However, Lord Bryce's observation is true only if it is understood to mean that public opinion is the major, but by no means the only, influence on public policy in this country. Its force is tempered by a number of other factors—for example, by interest groups.

Most importantly, however, remember that our system of constitutional government is not designed to give free, unrestricted play to public opinion—and especially not to majority opinion. In particular, the doctrines of separation of powers and of checks and balances, and the constitutional guarantees of civil rights and liberties are intended to protect minority interests against the excesses of majority views and actions.

**Interpreting Political Cartoons (a) What is the cartoon's message?(b) Does the text support this message?**

Finally, polls are not elections, nor are they substitutes for elections. It is when faced with a ballot that voters must decide what is important and what is not. Voters must be able to tell the difference between opinions and concrete information, and should know the difference between personalities and platforms.

Democracy is more than a simple measurement of opinion. Democracy is about making careful choices among leaders and their positions on issues, and among the governmental actions that may follow. Ideally, democracy is the thoughtful participation of citizens in the political process.

## Section 2 Assessment

### Key Terms and Main Ideas

1. Why are **interest groups** uncertain gauges for measuring public opinion?
2. What is the major problem with the **straw vote** polling technique?
3. How is it that a **random sample** gives a fairly accurate representation of public opinion?
4. For what reasons is public opinion measured?

### Critical Thinking

5. **Determining Relevance** List two good reasons for following polls during a presidential campaign.
6. **Understanding Point of View** How might the Framers of the Constitution have viewed public opinion polls?

7. **Predicting Consequences** What positive and/or negative effects might there be if polls were taken among student voters before a student government election?

 **Take It to the Net**

8. Read through some of the recent polls taken by the Harris Survey and analyze how the poll data are explained and presented. Then, using the Harris Surveys as a model, conduct and present your own poll on a public issue of your choice. Use the links provided in the Social Studies area at the following Web site for help in completing this activity. www.phschool.com

 **Take It to the Net**

8. Direct students to the Social Studies area at the Prentice Hall Web site. The *Magruder's American Government* companion Web site includes the directions and links needed to complete the activity. It also provides a printable Internet activity worksheet with scoring rubrics for assessment. Polls should demonstrate an understanding of the methodology of the Harris Surveys.

7. Possible answers: Polls might help undecided students become more familiar with the candidates and the issues; however, they could have a negative influence on students in terms of peer pressure.

### Answers to . . .

### Section 2 Assessment

1. They are uncertain because the number of people represented by the group is unknown, as well as how strongly these people hold the views the group espouses.
2. Straw votes rely on quantity of answers rather than quality of questions asked, and thus can never be accurate.
3. Random samples are more accurate because they rely on the law of probability, which says that a properly selected random sample will yield results with a small and predictable margin of error.
4. For public opinion to have an influence on public policy—as it is supposed to have in a democracy—it must be measured.
5. Possible reasons: To know how a candidate is perceived by most Americans, and to gauge important policy issues by being aware of the kinds of questions asked.
6. Possible answer: They may have been suspicious of the value of a poll in reflecting true public sentiment.

### Answer to . . .

**Interpreting Political Cartoons (a)** That people see responding to polls as more important than voting.
**(b)** Possible answer: It refutes it, by saying that public opinion can never replace voting in a democracy.

### Taking a Poll

**Focus** Lead a class project in which groups of students design, critique, and conduct a poll, analyzing and publishing the results.

**Instruct** As a class, brainstorm and decide on two topics on which to poll the student body. Then divide the class into two groups. Group A will design the first survey, deciding on the sample size and composition as well as drafting the questions. Group B will critique the polling method and the questions, make revisions as needed, and conduct the poll. Group A will compile and interpret the results. Then the groups will switch roles, with Group B designing the next survey.

**Close/Reteach** As an alternative, have both groups of students conduct identical surveys, and then compare and contrast the results. Or have students analyze polls and polling techniques used by major independent polling organizations. For links to their Web sites, see the *Magruder's* companion Web site. **www.phschool.com**

### *Answers . . .*

**1.** Population will probably be the student body, but students could limit to a particular grade.
**2.** Caution students not to make their sample too small, or it will be difficult to draw generalizations from the responses.
**3.** Survey questions should be short and simple. Ask only enough questions to get the information needed. Avoid open-ended questions.
**4.** Polling methods may include: (1) Random one-on-one interviews in which interviewers poll whoever comes along and is willing to participate; or (2) Written surveys, which are distributed to randomly selected respondents according to certain criteria.
**5.** Make sure the conclusions drawn reflect the data gathered and are not too far-reaching.

# SKILLS FOR LIFE

# Taking a Poll

Politicians have a love/hate relationship with public opinion polls. When a poll shows them gaining public approval, they hail the results as an endorsement of their views. When it shows their popularity slipping, they claim that they never pay attention to polls!

Indeed, a poorly constructed survey can deliver invalid information that can mislead decision makers or can be used to make false claims. Whether a poll is nationwide or within your classroom, certain standards of poll-taking apply. For instance:

**1. Define the population to be polled.** Decide what group you need to poll in order to find the answer to your question. For example, if you want to learn what percentage of registered voters in Tyler, Texas, voted in the last election, then it would not make sense to poll people who had not registered to vote.

**2. Construct a sample.** Within the group that you're polling, you can take a random sample—people chosen purely by chance. Or you can take a quota sample—a representative number of people from each subgroup in your survey.

**3. Prepare valid questions.** Ask objective questions rather than ones that lead the subject toward a particular answer. Try to ask questions that can be answered in one word, so your results will be easy to tally. Avoid wording that is difficult to understand, especially if your subjects are young or not fluent in English.

**4. Select and control the means by which the poll will be taken.** Decide whether you will conduct an in-person interview, a telephone interview, a mail interview, or an online interview. Be sure to interview all members of a group in the same manner. Choose interviewers who are careful not to influence the responses by their dress, attitude, or tone of voice.

**5. Report your findings.** Make a table of the results of your poll. Analyze the data to determine the answer to your original question.

### Test for Success

Work individually or in small groups to design, conduct, and present the findings from a poll of your class. Create a topic, or choose from one of the following: (a) television viewing habits; (b) career plans; (c) consumption of genetically engineered foods.

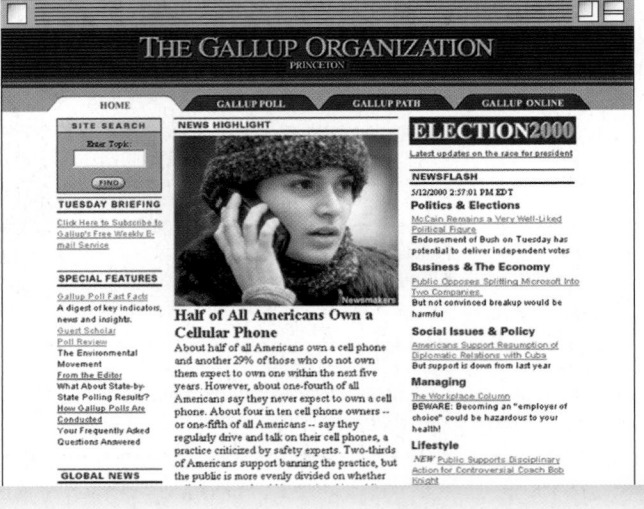

▲ Above, a student conducts a survey. At right is the Web site of a major national polling service, the Gallup Organization.

### Test for Success

Have students publish their survey results either on a bulletin board at school, in the school newspaper, or on the Web.

🔘 **Social Studies Skills Tutor CD-ROM** Provides interactive practice in geographic literacy, critical thinking and reading, visual analysis, and communications.

### Point-of-Use Resources

📁 **Skills for Life Activity** Unit 2 booklet, p. 35 provides an additional skill activity for this chapter.

# 3 The Mass Media

3 The Mass Media

## Section Preview

### OBJECTIVES

1. **Examine** the role of the mass media in providing the public with political information.
2. **Give examples of** the processes used by the media to affect public policy.
3. **Understand** the factors that limit the influence of the media.

### WHY IT MATTERS

How often do you watch television, read a newspaper or magazine, listen to the radio? While these media provide entertainment, they are also our most important sources of political information.

### POLITICAL DICTIONARY

★ medium
★ public agenda
★ sound bite

How much television do you watch each day? Little or none? Two hours a day? Three hours? More? However much you watch, you no doubt know that your peers spend a great deal of time in front of the TV. Studies show that by the time the average person graduates from high school today, he or she has spent nearly 11,000 hours in classrooms and nearly 14,000 hours watching television.

Television has an extraordinary impact on the lives of everyone in this country. As you will see in this section, so do the other elements of the mass media.

## The Role of Mass Media

A **medium** is a means of communication; it transmits some kind of information. *Media* is the plural of medium. As you have read, the mass media include those means of communication that can reach large, widely dispersed audiences simultaneously.

Four major mass media are particularly important in American politics. Ranked in terms of impact, they are television, newspapers, radio, and magazines. Other media—books, films, and audio- and videocassettes, for example—play a lesser role. So, too, does the Internet, though its communicating capabilities are becoming increasingly important.

The mass media are not a part of government. Unlike political parties and interest groups, they do not exist primarily to influence government. They are, nonetheless, an important force in politics.

Besides providing entertainment, the media present people with political information. They do so directly when they report the news, in a newscast or in the news columns of a newspaper, for example. The media also provide a large amount of political information less directly—for example, in radio and television programs, newspaper stories, and magazine articles. These venues often deal with such public topics as crime, health care, or some aspect of American foreign policy. Either way, people acquire most of the information they know about government and politics from the various forms of media.

### Television

Politics and television have gone hand in hand since the technology first appeared. The first public demonstration of television occurred at the New York World's Fair in 1939. President Franklin Roosevelt opened the fair on camera,

◀ *The "Wireless Web"* Some mobile phones provide access to the Internet, an increasingly important form of mass media.

## Reading Strategy

### Accessing Prior Knowledge

Before students begin reading, ask them to recall any political information they have acquired recently via television, radio, newspapers, and magazines. Have them think about the information and how it was presented. Tell them that they will learn more about the role of the mass media in politics as they read the section.

---

## Background Note

### Common Misconceptions

Most Americans know that the television networks are private businesses which make money by selling time for commercials, and that they are free, under the First Amendment, to broadcast a stunning variety of shows. But few Americans realize that the networks are required, by law, to broadcast news. Under the Communications Act of 1934, the Federal Government granted broadcast licenses on the condition that the networks serve the "public interest, convenience, and necessity"—which, for decades, meant airing news shows.

---

## Point-of-Use Resources

📁 **Guided Reading and Review** Unit 2 booklet, p. 33 provides students with practice identifying the main ideas and key terms of this section.

📁 **Lesson Plans** For lesson planning suggestions, see p. 40 of the Lesson Plans booklet.

---

*Answer to . . .*

**Critical Thinking** Directly, by showing debates, press conferences, and political shows; indirectly, through advertisements and by airing entertainment with political content.

---

and viewers watched him on tiny five- and seven-inch screens.

World War II interrupted the development of the new medium, but it began to become generally available in the late 1940s. Television boomed in the 1950s. The first transcontinental broadcast came in 1951, when President Harry Truman, speaking in Washington, addressed the delegates attending the Japanese Peace Treaty Conference in San Francisco.

Today, television is all-pervasive. As you read earlier, there is at least one television set in 98 percent of the nation's 120 million households. In fact, there are more homes in this country today with a television set than with indoor plumbing facilities!

Television replaced newspapers as the principal source of political information for a majority of Americans in the early 1960s. Today, television is the principal source of news for an estimated 80 percent of the population.

The more than 1,400 television stations in this country include more than 1,000 commercial outlets and over 300 public broadcasters. Three major national networks have dominated television from its infancy: the Columbia Broadcasting System (CBS), the American Broadcasting Company (ABC), and the National Broadcasting Company (NBC). Those three giants furnish about 90 percent of the programming for some 700 local stations. That programming accounts for about 45 percent of all television viewing time today.

The major networks' audience share has been declining in recent years, however. The main challenges to their domination have come from three sources: (1) several independent broadcasting groups—for example, the Fox Network; (2) cable broadcasters[4]—for example, Turner Broadcasting, and especially its Cable News Network (CNN); and (3) the Public Broadcasting System (PBS) and its more than 350 local stations.

Some of the most highly touted presentations on television—a Super Bowl game, for example, or a debate between the major presidential candidates—are seen by as many as 100 million people. From 15 to 40 million watch the more popular sitcoms. Each of the three major network's nightly news programs draws 7 to 10 million viewers. In addition, more than 75 million places, including nearly two thirds of the nation's households, are now hooked up to cable systems.

---

[4]C-SPAN, the Cable-Satellite Public Affairs Network, is sponsored by the cable industry. C-SPAN and C-SPAN II present both live and taped coverage of a broad range of public events—including major floor debates and committee hearings in Congress, presidential and other press conferences, and speeches by notable public figures.

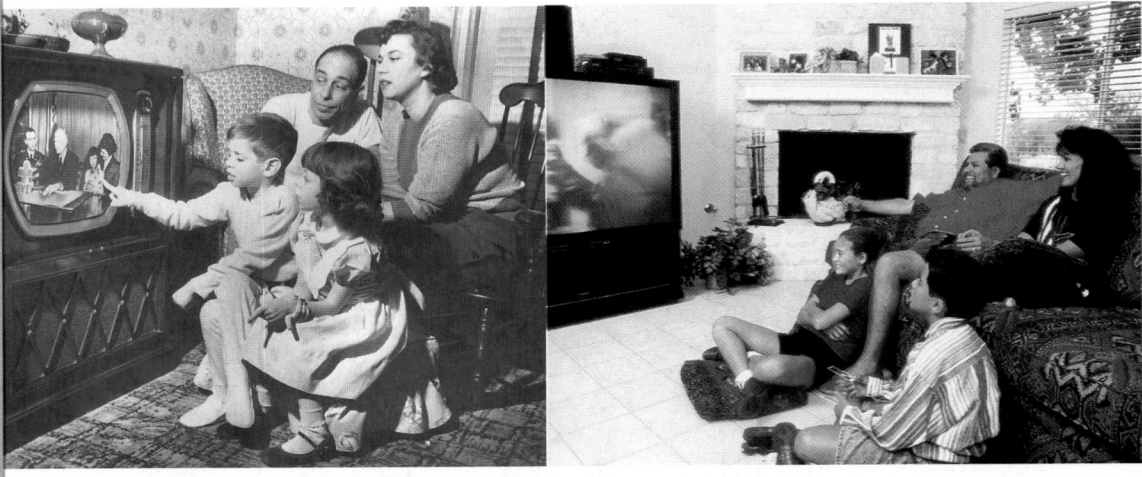

▲ Television viewing boomed during the 1950s. Today 98 percent of American households have at least one set. *Critical Thinking How does television provide political information both directly and indirectly?*

---

## Organizing Information

To make sure students understand the main points of this section, you may wish to use the tree map graphic organizer to the right.

Tell students that a tree map shows a main topic, its main ideas, and its supporting details. Have students use the tree map to record information about each of the types of mass media.

**Teaching Tip** A template for this graphic organizer can be found in the Section Support Transparencies, Transparency 3.

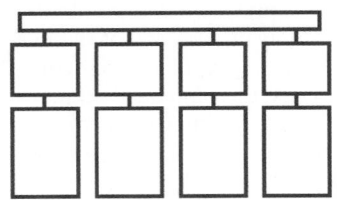

## Newspapers

The first regularly published newspaper in America, the *Boston News-Letter,* appeared in 1704.[5] Other papers soon followed, in Boston and then in Philadelphia, New York, Annapolis, and elsewhere. By 1775, 37 newspapers were being published in the colonies. All of them were weekly papers, and they were printed on one sheet that was usually folded to make four pages. The nation's first daily newspaper, the *Pennsylvania Evening Post and Daily Advertiser,* began publication in 1783.

Those first papers regularly carried political news. Several spurred the colonists to revolution, carrying the news of independence and the text of the Declaration to people throughout the colonies. Thomas Jefferson marked the vital role of the press in the earliest years of the nation when, in 1787, he wrote to a friend:

**"** *. . . were it left to me to decide whether we should have a government without newspapers or newspapers without a government, I should not hesitate a moment to prefer the latter.* **"**

—Letter to Colonel Edward Carrington, January 16, 1787

The 1st Amendment, added to the Constitution in 1791, made the same point regarding the importance of newspapers with its guarantee of the freedom of the press.

Today, more than 10,000 newspapers are published in the United States, including almost 1,500 dailies, more than 7,200 weeklies, some 550 semi-weeklies, and several hundred foreign-language papers. Those publications have a combined circulation of about 150 million copies per issue. About 45 percent of the nation's adult population read a newspaper every day.

The number of daily newspapers has been declining for decades, however, from more than 2,000 in 1920 to 1,745 in 1980 and to not quite 1,500 today. Radio and television, and more

---

[5]The world's first newspaper was almost certainly the *Acta Diurna,* a daily gazette in Rome dating from 59 B.C. Another very early forerunner of today's newspapers was *Tsing Pao,* a court journal in Beijing. Press historians believe that its first issues, printed from stone blocks, were published beginning in A.D. 618; its last issue appeared in 1911.

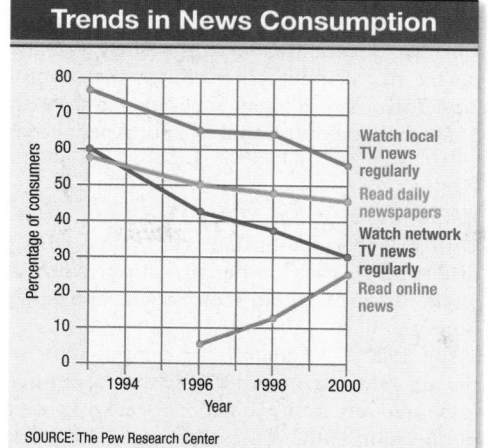

### Trends in News Consumption

Percentage of consumers (vertical axis: 0–80)
Year (horizontal axis: 1994, 1996, 1998, 2000)

Watch local TV news regularly
Read daily newspapers
Watch network TV news regularly
Read online news

SOURCE: The Pew Research Center

*Interpreting Graphs* While television and newspapers have declined as sources for news, use of the Internet as a news source is rising. **Briefly explain what you see as the reasons behind these trends.**

recently the Internet, have been major factors in that downward trend.

So, too, have been the battles over readers and advertisers that competing papers have fought in many places nationwide. Often, those struggles have left only one survivor. Competing daily papers exist in fewer than 50 cities today. This represents a major change from only a few decades ago, when at least two and sometimes three, four, or five newspapers existed in most major cities.

Nevertheless, newspapers rank second only to television as the public's primary source of information about government and politics. Most newspapers cover stories in greater depth than television does, and many try to present various points of view in their editorial sections. Those newspapers that have the most substantial reputations and national influence today include the *New York Times,* the *Washington Post,* the *Chicago Tribune,* the *Los Angeles Times,* the *Wall Street Journal, USA Today,* and the *Christian Science Monitor.*

Most newspapers are local papers. That is, most of their readers live in or near the communities in which they are published. While local papers do carry national and international news, most focus on their own locales.

Advances in telecommunications and computerized operations are changing that basic fact,

---

---

## Preparing for Standardized Tests

Have students read the passages under *Newspapers* and then answer the question below.

What is the main reason for the decline in the number of newspapers published?

**A** People are not interested in local papers.

**B** Newspapers are too political.

**C** Newspapers only express one point of view.

**D** Newspapers must compete with television and other media.

## Customize for
### English Language Learners

Have students prepare a two-page "Guide for Using the Mass Media to Find Out About Public Issues" that would be useful for a newcomer to the United States. Ask them to include the names of newspapers, magazines, and TV and radio networks with local channels and radio frequencies. The guide should provide brief descriptions of what each source offers relating to public issues.

### Make It Relevant

#### Students Make a Difference

Sheryl Anayas calls her internship at the Teen Environmental Media Network "an amazing experience." At TEMN, Sheryl got to try just about all aspects of radio journalism, including interviewing, writing scripts, selecting "cuts" for 90-second audio reports, recording her own narration, and editing audio digitally. "I learned to produce environmental audio and text reports independently," Sheryl says, and her audio reports were broadcast on the San Francisco Unified School District's radio station.

Science Interchange, Inc., which sponsors TEMN, uses radio and the Internet to inform the public about environmental issues. According to executive director Jerry Kay, Science Interchange hopes to contribute to "training the next generation of science and environmental journalists."

---

however. Today, each day's editions of the *New York Times,* the *Wall Street Journal,* and the *Christian Science Monitor* are generally available on the day of publication around the country, *USA Today,* which began publication in the early 1980s, has become a popular national newspaper.

### Radio

Radio as it exists today began in 1920. On November 2nd of that year, station KDKA in Pittsburgh went on the air with presidential election returns. Radio soon became immensely popular.

By 1927, 733 commercial stations were on the air, Americans owned more than seven million radio sets, and two national networks were in operation. NBC was established in 1926 and

### U.S. Radio Stations and Sales

| Year | Radio stations on air | Unit sales |
|------|------------------------|------------|
| 1946 | 961 | N.A. |
| 1950 | 2,773 | N.A. |
| 1955 | 3,211 | 7,327 |
| 1960 | 4,133 | 18,031 |
| 1965 | 5,249 | 31,689 |
| 1970 | 6,760 | 34,049 |
| 1975 | 7,744 | 25,276 |
| 1980 | 8,566 | 27,104 |
| 1985 | 10,359 | 21,575 |
| 1990 | 10,788 | 21,585 |
| 1991 | 10,989 | 18,530 |
| 1992 | 11,118 | 21,553 |
| 1993 | 11,371 | 19,697 |
| 1994 | 11,565 | 18,323 |
| 1995 | 11,834 | 17,051 |
| 1996 | 12,295 | 17,581 |
| 1997 | 12,482 | 17,664 |
| 1998 | 12,641 | 18,734 |
| 1999 | 12,641 | 19,178* |

*Estimate

SOURCE: *The New York Times Almanac*

**Interpreting Tables** The number of radio stations on the air has risen steadily since the 1940s. **(a) Describe trends in radio sales as shown on the table. (b) How can you explain the reasons behind these trends?**

---

CBS in 1927. The Mutual Broadcasting System was formed in 1934, and ABC was formed in 1943. The advent of networks made it possible for broadcasters to present their programs and advertising messages to millions of people all over the country.

By the 1930s, radio had assumed much of the role in American society that television has today. It was a major entertainment medium, and millions of people planned their daily schedules around their favorite programs. The networks also provided the nation with dramatic coverage of important events, and radio exposed the American people to national and international politics as never before.

President Franklin Roosevelt was the first major public figure to use radio effectively. Author David Halberstam has described the impact of FDR's famous fireside chats:

**PRIMARY Sources** *"He was the first great American radio voice. For most Americans of [that] generation, their first memory of politics would be of sitting by a radio and hearing that voice, strong, confident, totally at ease. . . . Most Americans in the previous 160 years had never even seen a President; now almost all of them were hearing him, in their own homes. It was literally and figuratively electrifying.* **"**
—David Halberstam, *The Powers That Be*

Many people thought that the arrival of television would bring the end of radio as a major medium. Radio has survived, however, in large part because it is so conveniently available. People can hear music, news, sports, and other radio programs in many places where they cannot watch television—in their cars, at work, in the country, and in a number of other places and situations.

Radio remains a major source of news and other political information. The average person hears 20 hours of radio each week. No one knows how many radios there are in this country—in homes, offices, cars, backpacks, and a great many other places. Those radios can pick up more than 12,000 stations on the AM and FM dials.

Many AM stations are affiliated with one or another of the national networks.

---

### Answer to . . .

**Interpreting Tables (a)** They peaked in 1970, remained relatively strong during the 1970s and 1980s, and began to decline in the 1990s. **(b)** Competition with television and the Internet.

Unlike television, however, most radio programming is local. There are also some 700 public radio stations, most of them on the FM dial. These noncommercial outlets are part of National Public Radio (NPR), which is radio's counterpart of television's PBS.

In most large cities there is at least one station that broadcasts nothing but news and public affairs programs. In addition, many stations serve the preferences of African American, Latino, or other minority audiences.

## Magazines

Several magazines were published in colonial America. Benjamin Franklin began one of the very first, his *General Magazine,* in Philadelphia in 1741. On into the early 1900s, most magazines published in the United States were generally devoted to literature and the social graces. The first political magazines—among them, *Harper's Weekly* and the *Atlantic Monthly*—appeared in the mid-1800s.

The progressive reform period in the early 1900s spawned several journals of opinion, including a number that featured articles by the day's leading muckrakers.[6] For decades before radio and television, magazines constituted the only national medium.

Some 12,000 magazines are published in the United States today. Most are trade publications, such as *Veterinary Forum* and the *Automotive Executive,* or periodicals that target some special personal interest, such as *Golf Digest, Teen,* and *American Rifleman.* Magazines with the highest circulation today are *Modern Maturity, TV Guide,* and *Reader's Digest.* They each sell some 10 to 20 million or more copies per issue.

Three news magazines, *Time, Newsweek,* and *U.S. News & World Report,* rank in the top

---

[6]The muckrakers were journalists who exposed wrongdoing in politics, business, and industry. The term was coined by Theodore Roosevelt in 1906 and is derived from the raking of muck—that is, manure and other barnyard debris. The muckrakers set the pattern for what is now called investigative reporting.

### Comparative Government

#### Access to Media in Selected Countries

| Country | Population in millions | Television sets per 1,000 persons | Radios per 1,000 persons | Daily newspaper circulation per 1,000 persons |
|---|---|---|---|---|
| United States | 281.0 | 847 | 2,115 | 215 |
| Japan | 126.5 | 708 | 957 | 578 |
| Bangladesh | 129.2 | 5 | 63 | 9 |
| Nigeria | 123.3 | 61 | 197 | 24 |
| Mexico | 100.3 | 257 | 329 | 97 |
| Italy | 57.6 | 483 | 874 | 104 |
| India | 1,014.0 | 68 | 117 | 21 |
| Chile | 15.1 | 280 | 305 | 101 |
| Canada | 31.3 | 708 | 1,078 | 157 |
| Nicaragua | 4.8 | 48 | 206 | 31 |

SOURCE: *The World Almanac,* 2001

*Interpreting Tables* Access to media varies considerably from country to country. *(a) In which countries shown in the table do people have the least access to the media? (b) How might people in these countries become informed about public affairs?*

## CONSTITUTIONAL PRINCIPLES

### Judicial Review

The role of the American media has long been controversial. In 1734, Peter Zenger was arrested for seditious libel and tried for publishing a newspaper with strong political opinions. Zenger was found not guilty, but this was not the last time that the press was "put on trial." In 1971, the Defense Department issued an injunction against the *New York Times,* directing the newspaper not to print government documents stolen during the Vietnam War. The *Times* appealed the injunction, and won.

### Activity

Have students read the *New York Times* v. *United States* case in the Close Up on the Supreme Court booklet in the Teaching Resources. Remind them that the government's reason for the injunction was that disclosing the papers would risk national security. Ask students whether they agree with the Court's decision. Had the Court ruled differently, how might the mass media be different today?

25 periodicals in terms of circulation. They have a combined circulation of nearly 10 million copies a week, and they are important sources of political news and comment. There are several other magazines devoted to public affairs, most of them vehicles of opinion, including the *Nation,* the *New Republic,* the *National Review,* and the *Weekly Standard.*

## The Media and Public Policy

Clearly, the media play a significant role in American politics. Just how significant that role is, and just how much the media affect public policy, has long been the subject of debate.

Whatever its weight, the media's influence can be seen in any number of situations. It is most visible in two areas: (1) the public agenda and (2) electoral politics.

### The Public Agenda

The media play a very large role in shaping the **public agenda,** the societal problems that political leaders and citizens agree need government attention. As they report and comment on events, the media determine to a very large extent what public issues the people will think and talk

▲ *Power of the Press* The media transmit information across the country and around the world instantly. They thus help to shape the public agenda and affect the outcome of elections. Shown here is a CNN newsroom.

about—and, so, those matters that public-policy makers will be concerned about. As a result, the media ultimately influence those matters of concern to public-policy makers.

To put the point another way, the media have the power to focus the public's attention on a particular issue. They do so by emphasizing some things and ignoring or downplaying others. For example, they feature certain items on the front page or at the top of the newscast and bury others.

It is not correct to say that the media tell the people *what* to think; but it is clear that they tell the people what to think *about.* A look at any issue of a daily newspaper or a quick review of the content of any television news program will demonstrate that point. Remember, people rely on the media for most of the information they receive on public issues.

The mass media also has a direct impact on the nation's leaders. Some years ago, Stephen Hess, a widely respected authority on the media, identified several news organizations that form the "inner ring" of influence in Washington, D.C. He cited the three major television networks, CBS, ABC, and NBC; three newspapers, the *New York Times,* the *Washington Post,* and the *Wall Street Journal;* the leading news wire service, the Associated Press (AP); and the three major news weeklies, *Time, Newsweek,* and *U.S. News & World Report.* CNN, MSNBC, Fox News, Reuters and *USA Today* have since joined that select group.

Top political figures in and out of government pay close attention to these sources. In fact, the President receives a daily digest of the news reports, analyses, and editorial comments that these and other sources broadcast and publish.

### Electoral Politics

You have seen several illustrations of the media's importance in electoral politics as you have read in this book. Recall, for example, the fact that the media, and in particular television, have contributed to a decline in the place of parties in American politics.

Television has made candidates far less dependent on party organizations than they once were. Before television, the major parties generally dominated the election process. They recruited most candidates who ran for office, and they ran those candidates' campaigns. The candidates depended on party organizations in order to reach the voters.

Now, television allows candidates to appeal directly to the people, without the help of a party organization. Candidates for major office need not be experienced politicians who have worked their way up a party's political ladder over the course of several elections. Today it is not at all unusual for candidates to assemble their own campaign organizations and operate with only loose connections to their political parties.

Remember, too, that how voters see a candidate—the impressions they have of that candidate's personality, character, abilities, and so on—is one of the major factors that influence voting behavior. Candidates and professional campaign managers are quite aware of this fact. They know that the kind of "image" a candidate projects in the media can have a telling effect on the outcome of an election.

Candidates regularly try to manipulate media coverage to their advantage. Campaign strategists understand that most people learn almost everything they know about a candidate from television. They therefore plan campaigns that emphasize television exposure. Such technical considerations as timing, location, lighting, and camera angles loom large, often at the expense of such substantive matters as the issues involved in an election or a candidate's qualifications for public office.

Good campaign managers also know that most television news programs are built out of stories that (1) take no more than a minute or two of air time, and (2) show people doing something interesting or exciting. Newscasts seldom feature "talking heads," speakers who drone on and on about some complex issue.

Instead, newscasts featuring candidates are usually short, sharply focused **sound bites**—snappy reports that can be aired in 30 or 45 seconds or so. Staged and carefully orchestrated visits to historic sites, factory gates, toxic-waste dumps, football games, and the like have become a standard part of the electoral scene.

## Limits on Media Influence

Having said all this, it is all too easy to overstate the media's role in American politics. A number of built-in factors work to limit the media's impact on the behavior of the American voting public.

For one thing, few people follow international, national, or even local political events very closely. Many studies of voting behavior show that in the typical election, only about 10 percent of those who can vote and only about 15 percent of those who do vote are well informed on the many candidates and issues under consideration in that election. In short, only a small part of the public actually takes in and understands much of what the media have to say about public affairs.

Moreover, most people who do pay some attention to politics are likely to be selective about it. That is, they most often watch, listen to, and read those sources that generally agree with their own viewpoints. They regularly ignore those sources with which they disagree. Thus, for example, many Democrats do not watch the televised campaign appearances of Republican candidates. Nor do many Republicans read newspaper stories about the campaign efforts of Democratic candidates.

---

## Voices on Government

**Joseph Turow,** a professor at the Annenberg School of Communications, studies the ways in which the media influence our political perspectives. Turow examines the mass media—from radio to the Internet—and their impact on people.

❝ *We have to make people a little more sophisticated about video images. . . . News and entertainment are, essentially, a battle over the definition of the world. You've got various sources in public relations, and interest groups and political organizations are always maneuvering to have a reporter write this or that, and we don't know, for example, why this person is on this television show. One of the things I tell my students is to interrogate the newspaper, interrogate the television show.* ❞

### Evaluating the Quotation

*What do you think Turow means by "interrogating" a newspaper or a television news program? How would following his advice change you as a "consumer" of the news?*

---

## Spotlight on Technology

**Magruder's American Government Video Collection**

The Magruder's Video Collection explores key issues and debates in American government. Each segment examines an issue central to chapter content through use of historical and contemporary footage. Commentary from civic leaders in academics, government, and the media follow each segment. Critical thinking questions focus students' attention on key issues, and may be used to stimulate discussion.

Use the Chapter 8 video segment to examine how film, television, and political commercials are used to mold candidates' images and shape public opinion. (time: about 5 minutes) This segment uses examples from past and current presidential and other elections to analyze how appearances are manipulated—both in negative campaigning and to increase voter appeal.

---

### Background Note
### Recent Scholarship

What is the role of the mass media in American politics? Bartholomew W. Sparrow explores that question in *Uncertain Guardians: The News Media as a Political Institution.* Drawing on a number of respected studies of the media as well as firsthand accounts by well-known journalists, Sparrow examines the responsibilities and performance of those who cover politics and government. Sparrow pays special attention to market factors that have significantly influenced what is considered newsworthy, how events are covered, and the implications of recent developments on the democratic process. The specific cases used to support his generalizations can easily be adapted to a classroom setting—either as illustrations in a discussion or as cases for students themselves to consider.

*Answer to . . .*

**Evaluating the Quotation** By "interrogating," Turow means looking at programs and stories critically, noting bias and examining why they are presented the way they are. In so doing, people can interpret the media rather than just "consuming" it.

## Point-of-Use Resources

**Guide to the Essentials** Chapter 8, Section 3, p. 49 provides support for students who need additional review of section content. Spanish support is available in the Spanish edition of the Guide on p. 42.

**Quiz** Unit 2 booklet, p. 34 includes matching and multiple-choice questions to check students' understanding of Section 3 content.

**Presentation Pro CD-ROM** Quizzes and multiple-choice questions check students' understanding of Section 3 content.

## Answers to . . .

### Section 3 Assessment

**1.** The Internet is a means of communication that transmits information.
**2.** They help determine what public issues concern most people, and as a result, influence matters of concern to public-policy makers.
**3.** Limits include: Most people do not follow the media closely; most people are selective in what they do watch; media content is often determined by what will entertain people rather than by what will inform them; and the media often do not present in-depth coverage.
**4.** Radio has survived because is readily available to people in situations where television is not available.
**5.** Possible answer: By choosing a location or other factors that emphasize the candidate's best qualities; by presenting interesting sound bites rather than the entire debate.
**6.** Budgets will vary, but should demonstrate an understanding of each medium's advantages and disadvantages.

Another important limit on the media's impact is the content the media carries. This is especially true of radio and television. Most television programs, for example, have little or nothing to do with public affairs, at least not directly. (A number of popular programs do relate to public affairs in an indirect way, however. Thus, many are "crime shows," and crime is certainly a matter of public concern. Many also carry a political message—for example, that the police are hard-working public servants.)

▲ **News or Entertainment?** Newspapers offer a variety of information, much of it not about politics, in order to appeal to the widest possible audience.

Advertisers who pay the high costs of television air time want to reach the largest possible audiences. Because most people are more interested in being entertained than in being informed about public issues, few public-affairs programs air in prime time. There are exceptions, however, such as *60 Minutes*, *20/20*, *Dateline*, and *Inside Politics*.

Radio and television mostly "skim" the news. They report only what their news editors judge to be the most important and/or the most interesting stories of the day. Even on widely watched evening news programs, most reports are presented in 60- to 90-second time slots. In short, the broadcast media seldom give the kind of in-depth coverage that a good newspaper can supply.

Newspapers are not as hampered as many other media in their ability to cover public affairs. Still, much of the content of most newspapers is nonpolitical. Like nearly all of television and radio, newspapers depend on their advertising revenues, which in turn depend on producing a product with the widest possible appeal. Newspaper readers are often more interested in the sports pages and the social, travel, advertising, and entertainment sections of a newspaper than they are in its news and editorial pages.

In-depth coverage of public affairs is available in the media to those who want it and will seek it out. There are a number of good newspapers around the country. In-depth coverage can also be found in several magazines and on a number of radio and television stations, including public broadcast outlets. Remember, however, that there is nothing about democracy that guarantees an alert and informed public. Like voting and other forms of political participation, being an informed citizen requires effort.

## Section 3 Assessment

### Key Terms and Main Ideas

1. Why is the Internet considered a **medium**?
2. How do the media influence the **public agenda**?
3. What limits are there on media influence?
4. Why has radio survived despite television's enormous appeal?

### Critical Thinking

5. **Drawing Inferences** How might campaign managers use a presidential debate among the candidates to their client's advantage?
6. **Demonstrating Reasoned Judgment** You are a candidate for the presidency. Draw up an advertising plan that shows the percentages of your advertising budget that you will allocate to each type of media. Then write a rationale to back up your plan.

 **Take It to the Net**

7. Select an issue on the public agenda and follow links to read more about it. Then prepare an oral report in which you explain the issue to the rest of your class. What role have the media played in bringing this issue to the public's attention? Use the links provided in the Social Studies area at the following Web site for help in completing this activity. **www.phschool.com**

 **Take It to the Net**

**7.** Direct students to the Social Studies area at the Prentice Hall Web site. The *Magruder's American Government* companion Web site includes the directions and links needed to complete the activity. It also provides a printable Internet activity worksheet with scoring rubrics for assessment. Oral reports should clearly explain the issue and include specific examples.

# Do Candidates Deserve "Equal Time"?

*A free press plays an essential role in political campaigns. It not only informs voters of candidates' views on key issues but also provides analysis and commentary on those views and issues. Often, of course, candidates strongly disagree with the press's opinions. In such cases, does the press have an obligation to give candidates an equal opportunity to respond?*

## *Miami Herald Publishing Co.* v. *Tornillo* (1974)

In 1972, while Pat Tornillo was running for a seat in the Florida House of Representatives, the *Miami Herald* published a series of editorials that were critical of his candidacy. Tornillo demanded that the newspaper print his responses to the editorials. He based his demand on a Florida "right of reply" law, which provided that if a newspaper attacked a political candidate's personal character or political record, the candidate could require the paper to print his or her reply. Under the law, the reply had to appear in as prominent a place and in the same kind of type as the criticisms themselves, so long as the reply was no longer than the original criticisms. The newspaper could not charge the candidate for publishing the reply.

The *Herald* refused to print Tornillo's reply, and instead sought a court ruling that the right of reply law was unconstitutional. The State circuit court ruled that the law unconstitutionally limited freedom of the press. The Florida Supreme Court then reversed that opinion, and the paper appealed the Florida decision to the Supreme Court.

### Arguments for Miami Herald Publishing Co.

1. The right of reply law is unconstitutional. It violates the First Amendment by regulating the content of a newspaper.
2. The law is so broadly worded that it cannot be enforced. A newspaper editor would not be able to determine which words in an editorial might create an obligation for the paper to print the candidate's reply.
3. The law unconstitutionally restricts the right of a newspaper to make critical comments on matters of public importance.

### Arguments for Tornillo

1. Since many local newspapers are owned by a small number of national news organizations, those few organizations have great power to select and shape the news that is distributed to the public. Furthermore, it is economically difficult for opponents of those newspapers to create competing papers. Measures like the right of reply law are therefore necessary to ensure that the public receives a full range of views.
2. The right of reply law does not restrict the *Herald's* right of free speech because it does not prevent the paper from saying anything it wants to. The law merely provides a balancing mechanism for presenting opposing points of view.
3. The right of reply is an appropriate way to protect an individual's interest in his or her reputation, and presents an acceptable method of correcting harm to a person's reputation when it occurs.

### Decide for Yourself

1. Review the constitutional grounds on which each side based its arguments and the specific arguments each side presented.
2. Debate the opposing viewpoints presented in this case. Which viewpoint do you favor?
3. Predict the impact of the Court's decision on press coverage of campaign issues and on the extent to which Americans will be adequately informed on political matters. (To read a summary of the Court's decision, turn to the Supreme Court Glossary on page 799.)

---

 **CLOSE·UP** FOUNDATION *Corner*

📁 **Close Up on the Supreme Court** *Miami Herald Publishing Co.* v. *Tornillo*, p. 9 provides an activity to extend coverage of this case.

 **CLOSE UP** FOUNDATION | Online

To keep up-to-date on Close Up news and activities, visit Close Up Online at

**www.closeup.org**

---

 **CLOSE·UP** FOUNDATION

## Do Candidates Deserve "Equal Time"?

**Focus** Explain that one of the rationales for the First Amendment is that a "free marketplace of ideas" promotes informed discussion of governmental affairs. Thus, some critics argue that the mass media should devote more coverage to elections and political candidates. Discuss the pros and cons of a law requiring the media to provide such coverage. How might such a law violate the media's First Amendment rights?

**Instruct** Divide the class into two groups. Have one group discuss the arguments for the *Miami Herald* and the other group the arguments for Tornillo. Next, have each group choose three students to debate the arguments. Have the class vote on which arguments they find more convincing.

**Close/Reteach** Explain that keeping informed about political issues sometimes requires looking beyond television, newspapers, and radio. Have students brainstorm a list of alternatives to those forms of mass media. *(books, the Internet, and public interest groups)*

💿 **Keep It Current CD-ROM** includes government-related projects by unit. The CD-ROM links to the Prentice Hall School Web site and may be used for daily updates.

### *Answers to . . .*
**Decide for Yourself**
1. The *Miami Herald* cited the 1st Amendment protection of free press in arguing that the "right of reply" law was unconstitutional. Tornillo argued that the law did not hinder free speech, because the newspaper could still say whatever it wanted to; also, the "right of reply" protects individual reputations.
2. Answers will vary, but should be supported with valid reasoning.
3. The Court ruled that the "right of reply" law violated the First Amendment.

## Practicing the Vocabulary

1. peer group
2. medium
3. public opinion
4. opinion leader
5. sound bite
6. interest group
7. quota sample
8. mandate
9. random sample
10. mass media

## Reviewing Main Ideas

### Section 1

**11.** As not all people think alike or even express opinions on the same subjects, there can never be a single undivided view of all the people.
**12.** Family and schools begin the process of teaching children fundamental values, and influence how children will see the political world.
**13.** Peer groups, opinion leaders, historic events, and the mass media.
**14.** Ways include writing or e-mailing, holding a demonstration, voting, creating billboards, and so on.
**15. (a)** Public opinion involves only those views people hold on political and social issues. **(b)** Examples may include parties and candidates, taxes, welfare programs, unemployment, national defense, and foreign policy.

### Section 2

**16. (a)** Elections indicate voter preference; interest groups make public opinion known; the media express public issues to large numbers of people; personal contacts allow politicians to gauge people's reactions. **(b)** Elections only show broad and vague opinions; interest groups only indicate narrow views of a limited number of people; the media can be biased; personal contacts cannot gauge public opinion as a whole.
**17.** Polls; because when they are conducted scientifically, they are unbiased with a small margin of error.
**18.** Public opinion is only one influence on public policy, and is constantly checked by constitutional principles.
**19.** A straw vote asks the same questions of a large number of people, emphasizing quantity. A scientific poll uses the law of probability to find more reliable results with a smaller number of people.

**20.** Polls that do not take into account intensity, stability and relevance would be less accurate; also, polls that attempt to shape rather than gauge opinion are less accurate.

### Section 3

**21. (a)** Television, newspapers, radio, and magazines. **(b)** Television is pervasive and reaches the most people; newspapers cover stories in greater depth and present more points of view; radio is convenient and readily available; magazines are important sources of political news and have dedicated readerships.
**22.** Competition from other media and competition among the newspapers themselves.
**23.** The media determines what public issues people are concerned with, and have the power to focus the public's attention on particular issues. They also have an impact on the nation's leaders.
**24.** The media have lessened candidates' reliance on their party organizations; they also shape the public's perceptions of candidates in the way they present their information.
**25.** Most people do not follow news closely, or are selective in what they do follow; media content is selective and often nonpolitical.

---

## Political Dictionary

public affairs (p. 208)
public opinion (p. 209)
mass media (p. 211)
peer group (p. 212)
opinion leader (p. 212)

mandate (p. 216)
interest group (p. 216)
public opinion poll (p. 217)
straw vote (p. 217)
sample (p. 218)

random sample (p. 218)
quota sample (p. 219)
medium (p. 223)
public agenda (p. 228)
sound bite (p. 229)

## Practicing the Vocabulary

*Matching*  *Choose a term from the list above that best matches each description.*

1. The people with whom one usually associates
2. A means of communication
3. The attitudes held by a significant number of people on matters of government and politics
4. A person who has an unusual amount of influence on the views held by other people
5. News reports that are brief and sharply focused
6. An organization that tries to influence public policy

*Fill in the Blank*  *Choose a term from the list above that best completes each sentence.*

7. A type of sample that is carefully constructed to reflect the major characteristics of a particular universe is called a _____.
8. Winners of elections often claim that their victories at the polls represent a _____ to carry out their proposed programs.
9. A _____ is a type of sample in which each member of the sample universe has a mathematically equal chance of being included.
10. _____ are those means of communication that can reach large numbers of people.

## Reviewing Main Ideas

### Section 1

**11.** Why is it incorrect to say that public opinion represents the single, undivided view of the American people?
**12.** Why are the influences of education and family so powerful in the development of political attitudes?
**13.** Besides education and family, what other forces help influence public opinion in American society?
**14.** Name at least three ways in which public opinion can be expressed.
**15. (a)** Why is your opinion about a rock group not a public opinion? **(b)** Give at least three examples of topics on which a group of people may have a public opinion.

### Section 2

**16.** Elections, interest groups, the media, and personal contacts all are means of measuring public opinion. **(a)** Describe how each is used to measure public opinion. **(b)** What are the limitations of each?

**17.** What is the most reliable means of measuring public opinion? Explain your answer.
**18.** Why it is only partly correct to say that government in the United States is "government by public opinion"?
**19.** How does a straw vote differ from a scientific poll?
**20.** What factors can make a public opinion poll less than completely accurate?

### Section 3

**21. (a)** What are the four major sources of political information in the United States? **(b)** List at least one advantage of each source.
**22.** Name two reasons for the decline in the number of daily newspapers in the United States.
**23.** Explain the impact of the mass media on the public agenda.
**24.** What is the impact of the mass media on electoral politics?
**25.** What factors limit the impact of the mass media on American politics?

## Critical Thinking Skills

**26. Applying the Chapter Skill** Write five questions that you would ask if you were conducting a poll on the significance of mass media in the lives of American voters.

**27. Drawing Inferences** Political scientist V. O. Key, Jr., once described public opinion as those expressions that governments "find it prudent to heed." Do you agree with Key's definition? Explain your answer.

**28. Expressing Problems Clearly** You have read that schools are key agents of political socialization. What are the most important elements of citizenship in American society that you think students ought to learn in school?

**29. Distinguishing False From Accurate Images** In spite of its powerful and important role in American society, television is often criticized for its lack of content on important issues. **(a)** Considering what you have read in this chapter, do you feel that it is accurate to characterize television as lacking in real content? **(b)** If so, what do you think is to blame for the quality of television programming?

## Analyzing Political Cartoons

Using your knowledge of American government and this cartoon, answer the questions below.

The Great American Debate

AM NOT

ARE TOO

**30.** Who are the characters in the cartoon intended to represent?
**31.** What does the cartoon suggest about television coverage of candidate debates?

---

## Participation Activities

**32. Current Events Watch** Choose a current topic, such as the death penalty or prayer in public schools, and find two newspaper reports about it. One should be a factual report, and one should be an editorial. Summarize the main points of each report. Then contrast the language, selection of details, and point of view of the two reports to explain how an editorial differs from a news story.

**33. Time Line Activity** Create a time line showing events in the development of television, newspaper, radio, magazine, and Internet news and information reporting. Include a summary of the trends in the roles of the various media that your time line illustrates.

**34. It's Your Turn** Write a magazine article in which you analyze the impact of political changes brought about by individuals, interest groups, or the media. First, research an event from American history—such as a war, a Court decision, or a new law—that resulted in political change. Identify who pushed for the event and describe how it brought about political change. **(Writing an Article)**

 **Take It to the Net**

**Chapter 8 Self-Test** As a final review activity, take the Chapter 8 Self-Test in the Social Studies area at the Web site listed below, and receive immediate feedback on your answers.

**www.phschool.com**

---

## Critical Thinking Skills

**26.** Questions will vary, but should avoid emotionally charged words and difficult terms, and avoid questions that can shape answers.
**27.** Answers will vary. Students who agree should list the ways in which public opinion can influence policy; those who disagree might point out that public opinion is only one influence on policy, and is checked by other factors.
**28.** Answers will vary, but might suggest fundamental values such as loyalty, civic participation, and personal responsibility.
**29. (a)** Answers will vary, but should be supported with specific examples. **(b)** Students might suggest such factors as stressing entertainment over political content, the prevalence of sound bites, and the influence of advertisers.

## Analyzing Political Cartoons

**30.** Presidential candidates.
**31.** That it reduces debate to simple name-calling.

## You Can Make a Difference

Encourage students to consider all the advantages and disadvantages of each medium before choosing one.

## Participation Activities

**32.** Students' summaries should show an understanding of the difference between an editorial and a news story.
**33.** Time lines should accurately show the development of each medium, and evaluations should take into account the factors discussed in the text.
**34.** Magazine articles should demonstrate an understanding of the power of individuals, the media, or interest groups to effect political change.

---

 **Take It to the Net**

Additional support materials and activities for Chapter 8 of *Magruder's American Government* can be found in the Social Studies area at the Prentice Hall School Web site. **www.phschool.com**

## Point-of-Use Resources

 **Guide to the Essentials of American Government** Chapter 8 Test, page 50 provides multiple-choice questions to test students' knowledge of the chapter.

**Test Bank CD-ROM** Chapter 8 Test

**Chapter Test** Chapter Tests booklet

# Interest Groups

| Section Objectives | Print and Technology Resources |
|---|---|
| **1 The Nature of Interest Groups** *(pp. 236–240)* <br><br> **1.** Describe the role of interest groups in influencing public policy. <br> **2.** Compare and contrast political parties and interest groups. <br> **3.** Explain why people see interest groups as both good and bad for American politics. <br><br> **TEKS 3A, 3B, 16A, 16B, 21A, 21D, 22A, 22B, 23B** | • **Unit 2 booklet** Guided Reading and Review, p. 36; Section 1 Quiz, p. 37 <br> • **Lesson Plans booklet** Section 1, p. 41 <br> • **Political Cartoons booklet** Section 1, p. 33 <br> • **Block Scheduling with Lesson Strategies booklet** p. 23 <br> • **Section Reading Support Transparencies** <br> • **Close Up on Primary Sources booklet** *Democracy in America,* p. 59 <br> • **Government Assessment Rubrics booklet** p. 12 <br> • **Basic Principles of the Constitution Transparencies** 13, 45 <br> • **Section Support Transparencies** 36, 135 <br> • **Presentation Pro CD-ROM** Section 1 <br> • **Social Studies Skills Tutor CD-ROM** |
| **2 Types of Interest Groups** *(pp. 242–247)* <br><br> **1.** Explain how the American tradition of joining organizations has resulted in a wide range of interest groups. <br> **2.** Describe four categories of groups based on economic interests. <br> **3.** Outline the reasons why other interest groups have been created. <br> **4.** Identify the purpose of public-interest groups. <br><br> **TEKS 3A, 3B, 16B, 17A, 21A, 21E, 22A, 22B, 22D, 23A** | • **Unit 2 booklet** Guided Reading and Review, p. 38; Section 2 Quiz, p. 39 <br> • **Lesson Plans booklet** Section 2, p. 42 <br> • **Political Cartoons booklet** Section 2, p. 34 <br> • **Block Scheduling with Lesson Strategies booklet** p. 23 <br> • **Close Up on Primary Sources booklet** Native American Interests, p. 11; Organizing Farm Workers, p. 48 <br> • **Section Reading Support Transparencies** <br> • **Close Up on Participation booklet** Helping the Homeless, pp. 14–15 <br> • **The Living Constitution booklet** p. 4 <br> • **Government Assessment Rubrics booklet** p. 26 <br> • **Section Support Transparencies** 37, 136 <br> • **Presentation Pro CD-ROM** Section 2 <br> • **Simulations and Data Graphing CD-ROM** |
| **3 Interest Groups at Work** *(pp. 249–254)* <br><br> **1.** Explain interest groups' three major goals in influencing public opinion. <br> **2.** Describe how interest groups use propaganda to persuade people to their point of view. <br> **3.** Give examples of the processes used by interest groups to affect public policy. <br><br> **TEKS 3A, 3B, 16A, 17C, 21A, 21B, 21C, 21D, 21E, 22A, 22B, 22C, 22D** | • **Unit 2 booklet** Guided Reading and Review, p. 40; Section 3 Quiz, p. 41; Skills for Life Activity, p. 42 <br> • **Lesson Plans booklet** Section 3, p. 43 <br> • **Political Cartoons booklet** Section 3, p. 35 <br> • **Section Reading Support Transparencies** <br> • **Close Up on the Supreme Court booklet** *Flast* v. *Cohen,* p. 10 <br> • **The Basic Principles of the Constitution Posters** <br> • **Section Support Transparencies** 38, 137 <br> • **Presentation Pro CD-ROM** Section 3 |

# Block Scheduling Strategies

The *Magruder's American Government* program addresses block-scheduling strategies in a variety of ways. For easy reference, side-column activities that fit a block format are marked  **Block Strategy.** Each section also contains a **Block Scheduling Strategies** box describing at least two block-format activities that address and extend core content from the section. The **Block Scheduling with Lesson Strategies booklet** found in the Teaching Resources contains additional block-scheduling activities for each chapter.

## Take It to the Net

Visit the Social Studies area at the Prentice Hall School Web site. Once there, you can find additional links, current events connections, and activities to enrich chapter content for *Magruder's American Government,* as well as a Self-Test for students. Be sure to check out this month's **eTeach** online discussion with a Master Teacher.

### www.phschool.com

## Pressed for Time?

If you are running short on time to cover this chapter, consider one of the following options:
- Use the **Presentation Pro CD-ROM** to create an outline for this chapter.
- Use one of the **Pressed for Time** activities found on p. 235.
- Use the Section Summaries for Chapter 9, from **Guide to the Essentials of American Government (English and Spanish).**

## Video Connections

Prentice Hall offers two video programs to reinforce and extend chapter content. Show students *The Blessings of Liberty* from the **ABC News Civics and Government Videotape Library** and *Prayer in Schools: A Nationwide Debate* from the **Magruder's American Government Video Collection.**

## Assessment Options
- Section Quizzes, **Unit 2 booklet,** pp. 37, 39, 41
- Chapter 9 Assessment, pp. 256–257
- **Guide to the Essentials of American Government,** Chapter 9 Test, p. 54

## Core Assessment
Chapter 9 Test, Chapter Tests booklet
ExamView® Test Bank CD-ROM Chapter 9
Government Assessment Rubrics

## Standardized Test Preparation
### Diagnose and Prescribe
Diagnostic Tests for High School
Social Studies Skills

### Review and Reteach
Review Book for Government

### Practice and Assess
Test-Taking Strategies With
   Transparencies for High School
Test Prep Book for Government

# Interest Groups

## Introducing the Chapter

In this chapter, students will learn about interest groups—the many private organizations that seek to influence the shaping of American public policy.

### Make It Relevant

#### ★ You Can Make a Difference

The SAFE in SAFE Students stands for "Sane Alternatives to the Firearms Epidemic," an interest group that supports gun control. NRA stands for the National Rifle Association, which promotes the right to gun ownership. Point out that these organizations represent just two of the hundreds of interest groups in this country. Then direct a committee of students to consult each group's Web site (www.safestudents.org and www.nra.org) and evaluate SAFE Students and the NRA. They should compare and contrast each group's purposes and activities and make a presentation to the class.

## CONSTITUTIONAL PRINCIPLES

Emphasize the following basic principles as students read Chapter 9. Have the class respond to the questions, and then ask volunteers to explain which principle they think a new interest group might take as its founding philosophy, and why.

**Popular Sovereignty** Interest groups are groups of people with specific shared interests. How can such groups be seen as reflecting popular sovereignty?

**Limited Government** How do interest groups provide Americans with ways to influence and check government policy?

**Federalism** In what ways do interest groups balance national and local concerns and agendas?

# Interest Groups

*"We are a nation of communities, of tens and tens of thousands of ethnic, religious, social, business, labor union, neighborhood, regional and other organizations, all of them varied, voluntary, and unique. . . ."*
—George H.W. Bush (1988)

Do you think that interest groups represent only people with money, power, and influence? On the contrary, many interest groups serve as the voice of ordinary people who care passionately about a cause or policy. They represent the diversity of Americans and their opinions about issues.

◆ Minnesota farmers' protest

## CLOSE UP FOUNDATION *Corner*

The following resources are available only from the Close Up Foundation to support the concepts discussed in Chapter 9 "Interest Groups":

◆ *Perspectives: Readings on Contemporary American Government*
◆ *Trade is Everybody's Business*
◆ *Current Issues: Critical Policy Choices Facing the Nation and the World*

To keep up-to-date on Close Up news and activities, visit Close Up Online at

**www.closeup.org**

Close Up Foundation
44 Canal Center Plaza
Alexandria, VA 22314-1592
800-765-3131

## ★ You Can Make a Difference

**IN THE LATE 1990s,** gun violence became a serious issue for schools. In response, Ben Gelt and David Winkler, recent Denver high school graduates, postponed their college plans to start SAFE Students, a national youth movement. In July 1999, they led a group of 95 Colorado students to Washington to lobby Congress for gun control laws. The group's goal is to teach members "how to become involved in the political process, and that their voices do matter." SAFE Students works to educate students about the gun debate, organize local groups across the country, and lobby at the national party conventions.

### SECTION 1

## The Nature of Interest Groups (pp. 236–240)

★ Interest groups are private organizations that try to persuade public officials to respond to the shared attitudes of their members.
★ Unlike political parties, interest groups do not nominate candidates, focus on winning elections, or concern themselves with a broad range of issues.
★ Among their positive benefits, interest groups stimulate interest in public affairs and serve as a vehicle for participation in the political process.
★ Interest groups have been criticized for having influence disproportionate to their size and occasionally using unethical tactics.

### SECTION 2

## Types of Interest Groups (pp. 242–247)

★ Most people belong to several organizations that meet the definition of an interest group.
★ Most interest groups represent economic interests such as business, labor, agriculture, and certain professions.
★ Some interest groups are devoted to specific political and social causes, religious interests, or the welfare of a certain segment of the population.
★ Public-interest groups work for some aspect of the public good.

### SECTION 3

## Interest Groups at Work (pp. 249–254)

★ Interest groups supply the public with information favorable to the group's cause, work to build a positive image for the group, and promote the group's policies.
★ Interest groups frequently use propaganda to achieve their goals.
★ While most interest groups take a balanced approach to affecting public policy, single-interest groups focus on an individual issue and fight for this issue aggressively.
★ Lobbyists use a variety of techniques to try to persuade policy makers to share an interest group's point of view.

### Keep It Current

Items marked with this logo are periodically updated on the Internet. Keep up-to-date with what's happening in the news. To get current information on interest groups, go to **www.phschool.com**

### To Omit the Chapter

If you wish to skip Chapter 9, ask students to read the Chapter in Brief and assign the Guide to the Essentials before continuing to another chapter. You may also want to assign the Chapter 9 Test in the Chapter Test booklet. Then specific portions of Chapter 9 may be assigned to students needing reinforcement of key terms and concepts.

### To Preview the Chapter

To introduce students to key terms and concepts in each section, have them read the Chapter in Brief. You may also assign the Reading Strategy activities on pp. 237, 243, and 250 of this book.

### To Review the Chapter

When students have completed Chapter 9, you might want to assign the Guide to the Essentials or the Guided Reading and Review worksheets on pp. 36, 38, and 40 of the Unit 2 booklet.

### To Cover the Chapter Quickly

To cover the material in Chapter 9 quickly, use the following activity.

**Focus** Ask students to name any interest groups that they can. You might get them started by naming certain topics that might spark a group's name for students, such as religion, health care, or the debate over gun control. List any names that students offer on the chalkboard.

**Instruct** Explain the different kinds of interest groups—business and economic, professional, those relating to certain causes, public interest, etc. Then ask volunteers to identify the type of interest group for each of the names on the chalkboard.

**Close/Reteach** Lead a discussion on the techniques different interest groups use. Ask students which technique they think is most useful, or most likely to garner support.

▣ **Block Strategy (Average)**

## Keep It Current

### Internet Update

Use the Prentice Hall School Web site and the Keep It Current CD-ROM to find quick content updates.

Visit **www.phschool.com** for current events articles that are linked to Chapter 9. Critical Thinking questions are included.

**Keep It Current CD-ROM** includes government-related projects by unit. Students complete each project using current information that they obtain by linking to the Prentice Hall School Web site from the CD-ROM.

·1· # The Nature of Interest Groups

## Objectives
You may wish to call students' attention to the objectives in the Section Preview. The objectives are reflected in the main headings of the section.

## Bellringer
Have students suppose that they and their friends want a drinking fountain in the local park. Discuss whether it would be better for one of them to approach a public official to demand a fountain or for all of them to do so. Explain that in this section, they will learn about groups of people who band together to get what they want.

## Vocabulary Builder
Point out the terms in the Political Dictionary. Ask students to try to link the meanings of the terms by using them all in the same sentence.

## Pressed for Time?

### Quick Lesson Plan

**1. Focus** Tell students that interest groups play a role in the creation and content of laws and other public policies. Ask students to discuss what they know about criticisms of interest groups.

**2. Instruct** Ask students to explain the difference between interest groups and political parties. As part of the discussion, have students define interest groups and examine their good and bad points.

**3. Close/Reteach** Remind students that interest groups seek to influence public policy in various ways. Ask students to write a set of debating points on both sides of the issue of whether interest groups are good or bad.

## Point-of-Use Resources

📁 **Block Scheduling with Lesson Strategies** Activities for Chapter 9 are presented on p. 23.

---

## Section Preview

### OBJECTIVES

1. **Describe** the role of interest groups in influencing public policy.
2. **Compare and Contrast** political parties and interest groups.
3. **Explain** why people see interest groups as both good and bad for American politics.

### WHY IT MATTERS

If you have ever joined with others who share your views on an issue, you have probably been part of an interest group. You almost surely will be part of one or more interest groups in the future. Interest groups provide an important way for Americans to influence government policies.

### POLITICAL DICTIONARY

★ public policy
★ public affairs

---

An interest group is a private organization that tries to persuade public officials to respond to the shared attitudes of its members. You may not think that you belong to any interest groups, but as you read this section, you may well discover that you do. In fact, you might even belong to several of them. You will probably also realize that you will become a part of many more of these organizations in the years to come. This is because interest groups provide one of the most effective means by which Americans try to get government to respond to their wants and needs.

## The Role of Interest Groups

Where do you stand on the question of gun control? What about prayer in public schools? Abortion? An increase in the minimum wage? What can you do to lend support to your views on these and other issues? How can you increase the chance that your position on these issues will carry the day?

Joining with others who share your views is both practical and democratic. Organized efforts to protect group interests are a fundamental part of the democratic process. Moreover, the right to do so is protected by the Constitution. Remember that the 1st Amendment guarantees "the right of the people peaceably to assemble, and to petition the Government for a redress of grievances."

Interest groups are sometimes called pressure groups. They are also known as special interests, organized interests, and lobbies. They give themselves a variety of additional names, too, such as committees, clubs, associations, leagues, and federations.

However they label themselves, interest groups seek to influence public policy. Used in this general sense, **public policy** includes all of the goals a government sets and the various courses of action it pursues as it attempts to realize these goals. Laws governing speed limits and seat-belt

▲ Interest groups often send members items such as buttons and bumper stickers to help publicize their causes.

---

## 🔲 Block Scheduling Strategies

Consider these suggestions to manage extended class time:

■ Present students with the following debate question: Are interest groups useful, or are they detrimental to a democratic society? Have students reread the section, taking notes that relate to both sides of the debate. Then divide the class into two groups to carry out the debate. Encourage students to use examples of current interest groups in the media to support their arguments.

■ Divide students into several small groups. Ask students in each group to poll each other on their interests, and then select one that most group members share. Have them also choose a concern that they want specific government action on. Then have them form an interest group based on their interest and concern. Have groups give "press conferences," in which they deliver prepared philosophy statements and group goals. One group should act as journalists, and pose questions to the interest groups.

▲ Americans participate in a wide variety of interest groups. Families USA advocates for family health care (left). The Gray Panthers call attention to the special concerns of senior citizens (center). Students from the Texas School for the Deaf acted as members of an interest group when they marched on their State capital to protest funding cuts that affected their school (right). *Critical Thinking* **What do these groups have in common?**

## Reading Strategy
### Drawing Inferences

Tell students that interest groups have been widely criticized. Ask students to consider, as they read, whether the American political system would be better off without interest groups. Have them explain their reasoning.

## Point–of–Use Resources

📁 **Guided Reading and Review** Unit 2 booklet, p. 36 provides students with practice identifying the main ideas and key terms of this section.

📁 **Lesson Plans** For lesson planning suggestions, see p. 41 of the Lesson Plans booklet.

📁 **Political Cartoons** See p. 33 of the Political Cartoons booklet for a cartoon relevant to this section.

📖 **Section Support Transparencies** Transparency 36, *Visual Learning*; Transparency 135, *Political Cartoon*

use are examples of public policy. So is a President's decision to send military aid to a foreign country.

Because interest groups exist to shape public policy, they operate wherever those policies are made or can be influenced. They also function at every level of government. They therefore can be found on Capitol Hill and elsewhere in Washington, D.C., in every one of the 50 State capitals, in thousands of city halls and county courthouses, and in many other places at the local level all across the country. In short, as diplomat and historian Lord Bryce put it somewhat indelicately more than a century ago: "Where the body is, there will the vultures be gathered."

Remember, our society is a pluralistic one. It is not dominated by any single elite. It is, instead, composed of a number of distinct cultures and groups. Increasingly, the members of various ethnic, racial, religious, and other groups compete for and share in the exercise of political power in this country.

## Political Parties and Interest Groups

Interest groups are made up of people who unite for some political purpose. So, too, are political parties. These two types of political organizations

necessarily overlap in a number of ways. However, they differ from one another in three striking respects: (1) in the making of nominations, (2) in their primary focus, and (3) in the scope of their interests.

First, parties nominate candidates for public office; interest groups do not. Remember, making nominations is a major function of political parties. If an interest group were to nominate candidates, it would, in effect, become a political party.

Interest groups do, of course, try to affect the outcomes of primaries and other nominating contests. However, interest groups do not themselves pick candidates who then run under their labels. It may be widely known that a particular interest group actively supports a candidate, but that candidate seeks votes as a Republican or Democrat.[1]

Second, political parties are chiefly interested in winning elections and controlling government. Interest groups are chiefly concerned with controlling or influencing the *policies* of government. Unlike parties, interest groups do not face the problems involved in trying to appeal to the largest possible number of people. In short, political parties are mostly interested in the *who,*

---

[1]Note that this discussion centers on the differences between interest groups and major parties. There are some striking parallels between interest groups and most minor parties—for example, in terms of their scope of interest.

### Organizing Information

To make sure students understand the main points of this section, you may wish to use the Venn diagram graphic organizer to the right.

Tell students that a Venn diagram compares two groups by showing features they have independently and features they have in common. Have students use it to compare interest groups with political parties.

**Teaching Tip** A template for this graphic organizer can be found in the Section Support Transparencies, Transparency 6.

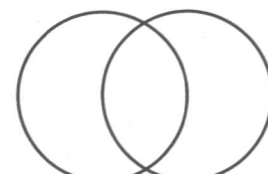

### Answer to . . .
**Critical Thinking** They are all trying to raise public awareness of issues that are important to them.

**237**

# UNIT 3

## The Legislative Branch

### Introducing the Unit

Unit 3 introduces students to both Congress as it was conceived over 200 years ago and Congress as it operates today. Chapter 10 explores the function of Congress as the national legislature, the structure of each house, and congressional membership. Chapter 11 analyzes the scope of the expressed, implied, and nonlegislative powers of Congress. Chapter 12 shows Congress in action: How it is organized, the role of committees, and how it turns bills into laws that affect everyone in the United States.

### Focus Activity

Concentrate students' attention on the United States Congress by writing the following quotation on the board:

*"Though the President is Commander in Chief, Congress is his commander. . . . this is not a Government of kings. . ., but a Government of the people, and. . .Congress is the people."*
—U.S. Representative Thaddeus Stevens (1867)

Have students consider the following after they have read the quotation.

◆ What does "Congress is the people" mean?
◆ Do you agree with this statement? Why or why not?
◆ Use these questions as springboards to a general class discussion about students' views of the United States Congress.

## IN THIS UNIT

★ **CHAPTER 10** *Congress*

★ **CHAPTER 11** *Powers of Congress*

★ **CHAPTER 12** *Congress in Action*

◆ The Capitol, Washington, D.C.

**CLOSE UP** *Corner*

The following Close Up features appear in this unit.
*Close Up on the Supreme Court* may be found on the following pages of this unit: 285, 315, 347
*Close Up on Primary Sources* may be found on the following pages of this unit: 274, 309, 328

**CLOSE UP** | **Online**

To keep up-to-date on Close Up news and activities, visit Close Up Online at

**www.closeup.org**

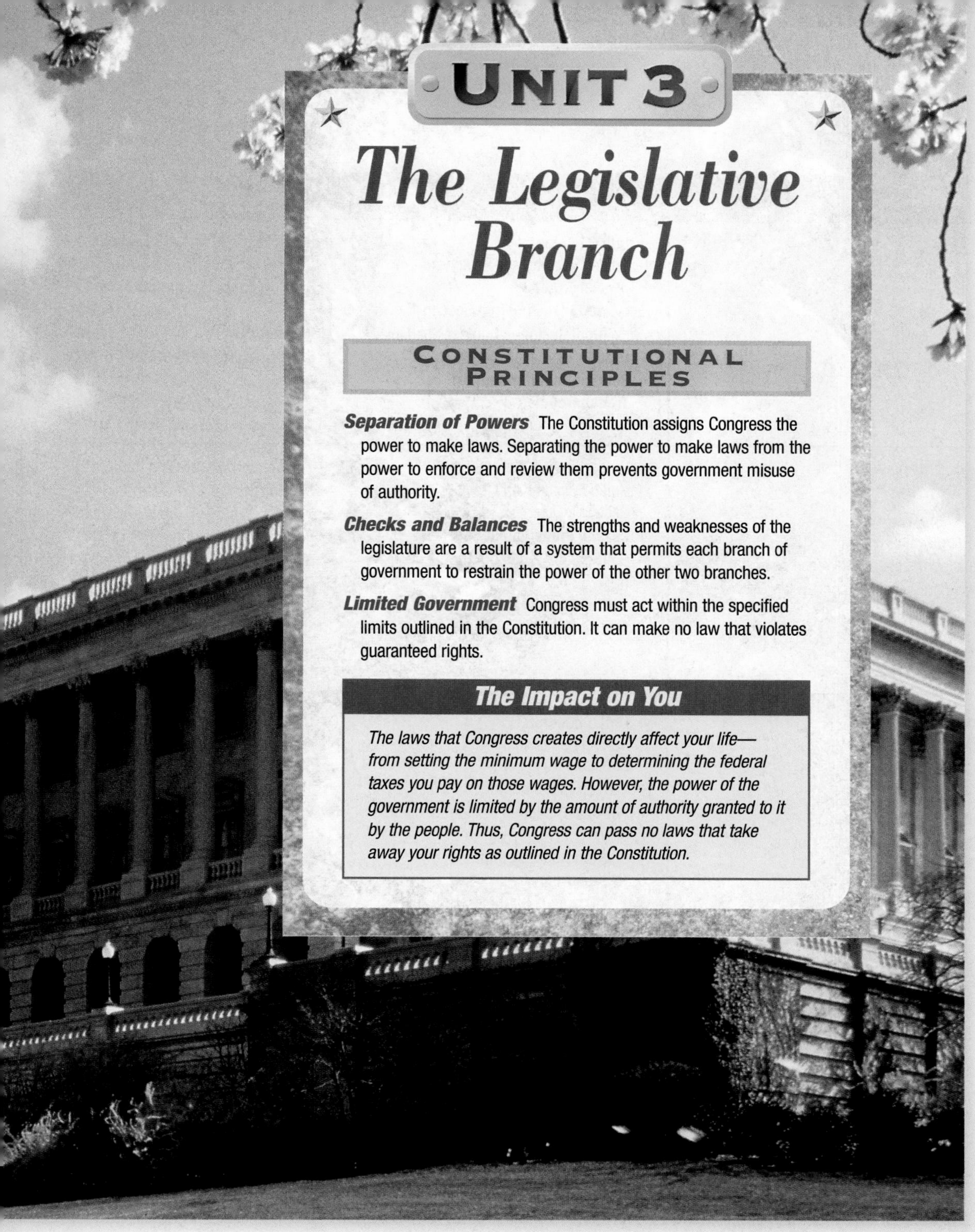

# UNIT 3

# The Legislative Branch

## Constitutional Principles

***Separation of Powers*** The Constitution assigns Congress the power to make laws. Separating the power to make laws from the power to enforce and review them prevents government misuse of authority.

***Checks and Balances*** The strengths and weaknesses of the legislature are a result of a system that permits each branch of government to restrain the power of the other two branches.

***Limited Government*** Congress must act within the specified limits outlined in the Constitution. It can make no law that violates guaranteed rights.

### The Impact on You

*The laws that Congress creates directly affect your life—from setting the minimum wage to determining the federal taxes you pay on those wages. However, the power of the government is limited by the amount of authority granted to it by the people. Thus, Congress can pass no laws that take away your rights as outlined in the Constitution.*

## Pressed for Time?

### Instruction Plus!

The resources you need to support your instruction of this chapter are conveniently located in a single box. This innovative package provides an instructional advantage in the classroom with its ready-to-use tools in a variety of formats.

- **Magruder's American Government Video Collection**
- **Keep It Current Web-based Activities Presentation Pro CD-ROM**
- **Section Support Transparencies**
- **Guide to the Essentials Current Issues**

## Spotlight on Technology

**Take it to the Net**
Offers student-appropriate Internet activities and links that extend core content. Visit us at the Social Studies area. **www.phschool.com**
Be sure to check out this month's **eTeach** online discussion with a Master Government Teacher.

**Keep It Current CD-ROM**
Includes government-related projects by unit. Use it to link to the Prentice Hall School Web site where you will find daily updates.

**Magruder's American Government Video Collection**
Chapter-by-chapter video selections bring key government concepts to life.

**ABC News Civics and Government Videotape Library**
These high-interest stories from ABC News relate to core content.

**Simulations and Data Graphing CD-ROM** Provides interactive federal budget and stock market simulations, and skills practice with statistical data.

**Prentice Hall Presentation Pro CD-ROM** Provides multimedia lecture notes for each chapter.

**ExamView® Test Bank CD-ROM**
Allows you to create, edit, and print out chapter level tests.

**Resource Pro® CD-ROM**
Teaching Resources that offer lesson planning flexibility, test-generation capability, and resource manageability.

**Social Studies Skills Tutor CD-ROM** Provides interactive practice in geographic literacy, critical thinking and reading, visual analysis, and communications.

**Section Support Transparencies**
Illustrates key government concepts through graphs, charts, photos, and cartoons.

**Basic Principles of the Constitution Transparencies**
Illustrates key principles of the Constitution.

**Section Reading Support Transparency System**
Delivers the main idea of each section in the student text through graphic organizers.

# Congress

| Section Objectives | Print and Technology Resources | |
|---|---|---|
| **1 The National Legislature** (pp. 262–265) | • **Unit 3 booklet** Guided Reading and Review, p. 2 Section 1 Quiz, p. 3 | • **Block Scheduling with Lesson Strategies booklet** p. 24 |
| 1. Analyze the bicameral structure of Congress. 2. Describe a term of Congress. 3. Identify how sessions of Congress have changed over time. | • **Lesson Plans booklet** Section 1, p. 44 • **Political Cartoons booklet** Section 1, p. 36 | • **Section Support Transparencies** 39, 138 • **Presentation Pro CD-ROM** Section 1 |
| **TEKS 2B, 8D, 9A, 21A, 21E, 22A, 22B** | • **Section Reading Support Transparencies** | • **Social Studies Skills Tutor CD-ROM** |
| **2 The House of Representatives** (pp. 267–273) | • **Unit 3 booklet** Guided Reading and Review, p. 4 Section 2 Quiz, p. 5 | • **The Living Constitution booklet** p. 8 • **Section Support Transparencies** 40, 139 |
| 1. Describe the size and terms of the House of Representatives. 2. Explain how House seats are reapportioned among the states after each census. 3. Describe a typical congressional election and congressional district. 4. Analyze the formal and informal qualifications for serving in the House. | • **Lesson Plans booklet** Section 2, p. 45 • **Political Cartoons booklet** Section 2, p. 37 • **Section Reading Support Transparencies** | • **Presentation Pro CD-ROM** Section 2 • **Simulations and Data Graphing CD-ROM** |
| **TEKS 9A, 17C, 21A, 21C, 21D, 21E, 22A, 22B** | | |
| **3 The Senate** (pp. 275–278) | • **Unit 3 booklet** Guided Reading and Review, p. 6 Section 3 Quiz, p. 7 | • **Close Up on Primary Sources booklet** What Is a Gerrymander?, p. 12 • **Section Support Transparencies** 41, 140 |
| 1. Compare the size of the Senate to the size of the House of Representatives. 2. Describe how States have elected Senators in the past and present. 3. Explain how and why a senator's term differs from a representative's term. 4. Identify the qualifications for serving in the Senate. | • **Lesson Plans booklet** Section 3, p. 46 • **Political Cartoons booklet** Section 3, p. 38 • **Section Reading Support Transparencies** | • **Presentation Pro CD-ROM** Section 3 |
| **TEKS 9A, 21A, 21D, 21E, 22A, 22B** | | |
| **4 The Members of Congress** (pp. 279–284) | • **Unit 3 booklet** Guided Reading and Review, p. 8 Section 4 Quiz, p. 9 Skills for Life Activity, p. 10 | • **Close Up on the Supreme Court booklet** *Hutchinson* v. *Proxmire*, p. 11 • **Government Assessment Rubrics booklet** p. 26 |
| 1. Compare and evaluate characteristics of the current members of Congress. 2. Compare and contrast the duties of the job of serving in Congress. 3. Describe the compensation and privileges given to members of Congress. | • **Lesson Plans booklet** Section 4, p. 47 • **Political Cartoons booklet** Section 4, p. 39 • **Block Scheduling with Lesson Strategies booklet** p. 24 • **Section Reading Support Transparencies** | • **The Basic Principles of the Constitution Posters** • **Section Support Transparencies** 42, 141 • **Presentation Pro CD-ROM** Section 4 |
| **TEKS 8D, 9A, 17C, 21A, 21C, 21D, 21E, 21F, 22A, 22B** | | |

# Block Scheduling Strategies

The *Magruder's American Government* program addresses block-scheduling strategies in a variety of ways. For easy reference, side-column activities that fit a block format are marked ▣ **Block Strategy.** Each section also contains a **Block Scheduling Strategies** box describing at least two block-format activities that address and extend core content from the section. The **Block Scheduling with Lesson Strategies booklet** found in the Teaching Resources contains additional block-scheduling activities for each chapter.

## Take It to the Net

Visit the Social Studies area at the Prentice Hall School Web site. Once there, you can find additional links, current events connections, and activities to enrich chapter content for *Magruder's American Government,* as well as a Self-Test for students. Be sure to check out this month's **eTeach** online discussion with a Master Teacher.

### www.phschool.com

## Pressed for Time?

If you are running short on time to cover this chapter, consider one of the following options:

- Use the **Presentation Pro CD-ROM** to create an outline for this chapter.
- Use one of the **Pressed for Time** activities found on p. 261.
- Use the Section Summaries for Chapter 10, from **Guide to the Essentials of American Government (English and Spanish).**

 ## Video Connections

Prentice Hall offers two video programs to reinforce and extend chapter content. Show students *The Blessings of Liberty* from the **ABC News Civics and Government Videotape Library** and *Prayer in Schools: A Nationwide Debate* from the **Magruder's American Government Video Collection.**

## Assessment Options

- Section Quizzes, **Unit 3 booklet,** pp. 3, 5, 7, 9
- Chapter 10 Assessment, pp. 286–287
- **Guide to the Essentials of American Government,** Chapter 10 Test, p. 59

### Core Assessment

Chapter 10 Test, Chapter Tests booklet
ExamView® Test Bank CD-ROM Chapter 10
Government Assessment Rubrics

### Standardized Test Preparation

#### Diagnose and Prescribe
Diagnostic Tests for High School
Social Studies Skills

#### Review and Reteach
Review Book for Government

#### Practice and Assess
Test-Taking Strategies With
Transparencies for High School
Test Prep Book for Government

# Chapter 10 Teacher's Edition Index

# Congress

## Introducing the Chapter

In this chapter, students will learn about the structure and functions of the two houses of Congress, as well as the backgrounds and roles of the members of Congress.

### Make It Relevant

#### ★ You Can Make a Difference

Many State and even local legislative bodies operate page programs that are quite similar to the one in the national Congress. Organize groups of students to investigate paging opportunities in your community and in your State. Students should summarize their findings in concise reports that answer these questions: *Who* sponsors the page program? *What* are a page's duties? *Where* does the page serve? *When* are the application deadlines? *Why* does the page program exist? Encourage interested students to apply to serve as pages.

**Service Learning**

## CONSTITUTIONAL PRINCIPLES

Emphasize the following basic principles as students read Chapter 10. Have the class respond to the questions, and then ask volunteers to explain which single principle they most closely associate with Congress, and why.

**Separation of Powers** What segment of the Constitution delegates legislative powers to Congress? Does the President have any powers relating to sessions of Congress?

**Judicial Review** How have the courts limited the power of the House of Representatives to create congressional districts?

**Federalism** In what way does the creation of congressional districts reflect the federal nature of the U.S. Government?

# Congress

*"Any one who is unfamiliar with what Congress actually does and how it does it, with all its duties and all its occupations, . . . is very far from a knowledge of the constitutional system under which we live."*

—Woodrow Wilson (1885)

Wilson saw Congress, the legislative branch, as the most basic part of a democratic, constitutional government. The men and women elected to the House and Senate give the people a voice in setting public policy and making laws.

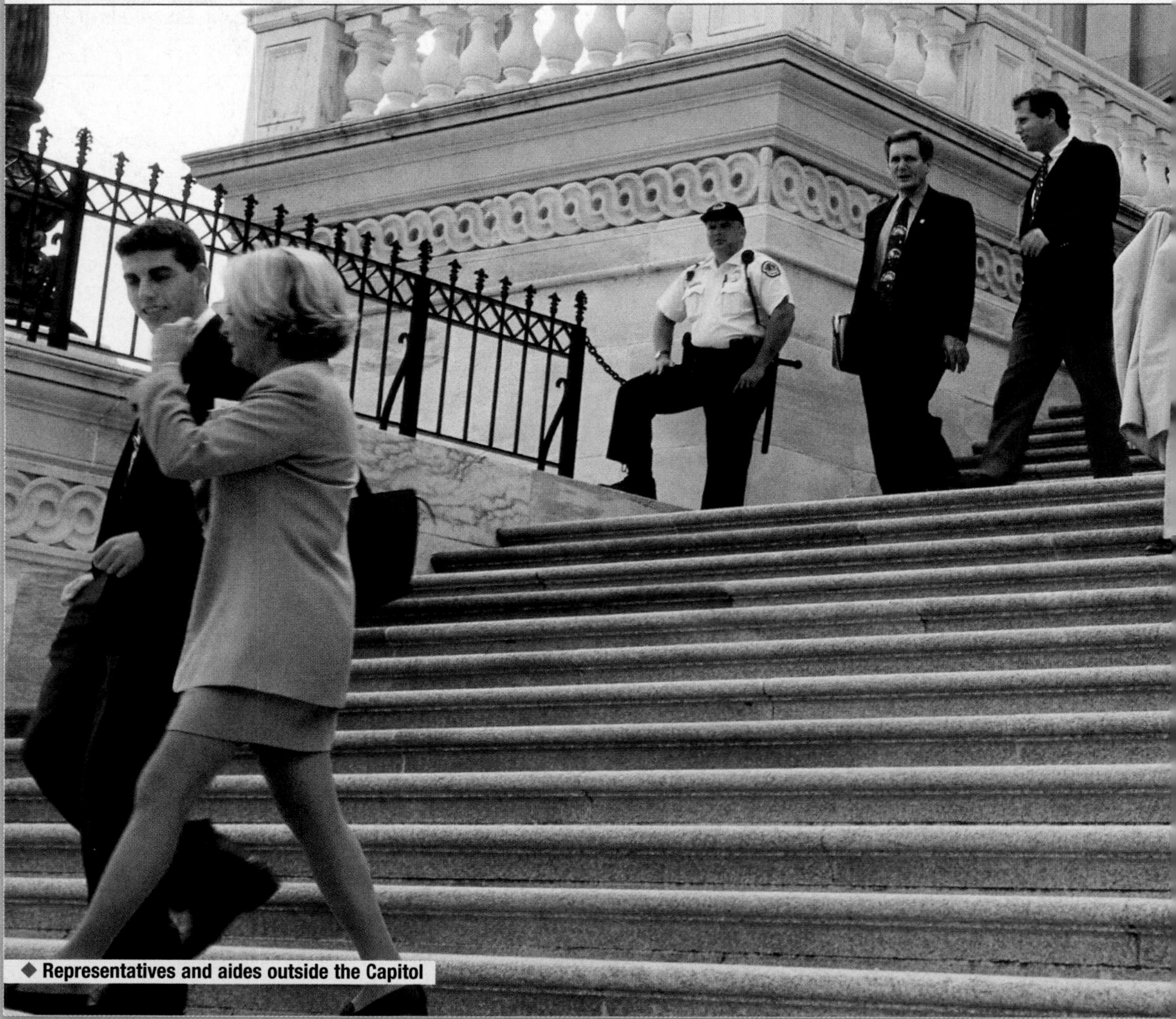

◆ **Representatives and aides outside the Capitol**

 **Corner**

The following resources are available only from the Close Up Foundation to support the concepts discussed in Chapter 10 "Congress":

◆ *Perspectives: Readings on Contemporary American Government*
◆ *U.S. Response: The Making of U.S. Foreign Policy*
◆ *The Active Citizenship Today Field Guide for Students*

 Online

To keep up-to-date on Close Up news and activities, visit Close Up Online at

**www.closeup.org**

Close Up Foundation
44 Canal Center Plaza
Alexandria, VA 22314-1592
800-765-3131

# Chapter 10 in Brief

## You Can Make a Difference

★

**PROBABLY THE BEST** way to learn about the day-to-day work of Congress is to be part of it. High school students who serve as congressional pages do just that—they carry messages between members of Congress and help staff members with office tasks. In 1971, Paulette Desell, a 16-year-old from Alexandria, Virginia, became the first female page. She was chosen by New York Senator Jacob Javits. In applying to be a page, Paulette wrote: "To have a thorough understanding of how the government operates is the best aid in encouraging young minds to want to learn."

### Keep It Current

Items marked with this logo are periodically updated on the Internet. Keep up-to-date with what's in the news. To get current information on Congress, go to **www.phschool.com**

## SECTION 1

### The National Legislature (pp. 262–265)

★ Congress is bicameral, or divided into two houses.
★ Each State has two members in the Senate.
★ In the House of Representatives, States are represented according to population.
★ Congress meets for two-year terms, divided into two one-year sessions.

## SECTION 2

### The House of Representatives (pp. 267–273)

★ Each member of the House of Representatives represents a district of roughly equal population and is up for reelection every two years.
★ Every ten years, following the census, seats in the House are redistributed among the States, and districts are redrawn to reflect changes in population.
★ Politicians frequently "gerrymander" districts into odd shapes to gain a political advantage.

## SECTION 3

### The Senate (pp. 275–278)

★ The Senate includes 100 members, two from each State, who are elected to six-year terms.
★ Senators usually have more experience, power, and prestige than their colleagues in the House.
★ Senators are protected from some political pressures because they serve for a long period between elections.

## SECTION 4

### The Members of Congress (pp. 279–284)

★ Members of Congress are likely to be older and wealthier than the average American, and most members are men.
★ Members bring a variety of viewpoints and career backgrounds to Congress.
★ Members of Congress juggle a number of roles by working as lawmakers, party members, and servants of the voters.
★ Congress sets its own pay and other compensations—and that fact poses peculiar problems for its members.

### Keep It Current

## Internet Update

Use the Prentice Hall School Web site and the Keep It Current CD-ROM to find quick content updates.

Visit **www.phschool.com** for current events articles that are linked to Chapter 10. Critical Thinking questions are included.

**Keep It Current CD-ROM** includes government-related projects by unit. Students complete each project using current information that they obtain by linking to the Prentice Hall School Web site from the CD-ROM.

## Objectives
You may wish to call students' attention to the objectives in the Section Preview. The objectives are reflected in the main headings of the section.

**Bellringer** Ask students to suppose that they have been chosen to design a huge mural for a wall in the middle of their town. Elicit design ideas. Then discuss how the mural design might change if their parents could check it and make changes to it. Explain that in this section, they will learn how the two houses of Congress act as a check on each other.

**Vocabulary Builder** Ask students the meaning of *adjourn*, and have them guess which word in the Political Dictionary is a synonym for *adjourn*. Then have students compare the meanings of the words *term, session,* and *special session.*

### Pressed for Time?

#### Quick Lesson Plan

**1. Focus** Tell students that the structure of Congress is designed to ensure that all States and the people who live in them are represented fairly. Ask students to discuss what they know about how Congress is structured.

**2. Instruct** Ask students how the States are represented differently in the House and Senate. Discuss why this structure is advantageous. Then have students compare the terms and sessions of the two houses.

**3. Close/Reteach** Remind students of the basic function of Congress—translating public will into public policy—and how the structure of Congress contributes to that function. Then have students list the three reasons for having a bicameral legislature, and provide two details for each.

### Point-of-Use Resources

📁 **Block Scheduling with Lesson Strategies** Activities for Chapter 10 are presented on p. 24.

---

# 1 The National Legislature

## Section Preview

### OBJECTIVES
1. **Analyze** the bicameral structure of Congress.
2. **Describe** a term of Congress.
3. **Summarize** how sessions of Congress have changed over time.

### WHY IT MATTERS
The Framers of the Constitution created a Congress with two bodies: a small Senate and a much larger House of Representatives. Each Congress since 1789 has met for a term of two years; those terms are now divided into two one-year sessions.

### POLITICAL DICTIONARY
★ **term**
★ **session**
★ **adjourn**
★ **prorogue**
★ **special session**

---

**Y**ou know that you live in a democracy, and in a democracy, the people rule. But what does that really mean? You are one of "the people," but you do not rule, at least not in the hands-on sense. You do not make laws, collect taxes, arrest criminals, or decide court cases.

You do not do those or all of the other things that government does because you live in a *representative* democracy. Here, it is the representatives of the people who are responsible for the day-to-day work of government.

Congress stands as a leading example of that fact. It is the legislative branch of the National Government. Congress, then, is charged with the most basic governmental function in a democratic society—that of translating the public will into public policy in the form of law.

James Madison called Congress "the first branch" of the National Government. Just how profoundly important he and the other Framers thought Congress to be can be seen in this fact: the very first and longest of the articles of the Constitution is devoted to it.

> **FROM THE Constitution** *All legislative Powers herein granted shall be vested in a Congress of the United States, which shall consist of a Senate and House of Representatives.*
> —Article I, Section 1, Clause 1

## A Bicameral Congress

As you have just read, the Constitution immediately establishes a bicameral legislature—that is, one made up of two houses. It does so for historical, practical, and theoretical reasons.

1. **Historical** The British Parliament had consisted of two houses since the 1300s. The Framers and most other Americans knew the British system of bicameralism quite well. Most of the colonial assemblies and, in 1787, all but two of the new State legislatures were also bicameral. Among the original thirteen colonies, only

▲ *Party Leaders* In the Senate, the two parties are led by Senator Tom Daschle (D., South Dakota) (left) and Senator Trent Lott (R., Mississippi) (right).

---

### 🖥 Block Scheduling Strategies

Consider these suggestions to manage extended class time:

■ Have students read about the reasons for having two houses of Congress. Then organize the class into groups of three with one student representing each of the following categories of arguments: historical, practical, and theoretical. Have students use the text and other resources to create a fact summary sheet on their assigned subject. Compile the information from each group into a class fact sheet.

■ Discuss the terms and sessions of Congress with the class. Then ask students to research the activities of their current congressional representatives during the most recent term. Have students identify at least one piece of legislation that each of their representatives has been involved with, describe their representatives' actions regarding the legislation, and state whether they agree with each of these actions. Links to Internet sites with congressional information are provided at **www.phschool.com**

Georgia and Pennsylvania had unicameral colonial and then State legislatures. Georgia's legislature became bicameral in 1789 and Pennsylvania's in 1790.[1]

2. **Practical** The Framers had to create a two-chambered body to settle the conflict between the Virginia and the New Jersey Plans at Philadelphia in 1787. As you have read in Chapter 2, the most populous States wanted to distribute seats in Congress in proportion to the population of each State, while smaller States demanded an equal voice in Congress. Bicameralism is a reflection of federalism. Each of the States is equally represented in the Senate and represented proportional to its population in the House.

3. **Theoretical** The Framers favored a bicameral Congress in order that one house might act as a check on the other.

A leading constitutional historian recounts a breakfast-table conversation between Thomas Jefferson and George Washington. Jefferson, who had just returned from France, told Washington that he was opposed to a two-chambered legislature. As he made his point, he poured his coffee into his saucer, and Washington asked him why he did so. "To cool it," replied Jefferson. "Even so," said Washington, "we pour legislation into the senatorial saucer to cool it."

The Framers were generally convinced that Congress would dominate the new National Government. As Madison wrote,

**PRIMARY Sources** *❝In a republican government, the legislative authority necessarily predominates. The remedy for this inconveniency is to divide the legislature into different branches. ❞*

—*The Federalist* No. 51

The Framers saw bicameralism as a way to diffuse the power of Congress and so prevent it from overwhelming the other two branches of government.

For more than 200 years now, some people have argued that the Senate should be abolished.[2] They say that because the States, not the

---

[1]Today, only Nebraska (since 1937) has a unicameral legislative body.

[2]There is not the remotest chance that that would ever be done. Recall, the Constitution provides in Article V that "no State, without its Consent, shall be deprived of its equal Suffrage in the Senate."

---

## Representation in Congress

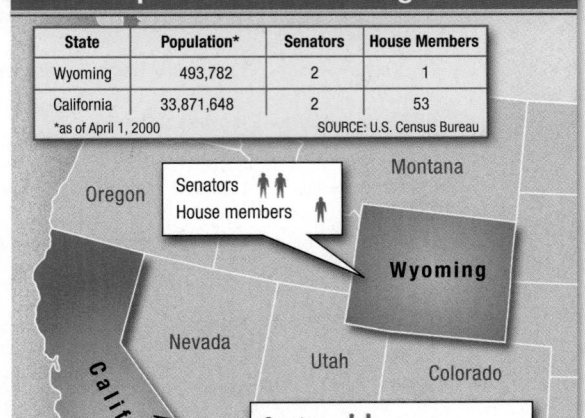

| State | Population* | Senators | House Members |
|-------|-----------|----------|---------------|
| Wyoming | 493,782 | 2 | 1 |
| California | 33,871,648 | 2 | 53 |

*as of April 1, 2000     SOURCE: U.S. Census Bureau

*Interpreting Maps* California and Wyoming each elect two senators, despite a huge difference in their populations. ***How does the distribution of Senate seats among the States illustrate the principle of federalism?***

people, are equally represented in the Senate, that body is undemocratic. Those critics often point to the two extremes to make their case. The State with the least population, Wyoming, has only some 500,000 residents. The largest State, California, now has more than 34 million. Yet each of these States has two senators.

Those who argue against State equality in the Senate ignore a vital fact. The Senate was purposely created as a body in which the States would be represented as coequal members and partners in the Union. Remember, had the States not been equally represented in the Senate, there might never have been a Constitution.

## Terms and Sessions

Some years ago, a woman, incensed at something her senator had just done, said to him: "You know, 535 of you people in Congress meet every two years. There are some of us who think that it would be much better if just two of you met every 535 years."

---

---

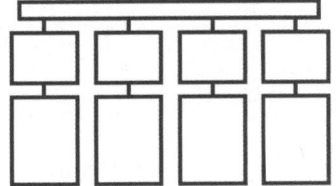

---

ACTIVITY

### American Government, American Humor

Share the following quotation with students:

*"There are two periods when Congress does no business: one is before the holidays, and the other after."*

—George D. Prentice

**Discussion** Ask students what Prentice means by his joke. Then ask: How do the sessions of Congress as dictated by the Constitution help ensure that Congress *does* complete its business?

**(Average)**

---

## Comparative Government

### Legislative Bodies

| Country | Legislative Body | Houses if Bicameral | Number of Members | How Elected | Term of Office |
|---|---|---|---|---|---|
| United States | Congress | House of Representatives | 435 | Direct popular vote | 2 years |
| | | Senate | 100 | Direct popular vote | 6 years |
| Costa Rica | Legislative Assembly | | 57 | Direct popular vote | 4 years |
| France | Parlement | National Assembly | 577 | Direct popular vote | 5 years |
| | | Senate | 321 | Local electoral colleges | 9 years |
| Israel | Knesset | | 120 | Direct popular vote | 4 years |
| Japan | Diet | House of Councillors | 252 | Direct popular vote | 6 years |
| | | House of Representatives | 500 | Direct popular vote | 4 years |
| Saudi Arabia | Consultative Council | | 90 | Appointed by the king | 4 years |

*Interpreting Tables* The size and makeup of legislative bodies vary widely among countries. *Why might the legislatures of Israel and Costa Rica have fewer members than the House of Representatives in the United States?*

While that story may or may not be true, the government has never followed this woman's advice. Ever since 1789, Congress has met for two-year terms.

### Terms of Congress

Each **term** of Congress lasts for two years, and each term is numbered consecutively.[3] Congress began its first term on March 4, 1789, and that term ended two years later, on March 4, 1791.

The date for the start of each new term was changed by the 20th Amendment in 1933. In the 1790s, the four-month gap between elections in November and the start of a new term in March allowed for delays in communicating election results around the country. It also allowed for the arrival of new lawmakers to Washington, D.C. However, the March starting date restricted the amount of work Congress could accomplish, and by the 1930s communications and travel were no longer an issue. The start of a new term is now "noon of the 3d day

---

[3]Article I, Section 2, Clause 1 dictates a two-year term for Congress by providing that members of the House "shall be . . . chosen every second Year."

of January" of every odd-numbered year. So the term of the 107th Congress began on January 3, 2001, and it will end at noon on January 3, 2003.

### Sessions

A **session** of Congress is that period of time during which, each year, Congress assembles and conducts business. There are two sessions to each term of Congress—one session each year. The Constitution provides

FROM THE *Constitution*
*"The Congress shall assemble at least once in every year, and such meeting shall begin at noon on the 3d day of January, unless they shall by law appoint a different day."*
—20th Amendment, Section 2

In fact, Congress often does "appoint a different day." The second session of each two-year term frequently begins a few days or even two or three weeks after the third of January.

Congress **adjourns,** or suspends until the next session, each regular session as it sees fit. Until World War II, a typical session lasted four or five months. Today, however, the many pressing issues facing Congress force it to remain in

---

*Answer to . . .*

**Interpreting Tables** Possible answer: The populations of those countries are smaller.

session through most of each year. Both houses recess for several short periods during a session.

Neither house may adjourn *sine die* (finally, ending a session) without the consent of the other. The Constitution provides that

> FROM THE *Constitution* **"** *Neither House . . . shall, without the Consent of the other, adjourn for more than three days, nor to any other Place than that in which the two Houses shall be sitting.* **"**

—Article I, Section 5, Clause 4

Article II, Section 3 of the Constitution does give the President the power to **prorogue,** or adjourn, a session, but only when the two houses cannot agree on a date for adjournment. No President has ever had to use that power.

## Special Sessions

Only the President may call Congress into **special session**—a meeting to deal with some emergency situation.[4] Only 26 special sessions of Congress have ever been held. President Harry Truman called the most recent one in 1948, to consider anti-inflation and welfare measures in the aftermath of World War II.

Note that the President can call Congress *or* either of its houses into a special session. The Senate has been called into special session alone

---

[4]Article II, Section 3 says that the President "may, on extraordinary Occasions, convene both Houses, or either of them. . . ."

▲ *Outside Washington* Members of Congress have many responsibilities outside the regular legislative session in Washington. Senator John Edwards (D., North Carolina) meets with constituents after devastating floods hit his State.

on 46 occasions, to consider treaties or presidential appointments, but not since 1933. The House has never been called alone.

Of course, the fact that Congress now meets nearly year-round reduces the likelihood of special sessions. That fact also lessens the importance of the President's power to call one. Still, as Congress nears the end of a session, the President sometimes finds it useful to *threaten* a special session if the two chambers do not act on some measure high on his legislative agenda.

## Section 1 Assessment

### Key Terms and Main Ideas

1. How long does a **term** of Congress last?
2. How does a **special session** differ from a regular session of Congress?
3. When does Congress **adjourn?**
4. Who has the power to **prorogue** a session of Congress?

### Critical Thinking

5. **Determining Cause and Effect** What are the historical, practical, and theoretical reasons for bicameralism in Congress?
6. **Expressing Problems Clearly** Why do some people believe the Senate is undemocratic?

7. **Making Comparisons** Use the chart on page 264 to compare the length of a term in the House of Representatives to terms in other legislatures. How does the House of Representatives differ from other legislatures? What might this indicate about the United States government?

 **Take It to the Net**

8. A one-house system of government works very differently from a bicameral system of representation. Select five differences and summarize them in a paragraph. Use the links provided in the Social Studies area at the following Web site for help in completing this activity. **www.phschool.com**

 **Take It to the Net**

8. Direct students to the Social Studies area at the Prentice Hall School Web site. The *Magruder's American Government* companion Web site includes the directions and links needed to complete the activity. It also provides a printable Internet activity worksheet with scoring rubrics for assessment. Paragraphs should include all relevant differences.

## Analyzing Maps

**Focus** Have students collect various types of maps and analyze them.

**Instruct** Ask each student to bring in at least one map from any of the following sources: atlases, newspapers, magazines, textbooks, the Internet. For each map, have the student identify **(a)** the purpose of the map; **(b)** what conclusions can be drawn from the map; and **(c)** possible real-world applications for the data in the map, such as agriculture, travel and tourism, interstate commerce, economic research, or historical research.

**Close/Reteach** Ask for volunteers to show their map(s) to the class and explain the possible uses for them.

# SKILLS FOR LIFE

TECHNOLOGY
CITIZENSHIP
CRITICAL THINKING
CHARTS and GRAPHS

# Analyzing Maps

Maps bring information to life in a way that words alone cannot. Maps are particularly useful to people who grasp concepts better when they are illustrated. To analyze a map and draw information from it, try these steps:

**1. Identify the purpose of the map.** The map shown here is a cartogram. It is a special-purpose map used to present statistics geographically. Here, the original 13 States are shown not in proportion to their land area, but according to the relative sizes of their populations in 1770. The cartogram intentionally distorts the sizes and shapes of territories in order to compare them visually. Compare this map with the one on page 31. (a) Which States had a large population for their small physical size? (b) Which States had a rather small population for their large size?

**2. Apply prior knowledge to draw conclusions from the map.** You read on page 263 about the debate, ongoing since the nation's founding, over whether to have equal representation in the Senate for every State, regardless of its size or population. Knowing

this, study the cartogram again. (a) At the nation's founding, which States stood to gain from having equal representation? (b) Which would gain from proportional representation tied to population? (c) How did the Constitution reconcile this problem?

### Test for Success

In the library or on the Internet, find a present-day population map of the United States. (a) List three States that would be awarded a large number of senators if they were apportioned according to population size, as in the House of Representatives. (b) List at least three States that would fare poorly with proportional representation in the Senate.

▲ Above, engraving of a map of the United States; at right, cartogram of the colonies

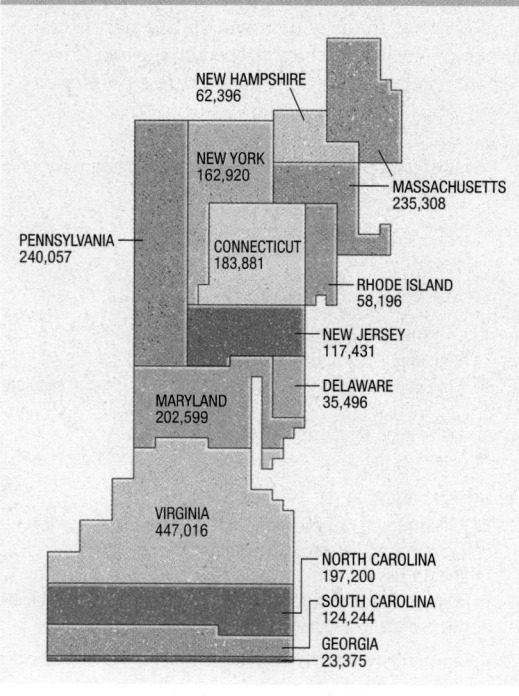

**Cartogram: Population of the Thirteen Colonies, 1770**

NEW HAMPSHIRE 62,396
NEW YORK 162,920
MASSACHUSETTS 235,308
PENNSYLVANIA 240,057
CONNECTICUT 183,881
RHODE ISLAND 58,196
NEW JERSEY 117,431
DELAWARE 35,496
MARYLAND 202,599
VIRGINIA 447,016
NORTH CAROLINA 197,200
SOUTH CAROLINA 124,244
GEORGIA 23,375

## Answers . . .

**1.** Possible answers:
**(a)** Massachusetts, Connecticut.
**(b)** Georgia, South Carolina.
**2. (a)** Rhode Island, Delaware, New Hampshire, Georgia. **(b)** Virginia, Pennsylvania, Massachusetts, Maryland. **(c)** It created a bicameral Congress, one (the Senate) with fixed apportionment and the other (the House) apportioned according to population size.

### Test for Success

Possible answers: **(a)** Texas, California, New York, Florida, Illinois. **(b)** Wyoming, Alaska, Delaware, Montana, Rhode Island.

🖫 **Social Studies Skills Tutor CD-ROM** Provides interactive practice in geographic literacy, critical thinking and reading, visual analysis, and communications.

## Point-of-Use Resources

📁 **Skills for Life Activity** Unit 3 booklet, p. 10 provides an additional skill activity for this chapter.

## Section Preview

### OBJECTIVES

1. **Describe** the size and terms of the House of Representatives.
2. **Explain** how House seats are reapportioned among the States after each census.
3. **Describe** a typical congressional election and congressional district.
4. **Analyze** the formal and informal qualifications for serving in the House.

### WHY IT MATTERS

The 435 members of the House of Representatives represent districts of roughly equal populations but very different characters. House members can serve for an unlimited number of two-year terms.

### POLITICAL DICTIONARY

★ **apportion**
★ **reapportion**
★ **off-year election**
★ **single-member district**
★ **at-large**
★ **gerrymander**

Every other autumn, all across the country, hundreds of men and women seek election to the House of Representatives. Most of them try to attract supporters and win votes with banners and posters, yard signs, billboards, flyers, buttons, and other eye-catching campaign materials. Nearly all of them make their "pitches" with radio and television spots, newspaper ads, and now in cyberspace. In this section, you will discover the general shape of the office that all of those candidates so eagerly pursue.

## Size and Terms

The exact size of the House of Representatives—today, 435 members—is not fixed by the Constitution. Rather, it is set by Congress. The Constitution provides that the total number of seats in the House of Representatives shall be **apportioned** (distributed) among the States on the basis of their respective populations.[5]

Each State is guaranteed at least one seat in the House, no matter what its population. Today, seven States—Alaska, Delaware, Montana, North Dakota, South Dakota, Vermont, and Wyoming—have only one representative apiece.

The District of Columbia, Guam, the Virgin Islands, and American Samoa each elect a delegate to represent them in the House and Puerto Rico chooses a resident commissioner. Those

officials are not, however, full-fledged members of the House of Representatives.

Article I, Section 2, Clause 1 of the Constitution provides that "Representatives shall be . . . chosen every second Year"—that is, for two-year terms. This rather short term means that, for House members, the next election is always just around the corner. That fact tends to make them pay close attention to "the folks back home."

There is no constitutional limit on the number of terms any member of Congress may serve. In the 1990s, people tried to persuade Congress to offer a constitutional amendment to limit congressional terms. Most versions of such an amendment would put a three- or four-term limit (six or eight years) on service in the House and a two-term limit (twelve years) for the Senate.[6]

## Reapportionment

Article I of the Constitution directs Congress to **reapportion**—redistribute—the seats in the House after each decennial census.[7] Until a first census could be taken, the Constitution set the size of the House at 65 seats. That many members served in the First and Second Congresses (1789–1793). The census of 1790 showed a national population of 3,929,214 persons;

---

[5]Article I, Section 2, Clause 3.

[6]The States do not have the power to limit the number of terms their members of Congress may serve, *United States* v. *Thornton*, 1995.
[7]Article I, Section 2, Clause 3. A decennial census occurs every ten years.

## Block Scheduling Strategies

Consider these suggestions to manage extended class time:
■ Discuss the processes of reapportioning, redistricting, and gerrymandering with the class. Refer students to the graphs on p. 280 of their textbooks. Ask them what the graphs show about diversity in Congress. Have students debate this question: Should reapportionment, redistricting, and gerrymandering be used to create diversity in Congress?

■ Organize the class into several small groups and have each group write a "want ad" for a representative. Want ads should include formal and informal qualifications, duties that the representative will fulfill, and any interesting supplementary information such as the terms and sessions the representative will take part in. You might want to have students skim the material in Section 4 to find other information to incorporate in their want ads.

**Objectives** You may wish to call students' attention to the objectives in the Section Preview. The objectives are reflected in the main headings of the section.

**Bellringer** Tell students to suppose that they and two friends have 10 free tickets to a play. They want to distribute the tickets fairly among their families. Ask them what criteria they would use to determine how many tickets each family gets. Explain that in this section, they will learn about how the seats in the House of Representatives are distributed among the States.

**Vocabulary Builder** Have students draw, on a scrap of paper, any odd geometrical shape—the odder the better. Ask them which Political Dictionary term could relate to their drawing. Have them find the term in the text to check their answer.

## Pressed for Time?

### Quick Lesson Plan

1. **Focus** Tell students that several rules and procedures determine the makeup of the House of Representatives. Ask students to discuss what they know about how the Constitution affects the composition of the House.
2. **Instruct** Ask students how reapportionment can alter the makeup of the House. Then discuss how seats were reapportioned before and after 1929. Extend the discussion to changes in the rules governing Congressional elections.
3. **Close/Reteach** Remind students that the Constitution and Congress both influence the makeup of the House. Have students make a chart to show how each affects the size and reapportionment of the House and the terms and election of its members.

**267**

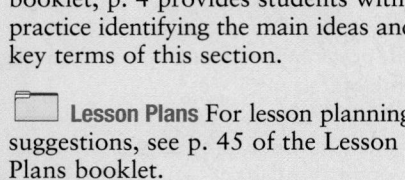

## Reading Strategy

### Getting the Main Idea

Ask students to write down the main ideas and important supporting details as they read the section. Encourage them to use the list of objectives in the Section Preview to help them determine the main ideas.

## Point-of-Use Resources

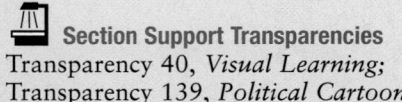

**Guided Reading and Review** Unit 3 booklet, p. 4 provides students with practice identifying the main ideas and key terms of this section.

**Lesson Plans** For lesson planning suggestions, see p. 45 of the Lesson Plans booklet.

**Political Cartoons** See p. 37 of the Political Cartoons booklet for a cartoon relevant to this section.

**Section Support Transparencies** Transparency 40, *Visual Learning;* Transparency 139, *Political Cartoon*

### Congressional Apportionment, 2003–2013

**KEY**
- Gained representation
- Lost representation
- No change
- **2** Number of Representatives

| Gained Seats | |
|---|---|
| Arizona | +2 |
| Florida | +2 |
| Georgia | +2 |
| Texas | +2 |
| California | +1 |
| Colorado | +1 |
| Nevada | +1 |
| North Carolina | +1 |

| Lost Seats | |
|---|---|
| New York | –2 |
| Pennsylvania | –2 |
| Connecticut | –1 |
| Illinois | –1 |
| Indiana | –1 |
| Michigan | –1 |
| Mississippi | –1 |
| Ohio | –1 |
| Oklahoma | –1 |
| Wisconsin | –1 |

SOURCE: Census 2000

*Interpreting Maps* This map shows the changes in State representation due to the reapportionment of the House after the 2000 Census, and in effect from January 3, 2003 to January 3, 2013. The next reapportionment will be based on the census to be taken in 2010. ***What general trend in population growth around the country does this map show?***

thus, in 1792 Congress increased the number of House seats by 41, to 106.

### A Growing Nation

As the nation's population grew, and as the number of States increased, so did the size of the House. It went to 142 seats after the census of 1800, to 186 seats 10 years later, and so on.[8] By 1912, following the census of 1910 and the admission of Arizona and New Mexico, the House had grown to 435 seats.

With the census of 1920, Congress found itself in a painfully difficult political position. The House had long since grown too large for effective floor action. To reapportion without adding more seats to the House, however, would mean that some States would have to lose seats if every State were to be represented according to its population.

Congress met the problem by doing nothing. So, despite the Constitution's command, there

---

[8]Once, following the census of 1840, the size of the House was reduced from 242 to 232 seats.

was no reapportionment on the basis of the 1920 census.

### The Reapportionment Act of 1929

Faced with the 1930 census, Congress avoided repeating its earlier lapse by passing the Reapportionment Act of 1929. That law, still on the books, sets up what is often called an "automatic reapportionment." It provides:

(1) The "permanent" size of the House is 435 members. Of course, that figure is permanent only so long as Congress does not decide to change it. Congress did enlarge the House temporarily in 1959 when Alaska and then Hawaii became States. Today each of the 435 seats in the House represents an average of some 650,000 persons.

(2) Following each census, the Census Bureau is to determine the number of seats each State should have.

(3) When the Bureau's plan is ready, the President must send it to Congress.

(4) If, within 60 days of receiving it, neither house rejects the Census Bureau's plan, it becomes effective.

## Answer to . . .

**Interpreting Maps** Most of the States that gained seats were located in the South and Southwest, indicating regional population shifts.

The plan set out in the 1929 law has worked quite well through eight reapportionments. The law leaves to Congress its constitutional responsibility to reapportion the House, but it gives to the Census Bureau the mechanical chores (and political "heat") that go with that task.

## Congressional Elections

According to the Constitution, any person whom a State allows to vote for members of "the most numerous Branch" of its own legislature is qualified to vote in congressional elections.[9] The Constitution also provides that

> *FROM THE Constitution* ❝*The Times, Places and Manner of holding [Congressional] Elections . . . shall be prescribed in each State by the Legislature thereof; but the Congress may at any time by Law make or alter such Regulations. . . .* ❞[10]
>
> —Article I, Section 4, Clause 1

### Date

Congressional elections are held on the same day in every State. Since 1872 Congress has required that those elections be held on the Tuesday following the first Monday in November of each even-numbered year. Congress has made an

---

[9]Article I, Section 2, Clause 1.
[10]The Constitution allows only one method for filling a vacancy in the House—by a special election, which may be called only by the governor of the State involved; Article I, Section 2, Clause 4.

exception for Alaska, which may hold its election in October. To date, however, Alaskans have chosen to use the November date.

In that same 1872 law, Congress directed that representatives be chosen by written or printed ballots. The use of voting machines was approved in 1899. Today, well over half of all the votes cast in congressional elections are cast on some type of voting machine.

### Off-Year Elections

Those congressional elections that occur in the nonpresidential years—that is, between presidential elections—are called **off-year elections.** The most recent ones were held in 2002, and the next ones are in 2006.

Far more often than not, the party in power—the party that holds the presidency—loses seats in the off-year elections. The time line below illustrates that point. It sets out the House and Senate seats gained (+) or lost (−) by the President's party in the off-year elections from 1970 through 1998. The President's party did particularly poorly in 1974, after President Nixon resigned due to the Watergate Scandal, and in 1994, during President Clinton's first term. The 1998 off-year elections were an exception to the rule. That summer and fall, the Republican Congress held hearings to prepare to impeach President Clinton. Public opinion polls showed weak support for the impeachment, and many believed the hearings encouraged Clinton's supporters to vote for Democratic candidates for Congress.

### Gains and Losses in Off-Year Elections

| Congressional Elections | 1970 seats: | 1974 seats: | 1978 seats: | 1982 seats: | 1986 seats: | 1990 seats: | 1994 seats: | 1998 seats: |
|---|---|---|---|---|---|---|---|---|
| | −12 House +2 Senate | −48 House −5 Senate | −15 House −3 Senate | −26 House +1 Senate | −5 House −8 Senate | −8 House −1 Senate | −53 House −8 Senate | +5 House 0 Senate |

| Presidential Elections | 1968 Richard Nixon elected | 1972* Richard Nixon reelected | 1976 Jimmy Carter elected | 1980 Ronald Reagan elected | 1984 Ronald Reagan reelected | 1988 George Bush elected | 1992 Bill Clinton elected | 1996 Bill Clinton reelected |
|---|---|---|---|---|---|---|---|---|

*Nixon resigned in August 1974 and was replaced by Gerald Ford.  KEY: 🐘 Republican  🐴 Democrat

*Interpreting Time Lines* The President's party frequently loses seats in the House and Senate in an off-year election. *In which two election years above did the President's party lose the most seats in the House?*

*Answer to . . .*
**Interpreting Time Lines** 1974 and 1994.

## Districts

The 435 members of the House are chosen by the voters in 435 separate congressional districts across the country. Recall that seven States now each have only one seat in the House of Representatives. There are, then, 428 congressional districts within the other 43 States.

The Constitution makes no mention of congressional districts. For more than half a century, Congress allowed each State to decide whether to elect its members by a general ticket system or on a single-member district basis. Under the **single-member district** arrangement, the voters in each district elect one of the State's representatives from among a field of candidates running for a seat in the House from that district.

Most States quickly set up single-member districts. Several States used the general ticket system, however. Under that arrangement, all of the State's seats were filled **at-large**—that is, elected from the State as a whole, rather than from a particular district. Every voter could vote for a candidate for each one of the State's seats in the House.

At-large elections proved grossly unfair. A party with even a very small plurality of voters Statewide could win all of a State's seats in the House. Congress finally did away with the general ticket system in 1842. Thereafter, all of the seats in the House were to be filled from single-member districts in each State. Since the seven States with the fewest residents each have only one representative in the House, these representatives are said to be elected "at-large." Although each representative represents a single-member district, that district covers the entire State.

The 1842 law made each State legislature responsible for drawing any congressional districts within its own State. It also required that each congressional district be made up of "contiguous territory," meaning that it must be all one piece. In 1872 Congress added the command that the districts within each State have "as nearly as practicable an equal number of inhabitants." In 1901 it further directed that all the districts be of "compact territory"—in other words, a comparatively small area.

These requirements of contiguity, population equality, and compactness were often disregarded by State legislatures, and Congress made no real effort to enforce them. The requirements were left out of the Reapportionment Act of 1929. In 1932 the Supreme Court held (in *Wood* v. *Broom*) that they had therefore been repealed. Over time, then, and most notably since 1929, the State legislatures have drawn many districts

*Interpreting Maps* The Texas Legislature was responsible for redrawing district lines following the 2000 Census. ***Does it make any real difference which party controls a State legislature and governorship during the redistricting process?***

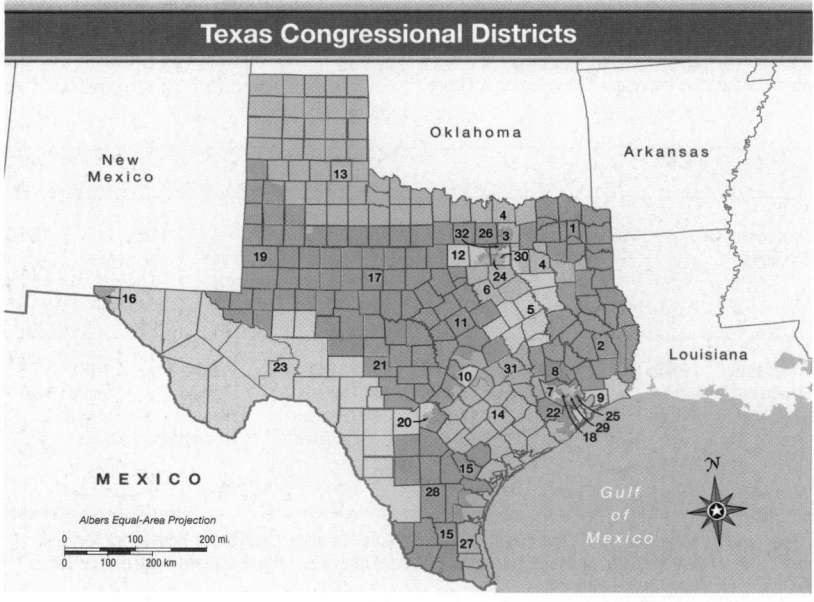

Texas Congressional Districts

with very peculiar geographic shapes. Moreover, until fairly recently, many districts were also of widely varying populations.

## Gerrymandering

Congressional district maps in several States show one and sometimes several districts of very odd shapes. Some look like the letters S or Y, some bear a resemblance to a dumbbell or a squiggly piece of spaghetti, and some defy description. Those districts have usually been **gerrymandered.** That is, they have been drawn to the advantage of the political party that controls the State's legislature.

Gerrymandering is widespread today—and not just at the congressional district level. Districts for the election of State legislators are regularly drawn for partisan advantage. In fact, gerrymandering can be found in most places where lines are drawn for the election of public officeholders—in cities, counties, school districts, and elsewhere.

Most often gerrymandering takes one of two forms. The lines are drawn either (1) to concentrate the opposition's voters in one or a few districts, thus leaving the other districts comfortably safe for the dominant party; or (2) to spread the opposition as thinly as possible among several districts, limiting the opposition's ability to win anywhere in the region. Gerrymandering's main goal is to create as many "safe" districts as possible—districts almost certain to be won by the party in control of the line-drawing process. And the computer-driven map-making techniques of today make the practice more effective than ever in its storied past.

For decades, gerrymandering produced congressional districts that differed widely in the number of people they included. State legislatures were responsible for this situation. A number of them regularly drew district lines on a partisan basis—with the Republicans gouging the Democrats in those States where the GOP controls the legislature, and the

---

[11]The pattern of rural over-representation in the State legislatures has now all but disappeared as a consequence of the Supreme Court's several "one-person, one-vote" decisions of the 1960s and 1970s. In the leading case, *Reynolds* v. *Sims,* 1964, the Court held that the 14th Amendment's Equal Protection Clause commands that the seats in both houses of a State's legislature must be apportioned on the basis of population equality.

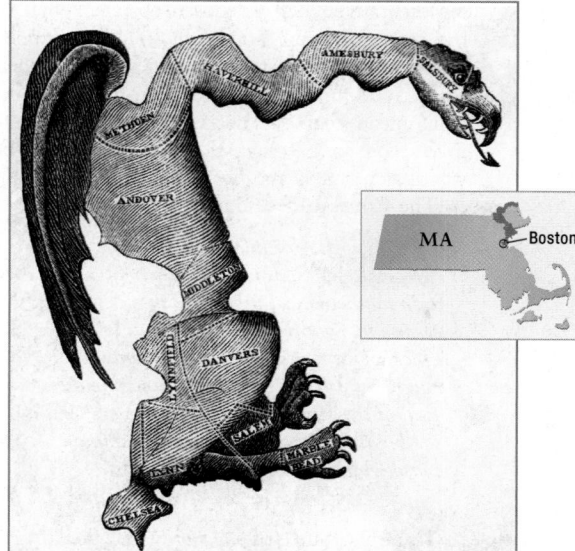

**▲ *The original Gerrymander*** Gerrymandering takes its name from Governor Elbridge Gerry of Massachusetts, who in 1812 drew the State's legislative districts to favor the Democratic-Republicans. It is said that the painter Gilbert Stuart added a head, wings, and claws on a district map hanging over the desk of a Federalist newspaper editor. "That," he said, "will do for a salamander." "Better say Gerrymander," growled the editor.

Democrats doing the same thing to the Republicans where they hold sway. In fact, that circumstance exists in several States today. Historically, most State legislatures were carved up on a rural versus urban as well as a partisan basis—because, through much of history, the typical State legislature was dominated by the less-populated (and over-represented) rural areas of the State.[11]

### *Wesberry* v. *Sanders,* 1964

Suddenly, and quite dramatically, these long-standing patterns of wide population variations among House districts and of rural over-representation in the chamber came to an end in the mid- to late 1960s. These abrupt changes were the direct result of a historic decision by the Supreme Court in 1964. In *Wesberry* v. *Sanders,* the Court held that the population differences among Georgia's congressional districts were so great as to violate the Constitution.

In reaching its landmark decision, the Supreme Court noted that Article I, Section 2 declares that

**RESOURCE ● PRO®**

**Resource Pro® CD-ROM** contains an electronic version of each activity found in the Teaching Resources as well as additional resources such as Supreme Court cases. The Planning Express® feature allows you to customize and create daily lesson plans within minutes.

## Background Note

### Political Talk

While the House has expelled only four members in its history, it has been common practice for a party to put enough pressure on a House member to cause that member to resign—as in the case of Jim Wright (D., Tex.), who resigned in 1989. The member responsible for pressuring Wright to resign was Newt Gingrich (R., Ga) who became Speaker of the House in 1994. Despite the popularity and respect he gained for his leadership of the "Contract With America" campaign, Gingrich was not immune to the very pressures that had forced Wright's resignation. Attacked by Democrats for a questionable book deal and facing ethics charges and a rare House reprimand, Gingrich followed Wright's example and resigned the speakership in 1999.

## Point-of-Use Resources

**The Living Constitution**
Federalism, p. 8

**Simulations and Data Graphing CD-ROM** offers data graphing tools that give students practice with creating and interpreting graphs.

**Basic Principles of the Constitution Transparencies** Transparencies 44–50, *Federalism*

## Answer to . . .

**Interpreting Tables** The House is too big to debate all bills on the floor of the House.

---

representatives shall be chosen "by the People of the several States" and shall be "apportioned among the several States . . . according to their respective Numbers. . . ." These words, the Court held, mean that "as nearly as practicable one man's vote in a congressional election is to be worth as much as another's."

The Court added that

**PRIMARY Sources** *"While it may not be possible to draw congressional districts with mathematical precision, that is no excuse for ignoring our Constitution's plain objective of making equal representation for equal numbers of people the fundamental goal of the House of Representatives. That is the high standard of justice and common sense which the Founders set for us."*

—Justice Black, *Opinion of the Court*

The importance of *Wesberry* and the Court's later "one person, one vote" decisions cannot be overstated. They had an extraordinary impact on the makeup of the House, on the content of public policy, and on electoral politics in general. The nation's cities and suburbs now speak with a much larger voice in Congress than ever before. Notice, however, that it is quite possible

### Major Differences Between the House and Senate

| HOUSE | SENATE |
|---|---|
| Larger body (435 members) | Smaller body (100 members) |
| Shorter term (2 years) | Longer term (6 years) |
| Smaller constituencies (elected from districts within States) | Larger constituencies (elected from entire State) |
| Younger membership | Older membership |
| Less prestige | More prestige |
| Lower visibility in the news media | Higher visibility in the news media |
| Strict rules, limited debate | Flexible rules, nearly unlimited debate |
| Most work is done in committees, not on the floor | Work is split more evenly between committees and the floor |
| No power over treaties and presidential appointments | Approves or rejects treaties and presidential appointments |

*Interpreting Tables* Members of the House and Senate work under very different rules and conditions. **Why do House members debate most bills in committees before bringing them to the House floor?**

to draw congressional (or any other) district lines in accord with the "one person, one vote" rule and, at the same time, to gerrymander them.

Gerrymandering based solely on race, however, is a violation of the 15th Amendment, *Gomillion* v. *Lightfoot,* 1960. So-called "majority-minority districts" were drawn in some States following the census in 1990 and again in 2000—districts crafted to include a majority of African Americans and/or Latinos and so likely to send African Americans and Latinos to Congress. The Supreme Court struck down those race-based districts in several cases—most notably, in a case from Texas, *Bush* v. *Vera,* 1996. But, most recently, the Court has held this: while race cannot be the controlling factor in drawing district lines, race can be one of the mix of factors that shape that process. It did so in a case from North Carolina, *Hunt* v. *Cromartie,* in 2001.

## Qualifications for House Members

You know that there are 435 members of the House of Representatives, and that each one of them had to win an election to get there. Each one of them also had to meet two quite different sets of qualifications to win office: the formal qualifications for membership in the House set out in the Constitution and a number of informal qualifications imposed by the realities of politics.

### Formal Qualifications

The Constitution says that a member of the House

(1) must be at least 25 years of age,

(2) must have been a citizen of the United States for at least seven years, and

(3) must be an inhabitant of the State from which he or she is elected.[12]

Longstanding custom, not the Constitution, also requires that a representative must live in the district he or she represents. The custom is based on the belief that the legislator should be closely familiar with the locale he or she represents, its people, and its problems. Rarely, then, does a district choose an outsider to represent it.

[12]Article I, Section 2, Clause 2; see also Article I, Section 6, Clause 2.
[13]Article I, Section 5, Clause 1.
[14]Article I, Section 5, Clause 2.

---

# CONSTITUTIONAL PRINCIPLES

### Federalism

State legislatures are responsible for creating their own legislative districts. At times, they have purposely created districts that favor one political party over another. In *Wesberry* v. *Sanders, Gomillion* v. *Lightfoot,* and other cases, the courts have tried to limit the practice of gerrymandering. Yet, the gerrymandering of congressional districts still makes headlines.

### Activity

Have students research court cases involving gerrymandering, and ask them to determine the cause for the investigation. Then, ask students to consider the importance of federalism to the U.S. government, and to report on the cases they researched, explaining the action the federal court(s) took to resolve the claim of gerrymandering.

The Constitution makes the House "the Judge of the Elections, Returns and Qualifications of its own Members."[13] Thus, when the right of a member-elect to be seated is challenged, the House has the power to decide the matter. Challenges are rarely successful.

The House may refuse to seat a member-elect by majority vote. It may also "punish its Members for disorderly Behavior" by majority vote, and "with the Concurrence of two thirds, expel a Member."[14]

Historically, the House viewed its power to judge the qualifications of members-elect as the power to impose additional standards. It did so several times. In 1900 it refused to seat Brigham H. Roberts of Utah because he was a polygamist—that is, he had more than one wife. In *Powell* v. *McCormack,* 1969, however, the Supreme Court held that the House could not exclude a member-elect who meets the Constitution's standards of age, citizenship, and residence. The House has not excluded anyone since that decision.

Over more than 200 years, the House has expelled only four members. Three were ousted in 1861 for their "support of rebellion." More recently, Michael Myers (D., Pennsylvania) was expelled in 1980 for corruption. Myers had been caught up in the Abscam probe, an undercover FBI investigation of corruption. Over time, a few members have resigned to avoid almost certain expulsion.

The House has not often punished a member for "disorderly Behavior," but such actions are not nearly so rare as expulsions. Most recently, the House voted to "reprimand" Barney Frank (D., Massachusetts) in 1990 for conduct stemming from his relationship with a male prostitute. Mr. Frank, an avowed homosexual, has been easily reelected by the voters in his congressional district every two years since then.

The Speaker of the House left Congress under a cloud in 1989. Jim Wright (D., Texas) resigned his seat after the House Ethics Committee charged him with a number of violations of House rules. Most of those allegations centered around Mr. Wright's financial dealings with individuals and companies with an interest in legislation before the House.

## Informal Qualifications

The realities of politics produce a number of informal qualifications for membership in the House—beyond those qualifications set out in the Constitution. These additional qualifications vary somewhat from time to time and from State to State, and sometimes from one congressional district to another within the same State.

Informal qualifications have to do with a candidate's vote-getting abilities. They include such factors as party identification, name familiarity, gender, ethnic characteristics, and political experience. The "right" combination of these factors will help a candidate win nomination and then election to the House. The "wrong" ones, however, will almost certainly spell defeat.

### Answers to . . .

### Section 2 Assessment

**1.** By the Census Bureau after each census is taken based on the population of each State.
**2.** In 2006 and 2010.
**3.** In a single-member district arrangement, voters elect a representative from candidates running from a particular district; in an at-large arrangement, voters elect a representative from the State as a whole.
**4.** To create districts that their party is almost certain to win in an election.
**5.** By basing apportionment on numbers of people, it ensured that populous areas such as cities and suburbs had a greater voice than before in Congress.
**6.** Answers will vary. Students might suggest that it makes it more difficult for members of Congress to stay in touch with their constituents.
**7.** Answers will vary, but opinions should be supported with relevant facts.

## Section **2** Assessment

**Key Terms and Main Ideas**

**1.** How are the seats in the House of Representatives **apportioned**?
**2.** When will the next two **off-year elections** occur?
**3.** Explain the difference between a **single-member district** seat and an **at-large** seat.
**4.** Why do politicians **gerrymander** districts?

**Critical Thinking**

**5. Drawing Inferences** How did *Wesberry* v. *Sanders* change the makeup of Congress?
**6. Predicting Consequences** Since 1910, the average number of people in a congressional district has tripled from 210,000 to well over 650,000. How might this have affected the ability of members of Congress to represent their constituents?
**7. Understanding Point of View** List four informal qualifications that you would look for in a candidate for Congress. Which qualification on your list do you think is most important? Explain your reasoning.

### Take It to the Net

**8.** Politicians have used gerrymandering for nearly 200 years to control the outcome of elections. Read about this practice and write a paragraph explaining at least two methods of gerrymandering. Use the links provided in the Social Studies area at the following Web site for help in completing this activity. www.phschool.com

### Take It to the Net

**8.** Direct students to the Social Studies area at the Prentice Hall School Web site. The *Magruder's American Government* companion Web site includes the directions and links needed to complete the activity. It also provides a printable Internet activity worksheet with scoring rubrics for assessment. Paragraphs should be supported with specific examples.

## Redistricting and Race

**Focus** Draw a square on the chalk-board and ask students to divide it into three segments. Have volunteers explain how they divided the square. Explain to students that just as there are many ways to divide the square, there are many ways to organize congressional districts.

**Instruct** Have students read the Primary Source selection, identifying reasons why the Supreme Court rejected the boundaries established for North Carolina's District 12. Ask students to suppose that they were one of the judges hearing the case. Have them write either con-senting or dissenting opinions based on what they've read.

**Close/Reteach** Have students share their opinions with the class. Then ask them to write paragraphs describing alternative ways to increase minority representation without redistricting.

**Keep It Current CD-ROM** includes government-related projects by unit. The CD-ROM links to the Prentice Hall School Web site and may be used for daily updates.

### Answers to . . .

**Analyzing Primary Sources**
**1.** The legislature wanted to create a district with an African American majority.
**2.** Because it unconstitutionally divided voters based on race.
**3.** It can perpetuate racial stereo-types by assuming all African Americans share the same political interests, promote the appearance of racial segregation, encourage other races to vote as a bloc, and lead elected officials to represent the needs of a racial group instead of all of a district's constituents.
**4.** Answers will vary, but should suggest that the main difference between parties and racial groups is that parties are organized around common interests, while racial groups do not necessarily hold common interests.

---

# Redistricting and Race

*African Americans and Latinos have historically been under-represented in the House of Representatives. After the 1990 Census, several States designed "majority-minority" congressional districts to elect more minority members to Congress. The Supreme Court rejected one such district, North Carolina's 12th, in Shaw v. Reno in 1993. Writing for the majority, Justice Sandra Day O'Connor outlined the problems with the redistricting plan.*

The second majority black district, District 12, is . . . unusually shaped. It is approximately 160 miles long and, for much of its length, no wider than the I-85 corridor. It winds in snake-like fashion through tobacco country, financial centers, and manufacturing areas "until it gobbles in enough enclaves [culturally distinct units] of black neighborhoods."

*What does the cartoon suggest about the process of redistricting?*

. . . One state legislator has remarked that "[i]f you drove down the interstate with both car doors open, you'd kill most of the people in the district.". . .

In some exceptional cases, a reapportionment plan may be so highly irregular that, on its face, it rationally cannot be understood as anything other than an effort to "segregat[e] . . . voters" on the basis of race. . . .

We believe that reapportionment is one area in which appearances do matter. A reapportionment plan that includes in one district individuals who belong to the same race, but who are otherwise widely separated by geographical and political boundaries, and who may have little in common with one another but the color of their skin, bears an uncomfortable resemblance to political apartheid [racial segregation]. It reinforces the perception that members of the same racial group—regardless of their age, education, economic status, or the community in which they live—think alike, share the same political interests, and will prefer the same candidates at the polls. We have rejected such

perceptions elsewhere as imper-missible racial stereotypes. . . .

By perpetuating such no-tions, a racial gerrymander may exacerbate [make more severe] the very patterns of racial bloc voting that majority-minority districting is sometimes said to counteract. . . .

The message that such districting sends to elected representatives is equally per-nicious [destructive]. When a district obviously is created solely to effectuate the perceived common interests of one racial group, elected officials are more likely to believe that their primary obligation is to represent only the members of that group, rather than their constituency as a whole. This is altogether antithetical [in oppositon] to our system of representative democracy.

### Analyzing Primary Sources

1. Why was the 12th Congressional District drawn in such an unusual shape?
2. Why did the Supreme Court order North Carolina to redraw the 12th district?
3. According to this opinion, what are the dangers of dividing congressional districts by race?
4. The Supreme Court has ruled that States can group voters into districts by party, but not by race. Do you agree or disagree with this decision? Give reasons for your position.

---

 *Corner*

📁 **Close Up on Primary Sources** What Is a Gerrymander?, p. 12, extends this feature with a primary source activity.

 **Online**

To keep up-to-date on Close Up news and activities, visit Close Up Online at

**www.closeup.org**

# 3 The Senate

## Section Preview

### OBJECTIVES

1. **Compare** the size of the Senate to the size of the House of Representatives.
2. **Describe** how States have elected senators in the past and present.
3. **Explain** how and why a senator's term differs from a representative's term.
4. **Identify** the qualifications for serving in the Senate.

### WHY IT MATTERS

Each State has two seats in the Senate, the smaller and more prestigious house of Congress. Senators are generally older and more experienced than representatives, and their long terms protect them from political pressure.

### POLITICAL DICTIONARY

★ continuous body
★ constituency
★ colleague

You should not be very much surprised by these facts: Nearly a third of the present members of the Senate once served in the House of Representatives; none of the current members of the House has ever served in the Senate. Indeed, many of the men and women who now serve in the House look forward to the day when, they hope, they will sit in the Senate. As you read this section, you will come to see why the Senate is often called the "upper house."

## Size, Election, and Terms

Why are there 100 members of the United States Senate? Have the members of the Senate always been elected by the voters of their States? Why do senators serve six-year terms? The organization of the Senate has changed some over time, but it remains a vital part of our government.

### Size

The Constitution says that the Senate "shall be composed of two Senators from each State," and so the Senate is a much smaller body than the House of Representatives.[15] The Senate had only 22 members when it held its first session in March of 1789, and 26 members by the end of the First Congress in 1791. Like the House, the size of the upper chamber has grown with the country. Today 100 senators represent the 50 States.

---
[15] Article I, Section 3, Clause 1 and the 17th Amendment.

The Framers hoped that the smaller Senate would be a more enlightened and responsible body than the House. Many of them thought that the House would be too often swayed by the immediate impact of events and by the passions of the moment. The Framers reinforced that hope by giving senators a longer term and by setting the qualifications for membership in the Senate a cut above those they set for the House.

James Madison saw those provisions as "a necessary fence" against the "fickleness and passion" of the House of Representatives. Nearly a century later, Woodrow Wilson agreed with Madison:

▲ Senator Blanche K. Bruce (R., Mississippi) was one of the first two African Americans to serve in the Senate. He served one term from 1875 to 1881.

**PRIMARY Sources** " It is indispensable that besides the House of Representatives which runs on all fours with popular sentiment, we should have a body like the Senate which may refuse to run with it at all when it seems to be wrong—a body which has time and security enough to keep its head, if only now and then and but for a little while, till other people have had time to think. "
—Woodrow Wilson, *Congressional Government*

## Reading Strategy

### Drawing Inferences

Have students consider the structure and rules of the Senate. Why are senators rarely punished for "disorderly behavior"?

## Background Note

### Roots of Democracy

The institution of the senate first appeared in ancient Rome, where Romulus established an advisory council comprised of the heads of 100 prominent families. By 500 B.C. the senate had come to represent the patrician—or aristocratic—members of Roman society. Its membership increased to 300 and later to 600 as the aristocracy grew. The principal political institution of the Roman Republic (509–31 B.C.), the senate functioned as the municipal government during the Roman Empire but declined as did other Roman institutions in the 4th and 5th centuries A.D.

## Point-of-Use Resources

📁 **Guided Reading and Review** Unit 3 booklet, p. 6 provides students with practice identifying the main ideas and key terms of this section.

📁 **Lesson Plans** For lesson planning suggestions, see p. 46 of the Lesson Plans booklet.

📁 **Political Cartoons** See p. 38 of the Political Cartoons booklet for a cartoon relevant to this section.

📽 **Section Support Transparencies** Transparency 41, *Visual Learning;* Transparency 140, *Political Cartoon*

## Answer to . . .

**Interpreting Diagrams** A bill in committee can still be changed. Also most bills die in committee, so the opportunity to make one's voice heard needs to be taken early in the life of the bill.

---

### How to Write to Your Lawmakers

**Choose a method.** You can write to your representative's local address or to their Washington address. Check your telephone directory's blue pages to find local addresses. Letters can be sent to representatives in Washington at the following addresses:

Representative _____
House Office Building
Washington, D.C. 20515

Senator _____
Senate Office Building
Washington, D.C. 20510

**Write while your issue is still current.** Don't wait until a bill is out of the committee or has passed the House (or Senate).

**Be specific.** Identify the issue that prompted you to write, preferably in your first paragraph. Give the bill number or mention its popular title - e.g. the Minimum Wage Bill, the Child Care Bill.

**Be brief, but give the reasons for your position.** Avoid these don'ts:
- Don't make threats or promises.
- Don't berate your lawmaker.
- Don't pretend to wield vast political power.
- Don't try to instruct your lawmaker on every issue.

> 9 Robin Court
> New Carrollton, MD 20784
> September 17, 2001
>
> Rep. Albert Wynn
> House Office Building
> Washington, D.C. 20515
>
> Dear Mr. Wynn:
>
> I am writing to express my support for H.R. 113, which would provide $14.2 billion to public high schools for repairs and construction. Since H.R. 113 will be debated next month, I would like to explain why I believe this bill is important to my school and others in the 4th district.
>
> I am a junior at Stevens High School, a public high school in New Carrollton. Like many schools in the United States, Stevens High School was built more than forty years ago and needs major repairs. This year the entire heating system had to be replaced, the roof is in poor condition, and the science laboratories are outdated. Our district simply does not have the money to make all of the repairs that are needed. As you can understand, students find it difficult to learn in this environment.
>
> I understand that lawmakers must make difficult decisions about the federal budget. However, I believe that school funding is crucial and I encourage you to vote "yes" on H.R. 113.
>
> Sincerely,
> *Ethan Locker*
> Ethan Locker

SOURCE: *Congressional Quarterly*

**Interpreting Diagrams** These guidelines were suggested by former Representative Morris Udall (D., Arizona).
*Why is it important to write while a bill is still in committee?*

Members of the Senate represent entire States. So nearly all of them represent a larger, more diverse population and a broader range of interests than do the representatives from their State. If you look at your own State—at the size, diversity, and major characteristics of its population and at its history, geography, and economy—you will see the point.

### Election

Originally, the Constitution provided that the members of the Senate were to be chosen by the State legislatures. Since the ratification of the 17th Amendment in 1913, however, senators have been picked by the voters in each State at the regular November elections. Only one senator is elected from a State in any given election, except when the other seat has been vacated by death, resignation, or expulsion.[16]

Before the coming of popular election, the State legislatures often picked popular and qualified senators. On other occasions, however, their choice was the result of maneuvering and in-fighting among the leaders of various factions in the State. These leaders all spent a great deal of energy trying to gain (and sometimes buy) enough legislators' votes to win a seat in the United States Senate. By the late 1800s, the Senate was often called the "Millionaires' Club," because so many wealthy party and business leaders sat in that chamber.

The Senate twice defeated House-passed amendments to provide for popular election. In 1912, it finally bowed to public opinion and agreed to what became the Seventeenth Amendment. The Senate was also persuaded by the fact that several States had already devised ways to ensure that their legislatures would choose senators who were supported by the people of the State.

---

[16]The 17th Amendment gives each State a choice of methods for filling a Senate vacancy. A State may (1) fill the seat at a special election called by the governor, or (2) allow the governor to appoint someone to serve until the voters fill the vacancy at such a special election or at the next regular (November) election. Most States use the appointment-special election method.

---

### Organizing Information

To make sure students understand the main points of this section, you may wish to use the web graphic organizer to the right.

Tell students that a web provides an outline of a main idea and its supporting details. Ask students to use the web to list details about the Senate. The word *Senate* should appear in the center circle.

**Teaching Tip** A template for this graphic organizer can be found in the Section Support Transparencies, Transparency 1.

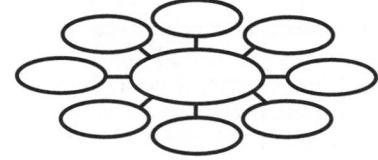

Each senator is elected from the State at-large. The Seventeenth Amendment declares that all persons whom the State allows to vote for members of "the most numerous Branch" of its legislature are qualified to vote for candidates for the United States Senate.

## Term

Senators serve for six-year terms, three times the length of those for which members of the House are chosen.[17] Senators may be elected to any number of terms. Strom Thurmond was elected to the Senate nine times, and served there for nearly 50 years. First elected as a Democrat, he became a Republican in 1964 and finally retired in 2003.

Senators' terms are staggered. Only a third of them—33 or 34 terms—expire every two years. The Senate is, then, a **continuous body.** That is, all of its seats are never up for election at the same time.

The six-year term gives senators a somewhat greater degree of job security than members of the lower house have. Those six years give senators some insulation from the rough-and-tumble of day-to-day politics. The six-year term is also intended to make senators less subject to the pressures of public opinion and less susceptible to the pleas of special interests than are members of the House.

The larger size and the geographic scope of their **constituencies**—the people and interests the senators represent—are designed to have much the same effect. In other words, senators are supposed to be less concerned with the interests of a specific small locality and more focused on the "big picture" of the national interest. Indeed, senators are in general more likely to be regarded as national political leaders than most House members.

The large size of the House generally prevents representatives from gaining as much notice and public exposure as members of the Senate attract. Senators, and especially those who have presidential ambitions, are better able to capture national media attention. Over the past several elections, the Senate has emerged as a prime source of candidates for the presidential nomination in both parties. Senators also find it easier to establish themselves as the champions of public policies that appeal to large

---

[17]Article I, Section 3, Clause 1.

segments of the American people—areas such as social security or national health care.

Senators are also more likely to be covered by the media in their States. They tend to have more clout in their State's politics than their **colleagues,** or coworkers, in the House.

## Qualifications for Senators

A senator must meet a higher level of qualifications than those the Constitution sets for a member of the House. A senator must be at least 30 years of age, must have been a citizen of the United States for at least nine years, and must be an inhabitant of the State from which he or she is elected.[18]

---

[18]Article I, Section 3, Clause 3. Under the inhabitant qualification, a senator need not have lived in the State for any particular period of time. Most often, of course, senators have been longtime residents of their States.

### *Spotlight* on Texas Government

**Congressional Leaders** Two Texas leaders, Sam Rayburn (1882–1961) and Lyndon Baines Johnson (1908–1973) had a major impact on American politics during the mid-1900s. Texas sent Sam Rayburn to the U.S. House of Representatives in 1912 and kept him in Congress for the next 48 years. Rayburn became Speaker of the House in 1940. He held this position in every Democratically-controlled Congress, and served as minority leader during the periods of Republican majorities.

Lyndon Johnson served in the United States House of Representatives for 11 years. He ran for the Senate against popular former governor Coke Stevenson in 1948, and after a long legal battle was declared the Democratic nominee. He won the general election easily, became the majority whip in 1951, and in 1953 became the youngest minority leader in Senate history. Johnson was reelected in 1954 and became the majority leader.

As majority leader, Johnson worked closely with Speaker of the House Rayburn. In 1960, the Texas legislature passed a special law allowing Johnson to run for President and for reelection to the Senate at the same time. His bid to lead the Democratic ticket failed, but he accepted the Vice President position on John F. Kennedy's ticket and ultimately became President after the Kennedy assassination.

**Analyzing Texas Government**

*What Texas issues and perspectives might Rayburn and Johnson have brought to Congress during the mid-1900s?*

## Point-of-Use Resources

**Guide to the Essentials** Chapter 10, Section 3, p. 57 provides support for students who need additional review of section content. Spanish support is available in the Spanish edition of the Guide on p. 50.

**Quiz** Unit 3 booklet, p. 7 includes matching and multiple-choice questions to check students' understanding of Section 3 content.

**Presentation Pro CD-ROM** Quizzes and multiple-choice questions check students' understanding of Section 3 content.

## Answers to . . .

### Section 3 Assessment

**1.** Because senators' terms are staggered, all of its seats are never up for election at the same time.
**2.** A senator's constituency is generally much larger than that of a representative, because a senator represents an entire State while a representative usually represents just a district within a State.
**3.** Because there are far fewer senators than representatives, each senator is more visible and tends to get more attention.
**4.** The 17th Amendment stipulated that senators be elected by the voters of each State; prior to the Amendment, they were elected by State legislatures.
**5.** They believed a six-year term would make senators less subject to pressure by public opinion or special interest groups.
**6.** Possible answer: If the required majority were less than two thirds, the vote could be dominated by a single party, which would not be fair.

## Answer to . . .

**Interpreting Political Cartoons** Possible answer: The candidate increases his chances of being elected by buying the votes of State legislators.

---

*Interpreting Political Cartoons* This 1890 cartoon depicts a candidate for the Senate. **Why does the candidate deposit his money in a box labeled "State Legislature"?**

"THE WAY WE BECOME SENATORS NOWADAYS"

The Senate, like the House, judges the qualifications of its members, and it may exclude a member by a majority vote.[19] As has the House, the Senate has at times refused to seat a member-elect. The Senate may also "punish its Members for disorderly Behavior" by majority vote and "with the Concurrence of two thirds, expel a Member."[20]

Fifteen members of the Senate have been expelled by that body, one in 1797 and 14 during

[19] Article I, Section 5, Clause 1.
[20] Article I, Section 5, Clause 2.

the Civil War. Senator William Blount of Tennessee was expelled in 1797 for conspiring to lead two Native American tribes, supported by British warships, in attacks on Spanish Florida and Louisiana. The 14 senators ousted in 1861 and 1862 were all from States of the Confederacy and were expelled for supporting secession.

Since the country was founded, a few senators have resigned in the face of almost certain expulsion. Most recently, the Senate's Ethics Committee had recommended that Senator Bob Packwood (R., Oregon) be expelled from the Senate because of several episodes of sexual harassment and other personal misconduct. Packwood, in his fifth term in the upper house, had fought the charges for years. But the Ethics Committee's chairman, Senator Mitch McConnell (R., Kentucky), noted that lengthy committee investigations had shown "a habitual pattern of aggressive, blatantly sexual advances." Such behavior, McConnell declared, "cannot be tolerated in the United States Senate." Senator Packwood resigned effective October 1, 1995.

The punishing of a senator for "disorderly Behavior" has also been rare. In the most recent case, in 1990, the Senate formally "denounced" Senator David Durenberger (R., Minnesota). The Ethics Committee had found him guilty on several counts of financial misconduct. The Senate called Durenberger's conduct "reprehensible" and declared that he had "brought the Senate into dishonor and disrepute." Senator Durenberger chose not to seek reelection to a third term in 1994.

---

## Section 3 Assessment

### Key Terms and Main Ideas

1. Why is the Senate called a **continuous body**?
2. How does a typical senator's **constituency** differ from that of a typical representative in the House?
3. Why do most senators receive more public attention than their **colleagues** in the House of Representatives?

### Critical Thinking

4. **Determining Cause and Effect** Why did the 17th Amendment change the way that senators are chosen?
5. **Making Comparisons** Why did the Framers set each senator's term at six years instead of two years?

6. **Drawing Inferences** In order to expel a senator from the Senate, two thirds of the Senate must agree. Why do you think the Constitution sets such a high requirement?

 **Take It to the Net**

7. In 1955, the Senate selected five former members who had been significant contributors to the nation. Choose one of the five senators and write a paragraph that explains why the senator you chose is included in the famous five. Use the links provided in the Social Studies area at the following Web site for help in completing this activity. **www.phschool.com**

---

**Take It to the Net**

**7.** Direct students to the Social Studies area at the Prentice Hall School Web site. The *Magruder's American Government* companion Web site includes the directions and links needed to complete the activity. It also provides a printable Internet activity worksheet with scoring rubrics for assessment. Paragraphs should be clearly organized and supported with relevant examples.

# 4 The Members of Congress

## Section Preview

### OBJECTIVES

1. **Compare and evaluate** characteristics of the current members of Congress.
2. **Compare and contrast** the duties of the job of serving in Congress.
3. **Describe** the compensation and privileges given to members of Congress.

### WHY IT MATTERS

Members of Congress must fill several roles as lawmakers, politicians, and servants of the voters. For their work, they receive fairly generous pay and benefits.

### POLITICAL DICTIONARY

★ **trustee**
★ **partisan**
★ **politico**
★ **oversight function**
★ **franking privilege**

You have seen help wanted ads in the newspaper—ads that describe jobs to be filled, listing their pay and so on. But you have never seen one that reads: "Wanted: Members of Congress. . . ." How would such an ad describe the duties, the pay, and other aspects of the position? This section will help you answer that question.

## Characteristics of Members of Congress

Whatever else they may be, the 535 members of Congress are *not* a representative cross section of the American people. Rather, the "average" member is a white male in his mid-50s. The median age of the members of the House is just over 54 and of the Senate, 60.

The composition of both chambers of Congress has been changing fairly rapidly over recent years. More women now sit in Congress than ever before: 59 of them are members of the House and 13 serve in the Senate. There are 39 African American members of Congress today—only one of them is a Republican, Representative J. C. Watts of Oklahoma. There are also 21 Hispanics and 6 Asian Americans and Pacific Islanders in the lower house. The House also now includes its first-ever Chinese American member, David Wu (D., Oregon), first elected in 1998, and reelected in 2000. The Senate's first full-blooded Native American, Ben Nighthorse Campbell (R., Colorado), was elected in 1992 and reelected in 1998.

Nearly all members are married, a few are divorced, and they have, on the average, two children. Only a few members say they have no religious affiliation. Just about 60 percent are Protestants, 25 percent are Roman Catholics, and some 8 percent are Jewish.

Well over a third of the members of the House and well over half the senators are lawyers. Nearly all went to college. More than four out of five have a college degree and a number have advanced degrees.

Most senators and representatives were born in the States they represent. Only a handful were born outside the United States. Sprinkled among the members of Congress are several millionaires. A surprisingly large number of representatives, however, depend on their congressional salaries as their major source of income.

Most members of Congress have had considerable political experience. The average senator is serving a second term, and the typical representative has served four terms. Nearly a third of the senators once sat in the House. Several senators are former governors. A few senators have held Cabinet seats or other high posts in the executive branch of the Federal Government. The House has a

▲ Representative J. C. Watts (R., Oklahoma) played professional football in Canada years before joining the House in 1995.

## Reading Strategy

### Predicting Content

Ask students to write a description of an average member of Congress, supplying as many details as they can, such as age, gender, education, job background, pay, and work requirements. Tell students to adjust their descriptions as they read the section.

## Customize for

### Less Proficient Readers

Remind students of the five major roles played by members of Congress: *legislator, representative, committee member, servant,* and *politician.* Assign students one of the roles and ask them to create a political cartoon that illustrates that aspect of a congressperson's job. Ask for volunteers to share their cartoons with the class.

## Point–of–Use Resources

**Guided Reading and Review** Unit 3 booklet, p. 8 provides students with practice identifying the main ideas and key terms of this section.

**Lesson Plans** For lesson planning suggestions, see p. 47 of the Lesson Plans booklet.

**Political Cartoons** See p. 39 of the Political Cartoons booklet for a cartoon relevant to this section.

**Section Support Transparencies** Transparency 42, *Visual Learning;* Transparency 141, *Political Cartoon*

### Answer to . . .

**Interpreting Graphs** The House has a higher percentage of non-Caucasian members.

large number of former State legislators and prosecuting attorneys among its members.

Again, Congress is not an accurate cross section of the nation's population. Rather, it is made up of upper-middle-class Americans, who are, on the whole, quite able and hard-working people.

## The Job

One leading commentary on American politics describes Congress and the job of a member of Congress this way:

> **PRIMARY Sources** ❝ Congress has a split personality. On the one hand, it is a lawmaking institution and makes policy for the entire nation. In this capacity, all the members are expected to set aside their personal ambitions and perhaps even the concerns of their constituencies. Yet Congress is also a representative assembly, made up of 535 elected officials who serve as links between their constituents and the National Government. The dual roles of making laws and responding to constituents' demands forces members to balance national concerns against the specific interests of their States or districts. ❞
> —Burns, et al., *Government by the People*

Members of Congress play five major roles. They are most importantly (1) legislators and (2) representatives of their constituents. Beyond these roles, they are also (3) committee members, (4) servants of their constituents, and (5) politicians. You will take a close look at their lawmaking function in the next two chapters. Here, we consider their representative, committee member, and servant functions.

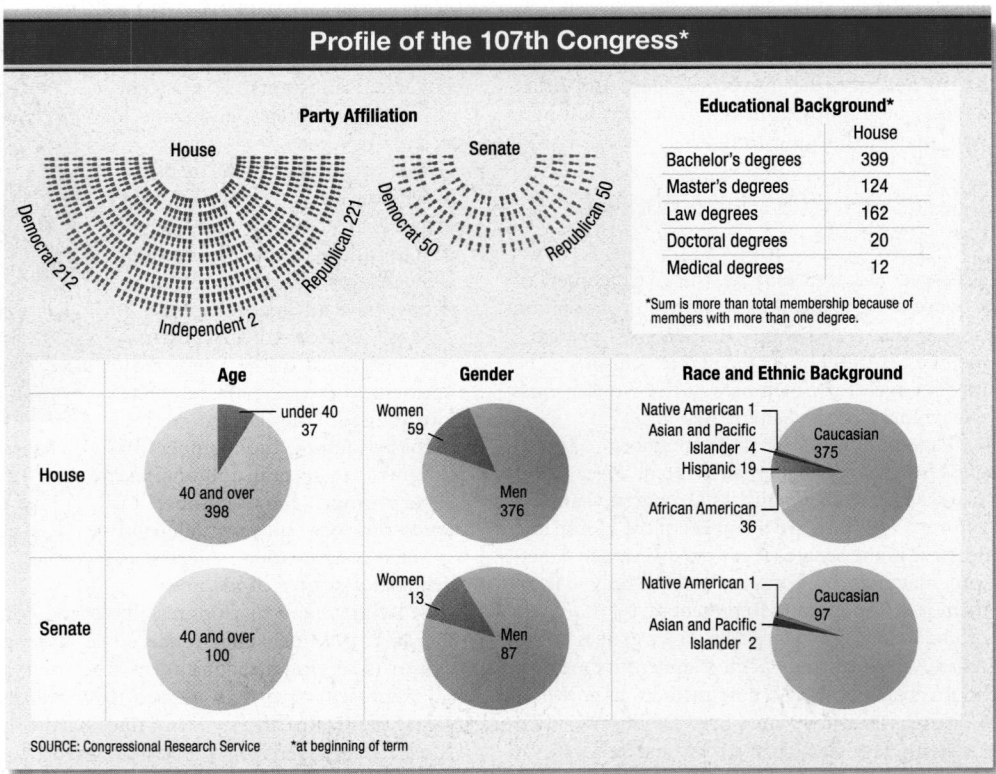

### Profile of the 107th Congress*

**Party Affiliation**

House — Democrat 212, Republican 221, Independent 2

Senate — Democrat 50, Republican 50

**Educational Background***

| | House |
|---|---|
| Bachelor's degrees | 399 |
| Master's degrees | 124 |
| Law degrees | 162 |
| Doctoral degrees | 20 |
| Medical degrees | 12 |

*Sum is more than total membership because of members with more than one degree.

**Age** — House: under 40 = 37; 40 and over = 398. Senate: 40 and over = 100.

**Gender** — House: Women 59, Men 376. Senate: Women 13, Men 87.

**Race and Ethnic Background** — House: Native American 1, Asian and Pacific Islander 4, Hispanic 19, African American 36, Caucasian 375. Senate: Native American 1, Asian and Pacific Islander 2, Caucasian 97.

SOURCE: Congressional Research Service    *at beginning of term

 **Interpreting Graphs** Members of Congress come to Washington, D.C., with a wide variety of backgrounds. **How does racial and ethnic diversity differ between the House and the Senate?**

## Spotlight on Technology

 **Magruder's American Government Video Collection**

The Magruder's Video Collection explores key issues and debates in American government. Each segment examines an issue central to chapter content through use of historical and contemporary footage. Commentary from civic leaders in academics, government, and the media follow each segment. Critical-thinking questions focus students' attention on key issues, and may be used to stimulate discussion.

Use the Chapter 10 video segment to explore the dynamics of the legislative branch. (time: about 5 minutes) This segment takes a look at the inner workings of Congress, including floor debates, roll call votes, and committee hearings. A filibuster clip from the 1950s adds historical perspective.

## Representatives of the People

Senators and representatives are elected to represent people. But what does that really mean? They cast hundreds of votes during each session of Congress. Many of those votes involve quite routine, relatively unimportant matters; for example, a bill to designate a week in May as National Wild Flower Week. But many of those votes, including some on matters of organization and procedure, are cast on matters of far-reaching import.

So, no questions about the lawmaking branch can be more vital than these: How do the people's representatives represent the people? On what basis do they cast their votes?

In broad terms, each lawmaker has four voting options. He or she can vote as a trustee, as a delegate, as a partisan, or as a politico.

**Trustees** believe that each question they face must be decided on its merits. Conscience and independent judgment are their guides. Trustees call issues as they see them, regardless of the views held by their constituents or by any of the other groups that seek to influence their decisions.

Delegates see themselves as the agents of those who elected them. They believe that they should vote the way they think "the folks back home" would want. They are willing to suppress their own views, ignore those of their party's leaders, and turn a deaf ear to the arguments of colleagues and of special interests from outside their constituencies.

Those lawmakers who owe their first allegiance to their political party are **partisans**. They feel duty-bound to vote in line with the party platform and the wishes of their party's leaders. Most studies of legislators' voting behavior show that partisanship is the leading factor influencing their votes on most important measures.

**Politicos** attempt to combine the basic elements of the trustee, delegate, and partisan roles. They try to balance these often conflicting factors: their own views of what is best for their constituents and/or the nation as a whole, the political facts of life, and the peculiar pressures of the moment.

## Committee Members

In every session of Congress, proposed laws (bills) are referred to committees in each chamber. As committee members, senators and representatives must screen those proposals. They decide which will go on to floor consideration—that is, be considered and acted upon by the full membership of the House or Senate.

Another vital part of their committee work involves the **oversight function.** Oversight is the process by which Congress, through its committees, checks to see that the various agencies in the executive branch are working effectively and acting in line with the policies that Congress has set by law.

## Servants

Members of the House and Senate also act as servants of their constituents. Most often, they do this as they (and, more particularly, their staff aides) try to help people who have various problems with the federal bureaucracy. Those problems may involve a Social Security benefit, a passport application, a small business loan, or any one of a thousand other issues.

Some of "the folks back home" believe that members of Congress are in Washington

---

# *Voices* on Government

For **Alan Simpson,** politics is a family business. His father was governor of Wyoming and a U.S. senator. Simpson began his political career at the State level, and was later elected to the U.S. Senate. His 18 years as a Republican senator gave him this perspective:

❝*I am a legislator. I never wanted to be governor or president or vice president. If you're thinking of politics, make up your mind. You're going to legislate or you want to be governor, president, emperor or king—what is it you're interested in? And make that choice. For me it was to take an idea and personally draft the bill. Which I would do. . . . I did my own amendments, would work the bill myself, manage it on the floor. And so I legislated.*❞

## Evaluating the Quotation

*Simpson sees a big difference between legislative and executive jobs. How does his description compare with what you have read about Congress in this chapter?*

---

---

## Take It to the Net

For career-related links and activities, visit the *Magruder's American Government* companion Web site in the Social Studies area at the Prentice Hall School Web site.

---

## Make It Relevant

# Careers in Government—Tour Guide

More than ten million people from around the world tour the Capitol every year, and benefit from the knowledge of members of the Capitol Guide Service. They and other government tour guides educate and delight as they make the American government accessible to everyone. They are a critical bridge between the people and their national treasures.

**Skills Activity** Direct pairs of students to create virtual tours of local historic or government sites using printed and/or Internet resources. Students should guide their classmates on these virtual tours, answering questions as they go. Then have individual students write paragraphs explaining why they would or would not be interested in a career as a government tour guide. **(Average)**

*Answer to . . .*
**Evaluating the Quotation** Answers will vary, but should be supported with facts from the chapter.

▲ Representative Ileana Ros-Lehtinen (R., Florida) must balance several different roles. Her jobs include publicizing important issues, meeting with constituents, and working with her fellow lawmakers in Washington. *Critical Thinking Why is it important for a representative to speak often with constituents?*

primarily to do favors for them. Most members are swamped with constituent requests from the moment they take office. The range of these requests is almost without limit—everything from help in securing a government contract or an appointment to a military academy, to asking for a free sightseeing tour of Washington or even a personal loan. Consider this job description offered only half-jokingly by a former representative:

**PRIMARY Sources** *A Congressman has become an expanded messenger boy, an employment agency, getter-outer of the Navy, Army, Marines, ward heeler, wound healer, trouble shooter, law explainer, bill finder, issue translator, resolution interpreter, controversy oil pourer, gladhand extender, business promoter, convention goer, civil ills skirmisher, veterans' affairs adjuster, ex-serviceman's champion, watchdog for the underdog, sympathizer with the upper dog, namer and kisser of babies, recoverer of lost luggage, soberer of delegates, adjuster for traffic violators, voters straying into Washington and into toils of the law, binder up of broken hearts, financial wet nurse, Good Samaritan, contributor to good causes—there are so many good causes—cornerstone layer, public building and bridge dedicator, ship christener—to be sure he does get in a little flag waving—and a little constitutional hoisting and*

*spread-eagle work, but it is getting harder every day to find time to properly study legislation—the very business we are primarily here to discharge, and that must be done above all things.*
—Rep. Luther Patrick (D., Alabama)

Most members of Congress know that to deny or fail to respond to these requests would mean to lose votes in the next election. This is a key fact, for all of the roles a member of Congress plays—legislator, representative, committee member, constituent servant, and politician—are related, at least in part, to their efforts to win reelection.

## Compensation

The Constitution says that members of Congress "shall receive a Compensation for their Services, to be ascertained by Law. . . ."[21] That is, the Constitution says that Congress fixes that "Compensation."

### Salary

Today, senators and representatives are paid a salary of $150,000 a year. A few members are paid somewhat more. The Speaker of the

[21] Article I, Section 6, Clause 1. The 27th Amendment modified this pay-setting authority. It provides that no increase in members' pay can take effect until after the next congressional election—that is, not until the voters have had an opportunity to react to the pay raise.

House makes $187,500 a year, the same salary that Congress has set for the Vice President. The Senate's president *pro tem* and the majority and minority floor leaders in both houses receive $162,000 a year.

## Nonsalary Compensation

Each member receives a number of "fringe benefits," some of which are quite substantial. For example, each member has a special tax deduction, not available to any other federal income tax payer. That deduction is designed to help members who must maintain two residences, one in his or her home State and another in Washington.

Generous travel allowances offset the costs of several round trips each year between home and Washington. Members pay relatively small amounts for life and health insurance and for outpatient care by a medical staff on Capitol Hill; they can get full medical care, at very low rates, at any military hospital. They also have a generous retirement plan, to which they contribute. The plan pays a pension based on years of service in Congress, and longtime members can retire with an income of $150,000 or more a year. Members of Congress are also covered by Social Security's retirement and medicare programs.

Members are also provided with offices in one of the several Senate and House office buildings near the Capitol and allowances for offices in their home State or district. Each member is given funds for hiring staff and for operation costs related to running those offices. The **franking privilege** is a well-known benefit that allows them to mail letters and other materials postage-free by substituting their facsimile signature (frank) for the postage.

Congress has also provided its members with the free printing—and through franking, the free distribution—of speeches, newsletters, and the like. Radio and television tapes can be produced at very low cost. Each member can choose among several fine restaurants in the Capitol. There are also two first-rate gymnasiums, with swimming pools, exercise rooms, and saunas. Members receive still more privileges, including such things as the help of the excellent services of the Library of Congress and free parking in spaces reserved for them at the Capitol and also at Washington's major airports.[22]

## The Politics of Pay

There are only two real limits on the level of congressional pay. One is the President's veto power. The other and more potent limit is the fear of voter backlash, an angry reaction by constituents at the ballot box. That fear of election-day fallout has always made most members reluctant to vote to raise their own salaries.

Congress has often tried to skirt the troublesome and politically sensitive pay question. Members have done so by providing for such fringe benefits as a special tax break, a liberal pension plan, more office and travel funds, and other perquisites, or "perks"—items of value that are much less apparent to "the folks back home."

The debate over congressional pay is not likely to end soon—at least not as long as the current method of establishing salaries remains in effect. All sides of the issue present reasonable arguments.

---

[22]For decades, many members of Congress supplemented their salaries with honoraria—speaking fees and similar payments from private sources, mainly special interest groups. Critics long attacked that widespread practice as at least unseemly and, at its worst, a form of legalized bribery. The House finally prohibited its members from accepting honoraria in 1989, and the Senate did so in 1991.

"*Congratulations on your raise, sir.*"

*Interpreting Political Cartoons* The salaries and benefits enjoyed by members of Congress have long been a sensitive political issue. **Why are voters reluctant to see members of Congress increase their benefits and pay?**

## Point-of-Use Resources

 **ABC News Civics and Government Videotape Library**
*The West Versus Washington* (time: about 21 minutes)

*Answer to . . .*

**Interpreting Political Cartoons** They may resent the fact that their tax dollars are used to pay members of Congress or resent that members make more than the average salary of most Americans.

## Point-of-Use Resources

**Guide to the Essentials** Chapter 10, Section 4, p. 58 provides support for students who need additional review of section content. Spanish support is available in the Spanish edition of the Guide on p. 51.

**Quiz** Unit 3 booklet, p. 9 includes matching and multiple-choice questions to check students' understanding of Section 4 content.

**Presentation Pro CD-ROM** Quizzes and multiple-choice questions check students' understanding of Section 4 content.

## Answers to . . .

### Section 4 Assessment

**1.** A delegate most values the opinions and wishes of his or her constituents.
**2.** A partisan most values the platform of his or her party and the wishes of that party's leader.
**3.** It allows them to mail letters and other materials postage-free.
**4.** To ensure that the various agencies in the executive branch are working effectively and are following congressional policies set by law.
**5.** Roles include: Legislators, committee members, representatives of their constituency, public servants, and politicians.
**6.** They fear that their constituents will not approve, which would affect their reelection chances.
**7.** Possible answer: The letter writer wants his or her message to be read and respected. Berating the congressperson won't achieve that end.

---

Clearly, decent salaries—pay in line with the responsibilities of the job—will not automatically bring the most able men and women to Congress, or to any other public office. But certainly, decent salaries can make public service much more appealing to qualified people.

### Membership Privileges

Beyond the matter of their salaries and other compensation, members of Congress enjoy several privileges. The Constitution commands that senators and representatives

 **FROM THE Constitution** *❝shall in all Cases, except Treason, Felony and Breach of the Peace, be privileged from Arrest during their Attendance at the Session of their respective Houses, and in going to and returning from the same. . . . ❞*
—Article I, Section 6, Clause 1

The provision dates from English and colonial practice, when the king's officers often harassed legislators on petty grounds. It has been of little importance in our national history, however.[23]

Another much more important privilege is set out in the same place in the Constitution. The Speech or Debate Clause of Article I, Section 6, Clause 1 declares ". . . for any Speech or Debate in either House, they shall not be questioned in any other Place." The words "any other Place" refer particularly to the courts.

The privilege is intended to "throw a cloak of legislative immunity" around members of Congress. The clause protects representatives and senators from suits for libel or slander arising out of their official conduct. The Supreme Court has held that the immunity applies "to things generally done in a session of the House [or Senate] by one of its members in relation to the business before it."[24] The protection goes, then, beyond floor debate, to include work in committees and all other things generally done by members of Congress in relation to congressional business.

The important and necessary goal of this provision of the Constitution is to protect freedom of legislative debate. Clearly, members must not feel restrained in their vigorous discussion of the sometimes contentious issues of the day. However, this provision is not designed to give members unbridled freedom to attack others verbally or in writing. Thus, a member is not free to defame another person in a public speech, an article, a conversation, or otherwise.

---

[23]The courts have regularly held that the words "Breach of the Peace" cover all criminal offenses. So the protection covers only arrest for civil (noncriminal) offenses while engaged in congressional business.

[24]The leading case is *Kilbourn* v. *Thompson*, 1881. The holding has been affirmed many times since. In *Hutchinson* v. *Proxmire*, 1979, however, the Court held that members of Congress may be sued for libel for statements they make in news releases or in newsletters.

## Section 4 Assessment

**Key Terms and Main Ideas**

1. What does a **delegate** value most when deciding how to vote on a bill?
2. What does a **partisan** value most when deciding how to vote on a bill?
3. How does the **franking privilege** help members of Congress?
4. What is the **oversight function**?

**Critical Thinking**

5. **Drawing Conclusions** What are the different roles that a member of Congress plays?
6. **Determining Cause and Effect** Why are members of Congress reluctant to pass laws that give them new benefits or higher pay?

7. **Drawing Inferences** Look again at the diagram on page 276. Why might it be a good idea for a letter writer to use a respectful tone?

### Take It to the Net

8. The Senate's oversight function is an important part of the system of checks and balances. Read about the oversight function and write a paragraph explaining why this is an essential power of the Senate. Use the links provided in the Social Studies area at the following Web site for help in completing this activity. **www.phschool.com**

 **Take It to the Net**

**8.** Direct students to the Social Studies area at the Prentice Hall School Web site. The *Magruder's American Government* companion Web site includes the directions and links needed to complete the activity. It also provides a printable Internet activity worksheet with scoring rubrics for assessment. Paragraphs will vary but should be supported with specific facts and examples.

# *on the Supreme Court*

## May Congresspersons Be Sued for Their Statements?

*The "Speech or Debate Clause" in Article I, Section 6 of the Constitution provides that senators and representatives "shall not be questioned in any other place" over "any speech or debate in either House." This has been interpreted to mean that they cannot be sued for anything they say in their legislative chambers. How far does this protection extend?*

### Hutchinson v. Proxmire (1979)

Senator William Proxmire of Wisconsin invented the "Golden Fleece of the Month Award" to publicize what he saw as examples of wasteful government spending. In 1975 he gave awards to various federal agencies for spending almost half a million dollars to fund Professor Ronald Hutchinson's research on emotional behavior. Hutchinson was trying to develop an objective measure of aggression, and his research focused on certain behavior patterns, such as clenching of the jaw.

In an "awards speech" to the Senate, Proxmire stated: "In view of the transparent worthlessness of Hutchinson's study of jaw-grinding and biting by angry . . . monkeys, it is time we put a stop to the bite [that] Hutchinson and the bureaucrats who fund him have been taking of the taxpayer." His remarks were published in the *Congressional Record* and in a press release and in various newsletters.

Hutchinson sued Proxmire, saying his professional reputation had been damaged. Proxmire responded that his remarks were protected by the Speech or Debate Clause and by the First Amendment. The district court and court of appeals ruled in favor of Proxmire, and the case went to the Supreme Court for review.

### Arguments for Hutchinson

1. The Speech or Debate Clause should not extend protection to comments that are made outside of the Senate chamber or are not part of the legislative function of the Senate.
2. The newsletters and press release about the Golden Fleece Award were aimed at persons outside Congress and thus are not part of the senator's official duties.
3. Since Professor Hutchinson is not a public figure, he does not have to prove as part of his lawsuit that the senator's remarks were made with actual malice (desire to harm).

### Arguments for Proxmire

1. The senator's comments in the Senate about matters of national importance were protected by the Speech or Debate Clause; the use of these comments in a press release and newsletters describing the Senate speech were part of the senator's official duty to inform the public about his activities.
2. The senator's criticisms of wasteful spending of public funds were also privileged under the Free Speech Clause of the First Amendment.
3. Professor Hutchinson is a public figure; therefore, he must prove as part of his suit that Proxmire acted with actual malice.

---

### Decide for Yourself

1. Review the constitutional grounds on which each side based its arguments and the specific arguments each side presented.
2. Debate the opposing viewpoints presented in this case. Which viewpoint do you favor?
3. Predict the impact of the Court's decision on activities and statements by members of Congress outside the House and Senate chambers. (To read a summary of the Court's decision, turn to the Supreme Court Glossary on page 799.)

---

*Corner*

📁 **Close Up on the Supreme Court** *Hutchinson* v. *Proxmire*, p. 11 provides an activity to extend coverage of this case.

To keep up-to-date on Close Up news and activities, visit Close Up Online at

**www.closeup.org**

---

## May Congresspersons Be Sued for Their Statements?

**Focus** Have the class read the Speech and Debate Clause of the Constitution. *(The final clause of Article I, Section 6 (1))* Call on a volunteer to explain its purpose. *(To protect freedom of legislative debate)* Then inform the class that this case considers the limits to the Speech and Debate privilege.

**Instruct** Ask a volunteer to explain how this case limits the Speech and Debate privilege. *(It only applies to speech directly related to the legislative function)* Then discuss why the law provides less protection for critical remarks about "public figures." *(Because public figures expect to have their opinions subjected to public debate and criticism)*

**Close/Reteach** Explain that the Speech and Debate Clause has been held to protect members of Congress from arrest, prosecution, or suit; however, it does not prohibit Congress from disciplining its own members. Ask students to explain how this arrangement is related to the Separation of Powers doctrine. *(It insures the independence of the legislative branch, but still provides a way to discipline legislators)*

💿 **Keep It Current CD-ROM** includes government-related projects by unit. The CD-ROM links to the Prentice Hall School Web site and may be used for daily updates.

---

### *Answers to . . .*

**Decide for Yourself**

**1.** Hutchinson argued that the senator made comments outside of his official role, and therefore cannot be protected by the Speech or Debate Clause. Proxmire argued that his comments were part of his official duties and were protected by the First Amendment.
**2.** Answers will vary, but should be supported with valid reasoning.
**3.** The Court ruled in favor of Hutchinson, saying that Proxmire's speech was not protected, and was thus not immune from being sued.

# Assessment

## Practicing the Vocabulary

1. reapportion
2. prorogue
3. franking privilege
4. oversight function
5. gerrymander
6. adjourn
7. constituency
8. term
9. at-large
10. partisan

## Reviewing Main Ideas

### Section 1

**11.** By giving each State equal representation in the Senate and representation proportional to its population in the House, bicameralism ensures a division of power.
**12. (a)** By population; the number of representatives each State has varies. **(b)** Equally; each State has two senators.
**13. (a)** A meeting of Congress called by the President to address an emergency situation. **(b)** As Congress now meets nearly year-round, it is less likely that the President would need to call a special session.

### Section 2

**14.** As seats are distributed according to each State's population, reapportionment must occur when the census is taken—every 10 years.
**15.** States have often gerrymandered districts; that is, they have re-drawn districts to the advantage of the party that controls the State legislature. They have also set up at-large systems of voting, which allow parties with even small pluralities to gain the entire State's seats.
**16. (a)** They must be 25 years of age, have been a U.S. citizen for at least seven years, and must be an inhabitant of the State from which they are elected. **(b)** They must be able to win votes.

### Section 3

**17.** Senators serve six-year terms rather than two-year terms; senators must meet a higher level of qualifications than those set for the House.
**18. (a)** Constituencies vary according to the size, diversity, and population characteristics of each State. **(b)** California.

## Political Dictionary

term (p. 264)
session (p. 264)
adjourn (p. 264)
prorogue (p. 265)
special session (p. 265)
apportion (p. 267)
reapportion (p. 267)

off-year election (p. 269)
single-member district (p. 270)
at-large (p. 270)
gerrymander (p. 271)
continuous body (p. 277)
constituency (p. 277)
colleague (p. 277)

trustee (p. 281)
partisan (p. 281)
politico (p. 281)
oversight function (p. 281)
franking privilege (p. 283)

## Practicing the Vocabulary

*Matching* Choose a term from the list above that best matches each description.

1. What happens to the seats in the House of Representatives every decade
2. What the President can do if the two houses of Congress cannot agree on a date to adjourn
3. The right of members of Congress to send mail postage-free by using a signature in place of a stamp
4. The function Congress is performing when it checks on the programs of the executive branch
5. How you might describe a congressional district that has been drawn by a legislature in a very odd shape

*Fill in the Blank* Choose a term from the list above that best completes the sentence.

6. Congress can _____, or suspend its meeting, whenever it chooses.
7. Each member of the House represents a _____ of about 630,000 people.
8. A member of the House of Representatives is elected for a two-year _____.
9. In States with a low population, members of the House of Representatives are chosen in _____ districts.
10. A _____ is a member of Congress who votes primarily according to the wishes of his or her party.

## Reviewing Main Ideas

### Section 1

11. How does bicameralism reflect the principle of federalism?
12. **(a)** How are States represented in the House of Representatives? **(b)** How are States represented in the Senate?
13. **(a)** What is a special session? **(b)** Why have special sessions lost their importance?

### Section 2

14. For what reasons must seats in Congress be reapportioned every 10 years?
15. In what ways has the redistricting of House seats been used for the political gain of certain groups and parties in the various States?
16. **(a)** What are the constitutional qualifications that all members of the House must meet? **(b)** What are the informal qualifications that members of the House should meet?

### Section 3

17. How do senators differ from their colleagues in the House of Representatives?
18. **(a)** How do constituencies vary within the Senate? **(b)** Which State's senators have the largest constituency?
19. **(a)** In what ways does the long six-year term affect how senators vote? **(b)** How does this confirm the Framers' intentions for the Senate?
20. What are the qualifications for senators?

### Section 4

21. **(a)** Do the members of Congress represent a cross section of the American people? **(b)** Why or why not?
22. **(a)** When deciding how to vote, what does a trustee consider? **(b)** When deciding how to vote, what does a politico consider?
23. How are members of Congress compensated for their work? List several examples.

**19. (a)** Senators are less likely to vote according to public or special interest pressure, as they have more job security with a six-year term. **(b)** The Framers wanted senators to be more enlightened and responsible than House members, and to serve national rather than local interests.
**20.** Senators must be 30 years of age; have been a U.S. citizen for at least nine years; and must be an inhabitant of the State from which they are elected.

### Section 4

**21. (a)** No; the average member of Congress is a white, well-educated, upper-class male in his mid-fifties. **(b)** Many Americans cannot meet the qualifications for members of Congress.
**22. (a)** Trustees consider the issue according to their conscience and independent judgment, regardless of party policies or their constituency. **(b)** Politicos consider all the elements of voter roles: their constituency, their party, and their own judgment.
**23.** In addition to set salaries, they receive a number of fringe benefits, including tax deductions, travel allowances, retirement plans, low-cost health insurance, offices and funds for staff, franking privileges, free printing, and other benefits.

## Critical Thinking Skills

**24.** *Applying the Chapter Skill* Study the map on page 263. **(a)** What does this map depict? **(b)** Write a summary explaining the information shown on the map. Which is the more effective way of conveying the information shown, the map or the written summary? Why?

**25.** *Predicting Consequences* Reread the conversation between Thomas Jefferson and George Washington on page 263. According to Washington, how would a unicameral (one-house) legislature produce different results than a bicameral Congress?

**26.** *Understanding Point of View* Congress is a frequent target of criticism in the media and elsewhere. Yet the text says that the members of Congress are on the whole hard-working and able people. How can you explain the existence of these two opposing viewpoints?

**27.** *Expressing Problems Clearly* Recall what you have read about the differences between the House and Senate. **(a)** Cite two benefits that flow from senators' six-year terms. **(b)** What are two drawbacks that arise out of those six-year terms?

## Analyzing Political Cartoons

Using your knowledge of American government and this cartoon, answer the questions below.

MEASURING POLITICAL CANDIDATES

**28.** According to this cartoonist, what factor plays an important role in determining who runs for office?

**29.** Based on your reading in this chapter, is the cartoonist correct? Explain your answer.

## You Can Make a Difference

Most congressional pages are nominated by the senator or representative from their home State. They are usually high school juniors with good grades and outstanding records in school and community service. Suppose that you want to spend a year in Washington, D.C., as a page in the House or Senate. Find out how to apply for this job. Then draft a letter to your senator or representative in which you explain why you want to be a page, what you think you would learn from the experience, and why you think your record and activities qualify you for the job.

## Participation Activities

**30.** *Current Events Watch* Choose one member of Congress named in a current news report and find out about a political action or decision made by the person while serving in Congress. Analyze the consequences of that action on American society.

**31.** *Graphing Activity* Turn to the map on page 268 and find the eight States with the greatest number of representatives in the House. Create a circle graph showing each State's representatives as a percentage of the 435 members of the House of Representatives. Remember to label the part of the circle graph that represents the other 42 States. What does this graph tell you about the influence of these States in the House of Representatives?

**32.** *It's Your Turn* Write a newspaper editorial expressing your views on the qualifications for membership in Congress. List the formal qualifications and those informal ones that you think members should satisfy. Suggest changes (if any) that you would make in those qualifications. Indicate why you think each of the informal qualifications you cite is important. Use standard grammar, spelling, sentence structure, and punctuation. Be sure to use social studies terminology correctly. **(Writing an Editorial)**

## Take It to the Net

*Chapter 10 Self-Test* As a final review activity, take the Chapter 10 Self-Test in the Social Studies area at the Web site listed below, and receive immediate feedback on your answers.

**www.phschool.com**

## Take It to the Net

Additional support materials and activities for Chapter 10 of *Magruder's American Government* can be found in the Social Studies area at the Prentice Hall School Web site.
**www.phschool.com**

## Point-of-Use Resources

**Guide to the Essentials of American Government** Chapter 10 Test, page 59 provides multiple-choice questions to test students' knowledge of the chapter.

**Test Bank CD-ROM** Chapter 10 Test

**Chapter Test** Chapter Tests booklet

## Critical Thinking Skills

**24. (a)** Every State has two senators, but population determines the number of House members. **(b)** The map is more concise. It is easy to visually compare quantities.

**25.** Possible answer: Washington thought a unicameral legislature would not provide the checks and balances called for by the principle of federalism.

**26.** Answers will vary. Students might suggest that members of Congress fill a number of roles in which they work ably and diligently, but these individual contributions are often overlooked by the public when blame is assigned for congressional actions.

**27. (a)** Possible benefits: Six-year terms make senators less likely to be pressured by special interests or public opinion and allow them to focus more on national interests. **(b)** Possible drawbacks: With six-year terms, a senator who is performing his or her job poorly cannot be voted out as quickly; with the focus on national interests, senators might not adequately take on the interests of their own States.

## Analyzing Political Cartoons

**28.** How much money the candidate has.

**29.** Answers will vary, but should be supported with relevant examples.

## You Can Make a Difference

Letters should be clear and well organized, and show an understanding of the qualifications for becoming a page.

## Participation Activities

**30.** Analyses should be well researched and clearly organized.

**31.** Graphs should accurately present the percentages of the eight States (California, Texas, New York, Florida, Illinois, Pennsylvania, Ohio, and Michigan); answers should suggest that these States would have great influence in the House.

**32.** Viewpoints expressed in students' editorials should be supported with specific facts and examples and should demonstrate an ability to use standard grammar, spelling, sentence structure, and punctuation. Social studies terminology should be used correctly.

# Powers of Congress

| Section Objectives | Print and Technology Resources |
|---|---|
| **1 The Scope of Congressional Powers** (pp. 290–292)<br><br>1. Identify the three types of Congressional power.<br>2. Compare strict construction of the U.S. Constitution on the subject of Congressional power to liberal construction.<br><br>🌐 **TEKS 2A, 8D, 9A, 17C, 21A, 21C, 22A, 22B, 22D** | • **Unit 3 booklet** Guided Reading and Review, p. 11 Section 1 Quiz, p. 12<br>• **Lesson Plans booklet** Section 1, p. 48<br>• **Political Cartoons booklet** Section 1, p. 40<br>• **Section Reading Support Transparencies**<br><br>• **Block Scheduling with Lesson Strategies booklet** p. 24<br>• **Basic Principles of the Constitution Transparencies** 17<br>• **Section Support Transparencies** 43, 142<br>• **Presentation Pro CD-ROM** Section 1<br>• **Social Studies Skills Tutor CD-ROM** |
| **2 The Expressed Powers of Money and Commerce** (pp. 294–300)<br><br>1. Summarize key points relating to Congress's power to tax.<br>2. Describe how Congress uses its power to borrow money.<br>3. Analyze the importance of Congress's commerce power.<br>4. Identify the reasons that the Framers gave Congress the power to issue currency.<br>5. Explain how the bankruptcy power works.<br><br>🌐 **TEKS 6B, 8D, 9A, 9E, 9G, 17C, 21A, 21C, 21D, 21E, 22A, 22B** | • **Unit 3 booklet** Guided Reading and Review, p. 13 Section 2 Quiz, p. 14<br>• **Lesson Plans booklet** Section 2, p. 49<br>• **Political Cartoons booklet** Section 2, p. 41<br>• **Close Up on the Supreme Court booklet** *Gibbons* v. *Ogden*, pp. 30–31<br>• **Section Reading Support Transparencies**<br><br>• **The Living Constitution booklet** p. 7<br>• **Basic Principles of the Constitution Transparencies** 24<br>• **Section Support Transparencies** 44, 143<br>• **Presentation Pro CD-ROM** Section 2<br>• **Simulations and Data Graphing CD-ROM** |
| **3 Other Expressed Powers** (pp. 301–304)<br><br>1. Identify the key sources of Congress's foreign relations powers.<br>2. Describe the power-sharing arrangement between Congress and the President on the issues of war and national defense.<br>3. List other key powers exercised by Congress.<br><br>🌐 **TEKS 8D, 9A, 9E, 9G, 17C, 21A, 21C, 21E, 22A, 22B, 22D** | • **Unit 3 booklet** Guided Reading and Review, p. 15 Section 3 Quiz, p. 16<br>• **Lesson Plans booklet** Section 3, p. 50<br>• **Political Cartoons booklet** Section 3, p. 42<br>• **Close Up on Primary Sources booklet** The Northwest Ordinance, p. 68<br>• **Section Reading Support Transparencies**<br><br>• **Basic Principles of the Constitution Transparencies** 36<br>• **Simulations and Debates booklet** pp. 53–55<br>• **Section Support Transparencies** 45, 144<br>• **Presentation Pro CD-ROM** Section 3 |
| **4 The Implied Powers** (pp. 305–308)<br><br>1. Explain how the Necessary and Proper Clause gives Congress flexibility in lawmaking.<br>2. Summarize the key developments in the battle over the implied powers of Congress.<br><br>🌐 **TEKS 2B, 8D, 9A, 9E, 21A, 21B, 21D, 22A, 22B, 22C** | • **Unit 3 booklet** Guided Reading and Review, p. 17 Section 4 Quiz, p. 18<br>• **Lesson Plans booklet** Section 4, p. 51<br>• **Political Cartoons booklet** Section 4, p. 43<br>• **Section Reading Support Transparencies**<br><br>• **The Living Constitution booklet** p. 13<br>• **Basic Principles of the Constitution Transparencies** 3<br>• **Section Support Transparencies** 46, 145<br>• **Presentation Pro CD-ROM** Section 4 |
| **5 The Nonlegislative Powers** (pp. 310–314)<br><br>1. Describe Congress's role in amending the Constitution and in deciding elections.<br>2. Describe Congress's power to impeach and summarize cases in which it has used that power.<br>3. Identify Congress's executive powers.<br>4. Explain how Congress uses its investigatory power.<br><br>🌐 **TEKS 8D, 9A, 9E, 17C, 21A, 21C, 21D, 22A, 22B** | • **Unit 3 booklet** Guided Reading and Review, p. 19 Section 5 Quiz, p. 20 Skills for Life Activity, p. 21<br>• **Lesson Plans booklet** Section 5, p. 52<br>• **Political Cartoons booklet** Section 5, p. 44<br>• **Block Scheduling with Lesson Strategies booklet** p. 24<br>• **Close Up on Primary Sources** Miranda Rights and Congressional Power, p. 13<br>• **Section Reading Support Transparencies**<br><br>• **Close Up on the Supreme Court booklet** *Heart of Atlanta Motel, Inc.* v. *U.S.*, p. 12; *United States* v. *Nixon*, pp. 54–55<br>• **Government Assessment Rubrics booklet** p. 20<br>• **The Basic Principles of the Constitution Posters**<br>• **Section Support Transparencies** 47, 146<br>• **Presentation Pro CD-ROM** Section 5 |

# Block Scheduling Strategies

The *Magruder's American Government* program addresses block-scheduling strategies in a variety of ways. For easy reference, side-column activities that fit a block format are marked ▦ **Block Strategy.** Each section also contains a **Block Scheduling Strategies** box describing at least two block-format activities that address and extend core content from the section. The **Block Scheduling with Lesson Strategies booklet** found in the Teaching Resources contains additional block-scheduling activities for each chapter.

## Take It to the Net

Visit the Social Studies area at the Prentice Hall School Web site. Once there, you can find additional links, current events connections, and activities to enrich chapter content for *Magruder's American Government*, as well as a Self-Test for students. Be sure to check out this month's **eTeach** online discussion with a Master Teacher.

### www.phschool.com

## Pressed for Time?

If you are running short on time to cover this chapter, consider one of the following options:

- Use the **Presentation Pro CD-ROM** to create an outline for this chapter.
- Use one of the **Pressed for Time** activities found on p. 27.
- Use the Section Summaries for Chapter 2, from **Guide to the Essentials of American Government (English and Spanish).**

 ## Video Connections

Prentice Hall offers two video programs to reinforce and extend chapter content. Show students *The Blessings of Liberty* from the **ABC News Civics and Government Videotape Library** and *Prayer in Schools: A Nationwide Debate* from the **Magruder's American Government Video Collection.**

## Assessment Options

- Section Quizzes, **Unit 3 booklet,** pp. 12, 14, 16, 18, 20
- Chapter 11 Assessment, pp. 316–317
- **Guide to the Essentials of American Government,** Chapter 11 Test, p. 65

### Core Assessment

Chapter 11 Test, Chapter Tests booklet
ExamView® Test Bank CD-ROM Chapter 11
Government Assessment Rubrics

### Standardized Test Preparation

#### Diagnose and Prescribe

Diagnostic Tests for High School
Social Studies Skills

#### Review and Reteach

Review Book for Government

#### Practice and Assess

Test-Taking Strategies With
    Transparencies for High School
Test Prep Book for Government

# Chapter 11 Teacher's Edition Index

# Powers of Congress

## Introducing the Chapter

In this chapter, students will learn about the expressed powers given to Congress by the Constitution. They will also explore how the many implied powers that Congress has assumed have expanded its role and caused intense debate.

### Make It Relevant

⭐ **You Can Make a Difference**

Although very few students can participate in the Senate Youth Program each year, most can participate in similar programs at the State or local level, or even develop programs of their own. Have the class list ways that they can participate in the legislative process within their State or community. Identify the three or four most promising entries on the list, and organize the same number of student groups. Each group will be responsible for developing a plan that maximizes student involvement.

**Service Learning**

## CONSTITUTIONAL PRINCIPLES

Emphasize the following basic principles as students read Chapter 11. Have the class respond to the questions, and then ask volunteers to explain which single principle might best justify the expansion of congressional powers.

**Limited Government** What are the expressed, implied, and inherent powers, and how do they limit the powers of Congress? What are some actions that Congress cannot take?

**Separation of Powers** How do the expressed, implied, and inherent powers of Congress maintain a clear separation of powers among the branches?

**Judicial Review** How did the case of *McCulloch* v. *Maryland* serve to expand the powers of Congress?

# Powers of Congress

❝*The range of issues that come before the United States Senate is infinite: from ratifying treaties, to confirming federal judges, . . . to appropriating the federal dollars that fund the programs upon which we all rely.*❞
— Senator Susan Collins (R.) of Maine (2000)

As Senator Collins points out, members of Congress must discuss an amazing array of issues as part of their lawmaking duties. How far the powers of Congress should extend has been a source of debate and controversy throughout the history of the nation.

◆ **Floor of the United States House**

CLOSE UP FOUNDATION *Corner*

The following resources are available only from the Close Up Foundation to support the concepts discussed in Chapter 11 "Powers of Congress":
◆ *Perspectives: Readings on Contemporary American Government*
◆ *U.S. Response: The Making of U.S. Foreign Policy*
◆ *Profiles of Freedom: A Living Bill of Rights*

CLOSE UP FOUNDATION **Online**

To keep up-to-date on Close Up news and activities, visit Close Up Online at

**www.closeup.org**

Close Up Foundation
44 Canal Center Plaza
Alexandria, VA 22314-1592
800-765-3131

## Pressed for Time?

## ★ You Can Make a Difference

**EACH YEAR, SENATORS** choose delegates for the U.S. Senate Youth Program, a week-long study of the Federal Government that focuses on the Senate. In 1999, Hawaii Senators Daniel Inouye and Daniel Akaka chose two outstanding students from their State to come to Washington, D.C., to participate. Gavin Maeda of Konawaena High School has worked on political campaigns, served as an election precinct official, and was his school's Senate president. His goal is to have his own criminal defense law firm. The other delegate, Daniel Evans, has participated in the debate club and other groups at Kahuku High School and served as a delegate to the Mock United Nations. He plans to work in government service.

### Keep It Current

Items marked with this logo are periodically updated on the Internet. Keep up-to-date with what's in the news. To get current information on issues related to the powers of Congress go to **www.phschool.com**

### SECTION 1

#### The Scope of Congressional Powers
*(pp. 290–292)*

★ Congress has only those powers delegated (granted) to it by the Constitution.

★ How those powers should be interpreted and applied—whether strictly or liberally—has been sharply debated throughout our history.

### SECTION 2

#### The Expressed Powers of Money and Commerce *(pp. 294–300)*

★ The Framers gave Congress the taxing power and the commerce power—two hugely important powers that it did not have under the Articles of Confederation.

★ Congress has the vital power to borrow money and to create a monetary system for the country.

### SECTION 3

#### Other Expressed Powers *(pp. 301–304)*

★ Congress shares power with the President in both defense and foreign affairs.

★ Congress regulates several matters that affect everyday life—including such things as mail, weights and measures, and copyrights and patents.

### SECTION 4

#### The Implied Powers *(pp. 305–308)*

★ Congress has a number of important powers not set out in so many words in the Constitution.

★ What Congress can and cannot do in the exercise of its implied powers has been and remains a subject of intense debate.

### SECTION 5

#### The Nonlegislative Powers *(pp. 310–314)*

★ Congress may propose amendments to the Constitution with a two-thirds vote in each house.

★ The House of Representatives decides a presidential election if no candidate wins a majority of electoral votes.

★ The House has the power to impeach (accuse) the President and the Senate may convict (remove) an impeached President. The House has impeached two Presidents—Andrew Johnson and Bill Clinton; neither was convicted by the Senate.

★ The Senate has the power to confirm or reject major presidential appointments and to approve or reject treaties.

★ Congress may investigate any matter that falls within the scope of its legislative powers.

## Pressed for Time?

### To Omit the Chapter

If you wish to skip Chapter 11, ask students to read the Chapter in Brief and assign the Guide to the Essentials before continuing to another chapter. You may also want to assign the Chapter 11 Test in the Chapter Test booklet. Then specific portions of Chapter 11 may be assigned to students needing reinforcement of key terms and concepts.

### To Preview the Chapter

To introduce students to key terms and concepts in each section, have them read the Chapter in Brief. You may also assign the Reading Strategy activities on pp. 291, 295, 302, 306, and 311 of this book.

### To Review the Chapter

When students have completed Chapter 11, you might want to assign the Guide to the Essentials or the Guided Reading and Review worksheets on pp. 11, 13, 15, 17, and 19 of the Unit 3 booklet.

### To Cover the Chapter Quickly

To cover the material in Chapter 11 quickly, use the following activity.

**Focus** Ask students to identify the powers of Congress. Many of these will be easy for students to identify, but some of them will not be obvious. Once students have finished answering, point out some of the powers that they missed and tell them that they will learn more about the powers of Congress in this chapter.

**Instruct** Have students create tables of congressional powers. The first column should list congressional powers that are discussed in this section. The second column should identify whether each power is expressed, implied, or inherent. The third column should point out whether the power is considered legislative or nonlegislative.

**Close/Reteach** For each power that students identify, have them state whether it is in keeping with the ideas of strict constructionists or liberal constructionists.

■ **Block Strategy**
**(Average)**

## Keep It Current

### Internet Update

Use the Prentice Hall School Web site and the Keep It Current CD-ROM to find quick content updates.

 Visit **www.phschool.com** for current events articles that are linked to Chapter 11. Critical Thinking questions are included.

**Keep It Current CD-ROM** includes government-related projects by unit. Students complete each project using current information that they obtain by linking to the Prentice Hall School Web site from the CD-ROM.

# 1 The Scope of Congressional Powers

**Objectives** You may wish to call students' attention to the objectives in the Section Preview. The objectives are reflected in the main headings of the section.

**Bellringer** Write on the chalkboard: "Students must be in class when the bell rings." Ask students how this rule could be interpreted. For example, does it mean students must be seated? Explain that in this section, students will learn about how the rules governing congressional powers are also subject to interpretation.

**Vocabulary Builder** Have students explain the difference between *expressed, implied,* and *inherent* and the difference between *strict* and *liberal.* Point out the first five terms in the Political Dictionary, and tell students that each is related to the Constitution. Then have them suggest what each term means.

## Section Preview

### OBJECTIVES

1. **Identify** the three types of congressional power.
2. **Compare** strict construction of the U.S. Constitution on the subject of congressional power to liberal construction.

### WHY IT MATTERS

The Constitution gives Congress certain limited powers. But what truly determines the extent of Congress's power is how Americans, Congress, and the courts interpret the Framers' intent.

### POLITICAL DICTIONARY

★ **expressed powers**
★ **implied powers**
★ **inherent powers**
★ **strict constructionist**
★ **liberal constructionist**
★ **consensus**

A typical day in either chamber of Congress might suggest that there is no limit to what Congress can do. On any given day, the House might consider bills dealing with such varying matters as inheritance and gift tax rates, the space shuttle program, and grazing on public lands. The Senate might be debating aid to a famine-stricken country in Africa, veterans' benefits, and dairy price supports. Senators might also be considering the President's nomination of a new Supreme Court justice.

At the same time, however, Congress operates under very real limits. Remember that (1) the government of the United States is limited government, and (2) the American system of government is federal in form. These two fundamental facts work both to shape and to limit the powers of Congress.

## Congressional Power

Remember, Congress has only those powers delegated (granted, given) to it by the Constitution. Large areas of power are denied to Congress—by the exact wording in the Constitution, by the Constitution's silence on many matters, and because the Constitution creates a federal system.

There is much that Congress cannot do. It cannot create a national public school system, require people to vote or attend church, or set a minimum age for marriage or drivers' licenses. It cannot abolish jury trials, confiscate all handguns, or censor the content of newspaper columns or radio or television broadcasts. Congress cannot do these and a great many other things because the Constitution does not allow it to do so.

Still, Congress *does* have the power to do many things. The Constitution grants it a number of specific powers—and, recall, it does so in three different ways: (1) explicitly, in its specific wording—the **expressed powers;** (2) by reasonable deduction from the expressed powers—the **implied powers;** and (3) by creating a national government for the United States—the **inherent powers.**

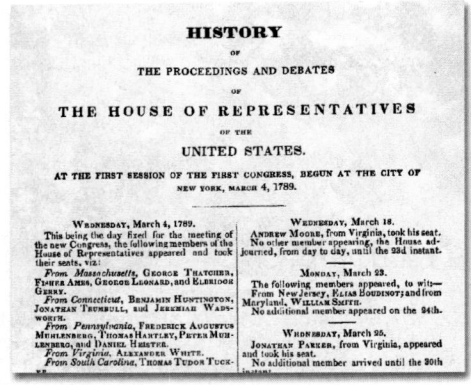

**HISTORY**
OF
THE PROCEEDINGS AND DEBATES
OF
**THE HOUSE OF REPRESENTATIVES**
OF THE
**UNITED STATES.**

AT THE FIRST SESSION OF THE FIRST CONGRESS, BEGUN AT THE CITY OF NEW YORK, MARCH 4, 1789.

▲ *Notes from the First Congress* The gavel came down on the first session of the House of Representatives on March 4, 1789, but the body lacked a quorum and had to adjourn every day until April 1, when enough members finally made it to New York City. The first order of business was to elect a Speaker.

### Pressed for Time?

#### Quick Lesson Plan

1. **Focus** Tell students that the Constitution gives Congress certain limited powers. Have them discuss what they know about the three ways in which the Constitution grants powers to Congress.

2. **Instruct** Ask students why the expressed powers are least open to interpretation. Then discuss how the interpretation of constitutional powers was historically split into strict and liberal construction and which type of interpretation dominates today.

3. **Close/Reteach** Remind students that the extent of Congress's power is open to interpretation. Have students create an informational brochure to explain the scope of congressional powers, including how those powers have been interpreted.

### Point-of-Use Resources

**Block Scheduling with Lesson Strategies** Activities for Chapter 11 are presented on p. 24.

## Block Scheduling Strategies

Consider these suggestions to manage extended class time:

■ Have groups of students draw up a "constitution" for a school administration that stipulates expressed, implied, and inherent powers. Then present groups with problems the administration needs to solve. For each, groups should provide a solution and indicate which of the three kinds of powers the action they will take falls under.

■ Remind students that the debate over how the Constitution should be interpreted has its roots in the early years of the nation. Have students refer to Chapters 2 and 4 of their textbooks, and summarize the debates of the Federalists and Anti-Federalists. Then ask students how these arguments relate to the debate of strict vs. liberal construction of the Constitution today. Have students look through recent magazines or newspapers for examples of politicians who take a side in the debate, and ask students whether that position would be supported by Federalists or Anti-Federalists.

## Strict Versus Liberal Construction

The Framers of the Constitution intended to create a new and stronger National Government. The ratification of their plan was opposed by many, and that opposition was not stilled by the adoption of the Constitution. Rather, the conflict that began with the Federalists and Anti-Federalists continued during the early years of the Republic. Much of that conflict centered on the powers of Congress. Just how broad, in fact, were those powers?

The **strict constructionists,** led by Thomas Jefferson, argued that Congress should be able to exercise only (1) its expressed powers and (2) those implied powers absolutely necessary to carry out those expressed powers. They wanted the States to keep as much power as possible. They agreed with Jefferson that "that government is best which governs least."

Most of these Jeffersonians did acknowledge a need to protect interstate trade, and they recognized the need for a strong national defense. At the same time, they feared the consequences of a strong National Government. They believed, for instance, that the interests of the people of Connecticut were not the same as those of South Carolinians or Marylanders or Pennsylvanians. They argued that only the States—not the far-off National Government—could protect and preserve those differing interests.

### Voices on Government

When President George W. Bush needed a Secretary of Education, he turned to Texan **Rod Paige.** As Superintendent of Schools in the Houston ISD, Paige created a system for getting recommendations from business and community leaders, set up charter schools, raised teachers' salaries, and established performance-based contracts for his staff. Secretary Paige responded to a proposal for giving federal funds to school libraries this way:

❝ *School libraries throughout America are filled with out-of-date books . . . Getting those kinds of books off the shelves and replacing them with new sources of information has to be a priority. In Houston, we decided to make an effort to replace some of those books with online resources and digital books, but we also decided we must put new, hardcover books into the libraries as well. Books were my best friends when I was growing up in rural Mississippi, and books can still be a child's best friend today.* ❞

#### Evaluating the Quotation

*Based on the quotation, what would you infer that Rod Paige sees as the role of the Secretary of Education?*

The **liberal constructionists,** led by Alexander Hamilton, had led the fight to adopt the

*Interpreting Illustrations* The debate over the scope of the powers of the Federal Government is as heated today as it was in early America. *What techniques does this illustration use to depict the conflict?*

Liberal Constructionists from Hamilton's time to today have favored a strong Federal Government...

while Strict Constructionists in the tradition of Jefferson have sought to limit the powers of the Federal Government.

### Organizing Information

To make sure students understand the main points of this section, you may wish to use the double web graphic organizer to the right.

Tell students that a double web compares and contrasts two ideas. Ask students to use the double web to compare the positions of strict and liberal constructionists.

**Teaching Tip** A template for this graphic organizer can be found in the Section Support Transparencies, Transparency 2.

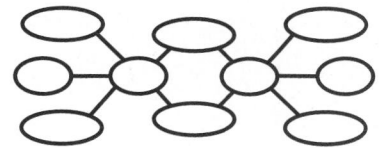

## Point-of-Use Resources

📖 **Guide to the Essentials** Chapter 11, Section 1, p. 60 provides support for students who need additional review of section content. Spanish support is available in the Spanish edition of the Guide on p. 53.

📁 **Quiz** Unit 3 booklet, p. 12 includes matching and multiple-choice questions to check students' understanding of Section 1 content.

💿 **Presentation Pro CD-ROM** Quizzes and multiple-choice questions check students' understanding of Section 1 content.

## Answers to . . .

### Section 1 Assessment

**1.** Expressed powers are stated explicitly in the Constitution; implied powers are those that can be reasonably deduced from the expressed powers; inherent powers are those traditionally held by national governments.
**2.** Strict: Congress should only have expressed powers and those implied powers necessary to carry them out. Liberal: the Constitution can be interpreted more liberally to give additional powers to Congress.
**3.** Allowed: Protect interstate trade, provide for a national defense, approve nominations of justices. Not allowed: Create a national public school system, set minimum ages for marriage or driver's licenses, use censorship.
**4.** Americans do not agree on whether the Constitution should be interpreted flexibly.
**5.** Because the powers of the National Government have expanded in a way that would have been unimaginable to all of the Framers.
**6.** While most Americans have supported expansion of congressional power because of crises and demand for services, the constitutionality of expansion is always debated.

## Answer to . . .

**Interpreting Political Cartoons** That if government gets too small, it becomes ineffectual. The fact that the tree now has no branches on which apples can grow.

**How much pruning can we do and still get apples?**

*Interpreting Political Cartoons* **What point is the cartoonist making about the big government/small government debate? What details in the drawing help to make the point?**

Constitution. Now they favored a liberal interpretation of the Constitution, a broad construction of the powers given to Congress. They believed that the country needed, as Hamilton put it, "an energetic government."

The liberal constructionists won several conflicts in the early years of the Republic, as you will see. Over the years, and particularly during the 20th century, however, the powers wielded by the National Government have grown to a point that even the most ardent supporters of liberal construction could not have imagined.

Several factors, working together with the liberal construction of the Constitution, have been responsible for that marked growth in national power. They have included wars, economic crises, and other national emergencies. Spectacular advances, especially in transportation and communication, have also had a real impact on the size and the scope of government. Equally important have been the demands of Americans themselves for more and more services from government.

Congress has been led by these and other factors to view its powers in broader and broader terms. Most Presidents have regarded their powers in like fashion. The Supreme Court has generally taken a similar position in its decisions in cases involving the powers of the National Government.

Today, United States politics is marked by a lack of **consensus,** or general agreement, over the proper limits of national power. Statists favor a liberal, or loose, construction, while constitutionalists favor a strict construction. This fundamental split is reflected, in general terms, in the different points of view of the Democratic and Republican parties.

## Section 1 Assessment

### Key Terms and Main Ideas

1. Explain the differences among Congress's **expressed powers, implied powers,** and **inherent powers.**
2. Compare the views of a **strict constructionist** and a **liberal constructionist.**
3. Give three examples of laws that Congress would be allowed to enact under the Constitution and three examples of laws that Congress would not be allowed to enact.
4. Explain this sentence: *Historically, there has been a lack of* **consensus** *in this country with regard to a liberal construction of the Constitution.*

### Critical Thinking

5. **Understanding Point of View** Why might Alexander Hamilton, a supporter of a strong National Government, be shocked at the power of the government today?
6. **Making Comparisons** Explain why these two seemingly contradictory statements both are true: (a) *Most Americans* agree with a liberal interpretation of the Constitution on the issue of congressional power. (b) *The issue of federal power is hotly debated in society today.*
7. **Determining Cause and Effect** How has consensus on the issue of congressional power helped provide stability to the country during the last two centuries?

 **Take It to the Net**

8. Recently, scholars have debated "originalism"—that is, the role the Framers' original intention should play in determining how much power the government should have. Check this debate on the Internet and write a brief comment in support of one of the views you find there. Use the links provided in the Social Studies area at the following Web site for help in completing this activity. **www.phschool.com**

**7.** Possible answer: In times of war, economic crisis, or national disaster, it has been easier to take action or provide necessary relief when the nation is in agreement on congressional power.

🌐 **Take It to the Net**

**8.** Direct students to the Social Studies area at the Prentice Hall School Web site. The *Magruder's American Government* companion Web site includes the directions and links needed to complete the activity. It also provides a printable Internet activity worksheet, with scoring rubrics for assessment. Paragraphs should accurately reflect the chosen scholar's position and be supported with examples.

# SKILLS FOR LIFE

TECHNOLOGY
CITIZENSHIP
CRITICAL THINKING
CHARTS and GRAPHS

## Evaluating Leadership

**W**hen you participate in representative government, you choose people to make decisions for you. What kind of person do you want representing you? Do you want someone who is full of new ideas? Who knows how to get things done? Who has experience? Which qualities are most important to you?

In an election, candidates compete to convince you that they have the stuff of leadership. Examine their claims carefully. Otherwise you'll be basing your decisions on criteria such as "She's really cool" or "He looks like my cousin."

Whether you're evaluating a candidate for President of the United States or for student council president, consider these steps:

**1. Establish your criteria for evaluating a leader.** Most people would agree on certain qualities that make a good leader, such as honesty and commitment to duty. Other characteristics may vary widely. Some jobs demand a person with a great deal of experience. Other positions are less dependent on experience, but require creative ideas. Are you looking for a "hands-on" leader (who personally

gets things done) or a skilled manager who inspires others to work productively? Make a list of criteria *you* look for in a leader. The table below lists some possible characteristics.

**2. Rate your subject.** Using the leadership criteria you've established, rate the person you are evaluating on a scale of 0 to 5 (with 5 being the highest), as shown in the table.

**3. Compare or contrast your subject with other leaders.** Use your checklist to compare candidates' leadership attributes. That might mean doing a little homework, such as calling campaign offices or doing other research on the candidates' views.

**4. Summarize your opinion.** When you finish, you should be able to say, "So-and-so would make a good leader <u>because</u> . . . ." If you *still* can't think of a reason, perhaps you should vote for somebody else.

### Test for Success

Choose someone in a leadership position or someone you think might make a good leader. Evaluate that person, and summarize your findings in a paragraph.

### Rating Sheet: Qualities of a Leader

| Qualities | Rating |
|---|---|
| Has fresh ideas | 4 |
| Has experience | 2 |
| Is honest | 5 |
| Takes charge | 5 |
| Encourages team building, cooperation | 3 |
| Is dynamic | 5 |
| Has strong sense of duty | 4 |
| Inspires others to excel | 3 |
| Is good decision maker | 4 |
| Shows political courage | 4 |
| Has steady personality, is dependable | 2 |
| Keeps promises | 4 |

## Point-of-Use Resources

📁 **Skills for Life Activity** Unit 3 booklet, p. 21 provides an additional skill activity for this chapter.

💿 **Social Studies Skills Tutor CD-ROM** Provides interactive practice in geographic literacy, critical thinking and reading, visual analysis, and communications.

### Test for Success

Students can work in small groups to do the evaluations, and then present their decisions to the class.

---

# SKILLS FOR LIFE

CITIZENSHIP

## Evaluating Leadership

**Focus** Work as a class to conduct a simulated "candidate search" for a school leadership position.

**Instruct** Explain to the class that when political parties want to field a candidate for an election, they sometimes need to conduct a candidate search. This is a systematic process of identifying the specific qualities a candidate would need to be viable and then trying to find someone who meets the criteria.

Simulate a candidate search for a class president or other class officer by brainstorming a list of desirable qualities for the job, as described in Step 1. Then try to reach a consensus on the most desirable candidate, following Steps 2 through 4.

**Close/Reteach** Try the same process for a different class officer, and compare the qualities needed. Hold a class discussion on whether the most desirable candidates for the jobs are also the most electable. If not, how do the criteria for a good candidate and an electable candidate differ?

### *Answers...*

**1.** Guide students to think about the desirable qualities in *any* good leader as well as the qualities needed for the specific position.
**2.** Students should be able to explain the reasoning behind their choices.
**3.** Many political candidates now have Web sites, but the information they provide will be self-promotional. News media sites often provide candidate profiles that are more objective.
**4.** Have students write a one- or two-sentence summary with specific reasoning.

**Objectives** You may wish to call students' attention to the objectives in the Section Preview. The objectives are reflected in the main headings of the section.

**Bellringer** Ask students how the designs of coins and bills have changed in recent years. Show an example of a newly designed dollar bill, dollar coin, or State quarter. Ask students who authorizes such changes in our currency. Tell students that the power to print and coin money is an expressed power of Congress.

**Vocabulary Builder** Have students read the terms in the Political Dictionary. Ask them which term is found on a dollar bill. *(legal tender)* Have a student read aloud, from a dollar bill, the sentence containing this term, and ask the class to discuss the term's meaning.

### Pressed for Time?

#### Quick Lesson Plan

**1. Focus** Tell students that the Constitution expressly gives Congress the power to regulate money and commerce. Ask students whether they know any examples of how Congress uses these powers.

**2. Instruct** Ask students to name the four limits on Congress's power to tax. Then have students describe Congress's other money and commerce powers and any limits on these powers.

**3. Close/Reteach** Remind students that the expressed powers of Congress include the power to regulate money and commerce. Have students draw a web diagram to organize the information in this section, starting with "the expressed powers of money and commerce" in the center circle.

### Point-of-Use Resources

**Section Support Transparencies** Transparency 44, *Visual Learning;* Transparency 143, *Political Cartoon*

---

# The Expressed Powers of Money and Commerce

## Section Preview

### OBJECTIVES

1. **Summarize** key points relating to Congress's power to tax.
2. **Describe** how Congress uses its power to borrow money.
3. **Analyze** the importance of Congress's commerce power.
4. **Identify** the reasons that the Framers gave Congress the power to issue currency.
5. **Explain** how the bankruptcy power works.

### WHY IT MATTERS

Congress fulfills a critical role in the American economy through its powers to regulate money and commerce. These powers cover everything from levying taxes, to printing money, to regulating interstate shipping.

### POLITICAL DICTIONARY

★ tax
★ direct tax
★ indirect tax
★ deficit financing
★ public debt
★ commerce power
★ legal tender
★ bankruptcy

---

Most, but not all, of the expressed powers of Congress are found in Article I, Section 8 of the Constitution. There, in 18 separate clauses, 27 different powers are explicitly given to Congress.[1]

These grants of power are brief. What they do and do not allow Congress to do often cannot be discovered by merely reading the few words involved. Rather, their meaning is found in the ways in which Congress has exercised its powers since 1789, and in scores of Supreme Court cases arising out of the actions taken by Congress.

As a case in point, take the Commerce Clause, which gives to Congress the power:

**FROM THE Constitution** *"To regulate Commerce with foreign Nations, and among the several States, and with the Indian Tribes."*

—Article I, Section 8, Clause 3

What do these words mean? Congress and the Court have had to answer hundreds of questions about the Commerce Clause. Here are but a few examples: Does "commerce" include people crossing State lines or entering or leaving the country? What about business practices?

▲ When they wrote the Commerce Clause, the Framers could not have envisioned this: a warehouse worker in Massachusetts filling orders for an online grocery service.

Working conditions? Radio and television broadcasts? Does the Commerce Clause give Congress the power to ban the shipment of certain goods from one State to another? To prohibit discrimination? To regulate the Internet? What trade is "foreign" and what is "interstate"? What trade is neither?

In answering these and dozens upon dozens of questions arising out of this one provision, Congress and the Court have defined—and are still defining—the meaning of the Commerce Clause. So it is with most of the other constitutional grants of power to Congress.

## The Power to Tax

The Constitution gives Congress the power:

**FROM THE Constitution** *"To lay and collect Taxes, Duties, Imposts and Excises, to pay the Debts and provide for the common Defense and general Welfare of the United States. . . ."*

—Article I, Section 8, Clause 1

---

[1]Several of the expressed powers of Congress are set out elsewhere in the Constitution. Thus, Article IV, Section 3 grants Congress the power to admit new States to the Union (Clause 1) and to manage and dispose of federal territory and other property (Clause 2). The 16th Amendment gives Congress the power to levy an income tax. The 13th, 14th, 15th, 19th, 24th, and 26th amendments grant Congress the "power to enforce" the provisions of the amendments "by appropriate legislation."

---

## Block Scheduling Strategies

Consider these suggestions to manage extended class time:

■ Describe the many expressed powers that Congress has regarding money. Then have student groups create two laws. One law should be based on these expressed powers. The other should be a law that Congress could not pass because of the limitations placed on expressed powers. Ask for volunteers to share their laws, and have the class determine whether Congress could or could not pass them.

■ Have students complete the Constitutional Principles activity on p. 297. Then ask students to consider why congressional powers and limitations regarding commerce are so important. Have student pairs create scenarios of what could happen if each power or limitation was not in place. Encourage volunteers to share their scenarios with the class.

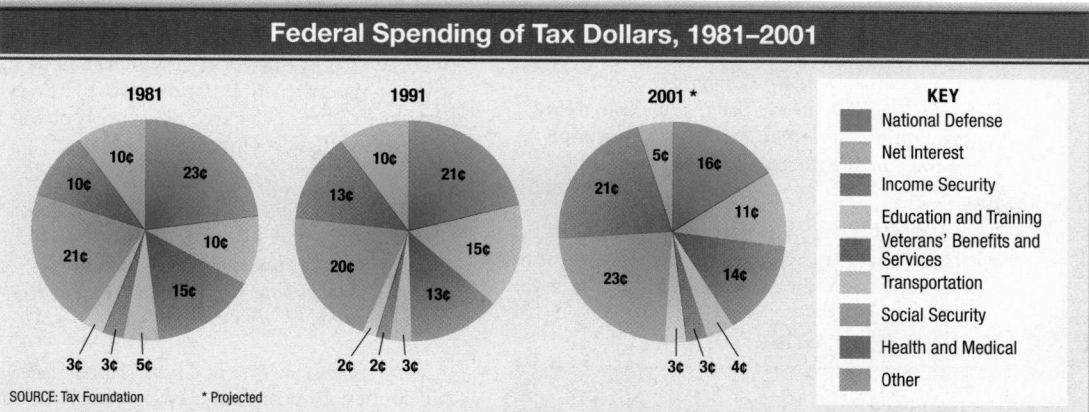

## Federal Spending of Tax Dollars, 1981–2001

**1981**
23¢, 10¢, 10¢, 21¢, 15¢, 3¢, 3¢, 5¢, 10¢

**1991**
21¢, 10¢, 13¢, 20¢, 13¢, 2¢, 2¢, 3¢, 15¢

**2001 ***
16¢, 5¢, 21¢, 11¢, 23¢, 14¢, 3¢, 3¢, 4¢

**KEY**
- National Defense
- Net Interest
- Income Security
- Education and Training
- Veterans' Benefits and Services
- Transportation
- Social Security
- Health and Medical
- Other

SOURCE: Tax Foundation      * Projected

*Interpreting Graphs* Congress's priorities can be seen in the way it spends tax revenues. These graphs show what proportions of a tax dollar were spent on what federal programs. *What major shifts in federal spending occurred (a) between 1981 and 1991 and (b) between 1991 and 2001?*

Recall that the Articles of Confederation had not given Congress the power to tax. Congress did have the power to requisition (request) funds from the States; that is, Congress could ask (in reality, beg) each of the thirteen States for money. But, through the 1780s, not a single State came even remotely close to meeting the requisitions Congress made, and some States paid nothing at all. The government was powerless, and the lack of a power to tax was a leading cause for the creation of the Constitution.

### The Purpose of Taxes

We shall take another and longer look at the taxing power in Chapter 16. But, here, a number of important points: The Federal Government will take in some $2 trillion in fiscal year 2002, and almost certainly an even larger sum in 2003. Most of that money—well over 90 percent of it—will come from the various taxes levied by Congress.

A **tax** is a charge levied by government on persons or property to meet public needs. Notice, however, that Congress sometimes imposes taxes for other purposes. The protective tariff is perhaps the oldest example of this point. Although it does bring in some revenue every year, its real goal is to "protect" domestic industry against foreign competition by increasing the cost of foreign goods.

Taxes are also sometimes levied to protect the public health and safety. The Federal Government's regulation of narcotics is a case in point. Only those who have a proper federal license can legally manufacture, sell, or deal in those drugs—and licensing is a form of taxation.

### Limits on the Taxing Power

Congress's power to tax is not unlimited, of course. As with all other powers, it must be used in accord with all other provisions of the Constitution. Thus, Congress cannot lay a tax on church services, for example—because such a tax would violate the 1st Amendment protection of the free exercise of religion. Nor could it lay a poll tax as a condition for voting in federal elections—because that tax would violate the 24th Amendment.

More specifically, the Constitution places four explicit limitations on the taxing power:

(1) Congress may tax only for public purposes, not for private benefit. Article I, Section 8, Clause 1 says that taxes may be levied only "to pay the Debts and provide for the common Defense and general Welfare of the United States. . . ."

(2) Congress may not tax exports. Article I, Section 9, Clause 5 declares "[n]o Tax or Duty shall be laid on Articles exported from any State." Thus, customs duties (tariffs), which are taxes, can be levied only on goods brought into the country (imports), not on those sent abroad (exports).

### Preparing for Standardized Tests

Have students read the passages under *The Power to Tax* on pp. 294–295 and then answer the question below.

What is a protective tariff?

**A** a low tax on imported goods to encourage their purchase by Americans

**B** a tax on exports

**C** a tax on cigarettes to make them more expensive and thus protect the public from the health risks of smoking

**D** a tax on imported goods to increase their price and make them less popular than American goods

ACTIVITY

## Learning Styles

**Linguistic** Have students write a position paper on the following topic: There is no constitutional limit on the amount of money that Congress can borrow. Encourage students to consider the pros (borrowing to finance war) and cons (deficit spending) of the issue before taking a stand. Ask them to provide specific examples of past government borrowing of money to support their position. Ask for volunteers to share their papers with the class.

**(Challenging)**

## Customize for

### Less Proficient Readers

Have students create charts or other graphic organizers that highlight the limits on both the commerce power and the taxing power. For each explicit limit placed on Congress by the Constitution, encourage students to provide a real-life example or illustration that further explains the limitation. Have students compare their charts for accuracy of information.

## Point–of–Use Resources

**Simulations and Data Graphing CD-ROM** offers data graphing tools that give students practice with creating and interpreting graphs.

---

(3) Direct taxes must be apportioned among the States, according to their populations:

> **FROM THE Constitution** ❝*No Capitation, or other direct, Tax shall be laid, unless in Proportion to the Census of Enumeration herein before directed to be taken.*❞
> —Article I, Section 9, Clause 4

A **direct tax** is paid by the person on whom it is imposed; for example, a tax on real estate or a capitation (head or poll) tax. It is a tax

### Comparative Government

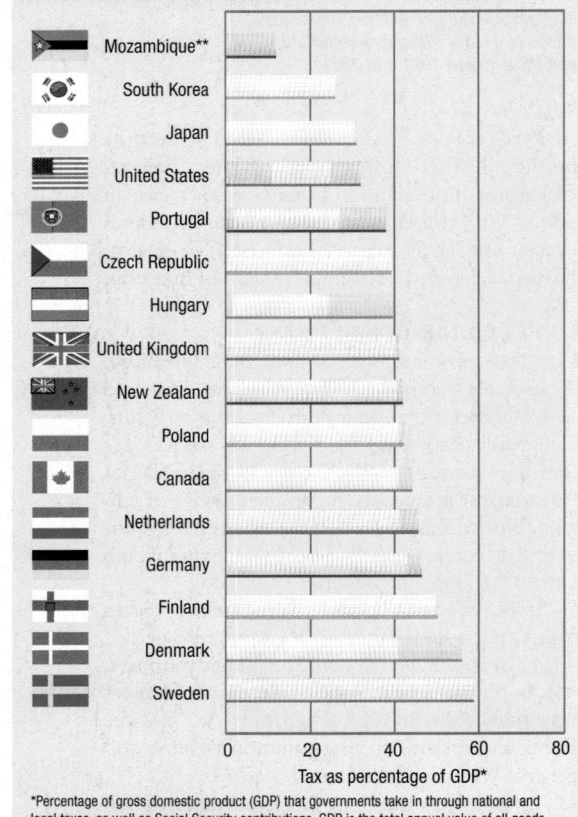

**The Tax Bite in Selected Countries, 1999**

Tax as percentage of GDP*

Countries listed: Mozambique**, South Korea, Japan, United States, Portugal, Czech Republic, Hungary, United Kingdom, New Zealand, Poland, Canada, Netherlands, Germany, Finland, Denmark, Sweden

(Scale: 0, 20, 40, 60, 80)

*Percentage of gross domestic product (GDP) that governments take in through national and local taxes, as well as Social Security contributions. GDP is the total annual value of all goods and services produced within a country.
**1998 data
SOURCE: *Statistical Abstract of the United States*: 1999

**Interpreting Graphs** As this bar graph shows, some nations tax their citizens much more heavily than do other nations. Often, countries with higher taxes also provide more government services. *How does the U.S. tax rate compare with that of other countries?*

---

that the individual payer cannot avoid by refraining from a transaction. A tax on wages (income tax) is a direct tax, which may be laid without regard to population. Note, however, that the Framers delegated no express power to Congress to levy such taxes.

> **FROM THE Constitution** ❝*The Congress shall have power to lay and collect taxes on incomes, from whatever source derived, without apportionment among the several States, and without regard to any census or enumeration.*❞
> —16th Amendment

(4) Article I, Section 8, Clause 1 provides that "all Duties, Imposts and Excises, shall be uniform throughout the United States." That is, all indirect taxes must be levied at the same rate in all parts of the country.

In practical terms, the question of whether a tax is direct or indirect is decided by Congress and the Supreme Court. As a general rule, however, an **indirect tax** is a tax that can be passed on to the ultimate consumer at a higher price, and which the consumer can avoid paying by avoiding the purchase of the product or service that includes the tax. It is indirectly paid by that second person. Take, for example, the federal tax on cigarettes. It is paid to the Treasury by the tobacco company that makes the cigarettes. But that company then passes the tax on through the wholesaler and retailer to the person who finally buys the cigarettes.

## The Borrowing Power

Article I, Section 8, Clause 2 gives Congress the power "[t]o borrow Money on the credit of the United States." There are no constitutional limits on the amount of money that Congress may borrow, or for what purposes.

Until recently, the Federal Government practiced **deficit financing.** That is, it spent more than it took in each year and borrowed to make up the difference. The government relied on deficit financing to deal with the Depression of the 1930s, to raise money for World War II, and to fund wars and social programs over the next several decades.

In fact, the government's books did not show a surplus (more income than spending) in any year from 1969 to 1998. As a result, the public debt rose year to year—to more than $5.5 trillion at the beginning of fiscal year 1999. The **public debt** is all of the money

---

**Answer to . . .**

**Interpreting Graphs** It is lower than all but three of the other selected countries.

borrowed by the government over the years and not yet repaid, plus the accumulated interest on that money.

With the passage of the Balanced Budget Act of 1997, Congress and President Clinton agreed to abandon deficit financing and to aim for a balanced budget by the year 2002. However, that goal was realized much more quickly than anyone anticipated. The nation's economy was so robust that the Federal Government's income rose dramatically, to the point where the Treasury Department reported a modest surplus at the end of fiscal year 1998, and larger ones for 1999, 2000, and 2001. Economic downturn and the war on terrorism mean that red ink has once again, at least temporarily, become the order of the day, however.

The fact that the Constitution gives Congress the power to borrow makes borrowing a national function. So, the interest the Federal Government pays to those who loan it money cannot be taxed by the States; that makes the Federal Government's notes and bonds quite attractive to investors. We shall return to this whole matter in Chapter 16, but for now remember this: Congress continues to borrow—in the form of bonds and securities issued by the Treasury Department—to service the public debt.

## The Commerce Power

The **commerce power**—the power of Congress to regulate interstate and foreign trade—is as vital to the welfare of the nation as is the taxing power. As you know, the commerce power played a major role in the formation of the Union. The weak Congress created under the Articles of Confederation had no power to regulate interstate trade and little authority over foreign commerce. The Critical Period of the 1780s was marked by intense commercial rivalries and bickering among the States. High trade barriers and spiteful State laws created chaos and confusion in much of the country.

Consequently, the Framers wrote the Commerce Clause. It gives Congress the power:

**FROM THE Constitution** " *To regulate Commerce with foreign Nations, and among the several States, and with the Indian Tribes.* "

—Article I, Section 8, Clause 3

▲ This engraving from the 1830s shows Robert Fulton's steamboat, the *Clermont*. **Critical Thinking** *If Fulton had held on to his riverboat monopoly in New York, what might have been the effects on interstate commerce?*

The Commerce Clause proved to be more responsible for the building of a strong and *United* States out of a weak confederation than any other provision in the Constitution. Its few words have prompted the growth in this country of the greatest open market in the world.

### *Gibbons* v. *Ogden*, 1824

The first case involving the Commerce Clause to reach the Supreme Court was *Gibbons* v. *Ogden*, decided in 1824. The case arose out of a clash over the regulation of steamboats by the State of New York, on the one hand, and the Federal Government, on the other. In 1807 Robert Fulton's steamboat, the *Clermont*, had made its first successful run up the Hudson River, from New York City to Albany. The State legislature then gave Fulton an exclusive, long-term grant to navigate the waters of the State by steamboat. Fulton's monopoly then gave Aaron Ogden a permit for steamboat navigation between New York City and New Jersey.

Thomas Gibbons, operating with a coasting license from the Federal Government, began to carry passengers on a line that competed with Ogden. Ogden sued him, and the New York courts held that Gibbons could not sail by steam in New York waters.

Gibbons appealed that ruling to the Supreme Court. He claimed that the New York grant conflicted with the congressional power to regulate commerce. The Court agreed. It rejected Ogden's argument that "commerce" should be defined narrowly, as simply "traffic" or the mere buying and selling of goods. Instead, it read the Commerce Clause in broad terms:

## Point-of-Use Resources

📁 **Close Up on the Supreme Court** *Gibbons* v. *Ogden* (1819), pp. 30–31

📁 **The Living Constitution** Judicial Review, p. 7

📖 **Basic Principles of the Constitution Transparencies** Transparencies 37–43, *Judicial Review*

## CONSTITUTIONAL PRINCIPLES

**Judicial Review**

The Supreme Court's decision in *Gibbons* v. *Ogden* helped to expand federal authority into many areas of American life, while its decision in *United States* v. *Lopez* effectively protected the reserved powers of the States. The differences between the decisions can be linked to the Court's interpretation of the Commerce Clause and how it applied to the laws in question.

**Activity**

Ask students to conduct additional research into *Gibbons* v. *Ogden* and *United States* v. *Lopez* to see how the Court's interpretation of the Commerce Clause and the purpose of the laws in question shaped its opinion. Have students summarize this information and explain why they agree or disagree.

*Answer to . . .*

**Critical Thinking** Possible answer: There would have been less competition, hampering the development of national transportation systems.

▲ Congress's commerce power affects the daily lives of many Americans, such as this worker in a fast-food sushi restaurant in New York City and this student on a school bus wheelchair lift in Berlin, Maryland. *Critical Thinking How might the Commerce Clause affect these people?*

**PRIMARY Sources** "*Commerce undoubtedly is traffic, but it is something more—it is intercourse. It describes the commercial intercourse between nations, and parts of nations, in all its branches, and is regulated by prescribing rules for carrying on that intercourse.*"

—Chief Justice John Marshall

The Court's ruling was widely popular at the time because it dealt a death blow to steamboat monopolies. Freed from restrictive State regulation, many new steamboat companies came into existence. As a result, steam navigation developed rapidly. Within a few years, the railroads, similarly freed, revolutionized transportation within the United States.

Over the decades, the Court's sweeping definition of commerce has brought an extension of federal authority into many areas of American life—a reach of federal power beyond anything the Framers could have imagined. As another of the many examples of the point, note this: It is on the basis of the commerce power that the Civil Rights Act of 1964 prohibits discrimination in access to or service in hotels, motels, theaters, restaurants, and in other public accommodations on grounds of race, color, religion, or national origin.[2]

Based on the expressed powers to regulate commerce and to tax, Congress and the courts have built nearly all of the implied powers.

Most of what the Federal Government does, day to day and year to year, it does as the result of legislation passed by Congress in the exercise of these two powers.

### Limits on the Commerce Power

Like Congress's taxing power, its commerce power is not unlimited. It, too, must be exercised in accord with all other provisions in the Constitution. Thus, the Supreme Court struck down the Gun-Free School Zone Act of 1990 in *United States* v. *Lopez,* 1995. That act had made it a federal crime for anyone other than a police officer to possess a firearm in or around a school. The Court could find no useful connection between interstate commerce and guns at school, and it held that Congress in this case had invaded the reserved powers of the States.

In more specific terms, the Constitution places four explicit limits on the use of the commerce power. Congress

(1) cannot tax exports, Article I, Section 9, Clause 5;

(2) cannot favor the ports of one State over those of any other in the regulation of trade, Article I, Section 9, Clause 6;

---

[2]The Supreme Court upheld this use of the commerce power in *Heart of Atlanta Motel* v. *United States* in 1964. The unanimous Court noted that there was "overwhelming evidence of the disruptive effect of racial discrimination on commercial intercourse." You will look at this case again in Chapter 21.

*Answer to . . .*

**Critical Thinking** The commerce power led to the prohibition of discrimination in public places; these people cannot be discriminated against because of their race or disability.

(3) cannot require that "Vessels bound to, or from, one State, be obliged to enter, clear or pay Duties in another," Article I, Section 9, Clause 6; and, finally,

(4) could not interfere with the slave trade, at least not until the year 1808, Article I, Section 9, Clause 1. This last limitation, part of the curious slave-trade compromise at the Constitutional Convention, has been a dead letter for nearly two centuries now.

## The Currency Power

Article I, Section 8, Clause 5 gives Congress the power "[t]o coin Money [and] regulate the Value thereof." The States are denied that power.[3]

Until the Revolution, the English money system, built on the shilling and the pound, was in general use in the colonies. With independence, that stable currency system collapsed. The Second Continental Congress and then the Congress under the Articles issued paper money. Without sound backing, and with no taxing power behind it, however, the money was practically worthless.

---

[3]Article I, Section 10, Clause 1 forbids the States the power to coin money, issue bills of credit (paper money), or make anything but gold and silver legal tender.

Each of the 13 States also issued its own currency. In several States, this amounted to little more than the State's printing its name on paper and calling it money. Adding to the confusion, people still used English coins, and Spanish money circulated freely in the southern States.

Nearly all the Framers agreed on the need for a single, national system of "hard" money. So the Constitution gave the currency power to Congress, and it all but excluded the States from that field. From 1789 on, among the most important of all of the many tasks performed by the Federal Government has been that of providing the nation with a uniform, stable monetary system.

From the beginning, the United States has issued coins—in gold, silver, and other metals. Congress chartered the first Bank of the United States in 1791 and gave it the power to issue bank notes—that is, paper money. Those notes were not legal tender, however. **Legal tender** is any kind of money that a creditor must by law accept in payment for debts. Congress did not create a national paper currency, and make it legal tender, until 1861.

At first, the new national notes, known as Greenbacks, could not be redeemed for gold or silver coin at the Treasury. Their worth fell to less than half of their face value. Then, in 1870,

### The Development of a National Currency

**CONTINENTAL CURRENCY**

**One third dollar, 1776** This "Continental" note, engraved by Benjamin Franklin, was issued to finance the American Revolution.

**U.S. COINAGE**

**United States half cent, 1834** On the face of this early American coin is a woman representing Liberty; on the reverse is a laurel wreath.

**DEMAND CURRENCY**

**$10 demand note, 1861** With metal badly needed for the Civil War, Congress issued this "Greenback," the first paper currency since the Continental.

**STATE CURRENCY**

**$5 Louisiana state bank note, 1862** From 1837 to 1863, just about anyone could issue currency—from States to stores to individuals— creating economic chaos.

**SILVER CERTIFICATE**

**$1 silver certificates, 1896** George Washington was not the only member of his family to have his face on a bill; this note, redeemable for silver, features his wife, Martha.

SOURCE: Federal Reserve Bank of San Francisco

*Interpreting Charts* The colonies, the States, and the young United States experimented with a variety of coins and paper notes in the effort to build a stable currency. For a long time, people trusted coins more than paper. ***Why do you think some forms of currency succeeded while others failed?***

**Resource Pro® CD-ROM** contains an electronic version of each activity found in the Teaching Resources as well as additional resources such as Supreme Court cases. The Planning Express® feature allows you to customize and create daily lesson plans within minutes.

## Customize for

### More Advanced Students

Have students choose one of the expressed powers of Congress listed in the Constitution. Ask them to research the history of this power, including major events or pieces of legislation that have been a direct result of it. Encourage students to find information about any Supreme Court cases that arose out of the actions taken by Congress and any decisions that were rendered. Allow student projects to be in the form of an oral report, written report, visual display, or multimedia presentation.

### Background Note
#### Economics

In 1997, Congress passed a bill requiring the creation of a new dollar coin to replace the Susan B. Anthony dollar, which had "flopped." Introduced in 1979, the Anthony dollar was unpopular with the public, partly because it was easily confused with a quarter. The Mint stopped producing it in 1981 due to lack of demand, but by the mid-1990s, dollar coins were called for because of increased use of vending machines. The United States One Dollar Coin Act of 1997 specified a new golden-colored coin with a distinctive edge (so it would not be confused with a quarter), the same size as the Anthony dollar. The Mint chose Sacagawea, Lewis and Clark's Shoshone guide, to appear on the new coin. Then, recalling the fate of the Anthony dollar, the Mint launched an unprecedented $40 million advertising campaign to promote the new "golden dollar."

### Answer to . . .

**Interpreting Charts** Possible answer: Forms of currency can only succeed if they have sound backing and are perceived as useful by the people.

## Point-of-Use Resources

 **Guide to the Essentials** Chapter 11, Section 2, p. 61 provides support for students who need additional review of section content. Spanish support is available in the Spanish edition of the Guide on p. 54.

**Quiz** Unit 3 booklet, p. 14 includes matching and multiple-choice questions to check students' understanding of Section 2 content.

**Presentation Pro CD-ROM** Quizzes and multiple-choice questions check students' understanding of Section 2 content.

## Answers to . . .

### Section 2 Assessment

**1.** A direct tax must be paid by the person on whom it is imposed; an indirect tax is paid by one person, but is in fact passed on to be paid by another. A tax on land ownership is an example of a direct tax, while a cigarette tax is an example of an indirect tax.

**2.** Because it led to public debt; when deficits are not paid back, the money borrowed to cover them accumulates interest and increases public debt.

**3.** Regulating commerce with foreign powers and between States; preventing monopolies and discrimination in access to public places.

**4.** The worthlessness of money that had no sound backing or taxing power; competition between State currencies; and the use of foreign currency.

**5.** Possible answer: They did not want Congress to be able to derive personal gain from taxes, nor did they want State competition.

**6.** Answers will vary, but should be supported with relevant facts and examples.

### Answer to . . .

**Interpreting Graphs** They nearly doubled, then began to decline.

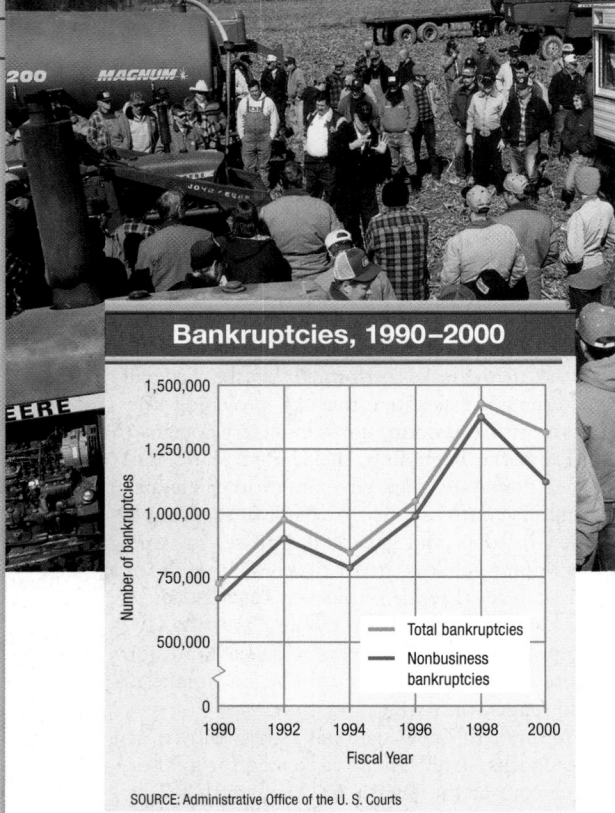

### Bankruptcies, 1990–2000

SOURCE: Administrative Office of the U. S. Courts

*Interpreting Graphs* Farmers—shown above auctioning off equipment in Manchester, Michigan—contributed to a sharp rise in U.S. bankruptcies during the 1990s. As a result, in 2000 Congress passed legislation making it more difficult for certain people to file for personal bankruptcy. *Describe the change in nonbusiness bankruptcies from 1990 to 2000 as shown in the graph.*

---

the Supreme Court held their issuance to be unconstitutional. In *Hepburn* v. *Griswold* it said "to coin" meant to stamp metal and so the Constitution did not authorize paper money.

The Court soon changed its mind, however, in *Knox* v. *Lee* and *Parker* v. *Davis*, both in 1871 (and after President Grant allegedly packed the Supreme Court), and again in *Juliard* v. *Greenman* in 1884. In these cases, it held the issuing of paper money as legal tender to be a proper use of the currency power. The Court also declared this a power properly implied from the borrowing and the war powers.

## The Bankruptcy Power

Article I, Section 8, Clause 4 gives Congress the power "[t]o establish . . . uniform Laws on the subject of Bankruptcies throughout the United States." A bankrupt individual or company or other organization is one a court has found to be insolvent—that is, unable to pay debts in full. **Bankruptcy** is the legal proceeding in which the bankrupt's assets—however much or little they may be—are distributed among those to whom a debt is owed. That proceeding frees the bankrupt from legal responsibility for debts acquired before bankruptcy.

The States and the National Government have concurrent power to regulate bankruptcy. Today federal bankruptcy law is so broad that it all but excludes the States. Bankruptcy cases are heard in bankruptcy courts, which are units of the U.S. district courts.

---

## Section **2** Assessment

**Key Terms and Main Ideas**

1. Explain the difference between a **direct tax** and an **indirect tax**, and give examples of each.
2. Why did the Federal Government finally eliminate **deficit financing**?
3. Give three examples of how Congress uses its **commerce power.**
4. What problems led the Framers to give Congress the power to coin money and make it **legal tender?**

**Critical Thinking**

5. **Making Inferences** Reread the four ways that the Constitution limits Congress's power to tax (pages 295–296). What can you infer about the Framers' reasons for limiting this power?

6. **Expressing Problems Clearly** This issue is hotly debated today: Should Congress regulate the Internet—for example, to ban false advertising? Do you think the Commerce Clause gives Congress the power to regulate Internet activity? Explain your reasoning.

 **Take It to the Net**

7. Read Chief Justice John Marshall's opinion for the Court in *McCulloch* v. *Maryland* and write a paragraph explaining how the decision interpreted Article 1, Section 8, Clause 18 of the Constitution. Use the links provided in the Social Studies area at the following Web site for help in completing this activity. **www.phschool.com**

---

**Take It to the Net**

**7.** Direct students to the Social Studies area at the Prentice Hall School Web site. The *Magruder's American Government* companion Web site includes the directions and links needed to complete the activity. It also provides a printable Internet activity worksheet, with scoring rubrics for assessment. Paragraphs should accurately demonstrate the points made in both the decision and Article 1.

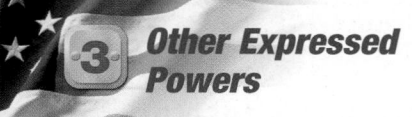

# **3** *Other Expressed Powers*

## Section Preview

### OBJECTIVES

1. **Identify** the key sources of Congress's foreign relations powers.
2. **Describe** the power-sharing arrangement between Congress and the President on the issues of war and national defense.
3. **List** other key powers exercised by Congress.

### WHY IT MATTERS

Congress has a broad range of powers that affect our lives, from international relations and warmaking to matters like daily mail service.

### POLITICAL DICTIONARY

★ naturalization
★ copyright
★ patent
★ eminent domain

We have just reviewed the several expressed powers that Congress has with regard to money and to foreign and interstate commerce. The Constitution grants a number of other very important powers to Congress. If, for example, you received a letter or magazine in the U.S. mail today, you were benefiting from just one of the other expressed powers of Congress.

## Foreign Relations Powers

The National Government has greater powers in the field of foreign affairs than in any other area. Congress shares power in this field with the President, who is primarily responsible for the conduct of our relations with other nations. Because the States in the Union are not sovereign, they have no standing in international law. The Constitution does not allow them to take part in foreign relations.[4]

The foreign relations powers of Congress come from two sources: (1) from various expressed powers, especially the war powers and the power to regulate foreign commerce, and (2) from the fact that the United States is a sovereign state in the world community. As the nation's lawmaking body, Congress has the inherent power to act on matters affecting the security of the nation. You will explore this vitally important subject at much greater length in Chapter 17.

---
[4]See Article I, Section 10, Clauses 1 and 3.

## War Powers

Eight of the expressed powers given to Congress in Article I, Section 8 deal with war and national defense.[5] Here, too, Congress shares power with the chief executive. The Constitution makes the President the commander in chief of the nation's armed forces,[6] and, as such, the President dominates the field.

The congressional war powers, however, are extensive and substantial. Only Congress may declare war. It has the power to raise and support armies, to provide and maintain a navy, and to make rules pertaining to the governing of land and naval forces. Congress also has the power to provide for "calling forth the Militia" and for the organizing, arming, and disciplining of it. Congress has the power to grant letters of marque and reprisal[7] and to make rules concerning captures on land and water.

With the passage of the War Powers Resolution of 1973, Congress claimed the power to restrict the use of American forces in

---
[5]The war powers of Congress are set out in Clauses 11 through 16.

[6]Article II, Section 2, Clause 1.

[7]A few of the expressed powers are of little importance today. Thus, Congress has the power to grant letters of marque and reprisal, Article I, Section 8, Clause 11, and the States are denied the power to issue them, Article I, Section 10, Clause 1. Letters of marque and reprisal are written grants of power authorizing private persons to outfit vessels to capture and destroy enemy vessels in time of war. In effect, they authorize a form of legalized piracy. Letters of marque and reprisal are forbidden by international law by the Declaration of Paris, 1856, and the United States honors the rule.

**301**

## Reading Strategy

### Getting the Main Idea

Tell students that Congress's expressed powers can often affect people's daily lives. Have students list, as they read the section, the expressed powers of Congress and note ways in which each power might affect them personally.

## Point-of-Use Resources

**Guided Reading and Review** Unit 3 booklet, p. 15 provides students with practice identifying the main ideas and key terms of this section.

**Lesson Plans** For lesson planning suggestions, see p. 50 of the Lesson Plans booklet.

**Political Cartoons** See p. 42 of the Political Cartoons booklet for a cartoon relevant to this section.

**Simulations and Debates** War Powers Resolution, pp. 53–55, helps students organize a debate on this controversial law.

**Section Support Transparencies** Transparency 45, *Visual Learning;* Transparency 144, *Political Cartoon*

### Take It to the Net

For career-related links and activities, visit the *Magruder's American Government* companion Web site in the Social Studies area at the Prentice Hall School Web site.

combat in areas where a state of war does not exist; see Chapters 14 and 17.

## Other Expressed Powers

The Constitution sets out a number of other expressed powers. Many of these powers have a direct influence on the daily lives of Americans.

### Naturalization

The process by which citizens of one country become citizens of another is called **naturalization.** Article I, Section 8, Clause 4 gives Congress the exclusive power "[t]o establish an uniform Rule of Naturalization." Today, our population includes more than nine million naturalized citizens; we shall return to this matter in Chapter 21.

### The Postal Power

Article I, Section 8, Clause 7 says that Congress has the power "[t]o establish Post Offices and post Roads." Post roads are all postal routes, including railroads, airways, and waters within the United States, during the time that mail is being carried on them.

The United States Postal Service traces its history back to the early colonial period. Benjamin Franklin is generally credited as the founder of the present-day postal system. Today some 39,000 post offices, branches, stations, and community post offices serve the nation. The Postal Service and its some 750,000 employees handle more than 180 billion pieces of mail a year.

Congress has established a number of crimes based on the postal power. Thus, it is a federal crime for anyone to obstruct the mails, to use the mails to commit any fraud, or to use the mails in the committing of any other crime.

Congress has also prohibited the mailing of many items. Any articles prohibited by a State's laws—for example, firecrackers or switchblade knives—cannot be sent into that State by mail. A great many other items, including chain letters and obscene materials, cannot be sent through the mails.

The States and their local governments cannot interfere with the mails unreasonably. Nor can they require licenses for Postal Service vehicles or tax the gas they use, or tax post offices or any other property of the United States Postal Service.

### Copyrights and Patents

The Constitution gives Congress the power

 **FROM THE Constitution** *" To promote the Progress of Science and useful Arts, by securing for limited Times to Authors and Inventors the exclusive Right to their respective Writings and Discoveries. "*

—Article I, Section 8, Clause 8

A **copyright** is the exclusive right of an author to reproduce, publish, and sell his or her creative work. That right may be assigned —transferred by contract—to

| Congressional Powers Expressed in Article 1, Section 8 ||||
| --- | --- | --- | --- |
| **PEACETIME POWERS** || **WAR POWERS** ||
| Clause | Provision | Clause | Provision |
| 1 | To impose and collect taxes, duties, and excises | 11 | To declare war; to make laws regarding captures on land and water |
| 2 | To borrow money | | |
| 3 | To regulate foreign and interstate commerce | 12 | To raise and support armies |
| 4 | To provide for naturalization; to create bankruptcy laws | | |
| 5 | To coin money and regulate its value; to regulate weights and measures | 13 | To provide and maintain a navy |
| | | 14 | To make laws governing land and naval forces |
| 6 | To punish counterfeiters of federal money and securities | 15 | To provide for summoning the militia to execute federal laws, suppress uprisings, and repel invasions |
| 7 | To establish post offices | | |
| 8 | To grant patents and copyrights | | |
| 9 | To create courts inferior to the Supreme Court | | |
| 10 | To define and punish crimes at sea and violations of international law | 16 | To provide for organizing, arming, and disciplining the militia and governing it when in the service of the Union |
| 17 | To exercise exclusive jurisdiction over the District of Columbia and other federal properties | | |
| 18 | To make all laws necessary and proper to the execution of any of the other expressed powers | | |

*Interpreting Tables* This table sets out the expressed powers of Congress. **Choose two war powers and two peacetime powers and explain why you think the Framers felt it important to give these powers to Congress.**

**Answer to . . .**

**Interpreting Tables** Answers will vary, but should demonstrate understanding that such powers—critical to the stability of the nation—were seen as falling within the domain of Congress.

## Make It Relevant

### Careers in Government—Capitol Police Officer

The mission of the United States Capitol Police has grown since 1828 from providing security at the Capitol to providing "the Congressional community and its visitors with the highest quality of a full range of police services. . . . Today's Capitol Police Officer has the primary responsibility for protecting life and property, preventing, detecting, and investigating criminal acts, and enforcing traffic regulations throughout a large complex of congressional buildings, parks, and thoroughfares." The Capitol Police have earned the nickname "The Nation's Finest." **Skills Activity** Direct pairs of students to write fictional descriptions of what they think a day in the life of a Capitol Police officer would be like. Then have them explain why they would or would not be interested in this career. **(Average)**

## Types of Intellectual Property

**Utility patents** protect useful processes, machines, articles of manufacture, and compositions of matter. Examples: fiber optics, computer hardware, medications.

**Design patents** prohibit the unauthorized use of new, original, and ornamental designs for manufactured articles. Examples: the look of an athletic shoe, a bicycle helmet, Star Wars characters.

**Plant patents** protect certain invented or discovered plant varieties. Examples: hybrid tea roses, Silver Queen corn, Better Boy tomatoes.

**Copyrights** protect works of authorship, such as writings, music, and works of art that have been "tangibly expressed"—that is, in some way published, written, recorded, or made. Examples: *Gone With the Wind* (book and film), Beatles recordings, video games.

**Trademarks** protect words, names, symbols, sounds, or colors that distinguish goods and services. Trademarks, unlike patents, can be renewed forever, as long as they are being used in business. Examples: the roar of the lion in MGM movies, the pink of the Owens-Corning Pink Panther, the word "three-peat"—coined by former Los Angeles Lakers basketball coach Pat Riley in 1989 in reference to record-setting three-in-a-row NBA championship victories.

**Trade secrets** are information that companies keep secret to give them an advantage over their competitors. Examples: the recipe for Coca-Cola, the recipe for Kentucky Fried Chicken.

SOURCE: United States Patent and Trademark Museum

**Interpreting Charts** In 2000, the government created a stir by granting an Internet store, Amazon.com, a patent on the structure of its Web page, which links to other merchants. *(a) Which type of patent listed above might have been given to Amazon? (b) Why do you think the granting of this patent was controversial?*

another, as to a publishing firm by mutual agreement between the author and the other party.

Copyrights are registered by the Copyright Office in the Library of Congress. Under present law they are good for the life of the author plus 70 years. They cover a wide range of creative efforts: books, magazines, newspapers, musical compositions and lyrics, dramatic works, paintings, sculptures, cartoons, maps, photographs, motion pictures, sound recordings, and much more.[8]

The Copyright Office does not enforce the protections of a copyright. If a copyright is infringed or violated, the owner of the right may sue for damages in the federal courts.

A **patent** grants a person the sole right to manufacture, use, or sell "any new and useful art, machine, manufacture, or composition of matter, or any new and useful improvement thereof." A patent is good for up to 20 years. The term of a patent may be extended only by a special act of Congress. The Patent and Trademark Office in the Department of Commerce administers patent laws.[9]

### Weights and Measures

Article I, Section 8, Clause 5 gives Congress the power to "fix the Standard of Weights and Measures" throughout the United States. The power reflects the absolute need for accurate, uniform gauges of time, distance, area, weight, volume, and the like.

In 1838 Congress set the English system of pound, ounce, mile, foot, gallon, quart, and so on, as the legal standards of weights and measures in this country. In 1866 Congress also legalized the use of the metric system of gram, meter, kilometer, liter, and so on.

In 1901, Congress created the National Bureau of Standards in the Commerce Department. Now known as the National Institute of Standards and Technology, the agency keeps the original standards for the United States. It is these standards by which all other measures in the United States are tested and corrected.

[8]Not all publications can be protected by copyright. Thus, the Supreme Court has held that such "factual compilations" as telephone directories "lack the requisite originality" for copyright protection, *Feist Publications, Inc.,* v. *Rural Telephone Service Co.,* 1991.

[9]The power to protect trademarks is an implied power, drawn from the commerce power. A trademark is some distinctive word, name, symbol, or device used by a manufacturer or merchant to identify his goods or services and distinguish them from those made or sold by others. A trademark need not be original, merely distinctive. The registration of a trademark carries the right to its exclusive use in interstate commerce for 10 years. The right may be renewed an unlimited number of times.

## Answers to . . .
### Section 3 Assessment

**1.** Foreign relations: the President has primary responsibility, but Congress has various expressed and inherent powers regarding foreign commerce and national security. War powers: the President is commander in chief of the armed forces, but only Congress can declare war, maintain armies and navies and make various rules pertaining to the military.
**2.** Naturalization is the process by which citizens of one country become citizens of another; Congress is given this power expressly in the Constitution.
**3.** A copyright is the exclusive right of an author to reproduce, sell, and publish his or her work, and is granted for the author's lifetime plus 70 years; a patent is the right to manufacture, use or sell any new invention and expires after 20 years.
**4.** Examples will vary, but inferences should relate to areas of national concern or foreign relations in which States are not sovereign.

## Answer to . . .
**Interpreting Maps (a)** Nevada, Arizona, and Utah. **(b)** Opinions should be supported with examples.

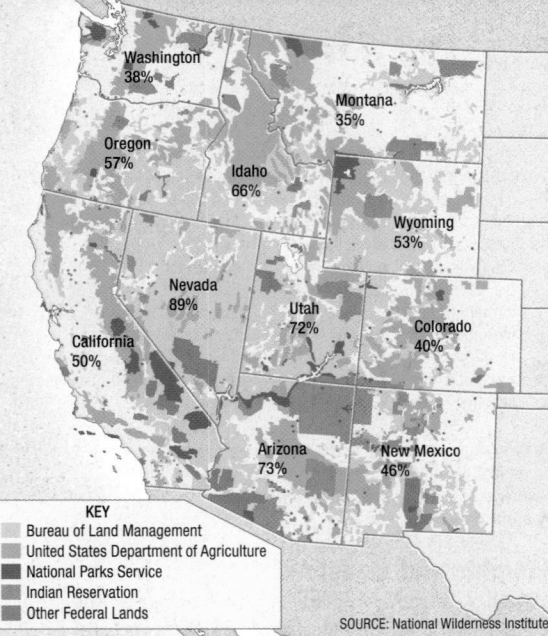

**Federal Land in the Western United States, 1998**

Washington 38%, Oregon 57%, Idaho 66%, Montana 35%, Wyoming 53%, Nevada 89%, Utah 72%, Colorado 40%, California 50%, Arizona 73%, New Mexico 46%

**KEY**
- Bureau of Land Management
- United States Department of Agriculture
- National Parks Service
- Indian Reservation
- Other Federal Lands

SOURCE: National Wilderness Institute

*Interpreting Maps* The Federal Government owns vast areas of the West. *(a) In which States is most of the land owned by the Federal Government? (b) Why do certain agencies own so much land?*

### Power Over Territories and Other Areas
Article I, Section 8, Clause 17 and Article IV, Section 3, Clause 2 give Congress the power to acquire, manage, and dispose of various federal areas. That power relates to the District of Columbia and to the several federal territories, including Puerto Rico, Guam, and the Virgin Islands. It also covers hundreds of military and naval installations, arsenals, dockyards, post offices, prisons, parks and forest preserves, and many other federal holdings.

The Federal Government may acquire property by purchase or gift. It may also do so through the exercise of **eminent domain,** the inherent power to take private property for public use.[10] Territory may also be acquired from a foreign state based on the power to admit new States, on the war powers, and on the President's treaty-making power.

### Judicial Powers
As a part of the system of checks and balances, Congress has several judicial powers. These include the expressed power to create all of the federal courts below the Supreme Court and to structure the federal judiciary.

Congress also has the power to define federal crimes and set punishment for violators of federal law. The Constitution mentions only four federal crimes:
  (1) counterfeiting;
  (2) piracies and felonies on the high seas;
  (3) offenses against the law of nations (in Article I, Section 8, Clauses 6 and 10); and
  (4) treason (in Article III, Section 3).

---
[10]The 5th Amendment restricts the government's use of the power with these words: "nor shall private property be taken for public use, without just compensation."

## Section 3 Assessment

**Key Terms and Main Ideas**
1. Explain how Congress and the President share power over issues regarding foreign relations and war.
2. Where does Congress get its power to regulate **naturalization?**
3. How does a **copyright** differ from a **patent?**

**Critical Thinking**
4. **Drawing Inferences** Choose three congressional powers discussed in this section and infer why the Framers gave these powers to Congress rather than to the States.
5. **Making Decisions** Some people suggest that the U.S. Postal Service be abolished because today's for-profit mail companies would do a better job and would compete for business, keeping prices low. Do you agree? Explain.

### Take It to the Net
6. At the U. S. Postal Service historical page, choose a specific innovation in mail service, and write a short essay explaining how it changed American life. Use the links provided in the Social Studies area at the following Web site for help in completing this activity. **www.phschool.com**

**5.** Answers will vary, but might suggest that postal power must come under the domain of the National Government as it concerns national and international laws and safety issues.

### Take It to the Net
6. Direct students to the Social Studies area at the Prentice Hall School Web site. The *Magruder's American Government* companion Web site includes the directions and links needed to complete the activity. It also provides a printable Internet activity worksheet, with scoring rubrics for assessment. Essays should be clearly organized and include relevant examples.

## Section Preview

### OBJECTIVES

1. **Explain** how the Necessary and Proper Clause gives Congress flexibility in lawmaking.
2. **Summarize** the key developments in the battle over the implied powers of Congress.

### WHY IT MATTERS

One clause in the Constitution was an early battleground over congressional power and led to the massive expansion of Congress's power today.

### POLITICAL DICTIONARY

★ appropriate
★ **Necessary and Proper Clause**
★ doctrine

---

What does the Constitution say about education? Nothing, not a word. Still, Congress **appropriates**—assigns to a particular use—more than $30 billion a year for the U.S. Department of Education to spend in various ways throughout the country. Look around you. What evidence of these federal dollars can you find in your school? If you attend a public school anywhere in the United States, those indications should not be hard to find.

How can this be? You know that Congress has only those powers delegated to it by the Constitution, and the Constitution says nothing about education. The answer lies in the implied powers of Congress.

### The Necessary and Proper Clause

Remember that the implied powers are those powers that are not set out in so many words in the Constitution but are implied by those that are. The constitutional basis for the implied powers is found in one of the expressed powers. The **Necessary and Proper Clause** gives to Congress the power:

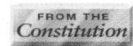 **FROM THE Constitution** *"To make all Laws which shall be necessary and proper for carrying into Execution the foregoing Powers and all other Powers vested by this Constitution in the Government of the United States, or in any Department or Officer thereof."*

—Article I, Section 8, Clause 18

Much of the vitality and adaptability of the United States Constitution can be traced directly to this provision—and even more so to the ways both Congress and the Supreme Court have interpreted and applied it over the years. For good reason, the Necessary and Proper Clause has often been called the "Elastic Clause," because it has been stretched so far and made to cover so much over the years.

### The Battle Over Implied Powers

The Constitution had barely come into force when the meaning of the Necessary and Proper Clause was called into question. In 1790

*Interpreting Political Cartoons* This cartoon depicts New York State's ratification of the Constitution in 1788. **(a) What does the ship represent? (b) What does the cartoon imply about the Federal Government? (c) Was the cartoonist a Federalist or an Anti-Federalist?**

---

**305**

## The *Living* Constitution

### Expansion of Congressional Power

By the beginning of the 20th century, America had transformed itself into a modern urban and industrial society. Americans had also begun to call on government to regulate their increasingly complex and impersonal society. This reform movement, called Progressivism, was an important factor in the expansion of congressional power. Antitrust, food and drug, and banking regulation all set important precedents for the broad regulatory powers of the Federal Government.

### Using the Time Line

Have students use library or Internet resources to fill in additional information about each event on the time line. Then, ask them to tie each event to another that occurred before or after it. How did one event set the precedent for another?

## Reading Strategy

### Finding Evidence

Have students find evidence, as they read, to support the idea that Congress and the Supreme Court have encouraged a broad interpretation of the Necessary and Proper Clause.

### A C T I V I T Y

### Heterogeneous Groups

**Enrichment** Tell students to assume the roles of newspaper reporters covering the case *McCulloch* v. *Maryland*. Ask them to write a brief newspaper report summarizing the key events and issues in the case, including its outcome. Student reports should conclude with a prediction about how the decision will affect the country in the future. Encourage students to be dramatic in their reporting.

**(Basic)**

Alexander Hamilton, as Secretary of the Treasury, urged Congress to set up a national bank. That proposal touched off one of the most important disputes in all of American political history.

The opponents of Hamilton's plan insisted that nowhere did the Constitution give to Congress the power to establish such a bank. Remember, those strict constructionists, led by Thomas Jefferson, believed that the new government had only (1) those powers expressly granted to it by the Constitution, and (2) those powers *absolutely* necessary to carrying out the expressed powers.

Hamilton and other liberal constructionists looked to the Necessary and Proper Clause. They said that it gave Congress the power to do anything that was reasonably related to the exercise of the expressed powers. As for the national bank, they argued that its creation was related to the execution of the taxing, borrowing, commerce, and currency powers.

The strict constructionists were sorely troubled by that broad view of the powers of Congress. They were sure that it would give the new government almost unlimited authority and all but destroy the reserved powers of the States.[11]

Reason and practical necessity carried the day for Hamilton and his side. Congress established the Bank of the United States in 1791. Its charter (the act creating it) was to expire in 1811. During those 20 years, the constitutionality of both the bank and the concept of implied powers went unchallenged in the courts.

### *McCulloch* v. *Maryland,* 1819

In 1816 Congress created the Second Bank of the United States. Its charter came only after

---

[11]In 1801 a bill was introduced in Congress to incorporate a company to mine copper. As Vice President, Jefferson ridiculed that measure with this comment: "Congress is authorized to defend the nation. Ships are necessary for defense; copper is necessary for ships; mines necessary for copper; a company necessary to work the mines; and who can doubt this reasoning who has ever played at 'This Is the House that Jack Built'?" While Jefferson himself was President (1801–1809), he and his party were many times forced to reverse their earlier stand. Thus, for example, it was only on the basis of the implied powers doctrine that the Louisiana Purchase in 1803 and the embargo on foreign trade in 1807 could be justified.

## The *Living* Constitution

### Expansion of Congressional Power   1875   1925

The powers and duties of the Federal Government have increased greatly over our nation's history. Congress's expressed powers are listed in the Constitution. Congress also has implied powers, which are based on Congress's right to make any laws that are "necessary and proper" to carry out those expressed powers. As the time line shows, the doctrine of implied powers has allowed Congress to pass laws that affect many areas of society, but there are limits to these implied powers.

**1890** Sherman Antitrust Act regulates monopolies and other practices that limit competition. (Expressed power: to regulate interstate commerce)

**1935** Wagner Act protects the right of labor unions and workers to engage in collective bargaining. (Expressed power: to regulate interstate commerce)

another hard-fought battle over the extent of the powers of Congress.

Having lost in Congress, opponents of the new bank now tried to persuade several State legislatures to cripple its operations. In 1818 Maryland placed a tax on all notes issued by any bank doing business in the State but not chartered by the State legislature. The tax was aimed directly at the Second Bank's branch in Baltimore. James McCulloch, the bank's cashier, purposely issued notes on which no tax had been paid. The State won a judgment against him in its own courts. Acting for McCulloch, the United States then appealed to the Supreme Court.

Maryland took the strict-construction position before the Court. It argued that the creation of the bank had been unconstitutional. The United States defended the concept of implied powers, and also argued that no State could lawfully tax any agency of the Federal Government.

In one of its most important decisions, the Court unanimously reversed the Maryland courts. It held that the Constitution need not expressly empower Congress to create a bank.

The creation of the Second Bank, said the Court, was "necessary and proper" to the execution of four of the expressed powers of Congress: the taxing, borrowing, currency, and commerce powers. In short, the Court gave sweeping approval to the concept of implied powers.[12]

Chief Justice John Marshall wrote the Court's opinion in the case. For the Court, he said:

**PRIMARY Sources** *"We admit, as all must admit, that the powers of the government are limited, and that its limits are not to be transcended. But we think the sound construction of the Constitution must allow to the national legislature that discretion, with respect to the means by which the powers it confers are to be carried into execution, which will enable that body to perform the high duties assigned to it, in the manner most beneficial to the people."*
—*McCulloch v. Maryland,* Opinion of the Court

[12]The Court also invalidated the Maryland tax. Because, said the Court, "the power to tax involves the power to destroy," no State may tax the United States or any of its agencies or functions.

---

**1947** U.S. Air Force is established as a separate branch of the military. (Expressed powers: to raise armies and provide a navy)

**1987** Supreme Court upholds law that cuts federal highway funds to States that fail to set 21 as minimum drinking age, *South Dakota* v. *Dole.* (Expressed power: to spend money for the general welfare)

**1950**          **1975**          **2000**

**1956** National Defense and Interstate Highway Act provides federal funds to build a national highway system. (Expressed Powers: to regulate interstate commerce and the War Powers Act)

**1995** Federal law establishing gun-free zones near schools, defended under the expressed power to regulate interstate commerce, is rejected by the Supreme Court, *United States* v. *Lopez.*

### Analyzing Time Lines

1. Which expressed power has been the basis for most of the expansion of Congress's powers? Why do you think this is so?
2. Why do you think the Supreme Court ruled against the federal law regarding gun-free zones?

**307**

## Point-of-Use Resources

**Guide to the Essentials** Chapter 11, Section 4, p. 63 provides support for students who need additional review of section content. Spanish support is available in the Spanish edition of the Guide on p. 56.

**Quiz** Unit 3 booklet, p. 18 includes matching and multiple-choice questions to check students' understanding of Section 4 content.

**Presentation Pro CD-ROM** Quizzes and multiple-choice questions check students' understanding of Section 4 content.

**Section Support Transparencies** Transparency 46, *Visual Learning*; Transparency 145, *Political Cartoon*

## Answers to . . .

### Section 4 Assessment

**1.** *Appropriate* means "to assign money to particular uses."
**2. (a)** The "Elastic Clause." **(b)** Because it has been interpreted in so many ways and expanded so much over the years.
**3.** It is the principle that implied powers are proper and useful if they may be reasonably drawn from the expressed powers.
**4. (a)** *McCulloch* v. *Maryland* was a debate between strict constructionism and the expansion of implied powers. **(b)** The State of Maryland; the Second Bank of the United States; the bank's cashier, James McCulloch; and John Marshall, Chief Justice. **(c)** The Court gave approval to the concept of implied powers. **(d)** It set the precedent for the broad interpretation of constitutional powers which would characterize government after the case.

## Answer to . . .

**Interpreting Charts** Answers will vary, but should demonstrate an understanding that such powers are necessary for Congress to carry out its expressed powers.

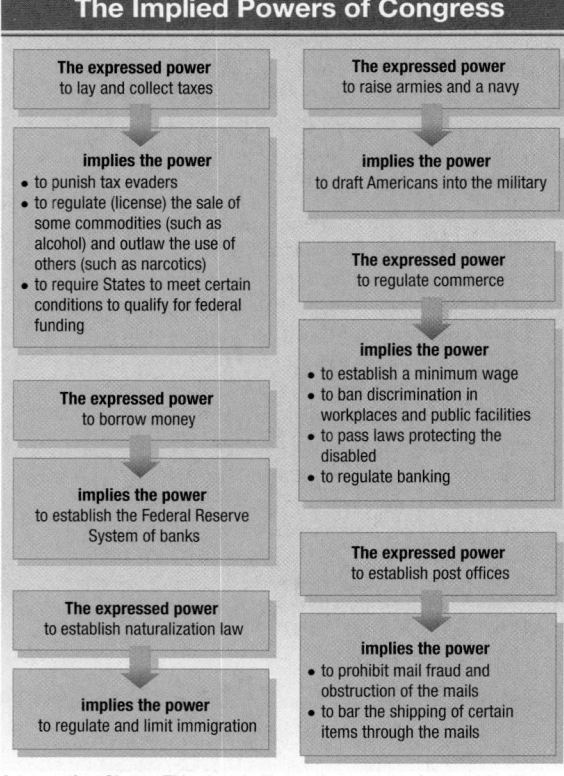

### The Implied Powers of Congress

| The expressed power to lay and collect taxes | The expressed power to raise armies and a navy |
|---|---|
| **implies the power** <br>• to punish tax evaders <br>• to regulate (license) the sale of some commodities (such as alcohol) and outlaw the use of others (such as narcotics) <br>• to require States to meet certain conditions to qualify for federal funding | **implies the power** <br>to draft Americans into the military |
| **The expressed power** to borrow money | **The expressed power** to regulate commerce |
| | **implies the power** <br>• to establish a minimum wage <br>• to ban discrimination in workplaces and public facilities <br>• to pass laws protecting the disabled <br>• to regulate banking |
| **implies the power** <br>to establish the Federal Reserve System of banks | **The expressed power** to establish post offices |
| **The expressed power** to establish naturalization law | **implies the power** <br>• to prohibit mail fraud and obstruction of the mails <br>• to bar the shipping of certain items through the mails |
| **implies the power** <br>to regulate and limit immigration | |

**Interpreting Charts** This chart indicates the sources of several implied powers, those that are not specifically spelled out in the Constitution but can be reasonably assumed. *Choose three of the implied powers listed above and explain why they are seen as implied by the expressed power cited. Do you agree that the powers you have chosen are implied by an expressed power?*

### Section 4 Assessment

**Key Terms and Main Ideas**
1. Explain what it means to **appropriate** funds.
2. **(a)** What is the **Necessary and Proper Clause** commonly called? **(b)** How did it get that name?
3. What is the **doctrine** of implied powers?

**Critical Thinking**
4. **Expressing Problems Clearly (a)** Write a one-sentence summary of the central dispute in the case of *McCulloch* v. *Maryland.* **(b)** Identify the key individuals and institutions involved in the case. **(c)** Summarize the outcome of the case. **(d)** Explain the long-term consequences of the decision.
5. **Evaluating the Quotation** Restate the first quotation from the *McCulloch* v. *Maryland* decision on page 307 in your own words.
6. **Drawing Conclusions** If the strict constructionists had won their battle to limit Congress's implied powers, how might our government be different today?

 **Take It to the Net**

7. Using examples from your text and from the Internet, write a paragraph explaining this statement: *The Commerce Clause has been used to greatly expand the powers of Congress.* Use the links provided in the Social Studies area at the following Web site for help in completing this activity. **www.phschool.com**

**5.** Statements will vary but should reflect an understanding that the National Government cannot carry out its responsibilities without implied powers.
**6.** Answers will vary, but should suggest that many of the powers of Congress could not have evolved without liberal constructionism.

### Take It to the Net

**7.** Direct students to the Social Studies area at the Prentice Hall School Web site. The *Magruder's American Government* companion Web site includes the directions and links needed to complete the activity. It also provides a printable Internet activity worksheet, with scoring rubrics for assessment. Paragraphs should list specific expansions of congressional power that stemmed from the commerce power.

---

Then he penned these deathless words:

**PRIMARY Sources** *"Let the end be legitimate, let it be within the scope of the Constitution, and all means which are appropriate, which are plainly adapted to that end, which are not prohibited, but consist with the letter and spirit of the Constitution, are constitutional."*
—*McCulloch* v. *Maryland*, Opinion of the Court

This broad interpretation of the powers granted to Congress has become firmly fixed in our constitutional system. Indeed, it is impossible to see how the United States could have developed as it has under the Constitution without the principle established by *McCulloch*.

### The Doctrine in Practice

A **doctrine** is a principle or fundamental policy. The doctrine of implied powers has been applied in instances almost too numerous to count. The way Congress has looked at and used its powers, along with the supporting decisions of the Supreme Court, have made Article I, Section 8, Clause 18 truly the Elastic Clause. Today the words "necessary and proper" really read "convenient and useful."

This is most especially true when applied to the power to regulate interstate commerce and the power to tax. Yet, recall, Congress cannot do something merely because it seems to promote the "general welfare" or be in the "public interest."

# on Primary Sources

## Reining in Congress

*Over recent years, the Supreme Court has appeared more willing to overturn federal laws when it felt that Congress had exceeded its authority. In this selection, Court observer Dan Carney discusses this trend and how it may impact the way in which Congress exercises its powers in the future.*

In early December [1996], Acting Solicitor General Walter E. Dellinger III argued before the U.S. Supreme Court on the merits of the Brady Act, which allows a police background check on people seeking to buy handguns. Almost in passing, he mentioned that the vast majority of sheriffs and police chiefs support the legislation.

This struck a raw nerve with Chief Justice William H. Rehnquist, who curtly informed Dellinger that the Supreme Court of the United States did not base its rulings on straw polls. If a person's constitutional rights are being violated by a popular statute, Rehnquist reasoned, the Court is not going to say: "Gee, plenty of other people obey this law and here you are complaining about it."

Under normal circumstances, this kind of statement might be dismissed as offhand. But in light of the Court's recent decisions—and cases it is now hearing—the remark illustrates the Court's growing willingness to strike down federal statutes on the grounds that Congress has overstepped its power.

The Supreme Court has undertaken a re-evaluation of Congress's legislative authority. . . .

The chief question in these cases is if Congress has ventured into areas where it has no right to be. . . . All of these cases involve limits to federal power, and most are likely to turn on interpretation of the 10th Amendment, which restricts the Federal Government to those powers specifically enumerated in the Constitution. For Congress, this is not some arcane legal debate taking place at the

*James Brady (right) and his allies speak in favor of gun control before the Supreme Court building.*

Court. It could have a dramatic effect on the type of legislation Congress can enact, and the way that it does it. "There are enough cases now where I think Congress ought to think of it as a wake-up call," says A. E. Dick Howard, a law professor at the University of Virginia. "Surely all this adds up to changing the way Congress does its business." . . . Orrin G. Hatch (R., Utah), chairman of the Senate Judiciary Committee, said he is "very happy with these decisions" because they indicate that "we have a Congress that operates under limited and enumerated powers."

At the very least, the Supreme Court's renewed interest in the 10th Amendment will likely mean more legislation based on the interstate commerce clause in Article I of the Constitution. Congress's authority to regulate such commerce is arguably its broadest and hardest-to-define power.

### Analyzing Primary Sources

1. On what basis has the Supreme Court challenged Congress?
2. How does the author suggest that Congress could respond to the Court?
3. What did Chief Justice Rehnquist mean when he said that the Supreme Court did not base its rulings on straw polls?
4. What change in federalism does this analysis suggest will occur?

## Reining In Congress

**Focus** Ask students to describe why the Supreme Court would rule an action of the legislative branch unconstitutional. Then have students read the article on this page and answer the questions.

**Instruct** Have students create a case in which a law that was ratified by Congress would be challenged in the courts based on the Commerce Clause in Article I of the Constitution. Ask them to create briefs detailing the circumstances of each case, and decide how the court would be likely to rule. Finally, ask how the Commerce Clause would affect that decision.

**Close/Reteach** Based on what they have learned thus far, have students consider whether the Internet could be regulated by Congress based on the Interstate Commerce Clause. After students have had time to form their arguments, carry on a brief debate on the topic.

💿 **Keep It Current CD-ROM** includes government-related projects by unit. The CD-ROM links to the Prentice Hall School Web site and may be used for daily updates.

### Answers to . . .

**Analyzing Primary Sources**

**1.** The Supreme Court has used the 10th Amendment to restrict Congress on the basis that it has overstepped its power.

**2.** The author suggests that Congress should pass more laws based on the Commerce Clause.

**3.** That the Supreme Court based its rulings on its interpretation of the Constitution, not on a law's popularity.

**4.** Answers will vary, but should suggest that using the 10th Amendment to limit congressional power will increase the power of the States, because that amendment delegates all remaining powers to the States or to the people.

**5** *The Nonlegislative Powers*

## Section Preview

### OBJECTIVES

1. **Describe** Congress's role in amending the Constitution and in deciding elections.
2. **Describe** Congress's power to impeach, and summarize presidential impeachment cases.
3. **Identify** Congress's executive powers.
4. **Describe** Congress's investigatory power.

### WHY IT MATTERS

Impeachment trials, close elections, far-reaching constitutional change, congressional committee investigations, presidential appointments—Congress has often captured the undivided attention of the American people as it has exercised one of its several non-legislative powers.

### POLITICAL DICTIONARY

★ successor
★ impeach
★ acquit
★ perjury
★ censure
★ subpoena

The Constitution gives Congress a number of other chores besides making laws. This section explores those other chores, the nonlegislative powers.

## Constitutional Amendments

Article V gives Congress the power to propose amendments by a two-thirds vote in each house. It has done so 33 times so far. Article V also provides that Congress may call a national convention of delegates from each of the States to propose an amendment if requested to do so by at least

▲ Suffragettes celebrate passage of the Nineteenth Amendment, giving women the right to vote. In 1972, Congress proposed an Equal Rights Amendment (ERA), but after a long, divisive battle, the effort to win ratification failed. *Critical Thinking* **Why did the Framers make the amendment process difficult, requiring State ratification in addition to congressional approval?**

two thirds of the State legislatures. No such convention has ever been called.

In recent years several State legislatures have petitioned Congress in behalf of amendments that would require that Congress balance the federal budget each year, prohibit flag burning, permit prayer in the public schools, and outlaw abortions. Today, the most vigorous efforts for a convention are being pushed by those who favor an amendment on congressional term limits.

## Electoral Duties

The Constitution gives certain electoral duties to Congress. But they are to be exercised only in very unusual circumstances.

The House of Representatives may be called on to elect a President. The 12th Amendment says that if no candidate receives a majority of the electoral votes for President, the House of Representatives, voting by States, must decide the issue. It must choose from among the three highest contenders in the electoral college balloting. Each State has but one vote to cast, and a majority of the States is necessary for election.

The Senate must also choose a Vice President when no candidate wins a majority of the electoral votes. The vote is not by States but by individual senators, with a majority of the full Senate necessary for election.[13]

---

[13]Notice that the 12th Amendment makes it possible for the President to be of one party and the Vice President another.

The House has twice chosen a President: Thomas Jefferson in 1801 and John Quincy Adams in 1825. The Senate has had to pick a Vice President only once: Richard M. Johnson in 1837.

Remember, too, that the 25th Amendment provides for the filling of a vacancy in the vice presidency. When one occurs, the President nominates a **successor**—a replacement, someone to fill the vacancy, subject to a majority vote in both houses of Congress. That process has been used twice: Gerald Ford was confirmed as Vice President in 1973 and Nelson Rockefeller in 1974.

## Impeachment

The Constitution provides that the President, Vice President, and all civil officers of the United States may "be removed from Office on Impeachment for and Conviction of, Treason, Bribery, or other high Crimes and Misdemeanors."[14] The House has the sole power to **impeach**—to accuse, bring charges. The Senate has the sole power to try—to judge, sit as a court—in impeachment cases.[15]

Impeachment requires only a majority vote in the House; conviction requires a two-thirds vote in the Senate. The Chief Justice presides over the Senate when a President is to be tried. The penalty for conviction is removal from office. The Senate may also prohibit a convicted person from ever holding federal office again; and he or she can be tried in the regular courts for any crime involved in the events that led to the impeachment. To date, there have been 17 impeachments and seven convictions; all seven persons removed by the Senate were federal judges.[16]

Two Presidents have been impeached by the House: Andrew Johnson in 1868 and Bill Clinton in 1998. The Senate voted to **acquit** both men—that is, it found them not guilty.

---

[14]Article II, Section 4. Military officers are not considered "civil officers," nor are members of Congress.
[15]Article I, Section 2, Clause 5; Section 3, Clause 6.
[16]Four other federal judges were impeached by the House but later acquitted by the Senate. Two federal judges impeached by the House resigned before the Senate could act in their cases. One of the seven judges removed from office was later elected to Congress. The only other federal officer ever impeached was William W. Bellknap, President Grant's Secretary of War. Bellknap had been accused of accepting bribes and, although he had resigned from office, was impeached by the House in 1876. He was then tried by the Senate and found not guilty.

▲ **Historical Drama** Political intrigue drew spectators to the impeachment trials of Presidents Andrew Johnson and Bill Clinton.

### Andrew Johnson

Andrew Johnson became the nation's 17th President when Abraham Lincoln was assassinated in 1865. Johnson soon became enmeshed in disputes with the Radical Republicans who controlled Congress. Many of those disagreements centered on the treatment of the defeated Southern States in the immediate post–Civil War period.

Matters came to a head when Congress passed the Tenure of Office Act, over the President's veto, in 1867. President Johnson's deliberate violation of that law triggered his impeachment by a House bent on political revenge. The table on the next page summarizes the episode.

### Bill Clinton

Bill Clinton was impeached by the House in 1998. In proceedings steeped in partisanship, the House voted two articles of impeachment against him on December 19. Both articles arose out of the President's admitted "inappropriate relationship" with a White House intern. As you can see in the table on the next page, the first article charged the President with **perjury,** or lying under oath. The second article accused him of obstruction of justice because he withheld information about his affair with the intern.

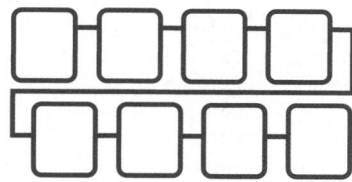

## Extended Class Periods

**Time** 90 minutes.
**Purpose** Write a "matching" quiz for Chapter 11.
**Grouping** Groups of four to six students.
**Activity** Have students in each group work together to compile a list of 25–30 terms discussed in the chapter. Then have group members divide the list and work independently to write a definition for each term.
**Roles** All group members will write definitions. Appoint one member of each group to act as recorder.
**Close** Have the recorder prepare the final quiz, listing all of the group's definitions in a "matching" format. Then have group members prepare an answer key. Duplicate quizzes and have groups exchange and complete them.

**Block Strategy (Basic)**

## Point-of-Use Resources

**Block Scheduling with Lesson Strategies** Additional activities for Chapter 11 appear on p. 24.

**Government Assessment Rubrics** Cooperative Learning Project: Process, p. 20

### Answer to . . .

**Interpreting Tables (a)** A majority of members is required to start the process, secure impeachment, and convict; witnesses are heard and evidence presented as in a regular trial; debate is present at every level of the process. **(b)** Possible answer: In both cases, conviction did not have the support of the majority of participants.

Members of the House who supported the articles of impeachment contended that lying under oath and withholding evidence were within the meaning of the Constitution's phrase "Other High Crimes and Misdemeanors," and justified the President's immediate removal from office.

Their opponents argued that the facts involved in the case did not justify either charge. They insisted that, while the President's conduct was deplorable and should be condemned, that conduct did not rise to the level of an impeachable offense. Many of them pressed for a resolution to **censure** the President—that is, for a formal condemnation of his behavior.

The Senate received the articles of impeachment when the new Congress convened in 1999, and it began to sit in judgment of the President on January 7. The Senate trial and its outcome are summarized in the table below.

### Richard Nixon

A few officeholders have resigned in the face of almost certain impeachment—most notably, Richard Nixon, who resigned the presidency in 1974. Nixon's second term in office was cut short by the Watergate scandal.

### The Impeachment Process

| THE PROCESS | PRESIDENT ANDREW JOHNSON IMPEACHMENT 1868 | PRESIDENT BILL CLINTON IMPEACHMENT 1998–1999 |
|---|---|---|
| **Step One** The House Judiciary Committee debates charges against the accused and votes on whether to send articles of impeachment to the full House. A simple majority vote is needed to start the process. | **Feb. 22, 1868** House committee votes to send to the full House articles of impeachment against Johnson for having violated the Tenure of Office Act, by firing Secretary of War Edwin Stanton. | **Dec. 11–12, 1998** After three months of hearings, the House Judiciary Committee approves four articles of impeachment against Clinton: two counts of perjury, obstruction of justice, and making false statements relating to his relations with a White House intern. |
| **Step Two** Acting much like a grand jury, the House considers the charge(s) brought by the Judiciary Committee. It can subpoena witnesses and evidence. It hears and debates arguments. | **Feb. 22–24, 1868** The House, led by the Radical Republicans, holds a raucous debate on charges against Johnson, a Democrat. The outcome is never in doubt. | **Dec. 18–19, 1998** The House holds 13 hours of bitter, partisan debate, in which more than 200 House members speak. Democrats briefly walk out to protest Republican leaders' refusal to consider the lesser punishment of censure. |
| **Step Three** The House votes on each article. If any article is approved by a majority vote, the official is impeached, which is similar to being indicted. The House sends the article(s) of impeachment to the Senate. | **Feb. 24, 1868** The House votes 126 to 47 to impeach. It drafts 11 articles of impeachment, including violation of the Tenure of Office Act and attempting to bring disgrace upon Congress. | **Dec. 19, 1998** The House votes to impeach Clinton on two counts. The votes are 228–206 on one count of perjury and 221–212 on obstruction of justice. Voting is mostly along party lines. |
| **Step Four** The Senate tries the case. If the President is to be tried, the Chief Justice of the United States presides. Selected members of the House act as managers (prosecutors). | **March 30, 1868** Opening statements begin in the Senate trial with Chief Justice Salmon P. Chase presiding. Johnson does not attend, but the gallery is packed with observers. | **January 7, 1999** Chief Justice William Rehnquist opens a televised trial. Rep. Henry Hyde of Illinois leads a team of 13 House managers. White House Counsel Charles Ruff leads Clinton defense. |
| **Step Five** Senators hear testimony and evidence. House prosecutors and lawyers for both sides present their cases. Additional witnesses may be called. Senators may also vote to curb testimony. | **March 30–May 15, 1868** The trial yields little new evidence. Votes are known from the start. The outcome rests on one swing vote, an undecided Republican, who is offered bribes by both sides. | **Jan. 7–Feb. 11, 1999** With public distaste for impeachment growing, the Senate limits testimony to four witnesses, the intern not among them. Closing arguments follow. For three days, the Senate deliberates in secret (despite Democrats' objections). |
| **Step Six** The Senate debates the articles, publicly or privately. It need not render a verdict. It could, for example, vote to drop the case or censure the official. A two-thirds vote is required for conviction. | **May 16, May 26, 1868** In voting on two days, 35 Republicans vote to convict, one vote short of two thirds. Twelve Democrats and seven Republicans, including the swing vote, support acquittal. | **Feb. 12, 1999** In a televised session, the Senate acquits Clinton on both charges, falling well short of the two-thirds vote needed for conviction. On perjury, 45 Democrats and 10 Republicans vote not guilty. On obstruction, the vote splits 50–50. |

**Interpreting Tables** This table details the complex process of impeaching a President.
**(a)** What measures did the Framers build into the impeachment process to try to make it fair?
**(b)** Why do you think both attempts to remove U.S. Presidents resulted in failure?

## Spotlight on Technology

**Magruder's American Government Video Collection**

The Magruder's Video Collection explores key issues and debates in American government. Each segment examines an issue central to chapter content through use of historical and contemporary footage. Commentary from civic leaders in academics, government, and the media follow each segment. Critical-thinking questions focus students' attention on key issues, and may be used to stimulate discussion.

Use the Chapter 11 video segment to explore the impact of congressional committees on daily life in the United States. (time: about 5 minutes) This video uses current events and contemporary footage to focus on a Senate committee. Students will view a committee firsthand as they follow the evolution of a piece of legislation.

The term *Watergate* comes from a June 1972 attempt by Republican operatives to break into the Democratic Party's national headquarters in the Watergate office complex in Washington, D.C. The reporting of that incident, by the *Washington Post* and then by other media, led to official investigations. Those investigations were led by the Department of Justice and by the Senate's Select Committee on Presidential Campaign Activities, known as the Senate Watergate Committee.

The probes unearthed a long list of illegal acts, including bribery, perjury, income tax fraud, and illegal campaign contributions. It was also revealed that Nixon had used the Federal Bureau of Investigation, the Internal Revenue Service, and other government agencies for personal and partisan purposes.

The House Judiciary Committee voted three articles of impeachment against President Nixon in late July 1974. He was charged with obstruction of justice, abuse of power, and failure to respond to the committee's subpoenas. A **subpoena** is a court order for a person to appear in court or to produce documents or other requested materials. Initially, Nixon had ignored the committee's subpoena of secret tape recordings he had made of Oval Office conversations.

It was quite apparent that the House would impeach Nixon and that the Senate would convict him. In the face of this threat, Nixon resigned the presidency on August 9, 1974.

Beyond doubt, the Watergate scandal involved the most extensive and the most serious known violations of public trust in the nation's history. Among its other consequences, several Cabinet officers, presidential assistants, and others were convicted of various felonies and misdemeanors.

## Executive Powers

The Constitution gives two executive powers to the Senate. One of those powers has to do with appointments to office, and the other with treaties made by the President.[17]

### Appointments

All major appointments made by the President must be confirmed by the Senate by majority vote. Each nomination is referred to the appropriate

[17]Article II, Section 2, Clause 2.

◀ *A Final Farewell* It was not impeachment but the threat of impeachment that forced a President from office. Richard Nixon resigned on August 9, 1974, giving a final wave from his helicopter before leaving the White House.

standing committee of the Senate. That committee may then hold hearings to decide whether or not to make a favorable recommendation to full Senate for that appointment. When that committee's recommendation is brought to the floor of the Senate, it may be, but seldom is, considered in executive (secret) session.

The appointment of a Cabinet officer or of some other top member of the President's "official family" is rarely turned down by the Senate. Only 12 of the more than 600 Cabinet appointments have been rejected.[18]

It is with the President's appointment of federal officers who serve in the various States (for example, U.S. attorneys and federal marshals) that the unwritten rule of "senatorial courtesy" comes into play. The Senate will turn down such a presidential appointment if it is opposed by a senator of the President's party from the State involved. The Senate's observance of this unwritten rule has a significant impact on the President's exercise of the power of appointment; in effect, some senators virtually dictate certain presidential appointments. The practice is often criticized. Those who defend it usually argue that a senator is more likely to be better informed about affairs in his/her State than is the President.

[18]The first was Roger B. Taney, Andrew Jackson's choice for secretary of the treasury. Two years later Jackson named Taney to succeed John Marshall as Chief Justice. The Senate confirmed him, and he served until his death in 1864.

## Preparing for Standardized Tests

Have students read the passages under *Richard Nixon* on pp. 312–313 and then answer the following question.

Which of the following was the first event in the chain of events leading to impeachment proceedings against Nixon?

**A** investigations by the Senate Watergate Committee

**B** the reporting of the Democratic national headquarters break-in by the *Washington Post*

**C** Nixon's resignation

**D** the subpoena of Nixon by the House Judiciary Committee

## Answers to . . .

### Section 5 Assessment

**1.** If the vice presidency becomes vacant mid-term, the President appoints a successor, which both houses of Congress must approve by a majority vote.
**2. (a)** The President, Vice President, and all civil officers. **(b)** Johnson and Clinton. **(c)** Both men were acquitted.
**3.** Many supporters believed that while Clinton had not broken any laws, he had behaved improperly, and thus should be censured.
**4.** To retrieve secret tape recordings Nixon had made in the White House as part of the impeachment investigation.
**5.** Answers will vary, but should be supported with relevant facts and examples. Students might suggest that an amendment is more difficult to overturn than a law.
**6. (a)** Republican Party members accused Democrats of not pressing impeachment simply because Clinton was a Democrat, while Democrats accused Republicans of pressing for impeachment simply because Clinton

### Answer to . . .

**Critical Thinking** They gather legislative information; oversee executive agencies; rouse public attention; expose questionable activities of public officials; and promote congressional interests.

▲ Teenagers testify in Congress about the December 1997 fatal shootings at West Paducah High School in Kentucky. Congress launched an investigation of school gun violence after a series of mass murders in public schools around the country. *Critical Thinking* **What purpose do congressional investigations serve?**

### Treaties

The President makes treaties "by and with the Advice and Consent of the Senate, . . . provided two thirds of the Senators present concur."[19] For a time after the adoption of the Constitution, the President asked the advice of the Senate when a treaty was being negotiated and prepared. Now the President most often consults the members of the Senate Foreign Relations Committee and other influential senators of both parties.

The Senate may accept or reject a treaty as it stands, or it may decide to offer amendments, reservations, or understandings to it. Treaties are sometimes considered in executive session. Because the House has a hold on the public purse strings, influential members of that body are often consulted in the treaty-making process, too.

## Investigatory Power

Congress has the power to investigate any matter that falls within the scope of its legislative powers. Congress exercises this authority through its standing committees, and their subcommittees, and often through special committees, as well.

Congress may choose to conduct investigations for several reasons. Most often, those inquiries are held to (1) gather information useful to Congress in the making of some legislation; (2) oversee the operations of various executive branch agencies; (3) focus public attention on a particular subject, from the drug war to movie violence; (4) expose the questionable activities of public officials or private persons; and/or (5) promote the particular interests of some members of Congress.

[19]Article II, Section 2, Clause 2. It is often said that the Senate "ratifies" a treaty. It does not. The Senate may give or withhold its "advice and consent" to a treaty made by the President. Once the Senate has consented to a treaty, the President ratifies it by exchanging "instruments of ratification" with other parties to the agreement.

## Section **5** Assessment

**Key Terms and Main Ideas**
1. Under what conditions does Congress help determine a vice presidential **successor**?
2. **(a)** What types of officials can the House **impeach**? **(b)** What two Presidents were impeached by the House? **(c)** Describe the outcomes of the two impeachment trials.
3. Why did some Clinton supporters want to **censure** him during his impeachment?
4. Why did a court serve **subpoenas** to President Nixon?

**Critical Thinking**
5. **Making Inferences** Why might a group supporting school prayer or some other issue press for a constitutional amendment, which is very difficult to win, rather than simply pressure Congress to pass a new law?

6. **Recognizing Bias** During the Clinton impeachment hearings and trial, members of Congress from both parties were accused of acting out of bias. **(a)** Explain this accusation. **(b)** What evidence might support this claim?

 **Take It to the Net**

7. Read about the impeachments of Presidents Andrew Johnson and Bill Clinton. Compare and contrast the impeachment charges, the trials, and the outcomes of the two cases. Use the links provided in the Social Studies area at the following Web site for help in completing this activity. **www.phschool.com**

was not of their party. **(b)** The vast majority of Republicans voted to approve both articles, while the vast majority of Democrats voted against them.

 **Take It to the Net**

7. Direct students to the Social Studies area at the Prentice Hall School Web site. The *Magruder's American Government* companion Web site includes the directions and links needed to complete the activity. It also provides a printable Internet activity worksheet, with scoring rubrics for assessment. Comparisons should include all relevant details of the two trials.

# Can Congress Prohibit Discrimination by Private Businesses?

*No provision in the Constitution gives Congress the expressed power to prohibit private acts of discrimination in the United States. Does Congress nevertheless have the right to outlaw such behavior by private persons and groups? If it does have that right, from which of its several constitutional powers is that authority drawn?*

## Heart of Atlanta Motel, Inc. v. United States (1964)

A provision of the Civil Rights Act of 1964 makes it unlawful for hotels, motels, restaurants, or any other place of "public accommodation" to discriminate in granting access or providing service because of a customer's race, sex, color, religion, or national origin. Congress passed the law after hearing testimony on the growing number of people of all races who were traveling from State to State and on African Americans' difficulties in finding accommodations in many parts of the country.

The Heart of Atlanta Motel was one facility that had regularly refused to rent rooms to African Americans. The motel was located in downtown Atlanta, Georgia, close to two State highways and two interstate freeways. It advertised in national media, and about 75 percent of its registered guests came from out of State.

The motel's owner filed suit in federal district court, claiming that the public accommodation provisions were unconstitutional. The court decided that the law was an acceptable use of Congress's power to regulate interstate commerce. The owner then appealed to the Supreme Court.

### Arguments for the Heart of Atlanta Motel, Inc.

1. The operation of privately-owned hotels, motels, and restaurants is essentially local. Therefore, Congress may not regulate these firms on the basis of its authority to regulate interstate commerce.
2. The Civil Rights Act prevents the motel owner from operating his business as he wishes. Thus

it deprives him of his liberty and property without due process, and takes his property without just compensation.
3. By requiring the motel owner to rent rooms to anyone against his will, Congress is subjecting him to involuntary servitude in violation of the Thirteenth Amendment.

### Arguments for the United States

1. The lack of adequate accommodations for African American travelers interferes significantly with interstate travel. Congress has the authority under the Commerce Clause to pass laws that correct that problem.
2. The Fifth Amendment prohibits the "taking" of property without just compensation, but does not prohibit reasonable regulations that affect the ways in which an owner may use his or her property.
3. The regulations do not constitute involuntary servitude under the Thirteenth Amendment.

### Decide for Yourself

1. Review the constitutional grounds on which each side based its arguments and the specific arguments each side presented.
2. Debate the opposing viewpoints presented in this case. Which viewpoint do you favor?
3. Predict the impact of the Court's decision on efforts to reduce discrimination in the United States. (To read a summary of the Court's decision, turn to the Supreme Court Glossary on page 799.)

---

---

## Can Congress Prohibit Discrimination by Private Businesses?

**Focus** In 1963, two events—Dr. Martin Luther King's "I Have a Dream" speech and the highly-publicized violent suppression of nonviolent protestors by police in Birmingham, Alabama— convinced Congress to use its power to regulate interstate commerce to pass a law prohibiting discrimination in public accommodations. Have the class brainstorm a list of the ways restaurants and motels are involved in interstate commerce.

**Instruct** Have the class identify the three constitutional provisions discussed in the case. *(The 5th and 13th Amendments and the Commerce Clause)* Have student pairs write a sentence for each provision explaining its relevance to the case.

**Close/Reteach** Remind the class of the Supreme Court's increased willingness to "rein in Congress." Discuss whether the present-day Supreme Court would favor a liberal or strict constructionist interpretation of the interstate commerce clause. *(Strict)*

💿 **Keep It Current CD-ROM** includes government-related projects by unit. The CD-ROM links to the Prentice Hall School Web site and may be used for daily updates.

## Answers to . . .

**Decide for Yourself**
1. Heart of Atlanta cited 5th and 13th Amendment violations in arguing that the Act unfairly restricted its right to run its business. The U.S. relied on the Commerce Clause to argue that the motel's refusal to rent rooms to African Americans interfered with interstate travel.
2. Answers will vary, but should be supported with valid reasoning.
3. The Court ruled in favor of the U.S., saying that the Commerce Clause upheld the constitutionality of the Act. This case opened up debate with its exemption for private clubs; later cases have been decided in favor of private clubs.

## Practicing the Vocabulary

1. appropriate
2. public debt
3. doctrine
4. expressed powers
5. consensus
6. legal tender
7. patent
8. tax
9.–15. Sentences should reflect an understanding of each term and how it relates to chapter content.

## Reviewing Main Ideas
### Section 1

16. (a) Power to tax. (b) Appropriation of funds for education.
17. Strict; he believed that Congress could exercise only expressed powers and those implied powers necessary to carry out the expressed powers.
18. It denies Congress large areas of power expressly by the Constitution, implicitly because the Constitution doesn't address many issues, and as a result of the system of federalism.

### Section 2

19. The power to tax, the power to borrow money, and the power to regulate interstate and foreign trade.
20. Without the power to tax, the National Government could not provide defense of the nation or other necessary services.
21. A direct tax is imposed on a person and must be made by that person. An indirect tax is imposed on one person, but is actually paid by other people that person passes the tax on to.
22. When the Government borrows money that it does not repay, that money accumulates interest over time and contributes to the public debt.

### Section 3

23. Regulates foreign commerce, declares war, raises and supports armies and navies, makes rules governing the military; provides for the organization of the militia.
24. It has established a number of crimes based on the postal power, prohibited the mailing of many materials, and prohibited unreasonable State and local interference with the mails.
25. It may acquire, manage, and dispose of federal areas, acquire prop-

## Political Dictionary

expressed powers (p. 290)
implied powers (p. 290)
inherent powers (p. 290)
strict constructionist (p. 291)
liberal constructionist (p. 291)
consensus (p. 292)
tax (p. 295)
direct tax (p. 296)
indirect tax (p. 296)

deficit financing (p. 296)
public debt (p. 296)
commerce power (p. 297)
legal tender (p. 299)
bankruptcy (p. 300)
naturalization (p. 302)
copyright (p. 302)
patent (p. 303)
eminent domain (p. 304)

appropriate (p. 305)
Necessary and Proper Clause (p. 305)
doctrine (p. 308)
successor (p. 311)
impeach (p. 311)
acquit (p. 311)
perjury (p. 311)
censure (p. 312)
subpoena (p. 313)

## Practicing the Vocabulary

*Matching* *Choose a term from the list above that best matches each description.*

1. To assign money to a particular purpose
2. The money owed by the Federal Government to its creditors
3. A principle
4. Powers of Congress that are specifically spelled out in the Constitution
5. A general agreement
6. Any kind of money that a creditor must, by law, accept in payment of debts
7. The sole right to sell an invention for a certain period of time
8. A charge levied by government on persons or property to meet public needs

*Using Words in Context* *For each of the terms below, write a sentence that shows how it relates to this chapter.*

9. direct tax
10. naturalization
11. Necessary and Proper Clause
12. implied powers
13. impeach
14. liberal constructionist
15. eminent domain

## Reviewing Main Ideas

### Section 1

16. Give an example of Congress's (a) expressed powers; (b) implied powers.
17. Was Thomas Jefferson a strict constructionist or a liberal constructionist? Explain.
18. In what ways does the Constitution limit Congress's power?

### Section 2

19. Give three examples of Congress's expressed powers relating to money and commerce.
20. The Articles of Confederation did not give Congress the power to tax. Why did the Framers of the Constitution decide to grant Congress this power?
21. Explain the difference between a direct tax and an indirect tax.
22. How does deficit financing lead to public debt?

### Section 3

23. What duties does Congress perform in the areas of foreign policy and defense?

24. What laws has Congress passed relating to the use of the U.S. mail system?
25. Give three examples of Congress's territorial powers.

### Section 4

26. Has the Necessary and Proper Clause been used to expand Congress's power, or to limit it? Explain.
27. What were the long-term consequences of the ruling in *McCulloch* v. *Maryland*?
28. Why is Congress's power to appropriate funds so important?

### Section 5

29. What kind of officials have most often been impeached by Congress?
30. (a) What body votes on impeachment? (b) What body conducts an impeachment trial? (c) Who presides at the trial of a President?
31. Under what circumstances may Congress choose a President or Vice President?
32. Why did Richard Nixon resign the presidency?

erty by purchase or gift, and use the exercise of eminent domain to take property for public use.

### Section 4

26. It has been used to expand Congress's power.
27. It set a precedent for broad interpretation of the constitutional powers granted to Congress.

28. Without the power of appropriation, Congress would be unable to provide many of the services necessary to run the country.

### Section 5

29. Federal judges.
30. (a) The House. (b) The Senate. (c) The Chief Justice of the Supreme Court.

31. If no presidential candidate receives a majority of the electoral votes, then the House may elect a President; similarly, in such a case, the Vice President is elected by the Senate.
32. He faced certain impeachment over the Watergate scandal.

## Critical Thinking Skills

**33. *Applying the Chapter Skill*** Brainstorm a list of the most important leadership qualities you think a member of Congress should have. Then choose any member of Congress, past or present from any State. Rate him or her on a scale of 0 to 5 for each of the qualities you listed, with 0 meaning "does not possess this quality" and 5 meaning "strongly possesses this quality."

**34. *Expressing Problems Clearly*** Why do you think it is difficult for Congress to reach consensus on many issues?

**35. *Evaluating the Quotation*** Reread the quotation from Article I, Section 9, Clause 4 on page 296 and the quotation from the 16th Amendment on page 296. Restate each passage in your own words and explain the difference between them.

## Analyzing Political Cartoons

Using your knowledge of American government and this cartoon, answer the questions below.

"THAT LAST ONE DIDN'T FLY AT ALL"

**36. (a)** In the cartoon above, why did the cartoonist choose to represent tax cuts as kites? **(b)** What does the caption at the top of the cartoon mean?

**37.** What is the central message of the cartoon?

---

## Participation Activities

**38. *Current Events Watch*** Scan news reports to find at least three stories about legislation that Congress is considering or has recently passed. **(a)** Summarize the key facts about each bill or law. **(b)** Explain what type of power Congress is exercising in writing each piece of legislation. **(c)** Show whether or not each is an example of Congress's expressed powers.

**39. *It's Your Turn*** The year is 1790. Alexander Hamilton has just made his proposal that Congress set up a national bank. Write an address to your colleagues in Congress, arguing for or against the proposal. Begin by summarizing the debate, explaining its importance to the country. Put forth your views on strict construction vs. liberal construction. Then make your specific arguments about the bank plan. Write a conclusion that you hope will rally support to your side.

**40. *Creating a Chart*** Write down all the powers of Congress that are mentioned in this chapter—from commerce powers to territorial powers. Use the information to create a chart that lists those powers, gives one or two examples of each, and tells whether it is an expressed, implied, or inherent power.

 **Take It to the Net**

***Chapter 11 Self-Test*** As a final review activity, take the Chapter 11 Self-Test in the Social Studies area at the Web site listed, and receive immediate feedback on your answers.

**www.phschool.com**

---

## Critical Thinking Skills

**33.** Answers will vary, but should touch on leadership qualities related to the President's roles discussed in this chapter.

**34.** Possible answer: Members of Congress have to consider their own viewpoints, those of their parties and constituents, and constitutional principles; given all of these factors, it is often difficult to reach consensus in Congress.

**35.** Answers will vary, but should suggest that the first quotation concerns taxes based on State populations, while the second concerns taxes levied without regard to population.

## Analyzing Political Cartoons

**36. (a)** To indicate that they are entertaining, but may or may not "fly."
**(b)** It was not acted on.
**37.** That the tax cuts considered by Congress are not consequential.

## You Can Make a Difference

Biographical sketches will vary, but should be comprehensive and answer all the questions presented.

## Participation Activities

**38.** Summaries will vary but should be well researched and supported with relevant facts, quotes, or examples.
**39.** Students' views should reflect an understanding of the difference between a strict and a liberal interpretation of the Constitution.
**40.** Charts should be clearly organized and accurate.

---

 **Take It to the Net**

Additional support materials and activities for Chapter 11 of *Magruder's American Government* can be found in the Social Studies area at the Prentice Hall School Web site. **www.phschool.com**

## Point-of-Use Resources

 **Guide to the Essentials of American Government** Chapter 11 Test, page 65 provides multiple-choice questions to test students' knowledge of the chapter.

**Test Bank CD-ROM** Chapter 11 Test

**Chapter Test** Chapter Tests booklet

# Congress in Action

| Section Objectives | Print and Technology Resources |
|---|---|
| **1 Congress Organizes** (pp. 320–327)<br><br>1. Describe how and when Congress convenes.<br>2. Compare the roles of the presiding officers in the Senate and the House.<br>3. Identify the duties of the party officers in Congress.<br>4. Describe how committee chairmen are chosen and explain their role in the legislative process.<br><br>TEKS 9A, 21A, 21D, 21E, 22A, 22B, 22C | • **Unit 3 booklet** Guided Reading and Review, p. 22 Section 1 Quiz, p. 23<br>• **Lesson Plans booklet** Section 1, p. 53<br>• **Political Cartoons booklet** Section 1, p. 45<br>• **Block Scheduling with Lesson Strategies booklet** p. 25<br>• **Section Reading Support Transparencies**<br><br>• **Close Up on Primary Sources booklet** A House Built on Compromise, p. 14<br>• **Government Assessment Rubrics booklet** p. 26<br>• **Section Support Transparencies** 48, 147<br>• **Presentation Pro CD-ROM** Section 1<br>• **Social Studies Skills Tutor CD-ROM** |
| **2 Committees in Congress** (pp. 329–333)<br><br>1. Analyze the role of committees in Congress.<br>2. Describe the duties and responsibilities of the House Rules Committee.<br>3. Compare the functions of joint and conference committees.<br><br>TEKS 9A, 21A, 21B, 21E, 22A, 22B, 22D | • **Unit 3 booklet** Guided Reading and Review, p. 24 Section 2 Quiz, p. 25<br>• **Lesson Plans booklet** Section 2, p. 54<br>• **Political Cartoons booklet** Section 2, p. 46<br>• **Section Reading Support Transparencies**<br><br>• **The Living Constitution booklet** p. 5<br>• **Section Support Transparencies** 49, 148<br>• **Presentation Pro CD-ROM** Section 2 |
| **3 How a Bill Becomes a Law: The House** (pp. 334–340)<br><br>1. Analyze the procedure in the House for enacting laws.<br>2. Describe what happens to a bill once it enters a committee.<br>3. Explain how the House leaders schedule debate on a bill.<br>4. Explain what happens to a bill on the House Floor, and identify the final step in passing a bill in the House.<br><br>TEKS 9A, 21A, 21D, 22A, 22B | • **Unit 3 booklet** Guided Reading and Review, p. 26 Section 3 Quiz, p. 27<br>• **Lesson Plans booklet** Section 3, p. 55<br>• **Political Cartoons booklet** Section 3, p. 47<br>• **Block Scheduling with Lesson Strategies booklet** p. 25<br>• **Section Reading Support Transparencies**<br><br>• **Government Assessment Rubrics booklet** p. 20<br>• **Close Up on Participation booklet** Kicking the Habit, p. 8<br>• **Section Support Transparencies** 50, 149<br>• **Presentation Pro CD-ROM** Section 3 |
| **4 The Bill in the Senate** (pp. 342–346)<br><br>1. Explain how a bill is introduced in the Senate.<br>2. Compare the Senate's rules for debate to the House rules.<br>3. Describe the role of conference committees in the legislative process.<br>4. Analyze the constitutional powers of the President after both houses have passed a bill.<br><br>TEKS 8D, 9A, 9B, 9E, 17C, 21A, 21B, 21C, 21D, 21E, 22A, 22B, 22C, 22D | • **Unit 3 booklet** Guided Reading and Review, p. 28 Section 4 Quiz, p. 29 Skills for Life Activity, p. 30<br>• **Lesson Plans booklet** Section 4, p. 56<br>• **Political Cartoons booklet** Section 4, p. 48<br>• **Close Up on the Supreme Court booklet** *Watkins* v. *U.S.*, p. 13<br>• **Simulations and Debates booklet** pp. 24–33<br>• **Section Reading Support Transparencies**<br><br>• **The Basic Principles of the Constitution Posters**<br>• **Basic Principles of the Constitution Transparencies** 30<br>• **Section Support Transparencies** 51, 150<br>• **Presentation Pro CD-ROM** Section 4<br>• **Simulations and Data Graphing CD-ROM** |

# Block Scheduling Strategies

The *Magruder's American Government* program addresses block-scheduling strategies in a variety of ways. For easy reference, side-column activities that fit a block format are marked  **Block Strategy.** Each section also contains a **Block Scheduling Strategies** box describing at least two block-format activities that address and extend core content from the section. The **Block Scheduling with Lesson Strategies booklet** found in the Teaching Resources contains additional block-scheduling activities for each chapter.

## Take It to the Net

Visit the Social Studies area at the Prentice Hall School Web site. Once there, you can find additional links, current events connections, and activities to enrich chapter content for *Magruder's American Government,* as well as a Self-Test for students. Be sure to check out this month's **eTeach** online discussion with a Master Teacher.

### www.phschool.com

## Pressed for Time?

If you are running short on time to cover this chapter, consider one of the following options:

- Use the **Presentation Pro CD-ROM** to create an outline for this chapter.
- Use one of the **Pressed for Time** activities found on p. 319.
- Use the Section Summaries for Chapter 12, from **Guide to the Essentials of American Government (English and Spanish).**

##  Video Connections

Prentice Hall offers two video programs to reinforce and extend chapter content. Show students *The Blessings of Liberty* from the **ABC News Civics and Government Videotape Library** and *Prayer in Schools: A Nationwide Debate* from the **Magruder's American Government Video Collection.**

## Assessment Options

- Section Quizzes, **Unit 3 booklet,** pp. 23, 25, 27, 29
- Chapter 12 Assessment, pp. 348–349
- **Guide to the Essentials of American Government,** Chapter 12 Test, p. 70

### Core Assessment

Chapter 12 Test, Chapter Tests booklet
ExamView® Test Bank CD-ROM Chapter 12
Government Assessment Rubrics

### Standardized Test Preparation

#### Diagnose and Prescribe

Diagnostic Tests for High School
Social Studies Skills

#### Review and Reteach

Review Book for Government

#### Practice and Assess

Test-Taking Strategies With
    Transparencies for High School
Test Prep Book for Government

# Chapter 12 Teacher's Edition Index

## Congress in Action

### CHAPTER 12

### Introducing the Chapter

In this chapter, students will learn about congressional leadership, the function of committees, and how proposed legislation is dealt with in both the House and Senate.

## Make It Relevant

### ★ You Can Make a Difference

Have groups of students think of and list problems that they feel confront their community. Write two headings on the board: *Solve Within the Community* and *Seek Solution in Congress.* Ask students to discuss each problem and assign it to one of the two headings. After they have made their assignments, students can work with community centers locally or contact appropriate groups related to Congress to pursue solutions.

**Service Learning**

## CONSTITUTIONAL PRINCIPLES

Emphasize the following basic principles as students read Chapter 12. Have the class respond to the questions, and then ask volunteers to explain which single principle they think gives Congress the most power.

**Limited Government** How is "Congress in action" an example of "limited government in action"? How does the legislative process itself limit Congress?

**Separation of Powers** How do conference committees illustrate this principle? How does the process through which a bill becomes a law demonstrate the separation of powers?

**Checks and Balances** How can Congress check and balance the powers of the judicial and executive branches? How do these two branches check and balance the powers of Congress?

# Congress in Action

*"It is very easy to defeat a bill in Congress. It is much more difficult to pass one."*
—John F. Kennedy (1962)

Making the nation's laws is the main job of Congress. Yet, as President Kennedy recognized, that is not an easy task. In trying to reach consensus, members of Congress draw on their own knowledge and experience. They also listen to other points of view, from both experts and ordinary citizens.

◆ **House Judiciary Committee**

 **Corner**

The following resources are available only from the Close Up Foundation to support the concepts discussed in Chapter 12 "Congress in Action":

◆ *Perspectives: Readings on Contemporary American Government*
◆ *U.S. Response: The Making of U.S. Foreign Policy*
◆ *The ACT Field Guide for Students*
◆ *We the People: The President and the Constitution*

To keep up-to-date on Close Up news and activities, visit Close Up Online at

**www.closeup.org**

Close Up Foundation
44 Canal Center Plaza
Alexandria, VA 22314-1592
800-765-3131

# Chapter 12 in Brief

## You Can Make a Difference

**IF YOU BELIEVE** strongly in a cause, you can make your voice heard in Congress. Jennifer Sussal carried her fight against drunk driving all the way to Washington, D.C. Her idea was simple—print warning labels on alcohol containers. Jennifer began her campaign in her hometown of Rockville Centre, New York. She worked with several groups that supported a bill proposing the idea. In 1988, Jennifer testified at a Senate hearing. She told senators about a 17-year-old who had been killed by a drunk driver. The thousands of teens killed each year "cannot speak for themselves," Jennifer said. A few months later, the Senate approved a bill requiring warning labels for alcohol.

### Keep It Current

Items marked with this logo are periodically updated on the Internet. Keep up-to-date with what's in the news. To get current information on issues involving Congress, go to **www.phschool.com**

## SECTION 1

### Congress Organizes (pp. 320–327)

★ Congress begins each new term on January 3 of every odd-numbered year; each new term follows the general election in November.
★ The Speaker of the House, usually the leader of the majority party, controls the agenda in the House of Representatives, while the Vice President and an experienced senator serve as largely ceremonial presidents in the Senate.
★ After the Speaker, the floor leaders and their whips in both houses are the most powerful members of Congress.
★ Committee chairmen, potent in their own domain, are chosen according to the seniority rule.

## SECTION 2

### Committees in Congress (pp. 329–333)

★ Most work in Congress is divided among committees that focus on special areas like national defense, the budget, agriculture, and the like.
★ The powerful House Rules Committee can speed, delay, or even prevent House action on a bill.
★ Both houses may create select committees, which are special, often temporary, bodies.
★ Joint committees are composed of members of both houses.

## SECTION 3

### How a Bill Becomes a Law: The House (pp. 334–340)

★ Only a member can introduce a bill in either house.
★ Bills are referred to standing committees, and are usually considered in subcommittees.
★ Bills approved by the appropriate committee and the Rules Committee are given floor consideration by the House.
★ Measures that win House approval are sent to the Senate.

## SECTION 4

### The Bill in the Senate (pp. 342–346)

★ Debate in the Senate is largely unrestricted.
★ The Senate's dedication to free debate gives rise to the filibuster—the tactic of "talking a bill to death."
★ After both houses approve a bill, it is sent to the President.
★ The President can sign the bill, allow it to become law without his signature, veto it, or apply a pocket veto.

### Keep It Current

## Internet Update

Use the Prentice Hall School Web site and the Keep It Current CD-ROM to find quick content updates.

Visit **www.phschool.com** for current events articles that are linked to Chapter 12. Critical Thinking questions are included.

**Keep It Current CD-ROM** includes government-related projects by unit. Students complete each project using current information that they obtain by linking to the Prentice Hall School Web site from the CD-ROM.

## Pressed for Time?

### To Omit the Chapter
If you wish to skip Chapter 12, ask students to read the Chapter in Brief and assign the Guide to the Essentials before continuing to another chapter. You may also want to assign the Chapter 12 Test in the Chapter Test booklet. Then specific portions of Chapter 12 may be assigned to students needing reinforcement of key terms and concepts.

### To Preview the Chapter
To introduce students to key terms and concepts in each section, have them read the Chapter in Brief. You may also assign the Reading Strategy activities on pp. 321, 330, 335, and 343 of this book.

### To Review the Chapter
When students have completed Chapter 12, you might want to assign the Guide to the Essentials or the Guided Reading and Review worksheets on pp. 22, 24, 26, and 28 of the Unit 3 booklet.

### To Cover the Chapter Quickly
To cover the material in Chapter 12 quickly, use the following activity.

**Focus** Have students describe a school group and the way it is organized. Ask them to point out what might happen if the group's organizational structure was not in place. Then explain to students that in this chapter, they will learn about the organizational structures of the House and Senate.

**Instruct** Organize the class into groups of four, assigning each student one of the following topics: Organization of the House, the path of a bill in the House, organization of the Senate, and the path of a bill in the Senate. Have students use graphic organizers to explain their assigned topics to the class.

**Close/Reteach** Finally, have each student write a summary of the similarities and differences between the organizational structures of the House and Senate and the process used by each house to deal with proposed legislation.

■ **Block Strategy (Average)**

**319**

## Section Preview

### OBJECTIVES

1. **Describe** how and when Congress convenes.
2. **Compare** the roles of the presiding officers in the Senate and the House.
3. **Identify** the duties of the party officers in Congress.
4. **Describe** how committee chairmen are chosen and explain their role in the legislative process.

### WHY IT MATTERS

How Congress is organized, and how its leaders are chosen and who they are, plays a large part in determining what the nation's lawmakers can and will do.

### POLITICAL DICTIONARY

★ Speaker of the House
★ president of the Senate
★ president *pro tempore*
★ party caucus
★ floor leader
★ whip
★ committee chairman
★ seniority rule

---

**W**hat comes to mind when you hear the word *Congress?* The Capitol? Some particular bill? Those senators and representatives you often see on the evening news? Of course, you know that Congress is much more than that. It is in fact a very complex enterprise, and much larger than most people realize.

Some 30,000 men and women work for the legislative branch; and Congress has appropriated more than $3 billion to finance its operations this year.[1] Given the large size and complexity of Congress, it must be well organized to conduct its business.

▲ Seal of Congress

### Congress Convenes

Congress convenes—begins a new term—every two years, on January 3 of every odd-numbered year. Each new term follows the general elections in November.

---

[1]More than 15,000 of those who work in the legislative branch have jobs in the House or Senate—in members' offices, as committee staff, or in some part of the congressional administrative organization. The other 15,000 or so work in the various agencies Congress has, over time, established within the legislative branch—especially the Library of Congress, the Government Printing Office, the Congressional Budget Office, and the General Accounting Office.

### Opening Day in the House

Every other January, the 435 men and women who have been elected to the House come together at the Capitol to begin a new term. At that point, they are, in effect, just so many representatives-elect. Because all 435 of its seats are up for election every two years, the House technically has no sworn members, no rules, and no organization until its opening-day ceremonies are held.

Representative Sherrod Brown (D., Ohio) remembers his first opening day, in 1993, this way:

**PRIMARY Sources** *"My first day on the House floor was thrilling—and a little scary. . . . Walking around the chamber . . . I was awed and nervous. . . . Questions gnawed at me when I walked into that august [majestic] room, when I met several members about whom I had read and whom I had seen on television. And then I thought about the President of the United States coming in to address us—'Do I deserve to be here with all these people? How did I get here? Will I measure up? How was I chosen for this privilege?'"*
—Sherrod Brown, *Congress From the Inside*

The clerk of the House in the preceding term presides, or chairs, at the beginning of the first

▲ Opening day in the House of Representatives follows a traditional routine of votes and speeches. The House chooses its Speaker and other officers for the coming term. *Critical Thinking* *Why are most of the votes on opening day only formalities?*

day's session.[2] The clerk calls the chamber to order and checks the roll of representatives-elect. Those members-to-be then choose a Speaker as their permanent presiding officer. By custom, the Speaker is a long-standing member of the majority party, and election on the floor is only a formality. The majority party's members in the House have settled the matter beforehand.

The Speaker then takes the oath of office. It is administered by the Dean of the House, the member-elect with the longest record of service in the House of Representatives.[3] With that accomplished, the Speaker swears in the rest of the members as a body. The Democrats take their seats to the left of the center aisle; the Republicans, to the right.

Next, the House elects its clerk, sergeant at arms, chief administrative officer, and chaplain. None of these people are members of the House, and the elections are also a formality. The majority party has already decided who these nonmember officers will be.

[2]The clerk, a nonmember officer of the House, is picked by the majority party and usually keeps the post until that party loses control of the chamber.

[3]Today, John D. Dingell (D., Michigan), who became a member of the House on December 13, 1955.

Then, the House adopts the rules that will govern its proceedings through the term. The rules of the House have been developing for over 200 years, and they are contained in a volume of about 400 pages. They are readopted, most often with little or no change, at the beginning of each term.

Finally, members of the 19 permanent committees of the House are appointed by a floor vote. With that, the House is organized.

## Opening Day in the Senate

The Senate is a continuous body. It has been organized without interruption since its first session in 1789. Recall that only one third of the seats are up for election every two years. From one term to the next, two thirds of the Senate's membership is carried over. As a result, the Senate does not face large organizational problems at the beginning of a term. Its first-day session is nearly always short and routine, even when the elections have brought a change in the majority party. Newly elected and reelected members must be sworn in, vacancies in Senate organization and on committees must be filled, and a few other details attended to.

**321**

ACTIVITY

## American Government, American Humor

Share the following quotation with students:

*"It could probably be shown by facts and figures that there is no distinctly native American criminal class except Congress."*

—Mark Twain (1897)

**Discussion** Have students contrast Twain's view of Congress with what they have learned in this unit. Ask: Why might a humorist such as Twain refer to members of Congress as "criminals"?

**(Average)**

---

### Background Note

## Government in History

Although Presidents Washington and Adams addressed Congress in person, Thomas Jefferson broke that precedent and sent his address in writing. It was not until 1913, when Woodrow Wilson delivered his State of the Union address in person, that the tradition begun by Jefferson was broken. From Wilson to Clinton, all Presidents, except Herbert Hoover, have appeared before Congress to deliver their State of the Union addresses in person.

---

## *Answers to . . .*

**Interpreting Political Cartoons** Possible answer: That it does not accurately reflect the political sentiment of the nation.

**Interpreting Charts** Possible answer: A President without the support of the majority party would likely face more opposition from Congress.

---

*Interpreting Political Cartoons* **What is the cartoonist suggesting about the annual State of the Union address?**

### State of the Union Checklist

| | |
|---|---|
| ✔ | Raise income tax rate on people earning over $180,000 a year |
| ✘ | Complete reform of the health care system |
| ✔ | Pass free trade pact with Canada and Mexico |
| ✔ | Free child immunizations to prevent disease |
| ✘ | $30 billion to build roads and repair buildings |
| ✔ | Create 700,000 summer jobs for young people |
| ✔ | Put 100,000 more police officers on the street |
| ✘ | New tax on energy from non-renewable sources |

KEY: ✔ Succeeded ✘ Failed

*Interpreting Charts* The President presents his plans for the year in the State of the Union address. President Clinton offered the proposals above in his first State of the Union address, given on February 17, 1993, but not all became law. *How does party control of Congress determine whether the President's proposals become law?*

## State of the Union Message

When the Senate is notified that the House is organized, a joint committee of the two is appointed and instructed "to wait upon the President of the United States and inform him that a quorum of each House is assembled and that the Congress is ready to receive any communication he may be pleased to make."

Within a few weeks, the President delivers the annual State of the Union message to a joint session of Congress. The President's speech is a major political event based on this constitutional command:

> **FROM THE Constitution** *"He shall from time to time give to the Congress Information on the State of the Union, and recommend to their Consideration such Measures as he shall judge necessary and expedient . . ."*
>
> —Article II, Section 3

The members of both houses, together with the members of the Cabinet, the justices of the Supreme Court, the foreign diplomatic corps, and other dignitaries, assemble in the House chamber to listen.

In his address, the President reports on the state of the nation as he sees it, in both domestic and foreign policy terms. The message is televised live, and it is followed very closely, both here and abroad. In fact, the President's speech is as much a message to the American people, and to the world, as it is an address to Congress. In it, the President lays out the broad shape of the policies his administration will follow and the course he has charted for the nation. His message regularly includes a number of specific legislative recommendations.

With the conclusion of the President's speech, the joint session is adjourned. Each house turns to the legislative business before it.

## The Presiding Officers

The Constitution provides for the presiding officers of each house—the Speaker of the House and the president of the Senate. Article I, Section 2, Clause 5 says "The House of Representatives shall choose their Speaker and other Officers. . . ." And Article I, Section 3, Clause 4 declares: "The Vice President of the United States shall be President of the Senate. . . ."

### The Speaker of the House

Of the two positions, the **Speaker of the House** is by far the more important and more powerful within the halls of Congress. This is largely because the Speaker is both the elected presiding officer of the House and the acknowledged leader of its majority party.

Although neither the Constitution nor its own rules require it, the House has always

---

## Spotlight on Technology

**Magruder's American Government Video Collection**

The Magruder's Video Collection explores key issues and debates in American government. Each segment examines an issue central to chapter content through use of historical and contemporary footage. Commentary from civic leaders in academics, government, and the media follow each segment. Critical-thinking questions focus students' attention on key issues, and may be used to stimulate discussion.

Use the Chapter 12 video segment to explore Congress in action. (time: about 5 minutes) This segment follows the day-to-day activities of a congressional staffer, and uses her perspective to focus on what goes on behind the scenes in the Senate.

chosen the Speaker from among its own members. Today, the post is held by Dennis Hastert (R., Illinois). He was first elected to the House in 1986, and he became Speaker in 1999.[4]

The Speaker is expected to preside in a fair and judicious manner, and he regularly does. He is also expected to aid the fortunes of his party and its legislative goals, and he regularly does that too.

Nearly all of the Speaker's specific powers revolve around two duties: to preside and to keep order. The Speaker presides over every session of the House, or occasionally appoints a member as the temporary presiding officer. No member may speak until he or she is recognized by the Speaker. He also interprets and applies the rules, refers bills to the standing committees, rules on points of order (questions of procedure raised by members), puts motions to a vote, and decides the outcome of most votes taken in the House. (The Speaker can be overridden by a vote of the House, but that almost never happens.) He also names the members of all select and conference committees and signs all bills and resolutions passed by the House.

As a member, the Speaker may debate and vote on any matter before the House. If he chooses to do so, however, he must appoint a temporary presiding officer and that member then occupies the Speaker's chair. The Speaker does not often vote, and the House rules say only that he must vote to break a tie. Notice then, that because a tie vote defeats a question, the Speaker occasionally votes to cause a tie and so defeat a proposal.

The Speaker of the House follows the Vice President in the line of succession to the presidency. This status is a considerable testimony to the power and importance of both the office and the person who holds it.

### The President of the Senate

The **president of the Senate,** the Senate's presiding officer, is not a member of the body over which

▲ Dennis Hastert (R., Illinois), who became Speaker of the House in 1999, has maintained a relatively low profile in public. *Critical Thinking How does the role of the Speaker differ from the role of the president of the Senate?*

he presides. Instead, the Constitution assigns the office to the Vice President of the United States. Because he is not a member of the chamber, the president of the Senate occupies a much less powerful chair than the Speaker's in the House.

The Vice President's route to his post is much different from the one the Speaker has traveled. In fact, the Senate's president is sometimes not even a member of the party with a majority of the seats in the upper chamber.

The president of the Senate does have the usual powers of a presiding officer: to recognize members, put questions to a vote, and so on. However, the Vice President cannot take the floor to speak or debate and may vote *only* to break a tie.

Any influence a Vice President may have in the Senate is largely the result of personal abilities and relationships. Several of the more recent Vice Presidents came to that office from the Senate: Harry Truman, Alben Barkley, Richard Nixon, Lyndon Johnson, Hubert Humphrey, Walter Mondale, Dan Quayle, and Al Gore. Each of them was able to build at least some power into the position out of that earlier experience.

The Senate does have another presiding officer, the **president** *pro tempore,* who serves in the Vice President's absence. The president *pro tempore,* or president *pro tem* for short, is elected by the Senate itself and is always a leading member of the majority party—usually its longest serving member. Today, Senator Robert C. Byrd (D.,

---

[4]Speaker Hastert is the 51st person to hold the post. The first Speaker, elected by the House in 1789, was Frederick A. C. Muhlenburg, a Federalist from Pennsylvania. Sam Rayburn (D., Texas) held the office for a record 17 years, 62 days in the period from 1940 to 1961. Mr. Hastert succeeded Newt Gingrich (R., Georgia) whose tenure (1995–1999) marked the first time a Republican had held the post in more than forty years.

## Make It Relevant

### Careers in Government—Web Site Developer

A C T I V I T Y

## Heterogeneous Groups

**Reteaching** Have students review material on the Speaker of the House in *The Presiding Officers* section of the text. Then have them list powers the Speaker possesses that make that position influential.

**(Basic)**

---

## Background Note

### Behind the Scenes

People often believe that the two major parties are the only caucuses in Congress. In fact, other groups also convene caucuses. One of the most widely known caucuses is the Congressional Black Caucus. Established in 1971, the Congressional Black Caucus provides a forum for discussing and formulating positions on important legislative issues of significant interest to African Americans.

---

### Leadership in the 107th Congress

| HOUSE | | SENATE | |
|---|---|---|---|
| **PRESIDING OFFICER AND PARTY LEADER** | | **PRESIDING OFFICERS** | |

| **Speaker of the House** Dennis Hastert (R., Illinois) Year Elected 1986 | | **President of the Senate** Dick Cheney (Vice President) Year Elected 2000 | **President Pro Tempore** Robert C. Byrd (D., West Virginia) Year Elected 1958 |

| **PARTY OFFICERS** | | **PARTY OFFICERS** | |

| **Majority Floor Leader** Richard Armey (R., Texas) Year Elected 1984 | **Minority Floor Leader** Dick Gephardt (D., Missouri) Year Elected 1976 | **Majority Floor Leader** Tom Daschle (D., South Dakota) Year Elected 1986 | **Minority Floor Leader** Trent Lott (R., Mississippi) Year Elected 1988 |
| **Majority Whip** Tom DeLay (R., Texas) Year Elected 1984 | **Minority Whip** Nancy Pelosi (D., California) Year Elected 1986 | **Majority Whip** Harry Reid (D., Nevada) Year Elected 1986 | **Minority Whip** Don Nickles (R., Oklahoma) Year Elected 1980 |

**Interpreting Charts** This chart shows the major leadership posts, both official and party, in both houses of Congress and the people who hold these positions today. ***How can you tell which party holds power in the Senate?***

---

West Virginia) holds the post. Senator Byrd was first elected to the upper house in 1958. He served as president *pro tem* from 1989 to 1995 and was returned to the office when the Democrats regained control of the Senate in 2001.

The president *pro tem* follows the Speaker in the line of presidential succession. Other members of the Senate occasionally preside over the chamber, on a temporary basis.

## Party Officers

Congress is a political body. This is so for two leading reasons: (1) because Congress is the nation's central policy-making body, and (2) because of its partisan makeup. Reflecting its political complexion, both houses of Congress are organized along party lines. This organization creates some very powerful positions.

### The Party Caucus

The **party caucus** is a closed meeting of the members of each party in each house. It meets just before Congress convenes in January and occasionally during a session. In recent years the Republicans have called their caucus in each house the party conference, and the Democrats now use this term in the Senate, too.

The caucus deals mostly with matters of party organization, such as the selection of the party's floor leaders and questions of committee membership. It sometimes takes stands on particular bills, but neither party tries to force its members to follow its caucus decisions, nor can it.[5]

The policy committee, composed of the party's top leadership, acts as an executive committee for the caucus. Strictly speaking, that body is known as the policy committee in each party's structure in the Senate and in the Republicans' organization in the House. However, it is called the steering and policy committee by the Democrats in the lower chamber.

### The Floor Leaders

Next to the Speaker, the majority and minority **floor leaders** in the House and Senate are the most important officers in Congress. They do

---

[5]A number of informal groupings of members of Congress meet to discuss matters of mutual interest. Some are partisan, others are bipartisan, and several use the word *caucus* in their titles. Some of these informal groups include, for example, the Congressional Black Caucus, the House Republican Study Committee, the Pro-Life Caucus, and the Congressional Hispanic Caucus.

---

### Answer to . . .

**Interpreting Charts** The Republican party has more major leadership posts, including president *pro tempore*.

---

## Preparing for Standardized Tests

Have students read the passages under *The President of the Senate* on pp. 323–324 and then complete the sentence below.

From the passages, you can infer that a Vice President will have more influence as president of the Senate if

**A** he or she is a powerful orator.

**B** he or she has a good relationship with the president *pro tempore*.

**C** he or she is from the same party as the majority party of the Senate.

**D** the Speaker of the House is not popular.

not hold official positions in either chamber. Rather, they are party officers, picked for their posts by their party colleagues.

The floor leaders are legislative strategists. They try to carry out the decisions of their parties' caucuses and steer floor action to their parties' benefit. Each of them is also the chief spokesman for his party in his chamber. All of that calls for political skills of a high order.

The majority leader's post is the more powerful in each house—for the obvious reason that the majority party has more seats (more votes) than the other party has. And, the majority leader very largely controls the order of business on the floor in his chamber.

The two floor leaders in each house are assisted by party **whips.** The majority whip and the minority whip are, in effect, assistant floor leaders. Each of them is chosen by the party caucus, almost always at the floor leader's recommendation. A number of assistant whips serve in the House, and the floor leaders in both houses have a paid staff.

Whips serve as a liaison—a two-way link—between the party's leadership and its rank-and-file members.[6] The whips check with party members and tell the floor leader which members,

and how many votes, can be counted on in any particular matter. The whips also see that all members of the party are present for important votes and that they vote with the party leadership. If a member must be absent for some reason, a whip sees that that member is paired with a member of the other party who will also be absent that day or who agrees not to vote on certain measures. In this way, one nonvote cancels out another.

## Committee Chairmen

The bulk of the work of Congress, especially in the House, is really done in committee. Thus, **committee chairmen**—those members who head the standing committees in each chamber—also hold strategic posts. The chairman[7] of each of

---

[6]The term was borrowed from British politics. There, it came from the "whipper-in" in a fox hunt, the rider who is supposed to keep the hounds bunched in a pack.

[7]The title *chairman*, rather than *chairperson*, is used here because this is the form used in both houses of Congress, both officially and informally. Only six women have ever chaired a standing committee. None does so today. The most recent: Nancy Johnson (R., Connecticut), who chaired the House Ethics Committee (1995 to 1997), and Nancy Landon Kassebaum (R., Kansas), the only woman ever to chair a Senate committee, who headed the Senate's Labor and Human Resources Committee (1995–1997).

### Party Strength (at beginning of term)

| HOUSE 435 MEMBERS | | | Years | SENATE 100 MEMBERS | | | |
|---|---|---|---|---|---|---|---|
| | 291 | 144 | | 1975 – 1977 | 61 | 37 | 2 |
| | 292 | 143 | | 1977 – 1979 | 61 | 38 | 1 |
| | 277 | 158 | | 1979 – 1981 | 58 | 41 | 1 |
| | 242 | 192 | 1 | 1981 – 1983 | 46 | 53 | 1 |
| | 269 | 166 | | 1983 – 1985 | 46 | 54 | |
| | 253 | 182 | | 1985 – 1987 | 47 | 53 | |
| | 258 | 177 | | 1987 – 1989 | 55 | 45 | |
| | 260 | 175 | | 1989 – 1991 | 55 | 45 | |
| | 267 | 167 | 1 | 1991 – 1993 | 56 | 44 | |
| | 258 | 176 | 1 | 1993 – 1995 | 57 | 43 | |
| 204 | 230 | | 1 | 1995 – 1997 | 48 | 52 | |
| 207 | 227 | | 1 | 1997 – 1999 | 45 | 55 | |
| 211 | 223 | | 1 | 1999 – 2001 | 45 | 55 | |
| 212 | 221 | | 2 | 2001 – 2003* | 50 | 50 | |
| 204 | 230 | | 1 | 2003 – 2005 | 48 | 51 | 1 |

SOURCES: Clerk of the House; *Congressional Quarterly*

*Democrats gained control of the Senate (50 Democrats, 49 Republicans, 1 Independent) in July 2001.

†Projected

KEY ■ Democrat ■ Republican ■ Other

*Interpreting Graphs* This graph indicates party strength in Congress over recent years. **Which party controlled the House of Representatives for most of the 1980s? Which party controlled the House of Representatives for the second half of the 1990s?**

## ACTIVITY

### Extended Class Periods

**Time** 90 minutes.

**Purpose** Analyze and compare leadership in the House with leadership in the Senate.

**Grouping** Three groups, each including a third of the class.

**Activity** Assign one group the topic "Leadership Positions in the House of Representatives" and a second group "Leadership Positions in the Senate." Direct each of these two groups to create a poster that illustrates their assigned topic. Explain that the posters can take any form, but should be comprehensive and include detailed descriptions. Assign the third group the topic "Comparing Leadership Positions in the House and Senate." Direct this group to create a poster that compares and contrasts leadership positions in the House and Senate. Again, the form of the poster should be determined by students, but it must clearly indicate similarities and differences.

**Roles** Art designers, writers, facilitators.

**Close** When groups have completed their tasks, conduct a class discussion on the organization of Congress, using students' posters as visual aids. Amend and correct the posters during the discussion, as needed.

■ **Block Strategy**
**(Average)**

### Point-of-Use Resources

📁 **Government Assessment Rubrics** Class Discussion, p. 26

📁 **Block Scheduling with Lesson Strategies** Additional activities for Chapter 12 appear on p. 25.

---

these permanent committees is chosen from the majority party by the majority party caucus. Committee chairmen decide when their committees will meet, which bills they will take up, whether they will hold public hearings, and what witnesses the committee should call. When a committee's bill has been reported to the floor, the chairman usually manages the debate and tries to steer it to final passage.

You will take a closer look at committees and their chairs in a moment. But, first, consider the fabled seniority rule.

### Seniority Rule

The **seniority rule** is, in fact, an unwritten custom. It dates from the late 1800s, and is still closely followed in both houses today. The seniority rule provides that the most important posts, in both the formal and the party organization, will be held by those party members with the longest records of service in Congress.

The rule is applied most strictly to the choice of committee chairmen. The head of each committee is almost always the longest-serving majority party member of that committee.

### Representation by State, 107th Congress

| | House D | House R | Senate D | Senate R | | House D | House R | Senate D | Senate R | | House D | House R | Senate D | Senate R |
|---|---|---|---|---|---|---|---|---|---|---|---|---|---|---|
| Alabama | 2 | 5 | 0 | 2 | Louisiana | 2 | 5 | 2 | 0 | Ohio | 8 | 11 | 0 | 2 |
| Alaska | 0 | 1 | 0 | 2 | Maine | 2 | 0 | 0 | 2 | Oklahoma | 1 | 5 | 0 | 2 |
| Arizona | 1 | 5 | 0 | 2 | Maryland | 4 | 4 | 2 | 0 | Oregon | 4 | 1 | 1 | 1 |
| Arkansas | 3 | 1 | 1 | 1 | Massachusetts | 10 | 0 | 2 | 0 | Pennsylvania | 10 | 11 | 0 | 2 |
| California | 32 | 20 | 2 | 0 | Michigan | 9 | 7 | 2 | 0 | Rhode Island | 2 | 0 | 1 | 1 |
| Colorado | 2 | 4 | 0 | 2 | Minnesota | 5 | 3 | 2 | 0 | South Carolina | 2 | 4 | 1 | 1 |
| Connecticut | 3 | 3 | 2 | 0 | Mississippi | 3 | 2 | 0 | 2 | South Dakota | 0 | 1 | 2 | 0 |
| Delaware | 0 | 1 | 2 | 0 | Missouri | 4 | 5 | 1 | 1 | Tennessee | 4 | 5 | 0 | 2 |
| Florida | 8 | 15 | 2 | 0 | Montana | 0 | 1 | 1 | 1 | Texas | 17 | 13 | 0 | 2 |
| Georgia | 3 | 8 | 2 | 0 | Nebraska | 0 | 3 | 1 | 1 | Utah | 1 | 2 | 0 | 2 |
| Hawaii | 2 | 0 | 2 | 0 | Nevada | 1 | 1 | 1 | 1 | Vermont | 0 | * 0 | 1 | * 0 |
| Idaho | 0 | 2 | 0 | 2 | New Hampshire | 0 | 2 | 0 | 2 | Virginia | 4 | * 6 | 0 | 2 |
| Illinois | 10 | 10 | 1 | 1 | New Jersey | 7 | 6 | 2 | 0 | Washington | 6 | 3 | 2 | 0 |
| Indiana | 4 | 6 | 1 | 1 | New Mexico | 1 | 2 | 1 | 1 | West Virginia | 2 | 1 | 2 | 0 |
| Iowa | 1 | 4 | 1 | 1 | New York | 19 | 12 | 2 | 0 | Wisconsin | 5 | 4 | 2 | 0 |
| Kansas | 1 | 3 | 0 | 2 | North Carolina | 5 | 7 | 1 | 1 | Wyoming | 0 | 1 | 1 | 1 |
| Kentucky | 1 | 5 | 0 | 2 | North Dakota | 1 | 0 | 2 | 0 | | | | | |

\* 1 Independent

**House**

Democratic majority ■
Equally divided ▨
Republican majority ■
Independent □

**Senate**

Democratic ■
Equally divided ▨
Republican ■
1 Democrat, 1 Independent □

SOURCE: Clerk of the House and Secretary of the Senate

 **Interpreting Maps** The map and the chart show State-by-State representation in the House and Senate. *Name five States that primarily send Republicans to both houses of Congress, and five States that primarily send Democrats to both houses of Congress.*

---

### Answer to ...

**Interpreting Maps** Possible answers: Republicans: Alaska, Idaho, Kansas, Oklahoma, Utah; Democrats: Hawaii, Massachusetts, North Dakota, Washington, West Virginia.

◀ John Conyers, Jr. (D., Michigan) is the second-most senior member of the House and the ranking Democratic member of the House Judiciary Committee. He served on that committee during both the 1974 hearings on the Watergate scandal and the 1999 impeachment of President Clinton. *Critical Thinking* ***What are the benefits and drawbacks of the seniority rule?***

## Criticism of the Seniority Rule

Critics of the seniority rule are many, and they do make a strong case. They insist that the seniority system ignores ability and discourages younger members. Critics also note that the rule means that a committee head often comes from a "safe" constituency—a State or district in which, election after election, one party regularly wins. With no play of fresh and conflicting forces in those places, critics claim, the chairman of a committee is often out of touch with current public opinion.

Defenders of the seniority rule argue that it ensures that a powerful and experienced member will head each committee. They maintain that the rule is easy to apply, and that it very nearly eliminates the possibility of fights within the party.

Opponents of the rule have gained some ground in recent years. Thus, the House Republican Conference (caucus) now picks several GOP members of House committees by secret ballot. House Democrats use secret ballots to choose a committee chairman whenever 20 percent of their caucus requests that procedure.

House Republicans forged a major change in the seniority rule when they took control of the lower chamber in 1995. They adopted a party rule that limits the tenure of their committee chairmen. Now, no GOP chairman can serve more than six years (three terms of Congress) in his or her post. The rule produced a much larger than usual turnover in chairmanships at the beginning of the 107th Congress in 2001. It was also a factor in the decision of some senior Republicans to retire from the House in 2001, following their sixth (and final) year as chairmen.

Whatever the arguments against the seniority rule, it is unlikely to be eliminated. Those members with the real power to abolish it also reap the largest benefits from it.

## Section **1** Assessment

### Key Terms and Main Ideas

1. What role does the **Speaker of the House** play?
2. What is the function of the **president of the Senate**?
3. Explain the importance of the party **whips**.
4. Identify the purpose of a **party caucus**.

### Critical Thinking

5. **Making Comparisons** Analyze the organizational structures of both houses of Congress. Create a Venn diagram showing similarities and differences between the two houses.
6. **Synthesizing Information** What powers make committee chairmen influential?

7. **Predicting Consequences** What might happen if the president of the Senate were given the same powers as the Speaker of the House? What problems could arise?

 **Take It to the Net**

8. Read an article about the seniority rule and write five questions about its origins and effects. Then pick three of these questions and answer them as fully as possible. Use the links provided in the Social Studies area at the following Web site for help in completing this activity. **www.phschool.com**

 **Take It to the Net**

8. Direct students to the Social Studies area at the Prentice Hall School Web site. The *Magruder's American Government* companion Web site includes the directions and links needed to complete the activity. It also provides a printable Internet activity worksheet with scoring rubrics for assessment. Answers should be comprehensive and include examples wherever possible.

6. The power to decide when a committee will meet and what bills it will address; whether the committee will hear witness testimony; and whether public hearings will be held.
7. Answers will vary but might suggest that the president of the Senate would have a disproportionate amount of power given that he or she is also the Vice President.

## Point-of-Use Resources

📖 **Guide to the Essentials** Chapter 12, Section 1, p. 66 provides support for students who need additional review of section content. Spanish support is available in the Spanish edition of the Guide on p. 59.

📁 **Quiz** Unit 3 booklet, p. 23 includes matching and multiple-choice questions to check students' understanding of Section 1 content.

💿 **Presentation Pro CD-ROM** Quizzes and multiple-choice questions check students' understanding of Section 1 content.

## Answers to . . .

### Section 1 Assessment

**1.** Serves as the presiding officer of the House; presides over the proceedings and keeps order. As a member of the House, the Speaker also has regular member duties.

**2.** To preside over the proceedings of the Senate. As the president is not a member of the Senate (it is always the Vice President), he or she does not have the usual member duties and may not vote except to break a tie.

**3.** The party whips assist the floor leaders and serve as liaisons between the party's leadership and its members. They help arrange and track voting and member attendance.

**4.** The party caucus selects floor leaders and deals with other matters of party organization.

**5.** Differences: The House's presiding officer is the Speaker while the Senate's is the president (who is also the Vice President); the Senate has a president *pro tempore* who serves in the Vice President's absence. Diagrams should show that both houses have majority and minority floor leaders and whips.

### Answer to . . .

**Critical Thinking** Benefits: Ensures experienced leaders and easy to apply. Drawbacks: Ignores younger members and encourages favoritism.

## Organizing Congressional Committees

**Focus** Ask students to identify any congressional committees that they can. Point out that much of the work of Congress is done in committees. Ask students to list reasons why they think the committee system is used.

**Instruct** After students have finished reading the selection, ask them to summarize Pat Schroeder's experience on the Armed Services Committee. Then have students refer to the lists they made. For each reason on their list, have them decide if the committee described in the selection would be a good example of why committees are used. Why or why not? Can Schroeder's description be taken as indicative of all committees? Why or why not?

**Close/Reteach** Call on volunteers to read their lists and explain their decisions to the class. Then have the entire class debate the usefulness of the committee system.

**Keep It Current CD-ROM** includes government-related projects by unit. The CD-ROM links to the Prentice Hall School Web site and may be used for daily updates.

### Answers to . . .
**Analyzing Primary Sources**
**1.** Because it was powerful and controlled approximately sixty-five cents out of every dollar allocated to Congress.
**2.** Schroeder faced many difficulties such as her status as a freshman senator and a woman, and opposition from the Armed Services chairman. Some of these problems were caused by her lack of experience as a senator, while other problems were caused by prejudices against women.
**3.** He required her to literally share a chair with the committee's only African American because he was unhappy that they had been added to the committee over his veto.
**4.** Under the seniority system, it is unusual for a freshman to win a seat on a prestigious committee.

**328**

---

 *on Primary Sources*

# Organizing Congressional Committees

*Pat Schroeder retired from public office in 1996, after 12 terms in Congress. In her memoir,* 24 Years of House Work . . . and the Place Is Still a Mess, *she relates her experiences in the House of Representatives. In this excerpt, Schroeder recalls her appointment, as a newly elected representative and a woman, to the powerful House Armed Services Committee.*

In a setup typical of Congress, where everything is done by committee, there is a committee to decide committee assignments for incoming freshmen. In 1973 it was headed by Representative Wilbur Mills of Arkansas. . . .

Considering that no senior member was going to fall on his sword for me, I expected to be assigned to something like Merchant Marine and Fisheries. Since my Denver district is landlocked . . . it would have meant sudden death for a new congressional career. I wanted to be on the Armed Services Committee. I wanted to be part of the committee that controlled approximately sixty-five cents out of every dollar allocated to Congress. . . .

The Armed Services chairman, F. Edward Hébert, was a seventy-two-year-old Louisiana Democrat who was dead set against my appointment. . . . Even though Mills chaired the [assignments] committee, I couldn't understand why he would override Hébert's veto. There was an unspoken rule that old congressional barons never cross each other. . . . Unbeknownst to me, Mills' wife had taken an interest in my career and apparently kept telling her husband that he should do whatever he could to help me. . . . Mills . . . performed the necessary arm-twisting.

Although I was [put] on the committee, I did not get a seat. Hébert was patronizingly contemptuous [lacking respect] of women in politics. . . . He also objected to the appointment of Congressman Ron

*Pat Schroeder, former Democratic representative of Colorado*

Dellums (Democrat from California). Ron had been in the House only one term when it was decided that it was time for an African-American to be on the Armed Services Committee. Hébert didn't appreciate the idea of a girl and a black forced on him. He was outraged that for the first time a chairman's veto of potential members was ignored. He announced that while he might not be able to control the makeup of the committee, he could . . . control the number of chairs in his hearing room, where he was enthroned on a carpet of stars, surrounded by military flags. He said that women and blacks were worth only half of one "regular" member, so he added only one seat to the committee room and made me and Ron share it. Nobody else objected, and nobody offered to scrounge up another chair. . . .

Ron and I had two choices: to go ballistic or to hang in. We decided to hang [in].

### Analyzing Primary Sources

1. Why did Schroeder want to serve on the Armed Services Committee?
2. What difficulties did Schroeder face and why?
3. How and why did Hébert embarrass Schroeder?
4. Aside from her gender, why is it surprising that Schroeder was assigned to the Armed Services Committee?

---

 *Corner*

**Close Up on Primary Sources** A House Built on Compromise, p. 14, extends this feature with a primary source activity.

 **Online**

To keep up-to-date on Close Up news and activities, visit Close Up Online at

**www.closeup.org**

# 2 Committees in Congress

## Section Preview

### OBJECTIVES

1. **Analyze** the role of committees in Congress.
2. **Describe** the duties and responsibilities of the House Rules Committee.
3. **Compare** the functions of joint and conference committees.

### WHY IT MATTERS

Congress divides into committees to manage the huge task of running the government. Committee leaders decide which pieces of legislation will receive attention in Congress.

### POLITICAL DICTIONARY

★ **standing committee**
★ **select committee**
★ **joint committee**
★ **conference committee**

---

**D**o you know the phrase "a division of labor"? Roughly explained, it means dividing the work to be done, assigning the several parts of the overall task to various members of the group.

The House and the Senate are both so large, and the business they each face is so great, that both chambers must rely on a division of labor. That is to say, much of the work that Congress does is in fact done by committees. Indeed, Representative Clem Miller (D., Calif.) once described Congress as "a collection of committees that comes together periodically to approve one another's actions."

## The Role of Committees

In 1789 the House and Senate each adopted the practice of naming a special committee to consider each bill as it was introduced. By 1794 there were more than 300 committees in each chamber. Each house then began to set up permanent panels, known as **standing committees,** to which all similar bills could be sent.

### Committee Assignments

The number of these committees has varied over the years. The graphic on page 330 lists the current 19 standing committees in the House and the 17 in the Senate. Each House committee has from 9 to as many as 75 members, and each Senate committee has from 12 to 28. Representatives are normally assigned to one or two standing committees and senators to three

or four. The pivotal role these committees play in the lawmaking process cannot be overstated. Most bills receive their most thorough consideration in these bodies. Members of both houses regularly respect the decisions and follow the recommendations they make. Thus, the fate of most bills is decided in the various standing committees, not on the floor of either house. More than a century ago, Woodrow Wilson described "Congress in its committee rooms" as "Congress at work," and that remains the fact of the matter today.

Some panels are more prominent and more influential than others. As you would expect, most members try to win assignments to these important panels. The leading committees in the House include the Rules, Ways and Means, Appropriations, Armed Services, Judiciary, International Relations, and Agriculture committees. In the Senate, senators compete for places on the Foreign Relations, Appropriations, Finance, Judiciary, Armed Services, and Banking, Housing, and Urban Affairs committees. Of course, some of the other committees are particularly attractive to some members. Thus, a representative whose district lies wholly within a major city might want to sit

► The House Committee on Banking and Financial Services considers bills that affect finance, including the proposal that led to the golden dollar coin.

---

### 2 Committees in Congress

**Objectives** You may wish to call students' attention to the objectives in the Section Preview. The objectives are reflected in the main headings of the section.

**Bellringer** Ask students for examples of committees with which they have first-hand experience. Have students discuss how these committees worked and how effective they were at reaching their goals. Explain that in this section they will explore the role of committees in Congress.

**Vocabulary Builder** Point out the terms in the Political Dictionary, and ask students to write a sentence predicting the role of each type of committee. Have them revise their predictions as they encounter each term in the section.

### Pressed for Time?

#### Quick Lesson Plan

**1. Focus** Tell students that in Congress, committees do the bulk of the work. Ask students to consider why Congress prefers to use committees, rather than the full House or Senate, to hammer out bills.

**2. Instruct** Ask students to state the difference between a standing committee and a select committee. Then have students describe the role of the House Rules Committee and tell the story of some historical select committees. Complete the discussion by comparing joint and conference committees.

**3. Close/Reteach** Remind students that committees are the workhorses of Congress. Have them list the various types of committees and, next to each, write a brief description of it along with two examples.

---

### 🔲 Block Scheduling Strategies

Consider these suggestions to manage extended class time:

■ Have students explain the reasons for the dramatic increase in the number of congressional committees and subcommittees. Group students and have each group identify and classify *social, economic, demographic,* and *political* reasons for the change. Finally, have each student research a committee or subcommittee and report on recent actions the committee has taken.

■ Have students focus on material from the text dealing with the House Rules Committee. Ask students to consider whether the House Rules Committee is too powerful. Organize the class into two debate teams: one will argue that the Rules Committee is too powerful, and the other will argue that it is not. Allow the teams time to prepare arguments and evidence, and then hold a class debate on the issue.

## Reading Strategy

### Organizing Information/ Graphic Organizer

Have students use a web graphic organizer to organize the information in this section as they read. Suggest that they start by writing *Committees in Congress* in the center circle.

## Point–of–Use Resources

📁 **Guided Reading and Review** Unit 3 booklet, p. 24 provides students with practice identifying the main ideas and key terms of this section.

📁 **Lesson Plans** For lesson planning suggestions, see p. 54 of the Lesson Plans booklet.

📁 **Political Cartoons** See p. 46 of the Political Cartoons booklet for a cartoon relevant to this section.

## Background Note

### Ranking Minority Members

The chairmanship of the House and Senate committees is determined by the majority party in each chamber. Thus, the committee chairs in the House in 2002 were all Republicans (as the table on page 331 shows). The committee chairs in the Senate in 2002 (after James Jeffords became an Independent) were all Democrats (as the table on page 332 shows). Yet each committee also has minority members. A committee member of the minority party with the greatest seniority is referred to as the "ranking minority" member of the committee. (For example, the "ranking Democrat" of the House Agricultural Committee was Charlie Stenholm of Texas.) The ranking minority position is important: should control of Congress transfer to the other major party, the ranking minority members are the likely new committee chairmen.

### *Answer to . . .*

**Interpreting Tables** Personal background; importance or influence of the committee.

## Permanent Committees of Congress

| HOUSE STANDING COMMITTEES | JOINT COMMITTEES OF CONGRESS | SENATE STANDING COMMITTEES |
|---|---|---|
| Agriculture | Economic | Agriculture, Nutrition, and Forestry |
| Appropriations | The Library | Appropriations |
| Armed Services | Printing | Armed Services |
| Budget | Taxation | Banking, Housing, and Urban Affairs |
| Education and the Workforce | | Budget |
| Energy and Commerce | | Commerce, Science, and Transportation |
| Financial Services | | Energy and Natural Resouces |
| Government Reform | | Environment and Public Works |
| House Administration | | Finance |
| International Relations | | Foreign Relations |
| Judiciary | | Governmental Affairs |
| Resources | | Indian Affairs |
| Rules | | Judiciary |
| Science | | Health, Education, Labor, and Pensions |
| Small Business | | Rules and Administration |
| Standards of Official Conduct | | Small Business and Entrepreneurship |
| Transportation and Infrastructure | | Veterans Affairs |
| Veterans Affairs | | |
| Ways and Means | | |

*Interpreting Tables* Most legislation is considered in standing committees, and party politics can shape those panels. ***What considerations might lead a member of Congress to want to serve on a particular committee?***

on the House Committee on Education and the Workforce. A senator from one of the western States might angle for assignment to the Senate's Committee on Energy and Natural Resources.

Most of the standing committees handle bills dealing with particular policy matters, such as veterans' affairs or foreign relations. There are three standing committees that do not operate as subject-matter bodies, however: in the House the Rules Committee and the Committee on Standards of Official Conduct, and in the Senate the Committee on Rules and Administration.

When a bill is introduced in either house, the Speaker or the president of the Senate refers the measure to the appropriate standing committee. Thus, the Speaker sends all tax measures to the House Ways and Means Committee; in the Senate tax measures go to the Finance Committee. A bill dealing with, say, enlistments in the armed forces goes to the Armed Services Committee in the House *and* to the Armed Services Committee in the Senate.

Recall that the chairman of each of the standing committees is chosen according to the seniority rule. To see the point, look at the tables on pages 331 and 332. Notice that most committee chairmen have served in Congress for at least 15 years and some much longer. The seniority rule is also applied closely in each house when it elects the other members of each of its committees.

The members of each standing committee are formally elected by a floor vote at the beginning of each term of Congress. In fact, each party has already drawn up its own committee roster before the vote, and the floor vote merely ratifies those party choices.

The majority party always holds a majority of the seats on each standing committee.[8] The other party is well represented, however.

---

[8]The only exception is the House Committee on Standards of Official Conduct, with five Democrats and five Republicans. Often called the House Ethics Committee, it investigates allegations of misconduct by House members. In the Senate, a six-member bipartisan Select Committee on Ethics plays a similar role.

## Organizing Information

To make sure students understand the main points of this section, you may wish to use the Venn diagram graphic organizer to the right.

Tell students that a Venn diagram compares two things by showing characteristics that they have in common and those that they have alone. Ask students to use the Venn diagram to compare standing committees with select committees.

**Teaching Tip** A template for this graphic organizer can be found in the Section Support Transparencies, Transparency 6.

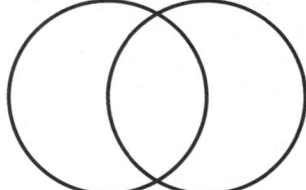

Most standing committees are divided into subcommittees, and each subcommittee is responsible for a particular slice of the committee's overall workload. There are now some 150 subcommittees in the two houses; nearly 70 in the Senate and 80 in the House.

To illustrate, the Senate's 25-member Committee on Armed Services does much of its work in six subcommittees. Each member serves on at least two of them, and the subcommittee titles generally describe their focus: the Subcommittee on Emerging Threats and Capabilities; the Subcommittee on Airland Forces; the Subcommittee on Personnel; the Subcommittee on Readiness and Management Support; the Subcommittee on Seapower; and the Subcommittee on Strategic Forces.

### The House Rules Committee

The House Committee on Rules is sometimes called the "traffic cop" in the lower house. So many measures are introduced in the House each term that some sort of screening is necessary.

Most bills die in the committees to which they are referred. Still, several hundred are reported out every year. So, before most of these bills can reach the floor of the House, they must also clear the Rules Committee.

Normally, a bill gets to the floor only if it has been granted a rule—been scheduled for floor consideration—by the Rules Committee. The committee decides whether and under what conditions the full House will consider a measure. This means that the powerful 13-member Rules Committee can speed, delay, or even prevent House action on a measure.

In the Senate, where the process is not so closely regulated, the majority floor leader controls the appearance of bills on the floor.

### Select Committees

At times, each house finds need for a **select committee.** These groups are sometimes called special committees; they are panels set up for some specific purpose and, most often, for a

---

### House Committee Chairs, 2002

| Committee | Name | Age* | Year Elected to House | Party Affiliation and State |
|---|---|---|---|---|
| Agriculture | Larry Combest | 57 | 1984 | R., Texas |
| Appropriations | C.W. "Bill" Young | 72 | 1970 | R., Florida |
| Armed Services | Bob Stump | 75 | 1976 | R., Arizona |
| Budget | Jim Nussle | 42 | 1990 | R., Iowa |
| Education and the Workforce | John Boehner | 53 | 1990 | R., Ohio |
| Energy and Commerce | W.J. "Billy" Tauzin | 59 | 1980 | R., Louisiana |
| Financial Services | Michael G. Oxley | 58 | 1981 | R., Ohio |
| Government Reform | Dan Burton | 64 | 1982 | R., Indiana |
| House Administration | Robert W. Ney | 48 | 1994 | R., Ohio |
| International Relations | Henry J. Hyde | 78 | 1974 | R., Illinois |
| Judiciary | F. James Sensenbrenner, Jr. | 59 | 1978 | R., Wisconsin |
| Resources | James V. Hansen | 70 | 1980 | R., Utah |
| Rules | David Dreier | 50 | 1980 | R., California |
| Science | Sherwood L. Boehlert | 66 | 1982 | R., New York |
| Small Business | David A. Manzullo | 58 | 1992 | R., Illinois |
| Standards of Official Conduct | Joel Hefley | 67 | 1986 | R., Colorado |
| Transportation and Infrastructure | Don Young | 69 | 1973 | R., Alaska |
| Veterans Affairs | Christopher H. Smith | 49 | 1980 | R., New Jersey |
| Ways and Means | Bill Thomas | 61 | 1978 | R., California |

SOURCE: *Congressional Directory* and the Clerk of the House          *As of birth date in 2002.

*Interpreting Tables* Committee chairmen have the power to schedule meetings, decide which bills to address, arrange public hearings, and decide which witnesses are to be called. ***What do their ages, years in the House, and party affiliation tell you about the post each of these members holds?***

limited time. The Speaker of the House or the president of the Senate appoints the members of these special committees, with the advice of the majority and minority leaders.

Most select committees are formed to investigate a current matter. The congressional power to investigate is an essential part of the lawmaking function. Congress must decide on the need for new laws and gauge the adequacy of those already on the books. It also must exercise its vital oversight function, to ensure that federal agencies are following the laws it has already passed. At times, too, a committee may conduct an investigation of an issue—for example, the threat of domestic terrorism—in order to focus public attention on that matter.

Most investigations are conducted by standing committees or by their subcommittees. Select committees occasionally do that work, however. Thus, the Senate's Select Committee on Aging conducts an ongoing study of the elderly. It holds hearings in Washington and around the country, issues reports and press releases, and otherwise tries to bring greater public and governmental attention to the problems facing older Americans.

At times, a select committee becomes a spectacularly important body. This happened, for example, with the Senate's Select Committee on Presidential Campaign Activities, popularly known as the Senate Watergate Committee. As the Watergate scandal began to unfold in 1973, the Senate created that committee. Chaired by Senator Sam Ervin (D., North Carolina), its job was to investigate "the extent, if any, to which illegal, improper, or unethical activities were engaged in by any persons . . . in the presidential election of 1972." Its sensational hearings riveted the nation for months. Eventually, they formed a key link in the chain of events that led to President Richard Nixon's resignation from office in 1974.

Since then, the most notable instance came in 1987, with the work of two panels: the Senate's Select Committee on Secret Military Assistance to Iran and the Nicaraguan Opposition, and the House Select Committee to Investigate Covert Arms Transactions with Iran. These twin committees, often referred to as the Iran-Contra Committee, probed the Reagan administration's conduct of two highly secret projects abroad:

### Senate Committee Chairs, 2002

| Committee | Name | Age* | Year Elected to Senate | Party Affiliation and State |
|---|---|---|---|---|
| Agriculture, Nutrition, and Forestry | Tom Harkin | 63 | 1984 (5) | D., Iowa |
| Appropriations | Robert C. Byrd | 85 | 1958 (4) | D, West Virginia |
| Armed Services | Carl Levin | 68 | 1978 | D., Michigan |
| Banking, Housing, and Urban Affairs | Paul S. Sarbanes | 69 | 1976 (3) | D., Maryland |
| Budget | Kent Conrad | 54 | 1986 | D., North Dakota |
| Commerce, Science, and Transportation | Ernest F. Hollings | 80 | 1966 | D., South Carolina |
| Energy and Natural Resources | Jeff Bingaman | 59 | 1982 | D., New Mexico |
| Environment and Public Works | James M. Jeffords | 68 | 1988 (7) | I., Vermont |
| Finance | Max S. Baucus | 61 | 1978 (2) | D, Montana |
| Foreign Relations | Joseph R. Biden | 60 | 1972 | D., Delaware |
| Governmental Affairs | Joseph I. Lieberman | 60 | 1988 | D., Connecticut |
| Health, Education, Labor, and Pensions | Edward M. Kennedy | 70 | 1962 | D., Massachusetts |
| Indian Affairs | Daniel K. Inouye | 78 | 1962 (2) | D., Hawaii |
| Judiciary | Patrick Leahy | 62 | 1974 | D., Vermont |
| Rules and Administration | Christopher J. Dodd | 58 | 1980 (3) | D., Connecticut |
| Small Business and Entrepreneurship | John F. Kerry | 59 | 1984 | D., Massachusetts |
| Veterans Affairs | John D. Rockefeller, IV | 65 | 1984 | D., West Virginia |

SOURCES: *Congressional Directory* and Secretary of the Senate

\* As of birth date in 2002

Number in parentheses indicates terms served in House.

**Interpreting Tables** Critics complain that the seniority system discourages younger members of Congress. ***How does this table demonstrate the importance of seniority in the United States Senate?***

## CONSTITUTIONAL PRINCIPLES

### Separation of Powers
Although the House of Representatives and the Senate are separate bodies that usually carry out their own business, they sometimes form joint committees and conference committees to handle work that affects both houses. These types of committees save Congress time by allowing both houses to work on the same issue at the same time, but they also diminish the distinction between the powers and duties of the House of Representatives and the Senate.

### Activity
Have each student choose a joint committee from the chart on page 330 of the text. Ask students to research the activities of the committee they choose. Have them create presentations highlighting the purpose of the committee, significant actions it has taken, and how it has saved Congress time. Encourage students to present their research to the class.

the covert sale of arms to Iran and clandestine efforts to give military aid to the Contra rebels in Nicaragua. The operation in Iran was intended, at least in part, as an arms-for-hostages deal, and it failed. The aid to the Contras was funded in part with money from the Iranian arms sales, despite an act of Congress that expressly prohibited such aid by the United States.

Most congressional investigations are not nearly so visible, nor so historic. Their more usual shape can be seen when, for example, the House Committee on Agriculture looks at the spruce budworm problem, an infestation affecting trees in the Pacific Northwest.

## Joint and Conference Committees

A **joint committee** is one composed of members of both houses. You may recall them from the chart on page 330. Some are select committees set up to serve some temporary purpose. Most are permanent groups that serve on a regular basis. Because the standing committees of the two houses often duplicate one another's work, many have long urged that Congress make much greater use of the joint committee device.

Some joint committees are investigative in nature and issue periodic reports to the House and Senate—for example, the Joint Economic Committee. Most joint committees have routine duties, however—for example, the Joint Committee on Printing and the Joint Committee on the Library of Congress.

Before a bill may be sent to the President, each house must pass it in identical form. If the two houses pass differing versions and cannot agree, a **conference committee**—a temporary, joint body—is created to iron out the differences in the bill. Its job is to produce a compromise bill that both houses will accept.

### Spotlight on Texas Government

**Committee Work** Bill Archer was born in Houston in 1928. He served in the Texas House of Representatives (1967–1970) before being elected to Congress in 1971. Texas returned him to Washington for fourteen successive terms, until he retired at the end of 2000.

When the Republicans took control of the House in 1994, Archer became the chariman of the House Ways and Means Committee. One of the Republican Party's major campaign promises had been a "Contract with America" that promised major congressional reforms within the first 100 days of the new term. Many of these changes came under the jurisdiction of Ways and Means. Archer restructured the committee and gained bi-partisanship respect for his fairness and for his frugality that helped save the country millions of dollars. He was a leader in the legislation for a balanced budget, for the first tax cut in 16 years, for welfare reform, and for fairer rules for the IRS.

In 2001, shortly after his retirement, the Woodrow Wilson International Center for Scholars awarded Archer its prestigious Woodrow Wilson Award for Public Services in recognition of "his years of service to our nation and his principled representation of the people of Houston."

**Analyzing Texas Government**

*Explain why the position of chairman of the House Ways and Means Committee is an influential post.*

### Section 2 Assessment

**Key Terms and Main Ideas**

1. What is a **standing committee** and why are such committees called "subject-matter" committees?
2. What is the role of **select committees** in the lawmaking process?
3. How do **joint committees** differ from **conference committees?**

**Critical Thinking**

4. **Testing Conclusions** Explain why you agree or disagree with the following statement: The Committee on Rules is the most powerful committee in the House.

5. **Drawing Conclusions** Woodrow Wilson once noted that Congress in its committee rooms is Congress at work. Explain the meaning of this statement in your own words.
6. **Recognizing Cause and Effect** How does the majority party manage to control all the committees in its house, and why does it do so?

#### Take It to the Net

7. The committees in Congress do much of the important work. Visit the Web page of one committee from the House of Representatives and make a list of five things that committee does. Use the links provided in the Social Studies area at the following Web site for help in completing this activity. **www.phschool.com**

#### Take It to the Net

7. Direct students to the Social Studies area at the Prentice Hall School Web site. The *Magruder's American Government* companion Web site includes the directions and links needed to complete the activity. It also provides a printable Internet activity worksheet with scoring rubrics for assessment. Lists should be comprehensive and accurate.

5. Possible answer: The major work of Congress is done in committees—they study the issues pertaining to specific bills, make changes to bills, and resolve differences between versions of bills prior to their passage.
6. The majority party always has the majority of seats on committees; parties want the majority to influence the kinds of bills that are considered and set conditions for their passage.

*Answers to . . .*

## Section 2 Assessment

1. Standing committees are permanent panels; because they deal only with bills that concern a particular subject matter, they are known as "subject-matter committees."
2. They are set up to investigate specific current matters for a limited amount of time; they usually investigate new laws, determine the adequacy of old ones, and exercise Congress's oversight function.
3. Both are composed of members from both houses, but joint committees are either select or standing committees while conference committees are temporary committees that deal only with resolving differences between House and Senate versions of a bill before the bill passes.
4. Answers will vary; those who agree might point out that the Rules Committee has the ability to speed, delay, or halt House actions; those who disagree might say that most of the screening of bills is actually done by other committees, not the Rules Committee.

*Answers to . . .*

**Analyzing Texas Government**
The House Ways and Means Committee has far-reaching responsibilities, including the handling of all tax measures and congressional reform proposals.

**3** # How a Bill Becomes a Law: The House

## Teacher Notes (left margin)

**Objectives** You may wish to call students' attention to the objectives in the Section Preview. The objectives are reflected in the main headings of the section.

**Bellringer** Ask students to estimate the percentage of daily news stories devoted to laws proposed in or passed by Congress. Lead a discussion of why so much news coverage is devoted to the legislative process. Explain that in this section, they will learn about the legislative process in the House of Representatives.

**Vocabulary Builder** Have students create three-column charts, with the terms from the Political Dictionary in the first column and what students think each term means in the second column. As they read, students should fill in the third column with the actual definitions.

### Pressed for Time?

#### Quick Lesson Plan

**1. Focus** Tell students that the process of passing a bill in the House is long and difficult. Ask students to discuss what they know about how the step-by-step process works.

**2. Instruct** Say: "A representative has an idea for a law. What happens next?" and call on a student. Continue asking for the next step until the class has thoroughly discussed the legislative process in the House.

**3. Close/Reteach** Remind students that the legislative process is complex. Write "A bill is introduced in the House" at the top of the chalkboard and "A page carries the bill to the Senate" at the bottom. Have students use these first and last steps to create a flowchart of the legislative process in the House.

### Point-of-Use Resources

📁 **Close Up on Participation** Kicking the Habit, pp. 8–9, uses the topic of smoking and public health to help students plan and carry out service learning projects.

---

## How a Bill Becomes a Law: The House

### Section Preview

**OBJECTIVES**

1. **Analyze** the procedure in the House for enacting laws.
2. **Describe** what happens to a bill once it enters a committee.
3. **Explain** how House leaders schedule debate on a bill.
4. **Explain** what happens to a bill on the House floor, and identify the final step in passing a bill in the House.

**WHY IT MATTERS**

A bill must go through reviews and committee hearings before coming to a vote on the House floor. Most bills never make it that far. Bills that are approved in the House move on to the Senate.

**POLITICAL DICTIONARY**

★ bill
★ joint resolution
★ concurrent resolution
★ resolution
★ rider
★ discharge petition
★ subcommittee
★ Committee of the Whole
★ quorum
★ engrossed

---

These numbers may surprise you: As many as 10,000 proposed laws are introduced in the House and Senate during a term of Congress. Fewer than 10 percent ever become law. Where do all those measures come from? Why are so few of them passed? By what process does Congress make law?

### Enacting Laws: First Steps

A **bill** is a proposed law presented to the House or Senate for consideration. Most bills introduced in either house do not originate with members of Congress themselves. Instead, most bills—the important as well as the routine—are born somewhere in the executive branch. Business, labor, agriculture, and other special interest groups often draft measures as well. Some bills, or at least the ideas for them, come from private citizens who think "there ought to be a law . . . ." Many others are born in the standing committees of Congress.

◄ A bill introduced in the House must be placed in the hopper.

According to the Constitution:

 **FROM THE Constitution** *❝ All Bills for raising Revenue shall originate in the House of Representatives; but the Senate may propose or concur with amendments as on other Bills. ❞*

—Article I, Section 7, Clause 1

Measures dealing with any other matter may be introduced in either chamber. Only members can introduce bills in the House, and they do so by dropping them into the "hopper," a box hanging on the edge of the clerk's desk. [9]

### Types of Bills and Resolutions

The thousands of measures—bills and resolutions—Congress considers at each session take several forms. To begin with, there are two types of bills: public bills and private bills.

Public bills are measures applying to the nation as a whole—for example, a tax measure or an amendment to the copyright laws. Private bills are measures that apply to certain persons or places

---

[9]Puerto Rico's resident commissioner and the delegates from the District of Columbia, Guam, the Virgin Islands, and American Samoa also may introduce measures in the House. Only a senator may introduce a measure in the upper house. He or she does so by addressing the chair.

---

### ▣ Block Scheduling Strategies

Consider these suggestions to manage extended class time:

■ Discuss with the class the process of how the House considers proposed legislation. Ask students to create graphic organizers depicting the process the House of Representatives uses when considering legislation. Have students create a visual for each step in the process. Ask them to write captions explaining each visual. Have volunteers explain their organizers to the class.

■ Explain to students that virtually all bills introduced in the House go to committee, and that most die there (are pigeonholed). Have them consider whether this demonstrates a fundamental problem in the House. Organize the class into two teams: one will argue that the pigeonholing of so many bills indicates a failure of the legislative process, and the other will argue that it indicates its success.

rather than to the entire nation. As an example, Congress recently passed an act to give an Idaho sheep rancher $85,000 for his losses resulting from attacks by grizzly bears, which had been moved from Yellowstone National Park onto nearby public lands on which he grazed his flock.

**Joint resolutions** are similar to bills, and when passed have the force of law. Joint resolutions most often deal with unusual or temporary matters. For example, they may be used to appropriate money for the presidential inauguration ceremonies or to correct an error in a statute already passed. Joint resolutions also are used to propose constitutional amendments and to annex territories, as well.

**Concurrent resolutions** deal with matters in which the House and Senate must act jointly. However, they do not have the force of law and do not require the President's signature. Concurrent resolutions are used most often by Congress to state a position on some matter—for example, in foreign affairs.

**Resolutions** deal with matters concerning either house alone and are taken up only by that house. They are regularly used for such things as the adoption of a new rule of procedure or the amendment of some existing rule. Like concurrent resolutions, a resolution does not have the force of law and is not sent to the President for approval.

A bill or resolution usually deals with a single subject, but sometimes a **rider** dealing with an unrelated matter is included. A rider is a provision not likely to pass on its own merit that is attached to an important measure certain to pass. Its sponsors hope that it will "ride" through the legislative process on the strength of the main measure.

Most riders are tacked onto appropriations measures, those in which Congress provides the money to pay for something. In fact, some money bills are hung with so many riders that they are called "Christmas trees." The opponents of those "decorations" and the President are almost always forced to accept them if they want the bill's major provisions to become law.

### The First Reading

The clerk of the House numbers each bill as it is introduced. Thus, H.R. 3410 would be the 3,410th measure introduced in the House during the congressional term. Bills originating in the Senate receive the prefix S.—such as S. 210.

## Types of Bills and Resolutions

| BILL | A proposed law or draft of a law; public bill applies to the entire nation; private bill applies only to certain people or places |
|---|---|
| JOINT RESOLUTION | A proposal for action that has the force of law when passed; usually deals with special circumstances or temporary matters |
| CONCURRENT RESOLUTION | A statement of position on an issue used by the House and Senate acting jointly; does not have the force of law; does not require the President's signature |
| RESOLUTION | A measure relating to the business of either house or expressing an opinion on a matter; does not have the force of law; does not require the President's signature |

*Interpreting Charts* To be considered by Congress, a measure must be introduced in either the House or the Senate in one of the above formats. *In what ways do joint resolutions and concurrent resolutions differ?*

Resolutions are similarly identified in each house in the order of their introduction.[10]

The clerk also gives each bill a short title—a brief summary of its principal contents. Having received its number and title, the bill is then entered in the House *Journal* and in the *Congressional Record* for the day.

The *Journal* contains the minutes, the official record, of the daily proceedings in the House or Senate. The *Congressional Record* is a voluminous account of the daily proceedings (speeches, debates, other comments, votes, motions, etc.) in each house. The *Record* is not quite a word-for-word account, however. Members have five days in which to make changes in each temporary edition. They often insert speeches that were in fact never made, reconstruct "debates," and revise thoughtless or inaccurate remarks.

With these actions the bill has received its first reading. All bills are printed immediately after introduction and distributed to the members.

---

[10] Thus, H.J. Res. 12 would be the 12th joint resolution introduced in the House during the term, and similarly in the Senate, S.J. Res. 19. Concurrent resolutions are identified as H. or S. Con. Res. 4, and other resolutions as H. or S. Res. 166.

## Reading Strategy
### Drawing Inferences

Have students suppose that they have proposed an idea for a new law to their representative in the House. Have students, as they read the section, determine at what stages in the legislative process they should contact their representative to push for passage of their proposal.

### Background Note
#### Ancient Roots

The use of the word *bill* for a proposed law is a reminder that the roots of American government are found in the classical world. Proposed laws are called *bills* today because of the ancient practice of placing official seals on documents. The Latin term for such a seal was *bulla,* which became *bull,* and, over the centuries, our word *bill.*

## Point–of–Use Resources

**Guided Reading and Review** Unit 3 booklet, p. 26 provides students with practice identifying the main ideas and key terms of this section.

**Lesson Plans** For lesson planning suggestions, see p. 55 of the Lesson Plans booklet.

**Political Cartoons** See p. 47 of the Political Cartoons booklet for a cartoon relevant to this section.

**Section Support Transparencies** Transparency 50, *Visual Learning;* Transparency 149, *Political Cartoon*

*Answer to . . .*

**Interpreting Charts** Unlike joint resolutions, concurrent resolutions do not have the force of law and are not signed by the President; they are meant to state a position.

## Customize for
### More Advanced Students

Have students conduct research to identify the subcommittees associated with three House committees. Have students report what they learn to the class, explaining the reason for each subcommittee's existence.

### Background Note
#### Junketeers

During congressional election campaigns, incumbents are routinely criticized for taking junkets. They are accused of wasting public funds, or, if a junket was paid for by a private group, for selling influence. The word "junketeer" is sometimes applied to representatives who take repeated junkets: it has an intentionally negative connotation, and is meant to be associated with words like *racketeer* and *profiteer*.

### ACTIVITY
#### Heterogeneous Groups

**Enrichment** Point out that sometimes new scientific discoveries raise issues of concern to society. In some cases, Congress proposes or enacts laws in response to the new discovery. For example, recent scientific research into the DNA of plants has led to the development of genetically modified plants. In this process, scientists can introduce a gene from one plant species into a different species to produce hardier, more productive crops. In 1999, a study was published in the journal *Nature* claiming that corn that had been modified to become poisonous to one specific pest also threatened monarch butterflies. In response to this and theories about food allergies, Rep. Dennis Kucinich (D., Ohio) introduced the Genetically Engineered Food Right to Know Act to require all genetically modified foods to be labeled before being sold.

During the 106th Congress, the bill was introduced in the House of Representatives as H.R. 3377 and in the Senate as S. 2080. Have students track the progress of these bills using the Internet and the "Links

Library" at **www.phschool.com.** Then, have them analyze these bills and explain how this scientific discovery prompted a reaction by the government.

**(Average)**

▲ *Testifying Before Congress* Committees often call upon citizens to give testimony at public hearings. Actor Michael J. Fox appeared before the Senate Appropriations Committee to discuss Parkinson's disease, a progressive disease with which he has been diagnosed.

Each bill that is finally passed in either house is given three readings along the legislative route. In the House, second reading comes during floor consideration, if the measure gets that far. Third reading takes place just before the final vote on the measure. Each reading is usually by number and title only: "H.R. 3410, A bill to provide. . . ." However, the more important or controversial bills are read in full and taken up line by line, section by section, at second reading.

The three readings, an ancient parliamentary practice, are intended to ensure careful consideration of bills. Today, the readings are little more than way stations along the legislative route. They were quite important in the early history of Congress, however, when some members could not read.

After the first reading, the Speaker refers the bill to the appropriate standing committee. That is, the proposal is sent to the committee that has jurisdiction over its subject matter.

## The Bill in Committee

The Constitution makes no mention of standing committees. These bodies play an absolutely essential role in the lawmaking process, however—and in both houses of Congress. Indeed, their place is so pivotal that they are sometimes called "little legislatures."

The standing committees act as sieves. They sift through all of the many bills referred to them—rejecting most, considering and reporting only those they find to be worthy of floor consideration. In short, the fate of most bills is decided in these committees rather than on the floor of either house of Congress.

Most of the thousands of bills introduced in each session of Congress are pigeonholed.[11] That is, they die in committee. They are simply put away, never to be acted upon.

Most pigeonholed bills deserve their fate. On occasion, however, a committee buries a measure that a majority of the House wants to consider. When that happens, the bill can be blasted out of the committee with a discharge petition.

A **discharge petition** enables members to force a bill that has remained in committee 30 days (7 in the Rules Committee) onto the floor for consideration. Any member may file a discharge motion. If that motion is signed by a majority (218) of House members, the committee has seven days to report the bill. If it does not, any member who signed the motion may, on the second and fourth Mondays of each month, move that the committee be discharged, or relieved, of the bill. If the motion carries, the House considers the bill at once. This maneuver is not often tried, and it seldom succeeds.

### Gathering Information

Those bills that a committee, or at least its chairman, does wish to consider are discussed at times chosen by the chairman. Today, most committees do most of their work through their several **subcommittees**—divisions of existing committees formed to address specific issues. There are now

---

[11]The term comes from the old-fashioned rolltop desks with pigeonholes—slots into which papers were put and often soon forgotten. Most "by request" bills are routinely pigeonholed; they are the measures that members introduce but only because some constituent or some interest group has asked them to do so.

some 80 of these committees within committees in the House, and nearly 70 in the Senate.

Where an important or controversial bill is involved, a committee, or more often one of its subcommittees, holds public hearings on the measure. Interested persons, special interest groups, and government officials are invited to testify at these information-gathering sessions.[12] If necessary, a committee can force a witness to testify under threat of imprisonment.

Occasionally, a subcommittee will make a junket (trip) to locations affected by a measure. Thus, members of the National Parks and Public Lands Subcommittee of the House Committee on Resources may take a firsthand look at a number of national parks. Or, the Water and Power Subcommittee of the Senate Energy and Natural Resources Committee may visit the Pacific Northwest to gather information on a public power bill.

These junkets are made at public expense, and members of Congress are sometimes criticized for taking them. Some junkets deserve criticism. But an on-the-spot investigation often proves to be the best way a committee can inform itself.

## Committee Actions

When a subcommittee has completed its work on a bill, the measure goes to the full committee. That body may do one of several things. It may:
1. Report the bill favorably, with a "do pass" recommendation. It is then the chairman's job to steer the bill through debate on the floor.
2. Refuse to report the bill—that is, pigeonhole it. Again, this is the fate suffered by most measures in both houses.
3. Report the bill in amended form. Many bills are changed in committee, and several bills on the same subject may be combined into a single measure.
4. Report the bill with an unfavorable recommendation. This does not often happen. Occasionally, however, a committee feels that the full House should have a chance to consider a bill or does not want to take the responsibility for killing it.

---

[12]If necessary, a committee may subpoena witnesses. A subpoena is an order compelling one to appear. Failure to obey a subpoena may lead the House or Senate to pass a resolution citing the offender for contempt of Congress—a federal crime punishable by fine and/or imprisonment.

5. Report a committee bill. This is an entirely new bill that the committee has substituted for one or several bills referred to it.

## Scheduling Floor Debate

Before it goes to the floor for consideration, a bill reported by a standing committee is placed on one of several calendars. A calendar is a schedule of the order in which bills will be taken up on the floor.

### Calendars

There are five calendars in the House:
(1) The Calendar of the Committee of the Whole House on the State of the Union, commonly known as the Union Calendar,

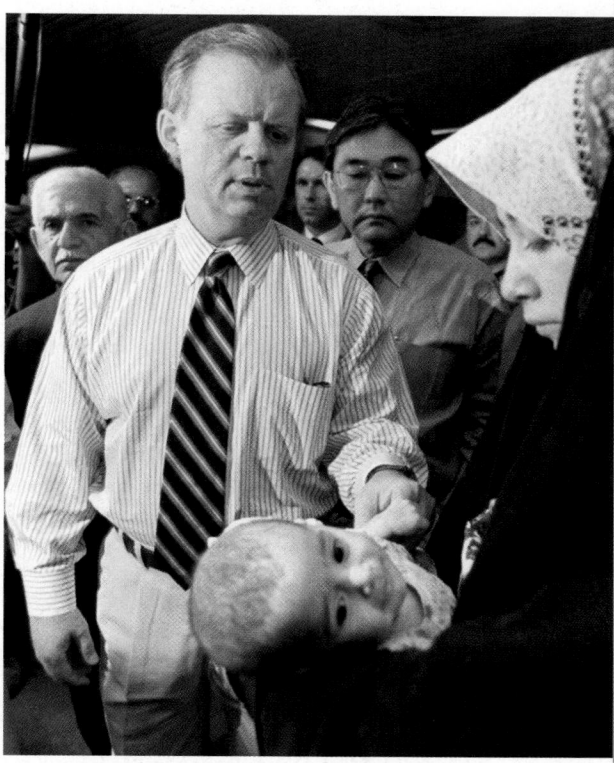

▲ Representative Tony Hall (D., Ohio) visited Iraq to study the effects of economic sanctions that were imposed to discourage that country from developing weapons. *Critical Thinking* **Which House committee would have been most likely to hear Representative Hall's testimony?**

*Answer to . . .*
**Critical Thinking** The Foreign Relations committee.

## Extended Class Periods

**Time** 90 minutes.
**Purpose** Simulate the legislative process in the House of Representatives.
**Grouping** Entire class.
**Activity** Have the class review current newspapers to identify a bill before the House. Create a simplified form of the bill for the class to consider. Assign students various House roles (representatives for and against the bill, committee members, etc.). You may assign the role of Speaker or assume it yourself. Guide students through the proper order of business, using proper House procedures.
**Roles** Representatives, committee members, Speaker.
**Close** After students have completed their mock House session, have them vote on the bill and tally their results.

■ **Block Strategy**
**(Average)**

## Point–of–Use Resources

📁 **Government Assessment Rubrics**
Cooperative Learning Project:
Process, p. 20

📁 **Block Scheduling with Lesson Strategies** Additional activities for Chapter 12 appear on p. 25.

*Answer to . . .*

**Interpreting Political Cartoons** That "debate" consists of politicians listening to their own opinions, rather than responding to those of others.

*Interpreting Political Cartoons* **What does this cartoon imply about political debate?**

for all bills having to do with revenues, appropriations, or government property.
(2) The House Calendar, for all other public bills.
(3) The Calendar of the Committee of the Whole House, commonly called the Private Calendar, for all private bills.
(4) The Corrections Calendar, for all bills from the Union or House Calendar taken out of order by unanimous consent of the House of Representatives. These are most often minor bills to which there is no opposition.
(5) The Discharge Calendar, for petitions to discharge bills from committee.

Under the rules of the House, bills are taken from each of these calendars for consideration on a regularly scheduled basis. For example, bills from the Corrections Calendar are considered on the first and third Mondays of each month. Measures relating to the District of Columbia are to be taken up on the second and fourth Mondays, and private bills every Friday. On "Calendar Wednesdays," the various committee chairmen may each call up one bill from the House or Union calendars that has cleared their committees.

### Rules

None of these arrangements is followed too closely, however. What often happens is even more complicated. First, remember that the Rules Committee plays a critical role in the legislative process of the House. It must grant a rule before most bills can in fact reach the floor. That is, before most measures can be taken from a calendar, the Rules Committee must approve that step and set a time for its appearance on the floor.

By not granting a rule for a bill, the Rules Committee can effectively kill it. Or, when the Rules Committee does grant a rule, it may be a special rule—one setting conditions under which the members of the House will consider the measure. A special rule regularly sets a time limit on floor debate. It may even prohibit amendments to certain, or even to any, of the bill's provisions.

Then, too, certain bills are privileged. They may be called up at almost any time, ahead of any other business before the House. The most highly privileged measures include major appropriations (spending) and general revenue (tax) bills, conference committee reports, and special rules from the Rules Committee.

On certain days, usually the first and third Mondays and Tuesdays, the House may suspend its rules. A motion to that effect must be approved by a two-thirds vote of the members present. When that happens, as it sometimes does, the House moves so far away from its established operating procedures that a measure can go through all the many steps necessary to enactment in a single day.

All of these—the calendars, the role of the Rules Committee, and the other complex procedures—have developed over time and for several reasons. In major part, they have developed because of the large size of the House and the sheer number and variety of bills its members introduce. In their own ways, the calendars, rules, and other complex procedures have developed to help members of the House manage their heavy workload. Without such help, no one member could possibly know the contents, let alone the merits, of every bill on which he or she has to vote.

### The Bill on the Floor

If a bill finally reaches the floor, it receives its second reading in the House. Many bills the House passes are minor ones, with little or no opposition. Most minor bills are called from the

Corrections Calendar, get their second reading by title only, and are quickly disposed of.

Nearly all the more important measures are dealt with in a much different manner, however. They are considered in the **Committee of the Whole,** an old parliamentary device for speeding business on the floor.

The Committee of the Whole includes all the members of the House. However, they sit as one large committee of the House, not as the House itself. The rules of the Committee of the Whole are much less strict than the rules of the House, and floor action moves along at a faster pace. For example, a **quorum,** or majority of the full membership (218), must be present in order for the House to do business. However, only 100 members need be present in the Committee of the Whole.

When the House resolves itself into the Committee of the Whole, the Speaker steps down because the full House of Representatives is no longer in session. Another member presides. General debate begins, and the bill receives its second reading, section by section. As each section is read, amendments may be offered. Under the five-minute rule, supporters and opponents of each amendment have just that many minutes to make their cases. Votes are taken on each section and its amendment as the reading proceeds.

When the bill has been gone through—and many run to dozens and sometimes hundreds of pages—the Committee of the Whole has completed its work. It then rises, that is, dissolves itself. The House is now back in session. The Speaker resumes the chair, and the House formally adopts the committee's work.

## Debate

Its large size has long since forced the House to impose severe limits on floor debate. A rule first adopted in 1841 forbids any member from holding the floor for more than one hour without unanimous consent to speak for a longer time. Since 1880 the Speaker has had the power to force any member who strays from the subject at hand to give up the floor.

The majority and minority floor leaders generally decide in advance how they will split the time to be spent on a bill. But at any time, any member may "move the previous question."

## *Voices* on Government

**Senator Kay Bailey Hutchison** (R., Texas) served two terms in the Texas House of Representatives and was elected Texas State Treasurer before going to Washington. As vice chairman of the Senate Republican Conference, she is now one of the top five Senate Republican leaders. Her experience in Texas informs her perspective on the role the Federal Government should play in local affairs.

❝ *The most effective federal programs are those that allow states enough flexibility and freedom to meet their individual situations and needs. One size fits all doesn't work for people, and it shouldn't be applied to the states, either. We learned this lesson with welfare reform. State legislatures took this new flexibility and created programs that suited our own needs. As a result, welfare rolls have been cut in half.* ❞

## Evaluating the Quotation

*Based on Senator Hutchison's statement, how would you expect her to vote on bills that seek to establish national policies?*

That is, any member may demand a vote on the issue before the House. If that motion passes, only 40 minutes of further debate are allowed before a vote is taken. This device is the only motion that can be used in the House to close (end) debate, but it can be a very effective one.

## Voting

A bill may be the subject of several votes on the floor. If amendments are offered, as they frequently are, members must vote on each of them. Then, too, a number of procedural motions may be offered, for example, one to table the bill (lay it aside), another for the previous question, and so on. The members must vote on each of these motions. These several other votes can be a better guide to a bill's friends and foes than is the final vote itself. Sometimes, a member votes for a bill that is now certain to pass, even though he or she supported amendments to it that would have scuttled the measure.

## Point-of-Use Resources

**Guide to the Essentials** Chapter 12, Section 3, p. 68 provides support for students who need additional review of section content. Spanish support is available in the Spanish edition of the Guide on p. 61.

**Quiz** Unit 3 booklet, p. 27 includes matching and multiple-choice questions to check students' understanding of Section 3 content.

**Presentation Pro CD-ROM** Quizzes and multiple-choice questions check students' understanding of Section 3 content.

## Answers to . . .

### Section 3 Assessment

**1.** Public bills apply to the nation as a whole, for example, taxes or copyright laws. Private bills apply to certain persons or places.

**2.** They attach a rider if they know the rider would not pass on its own; by attaching it to a bill that will pass, it can "ride" through the legislative process anyway.

**3.** The Committee of the Whole has rules that are much less strict than the rules of the House's general meetings, meaning that business may proceed much more quickly.

**4.** A discharge petition allows members to force bills that have remained in committee 30 days onto the floor for consideration.

**5.** Possible advantage: Each member would see each bill, making the process more democratic. Possible disadvantages: If all bills were sent directly to the complete House, the House would spend too much valuable time weeding out bills that would never obtain passage; also, with too many bills to consider, each member could not possibly become familiar with the contents of every bill.

**6.** The committee may not want the responsibility for killing the bill, or may want the entire House to consider it rather than taking their recommendation.

---

The House uses four different methods for taking floor votes:

1. Voice votes are the most common. The Speaker calls for the "ayes" and then the "noes," the members answer in chorus, and the Speaker announces the result.

2. If any member thinks the Speaker has erred in judging a voice vote, he or she may demand a standing vote, also known as a division of the House. All in favor, and then all opposed, stand and are counted by the clerk.

3. One fifth of a quorum (44 members in the House or 20 in the Committee of the Whole) can demand a teller vote. When this happens, the Speaker names two tellers, one from each party. The members pass between the tellers and are counted, for and against. Teller votes are rare today. The practice has been replaced by electronic voting, as you will see below.

4. A roll-call vote, also known as a record vote, may be demanded by one fifth of the members present.[13]

In 1973, the House installed a computerized voting system for all quorum calls and record votes to replace the roll call by the clerk. Members now vote at any of the 48 stations on the floor by inserting a personalized plastic card in a box and then pushing one of three buttons: "Yea," "Nay," or "Present." The "Present" button is most often used for a quorum call—a check to make sure that a quorum of the members is in fact present. Otherwise, it is used when a member does not wish to vote on a question but still wants to be recorded as present.[14]

A large master board above the Speaker's chair shows instantly how each member has voted. The House rules allow the members 15 minutes to answer quorum calls or cast record votes. Voting ends when the Speaker pushes a button to lock the electronic system, producing a permanent record of the vote at the same time. Under the former roll-call process, it took the clerk up to 45 minutes to call each member's name and record his or her vote. Before 1973, roll calls took up about three months of House floor time each session.

Voting procedures are much the same in the Senate. The upper house uses voice, standing, and roll-call votes, but does not take teller votes or use an electronic voting process. Only six or seven minutes are needed for a roll-call vote in the upper chamber.

### Final Steps

Once a bill has been approved at second reading, it is **engrossed.** This means the bill is printed in its final form. Then it is read a third time, by title, and a final vote is taken. If the bill is approved at third reading, the Speaker signs it. A page—a legislative aide—then carries it to the Senate and places it on the Senate president's desk.

---

[13]The Constitution (Article I, Section 7, Clause 2) requires a record vote on the question of overriding a presidential veto. No record votes are taken in the Committee of the Whole.

[14]A "present" vote is not allowed on some questions—for example, a vote to override a veto.

---

## Section **3** Assessment

**Key Terms and Main Ideas**

1. Explain the difference between the two types of **bills.**
2. Why do members of Congress attach **riders** to bills that are almost certain to pass?
3. How does the **Committee of the Whole** function differently from a general meeting of the House?
4. What is the purpose of a **discharge petition?**

**Critical Thinking**

5. **Predicting Consequences** What might happen if all proposed bills were sent directly to the complete House for a vote? What are the advantages and disadvantages of this system?

6. **Understanding Point of View** Why might members of a House committee choose to report a bill with an unfavorable recommendation rather than pigeonhole it?

 **Take It to the Net**

7. Read the thirteen steps a bill goes through before becoming a law. Based on your reading, explain why so many bills fail to become laws and which stages can stop a bill's progress. Use the links provided in the Social Studies area at the following Web site for help in completing this activity. **www.phschool.com**

---

 **Take It to the Net**

**7.** Direct students to the Social Studies area at the Prentice Hall School Web site. The *Magruder's American Government* companion Web site includes the directions and links needed to complete the activity. It also provides a printable Internet activity worksheet with scoring rubrics for assessment. Opinions should clearly express a point of view and should be backed by specific examples.

# SKILLS FOR LIFE

TECHNOLOGY
CITIZENSHIP
CRITICAL THINKING
CHARTS and GRAPHS

## Understanding Point of View

An old saying advises you to "walk a mile in your neighbor's shoes." That is, when you're evaluating or contradicting someone's opinion, think about how the issue looks from that person's perspective, or point of view. It might make you more tolerant of the other opinion, or it might help you strengthen your own argument.

Many factors can shape someone's perspective. Here are some guidelines for understanding point of view:
1. **Identify the source.** Find out whatever you can about the person whose views you are evaluating. Who are the sources of the excerpts below?
2. **Identify the view being presented.** In the excerpts below, the senators discuss different ways of dealing with the hostility between the North and the South over slavery. To preserve the Union, Senator John C. Calhoun favored nullification, giving Southern States the right to refuse to carry out federal laws that they opposed. Senator Jefferson Davis spoke nearly a decade later, advocating secession, withdrawal from the Union. (a) Summarize the main idea of each quotation. (b) Identify the intended audience for each speech. (c) Identify the purpose of each.
3. **List attributes that might influence the source's point of view.** Consider factors such as the person's origins, age, sex, ethnic group, education, socio-economic group, personal experiences, lifestyle, values, and priorities.

### Test for Success

Find background information on Calhoun and Davis. Compare and contrast the two points of view on the topic of *nullification* vs. *secession*.

> " . . . [W]hen the Constitution was ratified and the Government put in action, there was nearly a perfect equilibrium between the [North and South], which afforded ample means to each to protect itself against the aggression of the other; but, as it now stands, [the North] has the exclusive power of controlling the Government, which leaves [the South] without any adequate means of protecting itself against its encroachment and oppression. . . . How can the Union be saved? . . . [B]y adopting such measures as will satisfy the [southern states] that they can remain in the Union consistently with their honor and their safety. "
>
> —*South Carolina Senator John C. Calhoun, "Proposal to Preserve the Union," Senate speech, 1850*

> " It was because of his deep-seated attachment to the Union . . . that Mr. Calhoun advocated the doctrine of nullification, which he proclaimed to be peaceful, to be within the limits of State power, not to disturb the Union. . . . Secession belongs to a different class of remedies. It is to be justified upon the basis that the states are sovereign. There was a time when none denied it. I hope the time may come again when a better comprehension of the theory of our Government, and the inalienable rights of the people of the States, will prevent any one from denying that each State is a sovereign, and thus may reclaim the [agreements] which it has made to any [other government] whomsoever. "
>
> —*Mississippi Senator Jefferson Davis, Farewell speech to the Senate, 1861*

## Point-of-Use Resources

📁 **Skills for Life Activity** Unit 3 booklet, p. 30 provides an additional skill activity for this chapter.

💿 **Social Studies Skills Tutor CD-ROM** Provides interactive practice in geographic literacy, critical thinking and reading, visual analysis, and communications.

### Test for Success

Make sure students understand the difference between *nullification* and *secession* before they begin their research.

## SKILLS FOR LIFE
### CRITICAL THINKING
#### Understanding Point of View

**Focus** Analyze students' points of view on a contemporary issue.

**Instruct** Choose a topic, perhaps something in the news, on which students have strongly held, opposing views. Select one student on each side of the issue to state their views. Solicit comments from the class on what might influence each student's point of view.

**Close/Reteach** Repeat the exercise, having students argue a position *opposing* their own. This requires students to understand another's point of view in order to make the argument.

*Answers . . .*
1. South Carolina Senator John C. Calhoun and Mississippi Senator Jefferson Davis.
2. (a) Sample answers: Calhoun—Because the former balance of power between North and South has shifted in favor of the North, the Union must be preserved by taking steps to protect Southern interests; Jefferson—The States, as sovereign governments, may secede from the Union. (b) Both men were addressing the Senate. (c) Calhoun was trying to persuade both sides to work out their differences and preserve the Union. Davis was explaining the rationale for the secession of Southern States.
3. Both Calhoun and Davis were well-educated white Southerners, who believed passionately in the cause of the South. Yet their age differences and personal experiences may have influenced their different perspectives.

**341**

**4** *The Bill in the Senate*

**Objectives** You may wish to call students' attention to the objectives in the Section Preview. The objectives are reflected in the main headings of the section.

**Bellringer** Ask students whether they have ever seen a movie in which the hero struggles against all odds and finally seems to have won the day only to be faced with another major challenge at the end. Tell them that in this section, they will read about the final stages of the legislative process, where major challenges can arise.

**Vocabulary Builder** Tell students that the Political Dictionary includes several colorful terms related to the legislative process. Ask students to define *veto*, and then have them guess what *pocket veto* might mean. Have them check their guesses as they read the section.

## Pressed for Time?

### Quick Lesson Plan

**1. Focus** Tell students that the legislative process in the Senate differs in a few ways from that in the House. Ask students to discuss what they know about how the Senate differs from the House in general and how those differences affect the legislative process.

**2. Instruct** Ask students which house has more rules. Lead a discussion of how the Senate's rules, though limited, can have a great impact on the legislative process. Then discuss what can happen to a bill once the Senate has passed it.

**3. Close/Reteach** Remind students that the House and Senate both have to pass the same bill before it can become law. Ask students to draw a diagram to show the hurdles a bill can face both while it is in the Senate and after the Senate passes it.

## Section Preview

### OBJECTIVES

1. **Explain** how a bill is introduced in the Senate.
2. **Compare** the Senate's rules for debate with those in the House.
3. **Describe** the role of conference committees in the legislative process.
4. **Analyze** the constitutional powers of the President after both houses have passed a bill.

### WHY IT MATTERS

A bill that survives the legislative obstacle course in one house must still be passed in the other chamber—and face yet more hurdles before it can become law.

### POLITICAL DICTIONARY

★ filibuster
★ cloture
★ veto
★ pocket veto

The basic steps in the lawmaking process are much the same in the House and the Senate. There are a few critical differences, as you can see in the chart on page 345. Given the many similarities, there is no need here to trace a bill step-by-step through the Senate. However, it is important to look at those differences, and then at what happens to bills once they have passed in each house.

## Introducing the Bill

Bills are introduced by senators, who are formally recognized for that purpose. A measure is then given a number and short title, read twice, and referred to committee, where bills are dealt with much as they are in the House.

All in all, the Senate's proceedings are less formal and its rules less strict than those of the much larger House. For example, the Senate has only one calendar for all bills reported out by its committees. Bills are called to the floor at the discretion of the majority floor leader.[15]

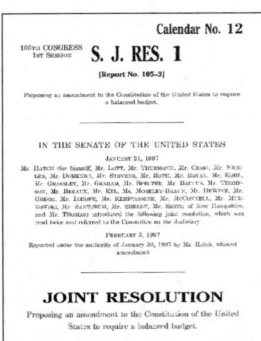

Calendar No. 12
105th CONGRESS
1st SESSION
**S. J. RES. 1**
[Report No. 105-3]

Proposing an amendment to the Constitution of the United States to require a balanced budget.

IN THE SENATE OF THE UNITED STATES

JANUARY 21, 1997

JOINT RESOLUTION
Proposing an amendment to the Constitution of the United States to require a balanced budget.

▲ **Senate bill**

---

[15]The Senate does have another, non-legislative calendar, the Executive Calendar, for treaties and appointments made by the President and awaiting Senate approval or, rarely, rejection. The majority leader controls that schedule, too.

## Rules for Debate

The major differences between House and Senate procedures involve debate. Floor debate is strictly limited in the House, but almost unrestrained in the Senate. In fact, most senators are intensely proud of belonging to what has often been called "the greatest deliberative body in the world."

As a general matter, senators may speak on the floor for as long as they please. Unlike the House, the Senate has no rule that requires a senator to speak only to the measure before the chamber; and the Senate's rules do not allow any member to move the previous question.

The Senate's consideration of most bills is brought to a close by unanimous consent agreements. That is, discussion ends and the chamber votes at a time previously agreed to by the majority and minority floor leaders. But if any senator objects—and so prevents unanimous consent—the procedure fails.

The Senate does have a "two-speech rule." Under this rule, no senator may speak more than twice on a given question on the same legislative day. By recessing—temporarily interrupting—rather than adjourning a day's session, the Senate can prolong a "legislative day" indefinitely. Thus, the two-speech rule can successfully limit the amount of time the Senate spends on some matters on its agenda.

The Senate's dedication to freedom of debate is almost unique among modern legislative bodies. That freedom is intended to encourage the

## Block Scheduling Strategies

Consider these suggestions to manage extended class time:

■ Ask students to consider whether the Senate filibuster is a valuable tool for debating proposed legislation or a political maneuver that diminishes congressional efficiency. Have students write editorials describing their points of view on the issue. Finally, have volunteers read segments of their editorials to the class. Make a class list of arguments for and against filibusters.

■ Prepare a number of flash cards on which are written various stages that a bill goes through in the Senate. For stages that can have more than one final outcome, write each possible outcome on separate cards and stack them. Have groups of students, taking turns, choose necessary cards to enact the path of a bill. For stages with several possible outcomes, students should choose cards randomly from the appropriate stack. After the class has finished, discuss the path the bill took and why it did so.

fullest possible discussion of matters on the floor. The great latitude it allows, however, can be abused by the filibuster.

## The Filibuster

Essentially, a **filibuster** is an attempt to "talk a bill to death." It is a stalling tactic, a process in which a minority of senators seeks to delay or prevent Senate action on a measure. The filibusterers try to so monopolize the Senate floor and its time that the Senate must either drop the bill or change it in some manner acceptable to the minority.

Talk—and more talk—is the filibusterers' major weapon. In addition, senators may use time-killing motions, quorum calls, and other parliamentary maneuvers. Indeed, anything to delay or obstruct is grist for the minority's mill as it works to block a bill that would very likely pass if brought to a vote.

Among the many better known filibusterers, Senator Huey Long (D., Louisiana) spoke for more than 15 hours in 1935. He stalled by reading from the Washington telephone directory and giving his colleagues his recipes for "potlikker," corn bread, and turnip greens. In 1947, Glen Taylor (D., Idaho) used more than eight hours of floor time talking of his children, Wall Street, baptism, and fishing. Senator Strom Thurmond (R., South Carolina) set the current filibuster record. He held the floor for 24 hours and 18 minutes in an unsuccessful, one-person effort against what later became the Civil Rights Act of 1957.

No later efforts have come close to matching that one. Still, the practice is often used and to great effect in the Senate. Over the past century and more, well over 200 measures have been killed by filibusters. Just the *threat* of a filibuster alone has resulted in the Senate's failure to consider a number of bills and the amending of many more.

The Senate often tries to beat off a filibuster with lengthy, even day-and-night, sessions to wear down the participants. At times, some little-observed rules are quite strictly enforced. Among them are the requirements that senators stand—not sit, lean on their desks, or walk about—as they speak and that they not use "unparliamentary language." These counter-measures seldom work, however.

▲ Senators rest on cots set up in the old Supreme Court Chamber during the filibuster that attempted to prevent passage of the Civil Rights Act of 1957. *Critical Thinking Why is a filibuster an effective way to kill legislation?*

## The Cloture Rule

The Senate's real check on the filibuster is its Cloture Rule, Rule XXII in the Standing Rules of the Senate. It was first adopted in 1917, after one of the most notable of all filibusters in Senate history. That filibuster lasted for three weeks, and took place less than two months before the United States entered World War I on April 6, 1917.

German submarines had renewed their attacks on shipping in the North Atlantic, so President Wilson asked Congress for legislation to permit the arming of American merchant vessels. The bill, widely supported in the country, was quickly passed by the House by a vote of 403–12. The measure died in the Senate, however, because twelve senators filibustered it until the end of the congressional term on March 4th.

The public was outraged. President Wilson declared: "A little group of willful men, representing no opinion but their own, has rendered the great Government of the United States helpless

## Reading Strategy

### Summarizing

Have students read the description of the filibuster on this page. Then ask them to summarize the process in their own words.

### A C T I V I T Y

### Learning Styles

**Logical/Linguistic** Present students with this quotation from the section: "All in all the Senate's proceedings are less formal than those of the much larger House." Direct students to use the quotation as the thesis statement for a brief essay. Students' essays should explain why the statement is true, referring to specific House and Senate procedures. They should also explain *why* this is the case, and identify implications of this situation to the legislative process.

**(Average)**

## Point–of–Use Resources

📖 **Guided Reading and Review** Unit 3 booklet, p. 28 provides students with practice identifying the main ideas and key terms of this section.

📖 **Lesson Plans** For lesson planning suggestions, see p. 56 of the Lesson Plans booklet.

📖 **Political Cartoons** See p. 48 of the Political Cartoons booklet for a cartoon relevant to this section.

📽 **Section Support Transparencies** Transparency 51, *Visual Learning*; Transparency 150, *Political Cartoon*

## Organizing Information

To make sure students understand the main points of this section, you may wish to use the double web graphic organizer to the right.

Tell students that a double web can be used to compare and contrast information about two main ideas. Ask students to use it to compare legislative processes in the House and the Senate.

**Teaching Tip** A template for this graphic organizer can be found in the Section Support Transparencies, Transparency 2.

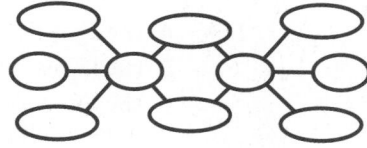

### Answer to . . .

**Critical Thinking** It prevents a bill from reaching the floor for consideration.

## Background Note

### Pirates in the Senate

The word *filibuster* shares its origin with the word *freebooter*—a pirate. This is understandable, since a filibustering Senator is attempting to "pirate" legislation: to intercept it before it reaches its intended destination. In fact, the phrase "pirating legislation" is often used to describe filibusters and other techniques designed to keep bills from passing.

## Point-of-Use Resources

📁 **Simulations and Debates** Senate Debate, pp. 24–33 helps students simulate mock senators as they debate and enact legislation.

📼 **ABC News Civics and Government Videotape Library** *The Federal Budget* (time: 2 minutes, 11 seconds)

💿 **Simulations and Data Graphing CD-ROM** offers data graphing tools that give students practice with creating and interpreting graphs.

### The Number of Bills that Become Laws*

| | |
|---|---|
| 10,238 | Bills introduced |
| 10,178 | Referred to or originated in committee |
| 1,205 | Reported or discharged by committee |
| 1,201 | Floor consideration |
| 1,184 | Passed one chamber |
| 667 | Passed both chambers |
| 590 | **Public laws** |

*Statistics represent only measures that can become public laws (bills and joint resolutions) and exclude simple and concurrent resolutions and private bills.

SOURCE: Ilona B. Nickels, Congressional Research Service, Library of Congress, Washington, D.C. Figures are for the 102nd Congress.

*Interpreting Charts* This chart illustrates the many stages through which a bill must pass before it becomes a law. *After which step do most bills "die"?*

and contemptible." The Senate passed the Cloture Rule at its next session, later that same year.

Rule XXII provides for **cloture,** or limiting debate. The rule is not in regular, continuing force; it can be brought into play only by a special procedure. A vote to invoke the rule must be taken two days after a petition calling for that action has been submitted by at least 16 members of the Senate. If at least 60 senators—three fifths of the full Senate—then vote for the motion, the rule becomes effective. From that point, no more than another 30 hours of floor time may be spent on the measure. Then it *must* be brought to a final vote.

Invoking the rule is no easy matter. So far, more than 400 attempts have been made to invoke the rule, and only about one third have succeeded. Many senators hesitate to support cloture motions for two reasons: (1) their

dedication to the Senate's tradition of free debate, and (2) their practical worry that the frequent use of cloture will undercut the value of the filibuster that they may some day want to use.

## Conference Committees

If you have ever watched a marathon, you know that no matter how well a runner covers the first 25 miles or so, he or she still has some distance to go in order to finish the race. So it is for bills in the legislative process. Even those that survive the long route through committees and rules and the floor in both houses still face some important steps before they can finally become law. Some of those final steps can be very difficult.

Any measure enacted by Congress *must* have been passed by both houses in identical form. Most often, a bill passed by one house and then approved by the other is not amended in the second chamber. When the House and Senate do pass different versions of the same bill, the first house usually concurs in the other's amendments, and congressional action is completed.

There are times when the House or the Senate will not accept the other's version of a bill. When this happens, the measure is turned over to a conference committee, a temporary joint committee of the two houses. It seeks to iron out the differences and come up with a compromise bill.

The conferees, or managers, are named by the respective presiding officers. Mostly, they are leading members of the standing committee that first handled the measure in each house.

Both the House and Senate rules restrict a conference committee to the consideration of those points in a bill on which the two houses disagree. The committee cannot include any new material in its compromise version. In practice, however, the conferees often make changes that were not even considered in either house.

Once the conferees agree, their report, the compromise bill, is submitted to both houses. It must be accepted or rejected without amendment. Only rarely does either house turn down a conference committee's work. This is not surprising, for two major reasons: (1) the powerful membership of the typical conference committee, and (2) the fact that its report usually comes in

## Answer to . . .

**Interpreting Charts** After the bills are referred to or originated in committees.

### Preparing for Standardized Tests

Have students read the passages under *Conference Committees* and then answer the question below.

Which statement best expresses the constitutional reason for conference committees in Congress?

**A** The Constitution requires such committees.

**B** The Constitution requires that both houses pass identical bills.

**C** The Constitution requires members of both houses to consult each other on issues of national concern.

**D** The Constitution requires that the President participate in committees.

## How a Bill Becomes a Law

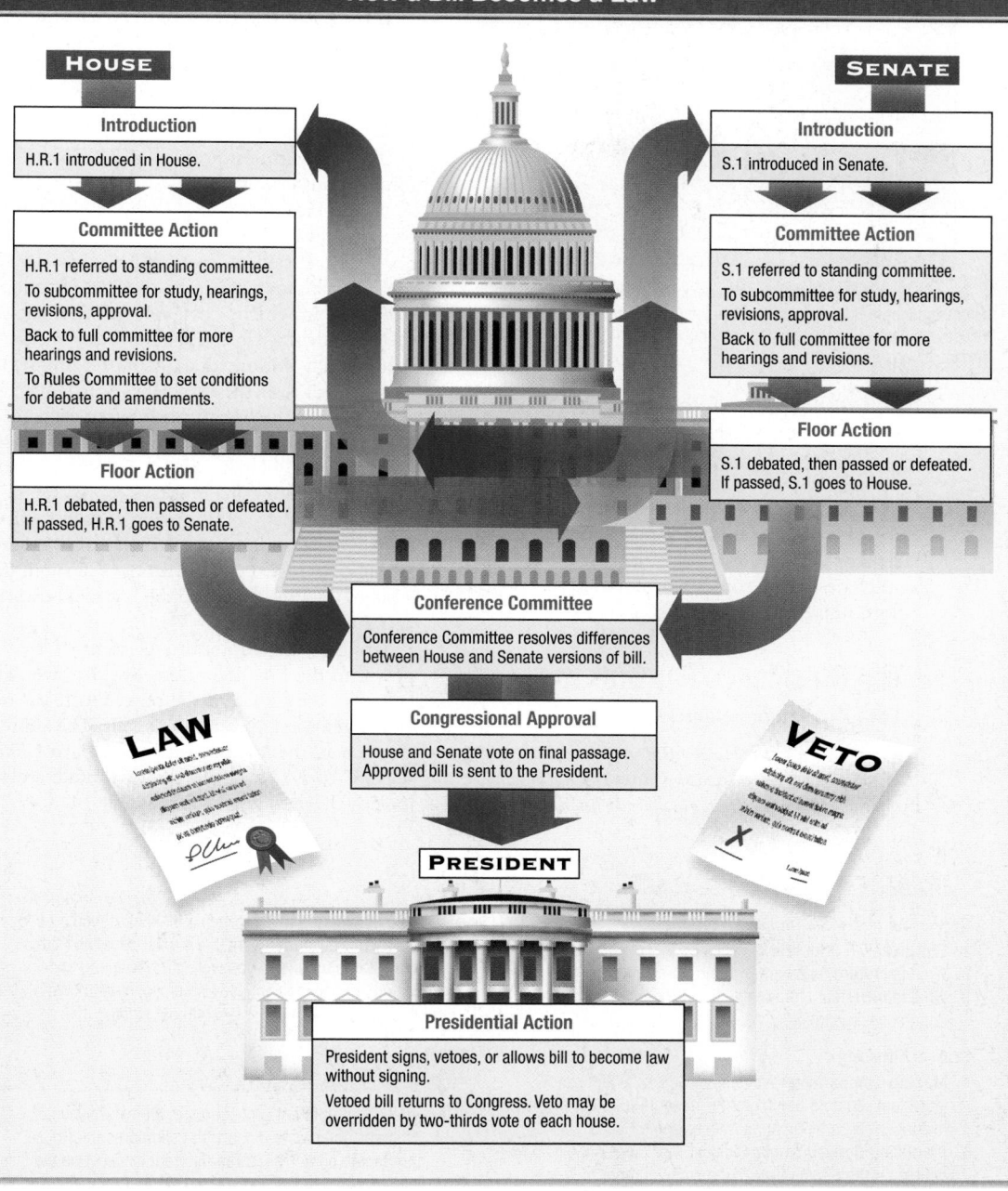

**HOUSE**

**Introduction**
H.R.1 introduced in House.

**Committee Action**
H.R.1 referred to standing committee.
To subcommittee for study, hearings, revisions, approval.
Back to full committee for more hearings and revisions.
To Rules Committee to set conditions for debate and amendments.

**Floor Action**
H.R.1 debated, then passed or defeated.
If passed, H.R.1 goes to Senate.

**SENATE**

**Introduction**
S.1 introduced in Senate.

**Committee Action**
S.1 referred to standing committee.
To subcommittee for study, hearings, revisions, approval.
Back to full committee for more hearings and revisions.

**Floor Action**
S.1 debated, then passed or defeated.
If passed, S.1 goes to House.

**Conference Committee**
Conference Committee resolves differences between House and Senate versions of bill.

**Congressional Approval**
House and Senate vote on final passage.
Approved bill is sent to the President.

**LAW**

**VETO**

**PRESIDENT**

**Presidential Action**
President signs, vetoes, or allows bill to become law without signing.
Vetoed bill returns to Congress. Veto may be overridden by two-thirds vote of each house.

*Interpreting Charts* A typical bill may be introduced in either house. It must be passed by each house before going to the President. ***In what way does the process of moving a bill through the House differ from the process in the Senate?***

## Answers to . . .

### Section 4 Assessment

**1.** It is meant to be a stalling tactic, whereby a minority of senators can monopolize the Senate floor until the bill is dropped or until the bill is changed to suit the minority.
**2.** Cloture is a measure for limiting debate; it is hard to achieve because it requires a three-fifths vote of the full Senate. Most senators are reluctant to invoke it because the use of filibusters is both useful and traditional.
**3.** When a President vetoes a bill, it must be returned to the house in which it originated. Congress may respond by passing the bill over the President's veto with a two-thirds vote of the members in each house.
**4.** Possible answer: Because the Senate has the final vote on whether a bill will be passed or killed, senators' unlimited debate privileges ensure that issues receive the fullest possible consideration before they are resolved.
**5.** Possible answer: It would be harder, because the minority group in the Senate can use the tactic of the filibuster, while the same group in the House could not.
**6.** Answers will vary; students might suggest that by allowing a bill to become law without signing it, or by using a pocket veto, the President can make a decision on a bill that he or she doesn't feel strongly enough about to either sign or veto outright.

▲ **Tax Cut Proposal** President Bush transmitted his tax cut proposal to Congress during a Rose Garden ceremony on February 8, 2001. The President is flanked by Hispanic businesspersons Maria Taxman, Hector Barreto, Jr., and Anna Cablik.

the midst of the rush to adjournment at the end of a congressional session.

The conference committee stage is a most strategic step in the legislative process. A number of major legislative decisions and compromises are often made at that point. Indeed, the late Senator George Norris (R., Nebraska) once quite aptly described conference committees as "the third house of Congress."

## The President's Powers

The Constitution requires that

 **Constitution** *"Every Bill which shall have passed the House of Representatives and the Senate, . . . [and] Every Order,* Resolution, or Vote to which the Concurrence of the Senate and House of Representatives may be necessary (except on a question of Adjournment) shall be presented to the President. . . . *"*
—Article I, Section 7, Clauses 2 and 3

The Constitution presents the President with four options at this point:

1. The President may sign the bill, and it then becomes law.
2. The President may **veto**—refuse to sign the bill. The measure must then be returned to the house in which it originated, together with the President's objections (a veto message). Although it seldom does, Congress may then pass the bill over the President's veto, by a two-thirds vote of the full membership of each house.
3. The President may allow the bill to become law without signing it—by not acting on it within 10 days, not counting Sundays, of receiving it.
4. The fourth option is a variation of the third, called the **pocket veto.** If Congress adjourns its session within 10 days of submitting a bill to the President, and the President does not act, the measure dies.

Congress added another element to the veto power in the Line Item Veto Act of 1996. That law gave the President the power to reject individual items in appropriations bills. The Supreme Court held the law unconstitutional, in *Clinton v. New York City,* 1998. You will take a closer look at the veto power in Chapter 14.

## Section **4** Assessment

**Key Terms and Main Ideas**
1. Explain how a **filibuster** is designed to work.
2. What is **cloture,** and why is it hard to achieve?
3. What is the effect of a President's **veto,** and how can Congress respond?

**Critical Thinking**
4. **Making Comparisons** Why do the Senate's rules allow individual senators much greater freedom to affect the law-making process than can members of the House?
5. **Predicting Consequences** Suppose that there is a bill up for debate on the Senate floor, but a small number of determined members oppose it. Would it be easier or harder for a majority of senators to pass such a bill than it would be for a majority of House members in a similar situation? Why?
6. **Drawing Conclusions** If you were the President, under what circumstances might you use a pocket veto? Why might you let a bill become law without signing it?

 **Take It to the Net**

7. Read about different procedures in the two houses of Congress and create a chart that compares the House and Senate on at least three different issues. Use the links provided in the Social Studies area at the following Web site for help in completing this activity. **www.phschool.com**

 **Take It to the Net**

7. Direct students to the Social Studies area at the Prentice Hall School Web site. The *Magruder's American Government* companion Web site includes the directions and links needed to complete the activity. It also provides a printable Internet activity worksheet with scoring rubrics for assessment. Charts should be clearly organized and should accurately contrast the two houses.

# on the Supreme Court

# How Broad Is Congress's Power to Investigate?

*Congress has broad authority to conduct investigations as part of the legislative process. Through investigations, Congress can evaluate existing laws and determine whether new laws are needed. How far can Congress go in these investigations?*

## *Watkins v. United States* (1957)

During the 1950s, the House Un-American Activities Committee (HUAC) investigated possible communist activities and influence in various areas of American life. John Watkins, a leader in the labor movement, was called to testify before a subcommittee of HUAC. In response to questions, he described his background in union activities and his connections with the Communist Party.

A lawyer for the committee then read a list of names to Watkins and asked him to identify the ones he knew to have been members of the Communist Party. Watkins stated that he was willing to answer questions about people who he believed were currently party members, but that he would not identify or answer questions about those who he believed had withdrawn from party membership.

The House requested that the United States attorney prosecute Watkins for his refusal to answer these questions. He was tried, found guilty, and fined $100. His prison sentence (one year) was suspended and he was placed on probation. A three-judge panel of the court of appeals reversed the conviction, but the full court of appeals later approved the conviction. The case then went to the Supreme Court.

## Arguments for Watkins

1. Congressional investigations must relate to legitimate subjects of legislative concern. Congress may not force witnesses to testify merely to embarrass or punish people whose beliefs may be unpopular.
2. The questions to Watkins interfered with his First Amendment rights of speech, political belief, and association.

3. The subject matter of a congressional investigation must be stated so that witnesses can decide whether the questions posed to them are relevant to the investigation.

## Arguments for the United States

1. Congress has broad authority to investigate matters of national concern, and may require citizens to provide information that may be relevant to these investigations. The Court may not dictate the manner in which Congress conducts its investigations.
2. The questions Watkins refused to answer were sufficiently related to the subject of communist influence in labor organizations. Witnesses should not be permitted to pick and choose which questions they will answer.
3. Although some individuals may be "exposed" as a result of witness testimony, there is no violation of First Amendment rights when Congress has a legitimate reason to ask its questions.

### Decide for Yourself

1. Review the constitutional grounds on which each side based its arguments and the specific arguments each side presented.
2. Debate the opposing viewpoints presented in this case. Which viewpoint do you favor?
3. Predict the impact of the Court's decision on other types of congressional investigations. (To read a summary of the Court's decision, turn to the Supreme Court Glossary on page 799.)

---

## *Corner*

📁 **Close Up on the Supreme Court** *Watkins* v. *United States,* p. 13 provides an activity to extend coverage of this case.

 **Online**

To keep up-to-date on Close Up news and activities, visit Close Up Online at

**www.closeup.org**

---

## How Broad is Congress's Power to Investigate?

**Focus** Review Congress's nonlegislative powers. *(See Chapter 11, Section 4.)* Then explain that impeachment and investigation involve powers similar to those held by the judicial branch, such as the power to call and question witnesses. Discuss whether Congress should be required to follow the same constitutional safeguards as courts when it performs these functions. Then explain that this case considers whether Congress may punish a witness who refuses to cooperate with a congressional investigation.

**Instruct** Have students identify the constitutional provisions relevant to the case. *(The Fifth Amendment Due Process Clause and the First Amendment)* Then have the class read and discuss the Court's decision and outline it on the blackboard using the briefing technique discussed in the Chapter 3 *Close Up on the Supreme Court* feature.

**Close/Reteach** Have a volunteer define the term *select committee. (A legislative committee created for a limited time and some specific purpose)* For homework, have students research the activities of a recent select committee.

💿 **Keep It Current CD-ROM** includes government-related projects by unit. The CD-ROM links to the Prentice Hall School Web site and may be used for daily updates.

### *Answers to . . .*
**Decide for Yourself**
**1.** Watkins cited the First Amendment rights of speech, political belief, and association in his argument that the committee asked him irrelevant questions. The United States cited Congress's authority to investigate matters of national concern as it sees fit, as long as questions are legitimate.
**2.** Answers will vary, but should be supported with valid reasoning.
**3.** The Court ruled in favor of Watkins, saying that the questions violated his due process right.

## Practicing the Vocabulary

1. party caucus
2. discharge petition
3. quorum
4. rider
5. select committee
6. *Resolution*; Resolution does not relate to issues of selecting committee leaders or other posts; a resolution is a measure passed by Congress.
7. *Whip*; Items *a, c,* and *d* are measures that affect the handling of bills; a whip is a party officer.
8. *Committee chairman*; Items *a, b,* and *c* are all presiding officers in Congress; committee chairs do not preside over Congress.
9. *Discharge petition*; Items *b, c,* and *d* are types of congressional measures; a discharge petition forces a bill onto the floor.
10. *Cloture*; Items *b, c,* and *d* all relate to the passage of bills; cloture is a means to limit debate.

## Reviewing Main Ideas
### Section 1

11. **(a)** House: all members must be sworn in; presiding officers and other officials are elected; rules are adopted; committees members are appointed. Senate: newly elected and reelected members are sworn in. **(b)** As the Senate is a continuous body, it does not need much reorganization.
12. Both officers preside over their houses; the Speaker of the House also carries out the goals of his or her party, keeps order, and carries out the duties of regular House members.
13. **(a)** It provides that the most important posts in Congress are held by those party members with the longest records of service. **(b)** That it ignores ability, discourages younger members, and draws from "safe" districts.

### Section 2
14. They investigate the issues, get the bill placed on the floor, and resolve conflicts in versions of bills.
15. **(a)** Standing, select, House Rules, joint, and conference. **(b)** Standing: study bills on particular subjects; House Rules: screen the bills prior to putting them on the floor; select: handle particular, temporary purposes; joint and conference: resolve disputes and make compromise bills.
16. Committees.

## Political Dictionary

Speaker of the House (p. 322)
president of the Senate (p. 323)
president *pro tempore* (p. 323)
party caucus (p. 324)
floor leader (p. 324)
whip (p. 325)
committee chairman (p. 325)
seniority rule (p. 326)
standing committee (p. 329)

select committee (p. 331)
joint committee (p. 333)
conference committee (p. 333)
bill (p. 334)
joint resolution (p. 335)
concurrent resolution (p. 335)
resolution (p. 335)
rider (p. 335)
discharge petition (p. 336)

subcommittee (p. 336)
Committee of the Whole (p. 339)
quorum (p. 339)
engrossed (p. 340)
filibuster (p. 343)
cloture (p. 344)
veto (p. 346)
pocket veto (p. 346)

## Practicing the Vocabulary

**Matching** *Choose a term from the list above that best matches each description.*

1. Selects the party's leaders in each house of Congress
2. Can force a committee to bring a bill to the floor of the House or Senate
3. The minimum number of legislators needed to perform official business
4. A provision added to a popular bill because it is unlikely to succeed on its own
5. A legislative committee created for a limited time and specific purpose

**Word Relationships** *Three of the terms in each of the following sets are related. Choose the term that does not belong and explain why it does not.*

6. **(a)** committee chairman **(b)** seniority rule **(c)** party caucus **(d)** resolution
7. **(a)** filibuster **(b)** whip **(c)** cloture **(d)** discharge petition
8. **(a)** Speaker of the House **(b)** president of the Senate **(c)** president *pro tempore* **(d)** committee chairman
9. **(a)** discharge petition **(b)** resolution **(c)** bill **(d)** concurrent resolution
10. **(a)** rider **(b)** bill **(c)** quorum **(d)** resolution

## Reviewing Main Ideas

### Section 1
11. **(a)** What happens at the opening sessions in the House and the Senate? **(b)** What makes those events different in the two houses?
12. What are the duties of the presiding officers in the House and Senate?
13. **(a)** How does the seniority rule function? **(b)** What are two criticisms of the seniority rule?

### Section 2
14. What role do committees play in turning bills into laws?
15. **(a)** What are the different types of committees? **(b)** What are the duties of each type of committee?
16. What are the sources of the bills introduced into Congress?

### Section 3
17. What happens to a bill once it enters the House?
18. **(a)** How is a resolution different from a bill? **(b)** Describe the different types of resolutions.
19. What options does a committee have when reviewing a bill?
20. **(a)** How have debate and voting rules in the House changed in the past two centuries? **(b)** What are the benefits of these changes?

### Section 4
21. **(a)** What are the rules of a filibuster? **(b)** How can the Senate defeat a filibuster?
22. What is the purpose of a conference committee?
23. What are the President's options when he receives a bill from Congress?

### Section 3
17. It is given a title and a number, printed, and distributed to House members; sent to the appropriate standing committee; debated on the House floor; and voted on.
18. **(a)** Joint resolutions usually deal with unusual or temporary matters; concurrent resolutions do not have the force of law; resolutions only involve one house. **(b)** Joint: deal with unusual or temporary matters and have the force of law; concurrent: require the houses to act jointly, usually to state a position, and do not have the force of law.
19. Report it favorably; pigeonhole it; amend it; report it unfavorably; or report a new bill.
20. **(a)** Rules have been instituted that place severe limits on floor debate; also, a computerized voting system has replaced the traditional roll call. **(b)** They have saved time and streamlined procedures.

### Section 4
21. **(a)** Senators must stand as they speak and not use "unparliamentary language." **(b)** It can invoke cloture, or wear down the participants.
22. To resolve differences between versions of the same bill.
23. Sign the bill into law; veto the bill; allow the bill to become law without signing it; or use a pocket veto.

**348**

## Critical Thinking Skills

**24.** *Applying the Chapter Skill* Analyze the validity of a primary source for point of view. Find a recent newspaper editorial dealing with a bill or debate in Congress. After reading the editorial, do your own research to learn more about the writer. What is the writer's point of view? Who is the intended audience?

**25.** *Drawing Inferences* Why does the President's State of the Union address play an important part in each congressional session? What are some possible ways that Congress can react to the speech?

**26.** *Expressing Problems Clearly* In your opinion, should the steps needed for a bill to become law be simplified? Support your argument with examples of bills that have been defeated and/or passed into law.

**27.** *Identifying Assumptions* Consider what you have read about the seniority rule. What does the seniority rule imply about qualifications for leadership?

## Analyzing Political Cartoons

Using your knowledge of American government and this cartoon, answer the questions below.

**28. (a)** If the flowers and gift represent new legislation, what might the pigs represent? **(b)** What legislative practice is represented by tying the pigs to the flowers and the gift?

**29.** How might a representative respond to the cartoonist to defend this legislative practice?

---

### ★ You Can Make a Difference

What would you say to a roomful of senators and news reporters? Use the opportunity to express and defend a point of view on an issue of contemporary interest in the United States. First identify a cause or issue about which you feel strongly. Then write a proposed bill that presents a way to address that problem. Your bill would be sent to Congress in hopes of becoming a law. Finally, prepare a statement that you would make at a Senate hearing, introducing and defending your proposal. Practice reading your statement aloud as you get ready to "testify" before your class.

## Participation Activities

**30.** *Current Events Watch* Scan news reports for examples of two of the following: a bill that dies in Congress, a bill that passes Congress but is vetoed by the President, and a bill that passes Congress and is signed by the President. Clip two articles and create a wall chart with each class member's contributions.

**31.** *Graphing Activity* Create a circle graph showing the percentage of bills introduced in Congress that actually became laws during the current session. Then create a second graph showing the same information from the 106th Congress, when a Democratic President governed with a Republican Congress, and the 103rd Congress, when a Democratic President governed with a Democratic Congress. Who controls these branches today, and how do the rates of passage compare?

**32.** *It's Your Turn* You have just been elected to the House. Write a letter to your local newspaper in which you talk about the bills you would like to see Congress pass and what steps you will take to make that happen. Also, describe the committees on which you would like to serve and how they will meet the needs of your district. Conclude your letter by listing three challenges you expect to encounter in the House. Did you use standard grammar, spelling, sentence structure, and punctuation? Proofread and revise to correct errors. Then draft a final copy. **(Writing a Letter)**

###  Take It to the Net

**Chapter 12 Self-Test** As a final review activity, take the Chapter 12 Self-Test in the Social Studies area at the Web site listed below, and receive immediate feedback on your answers.

**www.phschool.com**

---

 **Take It to the Net**

Additional support materials and activities for Chapter 12 of *Magruder's American Government* can be found in the Social Studies area at the Prentice Hall School Web site. **www.phschool.com**

---

## Critical Thinking Skills

**24.** Answers will vary, but should comment on the validity of the source by accurately assessing the writers' point of view and intended audience, and should be supported with specific examples.
**25.** The State of the Union address is important because it shares the policies the President intends to pursue that year with Congress, the American public, and the world. Congressional members or party leaders may respond to the address by publicizing their own agendas for the year.
**26.** Answers will vary, but should show an understanding of the steps by which a bill becomes a law, and should be supported with specific examples.
**27.** The seniority rule suggests that one of the most important qualifications for leadership is experience.

### Analyzing Political Cartoons
**28. (a)** Possible answer: Legislation that is not likely to be received as well as that represented by the flowers and gift. **(b)** The use of riders.
**29.** Answers will vary, but should demonstrate an understanding of the legislative practices discussed in this chapter.

### You Can Make a Difference
Proposed bills should clearly identify a problem and a solution; statements should be convincing and well delivered.

### Participation Activities
**30.** Wall charts should be clearly organized and contain several examples from each category.
**31.** Graphs should accurately reflect the percentages and should be clear and easy to read.
**32.** Letters will vary but should demonstrate a basic understanding of the responsibilities of a representative and of the committee system.

## Point–of–Use Resources

 **Guide to the Essentials of American Government** Chapter 12 Test, page 70 provides multiple-choice questions to test students' knowledge of the chapter.

**Test Bank CD-ROM** Chapter 12 Test

**Chapter Test** Chapter Tests booklet

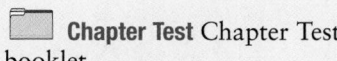

## The Executive Branch

### Introducing the Unit

Unit 4 introduces students to the powers and responsibilities of the President. Chapter 13 examines the duties of the President, the presidential succession process, the qualifications for the office, the nominating process, the presidential campaign, and the role of the electoral college. Chapter 14 explores the nature and extent of the executive power, the diplomatic, military, legislative, and judicial powers of the President, and the functions of the executive agencies and the Cabinet. Chapter 15 explores the federal bureaucracy, the function of the executive departments and independent agencies, and the civil service. Chapter 16 analyzes how the Federal Government raises, borrows, and spends money. Chapter 17 examines the past and present goals, features, and structure of America's foreign and defense policies, the purposes of American foreign aid and defense alliances, as well as the role of the United Nations.

### Focus Activity

Concentrate students' attention on the executive branch by writing the following quotation on the board:

*"When I ran for the presidency...I knew this country faced serious challenges, but I could not realize—nor could any man who does not bear the burdens of this office—how heavy and constant would be those burdens."*
—President John F. Kennedy

Have students consider the following after they have read the quotation.

◆ What "challenges" might Kennedy have been referring to?
◆ If it were possible for presidential candidates to be fully aware of the "burdens" of the presidency, do you think that they would still run for office? Why or why not?
◆ Use these questions as springboards to a general class discussion about students' views of the executive branch.

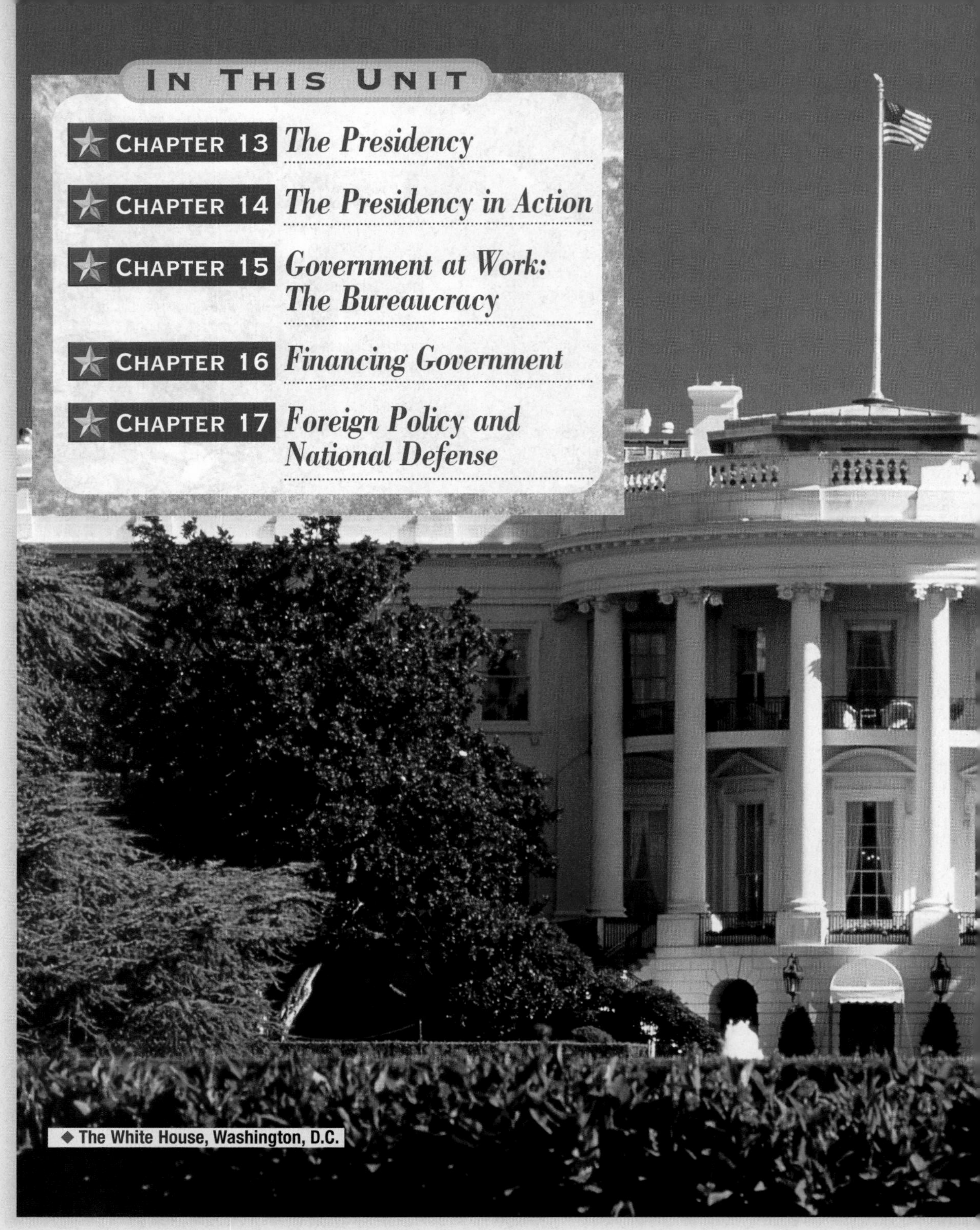

◆ The White House, Washington, D.C.

 *Corner*

The following Close Up features appear in this unit.
*Close Up on the Supreme Court* may be found on the following pages: 385, 409, 441, 463, 499
*Close Up on Primary Sources* may be found on the following pages: 364, 404, 423, 457, 476

 **Online**

To keep up-to-date on Close Up news and activities, visit Close Up Online at
**www.closeup.org**

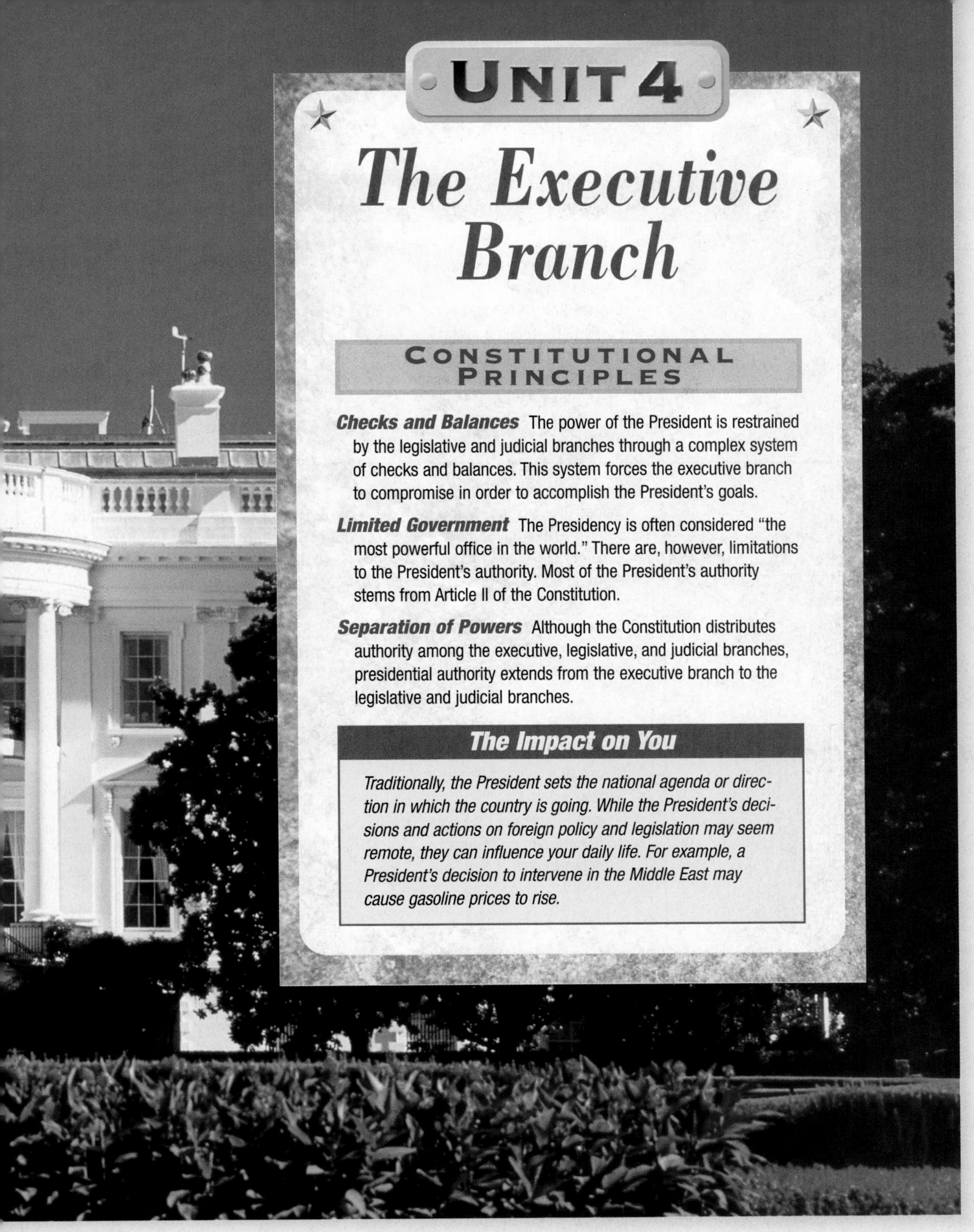

# UNIT 4

# The Executive Branch

## CONSTITUTIONAL PRINCIPLES

***Checks and Balances*** The power of the President is restrained by the legislative and judicial branches through a complex system of checks and balances. This system forces the executive branch to compromise in order to accomplish the President's goals.

***Limited Government*** The Presidency is often considered "the most powerful office in the world." There are, however, limitations to the President's authority. Most of the President's authority stems from Article II of the Constitution.

***Separation of Powers*** Although the Constitution distributes authority among the executive, legislative, and judicial branches, presidential authority extends from the executive branch to the legislative and judicial branches.

### The Impact on You

*Traditionally, the President sets the national agenda or direction in which the country is going. While the President's decisions and actions on foreign policy and legislation may seem remote, they can influence your daily life. For example, a President's decision to intervene in the Middle East may cause gasoline prices to rise.*

## Pressed for Time?

### Instruction Plus!

The resources you need to support your instruction of this chapter are conveniently located in a single box. This innovative package provides an instructional advantage in the classroom with its ready-to-use tools in a variety of formats.

- **Magruder's American Government Video Collection**
- **Keep It Current Web-based Activities Presentation Pro CD-ROM**
- **Section Support Transparencies**
- **Guide to the Essentials Current Issues**

## Spotlight on Technology

**Take it to the Net**
Offers student-appropriate Internet activities and links that extend core content. Visit us at the Social Studies area. **www.phschool.com**
Be sure to check out this month's **eTeach** online discussion with a Master Government Teacher.

**Keep It Current CD-ROM** Includes government-related projects by unit. Use it to link to the Prentice Hall School Web site where you will find daily updates.

**Magruder's American Government Video Collection**
Chapter-by-chapter video selections bring key government concepts to life.

**ABC News Civics and Government Videotape Library**
These high-interest stories from ABC News relate to core content.

**Simulations and Data Graphing CD-ROM** Provides interactive federal budget and stock market simulations, and skills practice with statistical data.

**Prentice Hall Presentation Pro CD-ROM** Provides multimedia lecture notes for each chapter.

**ExamView® Test Bank CD-ROM** Allows you to create, edit, and print out chapter level tests.

**Resource Pro® CD-ROM** Teaching Resources that offer lesson planning flexibility, test-generation capability, and resource manageability.

**Social Studies Skills Tutor CD-ROM** Provides interactive practice in geographic literacy, critical thinking and reading, visual analysis, and communications.

**Section Support Transparencies** Illustrates key government concepts through graphs, charts, photos, and cartoons.

**Basic Principles of the Constitution Transparencies**
Illustrates key principles of the Constitution.

**Section Reading Support Transparency System**
Delivers the main idea of each section in the student text through graphic organizers.

# The Presidency

| Section Objectives | Print and Technology Resources |
|---|---|
| **1 The President's Job Description** (pp. 354–358) 1. Identify the President's many roles. 2. Understand the formal qualifications necessary to become President. 3. Discuss issues involving the length of the President's term. 4. Describe the President's pay and benefits. **TEKS 9B, 21A, 21E, 22A, 22B** | • **Unit 4 booklet** Guided Reading and Review, p. 2 Section 1 Quiz, p. 3 • **Lesson Plans booklet** Section 1, p. 57 • **Political Cartoons booklet** Section 1, p. 49 • **Block Scheduling with Lesson Strategies booklet** p. 25 • **Close Up on Primary Sources booklet** *The Federalist*, No. 71, p. 67 • **Government Assessment Rubrics booklet** p. 22 • **Section Support Transparencies** 52, 151 • **Presentation Pro CD-ROM** Section 1 • **Section Reading Support Transparencies** |
| **2 Presidential Succession and the Vice Presidency** (pp. 359–363) 1. Explain how the Constitution provides for presidential succession. 2. Understand the Constitutional provisions for presidential disability. 3. Describe the role of the Vice President. **TEKS 9B, 21A, 21B, 21C, 21D, 21E, 22A, 22B, 22D** | • **Unit 4 booklet** Guided Reading and Review, p. 4 Section 2 Quiz, p. 5 • **Lesson Plans booklet** Section 2, p. 58 • **Political Cartoons booklet** Section 2, p. 50 • **Close Up on Primary Sources booklet** The Office of Vice President, p. 15; George Washington, Farewell Address, p. 33 • **The Living Constitution booklet** p. 15 • **Basic Principles of the Constitution Transparencies** 4 • **Section Support Transparencies** 53, 152 • **Presentation Pro CD-ROM** Section 2 • **Section Reading Support Transparencies** |
| **3 Presidential Selection: The Framer's Plan** (pp. 365–367) 1. Explain the Framers' original provisions for choosing the President. 2. Outline how the rise of political parties changed the original provisions set out in the Constitution. **TEKS 2B, 9B, 11B, 12C, 21A, 21E, 22A, 22B** | • **Unit 4 booklet** Guided Reading and Review, p. 6 Section 3 Quiz, p. 7 • **Lesson Plans booklet** Section 3, p. 59 • **Section Reading Support Transparencies** • **Political Cartoons booklet** Section 3, p. 51 • **Section Support Transparencies** 54, 153 • **Presentation Pro CD-ROM** Section 3 |
| **4 Presidential Nominations** (pp. 368–375) 1. Describe the role of conventions in the presidential nominating process. 2. Evaluate the importance of presidential primaries. 3. Understand the role of the caucus-convention process. 4. Outline the events that take place during a national convention. 5. Examine the characteristics that determine who is nominated as a presidential candidate. **TEKS 11B, 12C, 12D, 16D, 20A, 21A, 21B, 21C, 21D, 21E, 22A, 22B, 22D, 23A, 23B** | • **Unit 4 booklet** Guided Reading and Review, p. 8 Section 4 Quiz, p. 9 • **Lesson Plans booklet** Section 4, p. 60 • **Political Cartoons booklet** Section 4, p. 52 • **Block Scheduling with Lesson Strategies booklet** p. 25 • **Close Up on Primary Sources booklet** Barbara Jordan: Keynote Address to the Democratic National Convention, p. 49 • **The Living Constitution booklet** p. 3 • **Government Assessment Rubrics booklet** p. 24 • **Simulations and Debates booklet** pp. 42–43 • **Section Support Transparencies** 55, 154 • **Presentation Pro CD-ROM** Section 4 • **Simulations and Data Graphing CD-ROM** • **Section Reading Support Transparencies** • **Social Studies Skills Tutor CD-ROM** |
| **5 The Election** (pp. 377–384) 1. Understand the function of the electoral college today. 2. Describe the flaws in the electoral college system. 3. Outline the advantages and disadvantages of proposed reforms in the electoral college. **TEKS 11A, 17C, 21A, 21B, 21C, 21E, 22A, 22B, 22C, 22D, 23A** | • **Unit 4 booklet** Guided Reading and Review, p. 10 Section 5 Quiz, p. 11 Skills for Life Activity, p. 12 • **Lesson Plans booklet** Section 5, p. 61 • **Political Cartoons booklet** Section 5, p. 53 • **Close Up on the Supreme Court booklet** *Nixon* v. *Fitzgerald*, p. 14 • **Simulations and Debates booklet** pp. 56–58 • **The Basic Principles of the Constitution Posters** • **Section Support Transparencies** 56, 155 • **Presentation Pro CD-ROM** Section 5 • **Section Reading Support Transparencies** |

# Block Scheduling Strategies

The *Magruder's American Government* program addresses block-scheduling strategies in a variety of ways. For easy reference, side-column activities that fit a block format are marked ■ **Block Strategy.** Each section also contains a **Block Scheduling Strategies** box describing at least two block-format activities that address and extend core content from the section. The **Block Scheduling with Lesson Strategies booklet** found in the Teaching Resources contains additional block-scheduling activities for each chapter.

## Take It to the Net

Visit the Social Studies area at the Prentice Hall School Web site. Once there, you can find additional links, current events connections, and activities to enrich chapter content for *Magruder's American Government,* as well as a Self-Test for students. Be sure to check out this month's **eTeach** online discussion with a Master Teacher.

### www.phschool.com

## Pressed for Time?

If you are running short on time to cover this chapter, consider one of the following options:
- Use the **Presentation Pro CD-ROM** to create an outline for this chapter.
- Use one of the **Pressed for Time** activities found on p. 353.
- Use the Section Summaries for Chapter 13, from **Guide to the Essentials of American Government (English and Spanish).**

## Video Connections

Prentice Hall offers two video programs to reinforce and extend chapter content. Show students *The Blessings of Liberty* from the **ABC News Civics and Government Videotape Library** and *Prayer in Schools: A Nationwide Debate* from the **Magruder's American Government Video Collection.**

## Assessment Options
- Section Quizzes, **Unit 4 booklet,** pp. 3, 5, 7, 9, 11
- Chapter 13 Assessment, pp. 386–387
- **Guide to the Essentials of American Government,** Chapter 13 Test, p. 76

PRENTICE HALL ASSESSMENT SYSTEM

### Core Assessment
Chapter 13 Test, Chapter Tests booklet
ExamView® Test Bank CD-ROM Chapter 13
Government Assessment Rubrics

### Standardized Test Preparation
#### Diagnose and Prescribe
Diagnostic Tests for High School
Social Studies Skills

#### Review and Reteach
Review Book for Government

#### Practice and Assess
Test-Taking Strategies With
    Transparencies for High School
Test Prep Book for Government

# Chapter 13 Teacher's Edition Index

# CHAPTER 13

## The Presidency

### Introducing the Chapter

In this chapter students will learn about the eight roles the President has, and the processes by which he or she is elected.

### Make It Relevant

**You Can Make a Difference**

Have the class develop a plan for a program similar to "Grandma's Gifts." Students should identify a segment of the population they wish to help, determine how to obtain the needed goods or services, decide how to contact and screen potential recipients, and develop a distribution program. Consider organizing the class into separate work groups to address each task, and guiding them as they implement their program.

**Service Learning**

### Constitutional Principles

Emphasize the following basic principles as students read Chapter 13. Have the class respond to the questions, and then ask volunteers to explain which single principle they most closely associate with the presidency, and why.

**Popular Sovereignty** How were U.S. Presidents originally selected? What event(s) led to a change in this system?

**Separation of Powers** How do the various roles that the President fulfills blur the separation of powers that exist between the three branches of the U.S. government? What role does the President have in setting the legislative agenda?

CHAPTER 13

# The Presidency

*"The presidency has made every man who occupied it, no matter how small, bigger than he was, and no matter how big, not big enough for its demands."*

—Lyndon B. Johnson (1972)

As President Johnson knew, the responsibilities of the President can be overwhelming. The President not only leads the government and the nation, but also heads a political party. Even before he or she reaches the White House, the long and arduous campaign process tests the President's mettle.

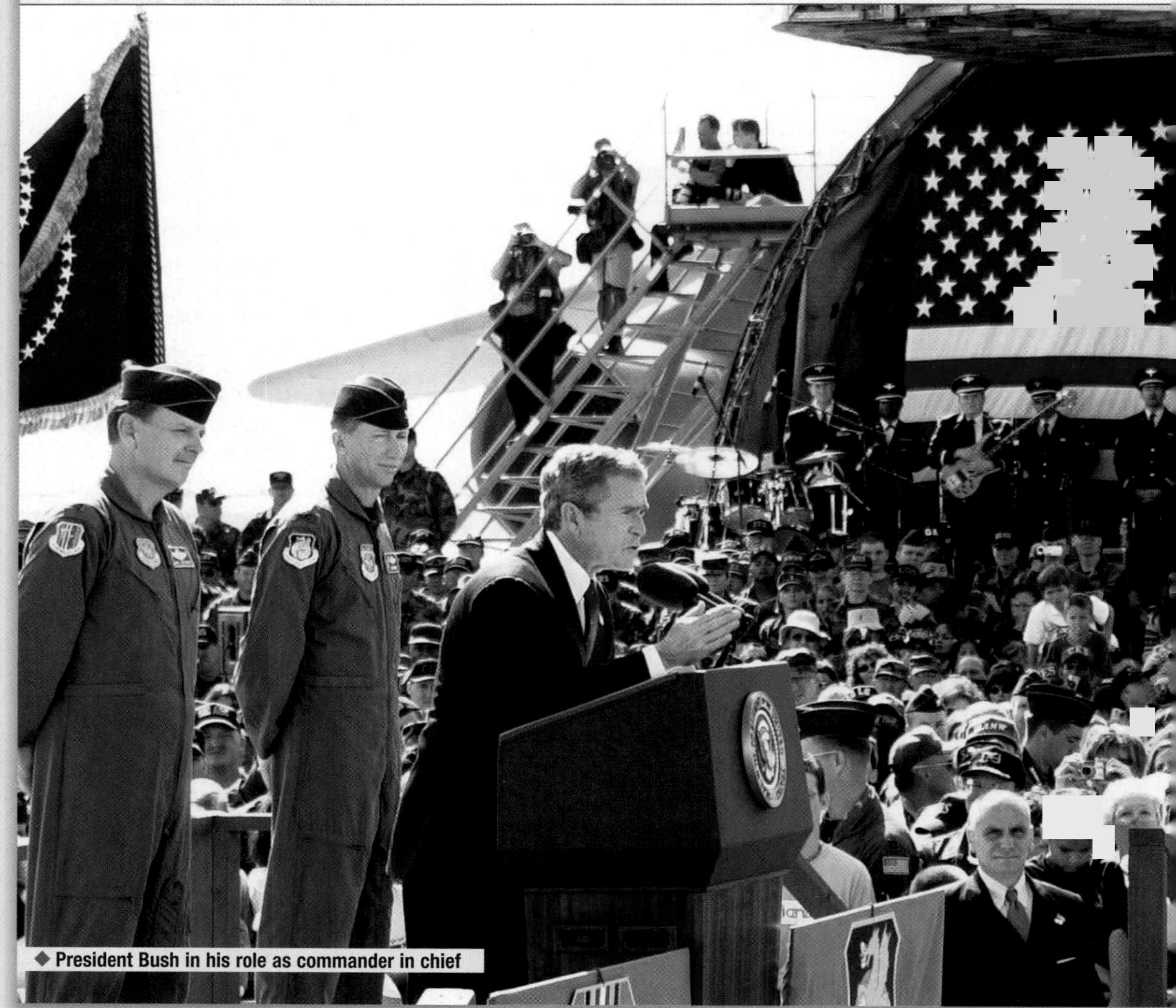

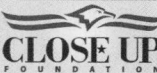

◆ President Bush in his role as commander in chief

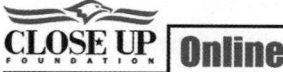

### CLOSE UP FOUNDATION Corner

The following resources are available only from the Close Up Foundation to support the concepts discussed in Chapter 13 "The Presidency":

- *Perspectives: Readings on Contemporary American Government*
- *Talking Peace: A Vision for the Next Generation*
- *We the People: The President and the Constitution*

**CLOSE UP FOUNDATION Online**

To keep up-to-date on Close Up news and activities, visit Close Up Online at

**www.closeup.org**

Close Up Foundation
44 Canal Center Plaza
Alexandria, VA 22314-1592
800-765-3131

## ★ You Can Make a Difference

AS **"CHIEF CITIZEN"** of the United States, the President recognizes other citizens for their volunteer service. In 1999, the winners of the President's Service Award included one teenager— Emily Douglas, 17, of Powell, Ohio. Eight years earlier, Emily started "Grandma's Gifts," inspired by her grandmother's stories of growing up poor in Appalachia. Emily's organization began small, with holiday presents for poor families. Soon it was giving food, clothing, books, and toys to children in Ohio, Kentucky, and West Virginia. With support from corporations and others, "Grandma's Gifts" has helped more than 18,500 children.

### Keep It Current

Items marked with this logo are periodically updated on the Internet. Keep up-to-date with what's in the news. To get current information on the presidency and the election process, go to **www.phschool.com**

### SECTION 1
### The President's Job Description (pp. 354–358)

★ The President has eight major roles, which are exercised simultaneously.
★ The Constitution outlines the formal qualifications for the presidency.
★ Presidents are limited to two four-year terms.
★ Congress determines the President's salary.

### SECTION 2
### Presidential Succession and the Vice Presidency (pp. 359–363)

★ The Constitution provides for an orderly succession of power if the President dies or leaves office.
★ The Constitution provides for the transfer of power should the President become disabled.
★ Although the vice presidency is often belittled, the Vice President is "a heartbeat away" from becoming President.

### SECTION 3
### Presidential Selection: The Framers' Plan (pp. 365–367)

★ The Framers created the electoral college for choosing the President and Vice President.
★ With the election of 1800, political parties began to control the nominating process.

### SECTION 4
### Presidential Nominations (pp. 368–375)

★ National conventions play a key role in the presidential nominating process.
★ Most States hold presidential primaries to determine convention delegates.
★ A few States select delegates through the caucus-convention process.
★ National conventions follow a schedule, culminating in the candidate's acceptance speech.
★ The candidate who is considered most electable usually wins the nomination.

### SECTION 5
### The Election (pp. 377–384)

★ Presidential electors today mainly "rubber-stamp" their party's candidate.
★ The electoral college is plagued by three major flaws.
★ Critics of the electoral college have proposed a variety of reforms.

## Keep It Current

### Internet Update

Use the Prentice Hall School Web site and the Keep It Current CD-ROM to find quick content updates.

Visit **www.phschool.com** for current events articles that are linked to Chapter 13. Critical Thinking questions are included.

**Keep It Current CD-ROM** includes government-related projects by unit. Students complete each project using current information that they obtain by linking to the Prentice Hall School Web site from the CD-ROM.

## Pressed for Time?

### To Omit the Chapter
If you wish to skip Chapter 13, ask students to read the Chapter in Brief and assign the Guide to the Essentials before continuing to another chapter. You may also want to assign the Chapter 13 Test in the Chapter Test booklet. Then specific portions of Chapter 13 may be assigned to students needing reinforcement of key terms and concepts.

### To Preview the Chapter
To introduce students to key terms and concepts in each section, have them read the Chapter in Brief. You may also assign the Reading Strategy activities on pp. 355, 360, 366, 369, and 378 of this book.

### To Review the Chapter
When students have completed Chapter 13, you might want to assign the Guide to the Essentials or the Guided Reading and Review worksheets on pp. 2, 4, 6, 8, and 10 of the Unit 4 booklet.

### To Cover the Chapter Quickly
To cover the material in Chapter 13 quickly, use the following activity.

**Focus** Ask students to describe the method used to elect the President and have them provide a job description of the position. Then point out that in this chapter they will learn about the original and current methods of electing the President as well as what the job entails.

**Instruct** Organize the class into five groups, assigning each group a section from the chapter. Have each group create a presentation detailing the main points of its assigned section. Ask each group to create a study guide for other students to fill out. Allow time for each group to make its presentation and for students to complete their study guides.

**Close/Reteach** Ask each group to create a quiz based on its presentation. Then allow groups time to prepare to take the other groups' quizzes by studying their completed study guides. Finally, have students take each of the other groups' quizzes.

■ **Block Strategy (Average)**

**1** # The President's Job Description

## Objectives
You may wish to call students' attention to the objectives in the Section Preview. The objectives are reflected in the main headings of the section.

**Bellringer** Ask students whether they have ever had a job with multiple duties. Lead a discussion of conflicts that can arise (such as scheduling or completing tasks) when a person has more than one area of responsibility. Explain that, in this section, students will learn about the President's multiple duties and roles.

**Vocabulary Builder** Point out the terms in the Political Dictionary. Tell students that these are the President's roles, and ask them what duties might be involved with each. Have them verify their answers as they read through the section.

### Pressed for Time?

#### Quick Lesson Plan

**1. Focus** Tell students that the formal qualifications for the job of President are not too difficult to meet. Ask students to discuss what they know about these formal qualifications.

**2. Instruct** Ask students to identify the greatest number of years a President can serve. Have them explain their answer and discuss the debate over this limit. Then have students identify the informal qualifications, roles, and pay of the President.

**3. Close/Reteach** Remind students that the job of President has formal and informal qualifications. Have students write a classified employment ad for a presidential candidate, including the qualifications and also the roles he or she must fulfill.

## Point-of-Use Resources

📁 **Block Scheduling with Lesson Strategies** Activities for Chapter 13 are presented on p. 25.

**354**

## Section Preview

### OBJECTIVES

1. **Identify** the President's many roles.
2. **Understand** the formal qualifications necessary to become President.
3. **Discuss** issues involving the length of the President's term.
4. **Describe** the President's pay and benefits.

### WHY IT MATTERS

Every four years, Americans participate in electing a new President. You will soon be able to participate in this process, if you have not already done so. Before your first vote in a presidential election, you will want to know as much as possible about the office and what it entails.

### POLITICAL DICTIONARY

★ chief of state
★ chief executive
★ chief administrator
★ chief diplomat
★ commander in chief
★ chief legislator
★ chief of party
★ chief citizen

Do you know who was the youngest person ever to be President? The oldest? Who held the presidency for the longest time? How long a person must live in the United States in order to run for President? You will find the answers to these questions and many more in this section, which provides a basic overview of the presidential office.

## The President's Roles

At any given time, of course, only one person is President of the United States. The office, with all of its powers and duties, belongs to that one individual. Whoever that person may be, he—and

► These cowboy boots, a gift to President Eisenhower, are an example of the many gifts that a President receives.

most likely someday she[1]—must fill a number of different roles, and all of them at the same time. The President is simultaneously (1) chief of state, (2) chief executive, (3) chief administrator, (4) chief diplomat, (5) commander in chief, (6) chief legislator, (7) party chief, and (8) chief citizen.

1. To begin with, the President is **chief of state.** This means he is the ceremonial head of the government of the United States, the symbol of all the people of the nation. He is, in President William Howard Taft's words, "the personal embodiment and representative of their dignity and majesty."

In many countries, the chief of state reigns but does not rule. That is certainly true of the queens of England and Denmark, the emperor of Japan, the kings of Norway and Sweden, and the presidents of Italy and Germany. It is most certainly not true of the President of the United States, who both reigns and rules.

2. The President is the nation's **chief executive;** he is vested by the Constitution with "the executive Power" of the United States. That power is immensely broad in both domestic and foreign affairs. Indeed, the American presidency is often described as "the most powerful office in the world."

---

[1]To this point all of the Presidents have been men, but nothing in the Constitution prevents the election of a woman to that office.

## 🔲 Block Scheduling Strategies

Consider these suggestions to manage extended class time:

■ Discuss with students the many different roles that the President must fulfill. Ask students to read about these roles in the text. Then have them conduct research using newspapers, magazines, and other resources to find examples of the President fulfilling each role. Ask students to use the information they find to explain how the President has fulfilled each role.

■ To build on the previous block scheduling activity, divide the class into eight groups, assigning each group one of the eight presidential roles. Ask each group to collect materials (copies of photographs, cuttings from magazines, quotes, etc.) showing the President fulfilling its assigned role. Have them use these materials to create visual presentations of the importance of their assigned roles. After each group has finished, hold a class discussion on which role students feel is the most important.

3. The President is also the **chief administrator,** or director, of the Federal Government, heading one of the largest governmental machines the world has known. Today, the President directs an administration that employs more than 2.7 million civilians and spends nearly $2 trillion a year.

4. The President is also the nation's **chief diplomat,** the main architect of American foreign policy and the nation's chief spokesperson to the rest of the world. "I make foreign policy," President Harry Truman once said—and he did. What the President says and does is carefully followed in this country and abroad.

5. In close concert with the President's role in foreign affairs, the Constitution also makes the President the **commander in chief** of the nation's armed forces. The 1.4 million men and women in uniform and the nation's entire military arsenal are subject to the President's direct and immediate control.

6. The President is also the nation's **chief legislator,** the main architect of its public policies. Most often it is the President who sets the overall shape of the congressional agenda. As chief legislator, the President initiates, suggests, requests, insists, and demands that Congress enact much of its major legislation.

These six presidential roles all come directly from the Constitution. Yet they do not complete the list. The President must fill still other vital roles.

7. The President acts as the **chief of party,** the acknowledged leader of the political party that controls the executive branch. As you know, parties are not mentioned in the Constitution, yet they play a vital role in the workings of the American governmental system. Thus, much of the real power and influence wielded by the President depends on the manner in which he or she plays this critical role.

8. The office also automatically makes its occupant the nation's **chief citizen.** The President is expected to be "the representative of all the people." As chief citizen, the President is expected to work for and represent the public interest against the many private interests.

"The presidency," said Franklin Roosevelt, "is not merely an administrative office. That is the least of it. It is preeminently a place of moral leadership." Listing the President's

several roles is a very useful way to describe the President's job. But, remember, the President must play all of these roles simultaneously. None of them can be performed in isolation. The manner in which a President plays any one role can have a powerful effect on his ability to play the others.

As two illustrations, take the experiences of Presidents Lyndon Johnson and Richard Nixon. Each was a strong and relatively effective President during his first years in office. Johnson's actions as commander in chief during the agonizing and increasingly unpopular war in Vietnam seriously damaged his effectiveness in the White House, however. In fact the damage was so great that it persuaded the President not to run for reelection in 1968.

The many-sided, sordid Watergate scandal proved to be President Nixon's downfall. During that time, the manner in which he filled the roles of party leader and chief citizen so destroyed Mr. Nixon's presidency that he was forced to leave office in disgrace in 1974.

## Voices on Government

Robert Reich was a professor at Harvard's John F. Kennedy School of Government before he became President Clinton's Secretary of Labor in 1993. As a member of the Cabinet for four years, Reich was in a good position to observe the presidency:

❝ Unlike Britain and other democratic monarchies, we ask our country's leader to do two jobs simultaneously, to act both as head of government and as the symbol of the nation. It's a hard act. Governing involves tough compromises and gritty reality. Symbolism requires nobility and grandeur. We demand a street-smart wheeler-dealer, but we also want a king and a royal family. ❞

### Evaluating the Quotation

*What other jobs do Americans expect the President to do? Use Reich's observation and what you read in this chapter to compile a full "job description."*

## Spotlight on Technology

► John F. Kennedy was the youngest person elected President. He is shown here with his son, John F. Kennedy, Jr. *Critical Thinking* **Why do you think that the Framers required that a President be at least 35 years old?**

## Formal Qualifications

The Constitution says that the President must:[2]

1. Be "a natural born Citizen." Under the doctrine of *jus sanguinis* it is apparently possible for a person born abroad as an American citizen to become President. Some dispute that view, and the real meaning of this requirement cannot be known until someone born a citizen, but born abroad, does in fact become President.[3]

2. Be at least 35 years of age. John F. Kennedy, at 43, was the youngest person ever to be elected President. Theodore Roosevelt reached the presidency by succession at age 42. Ronald Reagan, who was 69 when he was first elected in 1980, was the oldest man ever elected to the office; and, when he completed his second term eight years later, he was the oldest person ever to hold the office. Most Presidents, though,

---

[2]Article II, Section 1, Clause 5.
[3]Martin Van Buren, who was born December 5, 1782, was the first President actually born in the United States. His seven predecessors (and his immediate successor) were each born in the colonies, before the Revolution—that is, before there was a United States. But notice that the Constitution anticipated that situation with these words: "or a citizen of the United States at the time of the adoption of this Constitution."
[4]Given Herbert Hoover's election in 1928 and Dwight Eisenhower's in 1952, the 14-year requirement means any 14 years in a person's life. Both Hoover and Eisenhower spent several years before election outside the United States.
[5]Article II, Section 1, Clause 1.

---

have been in their 50s when they reached the White House. George W. Bush was 54 when he became President in 2001.

3. Have lived in the United States for at least 14 years.[4]

While these formal qualifications do have some importance, they are really not very difficult to meet. In fact, more than 100 million people in this country today do so. Clearly, there are other and much more telling *informal* qualifications for the presidency—as you will see shortly.

## The President's Term

The Framers considered a number of different limits on the length of the presidential term. Most of their debate centered on a four-year term, with the President eligible for reelection, versus a single six-year or seven-year term. They finally settled on a four-year term.[5] They agreed, as Alexander Hamilton wrote in *The Federalist* No. 71, that four years was a long enough period for a President to have gained experience, demonstrated his abilities, and established stable policies.

Until 1951, the Constitution placed no limit on the number of terms a President might

▲ This poster urged President Roosevelt to run for his third term. F.D.R. was the only President to serve more than two terms in office. *Critical Thinking* **Do you agree that a President should serve for no more than two terms? Explain your answer.**

## Careers in Government—Interpreter

As the nation's chief diplomat, the President must communicate with leaders of scores of nations—many of whom do not speak English. The many interpreters employed by the executive branch do more than translate what is said; they note figures of speech and other subtle clues that can help the President understand not only what foreign leaders say, but what they actually mean.

**Skills Activity** Have students simulate a summit meeting on a topic of current international interest. If possible, have students who speak or are learning a second language play the roles of foreign leaders and interpreters. Then have individual students write paragraphs explaining why they would or would not be interested in a career as an interpreter. **(Average)**

serve. Several Presidents, beginning with George Washington, refused to seek more than two terms, however. Soon, the "no-third-term tradition" became an unwritten rule in presidential politics.

Franklin D. Roosevelt broke this tradition by seeking and winning a third term in 1940, and then a fourth in 1944. To prevent future Presidents from following this precedent, the 22nd Amendment made the unwritten custom limiting presidential terms a part of the written Constitution. This amendment, adopted in 1951, reads in part:

> FROM THE Constitution " No person shall be elected to the office of the President more than twice, and no person who has held the office of President, or acted as President, for more than two years of a term to which

some other person was elected President shall be elected to the office of the President more than once. "

—22nd Amendment

As a general rule, then, each President may now serve a maximum of two full terms—eight years—in office. A President who succeeds to the office after the midpoint in a term could possibly serve for more than eight years. In that circumstance, the President may finish out the predecessor's term and then seek two full terms of his or her own. However, no President may serve more than 10 years in the office.

Many people, including Presidents Truman, Eisenhower, and Reagan, have called for the repeal of the 22nd Amendment and its limit on presidential service. They argue that the two-term rule

## Comparative Government

### Heads of State in Selected Countries

| Country | Title | Name | Date Acquired Office | Previous Profession/Title |
|---------|-------|------|---------------------|---------------------------|
| Poland | President | Aleksander Kwasniewski | December 23, 1995 | Former communist offical |
| China | State President | Jiang Zemin | March 27, 1993 | General Secretary, Communist Party |
| Panama | President | Mireya Moscoso | September 1, 1999 | Businesswoman, civil servant |
| South Africa | President | Thabo Mbeki | June 16, 1999 | Deputy President |
| Canada | Governor-General | Adrienne Clarkson | October 7, 1999 | Writer and producer |
| Spain | King | Juan Carlos I | November 22, 1975 | Crown Prince |
| Mexico | President | Vicente Fox | December 1, 2000 | Governor, businessman |
| Jordan | King | Abdullah II | August 20, 1998 | Crown Prince |
| Japan | Emperor | Akihito | January 7, 1989 | Crown Prince |
| Philippines | President | Gloria Macapagal-Arroyo | January 20, 2001 | Vice President |
| United States | President | George W. Bush | January 20, 2001 | Governor |

SOURCE: CIA Publications

*Interpreting Tables* The position or occupation from which a head of state came to his or her current office often suggests something about the political system in that country. **What does the table suggest about the governments of Jordan, China, and South Africa?**

Chapter **13** • Section **1**

ACTIVITY

## American Government, American Humor

Share the following quotation with students:

*"Within the first few months I discovered that being a president is like riding a tiger. A man has to keep riding or be swallowed."*

—Harry S Truman

**Discussion** Have students explain what Truman meant by his remark. Ask: How does Truman's description of the job compare with the "job description" in their textbooks? **(Average)**

## Customize for

### More Advanced Students

Have students choose one of the people who have served as President of the United States. Ask them to research the major events that took place during this President's term, including noteworthy personal characteristics, public opinion polls, and political successes and failures. After researching their subject, students should write a poem or song about the President they have chosen that highlights his years in the White House. Encourage students to share their work with their peers.

## Point-of-Use Resources

📁 **Close Up on Primary Sources** *The Federalist* No. 71 (1787–1788), p. 67

📼 **ABC News Civics and Government Videotape Library** *The Federal Budget* (time: about two minutes)

*Answer to . . .*

**Interpreting Tables** That people with political experience or from ruling families are often favored for heads of state.

### Answers to . . .

### Section 1 Assessment

**1.** As chief of state, the President is the ceremonial head of the United States government.

**2.** As chief of party, the President acts as the leader of the political party in control of the executive branch; as chief citizen, the President acts as the representative of all the people and defender of the public interest.

**3.** The President must be a natural born citizen, at least 35 years of age, and have lived in the United States for 14 years.

**4.** To limit the tenure of any President to two terms, or, in the case of a President who succeeded to the office mid-term, 10 years total.

**5.** Answers will vary, but should demonstrate an understanding of the President's various roles.

**6.** Lists will vary, but may include characteristics such as intelligence, character, moral convictions, and credibility.

**7.** Answers will vary but opinions should be supported with facts.

▲ **Benefits of the Presidency** President Jimmy Carter and his wife, Rosalynn, enjoying the White House and its grounds.

is undemocratic because it places an arbitrary limit on the right of the people to decide who should be President. Some critics also say that the amendment undercuts the authority of a two-term President, especially in the latter part of his second term. Supporters of the amendment defend it as a reasonable safeguard against "executive tyranny."

Several Presidents, most recently Lyndon Johnson and Jimmy Carter, have urged a single six-year term. They and others have argued that a single, nonrenewable term would free a President from the pressures of a campaign for a second term. This freedom would allow the chief executive to focus on the pressing demands of the office.

## Pay and Benefits

Congress determines the President's salary. It can neither be increased nor decreased during a presidential term.[6] The President's pay was first set at $25,000 a year, in 1789. It is now $400,000 a year. Congress set that figure in 1999, and it became effective on January 20, 2001.

Congress has also provided the President with a $50,000-a-year expense allowance. That money may be spent however the President chooses; it is, in effect, a part of his pay, and it is taxed as part of his income.

The Constitution forbids the President "any other emolument from the United States, or any of them." This clause does not prevent the President from being provided with a great many benefits, however. These include the White House, a magnificent 132-room mansion set on an 18.3-acre estate in the heart of the nation's capital; a sizable suite of offices and a large staff; a fleet of automobiles, the lavishly fitted *Air Force One* and several other planes and helicopters; Camp David, the resort hideaway in the Catoctin Mountains in Maryland; the finest medical, dental, and other health care available; generous travel and entertainment funds; and many other fringe benefits.

---

[6]Article II, Section 1, Clause 7. At Philadelphia, Benjamin Franklin argued that, as money and power might corrupt a man, the President ought to receive nothing beyond his expenses; his suggestion was not put to a vote at the Convention.

## Section 1 Assessment

**Key Terms and Main Ideas**

1. Explain the President's role as **chief of state.**
2. How does the President function as **chief of party** and **chief citizen?**
3. What are the three formal qualifications necessary to become President?
4. What is the purpose of the 22nd Amendment?

**Critical Thinking**

5. **Synthesizing Information** Admiral George Dewey once said, "the office of President is not such a very difficult one to fill, his duties being mainly to execute the laws of Congress." Do you agree or disagree with this statement? Explain why.
6. **Demonstrating Reasoned Judgment** Create a list of five informal qualifications that you believe are necessary for a

candidate to have in order to become President. Explain your choices.

7. **Making Decisions** At $400,000 a year, the President's salary is far more than that of the average American, yet less than the yearly income of the wealthiest Americans. Do you think that this is fair compensation? Explain your reasoning.

 **Take It to the Net**

8. Select one President and follow links to specific information regarding his term of office. Write an evaluation of how well he fulfilled at least three of the roles listed on page 354. Use the links provided in the Social Studies area at the following Web site for help in completing this activity. **www.phschool.com**

 **Take It to the Net**

**8.** Direct students to the Social Studies area at the Prentice Hall School Web site. The *Magruder's American Government* companion Web site includes the directions and links needed to complete the activity. It also provides a printable Internet activity worksheet with scoring rubrics for assessment. Evaluations should answer the questions presented.

# Presidential Succession and the Vice Presidency

## Section Preview

### OBJECTIVES

1. **Explain** how the Constitution provides for presidential succession.
2. **Understand** the constitutional provisions for presidential disability.
3. **Describe** the role of the Vice President.

### WHY IT MATTERS

Should the President die, be removed from office, or resign, the Vice President will succeed to the presidency. The Vice President is, indeed, just a heartbeat away from the President.

### POLITICAL DICTIONARY

★ presidential succession
★ Presidential Succession Act of 1947
★ balance the ticket

---

Consider these facts. Forty-six men have served as Vice President.[7] Fourteen of them later reached the White House—most recently, George Bush in 1989. Indeed, five of our last eleven Presidents were once Vice President.

## The Constitution and Succession

**Presidential succession** is the scheme by which a presidential vacancy is filled. If a President dies, resigns, or is removed from office by impeachment, the Vice President succeeds to the office.

Originally, the Constitution did not provide for the succession of the Vice President. Rather, it declared that "the powers and duties" of the office—not the office itself—were to "devolve on [transfer to] the Vice President."[8]

In practice the Vice President did succeed to the office when it became vacant. Vice President John Tyler set this precedent in 1841 when he succeeded President William Henry Harrison, who died of pneumonia just one month after taking office. This practice became a part of the Constitution with the adoption of the 25th Amendment in 1967. The amendment provides:

> FROM THE **Constitution**
>
> *"In case of the removal of the President from office or of his death or resignation, the Vice President shall become President."*
>
> —25th Amendment, Section 1

---

[7]No woman has yet held the office, but nothing in the Constitution bars that possibility.
[8]Article II, Section 1, Clause 6.

### Presidential Succession

| | |
|---|---|
| 1 | Vice President |
| 2 | Speaker of the House |
| 3 | President *pro tempore* of the Senate |
| 4 | Secretary of State |
| 5 | Secretary of the Treasury |
| 6 | Secretary of Defense |
| 7 | Attorney General |
| 8 | Secretary of the Interior |
| 9 | Secretary of Agriculture |
| 10 | Secretary of Commerce |
| 11 | Secretary of Labor |
| 12 | Secretary of Health and Human Services |
| 13 | Secretary of Housing and Urban Development |
| 14 | Secretary of Transportation |
| 15 | Secretary of Energy |
| 16 | Secretary of Education |
| 17 | Secretary of Veterans Affairs |

*Interpreting Charts* The Vice President is first in line to succeed to the presidency should the office become vacant. Such was the case when Lyndon Johnson took the oath of office aboard *Air Force One* after the assassination of President Kennedy in 1963. ***How does the chart demonstrate the importance of the positions of the Vice President and the Speaker of the House?***

---

## Block Scheduling Strategies

Consider these suggestions to manage extended class time:

■ Discuss the constitutional provisions for presidential succession and presidential disability with the class. Then ask students to read about these topics in the text. Have students work to create graphic organizers depicting information about each topic. Then call on volunteers to explain the information that they depicted to the class.

■ Once students have read about the role of the Vice President, point out that people are generally divided about the importance of the job. Some find it to be an important job while others think it is insignificant. Have students read the various quotations about the vice presidency in this section. Ask them to explain which ones reflect their own opinions of the Vice President's job, or offer their own quotations.

---

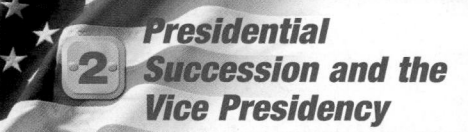

## Presidential Succession and the Vice Presidency

**Objectives** You may wish to call students' attention to the objectives in the Section Preview. The objectives are reflected in the main headings of the section.

**Bellringer** Have students discuss what their job would be like if they were the backup goalie on a soccer team whose starting goalie was a star player. Elicit that they might get to play only if the starter is injured. Explain that, in this section, they will learn about the circumstances in which the Vice President could take over the presidency.

**Vocabulary Builder** Tell students that the word *succession,* as it is used in the Political Dictionary, has nothing to do with being successful. Lead them to see that it actually relates to a sequence.

### Pressed for Time?

#### Quick Lesson Plan

1. **Focus** Tell students that the Constitution provides for replacing the President if necessary. Ask students to discuss what they know about who is in line to succeed to the presidency.
2. **Instruct** Ask students to list the duties of the Vice President, according to the Constitution. Lead a discussion of why the Vice President has but two formal duties besides being a "President-in-waiting." Turn the discussion toward presidential succession and the changing role of the Vice President.
3. **Close/Reteach** Remind students that the Constitution provides for presidential succession. Have students write questions about this succession on cards, with the answers on the reverse side of the cards. Ask pairs of students to quiz each other.

*Answer to ...*

**Interpreting Charts** As they are second and third in the line of succession, the possibility of them becoming President is quite high.

---

**359**

## Reading Strategy

### Finding Evidence

Tell students that the government does not cease to function if the President dies in office or is otherwise unable to serve. Have students read to find out how the Constitution guarantees that the nation continues to have a President under such circumstances.

## The *Living* Constitution

### Changes in the Presidency

In the early months of 1940, President Franklin D. Roosevelt gave every appearance of following President Washington's two-term precedent. Roosevelt was already planning the first presidential library and had signed a contract to write a series of magazine articles upon his retirement. However, with Germany's air invasion of Britain, the growing threat of world war convinced Roosevelt to try to stay in office. Four years later, with America at war, Roosevelt sought and won a fourth term.

### Using the Time Line

Have students use the time line to create an outline of the changing presidency. Then have them use their outlines to write a script for a documentary film about those changes.

## Point–of–Use Resources

📖 **Basic Principles of the Constitution Transparencies** Transparency 4, *The Living Constitution: The Executive Branch*

📁 **The Living Constitution** Two extension activities for this time line can be found on pp. 15–16.

---

Congress fixes the order of succession following the Vice President.[9] The present law on the matter is the **Presidential Succession Act of 1947.** By its terms, the Speaker of the House and then the President *pro tem* of the Senate are next in line. They are followed, in turn, by the secretary of state and then by each of the other 13 heads of the Cabinet departments, in order of precedence—the order in which the offices were created by Congress.[10]

## Presidential Disability

Before the passage of the 25th Amendment, there were serious gaps in the arrangement for presidential succession. Neither the Constitution nor Congress had made any provision for deciding when a President was disabled. Nor was there anything to indicate by whom such a decision was to be made.

For nearly 180 years, then, the nation played with fate. President Eisenhower suffered three serious but temporary illnesses while in office: a heart attack in 1955, ileitis in 1956,

and a mild stroke in 1957. Two other Presidents were disabled for much longer periods. James Garfield lingered for 80 days before he died from an assassin's bullet in 1881. Woodrow Wilson suffered a paralytic stroke in 1919 and was an invalid for the rest of his second term. He was so ill that he could not meet with his Cabinet for seven months after his stroke.

Sections 3 and 4 of the 25th Amendment fill the disability gap, and in detail. The Vice President is to become Acting President if (1) the President informs Congress, in writing, "that he is unable to discharge the powers and duties of his office," or (2) the Vice President and a majority of the members of the Cabinet inform

---

[9] Article II, Section 1, Clause 6. On removal of the President by impeachment, see Chapter 11.

[10] A Cabinet member is to serve only until a Speaker or a president *pro tem* is available and qualified. Notice that the 25th Amendment also provides for the filling of any vacancy in the vice presidency. In effect, that provision makes the Presidential Succession Act a law with little real significance—except in the highly unlikely event of simultaneous vacancies in the presidency and vice presidency.

---

# The *Living* Constitution

## Changes in the Presidency                                          1800 ❯

While historians have often noted the changes in the *power* of the presidency, other important aspects of the office have changed as well. These include how the President is selected, when the President takes office, how many terms the President may serve, and how the office of the President is to be filled when vacant. The time line lists some of the most important amendments, laws, and other developments concerning these areas of the nation's highest office.

**1796**
George Washington does not run for a third term, setting the precedent of a two-term limit.

**1804**
12th Amendment requires separate ballots for President and Vice President.

---

## Organizing Information

To make sure students understand the main points of this section, you may wish to use the flowchart to the right.

Tell students that a flowchart shows a sequence of events. Ask students to use the flowchart to record the steps of presidential succession. The first event on the chart should be the death, resignation, or removal of the President from office.

**Teaching Tip** A template for this graphic organizer can be found in the Section Support Transparencies, Transparency 4.

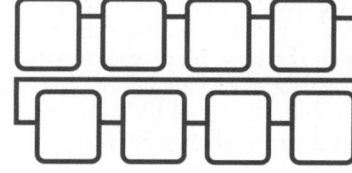

Congress, in writing, that the President is so incapacitated.[11]

In either case, the President may resume the powers and duties of the office by informing Congress that no inability exists. However, the Vice President and a majority of the Cabinet may challenge the President on this score. Congress then has 21 days in which to decide the matter.

To this point, the disability provisions of the 25th Amendment have come into play only once, and then only for a few hours. On July 13, 1985, surgeons removed a malignant tumor from President Reagan's large intestine. Just before surgery, Mr. Reagan transferred the powers of the presidency to Vice President Bush. President Reagan reclaimed those powers immediately after he awoke, seven hours and 54 minutes later. For that very brief period, George Herbert Walker Bush was the Acting President of the United States.

---

[11]The 25th Amendment gives this authority to the Vice President and the Cabinet or to "such other body as Congress may by law provide." To date, no "such other body" has been established.

## The Vice Presidency

"I am Vice President. In this I am nothing, but I may be everything." So said John Adams, the nation's first Vice President. Those words could have been repeated, very appropriately, by each of the 45 Vice Presidents who have followed him in that office.

### Importance of the Office

The Constitution pays little attention to the office of the Vice President. It assigns the position only two formal duties: (1) to preside over the Senate[12] and (2) to help decide the question of presidential disability.[13] Beyond those duties, the Constitution makes the Vice President a "President-in-waiting."

Through much of the nation's history, in fact, the vice presidency has been treated as an office of little real consequence and, often, as the butt of jokes. Many Vice Presidents themselves have

---

[12]Article I, Section 3, Clause 4; see Chapter 12, Section 1.
[13]25th Amendment, Sections 3 and 4.

---

### Point–of–Use Resources

☐ **Guided Reading and Review** Unit 4 booklet, p. 4 provides students with practice identifying the main ideas and key terms of this section.

☐ **Lesson Plans** For lesson planning suggestions, see p. 58 of the Lesson Plans booklet.

☐ **Political Cartoons** See p. 50 of the Political Cartoons booklet for a cartoon relevant to this section.

☐ **Close Up on Primary Sources** George Washington, Farewell Address (1796), p. 33

---

| 1944 | 1947 | 1967 | 1985 |
|---|---|---|---|
| FDR wins a fourth term; and Congress later acts (1947) to limit a President to two terms in office (22nd Amendment, ratified in 1951) | Presidential Succession Act lists officials who would succeed to the presidency after the Vice President. | 25th Amendment sets up procedures to follow when a President is disabled or vice presidency is vacant. | Disability provision of the 25th Amendment first used when Vice President Bush becomes acting President while President Reagan is in surgery. |

**1925** **1950** **1975** **2000**

| 1933 | 1973 |
|---|---|
| 20th Amendment moves President's inauguration from March to January. | President Nixon, following the 25th Amendment, nominates Gerald Ford to replace Vice President Agnew, who had resigned. |

*The Inaugural Ball 1957*

### Analyzing Time Lines

1. Which amendment deals with a vacancy in the office of Vice President? When and why was this provision first used?
2. For what reason do you think the 20th Amendment was passed?

---

### Answers to . . .

**Analyzing Time Lines 1.** The 25th Amendment; it was first used when President Nixon nominated Gerald Ford to replace Vice President Agnew, who had resigned. **2.** Answers will vary. Possible answers include: In order to hasten replacement of the old "lame duck" administration with the newly elected one; because improvements in communication and transportation have reduced the time it takes to switch over to a new administration.

had a hand in this. John Adams described his post

# 4 *Presidential Nominations*

## Section Preview

### OBJECTIVES

1. **Describe** the role of conventions in the presidential nominating process.
2. **Evaluate** the importance of presidential primaries.
3. **Understand** the role of the caucus-convention process in States that do not hold primaries.
4. **Outline** the events that take place during a national convention.
5. **Examine** the characteristics that determine who is nominated as a presidential candidate.

### WHY IT MATTERS

Presidential primaries and party caucuses lead up to the Democratic and Republican national conventions. At these conventions, which take place every four years during the summer before the fall election, each party officially selects its presidential candidate.

### POLITICAL DICTIONARY

★ **presidential primary**
★ **winner-take-all**
★ **proportional representation**
★ **national convention**
★ **platform**
★ **keynote address**

The Constitution makes no provision for the nomination of candidates for the presidency. Rather, as you have just seen, the Framers designed a system in which presidential electors would, out of their own knowledge, select the "wisest and best man" to be President. Later, the rise of parties altered that system dramatically.

## The Role of Conventions

The first method the parties developed to nominate their presidential candidates was the congressional caucus. As you may recall from Chapter 7, that method was regularly used in the elections of 1800 to 1824. However, the closed, nonrepresentative character of this system led to its downfall in the mid-1820s. For the election of 1832, both major parties turned to the national convention as their nominating device, and it has continued to serve them ever since.

### Convention Arrangements

Not only does the Constitution say nothing about presidential nominations; there is, as well, almost no federal or State statutory law on the matter. The convention system has been built almost entirely by the two major parties in American politics.

In both parties, the national committee makes the arrangements for the party's convention. This means, for example, setting the date and

picking the place for that meeting. In recent years, the party out of power has held its convention first, usually in July, and the President's party has met some three weeks later, in the early part of August.

Many of the nation's largest cities bid for the honor—and the financial return to local business—of hosting a convention. The map on the next page shows where the Democratic and Republican national conventions have been held since 1856. In 2000, the Republican convention was held in Philadelphia and the Democratic convention in Los Angeles.

### The Apportionment of Delegates

With the date and the location set, the national committee issues its "call" for the convention. That formal announcement names the time and place. It also tells the party's organization in each State how many delegates it may send to the national gathering.

By tradition, both parties give each State party a certain number of delegates based on that State's electoral vote. Over the past several conventions, both parties have developed complicated formulas that also award bonus delegates to those States that have supported the party's candidates in recent elections.

For 2000, the Republicans' formula produced a convention of 2,067 delegates. The Democrats'

## National Convention Sites

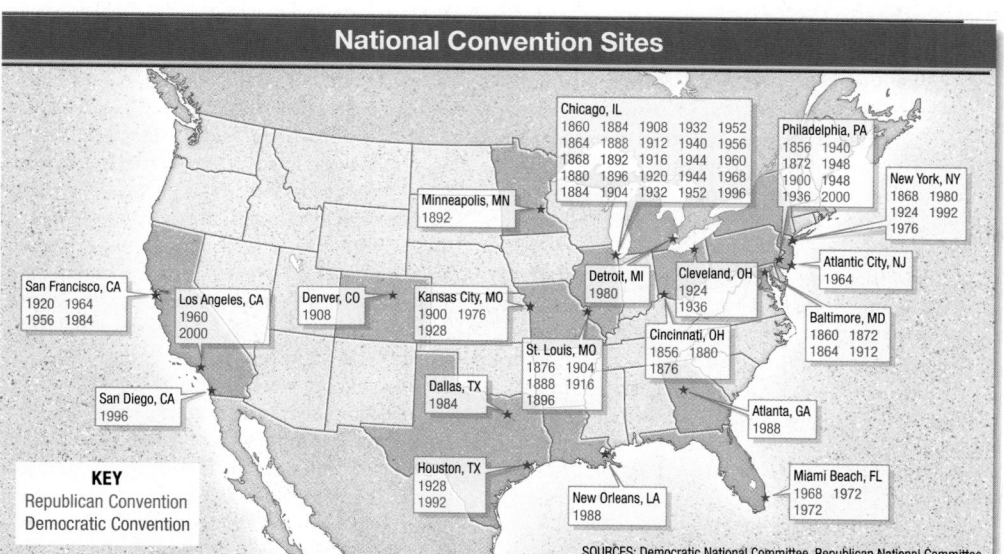

| | |
|---|---|
| **Chicago, IL** | **Philadelphia, PA** |
| 1860 1884 1908 1932 1952 | 1856 1940 |
| 1864 1888 1912 1940 1956 | 1872 1948 |
| 1868 1892 1916 1944 1960 | 1900 1948 |
| 1880 1896 1920 1944 1968 | 1936 2000 |
| 1884 1904 1932 1952 1996 | |

**New York, NY**
1868 1980
1924 1992
1976

**Minneapolis, MN**
1892

**Atlantic City, NJ**
1964

**San Francisco, CA**
1920 1964
1956 1984

**Los Angeles, CA**
1960
2000

**Denver, CO**
1908

**Kansas City, MO**
1900 1976
1928

**Detroit, MI**
1980

**Cleveland, OH**
1924
1936

**Cincinnati, OH**
1856 1880
1876

**Baltimore, MD**
1860 1872
1864 1912

**St. Louis, MO**
1876 1904
1888 1916
1896

**San Diego, CA**
1996

**Dallas, TX**
1984

**Atlanta, GA**
1988

**Houston, TX**
1928
1992

**New Orleans, LA**
1988

**Miami Beach, FL**
1968 1972
1972

**KEY**
Republican Convention
Democratic Convention

SOURCES: Democratic National Committee, Republican National Committee

*Interpreting Maps* Democrats held their first convention in Baltimore in 1832, and met there through 1852. The Republicans held their convention in Philadelphia in 1856. ***How can you explain the popularity of such cities as Chicago, New York, and Philadelphia as convention sites?***

more complex plan called for 4,337.[18] Given those large numbers, it should be fairly clear that neither party's national convention can be called "a deliberative body" that is able to give each of its decisions thoughtful consideration.

### Selection of Delegates

There are really *two* campaigns for the presidency. One is the contest between the Republican and Democratic candidates in the fall. The other is earlier and quite different. It takes place *within* each party: the struggle for convention delegates.

State laws and/or party rules fix the procedures for picking delegates in each State. That fact is a reflection of federalism, and it has produced a jigsaw puzzle of presidential primaries, conventions, and caucuses among the 50 States.

To a large extent, the Republican Party leaves the matter of delegate selection to its State organizations and to State law. The Democrats, on the other hand, have adopted several national rules to govern the process. Most of those rules reflect attempts to broaden participation in the delegate selection process, especially by the young, African Americans, other minorities, and women.

## Presidential Primaries

More than three fourths of all the delegates to both parties' conventions come from States that hold presidential primaries. Many of those primaries are major media events. Serious contenders in both parties must make the best possible showing in at least most of them.

Depending on the State, a **presidential primary** is an election in which a party's voters (1) choose some or all of a State party organization's delegates to their party's national convention, and/or (2) express a preference among various contenders for their party's presidential nomination.

---

[18]Both parties allot delegates to the District of Columbia, Puerto Rico, the Virgin Islands, Guam, and American Samoa; the Democrats also provide for delegates who represent Democrats Abroad. The Democratic convention also includes a large number of "superdelegates"—mostly party officers and Democrats who hold major elective offices. They are automatically members of their respective State delegations. More than 750 superdelegates were seated at the 2000 Democratic convention; their number included all of the members of the Democratic National Committee, all Democratic State governors (19), and nearly all of the Democratic members of the House and Senate.

## Reading Strategy

### Getting the Main Idea

Tell students that political parties use various procedures to nominate a presidential candidate. Have students judge, as they read, which procedures seem to offer voters the greatest chance to participate in the nomination process.

## Point–of–Use Resources

🗀 **Guided Reading and Review** Unit 4 booklet, p. 8 provides students with practice identifying the main ideas and key terms of this section.

🗀 **Lesson Plans** For lesson planning suggestions, see p. 60 of the Lesson Plans booklet.

🗀 **Political Cartoons** See p. 52 of the Political Cartoons booklet for a cartoon relevant to this section.

📖 **Section Support Transparencies** Transparency 55, *Visual Learning*; Transparency 154, *Political Cartoon*

*Answer to . . .*

**Interpreting Maps** They are bustling cities with good convention facilities, transportation, and entertainment possibilities.

## History of the Presidential Primary

The presidential primary first appeared in the early 1900s as part of the reform movement aimed at the boss-dominated convention system. Wisconsin passed the first presidential primary law in 1905, providing for the popular election of national convention delegates. Several States soon followed that lead, and Oregon added a preference primary in 1910. By 1916 nearly half the States had adopted presidential primary laws.

For a time, the primary system fell into disfavor so that by 1968, primaries were found in only 16 States and the District of Columbia. Efforts to reform the national convention process, especially in the Democratic Party, reversed that downward trend in the 1970s, however. The number of presidential primary States is now at an all-time high. For 2000, some form of presidential primary was in place in 44 States, and in the District of Columbia and Puerto Rico, as well.[19]

---

[19] In every State except Alaska, Hawaii, Iowa, Minnesota, Nevada, and North Dakota. In some States, the law permits but does not require a major party to hold a primary. In South Carolina the presidential primary is a product of party rules, not State law.

◀ **Campaigning Then and Now**
Campaigning for the presidency has changed dramatically since Harry S Truman's 1948 whistle-stop train tours were one of the best ways to reach voters. Today's candidates can use the Internet to reach potential voters.

georgewbush.com
▸ George & Laura Bush

**BUSH**
FOR PRESIDENT
George & Laura Bush
En Español
On The Road
News
Speeches
Issues
Volunteer
Contribute
Supporters
Youth Zone
Contact
★ ★ ★
Get Active in

George W. Bush
▸ 1946 to the Present
▸ Professional Biography
▸ Accomplishments (.pdf format)
Laura Welch Bush
▸ Biography
▸ Texas' First Lady - Working For Education & Children

Governor Bush Welcomes You To His Virtual Campaign Headquarters

[Video | Audio]

## Primaries Today

Again, a presidential primary is either or both of two things: a delegate-selection process and/or a candidate preference election. Once that much has been said, however, the system becomes very hard to describe, except on a State-by-State basis.

The difficulty comes largely from two sources: (1) the fact that in each State the details of the delegate-selection process are determined by that State's own law—and those details vary from one State to the next, and (2) the ongoing reform efforts in the Democratic Party. Since 1968, when the Democrats were shattered by disputes over Vietnam and civil rights policies, the Democratic National Committee has written and rewritten the party's rules to promote greater grassroots participation in the delegate-selection process. Those new rules have prompted many changes in most States' election laws.

Even a matter that seems as simple as the date for the primary illustrates the crazy-quilt pattern of State laws. New Hampshire holds the first of the presidential primaries every four years, and it has done so since 1940. New Hampshire guards its first-in-the-nation title with a law that sets the date for its primary as the Tuesday of the week before the date on which any other State schedules its contest. For the 2000 presidential election, the New Hampshire primary was held on February 1, 2000, and all of the others were held at various times over the next four months.

Most States prefer an early date, and so the primary schedule has become heavily "front-loaded." More than half of the primaries, including the contests in most of the larger States, now come in March and early April.

Name recognition and money have always been important factors in the presidential primary process, and front-loading has multiplied their significance. Until lately, a candidate who was not very well known nationally could hope to build a following from primary to primary—as, for example, Bill Clinton did in 1992. The process leaves little or no time for that strategy today, however. Candidates now have to mount (and pay for) campaigns in a number of widely separated States that hold their primaries on the same day or within only a few days of one another.

## Proportional Representation

Until fairly recently, most primaries were both delegate-selection and preference exercises. Several primaries were also **winner-take-all** contests. That is, the candidate who won the preference vote automatically won the support of all delegates chosen at the primary.

Winner-take-all primaries have now all but disappeared. The Democratic Party rules now prohibit them. Instead, the Democrats have a complex **proportional representation** rule. Any candidate who wins at least 15 percent of the votes cast in a primary gets the number of State Democratic convention delegates that corresponds to his or her share of that primary vote. Take, for example, a State that has 40 convention delegates. If a candidate wins 45 percent of the primary vote, he automatically gains the support of at least 18 of the delegates.

Most States had to change their primary laws to account for the Democrats' proportional representation rule. So in many States, Republican delegates are also chosen on a proportional representation basis. Still, a few States do permit winner-take-all primaries, and the Republicans hold them where they can.

The Democrats' proportional representation rule had yet another major impact on the shape of presidential primaries. It led several States—among them Oregon and Wisconsin, the States that had pioneered the presidential primary idea—to give up the popular selection of delegates.

More than half of the presidential primary States now hold only a preference primary. The delegates themselves are chosen later, at party conventions. In most of these States, the delegates must be picked to line up with the results of the preference primary—for example, for the Republicans in 2000, so many delegates for John McCain, so many for Steve Forbes, so many for George W. Bush, and so on. In some States, however, the preference vote does not govern the choice of the delegates. In

▲ **New Hampshire Primary** Because New Hampshire holds the first-in-the-nation primary, most presidential candidates target the State as essential to their campaigns. Here Al Gore meets a group of future voters during the 2000 primary season.

those States, the preference primary is often called simply a "beauty contest."

Most of the preference contests are also "all-candidate" primaries. These are contests in which all generally recognized contenders for a party's presidential nomination must be listed on that party's preference ballot.

## Evaluation of the Primary

No one who surveys the presidential primary system needs to be told that it is complicated, nor that it is filled with confusing variations. Still, these primaries are vital. Over recent years they have played the major part in deciding the presidential nominating contests in both parties—especially the party out of power.

Presidential primaries tend to democratize the delegate-selection process. And, importantly, they force would-be nominees to test their candidacies in actual political combat. For the party out of power, especially, the primaries are often "knock-down, drag-out" battles. Without the unifying force of the President as party leader, the leaders and factions in the party vie with one another, vigorously, for the presidential nomination. In this way, the screening out of the lesser possibilities takes places until only a few contenders for the presidential nomination remain.

Such hard-fought contests occur but are not common in the party in power. This tends to be true either because the President (1) is himself seeking reelection, or (2) has given his backing to someone he favors for the nomination. In either case the President almost always gets his way.

## Make It Relevant

### Students Make a Difference

In August 1996, 17-year-old Dan Lesh was a delegate to a Chicago political convention. Held in conjunction with the Democratic National Convention, Dan's meeting was a National Youth Convention, where 14- to 18-year-olds gathered to submit platforms to the presidential candidates. Tom Kremer, youth organizer for the Chicago host committee, explained that the convention's purpose was to convince politicians to "give young people a stronger voice in solving the problems that affect us."

After developing their platforms on the Internet, 150 student delegates met at each convention site and formed groups that focused on different issues. Groups suggested "one or two solutions that could be implemented," said Andrew Skora, who was at the Republican site in San Diego. Then it was up to 30 issue panelists to present the platform to officials and the press.

*Interpreting Political Cartoons* **What does the cartoon suggest about the significance of the Iowa caucus and the New Hampshire primary?**

There are exceptions, of course. Ronald Reagan made a stiff run at President Ford in the Republican Party in 1976; and Senator Edward Kennedy gave President Carter a real fight in the Democratic Party in 1980. The 2000 election provided another exception: Former Senator Bill Bradley's heated battle with President Clinton's choice for the Democratic nod, Vice President Al Gore.

### Reform Proposals

The fact that so many States now hold presidential primaries places great demands on candidates in terms of time, effort, money, scheduling, and fatigue. Primary season also tests the public's endurance.

For these and other reasons, many critics of the current system think that each of the major parties should hold a single, nationwide presidential primary. Some of those critics would have both parties nominate their presidential candidates in those contests. They would therefore do away with conventions, except perhaps to pick vice-presidential nominees or to write platforms.

Other critics favor a series of regional primaries, held at two- or three-week intervals in groups of States across the country. Hope for these plans is dim at best, as each plan would require joint action by Congress, the States, and both major parties.

## The Caucus-Convention Process

In those States that do not hold presidential primaries, delegates to the national conventions are chosen in a system of caucuses and conventions.[20] The process works basically as described here, although the details differ from State to State.

The party's voters meet in local caucuses, generally at the precinct level. There they choose delegates to a local or district convention, where delegates to the State convention are picked. At the State level, and sometimes in the district conventions, delegates to the national convention are chosen.

The caucus-convention process is the oldest method for picking national convention delegates. Its use has declined significantly over the years, however. In 2000, less than one fifth of all delegates to either party's convention came from those States that still use the caucus-convention process.

The Iowa caucuses generally get the most attention, largely because they are now the first delegate-selection event held in every presidential election season. Iowa purposely schedules the start of its caucus process early. In 2000 the event took place on January 24, eight days before New Hampshire held its first-in-the-nation presidential primary.

## The National Convention

Once all of the primaries and caucuses have been held and all of the delegates have been chosen, another event looms large. The two major parties hold their **national conventions,** the meetings at which the delegates vote to pick their presidential and vice-presidential candidates.

For a century and more, those party gatherings were highly dramatic, often chaotic and even stormy affairs at which, after days of heated bargaining, the party finally nominated its presidential candidate. Both parties' conventions have become much tamer in recent years. In large part, this is because there is now little doubt about who will win the convention's grand prize. Regularly, the leading contender has won enough delegates

---

[20]In 2000, national convention delegates were chosen by the caucus-convention method by both major parties in Alaska, Hawaii, Iowa, Minnesota, Nevada, and North Dakota. In a few other States, one party picked delegates through the caucus process while the other held a presidential primary.

RESOURCE○PRO®

**Resource Pro® CD-ROM** contains an electronic version of each activity found in the Teaching Resources as well as additional resources such as Supreme Court cases. The Planning Express® feature allows you to customize and create daily lesson plans within minutes.

*Answer to . . .*

**Interpreting Political Cartoons** Possible answer: That they get a disproportionate amount of attention.

in the primaries and caucuses to lock up the nomination before the convention meets.

Each party's convention remains a major event, nonetheless. Party conventions accomplish three main goals: (1) to officially name the party's presidential and vice-presidential candidates, (2) to bring the various factions and the leading personalities in the party together in one place for a common purpose, and (3) to adopt the party's **platform**—its formal statement of basic principles, stands on major policy matters, and objectives for the campaign and beyond.

If the meeting is successful, the convention also does several other things. It promotes party unity, mobilizes support for the party ticket, and captures the interest and attention of the country.

## The First Two Days

Both parties' conventions usually meet in one or two daily sessions over a four-day period, and they follow a fairly standard pattern. The first day is devoted to organizing the convention and to rousing speeches. The **keynote address** is almost always the high point of the first session. Traditionally, that speech is delivered by one of the party's most accomplished orators. The keynoter's remarks, and nearly all of the many other speeches made during the convention, follow a predictable form. They glorify the party, its history, its leaders, and its programs; condemn the opposition; underscore the virtues of party harmony; and predict a smashing victory in November.

The presentation and adoption of committee reports take up the better part of the second day's sessions. These sessions can be quite spirited. The convention's committee on rules proposes whatever changes it thinks should be made in the rules that guide the convention itself and in the rules that govern the national party's operations. The committee on platform and resolutions also makes its report. The platform emerges from a draft drawn up by the party's leadership before the convention.

Platform-writing is a fine art. Not only is a platform a statement of party principles and stands on policy matters, it is also a campaign document. Its more controversial planks often prompt arguments in the committee, and that debate may spill over to the convention floor.

However, a platform aims to appeal to as many people and as many groups as possible. So, both parties tend to produce somewhat generalized comments on some of the hard questions of the day. Platforms are regularly criticized for what their critics see as their blandness. Listen to this comment, made by the Republican presidential nominee in 1964:

> **PRIMARY Sources** *"Platforms are written to be ignored and forgotten. . . . Like Jell-O shimmering on a dessert plate, there is usually little substance and nothing you can get your teeth into."*
>
> —Barry Goldwater

Still, the platforms are important. They set out a number of hard and fast stands in many policy areas. They also reflect the compromise nature of American politics and of the two major parties.

## The Last Two Days

The convention turns to its chief task on the third day: the nomination of the party's candidate for the presidency. The names of any number of contenders may be offered to the delegates.[21] Once their nominating (and several seconding) speeches have been made, the convention begins to vote. The secretary calls the States in alphabetical order. The chair of each delegation announces how that delegation's

---

[21]Most of them have no real chance of becoming the party's nominee, but they are put forward for some other reason. Thus a "favorite son" may be touted because a State delegation wants to honor one of its own.

◀ **Keynote Speaker**
Representative Harold Ford, Jr.'s (D., Tennessee) image is projected on a large-screen monitor as he speaks at the 2000 Democratic National Convention.

## Background Note
### Political Talk
The word *caucus*, used today to describe the political party meetings at which delegates or candidates are selected, is an original American term dating from the eighteenth century. Nobody is exactly sure where the word comes from. Some believe it derives from the Algonquin "caucauasu," meaning counselor or promoter. Others trace it to a local political club of the 1760s, the Caucus Club of Boston, whose members may have taken their group's name from the Latin word meaning "drinking vessel." One interesting, though unlikely, theory is that the word is an acronym for the names of six eighteenth-century politicians—Cooper, Adams, Urann, Coulson, Urann, and Symmes.

## Point-of-Use Resources

📁 **The Living Constitution** Popular Sovereignty, p. 3

📁 **Close Up on Primary Sources** Barbara Jordan, Keynote Address to the Democratic National Convention (1976), p. 49

📁 **Simulations and Debates** Platform Committee, pp. 42–43, helps students prepare platforms for a new party as part of a political simulation.

📖 **Basic Principles of the Constitution Transparencies** Transparencies 9–15, *Popular Sovereignty*

# CONSTITUTIONAL PRINCIPLES

## Popular Sovereignty

The methods used to nominate presidential candidates and to choose delegates to the national conventions vary among the States. Some States use primaries, while others use caucuses. There are even differences in the types of primaries and caucuses that are held. Of course, this can be confusing for people who have just moved to a State and are unfamiliar with its methods for nominating presidential candidates and choosing delegates.

## Activity

Assign each student one of the 50 States. Ask each student to conduct research into the assigned State's method of nominating presidential candidates and choosing convention delegates. Have each student create a brief public-service announcement detailing the State's nominating process for presidential candidates as well as how it chooses delegates to the national conventions. Allow time for students to present their public-service announcements.

## Background Note
### Recent Scholarship

How do Presidents effectively combine political skills with intellectual and moral leadership? Erwin C. Hargrove attempts to answer this question in *The President as Leader: Appealing to the Better Angels of our Nature.* After analyzing classical and contemporary studies of political leadership, Hargrove describes three alternative leadership styles, exemplified by Presidents Franklin D. Roosevelt, Lyndon B. Johnson, and Ronald Reagan. He then contends that the element common to these styles is that of cultural leadership. By tailoring his skills and ideas to cultural mores, Hargrove argues, all of these Presidents were effective leaders—even if their leadership styles varied dramatically.

## Point–of–Use Resources

**Simulations and Data Graphing CD-ROM** offers data graphing tools that give students practice with creating and interpreting graphs.

## Spotlight on Texas Government

**Presidential Conventions** Two presidential conventions have been held in Houston, Texas. The first, in 1928, took place in Sam Houston Hall, which was built especially for the occasion in only sixty-four working days. Franklin Delano Roosevelt nominated Al Smith of New York.

Roosevelt's speech was carried to millions of Americans by a relatively new device, radio, that he would use effectively in his Fireside Chats when he later became President. At the first roll call, Smith fell short of the nomination by ten votes. Ohio then switched its votes to Smith, and other States followed suit. Texas, however, cast its forty votes for Texan Jesse H. Jones. The Democrats split over their support for Prohibition, which the party at large favored but Smith opposed. Smith was defeated in the general election, losing to Herbert Hoover.

The 1992 Republican National Convention was held at the Houston Astrodome. After a bitter battle over the party platform, the party renominated George Bush of Texas for President and Dan Quayle for Vice President. In the election, Clinton won with a plurality of 43% to Bush's 38%. Independent Ross Perot received 19% of the vote.

### Analyzing Texas Government

*What are the advantages and disadvantages for a city of hosting a presidential convention?*

votes are cast. Occasionally, a delegation passes and its votes are reported after the rest of the States have been called.

Most often, the first ballot produces a candidate. In the 26 conventions held by each party from 1900 through 2000, the Republicans have made a first ballot nomination 22 times and the Democrats 21 times. Indeed, the GOP has not had to take a second ballot since its 1948 convention, and the Democrats not since 1952. A convention can, however, become deadlocked, unable to make a choice between the top contenders. In that case, a "dark horse"—that is someone who did not seem a likely choice before the convention—may finally emerge as the nominee. [22]

The fourth day brings the nomination of the party's vice-presidential candidate. Whomever the presidential nominee's running mate turns out to be, he or she is almost invariably the hand-picked choice of the party's newly nominated presidential candidate.

With its candidates named, the convention comes to the final major item on its agenda: the presidential candidate's acceptance speech. As that speech ends, the delegates erupt in wild, elated celebration.

## Who Is Nominated?

If an incumbent President wants another term, the convention's choice of a nominee is easy. The President is almost certain to get the nomination, and usually with no real opposition from within the party. The President's advantages are immense: the majesty and publicity of the office and the close control of the party's machinery. [23]

When the President is not in the field, up to a dozen or so contenders may surface in the pre-convention period. At most, two or three of them may survive to contest the prize at the convention.

### Political Experience

Who among the contenders will win the nomination? The historical record argues this answer: the one who is, in the jargon of politics, the most available—that is, the most electable. Conventions want to pick candidates who can win, those with the broadest possible appeal within the party and to the electorate.

Most presidential candidates come to their nominations with substantial and well-known records in public office. But those records have to be free of controversies that could have antagonized important elements within the party or among the voting public. Generally, presidential candidates have served in elective office, where they have shown vote-getting ability. Seldom does a candidate step from the business world or from the military directly into the role of candidate, as did Wendell Willkie in 1940 or Dwight Eisenhower in 1952.

Historically, the governorships of larger States have produced the largest number of presidential candidacies. Of the 20 men nominated by the two

---

[22] The most spectacular deadlock in convention history occurred at the Democratic convention in New York in 1924. That convention took 103 ballots before John W. Davis of West Virginia won the nomination.

[23] In fact, only four sitting Presidents have ever been denied nomination: John Tyler by the Whigs in 1844; Millard Fillmore by the Whigs in 1852; Franklin Pierce by the Democrats in 1856; and Chester Arthur by the Republicans in 1884.

## Answers to . . .

**Analyzing Texas Government**
Advantages might include revenue for city businesses and national recognition. Disadvantages might include overcrowding and disruption of normal services.

major parties between 1900 and 1956, eleven were either then serving or had once served as a governor.

For a time the Senate became the prime source of major party presidential candidates. In the four elections from 1960 through 1972, each major party nominee had been a senator. None had ever been a governor.

More recently, however, the old pattern has been restored. Jimmy Carter, the former governor of Georgia, was nominated by the Democrats in 1976 and 1980. Ronald Reagan, former governor of California, was the GOP choice in 1980 and again in 1984. The Democrats nominated the governor of Massachusetts, Michael Dukakis, in 1988, and they picked Governor Bill Clinton of Arkansas in 1992 and renominated him in 1996. The Republicans nominated Governor George W. Bush of Texas in 2000.

### Other Characteristics

Most leading contenders for presidential nominations have been Protestants. The most notable exceptions, all Democrats and all Catholics, are Alfred E. Smith in 1928, John F. Kennedy in 1960, Eugene McCarthy and Robert F. Kennedy in 1968, and Michael Dukakis (Eastern Orthodox) in 1988.

Most presidential candidates have come from the larger States. Thus, hopefuls from such pivotal States as New York, Ohio, Illinois, Texas, and California have usually been seen as more electable than candidates from smaller States.

Television has reshaped this matter over the past several elections, however. The Republicans picked Barry Goldwater of Arizona in 1964 and Bob Dole of Kansas in 1996. And the Democrats nominated George McGovern of South Dakota in 1972, Jimmy Carter of Georgia in 1976, and Bill Clinton of Arkansas in 1992 and 1996.

Both parties' nominees usually have a pleasant and healthy appearance, seem to be happily married, and have an attractive (and exploitable) family. To this point, only three nominees have been divorced: Adlai Stevenson, the Democratic nominee in 1952 and 1956; Ronald Reagan, the Republican candidate in 1980 and 1984; and Bob Dole, the Republicans' choice in 1996.

A well-developed speaking ability has always been a major factor of availability (electability) in American politics. Of course, being able to project well over television has become a must, as well.

Neither party has, to this point, seriously considered a woman as its candidate for the presidency—or, until 1984 with the Democratic Party's nomination of Geraldine Ferraro, for the vice presidency. Nor has either party yet nominated a member of any minority group for President, although the Democrats nominated an Orthodox Jew, Senator Joseph Lieberman of Connecticut, for Vice President in 2000.

---

## Section 4 Assessment

### Key Terms and Main Ideas

1. What are the two major processes used to select delegates to **national conventions?**
2. How does **proportional representation** differ from the **winner-take-all** system?
3. Why are hard-fought **presidential primaries** fairly common in the party out of power and rare for the President's party?

### Critical Thinking

4. **Expressing Problems Clearly** Compare different methods of filling public offices. How does the current, Statewide presidential primary system stack up against a single, nationwide primary for each party, or a series of regional primaries?

5. **Demonstrating Reasoned Judgment** Presidential contender Adlai Stevenson once said "The hardest thing about any political campaign is how to win without proving that you are unworthy of winning." What do you think he meant?

### Take It to the Net

6. Read about the history of presidential campaign advertising and the ads that ran during a recent primary season. Based on this information and campaign ads you have seen, write a letter to an advertising agency describing the types of ads you think should be made for future campaigns. Use the links provided in the Social Studies area at the following Web site for help in completing this activity. **www.phschool.com**

### Take It to the Net

6. Direct students to the Social Studies area of the Prentice Hall School Web site. The *Magruder's American Government* companion Web site includes the directions and links needed to complete the activity. It also provides a printable Internet activity worksheet with scoring rubrics for assessment. Letters should include examples and demonstrate why they are useful.

## Point-of-Use Resources

**Guide to the Essentials** Chapter 13, Section 4, p. 74 provides support for students who need additional review of section content. Spanish support is available in the Spanish edition of the Guide on p. 67.

**Quiz** Unit 4 booklet, p. 9 includes matching and multiple-choice questions to check students' understanding of Section 4 content.

**Presentation Pro CD-ROM** Quizzes and multiple-choice questions check students' understanding of Section 4 content.

## Answers to . . .

### Section 4 Assessment

1. Primaries or caucus-conventions.
2. The proportional representation rule says that any candidate who wins at least 15 percent of the votes cast in a primary gets the number of State Democratic convention delegates that corresponds to his or her share of that primary vote; the winner-take-all rule says that the candidate who won the preference vote automatically wins the support of all the delegates chosen at the primary.
3. Because in the President's party, the President will usually get his or her way, either by running for reelection or backing a successor.
4. Nationwide primary would reduce the time, effort, money, scheduling, and fatigue of the current system. Regional primaries would offer easier scheduling and less effort by candidates and the public, but coordination of regional events and regulations by disparate States might be difficult.
5. Possible answer: Facing stiff competition, many candidates resort to mud-slinging, which causes them a loss of respect.

## SKILLS FOR LIFE

### CRITICAL THINKING

### Making Decisions

**Focus** Role-play President Kennedy's staff during the Cuban Missile Crisis. Present to the President a series of possible decisions with the pros and cons of each.

**Instruct** As a class or in small groups, brainstorm a decision-making chart that identifies possible options for dealing with the threat of a new Soviet nuclear arsenal in Cuba. Combine the ideas into a chart as described in Test for Success.

**Close/Reteach** Hold a simulated Cabinet debate on the various options presented to Kennedy and his advisors. Have students represent a variety of roles—national security, intelligence, defense, diplomacy, as well as those concerned with domestic politics—each with particular interests and opinions on how to respond to the crisis.

### Answers . . .

**1.** Because the new construction was going on so close to the mainland United States.

**2.** The paragraph numbered 5, which requests information on how missile development would affect the United States.

**3.** The paragraphs numbered 6 through 8, which request a study of three options: Issuing threats to the Soviets; destroying the bases by various means; and by blockading or invading Cuba.

**4.** Paragraphs numbered 6 through 8 request a study to identify the possible consequences of various courses of action.

**5.** Possible answer: Because it was less likely to provoke a nuclear war than was an invasion.

# SKILLS FOR LIFE

# Making Decisions

In 1962, U.S. intelligence reports revealed that the Soviet Union was building missile bases in Cuba. An infuriated President John F. Kennedy had to decide how to respond to this new nuclear threat in America's backyard.

President Kennedy summoned his top national security and military advisors to discuss the crisis. What followed is an example of the decision-making process:

**1. Identify the issue to be decided.** The first step in good decision making is to figure out *whether* a decision is needed and to clarify *what* ultimately needs to be decided. Reports of the Soviet activity in Cuba immediately raised two questions:

(a) Should the United States respond?

(b) If so, how can the Soviet Union be made to withdraw its arsenal without triggering a catastrophic nuclear war?

The two superpowers already had scores of long-range nuclear weapons aimed at each other's cities. Yet Kennedy felt that the Cuba buildup required a swift response. Why do you think he felt that strong action was needed?

**2. Gather information.** In a memo, National Security Advisor McGeorge Bundy outlined President Kennedy's orders on how to proceed. Read the excerpts from the memo, above right. What part instructs the staff to collect more information on the situation?

**3. Identify options.** A decision requires choosing among two or more options. What part of the memo concerns identifying options?

**4. Predict consequences.** What part of the memo concerns predicting consequences of various courses of action?

**5. Make a decision.** On October 22, President Kennedy announced his decision to launch a naval blockade of Cuba to prevent more missiles from reaching the island. Tense days followed, as the

### THE WHITE HOUSE
#### WASHINGTON

TOP SECRET AND SENSITIVE

August 23, 1962

NATIONAL SECURITY ACTION MEMORANDUM NO. 181

To: Secretary of State / Secretary of Defense / Attorney General / Acting Director, CIA / General Taylor

The President has directed that the following actions and studies be undertaken in the light of the new . . . activity in Cuba. . . .

5. An analysis should be prepared of the probable military, political, and psychological impact of the establishment in Cuba of either surface-to-air missiles or surface-to-surface missiles which could reach the U.S.

6. A study should be made of the advantages and disadvantages of making a statement that the U.S. would not tolerate the establishment of military forces . . . which might launch a nuclear attack from Cuba against the U.S.

7. A study should be made of the various military alternatives which might be adopted in executing a decision to eliminate any installations in Cuba. . . . What would be the pros and cons, for example of pinpoint attack, general counter-force attack, and outright invasion.

8. A study should be made of the advantages and disadvantages of action to liberate Cuba by blockade or invasion or other action . . . .

—Memo from National Security Advisor McGeorge Bundy

superpowers came to the brink of nuclear war. In the end, the Soviets backed down, called back their ships, and dismantled the Cuban bases. Why do you think the President chose the option of blockading Cuba?

### Test for Success

Make a decision-making chart on the Cuban Missile Crisis. Identify two or more courses of action that President Kennedy could have taken, and describe the possible consequences (pro and con) of each course of action.

### Test for Success

Possible answers: Issuing threats would be less confrontational (pro) but also less likely to force the Soviets to back down (con); destroying the bases by air attack or invasion would eliminate the missile threat (pro) but would be likely to provoke a war (con); blockading the island would be less confrontational (pro) and likely to force a Soviet withdrawal (pro) but still risked Soviet retaliation (con).

### Point-of-Use Resources

📁 **Skills for Life Activity** Unit 4 booklet, p. 12 provides an additional skill activity for this chapter.

💿 **Social Studies Skills Tutor CD-ROM** Provides interactive practice in geographic literacy, critical thinking and reading, visual analysis, and communications.

## Section Preview

### OBJECTIVES

1. **Understand** the function of the electoral college today.
2. **Describe** the flaws in the electoral college.
3. **Outline** the advantages and disadvantages of proposed reforms of the electoral college.

### WHY IT MATTERS

Most people do not understand the workings of the electoral college system. They do not understand that, no matter what the popular vote results may be, the electoral votes determine the outcome of a presidential election.

### POLITICAL DICTIONARY

★ district plan
★ proportional plan
★ direct popular election
★ electorate
★ national bonus plan

The presidential campaign—the all-out effort to win the votes of the people—begins soon after the conventions. Each candidate's campaign organization works to present its candidate in the best possible light. Voters are bombarded by radio and television speeches; "whistle-stop" tours; press conferences and press releases; public rallies; party dinners; newspaper, radio, and television advertisements; stickers and buttons; placards and pamphlets; billboards and match-covers; Web sites and e-mail. The candidates pose for hundreds of photographs and shake thousands of hands as each of them tries to convince the people that he is best for the country.

The presidential campaign ends on election day. Millions of voters go to the polls in all 50 States and the District of Columbia. But the President, whoever that is to be, is not formally elected until the presidential electors cast their votes, several weeks later.

### The Electoral College Today

You have arrived at one of the least understood parts of the American political process. As the people vote in the presidential election, they do not cast a vote directly for one of the contenders for the presidency. Instead, they vote to elect presidential electors.

Remember, the Constitution provides for the election of the President by the electoral college, in which each State has as many electors as it has members of Congress. The Framers expected the electors to use their own judgment in selecting a President. But today the electors, once chosen, are really just "rubber stamps." They are expected to vote automatically for their party's candidates for President and Vice President. In short, the electors go through the form set out in the Constitution in order to meet the letter of the Constitution, but their behavior is a far cry from its original intent.

◄ Delegates on the floor of the 2000 Democratic and Republican National Conventions are walking advertisements for their candidate.

## Choosing Electors

The electors are chosen by popular vote in every State[24] and on the same day everywhere: the Tuesday after the first Monday in November every fourth year. So the next presidential election will be held on November 2, 2004. In every State except Maine and Nebraska, the electors are chosen at-large.[25] That is, they are chosen on a winner-take-all basis. The presidential candidate—technically, the slate of elector-candidates nominated by his party—receiving the largest popular vote in a State regularly wins all of that State's electoral votes.

Today, the names of the individual elector-candidates appear on the ballot in only a handful of States. In most States, only the names of the presidential and vice-presidential candidates are listed. They stand as "shorthand" for the elector slates.

[24]The Constitution (Article II, Section 1, Clause 2) says that the electors are to be chosen in each State "in such Manner as the Legislature thereof may direct." In several States the legislatures themselves chose the electors in the first several elections. By 1832, however, every State except South Carolina had provided for popular election. The electors were picked by the legislature in South Carolina through the elections of 1860. Since then, all presidential electors have been chosen by popular vote in every State, with two exceptions. The State legislatures chose the electors in Florida in 1868 and in Colorado in 1876.

## Counting Electoral Votes

The Constitution provides that the date Congress sets for the electors to meet "shall be the same throughout the United States."[26] The 12th Amendment provides that "the electors shall meet in their respective states." The electors thus meet at their State capitol on the date set by Congress, now the Monday after the second Wednesday in December. There they each cast their electoral votes, one for President and one for Vice President. The electors' ballots, signed and sealed, are sent by registered mail to the president of the Senate in Washington.

Which party has won a majority of the electoral votes, and who then will be the next President of the United States, is usually known by midnight of election day, more than a month before the electors cast their ballots. But the

[25]Maine (beginning in 1972) and Nebraska (1992) use the "district plan." In those States, two electors are chosen from the State at-large and the others are picked in each of the State's congressional districts. The district plan was used by several States in the first few presidential elections, but every State except South Carolina had provided for the choice of the electors from the State at large by 1832. Since then, the district plan has been used only by Michigan in 1892 and by Maine and Nebraska.

[26]Article II, Section 1, Clause 4

---

### The Presidential Election Process

**January–June**
**Primaries** In States with presidential primaries, voters select their party's national convention delegates and/or express a preference among the candidates.

**Caucuses** In States with caucuses, voters in local meetings choose delegates to conventions at the congressional district or State levels.

| January | February | March | April | May | June | July | August |
|---|---|---|---|---|---|---|---|

**July–August**
**National Conventions** Delegates choose the nominee for each major party.

*Interpreting Charts* The Framers of the Constitution established the electoral college to allow the most capable citizens in each State to select the President. ***Is that how that electoral process works today? Why or why not?***

---

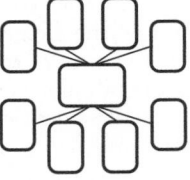

formal election of the President and Vice President finally takes place on January 6.[27]

On that date, the president of the Senate opens the electoral votes from each State and counts them before a joint session of Congress. The candidate who receives a majority of the electors' votes for President is declared elected, as is the candidate with a majority of the votes for Vice President.

If no candidate has won a majority—at least 270 of the 538 electoral votes today—the election is thrown into the House of Representatives. This happened in 1800 and again in 1824. The House chooses a President from among the top three candidates in the electoral college. Each State delegation has one vote, and it takes a majority of 26 to elect. If the House fails to choose a President by January 20, the 20th Amendment provides that the newly elected Vice President shall act as President until a choice is made.[28]

If no person receives a majority of votes for Vice President, the Senate decides between the top two candidates. It takes a majority of the whole Senate to elect. The Senate has had to choose a Vice President only once, when it elected Richard M. Johnson in 1837.

## Flaws in the Electoral College

The electoral college system is plagued by three major concerns: (1) the winner of the popular vote is not guaranteed the presidency; (2) electors are not required to vote in accord with the popular vote; and (3) any election might have to be decided in the House of Representatives.

### The First Major Concern

There is the ever-present threat that the winner of the popular vote will not win the presidency. This continuing danger is largely the result of two factors. The most important is the winner-take-all feature of the electoral college system. That is, the winning candidate customarily receives all of a State's electoral votes. Thus in 2000 George W.

---

[27]If that day falls on a Sunday, as it did most recently in 1985 (but will not again until 2013), then the ballot-counting is held the following day.

[28]The 20th Amendment further provides that "the Congress may by law provide for the case wherein neither a President-elect nor a Vice President-elect shall have qualified" by inauguration day. Congress has done so in the Succession Act of 1947; see Section 2. The Speaker of the House would "act as President … until a President or Vice President shall have qualified."

## ACTIVITY

### Heterogeneous Groups

**Enrichment** Have students create a time line of events that would take place for a presidential hopeful in the months or years leading up to the national election. Ask them to list all of the important events in the process, from the declaration of candidacy to the counting of electoral votes in the fall election, in which a candidate must participate on the road to the White House. Encourage students to include the location of events when possible to illustrate the exhaustive traveling schedule candidates must endure.

**(Average)**

**January 6** Electoral votes are counted before a joint session of Congress.

**January 20** **Inauguration** Candidate receiving majority of electoral votes is sworn in as President of the United States.

| September | October | November | December | January | February | March | April |

**Tuesday after first Monday in November** **Election Day** Voters cast ballot for a slate of electors pledged to a particular presidential candidate.

**Monday after second Wednesday in December** **Electoral College Vote** Winning electors in each State meet in their State capitals to cast votes for President and Vice President. Statement of their vote is sent to Washington, D.C. and opened in early January.

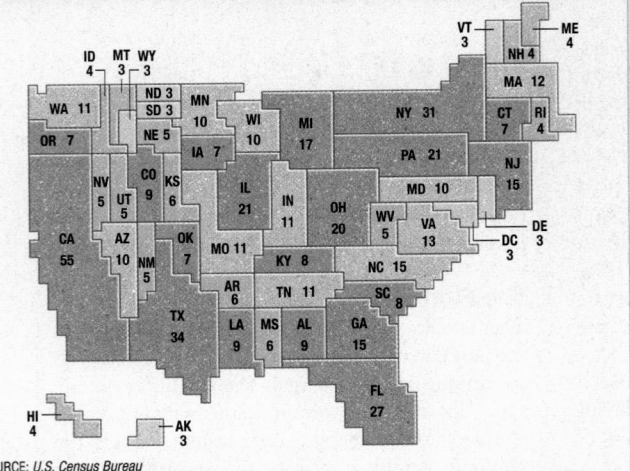

**Electoral Votes of Each State, 2004**

SOURCE: *U.S. Census Bureau*

*Interpreting Maps* This pictogram shows the number of electoral votes each State will have in the 2004 election. **Why are those states in which the election outcome is doubtful called "pivotal" States?**

Bush won 49.99 percent of the popular vote in Ohio. Still, he won all of that State's 21 electoral votes—even though some 2.3 million Ohioans voted for Democrat Al Gore and another 118,000 voted for the Green Party's Ralph Nader.

The other major culprit here is the way the electoral votes are distributed among the States. Remember, two of the electors in each State are allotted because of a State's Senate seats, regardless of population. So the allotment of electoral votes does not match the facts of population and voter distribution.

Take the extreme case to illustrate this point: California, the country's most populous State, has 55 electoral votes, one for each 615,848 persons in the State, based on its 2000 population of 33,871,698 residents. Wyoming has three electoral votes, one for each 164,594 persons, based on its 2000 population of 493,782 residents.

The popular vote winner has, in fact, failed to win the presidency four times: in 1824, 1876, 1888, and most recently in 2000. In 1824, Andrew Jackson won the largest share (a plurality, but not a majority) of the popular votes: 151,271, or 41.3 percent of the total. Jackson's nearest rival, John Quincy Adams, received

113,122 votes, or 30.9 percent. Ninety-nine of the 261 electors then voted for Jackson, again more than any other candidate but far short of a majority. The election thus went to the House and, early in 1825, it elected Adams to the presidency.

In the election of 1876, Republican candidate Rutherford B. Hayes received 4,034,311 popular votes and his Democratic opponent, Samuel J. Tilden, won 4,288,546. Tilden received 184 electoral votes. Hayes won 185 electoral votes and so became President.[29]

In 1888 President Grover Cleveland won 5,534,488 popular votes, 90,596 more than his Republican opponent, Benjamin Harrison. Harrison, however, received 233 electoral votes to Cleveland's 168, and so became the 23rd President.

In the most recent presidential election, the Democratic candidate, Vice President Al Gore, won 50,992,335 popular votes—537,179 more votes than his Republican opponent, then-Governor of Texas, George W. Bush. However, Mr. Bush received 271 electoral votes—one more than the bare majority in the electoral college, and so he became the nation's 43rd President.

Florida's 25 electoral votes proved to be decisive in the extraordinarily close 2000 election. The popular vote results in several Florida counties were challenged immediately after the polls closed there. The next five weeks were filled with partisan infighting, several recounts, and a number of court disputes. The United States Supreme Court finally brought an end to the bitter contest on December 12. It ruled, in *Bush* v. *Gore*, that the differing ways in which various counties were recounting votes violated the 14th Amendment's Equal Protection Clause. The Court's 5–4 decision ended those recounts. It also

[29]The election of 1876 is often called the "Stolen Election." Two conflicting sets of electoral votes were received from Florida (4 votes), Louisiana (8 votes), and South Carolina (7 votes), and the validity of one vote from Oregon was disputed. Congress set up an Electoral Commission with five senators, five representatives, and five Supreme Court justices to decide the matter. The Commissioners, eight Republicans and seven Democrats, voted on strict party lines, awarding all of the disputed votes, and so the presidency, to Hayes.

preserved George W. Bush's 537-vote lead in the Statewide count, resulting in Bush receiving Florida's 25 electoral votes. The Court's split decision in *Bush* v. *Gore* remains highly controversial.

Altogether, 15 Presidents have been elected who did not receive a majority of the popular vote. As you have just seen, four won despite the fact that their opponents received more popular votes than they did. Eleven others have won office with a *plurality*, but not a majority, of the popular vote. These "minority Presidents" were James K. Polk (1844), Zachary Taylor (1848), James Buchanan (1856), Abraham Lincoln (1860), James A. Garfield (1880), Grover Cleveland (1884, 1892), Woodrow Wilson (1912, 1916), Harry S Truman (1948), John F. Kennedy (1960), Richard Nixon (1968), Bill Clinton (1992, 1996), and George W. Bush (2000).

By now, you see the point: The "winner-take-all" factor produces an electoral vote that is, at best, only a distorted reflection of the popular vote.

### The Second Major Concern

Nothing in the Constitution, nor in any federal statute, requires the electors to vote for the candidate favored by the popular vote in their States. Several States do have such laws, but they are of doubtful constitutionality, and none has ever been enforced.

The electors are expected to vote for the candidate who carries their State and, as loyal members of their parties, they almost always do. Thus far, electors have "broken their pledges"—voted for someone other than their party's presidential nominee—on only nine occasions: in 1796, 1820, 1948, 1956, 1960, 1968, 1972, 1976, and 1988. In 2000, one elector from the District of Columbia refused to cast her vote for someone for President. Had that vote been cast, it would have gone to Al Gore. The elector said she acted as she did to protest the fact that the District of Columbia is not represented in Congress.

In no case has the vote of a "faithless elector" had a bearing on the outcome of a presidential election. But potential is certainly there.

### The Third Major Concern

In any presidential election, it is possible that the contest will be decided in the House. This has happened only twice, and not since 1824.

In several other elections, however—especially in 1912, 1924, 1948, and 1968—a strong third-party bid has threatened to make it impossible for either major party candidate to win a majority in the electoral college.

In 1968, George Wallace, the American Independent Party candidate, won five States and 46 electoral votes. If Democrat Hubert Humphrey had carried Alaska, Delaware, Missouri, Nevada, and Wisconsin—States where Richard Nixon's margin was thin and in which Wallace had a substantial vote—Nixon's electoral vote would have been 268, Humphrey's 224. Neither would have had a majority. The House would then have had to decide the election.

Three serious objections can be raised regarding election by the House. First, the voting in such cases is by States, not by individual members. A State with a small population, such as Alaska or Nevada, would have as much weight as the most populous State. Second, if the representatives from a State were so divided that no candidate was favored by a majority, the State would lose its vote. Third, the

## Popular Vote vs. Electoral Vote

| States | Popular Vote | % Popular Vote | Electoral Vote | % of Total National Electoral Vote |
|---|---|---|---|---|
| **Florida** | | | | |
| Bush | 2,912,790 | 48.85 | 25 | 4.6 |
| Gore | 2,912,253 | 48.84 | | |
| Nader | 97,488 | 1.63 | | |
| **Iowa** | | | | |
| Bush | 634,373 | 48.22 | | |
| Gore | 638,517 | 48.54 | 7 | 1.3 |
| Nader | 29,374 | 2.23 | | |
| **New Mexico** | | | | |
| Bush | 286,417 | 47.85 | | |
| Gore | 286,783 | 47.91 | 5 | .9 |
| Nader | 21,251 | 3.55 | | |
| **Oregon** | | | | |
| Bush | 713,577 | 46.52 | | |
| Gore | 720,342 | 46.96 | 7 | 1.3 |
| Nader | 77,357 | 5.04 | | |

SOURCE: Federal Election Commision

*Interpreting Tables* This table shows the election results in the four States where the 2000 presidential race was the closest. ***(a) How do these results illustrate the significance of the "winner-take-all" factor? (b) How did Ralph Nader's third-party candidacy affect these results?***

A C T I V I T Y

## Heterogeneous Groups

**Reteaching** Divide the class into four teams. On the chalkboard, draw a five-column chart. Label each column with the heading of each section from this chapter (column 1 heading = Section 1, column 2 heading = Section 2, etc.). Take the questions students developed in the English Language Learners Activity and categorize them into the appropriate sections. Using these questions, and any additional ones you choose to include, conduct a review session with the class. For students who created a visual rather than a question, write *visual* in the appropriate square and hold up the visual at that point in the review.

**(Average)**

Constitution requires a majority of the States for election in the House—today, 26 States. If a strong third-party candidate were involved, there is a real possibility that the House could not make a decision by Inauguration Day.[30]

## Proposed Reforms

Observers have long recognized the defects in the electoral college system. In fact, constitutional amendments to change the process have been introduced in every term of Congress since 1789. Most of the reforms people have offered fall under three headings: the district plan, the proportional plan, and direct popular election.

### The District Plan

Over time, many people have proposed the **district plan,** in which the electors would be chosen in each State in the same way as members of Congress. That is, two electors would be chosen from the State at large, and they would cast their electoral votes in line with the result of the Statewide popular vote. The other electors would be elected, separately, in each of the State's congressional districts. Their votes would be cast in accordance with the result of the popular vote in their district.[31]

The district plan would do away with the winner-take-all problem in the present system. Its supporters have argued that it would make the electoral vote a more accurate reflection of the popular returns.

The strongest argument against the plan is that it would not eliminate the possibility that the loser of the popular vote could still win the electoral vote. In fact, had it been in effect in 1960, Richard Nixon would have received 278 electoral votes, and he, not John Kennedy, would have won the presidency.

Further, the results under the district plan would depend very much on how the congressional districts were drawn in each State. Its use would be yet another motive for gerrymandering, or drawing electoral district lines for the advantage of a particular party.

### The Proportional Plan

Under the **proportional plan,** each presidential candidate would receive the same share of a State's electoral vote as he or she received in the State's popular vote. Thus, if a candidate won 40 percent of the votes cast in a State with 20 electoral votes, he or she would get 8 of that State's electoral votes.

This plan would cure the winner-take-all problem and eliminate faithless electors. It also would yield an electoral vote more in line with the popular vote, at least for each State.

The proportional plan would not necessarily produce the same result nationally. Because each of the smaller States is overweighted by its two Senate-based electors, the proportional plan would still make it possible for the loser of the popular vote to win the presidency in the electoral vote. In fact, this would have happened in 1896. William Jennings Bryan would have defeated William McKinley, although McKinley had a comfortable popular vote margin of 596,985 (4.3 percent).[32]

Many critics of the proportional plan worry about its effect on the two-party system. Certainly, its adoption would bring an increase in the number and vigor of minor parties. Third parties would no longer need to win entire States in order to get electoral votes. In addition, third-party candidates would regularly win at least some share of the electoral vote. Then the odds that a presidential election would have to go to the House would be increased.

Most of the plan's backers agree that an increase in minor party clout would mean that the winner of the popular vote would often fail to gain a clear majority of the electoral vote. Hence, advocates of this plan would lower the

---

[30]In such a case, Section 3 of the 20th Amendment states that "the Vice President-elect shall act as President until a President shall have qualified." If no Vice President-elect is available, the Presidential Succession Act would come into play. It is even mathematically possible for the minority party in the House to have control of a majority of the individual State delegations. That party could then elect its candidate, even though he or she may have run second or even third in both the popular and the electoral vote contests.

[31]Maine and Nebraska now use the district plan, as noted earlier. Any other State could do so, but it would take a constitutional amendment to make its use mandatory in all States.

[32]In the closest of all the presidential elections, Winfield S. Hancock would have defeated James A. Garfield in 1880, even though Garfield had a popular plurality of only 1,898 votes, 0.0213 percent. On the other hand, there would have been no "Stolen Election" in 1876, and Cleveland would have defeated Harrison in 1888.

---

## Preparing for Standardized Tests

Have students read the passages under *Proposed Reforms* on pp. 382–384 and then answer the question below.

Which plan might encourage gerrymandering?

**A** the district plan

**B** the national bonus plan

**C** the proportional plan

**D** the direct popular election plan

present requirement of a majority of the electoral votes to a plurality of at least 40 percent. If no candidate won 40 percent of the electoral votes, the two frontrunners would face one another in a runoff election.

## Direct Popular Election

The most common and widely supported proposal is the most obvious one: Do away with the electoral college system altogether and allow **direct popular election** of the President. The arguments for direct election seem overpowering. The strongest one is that it would support the democratic ideal: Each vote would count equally in the national result. The winner would always be the majority or plurality choice. The dangers and confusions of the present system would be eliminated, replaced by a simple and easily understood process.

The fact that the loser of the popular vote nevertheless won the presidency in the most recent election has given added weight to the case of direct election. Several obstacles stand in the way of the reform, however.[33]

The constitutional amendment process itself is a major stumbling block. It is time-consuming, difficult, and cumbersome. Second, the smaller States are greatly overrepresented in the electoral college. They would lose that advantage in a direct election. It is likely that enough senators or representatives of small States would oppose a direct election amendment to kill it.

Some opponents argue that direct election would weaken the federal system because the States, as States, would lose their role in the choice of a President. Others believe that direct election would put too great a load on the election process. They say that because every vote cast in each State would count in the national result, the candidates would have to campaign strenuously in every State. The impact that

Interpreting Political Cartoons *What details in the cartoon suggest that the electoral college is one of the most complex parts of the political process?*

would have on campaign time, effort, and finances would be huge and, opponents argue, probably unmanageable.[34]

Some say that direct election would spur ballot-box stuffing and other forms of voting fraud. That, they predict, would lead to lengthy, bitter, highly explosive post-election challenges.

In many States, a State-wide election often hangs on the behavior of a specific group in the **electorate**—the mass of people who can cast votes in an election. The result depends on how those voters cast their ballots or, even more importantly, on how heavily they do or do not turn out to vote. Thus, for example, the African American vote in Chicago is often decisive in the presidential election in Illinois. In a direct election, these groups would not hold the balance of power they now have, so many of them oppose the direct election plan.

Given all this and despite the current efforts on behalf of direct election, there seems little real chance that that reform will become fact any time soon.

[33]The House of Representatives did approve a direct election amendment by the necessary two-thirds vote in 1969. A Senate filibuster killed the measure in 1970. President Carter championed a similar proposal, but it was rejected by a Senate floor vote in 1979.

[34]In fact, it is possible for a candidate to win the presidency by carrying only the 11 largest States, because they now have a total of 271 electoral votes, one more than the minimum number needed to win the presidency.

ACTIVITY

## Learning Styles

**Verbal/Linguistic** Assign each student one of the following systems of presidential election: *electoral college, district plan, proportional plan, direct popular election,* and *national bonus plan.* Tell them that they have been asked to write an editorial for a national newspaper in an attempt to garner support for the presidential election system they have been assigned. Since the article will be printed as a column in the paper, the editorial cannot exceed 300 words. Ask for volunteers to share their columns with the class.

**(Challenging)**

## Background Note
### Global Awareness

Finland, which had used the electoral college system for electing its President since the founding of its Constitution in 1919, made the change to direct popular election in the1980s. By the election of 1994, the nation had adopted a two-round system of direct popular election. In the first round, political parties or civic groups name candidates (non-party groups are required to have the support of at least 20,000 registered voters in order to put forth a candidate). The candidate winning more than half of the votes cast becomes President. If no candidate wins more than half of the votes, a second round takes place, in which only the two leading candidates from the first round compete. The one who then receives the most votes is declared President. Direct popular election seems to be a success in terms of voter turnout; in 1994, more than 80 per cent of the electorate voted in both rounds. In the 2000 election—with an 80.2% voter turnout for the second round—Finland's first female President, Tarja Halonen, was elected.

*Answer to . . .*

**Interpreting Political Cartoons**
Possible answer: The diagrams on the chalkboard, the many plans and outlines strewn about the room, and the baffled or exhausted students.

## Point-of-Use Resources

 **Guide to the Essentials** Chapter 13, Section 5, p. 75 provides support for students who need additional review of section content. Spanish support is available in the Spanish edition of the Guide on p. 68.

**Quiz** Unit 4 booklet, p. 11 includes matching and multiple-choice questions to check students' understanding of Section 5 content.

**Presentation Pro CD-ROM** Quizzes and multiple-choice questions check students' understanding of Section 5 content.

## Answers to . . .

### Section 5 Assessment

**1.** Today electors serve as a "rubber stamp" by voting for their party's candidates; the Framers, in contrast, saw them as "free agents" who deliberated on each candidate's merits.

**2.** The winner of the popular vote is not guaranteed the presidency, electors are not required to vote in accord with the popular vote, and any election has the potential to be decided in the House.

**3.** District: Electors are chosen in each State in the same way as members of Congress. Proportional: Each candidate receives the same share of a State's electoral vote as he or she receives in the popular vote. Direct popular election: The people vote directly for the President and Vice President. National bonus: A national pool of electoral votes would be awarded to the winner of the popular vote and added to the regular electoral votes.

**4.** For: It would be democratic, easy to understand, and easy to carry out. Against: It would lessen the role of the States, could lead to vote fraud, and would require a hard-to-pass constitutional amendment.

**5.** Methods should be clearly explained and supported with relevant facts.

**6. (a)** Because of the winner-take-all feature and the fact that electoral votes are not based on population or voter distribution. **(b)** Answers will vary, but should be supported with relevant examples.

### The National Bonus Plan

Another and very different plan, called the **national bonus plan,** has recently surfaced. At first glance, the plan seems quite complicated and "off the wall." In fact, it is neither.

The national bonus plan would keep much of the electoral college system intact, especially its winner-take-all feature. It would weight that feature in favor of the winner of the popular vote, however.

Under this plan, a national pool of 102 electoral votes would be awarded, automatically, to the winner of the popular vote. This bloc of electoral votes would be added to the electoral votes that the candidate won in the election. If all those votes added up to a majority of the electoral college—at least 321—the candidate would be declared President. In the unlikely event that they did not add up to a majority, a runoff election between the two front runners in the popular vote would then be held.

The advocates of this plan see the electors themselves as unnecessary, and so would do away with them. They say that their plan meets all of the major objections to the present system and all of those raised against the other proposals for its reform. They also claim that their plan would almost guarantee that the winner of the popular vote would always be the winner of the electoral vote.

To date, the national bonus plan has not attracted much public attention. Nor has it attracted much understanding, interest, or support.

### Electoral College Supporters

Their case is not often heard, but the present electoral college system does have its defenders. They react to the several proposed reforms by raising the various objections you have just read. Beyond that they argue that critics exaggerate the "dangers" in the system. Only two elections have ever gone to the House of Representatives and none in more than 175 years. They grant the point that the loser of the popular vote has in fact won the presidency four times. But, they note, that has happened *only* four times over the course of now 54 presidential elections; and they add, it has happened only once in the last 120 years.

Supporters also say that the present arrangement, whatever its warts, has two major strengths:

1. It is a known process. Each of the proposed, but untried, reforms may very well have defects that could not be known until they appeared in practice.

2. In most cases, it identifies the winner of the presidential election quickly and certainly. With the exception of the 2000 election, the nation does not have to wait for very long to know the outcome.

## Section **5** Assessment

### Key Terms and Main Ideas

1. How does the way the electoral college functions today differ from the Framers' intentions?
2. What are the three main weaknesses of the electoral college system?
3. Explain the **district plan,** the **proportional plan,** the **direct popular election plan,** and the **national bonus plan** for reforming the electoral college.
4. What are the arguments for and against **direct popular election?**

### Critical Thinking

5. **Identifying Alternatives** Suppose you have been asked to draft a plan for reforming the electoral college. Choose one of the methods discussed in this section, or write one of

your own. Explain how your plan will work and why it is superior to other proposed plans.
6. **Expressing Problems Clearly (a)** How it is possible for the winner of the popular vote to fail to win the presidency? **(b)** How do you think the Framers might reply to this defect in the electoral college system?

 **Take It to the Net**

7. Read more about the electoral college today. Then plan a debate in which you argue for or against keeping the present system. Include at least three arguments in defense of your position. Use the links provided in the Social Studies area at the following Web site for help in completing this activity. **www.phschool.com**

**Take It to the Net**

**7.** Direct students to the Social Studies area at the Prentice Hall School Web site. The *Magruder's American Government* companion Web site includes the directions and links needed to complete the activity. It also provides a printable Internet activity worksheet with scoring rubrics for assessment. Positions should be clearly stated and backed with examples.

# on the Supreme Court

## May the President Be Sued?

*The Constitution contains no specific protection of the President against lawsuits. What kind of protection is appropriate for the President? Are all his actions protected, or only those that are taken in good faith and fall within the scope of his official duties?*

### Nixon v. Fitzgerald (1982)

In November 1968, A. Ernest Fitzgerald, a management analyst with the Department of the Air Force, revealed in testimony before Congress that development of the Air Force's C-5A transport plane would cost about $2 billion more than had been predicted. He also disclosed unexpected technical problems that had developed with the plane.

Just over a year later, in January of 1970, Fitzgerald's department was reorganized and he was laid off, along with some other employees. Fitzgerald complained to the Civil Service Commission, which found that he had been terminated for "purely personal" reasons but not in retaliation for his testimony. Fitzgerald then sued various Defense Department officials and White House aides who, he said, were responsible for his firing.

Fitzgerald later named President Richard M. Nixon as a defendant in his suit because Fitzgerald believed that the President had played a direct role in his firing. Nixon argued that as President, he had absolute immunity—complete protection—against lawsuits over actions he took while in office. The trial court and then the court of appeals both rejected this immunity defense. Nixon then appealed to the Supreme Court, which had never before ruled on the question of how far a President's immunity against lawsuits extended.

### Arguments for Nixon

1. The President occupies a unique position under our Constitution, because he serves as chief executive, policymaker, and law enforcement official. For the President to have to deal with private lawsuits as well would harm the effective operation of our government.

2. Judges and prosecutors have received absolute immunity in order to allow them to deal "fearlessly and impartially" with their official duties. The President should receive similar protection.

3. The President's immunity should cover all of his official functions. Otherwise, courts would have to review his motives in each case in order to determine whether particular actions were covered by the immunity.

### Arguments for Fitzgerald

1. Past Supreme Court cases have granted governors and Cabinet officials only partial immunity from lawsuits, which protects them only for actions taken in good faith.

2. If the President did in fact order the firing of an employee who was lawfully entitled to retain his job, then he acted outside the boundary of his proper duties and should be subject to a lawsuit for his actions.

3. Absolute immunity would place the President above the law.

---

### Decide for Yourself

1. Review the constitutional grounds on which each side based its arguments and the specific arguments each side presented.

2. Debate the opposing viewpoints presented in this case. Which viewpoint do you favor?

3. Predict the impact of the Court's decision on other situations in which a President might be sued. (To read a summary of the Court's decision, turn to the Supreme Court Glossary on page 799.)

---

**Close Up on the Supreme Court** *Nixon* v. *Fitzgerald,* p. 14 provides an activity to extend coverage of this case.

 **Corner**

 **Online**

To keep up-to-date on Close Up news and activities, visit Close Up Online at

**www.closeup.org**

---

## May the President Be Sued?

**Focus** Explain the difference between a civil lawsuit and a criminal case. *(Criminal cases are brought by the government against persons who commit crimes. Civil lawsuits settle disputes)* The Constitution provides for the threat of criminal prosecution after removal from office for dealing with Presidents accused of a crime. Explain that this case addresses whether a *civil* lawsuit may be filed against a President for actions taken while in office.

**Instruct** Ask students their opinion of the decision in this case. Then have students compose an editorial expressing their opinion regarding Nixon's "unique position" argument.

**Close/Reteach** In a recent case, an Appeals Court has held that the President may be sued while in office for unofficial actions occurring before entering office. (Nixon *concerns official actions as President*) Discuss the pros and cons of this decision. *(Pro: Presidents are not above the law; con: it may encourage frivolous lawsuits by political opponents)*

**Keep It Current CD-ROM** includes government-related projects by unit. The CD-ROM links to the Prentice Hall School Web site and may be used for daily updates.

### Answers to . . .

**Decide for Yourself**

**1.** Nixon argued that Presidents have special immunity from being sued. Fitzgerald cited past Supreme Court cases to argue that government officials should have only partial immunity and that Presidents cannot be above the law.

**2.** Answers will vary, but should be supported with valid reasoning.

**3.** The Court ruled that the President is entitled to absolute immunity from liability in connection with his official acts. This immunity did not extend to acts not connected with the President's role, which was addressed by the 1997 *Clinton* case.

## Practicing the Vocabulary

1. electoral college
2. chief of party
3. chief legislator
4. presidential primary
5. electorate
6. winner-take-all
7. chief citizen
8. chief administrator
9. platform
10. keynote address

## Reviewing Main Ideas

### Section 1

**11.** As the chief executive, the President is vested with the executive power of the nation; as the chief diplomat, the President is the main architect of American foreign policy; as commander in chief, the President is the leader of the nation's armed forces.
**12. (a)** George Washington's refusal to serve a third term lead to this tradition. **(b)** Franklin D. Roosevelt. **(c)** Two full terms.
**13.** They feel it places an arbitrary limit on the right of the people to choose their President.

### Section 2

**14.** The 25th Amendment provides specific rules for the Vice President to become Acting President.
**15.** The Constitution says only that the powers of the office—not the office itself—would transfer to the Vice President. The 1947 act stipulates the exact series of succession.
**16. (a)** The Constitution does not pay much attention to the role, assigning it just two duties: To preside over the Senate and to help decide presidential disability. **(b)** It enhances the office's reputation of being ineffectual and insignificant.

### Section 3

**17.** The plan called for a special body of electors to cast two votes, each for a different candidate; the candidate with the most would become President and the second most, Vice President.
**18.** The system broke down with the rise of political parties and more partisan politics.
**19.** The 12th Amendment ensures that an election will not result in a tie.

CHAPTER 13 Assessment

## Political Dictionary

chief of state (p. 354)
chief executive (p. 354)
chief administrator (p. 355)
chief diplomat (p. 355)
commander in chief (p. 355)
chief legislator (p. 355)
chief of party (p. 355)
chief citizen (p. 355)
presidential succession (p. 359)

Presidential Succession Act of 1947 (p. 360)
balance the ticket (p. 362)
presidential electors (p. 365)
electoral votes (p. 365)
electoral college (p. 366)
presidential primary (p. 369)
winner-take-all (p. 371)
proportional representation (p. 371)

national convention (p. 372)
platform (p. 373)
keynote address (p. 373)
district plan (p. 382)
proportional plan (p. 382)
direct popular election (p. 383)
electorate (p. 383)
national bonus plan (p. 384)

## Practicing the Vocabulary

***Matching*** *Choose a term from the list above that best matches each description.*

1. The group chosen every four years to make the formal selection of the President and Vice President
2. The role in which the President exercises leadership over his or her political party
3. The role in which the President acts as the main architect of the nation's public policies
4. An election at which a party's voters choose delegates to the party's national convention and/or express a preference for candidates for the party's nomination
5. All the people entitled to vote in a given election

***Word Recognition*** *Replace the underlined definition with the correct term from the list above.*

6. In the past, some presidential primaries were <u>contests in which the winner of the preference vote won the support of all the delegates</u>.
7. As <u>the representative of all the people</u>, the President speaks for the people of the nation and offers important moral leadership.
8. As <u>the head of a large organization that employs nearly three million people</u>, the President leads one of the world's largest governmental machines.
9. The <u>written declaration of principles and policy decisions</u> of a party is an important product of each national convention.
10. The <u>speech given at a party convention to set the tone for the convention and the campaign to come</u> is usually delivered by one of the party's best orators.

## Reviewing Main Ideas

### Section 1

11. Explain the significance of each of the following presidential roles: chief executive, chief diplomat, commander in chief.
12. **(a)** What is the origin of the no-third-term tradition? **(b)** Which President broke with this tradition? **(c)** What is the maximum number of terms that today's Presidents may serve?
13. Why have some critics called for a repeal of the 22nd Amendment?

### Section 2

14. How does the Constitution ensure a smooth transition of power in the event of a presidential disability?
15. Explain how the Constitution and the Presidential Succession Act of 1947 address the issue of presidential succession.
16. **(a)** How does the Constitution describe the role of the Vice President? **(b)** How does this description relate to the office's reputation?

### Section 3

17. Describe the Framers' plan for the selection of the nation's President.
18. Why did the electoral college cease to function as the Framers had intended?
19. What was the purpose of the 12th Amendment?

### Section 4

20. How do presidential primaries differ from the caucus-convention process?
21. For what major purposes do parties hold national conventions?
22. What have been the effects of the Democrats' proportional representation rule?

### Section 5

23. **(a)** How are electors chosen for the electoral college? **(b)** How are electoral votes counted?
24. On what grounds is the electoral college system criticized?

### Section 4

**20.** In a presidential primary, voters directly choose delegates to the party's national convention and/or express a preference for their party's presidential nomination. In a caucus-convention there are more stages: Voters choose delegates to a local or district convention, at which delegates for a State convention are chosen, at which delegates to the national convention are chosen.

**21.** To nominate presidential and vice-presidential candidates, to put forward a party platform, and to unite the party for the upcoming elections.
**22.** Several States have given up the process of popular selection of delegates.

### Section 5

**23. (a)** They are chosen by popular vote in every State, usually on a winner-take-all basis. **(b)** On January 6, the president of the Senate opens the electoral votes and counts them before a joint session of Congress.
**24.** Critics complain that the winner of the popular vote is not guaranteed the presidency, that electors are not required to vote in accord with the popular vote, and that any election has the potential to be decided in the House.

## Critical Thinking Skills

**25.** *Applying the Chapter Skill* Suppose the next presidential election is a week away, and you have not yet made up your mind for whom to vote. Describe how you will use the decision-making process to identify the situation that requires the decision, gather information, identify options, predict consequences, and take action to implement your decision.

**26.** *Distinguishing False from Accurate Images* The following quotation from John Adams appeared earlier in this chapter: "I am Vice President. In this I am nothing, but I may be everything." **(a)** Explain what Adams meant. **(b)** Do you think that a modern Vice President would agree with Adams?

**27.** *Identifying Alternatives* Review the formal qualifications for President in Section 1. **(a)** Why do you think the Framers chose these particular qualifications? **(b)** Do you think that any of these qualifications should be changed?

**28.** *Understanding Point of View* Should the major parties make a special effort to recruit a presidential nominee who is a woman or a member of a minority group? Explain your answer.

## Analyzing Political Cartoons

Using your knowledge of American government and this cartoon, answer the questions below.

"Hi there. I'm governor of a large State somewhere out West, and I'm running for President."

**29.** Why is it significant that the candidate in the cartoon is a governor of a large western state?

**30.** How accurate is the cartoon in portraying the qualifications necessary for a presidential candidate?

 **Take It to the Net**

Additional support materials and activities for Chapter 13 of *Magruder's American Government* can be found in the Social Studies area at the Prentice Hall School Web site. **www.phschool.com**

## ★ You Can Make a Difference

What organizations in your community provide help for children and their families who lack books, food, or clothing? Are these groups privately run or sponsored by government agencies? With your classmates, prepare a guidebook of the resources available in your community, what services they provide, and how they are funded. Organize the guide by services and location. Then look into the volunteer opportunities available for you and your friends.

## Participation Activities

**31.** *Current Events Watch* Follow news reports of the President's activities and find examples of the President filling any four of the eight roles outlined on pages 354–355. For each of the four roles, hand in a newspaper or magazine clipping or an Internet printout of the report, along with your explanation of which roles the President is filling.

**32.** *Chart Activity* Create a chart showing the advantages and disadvantages of the various plans for reforming the electoral college. Include the advantages and disadvantages of keeping the current system. Which, in your opinion, are the weakest and the strongest plans?

**33.** *It's Your Turn* Draw a political cartoon on one of the following topics: the plight of the Vice President, the flaws of the electoral college, the many roles of the President, the Framers' view of today's election process, or a topic of your own choosing. After you have made a rough sketch, be sure that the point you want to make will be clear to your viewers. Then create a final drawing to display in your classroom. **(Drawing a Cartoon)**

 **Take It to the Net**

*Chapter 13 Self-Test* As a final review activity, take the Chapter 13 Self-Test in the Social Studies area at the Web site listed below, and receive immediate feedback on your answers.

**www.phschool.com**

## Point-of-Use Resources

 **Guide to the Essentials of American Government** Chapter 13 Test, page 76 provides multiple-choice questions to test students' knowledge of the chapter.

**Test Bank CD-ROM** Chapter 13 Test

**Chapter Test** Chapter Tests booklet

## Critical Thinking Skills

**25.** Answers will vary, but should demonstrate an understanding of the decision-making process. Students might suggest reviewing the qualifications of each candidate and consulting media sources about each candidate.

**26. (a)** Possible answer: Adams meant that although the vice presidency is not a particularly important role, any Vice President has the potential to succeed to the presidency at any time. **(b)** Possible answer: They may agree that the role still has few formal duties, but feel that Vice Presidents today have assumed many informal political and diplomatic roles.

**27. (a)** Possible answer: They wanted to ensure that any President would be a mature adult who had experienced American culture for many years. **(b)** Answers will vary.

**28.** Answers will vary, but should be supported with relevant facts and examples, and express a firm opinion.

## Analyzing Political Cartoons

**29.** Possible answer: The candidate is playing up qualities that he thinks are important in the current race.

**30.** Possible answer: That sometimes the qualifications are not as important to a race as are factors such as regional location.

## You Can Make a Difference

Guidebooks should be well-organized and easy to navigate, and present all relevant information.

## Participation Activities

**31.** The news reports chosen and the students' written explanations should reflect an understanding of the four roles.

**32.** Charts should be clearly organized; opinions should be backed with facts and examples.

**33.** Cartoons should express a point in an easy-to-grasp manner.

# The Presidency in Action

| Section Objectives | Print and Technology Resources |
|---|---|

**1 The Growth of Presidential Power**

*(pp. 390–392)*

1. Summarize the content of Article II of the Constitution, and explain why it is controversial.
2. Analyze the growth of presidential power.
3. Explain how Presidents' own views on the presidency have affected the power of the office.

TEKS 2B, 9B, 17C, 21A, 21B, 21C, 21D, 22A, 22B, 22D

- **Unit 4 booklet**
  Guided Reading and Review, p. 13
  Section 1 Quiz, p. 14
- **Lesson Plans booklet** Section 1, p. 62
- **Political Cartoons booklet** Section 1, p. 54
- **Section Reading Support Transparencies**

- **Block Scheduling with Lesson Strategies booklet** p. 26
- **Basic Principles of the Constitution Transparencies** 18
- **Section Support Transparencies** 57, 156
- **Presentation Pro CD-ROM** Section 1

**2 The President's Executive Powers**

*(pp. 393–397)*

1. Analyze the constitutional powers of the President.
2. Define *ordinance power,* and explain where it comes from.
3. Explain how the appointing power works.
4. Summarize the historical debate over the removal power.

TEKS 8D, 9B, 9E, 9G, 11A, 17C, 21A, 21B, 21C, 21D, 21E, 22A, 22B, 22D

- **Unit 4 booklet**
  Guided Reading and Review, p. 15
  Section 2 Quiz, p. 16
- **Lesson Plans booklet** Section 2, p. 63
- **Political Cartoons booklet** Section 2, p. 55
- **Social Studies Skills Tutor CD-ROM**
- **Basic Principles of the Constitution Transparencies** 25

- **Section Support Transparencies** 58, 157
- **Presentation Pro CD-ROM** Section 2
- **Simulations and Data Graphing CD-ROM**
- **Section Reading Support Transparencies**

**3 Diplomatic and Military Powers**

*(pp. 399–403)*

1. Explain how treaties are made and approved.
2. Explain why and how executive agreements are made.
3. Summarize how and for what purposes the power of recognition is used, and give historic examples.
4. Describe the powers that the President has in the role of commander in chief.

TEKS 8D, 9B, 9E, 9G, 16D, 21A, 21B, 21D, 21E, 21F, 22A, 22B, 22C, 22D

- **Unit 4 booklet**
  Guided Reading and Review, p. 17
  Section 3 Quiz, p. 18
- **Lesson Plans booklet** Section 3, p. 64
- **Political Cartoons booklet** Section 3, p. 56
- **Close Up on Primary Sources booklet**
  The Monroe Doctrine and United States Foreign Policy, p. 16; John F. Kennedy, Inaugural Address, p. 43; War Powers

Resolution, p. 62
- **Simulations and Debates booklet** p. 53
- **Basic Principles of the Constitution Transparencies** 31
- **Section Support Transparencies** 59, 158
- **Presentation Pro CD-ROM** Section 3
- **Section Reading Support Transparencies**

**4 Legislative and Judicial Powers**

*(pp. 405–408)*

1. Describe the President's two major legislative powers, and explain how these powers are an important part of the system of checks and balances.
2. Describe the President's major judicial powers.

TEKS 8D, 9B, 9E, 9G, 17C, 21A, 21C, 21D, 21E, 22A, 22B, 22D

- **Unit 4 booklet**
  Guided Reading and Review, p. 19
  Section 4 Quiz, p. 20
  Skills for Life Activity, p. 21
- **Lesson Plans booklet** Section 4, p. 65
- **Political Cartoons booklet** Section 4, p. 57
- **Block Scheduling with Lesson Strategies booklet** p. 26
- **Section Reading Support Transparencies**

- **Close Up on the Supreme Court booklet** *Korematsu* v. *U.S.,* p. 15
- **The Living Constitution booklet** p. 4
- **Government Assessment Rubrics booklet,** p. 10
- **The Basic Principles of the Constitution Posters**
- **Section Support Transparencies** 60, 159
- **Presentation Pro CD-ROM** Section 4

# Block Scheduling Strategies

The *Magruder's American Government* program addresses block-scheduling strategies in a variety of ways. For easy reference, side-column activities that fit a block format are marked ■ **Block Strategy.** Each section also contains a **Block Scheduling Strategies** box describing at least two block-format activities that address and extend core content from the section. The **Block Scheduling with Lesson Strategies booklet** found in the Teaching Resources contains additional block-scheduling activities for each chapter.

## Take It to the Net

Visit the Social Studies area at the Prentice Hall School Web site. Once there, you can find additional links, current events connections, and activities to enrich chapter content for *Magruder's American Government,* as well as a Self-Test for students. Be sure to check out this month's **eTeach** online discussion with a Master Teacher.

### www.phschool.com

## Pressed for Time?

If you are running short on time to cover this chapter, consider one of the following options:
- Use the **Presentation Pro CD-ROM** to create an outline for this chapter.
- Use one of the **Pressed for Time** activities found on p. 27.
- Use the Section Summaries for Chapter 2, from **Guide to the Essentials of American Government (English and Spanish).**

## Video Connections

Prentice Hall offers two video programs to reinforce and extend chapter content. Show students *The Blessings of Liberty* from the **ABC News Civics and Government Videotape Library** and *Prayer in Schools: A Nationwide Debate* from the **Magruder's American Government Video Collection.**

## Core Assessment

Chapter 14 Test, Chapter Tests booklet
ExamView® Test Bank CD-ROM Chapter 14
Government Assessment Rubrics

## Standardized Test Preparation

### Core Assessment

Chapter 14 Test, Chapter Tests booklet
ExamView® Test Bank CD-ROM Chapter 14
Government Assessment Rubrics

### Standardized Test Preparation

**Diagnose and Prescribe**

Diagnostic Tests for High School
Social Studies Skills

**Review and Reteach**

Review Book for Government

**Practice and Assess**

Test-Taking Strategies With
    Transparencies for High School
Test Prep Book for Government

# Chapter 14 Teacher's Edition Index

# The Presidency in Action

## Introducing the Chapter

In this chapter, students will read about the many powers held by the President. They will also learn how the expansion of the power of the executive branch over the years has brought intense debate.

### Make It Relevant

★ *You Can Make a Difference*

Have the class develop a public information campaign that demonstrates to their fellow citizens that, as Dawn Smalls said, "[t]he divide that they see between them and their government . . . is not as great as they think it is." The goal of the campaign will be to increase citizen participation in government. Students should (1) choose a logo and a slogan; (2) create posters, brochures, news releases, a Web site, or other media; and, (3) develop their campaign in other appropriate ways.

**Service Learning**

### CONSTITUTIONAL PRINCIPLES

Emphasize the following basic principles as students read Chapter 14. Have the class respond to the questions, and then ask volunteers to explain how these principles ensure that a President cannot be tyrannical.

**Limited Government** How have presidential powers changed since the writing of the Constitution?

**Separation of Powers** What power does the President lack when negotiating treaties? How are the President's war powers different from those of Congress?

**Checks and Balances** What types of vetoes can the President use? How are pardons and reprieves checks on the judicial branch?

# The Presidency in Action

*"The President hears a hundred voices telling him that he is the greatest man in the world. He must listen carefully indeed to hear the one voice that tells him he is not."*

—Harry S Truman (1964)

Presidents today do have great power—to carry out laws, make policies, choose officials, command the military, and conduct foreign affairs. The Framers gave the President certain "executive powers," which have grown greatly over time. How much power a President actually exercises depends on the person and on the times.

◆ Vice President Dick Cheney, President George W. Bush, and Secretary of State Colin Powell

 **CLOSE UP** FOUNDATION *Corner*

The following resources are available only from the Close Up Foundation to support the concepts discussed in Chapter 14 "The Presidency in Action":

◆ *Perspectives: Readings on Contemporary American Government*
◆ *Talking Peace: A Vision for the Next Generation*
◆ *We the People: The President and the Constitution*

 **CLOSE UP** FOUNDATION **Online**

To keep up-to-date on Close Up news and activities, visit Close Up Online at

**www.closeup.org**

Close Up Foundation
44 Canal Center Plaza
Alexandria, VA 22314-1592
800-765-3131

### You Can Make a Difference

**At age 20, Dawn Smalls,** a Boston University honor student, became part of the busy "nerve center" of the United States government, as assistant to the White House chief of staff. She handled complaints, answered phone calls to the President, and dealt with senators and Cabinet members. Government service was not new to Dawn, who had interned in the West Wing of the White House. She also has worked with community groups in Washington and Boston, trying to show other young African Americans that "The divide that they see between them and their government . . . is not as great as they think it is."

### Keep It Current

Items marked with this logo are periodically updated on the Internet. Keep up-to-date with what's in the news. To get current information on the power of the President, go to **www.phschool.com**

### SECTION 1

#### The Growth of Presidential Power
(pp. 390–392)

★ Article II of the Constitution created the presidency and gives the President certain expressed powers.
★ Yet Article II is remarkably brief, leaving Americans to debate whether the Framers intended the presidency to be relatively strong or weak.
★ Since the nation's founding, the power of the presidency has grown significantly.
★ The power a President exercises depends on his views about the office and how he interprets Article II.

### SECTION 2

#### The President's Executive Powers
(pp. 393–397)

★ Article II gives the President the power and responsibility to "execute the laws."
★ This executive power gives the President a great deal of flexibility in deciding how laws are carried out.
★ Among the President's key powers are those to appoint and remove top federal officials.

### SECTION 3

#### Diplomatic and Military Powers (pp. 399–403)

★ The President shares treaty-making and other powers with Congress.
★ Certain diplomatic powers may be carried out without the approval of Congress; increasingly, Presidents have made use of these powers.
★ As commander in chief of the armed forces, the President possesses almost unlimited military power.

### SECTION 4

#### Legislative and Judicial Powers (pp. 405–408)

★ The Constitution gives the President important legislative and judicial powers as part of the system of checks and balances in the Federal Government.
★ The President's key legislative powers are to submit legislation for Congress to consider and to reject legislation that he opposes.
★ The Constitution gives the President several powers of clemency—powers with which he can show mercy to those convicted of federal crimes.

### To Omit the Chapter

If you wish to skip Chapter 14, ask students to read the Chapter in Brief and assign the Guide to the Essentials before continuing to another chapter. You may also want to assign the Chapter 14 Test in the Chapter Test booklet. Then specific portions of Chapter 14 may be assigned to students needing reinforcement of key terms and concepts.

### To Preview the Chapter

To introduce students to key terms and concepts in each section, have them read the Chapter in Brief. You may also assign the Reading Strategy activities on pp. 391, 394, 400, and 406 of this book.

### To Review the Chapter

When students have completed Chapter 14, you might want to assign the Guide to the Essentials or the Guided Reading and Review worksheets on pp. 13, 15, 17, and 19 of the Unit 4 booklet.

### To Cover the Chapter Quickly

To cover the material in Chapter 14 quickly, use the following activity.

**Focus** Explain to students that the presidency is often called "the most powerful office in the world," and the President's power continues to grow. Ask students to offer reasons for why this is so. Tell students that in this chapter they will learn more about the President's job.

**Instruct** Discuss the expanding role of the presidency with the class. Then organize students into groups of three, with one person covering the President's executive powers, another the diplomatic and military powers, and the third the legislative and judicial powers. Have each group create a set of guidelines outlining the President's powers in each of the categories listed above.

**Close/Reteach** Have students consider the President's powers and write themes based on the following question: "Is the U.S. presidency the most powerful office in the world?" Have volunteers share their opinions with the class.

■ **Block Strategy (Average)**

### Keep It Current

#### Internet Update

Use the Prentice Hall School Web site and the Keep It Current CD-ROM to find quick content updates.

Visit **www.phschool.com** for current events articles that are linked to Chapter 14. Critical Thinking questions are included.

**Keep It Current CD-ROM** includes government-related projects by unit. Students complete each project using current information that they obtain by linking to the Prentice Hall School Web site from the CD-ROM.

# 1 The Growth of Presidential Power

**Objectives** You may wish to call students' attention to the objectives in the Section Preview. The objectives are reflected in the main headings of the section.

**Bellringer** Have students compare the dominance of the Internet in people's lives today and 10 years ago. Ask students whether the increased power and influence of the Internet is controversial. Explain that in this section, they will learn about the controversy over the growth of presidential power.

**Vocabulary Builder** Ask students which term in the Political Dictionary relates to the Constitution. Have them explain their answer, and then briefly discuss the possible meanings of the other two terms.

## Pressed for Time?

### Quick Lesson Plan

**1. Focus** Tell students that over the years, the power of the President has grown significantly. Ask students to discuss what they know about this growth and what is responsible for it.

**2. Instruct** Ask students to explain how Article II of the Constitution has contributed to the growth of presidential power. Use their answers to start a list on the chalkboard of factors that have worked to strengthen the presidency. Then discuss why the growth of presidential power is controversial.

**3. Close/Reteach** Remind students that presidential power continues to grow, as social and economic life becomes more complex. Ask students to list five reasons for the growth of presidential power, putting them in order from most to least significant. Have them explain why their number one choice is the most significant.

## Point–of–Use Resources

📁 **Block Scheduling with Lesson Strategies** Activities for Chapter 14 are presented on p. 26.

## Section Preview

### OBJECTIVES

1. **Explain** why Article II of the Constitution can be described as "an outline."
2. **Analyze** the growth of presidential power.
3. **Explain** how Presidents' own views have affected the power of the office.

### WHY IT MATTERS

The Constitution establishes the office of the President in Article II. The interpretation of that article continues to be a battleground for people who want a powerful President and those who want to curb presidential powers.

### POLITICAL DICTIONARY

★ **Executive Article**
★ **mass media**
★ **imperial presidency**

The presidency is often called "the most powerful office in the world." Is this what the Framers had in mind when they created the post in 1787? At Philadelphia, they purposely created a single executive with broad powers. They also agreed with Thomas Jefferson, who wrote in the Declaration of Independence that "a Tyrant is unfit to be the ruler of a free people." So, just as purposely, they constructed a "checked," or limited, presidency.

## Article II

Article II, the Constitution's **Executive Article,** begins this way:

▲ President Reagan met with Soviet leader Mikhail Gorbachev in Geneva, Switzerland, in 1985.

**FROM THE Constitution** *"The executive Power shall be vested in a President of the United States of America. "*

With those few words, the Framers established the presidency. The Constitution sets out other, somewhat more specific grants of presidential power as well. Thus, the President is given the power to command the armed forces, to make treaties, to approve or veto acts of Congress, to send and receive diplomatic representatives, to grant pardons and reprieves, and "to take Care that the Laws be faithfully executed."[1]

Still, the Constitution deals with the powers of the presidency in a very sketchy fashion. Article II reads almost as an outline. It has been called "the most loosely drawn chapter" in the nation's fundamental law. It does not define "the executive power." The other grants of presidential authority are stated in equally broad terms.

A large part of America's political history has revolved around the struggle over the meaning of the constitutional phrase "executive power." That struggle has pitted those who have argued for a weaker presidency, subordinate to Congress, against those who have pressed for a stronger, independent, co-equal chief executive.

That never-ending contest began at the Philadelphia Convention in 1787. At that time, several Framers agreed with Roger Sherman of Connecticut, who, according to James Madison,

**PRIMARY Sources** *"considered the executive magistracy as nothing more than an institution for carrying the will of the legislature into effect, that the person or persons [occupying the presidency] ought to be appointed by and accountable to the legislature only, which was the depository of the supreme will of the Society. "*

—Notes of Debates in the Federal Convention of 1787, James Madison

---

[1]Most of the specific grants of presidential power are found in Article II, Sections 2 and 3. A few are elsewhere in the Constitution, such as the veto power, in Article I, Section 7, Clause 2.

## 📖 Block Scheduling Strategies

Consider these suggestions to manage extended class time:

■ Explain to students that U.S. Presidents are becoming increasingly more powerful. Have each student identify the factors that have brought additional power to the U.S. presidency. For each factor, have students summarize how it has done so. Then have students use the links at the *Magruder's American Government* Web site (**www.phschool.com**) to research recent Presidents who have brought additional power to the office. Call on volunteers to report their findings to the class.

■ Have students read the quote by Theodore Roosevelt and the quote by William Howard Taft found on page 392. Ask students to decide which view of the presidency they agree with and create arguments to support their side. Then organize the class into two groups, based on which side they support, and have them debate the issue. After the debate, encourage the class to analyze the arguments that were used.

As you know, those who argued for a stronger executive—led by Alexander Hamilton, James Wilson, and James Madison—carried the day. They persuaded the convention to establish a single executive, chosen independently of Congress and with its own distinct powers.

## Why Presidential Power Has Grown

Over the course of American history, the champions of a stronger presidency have almost always prevailed. One of the leading reasons they have is the unity of the presidency. The President is the single, commanding head of the executive branch. On the other hand, Congress consists of *two* houses. Both of them must agree on a matter before Congress can do anything. Moreover, one of those two houses is made up of 100 separately elected members, and the other has 435 of them.

Several other factors have strengthened the presidency—not least the Presidents themselves. The nation's increasingly complex social and economic life also has influenced the growth of presidential power. As the United States has become more industrialized and technologically advanced, the Federal Government has played an increasingly larger role in transportation, labor, civil rights, health, welfare, communication, education, the environment, and a host of other fields. Americans have looked especially to the President for leadership in these matters.

Another of these closely related factors has been the frequent need for extraordinary and decisive action in times of national emergency, most notably in times of war. The ability of the President—the single, commanding chief executive—to act in such situations has done much to strengthen the executive power.

Congress has also strengthened the presidential hand, as it has passed thousands of laws that have been an essential part of the historic growth of the Federal Government. Congress lacks the time and technical knowledge to provide more than the basic outlines of public policy. It has been forced to delegate authority to the executive branch to carry out its laws.

The President has a unique ability to attract public attention and build support for policies and actions. Every President since Franklin Roosevelt has purposely used the **mass media**—

## Presidents on the Presidency

**THOMAS JEFFERSON**

1801–1809

*"[The presidency] is a place of splendid misery."*

**JOHN QUINCY ADAMS**

1825–1829

*"The four most miserable years of my life were my four years in the presidency."*

**RUTHERFORD B. HAYES**

1877–1881

*"Nobody ever left the presidency with less regret."*

**JAMES A. GARFIELD**

1881

*"What is there in this place that a man should ever want to get into it!"*

**WILLIAM McKINLEY**

1897–1901

*"I have had all the honor there is in this place and have had responsibilities enough to kill any man."*

**WILLIAM H. TAFT**

1909–1913

*"I'm glad to be going—this is the loneliest place in the world."*

**WARREN G. HARDING**

1921–1923

*"[The presidency is] a prison."*

**HARRY S TRUMAN**

1945–1953

*"There is no exaltation in the office of the President of the United States—sorrow is the proper word."*

**DWIGHT D. EISENHOWER**

1953–1961

*"Oh, that lovely title, ex-president."*

**LYNDON B. JOHNSON**

1963–1969

*"No one can experience with the President of the United States the glory and agony of his office."*

*Interpreting Charts* Not everyone who occupied the Oval Office has always enjoyed the job. **(a) In the quotations above, what is the common message? (b) What do you think are some of the good and bad aspects of serving as President?**

## Reading Strategy

### Organizing Information/ Graphic Organizer

Tell students that the growth of presidential power could be likened to the growth of a tree. Have them draw a diagram in the shape of a tree. The diagram should show the roots of presidential power as well as factors that have enlarged that power throughout the nation's history.

## Customize for

### Less Proficient Readers

Remind students of the enormous growth of the powers of the presidency since the Framers of the Constitution created the position in 1787. Ask students to create political cartoons that illustrate this change in the balance of power in the Federal Government. Ask for volunteers to share their cartoons with the class.

## Point-of-Use Resources

**Guided Reading and Review** Unit 4 booklet, p. 13 provides students with practice identifying the main ideas and key terms of this section.

**Lesson Plans** For lesson planning suggestions, see p. 62 of the Lesson Plans booklet.

**Political Cartoons** See p. 54 of the Political Cartoons booklet for a cartoon relevant to this section.

**Section Support Transparencies** Transparency 57, *Visual Learning*; Transparency 156, *Political Cartoon*

**Resource Pro® CD-ROM** contains an electronic version of each activity found in the Teaching Resources as well as additional resources such as Supreme Court cases. The Planning Express® feature allows you to customize and create daily lesson plans within minutes.

### Answer to . . .

**Interpreting Charts (a)** Possible answer: That the presidency is difficult and demanding. **(b)** Answers will vary.

**391**

## Point-of-Use Resources

 **Guide to the Essentials** Chapter 14, Section 1, p. 77 provides support for students who need additional review of section content. Spanish support is available in the Spanish edition of the Guide on p. 70.

**Quiz** Unit 4 booklet, p. 14 includes matching and multiple-choice questions to check students' understanding of Section 1 content.

**Presentation Pro CD-ROM** Quizzes and multiple-choice questions check students' understanding of Section 1 content.

## Answers to . . .

### Section 1 Assessment

**1.** Article II defines the executive powers of the presidency.
**2.** Reasons include: Power is invested in one person, rather than shared among many; the public has demanded that the Federal Government take on larger roles; national emergencies have called for decisive action; Congress has expanded the role through the passage of laws; Presidents have expanded their role in the face of increased technology and urbanization and used the mass media to gain support for their actions.
**3.** The broad view is that the President has a responsibility to do whatever the nation needs done, with or without guidance from Congress. The narrow view is that the President may only take actions granted by Congress or the Constitution.
**4.** They think some Presidents have become isolated policymakers who do not listen to Congress or the public.
**5.** Examples will vary; answers might suggest that with such a large population, using the mass media is the only way for a President to inform the public about his or her intended actions.
**6.** Answers will vary, but should be supported with specific examples.

---

forms of communication, including printed publications, radio, television, and, most recently, the Internet—for that purpose.

## The Presidential View

The nature of the presidency depends on how each President views the office and exercises its powers. Historically, Presidents have held one of two contrasting views. The stronger and more effective of them have taken a broad view of their powers—a view that Theodore Roosevelt called "the stewardship theory":

>  **PRIMARY Sources** "I declined to adopt the view that what was imperatively necessary for the Nation could not be done by the President unless he could find some specific authorization to do it. My belief was that it was not only [a President's] right but his duty to do anything that the needs of the Nation demanded unless such action was forbidden by the Constitution or by the laws. . . . I did not usurp power, but I did greatly broaden the use of executive power. In other words, I acted for the public welfare . . . unless prevented by direct constitutional or legislative prohibition."
> —Theodore Roosevelt,
> *Theodore Roosevelt: An Autobiography,* 1913

Ironically, the strongest presidential statement of the opposing view came from Roosevelt's handpicked successor in the office, William Howard Taft.

> **PRIMARY Sources** "The true view of the Executive function is, as I conceive it, that the President can exercise no power which cannot be fairly and reasonably traced to some specific grant of power or justly implied and included within such express grant. . . . Such specific grant must be either in the Federal Constitution or in an act of Congress passed in pursuance thereof. There is no undefined residuum of power which he can exercise because it seems to him to be in the public interest."
> —William Howard Taft,
> *Our Chief Magistrate and His Powers,* 1916

In recent decades, critics of strong presidential power have condemned what is called the **imperial presidency.** The term paints a picture of the President as emperor, taking strong actions without consulting Congress or seeking its approval—sometimes acting in secrecy to evade or even to deceive Congress. Critics of the imperial presidency worry that Presidents have become isolated policymakers who are unaccountable to the American people through their representatives in Congress. The term *imperial presidency* has been used frequently in reference to President Richard Nixon and the political tactics that brought about his downfall.

Assertive Presidents, frustrated with the often slow pace and divided membership in Congress, have indeed taken policy matters into their own hands many times in recent history, as you will see in the sections that follow. It is a trend that has supporters as well as critics.

---

## Section 1 Assessment

**Key Terms and Main Ideas**
1. Why is Article II often called the **Executive Article**?
2. Give three reasons for the growth of presidential power.
3. Summarize the two competing views of the constitutional phrase "executive power."
4. Why do some people worry about an **imperial presidency**?

**Critical Thinking**
5. **Understanding Point of View** Give two examples of how a President might use the mass media to influence public opinion and increase his power. Do you think there are any legitimate reasons for a President to do so? Explain.

6. **Making Comparisons** Compare and contrast the quotations from Presidents Roosevelt and Taft on this page. **(a)** Whose view do you favor? Why? **(b)** Which view do you think most modern Presidents have favored? Explain.

 **Take It to the Net**

7. Read about the President's various roles as the leader of the executive branch. Then write an opinion column on how the President's power has increased or decreased. Use the links provided in the Social Studies area at the following Web site for help in completing this activity. **www.phschool.com**

---

 **Take It to the Net**

**7.** Direct students to the Social Studies area at the Prentice Hall School Web site. The *Magruder's American Government* companion Web site includes the directions and links needed to complete the activity. It also provides a printable Internet activity worksheet with scoring rubrics for assessment. Students should present clear opinions and support them with examples.

# **2** The President's Executive Powers

## Section Preview

### OBJECTIVES

1. **Analyze** the constitutional powers of the President.
2. **Define** *ordinance power,* and explain where it comes from.
3. **Explain** how the appointing power works.
4. **Summarize** the historical debate over the removal power.

### WHY IT MATTERS

The President has enormous powers to give orders, to decide how laws are carried out, and to appoint federal officials.

### POLITICAL DICTIONARY

★ **oath of office**
★ **executive order**
★ **ordinance power**

Thomas Jefferson wrote this to a friend in 1789: "The execution of the laws is more important than the making of them." Whether Jefferson was altogether right about that or not, in this section you will see that the President's power to execute the law endows him with an enormous amount of authority.

## Powers to Execute the Law

As chief executive, the President executes (enforces, administers, carries out) the provisions of federal law. The power to do so rests on two brief constitutional provisions. The first of them is the **oath of office** sworn by the President on the day he takes office:

> FROM THE *Constitution* **"***I do solemnly swear (or affirm) that I will faithfully execute the Office of President of the United States, and will to the best of my Ability, preserve, protect and defend the Constitution of the United States.* **"**
>
> —Article II, Section 1, Clause 8

The other provision is the Constitution's command that "he shall take care that the laws be faithfully executed."[2]

The President's power to execute the law covers all federal laws. Their number, and the different subject matters they cover, nearly boggle

the mind. The armed forces, social security, the minimum wage law, gun control, affirmative action, environmental protection, air traffic safety, immigration, housing, taxes—these only begin the list. There are scores of others.

The President and the President's subordinates have much to say about the meaning of the law, just as Congress and the courts do. In executing and enforcing law, the executive branch also interprets it. The Constitution requires the President to execute *all* federal laws, unless and until he or a court finds them to be unconstitutional. Still, the President may, and does, use some discretion as to how vigorously and in what particular way any given law will be applied in practice.

To look at the point more closely: Many laws that Congress passes are written in fairly broad

▲ President George Washington took the oath of office on this borrowed Bible on April 30, 1789.

[2]Article II, Section 3; this provision gives the President what is often called the "take care" power.

**393**

## Reading Strategy

### Drawing Inferences

Have students suppose that they are President. They have just learned that the head of the Environmental Protection Agency has decided, against their wishes, to ease enforcement of certain antipollution laws. They have already had many conflicts with this official. Tell students to look for ways to solve this problem as they read the section.

---

### Background Note

#### Common Misconceptions

Most people think that, as of January 2001, the United States has had 43 Presidents. In fact, that number should be increased by one. David Rice Atchison was President of the United States from noon on March 4, 1849, when James Polk's term officially ended, until the next day, when Zachary Taylor was sworn in. Polk's Vice President had resigned as President of the Senate, and the President *pro tem*, Senator Atchison, assumed the presidency, being next in line. Thus, Atchison was officially President—if even only for a day.

---

## Point-of-Use Resources

📁 **Guided Reading and Review** Unit 4 booklet, p. 15 provides students with practice identifying the main ideas and key terms of this section.

📁 **Lesson Plans** For lesson planning suggestions, see p. 63 of the Lesson Plans booklet.

📁 **Political Cartoons** See p. 55 of the Political Cartoons booklet for a cartoon relevant to this section.

---

### Answers to . . .

**Critical Thinking** Possible answer: Execution of such a power might take too much time if it had to go through Congress.

**Critical Thinking** It is typical of the kind of day-to-day administrative tasks the executive branch is required to oversee.

terms. Congress sets out the basic policies and standards. The specific details—much of the fine print necessary to the actual, day-to-day administration of the law—are usually left to be worked out by the executive branch.

For example, immigration laws require that all immigrants seeking permanent admission to this country must be able to "read and understand some dialect or language." That seems very straightforward, but what does this literacy requirement mean in everyday practice? How well must an alien be able to read and write? What words in some language must he or she know, and how many of them? The law does not say. Rather, such answers come from within the executive branch; in this case, from the Immigration and Naturalization Service in the Department of Justice.

## The Ordinance Power

From what has just been said, the President clearly deserves the title of chief administrator as well as chief executive. The job of administering and applying most federal law is the day-to-day work of all of the many departments, bureaus, offices, boards, commissions, councils, and other agencies that make up the huge executive branch of the Federal Government. All of the some 2.7 million

▲ One of the day-to-day jobs of the executive branch is the management of herds of wild ponies on Assateague Island, off the Virginia coast. To keep their numbers at levels the island can sustain, the Park Service holds an annual roundup and sale of the ponies. *Critical Thinking Why does this task fall to the executive branch?*

▲ During World War II, President Franklin D. Roosevelt issued executive orders requiring gasoline and other strategic war supplies to be rationed—sold in limited quantities. *Critical Thinking Why is it important that the President have such a power, instead of Congress?*

men and women who staff those agencies are subject to the President's control and direction.

The President has the power to issue executive orders. An **executive order** is a directive, rule, or regulation that has the effect of law. The power to issue these orders, the **ordinance power,** arises from two sources: the Constitution and acts of Congress.[3]

The Constitution does not mention the ordinance power in so many words, but that power is clearly intended. In granting certain powers to the President, the Constitution obviously anticipates their use. In order to exercise those powers, the President must have the power to issue the necessary orders, as well as the power to implement them. The President must also have the power to authorize his subordinates to issue such orders.

The number, the scope, and the complexity of governmental problems has grown over the years. As a result, Congress has found it necessary to delegate more and more discretion to the President

---

[3]The ordinance power applies only to parties to a contract that subjects them to it, such as employees, contractors, users of government assets, or visitors to government-owned facilities. However, it has been extended beyond its strict constitutional limits to apply to citizens not subject to supervision in that way.

---

## Organizing Information

To make sure students understand the main points of this section, you may wish to use the tree map graphic organizer to the right.

Tell students that a tree map provides an outline for a topic, its main ideas, and its supporting details. Have students use the tree map to supply information about the President's executive powers.

**Teaching Tip** A template for this graphic organizer can be found in the Section Support Transparencies, Transparency 3.

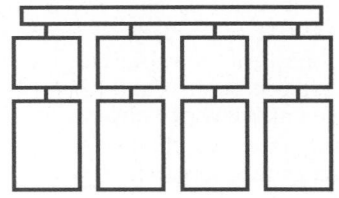

and to presidential subordinates to spell out the policies and programs it has passed. Members of Congress are not, and cannot be expected to be, experts in all of the fields in which they must legislate.

## The Appointment Power

A President cannot hope to succeed without loyal subordinates who support the policies of the President's administration. The Constitution provides that the President

 *"by and with the Advice and Consent of the Senate . . . shall appoint Ambassadors, other public Ministers and Consuls, Judges of the Supreme Court, and all other Officers of the United States, whose Appointments are not herein otherwise provided for[4] . . . but the Congress may by Law vest the Appointment of such inferior Officers, as they think proper, in the President alone, in the Courts of Law, or in the Heads of Departments."*
—Article II, Section 2, Clause 2

Acting alone, the President names only a handful of the 2.7 million federal civilian employees. Many of that handful fill the top spots in the White House Office.

With Senate consent, the President names most of the top-ranking officers of the Federal Government. Among them are:

(1) ambassadors and other diplomats;

(2) Cabinet members and their top aides;

(3) the heads of such independent agencies as the Environmental Protection Agency and the National Aeronautics and Space Administration;

(4) all federal judges, U.S. marshals, and attorneys;

(5) all officers in the armed forces.

When the President makes one of these appointments, the nomination is sent to the Senate. There, the support of a majority of the senators present and voting is needed for confirmation.

The unwritten rule of senatorial courtesy plays an important part in this process. That rule applies to the choice of those federal officers who serve within a State—a federal district

judge or a federal marshal, for example. The rule holds that the Senate will approve only those federal appointees acceptable to the senator or senators of the President's party from the State involved. The practical effect of this custom, which is closely followed in the Senate, is to place

---

[4]Those whose appointments are "otherwise provided for" are the Vice President, senators, representatives, and presidential electors.

### The Confirmation Process

For nominees who must be approved by the Senate, a multi-step process leads to their acceptance or rejection. Here are the steps involved in the confirmation of a high-level official nominated by the President, such as a Supreme Court justice.

**Nomination**
President's staff conducts a thorough search for a competent and acceptable candidate, getting input from key experts inside and outside of government. The President submits his choice to the Senate.

In 1993, President Clinton nominated Ruth Bader Ginsburg (shown below), a federal Court of Appeals judge for the District of Columbia Circuit, to serve on the Supreme Court.

**Senate Committee Hearings**
The nomination goes to the appropriate Senate committee. The nominee testifies before the committee—a sometimes grueling process if there is strong opposition to the candidate. The committee calls other experts to testify for and against the nominee. A majority vote is needed to recommend the nominee to the Senate.

Ginsburg's past doubts about the *Roe* v. *Wade* abortion ruling stirred initial resistance. She had favored a gradual legalization of abortion. But in the hearings she affirmed her support for abortion rights.

**Senate Debate**
The full Senate considers the nomination. Senators express their views before a floor vote is taken.

The White House had consulted key senators of both parties before submitting Ginsburg's nomination. Thus, debate was minimal.

**Confirmation**
If a simple majority votes to approve the nominee, he or she is confirmed.

On August 3, 1993, by a vote of 97 to 3, the Senate confirmed Ginsburg's nomination. She became the second woman ever to serve on the Supreme Court.

**Rejection**
If the nominee is rejected, another nomination is made. If strong opposition arises during the process, the President may withdraw the nomination or the nominee bows out to avoid the embarrassment of rejection.

*Interpreting Diagrams* In recent years, some nominees for top-level jobs have been subjected to bitter, hostile questioning at Senate hearings. Critics worry that the grueling process causes some talented people to shun public service. ***Why, do you think, did the Framers create this multi-step process?***

### Make It Relevant

### Careers in Government—Architect

The more than one million people who tour the White House each year marvel at the beauty of the building, but few realize that it has its own architect. Indeed, architects play an important role at all levels of government, for thousands of buildings all around the country. More than just building designers, architects oversee renovations, ensure buildings' soundness, and maintain the

historical integrity of the concrete symbols of American government.
**Skills Activity** Have student pairs draw rough plans for a government monument or building they would like to see erected or repaired. Then have individual students write paragraphs explaining why they would or would not be interested in a career as a government architect. **(Average)**

## Heterogeneous Groups

**Reteaching** List the President's executive powers on the chalkboard *(Ordinance, Appointment,* and *Removal).* Divide the class into three groups, assigning each group one of these executive powers. Ask each group to develop a list of examples of the power and write them on a sheet of paper. When finished, collect each group's list of examples. Call out an example from a list at random, and have students place the example under its appropriate heading.

**(Basic)**

---

## Background Note

### Recent Scholarship

In *The Strategic Presidency: Hitting the Ground Running,* James P. Pfiffner argues convincingly that the transition period between election and inauguration is crucial to the long-term success of an administration. Pfiffner draws on his own experience in the Office of Personnel Management as well as interviews with over 50 individuals who have served in presidential administrations. He focuses on the selection of White House staff, organization of the Cabinet, establishment of policies and procedures for working with the federal bureaucracy, mastering the budget process, and developing a legislative agenda. After comparing the Reagan, Bush, and Clinton administrations, Pfiffner asserts that when it comes to the presidency, "… power is not automatically transferred, it must be seized."

---

a meaningful part of the President's appointing power in the hands of particular senators.

Of course, not all executive branch employees are chosen by the President and Senate. Well over half of all the federal civilian work force is selected on the basis of competitive civil service examinations. Today, the Office of Personnel Management examines applicants for some 1.7 million positions.

## The Removal Power

The power to remove is the other side of the appointment coin, and it is as critically important to presidential success as the power to appoint. Yet except for mention of the little-used impeachment process,[5] the Constitution does not say how or by whom appointed officers may be dismissed, whether for incompetence, for opposition to presidential policies, or for any other cause.

### The Historical Debate

The question was hotly debated in the first session of Congress in 1789. Several members argued that for those offices for which appointment required Senate approval, Senate

---

[5]Article II, Section 4.

► The only removal power outlined in the Constitution is presidential impeachment, the threat of which caused Richard Nixon to step down and transfer power to Gerald Ford in 1974.

---

consent should also be required for removal. They insisted that this restriction on presidential authority was essential to congressional supervision (oversight) of the executive branch. Others argued that the President could not "take care that the laws be faithfully executed" without a free hand to dismiss those who were incompetent or otherwise undesirable.

The latter view prevailed. The First Congress gave to the President the power to remove any officer he appointed, except federal judges. Over the years since then, Congress has sometimes tried, with little success, to restrict the President's freedom to dismiss.

One notable instance came in 1867. Locked with Andrew Johnson in the fight over Reconstruction, Congress passed the Tenure of Office Act. The law's plain purpose was to prevent President Johnson from removing several top officers in his administration, especially the secretary of war, Edwin M. Stanton. The law provided that any person holding an office by presidential appointment with Senate consent should remain in that office until a successor had been confirmed by the Senate.

The President vetoed the bill, charging that it was an unconstitutional invasion of executive authority. Johnson's veto was overridden, but he ignored Congress and fired Stanton anyway. The veto and Stanton's removal sparked the move for Johnson's impeachment. Ultimately, the President was acquitted, and the law was ignored in practice. It was finally repealed in 1887.

### Removal and the Court

The question of the President's removal power did not reach the Supreme Court until *Myers* v. *United States,* 1926. In 1876, Congress had passed a law requiring Senate consent before the President could dismiss any first-class, second-class, or third-class postmaster.

In 1920, without consulting the Senate, President Woodrow Wilson removed Frank Myers as the postmaster at Portland, Oregon. Myers then sued for the salary for the rest of his four-year term. He based his claim on the point that he had been removed in violation of the 1876 law.

The Court found the law unconstitutional. The majority opinion was written by Chief Justice William Howard Taft, himself a former

President. The Court held that the power of removal was an essential part of the executive power, clearly necessary to the faithful execution of the laws.

The Supreme Court did place some limits on the President's removal power in 1935, in *Humphrey's Executor* v. *United States*. President Herbert Hoover had appointed William Humphrey to a seven-year term on the Federal Trade Commission (FTC) in 1931. When Franklin D. Roosevelt entered office in 1933, he found Humphrey to be in sharp disagreement with many of his policies. He asked Humphrey to resign, saying that his administration would be better served with someone else on the FTC. When Humphrey refused, Roosevelt removed him. Humphrey soon died, but his heirs filed a suit for back salary.

The Supreme Court upheld the heirs' claim. It based its decision on the act creating the FTC. That law provides that a member of the commission may be removed only for "inefficiency, neglect of duty, or malfeasance in office."[6] The President had given none of these reasons when he removed Humphrey.

The Court further held that Congress does have the power to set the conditions under which

---
[6]*Malfeasance* is wrongful conduct, especially by someone holding a public office.

**Interpreting Political Cartoons** Reagan's young budget director, David Stockman, cleverly and swiftly pushed through Congress severe budget cuts based on uncertain budget figures. When Stockman admitted as much in a famous magazine interview, Reagan fired him. *How does this cartoon reflect this newsmaking episode?*

a member of the FTC and other such agencies might be removed by the President. It did so because those agencies, the independent regulatory commissions, are not purely executive agencies—a rather complicated point covered in the next chapter.

As a general rule, the President may remove those whom the President appoints. Occasionally, the President does have to remove someone. Most often, however, what was in fact a dismissal is called a "resignation."

## Section 2 Assessment

**Key Terms and Main Ideas**

1. In taking the **oath of office,** what does the President promise to do?
2. How does the President affect the application of a law passed by Congress?
3. What is an **executive order,** and in what ways does it give the President great power?
4. What is the **ordinance power,** and where does the President get this power?
5. **(a)** Which officials does the President appoint? **(b)** What is the Senate's role in the appointment process?

**Critical Thinking**

6. **Making Decisions** Should the President have the sole power to remove all officials he appoints? Or should the

Senate have a role in deciding whether to remove officials that it confirmed? Summarize the arguments on both sides of this debate. Then decide which side you favor, and explain why.
7. **Making Comparisons** Compare and contrast the Supreme Court rulings in *Myers* v. *United States* and *Humphrey's Executor* v. *United States*.

 **Take It to the Net**

8. Do Presidents make too many appointments with an eye to politics? Read an Internet article on the topic and write a brief pro or con response. Use the links provided in the Social Studies area of the following Web site for help in completing this activity. **www.phschool.com**

 **Take It to the Net**

8. Direct students to the Social Studies area at the Prentice Hall School Web site. The *Magruder's American Government* companion Web site includes the directions and links needed to complete the activity. It also provides a printable Internet activity worksheet with scoring rubrics for assessment. Responses should clearly support or oppose the article.

7. In *Myers,* the Court ruled that the power of removal was essential to executive power. In *Humphrey's Executor,* the Court ruled that Congress could set the conditions under which officers in non-executive agencies could be removed.

## Answers to . . .

### Section 2 Assessment

**1.** To faithfully execute the office of President and preserve, protect, and defend the Constitution.
**2.** It is the duty of the President and various departments within the executive branch to work out the details of the laws.
**3.** An executive order is a directive, rule, or regulation issued by the President that has the effect of law.
**4.** The ordinance power is the power for the President to issue executive orders; the ordinance power is implied in the Constitution and has also arisen from acts of Congress.
**5. (a)** Ambassadors and diplomats; Cabinet members and their top aides; the heads of certain independent agencies; federal judges, attorneys, and marshals; all officers in the armed forces. **(b)** A majority of the the senators present must confirm all nominations.
**6.** Summaries and opinions should include several examples of the debate from the text.

### Answer to . . .

**Interpreting Political Cartoons** The budget cuts being pushed through Congress are reflected in the makeshift furniture of Reagan's office.

# SKILLS FOR LIFE

## CHARTS and GRAPHS

### Using Time Lines

**Focus** Work as a class to make a time line of major events that occurred during the students' lifetime.

**Instruct** Using the birth year of the oldest student as a starting point and the current year as an end point, construct a world history time line on the chalkboard. Break the class into small groups to research different segments of the time period and create entries, following the steps on this page. Then hold a discussion about the events on the time line. Are there more domestic events on the time line, or foreign ones? Why? Which events affected the students' lives the most?

**Close/Reteach** After students create their own time lines in the Test for Success exercise, have them compare those time lines to the one that the class constructed. Look for related or influential events.

## SKILLS FOR LIFE

# Using Time Lines

Even if you have a fantastic memory, it's difficult to keep a lot of dates in your head in the right order. A time line lets you visualize a sequence of events so that you can see relationships among dates and events. Often a time line reveals causes and effects as well as events that recur in time.

The time line below presents key events in the presidency of Richard Nixon. Use the steps below to analyze the time line:

**1. Identify the time period covered by the time line.** The upper time line shown here spans the years of Richard Nixon's presidency, from his first election in 1968 to his resignation in 1974. (a) How many years does the upper time line cover? A secondary time line appears to pop out from the upper line. This lower time line magnifies in detail the events on a certain segment of the upper time line. (b) How many years does the lower time line cover?

**2. Determine how the time line is divided.** Most time lines are divided into equal periods, or increments, of time: years, decades, or centuries. (a) What increments of time are used in the upper line? (b) What increments are used in the lower line?

**3. Study the time line to see how events are related.** (a) State what content is shown in the upper time line. (b) State the content of the lower time line.

**4. Use the time line to help you draw conclusions about the period you are studying.** What do you think happened to Nixon's popularity between his landslide reelection and his resignation? Explain.

### Test for Success

Construct a time line of your life or the life of someone you know. Make a secondary time line of a particular year or grade in school that shows some details from that period.

## Time Line of Nixon's Presidency

**November 1968** Nixon wins presidential election.

**July 1969** U.S. astronauts land on the moon.

**February 1972** Nixon becomes first President to visit China.

**November 1972** Nixon reelected in a landslide.

**January 1973** U.S. withdraws from Vietnam.

**August 1974** Nixon resigns.

| 1968 | 1969 | 1970 | 1971 | 1972 | 1973 | 1974 |

**1972**

**1973**

**1974**

**June 17, 1972** Five men arrested for breaking into Democratic Party Headquarters in the Watergate building. The burglars had close ties to the White House and to CREEP (Committee to Re-Elect the President).

**April 30, 1973** White House counsel John Dean fired after agreeing to testify against Nixon. Other close aides resign.

**August 1973** Judge orders Nixon to hand over secret and incriminating Oval Office tape recordings.

**March 1, 1974** Seven Nixon aides indicted for attempting to cover up the break-in; Nixon named as co-conspirator.

**August 9, 1974** Nixon resigns; Gerald Ford becomes President.

**July 27, 1974** House prepares articles of impeachment against Nixon.

### Answers . . .

**1. (a)** About 6 years. **(b)** About 3 years.
**2. (a)** 1-year increments. **(b)** 1-year increments.
**3. (a)** Nixon's presidency. **(b)** The Watergate scandal.
**4.** Possible answer: His popularity, although high at the time of his 1972 reelection, plummeted during the next two years, as the details of the Watergate scandal became public.

## Test for Success

Students should use equal time increments on their time lines and demonstrate an understanding of the function of the main and secondary time lines.

## Point–of–Use Resources

**Skills for Life Activity** Unit 4 booklet, p. 21 provides an additional skill activity for this chapter.

**Social Studies Skills Tutor CD-ROM** Provides interactive practice in geographic literacy, critical thinking and reading, visual analysis, and communications.

# Diplomatic and Military Powers

## Section Preview

### OBJECTIVES

1. **Explain** how treaties are made and approved.
2. **Explain** why and how executive agreements are made.
3. **Summarize** for what purposes the power of recognition is used, and give historic examples.
4. **Describe** the powers that the President has in the role of commander in chief.

### WHY IT MATTERS

The President shares various diplomatic and military powers with Congress, but in some areas the President's power is almost unlimited.

### POLITICAL DICTIONARY

★ treaty
★ executive agreement
★ recognition
★ *persona non grata*

---

John F. Kennedy once described the pressures of the presidency in these words:

**PRIMARY Sources** " *When I ran for the presidency . . . I knew the country faced serious challenges, but I could not realize— nor could any man who does not bear the burdens of this office—how heavy and constant would be those burdens.* "
—President John F. Kennedy, radio and TV broadcast on the Berlin crisis, July 25, 1961

When President Kennedy made that comment, he had in mind the subject of this section: the President's awesome responsibilities as chief diplomat and as commander in chief.

## The Power to Make Treaties

A **treaty** is a formal agreement between two or more sovereign states. The President, usually acting through the secretary of state, negotiates these international agreements. The Senate must give its approval, by a two-thirds vote of the members present, before a treaty made by the President can become effective. Recall, the Constitution makes treaties a part of the "supreme Law of the Land."

Contrary to popular belief, the Senate does not ratify treaties. The Constitution requires the Senate's "Advice and Consent" to a treaty made by the President. Once the Senate has approved a treaty, the President ratifies it by the exchange of formal notifications with the other party or parties to the agreement.

Treaties have the same legal standing as do acts passed by Congress. Congress may abrogate (repeal) a treaty by passing a law contrary to its provisions, and an existing law may be repealed by the terms of a treaty. When a treaty and a federal law conflict, the courts consider the latest enacted to be the law (*The Head Money Cases*, 1884). The terms of a treaty cannot conflict with the higher law of the Constitution (*Missouri v. Holland*, 1920), but the Supreme Court has never found a treaty provision to be unconstitutional.

▲ In 1945, the ailing President Franklin D. Roosevelt (right) undertook an ambitious trip to meet at sea with Saudi Arabia's King Ibn Saud, a key ally in the Middle East. *Critical Thinking* **In what way are the President's diplomatic powers among his strongest?**

---

---

**399**

## Reading Strategy
### Finding Evidence

Tell students that the President shares diplomatic and military powers with Congress. As they read, have students find evidence supporting and disputing this statement.

## Point-of-Use Resources

📁 **Guided Reading and Review** Unit 4 booklet, p. 17 provides students with practice identifying the main ideas and key terms of this section.

📁 **Lesson Plans** For lesson planning suggestions, see p. 64 of the Lesson Plans booklet.

📁 **Political Cartoons** See p. 56 of the Political Cartoons booklet for a cartoon relevant to this section.

📇 **Section Support Transparencies** Transparency 59, *Visual Learning*; Transparency 158, *Political Cartoon*

▲ *The Panama Canal* Former President Jimmy Carter attended the ceremony transferring control of the Panama Canal to Panama on December 14, 1999.

The Framers considered the Senate—with, originally, only 26 members—a suitable council to advise the President in foreign affairs. Secrecy was thought to be necessary and was seen as an impossibility in a body as large as the House.

The two-thirds rule creates the possibility that a relatively small minority in the Senate can kill a treaty. Take one of the most dramatic examples: In 1920 the Senate rejected the Treaty of Versailles, the general peace agreement to end World War I. The treaty included provisions for the League of Nations. Forty-nine senators voted for the pact and 35 against, but the vote was 7 short of the necessary two thirds. More than once a President has been forced to bow to the views of a few senators in order to get a treaty approved, even when this has meant making concessions opposed by the majority.

At times, a President has had to turn to roundabout methods in order to achieve his goals. When a Senate minority defeated a treaty to annex Texas, President Tyler was able to bring about annexation in 1845 by encouraging passage of a joint resolution—a move that required only a majority vote in each house. In 1898 President McKinley used the same tactic to annex Hawaii, again after a treaty his administration had negotiated had failed in the Senate.

## Executive Agreements

Many international agreements, especially routine ones, are made as executive agreements. An **executive agreement** is a pact between the President and the head of a foreign state, or between their subordinates. Unlike treaties, executive agreements do not require Senate consent.

Most executive agreements flow out of legislation already passed by Congress or out of treaties to which the Senate has agreed. However, the President can make these executive agreements without any congressional action.[7]

A few executive agreements have been extraordinary—most notably, the destroyers-for-bases deal of 1940. That pact was struck in the first year of World War II, more than a year before the United States became directly involved in the conflict. Under its terms, the United States gave Great Britain 50 "over-age" U.S. destroyers, naval vessels that the British desperately needed to combat German submarine attacks in the North Atlantic. In return, the United States received 99-year leases to a string of air and naval bases extending from Newfoundland to the Caribbean.

## The Power of Recognition

When the President receives the diplomatic representatives of another sovereign state, the President exercises the power of **recognition.** That is, the President, acting for the United States, acknowledges the legal existence of that country and its government. The President indicates that the United States accepts that country as an equal in the family of nations. Sovereign states generally recognize one another through the exchange of diplomatic representatives.[8]

Recognition does not mean that one government approves of the character and conduct of another. The United States recognizes several governments about which it has serious misgivings. Among the most notable examples today is the People's Republic of China. The facts of

---

[7]The Supreme Court has held executive agreements to be as binding as treaties and to be a part of the supreme law of the land, *United States* v. *Belmont*, 1937; *United States v. Pink*, 1942.

[8]Recognition may be carried out by other means, such as proposing to negotiate a treaty, since under international law only sovereign states can make such agreements.

## Spotlight on Technology

📼 **Magruder's American Government Video Collection**

The Magruder's Video Collection explores key issues and debates in American government. Each segment examines an issue central to chapter content through use of historical and contemporary footage. Commentary from civic leaders in academics, government, and the media follow each segment. Critical-thinking questions focus students' attention on key issues, and may be used to stimulate discussion.

Use the Chapter 14 video segment (time: about 5 minutes) to explore how Presidents have used their power to take far-reaching actions—without the consent of Congress. From FDR's creation of the Lend-Lease program to Carter's initiation of the Camp David Accords, this segment highlights several Presidents who turned their prerogatives into policy.

life in world politics make relations with these governments necessary.

Recognition is often used as a weapon in foreign relations, too. Prompt recognition of a new country or government may do much to guarantee its life—and withholding of recognition may seriously affect its continued existence.

President Theodore Roosevelt's quick recognition of the Republic of Panama in 1903 is a classic example of the use of the power as a diplomatic weapon. He recognized the new state less than three days after the Panamanians had begun a revolt against Colombia, of which Panama had been a part. Roosevelt's quick action guaranteed their success. Similarly, President Truman's recognition of Israel, within 24 hours of its creation in 1948, helped that new state to survive among its hostile Arab neighbors.

The President may show American displeasure with the conduct of another country by asking for the recall of that nation's ambassador or other diplomatic representatives in this country. The official recalled is declared to be ***persona non grata,*** an unwelcome person. The same point can be made by the recalling of an American diplomat from a post in another country. The withdrawal of recognition is the sharpest diplomatic rebuke one government may give to another and has often been a step on the way to war.

## Commander in Chief

The Constitution makes the President the commander in chief of the nation's armed forces.[9] Although Congress shares the war powers,[10] the President's position in military affairs is as dominant as it is in the field of foreign affairs. In fact, it does not stretch the matter too far to say that the President's powers as commander in chief are almost without limit.

Consider this illustration of the point: In 1907 Theodore Roosevelt sent the Great White Fleet around the world. He did so partly as a training exercise for the Navy, but mostly to impress other nations with America's naval might. Several members of Congress objected to the cost and threatened to block funds for the

[9]Article II, Section 2, Clause 1; see also Chapter 17.
[10]Article I, Section 8, Clauses 11–17; see also Chapter 11.

President's project. To this Roosevelt replied: "Very well, the existing appropriation will carry the Navy halfway around the world and if Congress chooses to leave it on the other side, all right." Congress was forced to give in.

Presidents delegate much of their command authority to military subordinates. They are not required to do so, however. George Washington actually took command of federal troops and led them into Pennsylvania during the Whiskey Rebellion of 1794. Abraham Lincoln often visited the Army of the Potomac and instructed his generals in the field during the Civil War.

Most Presidents have not become so directly involved in military operations. Still, the President always has the final authority over and responsibility for all military matters.

### Making Undeclared War

Presidents have used the armed forces abroad, in combat, without a declaration of war by Congress. In fact, most Presidents have done so, and on several hundred occasions.

John Adams was the first to do so, in 1798. At his command, the Navy fought and won a number of battles with French warships that were harassing American merchantmen in the Atlantic and the Caribbean. Thomas Jefferson and then James Madison followed that precedent in the war against the Barbary Coast pirates of North Africa in the early 1800s. There have been a great many other foreign adventures over the past two centuries. The long military conflicts in Korea (from 1950 to 1953) and in Vietnam

Lincoln, Civil War, 1862

Truman, post-World War II, 1946

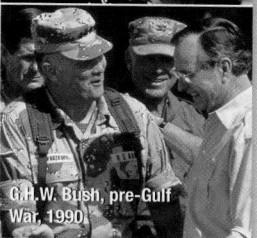
Johnson, Vietnam War, 1967

G.H.W. Bush, pre-Gulf War, 1990

G.W. Bush, War on Terrorism, 2001

▲ Presidents have sent the nation's armed forces into combat on more than 200 occasions. *Critical Thinking Why did the Framers choose the President, rather than a military officer, to be commander in chief?*

ACTIVITY

## Learning Styles

**Linguistic** Have students explore how the growth in presidential power has affected both the system of checks and balances and the separation of powers as outlined by the Framers of the Constitution. Ask students to prepare a written report that critically examines the impact of the increased presidential powers. Encourage students to draw on examples from history and current events to support their arguments. Ask for volunteers to share their reports with the class.

**Block Strategy
(Challenging)**

## Customize for

### More Advanced Students

Ask students to prepare a report that illustrates the use of presidential powers in action. Using magazine and newspaper articles or other resources, have students identify President Clinton's use of diplomatic and military powers in the Middle East in 1999. Ask for volunteers to present their reports to the class.

## Point–of–Use Resources

**Simulations and Debates** War Powers Resolution, p. 53 helps students debate the constitutionality and ramifications of this controversial law.

**Close Up on Primary Sources** War Powers Resolution (1973), p. 62

**ABC News Civics and Government Videotape Library** *The Volunteer Summit* (time: about 6 minutes)

*Answer to . . .*

**Evaluating the Quotation** The attack of September 11 and the events that followed have shown that President Bush's concerns were justified and his focus correct.

## *Voices* on Government

One of the most important roles of an American President is that of world leader and diplomat. **George W. Bush** spoke about the importance of a strong United States military during a speech at the Reagan Presidential Library in 1999, while he was still Governor of Texas.

❝*American defense . . . must be the first focus of a president, because it is his first duty to the Constitution. Even in this time of pride and promise, America has determined enemies, who hate our values and resent our success—terrorists and crime syndicates and drug cartels and unbalanced dictators. The Empire has passed, but evil remains. We must protect our homeland and our allies against missiles and terror and blackmail. We must restore the morale of our military. . . .*❞

### Evaluating the Quotation

*How have events during the George W. Bush presidency affected the sentiments expressed in the quotation?*

(from 1965 to 1973) were until now the largest of those "undeclared wars."

The most recent presidential uses of military forces have come with the war on terrorism. They began on October 7, 2001, when President George W. Bush ordered air strikes against Afghanistan. Those attacks were aimed at destroying (1) the training camps of Osama bin Laden's al Qaida terrorist network and (2) the Taliban regime, which had harbored bin Laden and his cohorts in Afghanistan. The devastating air strikes marked the beginning of what the President has called "a sustained, comprehensive, and relentless campaign" against terrorists and every government that sponsors them.

George H. W. Bush sent the armed forces into battle twice, first in Panama in late 1989 and then into Kuwait and Iraq in early 1991. He ordered the invasion of Panama to oust dictator Manuel Noriega and to safeguard American interests there, notably the Panama Canal.

President Bush also dispatched the armed forces to the Persian Gulf region in mid-1990—as the major part of an international response to Iraq's invasion of oil-rich Kuwait. The Persian Gulf War began in January 1991, with allied air attacks on Iraqi targets in Kuwait and within Iraq itself. In late February an American-led ground attack destroyed the Iraqi army. More than 500,000 Americans saw duty in the Gulf War, and the Air Force continues to patrol the skies above Iraq today.

In 1994, President Bill Clinton used the threat of military force to restore at least the beginnings of democratic government to Haiti. In 1991 a military coup had deposed President Jean-Baptiste Aristide, the first popularly elected leader in Haiti's history. Faced with invasion by the United States, the military dictatorship collapsed.

Mr. Clinton committed military forces to the Balkans—to what was once Yugoslavia—in 1995 and again in 1999. Yugoslavia had collapsed in 1992, shattered by bitter nationalistic rivalries and by longstanding ethnic conflicts in its six individual republics. Bosnia-Herzegovina, Croatia, Macedonia, and Slovenia became independent countries. The other two pieces of the old Yugoslavia, Serbia and Montenegro, formed a new Yugoslav state dominated by Serbia.

For four years, the ethnic Serb, Muslim, and Croat factions of the Bosnian population waged vicious war against one another. That conflict was fueled by Serbia and its president, Slobodan Milosevic. Finally, American-led efforts by the North Atlantic Treaty Organization (NATO) and the UN brought a cease-fire in 1995. Serbian-backed forces in Bosnia agreed to stop fighting only in the face of threatened air strikes by the NATO countries. At that point, President Clinton ordered 20,000 American troops to Bosnia, as part of a NATO peacekeeping force. They remain on duty there today.

A long-smoldering ethnic conflict in Kosovo, a province of Serbia, erupted into full-scale civil war in late 1997. Most Kosovars are ethnic Albanians, and they had resisted Serbian control for decades. In 1998 Serbia began an "ethnic cleansing" campaign—a deliberate effort to eliminate the ethnic Albanians by expulsion and slaughter.

The Milosevic government rebuffed repeated protests by the United States and its NATO allies. Finally, in March 1999, NATO launched an air war against Serbia. A 78-day bombing campaign, by mostly American and British aircraft, and Russian influence forced the Serbs to withdraw from Kosovo. Some 10,000 U.S. troops are now part of yet another NATO peacekeeping force in what was once Yugoslavia.

## Wartime Powers

The President's powers as commander in chief are far greater during a war than they are in more normal times. In fact, presidential wartime authority goes far beyond the traditional military field. During World War II, for example, Congress gave the President the power to ration food and gasoline, control wages and prices, and seize and operate private industries vital to the nation's war effort.

The President may use the armed forces to keep the domestic peace.[11] When necessary, the President also has the power to call any State's militia, or all of them, into federal service.[12]

## The War Powers Resolution

In today's world, no one can doubt that the President must be able to respond rapidly and effectively to threats to this nation's security. Still,

[11]Article IV, Section 4.
[12]Article I, Section 8, Clause 15; Article II, Section 2, Clause 1.

many people have long warned of the dangers inherent in the President's power to involve the nation in undeclared wars. They insist that the Constitution never intended the President to have such power.

The nation's frustrations and growing anguish over the war in Vietnam finally moved Congress to pass the War Powers Resolution of 1973. The act is designed to place close limits on the President's war-making powers. President Nixon vetoed the measure, calling it "both unconstitutional and dangerous to the best interest of our nation." Congress overrode the veto.

The resolution's central provisions require that:

(1) Within 48 hours after committing American forces to combat abroad, the President must report to Congress, detailing the circumstances and the scope of his actions.

(2) Combat commitment must end within 60 days, unless Congress agrees to a longer period. That 60-day deadline may be extended for up to 30 days, however, to allow for the safe withdrawal of the American forces involved.

(3) Congress may end the combat commitment at any time, by passing a concurrent resolution to that effect.

The constitutionality of the War Powers Resolution remains in dispute. A determination of the question must await a situation in which Congress demands that its provisions be obeyed but the President refuses to do so.

## Section 3 Assessment

### Key Terms and Main Ideas

1. Summarize the process by which treaties are negotiated and approved.
2. What is the difference between a **treaty** and an **executive agreement?**
3. Explain this statement: *The President's power of recognition can be used positively or negatively.*
4. Under what circumstances might the President declare a country's diplomat to be *persona non grata?*
5. Which of the President's powers is almost unlimited? Why?

### Critical Thinking

6. **Making Inferences** Why might a new country eagerly seek diplomatic recognition from the United States?

7. **Drawing Conclusions** Framer George Mason said, "The purse and the sword must never be in the same hands." How is this idea reflected in the War Powers Resolution?

### Take It to the Net

8. Read an online discussion of the use of executive agreements and treaties. Create bar charts showing the number of executive agreements made and treaties made in three time periods: (1) the first 50 years since independence (1776–1826); (2) from that early period, up to World War II (1827–1940); and (3) recent decades (1940–1989). **a)** What trend do the graphs show? **(b)** What are some reasons for the trend? Use the links provided in the Social Studies area at the following Web site for help in completing this activity. www.phschool.com

### Take It to the Net

8. Direct students to the Social Studies area at the Prentice Hall School Web site. The *Magruder's American Government* companion Web site includes the directions and links needed to complete the activity. It also provides a printable Internet activity worksheet with scoring rubrics for assessment. Charts should be clear and accurately show the trends.

## Point-of-Use Resources

**Guide to the Essentials** Chapter 14, Section 3, p. 79 provides support for students who need additional review of section content. Spanish support is available in the Spanish edition of the Guide on p. 72.

**Quiz** Unit 4 booklet, p. 18 includes matching and multiple-choice questions to check students' understanding of Section 3 content.

**Presentation Pro CD-ROM** Quizzes and multiple-choice questions check students' understanding of Section 3 content.

## Answers to...

### Section 3 Assessment

1. The President, usually through the secretary of state, negotiates a treaty. The Senate must approve the treaty by a two-thirds vote of members present, then the President ratifies it.
2. A treaty is a formal agreement that requires Senate approval. An executive agreement is a pact that does not require Senate approval.
3. When a President recognizes a new country or government quickly, it is a sign of approval that will help ensure the government's survival. Withholding recognition, in contrast, is a sign of disapproval that can challenge the new government's existence.
4. If that country has taken an economic, diplomatic, or military action unfavorable to United States policy.
5. The President's powers as commander in chief are almost unlimited, because the President always has the final authority over all military matters, and may exert it without the approval of Congress.
6. Possible answer: Recognition from the world's most powerful nation would help ensure the new country's survival.
7. The War Powers Resolution gives Congress (the purse) the power to end combat initiated by the President (the sword).

## The Monroe Doctrine

**Focus** Discuss the Monroe Doctrine with the class. Ask students to describe why it was such a bold doctrine for the President of the United States to declare in 1823. Be sure that students realize that the United States wasn't yet considered a world power and that colonization of foreign lands had become a common practice for European powers.

**Instruct** Have each student assume the role of President in the following scenario. A European nation has threatened to violate the Monroe Doctrine by invading a country in South America. Ask students to create a step-by-step plan for how they would deal with the crisis. Remind students to consider the President's military powers as discussed in the section.

**Close/Reteach** Have students discuss their plans with the class. If a plan would require the approval of Congress, have the class vote on it. If a plan doesn't require congressional approval, have students act as the press and ask the President questions about the plan.

**Keep It Current CD-ROM** includes government-related projects by unit. The CD-ROM links to the Prentice Hall School Web site and may be used for daily updates.

 *on Primary Sources*

# The Monroe Doctrine

*In the early 1800s, Spain's Central and South American colonies rebelled and gained their independence. U.S. leaders applauded these successful revolutions, but worried that Spain and its allies would reconquer the region. In 1823, President James Monroe discussed these concerns in a message to Congress. That part of his address, known as the Monroe Doctrine, became a cornerstone of American foreign policy.*

The occasion has been judged proper for asserting, as a principle in which the rights and interests of the United States are involved, that the American continents, by the free and independent condition which they have assumed and maintain, are henceforth not to be considered as subjects for future colonization by any European powers. . . .

United States military might upholds the Monroe Doctrine against European powers in this early twentieth-century cartoon.

In the wars of the European powers, in matters relating to themselves, we have never taken any part, nor does it comport with our policy so to do. It is only when our rights are invaded or seriously menaced that we resent injuries or make preparation for our defense.

With the movements in this hemisphere we are of necessity more immediately connected. . . . The political system of the [European] powers is essentially different . . . from . . . our own, which has been achieved by the loss of so much blood and treasure. . . . We owe it, therefore, to candor and to the amicable [friendly] relations existing between the United States and those powers to declare that we should consider any attempt on their part to extend their system to any portion of this hemisphere as dangerous to our peace and safety.

With the existing colonies or dependencies of any European power we have not interfered and shall not interfere. But with the governments who have declared their independence and maintained it, . . . we could not view any interposition [intervention]

for the purpose of oppressing them . . . in any other light than as the manifestation of an unfriendly disposition [attitude] toward the United States. . . .

Our policy in regard to Europe . . . remains the same, which is, not to interfere in the internal concerns of any of its powers; . . . to cultivate friendly relations with it, and to preserve those relations by a frank, firm, and manly policy. . . . But, in regard to [the American] continents, circumstances are eminently and conspicuously different. It is impossible that the allied powers should extend their political system to any portion of either continent without endangering our peace and happiness; nor can anyone believe that our southern brethren, if left to themselves, would adopt it of their own accord. . . . It is still the true policy of the United States to leave the parties to themselves in the hope that other powers will pursue the same course.

### Analyzing Primary Sources

1. According to Monroe, what is the foreign policy of the United States toward the nations of Europe?
2. Why is Monroe concerned about European expansion in Central and South America?
3. Monroe's statement suggests he is most concerned about whose independence, the South American nations or the United States? Explain.

 *Corner*

**Close Up on Primary Sources** The Monroe Doctrine and United States Foreign Policy, p. 16, extends this feature with a primary source activity.

 **Online**

To keep up-to-date on Close Up news and activities, visit Close Up Online at

**www.closeup.org**

# 4 Legislative and Judicial Powers

## Section Preview

### OBJECTIVES

1. **Describe** the President's two major legislative powers, and explain how these powers are an important part of the system of checks and balances.
2. **Describe** the President's major judicial powers.

### WHY IT MATTERS

The Constitution gives the President strong legislative and judicial powers as a part of the system of checks and balances.

### POLITICAL DICTIONARY

★ line-item veto
★ reprieve
★ pardon
★ clemency
★ commutation
★ amnesty

A s you know, the Federal Government is built on the principles of separation of powers and checks and balances. The Constitution gives to each of the three branches its own powers. It also gives to each of them powers with which to check—to delay or block—actions by the other two branches. As James Madison put it in *The Federalist* No. 51, each branch of the Federal Government has "the necessary constitutional means and personal motives to resist encroachments of the others."

## Legislative Powers

With his legislative powers, and the skillful playing of his roles as chief of party and chief citizen, the President can (and often does) have a considerable influence on the actions of Congress. The President is, in effect, the nation's chief legislator.

### Recommending Legislation

The Constitution says that the President

> **FROM THE Constitution** *❝shall from time to time give to the Congress Information on the State of the Union, and recommend to their Consideration such Measures as he shall judge necessary and expedient. . . . ❞*
>
> —Article II, Section 3

---

[13]Article I, Section 7, Clauses 2 and 3. Recall that, despite these words, joint resolutions proposing constitutional amendments and concurrent resolutions, which do not have the force of law, are not sent to the President.

This provision gives the President what is often called the *message power*.

The Chief Executive regularly sends three major messages to Capitol Hill each year. The first is the State of the Union message, a speech he almost always delivers in person to a joint session of Congress. The President's budget message and the annual Economic Report follow that speech soon after. The President often sends the lawmakers a number of other messages on a wide range of topics. In each of them, he calls on Congress to enact those laws he thinks to be necessary to the welfare of the country.

### The Veto Power

The Constitution says that "Every Bill" and "Every Order, Resolution, or Vote to which the Concurrence of the Senate and House of Representatives may be necessary (except on a question of Adjournment) shall be presented to the President."[13]

▲ Every year, huge bound volumes of the President's budget plan arrive at the Capitol, where they are distributed for Congress's consideration.

**405**

## Reading Strategy

### Questioning

Ask students to scan the title and headings in the section and then write three questions that they hope to have answered in this section. As they read, they should look for the answers.

### A C T I V I T Y

### Heterogeneous Groups

**Enrichment** Assign all students a number from 1 to 5. Create groups of five students so that members with the same numbers are together (a group of 1's, a group of 2's, etc.). Assign each group a different presidential power, including *executive, diplomatic, military, legislative,* and *judicial.* Ask groups to show how the current President is fulfilling these roles through a discussion of current events. Then have students return to their original groups to share the information they have gathered about presidential powers.

**📖 Block Strategy (Average)**

## Point–of–Use Resources

📁 **Guided Reading and Review** Unit 4 booklet, p. 19 provides students with practice identifying the main ideas and key terms of this section.

📁 **Lesson Plans** For lesson planning suggestions, see p. 65 of the Lesson Plans booklet.

📁 **Political Cartoons** See p. 57 of the Political Cartoons booklet for a cartoon relevant to this section.

📼 **ABC News Civics and Government Videotape Library** *The Federal Budget* (time: about 2 minutes)

### Answer to . . .

**Interpreting Tables (a)** The amount of time the person has spent in office; his relationship with Congress.
**(b)** Possible answer: They only vetoed bills they knew Congress would not try to overturn.

Remember, the Constitution presents the President with four options when he receives a measure passed by Congress. First, he may sign the bill, making it law. Or he can veto it, and the measure must then be returned to Congress. Of course, Congress can override a presidential veto by a two-thirds vote in each of its two chambers—but it seldom does.

As a third option, the President may allow the bill to become law by not acting on it, neither signing nor vetoing it, within 10 days (not counting Sundays). This rarely happens.

The fourth option, the pocket veto, can be used only at the end of a congressional session. If Congress adjourns within 10 days of sending a bill to the President and the chief executive does not act on it, the measure dies. Most Presidents have used the pocket veto with some frequency, because Congress regularly passes a large number of measures in the closing days of its annual sessions.

The fact that Congress is seldom able to muster the two-thirds majority needed to overturn a presidential veto makes the veto a significant weapon in the Chief Executive's dealings with the legislative branch. The weight that this power has in the executive–legislative relationship is underscored by this important point: The mere threat of a veto is often enough to defeat a bill or to prompt changes in its provisions as it moves through the legislative process. The record of presidential vetoes over the years, and the fact that they are not often overturned, can be seen in the table below.

### The Line-Item Veto

If the President decides to veto a bill, he must reject the *entire* measure. He cannot veto only a portion of it.

Since Ulysses S. Grant's day, most Presidents have favored the expansion of the veto power to include a **line-item veto.** That is, they have urged that the President be given the power to cancel specific dollar amounts (line items) in spending bills enacted by Congress. Those Presidents, and the many who have supported their position, have argued over the years that the line-item veto would be a potent weapon against wasteful and unnecessary federal spending.

Over time, opponents of the line-item veto—and there have been many of them—have said that to grant the President such authority would bring a massive and dangerous shift of power to

► Presidential signings of legislation are commemorated with special pens, like this one from a Reagan signing.

| Presidential Vetoes 1933–2001 | | | | |
|---|---|---|---|---|
| | Regular Vetoes | Pocket Vetoes | Total Vetoes | Vetoes Overridden |
| Franklin Roosevelt (1933–1945) | 372 | 263 | 635 | 9 |
| Harry Truman (1945–1953) | 180 | 70 | 250 | 12 |
| Dwight Eisenhower (1953–1961) | 73 | 108 | 181 | 2 |
| John Kennedy (1961–1963) | 12 | 9 | 21 | — |
| Lyndon Johnson (1963–1969) | 16 | 14 | 30 | — |
| Richard Nixon (1969–1974) | 26 | 14 | 43 | 7 |
| Gerald Ford (1974–1977) | 48 | 18 | 66 | 12 |
| Jimmy Carter (1977–1981) | 13 | 18 | 31 | 2 |
| Ronald Reagan (1981–1989) | 39 | 39 | 78 | 9 |
| George H. W. Bush (1989–1993) | 29 | 15 | 44 | 1 |
| Bill Clinton (1993–2001) | 36 | 1 | 37 | 2 |

SOURCE: Congressional Research Service, Library of Congress

*Interpreting Tables* Some Presidents have used their veto power more often than others. *(a) What might explain the huge variations in numbers of total vetoes? (b) Why, do you think, did some Presidents have fewer vetoes overridden?*

the executive branch. To this point, efforts to persuade Congress to propose a line-item veto amendment to the Constitution have failed.

In 1996, however, Congress did pass the Line Item Veto Act. That law gave the President the power to reject individual items in spending bills, and to eliminate any provision of a tax bill that benefited fewer than 100 people. President Clinton hailed the statute as a major step against "special interest boondoggles, tax loopholes, and pure pork."

Opponents of the measure challenged it in the courts, and they won their case in *Clinton* v. *New York City*, 1998. There, the Supreme Court struck down the law. By a 6–3 vote, it held that Congress lacked the authority to give the President a line-item veto by statute. If the President is to have such power, said the Court, it must come via an amendment to the Constitution.

## Other Legislative Powers

According to Article II, Section 3 of the Constitution, only the President can call Congress into special session. Most recently, President Truman did so in 1948, to have Congress consider post-World War II economic measures. The same constitutional provision also gives the President the power to prorogue (adjourn) Congress whenever the two houses cannot agree on a date for their adjournment—something that has never happened.

## Judicial Powers

The Constitution gives the President the power to

 **FROM THE Constitution** " . . . *Grant Reprieves and Pardons for Offenses against the United States, except in Cases of Impeachment.* "

—Article II, Section 2, Clause 1

A **reprieve** is the postponement of the execution of a sentence. A **pardon** is legal forgiveness of a crime.

The President's power to grant reprieves and pardons is absolute, except in cases of impeachment, where they may never be granted. These powers of **clemency** (mercy or leniency) may be used only in cases involving federal offenses. The President has no such authority with regard to those who violate State law.

KINDA PINCHES ACROSS THE TOES — GIMME A SIZE LARGER.

CONGRESS

VAST PRESIDENTIAL AUTHORITY

*Interpreting Cartoons* This cartoon comments on the increasing power of the President—in this case, Harry Truman, a former haberdasher, or clothier. ***According to the cartoonist, who is responsible for this growth in power?***

Presidential pardons are usually granted after a person has been convicted in court. Yet the President may pardon a federal offender before that person is tried, or even before that person has been formally charged.

Pardons in advance of a trial or charge are rare. The most noteworthy pardon, by far, was granted in 1974. In that year, President Gerald Ford gave "a full, free and absolute pardon unto Richard Nixon for all offenses against the United States which he . . . has committed or may have committed or taken part in during the period from January 20, 1969, through August 9, 1974." Of course, that pardon referred to the Watergate scandal—the many and sordid events that ultimately forced Nixon to resign the presidency.

To be effective, a pardon must be accepted by the person to whom it is granted. When one is granted before charge or conviction, as in Nixon's case, its acceptance is regularly seen as an admission of guilt by the person to whom it is given.

Nearly all pardons are accepted, of course, and usually gratefully. A few have been rejected, however. One of the most dramatic refusals led to a Supreme Court case, *Burdick* v. *United States*, 1915. George Burdick, a New York newspaper editor, had refused to testify before a federal grand jury regarding the sources for certain news stories his paper had printed. Those stories

## Point-of-Use Resources

📖 **Guide to the Essentials** Chapter 14, Section 4, p. 80 provides support for students who need additional review of section content. Spanish support is available in the Spanish edition of the Guide on p. 73.

📁 **Quiz** Unit 4 booklet, p. 20 includes matching and multiple-choice questions to check students' understanding of Section 4 content.

💿 **Presentation Pro CD-ROM** Quizzes and multiple-choice questions check students' understanding of Section 4 content.

## Answers to . . .

### Section 4 Assessment

**1.** The message power and the power to veto legislation passed by Congress.
**2.** The Line Item Veto Act was passed by Congress in 1996, but it was struck down by the Supreme Court in the 1998 case *Clinton v. New York City.* The Court ruled that only a constitutional amendment can provide for the line-item veto.
**3.** A reprieve postpones an execution of a sentence; a pardon is legal forgiveness of a crime; clemency describes powers of mercy, including pardons and reprieves, that may only be used in cases of federal offenses; commutation means the reduction of a sentence or fine; amnesty is a general pardon issued to a group of law violators rather than an individual.
**4.** Summaries will vary; arguments for should include that it would be a weapon against wasteful federal spending, while arguments against should mention that such a veto would give too much power to the executive branch.
**5.** Possible answer: As Congress meets nearly year-round, the need for a formal adjournment has been lessened.

### Answer to . . .

**Critical Thinking** Possible answer: To bring closure to a controversial time in American history.

▲ Some men called to serve in the Vietnam War burned their draft cards in protest. Others went into hiding, many fleeing to Canada. In 1977 President Carter pardoned them. *Critical Thinking* **What might have been Carter's motive for using his presidential power to pardon the draft evaders?**

reported fraud in the collection of customs duties. He invoked the 5th Amendment, claiming that his testimony could incriminate him. President Woodrow Wilson then granted Burdick "a full and unconditional pardon for all offenses against the United States" that he might have committed in obtaining material for the news stories.

Interestingly, Burdick refused to accept the pardon, and he continued to refuse to testify. With that, the federal judge in that district fined and jailed him for contempt. The judge ruled that (1) the President's pardon was fully effective, with or without Burdick's acceptance and (2) there was, therefore, no basis for Burdick's continued claim of protection against self-incrimination.

The Supreme Court overturned the lower court's action. It unanimously upheld the rule that a pardon must be accepted in order to be effective, and it ordered Burdick's release from jail.

The pardoning power includes the power to grant conditional pardons, provided the conditions are reasonable. It also includes the power of **commutation**—that is, the power to commute (reduce) the length of a sentence or a fine imposed by a court.

The pardoning power also includes the power of **amnesty,** in effect a blanket pardon offered to a group of law violators. Thus, in 1893 President Benjamin Harrison issued a proclamation of amnesty forgiving all Mormons who had violated the antipolygamy (multiple marriage) laws in the federal territories. In 1977 President Jimmy Carter granted amnesty to Vietnam War draft evaders.

## Section 4 Assessment

**Key Terms and Main Ideas**

**1.** What are the President's two major legislative powers?
**2.** What happened to the **line-item veto** law passed by Congress?
**3.** Explain how these judicial powers of the President differ: **reprieve, pardon, clemency, commutation, amnesty.**

**Critical Thinking**

**4. Expressing Problems Clearly** Write two paragraphs summarizing the arguments for and against the line-item veto.
**5. Predicting Consequences** Why, do you think, has no President had to use the power to prorogue Congress?

**6. Making Inferences** In giving the President several important judicial powers, what kinds of situations might the Framers have been anticipating?

 **Take It to the Net**

**7.** Read about the types of presidential vetoes and what actions Congress can take once the President vetoes a bill. Create a flowchart that shows the steps in the process and the possible outcomes. Use the links provided in the Social Studies area at the following Web site for help in completing this activity. **www.phschool.com**

**6.** Possible answer: Situations in which a law was broken but popular opinion dictates that the offender is not really guilty.

 **Take It to the Net**

**7.** Direct students to the Social Studies area at the Prentice Hall School Web site. The *Magruder's American Government* companion Web site includes the directions and links needed to complete the activity. It also provides a printable Internet activity worksheet with scoring rubrics for assessment. Flowcharts should be clear and accurate.

# *on the Supreme Court*

## Can Groups' Liberties Be Limited During Wartime?

*Many difficult questions concerning personal freedoms arise during national emergencies. When the survival of the nation is threatened, strong government action may be necessary to confront the threat. Such action might harm individuals or groups. May government impose limits on civil rights in case of emergencies?*

### *Korematsu* v. *United States* (1944)

Japan's attack on Pearl Harbor, Hawaii, on December 7, 1941, prompted widespread fear that Japan might try to invade the West Coast, and that persons of Japanese ancestry living there might aid the invasion. At that time, about 120,000 persons of Japanese descent lived in the West Coast States; some 70,000 of these were *Nisei* (Japanese Americans whose parents were born in Japan).

On February 19, 1942, President Franklin Roosevelt issued Executive Order No. 9066 authorizing the military to designate military areas and to exclude "any or all persons" from them. This order was intended to help protect the country from espionage or sabotage. Congress then passed a law requiring that all persons excluded from those military areas be sent to "war relocation camps" outside the sensitive military areas.

On March 2, 1942, the general in charge of the West Coast Defense Command issued the first of a series of orders that identified the entire Pacific Coast as Military Area No. 1. Soon, all persons of Japanese descent were ordered out of that area.

Fred Korematsu, a native-born American citizen, refused to leave his home in San Leandro, across the bay from San Francisco. He was arrested, charged with failure to report for relocation, and convicted in federal district court. After losing in the court of appeals, he appealed to the Supreme Court.

### Arguments for Korematsu

1. Executive Order 9066 denied Korematsu his liberty without due process of law, in violation of the Fifth Amendment.

2. The military does not have the authority to regulate civilian conduct, and the President cannot delegate that power to the military when martial law has not been declared.
3. The order of exclusion created a classification based on race, in violation of the Constitution.

### Arguments for the United States

1. Although the relocation would not be proper in peacetime, the danger of espionage and sabotage justified this denial of liberty to American citizens under wartime circumstances.
2. Because war had been declared, the President had the authority as commander in chief to issue such orders to the military.
3. The United States had been attacked by Japan, so it was logical that people of Japanese ancestry were suspect. The decision to relocate people from sensitive military areas was based on security concerns and not on racial prejudice.

### Decide for Yourself

1. Review the constitutional grounds on which each side based its arguments and the specific arguments each side presented.
2. Debate the opposing viewpoints presented in this case. Which viewpoint do you favor?
3. Predict the impact of the Court's decision on discrimination based on race and national ancestry in the United States. (To read a summary of the Court's decision, turn to the Supreme Court Glossary on page 799.)

---

 **CLOSE UP** FOUNDATION *Corner*

📁 **Close Up on the Supreme Court** *Korematsu* v. *United States,* p. 15 provides an activity to extend coverage of this case.

 **CLOSE UP** FOUNDATION | Online

To keep up-to-date on Close Up news and activities, visit Close Up Online at

**www.closeup.org**

---

 **CLOSE UP** FOUNDATION

## Can Groups' Liberties Be Limited During Wartime?

**Focus** Review the scope of the President's wartime powers. Explain that those powers have often been controversial. For instance, during the Civil War, many persons objected to President Lincoln's decision to suspend the constitutional right to a writ of habeas corpus, which guarantees arrested persons a prompt court hearing on the legality of their arrest and detention.

**Instruct** Tell students that since World War II Congress has passed two laws compensating relocated Japanese-Americans—a 1948 law which compensated for lost property, and a 1988 law which paid each survivor $20,000.

**Close/Reteach** Divide the class into small groups. Have each group suppose they are a Japanese-American family awaiting relocation, and then have them present a skit about the family's reaction to the order. The skit should address the arguments for and against relocation discussed in the feature.

💿 **Keep It Current CD-ROM** includes government-related projects by unit. The CD-ROM links to the Prentice Hall School Web site and may be used for daily updates.

### *Answers to . . .*
**Decide for Yourself**
1. Korematsu cited the Fifth Amendment in his argument that "war relocation camps" were unconstitutional. The United States cited the President's authority as commander in chief and the wartime circumstances in its argument that Executive Order No. 9066 was constitutional.
2. Answers will vary, but should be supported with valid reasoning.
3. The Court upheld the order, ruling in favor of the United States, citing wartime conditions. However, this case was revisited over the years, and in 1983 Korematsu's conviction was overturned.

## Practicing the Vocabulary

1. mass media
2. treaty
3. clemency
4. executive order
5. ordinance power
6. imperial presidency
7. line-item veto
8. executive agreement
9. Executive Article
10. *persona non grata*
11. pardon; amnesty
12. recognition

## Reviewing Main Ideas

### Section 1

**13. (a)** Because it outlines the presidency in a sketchy manner, there has been an ongoing argument about what "executive power" means. **(b)** Some felt the President(s) should carry out only those powers delegated by the legislature; others felt the President should be a strong single executive with distinct powers.

**14.** As a result of increased urbanization and technological advances, the public has demanded that the Federal Government—including the President—play a larger role in many areas of American life.

**15.** Some have seen themselves as protectors of the public interest, duty-bound to use whatever power necessary for the common good. Others have wanted only to fulfill the roles specified by the Constitution.

### Section 2

**16.** The President's power covers all federal laws. In addition, the executive branch works out the details of laws, and thus has influence over them.

**17.** Because the powers the Constitution does directly grant the presidency depend on the President's ability to issue and implement orders, or to authorize subordinates to do so.

**18.** In order for an administration to function successfully, a President requires loyal subordinates who support the administration's policies.

**19.** It mandates that when a President appoints an official who serves within a particular State, the candidate will be approved by that State's senators.

**20.** When Congress passed a law intended to block Johnson's power of removal, he ignored the law, thus leading to his impeachment.

## Political Dictionary

Executive Article (p. 390)
mass media (p. 391)
imperial presidency (p. 392)
oath of office (p. 393)
executive order (p. 394)
ordinance power (p. 394)

treaty (p. 399)
executive agreement (p. 400)
recognition (p. 400)
*persona non grata* (p. 401)
line-item veto (p. 406)
reprieve (p. 407)

pardon (p. 407)
clemency (p. 407)
commutation (p. 408)
amnesty (p. 408)

## Practicing the Vocabulary

**Matching** *Choose a term from the list above that best matches each description.*

1. Forms of communication, including printed publications, radio, television, and, most recently, the Internet
2. A formal agreement between two or more nations that requires the approval of two thirds of the Senate
3. The President's power to grant reprieves and pardons in cases involving federal offenses
4. A directive, rule, or regulation from the President that has the effect of law
5. The President's constitutional power to issue executive orders
6. Critics' term for the strong use of presidential power in ways that enable the President to evade the will of Congress

**Fill in the Blanks** *Choose a term from the list above that best completes the sentence.*

7. The _____ had been sought by many Presidents, but it was struck down by the Supreme Court as unconstitutional.
8. Unlike a treaty, a _____ does not need congressional approval.
9. The part of the Constitution that establishes the presidency is called the _____.
10. To show displeasure with another country, the President can declare its diplomatic representative to be _____.
11. A _____ is the legal forgiveness of a crime, whereas _____ is a general pardon of a group of lawbreakers.
12. _____ can be used as a weapon in foreign relations.

## Reviewing Main Ideas

### Section 1

**13. (a)** Why has the wording of Article II, Section I caused problems? **(b)** What differing views did the Framers hold about the power of the presidency?
**14.** How has the growing complexity of the nation's social and economic life affected presidential power?
**15.** What opposing views have Presidents had regarding their proper role in the job?

### Section 2

**16.** How does the responsibility for executing the law give the President great power?
**17.** Why do we know that the Framers intended the President to have ordinance power?
**18.** Why is it important that the President have the power to appoint officials?
**19.** What role does senatorial courtesy have in the appointment process?
**20.** How did the issue of the removal power result in the impeachment of President Andrew Johnson?

### Section 3

**21.** What types of agreements can the President make with foreign countries?
**22.** Why did the Framers include the Senate, but not the House, in the treaty-making process?
**23.** What is the power of recognition, and how can the President use it as a diplomatic tool?
**24. (a)** Describe the President's role in military affairs. **(b)** Give examples of presidential use of the power of commander in chief.

### Section 4

**25.** How do the President's legislative and judicial powers support the system of checks and balances?
**26.** What are the President's primary legislative powers?
**27.** How could the line-item veto be added to the President's legislative powers?
**28.** What are the President's primary judicial powers?
**29.** What kind of clemency did President Gerald Ford give to former President Richard Nixon?

### Section 3

**21.** Treaties and executive agreements.

**22.** The Framers believed secrecy was necessary with regard to foreign affairs; the smaller Senate would be able to guard that secrecy more easily.

**23.** Recognition is the acknowledgment of a country or government's existence. Quick recognition serves as a diplomatic seal of approval, while withholding recognition is a diplomatic rebuke.

**24. (a)** As commander in chief, the President has final authority over all military matters. **(b)** Using the armed forces without a declaration of war from Congress; using military forces as "peacekeeping forces."

### Section 4

**25.** Presidents check the legislative branch by recommending legislation through the message power and vetoing legislation; they check the judicial branch through the powers of clemency.

**26.** Recommending and vetoing legislation.

**27.** An amendment would have to be added to the Constitution.

**28.** To grant reprieves and pardons.

**29.** He granted Nixon a full pardon for the Watergate scandal.

## Critical Thinking Skills

**30. *Applying the Chapter Skill*** Using the information in the diagram on page 312, create a time line of either the Johnson or Clinton impeachment. How do the time line and the diagram differ in the way they present information? Which method of sequencing provides the better way to analyze information? Explain your answer.

**31. *Drawing Conclusions*** Why, do you think, have so many Presidents decided to make undeclared war?

**32. *Predicting Consequences*** **(a)** If the Supreme Court someday were to declare the War Powers Act unconstitutional, on what grounds might the law be struck down? **(b)** What might be the effect of such a ruling on presidential power?

**33. *Drawing Inferences*** Article II of the Constitution, which covers the powers of the executive, has been called the most loosely drawn chapter in the Constitution. Why might the Framers have created Article II in this way?

## Analyzing Political Cartoons

Using your knowledge of American government and this cartoon, answer the questions below.

**34.** In the cartoon above, what point is being suggested about how the President and Congress carry out foreign relations? (Note: NATO is the North Atlantic Treaty Organization, which coordinates military defense in Europe.)

## Participation Activities

**35. *Current Events Watch*** Presidents regularly meet with officials from other countries. Find a recent news report of such a meeting and become familiar with the main topic of their discussions. Summarize the main topic and goal of the meeting. Analyze the President's role in the discussions, and describe the outcome. What powers of the presidency did the President use during this event?

**36. *Chart Activity*** Create a visual presentation of social studies information by making a chart that lists the various powers of the President and the sources of each power. Write a summary statement contrasting the power of the President today with the power that the Framers intended the President to have when they created the position in 1787.

**37. *It's Your Turn*** You have completed your first year as President. Write the opening paragraphs of a State of the Union address. Explain how you intend to lead the nation in the year ahead. Open with a statement in which you summarize your beliefs about the role of the President. Explain what you predict will be your greatest upcoming challenge and how you will attempt to address it, using your constitutional powers. **(Writing a Speech)**

## Point-of-Use Resources

## Critical Thinking Skills

**30.** Answers will vary, but should show that students understand the concept of sequencing and that the time line emphasizes the linear nature of the impeachment, while the diagram emphasizes each distinct event.

**31.** Possible answer: In situations where a President feels immediate action is necessary, he or she may not want to wait for a declaration of war from Congress.

**32. (a)** On the grounds that its limiting of the executive branch is unconstitutional. **(b)** It would give the President more power as commander in chief.

**33.** Some students might suggest that the Framers wanted to create a presidency in which the officeholder was free to respond to the particular needs of the time. Others might say that the Framers simply could not agree on the proper definition of the chief executive.

## Analyzing Political Cartoons

**34.** That they carry out foreign relations in a secretive, yet haphazard way.

## You Can Make a Difference

Polls should include relevant questions; discussions should address all issues brought up by people polled.

## Participation Activities

**35.** Summaries should reflect an understanding of the main points of the report and accurately identify the presidential powers reported on.

**36.** Charts should include each power mentioned in the section and its source in the Constitution. Summaries should reflect an understanding of the changing nature of the presidency.

**37.** Speeches should include beliefs about the speaker's role as President, predictions about the President's greatest upcoming challenge, and ways in which the President will address this challenge.

# Government at Work: The Bureaucracy

| Section Objectives | Print and Technology Resources |
|---|---|
| **1 The Federal Bureaucracy**<br>(pp. 414–418)<br><br>1. Define a bureaucracy.<br>2. Identify the major elements of the federal bureaucracy.<br>3. Explain how groups within the federal bureaucracy are named.<br>4. Describe the difference between a staff agency and a line agency.<br><br>**TEKS 9B, 9D, 21A, 21B, 21E, 22A, 22B, 22C, 22D** | • **Unit 4 booklet** Guided Reading and Review, p. 22<br>Section 1 Quiz, p. 23<br>• **Lesson Plans booklet** Section 1, p. 66<br>• **Political Cartoons booklet** Section 1, p. 58<br>• **Section Reading Support Transparencies**<br>• **Block Scheduling with Lesson Strategies booklet** p. 26<br>• **Basic Principles of the Constitution Transparencies** 47<br>• **Section Support Transparencies** 61, 160<br>• **Presentation Pro CD-ROM** Section 1 |
| **2 The Executive Office of the President**<br>(pp. 419–422)<br><br>1. Describe the Executive Office of the President.<br>2. Explain the duties of the White House Office and the National Security Council.<br>3. Identify additional agencies in the Executive Office of the President that assist the President.<br><br>**TEKS 9B, 9D, 9G, 21A, 21C, 21D, 21E, 22A, 22B, 23B** | • **Unit 4 booklet** Guided Reading and Review, p. 24<br>Section 2 Quiz, p. 25<br>• **Lesson Plans booklet** Section 2, p. 67<br>• **Political Cartoons booklet** Section 2, p. 59<br>• **Close Up on Primary Sources booklet** Reinventing the Government, p.17<br>• **Section Reading Support Transparencies**<br>• **Simulations and Debates booklet** p. 39<br>• **Section Support Transparencies** 62, 161<br>• **Presentation Pro CD-ROM** Section 2<br>• **Simulations and Data Graphing CD-ROM** |
| **3 The Executive Departments**<br>(pp. 424–429)<br><br>1. Describe the origin and development of the executive departments.<br>2. Analyze the structure and functions of the Cabinet.<br>3. Analyze the role of the Cabinet in the President's decisions.<br><br>**TEKS 2B, 9B, 9D, 9G, 11A, 21A, 21B, 21D, 21E, 22A, 22B, 22D** | • **Unit 4 booklet** Guided Reading and Review, p. 26<br>Section 3 Quiz, p. 27<br>• **Lesson Plans booklet** Section 3, p. 68<br>• **Political Cartoons booklet** Section 3, p. 60<br>• **Section Reading Support Transparencies**<br>• **Close Up on Participation booklet** Raising AIDS Awareness, pp. 6–7<br>• **Section Support Transparencies** 63, 162<br>• **Presentation Pro CD-ROM** Section 3 |
| **4 Independent Agencies**<br>(pp. 430–435)<br><br>1. Explain why the government creates independent agencies.<br>2. Analyze the functions of selected independent executive agencies and independent regulatory commissions.<br>3. Describe the structure of government corporations.<br><br>**TEKS 9B, 9D, 9G, 21A, 21E, 22A, 22B, 22D** | • **Unit 4 booklet** Guided Reading and Review, p. 28<br>Section 4 Quiz, p. 29<br>• **Lesson Plans booklet** Section 4, p. 69<br>• **Political Cartoons booklet** Section 4, p. 61<br>• **Social Studies Skills Tutor CD-ROM**<br>• **The Living Constitution booklet** p. 5<br>• **Basic Principles of the Constitution Transparencies** 26<br>• **Section Support Transparencies** 64, 163<br>• **Presentation Pro CD-ROM** Section 4<br>• **Section Reading Support Transparencies** |
| **5 The Civil Service**<br>(pp. 437–440)<br><br>1. Describe the development of the civil service.<br>2. Identify characteristics of the civil service as it exists today.<br>3. Analyze the restrictions on the political activities of members of the civil service.<br><br>**TEKS 9B, 9D, 9G, 11A, 17C, 21A, 21B, 21C, 21D, 21E, 22A, 22B, 22C, 22D** | • **Unit 4 booklet** Guided Reading and Review, p. 30<br>Section 5 Quiz, p. 31<br>Skills for Life Activity, p. 32<br>• **Lesson Plans booklet** Section 5, p. 70<br>• **Political Cartoons booklet** Section 5, p. 62<br>• **Close Up on the Supreme Court booklet** *Goldberg* v. *Kelly*, p. 16<br>• **Section Reading Support Transparencies**<br>• **The Basic Principles of the Constitution Posters**<br>• **Section Support Transparencies** 65, 164<br>• **Presentation Pro CD-ROM** Section 5<br>• **Simulations and Data Graphing CD-ROM** |

# Block Scheduling Strategies

The *Magruder's American Government* program addresses block-scheduling strategies in a variety of ways. For easy reference, side-column activities that fit a block format are marked ■ **Block Strategy.** Each section also contains a **Block Scheduling Strategies** box describing at least two block-format activities that address and extend core content from the section. The **Block Scheduling with Lesson Strategies booklet** found in the Teaching Resources contains additional block-scheduling activities for each chapter.

## Take It to the Net

Visit the Social Studies area at the Prentice Hall School Web site. Once there, you can find additional links, current events connections, and activities to enrich chapter content for *Magruder's American Government,* as well as a Self-Test for students. Be sure to check out this month's **eTeach** online discussion with a Master Teacher.

### www.phschool.com

## Pressed for Time?

If you are running short on time to cover this chapter, consider one of the following options:

- Use the **Presentation Pro CD-ROM** to create an outline for this chapter.
- Use one of the **Pressed for Time** activities found on p. 27.
- Use the Section Summaries for Chapter 2, from **Guide to the Essentials of American Government (English and Spanish).**

## ■ Video Connections

Prentice Hall offers two video programs to reinforce and extend chapter content. Show students *The Blessings of Liberty* from the **ABC News Civics and Government Videotape Library** and *Prayer in Schools: A Nationwide Debate* from the **Magruder's American Government Video Collection.**

## Assessment Options

- Section Quizzes, **Unit 4 booklet,** pp. 23, 25, 27, 29, 31
- Chapter 15 Assessment, pp. 442–443
- **Guide to the Essentials of American Government,** Chapter 15 Test, p. 87

### Core Assessment

Chapter 15 Test, Chapter Tests booklet
ExamView® Test Bank CD-ROM Chapter 15
Government Assessment Rubrics

### Standardized Test Preparation

#### Diagnose and Prescribe

Diagnostic Tests for High School Social Studies Skills

#### Review and Reteach

Review Book for Government

#### Practice and Assess

Test-Taking Strategies With Transparencies for High School
Test Prep Book for Government

# Chapter 15 Teacher's Edition Index

# Government at Work: The Bureaucracy

# Government at Work: The Bureaucracy

*"Bureaucracy is not an obstacle to democracy but an inevitable complement to it."*

—Joseph A. Schumpeter (1942)

People often criticize and poke fun at the federal bureaucracy. Schumpeter, an economist, knew that it takes millions of bureaucrats to make democratic government work. Americans depend on the civil servants—from accountants to Webmasters—who work in federal agencies throughout the country.

◆ Federal workers sort income tax forms

## CLOSE UP *Corner*

The following resources are available only from the Close Up Foundation to support the concepts discussed in Chapter 15 "Government at Work: The Bureaucracy":

◆ *Perspectives: Readings on Contemporary American Government*
◆ *Slicing the Pie: A Federal Budget Game*
◆ *We the People: The President and the Constitution*

**CLOSE UP Online**

To keep up-to-date on Close Up news and activities, visit Close Up Online at

**www.closeup.org**

Close Up Foundation
44 Canal Center Plaza
Alexandria, VA 22314-1592
800-765-3131

## You Can Make a Difference

**"SOMETHING THAT'S IMPORTANT** to you—just fight for it." With that attitude, Andrew Holleman became the youngest winner of a Regional Merit Award from the Environmental Protection Agency, the federal agency that guards the nation's land and water. At age 12, Andrew began a campaign to save a local wetland in Chelmsford, Massachusetts, from a developer's bulldozer. He studied geology, collected neighbors' signatures on a petition, spoke at meetings, and wrote to State and local officials. At last, the Zoning Board turned down the development. Andrew carried his activism on into high school, with plans to study environmental science in college.

### Keep It Current

Items marked with this logo are periodically updated on the Internet. Keep up-to-date with what's in the news. To get current information on issues involving bureaucracy, go to www.phschool.com

### SECTION 1

## The Federal Bureaucracy (pp. 414–418)

★ The federal bureaucracy is a large, highly organized group that carries out the work of the Federal Government.
★ The names given to agencies, including *commission, administration,* and *corporation,* may indicate an agency's nature.
★ Agencies include line agencies, which operate programs, and staff agencies, which support the line agencies.

### SECTION 2

## The Executive Office of the President (pp. 419–422)

★ The Executive Office of the President includes several important agencies staffed by the President's closest advisors.
★ The White House Office is the "nerve center" of the Executive Office of the President.
★ Other units of the Executive Office advise the President on domestic affairs and foreign policy.

### SECTION 3

## The Executive Departments (pp. 424–429)

★ Each of the 14 executive departments manages federal policy in a broad field of activity, such as education, labor, or defense.
★ The heads of the departments meet with the President and other advisors in a group called the Cabinet.
★ The President chooses his nominees to lead executive departments, but the Senate can reject any nominee.
★ The President decides how often to call Cabinet meetings.

### SECTION 4

## Independent Agencies (pp. 430–435)

★ Independent agencies are not part of the executive departments.
★ The three types of independent agencies are independent executive agencies, independent regulatory commissions, and government corporations.
★ Independence gives these agencies some freedom from political pressure.

### SECTION 5

## The Civil Service (pp. 437–440)

★ The people who work in the federal bureaucracy make up the civil service.
★ Early on, the spoils system infected the civil service.
★ Corruption was a serious problem until reformers began to reshape the civil service in the 1880s.
★ Today, the vast majority of civil servants are hired and promoted on the basis of merit, not party membership.

### Keep It Current

## Internet Update

Use the Prentice Hall School Web site and the Keep It Current CD-ROM to find quick content updates.

Visit **www.phschool.com** for current events articles that are linked to Chapter 15. Critical Thinking questions are included.

**Keep It Current CD-ROM** includes government-related projects by unit. Students complete each project using current information that they obtain by linking to the Prentice Hall School Web site from the CD-ROM.

**Objectives** You may wish to call students' attention to the objectives in the Section Preview. The objectives are reflected in the main headings of the section.

**Bellringer** Ask students what they would think if someone called them a bureaucrat. Should they be insulted? Explain that in this section, they will learn about the role bureaucrats play in their lives.

**Vocabulary Builder** Point out the terms in the Political Dictionary. Write this question on the board: "Who in the federal bureaucracy would play a more active role in the administration of public programs, a staff agency bureaucrat or a line agency bureaucrat?" Have students scan the section to find the answer.

### Pressed for Time?

#### Quick Lesson Plan

**1. Focus** Tell students that the federal bureaucracy does much of the day-to-day work of the government. Ask students to name some specific agencies in the bureaucracy and describe what they do.

**2. Instruct** Ask students to name the three features of a bureaucracy. Discuss why these features make a bureaucracy so effective. Then have students describe the makeup of the federal bureaucracy, including its major elements.

**3. Close/Reteach** Remind students that without the federal bureaucracy, the Federal Government could not function. Have students choose a federal agency, and then write a scenario showing what might happen to the operation of that agency if just one of the three features of a bureaucracy were missing.

### Point-of-Use Resources

📁 **Block Scheduling with Lesson Strategies** Activities for Chapter 15 are presented on p. 26.

## Section Preview

### OBJECTIVES

1. **Define** a bureaucracy.
2. **Identify** the major elements of the federal bureaucracy.
3. **Explain** how groups within the federal bureaucracy are named.
4. **Describe** the difference between a staff agency and a line agency.

### WHY IT MATTERS

The Federal Government is the nation's largest employer. Nearly 2.7 million men and women work in the federal bureaucracy, and they do nearly all of the day-to-day work of the government.

### POLITICAL DICTIONARY

★ bureaucracy
★ bureaucrat
★ administration
★ staff agency
★ line agency

Think about this for a moment: It is impossible for you to live through a single day without somehow encountering the federal bureaucracy. A **bureaucracy** is a large, complex administrative structure that handles the everyday business of an organization.[1] The Federal Government is the largest organization in the country. Federal employees deliver the mail, regulate business practices, collect taxes, manage the national forests, conduct American foreign policy, administer Social Security programs—the list goes on and on.

▲ Bureaucrats once used red ribbon, called "red tape" in Britain, to hold their files together. Today, people use the phrase "red tape" to describe the delays and paperwork they face when working with a bureaucracy.

## What Is a Bureaucracy?

To many Americans, the word *bureaucracy* suggests such things as waste, red tape, and delay. While that image is not altogether unfounded, it is quite lopsided. Basically, bureaucracy is an efficient and an effective way to organize people to do work.

Bureaucracies are found wherever there are large organizations. They are found in both the public sector and the private sector in this country. Thus, the United States Air Force, McDonald's, the Social Security Administration, MTV, your town or city government, and the Roman Catholic Church are all bureaucracies. Even your school is a bureaucracy.

### Three Features of a Bureaucracy

In dictionary terms, a bureaucracy is a system of organization built on these three principles: hierarchical authority, job specialization, and formalized rules.

1. *Hierarchical authority.* The word *hierarchical* describes any organization that is built as a pyramid, with a chain of command running from the top of the pyramid to the bottom. The few officials and units at the top of the organization have authority over those

---

[1] The term *bureaucracy* is a combination of the French word *bureau*, which originally referred to a desk of a government official and later to the place where an official works, and the suffix *–cracy*, signifying a type of governmental structure.

## 🔲 Block Scheduling Strategies

Consider these suggestions to manage extended class time:

■ Have students create a bureaucracy for an organization of their choice—a new school, a government, or a club. Using the features and benefits of a bureaucracy described in the text, students should outline how their organization is to be structured, what kinds of jobs it will offer, how they will be assigned, and how the organization will function. Details about the bureaucracy and visuals may be posted on the class bulletin board.

■ Discuss the differences between staff and line agencies with the class. Have each student conduct Internet research on several of the major independent agencies mentioned in the chart on page 417, then assign small groups of students five agencies each. Have groups work together to fill in a table about the agencies that includes the agency's name, its function, whether it is a staff or line agency, the name of its chief administrator, the number of employees, and the year founded.

officials and units at the larger middle level, who in turn direct the activities of the many at the bottom level.

2. *Job specialization.* Each **bureaucrat,** or person who works for the organization, has certain defined duties and responsibilities. There is a precise division of labor within the organization.

3. *Formalized rules.* The bureaucracy does its work according to a set of established regulations and procedures.

### Costs and Benefits of Bureaucracy

These three features—hierarchical authority, job specialization, and formalized rules—can make bureaucracy an effective way to accomplish large and complex tasks. The hierarchy can speed action by reducing conflicts over who has the power to make decisions. Job specialization can promote efficiency because each worker focuses on one particular job and thus gains a set of specialized skills and knowledge. Formalized rules can mean that workers act with some speed and precision because decisions are based on a set of known standards. These rules also enable work to continue even as some workers leave and new workers are hired.

On the other hand, bureaucracy's reputation for waste and inefficiency is not unfounded. Bureaucracies can be large, unwieldy organizations where hierarchy, specialization, and rules lead to seemingly endless paperwork and delays.

Recognize this very important point about public bureaucracies: their bureaucrats hold appointive offices. Bureaucrats are *unelected* public-policy makers. This is not to say that bureaucracies are undemocratic. However, in a democracy much depends on how effectively the bureaucracy is controlled by those whom the people *do* elect. Listen to James Madison on the point:

 *In framing a government which is to be administered by men over men, the great difficulty lies in this: you must first enable the government to control the governed; and in the next place oblige it to control itself.*
—*The Federalist* No. 51

▲ *The Reagan Building* Second only to the Pentagon in size, the Ronald Reagan Building and International Trade Center houses government offices in downtown Washington, D.C.

## Major Elements of the Federal Bureaucracy

The federal bureaucracy is all of the agencies, people, and procedures through which the Federal Government operates. It is the means by which the government makes and administers public policy—the sum of its decisions and actions. As the chart on page 417 shows, nearly all of the federal bureaucracy is located in the executive branch.

The Constitution makes the President the chief administrator of the Federal Government. Article II, Section 3 declares that "he shall take Care that the Laws be faithfully executed." But the Constitution makes only the barest mention of the administrative machinery through which the President is to exercise that power.

Article II does suggest executive departments by giving to the President the power to "require

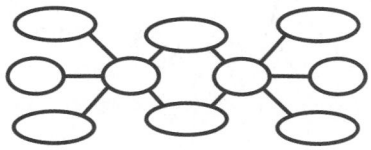

ACTIVITY

## Heterogeneous Groups

**Enrichment** Ask students to create a diagram or pictograph in their notebooks of the major components of the federal bureaucracy. Encourage them to be creative in their drawings and to include the Executive Office of the President, the 14 Cabinet positions, and some of the major independent agencies. Tell students that they will be learning more about each of these components as they read and discuss Chapter 15.

**(Average)**

## Background Note
### Common Misconceptions

When most people think of "those bureaucrats," they think of "those bureaucrats *in Washington.*" In fact, of the approximately 3 million federal civilian employees, only about 200,000—about 1 in 15—work in the District of Columbia. The rest work throughout the United States: 176,000 in Texas, 20,000 in Arkansas, 13,000 in Montana, and so on. The State with the greatest number of federal civilian workers is highly populated California (around 295,000 workers). The States with the fewest number (about 6,000 federal civilian employees)—Delaware and Vermont—have much smaller populations. Every major city in the country is home to at least some "Washington bureaucrats."

## Customize for
### Less Proficient Readers

Have students prepare a glossary defining the following terms: *bureaucracy, administration, department, staff agency,* and *line agency.* Then have them use each of these terms to formulate a response in support of the following statement: "The federal bureaucracy has grown steadily since the framing of the Constitution."

## *Answer to . . .*

**Critical Thinking** *Commission* is used for agencies that regulate business activities, as does the SEC.

▲ A federal agency can be called a *commission, bureau, administration,* or one of several other names. *Critical Thinking* **Why is commission** *an appropriate name for the SEC, which oversees stock markets?*

the Opinion, in writing, of the principal Officer in each of the executive Departments."[2]

Article II anticipates two departments in particular, one for military and one for foreign affairs. It does so by making the President the "Commander in Chief of the Army and Navy," and by giving him the power to make treaties and to appoint "Ambassadors, other public Ministers, and Consuls."[3]

Beyond those references, the Constitution is silent on the organization of the executive branch. The Framers certainly intended for administrative agencies to be created, however. They understood that no matter how wise the President and the Congress, their decisions still had to be acted upon to be effective. Without an **administration**—the government's many administrators and agencies—even the best policies would amount to just so many words and phrases. The President and Congress need millions of men and women to put policies into action in Washington, D.C., and in offices all around the country.

The chief organizational feature of the federal bureaucracy is its division into areas of specialization. As you can see on page 417, the executive branch is composed of three broad groups of agencies: (1) the Executive Office of the President, (2) the 14 Cabinet departments, and (3) a large number of independent agencies.[4]

## The Name Game

The titles given to the many units that make up the executive branch vary a great deal. The name *department* is reserved for agencies of Cabinet rank. Beyond the title of *department,* however, there is little standardized use of titles.

Common titles used in the executive branch include *agency, administration, commission, corporation,* and *authority.*

The term *agency* is often used to refer to any governmental body. It is sometimes used to identify a major unit headed by a single administrator of near-cabinet status, such as the Environmental Protection Agency. But so, too, is the title *administration;* for example, the National Aeronautics and Space Administration and the General Services Administration.

The name *commission* is usually given to agencies charged with the regulation of business activities, such as the Federal Communications Commission and the Securities and Exchange Commission. Top-ranking officers called commissioners head these units. The same title, however, is given to some investigative, advisory, and reporting bodies, including the Civil Rights Commission and the Federal Election Commission.

Either *corporation* or *authority* is the title most often given to those agencies that conduct business-like activities. Corporations and authorities are headed by a board and a manager. Examples include the Federal Deposit Insurance Corporation and the Tennessee Valley Authority.

---

[2] Article II, Section 2, Clause 1. There is also a reference to "Heads of Departments" in Clause 2, and to "any Department or Officer" of the government in Article I, Section 8, Clause 18.

[3] Article II, Section 2, Clauses 1 and 2.

[4] The chart is adapted from the current edition of the *United States Government Manual,* published each year by the Office of the Federal Register in the National Archives and Records Administration. The *Manual* includes a brief description of every agency in each of the three branches of the Federal Government. More than 750 of its now nearly 900 pages are devoted to the executive branch.

## Preparing for Standardized Tests

Have students read the passages under *The Name Game* and then answer the question below.

Which of the following titles may only be used in association with agencies of Cabinet rank?

**(A)** department

**B** bureau

**C** corporation

**D** authority

## The Government of the United States

### The Constitution creates three branches of government

#### THE LEGISLATIVE BRANCH

**CONGRESS**

**Houses of Congress**
Senate and House of Representatives

**Legislative Offices and Departments**
Architect of the Capitol
General Accounting Office
Government Printing Office
Library of Congress
United States Botanic Garden
Office of Technology Assessment
Congressional Budget Office
Copyright Royalty Tribunal
United States Tax Court

#### THE EXECUTIVE BRANCH

**THE PRESIDENT**

**The Administration**
1 Executive Office of the President
2 Executive Departments
3 Independent Agencies

#### THE JUDICIAL BRANCH

**THE SUPREME COURT OF THE UNITED STATES**

**Other Courts**
Courts of Appeals
District Courts
Federal Claims Court
Court of Appeals for the Federal Circuit
Court of International Trade
Territorial Courts
Court of Appeals for the Armed Forces
Court of Appeals for Veterans
Administrative Office of the United States
Federal Judicial Center

---

**1 Executive Office of the President**

White House Office
Office of Management and Budget
Council of Economic Advisers
National Security Council
Office of National Drug Control Policy
Office of the United States Trade Representative
Council on Environmental Quality
Office of Science and Technology Policy
Office of Administration
Office of the Vice President
Office of Faith-Based and Community Initiatives
Office of Homeland Security

**2 Executive Departments**

Department of State
Department of the Treasury
Department of Defense
Department of Justice
Department of the Interior
Department of Agriculture
Department of Commerce
Department of Labor
Department of Health and Human Services
Department of Housing and Urban Development
Department of Transportation
Department of Energy
Department of Education
Department of Veterans Affairs

**3 Independent Agencies\***

Central Intelligence Agency
Commission on Civil Rights
Commodity Futures Trading Commission
Consumer Product Safety Commission
Corporation for National and Community Service
Defense Nuclear Facilities Safety Board
Environmental Protection Agency
Equal Employment Opportunity Commission
Export-Import Bank of the U.S.
Farm Credit Administration
Federal Communications Commission
Federal Deposit Insurance Corporation
Federal Election Commission
Federal Emergency Management Agency

Federal Housing Finance Board
Federal Maritime Commission
Federal Mediation and Conciliation Service
Federal Reserve System
Federal Trade Commission
General Services Administration
National Aeronautics and Space Administration
National Archives and Records Administration
National Labor Relations Board
National Transportation Safety Board
Nuclear Regulatory Commission
Office of Personnel Management
Peace Corps
Securities and Exchange Commission
Selective Service System
Small Business Administration
Social Security Administration
Tennessee Valley Authority
U.S. Postal Service

\*Altogether, there are some 150 independent agencies in the executive branch.

**Interpreting Charts** The daily workings of government depend on these departments and agencies.
***According to this chart, which branch makes up the largest share of the federal bureaucracy?***

## American Government, American Humor

Share the following quotation with students:

*"Working for a federal agency was like trying to dislodge a prune skin from the roof of the mouth. More enterprise went into the job than could be justified by the result."*

—Caskie Stinnet,
American writer

**Discussion** Ask students what qualities of the federal bureaucracy might have led Stinnet to make such a remark. Do they think Stinnet's view is shared by most federal employees? Why or why not?

**(Average)**

### Background Note

#### The Federal Reserve

As the central bank of the United States, the twelve district banks that make up the core of the Federal Reserve System carry out several important functions. The Federal Reserve System does the following:

• Provides banking and fiscal services to the federal government;
• Provides banking services to member and nonmember banks;
• Regulates the banking industry;
• Tracks and manages the national money supply to meet current demand and to stabilize the economy.

Debates over the bank's constitutionality reach as far back as the early days of the Republic.

***Answer to . . .***

**Interpreting Charts** The executive branch.

## Point-of-Use Resources

**Guide to the Essentials** Chapter 15, Section 1, p. 82 provides support for students who need additional review of section content. Spanish support is available in the Spanish edition of the Guide on p. 75.

**Quiz** Unit 4 booklet, p. 23 includes matching and multiple-choice questions to check students' understanding of Section 1 content.

**Presentation Pro CD-ROM** Quizzes and multiple-choice questions check students' understanding of Section 1 content.

## Answers to . . .

### Section 1 Assessment

**1.** Students' descriptions should include hierarchical authority, job specialization, and formalized rules.
**2.** They are vital not only to running the day-to-day business of government, but also to carrying out all of the government's policies.
**3.** Staff agencies support the chief executive and other administrators by offering advice and assistance. Line agencies perform the organization's tasks.
**4.** Words will vary, but explanations should reflect an understanding that the naming system lacks uniformity and can be confusing.
**5.** Hierarchies increase efficiency by reducing conflicts over decision making; job specialization means that each worker is focused on the task he or she is most skilled to perform; formalized rules allow workers to base decisions on agreed-upon standards rather than interpretations.
**6.** Possible answer: Elected officials would have little influence on a particularly strong and independent bureaucracy.

---

Within each major agency, the same confusing lack of uniformity in the use of names is common. *Bureau* is the name often given to the major elements in a department, but *service, administration, office, branch,* and *division* are often used for the same purpose. For example, the major units within the Department of Justice include the Federal Bureau of Investigation, the Immigration and Naturalization Service, the Drug Enforcement Administration, the Office of the Pardon Attorney, and the Criminal Division.

Many federal agencies are often referred to by their initials. The EPA, IRS, FBI, CIA, FCC, and TVA are but a few of the dozens of familiar examples.[5] A few are also known by nicknames. For example, the Government National Mortgage Association is often called "Ginnie Mae," and the National Railroad Passenger Corporation is better known as Amtrak.

### Staff and Line Agencies

The several units that make up any administrative organization can be classified as either staff or line agencies. **Staff agencies** serve in a support capacity. They aid the chief executive and other administrators by offering advice and other assistance in the management of the organization. **Line agencies,** on the other hand, actually perform the tasks for which the organization exists. Congress and the President give the line agencies goals to meet, and the staff agencies help the line agencies meet these goals as effectively as possible through advising, budgeting, purchasing, management, and planning.

Two illustrations of this distinction are the several agencies that make up the Executive Office of the President and, in contrast, the Environmental Protection Agency. The agencies that make up the Executive Office of the President (the White House Office, the National Security Council, the Office of Management and Budget, and others, as you will read in the next section) each exist as staff support to the President. Their primary mission is to assist the President in the exercise of the executive power and in the overall management of the executive branch. They are not operating agencies. That is, they do not actually operate, or administer, public programs.

The Environmental Protection Agency (EPA), on the other hand, has a different mission. It is responsible for the day-to-day enforcement of the many federal antipollution laws. The EPA operates "on the line," where "the action" is.

This difference between staff agencies and line agencies can help you find your way through the complex federal bureaucracy. The distinction between the two can be oversimplified, however. For example, most line agencies do have staff units to aid them in their line operations. Thus, the EPA's Office of Civil Rights is a staff unit. It was established to ensure that the agency's personnel practices do not violate the Federal Government's antidiscrimination policies.

---

[5]The use of acronyms can sometimes cause problems. When the old Bureau of the Budget was reorganized in 1970, it was also renamed. It is now the Office of Management and Budget (OMB). However, it was for a time slated to be known as the Bureau of Management and Budget (BOMB).

## Section **1** Assessment

**Key Terms and Main Ideas**

1. Describe the three defining features of a **bureaucracy** in your own words.
2. Why does a government need an **administration**?
3. What is the role of a **staff agency**? A **line agency**?

**Critical Thinking**

4. **Drawing Conclusions** How would you describe the system of naming federal agencies in one word? Explain your answer.
5. **Drawing Inferences** Explain how the three defining characteristics of a bureaucracy can lead to an effective government.

6. **Predicting Consequences** How might a strong, independent bureaucracy weaken the power of elected representatives?

 **Take It to the Net**

7. Read how different parts of the federal bureaucracy deal with environmental issues. Then choose two agencies and create a diagram or graphic organizer comparing the different roles that they play in United States environmental policy. Use the links provided in the Social Studies area at the following Web site for help in completing this activity.
**www.phschool.com**

 **Take It to the Net**

**7.** Direct students to the Social Studies area at the Prentice Hall School Web site. The *Magruder's American Government* companion Web site includes the directions and links needed to complete the activity. It also provides a printable Internet activity worksheet with scoring rubrics for assessment. Graphic organizers should be clearly organized and accurately show the roles of the selected agencies.

# **2** The Executive Office of the President

**2** **The Executive Office of the President**

## Section Preview

### OBJECTIVES

1. **Describe** the Executive Office of the President.
2. **Explain** the duties of the White House Office, the National Security Council, and the Office of Homeland Security.
3. **Identify** additional agencies in the Executive Office of the President.

### WHY IT MATTERS

The Executive Office of the President is composed of the President's closest advisors and several support agencies. They aid the chief executive in the formation and execution of the nation's public policies.

### POLITICAL DICTIONARY

★ **Executive Office of the President**
★ **federal budget**
★ **fiscal year**
★ **domestic affairs**

---

Thomas Jefferson performed his presidential duties with the help of two aides, one a messenger and the other his secretary. Like other early Presidents, he paid their salaries out of his own pocket. Indeed, Congress did not provide any money for presidential staff until 1857, when it gave President James Buchanan $2,500 for one clerk.

The situation is remarkably different today. President Jefferson presided over an executive branch that employed only some 2,100 people. Now, some 2.7 million men and women work in the Bush administration. Two institutions—the Executive Office of the President and the President's Cabinet—are at the center of today's huge executive branch.

## The Executive Office of the President

Every officer, every employee, and every agency in the executive branch of the Federal Government is legally subordinate to the President. They all exist to help the President—the chief executive—in the exercise of the executive power.

The President's right arm, however, is the **Executive Office of the President** (the EOP). The Executive Office of the President is, in fact, an umbrella agency. It is a complex organization of several separate agencies staffed by most of the President's closest advisors and assistants.

The EOP was established by Congress in 1939. It has been reorganized in every administration since then.

## The White House Office

The "nerve center" of the Executive Office—in fact, of the entire executive branch—is the White House Office. It houses the President's key personal and political staff.

The two wings on either side of the White House hold the offices of most of the President's staff. These employees occupy most of the crowded West Wing, which the public seldom sees and where the legendary Oval Office and the Cabinet Room are located. Some staff members work in the East Wing, where public tours of the White House

▲ Federal workers in the West Wing

---

## Block Scheduling Strategies

Consider these suggestions to manage extended class time:

■ Have students use the text and other resources to create an organizational chart for the Executive Office of the President. Students should identify each agency that makes up this office, describe its purpose, and identify the year that it was created. Review the charts as a class to help students understand the function of each office.

■ Explain that political leaders around the world and throughout history have depended on advisors, but how they have used their advisors has varied dramatically. Leaders have relied on a single influential person, a group, or several groups; some have chosen advisors for their abilities in a certain subject matter, while others have chosen them because of religious backgrounds or family connections. Ask groups of students to discuss the merits of these different methods. Have them create a system of advisors and agencies that they think would be of most benefit to them were they to lead a country.

---

**419**

## Reading Strategy

### Self-Monitoring

Have students, as they read, note any facts of which they were previously unaware. For each fact, have them ask themselves, "Why did the author say that?" Ask students to re-read the text if they cannot answer this question.

### ACTIVITY

### Extended Class Periods

**Time** 90 minutes.
**Purpose** Prepare a federal budget proposal.
**Grouping** Several groups of 3 students, and 1 student acting as the President.
**Activity** Each group represents one of the major federal agencies. Another 3-person group serves as the OMB. Each agency should prepare a detailed list of estimated spending needs for the upcoming fiscal year. Upon completion, a spokesperson for each group should present the proposal to the OMB and the President.
**Roles** Discussion leader, recorder, spokesperson.
**Close** The OMB will review each proposal, allowing agencies to defend their requests. The President makes any final adjustments.

🔲 **Block Strategy (Challenging)**

### Point-of-Use Resources

📁 **Lesson Plans** For lesson planning suggestions, see p. 67 of the Lesson Plans booklet.

📁 **Simulations and Debates** National Security Council, p. 39 provides students with a simulation of a NSC meeting held to resolve a crisis.

💿 **Simulations and Data Graphing CD-ROM** The Federal Budget simulation lets students create federal budgets and submit them to Congress.

### Answer to . . .

**Interpreting Diagrams** Possible answer: Presidents and their Cabinets usually work closely together.

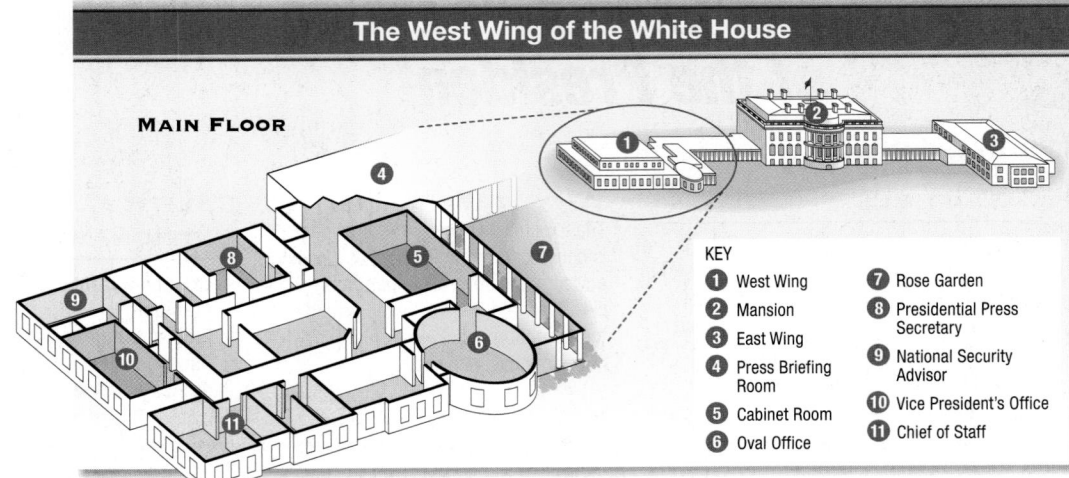

### The West Wing of the White House

**MAIN FLOOR**

**KEY**
1. West Wing
2. Mansion
3. East Wing
4. Press Briefing Room
5. Cabinet Room
6. Oval Office
7. Rose Garden
8. Presidential Press Secretary
9. National Security Advisor
10. Vice President's Office
11. Chief of Staff

*Interpreting Diagrams* The President's closest advisors work in the West Wing of the White House, near the Oval Office. **Why do you think the Cabinet Room is so close to the Oval Office?**

begin. Still others are housed in the historic Old Executive Office Building, across the street from the West Wing.

The chief of staff to the President directs all of the operations of the White House Office and is among the most influential of all the presidential aides. The counselor to the President and a number of senior advisors are also key members of the President's inner circle.

Several other top officials work in the White House Office. Assistants and deputy assistants to the President aid the chief executive in such vital areas as foreign policy, defense, the economy, political affairs, congressional relations, and contacts with the news media and the public.

The staff of the White House Office also includes such other major presidential aides as the press secretary, the counsel (legal advisor) to the President, and the President's physician. The first lady's very visible place in public life today is reflected by the fact that one of the assistants to the President serves as her chief of staff and one of the several deputy assistants is her press secretary. Altogether, the staff of the White House Office now numbers some 400 men and women who, in a very real sense, work for the President.

## The National Security Council

Most of the President's major steps in foreign affairs are taken in close consultation with the National Security Council (NSC). It meets at the President's call, often on short notice, to advise him in all domestic, foreign, and military matters that relate to the nation's security.

The President chairs the Council. Its other members are the Vice President and the secretaries of state and defense. The director of the Central Intelligence Agency (CIA) and the chairman of the Joint Chiefs of Staff also attend its meetings.

The NSC has a small staff of foreign and military policy experts. They work under the direction of the President's assistant for national security affairs, who is often called the President's national security advisor. The super-secret Central Intelligence Agency does much of its work at the direction of the NSC.

The National Security Council is a staff agency. That is, its job is to advise the President in all matters affecting the nation's security. However, during the Reagan administration in the 1980s, the NSC's staff actually conducted a number of secret operations. The most spectacular of these involved the sale of arms to Iran, and the use of some of the proceeds (money) from those sales to aid the Contra rebels in

Nicaragua. Congress had prohibited military aid to the Contras, and the disclosure of the NSC's role produced the Iran-Contra scandal of the mid-1980s.

## Office of Homeland Security

The Office of Homeland Security is the newest major agency in the EOP. It was created by President Bush immediately after terrorists struck the World Trade Center and the Pentagon on September 11, 2001.

The Office is headed by a director who has Cabinet rank. The President has ordered the Office to "lead, oversee, and coordinate a comprehensive national strategy to safeguard our country from terrorism." That means that the director and his 100-member staff must coordinate the anti-terrorist activities of more than forty federal agencies—the CIA, the FBI, the Coast Guard, the Federal Aviation Administration, and many others.

## Other EOP Agencies

The EOP's umbrella covers several other—and important—agencies. Each of them provides essential staff help to the Chief Executive.

### Office of Management and Budget

The Office of Management and Budget (OMB) is the largest and, after the White House Office, the most influential unit in the Executive Office. The OMB is headed by a director who is appointed by the President and confirmed by the Senate. The OMB's major task is the preparation of the federal budget, which the President must submit to Congress in January or February each year.

The **federal budget** is a detailed estimate of receipts and expenditures for the coming **fiscal year.** A fiscal year is the 12-month period used by government and business for record keeping, budgeting, and other financial management purposes. The Federal Government's fiscal year runs from October 1 through September 30.

The budget is more than just a financial document. It is a plan—a carefully drawn work plan for the conduct of government. It is an annual statement of the public policies of the United States, expressed in dollar terms.

The creation of each fiscal year's budget is a lengthy process that begins more than a year before the start of the fiscal year for which the budget is intended. In the first stages, each federal agency prepares detailed estimates of its spending needs for that 12-month period. The OMB reviews those proposals, usually in a series of budget hearings that give agency officials the opportunity to defend their dollar requests. Following that review, the revised (and usually lowered) spending estimates are fitted into the President's overall program.

The OMB also monitors the spending of the funds Congress appropriates. That is, it oversees the execution of the budget. The President's close control over the preparation and execution of the budget is a major factor in his ability to command the huge executive branch.

Beyond its budget chores, the OMB is a presidential odd-job agency. It studies the organization and management of the executive branch and keeps the President up-to-date on the work of all its agencies. The OMB checks agency stands on all legislative matters to make certain they agree with the President's positions. It also helps the President prepare the hundreds of executive orders he must issue and the veto messages he occasionally sends to Congress. In short, the OMB earns the word *management* in its title.

### Office of Faith-Based and Community Initiatives

The Office of Community and Faith-Based Initiatives was created by President Bush in 2001. Much of the best work being done today to combat drug abuse, homelessness, poverty, and similar problems is being done by private groups—by churches and church-related groups and other not-for-profit organizations. The Office of Faith-Based and Community Initiatives is charged with encouraging and expanding these private efforts.

### Office of National Drug Control Policy

The Office of National Drug Control Policy was established in 1989. Its existence dramatizes the nation's concern over drugs. The office is headed by a director who is appointed by the President, subject to the Senate's approval.

## Customize for

### More Advanced Students

Tell students that as investigative reporters for a national newspaper in 1987, they have been assigned the task of discovering the actual events that took place during the Iran-Contra scandal. Have them conduct research into the affair. As they uncover information about the sales and exchange of money and arms among the nations involved, ask them to write an article to be published on the front page of the newspaper. Encourage students to be thorough in their descriptions, as their primary goal is to let readers know what really happened behind the scenes.

### Background Note

### Census Policies on Race

Though the first U.S. census was taken in 1790, it looked quite different from those of today. Essentially just an inquiry into the total number of people in the United States, it did not include racial or social categories. As the nation grew more complex and more diverse, however, the government needed to know more and more about its citizens. In 1977, the OMB directed that persons taking the census were to check one of the following racial category boxes—White, Black, American Indian or Alaskan Native, or Asian or Pacific Islander. In 2000, again determining that the nation's racial makeup had grown more complex, the OMB set forth a new policy, in which persons may check more than one racial box. Under this policy, 63 racial combinations are possible. This policy—which greatly expands the total number of "minority" American citizens—is a current topic of interesting debate.

## Spotlight on Technology

**Magruder's American Government Video Collection**

The Magruder's Video Collection explores key issues and debates in American government. Each segment examines an issue central to chapter content through use of historical and contemporary footage. Commentary from civic leaders in academics, government, and the media follow each segment. Critical-thinking questions focus students' attention on key issues, and may be used to stimulate discussion.

Use the Chapter 15 video segment to explore the workings of the U.S. Census Bureau. (time: about 5 minutes) Students will see how the census does far more than tally the population—it affects government policies at every level.

## Point–of–Use Resources

**Guide to the Essentials** Chapter 15, Section 2, p. 83 provides support for students who need additional review of section content. Spanish support is available in the Spanish edition of the Guide on p. 76.

**Guided Reading and Review** Unit 4 booklet, p. 24 provides students with practice identifying the main ideas and key terms of this section.

**Political Cartoons** See p. 59 of the Political Cartoons booklet for a cartoon relevant to this section.

**Quiz** Unit 4 booklet, p. 25 includes matching and multiple-choice questions to check students' understanding of Section 2 content.

**Presentation Pro CD-ROM** Quizzes and multiple-choice questions check students' understanding of Section 2 content.

## Answers to . . .

### Section 2 Assessment

**1.** The chief of staff directs all White House operations; the counselor, aides, senior advisors, and assistants to the President provide vital advice and liaisons with the public and media; the first lady plays various and important public roles.
**2.** The Office of Policy Development.
**3.** Each federal agency prepares estimates of what it will need to spend; the OMB reviews them and hears arguments for these requests; revised estimates are produced and incorporated into a final budget document that goes to Congress.
**4.** Possible answer: Without the EOP, Presidents could not possibly manage all of the tasks they need to—including staying informed in all domestic and foreign affairs policies, staying in touch with the public, and informing the media.
**5.** Possible answer: Having one agency make and monitor the budget ensures that it is done rigorously; if these were tasks done by agencies responsible for other work, they could not be done as efficiently.

The news media regularly identify the director as "the nation's drug czar." To this point, the office has operated mostly as an advisory and planning agency, however.

### Council of Economic Advisers

Three of the country's leading economists, chosen by the President with the consent of the Senate, make up the Council of Economic Advisers. It is the chief executive's major source of information and advice on the nation's economy. The Council also helps the President prepare his annual Economic Report to Congress, which, together with a presidential message, goes to Capitol Hill in late January or early February each year.

### Other Units in the EOP

A number of other agencies in the Executive Office house key presidential aides. These men and women make it possible for the President to meet his many-sided responsibilities.

The Office of Policy Development advises the Chief Executive on all matters relating to the nation's **domestic affairs**—that is, all matters not directly connected to the realm of foreign affairs.

The Council on Environmental Quality aids the President in environmental policy matters and in the writing of the annual "state of the environment" report to Congress. It sees that federal agencies comply with the nation's many environmental laws and with the President's environmental policies.

The council's three members are appointed by the President, with the Senate's consent. They sometimes act as referees in disputes between or among executive branch agencies, such as a conflict between the Environmental Protection Agency and one or more agencies in the Departments of the Agriculture, Interior, or Energy.

The Office of the Vice President houses the Vice President's staff. It now includes more than 50 men and women who make it possible for the Vice President to perform the duties of his office.

The Office of United States Trade Representative advises the chief executive in all matters of foreign trade. The trade representative, appointed by the President and confirmed by the Senate, carries the rank of ambassador and represents the President in foreign trade negotiations.

The Office of Science and Technology Policy is the President's major advisor in all scientific, engineering, and other technological matters relating to national policies and programs. Its director is drawn from the nation's scientific community.

The Office of Administration is the general housekeeping agency for all the other units in the Executive Office. It provides them with the many support services they must have in order to do their jobs, including clerical help, data processing, library services, transportation, and much more.

## Section 2 Assessment

### Key Terms and Main Ideas

1. List and explain three duties of members of the **Executive Office of the President.**
2. Describe an executive agency that directly relates to **domestic affairs.**
3. What are the first two steps of writing the **federal budget?**

### Critical Thinking

4. **Testing Conclusions** Cite evidence to show that the Executive Office of the President is an essential part of the executive branch.
5. **Determining Cause and Effect** What are the benefits of having an agency, such as the OMB, write the federal budget and monitor spending?

6. **Understanding Point of View** If you could choose one executive agency for which to work, which would you choose? What would you like to accomplish in that agency?

### Take It to the Net

7. Look over statistics, graphs, and charts from the most recent federal budget. List five conclusions you can draw from looking at this data. Who will benefit from this budget? Use the links provided in the Social Studies area at the following Web site for help in completing this activity. www.phschool.com

**6.** Answers will vary, but should demonstrate an understanding of the chosen agency's structure and function.

### Take It to the Net

**7.** Direct students to the Social Studies area at the Prentice Hall School Web site. The *Magruder's American Government* companion Web site includes the directions and links needed to complete the activity. It also provides a printable Internet activity worksheet with scoring rubrics for assessment. Conclusions should be based on correct interpretation of the data.

# on Primary Sources

## The Making of the Modern Presidency

*As he began his second term in 1937, President Franklin D. Roosevelt asked Congress to authorize a major reorganization of the executive branch. Congress responded by creating the Executive Office of the President (EOP), in 1939.*

*President Franklin D. Roosevelt*
*1882–1945*

The time has come to set our house in order. . . . The executive structure of the Government is sadly out of date. I am not the first President to report to the Congress that anti-quated machinery stands in the way of effective administration and of adequate control by the Congress. . . .

Over a year ago. . . . I appointed a Committee on Administrative Management to examine the whole problem . . . .

They say what has been common knowledge for 20 years, that the President cannot adequately handle his responsibilities; that he is overworked; that it is humanly impossible under the system which we have, for him to carry out his constitutional duty as Chief Executive, because he is overwhelmed with minor details and needless contacts arising directly from the bad organization and equipment of the Government. I can testify to this. . . .

The Committee includes these major recommendations:

1. Expand the White House staff so that the President may have a sufficient group of able assistants to keep him in closer and easier touch with the widespread affairs of administration. . . .

2. Strengthen and develop the managerial agencies of the Government, particularly those dealing with the budget and efficiency research, with personnel and with planning, as management-arms of the Chief Executive. . . .

In placing this program before you I realize that it will be said that I am recommending the increase of the powers of the Presidency. This is not true. . . . What I am placing before you is not the request for more power, but for the tools of management and authority to distribute the work so that the President can effectively discharge those powers which the Constitution now places upon him. Unless we are prepared to abandon this important part of the Constitution, we must equip the Presidency with authority commensurate with his responsibilities under the Constitution.

### Analyzing Primary Sources

1. Why has the executive structure of government become out-of-date, according to Roosevelt?
2. According to Roosevelt, what problem does the existing executive structure create for the President?
3. What does it imply about the Federal Government that Roosevelt had to speak to Congress to reorganize his office?
4. Roosevelt claimed his request would not increase presidential power. Do you agree or disagree? Explain.

 *Corner*

**Close Up on Primary Sources** Reinventing the Government, p. 17, extends this feature with a primary source activity.

 **Online**

To keep up-to-date on Close Up news and activities, visit Close Up Online at

**www.closeup.org**

### The Making of the Modern Presidency

**Focus** Call on students to identify the President's responsibilities. Then ask students to read the article and consider why President Franklin D. Roosevelt made the recommendations that he did.

**Instruct** After students have read the article, point out to them that, in 1993, the Clinton administration created the National Partnership for Reinventing Government, which is dedicated to increasing the efficiency and responsiveness of the federal bureaucracy. One of its major goals is to reduce the size of the federal bureaucracy. Have students compare these goals to the recommendations that President Franklin D. Roosevelt made.

**Close/Reteach** Ask students to consider the debate between providing more government workers and reducing the size of the federal bureaucracy. Have them write an essay that supports one side of this argument.

**Keep It Current CD-ROM** includes government-related projects by unit. The CD-ROM links to the Prentice Hall School Web site and may be used for daily updates.

### Answers to . . .
**Analyzing Primary Sources**
1. The President could not carry out his duties because the current structure placed too many burdens on him that should have been handled by other people or departments.
2. It left too many day-to-day details in the hands of the President.
3. The nation's system of checks and balances prevents the executive branch from expanding its power without being "checked" by the legislative branch.
4. Some students may argue that the request allows the President to better manage the executive branch without increasing presidential power, while others may argue that his request increased the sources of power at the President's disposal.

**423**

**3** **The Executive Departments**

## Teacher Notes

**Objectives** You may wish to call students' attention to the objectives in the Section Preview. The objectives are reflected in the main headings of the section.

**Bellringer** Tell students to suppose that they are rich enough to hire any advisors they need. Ask whom they would hire to help them take better photographs or improve their violin playing or refine their basketball skills. Explain that in this section, they will read about the Cabinet, a group of advisors chosen by the President for their knowledge and skills in a variety of fields.

**Vocabulary Builder** Point out the terms in the Political Dictionary. Ask students what they think would be the responsibilities of the secretary of an executive department. Have them check their answers as they read the section.

### Pressed for Time?

#### Quick Lesson Plan

**1. Focus** Tell students that the 14 executive departments do much of the work of the Federal Government. Challenge students to name half of the executive, or Cabinet, departments.

**2. Instruct** Ask students to name the only department not headed by a secretary. Then have students name the 14 executive departments and list them on the chalkboard. Refer to the list as needed in discussing the various executive departments and the Cabinet, now and in the past.

**3. Close/Reteach** Have students create a crossword puzzle made up of words and phrases from the section. Students should choose mainly from the terms in the Political Dictionary and the names of the executive departments. Clues would be descriptions of those terms and names.

## Section Preview

### OBJECTIVES

1. **Describe** the origin and development of the executive departments.
2. **Analyze** the structure and functions of the Cabinet.
3. **Analyze** the role of the Cabinet in the President's decisions.

### WHY IT MATTERS

Fourteen executive departments carry out much of the Federal Government's work. The heads of these departments frequently meet with the President and other officials in a group called the Cabinet.

### POLITICAL DICTIONARY

★ executive departments
★ secretary
★ attorney general

---

In *The Federalist* No. 76, Alexander Hamilton declared that "the true test of a good government is its aptitude and tendency to produce a good administration." Given that comment, it seems strange that Hamilton and the other Framers of the Constitution spent so little time on the organization of the executive branch of the government they were creating. Instead, the machinery of federal administration has been built over time to meet the changing needs of the country.

### Executive Departments

Much of the work of the Federal Government is done by the 14 **executive departments.** Often called the Cabinet departments, they are the traditional units of federal administration, and each of them is built around some broad field of activity.

The First Congress created three of these departments in 1789: the Departments of State, Treasury, and War. As the size and the workload of the Federal Government grew, Congress added new departments. Some of the newer ones took over various duties originally assigned to older departments, and they gradually assumed new functions, as well. Over time, Congress has also created and later combined or abolished some departments.

### Chief Officers and Staff

Each department is headed by a **secretary,** except for the Department of Justice, whose work is directed by the **attorney general.** As you will see, these department heads serve in the President's Cabinet. However, the duties as the chief officer of their own department take up most of their time.

Each department head is the primary link between presidential policy and his or her own department. Just as importantly, each of them also strives to promote and protect his or her department with the White House, with Congress and its committees, with the rest of the federal bureaucracy, and with the media and the public.

An under secretary or deputy secretary and several assistant secretaries aid the secretary in his or her multidimensional role. These officials are also named by the President and confirmed by the Senate. Staff support for the secretary comes

► President George Washington's (right) first Cabinet included: Secretary of State Thomas Jefferson (second left); and Secretary of the Treasury Alexander Hamilton (second right).

---

### Block Scheduling Strategies

Consider these suggestions to manage extended class time:

■ Have students conduct library or Internet research to learn about the origins of the executive departments. Then organize the class into several small groups. Ask each group to create a mock documentary on how the current executive departments came into existence. Encourage students to point out significant historic events that led to the creation of each office. Finally, have each group present its documentary to the class.

■ Explain to students that the Cabinet's role has varied widely among Presidents. Some Presidents have relied heavily upon their Cabinets, while others have not. Assign each student a President. Then have students conduct research to determine the relationship between the President and his cabinet. Ask students to write a brief report documenting the relationship. Call on volunteers to present their research to the class.

## Federal Workers Around the Country

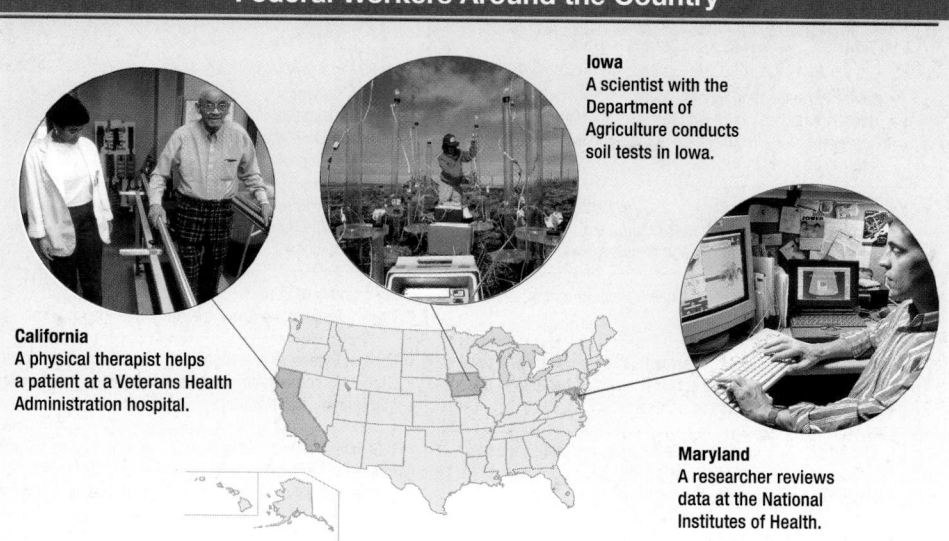

**Iowa**
A scientist with the Department of Agriculture conducts soil tests in Iowa.

**California**
A physical therapist helps a patient at a Veterans Health Administration hospital.

**Maryland**
A researcher reviews data at the National Institutes of Health.

*Interpreting Diagrams* Federal employees can be found wherever the Federal Government has work to do, including a Veterans Health Administration hospital in California, a farm in Iowa, or a federal office in Maryland. ***Why do only ten percent of federal employees work in the Washington, D.C., area?***

from assistants and aides with a wide range of titles in such areas as personnel, planning, legal advice, budgeting, and public relations.

### Subunits

Each department is made up of a number of subunits, both staff and line. Each of these subunits, or agencies, is usually further divided into smaller working units. Thus, the Criminal Division in the Department of Justice is composed of many sections, including, for example, the Terrorism and Violent Crime Section and the Narcotics and Dangerous Drugs Section. Approximately 80 percent of the men and women who head the bureaus, divisions, and other major units within each of the executive departments are career people, not political appointees.

Many of the agencies in executive departments are structured geographically. Much of the work is done through regional and/or district offices, which, in turn, direct the activities of the agency's employees in the field. In fact, nearly 90 percent of all of the men and women who work as civilian employees of the Federal

Government are stationed somewhere outside the nation's capital.

Take the Veterans Health Administration, part of the Department of Veterans Affairs, to illustrate the point. It does nearly all of its work providing medical care to eligible veterans at 173 medical centers, 376 outpatient clinics, and a large number of other facilities located throughout the country.

### The Departments Today

Today, the executive departments vary a great deal in terms of visibility, size, and importance. The Department of State is the oldest and the most prestigious department; but it is also among the smallest, with only about 25,000 employees. The Department of Defense is the largest, with nearly 670,000 civilian workers, and another 1.4 million men and women in uniform.

The Department of Health and Human Services has the largest budget; it accounts for approximately a third of all federal spending each year. The Department of Veterans Affairs became the newest of the departments when Congress created it in 1988.

## Reading Strategy

### Drawing Inferences

As students read the section of the text that describes the Cabinet, ask them what reasons the author gives for the President's choices. Then ask them, given the President's role as a politician, what other reasons they can infer that might guide a President's choice of Cabinet members.

## Point–of–Use Resources

**Guided Reading and Review** Unit 4 booklet, p. 26 provides students with practice identifying the main ideas and key terms of this section.

**Lesson Plans** For lesson planning suggestions, see p. 68 of the Lesson Plans booklet.

**Political Cartoons** See p. 60 of the Political Cartoons booklet for a cartoon relevant to this section.

**Section Support Transparencies** Transparency 63, *Visual Learning;* Transparency 162, *Political Cartoon*

## Organizing Information

To make sure students understand the main points of this section, you may wish to use the tree map graphic organizer to the right.

Tell students that a tree map can be used to record a topic, its main ideas, and its supporting details. Have students use the tree map to record information about the executive departments and the Cabinet.

**Teaching Tip** A template for this graphic organizer can be found in the Section Support Transparencies, Transparency 3.

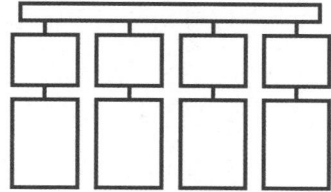

*Answer to . . .*

**Interpreting Diagrams** Although the seat of government is located in Washington, D.C., the majority of federal employees work in various governmental offices throughout the United States and abroad.

## Make It Relevant

### Students Make a Difference

Tara Church has given the old saying "tall oaks from little acorns grow" a new meaning. From the planting of Marcie the Marvelous Tree by Tara and her Brownie troop in 1987, a large and successful environmental organization—run for and by students—has sprouted. Tara founded Tree Musketeers to save the planet by planting trees, but it now includes environmental programs from local recycling in El Segundo, California, to the Youth Environmental Summit, which attracts delegates from around the world.

In 1991 Tara approached a National Forest Service official at a conference, and eventually convinced the Service to support her group. "The Forest Service contribution gave us credibility and was really the beginning of youth environmentalism," she says. In 1994, Tree Musketeers won the President's Volunteer Action Award, which Tara accepted from President Clinton at the White House.

### Point-of-Use Resources

📁 **Close Up on Participation** Raising AIDS Awareness, pp. 6–7 uses the topic of health care to help students plan and carry out service learning projects.

### The Fourteen Executive Departments

| DEPARTMENT (YEAR ESTABLISHED) | PRINCIPAL FUNCTIONS | IMPORTANT AGENCIES |
|---|---|---|
| **State** (1789) | • Advises President on foreign policy<br>• Negotiates agreements with foreign countries<br>• Represents the United States abroad and in international organizations | • Foreign Service<br>• Regional Bureaus<br>• Bureau of International Organization Affairs<br>• Bureau of Consular Affairs (Passport Office) |
| **Treasury** (1789) | • Produces coins and bills　• Collects taxes<br>• Borrows money and manages public debt<br>• Enforces alcohol, tobacco, and firearms laws | • Internal Revenue Service　• United States Mint<br>• Bureau of the Public Debt　• Customs Service<br>• Bureau of Alcohol, Tobacco, and Firearms　• Secret Service |
| **Defense** ᵃ (1789) | • Provides military forces to deter war and protects the nation's security | • Joint Chiefs of Staff<br>• Departments of the Army, the Navy, and the Air Force |
| **Justice** ᵇ (1870) | • Provides legal advice to President　• Enforces federal laws<br>• Represents United States in court　• Operates federal prisons<br>• Oversees immigration and naturalization | • Federal Bureau of Investigation　• Criminal Division<br>• Drug Enforcement Administration　• Civil Rights Division<br>• Immigration and Naturalization Service |
| **Interior** (1849) | • Manages public lands, wildlife refuges, and national parks<br>• Operates hydroelectric power plants<br>• Helps Native Americans manage their affairs | • U.S. Fish and Wildlife Service　• National Park Service<br>• Bureau of Land Management　• U.S. Geological Survey<br>• Bureau of Indian Affairs　• Bureau of Reclamation |
| **Agriculture** (1889) | • Manages national forests　• Inspects food<br>• Assists farmers and ranchers<br>• Administers food stamp and school lunch programs | • Agricultural Research Service　• Farm Service Agency<br>• Food and Nutrition Service　• Forest Service<br>• Food Safety and Inspection Service |
| **Commerce** ᶜ (1903) | • Conducts census<br>• Grants patents and registers trademarks<br>• Promotes international trade, economic growth, and technological development | • Bureau of the Census　• National Oceanic and<br>• Patent and Trademark Office　Atmospheric Administration<br>• International Trade Administration<br>• Economic Development Administration |
| **Labor** (1913) | • Enforces federal laws on minimum wages, maximum hours, and safe working conditions<br>• Operates job training programs<br>• Administers unemployment insurance and workers' compensation programs | • Employment Standards Administration<br>• Occupational Safety and Health Administration<br>• Employment and Training Administration<br>• Bureau of Labor Statistics |

*Interpreting Tables* Congress created the 14 Executive Departments over the years to handle the growing responsibilities of the Federal Government. ***How can the actions of Congress lead to the formation of new executive departments?***

The 14 departments are profiled in the table on these two pages. The principal functions they perform and the titles of their major agencies provide a fairly good description of each.

## The Cabinet

The Cabinet is an informal advisory body brought together by the President to serve his needs. The Constitution makes no mention of it, nor did Congress create it. Instead, the Cabinet is the product of custom and usage.⁶

At its first session in 1789, Congress established four executive posts: secretary of state, secretary of the treasury, secretary of war, and attorney general. By his second term, Washington was regularly seeking the advice of the four outstanding people he had named to those offices: Thomas Jefferson in the Department of State, Alexander Hamilton at the Treasury, Henry Knox in the War Department, and Edmund Randolph, the attorney general. So the Cabinet was born.

---

⁶The closest approach to it is in Article II, Section 2, Clause 1, where the President is given the power to "require the opinion, in writing, of the principal officer in each of the executive departments, upon any subject relating to the duties of their respective offices." The Cabinet was first mentioned in an act of Congress in 1907, well over a century after its birth.

*Answer to . . .*

**Interpreting Tables** Possible answer: Congressional actions determine areas of importance that require administrative attention.

| DEPARTMENT (YEAR ESTABLISHED) | PRINCIPAL FUNCTIONS | IMPORTANT AGENCIES |
|---|---|---|
| Health and Human Services [d] (1953) | • Funds health care research programs<br>• Conducts programs to prevent and control disease<br>• Enforces pure food and drug laws<br>• Administers Medicare and Medicaid | • Administration for Children and Families<br>• Administration on Aging<br>• Centers for Disease Control and Prevention<br>• Food and Drug Administration<br>• National Institutes of Health |
| Housing and Urban Development (1965) | • Operates home-financing and public housing programs<br>• Enforces fair housing laws | • Office of Housing<br>• Office of Fair Housing and Equal Opportunity<br>• Government National Mortgage Association |
| Transportation (1967) | • Administers programs to promote and regulate highways, mass transit, railroads, waterways, air travel, and oil and gas pipelines<br>• Enforces maritime (sea) law | • Federal Highway Administration<br>• Federal Aviation Administration<br>• Maritime Administration<br>• United States Coast Guard |
| Energy (1977) | • Promotes production of renewable energy, fossil fuels, and nuclear energy<br>• Transmits and sells hydroelectric power<br>• Conducts nuclear weapons research and production | • Office of Energy Efficiency and Renewable Energy<br>• Office of Nuclear Energy, Science and Technology<br>• Regional Power Administration<br>• Office of Defense Programs |
| Education (1979) | • Administers federal aid to schools<br>• Conducts educational research | • Office of Elementary and Secondary Education<br>• Office of Educational Research and Improvement |
| Veterans Affairs (1988) | • Administers benefits, pensions, and medical programs for veterans of the armed forces<br>• Oversees military cemeteries | • Veterans Benefits Administration<br>• Veterans Health Administration<br>• National Cemetery System |

a Congress created the National Military Establishment as an executive department, headed by the Secretary of Defense, in 1947. It was renamed the Department of Defense, in 1949. Since 1947 the department has included the former cabinet-level Departments of War (1789) and the Navy (1798), and the Department of the Air Force. The Secretaries of the Army, the Navy and the Air Force do not hold Cabinet rank.
b Congress created the office of Attorney General in 1789 but did not establish the Department of Justice until 1870.

c Congress created the Department of Commerce and Labor in 1903; it was replaced by the separate Departments of Commerce and of Labor in 1913.
d Congress created the Department of Health, Education, and Welfare in 1953. HEW's education functions were transferred to a new Department of Education in 1979, and HEW was renamed at that time.

By tradition, the heads of the now 14 executive departments form the Cabinet. Each of the last several Presidents has regularly added a number of other top officials to the group, including the director of the OMB, the director of the Office of Homeland Security, and the President's chief domestic policy advisor. Every Vice President since Alben Barkley, who served under President Truman (1949–1953), has also been a regular participant at Cabinet meetings. Several other major figures regularly attend Cabinet meetings in the Bush Administration—in particular the White House chief of staff, the United States trade representative, and the administrator of the Environmental Protection Agency.

## Choosing Cabinet Members

The President appoints the head of each of the 14 executive departments. Each of these appointments is subject to confirmation by the Senate, but rejections have been exceedingly rare. The Senate generally respects the personal choice of the President. Of the more than 600 presidential appointments made since 1789, only 12 have been turned down by the Senate. The most recent rejection occurred in 1989, when the Senate refused to confirm President Bush's selection of John Tower as secretary of defense.

President George W. Bush's nomination of John Ashcroft as Attorney General generated significant opposition in 2001; the Senate confirmed the President's choice by a narrow vote, however.

## Preparing for Standardized Tests

Have students read the passages under *The Cabinet* on pp. 426–429 and then complete the sentence below.

According to the passages, the Cabinet is mandated by

**A** the Constitution.

**B** tradition.

**C** an act of Congress.

**D** individual Presidents.

### Heterogeneous Groups

**Enrichment** Divide the class into four teams. Two competitions between two teams will run simultaneously. Prepare index cards of "clues" describing each of the 14 executive departments. The first clue on each card should be the name of the current person heading the department. (The remaining clues will vary.) Before reading the first clue, teams will state how many clues they think they will need to name the department being described. The team with the lowest "bid" will listen to that number of clues and write out their answer. Correct answers are awarded a point, while incorrect answers allow the opposition a chance to earn a point. Continue until each of the executive departments has been named.

**Block Strategy
(Average)**

▲ *The Bush Cabinet* The Cabinet includes the heads of 14 executive departments. Cabinet-rank members also include the Vice President and the heads of several additional agencies.

Many factors influence these presidential choices. Party is almost always important. Republican Presidents do not often pick Democrats, and vice versa. One or more of a new President's appointees usually come from among those who played a major role in the recent presidential campaign.

Of course, professional qualifications and practical experience are also taken into account in the selection of Cabinet secretaries. Geography also plays a part. In broad terms, each President tries to give some regional balance to the Cabinet. Thus, the secretary of the interior often comes from the West, where most of the department's work is carried out.

Many interest groups care about Cabinet secretary appointments, and they do influence some of the choices. Thus, the secretary of agriculture almost always has a background closely related to agriculture. The secretary of the treasury usually comes from the financial community, the secretary of commerce from the ranks of business, and so on.

Other considerations also guide the President's choices. Gender and race, an appointee's stand on the "hot" issues of the day, management abilities and experience, and other personal characteristics—these and a host of other factors play a part in selecting Cabinet members.

### Women and Minorities

Women and minorities have only gradually become represented in the Cabinet. Franklin Roosevelt appointed the first woman, Frances T. Perkins, secretary of labor from 1933 to 1945. Lyndon Johnson named the first African American, Robert C. Weaver, as the first secretary of housing and urban development (HUD) in 1966.

The Ford Cabinet was the first to include both a woman (Carla Hills, secretary of HUD) and an African American (William T. Coleman, secretary of transportation); both were appointed in 1975. Jimmy Carter appointed the first African American woman to the Cabinet when he named Patricia Roberts Harris secretary of HUD in 1977 and then secretary of health and human services (HHS) in 1979. Ronald Reagan appointed the first Hispanic Cabinet member; Lauro F. Cavazos became secretary of education in 1988.

President Clinton picked more women, African Americans, and Hispanics than any of his predecessors. Over his two terms, (1993–2001), the Cabinet included five women, six African Americans, four Hispanics, and its first Asian American, Norman Mineta, the Secretary of Commerce in Clinton's last year. Janet Reno became the first woman to serve as Attorney General and Madeleine Albright the first to be Secretary of State.

President George W. Bush's first Cabinet appointments included two African Americans: Secretary of State Colin Powell and Secretary of Education Rod Paige; three women: Secretary of Labor Elaine Chao, Secretary of the Interior Gale Norton, and Secretary of Agriculture Ann Veneman; and one Hispanic, Secretary of Housing and Urban Development Mel Martinez. Secretary Chao is the first Chinese American to hold a Cabinet office. Norman Mineta, a Democrat who also served in the Clinton Cabinet, was named Secretary of Transportation.

### The Cabinet's Role

Cabinet members have two major jobs. Individually, each is the administrative head of one of the executive departments. Together, they are advisors to the President.

A number of Presidents have given great weight to the Cabinet and to its advice; others have given it only a secondary role. George H. W. Bush's Cabinet (1989–1993) had more influence with the President than any Cabinet since the Eisenhower presidency in the 1950s. The Cabinet also played a prominent role in the Clinton administration (1993– 2001). On the other hand, John Kennedy described his Cabinet meetings as "a waste of time."

Kennedy's view notwithstanding, most Presidents have held regular Cabinet meetings—where reports are made and discussed, and advice is offered to the chief executive. That advice need not be taken, of course. Abraham Lincoln once laid a proposition he favored before his Cabinet. Each member opposed it, whereupon Lincoln declared: "Seven nays, one aye: the ayes have it."

William Howard Taft put the role of the Cabinet in its proper light years ago:

 **PRIMARY Sources** *"The Constitution . . . contains no suggestion of a meeting of all the department heads, in consultation over general governmental matters. The Cabinet is a mere creation of the President's will. . . . It exists only by custom. If the President desired to dispense with it, he could do so.*
—*Our Chief Magistrate and His Powers*

*Interpreting Political Cartoons* Madeleine Albright was President Clinton's second secretary of state. **According to this cartoon, why did President Clinton need a secretary of state?**

No President has ever suggested eliminating the Cabinet. However, several Presidents have leaned on other, unofficial advisory groups, and sometimes more heavily than on the Cabinet. Andrew Jackson began the practice when he became President in 1829. Several of his close friends often met with him in the kitchen at the White House and, inevitably, came to be known as the Kitchen Cabinet. Franklin Roosevelt's Brain Trust of the 1930s and Harry Truman's Cronies in the late 1940s were in the same mold.

## Section 3 Assessment

### Key Terms and Main Ideas

1. How were the **executive departments** created?
2. What is the role of the **secretary** of an executive department?
3. Which department does the **attorney general** lead?
4. Who decides how often the **Cabinet** meets?

### Critical Thinking

5. **Drawing Inferences** What are the two most important jobs of the head of an executive department?
6. **Drawing Conclusions** What can the President do to determine who serves in the Cabinet? How does a President shape the importance of the Cabinet?

7. **Determining Cause and Effect** How has the Cabinet changed over time? What factors have driven these changes?

 **Take It to the Net**

8. Select an executive department and follow a link to that department's Web site. Explore the Web site and write an essay explaining what the department is currently working on. Be sure to give examples of recent events. Use the links provided in the Social Studies area at the following Web site for help in completing this activity. **www.phschool.com**

**Take It to the Net**

8. Direct students to the Social Studies area at the Prentice Hall School Web site. The *Magruder's American Government* companion Web site includes the directions and links needed to complete the activity. It also provides a printable Internet activity worksheet with scoring rubrics for assessment. Essays should refer to recent events and show an understanding of each department's work.

## Answers to . . .

### Section 3 Assessment

1. By Congress.
2. The role of the secretary is to be a link between presidential policy and his or her own department; secretaries also strive to promote their departments within Congress and with the public.
3. The Department of Justice.
4. The President.
5. Possible answer: To serve as an advisor to the President and to oversee the functions of the department.
6. Presidents appoint department heads and thus decide who will serve in the Cabinet. Presidents decide the importance of a Cabinet by choosing to accept or ignore its advice; in addition, a President may choose to rely on unofficial advisors of his or her choice rather than on the Cabinet.
7. The Cabinet has come to include more minorities and women over time; the geographical origin of Cabinet members has changed with regional population shifts.

### Answer to . . .

**Interpreting Political Cartoons** To handle pressing matters of foreign affairs he didn't feel able to handle himself.

4 **Independent Agencies**

**Objectives** You may wish to call students' attention to the objectives in the Section Preview. The objectives are reflected in the main headings of the section.

**Bellringer** Have students suppose that they are a local police captain who suspects police corruption. Have them discuss whether it would be wise to assign someone from the local police force to investigate or hire an independent investigator. Explain that in this section, they will learn about independent agencies, some of which can investigate illegal activity.

**Vocabulary Builder** Tell students that independent regulatory commissions have the power to make rules and enforce them. Then ask students to find two other terms in the Political Dictionary that describe these commissions.

## Pressed for Time?

### Quick Lesson Plan

**1. Focus** Tell students that independent agencies exist outside of the Cabinet departments. Challenge them to name any of these agencies and explain what they do.

**2. Instruct** Ask students to explain what gives independent regulatory agencies their independence from the White House. Discuss the structure and role of this and the other two types of independent agencies. Extend the discussion to explore criticisms of independent regulatory agencies and government corporations.

**3. Close/Reteach** Remind students that independent agencies operate outside of the Cabinet departments, although some resemble Cabinet departments in structure and function. Have students make a chart showing the basic structure of the three types of independent agencies and providing examples of each.

## Section Preview

### OBJECTIVES

1. **Explain** why Congress has created independent agencies.
2. **Analyze** the functions of selected independent executive agencies and independent regulatory commissions.
3. **Describe** the structure of government corporations.

### WHY IT MATTERS

Some 150 executive branch agencies are not located within any of the 14 executive departments. Some of them rival Cabinet departments in size of their budgets, their functions, and the number of their employees.

### POLITICAL DICTIONARY

★ independent agencies
★ independent executive agencies
★ independent regulatory commissions
★ quasi-legislative
★ quasi-judicial
★ government corporation

Until the 1880s, nearly all that the Federal Government did was done through its Cabinet departments. Since then, however, Congress has created a large number of additional agencies—the **independent agencies**—located outside the departments. Today, they number nearly 150. Most of the more important ones are included in the chart on page 417.

Several independent agencies administer programs similar to those of the Cabinet departments. The work of the National Aeronautics and Space Administration (NASA), for example, is similar to that of a number of agencies in the Department of Defense. NASA's responsibilities are also not very far removed from those of the Department of Transportation.

Neither the size of an independent agency's budget nor the number of its employees provides a good way to distinguish between many of these agencies and the executive departments. The newest and largest of them, the Social Security Administration, became an independent agency in 1994. Since that time, its budget has been larger than that of any Cabinet department. The Administration now employs more than 64,000 people, and so by

itself has more workers and a larger payroll than several Cabinet departments.

## Why Independent Agencies?

The reasons these agencies exist outside the Cabinet departments are nearly as numerous as the agencies themselves. A few major reasons stand out, however. Some have been set up outside the regular departmental structure because they do not fit well within any department. The General Services Administration (GSA) is a leading example.

The GSA is the Federal Government's major housekeeping agency. Its main chores include the construction and operation of public buildings, purchase and distribution of supplies and equipment, management of real property, and a host of similar services to most other federal agencies. The Office of Personnel Management (OPM) is another example. It is the hiring agency for nearly all other federal agencies.

Congress has given some of these agencies an independent status to protect them from the influence of both partisan and pressure politics. Major examples include the OPM, the Social Security Administration, and the Federal Election Commission. The point can be turned on its head, too; some agencies are located outside any Cabinet department because that is exactly where certain pressure groups want them.

▲ **NASA** This special envelope celebrates NASA's *Apollo* missions to the moon.

---

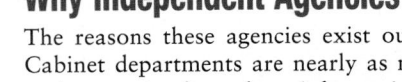

### Block Scheduling Strategies

Consider these suggestions to manage extended class time:

■ Have students read about independent agencies in the text. Then discuss the similarities and differences between independent executive agencies, independent regulatory commissions, and government corporations. Have students create graphic organizers that highlight the similarities and differences between independent agencies.

■ To extend the Block Scheduling activity from Section 3, place students in the same groups as when they made their documentaries. Ask each group to use the same format to explain how independent agencies came into existence. Have groups find the following information: Why the agency was created and when; its budget; its number of employees; and whether it is an executive agency, regulatory agency, or a government corporation.

Other federal agencies were born as independents largely by accident. No thought was given to future problems of administrative confusion when they were created. Finally, some agencies are independent because of the peculiar and sensitive nature of their functions. This is especially true of the independent regulatory commissions.

The label *independent agency* is a catchall. Most of these agencies are independent only in the sense that they are not located within any of the 14 Cabinet departments. They are not independent of the President and the executive branch. Some are independent in a much more concrete way, however. For most purposes, they do lie outside the executive branch and are largely free of presidential control.

Perhaps the best way to understand all of these independent agencies is to divide them into three main groups: (1) the independent executive agencies, (2) the independent regulatory commissions, and (3) the government corporations.

## The Independent Executive Agencies

The **independent executive agencies** include most of the independent agencies. Some are large, with thousands of employees, multimillion-dollar or even billion-dollar budgets, and extremely important public tasks to perform.

The GSA, NASA, and the EPA are three examples of larger independent executive agencies. They are organized much like the Cabinet departments; that is, they are headed by a single administrator with subunits operating on a regional basis, and so on. The most important difference between the independent executive agencies and the 14 executive departments is simply that they do not have Cabinet status.

Some of the agencies in this group are not administrative and policy giants. They do important work, however, and sometimes attract public notice. The Civil Rights Commission, the Peace Corps, the Federal Election Commission, and the National Transportation Safety Board all fall into this category.

Most independent executive agencies operate far from the limelight. They have few employees, small budgets, and rarely attract any attention. The American Battle Monuments Commission,

# Voices on Government

**Donna Shalala** became the secretary of health and human services from 1993 to 2001. Earlier, she taught political science, managed urban finances, and served as the president of the University of Wisconsin–Madison. In this position she was the first woman to head a Big Ten university. Shalala found an earlier experience, however, just as important for her career:

❝ *The Peace Corps is a voice for democracy and American values. . . . I know this from my own service as a Peace Corps volunteer in Iran in the 1960s, and from a trip I took to Thailand just last month where I met with Peace Corps volunteers doing AIDS prevention work. My Peace Corps service not only helped prepare me for my job as Secretary of Health and Human Services, it helped prepare me for life.* ❞

## Evaluating the Quotation

*What aspects of serving in the Peace Corps would provide useful background for a Cabinet post or other federal job?*

the Citizens' Stamp Advisory Committee, and the Migratory Bird Conservation Commission are typical of the dozens of these seldom seen or heard public bodies.

## Independent Regulatory Commissions

The **independent regulatory commissions** stand out among the independent agencies because they are largely beyond the reach of presidential direction and control. There are ten of these agencies today, each created to regulate, or police, important aspects of the nation's economy. Their vital statistics appear in the table on the next page.

### Structured for Independence

The independent regulatory commissions' large measure of independence from the White House comes mainly from the way in which Congress has structured them. Each is headed by a board or commission made up of five to

## Reading Strategy

### Organizing Information/Outline

Ask students to copy down the main headings and subheadings in outline form, leaving space for details. Have them fill in the details as they read the section.

## Point-of-Use Resources

📁 **Guided Reading and Review** Unit 4 booklet, p. 28 provides students with practice identifying the main ideas and key terms of this section.

📁 **Lesson Plans** For lesson planning suggestions, see p. 69 of the Lesson Plans booklet.

📁 **Political Cartoons** See p. 61 of the Political Cartoons booklet for a cartoon relevant to this section.

📑 **Section Support Transparencies** Transparency 64, *Visual Learning*; Transparency 163, *Political Cartoon*

📼 **ABC News Civics and Government Videotape Library** *Project HIRE* (time: 3 minutes, 14 seconds)

*Answer to . . .*

**Evaluating the Quotation** Such a background would provide not only specific job experience but experience with American foreign policy.

## The Independent Regulatory Commissions

| Agency | Date Established | Number of Members | Term of Members | Major Functions |
|---|---|---|---|---|
| Board of Governors, Federal Reserve System (the Fed) | 1913 | 7 | 14 years | Supervises banking system, practices; regulates money supply, use of credit in economy. |
| Federal Trade Commission (FTC) | 1914 | 5 | 7 years | Enforces antitrust, other laws prohibiting unfair competition, price-fixing, false advertising, other unfair business practices. |
| Securities and Exchange Commission (SEC) | 1934 | 5 | 5 years | Regulates securities, other financial markets, investment companies, brokers; enforces laws prohibiting fraud, other dishonest investment practices. |
| Federal Communications Commission (FCC) | 1934 | 5 | 5 years | Regulates interstate and foreign communications by radio, television, wire, satellite, and cable. |
| National Labor Relations Board (NLRB) | 1935 | 5 | 5 years | Administers federal labor-management relations laws; holds collective bargaining elections; prevents, remedies unfair labor practices. |
| Federal Maritime Commission (FMC) | 1936 | 5 | 5 years | Regulates waterborne foreign, domestic off-shore commerce of the United States; supervises rates, services. |
| Consumer Product Safety Commission (CPSC) | 1972 | 5 | 5 years | Sets, enforces safety standards for consumer products; directs recall of unsafe products; conducts safety research, information programs. |
| Nuclear Regulatory Commission (NRC) | 1974 | 5 | 5 years | Licenses, regulates all civilian nuclear facilities and civilian uses of nuclear materials.[a] |
| Commodity Futures Trading Commission (CFTC) | 1974 | 5 | 5 years | Regulates commodity exchanges, brokers, futures trading in agricultural, metal, other commodities. |
| Federal Energy Regulatory Commission (FERC) | 1977 | 5 | 4 years | Regulates, sets rates for transmission, sale of natural gas, electricity, oil by pipeline; licenses hydroelectric power projects.[b] |

[a] These functions performed by the Atomic Energy Commission from 1946 to 1974 (when the AEC was abolished); other AEC functions now performed by agencies in the Energy Department.

[b] These functions performed by the Federal Power Commission (created in 1930) until the FPC was abolished in 1977. The FERC is within the Energy Department, but only for administrative purposes; otherwise it is independent (except the Secretary of Energy may set reasonable deadlines for the FERC action in any matter before it). Under terms of National Energy Act of 1978, the FERC's authority to regulate natural gas prices ended in 1985.

*Interpreting Tables* Independent regulatory commissions are independent of all three branches of government, and are exceptions to the separation of powers rule. ***How do the functions listed above show that these commissions have legislative and judicial powers?***

seven members appointed by the President with Senate consent. However, those officials have terms of such length that it is unlikely a President will gain control over any of these agencies through the appointment process, at least not in a single presidential term.

Several other features of these boards and commissions put them beyond the reach of presidential control. No more than a bare majority of the members of each board or commission may belong to the same political party. Thus, several of those officers must belong to the party out of power.

Moreover, the appointed terms of the members are staggered so that the term of only one member on each board or commission expires in any one year. Finally, most of these officers can be removed by the President only for those causes Congress has specified.[7]

As with the other independent agencies, the regulatory commissions are executive bodies. That is, Congress has given them the power to

[7] Recall this point from Chapter 14, on page 397. The members of five of these bodies (the SEC, FCC, CPSC, NRC, and CFTC) are exceptions. Congress has provided that any of them may be removed at the President's discretion.

## Make It Relevant

### Careers in Government—Statistician

The Federal Government is the single largest collector of statistics in the world. Its various agencies compile and analyze statistics on almost anything imaginable, from the number of shipyard employees to the average age of farmers. Such information provides the basic picture of "where we are" as a nation, enabling government officials to adjust policies to a custom fit. Billions of dollars and

millions of lives depend on the critical knowledge that government statisticians collect.

**Skills Activity** Have small groups of students create statistical profiles of the class. They should share their results, explaining their data-gathering and analysis techniques. Then have individual students write paragraphs explaining why they would or would not be interested in this career. **(Challenging)**

administer the programs for which they were created. However, unlike those other independent agencies, the regulatory commissions are also **quasi-legislative** and **quasi-judicial** bodies.[8] That is, Congress has given them certain legislative-like and judicial-like powers.

These agencies exercise their quasi-legislative powers when they make rules and regulations. Those rules and regulations have the force of law. They implement, or spell out the details of, the laws that Congress has directed these regulatory bodies to enforce.

To illustrate the point: Congress has said that those who want to borrow money by issuing stocks, bonds, or other securities must provide a "full and fair disclosure" of all pertinent information to prospective investors. The Securities and Exchange Commission (SEC) makes that requirement effective and indicates how those who offer securities are to meet it by issuing rules and regulations.

The regulatory commissions exercise their quasi-judicial powers when they decide disputes in those fields in which Congress has given them policing authority. For example, if an investor in Iowa thinks a local stockbroker has defrauded (cheated) him, he may file a complaint with the SEC's regional office in Chicago. SEC agents will investigate and report their findings, and the agency will judge the merits of the complaint much as a court would do. Decisions made by the SEC, and by the other independent regulatory bodies, can be appealed to the United States courts of appeals.

In a sense, Congress has created these agencies to act in its place. Congress could hold hearings and set interest rates, license radio and TV stations and nuclear reactors, check on business practices, and do the many other things it has directed the regulatory commissions to do. These activities are complex and time-consuming, however, and they demand constant and expert attention. If Congress did all of this work, it would have no time for its other and important legislative work.

Note that these regulatory bodies possess all three of the basic governmental powers: executive, legislative, and judicial. They are

exceptions to the principle of separation of powers. Technically, they should not be grouped with the other independent agencies. Instead, they should somehow be located somewhere between the executive and legislative branches, and between the executive and judicial branches, too.

## Rethinking Regulation

Several authorities, and most recent Presidents, have urged that at least the administrative functions of the independent regulatory commissions be given to executive department agencies. Critics have raised other serious questions about these agencies and proposed to abolish or redesign them.

The most troubling questions are these: Have some of the independent regulatory commissions been captured by the special interests they are expected to regulate? Are all of the many and detailed rules created by these agencies really needed? Do some of these rules have the effect of stifling legitimate competition in the free enterprise system? Do some of them add unreasonably to the costs of doing business and therefore to the prices that consumers must pay?

Congress sets the basic policies of the regulatory agencies, and so it has a major responsibility to answer these questions. It has responded to some questions in recent years, particularly by deregulating much of the nation's transportation

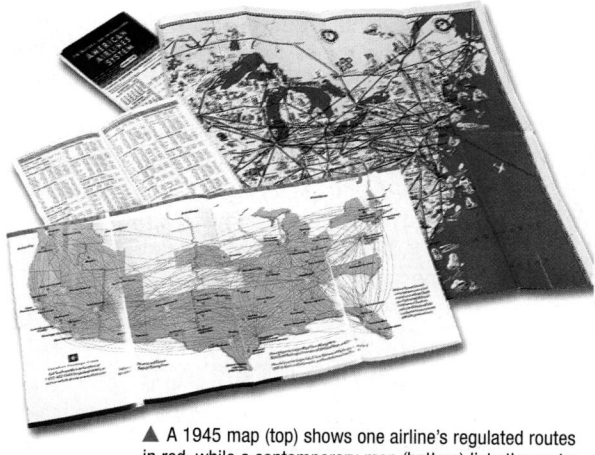

▲ A 1945 map (top) shows one airline's regulated routes in red, while a contemporary map (bottom) lists the routes freely chosen by a different airline. *Critical Thinking Why might the government have decided, under regulation, to require airlines to serve certain cities?*

---

[8]The prefix *quasi* is from the Latin, meaning "in a certain sense, resembling, seemingly."

## Chapter 15 • Section 4

ACTIVITY

## Learning Styles

**Visual** Remind students of some of the industries that the government has chosen to deregulate, including transportation and communications. Ask them to choose one of these industries, and then decide if they are in favor of or opposed to deregulation. Then have them create political cartoons that express their viewpoints. Display cartoons in the class, and have students explain the viewpoints being expressed.

(Average)

## Point-of-Use Resources

📁 **The Living Constitution** Separation of Powers, p. 5

📖 **Basic Principles of the Constitution Transparencies** Transparencies 23–29, *Separation of Powers*

## CONSTITUTIONAL PRINCIPLES

### Separation of Powers
Normally, when people think of separation of powers they think of the division of powers between the executive, legislative, and judicial branches. However, this can also apply to the separation of powers or duties within a branch of government. For instance, in the vast bureaucracy that makes up the executive branch, a separation of power exists between the Cabinet departments and the independent agencies and between the agencies themselves.

### Activity
Have students read through the section, focusing on the separation of powers between the independent agencies. Ask each student to create a summary of the differences between the three types of independent agencies and Cabinet departments. Once students have finished writing their summaries, call on volunteers to read them to the class. Consider creating a master list of differences on the chalkboard.

*Answer to . . .*

**Critical Thinking** Possible answer: The government might have wished to provide services to an isolated part of the country in order to serve the citizens and stimulate the economy.

▲ The government created Amtrak as a corporation to provide passenger train service. After years of losing money and relying on federal subsidies to stay afloat, Amtrak was told that Congress would not cover its losses after 2002. *Critical Thinking **What advantages might Amtrak enjoy as a government corporation?***

industry. Airlines, bus companies, truckers, and railroads have greater freedom to operate today than they did only a few years ago. The same trend can be seen in the field of communications, notably with regard to cable television.

Two major regulatory bodies have actually disappeared in recent years. The Civil Aeronautics Board was created in 1938 to oversee commercial air traffic in the United States. For decades it assigned the routes to be flown and the rates charged by airlines and other commercial air carriers, until it was abolished by Congress in 1985.

The Interstate Commerce Commission was the very first of the regulatory commissions to be established by Congress, in 1887. For a century it issued licenses and regulated the rates and routes and most other aspects of commercial transportation by rail, highway, and water. It, too, was abolished by Congress, in 1996.

## The Government Corporations

Several of the independent agencies are **government corporations.** Like most of the other independent agencies, government corporations are within the executive branch and subject to the President's direction and control. Unlike the other agencies, however, they were set up by Congress to carry out certain business-like activities.

Congress established the first government corporation when it chartered the Bank of the United States in 1791. Yet government corporations were little used until World War I and the Depression. In both periods Congress set up dozens of corporations to carry out emergency programs. Several still exist—among them, the Federal Deposit Insurance Corporation (FDIC), which insures bank deposits, and the Export-Import Bank of the United States (Eximbank), which makes loans to help the export and sale of American goods abroad.

There are now more than 50 of these corporations. They deliver the mail (the U.S. Postal Service); insure bank deposits (the FDIC); provide intercity rail passenger service (the National Railroad Passenger Corporation, Amtrak); protect pension benefits (the Pension Benefit Guaranty Corporation); and generate, sell, and distribute electric power (the Tennessee Valley Authority).[9]

---

[9]State and local governments maintain their own government corporations, most often called authorities, to operate airports, turnpikes, seaports, power plants, liquor stores, and housing developments, and to conduct many other corporate activities. The Port Authority of New York and New Jersey is one of the best known.

## Government v. Private Corporations

The typical government corporation is set up much like a corporation in the private sector. It is run by a board of directors, with a general manager who directs the corporation's operations according to the policies established by that board. Most government corporations produce income that is plowed back into the business.

There are several striking differences between government and private corporations, however. Congress decides the purpose for which the public agencies exist and the functions they can perform. Their officers are public officers; in fact, all who work for these corporations are public employees. The President selects most of the top officers of government corporations with Senate confirmation.

In addition, these public agencies are financed by public funds appropriated by Congress, not private investors. The Federal Government, representing the American people, owns the stock.

The advantage most often claimed is their flexibility. It is said that the government corporation, freed from the controls of regular departmental organization, can carry on its activities with the incentive, efficiency, and ability to experiment that make many private concerns successful.

Whether or not that claim is valid is open to question. At the very least, it raises this complex issue: Is a public corporation's need for flexibility compatible with the democratic requirement that all public agencies be held responsible and accountable to the people?

## Degrees of Independence

The degree of independence and flexibility government corporations have varies considerably. In fact, some corporations are not independent at all. They are attached to an executive department.

The Commodity Credit Corporation, for example, is the government's major crop-loan and farm-subsidy agency. It is located within the Department of Agriculture, and the secretary of agriculture chairs its seven-member board. The Commodity Credit Corporation carries out most of its functions through a line agency in the Department of Agriculture—the Farm Service Agency—which is also subject to the direct control of the secretary.

Some corporations do have considerable independence, however. The Tennessee Valley Authority (TVA) is a case in point. It operates under a statute that gives it considerable discretion over its own programs. Although its budget is subject to review by the OMB, the President, and Congress, the TVA has a large say in the uses of the income its several operations produce.[10]

---

[10]The TVA is a major example of government in business. Congress established the TVA in the Tennessee Valley Authority Act of 1933. The act called for the coordinated development and use of the natural resources of parts of seven southern States.

The TVA has had an extraordinary impact on the Tennessee River Valley and its approximately eight million residents. Its operations include electric power, flood control, reforestation, soil conservation, agricultural research, recreational facilities, and the promotion of industrial growth. The TVA's power program is self-supporting. Much of its other activities are supported by Congress. Still, it generates considerable revenues from sales of bonds, electricity, and fertilizer.

## Point-of-Use Resources

**Guide to the Essentials** Chapter 15, Section 4, p. 85 provides support for students who need additional review of section content. Spanish support is available in the Spanish edition of the Guide on p. 78.

**Quiz** Unit 4 booklet, p. 29 includes matching and multiple-choice questions to check students' understanding of Section 4 content.

**Presentation Pro CD-ROM** Quizzes and multiple-choice questions check students' understanding of Section 4 content.

## Answers to . . .

### Section 4 Assessment

**1.** Some lie outside of the executive branch and are largely free of presidential control; some carry out business-like functions; some have quasi-legislative and/or quasi-judicial powers.

**2.** To regulate important aspects of the nation's economy independent of Presidential influence or control.

**3.** A quasi-legislative body is an executive body that has been given legislative-like powers that have the force of law.

**4.** To resist influence from party politics or the public; because they serve umbrella regulatory functions and should be set apart; because they do not fit well with existing executive departments. They may choose to stay independent because they have increased flexibility and less government control.

**5.** Answers will vary; students might suggest that a good bureaucracy is one that allows the government to function properly, but does not become so independent that it cannot be checked.

---

## Section 4 Assessment

### Key Terms and Main Ideas

1. How do **independent agencies** differ from the other agencies in the executive branch?
2. What is the main purpose of the **independent regulatory commissions**?
3. What is the difference between a legislative body and a **quasi-legislative** body?

### Critical Thinking

4. **Drawing Inferences** Name three reasons why independent agencies operate outside the executive departments.
5. **Making Decisions** Economist Milton Friedman called bureaucracy "both a vehicle whereby special interests can achieve their objectives and an important special interest in its own right." What can the government do to minimize the situation Friedman describes?

### Take It to the Net

6. Read about the Federal Communications Commission. Then create an informational brochure or leaflet in which you analyze its functions and the issues with which it is involved. Use the links provided in the Social Studies area at the following Web site for help in completing this activity.
**www.phschool.com**

### Take It to the Net

6. Direct students to the Social Studies area at the Prentice Hall School Web site. The *Magruder's American Government* companion Web site includes the directions and links needed to complete the activity. It also provides a printable Internet activity worksheet with scoring rubrics for assessment. Brochures or leaflets will vary, but should reflect an understanding of the functions of the commission and the issues with which it is involved.

## SKILLS FOR LIFE

### CITIZENSHIP

### Gathering Information from Government Sources

**Focus** Have students work in pairs or small groups to create a plan for doing a research project.

**Instruct** Divide the class into pairs or into groups of three or four students. Each group should brainstorm a research topic and draft a list of possible government sources of information about the topic, following Steps 1 and 2 on this page. Topics should be either **(a)** something about the government itself or **(b)** something that can be researched using government sources.

**Close/Reteach** Have groups exchange their work and critique each other's research plans.

---

# SKILLS FOR LIFE

TECHNOLOGY
CITIZENSHIP
CRITICAL THINKING
CHARTS and GRAPHS

## Gathering Information from Government Sources

You might not know it, but if you're a U.S. citizen, you're a co-owner of a treasure-trove of information. The government uses a portion of the tax dollars it collects from its citizens to generate massive amounts of transcripts, research papers, legal records, maps, statistics, studies, videos, facsimiles, manuscripts, and music.

By far the best way to access federal information today is on the Internet. The growth of public and private Web sites containing government information has revolutionized the research process. If you don't have Internet access, however, many of the sources listed at right are available in print at large libraries. To seek out government information, try these steps:

**1. Define what information you're seeking.** Knowing what you need will help narrow your search. Do you need federal, regional, State, or local information? Are you looking for records, statistics, primary sources, or other media? Decide on a research objective, and write a question that summarizes it.

**2. Determine where to search.** What agency of the government is responsible for the topic you're researching? Information on water pollution, for example, might come from the Environmental Protection Agency, the Interior Department, the *Congressional Record*, and State and local sites. Using your question from Step 1, identify agencies that might provide relevant information.

**3. Gather information.** As you collect material, make note of the source: Is it public or private? Is it reliable? Steer clear of anonymous Web sites.

### Test for Success

Choose a government-related topic that interests you. Compile a list of at least five good places to search for the information.

---

### Searching Uncle Sam

**First Gov** is a government Web site that provides the public with easily accessible online U.S. government resources. http://www.firstgov.gov

**The National Archives and Records Administration (NARA)** manages and provides access to all federal records dating back to the Declaration of Independence —more than 4 billion pieces of paper and 6 million photographs. http://www.nara.gov

**The World Factbook** is the authoritative source for country-by-country information from the U.S. Central Intelligence Agency (CIA), published annually. http://www.odci.gov/cia/publications/factbook

**The Census Bureau** tracks where we live, where we work, what we earn, what we eat—you name it. http://www.census.gov

**The FedWorld Information Network** is a searchable database with links to government agencies. http://www.fedworld.gov

**FedStats** is a searchable database created by the Federal Interagency Council on Statistical Policy. Get federal, regional, State, and county statistics presented in tables, graphs, and maps. Contains the indispensible Statistical Abstracts. http://www.fedstats.gov

**The Library of Congress (LOC)**, created in 1800, is the world's largest library, the government's official storehouse of more than 115 million multimedia items. Any item ever copyrighted is here. http://www.loc.gov

**Thomas**, named after President Thomas Jefferson, is the official record of everything that happens in Congress. Thomas contains the *Congressional Record* as well as information on committee hearings and schedules. http://thomas.loc.gov

**FindLaw** is an online, private source of legal information: Supreme Court decisions, legal issues, news, and other resources. http://www.findlaw.com

---

### Answers . . .

**1.** Possible research objective: What major projects does the Federal Government fund to combat water pollution?
**2.** Types of research information and places to find them might include legislation (from the House and Senate Web sites), project funding (from specific agency sites), historical records (from the national archives), biographies (from the Library of Congress), statistics (from the Census Bureau), and maps (from the CIA World Factbook).
**3.** Government and university Web sites are usually reliable sources of information. However, the personal Web sites of some college academics may represent opinion rather than fact, so should be read and analyzed carefully.

### Test for Success

Besides government sources, students should consider news media archives as a good source of information about government activities.

### Point-of-Use Resources

**Skills for Life Activity** Unit 4 booklet, p. 32 provides an additional skill activity for this chapter.

**Social Studies Skills Tutor CD-ROM** Provides interactive practice in geographic literacy, critical thinking and reading, visual analysis, and communications.

## Section Preview

### OBJECTIVES

1. **Describe** the development of the civil service.
2. **Identify** characteristics of the civil service as it exists today.
3. **Analyze** the restrictions on the political activities of members of the civil service.

### WHY IT MATTERS

Most people who work for the Federal Government are members of the civil service. Over time, civil service reformers have worked to reduce corruption and political influence.

### POLITICAL DICTIONARY

★ civil service
★ spoils system
★ patronage
★ register
★ bipartisan

The **civil service** is composed of those civilian employees who perform the administrative work of government. Some 2.7 million men and women work for the Federal Government today.[11] Only about 300,000 of those work in the Washington area. The rest have jobs in regional, field, and local offices scattered throughout the country and around the world.

The President appoints the people who hold the highest ranking jobs in the executive branch. There are only about 2,500 of those positions—at the top levels of the Executive Office, the Cabinet departments, the independent agencies, and in American embassies and other diplomatic stations. All of the other jobs in the federal bureaucracy are covered by some aspect of the civil service system.

## Development of the Civil Service

The Constitution says very little about the staffing of the federal bureaucracy. The only direct reference is in Article II, which says that the President

FROM THE *Constitution* **"**shall nominate, and by and with the Advice and Consent of the Senate, shall appoint Ambassadors, other

*public Ministers and Consuls, Judges of the supreme Court, and all other Officers of the United States, whose appointments are not herein otherwise provided for, and which shall be established by law: but the Congress may by law vest the appointment of such inferior officers, as they think proper, in the President alone, in the Courts of Law, or in the Heads of Departments.* **"**

—Article II, Section 2, Clause 2

◀ The civil service includes people like this ranger who works at Grand Canyon National Park in Arizona.

[11]Another 1.5 million men and women serve in the armed forces; see Chapter 17. Altogether, there are now some 17.5 million civilian public employees in this country. More than 4 million work for the States, and another 11 million work for local governments (including 6.5 million persons employed by school districts). About 2.5 million of those who work for State and local governments are employed on a part-time basis.

## Block Scheduling Strategies

Consider these suggestions to manage extended class time:

■ Explain that many nations administer civil service exams to prospective federal employees. Have students discuss the pros and cons of having one exam for a variety of positions. Ask: what kinds of questions should be on the exam? Have groups of students create a 20-question exam, exchange them, and then take them. If possible, compare their exams to a copy of a real civil service exam.

■ Have students assume the role of a civil servant (government employee). A friend has asked about getting a job with the government. Have students write letters to their friend explaining how to get a federal job, and what the pay, benefits, and functions are. They should close by telling whether they like working for the government, and if they think their friend should apply.

## Chapter 16 Resource Manager

# Financing Government

| Section Objectives | Print and Technology Resources | |
|---|---|---|
| **1 Taxes** *(pp. 446–452)* <br><br> 1. Explain how and why the Constitution gives Congress the power to tax. <br> 2. Identify the sources of tax revenue of the U.S. Government and analyze their effect on the U.S. economy. <br> 3. Summarize why the Federal Government imposes taxes for nonrevenue purposes. <br><br> **TEKS 6A, 6B, 9G, 17C, 21A, 21C, 21D, 21E, 21F, 22A, 22B, 22C** | • **Unit 4 booklet** <br> Guided Reading and Review, p. 33 <br> Section 1 Quiz, p. 34 <br> • **Lesson Plans booklet** Section 1, p. 71 <br> • **Political Cartoons booklet** Section 1, p. 63 <br> • **Block Scheduling with Lesson Strategies booklet** p. 27 <br> • **The Living Constitution booklet** p. 8 <br> • **Section Reading Support Transparencies** | • **Government Assessment Rubrics booklet** p. 26 <br> • **Basic Principles of the Constitution Transparencies** 19, 46 <br> • **Section Support Transparencies** 66, 165 <br> • **Presentation Pro CD-ROM** Section 1 <br> • **Simulations and Data Graphing CD-ROM** <br> • **Social Studies Skills Tutor CD-ROM** |
| **2 Nontax Revenues and Borrowing** *(pp. 454–456)* <br><br> 1. Identify sources of nontax revenues of the U.S. Government and analyze their effect on the U.S. economy. <br> 2. Describe how the Federal Government borrows money. <br> 3. Analyze the causes and effects of the public debt. <br><br> **TEKS 6A, 6B, 17C, 21A, 21C, 21D, 21E, 22A, 22B, 22D** | • **Unit 4 booklet** <br> Guided Reading and Review, p. 35 <br> Section 2 Quiz, p. 36 <br> • **Lesson Plans booklet** Section 2, p. 72 <br> • **Political Cartoons booklet** Section 2, p. 64 <br> • **Section Reading Support Transparencies** | • **Close Up on Primary Sources booklet** History of the National Debt, p. 18 <br> • **Section Support Transparencies** 67, 166 <br> • **Presentation Pro CD-ROM** Section 2 |
| **3 Spending and the Budget** *(pp. 458–462)* <br><br> 1. Identify the key expenditures of the U.S. Government and analyze their effect on the U.S. economy. <br> 2. Explain how the President and Congress work together to create the federal budget. <br><br> **TEKS 6A, 6B, 9B, 9E, 9G, 17C, 21A, 21C, 21D, 21E, 22A, 22B** | • **Unit 4 booklet** <br> Guided Reading and Review, p. 37 <br> Section 3 Quiz, p. 38 <br> Skills for Life Activity, p. 39 <br> • **Lesson Plans booklet** Section 3, p. 73 <br> • **Political Cartoons booklet** Section 3, p. 65 <br> • **Block Scheduling with Lesson Strategies booklet** p. 27 <br> • **Close Up on the Supreme Court booklet** *Agostini* v. *Felton*, p. 17 <br> • **Section Reading Support Transparencies** | • **Government Assessment Rubrics booklet** p. 22 <br> • **The Basic Principles of the Constitution Posters** <br> • **Section Support Transparencies** 68, 167 <br> • **Presentation Pro CD-ROM** Section 3 <br> • **Simulations and Data Graphing CD-ROM** |

# Block Scheduling Strategies

The *Magruder's American Government* program addresses block-scheduling strategies in a variety of ways. For easy reference, side-column activities that fit a block format are marked ■ **Block Strategy.** Each section also contains a **Block Scheduling Strategies** box describing at least two block-format activities that address and extend core content from the section. The **Block Scheduling with Lesson Strategies booklet** found in the Teaching Resources contains additional block-scheduling activities for each chapter.

## Take It to the Net

Visit the Social Studies area at the Prentice Hall School Web site. Once there, you can find additional links, current events connections, and activities to enrich chapter content for *Magruder's American Government,* as well as a Self-Test for students. Be sure to check out this month's **eTeach** online discussion with a Master Teacher.

### www.phschool.com

## Pressed for Time?

If you are running short on time to cover this chapter, consider one of the following options:
- Use the **Presentation Pro CD-ROM** to create an outline for this chapter.
- Use one of the **Pressed for Time** activities found on p. 27.
- Use the Section Summaries for Chapter 2, from **Guide to the Essentials of American Government (English and Spanish).**

##  Video Connections

Prentice Hall offers two video programs to reinforce and extend chapter content. Show students *The Blessings of Liberty* from the **ABC News Civics and Government Videotape Library** and *Prayer in Schools: A Nationwide Debate* from the **Magruder's American Government Video Collection.**

## Assessment Options
- Section Quizzes, **Unit 4 booklet,** pp. 34, 36, 38
- Chapter 16 Assessment, pp. 464–465
- **Guide to the Essentials of American Government,** Chapter 16 Test, p. 91

### Core Assessment

Chapter 16 Test, Chapter Tests booklet
ExamView® Test Bank CD-ROM Chapter 16
Government Assessment Rubrics

### Standardized Test Preparation

#### Diagnose and Prescribe
Diagnostic Tests for High School
Social Studies Skills

#### Review and Reteach
Review Book for Government

#### Practice and Assess
Test-Taking Strategies With Transparencies for High School
Test Prep Book for Government

# Chapter 16 Teacher's Edition Index

# Financing Government

CHAPTER 16

## Introducing the Chapter
In this chapter, students will learn about how the Federal Government is financed, how it borrows and spends money, and how the federal budget is made.

### Make It Relevant

**★ You Can Make a Difference**

Have the class organize and conduct a "Challenge" tournament for younger students in their school or school district. The class should select a topic for the Challenge (it may be as specific as government finance, or as broad as American government), generate questions and answers, contact teachers, publicize the tournament to students, and arrange for a venue. Individual students in your class should create and fill specific roles during the tournament itself (e.g., moderator, judge, etc.).

**Service Learning**

## CONSTITUTIONAL PRINCIPLES

Emphasize the following basic principles as students read Chapter 16. Have the class respond to the questions, and then ask volunteers to suggest which principle has the most impact on how the Federal Government spends its money.

**Limited Government** In what ways is Congress's power to tax limited by the Constitution? How is the principle of limited government reflected in the process of making the federal budget?

**Separation of Powers** How does the system of direct taxation take into account a division between the operation of the National Government and that of the States?

# Financing Government

*"The power 'to lay and collect taxes, duties, imposts, and excises' was an indispensable one to...the Federal Government, which without it would possess no means of providing for its own support."*

—James Polk (1845)

To keep American institutions healthy and running well, the Federal Government depends on income from various types of taxes as well as some nontax sources. How government spends the money—the federal budget—has a major impact on society.

◆ The Bureau of Engraving and Printing

**CLOSE UP** *Corner*

The following resources are available only from the Close Up Foundation to support the concepts discussed in Chapter 16 "Financing Government":

◆ *Slicing the Pie: A Federal Budget Game*
◆ *The American Economy: Government's Role, Citizen's Choice*
◆ *Trade Is Everybody's Business*

**CLOSE UP Online**

To keep up-to-date on Close Up news and activities, visit Close Up Online at

**www.closeup.org**

Close Up Foundation
44 Canal Center Plaza
Alexandria, VA 22314-1592
800-765-3131

## ★ You Can Make a Difference

**THE WORKINGS OF** the Federal Reserve System may puzzle some people, but not the high school students who take the "Fed Challenge." To bring real-world economics into the classroom, Federal Reserve Banks in various districts sponsor this annual event. Student teams hold a mock Fed meeting and show their knowledge of economic issues. District winners then compete in Washington, D.C., for scholarship awards. In 2000, five Texas teens—the Midland High School team—won the Fed Challenge. They were Kelly Beall, Matt Josefy, Adam Martin, Ryan Myers, and Robin Nelson. Other finalists came from schools in Ohio, Missouri, Indiana, Virginia, and New Jersey.

### Keep It Current

Items marked with this logo are periodically updated on the Internet. Keep up-to-date with what's in the news. To get current information on issues involving government finance, go to **www.phschool.com**

### SECTION 1

#### Taxes (pp. 446–452)

★ The Framers put the power to tax first among the expressed powers of Congress.
★ The income taxes paid by individuals and corporations are the largest sources of federal revenue today.
★ Excise taxes, gift and estate taxes, customs duties, and social insurance taxes also support the Federal Government.
★ The power to tax is used, in large part, to raise revenue; however, it is also used to regulate and even discourage some activities.

### SECTION 2

#### Nontax Revenues and Borrowing (pp. 454–456)

★ The Federal Government receives a relatively small amount of revenue from nontax sources.
★ Between 1930 and 1998, the Federal Government borrowed tremendous sums of money to pay for federal spending.
★ For decades, the Federal Government practiced deficit financing; year after year, it spent more than it took in and then borrowed to make up the difference.
★ The public debt is composed of all of the money the government has borrowed over time and not yet repaid, plus all of the accrued interest on that money.

### SECTION 3

#### Spending and the Budget (pp. 458–462)

★ Federal spending—now some $2 trillion a year—has an enormous impact on the nation's economy.
★ The largest categories of federal spending include entitlements, defense, and interest on the public debt.
★ The federal budget is a major political document—a statement of the public policies of the United States, with dollar signs attached.

## Pressed for Time?

### To Omit the Chapter

If you wish to skip Chapter 16, ask students to read the Chapter in Brief and assign the Guide to the Essentials before continuing to another chapter. You may also want to assign the Chapter 16 Test in the Chapter Test booklet. Then specific portions of Chapter 16 may be assigned to students needing reinforcement of key terms and concepts.

### To Preview the Chapter

To introduce students to key terms and concepts in each section, have them read the Chapter in Brief. You may also assign the Reading Strategy activities on pp. 447, 455, and 459 of this book.

### To Review the Chapter

When students have completed Chapter 16, you might want to assign the Guide to the Essentials or the Guided Reading and Review worksheets on pp. 33, 35, and 37 of the Unit 4 booklet.

### To Cover the Chapter Quickly

To cover the material in Chapter 16 quickly, use the following activity.

**Focus** Have students recall any current debate on taxes they can from magazines or newspapers. Ask: What kinds of taxes stir up the most debate, and what are some of the arguments politicians and other people use to defend their viewpoints?

**Instruct** Explain the various sources of revenue the National Government receives, including taxes, nontax revenues, and loans. Then discuss with students the pros and cons of each source of revenue. Write these on the chalkboard as they are discussed. Ask: Is one form of revenue more "fair" than the others? Why or why not?

**Close/Reteach** Ask students to consider how a government could be run without one of the sources of revenue. Have them refer to the lists of pros and cons as they consider the question.
🖳 **Block Strategy (Average)**

## Keep It Current

### Internet Update

Use the Prentice Hall School Web site and the Keep It Current CD-ROM to find quick content updates.

Visit **www.phschool.com** for current events articles that are linked to Chapter 16. Critical thinking questions are included.

**Keep It Current CD-ROM** includes government-related projects by unit. Students complete each project using current information that they obtain by linking to the Prentice Hall School Web site from the CD-ROM.

**1 Taxes**

**Objectives** You may wish to call students' attention to the objectives in the Section Preview. The objectives are reflected in the main headings of the section.

**Bellringer** Tell students that they've won the lottery! Now they must make a choice: Take the entire $1 million today or receive it over the next 10 years. What's the difference? Explain that in this section, they will learn about income taxes and how they vary depending on annual income.

**Vocabulary Builder** Write the terms *income, imports, social insurance,* and *assets* on the board. Have students match these terms with as many terms as they can from the Political Dictionary and explain how the pairs of terms are related.

## Pressed for Time?

### Quick Lesson Plan

**1. Focus** Tell students that the money needed to run the Federal Government comes mainly from taxes. Ask students to discuss what they know about the various kinds of taxes.

**2. Instruct** Ask students which tax is the largest source of federal revenue. Discuss the income tax and its history. Briefly talk about the constitutional limitations on Congress's power to tax. Then have students identify the other kinds of taxes, including those imposed for nonrevenue purposes.

**3. Close/Reteach** Remind students that the Constitution gives Congress the power to tax, within limits. Ask them to consider, as they read, how the National Government could function without this power.

**Answer to . . .**

**Interpreting Political Cartoons** Possible answer: That the government is big, powerful, and domineering over its citizens.

## Section Preview

### OBJECTIVES

1. **Explain** how and why the Constitution gives Congress the power to tax.
2. **Identify** the sources of tax revenue of the U.S. government and analyze their effect on the U.S. economy.
3. **Summarize** why the Federal Government imposes taxes for nonrevenue purposes.

### WHY IT MATTERS

Article I of the Constitution and the 16th Amendment give Congress broad powers to set federal taxes. Today, Congress collects most of its revenue in the form of income taxes paid by individuals and corporations.

### POLITICAL DICTIONARY

* **progressive tax**
* **tax return**
* **payroll tax**
* **regressive tax**
* **excise tax**
* **estate tax**
* **gift tax**
* **custom duty**

According to Benjamin Franklin's oft-quoted comment, "in this world nothing is certain but death and taxes." In this section, you will consider the second of Franklin's certainties, taxes. More specifically, you will examine those taxes levied by the Federal Government.

During fiscal year 2003, which extends from October 1, 2002, through September 30, 2003, the Federal Government expects to spend just about $2 trillion. It will almost certainly take in even more than that stupendous sum. Those mind-boggling numbers tell you that, on average, it now costs every man, woman, and child in this country nearly $7,000 a year to support the Federal Government. Those figures should also tell you how important the subject of taxes really is.

### The Power to Tax

The Constitution underscores the central importance of the power to tax by listing it first among all of the many powers granted to Congress. The Constitution gives to Congress the power:

 **FROM THE Constitution** *"To lay and collect Taxes, Duties, Imposts and Excises, to pay the Debts and provide for the common Defense and general Welfare of the United States. . . ."*

—Article I, Section 8, Clause 1

First and foremost, Congress exercises the taxing power in order to raise the money needed to operate the Federal Government. However, Congress does levy some taxes for nonrevenue purposes, or reasons other than raising money.

### Constitutional Limitations

The power to tax is not unlimited. As with all of its other powers, Congress must exercise the taxing power in accord with the Constitution. Thus,

JIM BERRY ©NEA

"So then Tommy Taxpayer said to the big bully, Godzilla government, 'I am unwilling to pay the bill ...'"

**Interpreting Political Cartoons** Taxes are essential to government, but people disagree on how much the Federal Government should tax. **What is the speaker's attitude toward government?**

## Block Scheduling Strategies

Consider these suggestions to manage extended class time:

■ Explain that the income tax is one of the most hotly debated topics in American politics. Tell students that some politicians have proposed replacing the progressive income tax with a single "flat" tax on income; others have suggested a national sales tax on goods purchased. Call on students to list the benefits and drawbacks of each plan, and then have them write editorials in support or opposition. Students may also present their own alternate plans.

■ Have small groups of students work together to list all the kinds of taxes described in the section. Next to each, students should summarize on whom the tax is imposed and how it is supposed to work. Finally, have groups decide which tax on the list they find the least useful or most unfair, and cut it from the list. Ask groups to share their tax cuts with each other and explain their choices.

▲ The Federal Government draws revenue from many sources, including taxes on telephone calls, imported goods, and wages. *Critical Thinking* **Where does the Federal Government get the power to tax imports?**

for example, Congress cannot levy a tax on church services—clearly, such a tax would violate the 1st Amendment.

In more specific terms, the Constitution puts four expressed limits—and one very significant implied limit—on the power of Congress to tax. First, taxes must be used for public purposes only. That is, the Constitution says that Congress may levy taxes for public purposes, and not for the benefit of some private interest.

The second expressed limit is the prohibition of export taxes. Article I, Section 9, Clause 5 declares that "No Tax or Duty shall be laid on Articles exported from any State." Thus, customs duties (tariffs) can be applied only to imports—goods brought into the United States. They may not be applied to exports, or goods sent out of the country. This restriction was a part of the Commerce Compromise made by the Framers at Philadelphia in 1787.

While Congress cannot tax exports, it can and does prohibit the export of certain items. It does so under its expressed power to regulate foreign commerce, usually for reasons of national security. For example, Congress has banned the export of computer software that allows people to encrypt files in a code no government can crack.

The third expressed limit is that direct taxes must be equally apportioned, evenly distributed, among the States. The Constitution originally provided that:

**FROM THE Constitution** "*No Capitation, or other direct, Tax shall be laid, unless in Proportion to the Census of Enumeration herein before directed to be taken.*"
—Article I, Section 9, Clause 4

This restriction was a part of the Three-Fifths Compromise the Framers made at the Philadelphia Convention. In effect, delegates from the northern States insisted that if slaves were to be counted in the populations of the southern States, then those States would have to pay for them.

Recall that a direct tax is one that must be borne by the person upon whom it is levied. Examples include a tax on land or buildings, which must be paid by the owner of the property; or a capitation tax—a head or poll tax—laid on each person. Other taxes are indirect taxes, or levies that may be shifted to another for payment—as, for example, the federal tax on liquor. That tax, placed initially on the distiller, is ultimately paid by the person who buys the liquor.

The direct tax restriction means, in effect, that any direct tax that Congress levies must be apportioned among the States according to their populations. Thus, a direct tax that raised $1 billion would have to produce just about $120 million in California and $10 million in Mississippi, because California has just about 12 percent of the nation's population and Mississippi 1 percent.

Wealth is not evenly distributed among the States, of course. So, a direct tax laid in proportion to population would be grossly unfair; the

## Organizing Information

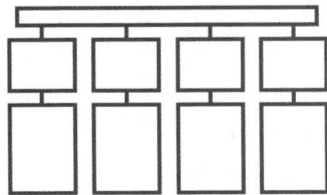

## ACTIVITY

### Learning Styles

**Visual/Spatial, Mathematical** Divide the class into groups of 2–3 students. Remind each group of the information from the text that stated the Federal Government's total collections from income tax in 1927 was $3.4 billion. Provide each group with copies of past federal revenues from income tax. (Some are provided in the table on this page.) Ask each group to create a graph that highlights how the amount of money collected by the Federal Government from income taxes has increased significantly over the past 75 years. Find space in the classroom for groups to display their work.

**(Challenging)**

## Customize for

### English Language Learners

Have pairs of students define and create visuals for the sources of taxes described in the section. Then have them find examples of each source.

## Point-of-Use Resources

 **Section Support Transparencies** Transparency 66, *Visual Learning;* Transparency 165, *Political Cartoon*

**Simulations and Data Graphing CD-ROM** offers data graphing tools that give students practice with creating and interpreting graphs.

*Answer to . . .*

**Interpreting Tables** From social insurance taxes and contributions.

tax would fall more heavily on the residents of some States than it would on others. As a result, Congress has not imposed a direct tax—except for the income tax—outside the District of Columbia since 1861.

An income tax is a direct tax, but it may be laid without regard to population:

> **FROM THE Constitution** *"The Congress shall have power to lay and collect taxes on incomes, from whatever source derived, without apportionment among the several States, and without regard to any census or enumeration. "*
>
> —16th Amendment

Congress first levied an income tax in 1861, to help finance the Civil War. The tax, which expired in 1873, was later upheld by the Supreme Court in *Springer* v. *United States,* 1881. A unanimous Court found that income tax to be an indirect rather than a direct tax.

However, a later income tax law, enacted in 1894, was declared unconstitutional in *Pollock* v. *Farmers' Loan and Trust Co.,* 1895. There, the Court held that the 1894 law imposed a direct tax that Congress should have apportioned among the several States. The impossibility of taxing incomes fairly in accord with any plan of apportionment led to the adoption of the 16th Amendment in 1913.

The fourth and final limit, in Article I, Section 8, Clause 1, declares that "all Duties, Imposts and Excises shall be uniform throughout the United States." That is, all of the indirect taxes levied by the Federal Government must be set at the same rate in all parts of the country.

### The Implied Limitation

The Federal Government cannot tax the States or any of their local governments in the exercise of their governmental functions. That is, federal taxes cannot be imposed on those governments when they are performing such tasks as providing public education, furnishing health care, or building streets and highways.

Recall, the Supreme Court laid down that rule in *McCulloch* v. *Maryland* in 1819, when it declared that "the power to tax involves the power to destroy." If the Federal Government could tax the governmental activities of the States or their local units, it could conceivably tax them out of existence and so destroy the federal system.

The Federal Government can and does tax those State and local activities that are of a nongovernmental character, however. Thus, in 1893, South Carolina created a State monopoly to sell

| The Federal Government's Income (in billions of dollars) | | | | | | |
|---|---|---|---|---|---|---|
| | **1980** | **1990** | **1995** | **2000** | **2001\*** | **2002\*** |
| Individual income taxes | $244.1 | $466.9 | $590.2 | $1,004.5 | $1,014.3 | $1,024.2 |
| Corporation income taxes | 64.6 | 93.5 | 157.0 | 207.3 | 155.4 | 229.1 |
| Social insurance taxes and contributions | 157.8 | 380.0 | 484.5 | 652.9 | 689.4 | 721.9 |
| Excise taxes | 24.3 | 35.3 | 57.5 | 68.9 | 67.6 | 70.4 |
| Estate and gift taxes | 6.4 | 11.5 | 14.8 | 29.0 | 30.0 | 28.0 |
| Customs duties | 7.2 | 16.7 | 19.3 | 19.9 | 19.8 | 21.5 |
| Miscellaneous receipts | 12.7 | 27.8 | 28.6 | 42.8 | 36.2 | 39.6 |
| Total receipts\*\* | $517.1 | $1,032.0 | $1,351.8 | $2,025.2 | $2,012.7 | $2,134.7 |

\*Estimated  \*\*Columns may not add to totals due to rounding and additional sources of income.

SOURCE: Office of Management and Budget

 *Interpreting Tables* Federal revenue comes from several different sources. *From which of these sources did the revenues collected increase by the greatest percentage from 1980 to 2002?*

---

## Preparing for Standardized Tests

Have students read the passages under *The Implied Limitation* and then answer the question below.

Which of the following State activities would have federal taxes imposed on it?

**A** the selling of liquor

**B** providing a police force

**C** running public hospitals

**D** building bridges

liquor, and it claimed that each of its liquor stores was exempt from the federal saloon license tax. But in *South Carolina* v. *United States,* 1905, the Supreme Court held that the State was liable for the tax, because the sale of liquor is not a necessary or usual governmental activity.

## Sources of Revenue

Oliver Wendell Holmes once described taxes as "what we pay for civilized society."[1] Society does not appear to be much more civilized today than it was when Justice Holmes made that observation in 1927. However, "what we pay" has certainly gone up. In 1927, the Federal Government's tax collections came to, altogether, less than $3.4 billion. Compare that figure with the figures in the table on page 448.

### The Income Tax

As the chart on page 448 shows, the income tax is the largest source of federal revenue today. It first became the major source in 1917 and 1918. And, except for a few years during the Depression of the 1930s, it has remained so.

Several features of the income tax fit its dominant role. It is a flexible tax, because its rates can be adjusted to produce whatever amount of money Congress thinks is necessary. The income tax is also easily adapted to the principle of ability to pay. It is a **progressive tax**—that is, the higher one's income, the higher the tax. The tax is levied on the earnings of both individuals and corporations.

### The Individual Income Tax

The tax on individuals' incomes regularly produces the largest amount of federal revenue. For fiscal year 2002, the individual income tax was expected to provide over $1 trillion.

The tax is levied on each person's taxable income—that is, one's total income in the previous year less certain exemptions and deductions. On returns filed in 2002, covering income received in 2001, each taxpayer had a personal exemption of $3,000, and another

---

[1]Holmes made this statement in a dissenting opinion in an insurance tax case, *Compania General de Tabacos de Filipinas* v. *Collector of Internal Revenue,* 1927.

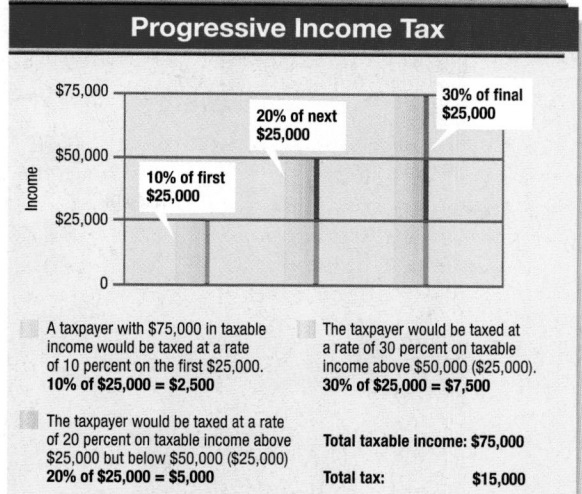

**Progressive Income Tax**

$75,000

$50,000

Income

$25,000

0

10% of first $25,000

20% of next $25,000

30% of final $25,000

A taxpayer with $75,000 in taxable income would be taxed at a rate of 10 percent on the first $25,000.
**10% of $25,000 = $2,500**

The taxpayer would be taxed at a rate of 20 percent on taxable income above $25,000 but below $50,000 ($25,000).
**20% of $25,000 = $5,000**

The taxpayer would be taxed at a rate of 30 percent on taxable income above $50,000 ($25,000).
**30% of $25,000 = $7,500**

**Total taxable income: $75,000**

**Total tax:          $15,000**

*Interpreting Diagrams* With a progressive income tax, the tax rate increases as total income increases. Today, federal income tax rates range from 10% to 39.1%. *How much would this taxpayer owe with a taxable income of $37,500, which is exactly half the income in the example?*

of the same amount for each dependent. Deductions are allowed for several things, including most medical care costs, most State and local taxes (except sales taxes), interest paid on home mortgages, and charitable contributions.

By April 15 of any given year, everyone who earned taxable income in the preceding calendar year must file a **tax return**—a declaration of that income and of the exemptions and deductions he or she claims. The returns are filed, by mail or online, with the Internal Revenue Service. The IRS now receives more than 120 million returns each year, more than 40 million of them e-filed.

President Bush urged Congress to enact major tax cuts in 2001, and it did so. Under the new law, all taxable income earned in 2001 was taxed (in 2002) at one of four rates (brackets). In the lowest bracket, the tax was 10 percent on incomes up to $12,000 for couples who filed joint returns, up to $10,000 for single parents, and up to $6,000 for other singles. Taxpayers in the highest bracket paid 39.1 percent on their taxable incomes in the $300,000 range and above.

## Customize for

### Less Proficient Readers

Bring in copies of an employee paycheck stub. Have students use it to identify each of the deductions listed. Ask them to identify each deduction as federal tax, State tax, Medicare, Social Security (OASDI), or other. In addition, have students state the type of tax each is (i.e. progressive, regressive, etc.). Students should share their answers with one another to check for accuracy.

---

### Background Note

#### Common Misconceptions

Most Americans think their taxes are too high, but few of them know exactly what their tax burden is. This is because they are more keenly aware of their income tax than they are of other taxes they pay, such as excise taxes. The Tax Foundation has developed a novel way of expressing the true tax burden. Each year, they calculate "Tax Freedom Day." Tax Freedom Day is calculated by assuming that, starting on January 1, taxpayers spend all of their earnings on taxes until their tax burden is met for the entire year. Most Americans estimate that Tax Freedom Day comes in February or March—that, after two to three months of working, they will have met their tax burden for the year. In reality, they would have to work into May: The average American spends more than one third of his or her income on taxes.

---

▲ **Social Security** If they have paid OASDI taxes for several years, Americans can retire at age 65 and receive financial support from OASDI taxes paid by people still in the work force.

Before the passage of the Tax Relief Act of 2001, the lowest tax bracket was set at 15 percent and the highest bracket at 39.6 percent. The law schedules additional rate cuts over the next several years.

Most people who pay income taxes do so through withholding, a pay-as-you-go plan. Employers are required to withhold a certain amount from each employee's paycheck and send that money to the IRS. When the employee files a tax return, he or she will receive a refund if the employer withheld more money than the employee owed in taxes. The employee must pay an additional amount if too little has been withheld. Those who earn income from sources not subject to withholding must estimate the income tax they will owe and make quarterly payments on that amount throughout the year.

### The Corporation Income Tax

Each corporation must pay a tax on its net income, that is, on all of its earnings above the costs of doing business. The corporate tax is the most complicated of all federal taxes because of the many deductions allowed. Nonprofit organizations such as churches and charitable foundations are not subject to the corporation income tax.

For 2002, the corporate tax rates ran from 15 percent on the first $50,000 of taxable earnings up to a top rate of 38 percent on taxable incomes of more than $18.33 million.

### Social Insurance Taxes

The Federal Government collects huge sums to finance three major social welfare programs: (1) the Old-Age, Survivors, and Disability Insurance (OASDI) program—the basic Social Security program, established by the Social Security Act of 1935; (2) Medicare—health care for the elderly, added to the Social Security program in 1965; and (3) the unemployment compensation program—benefits paid to jobless workers, a program also established by the Social Security Act in 1935.

OASDI and Medicare are supported by taxes imposed on nearly all employers and their employees, and on self-employed persons. These levies are often called **payroll taxes** because the amounts owed by employees are withheld from their paychecks. For 2001, employees paid an OASDI tax of 6.2 percent on the first $80,400 of their salary or wages for the year, and their employers had to match that amount. The self-employed were taxed at 12.4 percent on the first $80,400 of their income.

For Medicare, employees pay a 1.45 percent tax on their total annual income. Employers must match the amounts withheld from their employees' paychecks. The self-employed pay a 2.9 percent Medicare tax on their annual incomes.

The unemployment insurance program is a joint federal-State operation that makes payments to workers who lose their jobs for reasons beyond their control. The program now covers most workers in this country. Each State and the District of Columbia, Puerto Rico, and the Virgin Islands has its own unemployment compensation law. The amount of a worker's weekly benefits, and how many weeks they last, are determined by State law.

The unemployment compensation program is financed by both federal and State taxes. The federal tax is 6.2 percent of the first $7,000 an employer pays to each employee in a year. Each employer is given a credit of up to 5.4 percent against that tax for unemployment taxes that the employer pays to the State. So, the federal tax usually amounts to 0.8 percent on taxable wages.

Notice that social insurance taxes are **regressive taxes**. They are taxes levied at a flat rate, without regard to a taxpayer's income or ability to pay.

The IRS collects social insurance taxes. The money is credited to trust accounts maintained by the Treasury, and Congress appropriates funds for social insurance programs as needed. These funds are usually completely spent on an annual basis to help the government meet expenditures in other areas.

### Excise Taxes

An **excise tax** is a tax laid on the manufacture, sale, or consumption of goods and/or the performance of services. The Federal Government has imposed and collected excise taxes since Congress acquired its taxing power in 1789.

Today, federal excise taxes are imposed on a long list of things, including gasoline, oil, tires, tobacco, liquor, wine, beer, firearms, telephone services, airline tickets, and more. Many excise taxes are called "hidden taxes" because they are collected from producers who then figure them into the price that the retail customer finally pays. Some are called "luxury taxes" because they are imposed on goods not usually considered necessities. And some excise taxes are known as "sin taxes," particularly those laid on tobacco, beer, wine, liquor, and gambling.

### Estate and Gift Taxes

An **estate tax** is a levy imposed on the assets (the estate) of one who dies.[3] A **gift tax** is one imposed on the making of a gift by a living person. Congress first provided for the estate tax in 1916. It added the gift tax in 1932 to plug a loophole in the estate tax that allowed people to avoid the estate tax by giving away money or other property before death.

---

[3]An inheritance tax is another form of the so-called death tax. It is not levied on the entire net estate but, instead, on each portion inherited by each heir. Most States impose inheritance, not estate, taxes; most States also levy gift taxes.

[4]Since 1922, Congress has authorized the President to raise or lower any tariff by as much as 50 percent. The President can do so by an executive order, issued on the basis of recommendations made by the United States International Trade Commission, which studies the effect of tariffs and imports on the economy.

The first $1,000,000 of an estate is exempt from the federal tax. So, in fact, most estates are not subject to the federal levy. Deductions are allowed for such things as State death taxes and bequests to religious and charitable groups. Anything a husband or wife leaves to the other is taxed, if at all, only when the surviving spouse dies.

Any person may make up to $10,000 in tax-free gifts to any other person in any one year. Gifts that husbands/wives make to one another are not taxed, regardless of value.

The estate and gift taxes are separate federal taxes, but both are levied at the same rates. For 2002, those rates range from a minimum of 18 percent on an estate or a gift with a net value of less than $20,000, on up to a maximum of 50 percent on an estate or gift worth more than $3 million.

### Custom Duties

A **custom duty** is a tax laid on goods brought into the United States from abroad. Custom duties are also known as tariffs, import duties, or imposts. Congress decides which imports will be dutied and at what rates.[4] Most imports, some 30,000 different items, are dutied; but some are not—for example, Bibles, coffee, bananas, and up to $400 of a tourist's purchases abroad.

Custom duties were the major source of income for the Federal Government for more than a century. Now, they produce less than 1 percent of the money the government takes in.

▲ Duck hunters must buy a duck stamp from the Federal Government each year. The money is used for wildlife conservation programs. *Critical Thinking* **Explain why, other than to raise revenue, the Federal Government might require duck hunters to pay an annual fee.**

# Spotlight on Technology

### Magruder's American Government Video Collection

The Magruder's Video Collection explores key issues and debates in American government. Each segment examines an issue central to chapter content through use of historical and contemporary footage. Commentary from civic leaders in academics, government, and the media follow each segment. Critical-thinking questions focus students' attention on key issues, and may be used to stimulate discussion.

Use the Chapter 16 video segment to explore how taxes are conceived and collected. (time: about 5 minutes) This segment will show where specific tax revenues go and how they affect ordinary Americans. Finally, it will examine whether these taxes are fair, equitable, and justified.

**451**

## Point-of-Use Resources

**Guide to the Essentials** Chapter 16, Section 1, p. 88 provides support for students who need additional review of section content. Spanish support is available in the Spanish edition of the Guide on p. 81.

**Quiz** Unit 4 booklet, p. 34 includes matching and multiple-choice questions to check students' understanding of Section 1 content.

**Presentation Pro CD-ROM** Quizzes and multiple-choice questions check students' understanding of Section 1 content.

### Answers to . . .

### Section 1 Assessment

**1.** They are set according to how much income an individual or corporation has.

**2.** Individuals or corporations use tax returns to declare how much taxable income they have, so the government can assess how much they will pay in taxes.

**3.** Most goods that are brought into the United States from abroad.

**4.** An estate tax is levied on the estate of a person who has died, while a gift tax is levied on a gift made by a living person.

**5.** To provide a source of revenue for the Federal Government and to regulate or discharge an activity that the Federal Government finds harmful to the public.

**6.** Possible answer: Withholding year-round gives the Federal Government operating income year-round.

**7.** Answers will vary, but opinions should be supported with facts from the text.

# Taxing for Nonrevenue Purposes

Remember, the power to tax can be, and often is, used for purposes other than the raising of revenue. Usually, that other purpose is to regulate and even discourage some activity that Congress thinks is harmful or dangerous to the public.

Thus, much of the Federal Government's regulation of narcotics is based on the taxing power. Federal law provides that only those who hold a valid license may legally manufacture, sell, or otherwise deal in those drugs—and licensing is a form of taxation. The government also regulates a number of other things by licensing, including, for example, certain firearms, prospecting on public lands, and the hunting of migratory birds. The federal excise tax on gas-guzzling cars is intended to discourage their purchase.

The Supreme Court first upheld the use of the taxing power for nonrevenue purposes in *Veazie Bank* v. *Fenno* in 1869. Congress had established a national paper money system during the Civil War in 1863 to provide a single, sound currency for the country. Private bank notes, also used as paper money, soon interfered with the use of the government's new "greenbacks." So, in 1866, Congress imposed a 10 percent tax on the issuing of those private notes, and they soon disappeared. In upholding the tax, the Court declared:

 *"Having thus, in the exercise of undisputed constitutional powers, undertaken to provide a currency for the whole country, it cannot be questioned that Congress may, constitutionally, secure the benefit of it to the people by appropriate legislation."*
—*Veazie Bank* v. *Fenno,* Opinion of the Court

In 1912, Congress used its taxing power to destroy a part of the domestic match industry. It levied a tax of two cents per hundred on matches made with white or yellow phosphorus. These highly poisonous substances harmed workers who produced the matches. Matches made from other substances commonly sold for a penny a hundred. Thus, the two-cent tax drove the phosphorus matches from the market.

Congress cannot use its taxing power in any manner it wishes, however. As in all else, Congress is bound by the Constitution. Consider a 1951 tax law aimed at professional gamblers. The law imposed a $50-a-year license tax on bookies, and required them to register with and submit detailed reports to the IRS. The law did produce a small amount of income, but its real purpose was to force gamblers into the open for the benefit of State and local police. It also set a federal tax evasion trap for those who failed to comply.

The Supreme Court overturned the antigambling provisions in *Marchetti* v. *United States,* 1968. The Court did not hold that the taxes had been set for improper purposes, but that the tax, registration, and reporting provisions forced gamblers to give evidence against themselves, violating the 5th Amendment's protection against self-incrimination.

## Section 1 Assessment

**Key Terms and Main Ideas**

1. Describe how tax rates are set under a **progressive tax.**
2. What is the purpose of a **tax return?**
3. What items are subject to a **customs duty?**
4. What is the difference between a **gift tax** and an **estate tax?**

**Critical Thinking**

5. **Identifying Central Issues** List two distinct reasons why the Federal Government imposes taxes.
6. **Demonstrating Reasoned Judgment** What is one possible reason why the government asks employers to withhold tax money from each paycheck, instead of requiring taxpayers to pay a full year's taxes all at once?

7. **Expressing Problems Clearly** Some people claim that the federal income tax is a form of "forced labor" for the government. Explain the thinking behind this comparison, and why you agree or disagree.

### Take It to the Net

8. Read about the three possible options for surplus tax revenue, select one of the three different choices, and argue for or against it using examples. Use the links provided in the Social Studies area at the following Web site for help in completing this activity. www.phschool.com

### Take It to the Net

**8.** Direct students to the Social Studies area at the Prentice Hall School Web site. The *Magruder's American Government* companion Web site includes the directions and links needed to complete the activity. It also provides a printable Internet activity worksheet with scoring rubrics for assessment. Arguments should be persuasive and supported with examples.

# SKILLS FOR LIFE

# Paying Your Taxes

To some people, they are the three most dreaded letters in the English language: IRS—the Internal Revenue Service. The IRS, an agency within the Treasury Department, enforces tax laws made by Congress and collects federal income taxes.

Uncle Sam has been taking a bite out of Americans' paychecks since 1913, when the Sixteenth Amendment took effect. Every year of your working life you will probably file a federal tax return, the form on which you calculate how much tax you owe.

The federal tax system includes tax deductions for taxpayers with certain financial burdens, such as mortgages, college loans, or high medical bills. Such tax breaks can save you hundreds of dollars a year.

People in many places must pay federal, State, and local taxes. It is important, then, to prepare for tax time. For most people, these are the steps to follow:

**1. Fill out a W-4 form.** When you start a new job, the employer will give you IRS Form W-4, which you use to calculate how much of your pay you wish to have withheld for taxes. Tax laws require most people to have a certain minimum percentage withheld. At the end of the year, you figure out the amount of tax you owe. If you had too much money withheld, the Treasury gives that surplus back to you as a tax refund. If you did not have enough money withheld during the year, you must pay the balance you owe.

Fill out a W-4 and return it to your employer. If you need help, call the IRS or check out the "W-4 Calculator" on the IRS Web site.

## Tax Help

The IRS Web site is friendly and helpful, with loads of information. Try out TaxInteractive, an online information service. http://www.irs.ustreas.gov

Call the IRS toll-free at 1-800-829-1040. You can get help over the telephone, schedule an appointment, or use a walk-in service at some locations. Tax preparation services and tax accountants will prepare your tax return for a fee. They provide forms, make suggestions, and answer questions. Many will file your return for you.

**2. Collect important documents.** In January or early February you should receive IRS Form W-2, which shows the income you earned in the prior year. Employers must send out W-2s by January 31. If you have an interest-bearing account at a bank or other institution, you'll also receive a statement of interest you earned, which counts as income. Save these documents! W-2s and other documents must be attached to your tax return when you file.

**3. Calculate your taxes.** The tax "season" runs from January to April 15. During that time, you need to fill out and file your tax return. Tax forms and instruction books are free. You'll find them at post offices, public libraries, and banks. You can download forms at the IRS Web site, or get them via the IRS TaxFax Service.

Follow the directions on the forms to calculate how much tax you owe, or how much should be refunded to you. Never put false information on a tax form. If the IRS suspects you've cheated on your taxes, you'll be called in for an audit, a detailed review of your finances. Penalties for tax fraud or nonpayment are severe.

**4. Get help, if needed.** Each tax form has step-by-step instructions, but if you have questions, don't guess. Get help from one of the sources shown at left.

**5. File your tax return.** Your federal tax return must be postmarked by midnight on April 15. Late filers receive penalties and interest charges. If you prepare your return on paper, send it to an IRS Service Center listed in the instruction booklets and at the IRS Web site. To get a fast tax refund, file online. If you owe money, you can pay by check or credit card.

## Test for Success

What types of documents should you save to help you prepare your tax return?

## Point–of–Use Resources

**Skills for Life Activity** Unit 4 booklet, p. 39 provides an additional skill activity for this chapter.

**Social Studies Skills Tutor CD-ROM** Provides interactive practice in geographic literacy, critical thinking and reading, visual analysis, and communications.

## Test for Success

Answers include earnings statements, interest statements, records of charitable contributions, documents concerning real estate transactions, statements relating to Individual Retirement Accounts (IRAs), and records of out-of-pocket payments for medical, business, or child-care expenses.

## Paying Your Taxes

**Focus** Hold a "taxpayer seminar" for the class, using students as teachers, if applicable.

**Instruct** Assign a few students to gather various types of tax documents, as explained on this page. The documents are downloadable at the IRS Web site or, depending on the time of year, they may be available on paper at banks, libraries, and public offices. Find out if any students have prepared their own taxes before. If so, encourage them to conduct a brief seminar on tax preparation. Use a hypothetical teenage worker and calculate the earnings and tax for that worker using the available forms. In particular, spend some time reviewing the difference between exemptions and deductions.

**Close/Reteach** Hold a class discussion on why it is important that all citizens pay their taxes, completing the forms honestly and on time.

## Answers . . .

**1.** Review the withholding process, making sure students understand the pros and cons of having a large amount of pay withheld.
**2.** Ask for volunteers who have jobs to bring in copies (not originals) of a W-2 and interest statements, or download a sample W-2 from the IRS Web site.
**3.** You can download copies of a regular 1040 form and a 1040-EZ so students can compare the two. Most students will use the EZ form.
**4.** Remind students that tax laws change constantly, so they should always obtain an instruction book, because it contains a section on changes in tax law from the previous year. If taxpayers are not aware of changes, they may miss an opportunity to take advantage of new tax deductions.
**5.** Ask if any students have filed electronically, and find out how quickly they received a tax refund.

# ·2· Nontax Revenues and Borrowing

**Objectives** You may wish to call students' attention to the objectives in the Section Preview. The objectives are reflected in the main headings of the section.

**Bellringer** Ask students what would happen to them if, year in and year out, their spending was greater than their income, and they had to borrow more and more to pay their debts. Explain that in this section, they will learn about how the Federal Government's spending exceeded its income for many years.

**Vocabulary Builder** Ask students to name the two terms in the Political Dictionary that represent the difference between the Federal Government's income and its expenses. Have students verify their answers as they read the section.

## Pressed for Time?

### Quick Lesson Plan

**1. Focus** Tell students that government borrowing in the past two decades caused the public debt to soar. Have students discuss what they know about why the government has had to borrow money.

**2. Instruct** Ask students to name the Federal Government's largest source of nontax revenues. Then have them explain what happens when total revenues are less than total expenditures. Lead a discussion of federal borrowing and its end-product, the public debt.

**3. Close/Reteach** Remind students that in spite of increased revenues and a budget surplus in recent years, the public debt is still huge. Have students create two web diagrams, one for Nontax Revenues and one for Borrowing and Public Debt.

## Point-of-Use Resources

📁 **Lesson Plans** For lesson planning suggestions, see p. 72 of the Lesson Plans booklet.

## Section Preview

### OBJECTIVES

1. **Identify** sources of nontax revenues of the U.S. government and analyze their effect on the U.S. economy.
2. **Describe** federal borrowing.
3. **Analyze** the causes and effects of the public debt.

### WHY IT MATTERS

When the government spends more money than it takes in, it must borrow money from investors. Over time, government borrowing has created a public debt of more than $5 trillion.

### POLITICAL DICTIONARY

★ interest
★ deficit
★ surplus
★ public debt

In *Hamlet*, Shakespeare wrote: "Neither a borrower nor a lender be." That may be good advice in some situations. However, it certainly has not been followed by the government of the United States.

## Nontax Revenues

Large sums of money reach the federal treasury from a multitude of nontax sources. As the table on page 448 shows, these miscellaneous receipts now come to well over $30 billion a year.

These monies come from dozens of places. A large portion comes from the earnings of the Federal Reserve System, mostly in interest charges. **Interest** is a charge for borrowed money, generally a percentage of the amount borrowed. The interest on loans made by several other federal agencies, canal tolls, and fees for such items as passports, copyrights, patents, and trademarks also generate large sums. So do the premiums on veterans' life

► The United States Postal Service earns millions of dollars each year by selling commemorative stamps.

insurance policies, the sale or lease of public lands, the sale of surplus property, and such other items as the fines imposed by the federal courts.

The Treasury Department maintains a "conscience fund" for the several thousands of dollars a year that people send in to ease their minds over their past taxpaying mistakes. Another little-known source of nontax money is *seigniorage*—the profit the United States Mint makes in the production of coins. That profit is the difference between the value of the metals along with other costs of production and the monetary value of the minted coins. The Mint can produce a quarter for less than 25 cents and then "sell" the quarter at its face value. The difference adds up to more than $2 billion in most years.

The Philatelic Sales Branch of the United States Postal Service sells more than $100 million in mint-condition stamps to collectors each year. Stamp collectors spend untold millions more at local post offices. Most of the stamps they buy are never used on mail.

## Borrowing

Congress has the power "[t]o borrow Money on the credit of the United States" (Article I, Section 8, Clause 2). Historically, the power to borrow has been viewed as a way for the government (1) to meet the costs of short- and long-term crisis situations and (2) to finance large-scale projects that could not be paid for out of current income. For example, the Federal Government borrowed huge sums when the United States entered

## 🔲 Block Scheduling Strategies

Consider these suggestions to manage extended class time:

■ Have groups of three to four students search through magazines, newspapers, or the Internet for letters to the editors, editorials, or cartoons about the deficit or public debt. Then have each group make a presentation about what they found, drawing conclusions about how people view these topics.

■ Have students go to the Bureau of the Public Debt Web site within the Department of the Treasury site (links are provided at **www.phschool.com**). Ask them to use the "Public Debt" link to track the public debt for a week. At the end of the week, have them create a chart or graph showing how it has changed, and how it compares to prior months or years.

World War I, to combat the Great Depression of the 1930s, and again during World War II.

Over recent decades, the Federal Government has borrowed for yet another reason: deficit financing. Over those years, the government regularly spent more money than it collected in tax revenue. That is, it ran up an annual **deficit**—the yearly shortfall between income and outgo; and it borrowed heavily to make up the difference.

Indeed, the Federal Government's financial books did not show a **surplus,** more income than outgo, from 1969 until 1998.[5] The Treasury realized a surplus in the four years 1998–2001, mostly because of a robust economy in the 1990s. But an economic downturn, aggravated by the terrorist strikes of September 11, 2001, may well mean a return to deficits beginning in 2002.

Congress must authorize all federal borrowing. The borrowing itself is done by the Treasury Department, which issues various kinds of securities to investors. These investors are principally individuals and banks, investment companies, and other financial institutions. Securities usually take the form of Treasury notes or bills (T-bills) issued for short-term borrowing, or bonds for long-term purposes. They are, in effect, IOUs, promissory notes in which the government agrees to repay a certain sum, with interest, on a certain date.

The government is able to borrow money at lower rates of interest than those paid by private borrowers. This is true largely because investors can find no safer securities than those issued by the United States. If the United States could not pay its debts, no one else would be able to, either. Federal securities are also attractive because the interest they earn cannot be taxed by the States or their local governments.

## The Public Debt

Borrowing money produces a debt, of course. The public debt is the result of the Federal Government's borrowing over many years. More precisely, the **public debt** is the government's total outstanding indebtedness. It includes all of the money borrowed and not yet repaid, plus the accrued (accumulated) interest.[6]

The Federal Government has built up a huge debt over time. As you can see in the graphs on

page 456, the nation's debt more than doubled in the years 1981 through 1985 because of deficit financing. Continued deficit spending had quadrupled the debt by 1992.

The amounts involved here are absolutely mind-boggling. In 1981, when the debt was approaching $1 trillion, President Ronald Reagan said that he found "such a figure—a trillion dollars—incomprehensible." He then drew this verbal picture: "[I]f you had a stack of $1,000 bills in your hand only four inches high, you would be a millionaire. A trillion dollars would be a stack 67 miles high." Reagan's stack would have to be more than 400 miles high to equal the national debt today!

---

[5]In fact, from 1930 to 2001, the Federal Government ended only 11 fiscal years "in the black"—that is, with a surplus: fiscal years 1947, 1948, 1951, 1956, 1957, 1960, 1969, 1998, 1999, 2000, and 2001.
[6]The Treasury Department's Bureau of the Public Debt acts as the Federal Government's borrowing agent. It issues Treasury bills, notes, and bonds and manages the U.S. Savings Bond Program.

## *Voices* on Government

Economist **Alan Greenspan,** one of the most powerful voices in America, has held several government positions. Since 1987 he has been chairman of the Federal Reserve Board, which controls the country's monetary policy. In a lecture, Greenspan gave his view of the American economy:

❝ *The extraordinarily complex machine that we call the economy of the United States is, in the end, made up of human beings struggling to improve their lives. The individual values of those Americans . . . will continue to influence the structure of the institutions that support market transactions, as they have throughout our history. Without mutual trust and market participants abiding by a rule of law, no economy can prosper. Our system works fundamentally on individual fair dealing.* ❞

### Evaluating the Quotation

*How do Greenspan's thoughts about "mutual trust" and "fair dealing" apply to what you have learned about taxes in this chapter?*

## Make It Relevant

### Careers in Government—Clerk

Clerical jobs abound in American government, at every level and in every branch. Although they are not considered professional positions, government clerks do a professional job of keeping things running; without their contributions, government would grind to a halt. Advantages of working as a government clerk include job stability, opportunities to advance, and worthwhile work—every government clerk helps the country, and many help individual American citizens daily.

**Skills Activity** Have students observe work in a local government office, or in their school's administrative office, and report their experience to the class. Then have individual students write paragraphs explaining why they would or would not be interested in a career as a government clerk. **(Average)**

## Point-of-Use Resources

**Guide to the Essentials** Chapter 16, Section 2, p. 89 provides support for students who need additional review of section content. Spanish support is available in the Spanish edition of the Guide on p. 82.

**Guided Reading and Review** Unit 4 booklet, p. 35 provides students with practice identifying the main ideas and key terms of this section.

**Section Support Transparencies** Transparency 67, *Visual Learning*; Transparency 166, *Political Cartoon*

**Political Cartoons** See p. 64 of the Political Cartoons booklet for a cartoon relevant to this section.

**Quiz** Unit 4 booklet, p. 36 includes matching and multiple-choice questions to check students' understanding of Section 2 content.

**Presentation Pro CD-ROM** Quizzes and multiple-choice questions check students' understanding of Section 2 content.

## Answers to . . .

### Section 2 Assessment

**1.** Interest is a charge for the money borrowed, usually a set percentage.
**2.** It must take in more money than it spends.
**3.** A deficit is the yearly shortfall between income and spending; the public debt is the total amount of money the government owes.
**4.** While the amount of nontax revenues is much smaller than tax revenues, the Federal Government still depends on nontax sources as an important source of revenue.
**5.** From 1980 to about 1996, the debt increased sharply. Deficit spending caused the debt to rise.

### Answer to . . .

**Interpreting Graphs** Because the debt is the result of many years of borrowing with accumulated interest.

---

### Government Borrowing, 1940–2001

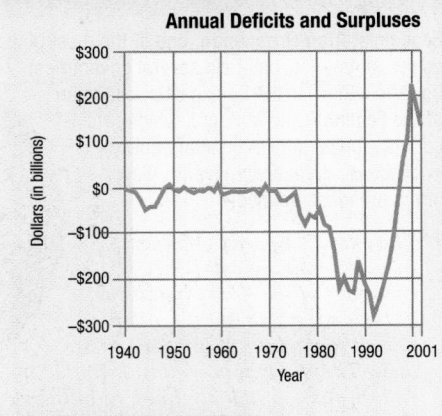

**Annual Deficits and Surpluses**

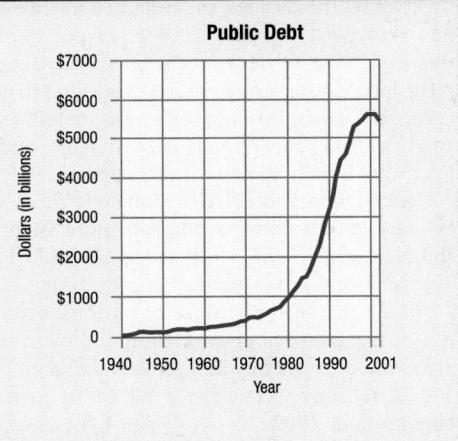

**Public Debt**

SOURCE: Office of Management and Budget

 *Interpreting Graphs* Public debt swelled with deficit spending in the 1980s and early 1990s. *Why hasn't the debt fallen as sharply as the deficit in recent years?*

There is no constitutional limit on the amount that may be borrowed, and so there is no constitutional limit on the public debt. Congress has put a statutory ceiling on the debt, but simply adjusts the ceiling upward whenever fiscal realities seem to call for it.

The debt has always been controversial, and its rapid rise in recent years has fueled the fire. The annual interest on the debt is the amount that must be paid each year to those from whom the government has borrowed. That interest came to nearly $400 billion in 2001 and will be even higher in 2002. More than one in every five dollars the Federal Government now spends goes just to service, or pay the interest on, the debt.

Most of those who are concerned about the size of the debt are worried about its impact on future generations of Americans. They say that years of short-sightedness and failure to operate government on a pay-as-you-go basis has produced huge debt and interest obligations that will have to be met by tomorrow's taxpayers.

## Section 2 Assessment

### Key Terms and Main Ideas

**1.** What is **interest,** in terms of borrowing money?
**2.** What must a government do to have a budget **surplus?**
**3.** Explain the difference between a budget **deficit** and the **public debt.**

### Critical Thinking

**4. Drawing Conclusions** Compare the government's annual nontax revenues with the annual tax revenues discussed in Section 1. How important are nontax revenues for funding the government?
**5. Drawing Inferences** Based on the graph above, which years saw the most rapid growth in the pubic debt? What events led to the increase in debt at that time?

**6. Making Decisions** Borrowing money enables the government to spend more in the present without having to make up the difference until years later. Why do you think that for many years politicians found it easier to borrow money than to cut the deficit?

 **Take It to the Net**

**7.** The current economic downturn and the war on terrorism will almost certainly have a major impact on the public debt. Write an editorial on the debt, commenting on its past, its present, and its future. Use the links provided in the Social Studies area at the following Web site for help in completing this activity. **www.phschool.com**.

**6.** Possible answer: There is no constitutional limit on borrowing and therefore it is easy to do; reaching consensus on how to cut the deficit is far more difficult.

### Take It to the Net

**7.** Direct students to the Social Studies area at the Prentice Hall School Web site. The *Magruder's American Government* companion Web site includes the directions and links needed to complete the activity. It also provides a printable Internet activity worksheet with scoring rubrics for assessment. Editorials should express a point of view and include relevant examples.

# The Meaning of a Balanced Budget

*In the late 1990s, the Federal Government ended decades of deficit spending. The President's announcement of a small budget surplus was hailed as a turning point in American government. Susan Dentzer, a commentator on* **The NewsHour With Jim Lehrer** *on PBS, suggests that the celebration of the balanced budget may be premature.*

RESUME FEDERAL OVERSPENDING!—ITS JUST A LITTLE ICE CUBE

TITANIC II

BUDGET SURPLUS

NATIONAL DEBT

*What does the cartoon suggest about those who celebrate the budget surplus?*

Although living within our means each year is a reasonable goal, we'd be even better off broadening our definition of fiscal responsibility to take into account the government's "balance sheet"—our assets and our long-term liabilities. For one thing, seeing the larger picture might minimize the temptation to propose silly steps for short-term budgetary gains. But more important, this broader look might help us focus on far tougher measures that will be needed to deal with massive liabilities in everything from nuclear-waste cleanup to Social Security. . . .

For example, take the costs we face for cleaning up radioactive waste from the production and testing of nuclear weapons. Rough estimates place these at $200 billion to $350 billion over a 75-year period. Throw in pension and other retirement benefits for the government's civilian workers and the military; as of 1995 those liabilities stood at nearly $1.6 trillion. Still other costs of an aging population weigh more heavily on the government's books. Social Security's long-term deficit over the next 75 years—what the system will pay out in benefits over and above currently projected taxes—is estimated at present at about $3 trillion. And these costs may pale beside rough estimates putting Medicare's unfunded costs at three times that level.

Only portions of these costs are captured in government budgets—for example, just one year's worth of benefits paid out and taxes paid in under Medicare. That suggests that our narrow focus on annual deficits is misguided; our broader problem is that we accumulate huge spending commitments years before the taxes come in to pay for them. . . . Since we don't focus on this "tax lag," we get budgets . . . that achieve a temporary balance on paper but neglect deeper concerns. . . .

Politicians might feel pressed to attack such problems more directly if the full scope of potential liabilities was better understood by the public. That's a key reason countries like Britain and Australia are moving to frame their budgets in similar "accrual," rather than cash-in, cash-out terms. So far, America is taking only baby steps in that direction. . . . We can only imagine what credible fiscal measures might ensue if balancing the budget yielded to a broader drive to clean up the government's balance sheet.

## Analyzing Primary Sources

1. Why does Dentzer believe that people should not focus solely on balancing the budget?
2. What future financial challenges does Dentzer foresee for the government? Why will they cause problems, according to Dentzer?
3. How does Dentzer suggest the government change its current method for calculating its finances?

 **Close Up on Primary Sources** History of the National Debt, p. 18, extends this feature with a primary source activity.

**CLOSE UP Corner**

 **Online**

To keep up-to-date on Close Up news and activities, visit Close Up Online at

**www.closeup.org**

---

## The Meaning of a Balanced Budget

**Focus** Ask students to look at the cartoon on this page and explain what it is saying about the current national debt of the United States in light of the recent budget surpluses.

**Instruct** Explain to students that in recent years some U.S. citizens have been calling for a balanced-budget amendment. Ask students to consider the proposal and create two charts, one describing the advantages of such an amendment and the other discussing the disadvantages of it. *(Advantages should include deficit reduction and increased pressure to reduce government waste. Disadvantages include reduced flexibility in meeting future public needs and the possibility that important programs will need to have their funding cut.)*

**Close/Reteach** Call on volunteers to share information from their lists. Then, as a class, debate the pros and cons of a balanced-budget amendment.

**Keep It Current CD-ROM** includes government-related projects by unit. The CD-ROM links to the Prentice Hall School Web site and may be used for daily updates.

### Answers to . . .
**Analyzing Primary Sources**
1. Dentzer believes that by only paying attention to balancing the yearly budget, the government ignores financial problems that will arise later from long-term commitments that aren't considered in yearly budgets.
2. Problems in paying for government pensions, Social Security, Medicare, and nuclear waste cleanup; because budgets only address short-term goals.
3. Dentzer suggests that the United States should frame its budgets in "accrual" rather than cash-in, cash-out terms so that it considers the scope of potential liabilities.

## 3 Spending and the Budget

## Section Preview

### OBJECTIVES

1. **Identify** the key expenditures of the U.S. government and analyze their effect on the U.S. economy.
2. **Explain** how the President and Congress work together to create the federal budget.

### WHY IT MATTERS

Federal spending has a huge effect on the economy. In the budget-making process, the President and Congress determine how the wide-ranging activities of the Federal Government will be financed.

### POLITICAL DICTIONARY

★ **entitlement**
★ **controllable spending**
★ **uncontrollable spending**
★ **continuing resolution**

The Federal Government will spend some $2 trillion in fiscal year 2002. If you placed 2 trillion dollar bills end to end, they would stretch some 175 million miles, just about the distance from Earth to the sun and back again. In this section, you will see how the government spends all that money, and how it plans for that spending through the budget process.

### Federal Expenditures

For more than half of our national history—from independence in 1776 to the mid-1930s—the Government's income and spending were so comparatively small that they had little real

▲ The government-run Food Stamp program provides coupons that recipients can exchange for food.

impact on the nation's economy. That situation changed dramatically with the coming of the Great Depression of the 1930s and then World War II in the early 1940s.

Today, the Federal Government takes tens of billions of dollars from some segments of the national economy. It then pumps those billions back into other segments of the economy—all, of course, with huge effects on the economy as a whole.

### Spending Priorities

Look at the table on page 460. As you can see, the independent Social Security Administration now spends more money than any other federal agency. Nearly all of Social Security's spending goes for OASDI (Old Age, Survivors, and Disability Insurance) benefit payments and similar entitlement programs.

**Entitlements** are benefits that federal law says must be paid to all those who meet the eligibility requirements, such as being at a certain age or income level. OASDI is the largest federal entitlement program today. Others include Medicare, Medicaid, food stamps, unemployment compensation, and veterans' pensions. The Federal Government guarantees assistance for all those who qualify. In effect, the law says that the people who receive those benefits are *entitled* (have a right) to them.

The Department of Health and Human Services will spend some $430 billion in 2002. Most of that money will pay for various welfare and public health programs. It will also

### ⬚ Block Scheduling Strategies

Consider these suggestions to manage extended class time:

■ Have small groups of students turn the figures in the Federal Spending table on p. 460 into a circle graph. (Or, ask students to create their own federal spending tables, giving them the total amounts to spend and areas on which to spend). Then present them with this challenge: A total of 10% must be cut from all federal spending. Ask them to choose how much will be cut from each department, and

then readjust their circle graphs. Call on volunteers to explain their reasoning for the specific cuts.

■ Explain to students that determining the federal budget is a continuous process. Ask students to track articles on the budgetary process for a few weeks. Have them clip the articles and add them to a portfolio. At the end of the allotted period, ask them to write summaries of the information they've tracked, and then share their portfolios with the class.

▲ The three largest categories of federal spending are entitlements, interest on the public debt, and defense. *Critical Thinking* *Which of these three categories is an example of controllable spending?*

cover the cutting-edge research projects of the National Institutes of Health and the vital work of the Centers for Disease Control and Prevention.

Interest on the public debt is now the third largest category of federal spending. Stoked by years of deficit financing, it has consumed a larger and still larger part of the federal budget over the last several years. In the table on page 460, interest on the debt is included in the Treasury Department's spending. For fiscal year 2001, that cost was nearly $390 billion.

Outlays for defense now account for a much larger share of the budget than they have over the past decade. Those expenditures came to some $281 billion in 2001. They will almost certainly top $350 billion in 2002—and they will continue to grow as the nation fights the global war on terrorism.

Note that the defense spending figures in the table are somewhat misleading. They do not include the defense-related expenditures of other federal agencies, such as the extensive nuclear weapons research and development work of the Department of Energy.

## Controllable and Uncontrollable Spending

What the Federal Government spends can be described in terms of **controllable** and **uncontrollable spending.** Most specific items in the federal budget are controllable. That is, Congress and the President decide how much will be spent each year on many of the individual expenditures the government makes. Controllable spending includes spending on environmental protection programs, military equipment, aid to education, and so on. Some people, most often economists, also use the term "discretionary spending" to describe spending on those budget items about which Congress and the President can make choices.

Much federal spending is uncontrollable, however. It is because "mandatory spending" was built into many public programs when Congress created them. The Office of Management and Budget estimates that nearly 80 percent of all federal spending falls into this category.

Take interest on the public debt as a leading example of uncontrollable spending. Paying the interest due cannot be avoided. That interest amounts to a fixed charge; once

ACTIVITY

## Extended Class Periods

**Time** 90 minutes.
**Purpose** Prepare a federal budget proposal.
**Grouping** Several groups of 3 to 4 students and 1 student acting as the President. Groups will include the OMB, the CBO, a Budget Committee, an Appropriations Committee, and Congress.
**Activity** The President, with the help of the OMB, prepares the budget and submits it to the Budget Committee. After receiving input from both the Appropriations Committee and the CBO, a spokesperson presents a budget resolution to Congress.
**Roles** Discussion leader, recorder, spokesperson.
**Close** Congress will review the proposal, make any necessary changes, and send an approved version of the budget to the President, who will make any final adjustments and present the budget to the class.

## Point-of-Use Resources

**Government Assessment Rubrics**
Cooperative Learning Project:
Product, p. 22

**Block Scheduling with Lesson Strategies** Additional activities for Chapter 16 appear on p. 27.

## Point-of-Use Resources

**Simulations and Data Graphing CD-ROM** The Federal Budget simulation lets students prepare a federal budget and submit it to Congress.

**ABC News Civics and Government Videotape Library**
*The International Monetary Fund* (time: 4 minutes, 27 seconds)

## Answer to . . .

**Interpreting Tables (a)** The Social Security Administration. **(b)** The EOP.

## Federal Spending (in billions of dollars)

| Category | 1997 | 1998 | 1999 | 2000 | 2001* | 2002* |
|---|---|---|---|---|---|---|
| Legislative Branch | $ 2.4 | $ 2.6 | $ 2.6 | $ 2.9 | $ 3.1 | $ 3.3 |
| Judicial Branch | 3.3 | 3.5 | 3.8 | 4.1 | 4.3 | 4.9 |
| Executive Office of the President | 0.2 | 0.2 | 0.4 | 0.3 | 0.3 | 0.3 |
| Department of Agriculture | 52.5 | 53.9 | 62.8 | 75.7 | 69.6 | 63.2 |
| Department of Commerce | 3.8 | 4.0 | 5.0 | 7.8 | 5.5 | 5.2 |
| Department of Defense–Military | 258.3 | 256.1 | 261.4 | 281.2 | 283.9 | 303.4 |
| Department of Defense–Other | 30.3 | 31.2 | 32.0 | 37.2 | 39.0 | 39.8 |
| Department of Education | 30.0 | 31.5 | 32.4 | 33.9 | 36.7 | 45.2 |
| Department of Energy | 14.5 | 14.4 | 16.0 | 15.0 | 16.7 | 17.2 |
| Department of Health and Human Services | 339.5 | 350.6 | 359.7 | 382.6 | 430.5 | 468.8 |
| Department of Housing and Urban Development | 27.5 | 30.2 | 32.7 | 30.8 | 37.3 | 34.8 |
| Department of the Interior | 6.8 | 7.3 | 7.8 | 8.0 | 8.7 | 9.3 |
| Department of Justice | 14.3 | 16.2 | 18.3 | 19.6 | 20.7 | 22.5 |
| Department of Labor | 30.5 | 30.0 | 32.5 | 31.4 | 38.2 | 42.0 |
| Department of State | 6.0 | 5.4 | 6.5 | 6.8 | 9.3 | 9.7 |
| Department of Transportation | 39.8 | 39.5 | 41.8 | 46.0 | 50.6 | 54.9 |
| Department of the Treasury | 379.3 | 390.1 | 386.7 | 391.2 | 388.5 | 381.5 |
| Department of Veterans Affairs | 39.3 | 41.8 | 43.2 | 47.1 | 45.2 | 51.5 |
| Environmental Protection Agency | 6.2 | 6.3 | 6.8 | 7.2 | 7.5 | 7.6 |
| National Aeronautics and Space Administration | 14.4 | 14.2 | 13.7 | 13.4 | 13.8 | 14.2 |
| Funds appropriated to the President (Mostly foreign economic/military aid) | 13.4 | 11.1 | 13.6 | 12.1 | 11.4 | 12.1 |
| Social Security Administration | 393.3 | 408.2 | 419.8 | 441.8 | 463.0 | 488.2 |
| Other | 50.7 | 65.3 | 62.6 | 69.8 | 101.6 | 120.3 |
| Deductions (undistributed offsetting receipts) | −155.0 | −161.0 | −159.1 | −172.8 | −190.2 | −201.8 |
| **Total Outlays** | **$ 1,601.3** | **$ 1,652.6** | **$ 1,703.0** | **$ 1,788.8** | **$ 1,856.2** | **$ 1,960.6** |
| Surplus (+) or Deficit (−) | −21.9 | 69.2 | 124.4 | 236.4 | 156.5 | 174.1 |

Note: Columns may not add to totals due to rounding.   *Estimated

SOURCES: Office of Management and Budget and Financial Management Service, Department of the Treasury.

*Interpreting Tables* **(a)** Which of the executive departments now spends the largest amount of money each year? **(b)** Which executive department spends the least?

the Federal Government borrows the money, the interest on that loan must be paid when it comes due and at the rate the government promised to pay.

Social Security benefits, food stamps, and most other entitlements are also largely uncontrollable. This is because once Congress has set the standards of eligibility for those programs, it has no control over how many people will meet those standards. Thus, Congress does not—really cannot—determine how many people covered by Social Security will become eligible for retirement benefits each year.

Those expenditures are not completely uncontrollable, however. Congress could redefine eligibility standards, or it could reduce the amount of money each beneficiary is to receive. But clearly those actions would be politically difficult.

In general, the percentage of federal spending that is uncontrollable has grown in recent years, while the percentage of controllable spending has decreased. These trends cause concern to politicians who are responsible for maintaining control of the budget.

## The Federal Budget

The Constitution declares that:

 " *No Money shall be drawn from the Treasury, but in Consequence of Appropriations made by Law.* . . . "

—Article I, Section 9, Clause 7

So, only Congress can provide the money upon which the Federal Government must depend. It is the President, however, who initiates the spending process by submitting a budget at the beginning of each congressional session.[7]

The federal budget is a hugely important document. It is, of course, a financial statement. As such, it is a detailed estimate, an anticipation, of federal income and outgo in the upcoming fiscal year. Yet it is much more than that. The federal budget is also a major political statement; a declaration of the public policies of the United States, with dollar signs attached. Put another way, the budget is the President's work plan for the conduct of government and the execution of public policy.

The annual budget-making process is a joint effort of the President and both houses of Congress. The President prepares the budget and submits (proposes) it to Congress soon after that body begins its annual session. Congress then reacts to the President's budget proposals, over a period of several months. It usually enacts most of those proposals, many of them in altered form, in appropriations measures.

### The President and the Budget

The process of building the budget is a lengthy one. In fact, that process begins some eighteen months before the start of the fiscal year for which the budget is intended. First, each federal agency prepares detailed estimates of its spending needs for that twelve-month period. Each agency then submits its spending plans to the Office of Management and Budget, the President's budget-making agency.

### Creating the Federal Budget

**Federal agencies** send their money requests to the Office of Management and Budget (OMB).

↓

**The OMB** reviews agency requests and melds them into the President's budget. In January or February, the President sends his budget to Congress.

↓

**Congress** reviews budget, enacts several appropriations measures.

↓

**The President** signs funding measures.

**OR**

**The President** vetoes one or more funding measures. If Congress cannot get a $\frac{2}{3}$ majority to override veto, Congress and the President must reach a compromise to resolve the dispute(s).

*Interpreting Diagrams* **When is compromise necessary to the budget process, according to the diagram?**

The OMB reviews all of the many agency proposals, often in budget hearings at which agency officials must defend their dollar requests. Following the OMB's review, revised and usually lowered spending plans for all of the agencies in the executive branch are fitted into the President's overall program. They become a part of the budget document the President sends to Capitol Hill.[8]

### Congress and the Budget

Remember that Congress depends upon and works through its standing committees. The President's budget is referred to the Budget Committee in each chamber. There, in both committees, the budget is studied and dissected with the help of the Congressional Budget Office.

The CBO is a staff agency created by Congress in 1974. It provides both houses of Congress and their committees with basic budget and economic data and analyses. The information that the CBO supplies is independent of the

---

[7]The word *budget* comes from the French *bougette,* meaning a small pouch or bag with its contents. In the eighteenth century, the budget was the bag in which the British Chancellor of the Exchequer carried financial documents.

[8]Congress enacts a separate budget for its own expenses. The spending requests for the judicial branch, prepared by the Administrative Office of the United States Courts, are included in the President's budget without OMB review.

**RESOURCE PRO®**

**Resource Pro® CD-ROM** contains an electronic version of each activity found in the Teaching Resources as well as additional resources such as Supreme Court cases. The Planning Express® feature allows you to customize and create daily lesson plans within minutes.

## Point-of-Use Resources

**Guide to the Essentials** Chapter 16, Section 3, p. 90 provides support for students who need additional review of section content. Spanish support is available in the Spanish edition of the Guide on p. 83.

**Political Cartoons** See p. 65 of the Political Cartoons booklet for a cartoon relevant to this section.

**Quiz** Unit 4 booklet, p. 38 includes matching and multiple-choice questions to check students' understanding of Section 3 content.

**Presentation Pro CD-ROM** Quizzes and multiple-choice questions check students' understanding of Section 3 content.

## Answers to . . .

### Section 3 Assessment

**1.** Entitlements are benefits that federal law says must be paid to all those who meet the eligibility requirements.
**2.** Examples may include: Military equipment, environmental protection programs, and aid to education.
**3.** A continuing resolution allows federal agencies to continue to function on the basis of previous appropriations during the time their new appropriations are being set.
**4.** Because if Congress wished to make them controllable, it could do so by changing eligibility requirements or amounts of payments.
**5.** Possible answer: The budget would be much larger, because requests are typically larger than the revised spending plans the OMB releases.
**6.** The President oversees the OMB—which reviews and revises budget proposals—and signs off on all appropriation measures. Congress holds hearings on measures, and develops and passes budget resolutions.

## Answer to . . .

**Interpreting Political Cartoons** The cartoonist implies that Social Security will run out in the near future.

**Interpreting Political Cartoons** The Social Security Administration accounts for the largest segment of the federal budget. **What is the cartoonist's view of the future of Social Security?**

information provided by the OMB, which, recall, is the President's budget agency.

The President's budget is also sent to the House and Senate Appropriations Committees.[9] Their subcommittees hold extensive hearings in which they examine agency requests, quiz agency officials, and take testimony from a wide range of interested parties. The two Appropriations Committees fashion measures that later are reported to the floor of each house. Those measures are the bills that actually appropriate the funds on which the government will operate.

---

[9]If the budget includes any tax proposals, they are referred to the House Ways and Means Committee and to the Senate's Finance Committee.

The two Budget Committees propose a concurrent resolution on the budget to their respective chambers. That measure, which must be passed by both houses by May 15, sets overall targets for federal receipts and spending in the upcoming fiscal year. The estimates are intended to guide the committees in both houses as they continue to work on the budget.

The two Budget Committees propose a second budget resolution in early September. Congress must pass that resolution by September 15, just two weeks before the beginning of the next fiscal year. The second budget resolution sets binding expenditure limits for all federal agencies in that upcoming year. No appropriations measure can provide for any spending that exceeds those limits.

Congress passes thirteen major appropriations bills each year. Recall, each of these measures must go to the White House for the President's action. Every year, Congress hopes to pass all thirteen of the appropriations measures by October 1 —that is, by the beginning of the fiscal year.

It seldom does so, however. Congress must then pass emergency spending legislation to avoid a shutdown of those agencies for which appropriations have not yet been signed into law. That legislation takes the form of a **continuing resolution.** When signed by the President, this measure allows the affected agencies to continue to function on the basis of the previous year's appropriations. Should Congress and the President fail to act, many agencies of the Federal Government would have to suspend their operations.

### Section 3 Assessment

**Key Terms and Main Ideas**

1. How are **entitlements** different from other types of benefits?
2. List two examples of **controllable spending** in the federal budget.
3. What is the purpose of a **continuing resolution**?

**Critical Thinking**

4. **Drawing Inferences** Why is the term "uncontrollable spending" not completely accurate for some entitlements?
5. **Predicting Consequences** What might happen if the OMB accepted all requests for funding without holding hearings? How would this affect the budget?

6. **Making Comparisons** What is the President's role in the budget-making process? What is the role of Congress in the budget-making process?

 **Take It to the Net**

7. Where does the money in the federal budget come from, and where does it go? Choose five items from a recent federal budget and describe how their funding affects communities like yours. Use the links provided in the Social Studies area at the following Web site for help in completing this activity. **www.phschool.com**

 **Take It to the Net**

**7.** Direct students to the Social Studies area at the Prentice Hall School Web site. The *Magruder's American Government* companion Web site includes the directions and links needed to complete the activity. It also provides a printable Internet activity worksheet with scoring rubrics for assessment. Descriptions should accurately reflect how federal spending affects individual communities.

# on the Supreme Court

# Can Federal Funds Be Used to Help Religious School Students?

*The First Amendment prohibits the government from establishing religion or interfering with the free exercise of religion. Because many students attend religious schools, States have tried to help with the secular (non-religious) parts of their education without violating the First Amendment. To what extent may government funds be used to support secular programs in religious schools?*

## Agostini v. Felton (1997)

In the 1985 case *Aguilar* v. *Felton*, the Supreme Court ruled that New York City public school teachers could not provide extra instruction to disadvantaged students at religious schools during regular school hours. Such instruction, the Court declared, violated the Establishment Clause of the First Amendment. Following that decision, the city's board of education used other methods to help religious school students, mostly by busing the students to public school buildings or other rented facilities after regular school hours.

In the years after *Aguilar*, the Supreme Court decided other cases involving government support of special education in religious schools. In *Zobrest* v. *Catalina Foothills School District* (1993), for example, the Court allowed a deaf student to bring his State-employed sign language interpreter with him to his parochial high school.

Twelve years after *Aguilar* v. *Felton*, New York City officials returned to court to ask that the decision in that case be reconsidered and reversed in light of the more-recent Supreme Court cases. The district court and court of appeals declined to do so, and the case then went to the Supreme Court.

### Arguments for Agostini

1. Government funding of secular instruction in religious schools violates the Establishment Clause by promoting religion. Because the instruction takes place in religious schools, the public school teachers might tailor their teaching to conform to the school's religious beliefs,

whether intentionally or not.
2. Government funding of secular instruction in religious schools entangles Church and State because the government has to monitor the ways in which the funds are used.

### Arguments for Felton

1. The board of education's program does not promote religion because the skills on which students will be helped are not related to students' religious beliefs or where they go to school. Therefore, recipients of aid have no incentive to change their religious beliefs or practices in order to obtain assistance.
2. The program requires only very limited government supervision of the ways in which funds are used, and thus does not result in excessive entanglement in religion.

---

### Decide for Yourself

1. Review the constitutional grounds on which each side based its arguments and the specific arguments each side presented.
2. Debate the opposing viewpoints presented in this case. Which viewpoint do you favor?
3. Predict the impact of the Court's decision on government-funded programs in religious schools. (To read a summary of the Court's decision, turn to the Supreme Court Glossary on page 799.)

---

## Corner

**Close Up on the Supreme Court** *Agostini* v. *Felton*, p. 17 provides an activity to extend coverage of this case.

To keep up-to-date on Close Up news and activities, visit Close Up Online at

**www.closeup.org**

---

**463**

## Practicing the Vocabulary

1. estate tax
2. regressive tax
3. public debt
4. entitlement
5. custom duty
6. deficit
7. continuing resolution
8. payroll tax
9. controllable spending
10. excise tax

## Reviewing Main Ideas

### Section 1

11. Taxes must be for public purposes only; export taxes are prohibited; direct taxes must be equally apportioned; and all indirect taxes must be levied at the same rates nationwide.
12. Federal taxes cannot be imposed on State governments carrying out vital government activities.
13. Income, corporate, payroll, excise, estate, and gift taxes; custom duties.
14. Regressive, because people would be paying a flat rate that does not take into account their ability to pay.
15. **(a)** The 16th Amendment gave Congress this power. **(b)** An earlier income tax law imposed the income tax according to population, which was ruled out by the 16th Amendment.

### Section 2

16. Interest, fines by courts, the "conscience fund," seigniorage, and stamps bought by stamp collectors that are not used.
17. **(a)** It can attract such investors as private individuals, banks, investment companies and other financial institutions; it can issue securities in the form of Treasury notes. **(b)** It can borrow at lower rates of interest and without taxation on the interest.
18. Historically, the Federal Government borrowed in crisis situations and to pay for particular large-scale projects; in recent decades, borrowing has been done to finance the deficit.
19. Future taxpayers will not only have the debt to pay, but the staggering amount of interest that the debt has accumulated.

## Political Dictionary

progressive tax (p. 449)
tax return (p. 449)
payroll tax (p. 450)
regressive tax (p. 451)
excise tax (p. 451)
estate tax (p. 451)

gift tax (p. 451)
custom duty (p. 451)
interest (p. 454)
deficit (p. 455)
surplus (p. 455)
public debt (p. 455)

entitlement (p. 458)
controllable spending (p. 459)
uncontrollable spending (p. 459)
continuing resolution (p. 462)

## Practicing the Vocabulary

**Matching** *Choose a term from the list above that best matches each description.*

1. Tax imposed on the assets of one who dies
2. Tax that falls most heavily on those who are least able to pay
3. The total amount of money owed by the United States, plus all interest
4. Payments that federal law says must be paid to all those who meet the eligibility requirements
5. Sometimes called tariffs, import duties, or imposts

**Fill in the Blank** *Choose a term from the list above that best completes the sentence.*

6. The Federal Government creates a budget _____ when it spends more money in one year than it takes in.
7. Congress passes a _____ to fund government agencies during long budget negotiations.
8. Employers withhold a(n) _____ from each paycheck.
9. Congress can decide how much money to spend each year on programs that are considered _____ (s).
10. The government lays a(n) _____ on the manufacture, sale, or consumption of goods.

## Reviewing Main Ideas

### Section 1

11. What are the four expressed limitations on the Federal Government's power to tax?
12. What is the implied limitation on the power to tax?
13. What are the different taxes by which the government raises revenue?
14. Are excise taxes regressive or progressive taxes? Explain your answer.
15. **(a)** How did the government gain the power to lay an income tax? **(b)** Describe how the role of the income tax in funding the government has changed since the Civil War.

### Section 2

16. List five of the nontax sources of revenue used by the Federal Government.
17. **(a)** Describe the different methods the Federal Government can use to borrow money. **(b)** What advantages does the Federal Government have when trying to borrow money from investors?

18. How does the historical use of borrowing differ from the practice of governmental borrowing in recent decades?
19. What is the significance of the public debt for future taxpayers?

### Section 3

20. How has federal spending changed over the past two centuries?
21. What is the largest item on which the Federal Government spends the money it raises?
22. **(a)** About what percentage of federal spending serves to pay interest on the national debt? **(b)** If the government enjoys a budget surplus each year, how will this percentage change in the future?
23. **(a)** What is the difference between uncontrollable and controllable spending? **(b)** About what percentage of the annual budget is controllable?
24. What are the roles of the Budget Committees and the Appropriations Committees?

### Section 3

20. Until the 1930s, spending, like income, was relatively small. Since the Great Depression and World War II, spending has increased dramatically.
21. Social Security.
22. **(a)** About 20 percent. **(b)** The percentage would stay the same, as interest on the debt remains a fixed charge.

23. **(a)** Controllable spending refers to items that Congress and the President can attach specific budgets to; uncontrollable spending refers to spending that Congress and the President have no direct control over. **(b)** About 20 percent.

24. The Appropriations Committees hold hearings on federal agencies' budget requests and then create appropriations measures; the Budget Committees propose concurrent resolutions on the budget to their respective chambers.

## Critical Thinking Skills

**25. Applying the Chapter Skill** Find a blank income tax form and review the questions asked. List ten pieces of information that a taxpayer would need to know in order to complete the form properly.

**26. Drawing Inferences** Consider the discussion of the purposes for which Congress can levy taxes. Do you think that the Framers of the Constitution intended for Congress to use its power to tax certain activities as a way of regulating or destroying those activities? Explain your answer.

**27. Making Decisions** Would you vote to amend the Constitution to require a balanced budget? Use a decision-making process to identify a situation that requires a decision, gather information, identify options, predict consequences, and take action to implement a decision.

**28. Drawing Conclusions** The text states that "the federal budget is a hugely important political document." Use evidence from the chapter to support and/or explain this statement.

## Analyzing Political Cartoons

Using your knowledge of American government and this cartoon, answer the questions below.

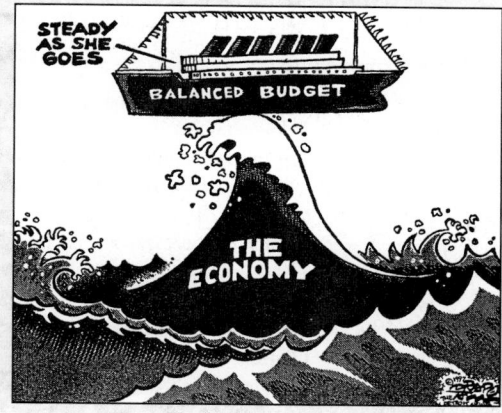

STEADY AS SHE GOES

BALANCED BUDGET

THE ECONOMY

**29. (a)** According to this cartoon, what factor has led to a balanced budget? **(b)** Based on your reading, how might this factor lead to the higher revenues and lower spending associated with a balanced budget?

**30.** Does the cartoon imply that the United States should expect a future of balanced budgets? Why or why not?

### Take It to the Net

Additional support materials and activities for Chapter 16 of *Magruder's American Government* can be found in the Social Studies area at the Prentice Hall School Web site.
**www.phschool.com**

---

### ★ You Can Make a Difference

How would you and your classmates do in the Fed Challenge? Find out in which Federal Reserve District your school is located. Then get in touch with the Bank itself or go to its Web site to find out about the coming year's Fed Challenge. Use the sample questions and topics that are supplied to conduct a mini-Fed Challenge in your class.

## Participation Activities

**31. Current Events Watch** Draw a time line showing the start and end of the next fiscal year and each month during that time period. Then use newspapers and magazines to find out which steps have already been completed in the creation of next year's federal budget. Show those steps on the time line. In the space next to the current month, tape an article that describes the current status of the budget.

**32. Graphing Activity** Choose one country from each of the following continents: Africa, Asia, Europe, and South America. Research the population, national budget, and national debt for each country and for the United States. Calculate national spending per person by dividing the national budget of each country by its population. Next, calculate the national debt per person by dividing the national debt by its population. Create a bar graph showing the population, national spending per person, and national debt per person for all five countries. Which country spends the most on each of its citizens? Which country owes the most money per person? How does the United States compare to the other countries you chose?

**33. It's Your Turn** Write a questionnaire you could use to determine people's views on federal taxes. To begin, create a list of questions that you hope will help you learn how people feel about federal taxes. Review each question to ensure that it is presented in an unbiased manner. Once you have refined your questions, reread them, correct any errors, and make a final draft. **(Writing a Questionnaire)**

### Take It to the Net

**Chapter 16 Self-Test** As a final review activity, take the Chapter 16 Self-Test in the Social Studies area at the Web site listed below, and receive immediate feedback on your answers.

**www.phschool.com**

### Point-of-Use Resources

**Guide to the Essentials of American Government** Chapter 16 Test, page 78 provides multiple-choice questions to test students' knowledge of the chapter.

**Test Bank CD-ROM** Chapter 16 Test

**Chapter Test** Chapter Tests booklet

---

## Critical Thinking Skills

**25.** Answers will vary, but should reflect an understanding of the many kinds of taxes as well as an understanding of exemptions.
**26.** Students might suggest that regulating or destroying certain activities falls within the constitutionally acceptable guideline that taxes be used to provide for the general welfare. Others might say that this use of taxation does not fit this guideline.
**27.** Answers will vary, but should demonstrate an ability to apply a decision-making process to the issue of a potential balanced budget amendment, and the possible consequences of such an amendment.
**28.** Answers should include the budget's importance as a political statement, its importance as a plan for the execution of public policy, and its relevance as a joint effort of the executive and legislative branches.

## Analyzing Political Cartoons

**29. (a)** A strong economy. **(b)** With a strong economy and high employment rate, government spending on certain programs can be reduced, bringing the budget more into balance.
**30.** It implies that the budget is rarely balanced; it may happen occasionally, but cannot really be planned.

## You Can Make a Difference

You might want to have different classes conduct their own Fed Challenges, and then compare their results.

## Participation Activities

**31.** Time lines should be clearly drawn, and reflect an understanding of the process of determining the federal budget.
**32.** Graphs should be clear and appropriately labeled; calculations and comparisons should be accurately tabulated.
**33.** Questions should be objective and touch on several of the issues in the text concerning federal taxes.

# Foreign Policy and National Defense

| Section Objectives | Print and Technology Resources |
|---|---|
| **1 Foreign Affairs and National Security**<br>(pp. 468–475)<br><br>1. Identify the difference between isolationism and internationalism.<br>2. Explain the major responsibilities of the Federal Government for foreign policy.<br>3. Explain the functions, components, and organization of the Department of State, the Department of Defense, and the military departments.<br><br>🏴 TEKS 2B, 7B, 8B, 9B, 9G, 21A, 21C, 21D, 21E, 22A, 22B | • **Unit 4 booklet**<br>Guided Reading and Review, p. 40<br>Section 1 Quiz, p. 41<br>• **Lesson Plans booklet** Section 1, p. 74<br>• **Political Cartoons booklet** Section 1, p. 66<br>• **Block Scheduling with Lesson Strategies booklet** p. 27<br>• **Section Reading Support Transparencies**<br><br>• **Close Up on Primary Sources booklet**<br>The Role of Congress in Foreign Policy, p. 19<br>• **The Living Constitution booklet** p. 5<br>• **Simulations and Debates booklet** pp. 39–41<br>• **Section Support Transparencies** 69, 168<br>• **Presentation Pro CD-ROM** Section 1 |
| **2 Other Foreign and Defense Agencies**<br>(pp. 477–480)<br><br>1. Describe the number of government agencies, besides the Departments of State and Defense, that are involved in foreign and defense policy.<br>2. Explain how the CIA, NASA, and the Selective Service System contribute to the nation's security.<br>3. Explore how the INS affects our relations with other nations and their citizens.<br><br>🏴 TEKS 9D, 9G, 17C, 21A, 21C, 21D, 22A, 22B, 22D, 23A | • **Unit 4 booklet**<br>Guided Reading and Review, p. 42<br>Section 2 Quiz, p. 43<br>• **Lesson Plans booklet** Section 2, p. 75<br>• **Political Cartoons booklet** Section 2, p. 67<br>• **Section Reading Support Transparencies**<br><br>• **Basic Principles of the Constitution Transparencies** 27<br>• **Section Support Transparencies** 70, 169<br>• **Presentation Pro CD-ROM** Section 2 |
| **3 American Foreign Policy Overview**<br>(pp. 481–489)<br><br>1. Summarize American foreign policy from independence through World War I.<br>2. Show how the two World Wars affected America's traditional policy of isolationism.<br>3. Explain the principles of collective security and deterrence.<br>4. Examine the United States policy of resisting Soviet aggression during the cold war.<br>5. Describe American foreign policy since the end of the cold war.<br><br>🏴 TEKS 4A, 4B, 9B, 9G, 16D, 21A, 21D, 21E, 22A, 22B, 22C, 22D | • **Unit 4 booklet**<br>Guided Reading and Review, p. 44<br>Section 3 Quiz, p. 45<br>• **Lesson Plans booklet** Section 3, p. 76<br>• **Political Cartoons booklet** Section 3, p. 68<br>• **Block Scheduling with Lesson Strategies booklet** p. 27<br>• **Close Up on Primary Sources booklet**<br>The Roosevelt Corollary to the Monroe Doctrine, p. 41; Franklin D. Roosevelt's "Four Freedoms" Speech, p. 42; George Bush on the Fall of the Berlin Wall, p. 50<br><br>• **Section Reading Support Transparencies**<br>• **The Living Constitution booklet** p. 3<br>• **Government Assessment Rubrics booklet** p. 22<br>• **Section Support Transparencies** 71, 170<br>• **Presentation Pro CD-ROM** Section 3<br>• **Simulations and Data Graphing CD-ROM**<br>• **Social Studies Skills Tutor CD-ROM** |
| **4 Foreign Aid and Defense Alliances**<br>(pp. 491–498)<br><br>1. Identify the two types of foreign aid and describe United States foreign aid policy.<br>2. Describe the major security alliances to which the United States belongs.<br>3. Summarize United States policy in the Middle East.<br>4. Examine the role, structure, and problems that face the United Nations.<br><br>🏴 TEKS 4A, 4B, 9G, 17C, 21A, 21C, 21D, 21E, 21F, 22A, 22B, 22C | • **Unit 4 booklet**<br>Guided Reading and Review, p. 46<br>Section 4 Quiz, p. 47<br>Skills for Life Activity, p. 48<br>• **Lesson Plans booklet** Section 4, p. 77<br>• **Political Cartoons booklet** Section 4, p. 69<br>• **Close Up on the Supreme Court booklet** *Rostker* v. *Goldberg*, p. 18<br><br>• **Close Up on Participation booklet**<br>Reducing Conflict, pp. 22–23<br>• **The Basic Principles of the Constitution Posters**<br>• **Section Support Transparencies** 72, 171<br>• **Presentation Pro CD-ROM** Section 4<br>• **Section Reading Support Transparencies** |

# Block Scheduling Strategies

The *Magruder's American Government* program addresses block-scheduling strategies in a variety of ways. For easy reference, side-column activities that fit a block format are marked ■ **Block Strategy.** Each section also contains a **Block Scheduling Strategies** box describing at least two block-format activities that address and extend core content from the section. The **Block Scheduling with Lesson Strategies booklet** found in the Teaching Resources contains additional block-scheduling activities for each chapter.

## Take It to the Net

Visit the Social Studies area at the Prentice Hall School Web site. Once there, you can find additional links, current events connections, and activities to enrich chapter content for *Magruder's American Government,* as well as a Self-Test for students. Be sure to check out this month's **eTeach** online discussion with a Master Teacher.

### www.phschool.com

## Pressed for Time?

If you are running short on time to cover this chapter, consider one of the following options:

- Use the **Presentation Pro CD-ROM** to create an outline for this chapter.
- Use one of the **Pressed for Time** activities found on p. 27.
- Use the Section Summaries for Chapter 2, from **Guide to the Essentials of American Government (English and Spanish).**

## Video Connections

Prentice Hall offers two video programs to reinforce and extend chapter content. Show students *The Blessings of Liberty* from the **ABC News Civics and Government Videotape Library** and *Prayer in Schools: A Nationwide Debate* from the **Magruder's American Government Video Collection.**

## Assessment Options

- Section Quizzes, **Unit 4 booklet,** pp. 41, 43, 45, 47
- Chapter 17 Assessment, pp. 500–501
- **Guide to the Essentials of American Government,** Chapter 17 Test, p. 96

### Core Assessment

Chapter 17 Test, Chapter Tests booklet
ExamView® Test Bank CD-ROM Chapter 17
Government Assessment Rubrics

### Standardized Test Preparation

#### Diagnose and Prescribe
Diagnostic Tests for High School
Social Studies Skills

#### Review and Reteach
Review Book for Government

#### Practice and Assess
Test-Taking Strategies With
    Transparencies for High School
Test Prep Book for Government

# Chapter 17 Teacher's Edition Index

## Foreign Policy and National Defense

### Introducing the Chapter

In this chapter, students will learn about the shaping and enacting of United States foreign policy, the organizations involved with American national defense, and the United States' role in foreign aid and defense alliances.

### Make It Relevant

#### ★ You Can Make a Difference

Have students identify a current foreign policy issue of importance, and then organize a panel discussion on the issue. The discussion should consist of presentations (background, options, consequences, etc.) and debate among the speakers. Students should research, prepare, rehearse, and then present their discussion to an appropriate school or community audience. Students should encourage their audience to ask questions or make comments.

**Service Learning**

### CONSTITUTIONAL PRINCIPLES

Emphasize the following basic principles as students read Chapter 17. Have the class respond to the questions, and then ask volunteers to brainstorm principles that guide nations' relations with one another in the "global village" that the text describes.

**Separation of Powers** How does the Constitution ensure that the military cannot be too powerful?

**Popular Sovereignty** In what ways can people's opinions bring about change in foreign policy?

# Foreign Policy and National Defense

*"A successful foreign policy in a nation where informed citizens have a free vote must be based on a public consensus."*

—Millicent Fenwick (1975)

American foreign policy guides all our dealings with the rest of the world—international trade, immigration, treaties, foreign aid, and defense. Civilian control over defense policy determines the role of the military in protecting national security.

◆ In the aftermath of the 2001 terrorist attacks, Americans show patriotism and a united front to the world.

 *Corner*

The following resources are available only from the Close Up Foundation to support the concepts discussed in Chapter 17 "Foreign Policy and National Defense":

◆ *International Relations: Understanding the Behavior of Nations*
◆ *The United Nations at Work*
◆ *U.S. Response: The Making of U.S. Foreign Policy*

To keep up-to-date on Close Up news and activities, visit Close Up Online at

**www.closeup.org**

Close Up Foundation
44 Canal Center Plaza
Alexandria, VA 22314-1592
800-765-3131

### ★ You Can Make a Difference

**COULD YOU NEGOTIATE** an international treaty? Debate about problems in Latin America? High school students who attend the Fulbright School of Public Affairs get a taste for diplomacy and learn about the complexities of world politics. In an intensive three-week session at the University of Arkansas (Fayetteville), students debate international issues, meet and question politicians about current events, and present their own ideas and proposals. One Fulbright student, Nicholas Norfolk, explained, "I'm so used to being in the United States that I forget how many problems other countries have and how come it's so hard for them to solve them. . . ."

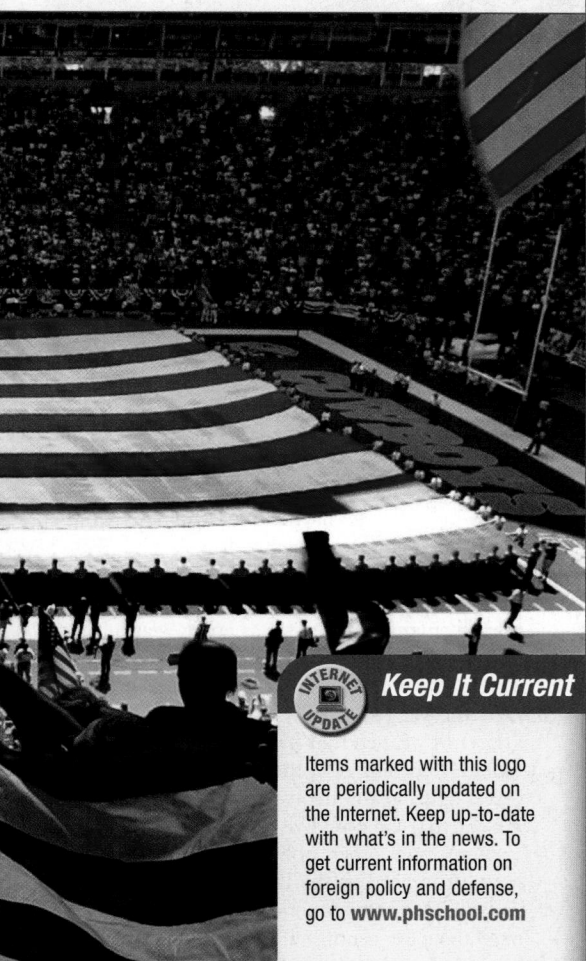

### Keep It Current

Items marked with this logo are periodically updated on the Internet. Keep up-to-date with what's in the news. To get current information on foreign policy and defense, go to **www.phschool.com**

---

#### SECTION 1
### Foreign Affairs and National Security
(pp. 468–475)

★ Foreign policy is all the actions and stands that a nation takes in its relations with other nations.

★ With World War II, the United States abandoned isolationism and became a full participant in world affairs.

★ The State Department, headed by the secretary of state, advises the President on foreign policy matters and carries out his policies through its diplomats abroad.

★ The secretary of defense is the President's chief aide and advisor on military matters and the head of the Defense Department.

#### SECTION 2
### Other Foreign and Defense Agencies
(pp. 477–480)

★ The CIA conducts worldwide intelligence operations.

★ The Office of Homeland Security is charged with protecting the nation against terrorist activities.

★ NASA runs the nation's space program. The Selective Service System is on standby.

#### SECTION 3
### American Foreign Policy Overview (pp. 481–489)

★ The Monroe Doctrine and Manifest Destiny shaped American foreign policy through World War I. During that time, the nation expanded and became a colonial power.

★ The two world wars ended America's traditional policy of isolationism and led to a policy of internationalism.

★ Victory in World War II made the United States one of two world superpowers, and led to the policies of collective security and deterrence.

★ U.S. policy during the cold war focused on resisting Soviet aggression through containment.

★ Although the cold war has ended, the world is still a dangerous place requiring continued vigilance.

#### SECTION 4
### Foreign Aid and Defense Alliances (pp. 491–498)

★ Both economic and military foreign aid are usually sent to countries regarded as most critical to this country's interests.

★ The United States belongs to a number of regional security alliances of which NATO is the most important.

★ Although the United States has no alliances in the Middle East, American administrations have worked hard to promote peace in this important region.

★ The purpose of the United Nations is to promote peace among nations, and to improve living conditions around the world.

---

### Keep It Current

### Internet Update

Use the Prentice Hall School Web site and the Keep It Current CD-ROM to find quick content updates.

Visit **www.phschool.com** for current events articles that are linked to Chapter 17. Critical thinking questions are included.

**Keep It Current CD-ROM** includes government-related projects by unit. Students complete each project using current information that they obtain by linking to the Prentice Hall School Web site from the CD-ROM.

---

### Pressed for Time?

#### To Omit the Chapter
If you wish to skip Chapter 17, ask students to read the Chapter in Brief and assign the Guide to the Essentials before continuing to another chapter. You may also want to assign the Chapter 17 Test in the Chapter Test booklet. Then specific portions of Chapter 17 may be assigned to students needing reinforcement of key terms and concepts.

#### To Preview the Chapter
To introduce students to key terms and concepts in each section, have them read the Chapter in Brief. You may also assign the Reading Strategy activities on pp. 469, 478, 482, and 492 of this book.

#### To Review the Chapter
When students have completed Chapter 17, you might want to assign the Guide to the Essentials or the Guided Reading and Review worksheets on pp. 40, 42, 44, and 46 of the Unit 4 booklet.

#### To Cover the Chapter Quickly
To cover the material in Chapter 17 quickly, use the following activity.

**Focus** Ask students to name all of the major players—individuals and government units—who have a role in shaping and carrying out foreign policy. Then describe the various roles of the Defense Department, the Office of Homeland Security, the CIA, and NASA.

**Instruct** Explain that foreign policy has become increasingly international. Briefly summarize each major war, the cold war, and important foreign policies of the last 150 years. Have students consider the change in American foreign policy from isolationist to internationalist. Ask why this change has occurred.

**Close/Reteach** Discuss the role of the United Nations. Explain the United States' involvement in NATO, and its participation in foreign aid and humanitarian efforts abroad. Explain the role of NATO in combating terrorism.

■ **Block Strategy (Average)**

## 1 Foreign Affairs and National Security

**Objectives** You may wish to call students' attention to the objectives in the Section Preview. The objectives are reflected in the main headings of the section.

**Bellringer** Ask students whether there are days that they would prefer just to stay at home, alone, and not take part in the outside world. Explain that in this section, students will learn about how the United States "stayed at home" for many years, avoiding relationships with other nations.

**Vocabulary Builder** Ask students which term in the Political Dictionary names a policy that the United States followed for more than 150 years. *(isolationism)* Discuss how the *-ism* ending adds meaning to the base word. (The suffix means "the practice of" or "a doctrine of.").

---

### Pressed for Time?

## Quick Lesson Plan

**1. Focus** Tell students that the President has the main responsibility for shaping United States policy toward other nations. Ask them to discuss what they know about the role of executive departments in making and carrying out foreign policy.

**2. Instruct** Ask students to explain what makes up a nation's foreign policy. Then have them discuss the role of the State Department and the Defense Department in United States foreign policy.

**3. Close/Reteach** Remind students that the President and other civilian authorities control the nation's military. Ask students to make a flowchart showing who has important power in the area of foreign policy and how that power is distributed.

---

## Point-of-Use Resources

📁 **Block Scheduling with Lesson Strategies** Activities for Chapter 17 are presented on p. 27.

---

## Section Preview

### OBJECTIVES

1. **Identify** the difference between isolationism and internationalism.
2. **Explain** the major responsibilities of the Federal Government for foreign policy.
3. **Explain** the functions, components, and organization of the Department of State, the Department of Defense, and the military departments.

### WHY IT MATTERS

Foreign policy includes all the stands and actions a nation takes in its relationships with other nations. The State Department carries out the President's diplomatic policies. The armed forces provide the nation's defense, but are under civilian control of the President.

### POLITICAL DICTIONARY

★ domestic affairs
★ foreign affairs
★ isolationism
★ foreign policy
★ right of legation
★ ambassador
★ diplomatic immunity

---

In *The Federalist* No. 72, Alexander Hamilton noted that the "actual conduct" of America's foreign affairs would be in the hands of "the assistants or deputies of the chief magistrate," the President. Today, most of the President's "assistants or deputies" in foreign affairs are in the State Department. Presidential aides in the closely related field of military affairs are located in the Department of Defense.

Foreign affairs have been of prime importance from the nation's very beginnings, more than a dozen years before Hamilton penned his comment in *The Federalist*. Indeed, it is important to remember that the United States would have been hard pressed to win its independence without the aid of its ally, France.

## Isolationism to Internationalism

With the coming of independence, and then for more than 150 years, the American people were chiefly concerned with **domestic affairs**—with events at home. **Foreign affairs**, the nation's relationships with other nations, were of little or no concern to them. Through that period, America's foreign relations were very largely shaped by a policy of **isolationism**—a purposeful refusal to become generally involved in the affairs of the rest of the world.

The past 60 years have been marked by a profound change in the place of the United States in world affairs, however. World War II finally convinced the American people that neither they nor anyone else can live in isolation—that, in many ways, and whether we like it or not, the world of today is indeed "one world." The well-being of everyone in this country—in fact, the very survival of the United States—is affected by much that happens elsewhere on the globe. If nothing else, the realities of ultra-rapid travel and instantaneous communications make it clear that we now live in a "global village."

Wars and other political upheavals abroad have an impact on the United States and on the daily lives of the American people. Four times over the past century the United States fought

▲ Benjamin Franklin (center), the first American diplomat, is received at the French court in 1778. Louis XVI and Marie Antoinette are seated at right.

---

## 🔲 Block Scheduling Strategies

Consider these suggestions to manage extended class time:

■ Ask students to monitor the news for several days, looking for articles or stories on foreign policy. Then have each student give a brief presentation to the class titled "Foreign Policy for the Week of …" Encourage students to include visuals in their presentations.

■ Divide students into small groups, assigning each either the State Department or Department of Defense. Assign each student one of the organizations or key people from each department. Students should prepare brief descriptions of their roles, or short skits. Have students read their descriptions or enact their skits, and then have the class guess which person or organization they are portraying.

major wars abroad; and in several other instances the nation committed its armed forces to lesser, but significant, foreign conflicts. The nation's security has also been threatened by terrorists in Europe and Asia, as well as at home, by racial strife in southern Africa, by Arab-Israeli conflicts in the Middle East, and by other events in many other places around the globe.

Economic conditions elsewhere also have a direct effect on and in this country. Japanese automobiles, European steel, oil from the Middle East, coffee from Brazil, Italian shoes, and expanding trade with China underscore the fact that every day Americans buy from other countries. American companies also sell their products in foreign markets, and often manufacture them abroad, as well. The American economy has become part of a truly global economy, linked by international banking, multinational corporations, and worldwide investments that transcend national boundaries.

Clearly, today's world cannot be described as "one world" in all respects, however. It remains, in many ways, a very fractured and dangerous place. Acts of international terrorism; civil wars in Sri Lanka, Colombia, Morocco, and the Congo; unrest in what was once the Soviet Union; drug cartels in Latin America and in Southeast Asia; the behavior of Iraq and other "rogue states"; the emerging dangers of chemical and of biological weapons—all of this, and more, make the point abundantly clear. In the interconnected yet divided world of today, only those polices that protect and promote the security of *all* nations can assure the security and the well-being of the United States.

## Conducting Foreign Policy

Every nation's **foreign policy** is actually many different policies on many different topics. It is made up of all of the stands and actions that a nation takes in every aspect of its relationships with other countries—diplomatic, military, commercial, and all others. To put the point another way, a nation's foreign policy is made up of all of its many foreign policies. In short, it includes everything that that nation's government says and everything that it does in world affairs.

Thus, American foreign policy consists of all of the Federal Government's official statements

▲ *Secretary of State* Diplomats meet with foreign leaders to negotiate treaties, discuss world problems, and promote national policies. Here, Secretary of State Colin Powell shakes hands with Chinese Vice Premier Qian Qichen (left).

and all of its actions as it conducts this nation's foreign relations. It involves treaties and alliances, international trade, the defense budget, foreign economic and military aid, the United Nations, nuclear weapons testing, and disarmament negotiations. It also includes the American position on oil imports, grain exports, immigration, space exploration, fishing rights in the Atlantic and Pacific oceans, cultural exchange programs, economic sanctions, computer technology exports, and a great many other matters.

Some aspects of foreign policy remain largely unchanged over time. For example, an insistence on freedom of the seas has been a basic part of American policy from the nation's beginnings. Other policies are more flexible. Only a few years ago, resisting the ambitions of the Soviet Union was a basic part of American foreign policy. Today, the United States and much of the former Soviet Union are seeking closer political, military, and economic ties.

The President is both the nation's chief diplomat and the commander in chief of its armed forces. Constitutionally and by tradition, the President bears the major responsibility for both the making and the conduct of foreign policy. The President depends on a number of officials and agencies—Hamilton's "assistants or deputies"—to meet the immense responsibilities that come with this dual role.

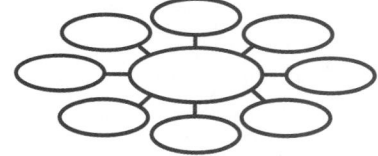

## ACTIVITY

### American Government, American Humor

Share the following quotation with students:

*"I have made more friends for American culture than the State Department. Certainly I have made fewer enemies, but that isn't very difficult."*

—Arthur Miller

**Discussion** Ask students what Miller meant by his remark. Ask: What foreign policies might it be applied to today, and historically? How does his comment embody a goal of American foreign policy?

**(Challenging)**

## Voices on Government

**Condoleezza Rice** was named National Security Advisor by President George W. Bush in 2001. During the administration of George H. W. Bush, she helped bring democratic reforms to Poland and played a vital role in crafting many of the Bush administration's policies with the former Soviet Union. In a speech regarding national security challenges for the George W. Bush administration, she had this to say:

❝ *Our interests and our values have to go hand in hand. In fact, our interests are reinforced by our values and vice versa. There is no doubt that American interests are better advanced today in a world in which more countries share our values of individual liberty, of freedom of the press, of human rights, and of human dignity.* ❞

### Evaluating the Quotation

*State in your own words what Rice means when she says, "Our interests and our values have to go hand in hand." In what circumstances might a nation's interests and values not go hand in hand?*

## The State Department

The State Department, headed by the secretary of state, is the President's right arm in foreign affairs. The President names the secretary of state, subject to confirmation by the Senate. It is to the secretary of state and to the Department of State that the President looks for advice on both the formulation and the conduct of the nation's foreign policy.

### The Secretary of State

The secretary of state ranks first among the members of the President's Cabinet. This ranking is because of the importance of the office, but also because the State Department was the first of the now 14 executive departments to be created by Congress.

The Department of Foreign Affairs had first been created in 1781 under the Articles of Confederation. It was re-created by Congress in 1789 as the first major unit in the executive branch under the Constitution. Later that year, its name was changed to the Department of State.

President Washington appointed Thomas Jefferson as the nation's first secretary of state. The first woman to hold the post, Madeleine Albright, was appointed by President Clinton in 1997. Colin Powell, secretary of state under President George W. Bush, is the first African American to hold the office. Today, the duties of the secretary relate almost solely to foreign affairs: to the making and conduct of policy and to managing the work of the department, its many overseas posts, and some 25,000 employees.[1]

Some Presidents have relied heavily on the secretary of state; others have chosen to keep foreign policy more tightly in their own hands. In either case, the secretary has been an important and influential officer in every administration.

### Organization and Components

The Department of State is organized along both geographic and functional lines. Some of its agencies, such as the Bureau of African Affairs and the Bureau of Near East Affairs, deal with matters involving particular regions of the world.

Other agencies have more broadly defined responsibilities, such as the Bureau of Arms Control and the Bureau for Political–Military Affairs. Most bureaus are headed by an assistant secretary and include several "offices." For example, both the Office of Passport Services and the Office of Visa Services are found in the Bureau of Consular Affairs.

### The Foreign Service

Some 6,000 men and women now represent the United States abroad as members of the Foreign Service. Under international law every nation has the **right of legation**—the right to send and receive diplomatic representatives.[2] The right of

---

[1]The secretary does have some domestic responsibilities. Thus, when Richard Nixon resigned the presidency on August 9, 1974, his formal, legal announcement of that fact had to be submitted to Secretary of State Henry Kissinger. Over the years, the secretary and the department have had (and been relieved of) various domestic functions—including publishing the nation's laws, issuing patents, and supervising the decennial census.

[2]International law consists of those rules and principles that guide sovereign states in their dealings with one another and in their treatment of foreign nationals (private persons and groups). Its sources include treaties, decisions of international courts, and custom. Treaties are the most important source today.

## Answer to . . .

**Evaluating the Quotation** Students should explain that the nation must not undermine its own values when pursuing its interests. For example, a financial interest in opening trade with another nation should not conflict with a stated commitment to human rights.

legation is an ancient practice. Its history can be traced back to the Egyptian civilization of 6,000 years ago.

The Second Continental Congress named this nation's first foreign service officer in 1778. That year, it chose Benjamin Franklin to be America's minister to France.

## Ambassadors

An **ambassador** is an official representative of the United States appointed by the President to represent the nation in matters of diplomacy. Today, the United States is represented by an ambassador stationed at the capital of each state the United States recognizes.[3] American embassies are found in more than 160 countries around the world today.

The United States also has some 120 consular offices abroad. There, Foreign Service officers promote American interests in a multitude of ways, such as encouraging trade, gathering intelligence data, advising persons who seek to enter this country, and aiding American citizens who are abroad and in need of legal advice or other help.

Some ambassadorships are much desired political plums. Too often, Presidents have appointed people to ambassadorships and other major diplomatic posts as a reward for their support—financial and otherwise—of the President's election to office.

President Truman named the first woman as an ambassador, to Denmark, in 1949. President Johnson appointed the first African American (also a woman), as ambassador to Luxembourg in 1965. Today, several women, African Americans, and other minority persons hold high rank in the Foreign Service.

## Special Diplomats

Those persons whom the President names to certain other top diplomatic posts also carry the rank of ambassador—for example, the United States representative to the UN and the American member of the North Atlantic Treaty Council.

---

[3]See page 400. An ambassador's official title is Ambassador Extraordinary and Plenipotentiary. When the office is vacant or the ambassador is absent, the post is usually filled by a next-ranking Foreign Service officer in the embassy. That officer, temporarily in charge of embassy affairs, is known as the chargé d'affaires.

▲ *From Here to There* Americans usually need passports to travel abroad. Nepal, shown here, is one nation that requires foreign visitors to have visas.

The President also gives the personal rank of ambassador to those diplomats who take on special assignments abroad, such as representing the United States at an international conference on arms limitations.

## Passports

A passport is a certificate issued by a government to its citizens who travel or live abroad. Passports entitle their holders to the privileges accorded to them by international custom and treaties. Few countries will admit persons who do not hold valid passports. Legally, no American citizen may leave the United States without a passport, except for trips to Canada, Mexico, and a few other nearby places.

The State Department's Passport Office now issues some six million passports to American citizens each year. Passports are not the same as visas. A visa is a permit to enter another state and must be obtained from the country one wishes to enter. Trips to most foreign countries require visas. Most visas to enter this country are issued at American consulates abroad.

## Diplomatic Immunity

In international law, every sovereign state is supreme within its own boundaries. All persons or things found within the state's territory are subject to its jurisdiction.

As a major exception to that rule, ambassadors are regularly granted **diplomatic immunity.**

## Background Note

### Common Misconceptions

Surprising to most Americans is the fact that the United States did not have ambassadors for nearly half of its history. True, the Constitution called for the establishment of embassies abroad, and the United States did in fact send representatives to many countries. But these were minister or consulate officials, not ambassadors. The first ambassador wasn't appointed until 1893, by President Grover Cleveland. Why the delay? Ambassadors in the early years of the country were associated with monarchies, and anything viewed as a tool of a monarchy was one thing the United States understandably tried to stay far away from.

## Point-of-Use Resources

**Simulations and Debates** National Security Council, pp. 39–41 provides students with a simulation of a NSC meeting.

## Background Note

### Political Talk

When the rights of U.S. citizens in foreign countries are violated without reason, the U.S. Government will intervene on the citizens' behalf. But most citizens do not get the kind of personal treatment from the President that Theodore Roosevelt delivered in one memorable case in 1904. Roosevelt authorized then Secretary of State Hay to send a rather undiplomatic message via telegram to Morocco, where one Ahmed ibn-Muhammed Raisuli had kidnapped a Greek-born United States citizen, Ion Perdicaris, and his British stepson. The message was brief: "We want Perdicaris alive or Raisuli dead." Perdicaris and his stepson were freed, unharmed.

## ACTIVITY

### Heterogeneous Groups

**Reteaching** Divide the class into small groups. Have each group create a chart that identifies the key members of the State Department and the Department of Defense, and describes the responsibilities of these members. Students should include the secretaries of each department and their principal deputies, as well as members of the Foreign Service, ambassadors, special diplomats, chief military aides, and members of the military departments. Encourage groups to include significant statistics when possible, such as the number of men and women participating in the various departments. **(Average)**

## Point-of-Use Resources

📁 **The Living Constitution**
Separation of Powers, p. 5

🏛 **Basic Principles of the Constitution Transparencies** Transparencies 23-29, *Separation of Powers*

### Answer to . . .

**Interpreting Charts** The Secretary of Defense and the Chairman of the Joint Chiefs of Staff.

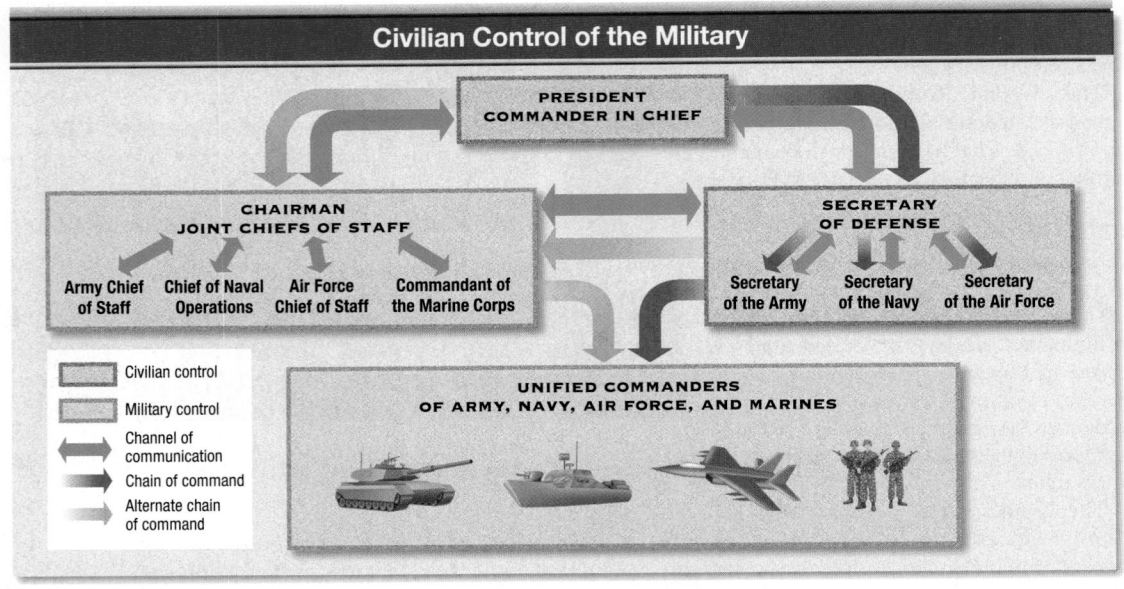

**Civilian Control of the Military**

PRESIDENT COMMANDER IN CHIEF

CHAIRMAN JOINT CHIEFS OF STAFF

Army Chief of Staff · Chief of Naval Operations · Air Force Chief of Staff · Commandant of the Marine Corps

SECRETARY OF DEFENSE

Secretary of the Army · Secretary of the Navy · Secretary of the Air Force

Civilian control
Military control
Channel of communication
Chain of command
Alternate chain of command

UNIFIED COMMANDERS OF ARMY, NAVY, AIR FORCE, AND MARINES

*Interpreting Charts* This chart shows the chain of command of the American military services. **Who advises the President on military matters?**

That is, they are not subject to the laws of the state to which they are accredited. They cannot be arrested, sued, or taxed. Their official residences (embassies) cannot be entered or searched without their consent, and their official communications, papers, and other properties are protected. All other embassy personnel and their families normally receive this same immunity.

Diplomatic immunity is essential to the ability of every nation to conduct its foreign relations. The practice assumes that diplomats will not abuse their privileged status. If a host government finds a diplomat's conduct unacceptable, that official may be declared *persona non grata* and expelled from the country. The mistreatment of diplomats is considered a major breach of international law.

Diplomatic immunity is a generally accepted practice. There are exceptions, however. The most serious breach in modern times occurred in Iran in late 1979. Militant followers of the Ayatollah Khomeini seized the American embassy in Teheran on November 4 of that year; 53 Americans were taken hostage and held for 444 days. The Iranians finally released the hostages moments after Ronald Reagan became President on January 20, 1981.

## The Defense Department

Congress established what is today called the Department of Defense in the National Security Act of 1947. It is the present-day successor to two historic Cabinet-level agencies: the War Department, created by Congress in 1789, and the Navy Department, created in 1798.

Congress created the Defense Department in order to unify the nation's armed forces. It wished to bring the then-separate army (including the air force) and the navy under the control of a single Cabinet department. Today, there are more than 1.4 million men and women in uniform, and nearly 700,000 civilians also work for the Defense Department.

### Civil Control of the Military

The authors of the Constitution understood the importance of the nation's defense. They emphasized that fact clearly in the Preamble, and they underscored it in the body of the Constitution by mentioning defense more frequently than any other governmental function.

The Framers also recognized the dangers inherent in military power. They knew that its very existence can pose a threat to free

## CONSTITUTIONAL PRINCIPLES

### Separation of Powers

The National Security Act of 1947, widely considered to be one of the most important pieces of defense legislation ever passed, was born at the end of World War II. America's experience in that war pointed to the need for a more coordinated and efficiently-run armed forces. President Truman spearheaded the effort to devise a plan that would not only coordinate all branches of the armed forces, but would ensure that the executive branch and Congress were given powers equal to those of

the military. Several plans were considered, but the act as written enjoyed wide bipartisan and military support, and was smoothly implemented.

### Activity

Ask students to consider how a recent conflict, such as the Persian Gulf War, might have played out if the Department of Defense had no civilian leaders and was not accountable to the President or Congress. Have students write paragraphs describing possible scenarios.

government. For that reason, the Constitution is studded with provisions to make sure that the military is always subject to the control of the nation's civilian authorities.

Thus, the Constitution makes the elected President the commander in chief of the armed forces. To the same end, it gives wide military powers to Congress—that is, to the elected representatives of the people.[4]

The United States has obeyed the principle of civilian control throughout its history. That principle has been a major factor in the making of defense policy, and in the creation and the staffing of the various agencies responsible for the execution of that policy. The importance of civilian control is clearly illustrated by this fact: The National Security Act of 1947 provides that the secretary of defense cannot have served on active duty in any of the armed forces for at least 10 years before being named to that post.

## The Secretary of Defense

The Department of Defense is headed by the secretary of defense, whose appointment by the President is subject to Senate confirmation. The secretary, who serves at the President's pleasure, has two major responsibilities. He is (1) the President's chief aide and advisor in making and carrying out defense policy, and (2) the operating head of the Defense Department.

The secretary's huge domain is often called the Pentagon—because of its massive five-sided headquarters building in Virginia, across the Potomac River from the Capitol. Year in and year out, its

---

[4]Recall that the Constitution makes defense a national function and practically excludes the States from that field. Each State does have a militia, which it may use to keep the peace within its own borders. Today, the organized portion of the militia is the National Guard. Congress has the power (Article I, Section 8, Clauses 15 and 16) to "provide for calling forth the Militia" and to provide for organizing, arming, and disciplining it. Congress first delegated to the President the power to call the militia into federal service in 1795, and the commander in chief has had that authority ever since. Today, the governor of each State is the commander in chief of that State's units of the Army and the Air National Guard, except when the President orders those units into federal service.

[5]The United States Marine Corps is a separate branch of the armed forces, but, for organizational purposes, it is located within the Navy Department. The Coast Guard is also a branch of the armed forces. It is organized as a military service, with a present strength of some 35,000 commissioned officers and enlisted personnel. Since 1967, the Coast Guard has been part of the Department of Transportation. In time of war or at any other time the President directs, the Coast Guard becomes a part of the United States Navy.

operations take a large slice of the federal budget—today, in fact, one sixth of all federal spending. The war on global terrorism has forced increased military outlays; total spending for the nation's defense will run to at least $350 billion in fiscal year 2003.

## Chief Military Aides

The five members of the Joint Chiefs of Staff serve as the principal military advisors to the secretary of defense, and to the President and the National Security Council. They are the chairman of the Joint Chiefs, the army chief of staff, the chief of naval operations, the commandant of the Marine Corps, and the air force chief of staff. The highest ranking uniformed officers in the armed services, the members of the Joint Chiefs are named by the President, subject to Senate approval.

## The Military Departments

The three military departments—the Departments of the Army, the Navy, and the Air Force—are major units and sub-Cabinet departments within the Department of Defense.[5] Each is headed by a civilian secretary, named by the

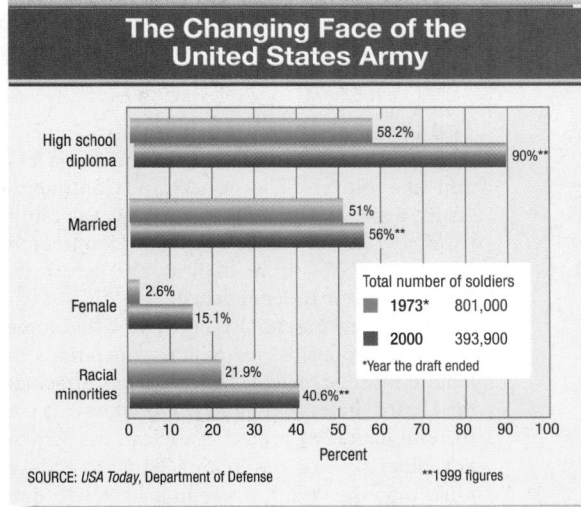

**The Changing Face of the United States Army**

High school diploma: 58.2%, 90%**
Married: 51%, 56%**
Female: 2.6%, 15.1%
Racial minorities: 21.9%, 40.6%**

Total number of soldiers
1973* 801,000
2000 393,900
*Year the draft ended

Percent (0 to 100)

SOURCE: *USA Today*, Department of Defense
**1999 figures

 *Interpreting Graphs* The make-up of the U.S. Army has changed since the draft ended and it became an all-volunteer force. *In what ways has the army become more diverse?*

## Make It Relevant

### Careers in Government—Armed Services Member

The men and women of the American armed services "stand on the wall" that separates the American people from foreign threats. Their occupations are as diverse as those of the people they protect: clerks, computer specialists, pilots, weapons designers, writers, architects, musicians, and many others. Enlistees enjoy the added advantages of service to their country, terrific benefits, education, training, and travel.

**Skills Activity** Have several pairs of students interview two current or former members of the military. Have students summarize and share their interviews with the class. Then have individual students write paragraphs explaining why they would or would not be interested in a career in the armed services.

**(Basic)**

### Take It to the Net

For career-related links and activities, visit the *Magruder's American Government* companion Web site in the Social Studies area at the Prentice Hall School Web site.

*"Wisht I could stand up an git some sleep."*

**Interpreting Political Cartoons** Bill Mauldin, who served in the U.S. Army during World War II, drew cartoons "for and about the soldiers because I knew what their life was like." His work appeared in the military newspaper *Stars and Stripes*. **According to this cartoon, what was it like to be a combat soldier?**

President and directly responsible to the secretary of defense. The nation's armed forces—the army, the navy, and the air force—operate within that unified structure.

### The Department of the Army
The army is the largest of the armed services, and the oldest. The American Continental Army, now the United States Army, was established by the Second Continental Congress on June 14, 1775—more than a year before the Declaration of Independence.

The army is essentially a ground-based force, and it is responsible for military operations on land. It must be ready (1) to defeat any attack on the United States itself, and (2) to take swift and forceful action to protect American interests in any other part of the world. To these ends, it must organize, train, and equip its active duty forces—the Regular Army—as well as its reserve units—the Army National Guard and the Army Reserve. All of its forces are under the direct command of the army's highest ranking officer, the army chief of staff.

The Regular Army is the nation's standing army, the heart of its land forces. There are now some 410,000 men and 71,000 women on active duty in the army—officers and enlisted personnel, professional soldiers, and volunteers. The army has been downsized dramatically in the post–cold war era. There were more than 700,000 men and women on active duty when the Soviet Union collapsed in 1991.

Women now serve in all of the Regular Army's units. Over recent years, their roles have come to include many combat-related duties in the army and in each of the other armed services, as well.

The army's combat units are made up of soldiers trained and equipped to fight enemy forces. The infantry takes, holds, and defends land areas. The artillery supports the infantry, seeks to destroy enemy concentrations with its heavier guns, and gives anti-aircraft cover. The armored cavalry also supports the infantry, using armored vehicles and helicopters to spearhead assaults and oppose enemy counteroffensives.

The other units of the army provide the many services and supplies in support of combat troops. Combat soldiers could not fight without the help of members of the engineer, quartermaster, signal, ordnance, transportation, chemical, military police, finance, and medical corps.

### The Department of the Navy
The United States Navy was first formed as the Continental Navy—a fledgling naval force created by the Second Continental Congress on October 13, 1775. From that day to this, its major responsibility has been sea warfare and defense.

The chief of naval operations is the navy's highest ranking officer and is responsible for its preparations and readiness for war and for its use in combat. The navy's ranks also have been thinned in the post–cold war period. Today, some 365,000 officers and enlisted personnel, including 50,000 women, serve in the navy.

The Second Continental Congress established the United States Marine Corps on November 10, 1775. Today, it operates as a separate armed service within the Navy Department, but it is not under the control of the chief of naval operations. Its commandant answers directly to the secretary of the navy.

The marines are a combat-ready land force for the navy. They have two major combat missions: (1) to seize or defend land bases from which the ships of the fleet and the air power of the navy and marines can operate, and (2) to carry out other land operations essential to a naval campaign. Today, some 160,000 men and 10,000 women serve in the USMC.

## Department of the Air Force

The air force is the youngest of the military services. Congress established the United States Air Force and made it a separate branch of the armed forces in the National Security Act of 1947. However, its history dates back to 1907, when the army assigned an officer and two enlisted men to a new unit called the Aeronautical Division of the army's Signal Corps. These three men were ordered to take "charge of all matters pertaining to military ballooning, air machines and all kindred subjects."

Today, the USAF is the nation's first line of defense. It has primary responsibility for military air and aerospace operations. In time of war, its major duties are to defend the United States; attack and defeat enemy air, ground,

▲ These Navy fighter pilots serve on the aircraft carrier USS *Dwight D. Eisenhower*. **Critical Thinking** *Do you think women should fly combat missions in wartime? Explain your answer.*

and sea forces; strike military and other war-related targets in enemy territory; and provide transport and combat support for land and naval operations.

The air force now has about 350,000 officers and enlisted personnel, including more than 65,000 women—all under the direct command of the chief of staff of the air force. The authorized strength of the USAF has been cut by more than 150,000 men and women since 1991.

### Answers to . . .

### Section 1 Assessment

**1.** Foreign affairs are a nation's relationships with other countries; domestic affairs are what is happening within the nation.
**2. (a)** Isolationism is a purposeful refusal to become involved in the affairs of the rest of the world.
**(b)** During the first 150 years of the nation.
**3.** Policies may include treaties and alliances, international trade, defense, foreign aid, the United Nations, nuclear weapons and disarmaments, environmental issues, exports, fishing rights, economic sanctions, cultural exchange programs, and so on.
**4.** The right of legation means that a nation may send and receive diplomatic representatives, including ambassadors who are representatives appointed by heads of state.
**5. (a)** Without civilian control, the military's powers would be unchecked and could threaten the government.
**(b)** Students might mention one of several Latin American countries.
**6.** Possible answer: Without diplomatic representatives, nations could not establish relationships.

### Answer to . . .

**Critical Thinking** Answers will vary; students might suggest that both men and women are capable of flying airplanes.

## Section 1 Assessment

### Key Terms and Main Ideas

1. What is the difference between **foreign affairs** and **domestic affairs**?
2. **(a)** What is the policy of **isolationism?** **(b)** During what period was this policy favored by most Americans?
3. Name five kinds of policies that are a part of United States **foreign policy**.
4. How does an **ambassador** exercise the **right of legation**?

### Critical Thinking

5. **Drawing Conclusions (a)** Explain how tyranny might result when the military is not kept under civilian control.
   **(b)** Name one nation where such a situation occurred.

6. **Analyzing Information** Why do you think the right of legation has been honored by nations for thousands of years?

 **Take It to the Net**

7. Read more on the debate about isolationism versus internationalism. Make a chart noting four or five points for each side of the argument, and rank each point on a scale of 1 (least convincing) to 5 (most convincing). Then state your own position on the issue. Use the links provided in the Social Studies area at the following Web site for help in completing this activity. **www.phschool.com**

**Take It to the Net**

7. Direct students to the Social Studies area at the Prentice Hall School Web site. The *Magruder's American Government* companion Web site includes the directions and links needed to complete the activity. It also provides a printable Internet activity worksheet with scoring rubrics for assessment. Charts should list several points, and rankings should be in accordance with students' opinions.

 *on Primary Sources*

# The State Department's Mission

*As the twentieth century drew to a close, Secretary of State Madeleine Albright testified before the congressional subcommittee that oversees her department. In reviewing the State Department's budget requests, she shared her thoughts on American foreign policy goals for the new century and her department's role in achieving those objectives.*

One of my highest goals upon becoming Secretary of State was to work with Members of Congress to restore both the spirit and substance of bipartisan support for American leadership around the globe. . . .

The accounts funded by this subcommittee determine whether we will have the right people in the right place with the right tools at the right time. And whether we will be able—through our bilateral and multilateral diplomacy effectively—to promote peace, halt the spread of deadly weapons, counter terror, fight international crime, enforce trade agreements, build democracy, raise core labor standards, protect the environment, increase respect for human rights, combat disease, and safeguard the rights of Americans who travel or do business overseas.

I have said that it is America's strategic objective, as we prepare for the new century, to seize the opportunity that history has presented to bring nations closer together around basic principles of democracy, free markets, respect for law, and a commitment to peace. America's place in this system is at the center. And our challenge is to keep the connections between regions and among the most prominent nations strong and sure. . . .

Mr. Chairman, American leadership is built on American ideals, backed by our economic and military might, and supported by our diplomacy. Unfortunately, . . . the resources we need to support our diplomacy are stretched thin. . . .

*Madeleine Albright served as Secretary of State from 1997 to 2001.*

There was a time, not that long ago, when State Department managers could afford to be guided by a "just in case" philosophy. Planning, acquisitions, and training could be based on what might be needed. Today, we are compelled by the pace of change and the tightness of budgets to practice "just in time" management. This requires putting personnel, resources, and infrastructure where they are required when they are required, and being prepared to reposition them rapidly and flexibly when they are not. . . .

Today, we have a responsibility . . . to reject the temptation of complacency and assume, not with complaint but welcome, the leader's role established by our forebears. For it is only by living up to the heritage of our past that we will fulfill the promise of our future—and enter the new century free and respected, prosperous, and at peace.

### Analyzing Primary Sources

1. According to Albright, how will the subcommittee's funding decisions affect her department?
2. What does Albright see as the goal of American foreign policy?
3. What are two possible reasons that Congress might choose not to increase the State Department's funding?

 *Corner*

📁 **Close Up on Primary Sources** The Role of Congress in Foreign Policy, p. 19, extends this feature with a primary source activity.

To keep up-to-date on Close Up news and activities, visit Close Up Online at

**www.closeup.org**

# 2 Other Foreign and Defense Agencies

## Section Preview

### OBJECTIVES

1. **Describe** a number of government agencies, besides the Departments of State and Defense, that are involved in foreign and defense policy.
2. **Explain** how the CIA, the Office of Homeland Security, NASA, and the Selective Service System contribute to the nation's security.

### WHY IT MATTERS

Besides the Departments of State and Defense, several other government agencies are closely involved with foreign policy. These agencies oversee such tasks as gathering and analyzing intelligence information, supervising the draft, exploring space, and strengthening homeland security.

### POLITICAL DICTIONARY

★ espionage
★ terrorism
★ draft

How many federal agencies, in addition to the Departments of State and Defense, are involved with the nation's foreign affairs? Dozens of them. For example, the Customs Service combats international smuggling. The Public Health Service works with the United Nations and foreign governments to conquer diseases and meet other health problems in many parts of the world. And the Coast Guard keeps an iceberg patrol in the North Atlantic to protect the shipping of all nations.

A recitation of this sort could go on and on. But, as you will see, this section deals with those agencies most directly involved in the areas of foreign and defense policy.

## The CIA

The Central Intelligence Agency (CIA) is a key part of the foreign policy establishment. Created by Congress in 1947, the CIA works under the direction of the National Security Council. A director heads "the agency," as it is often called. That director is appointed by the President and confirmed by the Senate.

On paper, the CIA has three major tasks: (1) to coordinate the information-gathering activities of all State, Defense, and other federal agencies involved in the areas of foreign affairs and national defense, (2) to analyze and evaluate all data collected by those agencies, and (3) to

brief the President and the National Security Council— that is, to keep them fully informed of all of that intelligence.

The CIA is far more than a coordinating and reporting body, however. It also conducts its own worldwide intelligence operations. In fact, it is a major "cloak-and-dagger" agency. Much of the information it gathers comes from more or less open sources, such as foreign newspapers and other publications, radio broadcasts, travelers, satellite photos, and the like. Still, a large share of information comes from the CIA's own secret, covert activities. Those operations cover the full range of **espionage,** or spying.

▲ The International Ice Patrol (IIP) of the U.S. Coast Guard tracks icebergs in the North Atlantic to help protect ships of all nations.

## Reading Strategy

### Organizing Information/Outline

Ask students to copy down the section's headings in outline form, leaving space for details. Have them fill in the details as they read the section.

ACTIVITY

### Heterogeneous Groups

**Kinesthetic, Logical** Separate the class into pairs. Provide students with a small set of note cards. Ask each student to create flash cards using the important terms from this section. (Include terms such as *START, espionage, Sputnik, Voice of America,* and the *draft.*) On the front of the note cards students should write the term; on the back they should write the agency associated with that term and a brief explanation of the association. After each pair has reviewed both sets of flash cards, have students rotate partners so they can pair up with someone new. Students should continue "quizzing" each other as time permits.

**(Basic)**

## Point-of-Use Resources

**Guided Reading and Review** Unit 4 booklet, p. 42 provides students with practice identifying the main ideas and key terms of this section.

**Lesson Plans** For lesson planning suggestions, see p. 75 of the Lesson Plans booklet.

**Political Cartoons** See p. 67 of the Political Cartoons booklet for a cartoon relevant to this section.

**Section Support Transparencies** Transparency 70, *Visual Learning;* Transparency 169, *Political Cartoon*

▲ *Increased Security* After the September 11, 2001, hijackings and attacks, the National Guard began patrolling airports. These members of the Florida National Guard march through Tampa International Airport.

Much of the CIA's work is shrouded in deepest secrecy. Even Congress has generally shied away from more than a surface check on the agency's activities. Indeed, the CIA's operating funds are disguised in several places in the federal budget each year.

When Congress established the CIA, it recognized the need for such an organization in a trouble-filled world. Most people agree that that need continues today. At the same time, Congress saw the dangers inherent in a supersecret intelligence agency that operates outside the realm of public scrutiny. Therefore, the National Security Act of 1947 expressly denies the CIA the authority to conduct any investigative, surveillance, or other clandestine activities within the United States. However, the agency has not always obeyed that command.

## Office of Homeland Security

The Office of Homeland Security is charged with the awesome task of protecting the United States against **terrorism.** Terrorism is the use of violence to intimidate a government or a society, usually for political or ideological reasons.

The Office was created immediately after the horrific assaults on the Pentagon and the World Trade Center on September 11, 2001. It was established by executive order and is located in the Executive Office of the President (pages 419–422). Its director, who is appointed by the President, has Cabinet rank and works in close concert with the National Security Council.

In the executive order creating the Office, President Bush assigned unprecedented responsibilities to the director. He must coordinate and direct the anti-terrorist activities of all of the federal, State, and local agencies that operate in the field of domestic security. As the order puts it, the director leads all of the nation's efforts "to detect, prepare for, prevent, protect against, respond to and recover from terrorist attacks within the United States."

The director oversees the anti-terrorist efforts of more than 40 federal agencies—among them the FBI, the CIA, the Secret Service, the Coast Guard, the Federal Aviation Administration, the Immigration and Naturalization Service, and the Federal Emergency Management Agency. And he also is charged with coordinating the work of thousands of State and local agencies across the country—thousands of police departments, fire departments, emergency medical and search and rescue units, and other disaster response agencies.

The threat of bioterrorism—the use of such biological agents as smallpox or anthrax as weapons—dramatizes the immensity of the problems facing the Office of Homeland Security. So, too, do these facts: There are nearly 600,000 bridges, 170,000 water systems, and more than 2,000 power plants (104 of them nuclear) in the United States. There are also 220,000 miles of railroad, 190,000 miles of natural gas pipelines, 25,000 miles of waterways, and 1,000 harbor channels. And there are 463 skyscrapers (each over 500 feet high), nearly 19,000 airports (including some 300 major facilities), thousands of stadiums and other large gathering places, and nearly 20,000 miles of border.

Add to all that such critical matters as the nation's food supply, its healthcare system, and its communications networks and this point becomes clear: This country cannot be protected—completely and absolutely—against terrorists. Terrorism thrives on unpredictability and uses it as a weapon to foment fear and anxiety.

Quite apparently, the best that can be hoped for in the current circumstances is that (1) most—nearly all—terrorist attacks will be thwarted or their impacts will at least be minimized and (2) those responsible for the attacks will be rooted out and brought to justice.

## NASA

The modern space age is only some forty years old. It began on October 4, 1957, when the Soviet Union put its first satellite, *Sputnik I,* in space. The first American satellite, *Explorer I,* was fired into orbit a few months later, on January 31, 1958. From that point on, a great number of space vehicles have been thrust into the heavens by both of the superpowers, and, more recently, by other nations as well.

The National Aeronautics and Space Administration (NASA) is an independent agency created by Congress in 1958 to handle this nation's space programs. Today, the scope of those programs is truly extraordinary. NASA's work ranges from basic research that focuses on the origin, evolution, and structure of the universe to explorations of outer space, and includes the development of a space station that will soon be occupied on a permanent basis.

The military importance of NASA's work can hardly be exaggerated. Congress has ordered the space agency to bend its efforts "to peaceful purposes for the benefit of all humankind," as well. NASA's research and development efforts have opened new frontiers in astronomy, physics, the environmental sciences, communications, medicine, and weather forecasting. NASA has shared a number of its scientific techniques with the private sector, leading to improved consumer products. Spinoffs include smoke detectors, cordless power tools, scratch-resistant lenses, football helmet padding, an artificial heart, and a vehicle tracking system.

NASA conducts its operations at a number of flight centers, laboratories, and other installations throughout the country. Among the best known are the Kennedy Space Center at Cape Canaveral in Florida; the Johnson Space Center near Houston, Texas; the Ames Research Center and the Jet Propulsion Laboratory, both in California; and the Goddard Space Flight Center in Greenbelt, Maryland.

▲ This NASA astronaut is working on the payload of a space shuttle as it orbits Earth. *Critical Thinking Should the U.S. government support and fund space exploration? Explain your answer.*

Over the years, NASA's accomplishments were so many, and its programs so successful, that space flights and space probes seemed to become almost routine. However, tragedy struck in 1986 when the space shuttle *Challenger* exploded moments after liftoff from Cape Canaveral. All seven crew members died, including Christa McAuliffe, a civilian and the first "teacher in space." NASA slowly recovered from that disaster and now tries to launch as many as ten space vehicles each year, some of them with secret military payloads.

Recently, NASA has had both successes and failures. The Hubble Space Telescope, built under NASA's supervision, was placed in orbit in 1990 to take clearer pictures of outer space than could be achieved on Earth. But its pictures were fuzzy; faulty testing procedures had resulted in an optical defect. NASA redeemed its reputation, however, with a space shuttle mission that successfully repaired the Hubble in 1993.

NASA had another huge success in 1997, when the Pathfinder landed safely on Mars. It then deployed the small rover, Sojourner, which did scientific experiments and beamed photos back to Earth. Millions of people watched the exploits of the little rover on television and online. In 1999, however, two other missions to Mars ended in spectacular failure: First the Mars Climate Orbiter was destroyed because of a mix-up of metric and English measurements; then the Mars Polar Lander disappeared, probably crashing into the surface. These failures have caused new scrutiny of the way NASA operates.

### Background Note
### A Diverse Nation

The Vietnam experience demonstrated the racial and class inequalities of the draft. Deferments were often granted based on college attendance, which resulted in more deferments for white, middle-class youths. Assignments once in the service were made in part on the basis of education. Thus, minorities were vastly overrepresented among frontline troops and suffered almost 50% of all U.S. ground casualties. African Americans made up 12% of the troops in Vietnam but accounted for 20% of all combat deaths. Hispanic losses were even higher—one of every two Hispanics in Vietnam saw combat; one in five Hispanics in Vietnam was killed; and one in every three was wounded.

## Customize for
### Less Proficient Readers

Have students create "Who am I?" riddles for a representative of one of the agencies discussed in the section. Each riddle should convey the purpose and one or more activities of the agency. Ask students to exchange papers and guess the answers to one another's riddles.

**RESOURCE PRO**

**Resource Pro® CD-ROM** contains an electronic version of each activity found in the Teaching Resources as well as additional resources such as Supreme Court cases. The Planning Express® feature allows you to customize and create daily lesson plans within minutes.

*Answer to ...*
**Critical Thinking** Answers will vary, but should be supported with thoughtful reasoning.

**479**

## Point–of–Use Resources

**Guide to the Essentials** Chapter 17, Section 2, p. 93 provides support for students who need additional review of section content. Spanish support is available in the Spanish edition of the Guide on p. 86.

**Quiz** Unit 4 booklet, p. 43 includes matching and multiple-choice questions to check students' understanding of Section 2 content.

**Presentation Pro CD-ROM** Quizzes and multiple-choice questions check students' understanding of Section 2 content.

## Answers to . . .

### Section 2 Assessment

**1.** To coordinate all federal agencies involved in foreign affairs and national defense; to analyze and evaluate all data collected by those agencies; and, to keep the President and National Security Council informed.
**2.** The use of violence to intimidate a government or society.
**3.** The draft.
**4.** Successes include many successful launches such as Pathfinder, research and development in many fields, and the pioneering of scientific techniques; failures include the explosion of *Challenger* and the initial failure of the Hubble Telescope.
**5.** Considerations are the unpredictable nature of terrorism, the variety of potential targets, and the role of fear. Opinions should be supported with valid reasoning.
**6. (a)** Answers will vary, but should reflect valid reasoning. **(b)** Possible answer: The benefits of the CIA's work are seen as outweighing its secrecy.

# The Selective Service System

Through most of American history, the armed forces have depended on voluntary enlistments to fill their ranks. From 1940 to 1973, however, the **draft**—also called conscription, or compulsory military service—was a major source of military manpower.

Conscription has a long history in this country. Several colonies and later nine States required all able-bodied males to serve in their militia. However, in the 1790s, Congress rejected proposals for national compulsory military service.

Both the North and the South did use limited conscription programs during the Civil War. It was not until 1917, however, that a national draft was first used in this country, even in wartime. More than 2.8 million of the 4.7 million men who served in World War I were drafted under the terms of the Selective Service Act of 1917.

The nation's first peacetime draft came with the Selective Service and Training Act of 1940, as World War II raged in Europe but before the United States entered the war. Eventually, more than 10 million of the 16.3 million Americans in uniform in World War II entered the service under that law.

The World War II draft ended in 1947. The crises of the postwar period, however, quickly moved Congress to revive the draft, which was reestablished by the Selective Service Act of 1948. From 1948 to 1973, nearly 5 million young men were drafted.

Mounting criticisms of compulsory military service, fed by opposition to our Vietnam policy, led many Americans to call for an end to the draft in the late 1960s. By 1972, fewer than 30,000 men were being drafted per year, and selective service was suspended in 1973. Nevertheless, the draft law is still on the books.

The draft law places a military obligation on all males in the United States between the ages of $18\frac{1}{2}$ and 26. During the years in which the draft operated, it was largely conducted through hundreds of local selective service boards. All young men had to register for service at age 18. The local boards then selected those who were to enter the armed forces.

As of 1980, the registration requirement was back in place. President Jimmy Carter reactivated it, and his executive order is still in force. All young males are required to sign up soon after they reach their 18th birthday. However, the President's power to order the actual induction of men into the armed forces expired on June 30, 1973. If the draft is ever to be reactivated, Congress must first renew that presidential authority.[6]

---

[6]The Supreme Court first upheld the constitutionality of the draft in the *Selective Draft Law Cases* in 1918. The Court also found its all-male features constitutional in *Rostker v. Goldberg* in 1981; see page 499.

## Section 2 Assessment

**Key Terms and Main Ideas**
1. What are the three major tasks of the CIA?
2. What is **terrorism**?
3. What was the major source of American military manpower from 1940 to 1973?
4. Name two successes and two failures of the NASA space programs.

**Critical Thinking**
5. **Demonstrating Reasoned Judgment** It seems clear that this country cannot be protected—completely and absolutely—against terrorist attacks. Give your reasons for agreeing or disagreeing with this statement.

6. **Checking Consistency (a)** Is an intelligence agency whose actions can be kept secret from the people consistent with the principle of popular sovereignty? Explain. **(b)** Why do you think the CIA is permitted to operate in this way?

 **Take It to the Net**

7. Visit NASA's *Spinoff* site to identify examples of government-assisted research that when shared with the private sector have resulted in improved consumer products. Identify computer and communications technologies in particular. Write a paragraph explaining the significance of one or more of these products. Use the links provided in the Social Studies area at the following Web site for help in completing this activity. **www.phschool.com**

 **Take It to the Net**

**7.** Direct students to the Social Studies area at the Prentice Hall Web site. The *Magruder's American Government* companion Web site includes the directions and links needed to complete the activity. It also provides a printable Internet activity worksheet with scoring rubrics for assessment. Paragraphs should identify one or more products and should offer specific reasons when explaining their significance.

# 3 American Foreign Policy Overview

## Section Preview

### OBJECTIVES

1. **Summarize** American foreign policy from independence through World War I.
2. **Show** how the two World Wars affected America's traditional policy of isolationism.
3. **Explain** the principles of collective security and deterrence.
4. **Examine** the United States policy of resisting Soviet aggression during the cold war.
5. **Describe** American foreign policy since the end of the cold war.

### WHY IT MATTERS

Understanding the origins of American foreign policy and the results of those stands and actions is essential to understanding foreign policy issues today. Over time, the United States changed from an isolationist nation to a world power. Although the United States is the only superpower today, the world remains a dangerous place, requiring a policy of constant vigilance.

### POLITICAL DICTIONARY

★ collective security
★ deterrence
★ cold war
★ containment
★ détente

**Objectives** You may wish to call students' attention to the objectives in the Section Preview. The objectives are reflected in the main headings of the section.

**Bellringer** Ask students what safety rules their parents made them follow when they were young. Then ask how those policies changed as they grew older. Explain that in this section, they will learn about how American foreign policy changed over time, although its goal remained the same.

**Vocabulary Builder** Tell students that the first, second, fourth, and fifth terms in the Political Dictionary name different post-World War II foreign policies. Have students suggest the meaning of each term, using any base words as clues.

## Pressed for Time?

### Quick Lesson Plan

1. **Focus** Tell students that the overriding goal of American foreign policy has always been to protect the security of the United States. Ask students to discuss what they know about when the United States ended its policy of isolationism.
2. **Instruct** Ask students what the Monroe Doctrine was. *(A warning to European nations not to interfere in Latin American affairs)* Discuss how that policy related to isolationism. Then have students find and discuss the various historical shifts in American foreign policy.
3. **Close/Reteach** Remind students that American foreign policy has changed over time. Ask students to create a time line of major events in the history of American foreign policy. On the time line, they should note changes in foreign policy.

The basic purpose of American foreign policy has always been to protect the security of the United States—and so it is today. It would be impossible to present a full-blown history of America's foreign relations in these pages, of course. But we can review its major themes and highlights here.

Why should you know as much as you can about the history of the United States? Because history is not "bunk," as automaker Henry Ford once described it. Let Robert Kelly, a leading historian, tell you what history really is: "History is our social memory. Our memories tell us who we are, where we belong, what has worked and what has not worked, and where we seem to be going."

## Foreign Policy From Independence Through WWI

From its beginnings, and for 150 years, American foreign policy was very largely built on a policy of isolationism. Throughout that period, the United States refused to become generally and permanently involved in the affairs of the rest of the world.

Isolationism arose in the earliest years of this nation's history. In his Farewell Address in 1796, George Washington declared that "our true policy" was "to steer clear of permanent alliances with any portion of the foreign world." Our "detached and distant situation," Washington said, made it desirable for us to have "as little political connection as possible" with other nations. In 1801, Thomas Jefferson added his own warning against "entangling alliances."

At the time, and for decades to come, isolationism seemed a wise policy to most Americans. The United States was a new and a relatively weak nation. We had a great many problems of our own, a huge continent to explore and settle, and two oceans to separate us from the rest of the world.

The policy of isolationism did not demand a complete separation from the rest of the world, however. From the first, the United States developed ties abroad—by exchanging diplomatic representatives with other nations, making treaties with many of them, and building an extensive foreign commerce. In fact, isolationism was, over time,

▲ This statue in Washington, D.C., honors the Marquis de Lafayette, a French nobleman who served in the Continental Army during the American Revolution.

## Block Scheduling Strategies

Consider these suggestions to manage extended class time:

■ Have students use the text, as well as an encyclopedia for supplemental material, to create annotated time lines showing U.S. foreign policy from 1796 to the present on the top and events around the world during that same time on the bottom. Assign different groups 25–30 years, and put finished time lines together to make one master time line.

■ Write the Primary Sources quotation from p. 486 by Harry S Truman on the board. Ask students to respond to the quotation. If they agree, they should write a short paragraph explaining why; if they disagree, have them rewrite the quotation in a way that makes more sense to them, and write a short paragraph explaining their reasoning. Ask for volunteers to share their paragraphs with the class.

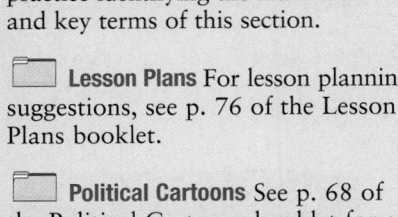
more a statement of our desire for noninvolvement outside the Western Hemisphere than a description of United States policy within our own hemisphere.

### The Monroe Doctrine

James Monroe gave the policy of isolationism a clearer shape in 1823. In a historic message to Congress, he proclaimed what has been known ever since as the Monroe Doctrine.

A wave of revolutions had swept Latin America, destroying the old Spanish and Portuguese empires there. The prospect that other European powers would now help Spain and Portugal to take back their lost possessions was seen as a threat to United States security and a challenge to this country's economic interests.

In his message, President Monroe restated America's intentions to stay out of European affairs. He also warned the nations of Europe—including Russia, then in control of Alaska—to stay out of the affairs of North and South America. He declared that the United States would look on

 **PRIMARY Sources** *"any attempt on their part to extend their system to any portion of this hemisphere as dangerous to our peace and safety. "*
—Speech by President James Monroe to Congress, December 2, 1823

At first, most Latin Americans took little notice of this doctrine. They knew that it was really the Royal Navy and British interest in Latin American trade that protected them from European domination. Later, as the United States became more powerful, many Latin Americans came to view the Monroe Doctrine as a selfish policy designed to protect the political and economic interests of the United States, not the independence of other nations in the Western Hemisphere.

### Continental Expansion

The Treaty of Paris officially ended the Revolutionary War in 1783. Under its terms, the United States held title to all of the territory from the Great Lakes in the north to Spanish Florida in the south, and from the Atlantic coast westward to the Mississippi.

The United States began to expand across the continent almost at once. Taking advantage of France's conflict with England in the early 1800s, President Jefferson negotiated the Louisiana Purchase in 1803. At a single stroke, the nation's size was doubled, with territory reaching from the mouth of the Mississippi up to what is now Montana. With the Florida Purchase in 1819, the nation completed its expansion to the south.

Through the second quarter of the nineteenth century, the United States pursued what most Americans believed was this nation's "Manifest Destiny": the mission to expand its boundaries across the continent to the Pacific Ocean. Texas was annexed in 1845. The United States obtained the Oregon Country by treaty with Great Britain in 1846. After its defeat in the Mexican War of 1846–1848, Mexico ceded what today makes up most of the southwestern quarter of the United States.

The Gadsden Purchase in 1853 rounded out the southwestern limits of the nation. By treaty, the United States bought a strip of territory from Mexico. This land in what is now the southern parts of Arizona and New Mexico was acquired to provide the best rail route to the Pacific.

In 1867, the United States bought Alaska from Russia. The treaty of purchase was negotiated by President Andrew Johnson's Secretary of State, William H. Seward. At the time, many Americans criticized the $7 million purchase as "Seward's Folly" and called Alaska "Seward's Icebox."

In that same year, the Monroe Doctrine got its first real test. While Americans were immersed in the Civil War, France had invaded Mexico. The French leader, Napoleon III, had installed Prince Maximilian of Austria as Mexico's puppet emperor. In 1867, the United States backed the Mexicans in forcing the French to withdraw, and the Maximilian regime fell.

### A World Power

The United States emerged as a first-class power in world politics by winning the Spanish-American War in 1898. With Spain's decisive defeat, America gained the Philippines and Guam in the Pacific, and Puerto Rico in the Caribbean. Cuba became independent, under American protection. Hawaii was also annexed in 1898.

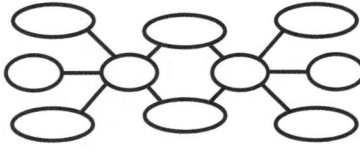

By 1900, the United States had become a colonial power. Its interests extended across the continent to Alaska, to the tip of Latin America, and across the Pacific to the Philippines.

## The Good Neighbor Policy

The threat of European intervention in the Western Hemisphere declined in the second half of the nineteenth century. That threat was replaced by problems within the hemisphere. Political instability, revolutions, unpaid foreign debts, and injuries to citizens and property of other countries plagued Central and South America.

Under what came to be known as the Roosevelt Corollary to the Monroe Doctrine, the United States began to police Latin America in the early 1900s. Several times, the marines were used to quell revolutions and other unrest in Nicaragua, Haiti, Cuba, and elsewhere.

In 1903, Panama revolted and became independent of Colombia, with American blessings. In the same year, the United States gained the right to build a canal across the Isthmus of Panama. In 1917, the United States purchased the Virgin Islands from Denmark to help guard the canal. These and other steps were resented by many in Latin America. They complained of "the Colossus of the North," of "Yankee imperialism," and of "dollar diplomacy"—and many still do.

This country's Latin American policies took an important turn in the 1930s. Theodore Roosevelt's Corollary was replaced by Franklin Roosevelt's Good Neighbor Policy, a conscious attempt to win friends to the south.

Today, the central provision of the Monroe Doctrine—the warning against foreign encroachments in the Western Hemisphere—is set out in the Inter-American Treaty of Reciprocal Assistance (the Rio Pact) of 1947. Still, the United States is, without question, the dominant power in the Western Hemisphere, and the Monroe Doctrine remains a vital part of American foreign policy.

## The Open Door in China

Historically, American foreign-policy interests have centered on Europe and on Latin America. But America has also had involvement in the Far East since the mid-1800s.

*Interpreting Political Cartoons* President Theodore Roosevelt's foreign policy was often described in his own famous statement, "Speak softly and carry a big stick." Here, TR is shown as the policeman of the Western Hemisphere. ***Do you think the cartoonist favors this policy or not? Explain your answer.***

Forty-five years before the United States acquired territory in the far Pacific, the U.S. Navy's Commodore Matthew Perry had opened Japan to American trade.

By the late nineteenth century, however, America's thriving trade in Asia was being seriously threatened. The British, French, Germans, and Japanese were each ready to take slices of the Chinese coast as their own exclusive trading preserves. In 1899, Secretary of State John Hay announced this country's insistence on an Open Door policy in China. That doctrine promoted equal trade access for all nations, and demanded that China's independence and sovereignty over its own territory be preserved.

The other major powers came to accept the American position, however reluctantly. Relations between the United States and Japan worsened from that point on, until the climax at Pearl Harbor in 1941. Over the same period, the United States built increasingly strong ties with China; but those ties were cut when communists won control of the Chinese mainland in 1949. For nearly 30 years, the United States and the People's Republic of China refused diplomatic recognition of one another.

The realities of world politics finally forced a reshaping of American-Chinese relations in the 1970s. President Nixon made a historic visit to Beijing in 1972, and full-fledged diplomatic ties were reestablished in 1979.

## Preparing for Standardized Tests

Have students read the passages under *The Good Neighbor Policy* on this page and then answer the question below.

From the passages, what can you infer that the phrase "dollar diplomacy" means?

**A** forcing a country to use the dollar as its national currency

**B** providing foreign aid to a country

**C** the use of economic policy to protect a country's business interests

**D** forming an economic alliance

## Point-of-Use Resources

☐ **Close Up on Primary Sources**
Franklin D. Roosevelt's "Four Freedoms" Speech (1941), p. 42

Still, the People's Republic is a totalitarian state, and American policy reflects that fact—though many argue that it does not do so strongly enough. The Chinese government's brutal response to pro-democracy demonstrations by thousands of students in Beijing's Tiananmen Square in 1989 has colored American-Chinese relations ever since.

## World War I and the Return to Isolationism

Germany's submarine campaign against American shipping in the North Atlantic forced the United States out of its isolationist cocoon in 1917. America entered World War I "to make the world safe for democracy."

With the defeat of Germany and the Central Powers, however, America pulled back from the involvements brought on by the war. The United States refused to join the League of Nations, which had been conceived by President Woodrow Wilson. Many Americans strongly believed that problems in Europe and the rest of the world need not concern them.

The rise of Mussolini in Italy (1922), Hitler in Germany (1933), and the militarists in Japan (1937) cast dark clouds over the world. Yet, for

▲ *A Hard-Fought Victory* This famous photograph shows U.S. Marines planting the American flag on the Pacific island of Iwo Jima during World War II.

more than 20 years after World War I, an isolationist United States remained aloof, protected by its two oceans.

## World War II

America's historic commitment to isolationism was finally ended by World War II. That massive conflict, which began in Europe in 1939, spread to engulf much of the world and lasted for nearly six years. The war involved 61 nations. By the time it ended in 1945, World War II had cost the lives of as many as 75 million people worldwide. The war's other costs, in human suffering and in physical destruction, were at least as appalling.

The United States became directly involved in the war when the Japanese attacked the American naval base at Pearl Harbor in Hawaii on December 7, 1941. From that point on—along with the British, the Russians, the Chinese, and our other Allies—the United States waged an all-out effort to defeat the Axis Powers (Germany, Italy, and Japan).

Under the direction of President Franklin Roosevelt, the United States became the "arsenal of democracy." American resources and industrial capacity supplied most of the armaments and other materials we and our Allies needed to win World War II. Within a very short time, the United States was also transformed into the mightiest military power in the world. American land, naval, and air forces fought and defeated the enemy in the Pacific, the Far East, North Africa, and Europe.

World War II finally ended in the middle of 1945 with the Allies victorious everywhere. In Europe, Germany—which had been devastated by the attacks of American and British forces from the west and by Russian troops from the east—surrendered unconditionally in May. The war in the Pacific came to a sudden end in August. Japan capitulated soon after the United States dropped two atomic bombs, which destroyed the Japanese cities of Hiroshima and Nagasaki.

## Two New Principles

World War II led to a historic shift from a position of isolationism to one of internationalism. This nation's foreign policy has been cast in that newer direction for more than 60 years now. Even so, the overall objective of that policy remains what it has always been: the protection of the security of the United States. As you will see, the major features of current American foreign policy are all reflections of that overriding goal.

## Collective Security

After World War II, the United States and most of the rest of a war-weary world looked to the principle of **collective security** to keep international peace and order. America hoped to forge a world community in which at least most nations would agree to act together against any nation that threatened the peace.

To that end, this country took the lead in creating the United Nations in 1945. The organization's charter declares that the UN was formed to promote international cooperation and so "to save succeeding generations from the scourge of war . . . and to maintain international peace and security" (see pages 494–498).

It soon became clear, however, that the future of the world would not be shaped in the UN. Rather, international security would depend largely on the nature of the relations between the two superpowers, the United States and the Soviet Union. These relations, never very close, quickly deteriorated—and for the next 40 years American foreign policy was built around that fact.

The United States is the only superpower in today's world. Still, collective security remains a cornerstone of American policy. The United States has supported the United Nations and other efforts to further international cooperation. In addition, because the UN did not immediately fulfill the dreams on which it was founded, the United States soon took another path to collective security—a network of regional alliances that you will read about in the next section.

## Deterrence

The policy of deterrence is another major plank of current American foreign policy. **Deterrence** is the policy of making America and its allies so militarily strong that their very strength will deter—discourage, or even prevent—any attack. The policy of deterrence was begun under President Truman, as the antagonisms between the United States and the Soviet Union grew

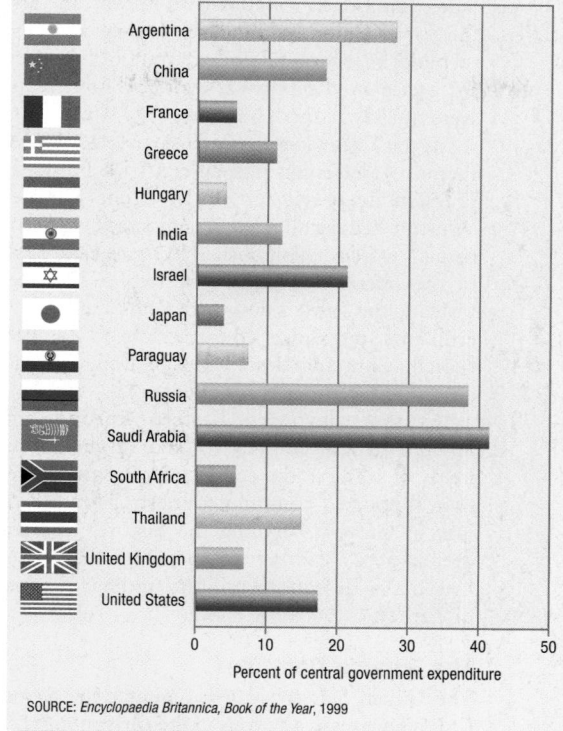

### Comparative Government

### Military Spending, Selected Countries

- Argentina
- China
- France
- Greece
- Hungary
- India
- Israel
- Japan
- Paraguay
- Russia
- Saudi Arabia
- South Africa
- Thailand
- United Kingdom
- United States

0  10  20  30  40  50

Percent of central government expenditure

SOURCE: *Encyclopaedia Britannica, Book of the Year*, 1999

*Interpreting Graphs* This graph shows how much of their budgets various nations spend on their military. *(a) Which nation spends the largest percentage? (b) Which two nations spend the least?*

after World War II. Every President since Truman has maintained it. The policy of deterrence can be summarized in this way: America's military might is most effective if, in fact, it does not have to be used.

## Resisting Soviet Aggression

One cannot hope to understand either recent or current American foreign policy without being familiar with the long years of the **cold war.** The cold war was a period of more than 40 years during which relations between the two superpowers were at least tense and, more often than not, distinctly hostile. It was, for

## CONSTITUTIONAL PRINCIPLES

**Popular Sovereignty**
At the height of the cold war, the anti-Communist crusade led by Senator McCarthy resulted in the loss of jobs and reputations for many Americans. Fearful of being labeled "radical" and suffering the same fate, many other Americans chose to remain silent on important issues. With popular sovereignty effectively silenced, the late 1950s and early 1960s were marked by a lack of social activism and cultural expression.

**Activity**
Have students explore McCarthyism at the Spartacus Internet Encyclopedia (links are provided at **www.phschool.com**). Encourage students to explore the links, choose one of the topics that interests them, and then explain how it relates to the historical context described in Section 3 of this chapter.

the most part, not a "hot war" of military action, but rather a time of threats, posturing, and military build-up.

Toward the end of World War II, the United States had hoped to work with its wartime ally the Soviet Union, particularly through the UN, to build international cooperation and to keep the peace in the postwar world. Those plans were quickly dashed, however.

At the Yalta Conference in early 1945, Soviet Premier Josef Stalin had agreed with President Franklin Roosevelt and British Prime Minister Winston Churchill that "democratic governments" would be established by "free elections" in the liberated countries of Eastern Europe. Instead, the Soviets imposed Communist governments on those countries. In a famous speech, Churchill described "an iron curtain" descending across the continent.

As they devoured Eastern Europe, the Soviets also attempted to take over the oil fields of Iran, to the south. At the same time, they supported communist guerrillas in a civil war in Greece. Pursuing the historic Russian dream of a "window to the sea," the Soviet Union also demanded military and naval bases in Turkey.

### The Truman Doctrine

The United States began to counter the Soviet Union's aggressive actions in the early months of 1947. The Truman Doctrine marked the first step in that long-standing process. Both Greece and Turkey were in danger of falling under the Soviet Union's control. At President Harry Truman's urgent request, Congress approved a massive program of economic and military aid, and both countries remained free of Soviet control. In his message to Congress, the President declared that it was now

**PRIMARY Sources** *"the policy of the United States to support free peoples who are resisting attempted subjugation by armed minorities or outside pressures."*
—Speech by President Harry S Truman to Congress, March 12, 1947

The Truman Doctrine soon became part of a broader American plan for dealing with the Soviet Union. From mid-1947 through the 1980s, the United States followed the policy of containment. That policy was rooted in the belief that if communism could be kept within its existing boundaries, it would collapse under the weight of its internal weaknesses.

The United States and the Soviet Union confronted one another often during the cold war years. Two of those confrontations were of major, near-war proportions: in Berlin in 1948–1949 and in Cuba in 1962. During this period, the United States also fought two wars against communist forces in Asia.

### The Berlin Blockade

At the end of World War II, the city of Berlin, surrounded by Soviet-occupied East Germany, was divided into four sectors. The Soviet Union controlled one sector, East Berlin. The United States, Britain, and France occupied the other three sectors, which made up West Berlin.

In 1948, the Soviets tried to force their former allies to withdraw from West Berlin. They clamped a land blockade around the city, stopping the shipment of food and supplies to the western sectors. The United States mounted a massive airlift that kept the city alive until the blockade was lifted, nearly a year and a half later.

### The Cuban Missile Crisis

The United States and the Soviet Union came perilously close to a nuclear conflict during the Cuban missile crisis in 1962. Cuba, just 90 miles off Florida's coast, had slipped into the Soviet orbit soon after Fidel Castro gained power there in 1959. By mid-1962, huge quantities of Soviet arms and thousands of Soviet "technicians" had been sent to Cuba. Suddenly, in October, the build-up became unmistakably offensive in character. Aerial photographs revealed the presence of several Soviet missiles that were capable of nuclear strikes against this country and much of Latin America.

President Kennedy immediately ordered a naval blockade of Cuba to prevent the delivery of any more missiles. Cuba and the Soviet Union were warned that the United States would attack Cuba unless the existing Soviet missiles were removed.

After several tense days, the Soviets backed down. Rather than risk all so far from home, they returned the weapons to the Soviet Union.

## Germany After World War II

**Interpreting Maps** The map shows how Germany was divided after World War II, and the division of its former capital into West Berlin and East Berlin. At right, German children watch an American transport plane land during the Berlin Airlift. **(a)Why was it so easy for the Soviets to block supplies to West Berlin? (b) Why do you think the United States made such a huge effort to break the blockade?**

### The Korean War

The Korean War began on June 25, 1950. South Korea (the UN-sponsored Republic of Korea) was attacked by communist North Korea (the People's Democratic Republic of Korea). Immediately, the UN's Security Council called on all UN members to help South Korea repel the invasion.

The war lasted for more than three years. It pitted the United Nations Command, largely made up of American and South Korean forces, against Soviet-trained and Soviet-equipped North Korean and communist Chinese troops. Cease-fire negotiations began in July 1951, but fighting continued until an armistice was signed on July 27, 1953. Final peace terms have never been agreed to.

The long and bitter Korean conflict did not end in a clear-cut UN victory. The war cost the United States 157,530 casualties, including 33,629 combat dead, and more than $20 billion. South Korea's military and civilian casualties ran into the hundreds of thousands. Much of Korea, north and south, was laid to waste.

Still, the invasion was turned back, and the Republic of Korea remained standing. Perhaps more importantly, for the first time in history, armed forces of several nations fought under an international flag against aggression. There is no telling how far that aggression might have carried had the United States not come to the aid of South Korea.

### The War in Vietnam

In the years following World War II, a nationalist movement arose in Vietnam. The Vietnamese nationalists were seeking independence from France. Made up mostly of communist forces led by Ho Chi Minh, the nationalists fought and defeated the French in a lengthy conflict. Under truce agreements signed in Geneva in 1954, what had been French Indochina was divided into two zones: a communist-dominated North Vietnam, with its capital in Hanoi, and an anticommunist South Vietnam, with Saigon as its capital.

Almost at once, communist guerrillas (the Viet Cong), supported by North Vietnamese, began a civil war in South Vietnam. The Eisenhower administration responded with economic and then military aid to Saigon. President Kennedy increased this aid. Even with stepped-up U.S. support to South Vietnam, the Viet Cong—and growing numbers of North Vietnamese supplied with mostly Soviet and

## Spotlight on Technology

**Magruder's American Government Video Collection**

The Magruder's Video Collection explores key issues and debates in American government. Each segment examines an issue central to chapter content through use of historical and contemporary footage. Commentary from civic leaders in academics, government, and the media follow each segment. Critical thinking questions focus students' attention on key issues, and may be used to stimulate discussion.

Use the Chapter 17 video segment to explore the President's role as commander in chief. (time: about 5 minutes) How is his power to make war balanced by congressional power to approve his actions? This segment takes a historical look at the War Powers Act and focuses on several recent case studies.

**A C T I V I T Y**

### Extended Class Periods

**Time** 90 minutes.
**Purpose** Create a storyboard of major events in the diplomatic history of the United States.
**Grouping** Four to five students.
**Activity** Provide groups with poster board and any necessary art supplies. Using information from the chapter, students will create a storyboard that highlights and summarizes, in chronological order, the important events in the history of America's foreign relations.
**Roles** Discussion leader, recorder, artists, spokesperson.
**Close** Have groups refer to their storyboards as you lead a discussion of the important consequences of each event described in the section.

■ **Block Strategy
(Average)**

### Point-of-Use Resources

▢ **Close Up on Primary Sources**
George Bush on the Fall of the Berlin Wall (1989), p. 50

▢ **Government Assessment Rubrics**
Cooperative Learning Project: Product, p. 22

▢ **Block Scheduling with Lesson Strategies** Additional activities for Chapter 17 appear on p. 27.

▲ *Remembering* The Vietnam Veterans Memorial in Washington, D.C., is inscribed with the names of Americans killed or missing in action in the Vietnam War.

some Chinese weapons—continued to make major gains.

It was President Johnson who, in early 1965, committed the United States to full-scale war. By 1968, more than 540,000 Americans were involved in a fierce ground and air conflict.

In 1969, President Nixon began what he called the "Vietnamization" of the war. Over the next four years, American troops were gradually pulled out of combat. Finally, a cease-fire agreement was signed in early 1973, and the last American units were withdrawn. (In spite of the cease-fire, the war between North and South Vietnam went on. By 1975, South Vietnam had been overrun, and the two Vietnams became the Socialist Republic of Vietnam.)

The ill-fated war in Vietnam cost the United States a staggering $165 billion and, irreplaceably, more than 58,000 American lives. As the war dragged on, millions of Americans came to oppose American involvement in Southwest Asia—and traces of the divisiveness of that period can still be seen in the politics of today.

### Détente and the Return to Containment

As the United States withdrew from Vietnam, the Nixon administration embarked on a policy of **détente.** The term is French, meaning "a relaxation of tensions." In this case, the policy of détente included a purposeful attempt to improve relations with the Soviet Union and, separately, with China.

President Nixon flew to Beijing in 1972 to begin a new era in American-Chinese relations. His visit paved the way for further contacts and, finally, for formal diplomatic ties between the United States and the People's Republic of China.

Less than three months later, Nixon journeyed to Moscow. There, he and Soviet Premier Leonid Brezhnev signed the first Strategic Arms Limitations Talks agreement, SALT. It was a five-year pact in which both sides agreed to a measure of control over their nuclear weapons.

Relations with mainland China have improved steadily since the 1970s. Efforts at détente with the Soviets, however, proved less successful. Moscow continued to apply its expansionist pressures and provided economic and military aid to revolutionary movements around the world.

The short-lived period of détente ended altogether when the Soviets invaded Afghanistan in 1979. After that act of aggression, first President Carter and then the Reagan administration placed a renewed emphasis on containing Soviet power.

### The End of the Cold War

Relations between the United States and the Soviet Union improved remarkably after Mikhail Gorbachev gained power in Moscow in 1985. Presidents Reagan and Gorbachev paved the way for the end of the cold war at four summit conferences. They met first in Geneva in 1985; and then in Reykjavik, Iceland, in 1986; in Washington in 1987; and in Moscow in 1988. Those meetings helped ease longstanding tensions, and they produced a major disarmament pact, the INF Treaty in 1987.

President Bush met with the Soviet leader in Malta in late 1989; in Washington in 1990; and in Washington, London, and Moscow in 1991. Those meetings reaffirmed the friendlier American-Soviet environment. They also produced commitments from both sides to eliminate a portion of their long-range nuclear missiles, to cut stockpiles of chemical weapons, and to reduce the levels of conventional military forces.

Clearly, Gorbachev deserves much of the credit for the fundamental change in the Soviets' approach to world affairs. However, another key factor was the economic and political chaos that ultimately caused the collapse of the Soviet Union itself in 1991. That the cold war is now relegated to history can and should be seen in this light: The American policy of containment, first put in place in 1947, finally realized its goal.

## The Persian Gulf War

Since the end of the cold war, some of the most important events shaping American foreign policy have occurred in the Middle East. In August of 1990, Iraqi President Saddam Hussein launched an invasion of small, oil-rich Kuwait. The invasion threatened the security of America's close ally, Saudi Arabia.

President Bush demanded the immediate withdrawal of Iraqi forces from Kuwait and the restoration of that country's legitimate government. He also ordered a huge deployment of American military might to the Persian Gulf region. By early 1991, American troop strength in the Gulf region amounted to more than 500,000—the largest massing of American power since Vietnam.

The American response was backed by most of the world community. A multinational (but mostly American) military force was established and the United Nations Security Council imposed economic sanctions on Iraq.

Iraq refused to withdraw from Kuwait, however; and Sadam Hussein's continued stubbornness finally triggered the Persian Gulf War. That brief conflict began in mid-January with sustained air attacks on Iraqi positions. By late February, the multinational force had driven Iraq's troops from Kuwait.

When Iraq posed a renewed threat to Kuwait in 1994 and again in 1996, President Clinton ordered a new deployment of American forces to the region, to reinforce the troops that have remained there since the end of the Gulf War.

## Maintaining Vigilance

American foreign policy at the start of the twenty-first century is shaped by one overriding conviction: The world remains a dangerous place—all the more dangerous following the September 11, 2001, attacks on the World Trade Center and the Pentagon. Terrorist attacks as well as drug trafficking, weapons proliferation, and cyber-terrorism are but a few of the dangers which our foreign policy must now address.

During the 2000 presidential campaign, George W. Bush noted that "peace is not ordained, it is earned. It is not a harbor where we rest, it is a voyage we must chart." Now, as throughout our history, constant vigilance is necessary to ensure the security of this nation and its people.

## Point-of-Use Resources

**Guide to the Essentials** Chapter 17, Section 3, p. 94 provides support for students who need additional review of section content. Spanish support is available in the Spanish edition of the Guide on p. 87.

**Quiz** Unit 4 booklet, p. 45 includes matching and multiple-choice questions to check students' understanding of Section 3 content.

**Presentation Pro CD-ROM** Quizzes and multiple-choice questions check students' understanding of Section 3 content.

## Answers to . . .
### Section 3 Assessment

**1.** The idea of collective security is that nations will unite to act together against any nation that threatens the peace of other nations.

**2.** Deterrence calls for spending large amounts on defense; by doing so, the nation would be so strong that it would deter attack by other nations.

**3.** Containment held that communism could be contained within its existing boundaries. It could be called a success because of the ultimate collapse of the Soviet Union, although it could be viewed as a failure with regard to Vietnam.

**4. (a)** Détente is a relaxation of tensions; in political terms, it implies an attempt to improve relations. **(b)** Their invasion of Afghanistan in 1979.

**5. (a)** Instability in Latin America was seen as a threat to United States' security and economic interests by President Monroe, who followed a policy of internationalism as set out in the Monroe Doctrine. **(b)** Possible answer: No; the U.S. has too many close economic and political ties to ever be isolationist again.

**6.** Answers should refer to the Monroe Doctrine and Roosevelt Corollary; the two world wars; the cold war policy in response to Soviet actions in Eastern Europe; and the Korean and Vietnam Wars.

---

## Section 3 Assessment

### Key Terms and Main Ideas

1. How does the phrase "United we stand, divided we fall" describe the concept of **collective security?**
2. Does the policy of **deterrence** call for the United States to spend large amounts on defense or to curtail spending unless the nation is threatened? Explain your answer.
3. Explain the policy of **containment.** Was it a success or a failure? Why?
4. **(a)** What is **détente? (b)** What Soviet action ended détente?

### Critical Thinking

5. **Identifying Central Issues (a)** Why did the United States change from a policy of isolationism to one of internationalism? **(b)** Could America ever successfully return to isolationism in today's world? Explain your answer.

6. **Synthesizing Information** America's foreign policy during the cold war was based partly on the "domino" theory, which held that if one small nation fell to the communists, nearby nations would likely follow. Explain how this belief was translated into policy and action. Give specific examples.

### Take It to the Net

7. Learn more about Harry Truman and the Truman Doctrine. Explore the site, and read some of the available documents. Then create a flowchart showing the chain of events that led to the issuing of the Truman Doctrine. Use the links provided in the Social Studies area at the following Web site for help in completing this activity. **www.phschool.com**

### Take It to the Net

7. Direct students to the Social Studies area at the Prentice Hall School Web site. The *Magruder's American Government* companion Web site includes the directions and links needed to complete the activity. It also provides a printable Internet activity worksheet with scoring rubrics for assessment. Flowcharts should include all relevant events, correctly ordered.

# SKILLS FOR LIFE

## CRITICAL THINKING

### Determining Cause and Effect

**Focus** Conduct research on the Korean War to create a cause-and-effect diagram of the war.

**Instruct** After students review the material in Chapter 17 on the Korean War, have them conduct additional research on the war's causes and its short-term and long-term effects. The causes could extend as far back as the start of the cold war, and the effects could reach as far as the recent diplomatic dialogue between North and South Korea. Have students work in small groups to make a chain-of-events diagram in which the war is both an effect and a cause. The diagram can be created on poster board or on several sheets of paper taped together, so the diagrams can be hung up and compared.

**Close/Reteach** Compare the diagrams to see how many causes and how many effects were identified. Hold a class discussion on how an understanding of the causes and effects of war could help prevent future wars.

### Answers . . .

**1.** (a), (c), and (d).
**2.** It shows multiple causes leading to a single effect.
**3.** It shows multiple causes leading to an effect that is also a cause of several effects.
**4.** Possible answer: From Diagram B we can conclude that Soviet military aggression after World War II set off a dangerous chain of events that brought the United States and the U.S.S.R. into increasingly hostile clashes.

# SKILLS FOR LIFE

TECHNOLOGY
CITIZENSHIP
CRITICAL THINKING
CHARTS and GRAPHS

## Determining Cause and Effect

Remembering individual facts, dates, and events might help you on a game show or test. But finding out why events happen helps you understand specific events in history and politics. To answer the question *Why?*, try these steps:

**1. Identify possible causes and effects.** A cause is an event or action that brings about an effect. For that reason, the cause must occur before the effect. Yet an event that precedes another does not necessarily cause it. Words such as *because, due to,* and *on account of* signal causes. Words such as *so, therefore,* and *as a result* signal effects. Which of these sentences describe a cause-effect relationship? (a) *Soviet aggression in the postwar era led to the cold war.* (b) *Within a short time, the United States was transformed into the world's mightiest military power.* (c) *Nixon's visit to China paved the way to further contacts and, finally, to formal diplomatic ties between the United States and China.* (d) *The growth of U.S.-Soviet tensions was due in part to the opposing post war goals of the two superpowers.*

**2. Diagram the cause-effect relationship.** Diagrams can help you analyze relationships among events. Diagrams can also help you identify multiple causes. Several causes can combine to create one effect, just as one cause can bring about several effects. What does Diagram A show?

**3. Diagram a chain of events.** A single event can be both a cause and an effect. Causes and effects can form a chain of events that continue over a period of time. How is Diagram B a chain of events?

**4. Draw conclusions based on your analysis.** What general statements can you make based on this analysis of cause and effect? Look for connected ideas and trends.

### Test for Success

Re-read the paragraphs about the Korean War on pages 486–487. Using the steps above, diagram the causes and effects of the war. Make sure that the events are truly causes, not just a series of events.

### Test for Success

Diagrams should be constructed according to the steps outlined in this skill.

### Diagram A

**Cause/Effect: The Cold War**

**CAUSES**

Soviets impose communism in Eastern Europe
Soviets try to seize Iranian oil fields
Soviets demand seaport in Turkey

**EFFECT**

U.S. and U.S.S.R. engage in the cold war

### Diagram B

**Cause/Effect: The Cold War**

**CAUSES**

Soviets impose communism in Eastern Europe
Soviets try to seize Iranian oil fields
Soviets demand seaport in Turkey

**EFFECT**

U.S. and U.S.S.R. engage in the cold war

**EFFECTS**

Truman Doctrine
Containment policy
Berlin blockade
Cuban missile crisis
Wars in Korea and Vietnam

### Point-of-Use Resources

📁 **Skills for Life Activity** Unit 4 booklet, p. 48 provides an additional skill activity for this chapter.

💿 **Social Studies Skills Tutor CD-ROM** Provides interactive practice in geographic literacy, critical thinking and reading, visual analysis, and communications.

# Foreign Aid and Defense Alliances

## Section Preview

### OBJECTIVES

1. **Identify** the two types of foreign aid and describe United States foreign aid policy.
2. **Describe** the major security alliances to which the United States belongs.
3. **Summarize** United States policy in the Middle East.
4. **Examine** the role, structure, and problems that face the United Nations.

### WHY IT MATTERS

The United States works with other nations to keep the peace and to ensure political stability around the world. American foreign aid strengthens the economies and security of nations important to the United States. Security alliances deter aggression and repel invasion.

### POLITICAL DICTIONARY

★ foreign aid
★ regional security alliance
★ UN Security Council

---

**D**o you know this ancient saying: "Those who help others help themselves"? You will see that that maxim underlies two basic elements of present-day American foreign policy: foreign aid and security alliances.

## Foreign Aid

**Foreign aid**—economic and military aid to other countries—has been a basic feature of American foreign policy for more than 50 years. It began with the Lend-Lease program of the early 1940s, through which the United States gave nearly $50 billion in food, munitions, and other supplies to its allies in World War II. Since then, this country has sent more than $500 billion in aid to more than 100 countries.

Foreign aid became an important part of the containment policy beginning with American aid to Greece and Turkey in 1947. The United States also helped its European allies rebuild after the devastation of World War II. Under the Marshall Plan, named for its author, Secretary of State George C. Marshall, the United States poured some $12.5 billion into 16 nations in Western Europe between 1948 and 1952.

Foreign aid policy has taken several different directions over the years. Immediately after World War II, American aid was primarily economic. Since that time, however, military assistance has assumed a large role in aid policy. Until the mid-1950s, Europe received the lion's

share of American help. Since then, the largest amounts have gone to nations in Asia, the Middle East, and Latin America.

On balance, most aid has been sent to those nations regarded as the most critical to the realization of this country's foreign policy objectives. Over recent years, Israel, Egypt, the Philippines, and various Latin American countries have been the major recipients of American help, both economic and military.

Most foreign aid money must be used to buy American goods and services. So, most of the billions spent for that aid amount to a

▲ CARE packages, like this one being sampled by Czech children, were sent to war-torn Europe after World War II through a joint effort of Canadian and American relief organizations.

---

---

### Block Scheduling Strategies

Consider these suggestions to manage extended class time:

■ Have students create study guides on regional security alliances, intended to be used by younger students. Guides should mention all alliances discussed in the text, and include reasons for founding, members, and philosophies. Guides should also include a map of the world, on which students use color coding or some other means to identify countries who are part of each alliance.

■ Have small groups of students, representing different countries, create an agenda for the UN for the year. First they should draft a philosophy statement for the organization that explains its overall ideals and goals, and how these ideals may have changed from those it had in the past. Then the agenda should list specific actions that the organization will take during the year, along with a rationale for each. Have groups exchange agendas and critique them.

## Reading Strategy

### Finding Evidence

Tell students that they will be reading about American assistance to other nations, alliances with other nations, and participation in the United Nations. Then point out to students the ancient saying quoted on page 491: "Those who help others help themselves." Have students, as they read, look for evidence that supports this saying.

## Point-of-Use Resources

📁 **Guided Reading and Review** Unit 4 booklet, p. 46 provides students with practice identifying the main ideas and key terms of this section.

📁 **Lesson Plans** For lesson planning suggestions, see p. 77 of the Lesson Plans booklet.

📁 **Political Cartoons** See p. 69 of the Political Cartoons booklet for a cartoon relevant to this section.

📓 **Section Support Transparencies** Transparency 72, *Visual Learning*; Transparency 171, *Political Cartoon*

---

substantial subsidy to both business and labor in this country. The independent Agency for International Development (AID) administers most of the economic aid programs, in close cooperation with the Departments of State and Agriculture. Most military aid is channeled through the Defense Department.

## Security Alliances

Over the past five decades, the United States has constructed a network of **regional security alliances,** built on mutual defense treaties. In each of those treaties, the United States and the other countries involved have agreed to take collective action to meet aggression in a particular part of the world.

### NATO

The North Atlantic Treaty, signed in 1949, established NATO, the North Atlantic Treaty Organization. The alliance was formed to promote the collective defense of Western Europe, particularly against the threat of Soviet aggression. Each of the 19 member countries has agreed that "an armed attack against one or more of them in Europe or in North America shall be considered an attack against them all."

NATO was originally composed of the United States and 11 other countries: Canada, the United Kingdom, France, Italy, Portugal, the Netherlands, Belgium, Luxembourg, Denmark, Norway, and Iceland. Greece and Turkey joined the alliance in 1952, West Germany in 1955, and Spain in 1982. When East and West Germany united in 1990, the new state of Germany became a member of NATO.

With the collapse of the Soviet Union, NATO's mutual security blanket was extended to cover much of Eastern Europe. Poland, Hungary, and the Czech Republic joined the alliance in 1999, and other one-time Soviet satellites will probably be admitted over the next few years, as well.

But the collapse of the Soviet Union has also suggested to some observers that NATO's purpose may have collapsed as well. The Secretary General of NATO addressed this perception in a millennium speech:

**PRIMARY** *Sources* ❝*By the early 1990s, the threat of massive attack on NATO territory was gone, to the great relief of us all. In those circumstances, however, some voices have called NATO's continuing purpose into question. . . . No institution*

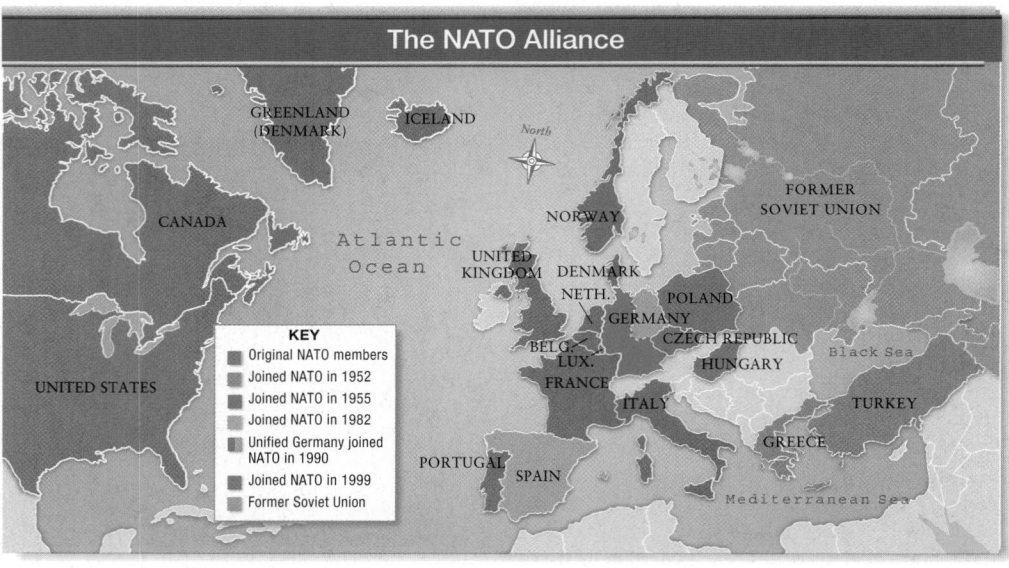

**The NATO Alliance**

KEY
- Original NATO members
- Joined NATO in 1952
- Joined NATO in 1955
- Joined NATO in 1982
- Unified Germany joined NATO in 1990
- Joined NATO in 1999
- Former Soviet Union

*Interpreting Maps* This map shows when each NATO member became part of the alliance. *Which nations joined most recently?*

---

## Answer to . . .

**Interpreting Maps** Poland, the Czech Republic, and Hungary.

*exists for its own sake. If it does not have a useful purpose, it will wither on the vine. And yet, a decade after the end of the Cold War, NATO is more vibrant than ever. . . . [and] still plays a crucial role in preserving the safety and security of all of its members. But today, that mission is being accomplished in a very different way. . .*

*[A]s we enter the new Millennium, NATO is engaged in a much broader range of activities, all designed with one fundamental goal—to address proactively the security challenges which could, or already do, affect the safety or the interests of its members and their populations.* **"**

—"NATO in the 21st Century," Secretary General Lord George Robertson

Secretary General Robertson gave three examples of NATO's new agenda:

(1) A different relationship between the West and Russia, which includes consultations on a regular basis as well as cooperation on certain security issues;

(2) NATO's enlargement, which has added to the stability of Europe;

(3) Partnership, including security relationships, with almost all the new democracies of Europe.

NATO was formed for defensive purposes more than 50 years ago and—if defense includes military intervention in conflicts that may destabilize Europe as well as the prevention of humanitarian disasters—defense remains its basic charge. The most obvious example of this role is NATO's intervention in the Balkan nations of the former Yugoslavia. Military intervention first in Bosnia and then in Kosovo put NATO in the news as well as planes in the air and troops on the ground. Robertson called Kosovo "a success story," praising the 1999 NATO actions that ensured the withdrawal of Serb troops, enabled the return of Kosovar refugees, and now contribute to a fragile peace.

## Other Alliances

The Rio Pact, or the Inter-American Treaty of Reciprocal Assistance, was signed in 1947. In this pact, the United States, Canada, and now 32 Latin American countries have agreed "that an armed attack by any state against an American state shall be considered as an attack against all

## *Spotlight* on Texas Government

**Texas and NAFTA** Nearly 60% of Texas's foreign trade exports go to America's two NAFTA trading partners, Mexico and Canada. Texas is America's largest exporter to Mexico, with nearly half of American exports to Mexico coming from the State. Texas's exports to both Canada and Mexico have grown substantially since NAFTA went into effect in 1994. Economists have estimated that about a quarter of a million jobs in Texas are supported by production of goods for export to these two countries.

The impact of NAFTA on Texans is not all positive, however. The U.S. Department of Labor certified 2,773 Texas workers for NAFTA Trade Adjustment Assistance in 2000, meaning that they lost their jobs at least partly because of increased imports that may have been due to NAFTA. In addition, Texas border towns have been struggling under the increase in shipping traffic along the roads connecting Mexico and the U.S. As NAFTA traffic increases, more trucks pass through the centers of small towns not accustomed to heavy traffic.

The Texas border area includes some of the poorest counties in America. Texas Secretary of State, Henry Cuellar, wrote in 2001 that "the passage of NAFTA . . . helped bring the importance of the border to the forefront." The border region may ultimately benefit from NAFTA, but it will need financial support from the rest of the State if that is to happen.

### Analyzing Texas Government
***Summarize the impact of NAFTA on the State of Texas.***

the American states." The treaty pledges those countries to the mutual peaceful settlement of all disputes. In effect, the Rio Pact is a restatement of the Monroe Doctrine.

In addition to NATO and the Rio Pact, the United States is party to several other regional security alliances. For example, the ANZUS Pact of 1951 unites Australia, New Zealand, and the United States to ensure their collective security in the Pacific region.

The Japanese Pact also dates from 1951. After six years of American military occupation, the allies of World War II (with the exception of the Soviet Union) signed a peace treaty with Japan. At the same time, the United States and Japan signed a mutual defense treaty. In return for American protection, Japan permitted the United States to maintain land, sea, and air forces in and about its territory.

The Philippines Pact was also signed in 1951. It, too, is a mutual defense agreement. The pact remains in force, but disagreements over its redrafting prompted the withdrawal of all

## Background Note
### The Korean Peninsula

After decades of hostility and suspicion following the Korean War, the leaders of North and South Korea met at a historic summit in 2000. The purpose of the summit was to resume cordial relations, and possibly open the way to a future reunification of the two nations. Kim Dae-jung of South Korea and Kim Jong Il of North Korea signed an agreement to work toward those goals. Though the agreement did not address many specific issues, it did call for the reunion of families separated during the war, who had had no contact for nearly fifty years. Other Asian leaders, hoping for stability in the region, met the agreement with enthusiasm—as did the United States. Ending five decades of hostility, Secretary of State Madeleine Albright met with North Korean leaders in Washington, D.C., to discuss the opening of relations between North Korea and the United States. Though the United States remains concerned about several issues—particularly North Korea's nuclear arsenal and the location of American POWs from the Korean War—Albright expressed enthusiasm and accepted an invitation to visit Pyongyang.

## Preparing for Standardized Tests

Have students read the Primary Sources quotation on pp. 492–493 and then answer the question below.

What is the best definition for the word *proactively* in this selection?

**A** completely

**B** strongly

**C** in the future

**(D)** in advance

*Answers to . . .*

**Analyzing Texas Government** The impact has been both positive and negative. Positive effects include an increased market for Texas goods, resulting in greater employment opportunities. Negative effects include a loss of jobs due to increased imports and heavy trucking traffic in small communities.

# The Judicial Branch

## Introducing the Unit

Unit 5 introduces students to the constitutional protections of individual rights and liberties. Chapter 18 explores the role of the judiciary, including the Supreme Court, the special courts in the federal court system, and the significance of judicial review. Chapter 19 examines the importance of freedom of religion, the scope of and limits on the freedoms of speech, press, assembly, and petition, and the relationship between individual liberties and national security. Chapter 20 analyzes the concepts of due process of law, the rights to freedom and security of the person, the right to a fair trial, and the constitutional limits on punishments for crime. Chapter 21 shows the diversity of the United States' population, the constitutional guarantees of equality before the law, civil rights laws, and how to become an American citizen.

## Focus Activity

Concentrate students' attention on the judicial branch of government by writing the following quotation on the board:

> "Our Constitution was not written in the sands to be washed away by each wave of new judges blown in by each successive political wind."
> —Justice Hugo L. Black (1970)

Have students consider the following after they have read the quotation.

◆ How does Justice Black view the role of the judiciary in interpreting the Constitution?

◆ Do you agree with this statement? Why or why not?

◆ Use these questions as springboards to a general class discussion about students' views of the judicial branch.

## IN THIS UNIT

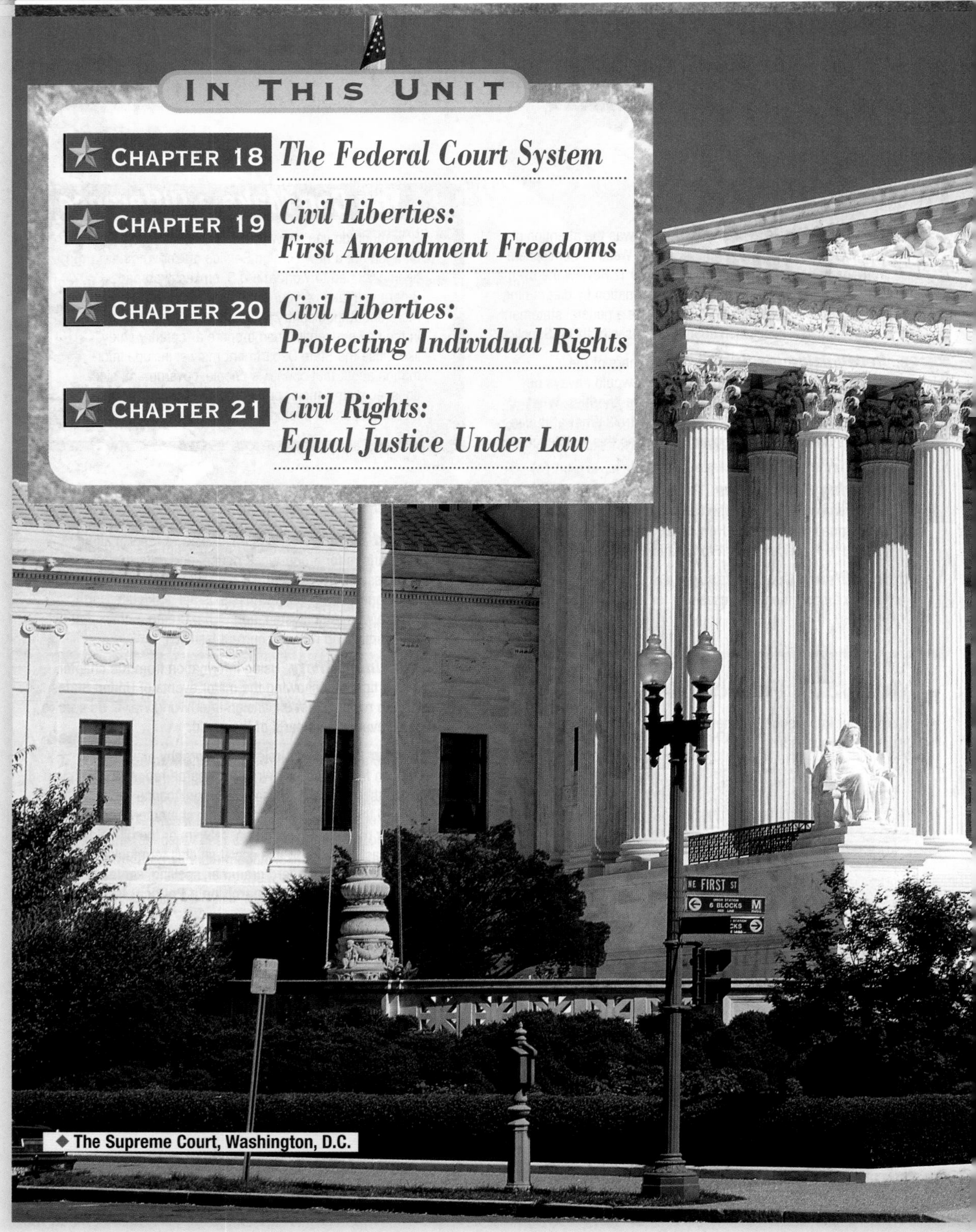

◆ The Supreme Court, Washington, D.C.

## Corner

The following Close Up features appear in this unit.
*Close Up on the Supreme Court* may be found on the following pages: 527, 559, 589, 619
*Close Up on Primary Sources* may be found on the following pages: 516, 545, 584, 607

To keep up-to-date on Close Up news and activities, visit Close Up Online at

**www.closeup.org**

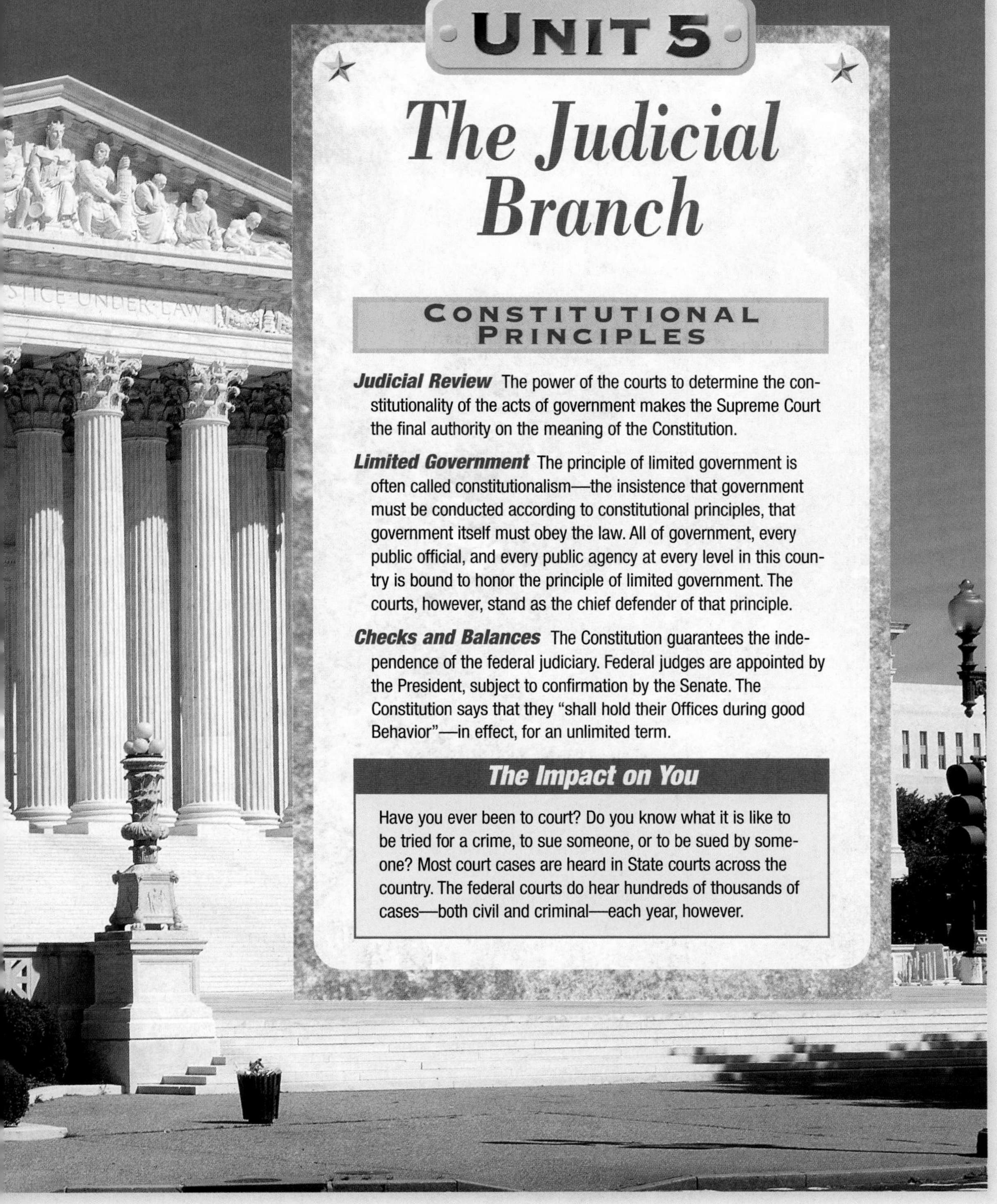

# The Judicial Branch

## CONSTITUTIONAL PRINCIPLES

**Judicial Review** The power of the courts to determine the constitutionality of the acts of government makes the Supreme Court the final authority on the meaning of the Constitution.

**Limited Government** The principle of limited government is often called constitutionalism—the insistence that government must be conducted according to constitutional principles, that government itself must obey the law. All of government, every public official, and every public agency at every level in this country is bound to honor the principle of limited government. The courts, however, stand as the chief defender of that principle.

**Checks and Balances** The Constitution guarantees the independence of the federal judiciary. Federal judges are appointed by the President, subject to confirmation by the Senate. The Constitution says that they "shall hold their Offices during good Behavior"—in effect, for an unlimited term.

### The Impact on You

Have you ever been to court? Do you know what it is like to be tried for a crime, to sue someone, or to be sued by someone? Most court cases are heard in State courts across the country. The federal courts do hear hundreds of thousands of cases—both civil and criminal—each year, however.

## Spotlight on Technology

**Take it to the Net** Offers student-appropriate Internet activities and links that extend core content. Visit us at the Social Studies area. **www.phschool.com** Be sure to check out this month's **eTeach** online discussion with a Master Government Teacher.

**Keep It Current CD-ROM** Includes government-related projects by unit. Use it to link to the Prentice Hall School Web site where you will find daily updates.

**Magruder's American Government Video Collection** Chapter-by-chapter video selections bring key government concepts to life.

**ABC News Civics and Government Videotape Library** These high-interest stories from ABC News relate to core content.

**Simulations and Data Graphing CD-ROM** Provides interactive federal budget and stock market simulations, and skills practice with statistical data.

**Prentice Hall Presentation Pro CD-ROM** Provides multimedia lecture notes for each chapter.

**ExamView® Test Bank CD-ROM** Allows you to create, edit, and print out chapter level tests.

**Resource Pro® CD-ROM** Teaching Resources that offer lesson planning flexibility, test-generation capability, and resource manageability.

**Social Studies Skills Tutor CD-ROM** Provides interactive practice in geographic literacy, critical thinking and reading, visual analysis, and communications.

**Section Support Transparencies** Illustrates key government concepts through graphs, charts, photos, and cartoons.

**Basic Principles of the Constitution Transparencies** Illustrates key principles of the Constitution.

**Section Reading Support Transparency System** Delivers the main idea of each section in the student text through graphic organizers.

## Pressed for Time?

### Instruction Plus!

The resources you need to support your instruction of this chapter are conveniently located in a single box. This innovative package provides an instructional advantage in the classroom with its ready-to-use tools in a variety of formats.

 **Magruder's American Government Video Collection**

 **Keep It Current Web-based Activities Presentation Pro CD-ROM**

 **Section Support Transparencies**

 **Guide to the Essentials Current Issues**

# The Federal Court System

| Section Objectives | Print and Technology Resources |
|---|---|

## 1 The National Judiciary
### (pp. 506–511)

1. Analyze the structure and functions of the federal court system.
2. Analyze the types of federal court jurisdiction.
3. Outline the selection process for federal judges.
4. List the terms of office for federal judges and explain how their salaries are determined.
5. Examine the roles carried out by federal court officers.

**TEKS 2B, 9C, 9E, 9F, 11A, 21A, 21E, 22A, 22B, 22D**

- **Unit 5 booklet**
  Guided Reading and Review, p. 2
  Section 1 Quiz, p. 3
- **Lesson Plans booklet** Section 1, p. 78
- **Political Cartoons booklet** Section 1, p. 70
- **Block Scheduling with Lesson Strategies booklet** p. 28
- **Section Reading Support Transparencies**

- **Close Up on Primary Sources booklet**
  Franklin D. Roosevelt: Fireside Chat, p. 61
- **Basic Principles of the Constitution Transparencies** 32, 48
- **Section Support Transparencies** 73, 172
- **Presentation Pro CD-ROM** Section 1
- **Simulations and Data Graphing CD-ROM**

## 2 The Inferior Courts
### (pp. 512–515)

1. Outline the structure and jurisdiction of the federal district courts.
2. Describe the structure and jurisdiction of the federal courts of appeals.
3. Outline the structure and jurisdiction of the two other constitutional courts.

**TEKS 9C, 9E, 21A, 21D, 21E, 22A, 22B, 22D**

- **Unit 5 booklet**
  Guided Reading and Review, p. 4
  Section 2 Quiz, p. 5
- **Lesson Plans booklet** Section 2, p. 79
- **Political Cartoons booklet** Section 2, p. 71
- **Section Reading Support Transparencies**

- **Close Up on Primary Sources booklet**
  The Selection of Supreme Court Justices, p. 20
- **Section Support Transparencies** 74, 173
- **Presentation Pro CD-ROM** Section 2
- **Unit 5 booklet**
  Guided Reading and Review, p. 6

## 3 The Supreme Court
### (pp. 517–522)

1. Define the concept of judicial review.
2. Outline the scope of the Supreme Court's jurisdiction.
3. Examine how cases reach the Supreme Court.
4. Summarize the way the Court operates.

**TEKS 9C, 9E, 9F, 21A, 21E, 22A, 22B, 22D**

- Section 3 Quiz, p. 7
- **Lesson Plans booklet** Section 3, p. 80
- **Political Cartoons booklet** Section 3, p. 72
- **Close Up on Primary Sources booklet**
  Marbury v. Madison, p. 64; Justice William J. Brennan: How the Supreme Court Arrives at Decisions, p. 65
- **Section Reading Support Transparencies**

- **The Living Constitution booklet** p. 7
- **Government Assessment Rubrics booklet** p. 26
- **Basic Principles of the Constitution Transparencies** 37
- **Section Support Transparencies** 75, 174
- **Presentation Pro CD-ROM** Section 3
- **Social Studies Skills Tutor CD-ROM**

## 4 The Special Courts
### (pp. 524–526)

1. List the conditions under which a citizen may sue the government in the U.S. Court of Federal Claims.
2. Examine the roles of the territorial courts and of the District of Columbia courts.
3. Describe the functions of the Court of Appeals for the Armed Forces, the Court of Appeals for Veterans Claims, and the Tax Court.
4. Explain the function of military tribunals.

**TEKS 9C, 9E, 10C, 10D, 21A, 21E, 22A, 22B**

- **Unit 5 booklet**
  Guided Reading and Review, p. 8
  Section 4 Quiz, p. 9
  Skills for Life Activity, p. 10
- **Lesson Plans booklet** Section 4, p. 81
- **Political Cartoons booklet** Section 4, p. 73
- **Close Up on Primary Sources booklet**
  The Cherokee Address the American People, p. 36
- **Section Reading Support Transparencies**

- **Close Up on the Supreme Court booklet** Reno v. Condon, p. 19
- **The Basic Principles of the Constitution Posters**
- **Section Support Transparencies** 76, 175
- **Presentation Pro CD-ROM** Section 4

# Block Scheduling Strategies

The *Magruder's American Government* program addresses block-scheduling strategies in a variety of ways. For easy reference, side-column activities that fit a block format are marked ▦ **Block Strategy.** Each section also contains a **Block Scheduling Strategies** box describing at least two block-format activities that address and extend core content from the section. The **Block Scheduling with Lesson Strategies booklet** found in the Teaching Resources contains additional block-scheduling activities for each chapter.

## Take It to the Net

Visit the Social Studies area at the Prentice Hall School Web site. Once there, you can find additional links, current events connections, and activities to enrich chapter content for *Magruder's American Government,* as well as a Self-Test for students. Be sure to check out this month's **eTeach** online discussion with a Master Teacher.

### www.phschool.com

## Pressed for Time?

If you are running short on time to cover this chapter, consider one of the following options:

- Use the **Presentation Pro CD-ROM** to create an outline for this chapter.
- Use one of the **Pressed for Time** activities found on p. 27.
- Use the Section Summaries for Chapter 2, from **Guide to the Essentials of American Government (English and Spanish).**

 ## Video Connections

Prentice Hall offers two video programs to reinforce and extend chapter content. Show students *The Blessings of Liberty* from the **ABC News Civics and Government Videotape Library** and *Prayer in Schools: A Nationwide Debate* from the **Magruder's American Government Video Collection.**

## Assessment Options

- Section Quizzes, **Unit 5 booklet,** pp. 3, 5, 7, 9
- Chapter 18 Assessment, pp. 528–529
- **Guide to the Essentials of American Government,** Chapter 18 Test, p. 101

### Core Assessment

Chapter 18 Test, Chapter Tests booklet
ExamView® Test Bank CD-ROM Chapter 18
Government Assessment Rubrics

### Standardized Test Preparation

#### Diagnose and Prescribe
Diagnostic Tests for High School
Social Studies Skills

#### Review and Reteach
Review Book for Government

#### Practice and Assess
Test-Taking Strategies With
    Transparencies for High School
Test Prep Book for Government

## Chapter 18 Teacher's Edition Index

# The Federal Court System

## Introducing the Chapter

In this chapter, students will learn about the establishment and function of the judicial branch of government—the Supreme Court, the inferior courts, and the special courts of the federal court system.

### Make It Relevant

★ *You Can Make a Difference*

The press is often called "the fourth branch of government" since it can check and balance the power of the actual three branches. Have students explore this "watchdog" function of the press by generating a list of local issues or possible injustices that bear investigating. Then direct students to select one of the issues, conduct research and interviews, and write news stories that shed light on the issue.

**Service Learning**

### CONSTITUTIONAL PRINCIPLES

Emphasize the following basic principles as students read Chapter 18. Have the class respond to the questions, and then ask volunteers to explain which single principle they most closely associate with the federal court system, and why.

**Federalism** How does the nation's judicial system reflect the concept of federalism? How does the exclusive jurisdiction of the federal courts reflect the concept of federalism?

**Checks and Balances** What checks and balances relate to the judicial branch? How does judicial review check the power of the legislative branch?

**Judicial Review** What court case established the concept of judicial review? Which courts have the power of judicial review?

CHAPTER 18

# The Federal Court System

*"It is emphatically the province and duty of the judicial department to say what the law is. . . . If two laws conflict with each other, the courts must decide on the operation of each."*

—Chief Justice John Marshall (1803)

The Framers provided for a national system of courts to correct a major weakness in the Articles of Confederation. The Constitution provides for a Supreme Court and for other courts created by Congress. The federal courts operate in a dual court system, alongside the courts of each of the fifty States.

Protesters argue in front of the Supreme Court Building

**CLOSE UP** FOUNDATION *Corner*

The following resources are available only from the Close Up Foundation to support the concepts discussed in Chapter 18 "The Federal Court System":

◆ *Perspectives: Readings on Contemporary American Government*
◆ *The Bill of Rights: A User's Guide*
◆ *Profiles of Freedom: A Living Bill of Rights*

**CLOSE UP** FOUNDATION **Online**

To keep up-to-date on Close Up news and activities, visit Close Up Online at

**www.closeup.org**

Close Up Foundation
44 Canal Center Plaza
Alexandria, VA 22314-1592
800-765-3131

## ★ You Can Make a Difference

**THE ROLE OF THE JUDICIAL BRANCH** is to interpret and apply the law. It is up to the courts to see that justice is done, but that sometimes takes a long time. In 1999, six journalism students at Northwestern University in Evanston, Illinois, helped the courts correct a 17-year-old injustice. The students in the investigative journalism class of Professor David Protess worked together to help free Anthony Porter, a death-row inmate who had been wrongfully convicted of a double murder. They asked questions, searched police records, and tracked down witnesses to find new evidence in the 1982 case. Finally, their work paid off, and another man confessed to the crime. Porter was freed after nearly 17 years in prison.

### Keep It Current

Items marked with this logo are periodically updated on the Internet. Keep up-to-date with what's in the news. To get current information on issues related to the federal court system, go to **www.phschool.com**

### SECTION 1

#### The National Judiciary (pp. 506–511)

★ The Framers created a national judiciary consisting of a Supreme Court and inferior courts to be created by Congress.
★ The federal courts have exclusive or concurrent and original or appellate jurisdiction over the cases they hear.
★ Federal judges are appointed by the President, subject to confirmation by the Senate.
★ Supreme Court and inferior court judges serve for life, removable only by impeachment, while special court judges serve 15-year terms; Congress sets the salaries of federal judges.
★ Federal court officers, such as magistrates, U.S. attorneys, bailiffs, and clerks, serve in administrative and judicial roles.

### SECTION 2

#### The Inferior Courts (pp. 512–515)

★ The 94 U.S. district courts handle about 80 percent of the federal caseload; they have original jurisdiction over most federal criminal and civil cases.
★ The 12 federal appeals courts have appellate jurisdiction only.
★ The Court of International Trade hears tariff and trade cases; the Court of Appeals for the Federal Circuit has nationwide appellate jurisdiction from various federal courts.

### SECTION 3

#### The Supreme Court (pp. 517–522)

★ All federal and most State courts have the power of judicial review, deciding the constitutionality of an act of government.
★ The U.S. Supreme Court has both original and appellate jurisdiction, but usually hears cases on appeal; the Court decides only a handful of cases each year.
★ The Supreme Court is in session from October through June; it hears oral arguments, studies written briefs, meets in conference to discuss the cases, and renders majority, concurring, and dissenting opinions.

### SECTION 4

#### The Special Courts (pp. 524–526)

★ The U.S. government may not be sued without its consent; those who seek damages must take their cases to the U.S. Court of Federal Claims.
★ Congress has created federal courts for U.S. territories, as well as for the District of Columbia.
★ The U.S. Court of Appeals for the Armed Forces is a civilian tribunal that hears appeals of court-martial cases.
★ The U.S. Court of Appeals for Veterans Claims hears claims regarding veterans' benefits.
★ The U.S. Tax Court hears civil cases concerning tax law.

## Pressed for Time?

### To Omit the Chapter

If you wish to skip Chapter 18, ask students to read the Chapter in Brief and assign the Guide to the Essentials before continuing to another chapter. You may also want to assign the Chapter 18 Test in the Chapter Test booklet. Then specific portions of Chapter 18 may be assigned to students needing reinforcement of key terms and concepts.

### To Preview the Chapter

To introduce students to key terms and concepts in each section, have them read the Chapter in Brief. You may also assign the Reading Strategy activities on pp. 508, 513, 518, and 525 of this book.

### To Review the Chapter

When students have completed Chapter 18, you might want to assign the Guide to the Essentials or the Guided Reading and Review worksheets on pp. 2, 4, 6, and 8 of the Unit 5 booklet.

### To Cover the Chapter Quickly

To cover the material in Chapter 18 quickly, use the following activity.

**Focus** Ask students to identify the number of people living in the United States. Then have them consider the types of courts that are needed to serve all of those people.

**Instruct** Ask students to identify any of the federal courts that they can. Have students list these courts and attempt to identify each court's function. Then, ask students to skim the chapter to identify any courts that they have forgotten and to describe the function of each court.

**Close/Reteach** Remind students of the various federal courts. Then have them create graphic organizers showing the various federal courts, their functions, and how they relate to one another (if there is a relation).

■ **Block Strategy (Average)**

## Keep It Current

### Internet Update

Use the Prentice Hall School Web site and the Keep It Current CD-ROM to find quick content updates.

Visit **www.phschool.com** for current events articles that are linked to Chapter 18. Critical Thinking questions are included.

**Keep It Current CD-ROM** includes government projects by unit. Students complete each project using current information that they obtain by linking to the Prentice Hall School Web site from the CD-ROM.

# 1 The National Judiciary

**Objectives** You may wish to call students' attention to the objectives in the Section Preview. The objectives are reflected in the main headings of the section.

**Bellringer** Have students imagine a scene in which two neighbors are arguing about who owns a tree on the boundary of their yards. Suddenly one of them shouts, "What are you trying to do—make a federal case out of it?" Ask students what this means. Explain that in this section, they will learn what constitutes a federal case.

**Vocabulary Builder** Have students look up the meaning of *jurisdiction*. Then ask them to suggest meanings for the other four terms in the Political Dictionary that contain the word *jurisdiction*. Have them check their meanings as they read.

## Section Preview

### OBJECTIVES

1. **Analyze** the structure and functions of the federal court system.
2. **Analyze** the types of federal court jurisdictions.
3. **Outline** the process for appointing federal judges.
4. **List** the terms of office for federal judges and explain how their salaries are determined.
5. **Examine** the roles of federal court officers.

### WHY IT MATTERS

The Framers of the Constitution believed in the need for a national judicial system. The Constitution outlines the structure of the federal judiciary, the jurisdiction of the courts, and the functions of federal judges.

### POLITICAL DICTIONARY

★ **inferior courts**
★ **jurisdiction**
★ **exclusive jurisdiction**
★ **concurrent jurisdiction**
★ **plaintiff**
★ **defendant**
★ **original jurisdiction**
★ **appellate jurisdiction**

---

Joe Smith steals a brand-new sports car, a bright red convertible, in Chicago. Two days later, he is stopped for speeding in Atlanta. Where, now, will he be tried for car theft? In Illinois, where he stole the car? In Georgia, where he was caught? In point of fact, Joe may be on the verge of learning something about the federal court system—and about the Dyer Act of 1925, which makes it a federal crime to transport a stolen automobile across a State line.

## The Federal Court System

During the years the Articles of Confederation were in force (1781–1789), there were no national courts and no national judiciary. The laws of the United States were interpreted and applied as each State saw fit, and sometimes not at all. Disputes between States and between persons who lived in different States were decided, if at all, by the courts in one of the States involved. Often, decisions by the courts in one State were ignored by the courts in the other States.

Alexander Hamilton spoke to the point in *The Federalist* No. 22. He described "the want of a judiciary power" as a "circumstance which crowns the defects of the Confederation." Arguing the need for a national court system, he added: "Laws are a dead letter without courts to expound and define their true meaning and operation."

The Framers created a national judiciary for the United States in a single sentence in the Constitution:

 **FROM THE Constitution** *"The judicial Power of the United States shall be vested in one supreme Court, and in such inferior Courts as the Congress may from time to time ordain and establish."*

—Article III, Section 1

Congress also is given the expressed power "to constitute Tribunals inferior to the supreme Court" in Article I, Section 8, Clause 9.

### A Dual Court System

Keep in mind this important point: There are *two* separate court systems in the United States.[1] On one hand, the national judiciary spans the country with its more than 120 courts. On the other hand, each of the 50 States has its own system of courts. Their numbers run well into the thousands. These State courts hear most of the cases in this country.

---

[1]Federalism does not require two court systems. Article III provides that Congress "may" establish lower federal courts. At its first session, in 1789, Congress decided to construct a complete set of federal courts to parallel those of the States. In most of the world's other federal systems, the principal courts are those of the states or provinces; typically, the only significant federal court is a national court of last resort, often called the supreme court.

---

### Pressed for Time?

## Quick Lesson Plan

1. **Focus** Tell students that federal courts have the authority to hear specific kinds of cases. Ask students to discuss what they know about how the national judiciary is organized and the kinds of cases it hears.
2. **Instruct** Ask students what court would be involved in the case of a boundary dispute between neighboring States. Have students describe the rest of the federal court system and its jurisdiction. Then discuss differences in the appointment, terms, and pay of federal judges.
3. **Close/Reteach** Remind students that the national judiciary has two types of courts. Have students make a table showing the differences between the functions of the two courts and the judges who sit on them.

## Point-of-Use Resources

📁 **Block Scheduling with Lesson Strategies** Activities for Chapter 18 are presented on p. 28.

---

## 🔲 Block Scheduling Strategies

Consider these suggestions to manage extended class time:

■ Discuss with the class the criteria for a case reaching a federal court. Then, provide students with blank Venn diagrams (one is provided in the Section Support Transparencies, Transparency 6). Have students use the Venn diagram to show which cases are referred to federal courts, which are referred to State courts, and which can be referred to either.

■ Ask students to assume the role of television news reporters. Have them work to create public-service announcements on federal judges. Their work should focus on the selection process, the terms of office, and how federal judges' salaries are determined. Have students enact their public-service announcements for the class.

## Types of Federal Courts

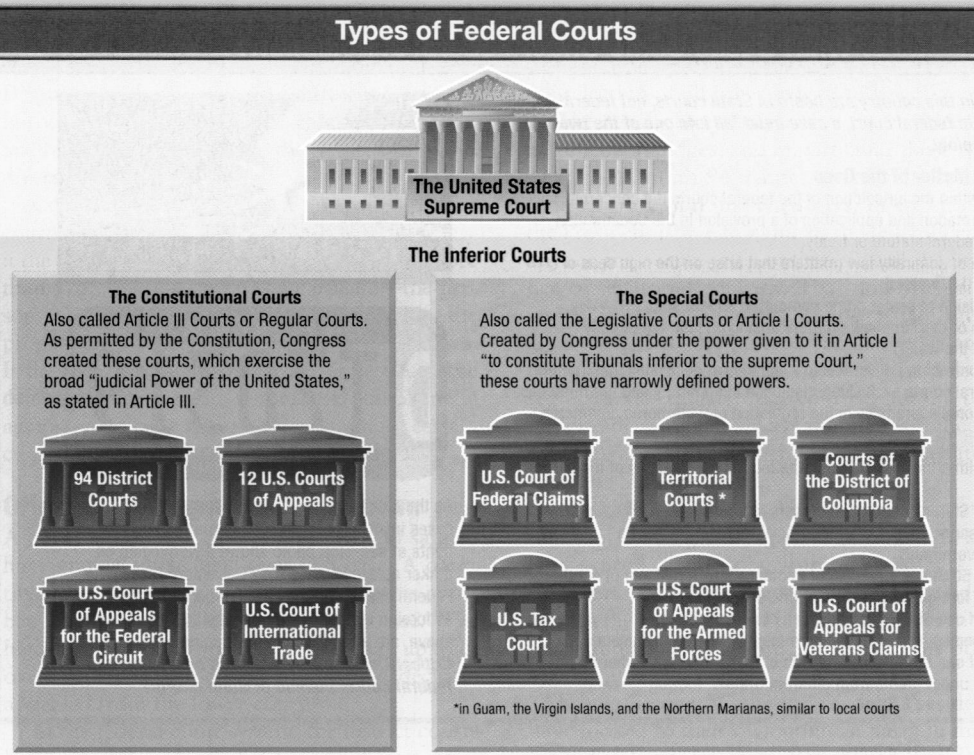

**The United States Supreme Court**

**The Inferior Courts**

**The Constitutional Courts**
Also called Article III Courts or Regular Courts. As permitted by the Constitution, Congress created these courts, which exercise the broad "judicial Power of the United States," as stated in Article III.

- 94 District Courts
- 12 U.S. Courts of Appeals
- U.S. Court of Appeals for the Federal Circuit
- U.S. Court of International Trade

**The Special Courts**
Also called the Legislative Courts or Article I Courts. Created by Congress under the power given to it in Article I "to constitute Tribunals inferior to the supreme Court," these courts have narrowly defined powers.

- U.S. Court of Federal Claims
- Territorial Courts *
- Courts of the District of Columbia
- U.S. Tax Court
- U.S. Court of Appeals for the Armed Forces
- U.S. Court of Appeals for Veterans Claims

*in Guam, the Virgin Islands, and the Northern Marianas, similar to local courts

*Interpreting Diagrams* The Constitution created only the Supreme Court, giving Congress the power to create any lower, or "inferior," courts, as needed. ***Using this diagram, compare and contrast the purpose of the constitutional courts and the special courts, as defined in the Constitution.***

## Two Kinds of Federal Courts

The Constitution creates the Supreme Court and leaves to Congress the creation of the **inferior courts**—the lower federal courts, those beneath the Supreme Court. Over the years, Congress has created two distinct types of federal courts: (1) the constitutional courts and (2) the special courts. The diagram on this page sets out these several federal courts.

The constitutional courts are the federal courts that Congress has formed under Article III to exercise "the judicial Power of the United States." Together with the Supreme Court, they now include the courts of appeals, the district courts, and the U.S. Court of International Trade. The constitutional courts are also called the regular courts or Article III courts.

The special courts do not exercise the broad "judicial Power of the United States." Rather, they have been created by Congress to hear cases arising out of some of the expressed powers given to Congress in Article I. The special courts hear a much narrower range of cases than those that may come before the constitutional courts.

These special courts sometimes are called the legislative courts. Today, they include the U.S. Court of Appeals for the Armed Forces, the U.S. Court of Appeals for Veterans Claims, the U.S. Court of Federal Claims, the U.S. Tax Court, the various territorial courts, and the courts of the District of Columbia. You will look at the unique features of these courts later in this chapter.

## Organizing Information

To make sure students understand the main points of this section, you may wish to use the tree map graphic organizer to the right.

Tell students that a tree map shows an outline of a topic, its main ideas, and its supporting details. Ask students to use the tree map to record details about the kinds of federal court jurisdiction.

**Teaching Tip** A template for this graphic organizer can be found in the Section Support Transparencies, Transparency 3.

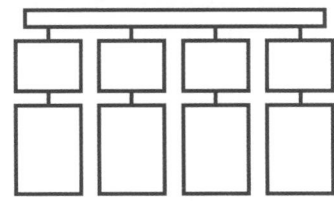

## Reading Strategy

### Getting the Main Idea

Tell students that the Supreme Court has greater powers than the other federal courts. Have students, as they read, note the powers of the Supreme Court and how the Court exercises those powers.

### A C T I V I T Y

### American Government, American Humor

Share the following quotation with students:

*"No matter whether th' consti-tution follows th' flag or not, th' supreme coort follows the iliction returns."*
—Mr. Dooley (character created by journalist and humorist Finley Peter Dunne)

**Discussion** Have students identify the view of the Supreme Court that Dunne is expressing. Then have students explain why they agree or disagree with this interpretation. Ask students how the Constitution seeks to guard against a Supreme Court that "follows the iliction returns."
**(Challenging)**

## Point-of-Use Resources

☐ **Guided Reading and Review** Unit 5 booklet, p. 6 provides students with practice identifying the main ideas and key terms of this section.

☐ **Lesson Plans** For lesson planning suggestions, see p. 80 of the Lesson Plans booklet.

☐ **Political Cartoons** See p. 72 of the Political Cartoons booklet for a cartoon relevant to this section.

### Answer to . . .

**Interpreting Charts** It expanded the judicial branch's role by introducing judicial review.

---

that the federal courts—and, in particular, the Supreme Court—should have this power.[11]

### Marbury v. Madison

The Court first asserted its power of judicial review in the classic case of *Marbury* v. *Madison* in 1803.[12] The case arose in the aftermath of the stormy elections of 1800. Thomas Jefferson and his Democratic-Republicans had won the presidency and control of both houses of Congress. The outgoing Federalists, stung by their defeat, then tried to pack the judiciary with loyal party members. Congress created several new federal judgeships in the early weeks of 1801; President John Adams quickly filled those posts with Federalists.

William Marbury had been appointed a justice of the peace for the District of Columbia. The Senate had confirmed his appointment and, late on the night of March 3, 1801, President Adams signed the commissions of office for Marbury and for a number of other new judges. The next day Jefferson became the President, and discovered that Marbury's commission and several others had not yet been delivered.

Angered by the Federalists' attempted court-packing, Jefferson at once told James Madison, the new secretary of state, not to deliver those commissions to the "midnight justices." William Marbury then went to the Supreme Court, seeking a writ of mandamus[13] to force delivery.

Marbury based his suit on a provision of the Judiciary Act of 1789, in which Congress had created the federal court system. That law gave the Supreme Court the right to hear such suits in its original jurisdiction (not on appeal from a lower court).

---

[11]See Article III, Section 2, setting out the Court's jurisdiction, and Article VI, Section 2, the Supremacy Clause.
[12]It is often mistakenly said that the Court first exercised the power in this case, but in fact the Court did so at least as early as *Hylton* v. *United States* in 1796. In that case it upheld the constitutionality of a tax Congress had laid on carriages.

[13]A writ of mandamus is a court order compelling a government officer to perform an act which that officer has a clear legal duty to perform.

---

### An Early Supreme Court Drama: *Marbury* v. *Madison*

| The Players | The Case | The Decision | The Impact |
| --- | --- | --- | --- |
| **John Adams,** outgoing Federalist President of the United States<br>**Thomas Jefferson,** incoming Democratic-Republican President of the United States<br>**James Madison,** incoming secretary of state<br>**William Marbury,** appointed a justice of the peace for the District of Columbia<br>**John Marshall,** Chief Justice of the United States Supreme Court | 1. The night before leaving office, Adams signs several judicial commissions.<br>2. Angered by Adams' actions, Jefferson orders Madison to withhold any commissions not yet delivered.<br>3. Hoping to force Jefferson to give him the judgeship, Marbury files suit in the Supreme Court. He argues that the Judiciary Act of 1789 allows him to take his case directly to the high court. | Marshall, writing for a unanimous court, declares that the Judiciary Act violates Article III, Section 2 and is therefore unconstitutional. Marbury loses, having based his case on an unconstitutional law. | The case established the Supreme Court's power of judicial review—its power to determine the constitutionality of a governmental action. The power extends to the actions of all governments in the United States—national, State and local. The Court's decision in *Marbury* assured the place of the judicial branch in the system of separation of powers. |

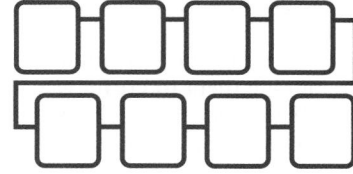

*Interpreting Charts* In the landmark case *Marbury* v. *Madison*, the Supreme Court ruled against William Marbury because he had based his case on a part of the Judiciary Act of 1789, which was found to be in conflict with the Constitution. *How did the Court's decision affect the role of the judicial branch in our system of government?*

---

## Organizing Information

To make sure students understand the main points of this section, you may wish to use the flowchart organizer to the right.

Tell students that a flowchart shows a sequence of events. Ask students to use the flowchart to describe how judicial review evolved and what its effects have been on the Supreme Court.

**Teaching Tip** A template for this graphic organizer can be found in the Section Support Transparencies, Transparency 4.

In a unanimous opinion written by Chief Justice John Marshall, the Court refused Marbury's request.[14] It did so because it found the section of the judiciary act on which Marbury had based his case to be in conflict with the Constitution and, therefore, void. Specifically, it found the statute in conflict with the section of the Constitution that reads:

> FROM THE *Constitution*
> "*In all Cases affecting Ambassadors, other public Ministers and Consuls, and those in which a State shall be Party, the supreme Court shall have original Jurisdiction. In all the other Cases before mentioned, the supreme Court shall have appellate Jurisdiction. . . .*"
> —Article III, Section 2, Clause 2

Marshall's powerful opinion was based on three propositions. First, the Constitution is, by its own terms, the supreme law of the land. Second, all legislative acts and other actions of government are subordinate (inferior) to the supreme law and cannot be allowed to conflict with it. Third, judges are sworn to enforce the provisions of the Constitution, and therefore must refuse to enforce any government action they find to be in conflict with it.

## The Effects of *Marbury*

The impact of the Court's decision goes far beyond the fate of an obscure individual named William Marbury. In this decision, Chief Justice Marshall claimed for the Supreme Court the right to declare acts of Congress unconstitutional, and so laid the foundation for the judicial branch's key role in the development of the American system of government.

The Court has used its power of judicial review in thousands of cases since 1803. Usually it has upheld the constitutionality of federal and State actions.

The dramatic and often far-reaching effects of the Supreme Court's exercise of the power of

---

[14]Marshall was appointed Chief Justice by President John Adams, and he took office on January 31, 1801. He served in the post for 34 years, until his death on July 6, 1835. He also served as Adams's secretary of state from May 13, 1800, to March 4, 1801. Thus, he served simultaneously as secretary of state and Chief Justice for more than a month at the end of the Adams administration. What is more, he was the secretary of state who had failed to deliver Marbury's commission in a timely fashion.

# *Voices* on Government

**David Souter** was named a Supreme Court justice by President George Bush in 1990. From his experience as New Hampshire attorney general and a State court judge, Souter knew that judges' decisions are more than abstract legal ideas. Here are his thoughtful insights on justice:

" *Whether we are on a trial court or an appellate court, at the end of our task some human being is going to be affected. . . . If indeed we are going to be trial judges, whose rulings will affect the lives of other people and who are going to change their lives by what we do, we had better use every power of our minds and our hearts and our beings to get those rulings right.* "

## Evaluating the Quotation

*Think of an issue that reflects the "human" effects of court decisions that Souter refers to. In what ways did a court decision affect the daily lives of Americans?*

judicial review tends to overshadow much of its other work. Each year it hears dozens of cases in which questions of constitutionality are not raised, but in which federal law is interpreted and applied. Thus, many of the more important statutes that Congress has passed have been brought to the Supreme Court time and again for decision. So, too, have many of the lesser ones. In interpreting those laws and applying them to specific situations, the Court has had a real impact on both their meaning and their effect.

## Supreme Court Jurisdiction

The Supreme Court has both original and appellate jurisdiction. Most of its cases, however, come on appeal—from the lower federal courts and from the highest State courts.

Article III, Section 2 of the Constitution spells out two classes of cases that may be heard by the High Court in its original jurisdiction: (1) those to which a State is a party and (2) those affecting ambassadors, other public ministers, and consuls.

Congress cannot enlarge on this constitutional grant of original jurisdiction. Recall, that

---

---

## Preparing for Standardized Tests

Have students read the passages under the heading *Supreme Court Jurisdiction* and then answer the question below.

What jurisdiction does the Supreme Court have?

**A** appellate jurisdiction

**B** original jurisdiction

**C** original and appellate jurisdiction

**D** any case it chooses to take

---

*Answer to . . .*
**Evaluating the Quotation** Answers will vary, but should be supported with relevant facts and examples.

## Background Note
### Recent Scholarship

Tinsley E. Yarborough's book *The Rehnquist Court and the Constitution* asks whether the Supreme Court under William Rehnquist has succeeded in challenging the federal civil liberties doctrine adopted by the Warren Court. The book begins by introducing the justices appointed by Presidents Reagan, Bush, and Clinton and examining the internal workings of the Supreme Court in recent years. The remainder of the book focuses on areas of constitutional decision making, the Federal Government's powers, States rights, the right to privacy, the religion clauses, freedom of expression, and criminal rights. What makes Yarborough's work particularly helpful is that he places recent decisions in context, explaining their significance and how they compare to rulings handed down by an earlier generation of justices.

## Point-of-Use Resources

📁 **The Living Constitution** Judicial Review, p. 7

📁 **Close Up on Primary Sources** *Marbury* v. *Madison* (1803), p. 64; Justice William J. Brennan, How the Supreme Court Arrives at Decisions, p. 65

📖 **Basic Principles of the Constitution Transparencies** Transparencies 37-43 *Judicial Review*

### Answer to ...

**Interpreting Diagrams** Possible answer: As the Supreme Court has time only to hear a limited number of cases, they must be of significance.

▶ **No Anonymous Tips**
In *Florida* v. *J.L.,* 2000, the Supreme Court ruled that under ordinary circumstances, an anonymous tip to police about a concealed firearm was not sufficient to prompt a legal "stop and frisk" search.

is what the Court held in *Marbury.* If Congress could do so, it would in effect be amending the Constitution. Congress can implement the constitutional provision, however, and it has done so. It has provided that the Court shall have original and exclusive jurisdiction over (1) all controversies involving two or more States, and (2) all cases brought against ambassadors or other public ministers, but not consuls.

The Court may choose to take original jurisdiction over any other case covered by the broad wording in Article III, Section 2 of the Constitution. Almost without exception, however, those cases are tried in the lower courts. The Supreme Court hears only a very small number of cases in its original jurisdiction—in fact, only a case or two each term.

## How Cases Reach the Court

Some 8,000 cases are now appealed to the Supreme Court each year. Of these, the Court accepts only a few hundred for decision. In most cases, petitions for review are denied, usually because most of the justices agree with the decision of the lower court or believe that the case involves no significant point of law. The Court selects those cases that it does hear according to "the rule of four": At least four of its nine justices must agree that a case should be put on the Court's docket.

More than half the cases decided by the Court are disposed of in brief orders. For example, an order may remand (return) a case to a lower court for reconsideration in the light of some other recent and related case decided by the High Court. All told, the Court decides, after hearing arguments and with full opinions, fewer than 100 cases a year.

Most cases reach the Supreme Court by **writ of certiorari** (from the Latin, meaning "to be made more certain"). This writ is an order by the Court directing a lower court to send up the record in a given case for its review. Either party

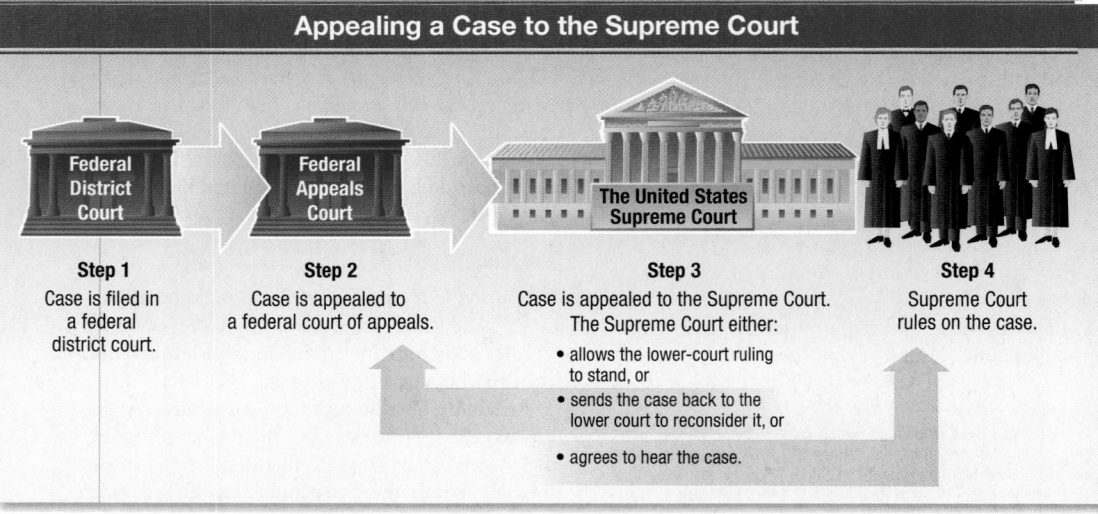

### Appealing a Case to the Supreme Court

**Federal District Court**

**Federal Appeals Court**

**The United States Supreme Court**

**Step 1**
Case is filed in a federal district court.

**Step 2**
Case is appealed to a federal court of appeals.

**Step 3**
Case is appealed to the Supreme Court. The Supreme Court either:
• allows the lower-court ruling to stand, or
• sends the case back to the lower court to reconsider it, or
• agrees to hear the case.

**Step 4**
Supreme Court rules on the case.

*Interpreting Diagrams* The diagram above shows the typical route (though not the only one) a case might take to the Supreme Court. ***Why do you think this process requires so many steps to reach the Supreme Court—often at great expense and time to the parties involved?***

## CONSTITUTIONAL PRINCIPLES

**Judicial Review**
It may seem odd that the power of judicial review, which has left the Supreme Court as the final authority on the constitutionality of U.S. laws, is not mentioned in the Constitution. However, statements from Framers of the Constitution, such as Alexander Hamilton in *The Federalist* No. 78, seem to suggest the need for the power of judicial review, and decisions made by the Supreme Court seem to suggest that the Court considered it one of its basic functions.

**Activity**
Have students conduct research on the legal system of at least two other countries to determine whether their courts have the power of judicial review. For countries that do allow for judicial review, ask students to determine whether it is a power granted by the country's constitution or if the power developed out of tradition.

to a case can petition the Court to issue a writ. But, again, "cert" is granted in a limited number of instances—typically, only when a petition raises some important constitutional question or a serious problem in the interpretation of a statute.

When certiorari is denied, the decision of the lower court stands in that particular case. Note, however, that the denial of cert is not a decision on the merits of a case. All that a denial means is that, for whatever reason, four or more justices could not agree that the Supreme Court should accept that case for review.

A few cases do reach the Court in yet another way, by **certificate**. This process is used when a lower court is not clear about the procedure or the rule of law that should apply in a case. The lower court asks the Supreme Court to certify the answer to a specific question in the matter.

Most cases that reach the Court do so from the highest State courts and the federal courts of appeals. A few do come, however, from the federal district courts and a very few from the Court of Appeals for the Armed Forces.

## How the Court Operates

The Court sits from the first Monday in October to sometime the following June or July. Each term is identified by the year in which it began. Thus, the 2002 term ran from October 1, 2002, into the early summer of 2003.

### Oral Arguments

Once the Supreme Court accepts a case, it sets a date on which that case will be heard. As a rule, the justices consider cases in two-week cycles from October to early May. They hear oral arguments in several cases for two weeks; then the justices recess for two weeks to consider those cases and handle other Court business.

While the Supreme Court is hearing oral arguments, it convenes at 10:00 A.M. on Mondays, Tuesdays, Wednesdays, and sometimes Thursdays. At those public sessions, the lawyers make their oral arguments. Their presentations are almost always limited to 30 minutes.[15]

### Briefs

Briefs are written documents filed with the Court before oral arguments begin. These detailed statements support one side of a case, presenting arguments built largely on relevant facts and the citation of previous cases. Some briefs run to hundreds of pages.

The Court may also receive *amicus curiae* (friend of the court) briefs. These are briefs filed by persons or groups who are not actual parties to a case but who nonetheless have a substantial interest in its outcome. Thus, for example, cases involving such highly charged matters as abortion or affirmative action regularly attract a large number of amicus briefs. Notice, however, that these briefs can be filed only with the Court's permission or at its request.

The solicitor general, a principal officer in the Department of Justice, is often called the Federal Government's chief lawyer. He—and, certainly, one day she—represents the United States in all cases to which it is party in the Supreme Court and may appear for the government for any federal State court.[16]

The solicitor general also has another extraordinary responsibility. He or she decides which cases the government should ask the Supreme Court to review and what position the United States should take in those cases it brings before the High Court.

### The Court in Conference

On most Wednesdays and Fridays through a term, the justices meet in conference. There, in closest secrecy, they consider the cases in which they have heard oral arguments.[17]

The Chief Justice presides over the conference. He speaks first on each case to be considered and usually indicates how he intends to vote. Then each associate justice summarizes his or her views. Those presentations are made in order of seniority, with the justice most recently named to the Court speaking last. After the justices are "polled," they usually debate the case.

---

[15]The justices usually listen closely to a lawyer's oral arguments and sometimes interrupt them with questions or requests for information. After 25 minutes, a white light comes on at the lectern from which the lawyer addresses the Court; five minutes later a red light signals the end of the presentation, even if the lawyer is in mid-sentence.

[16]The attorney general may argue the government's position before the Supreme Court but rarely does.

[17]At conference, the justices also decide which new cases they will accept for decision.

## Point-of-Use Resources

 **Guide to the Essentials** Chapter 18, Section 3, p. 99 provides support for students who need additional review of section content. Spanish support is available in the Spanish edition of the Guide on p. 92.

**Quiz** Unit 5 booklet, p. 7 includes matching and multiple-choice questions to check students' understanding of Section 3 content.

**Presentation Pro CD-ROM** Quizzes and multiple-choice questions check students' understanding of Section 3 content.

## Answers to . . .

## Section 3 Assessment

**1. (a)** Both are means for a case from a lower court to reach the Supreme Court. **(b)** A writ is requested by either party in the case, while a certificate is requested by the lower court.
**2.** Majority: the actual decision on a case and the reasoning on which it was based. Concurring: adds or emphasizes points; written by one or more justices who agree with the majority opinion. Dissenting: written by justices who disagree with the majority opinion.
**3. (a)** Precedents serve as examples for justices to follow in similar cases. **(b)** Sample sentence: *Marbury* v. *Madison* served as a precedent for the use of judicial review by the Supreme Court.
**4.** "Easy" cases involve simple points of law or their decisions are not appealed. The Supreme Court hears only those cases that it feels involve significant points of law or were not decided properly in the lower court.
**5.** Possible answer: Concurring and dissenting opinions are ways that all points of view can be expressed; in future cases, they may form the basis for majority opinions. This process suggests that the U.S. judicial system is flexible—always capable of reviewing and checking itself.
**6.** It ensures that the judicial branch has the authority to check the power of Congress, by declaring acts of Congress unconstitutional.

 ▲ The current members of the Supreme Court pose for their official photograph. Front row: Antonin Scalia, John Paul Stevens, Chief Justice William H. Rehnquist, Sandra Day O'Connor, Anthony Kennedy. Back Row: Ruth Bader Ginsburg, David Souter, Clarence Thomas, Stephen Breyer.

About a third of all the Court's decisions are unanimous, but most find the Court divided. The High Court is sometimes criticized for its split decisions. But, notice, its cases pose very difficult questions, and many also present questions on which lower courts have disagreed. In short, most of the Court's cases are controversial ones; the easy cases seldom get that far.

### Opinions

If the Chief Justice is in the majority on a case, he assigns the writing of the Court's opinion. When the Chief Justice is in the minority, the assignment is handled by the senior associate justice on the majority side.

The Court's opinion is often called the **majority opinion.** Officially called the Opinion of the Court, it announces the Court's decision in a case and sets out the reasoning on which it is based.[18]

The Court's written opinions are exceedingly valuable. The majority opinions stand as **precedents,** or examples to be followed in similar cases as they arise in the lower courts or reach the Supreme Court.

Often, one or more of the justices who agree with the Court's decision may write a **concurring opinion**—to add or emphasize a point that was not made in the majority opinion. The concurring opinions may bring the Supreme Court to modify its present stand in future cases.

One or more **dissenting opinions** are often written by those justices who do not agree with the Court's majority decision. Chief Justice Charles Evans Hughes once described dissenting opinions as "an appeal to the brooding spirit of the law, to the intelligence of a future day." On rare occasions, the Supreme Court does reverse itself. The minority opinion of today could become the Court's majority position in the future.

---

[18]Most majority opinions, and many concurring and dissenting opinions, run to dozens of pages. Some decisions are accompanied by very brief and unsigned opinions. These *per curiam* (for the court) opinions seldom run more than a paragraph or two and usually dispose of relatively uncomplicated cases.

## Section 3 Assessment

**Key Terms and Main Ideas**

1. **(a)** What does a **writ of certiorari** have in common with a **certificate? (b)** How do the two differ?
2. Explain how a **majority opinion,** a **concurring opinion,** and a **dissenting opinion** differ.
3. **(a)** Why are **precedents** important? **(b)** Write a sentence using the word *precedent* in a judicial context.
4. Why do "easy" cases seldom reach the Supreme Court?

**Critical Thinking**

5. **Drawing Conclusions** Why do you think the Supreme Court justices often write concurring and/or dissenting opinions in a case?

6. **Determining Cause and Effect** How does the Court's power of judicial review affect the balance of power in the Federal Government?

### Take It to the Net

7. Analyze issues raised by judicial activism and judicial restraint. Visit the Exploring Constitutional Conflicts site on the Internet and use the information provided to explore a case in which the Supreme Court was criticized for being activist. Then write an analysis of whether the Court's approach was justified. Use the links provided in the Social Studies area at the following Web site for help in completing this activity. **www.phschool.com**

### Take It to the Net

**7.** Direct students to the Social Studies area at the Prentice Hall School Web site. The *Magruder's American Government* companion Web site includes the directions and links needed to complete the activity. It also provides a printable Internet activity worksheet with scoring rubrics for assessment. Analyses should show an understanding of judicial activism and an understanding of the particular case chosen.

# SKILLS FOR LIFE

TECHNOLOGY
CITIZENSHIP
CRITICAL THINKING
CHARTS and GRAPHS

## Drawing Conclusions

A caravan of police cars converges on a Chicago neighborhood known for illegal drug trafficking. A man sees the police and flees the scene. Suspicious, the police chase him down and "frisk" him for weapons. They find a handgun. They arrest him.

Was this a legal search and seizure? The 4th Amendment to the Constitution protects U.S. citizens from "unreasonable searches and seizures." Did the police officers have sufficient reason to suspect that the fleeing man had committed a crime, even though they did not see him do anything wrong? In *Wardlow v. Illinois*, 2000, the Supreme Court ruled that the police acted legally when they drew this conclusion.

Drawing a conclusion means arriving at an idea or opinion that is suggested, indirectly, from given information. How did the officers reach their conclusion? Instinctively, within seconds, they used a process like this:

**1. Assess information.** Analyze a fact or set of facts to see if they suggest other ideas. Sometimes a given piece of information may imply a cause-effect relationship. In the Chicago case, what did police actually observe when they arrived on scene?

**2. Apply prior knowledge.** To come to a conclusion, you usually combine new information with facts you already know. What relevant information did the police already know when they arrived on scene?

**3. Reach a conclusion.** Often a conclusion can be stated in this form: *X, therefore Y*. Use this format to state the conclusion that the police drew from the scene.

**4. Test your conclusion.** It's possible to draw the wrong conclusion from a set of facts. Always test the validity of your conclusion by considering whether any other conclusion is possible from the information given. Is there another possible explanation for what the Chicago police saw? If so, is it a likely explanation? Explain.

What did the Supreme Court think of the police officers' conclusions? In a ruling in early 2000, the Court said that "An individual's presence in a 'high crime area,' standing alone, is not enough to support

a reasonable, particularized suspicion of criminal activity," but the man's "nervous, evasive behavior" and "unprovoked flight" were "sufficiently suspicious to warrant further investigation." The officers' conclusions, the Court found, were sufficiently valid to justify their actions.

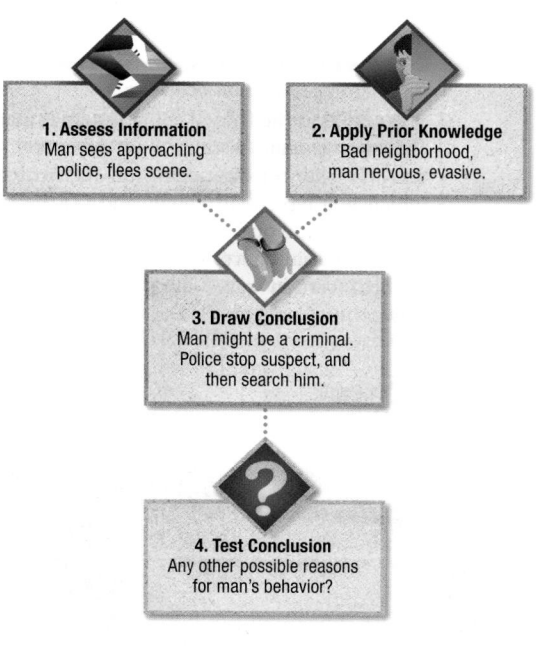

**1. Assess Information**
Man sees approaching police, flees scene.

**2. Apply Prior Knowledge**
Bad neighborhood, man nervous, evasive.

**3. Draw Conclusion**
Man might be a criminal. Police stop suspect, and then search him.

**4. Test Conclusion**
Any other possible reasons for man's behavior?

### Test for Success

Use the steps above and the facts in the following paragraph to draw a conclusion about *Plessy* v. *Ferguson*. State your conclusion as *X, therefore Y*.

*In* Plessy *v.* Ferguson *(1896) the Supreme Court ruled that racially segregated facilities were constitutional as long as the facilities were "separate but equal." In 1954 the Court overturned* Plessy *in* Brown *v.* Board of Education, *1954.*

## Point-of-Use Resources

📁 **Skills for Life Activity** Unit 5 booklet, p. 10 provides an additional skill activity for this chapter.

💿 **Social Studies Skills Tutor CD-ROM**
Provides interactive practice in geographic literacy, critical thinking and reading, visual analysis, and communications.

### Test for Success

Possible answers: (1) The Court in *Plessy* v. *Ferguson* decided that separate facilities could be equal, yet a later Court overturned the decision; therefore the 1954 ruling must have decided that segregated facilities were inherently unequal. (2) *Plessy* required "separate but equal" facilities, yet segregated schools remained unequal throughout the 1900s; therefore the ruling was not enforced properly.

---

★ ★ ★ ★ ★ ★ ★ ★

# SKILLS FOR LIFE

CRITICAL THINKING

## Drawing Conclusions

**Focus** Work as a class to formulate conclusions about a Supreme Court case.

**Instruct** Direct students to coverage of a landmark Supreme Court case, either in this book, a reference book, or online. (Landmark cases are also presented in the Close Up on the Supreme Court booklet in the *Teaching Resources*.) Have students study the details of the case. Guide students to use the steps on this page to draw conclusions about the case.

**Close/Reteach** Have students discuss whether their conclusions about the case were the same as the conclusions reached by either the majority or the minority on the Court.

### Answers...

**1.** They saw a man who, upon seeing the police, fled the scene.
**2.** They knew that illegal drug trafficking went on in the neighborhood.
**3.** Possible answer: In a high-crime area, a man saw the police and fled the scene, therefore he must be engaged in some criminal activity.
**4.** Possible answers: The man could have fled from the police because he feared police violence. He could have had bad experiences with the police in the past, or just didn't want to be stopped and questioned.

## Practicing the Vocabulary

1. concurrent jurisdiction
2. civilian tribunal
3. majority opinion
4. docket
5. plaintiff
6. precedent
7. court-martial
8. civil case
9. redress
10. writ of certiorari
11. inferior courts
12. concurring opinion

## Reviewing Main Ideas

### Section 1

**13.** They believed the new government needed a way to enforce its laws in a uniform way across the nation.

**14.** Possible answers: It creates the Supreme Court; it creates the inferior courts; it gives the federal courts jurisdiction over special cases.

**15.** State courts.

**16.** The President nominates federal judges and the Senate confirms the appointments. For most federal judges, the President bases his nominations on the advice of the Senate.

### Section 2

**17. (a)** The district courts have original jurisdiction over most cases, while the appeals courts have only appellate jurisdiction. **(b)** They handle nearly all cases tried in the federal courts, excepting special court cases.

**18.** Congress created the Court of Appeals.

**19.** A circuit is one of 12 geographic areas of the United States that has its own court of appeals.

**20.** Most come from the district courts.

**21.** It has nationwide jurisdiction.

### Section 3

**22. (a)** Judicial review is vital because it serves as a check on actions taken by all three branches of government. **(b)** *Marbury* v. *Madison*.

**23. (a)** The Supreme Court has both original and appellate jurisdiction. **(b)** Most of the cases the Supreme Court accepts are appeal cases from the highest State courts and the federal courts of appeals.

**24.** The "rule of four" means that four of the nine justices must agree to put a

case on the Supreme Court's docket before the case is heard.

**25.** Typically, the case is ended. It might be remanded to a lower court for reconsideration.

**26.** Lawyers from both sides of the case present oral arguments in public sessions. Each lawyer has 30 minutes to present his or her side, and typically focuses on the major points made in written briefs.

### Section 4

**27. (a)** Congress. **(b)** They are created to address cases that involve only certain expressed powers of Congress.

**28.** A citizen can sue the United States only if Congress has declared that the United States is open to suit. In that case, the citizen takes his or her plea to the Court of Federal Claims.

**29.** This court hears appeals from the decisions made by the Department of Veterans Affairs. In such cases an individual claims that the VA has denied or mishandled claims for veterans' benefits.

## Political Dictionary

inferior courts (p. 507)
jurisdiction (p. 508)
exclusive jurisdiction (p. 508)
concurrent jurisdiction (p. 508)
plaintiff (p. 509)
defendant (p. 509)
original jurisdiction (p. 509)

appellate jurisdiction (p. 509)
criminal case (p. 513)
civil case (p. 513)
docket (p. 513)
writ of certiorari (p. 520)
certificate (p. 521)
majority opinion (p. 522)

precedent (p. 522)
concurring opinion (p. 522)
dissenting opinion (p. 522)
redress (p. 524)
civilian tribunal (p. 525)
court-martial (p. 525)

## Practicing the Vocabulary

*Matching* *Choose a term from the list above that best matches each description.*

1. Jurisdiction shared by a State court and a federal court
2. A court made up of non-military judges
3. The Supreme Court's official decision of a case
4. A court's caseload
5. A person who initiated a lawsuit
6. An example to follow in similar cases in the future
7. A court of military personnel, used to try those accused of violating military law

*Fill in the Blank* *Choose a term from the list above that best completes the sentence.*

8. A _____ would be filed in a claim of patent infringement.
9. Satisfaction of a legal claim is called_____.
10. The Supreme Court issues a _____ when a case relates to the interpretation of law.
11. The Constitution left the creation of the _____ to Congress.
12. A Supreme Court justice may choose to write a _____ if he or she believes that a point in the Court's opinion needs additional emphasis.

## Reviewing Main Ideas

### Section 1

13. Why did the Framers see a need for a national judiciary?
14. Name two provisions that the Constitution makes regarding the federal courts and their jurisdictions.
15. Which courts hear most of the cases in this country, the State courts or the federal courts?
16. Describe the process by which most federal judges are nominated and approved.

### Section 2

17. **(a)** What jurisdiction do the inferior courts have? **(b)** What kinds of cases do they hear?
18. When the Supreme Court's docket became overloaded in the late 1800s, what did Congress do to ease the burden?
19. In the federal judicial system, what is a circuit?
20. Where do most of the cases that reach the federal courts of appeals come from?
21. How does the Court of Appeals for the Federal Circuit differ from other federal courts of appeals?

### Section 3

22. **(a)** Why is it so important for courts to have the power of judicial review? **(b)** What famous court case established the Supreme Court's right to exercise the power of judicial review?
23. **(a)** What kinds of jurisdiction does the Supreme Court have? **(b)** What kind of cases does it usually accept?
24. What is the "rule of four"?
25. If the Supreme Court decides not to hear a case, what happens to the case?
26. Describe how oral arguments are presented before the Supreme Court.

### Section 4

27. **(a)** Who creates the special courts? **(b)** Why have they been created?
28. Can the United States be sued by its own citizens? Explain.
29. What kind of claims are heard by the Court of Appeals for Veterans Claims?

## Critical Thinking Skills

**30. *Applying the Chapter Skill*** Appeals of certain court-martial cases go to a civilian tribunal, the Court of Appeals for the Armed Forces. Knowing this, what conclusion can you draw about the role of that court?

**31. *Drawing Inferences*** Why did the Framers create a system of appointing judges that required cooperation between the President and the Senate?

**32. *Making Decisions*** Occasionally the Supreme Court refuses to hear a certain case, then later agrees to hear a very similar case. Why might the Court decide to hear the later case?

## Analyzing Political Cartoons

Using your knowledge of American government and this cartoon, answer the questions below.

THAT COMPASS DOESN'T POINT THE WAY I WANT TO GO. CHANGE IT. NOW!

**33.** In 1937, President Roosevelt proposed a law that would have allowed him to appoint as many as six new justices to the Supreme Court. He was widely criticized for trying to "pack the court" with judges favorable to his New Deal programs. **(a)** Who is the captain of the ship? **(b)** Who does the smaller sailor represent? **(c)** How is the Supreme Court represented?

**34.** Does the cartoonist approve of FDR's plan? Explain.

### Take It to the Net

Additional support materials and activities for Chapter 18 of *Magruder's American Government* can be found in the Social Studies area at the Prentice Hall School Web site.
**www.phschool.com**

### You Can Make a Difference

Investigative reporters look into many different kinds of matters, from political scandals to questions of consumer health and safety. Probably you have seen their reports on television or in newspaper articles. Reporters often uncover issues that make people think "something should be done."

Identify a problem or issue involving people whom you think are being treated unfairly. Write a proposal for an investigative report that would track down the truth about this issue. In your proposal, clearly identify the issue. Explain what you expect to find out in your investigation. List the types of people and organizations, governmental or private, you plan to contact, and why. Write a concluding statement suggesting what type of court might hear a case resulting from your investigation.

## Participation Activities

**35. *Current Events Watch*** Find news reports of a recent major decision by the Supreme Court. Form a mock panel of justices and deliberate on the case, using detailed accounts of the case. When your panel reaches a decision, identify the arguments that most influenced you, and explain why your group agreed or disagreed with the Court.

**36. *Graphing Activity*** Construct a time line showing the dates when each of the current Supreme Court justices was appointed to the bench. Make a second time line showing the Presidents during that time span. Compare the two to see which President appointed each justice and who appointed the majority of the present-day Court.

**37. *It's Your Turn*** A justice of the Supreme Court has announced her retirement, giving you, the President, the opportunity to nominate someone to fill that seat. Explain how you would use a decision-making process to identify the situation that requires the decision, gather information, identify options, predict consequences, and take action to implement your decisions.

### Take It to the Net

***Chapter 18 Self-Test*** As a final review activity, take the Chapter 18 Self-Test in the Social Studies area at the Web site listed, and receive immediate feedback on your answers.

**www.phschool.com**

## Critical Thinking Skills

**30.** Possible answer: The role of this court is appellate; its job is to judge the accuracy of earlier decisions, not to decide on military issues.

**31.** Possible answer: If either the executive or legislative branch had the sole power to appoint a judge, the other branch would always suspect a lack of impartiality and would not support the work of the judge.

**32.** Possible answer: The justices may have agreed with the decision of lower court on the case they denied, but not agreed with the decision of the lower court on the later case—even though the cases were similar.

## Analyzing Political Cartoons

**33. (a)** Franklin D. Roosevelt **(b)** Congress **(c)** by the compass
**34.** Possible answer: Disapproves; the cartoonist depicts FDR as a tyrannical leader who wants to change the system because he can't get his own way.

## You Can Make a Difference

Proposals will vary, but subjects should be relevant and indicate an understanding of investigative techniques.

## Participation Activities

**35.** Jury debate should be well-reasoned and make use of relevant details from the chosen case. Decisions should be accurate based on the jury activity and should be backed up by clear arguments.
**36.** Time lines should be accurate and include all relevant dates and people.
**37.** Answers will vary, but should demonstrate a working knowledge of the decision-making process and an understanding that Presidents choose judges who agree with their own views.

## Point-of-Use Resources

**Guide to the Essentials of American Government** Chapter 18 Test, page 101 provides multiple-choice questions to test students' knowledge of the chapter.

**Test Bank CD-ROM** Chapter 18 Test

**Chapter Test** Chapter Tests booklet

# Civil Liberties: First Amendment Freedoms

| Section Objectives | Print and Technology Resources |
|---|---|
| **1 The Unalienable Rights**<br>*(pp. 532–536)*<br><br>1. Explain how Americans' commitment to freedom led to the creation of the Bill of Rights.<br>2. Evaluate constitutional provisions for limiting the role of government in regard to individual rights.<br>3. Show how federalism affects individual rights.<br>4. Describe how the 9th Amendment helps guarantee individual rights.<br><br>**TEKS 1A, 2A, 8D, 8F, 9C, 9E, 10D, 14A, 14B, 14D, 14E, 14F, 18C, 21A, 21C, 21E, 22A, 22B, 22D** | • **Unit 5 booklet**<br>Guided Reading and Review, p. 11<br>Section 1 Quiz, p. 12<br>• **Lesson Plans booklet** Section 1, p. 82<br>• **Political Cartoons booklet** Section 1, p. 74<br>• **Block Scheduling with Lesson Strategies booklet** p. 28<br><br>• **The Living Constitution booklet** p. 7<br>• **Basic Principles of the Constitution Transparencies** 33<br>• **Section Support Transparencies** 77, 176<br>• **Presentation Pro CD-ROM** Section 1<br>• **Section Reading Support Transparencies** |
| **2 Freedom of Religion**<br>*(pp. 537–544)*<br><br>1. Examine why a free society cannot exist without free expression.<br>2. Describe the "wall of separation between church and state" set up by the Establishment Clause of the First Amendment.<br>3. Analyze issues addressed in Supreme Court rulings on religion and education, such as *Engel* v. *Vitale*.<br>4. Explain how the Supreme Court has interpreted and limited the Free Exercise Clause.<br><br>**TEKS 8B, 8D, 8F, 9C, 9E, 10D, 14A, 14B, 14C, 14D, 14E, 14F, 15B, 15C, 18C, 21A, 21E, 22A, 22B, 22D** | • **Unit 5 booklet**<br>Guided Reading and Review, p. 13<br>Section 2 Quiz, p. 14<br>• **Lesson Plans booklet** Section 2, p. 83<br>• **Political Cartoons booklet** Section 2, p. 75<br>• **Block Scheduling with Lesson Strategies booklet** p. 28<br>• **Close Up on Primary Sources booklet** A Legacy of Religious Freedom, p. 21<br>• **Section Reading Support Transparencies**<br><br>• **Close Up on the Supreme Court booklet** *Engel* v. *Vitale*, pp. 46–47<br>• **Government Assessment Rubrics booklet** p. 24<br>• **Simulations and Debates booklet** pp. 62–64<br>• **Basic Principles of the Constitution Transparencies** 38<br>• **Section Support Transparencies** 78, 177<br>• **Presentation Pro CD-ROM** Section 2 |
| **3 Freedom of Speech and Press**<br>*(pp. 546–553)*<br><br>1. Analyze the importance of free speech and press in a democratic society.<br>2. Analyze issues that involve Supreme Court interpretations of free speech.<br>3. Examine the issues of prior restraint and press confidentiality, and describe the limits the Court has placed on the media.<br>4. Define symbolic speech and commercial speech, and describe the limits on their exercise.<br><br>**TEKS 3A, 3B, 8B, 8D, 8F, 9C, 9E, 14A, 14B, 14C, 14D, 14E, 14F, 15B, 17B, 17C, 18C, 21A, 21C, 21D, 22A, 22B, 23A, 23B** | • **Unit 5 booklet**<br>Guided Reading and Review, p. 15<br>Section 3 Quiz, p. 16<br>• **Lesson Plans booklet** Section 3, p. 84<br>• **Political Cartoons booklet** Section 3, p. 76<br>• **Close Up on the Supreme Court booklet** *Schenck* v. *United States*, pp. 38–39; *New York Times* v. *United States*, pp. 50–51<br><br>• **The Living Constitution booklet** p. 7<br>• **Simulations and Debates booklet** pp. 59–61<br>• **Basic Principles of the Constitution Transparencies** 39<br>• **Section Support Transparencies** 79, 178<br>• **Presentation Pro CD-ROM** Section 3<br>• **Section Reading Support Transparencies** |
| **4 Freedom of Assembly and Petition**<br>*(pp. 555–558)*<br><br>1. Explain the Constitution's guarantees of assembly and petition.<br>2. Summarize how the government can limit the time, place, and manner of assembly.<br>3. Compare and contrast the freedom-of-assembly issues that arise on public versus private property.<br>4. Explore how the Supreme Court has interpreted freedom of association.<br><br>**TEKS 3A, 3B, 8B, 8D, 8F, 9C, 9E, 10D, 14A, 14B, 14D, 14E, 14F, 15B, 17C, 21A, 21C, 22A, 22B, 22C, 22D** | • **Unit 5 booklet**<br>Guided Reading and Review, p. 17<br>Section 4 Quiz, p. 18<br>Skills for Life Activity, p. 19<br>• **Lesson Plans booklet** Section 4, p. 85<br>• **Political Cartoons booklet** Section 4, p. 77<br>• **Close Up on the Supreme Court booklet** *Tinker* v. *Des Moines School District*, p. 20<br><br>• **The Basic Principles of the Constitution Posters**<br>• **Basic Principles of the Constitution Transparencies** 40<br>• **Section Support Transparencies** 80, 179<br>• **Presentation Pro CD-ROM** Section 4<br>• **Section Reading Support Transparencies**<br>• **Social Studies Skills Tutor CD-ROM** |

# Block Scheduling Strategies

The *Magruder's American Government* program addresses block-scheduling strategies in a variety of ways. For easy reference, side-column activities that fit a block format are marked  **Block Strategy.** Each section also contains a **Block Scheduling Strategies** box describing at least two block-format activities that address and extend core content from the section. The **Block Scheduling with Lesson Strategies booklet** found in the Teaching Resources contains additional block-scheduling activities for each chapter.

## Take It to the Net

Visit the Social Studies area at the Prentice Hall School Web site. Once there, you can find additional links, current events connections, and activities to enrich chapter content for *Magruder's American Government,* as well as a Self-Test for students. Be sure to check out this month's **eTeach** online discussion with a Master Teacher.

### www.phschool.com

## Pressed for Time?

If you are running short on time to cover this chapter, consider one of the following options:
- Use the **Presentation Pro CD-ROM** to create an outline for this chapter.
- Use one of the **Pressed for Time** activities found on p. 27.
- Use the Section Summaries for Chapter 2, from **Guide to the Essentials of American Government (English and Spanish).**

##  Video Connections

Prentice Hall offers two video programs to reinforce and extend chapter content. Show students *The Blessings of Liberty* from the **ABC News Civics and Government Videotape Library** and *Prayer in Schools: A Nationwide Debate* from the **Magruder's American Government Video Collection.**

## Assessment Options

- Section Quizzes, **Unit 5 booklet,** pp. 12, 14, 16, 18
- Chapter 19 Assessment, pp. 560–561
- **Guide to the Essentials of American Government,** Chapter 19 Test, p. 106

### Core Assessment
Chapter 19 Test, Chapter Tests booklet
ExamView® Test Bank CD-ROM Chapter 19
Government Assessment Rubrics

### Standardized Test Preparation
#### Diagnose and Prescribe
Diagnostic Tests for High School
Social Studies Skills

#### Review and Reteach
Review Book for Government

#### Practice and Assess
Test-Taking Strategies With
   Transparencies for High School
Test Prep Book for Government

# Chapter 19 Teacher's Edition Index

# Civil Liberties: First Amendment Freedoms

## Introducing the Chapter

In this chapter, students learn about the basic rights and freedoms guaranteed by the Constitution, particularly the freedoms of religion, speech and press, and assembly and petition.

## CONSTITUTIONAL PRINCIPLES

Emphasize the following basic principles as students read Chapter 19. Have the class respond to the questions, and then ask volunteers to explain which is most vital to the protection of individual liberties.

**Limited Government** How does each of the freedoms guaranteed in the Constitution serve to limit the government?

**Federalism** How does the 14th Amendment ensure that States do not take away rights bestowed on people by the National Government?

**Judicial Review** How have Supreme Court decisions emphasized that rights may be relative?

● CHAPTER 19 ●

# Civil Liberties: First Amendment Freedoms

*"All through the years we have had to fight for civil liberty, and we know that there are times when the light grows rather dim, and every time that happens democracy is in danger."*
—Eleanor Roosevelt (1940)

Eleanor Roosevelt spoke at a time of widespread suppression of civil liberties around the world. Protecting our own freedoms of speech, press, religion, and assembly became especially important. Yet these First Amendment freedoms are often controversial, and the courts have set limits on them.

◆ **Americans enjoying their freedom of religion**

 *Corner*

The following resources are available only from the Close Up Foundation to support the concepts discussed in Chapter 19 "Civil Liberties: First Amendment Freedoms":

◆ *The Bill of Rights: A User's Guide*
◆ *The First Amendment: America's Blueprint for Tolerance*
◆ *Profiles of Freedom: A Living Bill of Rights*

**CLOSE UP** | **Online**

To keep up-to-date on Close Up news and activities, visit Close Up Online at

**www.closeup.org**

Close Up Foundation
44 Canal Center Plaza
Alexandria, VA 22314-1592
800-765-3131

## Chapter 19 in Brief

### You Can Make a Difference

**THE INTERNET RAISES** new free speech issues. Brandon Beussink, a high school junior in Marble Hill, Missouri, set up a home page on his home computer, where he criticized some teachers and made fun of the school's Web site. A link went to the school's home page, but not the other way. School administrators were furious. They ordered Brandon to shut his Web site down (which he did) and suspended him for 10 days. Then they used the suspension to calculate his absences, lower his grades, and fail him in all courses. Brandon and his parents sued, with the help of the ACLU. In December 1998, a federal court ruled that the school had violated Brandon's free speech rights.

### Keep It Current

Items marked with this logo are periodically updated on the Internet. Keep up-to-date with what's in the news. To get current information about First Amendment issues, go to **www.phschool.com**

### SECTION 1

#### The Unalienable Rights *(pp. 532–536)*

★ The guarantees in the Bill of Rights reflect Americans' long-held commitment to personal freedom as well as the principle of limited government.
★ Individual rights are not absolute; they can be restricted when they come into conflict with the rights of others.
★ The Bill of Rights restricts only the National Government, but the Due Process Clause of the 14th Amendment "nationalizes" most of those guarantees.

### SECTION 2

#### Freedom of Religion *(pp. 537–544)*

★ Free expression, including freedom of religion, is necessary to a free society.
★ The Establishment Clause sets up what Thomas Jefferson called "a wall of separation between church and state." The nature of this "wall," particularly as it applies to education, has been a matter of continuing controversy.
★ The Free Exercise Clause protects individuals' right to believe—but not to do—whatever they wish.

### SECTION 3

#### Freedom of Speech and Press *(pp. 546–553)*

★ The 1st and 14th amendments' guarantees of free speech and press protect a person's right to speak freely and to hear what others have to say.
★ These freedoms are not absolute: the Supreme Court has limited such expressions as seditious speech and obscenity, but seldom allows prior restraint of spoken or written words.
★ The media also can be limited: Reporters do not have an unlimited right of confidentiality, and radio and television are subject to more regulation because they use the public airwaves.
★ Symbolic and commercial speech enjoy constitutional protection but can be limited under certain circumstances.

### SECTION 4

#### Freedom of Assembly and Petition *(pp. 555–558)*

★ The 1st Amendment guarantees the right to assemble peaceably and to petition the government for a redress of grievances.
★ Government can reasonably regulate the time, place, and manner of assembly, but those regulations must be "content neutral."
★ The right of assembly does not give demonstrators a right to trespass on private property.
★ The guarantee of freedom of assembly and petition carries with it a right of association.

### Keep It Current

#### Internet Update

Use the Prentice Hall School Web site and the Keep It Current CD-ROM to find quick content updates.

Visit **www.phschool.com** for current events articles that are linked to Chapter 19. Critical thinking questions are included.

**Keep It Current CD-ROM** includes government-related projects by unit. Students complete each project using current information that they obtain by linking to the Prentice Hall School Web site from the CD-ROM.

### Pressed for Time?

#### To Omit the Chapter

If you wish to skip Chapter 19, ask students to read the Chapter in Brief and assign the Guide to the Essentials before continuing to another chapter. You may also want to assign the Chapter 19 Test in the Chapter Test booklet. Then specific portions of Chapter 19 may be assigned to students needing reinforcement of key terms and concepts.

#### To Preview the Chapter

To introduce students to key terms and concepts in each section, have them read the Chapter in Brief. You may also assign the Reading Strategy activities on pp. 533, 538, 547, and 556 of this book.

#### To Review the Chapter

When students have completed Chapter 19, you might want to assign the Guide to the Essentials or the Guided Reading and Review worksheets on pp. 11, 13, 15, and 17 of the Unit 5 booklet.

#### To Cover the Chapter Quickly

To cover the material in Chapter 19 quickly, use the following activity.

**Focus** Begin by asking students to name all the rights they believe that Americans have. Write them on the board, and then for each elicit from students whether the right should be considered absolute or relative, and why.

**Instruct** Ask for volunteers to read aloud the text of the 1st and 14th amendments from the back of their textbook. Explain that these two amendments established the bases for freedom of religion, speech, and assembly, and have been interpreted to cover many other basic freedoms as well. Describe some of the Supreme Court decisions that have expanded individual freedoms.

**Close/Reteach** Assign small groups of students the various freedoms discussed in this chapter. Have each group create a presentation that describes that freedom, citing Supreme Court decisions or historical events where applicable.

■ **Block Strategy (Average)**

**531**

**1** *The Unalienable Rights*

**Objectives** You may wish to call students' attention to the objectives in the Section Preview. The objectives are reflected in the main headings of the section.

**Bellringer** Ask students what kinds of things they have a right to do at a shopping mall. Then have them name some rights they do not have there. Explain that, in this section, they will learn about how each American's rights are relative to the rights of every other person.

**Vocabulary Builder** Point out the terms in the Political Dictionary. Discuss possible differences between civil liberties and civil rights. Then have students discuss what *due process* means. Ask them what the *Due Process Clause* in the Constitution might say.

### Pressed for Time?

#### Quick Lesson Plan

**1. Focus** Tell students that the Constitution protects the rights of individuals against government. Ask students to discuss what they know about individual rights in the Constitution.

**2. Instruct** Explore the historic process of extending the Due Process Clause to the Bill of Rights. Include discussion of the constitutional limits on government and on individual rights.

**3. Close/Reteach** Remind students that individuals can exercise their constitutional rights only as long as they do not infringe on the rights of other individuals. Ask students to create a diagram that illustrates how the Constitution protects the rights of individuals against the Federal Government, State governments, and other individuals.

### Point-of-Use Resources

📁 **Block Scheduling with Lesson Strategies** Activities for Chapter 19 are presented on p. 28.

## Section Preview

### OBJECTIVES

1. **Explain** how Americans' commitment to freedom led to the creation of the Bill of Rights.
2. **Evaluate** constitutional provisions for limiting the role of government in regard to individual rights.
3. **Show** how federalism affects individual rights.
4. **Describe** how the 9th Amendment helps guarantee individual rights.

### WHY IT MATTERS

The United States was founded, in part, to ensure individual rights against the power of government. However, these rights can be restricted when they come into conflict with the rights of others. The Due Process Clause of the 14th Amendment prevents the States from abridging rights guaranteed in the Constitution's Bill of Rights.

### POLITICAL DICTIONARY

★ **Bill of Rights**
★ **civil liberties**
★ **civil rights**
★ **alien**
★ **Due Process Clause**
★ **process of incorporation**

---

**H**ave you ever heard of Walter Barnette? Probably not. How about Toyosaburo Korematsu? Dolloree Mapp? Clarence Earl Gideon? Almost certainly, you have the same answer: No.

Walter Barnette was a Jehovah's Witness who told his children not to salute the flag or to recite the Pledge of Allegiance. Toyosaburo Korematsu was a citizen of the United States interned by the Federal Government during World War II. Dolloree Mapp was fined $25 for possessing "lewd and lascivious books." Finally, Clarence Earl Gideon was sentenced to prison for breaking into and entering a poolroom.

You will encounter these names again over the next few pages. Each of them played an important part in building and protecting the rights of all Americans.

### A Commitment to Freedom

A commitment to personal freedom is deeply rooted in America's colonial past. Over many centuries, the English people had waged a continuing struggle for individual rights, and the early colonists brought a dedication to that cause with them to America.

Their commitment to freedom took root here, and it flourished. The Revolutionary War was fought to preserve and expand these very rights:

the rights of the individual against government. In proclaiming the independence of the new United States, the founders of this country declared:

*We hold these truths to be self-evident, that all men are created equal, that they are endowed by their Creator with certain unalienable Rights, that among these are Life, Liberty and the pursuit of Happiness. That to secure these rights, Governments are instituted among Men. . . .*
—Declaration of Independence

The Framers of the Constitution repeated that justification for the existence of government in the Preamble to the Constitution.

The Constitution, as it was written in Philadelphia, contained a number of important guarantees. The most notable of these can be found in Article I, Sections 9 and 10, and in Article III. Unlike many of the first State constitutions, however, the United States Constitution did not include a general listing of the rights of the people.

That omission raised an outcry. The objections were so strong that several States ratified the Constitution only with the understanding that such a listing would be added immediately. The first session of the new Congress met that demand with a series of proposed amendments. Ten of them, known as the **Bill of Rights,**

---

### 🖵 Block Scheduling Strategies

Consider these suggestions to manage extended class time:
■ Have small groups of students list things that they think they have the right to do without government interference. Then ask groups to present their lists to the class. Other groups should decide whether each right listed is protected by the Constitution, not protected, or open to interpretation.

■ Have students reread the passages on p. 534 about Japanese internment. (They may also refer to the *Korematsu* v. *U.S.* case in the Close Up on the Supreme Court booklet in the *Teaching Resources*). Then pose this question: Are there any circumstances under which civil liberties may be suspended? Ask students to write short magazine articles expressing their views.

were ratified by the States and became a part of the Constitution on December 15, 1791. Later amendments, especially the 13th and the 14th, have added to the Constitution's guarantees of personal freedom.

The national Constitution guarantees both rights and liberties to the American people. The distinction between civil rights and civil liberties is at best murky. Legal scholars often disagree on the matter, and the two terms are quite often used interchangeably.

However, you can think of the distinction this way: In general, **civil liberties** are protections *against government*. They are guarantees of the safety of persons, opinions, and property from arbitrary acts of government. Examples of civil liberties include freedom of religion, freedom of speech and press, and the guarantee of a fair trial.

The term **civil rights** is sometimes reserved for those *positive acts of government* that seek to make constitutional guarantees a reality for all people. From this perspective, examples of civil rights include the prohibitions of discrimination on the basis of race, sex, religious belief, or national origin. These prohibitions are set out in the Civil Rights Act of 1964.

## Limited Government

Government in the United States is *limited* government. The Constitution is filled with examples of these limitations. Chief among them are its many guarantees of personal freedom. Each one of those guarantees is either an outright prohibition or a restriction on the power of government to do something.

All governments have and use authority over individuals. The all-important difference between a democratic government and a dictatorial one lies in the *extent* of that authority. In a dictatorial regime, the government's powers are practically unlimited. The government regularly suppresses dissent, often harshly. In the United States, however, governmental authority is strictly limited. As Justice Robert H. Jackson once put the point:

▲ **Celebrating the Bill of Rights** A crowd gathers for Bill of Rights Day in New York City, 1941.

**PRIMARY Sources** ❝ *If there is any fixed star in our constitutional constellation, it is that no official, high or petty, can prescribe what shall be orthodox in politics, nationalism, religion, or any other matter of opinion or force citizens to confess by word or act their faith therein.* ❞

—*West Virginia Board of Education v. Barnette*, 1943

### Rights Are Relative, Not Absolute

The Constitution guarantees many different rights to *everyone* in the United States. Still, *no one* has the right to do anything he or she pleases. Rather, all persons have the right to do as they please as long as they do not infringe on the rights of others. Thus, each person's rights are relative to the rights of every other person.

This example will illustrate the point: Everyone in the United States has a right of free speech, but no one enjoys absolute freedom of speech. A person can be punished for using obscene language, or for using words in a way that causes another person to commit a crime—for example, to riot or to desert the military. The Supreme Court dealt with this point in *ApolloMedia Corporation v. United States*, 1999. There, it unanimously upheld a federal law that makes it illegal for anyone to send obscene and intentionally annoying e-mail via the Internet.

Justice Oliver Wendell Holmes stated the relative nature of each person's rights this way:

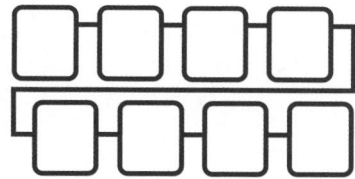

## American Government, American Humor

Share the following quotation with students:

*"One man's vulgarity is another's lyric."*
—Justice John M. Harlan

**Discussion** Ask students what Harlan meant by his remark. Ask: How does his comment capture the fundamental issue of freedom of speech?
**(Average)**

---

### Background Note

## Connections to Today

In the weeks and months following the September 11, 2001, terrorist attacks, historians and others began drawing a parallel between that event and the events surrounding other wars. The forced relocation of Japanese Americans during World War II was at the forefront of many of these discussions. President George W. Bush attempted to lead the nation away from the mistakes of the past when he stated: "We are in a fight for our principles, and our first responsibility is to live by them. No one should be singled out for unfair treatment or unkind words because of their ethnic background or religious faith."

---

 **PRIMARY Sources** "The most stringent [strict] protection of free speech would not protect a man in falsely shouting fire in a theatre and causing a panic."
—*Schenck v. United States*, 1919

### When Rights Conflict

Sometimes different guarantees of rights come into conflict with one another. One common example is freedom of the press versus the right to a fair trial.

In one famous case, Dr. Samuel Sheppard of Cleveland, Ohio, had been convicted of murdering his wife. His lengthy trial was widely covered in the national media. On appeal, Sheppard claimed that the highly sensational coverage had denied him a fair trial. The Supreme Court agreed. In *Sheppard* v. *Maxwell*, 1966, the Court rejected the free press argument, overturned Sheppard's conviction, and ordered a new trial.

### To Whom Are Rights Guaranteed?

Most constitutional rights are extended to all persons. The Supreme Court has often held that "persons" covers **aliens** as well as citizens. (Aliens are persons who are not citizens of the country in which they live.) Not all rights are given to aliens, however. Thus, the right to travel freely throughout the country is guaranteed to all citizens.[1] But the travel of aliens can be restricted.

After the bombing of Pearl Harbor by Japan, all persons of Japanese descent living on the

▲ *Trial and Trial Again* Although Dr. Sam Sheppard was acquitted in a retrial in 1966, his son Sam Reese Sheppard (shown here on the witness stand) filed a wrongful imprisonment suit in order to exonerate his father. In 2000, a jury ruled that the elder Sheppard could not be proved innocent by the greater weight of the evidence. Sheppard has appealed.

Pacific Coast were evacuated—forcibly moved—inland. Many suffered economic and other hardships as a result. In 1944 the Supreme Court reluctantly upheld the forced evacuation as a reasonable wartime emergency measure.[2] Still, the relocation was strongly criticized over the years. In 1988, the Federal Government admitted that the wartime relocation had been both unnecessary and unjust. Congress voted to pay $20,000 to each living internee. It also declared: "On behalf of the nation, the Congress apologizes."

Today's war on terrorism has created a political climate not unlike that of the early days of World War II. Did the treatment of Japanese Americans then teach us something for today? Will the rights of Muslims and others of Middle Eastern descent be respected by government as it fights terrorism here and abroad?

## Federalism and Individual Rights

Federalism is a complicated governmental arrangement. It produces any number of problems—including a very complex pattern of guarantees of individual rights in the United States.

### The Bill of Rights

Remember, the first ten amendments were originally intended as restrictions on the new National Government, not on the already existing States. And that remains the fact of the matter today.[3]

To illustrate this important point: The 5th Amendment says that no person can be charged with "a capital, or otherwise infamous crime" except by a grand jury. As a part of the Bill of Rights, this provision applies only to the National Government. The States are free to use the grand jury to bring accusations of serious crime—or, if they prefer, they can use some other process for that purpose. In fact, the grand jury is a part of the criminal

---

[1] See the two Privileges and Immunities clauses, in Article IV, Section 2, and the 14th Amendment. The guarantee does not extend to citizens under some form of legal restraint—for example, in jail or out on bail awaiting trial.

[2] *Korematsu* v. *United States*, 1944. However, on the same day the Court held, in *Ex parte Endo*, that once the loyalty of any citizen internee had been established, no restriction could be placed on that person's freedom to travel that was not legally imposed on all other citizens.

[3] The Supreme Court first held that the provisions of the Bill of Rights restrict only the National Government in *Barron* v. *Baltimore*, 1833. This was the first case in which the point was raised. The Court has followed that holding ever since.

▲ This part of *The Great Wall of Los Angeles,* a half-mile-long mural, depicts Japanese internment during World War II. *Critical Thinking* **How does the artist convey the conditions and feelings of the internees?**

justice system in only about half of the States today; see pages 577–578 and 704.

## The Modifying Effect of the 14th Amendment

Again, the provisions of the Bill of Rights apply against the National Government, not against the States. This does *not* mean, however, that the States can deny basic rights to the people.

In part, the States cannot do so because each of their own constitutions contains a bill of rights. In addition, they cannot deny these basic rights because of the 14th Amendment's **Due Process Clause.** It says:

> **FROM THE Constitution** ❝*No State shall . . . deprive any person of life, liberty, or property, without due process of law. . . .*❞
> —United States Constitution

The Supreme Court has often said that the 14th Amendment's Due Process Clause means this: No State can deny to any person any right that is "basic or essential to the American concept of ordered liberty."

But what specific rights are "basic or essential"? The Court has answered that question in a long series of cases. In those cases it has held that most (but not all) of the protections set out in the Bill of Rights are also covered by the 14th Amendment's Due Process Clause, and so apply against the States. In deciding those cases, the Court has engaged in what has come to be called the **process of incorporation.** It has

incorporated, or included, most of the guarantees in the Bill of Rights into the 14th Amendment's Due Process Clause.

The Court began that historic process in *Gitlow* v. *New York* in 1925. That landmark case involved Benjamin Gitlow, a communist, who had been convicted in the State courts of criminal anarchy. He had made several speeches and published a pamphlet calling for the violent overthrow of government in this country.

On appeal, the Supreme Court upheld Gitlow's conviction and the State law under which he had been tried, viewing Gitlow's conduct as a call to action. In deciding the case, however, the Court made this crucial point: Freedom of speech and press, which the 1st Amendment says cannot be denied by the National Government, are also "among the fundamental personal rights and liberties protected by the Due Process Clause of the 14th Amendment from impairment by the States."

Soon after *Gitlow,* the Court held each of the 1st Amendment's guarantees to be covered by the 14th Amendment. It struck down State laws involving speech (*Fiske* v. *Kansas,* 1927; *Stromberg* v. *California,* 1931), the press (*Near* v. *Minnesota,* 1931), assembly and petition (*DeJonge* v. *Oregon,* 1937), and religion (*Cantwell* v. *Connecticut,* 1940). In each of those cases, the Court declared a State law unconstitutional as a violation of the 14th Amendment's Due Process Clause.

In the 1960s, the Court extended the scope of the 14th Amendment's Due Process Clause even

## CONSTITUTIONAL PRINCIPLES

### Judicial Review

The *Gitlow* case established that the Due Process Clause prevented States from impairing personal freedoms; however, the decision upheld Gitlow's conviction. Justice Holmes, in dissent, went one step farther in arguing that the conviction be overturned. His dissent addressed New York attorneys' claim that Gitlow's actions were an incitement. "It is said that this manifesto was more than a theory, that it was an incitement. Every idea is an incitement.... The only difference between the expression

of an opinion and an incitement in the narrower sense is the speaker's enthusiasm for the result."

### Activity

Have students read more about *Gitlow* (links to Web sites are provided at **www.phschool.com**). Then have them read about the *Schenck* v. *United States* case in the Close Up on the Supreme Court booklet in the *Teaching Resources.* In what ways did Holmes' reasoning in *Schenck* concerning the "clear and present danger" rule expand on his thinking in *Gitlow?*

**535**

# Point-of-Use Resources

📄 **Guide to the Essentials** Chapter 19, Section 1, p. 102 provides support for students who need additional review of section content. Spanish support is available in the Spanish edition of the Guide on p. 95.

📁 **Quiz** Unit 5 booklet, p. 12 includes matching and multiple-choice questions to check students' understanding of Section 1 content.

💿 **Presentation Pro CD-ROM** Quizzes and multiple-choice questions check students' understanding of Section 1 content.

## Answers to . . .

## Section 1 Assessment

**1.** Civil rights are positive acts of government that seek to make constitutional guarantees for all people; civil liberties are protections against arbitrary acts of government.

**2.** The Bill of Rights is the first 10 amendments to the Constitution. It was added during the first session of the new Congress following public demand.

**3.** Federalism means that restrictions on the National Government concerning individual rights as set out in the Constitution do not apply to the States.

**4.** It used provisions from the 1st Amendment to strike down State laws as unconstitutional, saying that they violated the Due Process Clause.

**5.** Possible answer: The Supreme Court felt that ensuring a fair trial, in which a man's innocence would be decided, was more important than the press's right to cover that trial.

**6.** Possible answer: The incorporation doctrine strengthened the nation's commitment to individual rights and clarified the powers of the Federal Government in relation to those of the States.

## Answer to . . .

**Interpreting Tables** Possible answer: Cases involving these provisions might appear before the Supreme Court and result in incorporation.

## Process of Incorporation

### Provisions of the Bill of Rights Incorporated into the 14th Amendment's Due Process Clause

| Year | Amendment | Provision | Case |
|---|---|---|---|
| 1925 | 1st | Freedom of speech | *Gitlow* v. *New York* |
| 1931 | 1st | Freedom of the press | *Near* v. *Minnesota* |
| 1937 | 1st | Freedom of assembly, petition | *DeJonge* v. *Oregon* |
| 1940 | 1st | Free Exercise Clause | *Cantwell* v. *Connecticut* |
| 1947 | 1st | Establishment Clause | *Everson* v. *Board of Education* |
| 1961 | 4th | Unreasonable searches, seizures | *Mapp* v. *Ohio* |
| 1962 | 8th | Cruel, unusual punishments | *Robinson* v. *California* |
| 1963 | 6th | Right to counsel | *Gideon* v. *Wainwright* |
| 1964 | 5th | Self-incrimination | *Malloy* v. *Hogan* |
| 1965 | 6th | Confront witnesses | *Pointer* v. *Texas* |
| 1967 | 6th | Speedy trial | *Klopfer* v. *North Carolina* |
| 1967 | 6th | Obtain witnesses | *Washington* v. *Texas* |
| 1968 | 6th | Trial by jury in criminal cases | *Duncan* v. *Louisiana* |
| 1969 | 5th | Double jeopardy | *Benton* v. *Maryland* |

### Provisions NOT Incorporated into the 14th Amendment's Due Process Clause

| Amendment | Provision | |
|---|---|---|
| 2nd | Right to keep, bear arms | |
| 3rd | Quartering of troops | |
| 5th | Grand jury | |
| 7th | Trial by jury in civil cases | |

*Interpreting Tables* This table shows which rights the Supreme Court has "nationalized," by incorporating them into the Due Process Clause of the 14th Amendment. **How do you think the rights NOT incorporated might be nationalized in the future?**

further. The key cases are set out in the table at left. Due Process now covers nearly all of the guarantees set out in the Bill of Rights. In effect, the Supreme Court has "nationalized" them by holding that the Constitution guarantees them against the States through the 14th Amendment. You will look at each of the guarantees that are involved here shortly—the First Amendment rights in this chapter and the others in Chapter 20.

## The 9th Amendment

As you know, the Constitution contains many guarantees of individual rights. However, nowhere in the Constitution—and, indeed, nowhere else—will you find a complete catalog of all of the rights held by the American people.

The little-noted 9th Amendment declares that there are rights beyond those set out in so many words in the Constitution:

> FROM THE **Constitution** *"The enumeration in the Constitution, of certain rights, shall not be construed to deny or disparage others retained by the people."*
> —United States Constitution

Over the years, the Supreme Court has found that there are, in fact, a number of other rights "retained by the people." They include the guarantee that an accused person will not be tried on the basis of evidence unlawfully gained, and the right of a woman to have an abortion without undue interference by government.

## Section 1 Assessment

**Key Terms and Main Ideas**

1. What is the difference between **civil rights** and **civil liberties?**
2. What is the **Bill of Rights,** and how did it come to be added to the Constitution?
3. How does federalism affect the guarantees of individual rights?
4. How did the Supreme Court use the **process of incorporation** to expand the influence of the **Due Process Clause** of the 14th Amendment?

**Critical Thinking**

5. **Identifying Assumptions** For what reason(s) do you think the Supreme Court found that the right to a fair trial outweighed freedom of the press in *Sheppard?* Do you agree with this decision? Why or why not?
6. **Drawing Conclusions** Write a paragraph in which you analyze the impact of the incorporation doctrine on individual rights and federalism. Be sure to use social studies terminology correctly.

### 🌐 Take It to the Net

7. Read several current news articles relating to First Amendment rights. Choose two articles that deal with the same freedom (of religion, speech, press, assembly, or petition), and write a paragraph comparing the issues in the articles. Use the links provided in the Social Studies area at the following Web site for help in completing this activity. **www.phschool.com**

### 🌐 Take It to the Net

**7.** Direct students to the Social Studies area at the Prentice Hall School Web site. The *Magruder's American Government* companion Web site includes the directions and links needed to complete the activity. It also provides a printable Internet activity worksheet with scoring rubrics for assessment. Paragraphs should provide accurate and complete comparisons.

# 2 Freedom of Religion

## Section Preview

### OBJECTIVES

1. **Examine** why a free society cannot exist without free expression.
2. **Describe** the "wall of separation between church and state" set up by the Establishment Clause of the 1st Amendment.
3. **Analyze** issues addressed in Supreme Court rulings on religion and education, such as *Engel* v. *Vitale*.
4. **Explain** how the Supreme Court has interpreted and limited the Free Exercise Clause.

### WHY IT MATTERS

Freedom of religion is one component of the constitutional guarantee of free expression. The Establishment Clause sets up what Thomas Jefferson called "a wall of separation between church and state," but the nature of that separation is still being argued in American society and in the courts. The Free Exercise Clause protects Americans' right to believe—though not to do—whatever they wish.

### POLITICAL DICTIONARY

★ **Establishment Clause**
★ **parochial**
★ **Free Exercise Clause**

In the early 1830s, a Frenchman, Alexis de Tocqueville, came to this country to observe life in the young United States. He later wrote that he had searched for the greatness of America in many places: in its large harbors and its deep rivers, in its fertile fields and its boundless forests, in its rich mines and its vast world commerce, in its public schools and its institutions of higher learning, and in its democratic legislature and its matchless Constitution. Yet it was not until he went into the churches of America, that Tocqueville said he came to understand the genius and the power of this country.

## Freedom of Expression

A free society cannot exist without rights of free expression, without what has been called a "free trade in ideas." Freedom of expression is protected in the 1st Amendment:

> **FROM THE Constitution** *"Congress shall make no law respecting an establishment of religion, or prohibiting the free exercise thereof; or abridging the freedom of speech, or of the press; or the right of the people peaceably to assemble, and to petition the Government for a redress of grievances.* "
>
> —United States Constitution

Additionally, as you know, the 14th Amendment's Due Process Clause protects these freedoms from the arbitrary acts of States or their local governments.

It is not surprising that the Bill of Rights provides first for the protection of religious liberty. Religion has always played a large and important role in American life. Many of the early colonists, and many later immigrants, came here to escape persecution for their religious beliefs.

▲ Alexis de Tocqueville, author of *Democracy in America*

The 1st and 14th amendments set out two guarantees of religious freedom. These guarantees prohibit (1) an "establishment of religion" (the **Establishment Clause**), and (2) any arbitrary interference by government in "the free exercise" of religion (the Free Exercise Clause).[4]

---

[4]Also, Article VI, Section 3 provides that "no religious Test shall ever be required as a Qualification to any Office or public Trust under the United States." In *Torcaso* v. *Watkins*, 1961, the Supreme Court held that the 14th Amendment puts the same restriction on the States.

**537**

## Reading Strategy

### Organizing Information/ Graphic Organizer

Have students create, as they read, a graphic organizer in the form of two tree map graphic organizers. The trunk of one tree should be the Establishment Clause. The trunk of the other should be the Free Exercise Clause. Tell students to use as many branches as they need to list details that help them understand these two concepts.

## Point-of-Use Resources

📁 **Guided Reading and Review** Unit 5 booklet, p. 13 provides students with practice identifying the main ideas and key terms of this section.

📁 **Lesson Plans** For lesson planning suggestions, see p. 83 of the Lesson Plans booklet.

📁 **Political Cartoons** See p. 75 of the Political Cartoons booklet for a cartoon relevant to this section.

📺 **Section Support Transparencies** Transparency 78, *Visual Learning;* Transparency 177, *Political Cartoon*

▲ *Religious Freedom* Like all Americans, these church-goers are free to practice whatever religion they choose.

## Separation of Church and State

The Establishment Clause sets up, in Thomas Jefferson's words, "a wall of separation between church and state." That wall is not infinitely high, however, and it is not impenetrable. Church and government are constitutionally separated in this country, but that does not make them enemies or even strangers to one another.

Government has done much to encourage churches and religion in the United States. Nearly all property of and contributions to religious sects are free from federal, State, and local taxation. Chaplains serve with each branch of the armed forces. Most public officials take an oath of office in the name of God. Sessions of both houses of Congress, most State legislatures, and many city councils open with prayer. The nation's anthem and its coins and currency make reference to God.

The meaning of the Establishment Clause cannot be pinned down in precise terms. The exact nature of the wall of separation—how high it really is—remains a matter of continuing and often heated controversy.

The Supreme Court did not hear its first Establishment Clause case until 1947. A few earlier cases did involve government and religion, but none of them involved a direct consideration of the "wall of separation."

The most important of those earlier cases was *Pierce* v. *Society of Sisters,* 1925. There, the Court held an Oregon compulsory school attendance law unconstitutional. That law required parents to send their children to public schools. It was purposely intended to eliminate private and especially **parochial** (church-related) schools.

In striking down the law, the Court did not address the Establishment Clause question. Instead, it found the law to be an unreasonable interference with the liberty of parents to direct the upbringing of their children. As such, it was in conflict with the Due Process Clause of the 14th Amendment.

## Religion and Education

The first direct ruling on the Establishment Clause came in *Everson* v. *Board of Education,* a 1947 case often called the *New Jersey School Bus Case.* There the Court upheld a State law that provided for the public, tax-supported busing of students attending any school in the State, including parochial schools.

Critics attacked the law as a support of religion. They maintained that it relieved parochial schools of the need to pay for busing and so freed their money for other, including religious, purposes. The Court disagreed; it found the law to be a safety measure intended to benefit children, no matter what schools they might attend. Since that decision, the largest number of the Court's Establishment Clause cases have involved, in one way or another, religion and education.

### Released Time

"Released time" programs allow public schools to release students during school hours to attend religious classes. In *McCollum* v. *Board of Education,* 1948, the Court struck down the released time program in Champaign, Illinois, because the program used public facilities for religious purposes.

In *Zorach* v. *Clauson,* 1952, however, the Court upheld New York City's released time program. It did so because the New York program required that the religious classes be held in private places, for example, in private homes.

## Prayers and the Bible

The Court has now decided seven major cases involving the recitation of prayers and the reading of the Bible in public schools. In *Engel* v. *Vitale*, 1962, the Court outlawed the use, even on a voluntary basis, of a prayer written by the New York State Board of Regents. The prayer read:

 **PRIMARY Sources** *"Almighty God, we acknowledge our dependence upon Thee, and we beg Thy blessings upon us, our parents, our teachers, and our country."*

—Regents' prayer

In striking down the prayer, the Supreme Court held that:

 **PRIMARY Sources** *"[T]he constitutional prohibition against laws respecting an establishment of religion must at least mean that, in this country, it is no part of the business of government to compose official prayers for any group of the American people to recite as part of a religious program carried on by government."*

—Justice Hugo L. Black, Opinion of the Court

The Supreme Court extended that holding in two 1963 cases. In *Abington School District* v. *Schempp*, it struck down a Pennsylvania law requiring that each school day begin with readings from the Bible and a recitation of the Lord's Prayer. In *Murray* v. *Curlett*, the Court erased a similar rule in the city of Baltimore. In both of these cases, the Court found violations of "the command of the First Amendment that the government maintain strict neutrality, neither aiding nor opposing religion."

Since then, the Supreme Court has found unconstitutional:
- a Kentucky law that ordered the posting of the Ten Commandments in all public school classrooms, *Stone* v. *Graham*, 1980;
- Alabama's "moment of silence" law, *Wallace* v. *Jaffree*, 1985, which provided for a one-minute period of silence for "meditation or voluntary prayer" at the beginning of each school day;
- the offering of prayer as part of a public school graduation ceremony, in a Rhode Island case, *Lee* v. *Weisman*, 1992;
- a Texas school district's policy that permitted student-led prayer at high school football games, *Santa Fe Independent School District* v. *Doe*, 2000.

To sum up these rulings, the Court has held that public schools cannot sponsor religious exercises. It has not held that individuals cannot pray when and as they choose in schools or in any other place. Nor has it held that students cannot study the Bible in a literary or historical context in the schools.

These rulings have stirred strong criticism. Many individuals and groups have long proposed that the Constitution be amended to allow voluntary prayer in the public schools. Despite these decisions, both organized prayer and Bible readings are found in a great many public school classrooms today.

## Student Religious Groups

The Equal Access Act of 1984 declares that any public high school that receives federal funds (nearly all do) must allow student religious groups to meet in the school on the same terms that it sets for other student organizations.

The Supreme Court found that the law does not violate the Establishment Clause in a case from Nebraska, *Westside Community Schools*

▲ *Prayer and the Public Schools* The Supreme Court has ruled that public schools cannot sponsor prayer either in school or at school-related events.

## Learning Styles

**Kinesthetic** On slips of paper make a list of the Supreme Court cases discussed in this section. Separate the class into small groups and have each group pick two cases. Ask each group to perform a short skit in which they reenact the major events of the case. Encourage students to choose "characters" of the case that will best depict its political importance. After groups perform, ask other students to guess which case was being portrayed.

**(Average)**

v. *Mergens,* 1990. There, several students had tried to form a Christian club at Omaha's Westside High School. The students had to fight the school board in the federal courts in order to win their point.

The High Court has recently gone much further than it did in *Mergens*—in a case from New York, *Good News Club* v. *Milford Central School,* 2001. There, a school board had refused to allow a group of grade-school students to meet, after school, to sing, pray, memorize scriptures, and hear Bible lessons. The school board based its action on the Establishment Clause. *However,* the Court held that the board had violated Good News Club members' 1st and 14th amendment rights to free speech.

### Evolution

In *Epperson* v. *Arkansas,* 1968, the Court struck down a State law forbidding the teaching of the scientific theory of evolution. The Court held that the Constitution

> **PRIMARY Sources** **"**forbids alike the preference of a religious doctrine or the prohibition of theory which is deemed antagonistic to a particular dogma. . . . 'The State has no legitimate interest in protecting any or all religions from views distasteful to them.' **"**
>
> —Justice Abe Fortas, Opinion of the Court

The Court found a similar law to be unconstitutional in 1987. In *Edwards* v. *Aguillard,* it voided a 1981 Louisiana law that provided that whenever teachers taught the theory of evolution, they also had to offer instruction in "creation science."

### Aid to Parochial Schools

Most recent Establishment Clause cases have centered on this highly controversial question: What forms of State aid to parochial schools are constitutional? Several States give help to private schools, including schools run by church organizations, for transportation, textbooks, laboratory equipment, standardized testing, and much else.

Those who support this kind of aid argue that parochial schools enroll large numbers of students who would otherwise have to be educated at public expense. They also point out that the Supreme Court has held that parents have a legal right to send their children to those schools (*Pierce* v. *Society of Sisters*).

To give that right real meaning, they say, the State must give some aid to parochial schools in order to relieve parents of some of the double burden they carry because they must pay taxes to support the public schools their children do not attend. Many advocates also insist that schools run by religious organizations pose no real church-state problems because they devote most of their time to secular (nonreligious) subjects rather than to sectarian (religious) ones.

Opponents of aid to parochial schools argue that parents who choose to send their children to parochial schools should accept the financial consequences of that choice. Many of these critics also insist that it is impossible to draw clear lines between secular and sectarian courses in parochial schools. They say that religious beliefs are bound to have an effect on the teaching of nonreligious subjects in church-run schools.

### The *Lemon* Test

The Supreme Court has been picking its way through cases involving State aid to parochial schools for several years. In most of these cases, the Court now applies a three-pronged standard, the *Lemon* test: (1) The purpose of the aid must be clearly secular, not religious; (2) its primary effect must neither advance nor inhibit religion; and (3) it must avoid an "excessive entanglement of government with religion."

The test stems from *Lemon* v. *Kurtzman,* 1971. There, the Supreme Court held that the Establishment Clause is designed to prevent three main evils: "sponsorship, financial support, and active involvement of the sovereign in religious activity." In *Lemon,* the Court struck down a Pennsylvania law that provided for reimbursements (financial payments) to private schools to cover their costs for teachers' salaries, textbooks, and other teaching materials in nonreligious courses.

The Court held that the State program was of direct benefit to the parochial schools, and so to the churches sponsoring them. It also found that the Pennsylvania program required such close State supervision that it produced an excessive entanglement of government with religion.

## The *Lemon* Test

State aid to parochial schools is constitutional if...

★ its purpose is clearly secular, not religious.

★ its primary effect neither enhances nor inhibits religion.

★ it avoids an excessive entanglement of government with religion.

*Interpreting Charts* To be constitutional, State aid to parochial schools must meet all three of the criteria in the chart. *Which criterion do you think the courts would find most difficult to apply? Explain your answer.*

On the other hand, a number of State aid programs have passed the *Lemon* test over the past 30 years. Thus, the Court has held that a State can pay church-related schools what it costs them to administer the State's standardized tests. This decision was rendered in a New York case, *Committee for Public Education and Religious Liberty* v. *Regan,* 1980.

Public funds cannot be used to pay any part of the salaries of parochial school teachers, however, including those who teach only secular courses. In *Grand Rapids School District* v. *Ball,* 1985, the Court said that the way a teacher presents a course cannot easily be checked.

In *Bowen* v. *Kendrick,* 1988, the Court upheld a controversial federal statute, the Adolescent Family Life Act of 1981. That law provides for grants to both public and private agencies dealing with the problems of adolescent sex and pregnancy. Some of the grants were made to religious groups that oppose abortion, prompting the argument that those groups use federal money to teach religious doctrine.

The Supreme Court found the law's purpose—curbing "the social and economic problems caused by teenage sexuality, pregnancy, and parenthood"—to be a legitimate one. Even though some grants pay for counseling that "happens to coincide with the religious views" of some groups, this does not by itself mean that the federal funds are being used with "a primary effect of advancing religion," according to the Court.

In a 1993 Arizona case, *Zobrest* v. *Catalina Foothills School District,* the Court said that the use of public money to provide an interpreter for a deaf student who attends a Catholic high school does not violate the Establishment Clause. The Constitution, said the Court, does not lay down an absolute barrier to placing a public employee in a religious school.

In the most recent case, from Louisiana, *Mitchell* v. *Helms,* 2000, the Supreme Court upheld a federal law under which some material and equipment, including computer hardware and software, are loaned to public and private schools. Two facts were key to the Court's ruling: that those items (1) are loaned, not given to parochial schools, and (2) can be used only in "secular, neutral, and nonideological" programs.

In 1973, the Court struck down a New York law that reimbursed parents for the tuition they paid to religious schools, *Committee for Public Education and Religious Liberty* v. *Nyquist.* But in *Mueller* v. *Allen,* 1983, it upheld a Minnesota tax law that really accomplishes the same end.

The Minnesota law gives parents a State income tax deduction for the costs of tuition, textbooks, and transportation. Parents can claim the tax break no matter what schools their children attend. Most public school parents pay little or nothing for those items, so the law is of particular benefit to parents with children in private, mostly parochial, schools. The Court found that the law meets the *Lemon* test, and it relied on this point: The tax deduction is available to *all* parents with children in school, and they are free to decide which type of school their children attend.

### Make It Relevant

## Careers in Government—Attorney

Many of the battles over American freedoms have been conducted in America's courtrooms. Attorneys arguing before judges—themselves usually attorneys—have added to, subtracted from, and otherwise modified American freedoms innumerable times over the course of the nation's history. From arguing basic freedom issues in front of the Supreme Court to drafting local ordinances, the expertise of attorneys is fundamental to the operation of government in America.

**Skills Activity** Have students hold a mock Supreme Court session, arguing one of the landmark cases they read about in this chapter. Then have individual students write paragraphs explaining why they would or would not be interested in a career as a government attorney. **(Average)**

**Answer to ...**

Interpreting Charts Answers will vary. Students may suggest that "excessive entanglement of government with religion" would be most difficult to apply, as that is the least specific of the three criteria.

The High Court went much further in *Zelman* v. *Simmons-Harris* in 2002. There, it upheld Ohio's experimental "school choice" plan. Under that plan, parents in Cleveland can receive vouchers (grants for tuition payments) from the State and use them to send their children to private schools. Nearly all families who take the vouchers send their children to parochial schools. The Court found, 5–4, that the Ohio program is not intended to promote religion but, rather, to help children from low-income families.

## Other Establishment Clause Cases

Beyond the realm of education, the Supreme Court has ruled on many other important aspects of freedom of religious expression.

### Seasonal Displays

Many public organizations sponsor celebrations of the holiday season with street decorations, programs in public schools, and the like. Can these publicly sponsored observances properly include expressions of religious belief?

▲ This Christian nativity scene was displayed in front of the Massachusetts State House. *Critical Thinking* ***Does this seasonal display violate the separation of church and state? How might it be relocated or changed to avoid coming into conflict with the First Amendment?***

In *Lynch* v. *Donnelly*, 1984, the Court held that the city of Pawtucket, Rhode Island, could include the Christian nativity scene in its holiday display, which also featured nonreligious objects such as candy canes and Santa's sleigh and reindeer. That ruling, however, left open this question: What about a public display made up *only* of a religious symbol?

The Court faced that question in 1989. In *County of Allegheny* v. *ACLU*, it held that the county's seasonal display "endorsed Christian doctrine," and so violated the 1st and 14th amendments. The county had placed a large display celebrating the birth of Jesus on the grand stairway in the county courthouse, with a banner proclaiming "Glory to God in the Highest."

At the same time, the Court upheld another holiday display in *Pittsburgh* v. *ACLU*. The city's display consisted of a large Christmas tree, an 18-foot menorah, and a sign declaring the city's dedication to freedom.

### Chaplains

Daily sessions of both houses of Congress and most of the State legislatures begin with prayer. In Congress, and in many States, a chaplain paid with public funds offers the opening prayer.

The Supreme Court has ruled that this practice, unlike prayers in the public schools, is constitutionally permissible. The ruling was made in a case involving Nebraska's one-house legislature, *Marsh* v. *Chamber*, 1983.

The Court rested its distinction between school prayers and legislative prayers on two points. First, prayers have been offered in the nation's legislative bodies "from colonial times through the founding of the Republic and ever since." Second, legislators, unlike schoolchildren, are not "susceptible to religious indoctrination or peer pressure."

## The Free Exercise Clause

The second part of the constitutional guarantee of religious freedom is set out in the Constitution's **Free Exercise Clause,** which guarantees to each person the right to believe whatever he or she chooses to believe in matters of religion. No law and no other action by government can violate that absolute constitutional right. It is protected by the 1st and the 14th amendments.

No person has an absolute right to act as he or she chooses, however. The Free Exercise Clause does *not* give anyone the right to violate criminal laws, offend public morals, or otherwise threaten the health, welfare, or safety of the community.

The Supreme Court laid down the basic shape of the Free Exercise Clause in the first case it heard on the issue, *Reynolds* v. *United States,* 1879. Reynolds, a Mormon, had two wives. That practice, polygamy, was allowed by the teachings of his church, but it was prohibited by a federal law banning polygamy in any territory of the United States.

Reynolds was tried and convicted under the law. On appeal, he argued that the law violated his constitutional right to the free exercise of his religious beliefs. The Supreme Court disagreed. It held that the First Amendment does not forbid Congress the power to punish those actions that are "violations of social duties or subversive of good order."

### Limits on Free Exercise

Over the years, the Court has approved many regulations of human conduct in the face of free exercise challenges. For example, it has upheld laws that require the vaccination of schoolchildren, *Jacobson* v. *Massachusetts,* 1905; laws that forbid the use of poisonous snakes in religious rites, *Bunn* v. *North Carolina,* 1949; and laws that require businesses to be closed on Sundays ("blue laws"), *McGowan* v. *Maryland,* 1961.

A State can require religious groups to have a permit to hold a parade on the public streets, *Cox* v. *New Hampshire,* 1941; and organizations that enlist children to sell religious literature must obey child labor laws, *Prince* v. *Massachusetts,* 1944. The Federal Government can draft those who have religious objections to military service, *Welsh* v. *United States,* 1970.

The Court has made this last ruling many times. *Welsh* is the leading case from the Vietnam War period. There, the Court held that the only persons who could not be drafted were those "whose consciences . . . would give them no rest if they allowed themselves to become part of an instrument of war."

The Air Force can deny an Orthodox Jew the right to wear his yarmulke (skull cap) while on

▲ The rabbi at right, a Jewish chaplain at the U.S. Naval Academy, helps a midshipman study the Torah. *Critical Thinking Do you think military chaplains, especially at the service academies, violate the separation of church and state?*

active duty, *Goldman* v. *Weinberger,* 1986. The U.S. Forest Service can allow private companies to build roads and cut timber in national forests that Native Americans have traditionally used for religious purposes, *Lyng* v. *Northwest Indian Cemetery Protective Association,* 1988.

In addition, a State can deny unemployment benefits to a man fired by a private drug counseling group because he used peyote in violation of the State's drug laws. The Court made that finding even though the man ingested the hallucinogenic drug as part of a ceremony of his Native American Church, *Oregon* v. *Smith,* 1990.

### Free Exercise Upheld

Over time, however, the Court has also found many actions by governments to be incompatible with the free exercise guarantee. The Court did so for the first time in one of the landmark Due Process cases cited earlier in this chapter, *Cantwell* v. *Connecticut,* 1940. In that case, the Court struck down a law requiring a person to obtain a license before soliciting money for a religious cause.

The Supreme Court has decided a number of other cases in a similar way. Thus, Amish children cannot be forced to attend school beyond the 8th grade, because that sect's centuries-old "self-sufficient agrarian lifestyle

---

RESOURCE PRO

**Resource Pro® CD-ROM** contains an electronic version of each activity found in the Teaching Resources as well as additional resources such as Supreme Court cases. The Planning Express® feature allows you to customize and create daily lesson plans within minutes.

---

ACTIVITY

### Extended Class Periods

**Time** 90 minutes.
**Purpose** Examine opposing points of view in court cases.
**Grouping** Groups of four students.
**Activity** Have each group choose one of the Supreme Court cases from Section 2. Ask groups to develop a list of questions a reporter would ask both parties involved in the case. Responses should provide a general description of the case, defend each side's points of view, and comment on the final Court decision that was rendered.
**Roles** Reporter/interviewer, plaintiff, defendant, scriptwriter.
**Close** Each group should conduct the interview for the class.

 **Block Strategy
(Challenging)**

### Point–of–Use Resources

 **Government Assessment Rubrics** Oral Presentation, p. 24

 **Block Scheduling with Lesson Strategies** Additional activities for Chapter 19 appear on p. 28.

*Answer to . . .*
**Critical Thinking** Possible answer: Without access to military chaplains, military personnel would be denied their constitutional right to enjoy free exercise of religion.

## Point-of-Use Resources

📖 **Guide to the Essentials** Chapter 19, Section 2, p. 103 provides support for students who need additional review of section content. Spanish support is available in the Spanish edition of the Guide on p. 96.

📁 **Quiz** Unit 5 booklet, p. 14 includes matching and multiple-choice questions to check students' understanding of Section 2 content.

💿 **Presentation Pro CD-ROM** Quizzes and multiple-choice questions check students' understanding of Section 2 content.

## Answers to . . .

### Section 2 Assessment

**1.** The Establishment Clause is the part of the 1st Amendment that sets up the idea of the separation of church and state; examples not involving education include seasonal displays and chaplains leading prayer in legislative sessions.
**2.** Because parochial schools are private schools; in addition, they are structured around religious beliefs.
**3.** The *Lemon* test consists of three criteria for providing aid to parochial schools: That aid must be for secular reasons; that it have no affect on religion; and that it maintain a separation between church and state.
**4.** The Free Exercise Clause guarantees each person the right to believe whatever he or she wants to in matters of religion without interference. *Reynolds* v. *United States* limited this free exercise.
**5.** Possible answer: The guarantees of religion set up in 1791 set the precedent for the expansion of individual liberties that took place over the next 200 years; without it, the National Government and State governments may not have protected individual liberties to the same degree.
**6.** Possible answer: That the colonists viewed religion as a basic right that needed to be protected from government interference in every way possible.

---

essential to their religious faith is threatened by modern education," *Wisconsin* v. *Yoder,* 1972. On the other hand, the Amish, who provide support for their own people, must pay Social Security taxes, as all other employers do, *United States* v. *Lee,* 1982.

A State cannot forbid ministers to hold elected public offices, *McDaniel* v. *Paty,* 1978. Nor can it deny unemployment compensation benefits to a worker who quit a job because it involved a conflict with his or her religious beliefs, *Sherbert* v. *Verner,* 1963; *Thomas* v. *Indiana,* 1981; *Hobbie* v. *Florida,* 1987; *Frazee* v. *Illinois,* 1989.

The Court has often held that "only those beliefs rooted in religion are protected by the Free Exercise Clause" (*Sherbert* v. *Verner,* 1963). This leaves open the perplexing question of what beliefs are "rooted in religion"? Clearly, religions that seem strange or even bizarre to most Americans are as entitled to constitutional protection as are the more traditional ones. For example, in *Lukumi Babalu Aye* v. *City of Hialeah,* 1993, the High Court struck down a Florida city's ordinance that outlawed animal sacrifices as part of any church services.

The Jehovah's Witnesses have carried several important religious freedom cases to the Supreme Court. Perhaps the stormiest controversy resulting from these cases arose out of the Witnesses' refusal to salute the flag.

The Witnesses refuse to salute the flag because they see such conduct as a violation of the Bible's commandment against idolatry. In *Minersville School District* v. *Gobitis,* 1940, the Court upheld a Pennsylvania school board regulation requiring students to salute the flag at the beginning of each school day. Gobitis instructed his children not to do so, and the school expelled them. He went to court, basing his case on the constitutional guarantee.

Gobitis finally lost in the Supreme Court, which declared that the board's rule was not an infringement of religious liberty. Rather, the Court held that the rule was a lawful attempt to promote patriotism and national unity.

Three years later, the Court reversed that decision. In *West Virginia Board of Education* v. *Barnette,* 1943, it held a compulsory flag-salute law unconstitutional. Justice Robert H. Jackson's words on page 533 are from the Court's powerful opinion in that case. So are these:

 **PRIMARY Sources** ❝*To believe that patriotism will not flourish if patriotic ceremonies are voluntary and spontaneous, instead of a compulsory routine, is to make an unflattering estimate of the appeal of our institutions to free minds.*❞

—Opinion of the Court

## Section 2 Assessment

### Key Terms and Main Ideas

1. Explain the **Establishment Clause**. Give one example of an Establishment Clause issue that does not involve education.
2. Why does aid to **parochial** schools often pose a constitutional problem?
3. What is the *Lemon* test?
4. Explain the **Free Exercise Clause**. Give one example of a Supreme Court ruling that limits free exercise of religion.

### Critical Thinking

5. **Predicting Consequences** How do you think the guarantees of religious freedom ratified in 1791 affected the growth and development of the United States? In other words, how do you think the nation might be different today without these protections?

6. **Recognizing Ideologies** The 1st Amendment protects freedom of religion in two ways. What does this approach reveal about the beliefs and experiences of those Americans who insisted on these guarantees?

 **Take It to the Net**

7. Select at least three Supreme Court cases on religious freedom that you find interesting. Then search for and read the actual Supreme Court rulings. For each case, briefly explain the issue at stake, the Court's opinion, and the effect of that opinion. Finally, state which case you think was most important to American religious freedom. Use the links provided in the Social Studies area at the following Web site for help in completing this activity. www.phschool.com

---

**Take It to the Net**

**7.** Direct students to the Social Studies area at the Prentice Hall Web site. The *Magruder's American Government* companion Web site includes the directions and links needed to complete the activity. It also provides a printable Internet activity worksheet with scoring rubrics for assessment. Explanations should clearly describe the issue and the court's ruling, and students' statements should be persuasive.

# Religious Freedom in a Diverse Nation

*The Freedom Forum is a nonpartisan foundation dedicated to a free press, free speech, and other freedoms for people around the world. In 1999, the foundation completed a study of the status of First Amendment rights in the United States. Here, the foundation's report expresses concern for religious freedom in the United States.*

The First Amendment guarantee of religious freedom has been a binding force in this country for more than two centuries. It is a key element of the boldest political experiment the world has ever known. Today, however, there are disturbing signs in the United States that religious liberty—the

*Religious and ethnic diversity, as shown in this Los Angeles classroom, gives First Amendment discussions a new urgency.*

freedom to believe or not to believe and to practice one's faith openly and freely without government interference—is in danger. People undermining religious liberty include both those who seek to establish in law a "Christian America" and those who seek to exclude religion from public life entirely.

. . . Religion has become a source of divisiveness as people spar and sometimes resort to violence over issues of conscience and belief like abortion, school prayer, and public school curricula. . . . The situation is made more complicated by the fact that the religious composition of the United States is becoming more diverse than ever. Along with many groups of Christians and Jews, this country is now home to growing numbers of Muslims, Hindus, Buddhists, and other believers. . . . Religious diversity was made possible by the First Amendment. Now, ironically, religious diversity makes the First Amendment more necessary and urgent than at any time in our history. . . .

As [Freedom Forum scholar] Charles Haynes notes: ". . . An American is not defined by race or ethnicity, but by a commitment to the democratic first principles in our framing documents. Because

of our exploding religious diversity, there is an urgent need for all citizens to rethink our shared commitment to the guiding principles of religious liberty. These principles of the First Amendment provide a civic framework for living with our deepest differences. . . ."

Religious freedom is at the heart of this country's experiment with democracy. The continuing controversies are proof of continued passion for liberty of conscience, even as debates rage about whether religion receives sufficient attention from the media, educators, and the government. Disputes involving religious liberty reflect America's ambivalence about the limits of individual liberty. At present, the country's internationally recognized commitment to tolerance of all cultures and faiths is being tested and torn. The question to be answered is whether we can sustain this commitment to the religion clauses of the First Amendment into the next century.

## Analyzing Primary Sources

1. What defines an American, according to this report?
2. Describe recent changes in the nation's religious makeup identified in this report.
3. What benefit do the authors see in disputes that involve "issues of conscience"? What potential dangers do they see in such disputes?

# 3 Freedom of Speech and Press

## Section Preview

### OBJECTIVES

1. **Analyze** the importance of free speech and press in a democratic society.
2. **Analyze** issues that involve Supreme Court interpretations of free speech.
3. **Examine** the issues of prior restraint and press confidentiality, and describe the limits the Court has placed on the media.
4. **Define** symbolic speech and commercial speech, and describe the limits on their exercise.

### WHY IT MATTERS

The freedom to express ideas freely and to hear the ideas of others is fundamental to American democracy. However, some limitations on freedom of expression have been upheld by the Supreme Court. These include restrictions on certain kinds of speech, such as sedition and obscenity, and on speech in certain circumstances, such as when broadcast over the public airwaves.

### POLITICAL DICTIONARY

★ libel
★ slander
★ sedition
★ seditious speech
★ prior restraint
★ shield law
★ symbolic speech
★ picketing

▲ Free speech is essential to this rally planning the 2000 Million Mom March in support of gun control.

Think about this children's verse for a moment: "Sticks and stones may break my bones, but names will never hurt me." That rhyme says, in effect, that acts and words are separate things, and that acts can harm but words cannot.

Is that really true? Certainly not. You know that words can and do have consequences, sometimes powerful consequences. Words, spoken or written, can make you happy, sad, bored, informed, or entertained. They can also expose you to danger, deny you a job, or lead to other serious consequences.

## Free Speech and Press

The guarantees of free speech and press in the 1st and 14th amendments serve two fundamentally important purposes:

(1) to guarantee to *each* person a right of free expression, in the spoken and the written word, and by all other means of communication, as well;

(2) to guarantee to *all* persons a full, wide-ranging discussion of public affairs.

That is, the 1st and 14th amendments give to all people the right to have their say and the right to hear what others have to say.

The American system of government depends on the ability of the people to make sound, reasoned judgments on matters of public concern. Clearly, people can best make such judgments when they know all the facts and can hear all the available interpretations of those facts.

As you examine the Constitution's 1st and 14th amendments here, keep two other key points in mind: First, the guarantees of free speech and press are intended to protect the expression of unpopular views. Clearly, the opinions of the majority need little or no constitutional protection. These guarantees seek to ensure, as Justice Oliver Wendell Holmes put it, "freedom for the thought that we hate," (Dissenting Opinion, *Schwimmer v. United States*, 1929).

Second, some forms of expression are not protected by the Constitution. No person has an unbridled right of free speech or free press. Many reasonable restrictions can be placed on those rights. Think about Justice Holmes's comment about restricting the right to shout "Fire!" in a crowded theater. Or consider this restriction: No person has the right to libel or slander another. **Libel** is the false and malicious use of

---

printed words; **slander** is the false and malicious use of spoken words.[6]

Similarly, the law prohibits the use of obscene words, the printing and distributing of obscene materials, and false advertising. It also condemns the use of words to prompt others to commit a crime—for example, to riot or to attempt to overthrow the government by force.

## Free Speech or Sedition?

**Sedition** is the crime of attempting to overthrow the government by force or to disrupt its lawful activities by violent acts.[7] **Seditious speech** is the advocating, or urging, of such conduct. It is not protected by the 1st Amendment.

### The Alien and Sedition Acts

Congress first acted to curb opposition to government in the Alien and Sedition Acts of 1798. Those acts gave the President the power to deport undesirable aliens and made "any false, scandalous, and malicious" criticism of the government a crime. These laws were meant to stifle the opponents of President John Adams and the Federalists.

The Alien and Sedition Acts were undoubtedly unconstitutional, but that point was never tested in the courts. Some 25 persons were arrested for violating them; of those, ten were convicted. The Alien and Sedition Acts expired before Thomas Jefferson became President in 1801, and he soon pardoned those who had run afoul of them.

### The Sedition Act of 1917

Congress passed another sedition law during World War I, as part of the Espionage Act of 1917. That law made it a crime to encourage disloyalty, interfere with the draft, obstruct recruiting, incite insubordination in the armed forces, or hinder the sale of government bonds.

---

[6]Both libel and slander involve the use of words maliciously—with vicious purpose—to injure a person's character or reputation or expose that person to public contempt, ridicule, or hatred. Truth is generally an absolute defense against a libel or slander claim.

[7]Espionage, sabotage, and treason are often confused with sedition. Espionage is spying for a foreign power. Sabotage involves an act of destruction intended to hinder a nation's war or defense effort. Treason can be committed only in time of war and can consist only of levying war against the United States or giving aid and comfort to its enemies.

▲ This poster warned of the dangers of careless talk and espionage during World War II. *Critical Thinking How might careless conversation endanger ships during wartime?*

The act also made it a crime to "willfully utter, print, write, or publish any disloyal, profane, scurrilous, or abusive language about the form of government of the United States."

More than 2,000 persons were convicted for violating the Espionage Act. The constitutionality of the law was upheld several times, most importantly in *Schenck* v. *United States,* 1919. Charles Schenck, an officer of the Socialist Party, had been found guilty of obstructing the war effort. He had sent fiery leaflets to some 15,000 men who had been drafted, urging them to resist the call to military service.

The Supreme Court upheld Schenck's conviction. The case is particularly noteworthy because the Court's opinion, written by Justice Oliver Wendell Holmes, established the "clear and present danger" rule.

**PRIMARY Sources** *"Words can be weapons.... The question in every case is whether the words used are used in such circumstances and are of such nature as to create a clear and present danger that they will bring about the substantive evils that Congress has a right to prevent."*

—Opinion of the Court

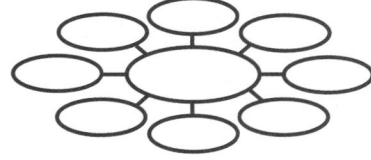

In short, the rule says that words can be outlawed. Those who utter them can be punished when the words they use trigger an immediate danger that criminal acts will follow.

### The Smith Act of 1940

Congress passed the Smith Act in 1940, just over a year before the United States entered World War II. That law is still on the books. It makes it a crime for anyone to advocate the violent overthrow of the government of the United States, to distribute any material that teaches or advises violent overthrow, or to knowingly belong to any group with such an aim.

The Court upheld the Smith Act in *Dennis* v. *United States,* in 1951. Eleven Communist Party leaders had been convicted of advocating the overthrow of the Federal Government. On appeal, they argued that the law violated the 1st Amendment's guarantees of freedom of speech and press. They also claimed that no act of theirs constituted a clear and present danger to this country. The Court disagreed, and modified Justice Holmes's doctrine as it did so:

**PRIMARY Sources** "*An attempt to overthrow the government by force, even though doomed from the outset because of inadequate numbers or power of the revolutionists, is a sufficient evil for Congress to prevent. . . .* "
—Chief Justice Fred M. Vinson, Opinion of the Court

Later, however, the Court modified that holding in several cases. In *Yates* v. *United States,* 1957, for example, the Court overturned the Smith Act convictions of several Communist Party leaders. It held that merely to urge someone to *believe* something, in contrast to urging that person to *do* something, cannot be made illegal. In *Yates* and other Smith Act cases, the Court upheld the constitutionality of the law, but interpreted its provisions so that their enforcement became practically impossible.

## Free Speech or Obscenity?

The 1st and 14th amendments do not protect obscenity, but in recent years the Court has had to wrestle with these questions: What language and images in printed matter, films, and other materials are, in fact, obscene? What restrictions can be properly placed on such materials?

Congress passed the first of a series of laws to prevent the mailing of obscene matter in 1872. The current law, upheld by the Court in *Roth* v. *United States,* 1957, excludes "every obscene, lewd, lascivious, or filthy" piece of material from the mails. The Court found the law a proper exercise of the postal power (Article I, Section 8, Clause 7), and so not prohibited by the 1st Amendment. *Roth* marked the Court's first attempt to define obscenity.

Today, the leading case is *Miller* v. *California,* 1973. There, the Court laid down a three-part test to determine what material is obscene and what is not.

A book, film, recording, or other piece of material is legally obscene if (1) "the average person applying contemporary [local] community standards" finds that the work, taken as a whole, "appeals to the prurient interest"—that is, tends to excite lust; (2) "the work depicts or describes, in a patently offensive way," a form of sexual conduct specifically dealt with in an antiobscenity law; and (3) "the work, taken as a whole, lacks serious literary, artistic, political, or scientific value."

A sampling of Supreme Court decisions involving local attempts to regulate so-called adult book stores and similar places shows how thorny the problem can be. Most of what those stores sell cannot be mailed, sent across State lines, or imported—at least not legally. Still, those shops are usually well-stocked.

The 1st and 14th amendments do not prevent a city from regulating the location of "adult entertainment establishments," said the Court in

"The Small Society," by Yates-Brickman. Washington Star Syndicate, Inc.

*Interpreting Political Cartoons* This kind of "free speech" is clearly not what is covered by the 1st Amendment. **What other kinds of speech are not protected by the Constitution?**

Young v. *American Mini Theaters,* 1976. In *City of Renton v. Playtimes Theaters, Inc.,* 1986, the Court ruled that a city can decide to bar the location of such places within 1,000 feet of a residential zone, church, park, or school. But a city cannot prohibit live entertainment in any and all commercial establishments, according to *Schad v. Borough of Mount Ephraim,* 1981 (a case that involved nude dancing in adult book stores).

The Supreme Court has upheld a State law that makes it a crime to possess or view child pornography, including films. In *Osborne v. Ohio,* 1990, the Court ruled that the State has a compelling interest in protecting the physical and the psychological well-being of minors and in the destruction of the market in which they are exploited.

In their most recent case involving obscenity and the First Amendment, *City of Erie v. Pap's A&M,* 2000, the Court upheld the power of cities to ban taverns, bars, and similar places that feature nude dancing. It found Erie's city ordinance constitutional because that law is not aimed at limiting free expression; instead, it limits the *means* of expression—that is, nude (as distinguished from other forms of) dancing.

## Prior Restraint

The Constitution allows government to punish some utterances *after* they are made. But, with almost no exceptions, government cannot place any **prior restraint** on spoken or written words. Except in the most extreme situations, government cannot curb ideas *before* they are expressed.

*Near* v. *Minnesota,* 1931, is a leading case in point. The Supreme Court struck down a State law that prohibited the publication of any "malicious, scandalous, and defamatory" periodical. Acting under that law, a local court had issued an order forbidding the publication of the *Saturday Press.* This Minneapolis paper had printed several articles charging public corruption and attacking "grafters" and "Jewish gangsters."

The Court held that the guarantee of a free press does not allow a prior restraint on publication, except in such extreme cases as wartime, or when a publication is obscene or incites violence. The Court said that even "miscreant purveyors of scandal" and anti-Semitism have this constitutional protection.

## *Voices* on Government

**Katharine Graham** was publisher of the *Washington Post* when the paper decided to print the "Pentagon Papers" despite the government's attempt to bar their publication. The case *New York Times* v. *United States,* 1971, was a strong challenge to freedom of the press. Graham wrote about it in her autobiography:

❝ *Basically, we were challenging the right of the executive branch to prevent a newspaper from publishing material we believed should be available to the public. In court, we had challenged the government's contention that the material in the Papers was too sensitive for the public eye. . . . Though the decision was in favor of allowing the newspapers to publish, there was . . . 'no ringing reaffirmation of First Amendment guarantees that all publishers yearn to hear.'* ❞

### Evaluating the Quotation
*From what you have read, who do you think should make the decision about what news should be published—the newspapers or the government? What would be the effects of your answer?*

The Constitution does not forbid any and all forms of prior censorship, but "a prior restraint on expression comes to this Court with a 'heavy presumption' against its constitutionality," according to *Nebraska Press Association* v. *Stuart,* 1976.[8] The Court has used that general rule several times—for example, in the famous Pentagon Papers Case, *New York Times* v. *United States,* 1971.

In that case, several newspapers had obtained copies of a set of classified documents, widely known as the Pentagon Papers. Officially titled *History of U.S. Decision-Making Process on Viet Nam Policy,* these documents had been stolen from the Defense Department and then leaked to the press.

[8]In this case a judge had ordered the media not to report certain details of a murder trial. The Court held the judge's gag order to be unconstitutional.

**The Living Constitution** Judicial Review, p. 7

### ACTIVITY
## Heterogeneous Groups
**Enrichment** Have students skim Section 3. When students understand the principles of the 1st and 14th amendments in regard to freedom of speech and press, have them conduct a mock debate. Pose a question for the group, such as: Do news reporters have a constitutional right to withhold certain information from government? Divide students into teams and allow them ample time to prepare their arguments. Encourage them to support their opinions with convincing arguments and specific examples. **(Average)**

## Point-of-Use Resources
**The Living Constitution** Judicial Review, p. 7

**Basic Principles of the Constitution Transparencies** Transparencies 37–43, *Judicial Review*

## CONSTITUTIONAL PRINCIPLES

### Judicial Review
The use of prior restraint in the process of judicial review has been limited and controversial—mainly because allowing prior restraint challenges one of the most cherished American freedoms, freedom of speech. Therefore the Supreme Court has only allowed it in a handful of cases, primarily relating to issues that are seen to endanger national security.

### Activity
The Supreme Court has held that the Internet has the same First Amendment rights as newspapers; however, a case concerning prior restraint and the Internet has not yet come before the Supreme Court. Have students create a theoretical case in which a person or group demands prior restraint of content on a Web site. Students should consider all the points of view, and together develop a Court decision.

### Answer to . . .
**Evaluating the Quotation** Answers will vary. Students may suggest that the 1st Amendment gives newspapers the right to decide what to publish; it is up to the courts to make judgments if conflicts arise after publication.

▶ These teenagers should not be admitted to R-rated movies. *Critical Thinking Does the 1st Amendment protect their right to see whatever movie they wish? Why or why not?*

The government sought a court order to bar their publication. The Court, however, held that the government had not shown that printing the Pentagon Papers would endanger the nation's security. The government thus had not overcome the "heavy presumption" against prior censorship.

The few prior restraints the Court has approved include:

• regulations prohibiting the distribution of political literature on military bases without the approval of military authorities, *Greer* v. *Spock*, 1976;

• a CIA rule that agents must agree never to publish anything about the agency without the CIA's permission, *Snepp* v. *United States*, 1980;

• a federal prison rule that allows officials to prevent an inmate from receiving publications considered "detrimental to the security, good order, or discipline" of the prison, *Thornburgh* v. *Abbott*, 1989.

The Court has also said that public school officials have a broad power to censor school newspapers and plays, as well as other "school-sponsored expressive activities." In *Hazelwood School District* v. *Kuhlmeier*, 1988, it held that educators can exercise "editorial control over the style and content of student speech in school-sponsored expressive activities so long as their actions are reasonably related to legitimate pedagogical concerns."

## The Media

The 1st Amendment stands as a monument to the central importance of the media in a free society. That raises this question: To what extent can the media—both print and electronic—be regulated by government?

### Confidentiality

Can news reporters be forced to testify before a grand jury in court, or before a legislative committee? Can these government bodies require journalists to name their sources and reveal other confidential information? Many reporters and news organizations insist that they must have the right to refuse to testify, the right to protect their sources. They argue that without this right they cannot assure confidentiality, and therefore many sources will not reveal information needed to keep the public informed.

Both State and federal courts have generally rejected the news media argument. In recent years several reporters have refused to obey court orders directing them to give information, and have gone to jail, thus testifying to the importance of these issues.

In the leading case, *Branzburg* v. *Hayes*, 1972, the Supreme Court held that reporters, "like other citizens, [must] respond to relevant questions put to them in the course of a valid grand jury investigation or criminal trial." If the media are to receive any special exemptions, said the Court, they must come from Congress and the State legislatures.

To date, Congress has not acted on the Court's suggestion, but some 30 States have passed so-called **shield laws.** These laws give reporters some protection against having to disclose their sources or reveal other confidential information in legal proceedings in those States.

### Motion Pictures

The Supreme Court took its first look at motion pictures early in the history of the movie industry. In 1915, in *Mutual Film Corporation* v. *Ohio*, the Court upheld a State law that barred the showing of any film that was not of a "moral, educational, or harmless and amusing character." The Court declared that "the exhibition of moving pictures is a business, pure and simple," and "not . . . part of the press of the country." With that decision, nearly every State and thousands of communities set up movie review (really movie censorship) programs.

The Court reversed itself in 1952, however. In *Burstyn* v. *Wilson,* a New York censorship case, it found that "liberty of expression by means of motion pictures is guaranteed by the 1st and 14th amendments."

Very few local movie review boards still exist. Most movie-goers now depend on the film industry's own rating system and on the comments of movie critics.

### Radio and Television

Both radio and television broadcasting are subject to extensive federal regulation. Most of this regulation is based on the often-amended Federal Communications Act of 1934, which is administered by the Federal Communications Commission. In *Red Lion Broadcasting Co.* v. *FCC,* 1969, the Supreme Court acknowledged, "Of all forms of communication, it is broadcasting that has received the most limited 1st Amendment protection."

The Court has upheld this wide-ranging federal regulation as a proper exercise of the commerce power several times. Unlike newspapers and other print media, radio and television use the public's property—the public airwaves—to distribute their materials. They have no right to do so without the public's permission in the form of a proper license, said the Court in *National Broadcasting Co.* v. *United States,* 1943.

The Court has regularly rejected the argument that the 1st Amendment prohibits such regulations. Instead, the Court claims that regulation of this industry actually implements the constitutional guarantee. In *Red Lion Broadcasting Co.* v. *FCC,* 1969, the Court held that there is no "unabridgeable 1st Amendment right to broadcast comparable to the right of every individual to speak, write, or publish." However, "this is not to say that the 1st Amendment is irrelevant to broadcasting. But . . . it is the right of the viewers and the listeners, not the right of the broadcasters, which is paramount."

Congress has forbidden the FCC to censor the content of programs before they are broadcast. However, the FCC can prohibit the use of indecent language, and it can take violations of this ban into account when a station applies for the renewal of its operating license, according to *FCC* v. *Pacifica Foundation,* 1978.

In several recent decisions, the Supreme Court has given the growing cable television industry broader 1st Amendment freedoms than those enjoyed by traditional television.

*United States* v. *Playboy Entertainment Group,* 2000, is fairly typical. There, the Court struck down an attempt by Congress to force many cable systems to limit sexually explicit channels to late night hours. The Court agreed that shielding children from such programming is a worthy goal; nevertheless, it found the 1996 law to be a violation of the 1st Amendment.

## Symbolic Speech

People also communicate ideas by conduct, by the way they do a particular thing. Thus, a person can "say" something with a facial expression or a shrug of the shoulders, or by carrying a sign or wearing an armband. This expression by conduct is known as **symbolic speech.**

Clearly, not all conduct amounts to symbolic speech. If it did, murder or robbery or any other crime could be excused on grounds that the person who committed the act meant to say something by doing so.

Just as clearly, however, some conduct does express opinion. Take picketing in a labor dispute as an example. **Picketing** involves patrolling of a business site by workers who are on strike. By their conduct, picketers attempt to inform the public of the controversy, and to persuade others not to deal with the firm involved. Picketing is, then, a form of expression. If peaceful, it is protected by the 1st and 14th amendments.

The leading case on the point is *Thornhill* v. *Alabama,* 1940. There, the Court struck down a State law that made it a crime to loiter about or to picket a place of business in order to influence others not to trade or work there. Picketing that is "set in a background of violence," however, can be prevented. Even peaceful picketing can be restricted if it is conducted for an illegal purpose, such as forcing someone to do something that is itself illegal.

## Spotlight on Technology

### Magruder's American Government Video Collection

The Magruder's Video Collection explores key issues and debates in American government. Each segment examines an issue central to chapter content through use of historical and contemporary footage. Commentary from civic leaders in academics, government, and the media follow each segment. Critical thinking questions focus students' attention on key issues, and may be used to stimulate discussion.

Use the Chapter 19 video segment to examine how the Internet challenges the American constitutional tradition of free speech protections. (time: about 5 minutes) This segment explores issues of free speech protection, then goes on to show how parents, schools, and the government have responded to controversial Internet materials.

## Background Note
### Recent Scholarship

John W. Johnson, author of *The Struggle for Student Rights:* Tinker *v.* Des Moines *and the 1960s,* does an excellent job of blending "details and personalities with legal analysis" in this case history. Careful to place the students' protest in the context of the Vietnam War, Johnson narrates the events leading up to the Supreme Court's landmark decision on February 24, 1969. He draws from a wide variety of sources—firsthand accounts, newspaper articles, school board records, legal briefs, court transcripts, and judicial opinions—in piecing together the story and explaining in clear and simple terms the steps in the legal process. The book concludes with a discussion of cases involving students' rights that have relied on the *Tinker* decision as a precedent.

## Point-of-Use Resources

**Simulations and Debates** Flag Burning, pp. 59–61 provides students with the opportunity to debate whether flag burning is protected by the First Amendment.

▲ These demonstrators were protesting the Vietnam War in 1971. *Critical Thinking* **Was this demonstration protected by the First Amendment? Why or why not?**

### Other Symbolic Speech Cases

Generally, the Supreme Court has been sympathetic to the symbolic speech argument. Still, it has not given blanket First Amendment protection to that means of expression.

*United States* v. *O'Brien,* 1968, involved four young men who had burned their draft cards to protest the war in Vietnam. A court convicted them of violating a federal law that makes that act a crime. O'Brien appealed, arguing that the First Amendment protects "all modes of communication of ideas by conduct." The Supreme Court disagreed. Said the Court: "We cannot accept the view that an apparently limitless variety of conduct can be labeled 'speech' whenever the person engaging in the conduct intends thereby to express an idea."

The Court also held that acts of dissent by conduct can be punished if: (1) the object of the protest (here, the war and the draft) is within the constitutional powers of the government; (2) whatever restriction is placed on expression is no greater than necessary in the circumstances; and (3) the government's real interest in the matter is not to squelch dissent.

Using that test, the Court has denied some other claims of symbolic speech. Thus, in *Kelley* v. *Johnson,* 1976, it held that a policeman does not have a constitutional right to protest a department dress code by growing long hair. This is true even if the officer believes his actions to be "a means of expressing his attitude and lifestyle." The Court felt that a government has a

reasonable stake in requiring a "similarity of garb and appearance" among its police officers.

*Tinker* v. *Des Moines School District,* 1969, on the other hand, is one of several cases in which the Court has come down on the side of symbolic speech. A small group of students in the Des Moines public schools had worn black armbands to publicize their opposition to the war in Vietnam. The school suspended them for it.

The Court ruled that school officials had overstepped their authority and violated the Constitution. Said the Court: "It can hardly be argued that either students or teachers shed their constitutional rights to freedom of speech or expression at the schoolhouse gate."[9]

In *Buckley* v. *Valeo,* 1976, the Court found that campaign contributions are "a symbolic expression of support" for candidates, and therefore the making of those contributions is entitled to constitutional protection. Both federal and State laws regulate campaign contributions, but the fact that in politics "money is speech" greatly complicates the whole matter of campaign finance regulation (see Chapter 7).

### Flag Burning

Burning the American flag as an act of political protest is expressive conduct protected by the 1st and 14th amendments—so a sharply divided Court has twice held. In *Texas* v. *Johnson,* 1989, a 5–4 majority ruled that State authorities had violated a protester's rights by prosecuting him under a law that forbids the "desecration of a venerated object." Johnson had set fire to an American flag during an anti-Reagan demonstration at the Republican National Convention in Dallas in 1984. Said the Court:

> **PRIMARY Sources** *If there is a bedrock principle underlying the 1st Amendment, it is that the government may not prohibit the expression of an idea simply because society finds the idea itself offensive. . . . We do not consecrate the flag by punishing its desecration, for in doing so we dilute the*

---

[9] Do not read too much into this, for the Court added, it "has repeatedly affirmed the comprehensive authority of the States and of school authorities, consistent with fundamental constitutional safeguards, to prescribe and control conduct in the schools." The fact that in *Tinker* the students' conduct did not cause a substantial disruption of normal school activities was an important factor in the Court's decision.

*Answer to . . .*

**Critical Thinking** Possible answer: Yes; it appears to be peaceful.

> *freedom that this cherished emblem represents.* **"**
>
> —William J. Brennan, Jr., Opinion of the Court

The Court's decision in *Johnson* set off a firestorm of criticism around the country and prompted Congress to pass the Flag Protection Act of 1989. It, too, was struck down by the Court, 5 to 4, in *United States* v. *Eichman,* 1990. The Court based its decision on the same grounds as those set out a year earlier in *Johnson.*

## Commercial Speech

Commercial speech is speech for business purposes; the term refers most often to advertising. Until the mid-1970s, it was thought that the 1st and 14th amendments did not protect such speech. In *Bigelow* v. *Virginia,* 1975, however, the Supreme Court held unconstitutional a State law that prohibited the newspaper advertising of abortion services. The following year, in *Virginia State Board of Pharmacy* v. *Virginia Citizens Consumer Council,* it struck down another Virginia law forbidding the advertisement of prescription drug prices.

Not all commercial speech is protected, however. Thus, government can and does prohibit false and misleading advertisements, and the advertising of illegal goods or services.

In fact, government can even forbid advertising that is neither false nor misleading. Thus, in 1970, Congress banned cigarette ads on radio

and television. In 1986, it extended the ban to include chewing tobacco and snuff.

In most of its commercial speech cases, the Court has struck down arbitrary restrictions on advertising. Thus, in *44 Liquormart, Inc.* v. *Rhode Island,* 1996, the Court voided a State law that prohibited ads in which liquor prices were listed. In *Greater New Orleans Broadcasting Ass'n* v. *United States,* 1999, it struck down a federal law that prohibited casino advertising on radio or television.

Most recently, the Court dealt with limits on smokeless tobacco and cigar advertising. Massachusetts had barred outdoor ads for these commodities within 1000 feet of any school or playground. The Court held that limit a violation of the 1st and 14th amendments' guarantee of free speech, *P. Lorillard Co.* v. *Reilly,* 2001.

One of the Court's first commercial speech cases had an interesting twist. In *Wooley* v. *Maynard,* 1977, the Court held that a State cannot force its citizens to act as "mobile billboards." At least, a State cannot do so when the words used conflict with its citizens' religious or moral beliefs. The Maynards, who were Jehovah's Witnesses, objected to the New Hampshire State motto on their automobile license plates. The words *Live Free or Die* clashed with their belief in everlasting life, and so they covered those words with tape. For this, Maynard was arrested three times. On appeal, the Supreme Court sided with Maynard.

# Chapter **19** • Section **3**

## Point-of-Use Resources

**Guide to the Essentials** Chapter 19, Section 3, p. 104 provides support for students who need additional review of section content. Spanish support is available in the Spanish edition of the Guide on p. 97.

**Quiz** Unit 5 booklet, p. 16 includes matching and multiple-choice questions to check students' understanding of Section 3 content.

**Presentation Pro CD-ROM** Quizzes and multiple-choice questions check students' understanding of Section 3 content.

## Answers to . . .

### Section 3 Assessment

**1.** Both terms refer to the false and malicious use of words; libel refers to printed words, while slander refers to spoken words.

**2.** Because the Supreme Court determined that seditious speech had the power to provide a "clear and present danger" to the government.

**3. (a)** Prior restraint is the placing of restrictions on spoken or written words before they are expressed. **(b)** It has usually disallowed prior restraint cases.

**4.** Picketing is a means of informing the public of a point of view on an issue, and thus is symbolic speech.

**5.** Answers will vary; a possible harmful instance could be protecting a source who later commits a terrible crime; a helpful instance could be providing the public with vital information that could not otherwise be obtained.

**6. (a)** Protecting unpopular views means that every citizen has a voice and can participate in public affairs. **(b)** and **(c)** Answers will vary, but should be supported with examples.

## Section **3** Assessment

**Key Terms and Main Ideas**

1. Compare **libel** with **slander**.
2. Why does the government restrict **seditious speech?**
3. **(a)** Define **prior restraint. (b)** How has the Supreme Court usually dealt with prior restraint cases?
4. In what way is **picketing symbolic speech?**

**Critical Thinking**

5. **Identifying Alternatives** Do you think journalists should have the right to protect their sources? Describe one instance where this right would benefit society and one instance where it might be harmful.
6. **Identifying Central Issues** The Constitution makes a particular effort to protect the expression of unpopular views.

**(a)** Why is this important? **(b)** Do you think even racist or sexist speech and publications should be protected? **(c)** Explain your answer.

 **Take It to the Net**

7. The States of Kentucky and Virginia passed resolutions in response to the Alien and Sedition Acts. Read the final version of the Kentucky resolution. Make an outline that shows Kentucky's objections to the Alien and Sedition Acts and the actions that the State took in response. Use the links provided in the Social Studies area at the following Web site for help in completing this activity. **www.phschool.com**

 **Take It to the Net**

7. Direct students to the Social Studies area at the Prentice Hall School Web site. The *Magruder's American Government* companion Web site includes the directions and links needed to complete the activity. It also provides a printable Internet activity worksheet with scoring rubrics for assessment. Outlines should include all objections and all State actions.

### Participating in Public Debates

**Focus** Have students work together to construct plans for participating in a public debate.

**Instruct** Have students individually write down one or two issues that interest them. Group students whose topics are similar. Then have each group make a plan for carrying out Steps 1 through 4. Make sure students' plans include both short-term and long-term goals.

**Close/Reteach** Ask for a volunteer from each group to present the plan to the class.

## SKILLS FOR LIFE

# Participating in Public Debates

The process of debating public issues has never been more "transparent" than it is today. That is, the process is more open to public scrutiny. The increase in media outlets, such as cable TV and the Internet, has created opportunities for people to register their opinions. Use your opportunities to voice your opinions by following these steps:

**1. Identify the issue(s) of concern to you.** Get in the habit of looking at the morning newspaper or the evening news. If you see something of interest, study the topic further rather than basing your opinions on short TV sound bites. What public issue is of most interest to you?

**2. Find out whom to contact.** Your opinion counts most when you express it to those people who have some authority or influence on the issue. That could be a government official, a private lobbying group, or a media outlet that reaches many voters. Who might you contact to express your views on your topic? Why?

**3. Decide on a strategy for publicizing your opinions.** Decide on the best way to get your ideas across. Consider your communications skills—do you express yourself better through speaking or through writing? Which of the strategies in the box at right would be best for you?

**4. Present your ideas.** Generally, a battle to win the hearts and minds of your fellow citizens is won on the strength of good ideas well presented. What short-term and long-term goals might you seek through participating in public debates?

Indiana teenager Ryan White became a nationally known political activist, speaking and lobbying on behalf of the rights of AIDS patients, prior to his death from AIDS in 1990, at age 19.

### Test for Success

Choose an issue that is being publicly debated right now. Follow the steps listed here to develop a strategy for airing your views about it. Write a brief letter to the editor or a newsgroup posting, or prepare an oral argument on the issue.

### Make Your Opinions Known

▶ Write a letter to the editor. Your letter should be brief, quickly stating the issue, your opinion, and facts to support your opinion. Letters that are well-reasoned may have more influence than hostile or insulting prose.

▶ Contact a government official or agency. Find out who the decision makers are on your issue.

▶ Join a public interest group or other lobbying organization. You might want to work for a cause you believe in. Find out if there are any requirements for joining, such as fees.

▶ Join an Internet chatroom or newsgroup. Live, "real time" chatrooms let you participate in actual conversations and debates. Consult with your teacher about appropriate groups.

▶ Address a government hearing on an issue of concern to you. Come prepared with facts and a few specific points to make. Be prepared to rebut any opposing arguments.

▶ Participate in a public protest or demonstration of support. Coming together with other activists to rally support and send a loud message can be an exciting way to participate in public debate, if the event is legal and orderly.

▶ Participate in a petition drive. A great way to register grassroots support for an issue or a specific bill is to gather signatures for a petition. You'll learn more about petitions in Chapter 24.

### Answers . . .

**1.** Possible prompts: First Amendment rights, U.S. involvement in international crises, environmental issues, social policies.
**2.** Best choices might be policymakers involved with the issue or media outlets that reach people most likely to rally to the cause.
**3.** Students with good speaking skills might consider direct telephone contact with public officials or participation in a public discussion or protest. Those who prefer writing might choose some of the other strategies listed.
**4.** Short-term goals might include acknowledgment of the receipt of a letter or e-mail, or a promise by a public official to investigate the matter. Getting real, measurable progress on a public issue is the ultimate long-term goal.

### Test for Success

Ask students to show their decision-making as they do Steps 1–3. They should identify where they learned about the issue and their rationale for whom to contact and in what manner.

### Point-of-Use Resources

**Skills for Life Activity** Unit 5 booklet, p. 19 provides an additional skill activity for this chapter.

**Social Studies Skills Tutor CD-ROM** Provides interactive practice in geographic literacy, critical thinking and reading, visual analysis, and communications.

# Freedom of Assembly and Petition

## Section Preview

### OBJECTIVES

1. **Explain** the Constitution's guarantees of assembly and petition.
2. **Summarize** how the government can limit the time, place, and manner of assembly.
3. **Compare and contrast** the freedom-of-assembly issues that arise on public versus private property.
4. **Explore** how the Supreme Court has interpreted freedom of association.

### WHY IT MATTERS

The constitutional guarantees of assembly and petition protect Americans' rights to gather peacefully in order to express their views and to influence public policy, by such means as demonstrations and written petitions. There are place, time, and manner limitations on these freedoms, however.

### POLITICAL DICTIONARY

★ assemble
★ content neutral
★ right of association

A noisy street demonstration by gay rights activists, or by neo-Nazis, or by any number of other groups; a candlelight vigil of opponents of the death penalty; the pro-life faithful singing hymns as they picket an abortion clinic; pro-choice partisans gathered on the steps of the State capitol . . . these are commonplace events today. They are also everyday manifestations of freedom of assembly and petition.

## The Constitution's Guarantees

The 1st Amendment guarantees

> FROM THE Constitution
> " . . . the right of the people peaceably to assemble, and to petition the Government for a redress of grievances. "
> —United States Constitution

The 14th Amendment's Due Process Clause also protects those rights of assembly and petition against actions by the States or their local governments.

The Constitution protects the right of the people to **assemble**—to gather with one another—to express their views on public matters. It protects their right to organize to influence public policy, whether in political parties, interest groups, or other organizations. It also protects the people's right to bring their views to the attention of public officials by such varied means as written petitions, letters, or advertisements; lobbying; or parades, marches, or other demonstrations.

Notice, however, the 1st and 14th amendments protect the rights of *peaceable* assembly and petition. The Constitution does not give people the right to incite others to violence, to block a public street, to close a school, or otherwise to endanger life, property, or public order.

◀ A silent vigil is one form of assembly protected by the 1st Amendment.

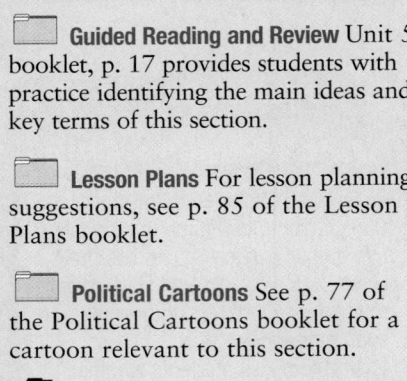
## Time-Place-Manner Regulations

Government can make and enforce reasonable rules covering the time, place, and manner of assemblies. Thus, in *Grayned* v. *City of Rockford,* 1972, the Supreme Court has upheld a city ordinance that prohibits making a noise or causing any other diversion near a school if that action disrupts school activities. It has also upheld a State law that forbids parades near a courthouse when they are intended to influence court proceedings, in *Cox* v. *Louisiana,* 1965.

Rules for keeping the public peace must be more than reasonable, however. They must also be precisely drawn and fairly administered. In *Coates* v. *Cincinnati,* 1971, the Court struck down a city ordinance that made it a crime for "three or more persons to assemble" on a sidewalk or street corner "and there conduct themselves in a manner annoying to persons passing by, or to occupants of adjacent buildings." The Court found the ordinance much too vague.

Government's rules must be **content neutral.** That is, while government can regulate assemblies on the basis of time, place, and manner, it cannot regulate assemblies on the basis of what might be said there. Thus, in *Forsyth County* v. *Nationalist Movement,* 1992, the Court threw out a Georgia county's ordinance that levied a fee of up to $1,000 for public demonstrations.

The law was contested by a white supremacist group seeking to protest the creation of a holiday to honor Martin Luther King, Jr. The Court found the ordinance not to be content neutral, particularly because county officials had unlimited power to set the exact fee to be paid by any group.

Notice that the power to control traffic or keep a protest rally from becoming a riot *can* be used as an excuse to prevent speech. The line between crowd control and thought control can be very thin, indeed.

## Public Property

Over the past several years, most of the Court's freedom of assembly cases have involved organized demonstrations. Demonstrations are, of course, assemblies.

Most demonstrations take place in public places, on streets and sidewalks, in parks or public buildings, and so on. Demonstrations take place in these locations because it is the public the demonstrators want to reach.

Demonstrations almost always involve some degree of conflict. Most often, they are held to protest something, and so there is an inherent clash of ideas. Many times there is also a conflict with the normal use of streets or other public facilities. It is hardly surprising, then, that the tension can sometimes rise to a serious level.

Given all this, the Supreme Court has often upheld laws that require advance notice and permits for demonstrations in public places. In an early leading case, *Cox* v. *New Hampshire,* 1941, it unanimously approved a State law that required a license to hold a parade or other procession on a public street.

Right-to-demonstrate cases raise many basic and thorny questions. How and to what extent can government regulate demonstrators and their demonstrations? Does the Constitution require that police officers allow an unpopular group to continue to demonstrate when its activities have excited others to violence? When, in the name of public peace and safety, can police properly order demonstrators to disband?

### *Gregory* v. *Chicago*

*Gregory* v. *Chicago,* 1969, is an illustrative case. While under police protection, Dick Gregory and others had marched, while singing, chanting, and carrying placards, from city hall to the mayor's home some five miles away. Marching in the streets around the mayor's house, they demanded the firing of the city's school superintendent and an end to de facto segregation in the city's schools.

A crowd of several hundred people, including many residents of the all-white neighborhood, quickly gathered. Soon, the bystanders began throwing insults and threats, as well as rocks, eggs, and other objects. The police tried to keep order, but after about an hour, they decided that serious violence was about to break out. At that point, they ordered the demonstrators to leave the area. When Gregory and the others failed to do so, the police arrested them and charged them with disorderly conduct.

The convictions of the demonstrators were unanimously overturned by the High Court. The Court noted that the marchers had done no

▲ *Peaceful Protest* Elian Gonzales, a five-year-old Cuban boy, was rescued after his boat sank while fleeing Cuba for the United States. These demonstrators gathered in Miami to show their support for Elian to remain in this country.

more than exercise their constitutional rights of assembly and petition. Neighborhood residents and others, not the demonstrators, had caused the disorder. So long as the demonstrators acted peacefully, they could not be punished for disorderly conduct.

### Recent Cases

Over recent years, many of the most controversial demonstrations have been those held by Operation Rescue and other anti-abortion groups. For the most part, the efforts of those groups have been aimed at discouraging women from seeking the services of abortion clinics, and those efforts have generated many lawsuits.

There have been two particularly notable cases to date. In the first one, *Madsen* v. *Women's Health Services, Inc.,* 1994, the Supreme Court upheld a Florida judge's order directing protesters not to block access to an abortion clinic. The judge's order had drawn a 36-foot buffer zone around the clinic. The High Court found that to be a reasonable limit on the demonstrators' activities.

The other major case is a more recent one, *Hill* v. *Colorado,* 2000. There, the Court upheld, 5–4, a State law that limits "sidewalk counseling" at clinics where abortions are performed. That statute creates an eight-foot buffer zone around anyone who is within 100 feet of the entrance to a health-care facility and wants to enter. No one may make an "unwanted approach" (invade that buffer zone) to talk or do such other things as hand out a leaflet or wave a sign.

The Court found that the Colorado law does not deal with the content of abortion protestors' speech. Instead it is aimed at where, when, and how their message is delivered.

### Private Property

What of demonstrations on private property— for example, at shopping centers? The Court has heard only a few cases raising this question. However, at least this much can be said: The rights of assembly and petition do not give people a right to trespass on private property, even if they wish to express political views.

Privately owned shopping centers are not public streets, sidewalks, parks, and other "places of public assembly." Thus, no one has a constitutional right to do such things as hand out political leaflets or ask people to sign petitions in those places.

These comments are based on the leading case here, *Lloyd Corporation* v. *Tanner,* 1972. However, since that case the Court has held this: A State supreme court may interpret the provisions of that State's constitution in such a way as to require the owners of shopping centers to allow the reasonable exercise of the right of petition on their private property.

In that event, there is no violation of the property owners' rights under any provision in the federal Constitution. A case in point is *PruneYard Shopping Center* v. *Robins,* 1980. Several California high school students had set up a card table in the shopping center. They passed out

ACTIVITY

## Heterogeneous Groups

**Reteaching** Divide students into four groups. Each group will cover a different 1st Amendment right discussed in this section. Groups will create a section for a citizen handbook that highlights the various 1st Amendment rights and limitations. Students should include text and illustrations for the portion of the handbook they are developing. When finished with their section, each group should present their information to the other groups so that a complete citizen handbook can be finalized.

**Block Strategy (Average)**

---

## Preparing for Standardized Tests

Have students read the passages under *Private Property* and then answer the question below.

Which of the following statements is most accurate?

**A** It is unconstitutional to petition in a shopping mall.

**B** All States prohibit petitioning at a shopping mall.

**C** Owners of shopping malls may allow petitioners on a case-by-case basis.

**D** Whether people can petition at a shopping mall depends on each State's constitution.

## Answers to . . .

### Section 4 Assessment

**1.** That people may gather together to express their views on public matters as long as they do not endanger life, property, or public order; examples include writing petitions or letters, advertising, lobbying, or holding marches or demonstrations.
**2.** It has upheld laws limiting activities near schools and courtrooms.
**3.** It stipulates the right to associate with others to promote political, economic, and social causes.
**4.** Assembling to promote causes is a primary means for people to express their opinions and influence policy, which is vital to any democracy.
**5.** Questions may include: Is our place too close to a school or courthouse, or is it on private property? Will the location disrupt public proceedings? Will our activities endanger anyone or any property?

Interpreting Political Cartoons **How do you think the Supreme Court might rule in a case like this: for the boys (freedom of association) or for the girl (anti-discrimination)? Explain your answer.**

pro-Israeli pamphlets and asked passersby to sign petitions to be sent to the President and Congress.

## Freedom of Association

The guarantees of freedom of assembly and petition include a **right of association.** That is, those guarantees include the right to associate with others to promote political, economic, and other social causes. That right is not set out in so many words in the Constitution. However, in *National Association for the Advancement of Colored People* v. *Alabama,* 1958, the Supreme Court said "it is beyond doubt that freedom to engage in association for the advancement of

beliefs and ideas is an inseparable aspect" of the Constitution's guarantees of free expression.

The case just cited is one of the early right-to-associate cases. There, a State law required the Alabama branch of the NAACP to disclose the names of all its members in that State. When the organization refused a court's order to do so, it was found in contempt of court and fined $100,000.

The Supreme Court overturned the contempt conviction. It said that it could find no legitimate reason why the State should have the NAACP's membership list.

The Court's most recent case bearing on freedom of association involved the Boy Scouts of America. In *Boy Scouts of America* v. *Dale,* 2000, it held that the Boy Scouts have a constitutional right to exclude gays from their organization. The High Court made that decision in a New Jersey case, noting that opposition to homosexuality is a part of the Boy Scout organization's "expressive conduct"—that is, what they stand for.

The decision overturned a ruling by the New Jersey Supreme Court. That court had applied the State's anti-discrimination law against the Scouts; it ordered a New Jersey troop to readmit James Dale, an Eagle Scout, whom the troop had dismissed when it learned he was gay.

The Court ruled that the Constitution's guarantee of freedom of association means that a State cannot force an organization like the Boy Scouts to accept members when that action would contradict what the organization professes to believe.

## Section 4 Assessment

### Key Terms and Main Ideas

1. What does the right to **assemble** peaceably mean? Give two examples of peaceful assembly for political purposes.
2. Summarize briefly how the Supreme Court has limited the time, place, and manner of assembly.
3. How does the **right of association** extend the right of assembly?

### Critical Thinking

4. **Identifying Central Issues** Why are the freedom to assemble peacefully and the freedom of association central to an open, democratic society?
5. **Formulating Questions** Not all assembly is protected by the 1st Amendment. Suppose you are helping to organize

a demonstration for a political cause. Make up three to five questions you should ask in order to determine if your demonstration would be considered constitutional by the Supreme Court.

 **Take It to the Net**

6. Read about the history of the right to assemble. Create a time line showing what you think are the most important events in the evolution of this right, first in England and later in the American colonies and the United States. Include at least seven events. Use the links provided in the Social Studies area at the following Web site for help in completing this activity. **www.phschool.com**

 **Take It to the Net**

**6.** Direct students to the Social Studies area at the Prentice Hall School Web site. The *Magruder's American Government* companion Web site includes the directions and links needed to complete the activity. It also provides a printable Internet activity worksheet with scoring rubrics for assessment. Time lines should include at least seven relevant events.

## Answer to . . .

**Interpreting Political Cartoons** Possible answer: For the boys, as their club house is a private organization.

# *on the Supreme Court*

## May Schools Ban Political Protests?

*In order to educate students and also to ensure their safety, school officials need broad authority to control what goes on in schools. Recognizing this fact, the courts have granted schools flexibility in certain areas, such as censorship. Can schools prevent students from peacefully expressing opinions on controversial political issues?*

### Tinker v. *Des Moines School District* (1969)

In December 1965, a group of students and adults in Des Moines, Iowa, met to discuss ways of publicizing their opposition to the war in Vietnam and their support for a truce in the fighting. The group included 15-year-old high school student John Tinker, his sister Mary Beth Tinker, and his friend Christopher Eckhardt. The three students decided to wear black armbands through the end of the holiday season and to fast on two days.

The principals of the Des Moines schools learned of the plans to wear armbands. They met on December 14 and adopted a policy that any student wearing an armband would be asked to remove it. Anyone refusing to comply would be suspended.

On December 16, Mary Beth and Christopher wore their armbands to school. John wore his the following day. All were sent home and were suspended until they returned without the armbands. They did not return to school until January, when the planned time for wearing the armbands had expired. The students' fathers filed suit in federal district court, seeking a court order to prevent enforcement of the school district's ban on armbands. They also asked that the school district not be allowed to discipline the students for wearing them. The court found that the school authorities' actions did not violate the Constitution. The court of appeals agreed with the district court, and the Tinkers appealed to the Supreme Court.

### Arguments for Tinker

1. Wearing an armband to express an opinion is symbolic speech that is protected under the Free Speech Clause of the 1st Amendment.

2. Students do not lose their 1st Amendment rights when they are in school. School authorities may restrict speech or action that interferes with the work of the school but may not prohibit silent, passive expressions of opinion that create no such interference.

3. Schools may not limit expressions of opinion to avoid confrontation or disagreement among students over politically sensitive issues.

### Arguments for Des Moines School District

1. States and school officials must have complete authority to control conduct in public schools in order to maintain discipline and good order.

2. The ban on armbands was reasonable because it was based upon fear of a disturbance in school.

3. The plaintiffs' wearing of armbands distracted other students from their classwork and diverted them to the highly emotional subject of the Vietnam War. Schools have the right to adopt reasonable regulations to keep students focused on school subjects.

### Decide for Yourself

1. Review the constitutional grounds on which each side based its arguments and the specific arguments each side presented.
2. Debate the opposing viewpoints presented in this case. Which viewpoint do you favor?
3. Predict the impact of the Court's decision on other issues relating to students' rights. (To read a summary of the Court's decision, turn to the Supreme Court Glossary on page 799.)

---

 **CLOSE·UP** FOUNDATION *Corner*

📁 **Close Up on the Supreme Court** *Tinker* v. *Des Moines School District,* p. 20 provides an activity to extend coverage of this case.

 **CLOSE·UP** FOUNDATION **Online**

To keep up-to-date on Close Up news and activities, visit Close Up Online at

**www.closeup.org**

---

## Practicing the Vocabulary

**1.–10.** Sentences should accurately reflect the meaning of each term in context of chapter content.
**11.** *c;* libel, slander, and seditious speech all concern maligning a person or country; symbolic speech expresses ideas.
**12.** *c;* the other terms are protections against government; civil rights are positive acts of government.
**13.** *d;* the other terms guarantee individual freedoms; prior restraint limits expression.
**14.** *a;* the other terms are forms of expression; parochial refers to private, church-related schools.

## Reviewing Main Ideas
### Section 1

**15. (a)** People wanted specific protection against abuses of government. **(b)** The first session of Congress added the Bill of Rights.
**16.** Federalism means that restrictions on the National Government concerning individual rights do not apply to the States.
**17. (a)** Rights apply to people so long as they do not infringe on those of others. **(b)** The Supreme Court decides which takes precedence.
**18.** By incorporation of most provisions.

### Section 2

**19.** Endorse or support a particular religion.
**20.** Issues include "released time" programs, prayers and the Bible in public schools, aid to parochial schools, the teaching of evolution in public schools, seasonal displays, and the use of chaplains in legislatures.
**21.** To qualify for aid, the aid must have a secular purpose; must have no intention of advancing or inhibiting religion; and must avoid entangling government and religion.
**22.** Religious groups must have permits to hold parades on public streets, religions must obey child labor laws, religious objectors are still subject to the draft, and religious beliefs cannot violate constitutional principles.

### Section 3

**23.** To guarantee free expression and to ensure all persons a full discussion

### Political Dictionary

Bill of Rights (p. 532)
civil liberties (p. 533)
civil rights (p. 533)
alien (p. 534)
Due Process Clause (p. 535)
process of incorporation (p. 535)
Establishment Clause (p. 537)

parochial (p. 538)
Free Exercise Clause (p. 542)
libel (p. 546)
slander (p. 547)
sedition (p. 547)
seditious speech (p. 547)
prior restraint (p. 549)

shield law (p. 550)
symbolic speech (p. 551)
picketing (p. 551)
assemble (p. 555)
content neutral (p. 556)
right of association (p. 558)

## Practicing the Vocabulary

**Using Terms in Context** *For each of the terms below, write a sentence that shows how it relates to this chapter.*

1. Bill of Rights
2. civil liberties
3. Due Process Clause
4. process of incorporation
5. Establishment Clause
6. Free Exercise Clause
7. prior restraint
8. symbolic speech
9. assemble
10. right of association

**Word Relationships** *Three of the terms in each of the following sets of terms are related. Choose the term that does not belong and explain why it does not.*

11. **(a)** libel **(b)** slander **(c)** symbolic speech **(d)** seditious speech
12. **(a)** civil liberties **(b)** shield law **(c)** civil rights **(d)** right of association
13. **(a)** Bill of Rights **(b)** Free Exercise Clause **(c)** Establishment Clause **(d)** prior restraint
14. **(a)** parochial **(b)** picketing **(c)** assemble **(d)** symbolic speech

## Reviewing Main Ideas

### Section 1

15. **(a)** Why was there an outcry when the Constitution did not originally contain a general listing of the rights of the people? **(b)** How was this remedied?
16. How does federalism affect the guarantees of individual rights?
17. **(a)** Explain this statement: Rights are relative, not absolute. **(b)** What happens when rights conflict?
18. How does the Due Process Clause of the 14th Amendment affect the guarantees in the Bill of Rights?

### Section 2

19. What does the Establishment Clause say that the government cannot do?
20. Describe three Establishment Clause issues regarding education that the Supreme Court has addressed.
21. What are the three elements of the *Lemon* test?
22. Identify three ways in which government may restrict the exercise of religious belief.

### Section 3

23. What are the two elements of the free exchange of ideas, and why are they both important in a democracy?

24. Why has the Supreme Court upheld prohibitions of **(a)** slander and libel, **(b)** seditious speech, and **(c)** obscenity.
25. What has generally been the Supreme Court's attitude toward prior restraint?
26. **(a)** What is the press argument in favor of shield laws? **(b)** How has the Supreme Court generally responded to press confidentiality issues?
27. Why can radio and television be regulated more strictly than other forms of the media?
28. Describe briefly one case in which the Supreme Court upheld a restriction on symbolic speech and one case where it struck down a restriction.

### Section 4

29. Describe the time, place, and manner limits that the government can put on freedom of assembly.
30. **(a)** What is the right of association? **(b)** Since it is not expressly granted in the Constitution, what is the origin of this right?

of public affairs; the ability to speak freely and participate in government are essential to democracy.
**24. (a)** It has placed reasonable restrictions on freedom of speech, to prevent injury to other persons. **(b)** It has set the "clear and present danger" precedent. **(c)** It has chosen a three-part test to determine obscenity, and placed regulations on the dissemination of pornography.

**25.** It has generally disallowed the use of prior restraint.
**26. (a)** That without the ability to protect its sources, it cannot keep the public informed. **(b)** It has generally rejected that argument.
**27.** Because they use the public's property (airwaves) to distribute their materials.
**28.** Answers will vary, but might mention the *Tinker* case for upholding, and the *Kelley* case for striking down.

### Section 4

**29.** Government has placed restrictions on where, how, and at what time people assemble, for the purpose of preventing violence or endangering life, property, or public order.
**30. (a)** A guarantee that people may associate with others to promote causes. **(b)** The 1958 Supreme Court case *NAACP* v. *Alabama* set the precedent.

## Critical Thinking

**31.** *Applying the Chapter Skill* There are a number of interest groups that focus on 1st Amendment issues. Contact a group that takes a stand on an issue that interests you, and find out what its position is, how it goes about promoting its cause, and how successful the group has been. Summarize this information, and state whether you think the group is one that you might wish to join.

**32.** *Determining Relevance* Analyze the 1st Amendment rights guaranteed by the Bill of Rights by exploring what Justice Holmes called protection of "thought that we hate."
**(a)** Explain briefly what this protection means, and why it is so important. **(b)** Then, from your knowledge of history or current affairs, discuss one example of a repressive government suppressing speech that it hates, and the repercussions of that repression.

**33.** *Drawing Conclusions* Your school newspaper wants to publish an article critical of one board member's speech at a school board meeting. The principal has forbidden publication of the article because it is disrespectful, misquotes the board member, and states a position that the school administration does not agree with. What constitutional issues does the principal's action raise? Explain how you think the Supreme Court would rule on each of these issues.

## Analyzing Political Cartoons

Using your knowledge of American government and this cartoon, answer the questions below.

*Since you have already been convicted by the media, I imagine we can wrap this up pretty quickly.*

**34. (a)** In the caption of this cartoon, what does "convicted by the media" mean? **(b)** How can this kind of conviction affect a trial?
**35.** What do you think the cartoonist feels about the right of a free press versus the right to a fair trial?

 **You Can Make a Difference**

How much freedom of speech do you think students should have, in or out of school? What issues of censorship and free speech have arisen in your school and community? Prepare a list of questions to use in interviewing the following people on this issue: computer science teachers, the editorial staff and faculty advisers of the school newspaper, the school librarian, and school administrators.

## Participation Activities

**36** *Current Events Watch* "Speech" on the Internet is unlike expression in other media. Find recent newspaper articles on this topic. List the types of Internet speech some people think should be regulated, the practical difficulties of regulating it, and the 1st Amendment issues raised by each type. Include court cases where applicable.

**37.** *Table Activity* Make a table of the important Supreme Court cases involving freedom of assembly. Include a very brief description of each case; indicate whether the issue was time, place, or manner of assembly; and give the Supreme Court's ruling.

**38.** *It's Your Turn* Explain a point of view on a government issue. Choose one of the controversial Supreme Court cases discussed in this chapter, and take a position on the issue. Prepare an argument (speech) that you would present to the Supreme Court—for the government or for the other party to the suit. Your argument should not only state and defend your position on the issue but also answer the opposing arguments. **(Writing a Speech)**

 **Take It to the Net**

*Chapter 19 Self-Test* As a final review activity, take the Chapter 19 Self-Test in the Social Studies area at the Web site listed below, and receive immediate feedback on your answers.

**www.phschool.com**

## Critical Thinking Skills

**31.** Answers will vary; students' decisions on whether they would or would not join should be explained with examples and clear reasoning for supporting the group or for not being interested in it.
**32. (a)** The provision means that even unpopular speech must be protected, because a nation that doesn't allow for the expressions of dissenting views can never be democratic. **(b)** Answers will vary, but should include relevant examples.
**33.** The principal's action raises the issue of prior restraint; students might suggest that the Supreme Court would disallow the use of prior restraint, as the article would not hurt the school or the person about whom it was written.

## Analyzing Political Cartoons

**34. (a)** The media's reports concerning the accused have been unfavorable.
**(b)** It can cause disruption and introduce bias.
**35.** That the right of a fair trial outweighs the right of a free press.

## You Can Make a Difference

Lists should include relevant questions that cover the issue of freedom of speech from several angles.

## Participation Activities

**36.** Lists should include several types of Internet speech, accurately defined, and identify the correct First Amendment issues.
**37.** Tables should be neatly organized and easy to read.
**38.** Arguments should clearly present a point of view on the issue, answer all opposing arguments, and if possible cite relevant Supreme Court cases.

## Point-of-Use Resources

**Guide to the Essentials of American Government** Chapter 19 Test, page 106 provides multiple-choice questions to test students' knowledge of the chapter.

**Test Bank CD-ROM** Chapter 19 Test

**Chapter Test** Chapter Tests booklet

# Civil Liberties: Protecting Individual Rights

| Section Objectives | Print and Technology Resources |
|---|---|

## 1 Due Process of Law

*(pp. 564–568)*

1. Explain the importance of due process rights to the protection of individual rights and to the limits on the powers of government.
2. Define police power and understand its relationship to civil rights.
3. Describe the right of privacy and its origins in constitutional law.

**TEKS 3A, 3B, 8B, 8D, 8F, 9C, 9E, 9G, 10D, 14A, 14B, 14D, 14E, 14F, 15B, 15C, 17C, 21A, 22A, 22B, 22D**

- **Unit 5 booklet**
  Guided Reading and Review, p. 20
  Section 1 Quiz, p. 21
- **Lesson Plans booklet** Section 1, p. 86
- **Political Cartoons booklet** Section 1, p. 78
- **Block Scheduling with Lesson Strategies booklet** p. 29

- **Close Up on the Supreme Court booklet** *Roe* v. *Wade,* pp. 52–53
- **Basic Principles of the Constitution Transparencies** 34
- **Section Support Transparencies** 81, 180
- **Presentation Pro CD-ROM** Section 1
- **Section Reading Support Transparencies**

## 2 Freedom and Security of the Person

*(pp. 569–574)*

1. Outline Supreme Court decisions regarding slavery and involuntary servitude.
2. Explain the intent and application of the 2nd Amendment's protection of the right to keep and bear arms.
3. Summarize the constitutional provisions designed to guarantee security of home and person.

**TEKS 3A, 3B, 8B, 8D, 8F, 9C, 9E, 9G, 10D, 14A, 14B, 14D, 14E, 14F, 15B, 15C, 17C, 18A, 18B, 18C, 21A, 21B, 21D, 21E, 22A, 22B, 22D**

- **Unit 5 booklet**
  Guided Reading and Review, p. 22
  Section 2 Quiz, p. 23
- **Lesson Plans booklet** Section 2, p. 87
- **Political Cartoons booklet** Section 2, p. 79
- **Close Up on the Supreme Court booklet** *The Civil Rights Cases,* pp. 34–35
- **The Living Constitution booklet** p. 8

- **Simulations and Debates booklet** pp. 65–70
- **Basic Principles of the Constitution Transparencies** 41
- **Section Support Transparencies** 82, 181
- **Presentation Pro CD-ROM** Section 2
- **Section Reading Support Transparencies**
- **Social Studies Skills Tutor CD-ROM**

## 3 Rights of the Accused

*(pp. 576–583)*

1. Define the writ of habeas corpus, bills of attainder, and ex post facto laws.
2. Outline how the right to a grand jury and the guarantee against double jeopardy help ensure the rights of the accused.
3. Describe issues that arise from the guarantee of a speedy and public trial.
4. Determine what constitutes a fair trial by jury.
5. Examine the right to an adequate defense and the guarantee against self-incrimination.

**TEKS 3A, 3B, 8B, 8D, 8F, 9C, 9E, 9G, 10D, 14A, 14B, 14C, 14D, 14E, 14F, 15B, 15C, 17C, 18A, 18B, 18C, 21A, 21B, 21C, 21D, 21E, 22A, 22B, 22D**

- **Unit 5 booklet**
  Guided Reading and Review, p. 24
  Section 3 Quiz, p. 25
- **Lesson Plans booklet** Section 3, p. 88
- **Political Cartoons booklet** Section 3, p. 80
- **Block Scheduling with Lesson Strategies booklet** p. 29
- **Close Up on Primary Sources booklet** The Right to Due Process, p. 22; The Sword and the Robe, p. 60

- **Close Up on the Supreme Court booklet** *Miranda* v. *Arizona,* pp. 48–49
- **The Living Constitution booklet** p. 4
- **Government Assessment Rubrics booklet** p. 24
- **Simulations and Debates booklet** pp. 2–23
- **Section Support Transparencies** 83, 182
- **Presentation Pro CD-ROM** Section 3
- **Section Reading Support Transparencies**

## 4 Punishment

*(pp. 585–588)*

1. Explain the purpose of bail and preventative detention.
2. Describe the Court's interpretation of cruel and unusual punishment.
3. Outline the history of the Court's decisions on capital punishment.
4. Define the crime of treason.

**TEKS 3A, 3B, 8B, 8D, 8F, 9C, 9E, 9G, 10D, 14A, 14B, 14D, 14E, 14F, 15B, 15C, 17C, 18A, 18B, 18C, 21A, 21C, 21E, 22A, 22B, 22C**

- **Unit 5 booklet**
  Guided Reading and Review, p. 26
  Section 4 Quiz, p. 27
  Skills for Life Activity, p. 28
- **Lesson Plans booklet** Section 4, p. 89
- **Political Cartoons booklet** Section 4, p. 81
- **Close Up on the Supreme Court booklet** *Illinois* v. *Wardlow,* p. 21

- **Simulations and Debates booklet** pp. 50–52
- **The Basic Principles of the Constitution Posters**
- **Section Support Transparencies** 84, 183
- **Presentation Pro CD-ROM** Section 4
- **Section Reading Support Transparencies**

# Block Scheduling Strategies

The *Magruder's American Government* program addresses block-scheduling strategies in a variety of ways. For easy reference, side-column activities that fit a block format are marked  **Block Strategy.** Each section also contains a **Block Scheduling Strategies** box describing at least two block-format activities that address and extend core content from the section. The **Block Scheduling with Lesson Strategies booklet** found in the Teaching Resources contains additional block-scheduling activities for each chapter.

## Take It to the Net

Visit the Social Studies area at the Prentice Hall School Web site. Once there, you can find additional links, current events connections, and activities to enrich chapter content for *Magruder's American Government,* as well as a Self-Test for students. Be sure to check out this month's **eTeach** online discussion with a Master Teacher.

### www.phschool.com

## Pressed for Time?

If you are running short on time to cover this chapter, consider one of the following options:

- Use the **Presentation Pro CD-ROM** to create an outline for this chapter.
- Use one of the **Pressed for Time** activities found on p. 27.
- Use the Section Summaries for Chapter 2, from **Guide to the Essentials of American Government (English and Spanish).**

##  Video Connections

Prentice Hall offers two video programs to reinforce and extend chapter content. Show students *The Blessings of Liberty* from the **ABC News Civics and Government Videotape Library** and *Prayer in Schools: A Nationwide Debate* from the **Magruder's American Government Video Collection.**

## Assessment Options

- Section Quizzes, **Unit 5 booklet,** pp. 21, 23, 25, 27
- Chapter 20 Assessment, pp. 590–591
- **Guide to the Essentials of American Government,** Chapter 20 Test, p. 111

PRENTICE HALL
ASSESSMENT
SYSTEM

## Core Assessment

Chapter 20 Test, Chapter Tests booklet
ExamView® Test Bank CD-ROM Chapter 20
Government Assessment Rubrics

## Standardized Test Preparation

### Diagnose and Prescribe

Diagnostic Tests for High School
Social Studies Skills

### Review and Reteach

Review Book for Government

### Practice and Assess

Test-Taking Strategies With
    Transparencies for High School
Test Prep Book for Government

# Civil Liberties: Protecting Individual Rights

## Introducing the Chapter

In this chapter, students will learn about the many individual rights guaranteed by the Bill of Rights, as well as the constitutional guidelines for trying and punishing Americans accused of committing crimes.

### Make It Relevant

★ *You Can Make a Difference*

Organize a group of students to plan, create, and operate a center in your school to resolve disputes between students. Those students who operate the dispute resolution center should develop plans and procedures for hearing cases, considering them with faculty advisors, and suggesting solutions. Consider having students invite a professional mediator to help them prepare and operate the center.

**Service Learning**

### CONSTITUTIONAL PRINCIPLES

Emphasize the following basic principles as students read Chapter 20. Have the class respond to the questions, and then ask volunteers to discuss whether individual rights would be endangered without any one of these principles.

**Limited Government** In what ways can the Due Process Clause be described as the ultimate statement of limited government?

**Checks and Balances** How does the judicial branch use the concept of due process to check the executive branch?

**Judicial Review** What impact have Supreme Court decisions made on the expansion or restriction of individual rights?

# Civil Liberties: Protecting Individual Rights

*"Most of all, we have got to remember that the law is people. . . . What we are trying to do is solve people's problems and protect their freedoms and protect their interests."*

—Janet Reno (1995)

As Attorney General Reno pointed out, the goal of the law is to serve people, to protect both the rights of individuals and the rights of those accused of crimes. Judges and lawmakers thus constantly debate the spirit of the law and how it applies in real life.

◆ **Courtroom with a trial in session**

 *Corner*

The following resources are available only from the Close Up Foundation to support the concepts discussed in Chapter 20 "Civil Liberties: Protecting Individual Rights":

◆ *The Bill of Rights: A User's Guide*
◆ *The Bill of Rights Video Series*
◆ *Profiles of Freedom: A Living Bill of Rights*
◆ *Democracy and Rights: One Citizen's Challenge*

To keep up-to-date on Close Up news and activities, visit Close Up Online at

**www.closeup.org**

Close Up Foundation
44 Canal Center Plaza
Alexandria, VA 22314-1592
800-765-3131

## You Can Make a Difference

**FOR CORY KADAMANI,** "real life" once meant drugs, dropping out, and run-ins with the New York City police. Then he turned his life around, earning a high school equivalency diploma and joining Youth Force, a community group. At age 17, Cory helped create the group's South Bronx Community Justice Center to resolve neighborhood issues before they led to crimes. Young people—including former gang members—worked with lawyers, community leaders, and probation officers. Cory also advised younger kids awaiting trial at a South Bronx detention facility. He hoped his story would keep them from making the same mistakes he had made.

### Keep It Current

Items marked with this logo are periodically updated on the Internet. Keep up-to-date with what's in the news. To get current information on protecting individual freedoms, go to **www.phschool.com**

## Due Process of Law (pp. 564–568)

★ The 5th and 14th amendments guarantee that the government cannot deprive a person of "life, liberty, or property, without due process of law."

★ The States' reserved powers include the police power—the power to protect and promote public health, public safety, public morals, and the general welfare.

★ The exercise of the police power can produce conflicts with individual rights.

★ The constitutional guarantees of due process create a right of privacy.

★ The most controversial applications of the right of privacy involve abortion.

## Freedom and Security of the Person (pp. 569–574)

★ The 13th Amendment was added to the Constitution in 1865 to end slavery and involuntary servitude.

★ The 2nd Amendment was added to the Constitution to preserve the right of States to keep a militia.

★ The 4th Amendment prohibits unreasonable searches and seizures, not those which are reasonable. The amendment has given rise to the controversial Exclusionary Rule.

## Rights of the Accused (pp. 576–583)

★ Rights of the accused include the writ of habeas corpus and a constitutional ban on bills of attainder and ex post facto laws.

★ The 5th Amendment says that one may be accused of a serious federal crime only by grand jury indictment.

★ Accused persons are guaranteed a speedy and public trial. They cannot, however, be tried twice for the same crime.

★ The accused also have the right to a trial by jury.

★ The right to an adequate defense and the guarantee against self-incrimination help safeguard the rights of the accused.

## Punishment (pp. 585–588)

★ A person accused of a crime is presumed innocent until proven guilty.

★ The accused must not face excessive bail or fines.

★ The Constitution prohibits cruel and unusual punishment.

★ The Supreme Court has consistently held that the death penalty is constitutional if it is applied fairly.

★ The crime of treason is specifically defined in the Constitution to prevent its use for political purposes.

## Keep It Current

### Internet Update

Use the Prentice Hall School Web site and the Keep It Current CD-ROM to find quick content updates.

Visit **www.phschool.com** for current events articles that are linked to Chapter 20. Critical thinking questions are included.

**Keep It Current CD-ROM** includes government-related projects by unit. Students complete each project using current information that they obtain by linking to the Prentice Hall School Web site from the CD-ROM.

## Pressed for Time?

### To Omit the Chapter

If you wish to skip Chapter 20, ask students to read the Chapter in Brief and assign the Guide to the Essentials before continuing to another chapter. You may also want to assign the Chapter 20 Test in the Chapter Test booklet. Then specific portions of Chapter 20 may be assigned to students needing reinforcement of key terms and concepts.

### To Preview the Chapter

To introduce students to key terms and concepts in each section, have them read the Chapter in Brief. You may also assign the Reading Strategy activities on pp. 565, 570, 577, and 586 of this book.

### To Review the Chapter

When students have completed Chapter 20, you might want to assign the Guide to the Essentials or the Guided Reading and Review worksheets on pp. 20, 22, 24, and 26 of the Unit 5 booklet.

### To Cover the Chapter Quickly

To cover the material in Chapter 20 quickly, use the following activity.

**Focus** Ask students what they know about the protection of civil liberties in the United States. Encourage them to name amendments that relate to these protections, and summarize them if they can. Refer them to the text of the amendments in the back of the book.

**Instruct** Write *Due Process* on the board; below it, write *5th Amendment* and *14th Amendment*. Explain how due process is covered in each of these amendments. Then ask students to create a table, using the head structure on the board, in their notebooks. Students should record information about these two amendments as they work through the chapters.

**Close/Reteach** Ask students to explain all they know about what happens when a person is accused of a crime. What are the person's rights and how is the person made aware of those rights? What guidelines apply to the sentencing of a person convicted of a crime? Have students write short paragraphs describing this process.

**Block Strategy (Average)**

## Point-of-Use Resources

**Guide to the Essentials** Chapter 20, Section 2, p. 108 provides support for students who need additional review of section content. Spanish support is available in the Spanish edition of the Guide on p. 101.

**Quiz** Unit 5 booklet, p. 23 includes matching and multiple-choice questions to check students' understanding of Section 2 content.

**Presentation Pro CD-ROM** Quizzes and multiple-choice questions check students' understanding of Section 2 content.

## Answers to . . .

### Section 2 Assessment

**1.** Recent Supreme Court decisions have acted against private parties who practiced race-based discrimination.
**2.** The 2nd Amendment was added to protect the right of each State to keep a militia.
**3.** Probable cause is the reasonable suspicion of a crime, which justifies the issuance of a warrant.
**4. (a)** The exclusionary rule says that evidence gained by an illegal police act cannot be used against the person from whom it was seized. **(b)** It has changed over time to extend to the States.
**5.** Possible answers: Yes: If constitutional protections are to have meaning, government cannot violate them; No: Those who have clearly violated the law must be punished.
**6.** Possible assumptions: Government's ability to provide for its national defense takes precedence over individual rights; civic duty is more important than individual rights.

---

apartment—the one for which they did not have a warrant.

### Drug Testing

Federal drug-testing programs involve searches of persons and so are covered by the 4th Amendment. To date, the Court has held that they can be conducted without either warrants or even any indication of drug use by those who must take them. It did so in two 1989 cases, *Skinner* v. *Federal Railway Labor Executives Association* and *National Treasury Employees Union* v. *Von Raab*.

The Court has also upheld an Oregon school district's drug-testing program, *Vernonia School District* v. *Acton*, 1995. That program required all students who take part in school sports to agree to be tested for drugs. Thus, all student athletes were tested at the beginning of a sports season. Ten percent of the students participating in school sports were chosen at random to be tested each week thereafter.

That ruling was extended in *Board of Education of Pottowatomie County* v. *Earls* in 2002. There, the Court upheld the random testing of students who want to participate in any competitive, extracurricular activity.

### Wiretapping

Wiretapping, electronic eavesdropping, videotaping, and other more sophisticated means of "bugging" are now quite widely used in the United States. They present difficult search and seizure questions that the authors of the 4th Amendment could not have begun to foresee.

The Supreme Court decided its first wiretap case in 1928. In *Olmstead* v. *United States*, federal agents had tapped a Seattle bootlegger's telephone calls. Their bugs produced evidence that led to Olmstead's conviction. The High Court upheld that conviction. It found that although the agents had not had a warrant, there had been no "actual physical invasion" of Olmstead's home or office—because the phone lines had been tapped *outside* those places.

The leading case today is *Katz* v. *United States*, 1967. There, the Court expressly overruled *Olmstead*. Katz had been convicted of transmitting gambling information across State lines. He had used a public phone booth in Los Angeles to call his contacts in Boston and Miami. Much of the evidence against him had come from an electronic tap planted on the roof—outside—the phone booth.

The Court held that the bugging evidence could not be used against Katz. Despite the fact that Katz was in a public, glass-enclosed phone booth, he was entitled to make a *private* call. Said the Court: the 4th Amendment protects "persons, not just places." It did go on to say, however, that the 4th Amendment can be satisfied in such situations if police obtain a proper warrant before they install a listening device.

---

## Section 2 Assessment

### Key Terms and Main Ideas

1. In what sense has the Supreme Court "breathed new life" into the 13th Amendment?
2. Why was the 2nd Amendment added to the Constitution?
3. Define **probable cause**.
4. **(a)** What is the **exclusionary rule**? **(b)** How has its application changed over time?

### Critical Thinking

5. **Expressing Problems Clearly** Discuss whether or not you think that people who have clearly committed crimes should be able to go free if their rights are violated during arrest or trial.
6. **Identifying Assumptions** In 1918, the Court ruled that the 13th Amendment's prohibition of involuntary servitude does not apply to the military draft. Identify the assumptions about the relative importance of individual rights and civic duty that underlie this decision.

 **Take It to the Net**

7. Read about probable cause and follow links to learn more about the cases that have shaped our understanding of it. Then choose three cases involving probable cause and prepare a brief oral report describing their importance. Use the links provided in the Social Studies area at the following Web site for help in completing this activity. **www.phschool.com**

---

 **Take It to the Net**

7. Direct students to the Social Studies area at the Prentice Hall Web site. The *Magruder's American Government* companion Web site includes the directions and links needed to complete the activity. It also provides a printable Internet activity worksheet with scoring rubrics for assessment. Oral reports should concisely describe each of the three cases.

# SKILLS FOR LIFE

## Creating a Multimedia Presentation

Maps help to orient your audience

Use written text for lengthy, complex topics

Add realism with audio/video passages

Create a Web site with quizzes and links

Photographs add visual interest

As chalkboards and typewriters make way for computer and TV monitors, there are many new ways to tell a story. A "report" can include written text, maps, charts, photographs, video clips, audio segments, and Web pages. Use these steps to create an exciting presentation:

**1. Define your topic.** This step determines the success of your project. Multimedia presentations lend themselves to topics that have a variety of aspects or subtopics. Choose carefully. A topic that's too broad—say, "Civil Liberties"—is difficult to cover thoroughly. How might you narrow that topic?

**2. Make a "blueprint"—a plan—for your project.** Create a blueprint by brainstorming ideas for covering your topic in various media. First, find out what media are available to you. Then make a detailed plan for how you want to tell your "story." Use the form at right as a model. Assign roles to others involved in the project, if needed. Set a deadline for each main task. Why do you think a blueprint is especially helpful for a multimedia presentation?

**3. Develop your presentation.** Carry out your project plan by doing research, writing scripts, and gathering materials. You may want to collect more material than you'll use. This gives you flexibility in editing and assembling your work. Aim for an accurate, lively, and logical flow of ideas with coordinated visual and audio content.

**4. Present your work.** The best presentations are interactive in some way. Try to involve your audience in the presentation.

### PROJECT BLUEPRINT

Topic/title:

Purpose:

Media to be used:

Main subtopics:
Key sources:

Sequence and description of segments:

List of elements (photos, video clips, audio segments):

### Test for Success

Choose a possible topic for a multimedia presentation, and create a project blueprint.

## Point-of-Use Resources

📁 **Skills for Life Activity** Unit 5 booklet, p. 28 provides an additional skill activity for this chapter.

💿 **Social Studies Skills Tutor CD-ROM**
Provides interactive practice in geographic literacy, critical thinking and reading, visual analysis, and communications.

### Test for Success

Blueprints should demonstrate a clear understanding of purpose, a narrow and manageable topic focus, and a coherent sequence that tells the story.

## Creating a Multimedia Presentation

**Focus** Work in production teams to produce a multimedia presentation on the topic "Protecting Individual Rights."

**Instruct** Organize teams of students that include at least one student for each type of media to be used in the project: Print, Internet, audio, and video. Have production teams meet initially to decide the scope of the project, the main topics, and which media will be used to cover each topic. Teams should create a production schedule that includes time for editing and revisions. They should consider the availability of audio/visual equipment for recording and presenting their work.

**Close/Reteach** Find a venue for presentations in which audio presentations can be heard well. Have teams critique each other's presentations.

### Answers . . .

**1.** Encourage teams to focus on a specific aspect of civil liberties, such as a free speech issue in the news.
**2.** Because of the multiple elements and many roles involved in the project, a blueprint helps organize time and resources.
**3.** Monitor student progress by reviewing drafts of scripts.
**4.** Opportunities for interactive presentations include videotaped debates and online quizzes.

## Customize for
### Less Proficient Readers

Have students create a time line that charts the development of the rights of the accused. Time lines should begin at the time of the Constitution and continue to the present. Encourage students to include key dates, including any Supreme Court cases discussed in the section, along with explanations of their significance. Find space in the classroom to display students' charts.

### Make It Relevant
#### Students Make a Difference

Daniel Beeman just graduated from high school and has already been a presiding judge in the Tulsa, Oklahoma, juvenile court system. He is member of the Tulsa Youth Court, a volunteer program coordinated by Youth Services of Tulsa and the Oklahoma Bar Association. This all-teen court gives first-time, misdemeanor juvenile offenders a trial by their peers. The roles of prosecuting and defense attorneys, bailiff, court clerk, and judge rotate among the teens, who have taken a seven-week training course. Daniel explains that first offenders feel they are treated more fairly when tried by those who can understand their situation. Although he participated in mock trials in high school, Daniel says that this is different: "I realized as presiding judge that every decision we make affects that person completely." Daniel and his peers must be doing something right: 97 percent of first-time offenders who go through this program do not commit a second offense.

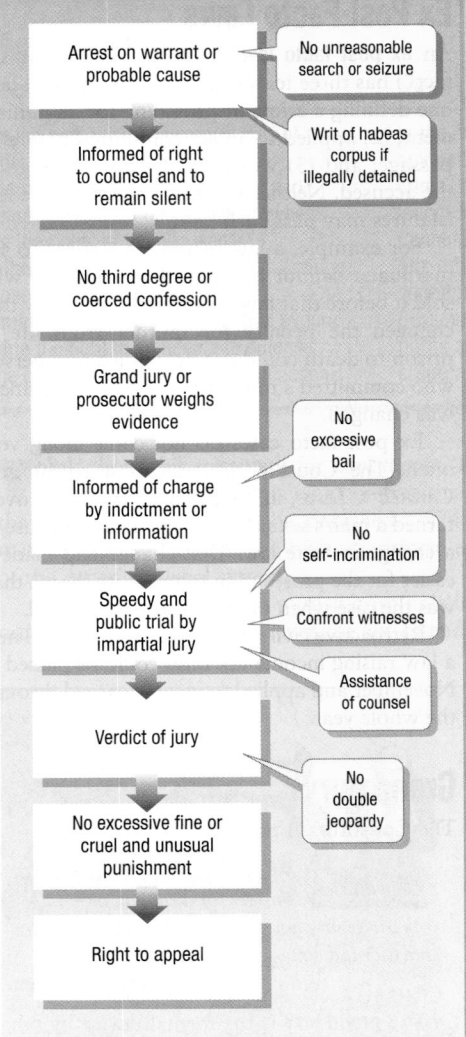

**Constitutional Protections for Persons Accused of a Crime**

- Arrest on warrant or probable cause → No unreasonable search or seizure
- Informed of right to counsel and to remain silent → Writ of habeas corpus if illegally detained
- No third degree or coerced confession
- Grand jury or prosecutor weighs evidence → No excessive bail
- Informed of charge by indictment or information → No self-incrimination
- Speedy and public trial by impartial jury → Confront witnesses
- → Assistance of counsel
- Verdict of jury → No double jeopardy
- No excessive fine or cruel and unusual punishment
- Right to appeal

*Interpreting Charts* Any person accused of a crime is presumed innocent until proven guilty. **What protections does the Constitution extend to those convicted of a crime?**

grand jurors are needed to return an indictment or to make a presentment.

An **indictment** is a formal complaint that the prosecutor lays before a grand jury. It charges the accused with one or more crimes. If the grand jury finds that there is enough evidence for a trial, it returns a "true bill of indictment." The accused is then held for prosecution. If the grand jury does not make such a finding, the charge is dropped.

A presentment is a formal accusation brought by the grand jury on its own motion, rather than that of the prosecutor. It is little used in federal courts.

A grand jury's proceedings are not a trial. Since unfair harm could come if they were public, its sessions are secret. They are also one-sided—in the law, *ex parte*. That is, only the prosecution, not the defense, is present.

The right to grand jury is intended as a protection against overzealous prosecutors. Critics say that it is too time-consuming, too expensive, and too likely to follow the dictates of the prosecutor.

The 5th Amendment's grand jury provision is the only part of the Bill of Rights relating to criminal prosecution that the Supreme Court has not brought within the coverage of the 14th Amendment's Due Process Clause. In most States today, most criminal charges are not brought by grand jury indictment. They are brought, instead, by an information, an affidavit in which the prosecutor swears that there is enough evidence to justify a trial (see Chapter 24).

### Double Jeopardy

The Fifth Amendment's guarantee against double jeopardy is the first of several protections in the Bill of Rights especially intended to ensure fair trial in the federal courts.[9] Fair trials are guaranteed in State courts by each State's own constitution and by the 14th Amendment's Due Process Clause.

The Fifth Amendment says in part that no person can be "twice put in jeopardy of life or limb." Today, this prohibition against **double jeopardy** means that once a person has been tried for a crime, he or she cannot be tried again for that same crime.

A person can violate both a federal *and* a State law in a single act, however—for example, by selling narcotics. That person can then be

---

[9]See the 5th, 6th, 7th, and 8th amendments and Article III, Section 2, Clause 3. The practice of excluding evidence obtained in violation of the 4th Amendment is also intended to guarantee a fair trial.

*Answer to . . .*

**Interpreting Charts** No excessive fine, no cruel and unusual punishment, and the right to appeal.

tried for the federal crime in a federal court and for the State crime in a State court. A single act can also result in the commission of several crimes. A person who breaks into a store, steals liquor, and sells it can be tried for illegal entry, theft, and selling liquor without a license.

In a trial in which a jury cannot agree on a verdict, there is no jeopardy. It is as though no trial had been held, and the accused can be tried again. Nor is double jeopardy involved when a case is appealed to a higher court.[10] Recall that the Supreme Court has held that the 5th Amendment's ban on double jeopardy applies against the States through the 14th Amendment, *Benton* v. *Maryland*, 1969.

Several States allow the continued confinement of violent sex predators after they have completed a prison term. The Court has twice (in 1987 and 2001) held that that confinement is not punishment—and so does not involve double jeopardy. Rather, the practice is intended to protect the public from harm.

## Speedy and Public Trial

The Constitution commands:

> FROM THE *Constitution* **❝** *In all criminal prosecutions, the accused shall enjoy the right to a speedy and public trial. . . .* **❞**
>
> —6th Amendment

### Speedy Trial

The guarantee of a speedy trial is meant to ensure that the government will try a person accused of crime without undue delay. But how long a delay is too long? The Supreme Court has long recognized that each case must be looked at on its own merits.

In a leading case, *Barker* v. *Wingo,* 1972, the Court listed four criteria for determining if a delay has violated the constitutional protection. They are (1) the length of the delay, (2) the reasons for it, (3) whether the delay has in fact harmed the defendant, and (4) whether the defendant asked for a prompt trial.

---

[10]The Organized Crime Control Act of 1970 allows federal prosecutors to appeal sentences they believe to be too lenient. The Supreme Court has held that such appeals do not violate the double jeopardy guarantee, *United States* v. *Di Francesco,* 1980.

*Interpreting Political Cartoons* The term "media circus" applies to trials that generate a great deal of publicity. *What are the dangers of a trial becoming too public?*

The Speedy Trial Act of 1974 says that the time between a person's arrest and the beginning of his or her federal criminal trial cannot be more than 100 days. The law does allow for some exceptions, however. Examples include a case where the defendant must undergo extensive mental tests, or when the defendant or a key witness is ill.

The 6th Amendment guarantees a prompt trial in *federal* cases. The Supreme Court first declared that this right applies against the States as part of the 14th Amendment's Due Process Clause in *Klopfer* v. *North Carolina,* 1967.

### Public Trial

The 6th Amendment says that a trial must also be public. The right to be tried in public is also part of the 14th Amendment's guarantee of procedural due process.

A trial must not be *too* speedy or *too* public, however. The Supreme Court threw out an Arkansas murder conviction in 1923 on just those grounds. The trial had taken only 45 minutes, and it had been held in a courtroom packed by a threatening mob.

Within reason, a judge can limit both the number and the kinds of spectators who may be present at a trial. Those who seek to disrupt a courtroom can be barred from it. A judge can order a courtroom cleared when the expected

---

## CONSTITUTIONAL PRINCIPLES

### Limited Government

A key component of limited government is the protection of individual rights. That assurance is particularly important in the holding of public trials, and explains why the televising of trials has become a topic of hot debate. An interesting part of the debate concerns whether media coverage skews the perception of certain cases. The 1995 *California* v. *Simpson* trial, in which O.J. Simpson was acquitted of murdering his ex-wife, has been called the "Trial of the Century" by some. Critics,

however, say the only big thing about the trial was the amount of TV coverage it received; it was a typical domestic murder case, and did not delve into any of the issues of other 20th-century cases such as the Scopes "Monkey Trial" of 1925.

### Activity

Have students research several 20th-century cases, including the Scopes trial, the Lindbergh kidnapping trial, the Scottsboro trials, and the Sacco and Vanzetti trial. Have them explain which trial should be labeled the "Trial of the Century," and why.

## Background Note
### Constitutional Issues

As another way to insure the justice of a law before a person could be punished for violating it, the Framers allowed for "jury nullification." This was an idea stemming back to the Magna Carta of 1215, when English citizens complained about the excessive power of King John. In jury nullification, a jury has the right to return a "not guilty" verdict for a prisoner, who is actually guilty of breaking a certain law, if they feel that the law is unjust or oppressive. In this way, no jury is forced to decide against a person for breaking a law with which they do not agree.

ACTIVITY

### American Government, American Humor

Share the following quotation with students:

*"A man who has never gone to school may steal from a freight car, but if he has a university education he may steal the whole railroad."*
—Franklin Delano Roosevelt

**Discussion** Ask students what Roosevelt meant by his remark. Ask: How does Roosevelt's comment relate to the day-to-day rights of accused persons in the United States? **(Challenging)**

▲ *Cameras in the Courtroom?* Friends and family watch the 1997 televised trial (above) of nanny Louise Woodward for the murder of a child in her care. In trials in which cameras are not allowed in the courtroom, lawyers and the public may "view" the trial through courtroom sketches (right).

testimony may be embarrassing to a witness or to someone else not a party to the case.

Many of the questions about how public a trial should be involve the media—especially newspapers and television. The guarantees of fair trial and free press, however, often conflict in the courts. On the one hand, a courtroom is a public place where the media have a right to be present. On the other hand, media coverage must not damage the right to a fair trial.

Champions of the public's right to know hold that the courts must allow the broadest possible press coverage of a trial. The Supreme Court has often held, however, that the media have only the same right as the general public to be present in a courtroom. The right to a public trial belongs to the defendant, not to the media.

What of televised trials? Television cameras are barred from all federal courtrooms. Most States do allow some form of in-court television reporting, however. Does televising a criminal trial violate a defendant's rights?

An early major case on the point was *Estes v. Texas*, 1965. Radio and television reporting of Estes' case had been allowed from within the courtroom and over the objections of Estes himself. The Court held that this reporting had been so disruptive that it had denied Estes a fair trial.

Sixteen years later, the Court held in *Chandler v. Florida*, 1981, that nothing in the Constitution prevents a State from allowing the televising of a criminal trial. At least, televising is not prohibited as long as steps are taken to avoid too much publicity and to protect the defendant's rights.

## Trial by Jury

The 6th Amendment also says that a person accused of a federal crime must be tried "by an impartial jury." This guarantee reinforces an earlier one set out in Article III, Section 2. The right to trial by jury is also binding on the States through the 14th Amendment's Due Process Clause, but only in cases involving "serious" crimes, *Duncan v. Louisiana*, 1968.[11] The trial jury is often called the petit jury. *Petit* is the French word for "small."

The 6th Amendment adds that the members of the federal court jury must be drawn from "the State and district wherein the crime shall have been committed, which district shall have been previously ascertained by law." This clause gives the defendant any benefit there might be in having a court and jury familiar with the people and problems of the area.

A defendant may ask to be tried in another place—seek a "change of venue"—on grounds that the people of the locality are so prejudiced in the case that an impartial jury cannot be drawn. The judge must decide whether a change of venue is justified.

A defendant may also waive (put aside or relinquish) the right to a jury trial. However, he or she can do so only if the judge is satisfied that the defendant is fully aware of his or her rights and understands what that action means. In fact, a judge can order a jury trial even when a defendant does not want one, *One Lot Emerald Cut Stones and One Ring v. United States*, 1972. If a defendant waives the right, a **bench trial** is held. That is, a judge

---

[11]In *Baldwin v. New York*, 1970, the Court defined those crimes as offenses for which imprisonment for more than six months is possible.

alone hears the case. (Of course, a defendant can plead guilty and so avoid a trial of any kind.)

In federal practice, the jury that hears a criminal case must have 12 members. Some federal civil cases are tried before juries of as few as six members, however. Several States now provide for smaller juries, often of six members, in both criminal and civil cases.

In the federal courts, the jury that hears a criminal case can convict the accused only by a unanimous vote. Most States follow the same rule.[12]

In a long series of cases, dating from *Strauder* v. *West Virginia,* 1880, the Supreme Court has held that a jury must be "drawn from a fair cross section of the community." A person is denied the right to an impartial jury if he or she is tried by a jury from which members of any groups "playing major roles in the community" have been excluded, *Taylor* v. *Louisiana,* 1975.

In short, no person can be kept off a jury on such grounds as race, color, religion, national origin, or sex. As the Court put it in one of its more recent decisions on the point: Both the 5th and the 14th amendments mean that jury service cannot be determined by "the pigmentation of skin, the accident of birth, or the choice of religion," *Georgia* v. *McCollum,* 1992.

## Right to an Adequate Defense

Every person accused of a crime has the right to the best possible defense that circumstances will allow. The 6th Amendment says that a defendant has the right (1) "to be informed of the nature and cause of the accusation," (2) "to be confronted with the witnesses against him" and question them in open court, (3) "to have compulsory process for obtaining witnesses in his favor" (that is, favorable witnesses can be subpoenaed, or forced to attend), and (4) "to have the Assistance of Counsel for his defense."

These key safeguards apply in the federal courts. Still, if a State fails to honor any of them, the accused can appeal a conviction on grounds

that the 14th Amendment's Due Process Clause has been violated. Recall from Chapter 19 that the Supreme Court protected the right to counsel in *Gideon* v. *Wainwright,* 1963; the right of confrontation in *Pointer* v. *Texas,* 1965; and the right to call witnesses in *Washington* v. *Texas,* 1967.

These guarantees are intended to prevent the cards from being stacked in favor of the prosecution. One of the leading right-to-counsel cases, *Escobedo* v. *Illinois,* 1964, illustrates this point.

Chicago police picked up Danny Escobedo for questioning in the death of his brother-in-law. On the way to the police station, and then while he was being questioned there, he asked several times to see his lawyer. The police denied these requests. They did so even though his lawyer was in the police station and was trying to see him, and the police knew the lawyer was there. Through a long night of questioning, Escobedo made several damaging statements. Prosecutors later used those statements in court as a major part of the evidence that led to his murder conviction.

The Supreme Court ordered Escobedo freed from prison four years later. It held that he had been improperly denied his right to counsel.

In *Gideon* v. *Wainwright,* 1963, the Court held that an attorney must be furnished to a defendant who cannot afford one. In many places, a judge still assigns a lawyer from the local community, or a private legal aid association provides counsel.

WE, THE JURY, AFTER POLLING FRIENDS AND NEIGHBORS, FIND THE DEFENDANT NOT GUILTY

*Interpreting Political Cartoons* **Would a poll of friends and neighbors produce a fair verdict? Explain your answer.**

[12]The 14th Amendment does not say that there cannot be juries of fewer than 12 persons, *Williams* v. *Florida,* 1970, but it does not allow juries of fewer than six members, *Ballew* v. *Georgia,* 1978. Nor does it prevent a State from providing for a conviction on a less than unanimous jury vote, *Apodaca* v. *Oregon,* 1972. But if a jury has only six members, it may convict only by a unanimous vote, *Burch* v. *Louisiana,* 1979.

A C T I V I T Y

## Heterogeneous Groups

**Enrichment** Divide the class into pairs of students. Begin this activity by presenting samples of newspaper editorials and discussing the nature of the writing in each. Then assign one of the following issues to each pair of students, asking partners to write opposing viewpoint editorials about the topic: (1) Federal Government drug testing programs; (2) the exclusionary rule; (3) limits on the right to bear arms; (4) the televising of criminal trials; (5) the Miranda Rule. Ask for pairs to volunteer to read their opposing viewpoint editorials to the class.
**(Average)**

## Point-of-Use Resources

☐ **Close Up on the Supreme Court** *Miranda* v. *Arizona* (1966), pp. 48–49

☐ **Simulations and Debates** Mock Trial, pp. 18–23 and Mock Jury Deliberation, pp. 2–17 provide students with simulations of a criminal trial and jury deliberation.

Since *Gideon,* however, a growing number of States, and many local governments, have established tax-supported public defender offices. In 1970, Congress authorized the appointment of federal public defenders or, as an alternative, the creation of community legal service organizations financed by federal grants.

## Self-Incrimination

The guarantee against self-incrimination is among the protections set out in the Fifth Amendment. That provision declares that no person can be "compelled in any criminal case to be a witness against himself." This protection must be honored in both the federal and State courts, *Malloy v. Hogan,* 1964.

In a criminal case, the burden of proof is always on the prosecution. The defendant does not have to prove his or her innocence. The ban on self-incrimination prevents the prosecution from shifting the burden of proof to the defendant. As the Court put it in *Malloy v. Hogan,* the prosecution cannot force the accused to "prove the charge against" him "out of his own mouth."

### Applying the Guarantee

The language of the 5th Amendment suggests that the guarantee against self-incrimination applies only to criminal cases. In fact, the guarantee covers any governmental proceeding in which a person is legally compelled to answer any question that could lead to a criminal charge. Thus, a person may claim the right ("take the Fifth") in a variety of situations: in a divorce proceeding (which is a civil matter), before a legislative committee, at a school board's disciplinary hearing, and so on.

The courts, not the individuals who claim it, decide when the right can be properly invoked. If the plea of self-incrimination is pushed too far, a person can be held in contempt of court.

The guarantee against self-incrimination is a personal right. One can claim it only for oneself.[13] It cannot be invoked in someone else's behalf; a person *can* be forced to "rat" on another.

The privilege does not protect a person from being fingerprinted or photographed, submitting a handwriting sample, or appearing in a police lineup. And, recall, it does not mean that

a person does not have to submit to a blood test in a drunk driving situation, *Schmerber* v. *California,* 1966.

A person cannot, however, be forced to confess to a crime under duress, that is, as a result of torture or other physical or psychological pressure. In *Ashcraft* v. *Tennessee,* 1944, for example, the Supreme Court threw out the conviction of a man accused of hiring another person to murder his wife. The confession on which his conviction rested had been secured only after some 36 hours of continuous, threatening interrogation. The questioning was conducted by officers who worked in shifts because, they said, they became so tired that they had to rest.

The gulf between what the Constitution says and what goes on in some police stations can be wide indeed. For that reason, the Supreme Court has come down hard in favor of the defendant in many cases involving the protection against self-incrimination and the closely related right to counsel.

Recall, for example, the Court's decision in *Escobedo* v. *Illinois,* 1964. There it held that a confession cannot be used against a defendant if it was obtained by police who refused to allow the defendant to see his attorney and did not tell him that he had a right to refuse to answer their questions.

### Miranda v. Arizona

In a truly historic decision, the Court refined the *Escobedo* holding in *Miranda* v. *Arizona,* 1966. A mentally retarded man, Ernesto Miranda, had been convicted of kidnapping and rape. Ten days after the crime, the victim picked Miranda out of a police lineup. After two hours of questioning, during which the police did not tell him of his rights, Miranda confessed.

The Supreme Court struck down Miranda's conviction. More importantly, the Court said that it would no longer uphold convictions in any cases in which suspects had not been told of their constitutional rights before police questioning. It thus laid down the **Miranda Rule.** Under the rule, before police may question a suspect, that person must be

---

[13]With this major exception: A husband cannot be forced to testify against his wife, or a wife against her husband, *Trammel* v. *United States,* 1980. One can testify against the other voluntarily, however.

(1) told of his or her right to remain silent;

(2) warned that anything he or she says can be used in court;

(3) informed of the right to have an attorney present during questioning;

(4) told that if he or she is unable to hire an attorney, one will be provided at public expense;

(5) told that he or she may bring police questioning to an end at any time.

The Miranda Rule has been in force for 35 years now and has been built into thousands of television programs and books over that period. As the Court put it in *Dickerson* v. *United States,* 2000, the rule "has become embedded in routine police practice to the point where the warnings have become part of our national culture."

The Supreme Court is still refining the rule on a case-by-case basis. Most often the rule is closely followed. But there are exceptions. Thus, the Court has held that an undercover police officer posing as a prisoner does not have to tell a cell mate of his Miranda rights before prompting him to talk about a murder, *Illinois* v. *Perkins,* 1990.

*Texas* v. *Cobb,* 2001, involved a man who had been read his rights in a burglary case. Later, out on bail, he confessed to killing a woman and her child during the burglary.

Cobb confessed to police voluntarily, but without consulting his attorney. He was convicted of the murders and sentenced to death. On appeal, Cobb argued that his confession should not have been used against him—because he had not had

▲ In 1966, the Court struck down the conviction of Ernesto Miranda (right), who had confessed to a crime without being told of his rights. *Critical Thinking* **What were the long-term effects of the Miranda decision on police procedures?**

the help of his attorney. But the High Court disagreed, 5–4; it held that his Miranda rights had not been violated.

The Miranda rule has always been controversial. Critics see it as a serious obstacle to effective law enforcement. Many contend that it "puts criminals back on the streets." Others applaud the rule, however. They hold that criminal law enforcement is most effective when it relies on independently secured evidence, rather than on confessions gained by questionable tactics from defendants who do not have the help of a lawyer.

## Section **3** Assessment

**Key Terms and Main Ideas**

1. What does the **writ of habeas corpus** seek to prevent?
2. Why are **bills of attainder** and **ex post facto laws** forbidden?
3. What does the 5th Amendment guarantee to the accused?
4. List the provisions of the 6th Amendment concerning the rights of the accused.

**Critical Thinking**

5. **Drawing Inferences** Consider the statement, "It is better that ten guilty persons go free than that one innocent person be punished." Use this statement as the first sentence in a paragraph in which you evaluate whether and/or when the

rights of individuals should ever be violated even against claims for the public good.

6. **Predicting Consequences** If the guarantee against self-incrimination were removed from the Bill of Rights, what might be the effect on the modern criminal justice system? Would justice be more or less likely to be carried out?

### Take It to the Net

7. Analyze issues that involve Supreme Court interpretations of constitutional rights by reading more about the Miranda Rule. Then work with a small group of classmates to write a paragraph summarizing the importance of the rule. Use the links provided in the Social Studies area at the following Web site for help in completing this activity. **www.phschool.com**

### Take It to the Net

7. Direct students to the Social Studies area at the Prentice Hall School Web site. The *Magruder's American Government* companion Web site includes the directions and links needed to complete the activity. It also provides a printable Internet activity worksheet with scoring rubrics for assessment. Paragraphs should clearly present all major points of the Miranda Rule.

## Answers to . . .

### Section 3 Assessment

**1.** The writ of habeas corpus seeks to prevent unjust arrests and imprisonments.

**2.** These laws are forbidden because they threaten individual freedom and the principle of separation of powers.

**3.** The 5th Amendment provides for grand juries and due process and prohibits double jeopardy.

**4.** The 6th Amendment guarantees a prompt trial in federal cases, calls for public trials and trial by an impartial jury, and gives defendants the right to know the charges against them and to have legal counsel.

**5.** Possible answer: The United States Government subordinates the public good to the rights of individuals. The guarantees that guide the courts in such matters can be found in the Constitution.

**6.** Possible answer: More people would be found guilty, because the burden of proof would be shifted to the defendant.

### Answer to . . .

**Critical Thinking** The Miranda Rule has become a routine part of police practice and is well-known to all citizens.

## The Right to an Attorney

**Focus** Ask students to describe the job of an attorney. Then have students identify reasons why people would want to have an attorney acting on their behalf when facing charges. Be sure that students realize that attorneys can often clear a defendant of charges or get the charges reduced.

**Instruct** Organize the class into several small groups. Ask each group to create a mock public-service announcement informing U.S. citizens of the rights of the accused. Be sure that students include the right to an attorney in their presentations. Have each group present its announcement to the class. Be sure to allow time for correction of ideas presented and general discussion.

**Close/Reteach** Ask students to reread the selection. Based on Clarence Gideon's letter, would they have voted to support his appeal? Have students discuss how the judicial process might be different today if accused people did not have the right to attorneys.

**Keep It Current CD-ROM** includes government-related projects by unit. The CD-ROM links to the Prentice Hall School Web site and may be used for daily updates.

### Answers to . . .

**Analyzing Primary Sources**

**1.** Gideon points out that he had keys to the building so he didn't need to break in, and he raises questions about the reliability of testimony of a witness against him.
**2.** They are less able to defend themselves, are more quickly convicted, and are more likely to receive harsh sentences.
**3.** Answers will vary, but students should recognize that he criticizes the legal system as flawed and unfair but also believes that it has improved over time.
**4.** Answers will vary, but students should recognize that he hopes that his appeal will improve the law.

**584**

 *on Primary Sources*

# The Right to an Attorney

*Clarence Gideon was an uneducated man who had to defend himself in court because he could not afford an attorney and the trial judge refused to provide one for free. Here, Gideon writes from prison to the attorney assigned to handle his Supreme Court appeal. Fourteen months after this letter, the Court ruled in* **Gideon v. Wainwright** *that every defendant has a right to an attorney.*

*Clarence Gideon
1910–1972*

On June 3rd 1961 I was arrested for the crime I am now doing time on. I was charged with Breaking & Entering to comitt a misdemeanor and was convicted in a trial August 4th 1961 [and] sentenced to State Prison August 27th 1961.

This charge growed out of gambling. . . . I worked in this place and did run a Poker game there. . . . I did not break into this building nor did I have to [because] I had the keys to the building. . . . The State witness Cook who was supposed to identify me. Had a bad police record and the Court would not let me bring that out. Nor that one time I had at the point of a pistal made him stop beating a girl[.]

I always believed that the primarily reason of a trial in a court of law was to reach the truth. My trial was far from the truth. One day when I was being arraigned [brought to court to be formally charged] I seen two trials of two different men tried without attorneys. One hour from the time they started they had two juries out and fifteen minutes later they were found guilty and sentenced. Is this a fair trial? This is common practiced through most of this state. . . . I am an electrician here [in prison] and one of my fellow workers has two years for drunk and resisting arrest. Most city Police courts would give a citizen a twenty-five dollar fine for the same charge he was tried without an attorney and convicted. . . .

There was not a crime committed in my case and I don't feel like I had a fair trial. If I had a attorney[,] he could brought out all these things in my trial.

When I was arrested I was put in solitary confinement and I was not allowed the papers not to use the telephone or write to everyone I should. I did get a speedy arraignment and . . . was allow more time to try and obtain a attorney[,] which I could not do. You know about the rest of my trial. . . .

I hope that [this letter] may help you in preparing this case. I am sorry I could not write better[.] I have done the best I could.

I have no illusions about the law and courts or the people who are involved in them. I have read the complete history of law ever since the Romans first started writing them down and[,] before[,] the laws of religions. I believe that each era finds a improvement in the law[.] Each year brings something new for the benefit of mankind. Maybe this will be one of those small steps forward. . . .

### Analyzing Primary Sources

1. What "proof" does Gideon offer to support his innocence?
2. In what three ways, according to Gideon, are defendants harmed by not having an attorney?
3. What attitude does Gideon show toward the law and the legal system?
4. What point is Gideon trying to make in the last paragraph of his letter?

 *Corner*

**Close Up on Primary Sources** The Right to Due Process, p. 22, extends this feature with a primary source activity.

 **Online**

To keep up-to-date on Close Up news and activities, visit Close Up Online at

**www.closeup.org**

# 4 *Punishment*

## Section Preview

### OBJECTIVES

1. **Explain** the purpose of bail and preventive detention.
2. **Describe** the Court's interpretation of cruel and unusual punishment.
3. **Outline** the history of the Court's decisions on capital punishment.
4. **Define** the crime of treason.

### WHY IT MATTERS

The 8th Amendment addresses the issue of punishment for crime. It bans excessive bail and cruel and unusual punishment. The Court has ruled that the death penalty does not constitute cruel and unusual punishment, although the question of capital punishment continues to be hotly debated.

### POLITICAL DICTIONARY

★ bail
★ preventive detention
★ capital punishment
★ treason

---

Once again, think about this statement: "It is better that ten guilty persons go free than that one innocent person be punished." What do you think of that notion after reading the previous section? Turn now to those guilty persons who do not go free but are instead punished. How should they be treated? The Constitution gives its most specific answers to that question in the 8th Amendment.

## Bail and Preventative Detention

The 8th Amendment says, in part:

FROM THE
Constitution

*"Excessive bail shall not be required, nor excessive fines imposed. . . ."*
—United States Constitution

Each State constitution sets out similar restrictions. The general rule is that the bail or fine in a case must bear a reasonable relationship to the seriousness of the crime involved.

### Bail

**Bail** is a sum of money that the accused may be required to post (deposit with the court) as a guarantee that he or she will appear in court at the proper time. The use of bail is justified on two grounds: (1) A person should not be jailed until his or her guilt is established. (2) A defendant is better able to prepare for trial outside of a jail.

Note that the Constitution does not say that all persons accused of a crime are automatically entitled to bail. Rather, it guarantees that, where bail is set, the amount will not be excessive.

The leading case on bail in the federal courts is *Stack* v. *Boyle*, 1951. There the Court ruled that "bail set at a figure higher than the amount reasonably calculated" to assure a defendant's appearance at a trial "is 'excessive' under the 8th Amendment."

A defendant can appeal the denial of release on bail or the amount of bail. Bail is usually set in accordance with the severity of the crime

BAIL SET AT $50 EACH, EXCEPT FOR THE DUCK, WHO SHOWS A TENDENCY TOWARD FLIGHT... BAIL DENIED!

*Interpreting Political Cartoons* **Under what circumstances may bail actually be denied?**

---

## Block Scheduling Strategies

Consider these suggestions to manage extended class time:

■ Have students as a class work together to frame a definition of "cruel and unusual punishment." Then have them read through the section and take notes about how the 8th Amendment defines the phrase, and how Supreme Court decisions have redefined it. After students have finished, have them revise their initial definition.

■ Remind students that capital punishment is one of the most controversial topics in politics. Hold a class debate by forming small teams of debaters. Ask students to take the viewpoint opposite to their own. Encourage students to refer to Supreme Court decisions in their arguments, whether to agree or refute.

---

**Objectives** You may wish to call students' attention to the objectives in the Section Preview. The objectives are reflected in the main headings of the section.

**Bellringer** Have students suppose that one night they arrived home 20 minutes after their curfew. As a result, for two months they were grounded, could watch no TV, and could not use the phone. How would they describe that punishment? In this section, they will learn about the constitutional prohibition against "cruel and unusual punishment."

**Vocabulary Builder** Point out the terms in the Political Dictionary. Ask students what they think preventive detention prevents. *(additional crimes)* Then have them define *capital punishment,* and ask what *capital* means. (head, *as in* beheading)

### Pressed for Time?

## Quick Lesson Plan

1. **Focus** Tell students that the 8th Amendment has generated several issues related to punishment. Ask students to discuss what they know about capital punishment and why it is controversial.

2. **Instruct** Ask students to explain why bail is justified. Write the two reasons on the board. In light of those answers, discuss why the Court has also sanctioned preventive detention. Conclude with a discussion of cruel and unusual punishment, focusing on the death penalty.

3. **Close/Reteach** Remind students that treason—the only crime defined in the Constitution—can be punished by death. Ask students to develop a set of debating points, including Court cases, on both sides of the death-penalty issue.

---

*Answer to . . .*

**Interpreting Political Cartoons** In the preventive detention of accused felons.

▶ Supporters for (right) and against (left) capital punishment make their views known. *Critical Thinking* Briefly summarize arguments for and against the death penalty.

charged and with the reputation and financial resources of the accused. People with little or no income often have trouble raising bail. The federal and most State courts thus release many defendants "on their own recognizance," that is, on their honor. Failure to appear for trial— "jumping bail"—is itself a punishable crime.

### Preventive Detention

In 1984, Congress provided for the **preventive detention** of some people accused of federal crimes. A federal judge can order that the accused be held, without bail, when there is good reason to believe that he or she will commit another serious crime before trial.

Critics of the law claim that preventive detention amounts to punishment before trial. They say it undercuts the presumption of innocence to which defendants are entitled.

The Supreme Court upheld the 1984 law, 6–3, in *United States* v. *Salerno,* 1987. The majority rejected the argument that preventive detention is punishment. Rather, it found the practice a legitimate response to a "pressing societal problem." The Court held that, "There is no doubt that preventing danger to the community is a legitimate regulatory goal." More than half the States have recently adopted preventive detention laws.

## Cruel and Unusual Punishment

The 8th Amendment also forbids "cruel and unusual punishment." The 14th Amendment extends that prohibition against the States, *Robinson* v. *California,* 1962.

The Supreme Court decided its first cruel and unusual case in *Wilkerson* v. *Utah,* 1879. There a territorial court had sentenced a convicted murderer to death by a firing squad. The Court held this punishment to be constitutional.

The kinds of penalties the Constitution intended to prevent, said the Court, were such barbaric tortures as burning at the stake, crucifixion, drawing and quartering, "and all others in the same line of unnecessary cruelty." It upheld electrocution for the first time in a case from New York, *In re Kemmler,* 1890.

Since then, the Court has heard only a handful of cruel and unusual cases, except for those relating to capital punishment. More often than not, the Court has rejected the cruel and unusual punishment claim.[14]

*Louisiana* v. *Resweber,* 1947, is typical. There the Court found that it was not unconstitutional to subject a convicted murderer to a second electrocution after the chair had failed to work properly on the first occasion.

In *Rummel* v. *Estelle,* 1980, a Texas court had imposed a mandatory life sentence on a "three-time loser." It did so even though the three crimes of which the individual had been convicted were all petty and nonviolent, and all together involved less than $230.

However, the Court has held some punishments to be cruel and unusual. In *Robinson* v. *California,* 1962, the Court held that a State law

---

[14]The prohibition of cruel and unusual punishment is limited to criminal matters. It does not forbid paddling or similar punishments in the public schools, *Ingraham v. Wright,* 1977.

defining narcotics addiction as a crime to be punished, rather than an illness to be treated, violated the 8th and 14th amendments.[15] In *Estelle* v. *Gamble*, 1976, it ruled that a Texas prison inmate could not properly be denied needed medical care.

Again, however, most cases have gone the other way. Thus, in *Rhodes* v. *Chapman*, 1981, the Court held that putting two prisoners in a cell built for one is not cruel and unusual.

## Capital Punishment

Is **capital punishment**—punishment by death—cruel and unusual and therefore unconstitutional?[16] For years, the Supreme Court was reluctant to face that highly charged issue.[17]

The Court met the issue indirectly in *Furman* v. *Georgia*, 1972. There it struck down all of the then existing State laws allowing the death penalty, but not because that penalty as such was cruel and unusual. Rather, the Court voided those laws because they gave too much discretion to judges or juries in deciding whether to impose the death penalty. The Court noted that out of all the people convicted of capital crimes, only "a random few," most of them African American or poor or both, were "capriciously selected" for execution.

Since that decision, Congress and 38 States have passed new capital punishment laws. At first, those laws took one of two forms. Several States made the death penalty mandatory for certain crimes, such as killing a police officer or murder committed during a rape, kidnapping, or arson. Other States provided for a two-stage process in capital cases: a trial to settle the issue of guilt or innocence, and then a second hearing to decide whether the circumstances justify a sentence of death.

In considering the scores of challenges to those State laws, the Supreme Court found the mandatory death penalty laws to be unconstitutional. In *Woodson* v. *North Carolina*, 1976, the Court ruled that such laws were "unduly harsh and rigidly unworkable." It saw the laws as attempts simply to "paper over" the decision in *Furman*.

The two-stage approach to capital punishment *is* constitutional, however. In *Gregg* v. *Georgia*, 1976, the Court held, for the first time, that the "punishment of death does not invariably violate the Constitution." It ruled that well-drawn two-stage laws can practically eliminate "the risk that [the death penalty] will be inflicted in an arbitrary or capricious manner."

However, the Court has ruled that a State can impose the death penalty only for "crimes resulting in the death of the victim," *Coker* v. *Georgia*, 1977. Moreover, a capital punishment law "must allow for whatever mitigating circumstances" may be present in a case, *Roberts* v. *Louisiana*, 1977.

Opponents of capital punishment continue to appeal cases to the Court, but to no real avail. The sum of the Court's many decisions over the past 25 years is this: The death penalty, fairly applied, is constitutional.

Current polls indicate that two of every three Americans support the death penalty. Still, many

---

[15]But, notice, that does not mean that buying, selling, or possessing narcotics cannot be made a crime. Such criminal laws are designed to punish persons for their behavior, not for being ill.

[16]The phrase "capital punishment" comes from the Latin *caput*, meaning "head"; in many cultures, the historically preferred method for executing criminals was beheading (decapitation).

[17]The Court did hold that neither death by firing squad (*Wilkerson* v. *Utah*, 1878) nor by a second electrocution *(Louisiana* v. *Resweber*, 1947) is unconstitutional. But in neither of those cases, nor in others, did it deal with the question of the death penalty as such.

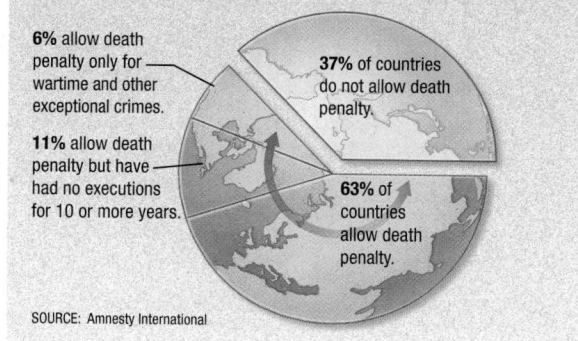

## Comparative Government

### Use of Capital Punishment Worldwide

**6%** allow death penalty only for wartime and other exceptional crimes.

**11%** allow death penalty but have had no executions for 10 or more years.

**37%** of countries do not allow death penalty.

**63%** of countries allow death penalty.

SOURCE: Amnesty International

*Interpreting Graphs* Over half of the world's countries allow the death penalty. *What percentage of these countries allow the death penalty only for "exceptional" crimes or have had no executions for ten years or longer?*

## Point-of-Use Resources

 **Guide to the Essentials** Chapter 20, Section 4, p. 110 provides support for students who need additional review of section content. Spanish support is available in the Spanish edition of the Guide on p. 103.

**Quiz** Unit 5 booklet, p. 27 includes matching and multiple-choice questions to check students' understanding of Section 4 content.

**Presentation Pro CD-ROM** Quizzes and multiple-choice questions check students' understanding of Section 4 content.

## Answers to . . .

### Section 4 Assessment

**1.** Excessive bail is an amount higher than that necessary to assure a defendant's appearance at a trial.
**2.** The Court has usually ruled that the punishment in question was not cruel and unusual.
**3.** The Court's view of capital punishment has been that as long as it is fairly applied, it is constitutional.
**4.** To prevent political leaders from using the charge of treason against their opponents.
**5. (a)** Mandatory death penalty sentences for certain crimes; a two-stage process with a trial and then a separate hearing for sentencing. **(b)** The Court has found mandatory sentencing unconstitutional because it is too rigid.
**6.** Possible answer: The Court assumes that protection of the community takes precedence over personal liberties in such cases.

### Answer to . . .

**Interpreting Graphs** The number of executions has risen dramatically, from 0 in 1976 to 98 in 1999 with a slight drop in 2000.

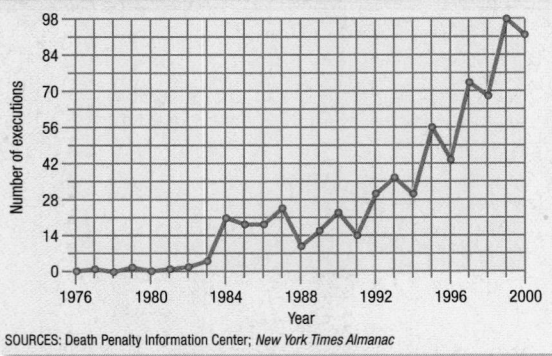

**Executions in the United States, 1976–2000**

SOURCES: Death Penalty Information Center; *New York Times Almanac*

 **Interpreting Graphs** In 1976, the Supreme Court upheld the constitutionality of the death penalty. ***Summarize the data shown on the graph.***

who favor it have some misgivings about the fairness with which death sentences are applied.

In January 2000, Governor George Ryan of Illinois, a longtime supporter of capital punishment, ordered a moratorium on (a suspension of) executions in his State. He did so, he said, because the death penalty process is "fraught with error."

From 1977 to 2000, 285 people were sentenced to death in Illinois. By 2000, 12 of them had been executed, but 13 others had been released from prison because they had been wrongly convicted. It appears that several other

death row inmates in Illinois may not in fact be guilty of the crimes for which they were sentenced to die. Governor Ryan's action set off a new and continuing debate over the use of the death penalty in this country.

## Treason

Treason against the United States is the only crime that is defined in the Constitution. The Framers provided a specific definition of the crime because they knew that the charge of treason is a favorite weapon in the hands of tyrants.

**Treason,** says Article III, Section 3, can consist of only two things: either (1) levying war against the United States or (2) "adhering to their Enemies, giving them Aid and Comfort." No person can be convicted of the crime "unless on the Testimony of two Witnesses to the same overt Act, or on Confession in open Court."

Congress has established the death penalty as the maximum penalty for treason against the United States, but no one has ever been executed for the crime. Note that a person can commit treason only in wartime. However, Congress has made it a crime, during times of either peace or war, to commit espionage or sabotage, to attempt to overthrow the government by force, or to conspire to do any of these things.

Most of the State constitutions also provide for treason. John Brown was hanged as a traitor to Virginia after his raid on Harpers Ferry in 1859. He is believed to be the only person ever to be executed for treason against a State.

## Section 4 Assessment

**Key Terms and Main Ideas**

1. What constitutes excessive **bail?**
2. In cases involving cruel and unusual punishment, how has the Court generally ruled?
3. What is the Supreme Court's view of **capital punishment?**
4. For what reason does the Constitution specifically define **treason?**

**Critical Thinking**

5. **Demonstrating Reasoned Judgment (a)** What two forms did State laws allowing capital punishment take after the Court's decision in *Furman* v. *Georgia?* **(b)** Why did the Court find one form of these laws "unduly harsh and rigidly unworkable"?

6. **Identifying Assumptions** What assumptions underlie the Court's decision that preventive detention is constitutional?

**Take It to the Net**

7. Browse through at least three Internet sites on the death penalty. Then answer the following: What are the most convincing arguments presented in favor of abolishing the death penalty? What arguments could you offer against abolishing the death penalty? Use the links provided at the Social Studies area of the following Web site for help in completing this activity. **www.phschool.com**

 **Take It to the Net**

**7.** Direct students to the Social Studies area at the Prentice Hall School Web site. The *Magruder's American Government* companion Web site includes the directions and links needed to complete the activity. It also provides a printable Internet activity worksheet with scoring rubrics for assessment. Answers should address both questions, and arguments should be persuasive.

# on the Supreme Court

## Does a Suspect's Flight From Police Justify a Stop and Search?

*The 4th Amendment prohibits "unreasonable searches and seizures," but it does not define the term "unreasonable." In **Terry v. Ohio**, 1968, the Supreme Court held that police officers may stop and frisk a person when they have good reason to believe that that person is armed and dangerous. May police stop a person simply because that person flees when the police approach?*

### Illinois v. Wardlow (2000)

William Wardlow was holding a white bag while in an area of Chicago known for heavy drug trafficking when he saw a caravan of police cars approaching. He fled, and the police pursued. When they caught up with him, one of the officers conducted a "pat-down" search for weapons. (In the police officer's experience, weapons were usually found in the vicinity of narcotics transactions.) The officer squeezed the bag Wardlow was carrying and felt a heavy, hard object shaped like a gun. He opened the bag and discovered a .38-caliber handgun with five live rounds of ammunition.

At his trial, Wardlow argued that he should not be prosecuted for possession of the gun because the officer did not have reasonable suspicion to stop and search him. The Illinois trial court ruled against him, and he was convicted of unlawful use of a weapon by a felon. The Illinois Appellate Court then reversed his conviction. The Illinois Supreme Court affirmed that ruling, holding that both the stop and the arrest violated the 4th Amendment. The case then went to the Supreme Court.

### Arguments for Illinois

1. The fact that a person fled from a police officer strongly indicates criminal behavior and provides reasonable grounds for stopping the suspect in order to conduct a brief investigation.
2. Even if flight alone is not sufficient to justify stopping and searching a suspect, the fact that the suspect was in a high-crime area, combined with the fact that the suspect fled upon the arrival of the police, provide reasonable grounds for stopping the suspect.
3. The standard that must be met to justify stopping a suspect, "reasonable suspicion," is less demanding than the standard of "probable cause" that must be met to justify arresting a suspect.

### Arguments for Wardlow

1. There can be many reasons for fleeing from police; the fact that a person fled does not by itself mean that he is guilty of a crime.
2. Even the combined circumstances of being in a high-crime area, carrying a white bag, and running from the police do not create reasonable suspicion to justify a search.
3. An individual has the right to ignore the police unless and until the police have sufficient grounds under the Constitution to detain or arrest him. No one is required to cooperate with the police.

---

### Decide for Yourself

1. Review the constitutional grounds on which each side based its arguments and the specific arguments each side presented.
2. Debate the opposing viewpoints presented in this case. Which viewpoint do you favor?
3. Predict the impact of the Court's decision on the conduct of police investigations and on relations between minority groups and the police. (To read a summary of the Court's decision, turn to the Supreme Court Glossary on page 799.)

---

## Corner

📁 **Close Up on the Supreme Court** *Illinois* v. *Wardlow*, p. 21 provides an activity to extend coverage of this case.

 **Online**

To keep up-to-date on Close Up news and activities, visit Close Up Online at

**www.closeup.org**

---

## Does a Subject's Flight from Police Justify a Stop and Search?

**Focus** Have the class skim the chapter's section on the Fourth Amendment. Then call on volunteers to explain the amendment's purpose *(to prevent unreasonable searches by the government)* and the main requirement for obtaining a search warrant. *(probable cause)*

**Instruct** Call on volunteers to explain the plain view, emergency, arrest, and automobile exceptions to the search warrant rule. Then explain that this case considers another exception to the search warrant requirement. After reading the feature, have the class identify the argument in the feature that they find most convincing and explain why.

**Close/Reteach** In President John Adams words, "the child Independence was born" in the colonists' opposition to writs of assistance issued to British customs officials. Have students suppose that they are colonists who opposed British threats to liberty. Have them write a petition to the king that explains why blanket search warrants pose a threat to the security of home and person.

💿 **Keep It Current CD-ROM** includes government-related projects by unit. The CD-ROM links to the Prentice Hall School Web site and may be used for daily updates.

---

*Answers to . . .*

**Decide for Yourself**

**1.** Illinois argued that police officers may stop a suspect providing that they have "reasonable suspicion." Wardlow argued that his Fourth Amendment rights were violated, and that the Constitution does not specify grounds under which a suspect may be detained.
**2.** Answers will vary, but should be supported with valid reasoning.
**3.** The Court ruled in favor of Illinois, holding that police did have reasonable suspicion and that was enough to justify a stop.

## Practicing the Vocabulary

1. grand jury
2. due process
3. police power
4. bail
5. bill of attainder
6. writs of assistance
7. Miranda Rule
8. double jeopardy
9. search warrant
10. ex post facto law

## Reviewing Main Ideas
### Section 1

**11.** *Rochin*—in which sheriffs broke into a suspect's home, pried open his mouth, and pumped his stomach—pointed to the need for procedural due process. *Pierce*—in which a law was passed with the purpose of destroying parochial schools—pointed to the need for substantive due process.
**12.** States' exercise of police power has sometimes led to conflicts with individuals; in general, courts have permitted the use of police power in cases of conflict.
**13.** To promote health, safety, morals, and general welfare.
**14.** The right of privacy.

### Section 2

**15.** With the *Civil Rights Cases*, the Court weakened the 13th Amendment by holding that racial discrimination was different from slavery; with *Jones*, the Court strengthened the amendment by holding that it had the power to abolish "the badges and incidents of slavery."
**16.** To provide for the security of people in their homes and on their persons.
**17.** The 3rd Amendment was made in response to the British practice of quartering soldiers in private homes; it is no longer significant, as the historical context from which it grew no longer exists.
**18.** It holds that if police obtain evidence illegally, it may not be used against the citizen from whom the evidence was taken.

### Section 3

**19.** One of the principles of the American legal system is that the protection of innocent people

outweighs the prosecution of the guilty.
**20.** By mandating writs of habeas corpus, grand juries, and public trials by jury, and by outlawing bills of attainder and ex post facto laws.
**21.** Trials must be speedy and public, and they must involve a jury—unless this right is waived by the defendant. Also, the accused cannot be exposed to double jeopardy.

### Section 4
**23.** No excessive bail or fines are allowed, and punishment cannot be cruel or unusual.
**24.** Mandatory death sentences have been found unconstitutional.

**22.** The 5th Amendment protects people against self-incrimination, and the Miranda Rule ensures that the accused are aware of their rights.

**25.** *Furman* struck down all State laws that allowed the death penalty, on the grounds that executions were random. This led to the passage of new State laws.
**26. (a)** Treason. **(b)** A court must have the testimony of two witnesses or an open confession by the accused in order to convict.

---

## Political Dictionary

| | | |
|---|---|---|
| due process (p. 564) | probable cause (p. 571) | bench trial (p. 580) |
| substantive due process (p. 565) | exclusionary rule (p. 573) | Miranda Rule (p. 582) |
| procedural due process (p. 565) | writ of habeas corpus (p. 576) | bail (p. 585) |
| police power (p. 566) | bill of attainder (p. 577) | preventive detention (p. 586) |
| search warrant (p. 566) | ex post facto law (p. 577) | capital punishment (p. 587) |
| involuntary servitude (p. 569) | grand jury (p. 577) | treason (p. 588) |
| discrimination (p. 570) | indictment (p. 578) | |
| writs of assistance (p. 571) | double jeopardy (p. 578) | |

## Practicing the Vocabulary

**Matching** *Choose a term from the list above that best matches each description.*

1. A group convened by a court to determine whether or not there is enough evidence against a person to justify a trial
2. A constitutional guarantee that a government will not deprive any person of life, liberty, or property by any unfair, arbitrary, or unreasonable action
3. The power of each State to act to protect and promote the public health, safety, morals, and general welfare
4. A sum of money that an accused person may be required to post as a guarantee that he or she will appear in court at the proper time
5. A legislative act that inflicts punishment without court trial

**Fill in the Blank** *Choose a term from the list above that best completes the sentence.*

6. During colonial times, British officials used _____ in order to search private homes for smuggled goods.
7. According to the _____, suspects must be advised of their rights before police questioning.
8. If a person is tried twice for the same crime, he or she may have been subjected to _____.
9. Police generally need a _____ in order search someone's house.
10. An _____ is a law applied to acts performed before the law was passed.

## Reviewing Main Ideas

### Section 1

11. Use the examples of *Rochin* v. *California* and *Pierce* v. *Society of Sisters* to explain why it is necessary to have both substantive and procedural due process.
12. Describe the relationship between the States' police power and due process of law.
13. What four goals may States use police power to promote?
14. What right did the Court first articulate in *Griswold* v. *Connecticut,* 1965?

### Section 2

15. Use the examples of the *Civil Rights Cases*, 1883, and *Jones* v. *Mayer*, 1968, to illustrate how the Court's interpretation of the 13th Amendment has changed over the years.
16. What is the aim of the 4th Amendment?
17. What are the roots of the 3rd Amendment, and why is it no longer significant?
18. How does the exclusionary rule help to protect citizens?

### Section 3

19. For what reason does the Constitution protect the rights of those accused of a crime?
20. In what ways does the Constitution protect the rights of the accused?
21. What are the key constitutional guarantees of a fair trial?
22. What guarantees and rules exist to ensure those accused of a crime the right not to incriminate themselves?

### Section 4

23. What are the key constitutional guarantees regarding punishment of the guilty?
24. Under what circumstances has the Supreme Court found death penalty laws to be unconstitutional?
25. What was the significance of *Furman* v. *Georgia*, 1972, in the history of the Supreme Court's rulings regarding capital punishment?
26. **(a)** What is the only crime defined in the Constitution? **(b)** What requirements must be met in order for a person to be convicted of this crime?

## Critical Thinking Skills

**27.** *Applying the Chapter Skill* You have been assigned to make a presentation on 4th Amendment implications of the use of wiretapping by law enforcement officials. How could you use various media to make your presentation more interesting? Following the instructions on page 575, create a blueprint for the project.

**28.** *Checking Consistency* Recall that an accused person can be held without bail when there is reason to believe that he or she will commit a crime. In your opinion, does this law violate the principle of presumed innocence until proven guilty? Explain your reasoning.

**29.** *Identifying Assumptions* What assumptions underlie the existence of the Miranda Rule and its specific provisions?

**30.** *Determining Relevance* How did the experiences of colonial Americans with British law enforcement and military practice influence the composition of the 2nd, 3rd, and 4th amendments?

**31.** *Making Comparisons* Analyze the role of each branch of government in protecting the rights of individuals. Which branch has the greatest responsibility? Explain.

## Analyzing Political Cartoons

Use your knowledge of American history and government and this cartoon to answer the questions below.

*"That was fun. What time does the next trial of the century start?"*

**32. (a)** Who are the people in the cartoon? **(b)** What are they watching on television?

**33.** What does the cartoon suggest about television cameras in the courtroom?

---

 **You Can Make a Difference**

Set up an interview with a representative of a local community group or law-enforcement agency that tries to keep young people from committing crimes or helps those who have already been in trouble with the law. Before you meet with this person, draw up a list of questions to ask him or her. Your questions should address issues of civil liberties, victims' rights, and the rights of the accused. If possible, make a tape-recording of your interview to play for the class.

## Participation Activities

**34.** *Current Events Watch* Scan the newspaper for stories concerning any guarantees of the rights of the accused shown on the chart on page 578. Be prepared to give an oral report summarizing the story.

**35.** *Time Line Activity* Choose an issue discussed in this chapter (for example, the constitutionality of the death penalty or abortion). Based on both the information in this chapter and your own research, make a list of the key Supreme Court decisions regarding this issue. Present these decisions in a time line that demonstrates the development of the Court's opinion over the years.

**36.** *It's Your Turn* Create a survey to gauge citizens' opinions of the Constitution's civil liberties protections. Begin by listing the rights discussed in this chapter, such as due process. Next, note some of the controversial aspects of these rights (for example, the fact that evidence gathered illegally cannot be used against a person). Compose a list of questions designed to gather opinions on these issues. Ask ten people to complete your survey and compile their answers. **(Conducting A Survey)**

---

 **Take It to the Net**

***Chapter 20 Self-Test*** As a final review activity, take the Chapter 20 Self-Test in the Social Studies area at the Web site listed below, and receive immediate feedback on your answers.

**www.phschool.com**

---

 **Take It to the Net**

Additional support materials and activities for Chapter 20 of *Magruder's American Government* can be found in the Social Studies area at the Prentice Hall School Web site. **www.phschool.com**

## Critical Thinking Skills

**27.** Blueprints should indicate that students read and followed the steps outlined in the Skills activity.

**28.** Answers will vary; students should question on what basis a person who is technically innocent can be considered a danger with the potential to commit a crime.

**29.** The Rule assumes that many people are unaware of the rights of the accused.

**30.** Anger about British colonial practices that infringed on colonists' rights brought about each of these amendments.

**31.** Students should identify each branch of government and its role as follows: legislative makes laws to protect individual rights; executive carries out the laws that protect rights; judicial interprets the laws that protect rights. Answers will vary as to which branch has the greatest responsibility, but should present a well-reasoned argument.

## Analyzing Political Cartoons

**32. (a)** Ordinary Americans.
**(b)** A well-publicized trial.
**33.** That they trivialize important trials.

## You Can Make a Difference

Students should ask valid questions that touch on the themes discussed in the chapter; encourage students to refer to specific cases in their questioning.

## Participation Activities

**34.** Summaries should be accurate and include all relevant points; opinions should be backed with precedents.
**35.** Time lines should be clearly constructed and show an obvious development of political thought.
**36.** Surveys should ask non-biased, non-leading questions.

---

## Point-of-Use Resources

 **Guide to the Essentials of American Government** Chapter 20 Test, page 111 provides multiple-choice questions to test students' knowledge of the chapter.

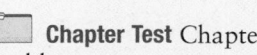 **Test Bank CD-ROM** Chapter 20 Test

📁 **Chapter Test** Chapter Tests booklet

# Civil Rights: Equal Justice Under Law

| Section Objectives | Print and Technology Resources | |
|---|---|---|
| **1 Diversity and Discrimination in American Society** (pp. 594–599)<br><br>1. Understand what it means to live in a heterogeneous society.<br>2. Summarize the history of race-based discrimination in the United States.<br>3. Examine discrimination against women in the past and present.<br><br>TEKS 3A, 3B, 8B, 9E, 16A, 16B, 17C, 18A, 18B, 18C, 21A, 21C, 21E, 22A, 22B, 22D | • **Unit 5 booklet** Guided Reading and Review, p. 29 Section 1 Quiz, p. 30<br>• **Lesson Plans booklet** Section 1, p. 90<br>• **Political Cartoons booklet** Section 1, p. 82<br>• **Block Scheduling with Lesson Strategies booklet** p. 29<br>• **Section Reading Support Transparencies**<br>• **Social Studies Skills Tutor CD-ROM** | • **Close Up on Primary Sources booklet** Petition by Free Negroes for Equality Under the Law, p. 32<br>• **Simulations and Debates booklet** pp. 44–45<br>• **Basic Principles of the Constitution Transparencies** 14<br>• **Section Support Transparencies** 85, 184<br>• **Presentation Pro CD-ROM** Section 1 |
| **2 Equality Before the Law** (pp. 601–606)<br><br>1. Explain the importance of the Equal Protection Clause.<br>2. Describe the history of segregation in America.<br>3. Examine how classification by sex relates to discrimination.<br><br>TEKS 3A, 3B, 8B, 8D, 9C, 9E, 9G, 10D, 14A, 14D, 16A, 16B, 18A, 18B, 18C, 21A, 21E, 22A, 22B | • **Unit 5 booklet** Guided Reading and Review, p. 31 Section 2 Quiz, p. 32<br>• **Lesson Plans booklet** Section 2, p. 91<br>• **Political Cartoons booklet** Section 2, p. 83<br>• **Block Scheduling with Lesson Strategies booklet** p. 29<br>• **Close Up on Primary Sources booklet** The Struggle for Integration, p. 23<br>• **Section Reading Support Transparencies** | • **Close Up on the Supreme Court booklet** *Plessy* v. *Ferguson*, pp. 36–37; *Powell* v. *Alabama*, pp. 40–41; *Brown* v. *Board of Education of Topeka*, pp. 42–43<br>• **The Living Constitution booklet** pp. 7; 17–18<br>• **Basic Principles of the Constitution Transparencies** 5, 35, 42<br>• **Section Support Transparencies** 86, 185<br>• **Presentation Pro CD-ROM** Section 2 |
| **3 Federal Civil Rights Laws** (pp. 608–612)<br><br>1. Outline the history of civil rights legislation from Reconstruction to today.<br>2. Explore the issues surrounding affirmative action.<br><br>TEKS 2D, 3A, 3B, 8B, 8D, 9E, 9G, 10D, 14A, 14D, 16A, 16B, 18A, 18B, 18C, 21A, 21E, 22A, 22B | • **Unit 5 booklet** Guided Reading and Review, p. 33 Section 3 Quiz, p. 34<br>• **Lesson Plans booklet** Section 3, p. 92<br>• **Political Cartoons booklet** Section 3, p. 84<br>• **Block Scheduling with Lesson Strategies booklet** p. 29 | • **Close Up on Primary Sources booklet** The Civil Rights Acts, p. 46<br>• **Government Assessment Rubrics booklet** p. 26<br>• **Section Support Transparencies** 87, 186<br>• **Presentation Pro CD-ROM** Section 3<br>• **Section Reading Support Transparencies** |
| **4 American Citizenship** (pp. 613–618)<br><br>1. Identify the questions surrounding American citizenship.<br>2. Describe how people become American citizens by birth and by naturalization.<br>3. Explain how an American can lose his or her citizenship.<br>4. Illustrate how the United States is a nation of immigrants.<br>5. Compare and contrast the status of undocumented aliens and legal immigrants.<br><br>TEKS 3A, 3B, 8B, 8D, 9E, 9G, 10D, 14A, 14D, 16A, 16B, 17C, 18A, 18B, 18C, 21A, 21C, 21D, 21E, 22A, 22B | • **Unit 5 booklet** Guided Reading and Review, p. 35 Section 4 Quiz, p. 36 Skills for Life Activity, p. 37<br>• **Lesson Plans booklet** Section 4, p. 93<br>• **Political Cartoons booklet** Section 4, p. 85<br>• **Close Up on Primary Sources booklet** The Dawes Act, p. 39<br>• **Section Reading Support Transparencies** | • **Close Up on the Supreme Court booklet** *Regents of the University of California* v. *Bakke*, p. 22<br>• **The Basic Principles of the Constitution Posters**<br>• **Section Support Transparencies** 88, 187<br>• **Presentation Pro CD-ROM** Section 4<br>• **Simulations and Data Graphing CD-ROM** |

# Block Scheduling Strategies

The *Magruder's American Government* program addresses block-scheduling strategies in a variety of ways. For easy reference, side-column activities that fit a block format are marked ▣ **Block Strategy.** Each section also contains a **Block Scheduling Strategies** box describing at least two block-format activities that address and extend core content from the section. The **Block Scheduling with Lesson Strategies booklet** found in the Teaching Resources contains additional block-scheduling activities for each chapter.

## Take It to the Net

Visit the Social Studies area at the Prentice Hall School Web site. Once there, you can find additional links, current events connections, and activities to enrich chapter content for *Magruder's American Government,* as well as a Self-Test for students. Be sure to check out this month's **eTeach** online discussion with a Master Teacher.

### www.phschool.com

## Pressed for Time?

If you are running short on time to cover this chapter, consider one of the following options:
- Use the **Presentation Pro CD-ROM** to create an outline for this chapter.
- Use one of the **Pressed for Time** activities found on p. 27.
- Use the Section Summaries for Chapter 2, from **Guide to the Essentials of American Government (English and Spanish).**

##  Video Connections

Prentice Hall offers two video programs to reinforce and extend chapter content. Show students *The Blessings of Liberty* from the **ABC News Civics and Government Videotape Library** and *Prayer in Schools: A Nationwide Debate* from the **Magruder's American Government Video Collection.**

## Assessment Options
- Section Quizzes, **Unit 5 booklet,** pp. 30, 32, 34, 36
- Chapter 21 Assessment, pp. 620–621
- **Guide to the Essentials of American Government,** Chapter 21 Test, p. 116

### Core Assessment
Chapter 21 Test, Chapter Tests booklet
ExamView® Test Bank CD-ROM Chapter 21
Government Assessment Rubrics

### Standardized Test Preparation
#### Diagnose and Prescribe
Diagnostic Tests for High School
Social Studies Skills

#### Review and Reteach
Review Book for Government

#### Practice and Assess
Test-Taking Strategies With
  Transparencies for High School
Test Prep Book for Government

# Chapter 21 Teacher's Edition Index

## Civil Rights: Equal Justice Under Law

# Civil Rights: Equal Justice Under Law

### Introducing the Chapter

In this chapter, students will learn about American citizenship—how it is acquired, how the Constitution guarantees equality for all citizens, and how all citizens are protected against discrimination.

### Make It Relevant

#### ★ You Can Make a Difference

Guide a group of students as they conceive and execute a mentoring program for younger, at-risk students in your school district or community. Students will work to tutor their younger peers and teach them academic and life skills that will enable them to succeed. Student-mentors should begin by creating a list of needed skills and the techniques they can use to teach them.

**Service Learning**

### CONSTITUTIONAL PRINCIPLES

Emphasize the following basic principles as students read Chapter 21. Have the class respond to the questions, and then ask volunteers to explain which principle has the biggest impact on civil rights.

**Popular Sovereignty** How has civil-rights legislation passed since 1957 reflected the principle of popular sovereignty?

**Judicial Review** What was the significance of the Supreme Court's decision in the case of *Brown* v. *Board of Education of Topeka*?

**Federalism** In what ways did State laws undermine the 14th Amendment, which guaranteed "equal protection under the laws" to all Americans?

> *"Our Constitution is color-blind, and neither knows nor tolerates classes among citizens. In respect of civil rights, all citizens are equal before the law."*
>
> —Justice John Marshall Harlan (1896)

Although Justice Harlan was speaking about the civil rights of African Americans, today his words apply to a much more diverse American society. Many groups have faced challenges in trying to get and keep the civil rights that the Constitution and civil rights legislation promise to all citizens.

◆ Demonstrators protest discrimination against African Americans at Woolworth's lunch counters, 1960

 *Corner*

The following resources are available only from the Close Up Foundation to support the concepts discussed in Chapter 21 "Civil Rights: Equal Justice Under Law":

◆ *Perspectives: Readings on Contemporary American Government*
◆ *Democracy and Rights: One Citizen's Challenge*
◆ *Exploring Race and Affirmative Action*
◆ *Words of Ages: Witnessing U.S. History Through Literature*

 **Online**

To keep up-to-date on Close Up news and activities, visit Close Up Online at

**www.closeup.org**

Close Up Foundation
44 Canal Center Plaza
Alexandria, VA 22314-1592
800-765-3131

## You Can Make a Difference

★ **CIVIL RIGHTS INEQUALITIES** still persist. In Boston, Kedesha Malcolm attended Boston Latin School, one of the city's prestigious "exam schools"—public high schools whose students must pass an entrance exam. Kedesha, 18, realized that there were not many students of color in her school, even though a large percentage of the city's overall student population is African American or Hispanic. "So I decided to do something to improve the school's diversity," Kedesha said. In response, she started Young Leaders of Color. Its members work with minority middle school students to help them pass the exams, and then offer mentoring to help them keep up with the challenging courses.

### Keep It Current

Items marked with this logo are periodically updated on the Internet. Keep up-to-date with what's in the news. To get current information on civil rights, go to **www.phschool.com**

### SECTION 1

#### Diversity and Discrimination in American Society (pp. 594–599)

★ The United States is a diverse nation made up of people from many different backgrounds and communities.
★ African Americans, Native Americans, Hispanic Americans, and Asian Americans are four large minority groups that have suffered from discrimination at the hands of government and private individuals.
★ Women of all backgrounds experience discrimination in much the same way as members of racial and ethnic minorities.

### SECTION 2

#### Equality Before the Law (pp. 601–606)

★ The 14th Amendment guaranteed "equal protection of the law" to all Americans in 1868, but States passed laws that segregated white Americans and African Americans.
★ The Supreme Court overturned many of these laws—and its own past decisions—during the 1950s and 1960s.
★ De facto segregation persists in public schools and housing.
★ Since 1971, most laws that treat women differently from men have been successfully challenged in court.

### SECTION 3

#### Federal Civil Rights Laws (pp. 608–612)

★ The Federal Government passed several acts in the 1960s to guarantee the civil rights of African Americans, other minorities, and women.
★ Affirmative action policies require the Federal Government and those who do business with the Federal Government to take positive steps to remedy past discrimination.
★ Supporters and critics of affirmative action have taken their debate to the Supreme Court, Congress, State legislatures, and the voting booth.

### SECTION 4

#### American Citizenship (pp. 613–618)

★ The vast majority of people living in the United States are American citizens who were born in this country or to parents with citizenship.
★ Several million Americans have become citizens through a difficult process called naturalization.
★ Americans can lose their citizenship by choice or, in rare cases, through a court order.
★ Most immigrants to the United States have come through official channels, but many arrive illegally and face special challenges to stay in this country.

## Keep It Current

### Internet Update

Use the Prentice Hall School Web site and the Keep It Current CD-ROM to find quick content updates.

Visit **www.phschool.com** for current events articles that are linked to Chapter 21. Critical thinking questions are included.

**Keep It Current CD-ROM** includes government-related projects by unit. Students complete each project using current information that they obtain by linking to the Prentice Hall School Web site from the CD-ROM.

## Pressed for Time?

### To Omit the Chapter

If you wish to skip Chapter 21, ask students to read the Chapter in Brief and assign the Guide to the Essentials before continuing to another chapter. You may also want to assign the Chapter 21 Test in the Chapter Test booklet. Then specific portions of Chapter 21 may be assigned to students needing reinforcement of key terms and concepts.

### To Preview the Chapter

To introduce students to key terms and concepts in each section, have them read the Chapter in Brief. You may also assign the Reading Strategy activities on pp. 595, 602, 609, and 614 of this book.

### To Review the Chapter

When students have completed Chapter 21, you might want to assign the Guide to the Essentials or the Guided Reading and Review worksheets on pp. 29, 31, 33, and 35 of the Unit 5 booklet.

### To Cover the Chapter Quickly

To cover the material in Chapter 21 quickly, use the following activity.

**Focus** Write the word *diversity* on the chalkboard and ask students to explain what it means. Have students provide examples of diversity in the United States. Then ask them to consider how diversity has brought challenges to government in terms of protecting individual rights.

**Instruct** Have students read the text of the 14th Amendment. Then describe the pieces of legislation—both State and federal—that challenged or expanded the 14th Amendment. End the historical discussion on civil and equal rights by debating the topic of affirmative action. Encourage students to support their stances with specific historical examples.

**Close/Reteach** Describe the process of naturalization to students, or encourage students with family members who have been naturalized to offer their experiences. Ask students if they think the naturalization process is appropriate for immigrants. How might they change it?

■ **Block Strategy (Average)**

**1** *Diversity and Discrimination in American Society*

**Objectives** You may wish to call students' attention to the objectives in the Section Preview. The objectives are reflected in the main headings of the section.

**Bellringer** Ask students to consider a group of 100 people who represent the population of the United States. Have them estimate how many African Americans, Hispanic Americans, Native Americans, and Asian Americans, as well as males and females, are in the group. Explain that in this section, they will learn about diversity in the United States.

**Vocabulary Builder** Tell students that the root word of one of the terms in the Political Dictionary means "to flee." Ask them which word that might be. *(refugee, from the Latin* fugere*)* Then have students suggest the meanings of the other terms.

---

## Pressed for Time?

### Quick Lesson Plan

**1. Focus** Tell students that the United States has a history of discrimination against its ethnic minorities and women. Ask students to name some forms that this discrimination has taken.

**2. Instruct** Ask students how the ethnic composition of the United States is changing. Discuss the increasing heterogeneity of the American population and the history of discrimination that nonwhite Americans have faced. Conclude by discussing discrimination against women.

**3. Close/Reteach** Remind students that for most of our history, the percentage of whites steadily rose. Ask students to make a time line of diversity and discrimination, with notes describing the details.

---

## Point-of-Use Resources

📁 **Block Scheduling with Lesson Strategies** Activities for Chapter 21 are presented on p. 29.

---

# Diversity and Discrimination in American Society

## Section Preview

### OBJECTIVES

1. **Understand** what it means to live in a heterogeneous society.
2. **Summarize** the history of race-based discrimination in the United States.
3. **Examine** discrimination against women in the past and present.

### WHY IT MATTERS

Although the Declaration of Independence declares that "all men are created equal," our nation has often struggled to meet that ideal. Members of ethnic minorities, as well as women, have historically faced discrimination in many aspects of their lives.

### POLITICAL DICTIONARY

★ **heterogeneous**
★ **immigrant**
★ **reservation**
★ **refugee**
★ **assimilation**

---

**H**ave you read George Orwell's classic, *Animal Farm?* Even if you have not, you may have heard its most infamous line: "All animals are created equal, but some animals are more equal than others." You might keep Orwell's words in mind, as well as the words of the Declaration of Independence, as you read the pages in this chapter.

## A Heterogeneous Society

The term **heterogeneous** is a compound of two Greek words: *hetero,* meaning "other or different," and *genos,* meaning "race, family, or kind." Something that is heterogeneous is composed of a mix of ingredients. "We the People of

► *A Diverse Nation*
Individuals like this attorney (right) have enjoyed great success, despite the fact that women and Native Americans, among others, are often discriminated against in our society.

the United States" are a heterogeneous lot, and we are becoming more so, year to year.

The population of the United States is predominantly white. It is today and, as you can see in the table on page 595, it has been historically. The first census in 1790 reported that there were 3,929,214 people living in this country. Four out of every five of them were white. African Americans made up the remaining 20 percent of the population counted in the census. As the nation's population grew over the decades, so, too, did the proportion of the American people who were white—until recently.

Today, the ethnic composition of the population is strikingly different from what it was only a generation ago. **Immigrants**—that is, those people legally admitted as permanent residents—have arrived in near-record numbers every year since the mid-1960s. Over that period, the nation's African American, Hispanic American, and Asian American populations have grown at rates several times that of the white population.

A look at gender balance in the population reveals that females are more numerous than males. This has been the case for more than half a century now.

As a result of these changes in the American population, the United States is more heterogeneous today than ever before in its history. That fact is certain to have a profound effect on the American social, political, and economic landscape in the twenty-first century.

---

## 🔲 Block Scheduling Strategies

Consider these suggestions to manage extended class time:

■ Have students explore the State-profiles link at the Statistical Abstract of the Census Bureau (links are provided at **www.phschool.com**). Ask students to find the State and county they live in and report on its population and ethnic composition. Have them compare the ethnic composition of their State and county with that of the nation as a whole, and present their findings in a table or series of pie charts.

■ Describe the history of the attempt to pass the Equal Rights Amendment. Ask students to decide whether they support or oppose such an amendment. Then have them write letters to their congressperson in which they urge appropriate action. Letters should cite some of the historical precedents and economic statistics discussed in this section.

## Ethnic Composition of the United States

### Ethnic Composition of the Population, 1790 – 2050*

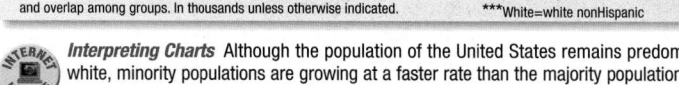

#### 1790 – 2000

| | White | % | African American | % | Hispanic Origin[1] | % | Native American[2] | Asian American[3] |
|---|---|---|---|---|---|---|---|---|
| 1790 | 3,172 | 80.7 | 757 | 19.3 | ** | ** | ** | ** |
| 1800 | 4,306 | 81.0 | 1,002 | 19.0 | ** | ** | ** | ** |
| 1850 | 19,553 | 84.3 | 3,639 | 15.7 | ** | ** | ** | ** |
| 1900 | 66,809 | 87.9 | 8,834 | 11.6 | ** | ** | 237 | 114 |
| 1950 | 135,150 | 89.3 | 15,045 | 9.9 | ** | ** | 343 | 259 |
| 1960 | 158,832 | 88.6 | 18,872 | 10.5 | ** | ** | 524 | 702 |
| 1970 | 178,098 | 87.6 | 22,581 | 11.1 | ** | ** | 793 | 1,026 |
| 1980*** | 180,906 | 79.9 | 26,683 | 11.8 | 14,609 | 6.4 | 1,420 | 3,729 |
| 1990*** | 188,306 | 75.7 | 29,986 | 12.1 | 22,354 | 9.0 | 1,959 | 7,274 |
| 2000*** | 194,552 | 69.1 | 34,658 | 12.3 | 35,306 | 12.5 | 2,476 | 10,243 |

#### 2000
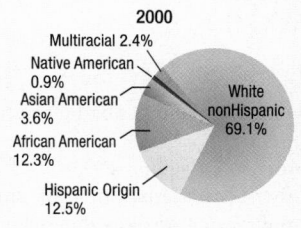

Multiracial 2.4%
Native American 0.9%
Asian American 3.6%
African American 12.3%
Hispanic Origin 12.5%
White nonHispanic 69.1%

#### 2050*
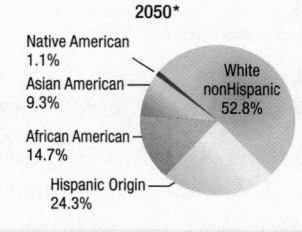

Native American 1.1%
Asian American 9.3%
African American 14.7%
Hispanic Origin 24.3%
White nonHispanic 52.8%

### Rate of Growth of Ethnic Populations

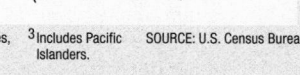

Percentage increase from 1990 to 2000*

- White 9.4%
- African American 15.5%
- Native American 26.4%
- Hispanic Origin 40.8%
- Asian American 57.9%

*Data for 2050 projected. Projections for multiracial not available. Totals may not add up to 100% due to rounding and overlap among groups. In thousands unless otherwise indicated.

**Not available

***White=white nonHispanic

[1] Persons of Hispanic origin may be of any race.

[2] Includes Alaska Natives, 1960 and later.

[3] Includes Pacific Islanders.

SOURCE: U.S. Census Bureau

*Interpreting Charts* Although the population of the United States remains predominantly white, minority populations are growing at a faster rate than the majority population. The 2000 census showed that more and more Americans trace their heritage to multiple groups or choose not to identify themselves by race. ***According to the data, which group will be the largest minority group in 2050?***

## Race-Based Discrimination

White Americans have been historically reluctant to yield to nonwhite Americans a full and equal place in the social, economic, and political life of this nation. Over time, the principal targets of that ethnic prejudice have been African Americans, Native Americans, Asian Americans, and Hispanic Americans. The white-male-dominated power structure has also been slow to recognize the claims of women to a full and equal place in American society.

### African Americans

Much of what you will read in these pages focuses on discrimination against African Americans. There are three reasons for this focus:

1. African Americans constitute the second largest minority group in the United States. They number more than 34 million today, over 12 percent of all the American people.

2. African Americans have been the victims of consistent and deliberate unjust treatment for a longer time than perhaps any other group of Americans.[1] The ancestors of most African Americans came to this country in chains. Tens of thousands of Africans were kidnapped, crammed aboard sailing vessels, brought to America, and then sold in slave markets. As slaves, they could be bought and

---

[1] Slavery began in what was to become the United States in 1619; in August of that year, 20 Africans were sold to white settlers at Jamestown.

## Reading Strategy
### Organizing Information/Outline
Ask students to copy down the main headings and subheadings in outline form, leaving space for details. Have them fill in the details as they read the section.

## Point-of-Use Resources

**Guided Reading and Review** Unit 5 booklet, p. 29 provides students with practice identifying the main ideas and key terms of this section.

**Lesson Plans** For lesson planning suggestions, see p. 90 of the Lesson Plans booklet.

**Political Cartoons** See p. 82 of the Political Cartoons booklet for a cartoon relevant to this section.

**Section Support Transparencies** Transparency 85, *Visual Learning*; Transparency 184, *Political Cartoon*

## Background Note
### Learning from History
Immigrants have long been vulnerable to attacks on their civil liberties. During the Red Scare that began in the late 1910s, U.S. Attorney General A. Mitchell Palmer relentlessly pursued "subversives." Thousands of people—mainly immigrants—were arrested and held without trial. In the aftermath of the September 11, 2001, terrorist attacks, Congress quickly acted in an attempt to lead the nation away from the mistakes of the past. Its members swiftly passed House Concurrent Resolution 227, declaring "that in the quest to identify, bring to justice and punish the perpetrators and sponsors of the terrorist attacks. . .the civil rights and civil liberties of all Americans, including Arab Americans, American Muslims, and Americans from South Asia, should be protected...."

*Answer to . . .*
**Interpreting Charts** Hispanic Americans.

## Organizing Information

To make sure students understand the main points of this section, you may wish to use the tree map graphic organizer to the right.

Tell students that a tree map can be used to record a topic, its main ideas, and supporting details. Have students use a tree map to record information about how African Americans, Native Americans, Hispanic Americans, and Asian Americans have been discriminated against.

**Teaching Tip** A template for this graphic organizer can be found in the Section Support Transparencies, Transparency 3.

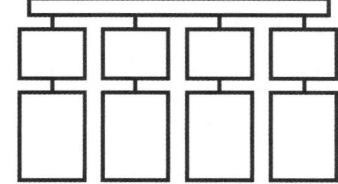

## Learning Styles

**Visual, Spatial** Have students use the graphs on p. 595 to make an illustrated time line of the ethnic breakdown of the U.S. population. Time lines should include all of the groups that appear in the graphs and should begin with the year 1790. Have students end their time lines in a year of their choice, but the end year should be no earlier than 2100. Students should make predictions for their end year, and support their predictions with valid reasoning based on the preceding information. Find space in the classroom to display students' work.

🔲 **Block Strategy
(Challenging)**

## Point-of-Use Resources

📁 **Simulations and Debates**
Discrimination, pp. 44–45 provides students with a simulation of a class run according to random rules of discrimination.

📁 **Close Up on Primary Sources**
Petition by Free Negroes for Equality Under the Law (1791), p. 32

📼 **ABC News Civics and Government Videotape Library**
*Mentor on the Court* (time: about 4 minutes)

▲ Before beginning the voyage to the Americas, many African men and women were imprisoned in European slave forts like San Sebastian in modern-day Ghana. Untold numbers of people died in terrible conditions in slave forts and slave ships. *Critical Thinking **How did the experiences of African men and women in slave forts typify the injustices of slavery?***

sold and forced to do their masters' bidding, however harsh the circumstances.

It took a civil war to end more than 200 years of slavery in this country. The 13th Amendment finally abolished slavery in 1865. Still, the Civil War and the ratification of that amendment did not end widespread racial discrimination in the United States.

3. Most of the gains the nation has made in translating the Constitution's guarantees of equality into a reality for all persons have come out of efforts made by and on behalf of African Americans. For example, the struggles of Martin Luther King, Jr., and others resulted in the Civil Rights Act of 1964 and then the Voting Rights Act of 1965; see pages 159–163.

America is now an inescapably multiracial society. Still, unlike whites, African Americans live with the consequences of America's history of racial discrimination every day of their lives. Of course, this is not to say that other groups of Americans have not also suffered the effects of discrimination. Clearly, many have.

### Native Americans

White settlers first began to arrive in America in relatively large numbers in the early middle years of the 17th century. At the time, some one million Native Americans were living in territory that was to become the United States.[2]

By 1900, however, their number had fallen to less than 250,000.

Diseases brought by white settlers had decimated those first Americans. So, too, did the succession of military campaigns that accompanied the westward expansion of the United States. To quote one historian, Thomas E. Patterson: "'The only good Indian is a dead Indian' is not simply a hackneyed expression from cowboy movies. It was part of the strategy of westward expansion, as settlers and U.S. troops mercilessly drove the eastern Indians from their ancestral lands to the Great Plains and then took those lands too."

Today, more than 2.4 million Native Americans live in this country. More than a third of them live on or near **reservations,** which are public lands set aside by a government for use by Native American tribes.

Like African Americans, Native Americans have been the victims of overwhelming discrimination. The consequences of that bias have been truly appalling, and they remain all too evident today. Poverty, joblessness, and alcoholism plague many reservations. The life expectancy of Native Americans living on reservations today is

---

[2]Most authorities estimate that there were some 8 to 10 million Native Americans living in all of North and South America in the mid-1600s.

## Answer to . . .

**Critical Thinking** They were kidnapped and imprisoned under horrible conditions; they were treated like animals.

10 years less than the national average, and the Native American infant mortality rate is three times that for white Americans.

## Hispanic Americans

Hispanic Americans are those in this country who have a Spanish-speaking background; many prefer to be called Latinos. Hispanics may be of any race. According to the Bilateral Commission on the Future of United States-Mexican Relations, Hispanic Americans "are among the world's most complex groupings of human beings. [The largest number] are white, millions . . . are mestizo, nearly half a million in the United States are black or mulatto."[3]

Hispanic Americans number more than 35 million. They now constitute the largest minority group of Americans. Hispanics replaced African Americans as the largest minority group in the United States around the year 2000.

Hispanic Americans can generally be divided into four main groups:

1. *Mexican Americans.* More than half of all Hispanics in the United States, at least 18 million persons, were either born in Mexico or trace their ancestry there. Those who were born in this country of Mexican parents are often called Chicanos.

The largest part of the Mexican American population lives in the States of California, Arizona, New Mexico, and Texas. Large cities such as El Paso and San Antonio, Texas, have Hispanic majorities, and smaller border cities such as Laredo and Brownsville, Texas, are over 90 percent Latino.

2. *Puerto Ricans.* Another large group of Hispanics has come to the mainland from the island of Puerto Rico. The population of the United States now includes some three million Puerto Ricans. Most of them have settled in New York, New Jersey, and in other parts of the Northeast.

3. *Cuban Americans.* The Hispanic population also includes some one million Cuban Americans. They are mostly people who fled the Castro dictatorship in Cuba and their descendants. A majority of Cuban Americans have settled in Miami and elsewhere in South Florida.

4. *Central and South Americans.* The fourth major subgroup of Hispanic Americans came here from Central and South America, many as **refugees.** A refugee is one who seeks protection (refuge) from war, persecution, or some other danger. More than three million persons have emigrated to the United States from Central and South American countries over the past 25 years; they have come in the largest numbers from Nicaragua, El Salvador, Guatemala, Colombia, and Chile. Many have also come from the Dominican Republic, an island nation in the Caribbean.

## Asian Americans

The story of white America's mistreatment of Asians is a lengthy one, too. They have faced discrimination from the first day they arrived in this country. As with all immigrant groups, assimilation into the white-dominated population has been difficult. **Assimilation** is the process by which people of one culture merge into and become part of another culture.

Chinese laborers were the first Asians to come to the United States in large numbers. They were brought here in the 1850s to 1860s as contract laborers to work in the mines and to

▲ Many Asian Americans, like this Vietnamese storeowner in Seattle, Washington, came to the United States from Southeast Asia in the 1970s and 1980s. People fled the turmoil of the Vietnam War and the Communist conquest of South Vietnam that followed. *Critical Thinking Did Vietnamese immigrants come to the United States for the same reasons as Chinese immigrants did a century earlier? Explain.*

---

[3]A mestizo is a person with both Spanish or Portuguese and Native American ancestry. A mulatto is a person with African and white ancestry.

## Customize for
### More Advanced Students

Divide students into four groups and assign each group the freshman, sophomore, junior, or senior class. Have each group conduct a poll to determine the ethnic composition of each class. Each group should create a pie chart to illustrate their findings. Display the graphs on a bulletin board and compare your school's composition with that of the United States as a whole.

## Background Note
### Common Misconceptions

Americans learn early that theirs is a diverse country. Yet, Americans travelling abroad for the first time are often surprised to learn that such diversity is not an American phenomenon. For example, Nigeria, the tenth most-populous country in the world, is home to 250 distinct ethnic groups. More than 800 languages are spoken in Papua New Guinea—a country with a population close to that of Los Angeles. Even countries that Americans view as especially homogenous, like France and Spain, are home to a wide variety of peoples, beliefs, religions, and languages. Developments in communications and transportation technology over the past century or so have made many parts of the world more diverse than they have ever been before—demographers note increasingly heterogeneous populations.

## Answer to . . .

**Critical Thinking** Possible answer: No; Chinese people in the mid-1800s were brought over specifically to labor on railroads.

### Background Note

#### Recent Scholarship

In the United States, "rights" have often been used to restrict rather than to enhance the status of women, asserts Linda Kerber in her book *No Constitutional Right to Be Ladies: Women and the Obligations of Citizenship.* Kerber relies on personal stories of real women—some heroic, many ordinary—in exploring the reasons for their dissatisfaction, the steps they took to challenge inequities, the legal barriers they encountered, and the achievements that resulted from their efforts. This thoughtful and engaging book deals specifically with property rights, obligations to work, restrictions on citizenship, taxation without representation, jury duty, and the benefits as well as responsibilities of military service.

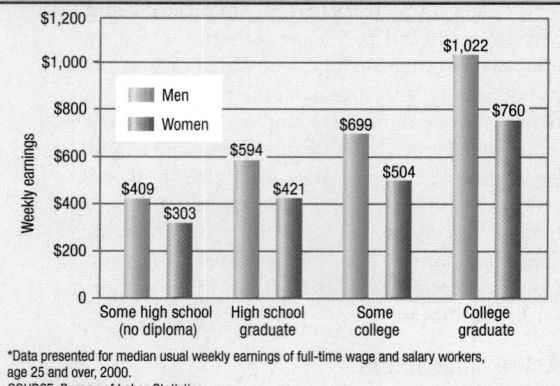

**Median Weekly Earnings of Men and Women***

*Data presented for median usual weekly earnings of full-time wage and salary workers, age 25 and over, 2000.
SOURCE: Bureau of Labor Statistics

*Interpreting Graphs* This graph illustrates how much money working men and women earned each week in 2000. **What does the graph show about equality in the workplace today?**

build railroads in the West. Many white Americans, native-born and immigrants, resented the competition of "coolie labor." Their resentments were frequently expressed in violence toward Asians.

Congress brought Chinese immigration nearly to a halt with the Chinese Exclusion Act of 1882. Because of this and other government actions, only a very small number of Chinese, Japanese, and other Asians were permitted to enter the United States for more than 80 years.

Early in World War II, the Federal Government ordered the evacuation of all persons of Japanese descent from the Pacific Coast. Some 120,000 people, two thirds of them native-born American citizens, were forcibly removed to inland "war relocation camps." Years later, the Government conceded that that action had been both unnecessary and unjust.

Congress made dramatic changes in American immigration policies in 1965. Since then, some four million Asian immigrants have come to this country, mostly from the Philippines, China, Korea, Vietnam, and India. The term "Asian American" describes an ever more diverse population. Asian Americans represent a tremendous variety of languages, religions, and cultures, and many recent immigrants from Asia have little in common with one another.

Today, the Asian American population exceeds 11 million, and it is the nation's fastest growing minority group. Today, Asian Americans live in every part of the United States. They are a majority of the population in Hawaii and more than 10 percent of that of California. New York City boasts the largest Chinese community outside of China itself.

## Discrimination Against Women

Unlike the several ethnic groups described here, women are not a minority in the United States. They are, in fact, a majority group. Still, traditionally in many instances in American law and public policy, women have not enjoyed the same rights as men. Their status was even lower, in many instances, than men who were themselves the target of virulent discrimination. Women have been treated as less than equal in a great many matters, including, for example, property rights, education, and employment opportunities.

Organized efforts to improve the place of women in American society date from July 19, 1848. On that date, a convention on women's rights, meeting in Seneca Falls, New York, adopted a set of resolutions that deliberately echoed the words of the Declaration of Independence. It began:

> **PRIMARY** **Sources** ❝*When, in the course of human events, it becomes necessary for one portion of the family of man to assume among the people of the earth a position different from that which they have hitherto occupied. . . . We hold these truths to be self-evident: that all men and women are created equal. . . .*❞
> —Declaration of Sentiments

Those who fought and finally won the long struggle for woman suffrage believed that, with the vote, women would soon achieve other basic rights. That assumption proved to be false. Although more than 51 percent of the population is female, women have held only a fraction of one percent of the nation's top public offices since 1789.

Even today, women hold little more than 10 percent of the 535 seats in Congress and little more than 20 percent of the 7,611 seats in the 50 State legislatures. Only five of the 50 State governors today are female. Women are also hugely underrepresented at the upper levels of corporate management and other power groups in the private sector. Fewer than 20 percent of the nation's doctors, lawyers, and college professors are women.

It is illegal to pay women less than men for the same work. The Equal Pay Act of 1963 requires employers to pay men and women the same wages if they perform the same jobs in the same establishment under the same working conditions. The Civil Rights Act of 1964 also prohibits job discrimination based on sex. Yet, nearly 40 years after Congress passed those laws, working women earn, on the average, less than 80 cents for every dollar earned by working men. See the graph on page 598.

Women earn less than men for a number of reasons—including the fact that the male work force is, over all, better educated and has more job experience than the female work force. (Note that these factors themselves can often be traced to discrimination.) In addition, some blame the so-called "Mommy track," in which women put their careers on hold to have children or work reduced hours to juggle child-care responsibilities. Others claim that a "glass ceiling" of discrimination in the corporate world and elsewhere, invisible but impenetrable, prevents women from rising to their full potential.

Certainly it is true that until quite recently women were limited to a narrow range of jobs. In many cases, women were encouraged to quit

▲ **Women's Work** Very few careers were open to women before the 1960s. Women with college degrees often took jobs as typists or secretaries, hoping for a rare opportunity to move up to better-paying jobs usually reserved for men.

working outside the house once they were married. Even now, more than three fourths of all jobs held by women are in low-paying clerical and service occupations. The Bureau of Labor Statistics reports that 98 percent of all secretaries today are women; so too are 96 percent of all child-care workers, 92 percent of all registered nurses, 89 percent of all waiters, 86 percent of all dieticians, and 89 percent of all bank tellers.

Efforts on behalf of equal rights for women have gained significant ground. However, that ground has not included the passage of an Equal Rights Amendment to the Constitution.

## Section 1 Assessment

**Key Terms and Main Ideas**

1. What defines a **heterogeneous** nation?
2. Name one factor that can lead a **refugee** to leave his or her country.
3. Who are **immigrants**?
4. What is the purpose of a **reservation**?

**Critical Thinking**

5. **Understanding Point of View** In what sense are women a unique group among those who have suffered discrimination?
6. **Drawing Inferences** Assimilation is a controversial issue for members of minority groups. List two reasons why a recent immigrant to the United States might try to assimilate. Then, list two reasons why an immigrant might choose to retain as much of his or her native land's culture as possible.

 **Take It to the Net**

7. Read about efforts to change discriminatory immigration laws in Congress. Select three different letters and write an essay that explains why people are criticizing the government and what is being done to respond. What do you think should be done? Use the links provided in the Social Studies area the at following Web site for help in completing this activity. **www.phschool.com**

## Point–of–Use Resources

**Guide to the Essentials** Chapter 21, Section 1, p. 112 provides support for students who need additional review of section content. Spanish support is available in the Spanish edition of the Guide on p. 105.

**Quiz** Unit 5 booklet, p. 30 includes matching and multiple-choice questions to check students' understanding of Section 1 content.

**Presentation Pro CD-ROM** Quizzes and multiple-choice questions check students' understanding of Section 1 content.

### Answers to . . .

### Section 1 Assessment

**1.** A heterogeneous nation has citizens of many different races and ethnic groups.
**2.** People legally admitted into a country as permanent residents.
**3.** Immigrants have to be legally admitted into the country as permanent residents.
**4.** To set aside public land for Native Americans to live on.
**5.** They constitute a majority of the population.
**6.** Answers will vary. For assimilation: To try to blend in and not feel different from other members of the community; to achieve social, educational, and economic mobility. Against: To maintain a sense of their family's history and identity; to preserve their national identities and pride; to retain the traditional values of their culture.

 **Take It to the Net**

7. Direct students to the Social Studies area at the Prentice Hall School Web site. The *Magruder's American Government* companion Web site includes the directions and links needed to complete the activity. It also provides a printable Internet activity worksheet with scoring rubrics for assessment. Essays should include examples and quotations from each of the letters.

# SKILLS FOR LIFE

## CHARTS and GRAPHS

### Reading Tables and Analyzing Statistics

**Focus** Have students find and evaluate census statistics and present them to the class.

**Instruct** Have students begin by writing a question that they might find the answer to in census data, such as "Which ethnic group had the largest increase in income in the 1990s?" Then have them collect census data in a library or online. (Links are provided at the *Magruder's* companion Web site. **www.phschool.com**) Use Steps 1 through 4 on this page to have them analyze the statistics they gather.

**Close/Reteach** Students should put their data on a poster or some other visible media for presenting it to the class. If appropriate, students may put the data into a line graph or bar graph. Have them briefly describe what the data show.

# Reading Tables and Analyzing Statistics

People have been collecting and analyzing statistics for a long time. For instance, the census—the practice of counting people—dates back at least to ancient Egypt. In our electronic age, collecting and storing data are becoming easier all the time. Therefore, reading and analyzing statistics are now much-needed skills. Use the steps below to help you interpret data tables:

**1. Determine the source of the information and decide if the source is reliable.** Faulty data produce faulty conclusions, so make sure your sources are accurate, complete, and trustworthy. A disreputable source might be sloppy in its data-gathering procedures, or it might edit out data that doesn't suit its purposes. Published government data are usually considered reliable. Be skeptical about information with an unfamiliar source or no source at all. (a) What is the source of the information in the table below? (b) Is the source reliable?

**2. Study the table to determine its purpose.** Information is collected for a variety of purposes: to compare and contrast, to show proportions, or to identify trends over time. What is the purpose of the table below?

**3. Identify relationships among the data.** Figure out percentage increases and decreases over time. (a) What ethnic group is expected to have the biggest percentage increase in number of households from 1995 to 2010? (b) Is the number of households of any ethnic group projected to decrease during that time?

**4. Draw conclusions.** The ethnic groups appear in order from the most households (white) to the fewest (American Indian, Eskimo, and Aleut) in 1995. (a) Is this ranking expected to change by 2010? (b) From this fact, state a one- or two-sentence conclusion.

### Test for Success

The number of Hispanic Americans is expected to surpass the number of African Americans within several years, making Hispanics the largest minority in the country. Given this fact, and using information from the table, what can you conclude about the size of households of these two groups?

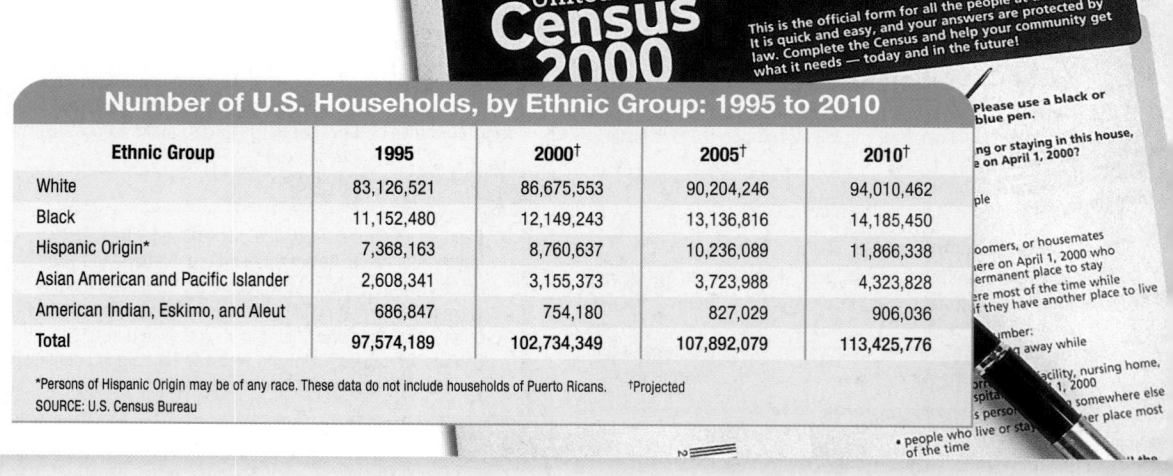

| Number of U.S. Households, by Ethnic Group: 1995 to 2010 | | | | |
|---|---|---|---|---|
| **Ethnic Group** | **1995** | **2000†** | **2005†** | **2010†** |
| White | 83,126,521 | 86,675,553 | 90,204,246 | 94,010,462 |
| Black | 11,152,480 | 12,149,243 | 13,136,816 | 14,185,450 |
| Hispanic Origin* | 7,368,163 | 8,760,637 | 10,236,089 | 11,866,338 |
| Asian American and Pacific Islander | 2,608,341 | 3,155,373 | 3,723,988 | 4,323,828 |
| American Indian, Eskimo, and Aleut | 686,847 | 754,180 | 827,029 | 906,036 |
| Total | 97,574,189 | 102,734,349 | 107,892,079 | 113,425,776 |

*Persons of Hispanic Origin may be of any race. These data do not include households of Puerto Ricans.   †Projected
SOURCE: U.S. Census Bureau

### Answers . . .

**1. (a)** The U.S. Census Bureau.
**(b)** Yes; it is considered a reliable source of information on American households and the economy.
**2.** To show in raw numbers how many U.S. households were made up of members of various ethnic groups in four different years.
**3. (a)** Asian American and Pacific Islander. **(b)** No.
**4. (a)** No. **(b)** Although U.S. households of every major ethnic group are expected to increase through the year 2010, the order from most (whites) to least (American Indian, Eskimo, and Aleut) is not expected to change.

### Test for Success

Since the *number* of Hispanics will surpass African Americans but the number of *households* will not, we might conclude that Hispanic households will have more members, on average, than black households.

### Point–of–Use Resources

📁 **Skills for Life Activity** Unit 5 booklet, p. 37 provides an additional skill activity for this chapter.

💿 **Social Studies Skills Tutor CD-ROM** Provides interactive practice in geographic literacy, critical thinking and reading, visual analysis, and communications.

# 2 Equality Before the Law

## Section Preview

### OBJECTIVES

1. **Explain** the importance of the Equal Protection Clause.
2. **Describe** the history of segregation in America.
3. **Examine** how classification by sex relates to discrimination.

### WHY IT MATTERS

The law includes safeguards to protect Americans from unfair discrimination on the basis of race or sex. The most important protections lie in the 5th and 14th amendments and the Civil Rights Act of 1964.

### POLITICAL DICTIONARY

★ segregation
★ Jim Crow law
★ separate-but-equal doctrine
★ integration
★ de jure segregation
★ de facto segregation

**Objectives** You may wish to call students' attention to the objectives in the Section Preview. The objectives are reflected in the main headings of the section.

**Bellringer** Ask students whether they think it would be reasonable for a police department to protect only those citizens under six feet tall. Have them briefly discuss their reasoning. Explain that in this section, they will learn about the Equal Protection Clause of the Constitution and how the government applies it.

**Vocabulary Builder** Ask students which term in the Political Dictionary fits best with the idea of equality before the law. *(integration)* Then have students try to differentiate among the remaining terms.

Records recently unearthed by the Architect of the Capitol show that at least 400 slaves worked on the building's construction from 1792 through 1800, and they likely did for several years thereafter.

Those records also indicate payments to a number of local slave owners—for example, "To Joseph Forest, for the hire of the Negro Charles." The slave owners were paid $5 a month for laborers. Slaves even cast the bronze statue of *Freedom* and hoisted it atop the Capitol in 1800.

## Equal Protection Clause

Nothing, not even a constitutional command, can *make* people equal in a literal sense. Individuals differ in strength, intelligence, height, and countless other ways. Still, the democratic ideal demands that government must treat all persons alike.

The equality of all persons, so boldly set out in the Declaration of Independence, is not proclaimed in so many words in the Constitution. Still, that concept pervades the document.

The closest approach to a literal statement of equality is to be found in the 14th Amendment's Equal Protection Clause. It declares:

> **FROM THE Constitution** "*No State shall . . . deny to any person within its jurisdiction the equal protection of the laws.*"
> —United States Constitution

The clause was originally intended to benefit newly freed slaves. Over time, it has acquired a broader meaning. Today, it forbids States and local governments to draw unreasonable distinctions between classes of persons. The Supreme Court has often held that the 5th Amendment's Due Process Clause puts the same restriction on the Federal Government.

### Reasonable Classification

Government must have the power to classify, to draw distinctions between persons and groups. Otherwise, it could not possibly regulate human behavior. That is to say, government must be able to discriminate—and it does. Thus, those who rob banks fall into a special class, and they receive special treatment by the law. That sort of discrimination is clearly reasonable.

Government may not discriminate *unreasonably,* however. Every State taxes the sale of cigarettes, and so taxes smokers but not nonsmokers. No State can tax only blonde smokers, however, or only male smokers.

Over time, the Supreme Court has rejected many equal protection challenges to the actions of government.

► *Freedom* atop the Capitol

### Pressed for Time?

### Quick Lesson Plan

1. **Focus** Tell students that the Constitution protects Americans from unfair discrimination. Ask students to discuss what they know about the history of segregation.
2. **Instruct** Ask students to explain what the Equal Protection Clause does. Lead a discussion about reasonable discrimination and how the Supreme Court tests for it. Then have students explore the history of discrimination against African Americans and women.
3. **Close/Reteach** Remind students that the Court has applied the Equal Protection Clause differently over time. Ask students to create a simple flowchart showing how discrimination against African Americans changed with various Court decisions and an act of Congress.

### ▣ Block Scheduling Strategies

Consider these suggestions to manage extended class time:
■ Divide the class into small groups. Ask each group to brainstorm a list of theoretical cases or laws that relate to equal protection. Then ask a member of each group to present each case or law to the rest of the class. The class should apply the rational basis and strict scrutiny test to each case, and then decide on its constitutionality.

■ After students have read about segregation and gender-based discrimination, have them consider whether there are any situations where these should be allowed. *(for example, private clubs, separate facilities in jails and hospitals, etc.)* Have students write short paragraphs explaining each situation or explaining why discrimination should never be allowed under any circumstances.

**601**

# *Voices* on Government

In 1955, **Rosa Parks** refused to give her seat to a white man on a bus in Montgomery, Alabama, and was subsequently arrested. That simple act led to a bus boycott by African Americans and helped the civil rights movement grow into a national cause. Parks, who had long worked for civil rights, later explained her brave action:

"*For half of my life there were laws and customs in the South that kept African Americans segregated from Caucasians and allowed white people to treat black people without any respect. I never thought this was fair, and from the time I was a child, I tried to protest against disrespectful treatment. But it was very hard to do anything about segregation and racism when white people had the power of the law behind them. Somehow we had to change the laws.*"

## Evaluating the Quotation

*From what you have read, how did court decisions combine with changes in the law to move the nation toward protecting civil rights?*

More often than not, the Supreme Court has found that what those governments have done is, in fact, constitutional.[4]

### The Rational Basis Test

The Supreme Court most often decides equal protection cases by applying a standard known as the rational basis test. This test asks: Does the classification in question bear a reasonable relationship to the achievement of some proper governmental purpose?

A California case, *Michael M. v. Superior Court*, 1981, illustrates that test. California law says that a man who has sexual relations with a girl under 18 to whom he is not married can be prosecuted for statutory rape. However, the girl

---

[4]The Court has voided a number of those actions on equal protection grounds, however. You will consider several of those cases in a moment, and you have encountered many others previously—for example, with regard to lengthy residence requirements for voting purposes and gerrymandering on the basis of race.

cannot be charged with that crime, even if she is a willing partner. The Court found the law to bear a reasonable relationship to a proper public policy goal: preventing teenage pregnancies.

### The Strict Scrutiny Test

The Supreme Court imposes a more demanding standard in some equal protection cases, however. This is especially true when a case deals with (1) such "fundamental rights" as the right to vote, the right to travel between the States, or 1st Amendment rights; or (2) such "suspect classifications" as those based on race, sex, or national origin.

In these instances, the Court has said that a law must meet a higher standard than the rational basis test. This standard is called the strict scrutiny test. The State must be able to show that some "compelling governmental interest" justifies the distinctions it has drawn.

An alimony case, *Orr v. Orr*, 1979, involved the use of that stricter test. An Alabama law that made women but not men eligible for alimony was held unconstitutional, as a denial of equal protection—because the law's distinction between men and women did not serve a compelling governmental interest.

## Segregation in America

Beginning in the late 1800s, nearly half of the States passed racial segregation laws. **Segregation** means the separation of one group from another. Most of those **Jim Crow laws**—laws that separate people on the basis of race—were aimed at African Americans. Some were also drawn to affect Mexican Americans, Asians, and Native Americans. These laws required segregation by race in the use of both public and private facilities: schools, parks and playgrounds, hotels and restaurants, streetcars, even public drinking fountains.

### Separate-but-Equal Doctrine

In 1896, the Supreme Court provided a constitutional basis for Jim Crow laws by creating the **separate-but-equal doctrine.** In *Plessy v. Ferguson,* it upheld a Louisiana law requiring segregation in rail coaches. The Court held that the law did not violate the Equal Protection Clause because the separate facilities provided for African Americans were equal to those for whites.

The separate-but-equal doctrine became the constitutional justification for segregation by race in several other fields for nearly 60 years. Indeed, until the late 1930s, little effort was made by government even to see that the separate accommodations for African Americans were, in fact, equal to those reserved to whites. More often than not, they were not.

### Brown v. Board of Education

The Supreme Court first began to chip away at the separate-but-equal doctrine in *Missouri ex rel. Gaines* v. *Canada* in 1938. Lloyd Gaines, an African American, was denied admission to the law school at the all-white University of Missouri. Gaines was fully qualified for admission—except for his race. The State did not have a separate law school for African Americans. However, it did offer to pay his tuition at a public law school in any of four neighboring States, which did not discriminate by race. Gaines, however, insisted on a legal education in his home State.

The Supreme Court held that the separate-but-equal doctrine left the State of Missouri with only two choices: It could either (1) admit Gaines to the State's law school or (2) establish a separate-but-equal school for him. The State gave in and admitted Gaines.

Over the next several years, the Court took an increasingly rigorous attitude toward the requirement of equal facilities. It began to insist on equality *in fact* between separate facilities. Finally, in an historic decision in 1954, the Court reversed *Plessy* v. *Ferguson*. In *Brown* v. *Board of Education of Topeka*, it struck down the laws of four States requiring or allowing separate public schools for white and African American students.[5]

Unanimously, the Supreme Court held that segregation by race in public education is unconstitutional:

> **PRIMARY Sources** "Does segregation of children in public schools solely on the basis of race, even though the physical facilities and other 'tangible' factors may be equal, deprive the children of the minority group of equal educational opportunities? We believe that it does.
>
> . . . To separate them from others of similar age and qualifications solely because of their race generates a feeling of inferiority

▲ **The Migrants Cast Their Ballots** Beginning in the last century, many African Americans left the South for jobs in northern cities. Migrants encountered fewer Jim Crow laws in the North, but faced discrimination that closed them out of good jobs, schools, and housing. Artist Jacob Lawrence captured the lives of African Americans in works such as *The Migrants Cast Their Ballots*.

> as to their status in the community that may affect their hearts and minds in a way unlikely ever to be undone. . . . We conclude that in the field of public education the doctrine of 'separate but equal' has no place. Separate educational facilities are inherently unequal. "
> —Chief Justice Earl Warren, Opinion of the Court

The Court in 1955 directed the States to make "a prompt and reasonable start" and to end segregation "with all deliberate speed." Federal district courts were ordered to supervise the desegregation process.

A "reasonable start" was made in Baltimore, Louisville, St. Louis, and elsewhere. In most of the Deep South, however, "massive resistance" soon developed. State legislatures passed laws and school boards worked to block **integration,** which is the process of bringing a group into equal membership in society. Most of these steps were clearly unconstitutional, but challenging them was costly and slow.

[5]Kansas, Delaware, South Carolina, and Virginia. On the same day, it also struck down racially segregated public schools in the District of Columbia, under the 5th Amendment, *Bolling* v. *Sharpe*, 1954.

## CONSTITUTIONAL PRINCIPLES

### Judicial Review
Judicial review has played an active role in the history of American civil rights. In the area of school segregation and integration, its role is still evolving. The 1971 *Swann* decision and the subsequent court-ordered busing across the nation resulted in a backlash from parents and educators who felt that forced integration actually emphasized racial discrimination. In 1999 in Massachusetts, the Boston School Committee, facing a federal lawsuit against its race-conscious admissions policies for schools, voted to end that city's 25-year-long "experiment" with school busing.

### Activity
Have students write letters to the school committee of their city or county in which they argue for or against school busing. Encourage students to cite historical precedents and relevant Supreme Court cases, and to express a strong opinion in their letters.

## The *Living* Constitution

### The Supreme Court and Civil Rights

In 1875 Congress passed a law guaranteeing equal access to public accommodations for all Americans of "every race or color." When many white-owned businesses refused to comply with the act, African Americans took their case to the courts. In 1883 the U.S. Supreme Court struck down the law. Justice John Marshal Harlan, who strongly disagreed with the decision, expressed his outrage by writing his dissent with the pen used to draft the notorious *Dred Scott* decision, which helped trigger the Civil War by denying citizenship to all black Americans.

### Using the Time Line

Discuss why Justice Harlan used the pen from *Dred Scott* to write his dissent. *(It symbolized his belief that the decision, like the* Dred Scott *decision, was an outrageous violation of African American civil liberties.)* Then have students classify the court decisions on the time line according to whether they supported or restricted civil rights.

### Point-of-Use Resources

📁 **The Living Constitution** Two extension activities for this time line are presented on pp. 17–18.

📇 **Basic Principles of the Constitution Transparencies** Transparency 5, *The Living Constitution: The Supreme Court and Civil Rights*

---

The pace of desegregation quickened after Congress passed the Civil Rights Act of 1964. That act forbids the use of federal funds to aid any State or local activity in which racial segregation is practiced. It directed the Justice Department to file suits to prompt desegregation actions.

The Supreme Court quickened the pace in 1969. In a case from Mississippi, *Alexander v. Holmes County Board of Education,* it ruled that, after 15 years, the time for "all deliberate speed" had ended. Said a unanimous Court: "The continued operation of segregated schools under a standard allowing for 'all deliberate speed' . . . is no longer constitutionally permissible."

### De Jure, De Facto Segregation

By fall 1970, school systems characterized by **de jure segregation** had been abolished. De jure segregation is segregation by law, with legal sanction. That is not to say that desegregation had been fully accomplished—far from it.[6]

Many recent integration controversies have come in places where the schools have never been segregated by law. They have occurred, instead, in communities in which **de facto segregation** has long been present, and continues. De facto segregation is segregation in fact, even if no law requires it. Housing patterns have most often been its major cause. The concentration of African Americans in certain sections of cities inevitably led to local school systems in which some schools are largely African American. That condition is apparent in many northern as well as southern communities.

Efforts to desegregate those school systems have taken several forms. School district lines have been redrawn and the busing of students out of racially segregated neighborhoods has been tried. These efforts have brought strong protests in many places and violence in some.

The Supreme Court first sanctioned busing in a North Carolina case, *Swann v. Charlotte-Mecklenburg Board of Education,* 1971. There it held that "desegregation plans cannot be limited to walk-in schools." Since then, busing has been used to increase the racial mix in many school districts across the country. In some cases busing is by court order; in others it is voluntary.

### Segregation in Other Fields

This nation has not yet achieved a complete integration of the public schools, but legally enforced racial segregation in all other areas of life has been eliminated. Many State and local laws have been repealed or struck down by the courts.

---

[6]Some States, several school districts, and many parents and private groups have sought to avoid integrated schools through established or, often, newly created private schools. On the point, see the Court's rulings in *Runyon* v. *McCrary,* 1976, page 570.

---

# The *Living* Constitution

## The Supreme Court and Civil Rights                                1900

The Constitution describes Americans' civil rights only in general terms. The courts, especially the Supreme Court, have had to decide how these constitutional guarantees apply to specific situations. As the time line entries show, some Court decisions have supported and broadened civil rights, while other decisions have restricted them.

**1883** In the *Civil Rights Cases,* the Court rules that the 14th Amendment does not ban racial discrimination by private individuals or businesses.

**1896** In *Plessy* v. *Ferguson,* the Court rules that "separate but equal" facilities for different races are acceptable.

The Supreme Court has found segregation by race to be as unconstitutional in other areas as it is in public education. It has held that the Equal Protection Clause forbids segregation in: public swimming pools or other recreational facilities, *Baltimore* v. *Dawson*, 1955; local transportation, *Gayle* v. *Browder*, 1956; and State prisons and local jails, *Lee* v. *Washington*, 1968. The High Court struck down all State miscegenation laws (laws that forbid interracial marriages) in *Loving* v. *Virginia*, 1967. It has held that race cannot be the basis for a child custody decision, *Palmore* v. *Sidoti*, 1984.

## Classification by Sex

The Constitution speaks of the civil rights of "the people," "persons," and "citizens." Nowhere does it make its guarantees only to "men" or separately to "women." The only reference to sex is in the 19th Amendment, which forbids denial of the right to vote "on account of sex."

Gender has long been used as a basis of classification in the law, however. By and large, that practice reflected society's historic view of the "proper" role of women. Most often, laws that treated men and women differently were intended to protect "the weaker sex." Over the years, the Supreme Court read that view into the 14th Amendment. It did not find *any*

sex-based classification to be unconstitutional until 1971.

In the first case to challenge sex discrimination, *Bradwell* v. *Illinois*, 1873, the Court upheld a State law barring women from the practice of law. In that case, Justice Joseph P. Bradley wrote that:

 **PRIMARY Sources** "*The civil law, as well as nature itself, has always recognized a wide difference in the respective spheres and destinies of man and woman. Man is, or should be, woman's protector and defender. The natural and proper timidity and delicacy of the female sex evidently unfits it for many of the occupations of civil life.*"
—Concurring Opinion

Even as late as 1961, in *Hoyt* v. *Florida*, the Court could find no constitutional fault with a law that required men to serve on juries, but gave women the choice of serving or not.

Matters are far different today. The Court now takes a very close look at cases involving claims of sex discrimination. The first such case was *Reed* v. *Reed*, 1971, in which the Court struck down an Idaho law that gave fathers preference over mothers in the administration of their children's estates.

Since then, the Supreme Court has found a number of sex-based distinctions to be unconstitutional. In *Taylor* v. *Louisiana*, 1975, the Court held that the Equal Protection Clause forbids the

ACTIVITY

## Extended Class Periods

**Time** 90 minutes.
**Purpose** Create graffiti boards.
**Grouping** Groups of four to six students.
**Activity** Divide chalkboards in the classroom so that each group has its own space. Have students use colored chalk to create graffiti boards illustrating their opinions about discrimination.
**Roles** All group members should participate as "artists" and express their opinions.
**Close** Allow students to discuss their boards and compare their work with other groups.

■ **Block Strategy (Basic)**

## Point-of-Use Resources

▱ **Block Scheduling with Lesson Strategies** Additional activities for Chapter 21 appear on p. 29.

▱ **Close Up on the Supreme Court** *Plessy* v. *Ferguson* (1896), pp. 36–37; *Powell* v. *Alabama* (1932), pp. 40–41; *Brown* v. *Board of Education of Topeka* (1954), pp. 42–43

**1944** In *Korematsu* v. *United States*, the Court upholds the internment of Japanese Americans during World War II.

**1954** In *Brown* v. *Board of Education*, the Court rules that "separate but equal" public schools are unconstitutional.

**1988** In *New York State Club Association* v. *City of New York*, the Court upholds a law that stops most private clubs from denying membership to women.

| 1925 | 1950 | 1975 | 2000 |
|---|---|---|---|

### Analyzing Time Lines

1. Which Supreme Court decision endorsed the principle of "separate but equal" facilities? Which decision rejected this idea?
2. Besides African Americans, what groups of people could be affected by the Supreme Court's recent civil rights rulings?

**1978** In *Regents of University of California* v. *Bakke*, the Court rules that affirmative action is acceptable but strict quotas are not.

**2001** In *Hunt* v. *Cromartie*, the Court holds that, while race cannot be the controlling factor in drawing electoral district lines, it can be one of the several factors that shape that process.

## Preparing for Standardized Tests

Have students read the passages under *Classification by Sex* on pp. 605–606 and then answer the question below.

Which of the following would be a valid reason for upholding a law that treats men and women differently?

**A** Gender discrimination is not unconstitutional.

**B** Men and women are fundamentally different.

Ⓒ The law serves a legitimate governmental objective.

**D** The Constitution does not mention gender.

### Answers to . . .

**Analyzing Time Lines 1.** *Plessy* v. *Ferguson*; *Brown* v. *Board of Education*. **2.** Recent rulings affect women and persons belonging to any minority group.

## Point-of-Use Resources

**Guide to the Essentials** Chapter 21, Section 2, p. 113 provides support for students who need additional review of section content. Spanish support is available in the Spanish edition of the Guide on p. 106.

**Quiz** Unit 5 booklet, p. 32 includes matching and multiple-choice questions to check students' understanding of Section 2 content.

**Presentation Pro CD-ROM** Quizzes and multiple-choice questions check students' understanding of Section 2 content.

## Answers to . . .

### Section 2 Assessment

**1.** Jim Crow laws discriminated against African Americans by separating them from whites.
**2.** *Brown* v. *Board of Education of Topeka.*
**3.** *De jure* means segregation by law; *de facto* means segregation in fact.
**4.** The Supreme Court created the separate-but-equal doctrine, which allowed for the establishment of separate but equal facilities for African Americans and whites.
**5.** Answers will vary. Students may suggest that de facto segregation would be harder to combat because it requires a change in behavior.
**6. (a)** That the civil law recognized different spheres for men and women.
**(b)** That nature recognizes different spheres and destinies for men and women; that men should be the protectors of women; that because women are naturally timid and delicate, they are unfit for certain jobs.

States to exclude women from jury service. It has also struck down an Oklahoma law that prohibited the sale of beer to males under 21 and to females under 18, *Craig* v. *Boren,* 1976. Also unconstitutional is the practice of refusing to admit women to the rigorous citizen-soldier program offered by a public institution, Virginia Military Institute, *United States* v. *Virginia,* 1996.

In the same vein, the Supreme Court has upheld a California law that prohibits community service clubs from excluding women from membership, *Rotary International* v. *Rotary Club of Duarte,* 1987. It also upheld a New York City ordinance that forbids sex discrimination in any place of public accommodation, including large private-membership clubs used by their members for business purposes, *New York State Club Association, Inc.* v. *City of New York,* 1988.

The Court's present attitude was put this way in *Frontiero* v. *Richardson,* 1973:

 **PRIMARY Sources** **"***There can be no doubt that our nation has had a long and unfortunate history of sex discrimination. Traditionally, such discrimination was rationalized by an attitude of 'romantic paternalism' which, in practical effect, put women, not on a pedestal, but in a cage.***"**[7]
—Justice William J. Brennan, Jr.,
Opinion of the Court

Not all sex-based distinctions are unconstitutional, however. The Supreme Court has

upheld some of them in several cases. You saw one example of this in *Michael M.* v. *Superior Court,* 1981. Similarly, the Court has upheld a Florida law that gives an extra property tax exemption to widows, but not to widowers, *Kahn* v. *Shevin,* 1974; an Alabama law forbidding women to serve as prison guards in all-male penitentiaries, *Dothard* v. *Rawlinson,* 1977; and the federal selective service law that requires only men to register for the draft and excludes women from any future draft, *Rostker* v. *Goldberg,* 1981.

In effect, these cases say this: Classification by sex is not in and of itself unconstitutional. However, laws that treat men and women differently will be overturned by the courts unless (1) they are intended to serve an "important governmental objective" and (2) they are "substantially related" to achieving that goal.

In upholding the all-male draft, the Court found that Congress did in fact have an important governmental objective: to raise and support armies and, if necessary, to do so by "a draft of combat troops." "Since women are excluded from combat," said the Supreme Court, they may properly be excluded from the draft.

---

[7]In this case the Court, for the first time, struck down a federal law providing for sex-based discrimination, as a violation of the 5th Amendment's Due Process Clause. That law gave various housing, medical, and other allowances to a serviceman for his wife and other dependents, but it made those same allowances available to a servicewoman only if her husband was dependent on her for more than half of his support.

## Section **2** Assessment

**Key Terms and Main Ideas**
1. What was the purpose of **Jim Crow laws?**
2. Which important Supreme Court case led to school **integration?**
3. Explain the difference between **de jure segregation** and **de facto segregation.**
4. Who developed the **separate-but-equal doctrine?** What does that doctrine say?

**Critical Thinking**
5. **Making Decisions** In your opinion, which would be harder to combat, de facto or de jure segregation? Why?

6. **Recognizing Bias** Read the quote from Justice Bradley on page 605. **(a)** What is the only statement that can be considered a fact, and not an opinion? **(b)** List three opinions included in the quote.

 **Take It to the Net**

7. Learn more about how the courts have handled discrimination cases. Select several cases and outline the major points of each one. Are the outcomes of the cases similar? Use the links provided in the Social Studies area at the following Web site for help in completing this activity. **www.phschool.com**

**Take It to the Net**

**7.** Direct students to the Social Studies area at the Prentice Hall School Web site. The *Magruder's American Government* companion Web site includes the directions and links needed to complete the activity. It also provides a printable Internet activity worksheet with scoring rubrics for assessment. Outlines should accurately compare the cases and include specific examples from each.

# on Primary Sources

## Breaking Down Barriers

*Ernest Green was the first black student to graduate from Central High School in Little Rock, Arkansas. Mr. Green recalls the historic days in 1957 when, as one of the "Little Rock Nine," he helped bring an end to school segregation in the United States.*

When the U.S. Supreme Court handed down its historic *Brown* v. *Board of Education of Topeka, Kansas,* decision in 1954, I was a student in Little Rock, Arkansas, finishing the eighth grade. Little Rock had one high school for blacks . . . and one for whites, Little Rock Central High School. . . .

The *Brown* decision made me feel that the U.S. Constitution was finally working for me. . . . I could believe I was a full citizen, not a second-class citizen as segregation had made me feel.

In the spring of 1957, I was asked, along with other black students in Little Rock, to consider attending Central High School the following fall. Initially, a number of students signed up to enroll, but when fall came, only nine of us had survived the pressure to quit. . . .

During the summer, rumors began to circulate that there might be violence if the "Little Rock Nine," as we became known, tried to attend school in the fall. I didn't pay much attention to what was going on. . . .

But when we tried to attend school, we were met by an angry white mob and armed soldiers. Arkansas Governor Orval Faubus had called out the National Guard to prevent us from enrolling, defying a federal court order to integrate Little Rock schools. Governor Faubus said he was doing this to protect the peace and tranquility of the community; obviously, my rights were secondary. . . .

Finally, President Dwight Eisenhower called out the U.S. Army's famous 101st Airborne Division to protect us and enforce the federal court's integration order. . . .

When we tried to attend school again, about 1,000 paratroopers were there to protect us. We rode to school in an army station wagon, surrounded by army jeeps that were loaded with soldiers holding machine guns and drawn bayonets. It was an exciting ride to school!

Once we got inside, it was like being in a war zone. We were harassed, our books were destroyed, and our lockers were broken into several times a day. . . .

I was a senior that year. As graduation neared, I was surprised at the number of students who signed my yearbook, saying they admired my courage in sticking it out. But on the night of graduation, there was an eerie silence when my name was called. I didn't care that no one clapped for me. I knew that not only had I achieved something for myself, but I had broken a barrier as well.

*Ernest Green shows his textbooks to children in Little Rock.*

### Analyzing Primary Sources

1. Why did Green decide to enroll in Central High School?
2. What resistance did the "Little Rock Nine" encounter when they tried to enroll at the school?
3. How was Green finally able to attend the school?
4. Why would attending Central High School have made Green feel that he was no longer a "second-class citizen"?

## Corner

📁 **Close Up on Primary Sources** The Struggle for Integration, p. 23, extends this feature with a primary source activity.

 **Online**

To keep up-to-date on Close Up news and activities, visit Close Up Online at

**www.closeup.org**

---

## Breaking Down Barriers

**Focus** Ask students to describe ways in which racial segregation existed in the United States during the mid-1950s. *(Answers will vary but should state that buses, drinking fountains, and even schools were segregated during this period.)*

**Instruct** Summarize the *Brown* case and decision for students, emphasizing its significance for civil rights. Then ask students to discuss the various viewpoints of the people involved in the "Little Rock Nine" integration. What was Governor Orval Faubus's reasoning for blocking the integration? What was President Eisenhower's reasoning for ordering U.S. Army protection? What was Ernest Green's reasoning for choosing to take part in the desegregation process?

**Close/Reteach** Have students consider Ernest Green's comments about graduation that are found in the last paragraph of the article. Ask students to explain the significance of the barrier he broke.

💿 **Keep It Current CD-ROM** includes government-related projects by unit. The CD-ROM links to the Prentice Hall School Web site and may be used for daily updates.

*Answers to . . .*

**Analyzing Primary Sources**

**1.** He wanted to be a "full citizen" rather than the "second-class citizen" he felt like under segregation.

**2.** They were harassed by an angry white mob, and the governor used the National Guard to keep them from enrolling.

**3.** The President used a division of the Army to enforce the integration order and to protect the students.

**4.** Answers will vary, but students should recognize that even if separate facilities were physically equal, segregation made black students feel inherently inferior. Therefore, attending Central High was a step up for Green.

## 3 Federal Civil Rights Laws

## Section Preview

### OBJECTIVES

1. **Outline** the history of civil rights legislation from Reconstruction to today.
2. **Explore** the issues surrounding affirmative action.

### WHY IT MATTERS

Federal laws passed in the 1960s and later ended long-standing discrimination in voting, housing, public accommodations, and many other areas. Affirmative action policies remain controversial.

### POLITICAL DICTIONARY

★ **affirmative action**
★ **quota**
★ **reverse discrimination**

You may have heard this oft-made argument: "You can't legislate morality." That is, racism, sexism, and other forms of discrimination cannot be eliminated merely with laws.

Martin Luther King, Jr., replied to that contention this way: "Laws," he said, "may not change the heart, but they can restrain the heartless." Congress has agreed with Dr. King—as it has enacted a number of civil rights laws over the past 40 years.

## Civil Rights: Reconstruction to Today

From the 1870s to the late 1950s, Congress did not pass a single piece of meaningful civil rights legislation. Several factors contributed to that sorry fact. First, through that period the nation's predominantly white population was generally unaware of or little concerned with the plight of African Americans, Native Americans, or other nonwhites in this country. Secondly, southern white Democrats, bolstered by such devices as the seniority system and the filibuster, held many of the most strategic posts in Congress.

◄ Martin Luther King, Jr.

That historic logjam was broken in 1957, very largely as a result of the pressures brought to bear by the civil rights movement led by Dr. King (see Chapter 6, pages 159–163). Beginning in that year, Congress passed a number of civil rights laws—notably, the Civil Rights Acts of 1957, 1960, 1964, and 1968 and the Voting Rights Acts of 1965, 1970, 1975, and 1982. The 1957 and 1960 laws set up modest safeguards for the right to vote.[8]

### The Civil Rights Act of 1964

The 1964 law is the most far-reaching of these statutes. It passed after the longest debate in the Senate's history (83 days), and only after the Senate had invoked cloture to kill a filibuster.

Beyond its voting rights provisions, the 1964 law outlaws discrimination in a number of areas. With its several later amendments, the law's major sections now:

(1) provide that no person may be denied access to or refused service in various "public accommodations" because of race, color, religion, or national origin (Title II).[9]

---

[8] You considered the voting rights provision in these statutes in Chapter 6. See pages 160–163. The 1957 law created the U.S. Civil Rights Commission. The commission is an independent eight-member agency that is supposed to monitor the enforcement of the various civil rights laws, investigate cases of alleged discrimination, and report its findings to the President, Congress, and the public.

[9] Congress based this section of the law on its commerce power; see Chapter 11, pages 294–300. Title II covers those places in which lodgings are offered to transient guests and those where a significant portion of the items sold have moved in interstate commerce. The Supreme Court upheld Title II and the use of the Commerce Clause as a basis for civil rights legislation in *Heart of Atlanta Motel, Inc.* v. *United States*, 1964.

(2) prohibit discrimination against any person on grounds of race, color, religion, national origin, sex, or physical disability in any program that receives any federal funding; require the cut-off of federal funds to any program that practices such discrimination (Title VI).

(3) forbid employers and labor unions to discriminate against any person on grounds of race, color, religion, sex, physical disability, or age in job-related matters (Title VII).[10]

## The Civil Rights Act of 1968

The Civil Rights Act of 1968 is often called the Open Housing Act. With minor exceptions, it forbids anyone to refuse to sell or rent a dwelling to any person on grounds of race, color, religion, national origin, sex, or disability. It also forbids refusal to sell or rent to a family with children. At first, the burden of enforcing the law fell on those persons who claimed to be the victims of housing discrimination. Congress finally strengthened the law in 1988, by allowing the Justice Department to bring criminal charges against those who violate its terms.

## Affirmative Action

These several civil rights statutes all come down to this: Discriminatory practices based on such factors as race, color, national origin, or sex are illegal. But what about the effects of past discrimination? Consider an African American who, for no reason of his or her own making, did not get a decent education and so today cannot get a decent job. Of what real help to that person are all of those laws that make illegal today what was done years ago?

So far, the Federal Government's chief answer to this troubling question has been a policy of **affirmative action.** That policy requires that most employers take positive steps (affirmative action) to remedy the effects of past discriminations. The policy applies to all the agencies of the Federal Government, to all the States and their local governments, and to all those private employers who sell goods or services to any agency of the Federal Government.

---
[10]The 1964 law also created the Equal Employment Opportunity Commission. The five-member EEOC's major responsibility is the enforcement of Title VII.

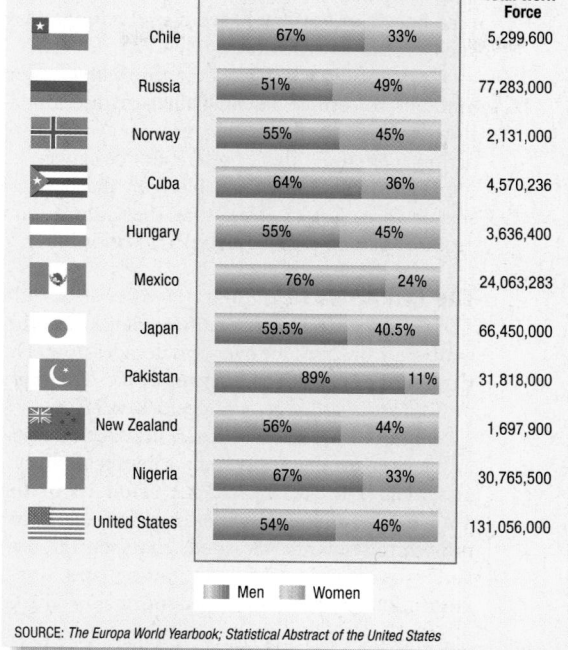

### Comparative Government

#### Men and Women in the Work Force, Selected Countries

| | | Men | Women | Total Work Force |
|---|---|---|---|---|
| ★ | Chile | 67% | 33% | 5,299,600 |
| | Russia | 51% | 49% | 77,283,000 |
| | Norway | 55% | 45% | 2,131,000 |
| | Cuba | 64% | 36% | 4,570,236 |
| | Hungary | 55% | 45% | 3,636,400 |
| | Mexico | 76% | 24% | 24,063,283 |
| ● | Japan | 59.5% | 40.5% | 66,450,000 |
| | Pakistan | 89% | 11% | 31,818,000 |
| | New Zealand | 56% | 44% | 1,697,900 |
| | Nigeria | 67% | 33% | 30,765,500 |
| | United States | 54% | 46% | 131,056,000 |

■ Men   ■ Women

SOURCE: *The Europa World Yearbook; Statistical Abstract of the United States*

**Interpreting Graphs** This graph shows the percentage of men and women in the work force in selected countries. *(a) In which two countries are the lowest percentages of women employed? (b) In which two countries are the highest percentages of women employed?*

The Federal Government began to demand the adoption of affirmative action programs in 1965. Some programs are simply plans that call for the wide advertisement of job openings. Most, however, establish guidelines and timetables to overcome past discriminations.

To illustrate the policy, take the case of a company that does business with the Federal Government. That private business must adopt an affirmative action plan designed to make its work force reflect the general makeup of the population in its locale. The company's program must also include steps to correct or prevent inequalities in such matters as pay, promotions, and fringe benefits.

For many employers this has meant that they must hire and/or promote more workers with

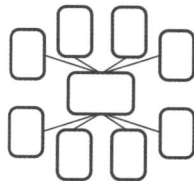

## Heterogeneous Groups

**Enrichment** Separate the class into small groups. Provide each group with a large piece of butcher paper, art supplies, magazines, newspapers, and other historical resources. Ask groups to make a collage that highlights the significance of Martin Luther King, Jr.'s quote about discrimination: "Laws may not change the heart, but they can restrain the heartless." Encourage students to use magazine clippings, copies of photographs, original drawings, or any other artwork to present their interpretation of Dr. King's message. Ask for volunteers to share their group's work with the class.

**(Basic)**

## Background Note

### Behind the Scenes

The Senate debate of the first Civil Rights Act of 1957 was a lengthy one, due in part to the efforts of Senator Strom Thurmond. Thurmond, a Democrat from South Carolina who opposed the bill, filibustered for 24 hours and 18 minutes—the longest filibuster in Senate history. Thurmond used his time to read the texts of the election laws for all 48 States. Other senators refused to help Thurmond because they believed that a filibuster would anger supporters of the bill and draw criticism of Southern Democrats opposing the bill. Despite this momentous one-person effort, the bill was eventually passed, paving the way for future civil rights legislation.

## Answer to . . .

**Critical Thinking** By holding that race could not be the *only* factor in affirmative action decisions but could be *a* factor, the Court left the door open to future interpretations.

minority backgrounds and more females. Such rules requiring certain numbers of jobs or promotions for members of certain groups are called **quotas.**

### Reverse Discrimination?

Affirmative action programs necessarily involve race-based and/or sex-based classifications. Are such programs constitutional?

Critics of the policy say that affirmative action amounts to **reverse discrimination,** or discrimination against the majority group. Affirmative action demands that preference be given to females and/or nonwhites solely on the basis of sex or race. Critics insist that the Constitution requires that all public policies be "color blind."

### The Bakke Case

The Supreme Court has been wrestling with affirmative action cases for over two decades now. The Court's first major case, *Regents of the University of California* v. *Bakke,* was decided in 1978.

Allan Bakke, a white male, had been denied admission to that university's medical school at Davis. The school had set aside 16 of the 100 seats in each year's entering class for nonwhite students. He sued, charging the university with reverse discrimination and, so, a violation of the 14th Amendment's Equal

▲ Allan Bakke (left) successfully challenged the admissions policies of the University of California. *Critical Thinking How did the* Bakke *case leave the legal status of affirmative action unsettled?*

Protection Clause. By a 5–4 majority, the Court held that Bakke had been denied equal protection and should be admitted to the medical school.

A differently composed 5–4 majority made the more far-reaching ruling in the case, however. Although the Constitution does not allow race to be used as the *only* factor in the making of affirmative action decisions, both the Constitution and the 1964 Civil Rights Act do allow its use as one among several factors in such situations.

### Later Cases

The Supreme Court has decided several affirmative action cases since *Bakke.* In some of them it has upheld quotas, especially when longstanding, flagrant discrimination was involved.

In *United Steelworkers* v. *Weber,* 1979, the Kaiser Aluminum Company had created training programs intended to increase the number of skilled African Americans in its work force. Trainees were chosen on the basis of race and seniority. Brian Weber, a white worker, was rejected for training three times. Each time, however, a number of African Americans with less seniority were picked.

Weber went to court. The Court found that the training programs, although built on quotas, did not violate the 1964 law. That law, it said, Congress had purposely designed to "overcome manifest racial imbalances."

*Fullilove* v. *Klutznick,* 1980, was another case in which the Court upheld quotas. That case centered on a law Congress had passed that provided $4 billion in grants to State and local governments for public works projects. It also contained a "minority set-aside" provision. The provision required that at least 10 percent of each grant had to be set aside for minority-owned businesses.

A white contractor challenged the set-asides. He argued that they were quotas and therefore unconstitutional—because they did not give white contractors an equal chance to compete for all of the available funds. The Court held the law to be a permissible attempt to overcome the effects of blatant and longstanding bias in the construction industry.

Note, however, that quotas can be used in only the most extreme situations. Thus, the Court rejected a city's minority set-aside policy in *Richmond v. Croson,* 1989. There the Court held, 6–3, that the city of Richmond, Virginia, had not shown that its ordinance was justified by past discrimination. Therefore, it had denied white contractors their right to equal protection.

*Johnson v. Transportation Agency of Santa Clara County,* 1987, marked the first time the Court decided a case of preferential treatment on the basis of sex. By a 6–3 vote, the justices held that neither the Equal Protection Clause nor Title VII of the 1964 law forbids the promotion of a woman rather than a man, even though he had scored higher on a qualifying interview than she did. The case arose in California, when a woman was promoted to a job that until then had always been held by a man.

The current Supreme Court's increasingly conservative bent is evident in some of its more recent affirmative action decisions. Thus, for example, in *Wards Cove Packing Co. v. Atonio,* 1989, the Court made it more difficult for those who charge discrimination to prove their point. There, a group of nonwhite cannery workers in Alaska produced statistical evidence to bolster their case. The data showed a longstanding pattern of employment practices by which their cannery company channeled nonwhites into low-paying jobs, while whites received the much more desirable positions.

The Court ruled against them, however. It held, 5–4, that such statistical evidence was not adequate proof of race discrimination. Instead, said the majority, Title VII requires that those who claim discrimination in employment must be able to show that the conditions they challenge are not the result of some legitimate "business necessity."

The Court's holding in *Wards Cove* was pointedly rejected by an act of Congress in 1991. In effect, Congress said that the Court had misread Title VII. The new law declares that Title VII means this: Any business practice that results in the unequal treatment of female or minority employees is permissible only if the employer can show that that practice is based on some legitimate business necessity. Note that in

▲ *Title IX* Title IX of the Educational Amendments of 1972 requires near-equal funding for men's and women's athletic teams at public schools and universities. This decision dramatically increased opportunities for women to participate in sports.

*Wards Cove* it was the *employees'* responsibility to show that the action did not serve a legitimate business necessity.

## The Adarand Case

*Adarand Constructors v. Pena,* 1995, is the most recent major affirmative action case. Its decision marked a major departure from the Supreme Court's previous rulings in such cases.

Until *Adarand,* the High Court had regularly accepted affirmative action laws, regulations, and programs as "benign" instances of "race-conscious policy-making." By this, the Court meant that it considered them mild but necessary. In *Adarand,* however, the Court made it much more difficult for the Federal Government to use affirmative action programs. It held that whenever government provides for any preferential treatment based on race, that action is almost certainly unconstitutional. This is likely to be true even when it is intended to benefit minority groups suffering from past injustices.

"The Constitution protects persons, not groups," wrote Justice Sandra Day O'Connor. "Whenever the government treats any person unequally because of his or her race, that person has suffered an injury" covered by "the Constitution's guarantee of equal treatment." Government can conduct affirmative action programs, said the Court, but only when they

## Spotlight on Technology

**Magruder's American Government Video Collection**

The Magruder's Video Collection explores key issues and debates in American government. Each segment examines an issue central to chapter content through use of historical and contemporary footage. Commentary from civic leaders in academics, government, and the media follow each segment. Critical-thinking questions focus students' attention on key issues, and may be used to stimulate discussion.

Use the Chapter 21 video segment to examine the rights of the disabled. (time: about five minutes) This segment explores the 1990 Americans with Disabilities Act and its ramifications for American society.

## Answers to . . .

### Section 3 Assessment

**1.** To require employers or educators to take positive steps to overcome past discriminations.
**2.** The policy has prompted employers to hire and/or promote more workers with minority backgrounds and more females.
**3.** Reverse discrimination affects members of the majority group, usually white males.
**4.** Some might argue that society must remedy damage caused by earlier government action or inaction; others argue that government cannot do anything more than prevent future harm.
**5.** Answers will vary. Students should be able to defend their answers based on a clear understanding of reverse discrimination and affirmative action.

## Answer to . . .

**Critical Thinking** Possible answer: As the decision resulted from a ballot initiative, students of voting age had the opportunity to vote for or against the initiative.

▲ Students at the University of California marched to defend affirmative action at their school. *Critical Thinking Did high school and college students have much say in the decision to end state-sponsored affirmative action in California?*

are "narrowly tailored" to overcome specific, clearly provable cases of discrimination.

*Adarand* arose when a white-owned Colorado company, Adarand Constructors, Inc., challenged an affirmative action policy of the Federal Highway Administration (FHA). Under that policy, the FHA gave bonuses to highway contractors if 10 percent or more of their construction work was subcontracted to "socially and economically disadvantaged" businesses, including those owned by racial minorities.

### Affirmative Action on the Ballot

The controversy surrounding affirmative action continues. In 1996, California's voters gave overwhelming approval to an initiative measure that eliminated nearly all of the affirmative action programs conducted by public agencies in that State.

The measure, Proposition 209, amended the State's constitution. It forbids all State and local agencies (including public schools, colleges, and universities) to discriminate against or give preferential treatment to any person or group on the basis of race, sex, color, ethnicity, or national origin. The measure covers matters of employment, education, or contracting. It only allows exceptions where necessary to satisfy some federal requirement.

A federal district court found Proposition 209 unconstitutional in late 1996. It held that the measure violated both the 14th Amendment's Equal Protection Clause and the Supremacy Clause in Article VI. That decision was overturned by the Court of Appeals for the 9th Circuit in 1997. The Supreme Court refused to hear an appeal of the Circuit Court's ruling.

In 1998, Washington's voters adopted an initiative measure almost identical to California's Proposition 209. Encouraged by their successes in California and Washington, opponents of affirmative action have launched campaigns to put similar measures on the ballot in other States.

## Section 3 Assessment

**Key Terms and Main Ideas**
1. What is the purpose of **affirmative action?**
2. How has government policy involving **quotas** affected particular racial or ethnic groups?
3. Who, in a general sense, is disadvantaged by **reverse discrimination?**

**Critical Thinking**
4. **Expressing Problems Clearly** In your opinion, is it society's responsibility to rectify the harm suffered by a group of people as a result of discrimination in the past?
5. **Making Decisions** Universities often extend preferences to "legacies"—students whose parents attended that school. Based on past discrimination at many universities, how do these policies support or weaken the case for affirmative action?

 **Take It to the Net**
6. Explore a time line of civil rights and affirmative action. Select four events that you feel were turning points in the struggle for equal rights. Explain why you chose these events and how they had an impact on society. Use the links provided in the Social Studies area at the following Web site for help in completing this activity. **www.phschool.com**

 **Take It to the Net**
6. Direct students to the Social Studies area at the Prentice Hall School Web site. The *Magruder's American Government* companion Web site includes the directions and links needed to complete the activity. It also provides a printable Internet activity worksheet with scoring rubrics for assessment. Explanations should include persuasive reasons for why the events chosen were pivotal.

# ·4· American Citizenship

## Section Preview

### OBJECTIVES

1. **Identify** the questions surrounding American citizenship.
2. **Describe** how people become American citizens by birth and by naturalization.
3. **Explain** how an American can lose his or her citizenship.
4. **Illustrate** how the United States is a nation of immigrants.
5. **Compare and contrast** the status of undocumented aliens and legal immigrants.

### WHY IT MATTERS

People can receive American citizenship through their parents or by undergoing a rigorous process of naturalization. As immigration to the United States has surged, record numbers of immigrants are becoming American citizens.

### POLITICAL DICTIONARY

★ **citizen**
★ **jus soli**
★ **jus sanguinis**
★ **naturalization**
★ **alien**
★ **expatriation**
★ **denaturalization**
★ **deportation**

A re you an American **citizen**—one who owes allegiance to the United States and is entitled to its protection? Very likely you are; more than 90 percent of all the people who live in this country are citizens of the United States. Many of those who are not citizens actively seek that distinction.

## The Question of Citizenship

As it was originally written, the Constitution mentioned both "citizens of the United States" and "citizens of the States." It did not define either of those phrases, however. Through much of America's early history, it was generally agreed that national citizenship followed that of the States.

The coming of the Civil War and the adoption of the 13th Amendment in 1865 raised the need for a constitutional definition.[11] That need was finally met in 1868 by the 14th Amendment, which begins with these words:

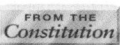 **"** *All persons born or naturalized in the United States and*

*subject to the jurisdiction thereof, are citizens of the United States and of the State wherein they reside.* **"**

—United States Constitution

Thus, the 14th Amendment declares that a person can become an American citizen either by birth or by naturalization. The chart on page 615 summarizes the means by which American citizenship can be acquired.

## Citizenship by Birth

Some 260 million Americans—over 90 percent of us—are American citizens because we were born in the United States. Another several million are also citizens by birth, even though they were born abroad. Citizenship by birth is determined in two ways: **jus soli** and **jus sanguinis.**

Jus soli is the law of the soil, or where one is born. The 14th Amendment confers citizenship according to the location of a person's birth: "All persons born . . . in the United States. . . ." Congress has defined the United States to include, for purposes of citizenship, the 50 States, the District of Columbia, Puerto Rico, Guam, the Virgin Islands, and the Northern Mariana Islands. It also includes American embassies and American public vessels abroad.

Until 1924, Native Americans born to tribal members living on reservations were not citizens,

---

[11]In the Dred Scott case *(Scott v. Sandford)* in 1857, the Supreme Court had ruled that neither the States nor the National Government had the power to confer citizenship on African Americans—slave or free. The dispute over that issue was one of the several causes of the Civil War.

---

## ⊡ Block Scheduling Strategies

Consider these suggestions to manage extended class time:

■ Have students prepare a citizenship and naturalization handbook that recent immigrants could use to help them prepare for American citizenship. Encourage students to illustrate their handbooks and provide the names and phone numbers of important local government resources. Handbooks should also include a citizenship study guide and test.

■ Remind students that immigration policy is a subject of intense political debate. Have small groups of students develop an immigration policy that outlines how immigrants should be admitted, which restrictions should apply, what the total number should be, and how aliens—both documented and undocumented—should be handled. Each group should present its policy to the class.

## Reading Strategy

### Self-Questioning

Ask students to look at every heading and subheading in the section and turn it into a question that begins with *What, How,* or *Why.* Have them read the section to answer their questions.

## Point-of-Use Resources

📁 **Guided Reading and Review** Unit 5 booklet, p. 35 provides students with practice identifying the main ideas and key terms of this section.

📁 **Lesson Plans** For lesson planning suggestions, see p. 93 of the Lesson Plans booklet.

📁 **Political Cartoons** See p. 85 of the Political Cartoons booklet for a cartoon relevant to this section.

📁 **Close Up on Primary Sources** The Dawes Act (1887), p. 39

🖥 **Section Support Transparencies** Transparency 88, *Visual Learning;* Transparency 187, *Political Cartoon*

## Rules of Naturalization

**To become a naturalized citizen, a person must:**

★ be at least 18 years old

★ have entered the country legally, lived in the United States for at least five years (for husbands or wives of citizens, three years)

★ file a petition for naturalization with the clerk of a Federal district court or a State court of record

★ be literate in the English language

★ be "of good moral character," "attached to the principles of the Constitution," and "well disposed to the good order and happiness of the United States"

★ have "a knowledge and understanding of the fundamentals of the history, and the principles and form of government, of the United States"

★ take an oath or affirmation in which he or she absolutely renounces any allegiance to any foreign power and promises to "support and defend the Constitution and laws of the United States against all enemies, foreign and domestic"

*Interpreting Charts* **Which of these requirements do you think is the most difficult to evaluate?**

but wards, persons under the legal guardianship, of the government. In that year, Congress granted citizenship to all Native Americans who did not already possess it.

Jus sanguinis is the law of the blood, or to whom one is born. A child born abroad can become an American citizen at birth under certain circumstances described in the chart on page 615. The child must be born to at least one parent who is a citizen, and who has at some time lived in the United States.

The 14th Amendment does not provide for jus sanguinis, but Congress has included it as a part of American citizenship law since 1790. The constitutionality of the rule has never been challenged.

## Citizenship by Naturalization

**Naturalization** is the legal process by which a person becomes a citizen of another country at some time after birth. Congress has the exclusive power to provide for naturalization. No State may do so.[12]

### Individual Naturalization

Naturalization is most often an individual process, conducted by a court. More than 800,000 aliens now become naturalized American citizens each year. An **alien** is a citizen or national of a foreign state living in this country.

Generally, any person who has come to the United States as an immigrant can be naturalized. The chart on page 615 describes the different ways that people can become American citizens.

The Immigration and Naturalization Service (INS) in the Department of Justice investigates each applicant, and then reports to the judge of the court overseeing the petition for naturalization. If the judge is satisfied, the oath or affirmation is administered in open court, and the new citizen receives a certificate of naturalization.

### Collective Naturalization

At various times in American history an entire group of persons has been naturalized *en masse.* This has most often happened when the United States has acquired new territory. As the chart on the next page indicates, those living in the areas involved were naturalized by a treaty or by an act or a joint resolution passed by Congress.

The largest single instance of collective naturalization came with the ratification of the 14th Amendment, however. The most recent instance occurred in 1977, when Congress gave citizenship to the more than 16,000 native-born residents of the Northern Mariana Islands.

## Loss of Citizenship

Although it rarely happens, every American citizen, whether native-born or naturalized, has the right to renounce, or voluntarily abandon, his or her citizenship. **Expatriation** is the legal process by which a loss of citizenship occurs.

The Supreme Court has several times held that the Constitution prohibits automatic expatriation. That is, Congress cannot take away a person's citizenship for something he or she has done. Thus, actions such as committing a crime, voting in a foreign election, or serving in the armed forces of another country are not grounds for automatic expatriation.[13]

---

[12]Article I, Section 8, Clause 4.

[13]A person convicted of a federal or a State crime may lose some of the privileges of citizenship, however, either temporarily or permanently—for example, the right to travel freely or to vote or hold public office.

*Answer to . . .*

**Interpreting Charts** Possible answer: To be of "good moral character."

## Acquiring Citizenship

### Naturalization

**Individually**

★ Naturalization of both parents (one parent if divorced or the other is dead) automatically naturalizes children under 16 who reside in the United States. Adopted children born abroad are automatically naturalized if under 18 when adoption becomes final.

★ Federal Courts: Any United States district court

★ State and Territorial Courts: Any general trial court

**Collectively**

Treaties:
★ Louisiana (1803)
★ Florida (1819)
★ Alaska (1867)

Joint Resolution of Congress:
★ Texas (1845)

Acts of Congress:
★ Hawaii (1898), Puerto Rico (1917), Native Americans (1924), Virgin Islands (1927), Guam (1950), Northern Mariana Islands (1977)

Constitutional Amendment:
★ African Americans and others by 14th Amendment (1868)

### Birth

*Jus Sanguinis*

A child born to an American citizen on foreign soil becomes a citizen if:

★ both parents are American citizens, and at least one has lived in the United States or an American territory at some time

★ one parent is an American citizen who has lived in the United States for at least 10 years, 5 of them after age 14, and the child has lived in the United States continuously for at least 5 years between the ages of 14 and 28

*Jus Soli*

A child becomes an American citizen if born in the United States, Puerto Rico, Guam, Virgin Islands, Northern Mariana Islands, any United States embassy, or aboard a United States public vessel anywhere in the world

*Interpreting Charts* Most Americans acquire citizenship at birth. **Name two additional ways that people can acquire American citizenship.**

Naturalized citizens can lose their citizenship involuntarily. However, this process—**denaturalization**—can occur only by court order and only after it has been shown that the person became a citizen by fraud or deception.

A person can neither gain nor lose American citizenship by marriage. The only significant effect that marriage has is to shorten the time required for the naturalization of an alien who marries an American citizen.

## A Nation of Immigrants

We are a nation of immigrants. Except for Native Americans—and even they may be the descendants of earlier immigrants—all of us have come here from abroad or are descended from those who did.

There were only some 2.5 million persons in the United States in 1776. Since then, the population has grown a hundredfold, to more than 285 million people today. That extraordinary population growth has come from two sources: births and immigration. About 70 million immigrants have come here since 1820, when figures were first recorded.

### Regulation of Immigration

Congress has the exclusive power to regulate immigration. Congress alone may decide who

may be admitted to the United States and under what conditions. The power to control the nation's borders is an inherent power of the United States (see Chapter 4, page 91). In an early leading case on the point, the Court ruled that the power of the United States to "exclude aliens from its territory . . . is not open to controversy," *Chae Chan Ping* v. *United States,* 1889. The States have no power in the field, *The Passenger Cases,* 1849.

Congress made no serious attempt to regulate immigration for more than a century after independence. As long as land was plentiful and expanding industry demanded more workers, immigration was encouraged.

By 1890, however, the open frontier was a thing of the past, and labor was no longer in short supply. Then, too, the major source of immigration had shifted. Until the 1880s, most immigrants had come from the countries of northern and western Europe. The "new immigration" from the 1880s onward came mostly from southern and eastern Europe. All these factors combined to bring major changes in the traditional policy of encouraging immigration.

Congress placed the first major restrictions on immigration with the passage of the Chinese Exclusion Act in 1882. At the same time, it barred the entry of convicts, "lunatics," paupers, and others likely to become public charges.

## Make It Relevant

### Careers in Government—Immigration Inspector

The first representative of the American government that millions of people meet is an Immigration Inspector. Immigration Inspectors interview potential immigrants and determine whether they are eligible for entry into the country. Inspectors must know and follow immigration laws, policies, and INS procedures. They work wherever people enter the United States (chiefly at seaports and airports),

and they have a huge role in determining who might be the nation's next citizens.

**Skills Activity** Have a small group of students brainstorm lists of the pros and cons of working as an Immigration Inspector. Then have individual students write paragraphs explaining why they would or would not be interested in a career as an Immigration Inspector. **(Average)**

ACTIVITY

## Learning Styles

**Linguistic** Have students consider the problems and challenges facing recent immigrants to the United States. Ask students to suppose they are recent immigrants and have them write letters to their families and friends back in their native country. Ask students to include in their letters the problems, challenges, setbacks, and opportunities immigrants may experience in the United States. Ask for volunteers to share their letters with the class.

**(Basic)**

## Background Note

### Dual Citizenship

Dual citizenship has become much more common in recent years. Although the U.S. State Department does not officially recognize dual citizenship, it does not specifically prohibit it under some circumstances. There are certain rules for becoming a legal citizen of the United States and another country. The most basic rule is that a person who has United States citizenship by birth may later apply for citizenship in another country, without losing his or her American citizenship. A naturalized citizen, however, is required to renounce his or her foreign citizenship when granted American citizenship.

## Point–of–Use Resources

**Simulations and Data Graphing CD-ROM** offers data graphing tools that give students practice with creating and interpreting graphs.

### Legal Immigration to the United States, 1820–1998*

Total (1820 to 1998) = 64,599,082

Europe 59%
Australia and Oceania 0.4%
Africa 0.9%
South America 3%
Asia 13%
North America** 23%

*Figures less than 18,000 not included. Percentages may not add up to 100% due to rounding.

**Includes Canada, Mexico, the Caribbean, and Central America

SOURCE: *1998 Statistical Yearbook of the Immigration and Naturalization Service*

 *Interpreting Graphs* Until the 1970s, Europeans dominated United States immigration figures. **Where do the two largest groups of immigrants come from now?**

Over the next several years a long list of "undesirables" was added to the law. Thus, contract laborers were excluded in 1885, immoral persons and anarchists in 1903, and illiterates in 1917. By 1920 more than 30 groups were denied admission on the basis of personal traits.

The tide of newcomers continued to mount, however. In the 10 years from 1905 through 1914, an average of more than a million persons, most of them from southern and eastern Europe, came to this country each year.

Congress responded to pressure for tighter regulation by adding quantitative limits (numerical ceilings) to the qualitative restrictions (personal characteristics) already in place. The Immigration Acts of 1921 and 1924 and the National Origins Act of 1929 assigned each country in Europe a quota—a limit on the number of immigrants who could enter the United States from that country each year. Altogether, only 150,000 quota immigrants could be admitted in any one year. The quotas were purposely drawn to favor northern and western Europe. The quota system was not applied to the Western Hemisphere, but immigration from Asia, Africa, and elsewhere was generally prohibited.

In 1952, Congress passed yet another basic law, the Immigration and Nationality Act. That statute modified the quota system to cover every country outside the Western Hemisphere.

Congress finally eliminated the country-based quota system in the Immigration Act of 1965. That law allowed as many as 270,000 immigrants to enter the United States each year, without regard to race, nationality, or country of origin. The 1965 law gave special preference to immediate relatives of American citizens or of aliens legally residing in this country.

### Present Immigration Policies

Today, the Immigration Act of 1990 governs the admission of aliens to the United States. The act became effective on October 1, 1991. Like its predecessors, it was adopted only after years of intense debate, and many of its provisions are the subject of continuing controversy.

The 1990 law provided for a substantial increase in the number of immigrants who may enter the United States each year. The annual ceiling is now set at 675,000. It also continues the family-preference policy first put in place in 1965; at least one third of those persons admitted under its terms must be the close relatives of American citizens or resident aliens. Those immigrants who have occupational talents in short supply in the United States (notably, highly skilled researchers, engineers, and scientists) also receive special preference.

Only those aliens who can qualify for citizenship can be admitted as immigrants. The law's list of "excludable aliens"—those barred because of some personal characteristic—is extensive. Among those excluded are: criminals, persons with communicable diseases, drug abusers and addicts, illiterates, and mentally disturbed persons who might pose a threat to the safety of others.

*Answer to . . .*

**Interpreting Graphs** North America and Asia.

More than 25 million nonimmigrants also come here each year for temporary stays. They are mostly tourists, students, and people traveling for business reasons.

## Deportation

Most of the civil rights set out in the Constitution are guaranteed to "persons." That term covers aliens as well as citizens. In one important respect, however, the status of aliens is altogether unlike that of citizens: Aliens may be subject to **deportation,** a legal process in which aliens are legally required to leave the United States.

The Supreme Court has long held that the United States has the same almost-unlimited power to deport aliens as it has to exclude them. In an early major case, the Court ruled that (1) deportation is an inherent power, arising out of the sovereignty of the United States, and (2) deportation is not criminal punishment, and so does not require a criminal trial, *Fong Yue Ting* v. *United States, 1893.*

Because deportation is a civil, not a criminal, matter, several constitutional safeguards do not apply—for example, bail and ex post facto laws. In *Immigration and Naturalization Service* v. *Lopez-Mendoza,* 1984, the Court held that illegally seized evidence, which under the exclusionary rule cannot be used in a criminal trial, can be used at a deportation hearing.

An alien may be deported on any one of several grounds. The most common today is illegal entry. Thousands of aliens who enter with false papers, sneak in by ship or plane, or slip across the border at night are caught each year. Most are apprehended by the Border Patrol, the police arm of the Immigration and Naturalization Service.

Conviction of any serious crime, federal or State, usually leads to a deportation order by the INS. In recent years, several thousand aliens have been expelled on the basis of their criminal records, especially narcotics violators.

## Undocumented Aliens

No one knows how many undocumented aliens reside in the United States today. The Census Bureau has put their number at somewhere between three and a half and five million, and the INS at four to six million. Some

believe that the actual figure is at least twice those estimates.

The number of undocumented aliens is increasing by at least half a million a year, according to the INS. Most of these "undocumented persons" enter the country by slipping across the Mexican or Canadian borders, usually at night. Some come with forged papers. Many are aliens who entered legally, as nonimmigrants, but overstayed their legal welcomes.

Well over half of all undocumented aliens have come from Mexico; most of the others come from other Latin American countries and from Asia. A majority of the Mexicans stay here only four to six months a year, working on farms or in other seasonal jobs. Most other illegal aliens hope to remain permanently.

### A Troublesome Situation

Once here, most undocumented aliens find it easy to become "invisible," especially in larger cities, and the understaffed INS finds it very difficult to locate them. Even so, immigration officials have apprehended more than a million undocumented aliens in each of the last several years. Nearly all are sent home. Most go voluntarily, but some leave only as the result of formal deportation proceedings.

The presence of so many undocumented persons has raised a number of difficult problems. Those problems have grown worse over the past several years and, until recently, not much had been done to meet them.

▲ This sign in southern California warns drivers that undocumented aliens may try to cross the busy highway. *Prohibido*—prohibited—discourages Spanish-speaking immigrants from taking that risk.

## Answers to . . .

### Section 4 Assessment

**1.** One or both parents are American citizens.

**2.** Aliens are not citizens of the state in which they live.

**3.** To legally become a citizen of another country.

**4.** Aliens.

**5.** Answers will vary. Students might suggest that employers be punished for hiring undocumented aliens because they will pay them unfairly, offer them poor working conditions, and place an added demand on welfare services that should be provided only to legal aliens.

**6.** Possible answer: The government believes that immigrants with certain needed skills will be more useful to American society.

**7.** Answers will vary. Students might suggest that because the majority of the population is made up of citizens by birth, it would be impossible to ensure that each person meets the same standards as naturalized citizens.

### Answer to . . .

**Interpreting Political Cartoons** The stereotypes of immigrants that the Native Americans are shown as having are similar to those Americans have about immigrants today.

By Don Wright, © 1980: Miami News. New York Times Syndicate.

*Interpreting Political Cartoons* Newcomers are greeted with suspicion by most cultures. **Why is this cartoon particularly effective?**

One example: Until 1987, it was legal to hire undocumented aliens. As a result approximately 3.5 million persons who now hold jobs in this country came here illegally. Some employers were more than willing to hire undocumented aliens, many of whom will work for substandard wages and under substandard conditions.

Hundreds of thousands of undocumented aliens have taken jobs on farms, often as laborers; thousands more have become janitors and dishwashers, or seamstresses in sweatshops, or found other menial work. The increase in population has also placed added stress on the public schools and welfare services of several States, notably California, Texas, and Florida.

### Current Law

Many groups have been troubled and divided by the problem of undocumented aliens. Those concerned include labor, farm, business, religious, ethnic, civil rights, and other groups. After wrestling with the issue for years, Congress passed the Immigration Reform and Control Act of 1986. Then, after another decade of debate and struggle, Congress passed the Illegal Immigration Restrictions Act of 1996.

The 1986 law did two major things. First, it established a one-year amnesty program under which many undocumented aliens could become legal residents. More than two million aliens used it to legalize their status here. Secondly, that law made it a crime to hire any person who is in this country illegally. An employer who knowingly hires an undocumented alien can be fined from $250 to $10,000. A repeat offender can be jailed for up to six months.

The 1996 law made it easier for the INS to deport illegal aliens by streamlining the deportation process. It also toughened the penalties for smuggling aliens into this country, prevented undocumented aliens from claiming Social Security benefits or public housing, and allowed State welfare workers to check the legal status of any alien who applies for any welfare benefit. The new law also doubled the size of the Border Patrol. It will have 10,000 uniformed officers by the year 2002.

## Section 4 Assessment

### Key Terms and Main Ideas

1. How does a person become a citizen through **jus sanguinis?**
2. What is the main difference between a **citizen** and an **alien?**
3. What is the purpose of the **naturalization** process?
4. Members of which group can be threatened by **deportation?**

### Critical Thinking

5. **Understanding Point of View** Should employers be punished for hiring undocumented aliens? Why or why not?
6. **Drawing Conclusions** Why do you think the current immigration law gives special preference to immigrants who have certain occupations?

7. **Decision Making** Review the chart on page 614. In your opinion, should citizens "by birth" be required to meet the same requirements as naturalized citizens? Why or why not?

 **Take It to the Net**

8. Read stories written by people who have become American citizens and explore the struggles they went through. Write your own fictional story in which you come to America and apply for citizenship. Use the links provided in the Social Studies area at the following Web site for help in completing this activity. **www.phschool.com**

 **Take It to the Net**

**8.** Direct students to the Social Studies area at the Prentice Hall School Web site. The *Magruder's American Government* companion Web site includes the directions and links needed to complete the activity. It also provides a printable Internet activity worksheet with scoring rubrics for assessment. Stories should allude to the processes of naturalization and citizenship as described in the section.

# on the Supreme Court

## May Public Universities Use Admissions Quotas?

When selecting students for admission, colleges and universities consider a number of factors, such as test scores and participation in extracurricular activities. Should they also be allowed to consider factors such as race?

### Regents of the University of California v. Bakke (1978)

Allan Bakke, a white NASA engineer with two degrees in engineering, decided that he wanted to be a doctor. He applied to the medical school of the State-run University of California at Davis. His application was rejected.

At that time, the medical school reserved 16 of the 100 spaces in each year's incoming class for "disadvantaged" applicants. This policy was intended to attract ethnic minority students to the school. Bakke discovered that several applicants with lower entrance exam scores, scholastic averages, and other qualifications had been admitted to the school under the set-aside policy.

Bakke sued the university, basing his case in part on the Civil Rights Act of 1964. The trial court found that the school's admissions policy violated the equal protection guarantees of the United States and California constitutions. The court also ruled, however, that Bakke had failed to prove that he would have been admitted to the school if there had been no set-aside program. Thus the court did not order the medical school to admit Bakke.

The California Supreme Court also found the medical school's set-aside program unconstitutional. It went a step further, ordering the school to admit Bakke to its next entering class. The Regents of the University of California then appealed to the United States Supreme Court.

### Arguments for the Regents of the University of California

1. State programs, including State medical schools, should be able to give certain minority applicants extra protection in order to undo the effects of past discrimination.
2. Discrimination is not unconstitutional when it is applied against members of majority groups in order to assist minorities.
3. A major purpose of the Civil Rights Act of 1964 was to overcome the effects of past discrimination. The law should therefore protect minority students who might otherwise be displaced by whites.

### Arguments for Bakke

1. The policy is unconstitutional under the Equal Protection Clause of the 14th Amendment, because it is based on the use of racial quotas.
2. Racial discrimination is unconstitutional, whether it is against minorities or "reverse discrimination" against members of majority groups.
3. The Civil Rights Act of 1964 also prohibits race-based discrimination in programs (such as this one) that receive federal financial aid.

### Decide for Yourself

1. Review the constitutional grounds on which each side based its arguments and the specific arguments each side presented.
2. Debate the opposing viewpoints presented in this case. Which viewpoint do you favor?
3. Predict the impact of the Court's decision on affirmative action programs in the United States. (To read a summary of the Court's decision, turn to the Supreme Court Glossary on page 799.)

 **Corner**

 **Online**

**Close Up on the Supreme Court** *Regents of the University of California* v. *Bakke,* p. 22 provides an activity to extend coverage of this case.

To keep up-to-date on Close Up news and activities, visit Close Up Online at

**www.closeup.org**

## May Public Universities Use Admissions Quotas?

**Focus** Ask students to explain the purpose of the Civil Rights Act of 1964. *(To outlaw public discrimination)* Then ask students to define affirmative action. *(The government policy of taking positive steps to overcome the effects of past discrimination)* Then ask students to explain the main criticism of affirmative action. *(Quotas are a form of reverse discrimination)*

**Instruct** Have students read the feature and work through the "Decide for Yourself" section. After discussing both sides of the debate, have students read the Supreme Court's decision and then write a short newspaper editorial, explaining the Court's decision and their reactions to it.

**Close/Reteach** Review the chapter's discussion of the Supreme Court's record on affirmative action since the *Bakke* decision. Have the class outline the Court's decisions on the blackboard. Then ask: Might the *Bakke* decision might be decided differently today? Have students draw a political cartoon expressing their opinion of the Court's handling of affirmative action in recent years.

**Keep It Current CD-ROM** includes government-related projects by unit. The CD-ROM links to the Prentice Hall School Web site and may be used for daily updates.

### Answers to . . .

**Decide for Yourself**
**1.** The Regents cited the Civil Rights Act of 1964 in its argument that universities had to use discrimination if the purpose was to assist minorities. Bakke argued that this practice was unconstitutional as it violated the 14th Amendment.
**2.** Answers will vary, but should be supported with valid reasoning.
**3.** The Court ruled in favor of Bakke, ordering his admission to the school. However, the Court established that race should be seen as an admission factor in future decisions.

**619**

## Practicing the Vocabulary

**1.** refugee
**2.** jus soli
**3.** Jim Crow law
**4.** expatriation
**5.** de jure segregation
**6.** quota
**7.** assimilation
**8.** affirmative action
**9.** denaturalization
**10.** segregation
**11.** heterogeneous

## Reviewing Main Ideas

### Section 1

**12.** The United States began as a predominantly white country and became more so over time. The last 40 years have seen a sharp rise in the rate of minority, nonwhite population growth.
**13.** Minority groups have been consistently discriminated against.
**14. (a)** They trace their roots to many different places and tend to live in certain geographic areas according to those roots. **(b)** Because it includes a huge diversity of cultures, and many Asian immigrants have little in common with each other.
**15.** Women have been the targets of discrimination.

### Section 2

**16.** Equal treatment of people under the law.
**17.** They must lead to the achievement of some legitimate governmental purpose and, in some cases, serve a compelling governmental interest.
**18.** In the late 1800s, many States passed Jim Crow laws. The Supreme Court put forth the separate-but-equal doctrine in 1896; it was finally overturned in 1954. In spite of the decline of de jure segregation, de facto segregation persists.
**19.** If the law serves an important governmental objective.

### Section 3

**20. (a)** From the 1870s to the 1950s, no meaningful civil rights legislation was passed. Since 1957, Congress has passed a number of important civil rights acts. **(b)** From the 1870s to the late 1950s, no meaningful civil rights laws were passed; from 1957 to 1964, a number of notable civil rights laws were passed, particularly the Civil Rights Act of 1964; from 1965 to

## Political Dictionary

heterogeneous (p. 594)
immigrant (p. 594)
reservation (p. 596)
refugee (p. 597)
assimilation (p. 597)
segregation (p. 602)
Jim Crow law (p. 602)
separate-but-equal doctrine (p. 602)

integration (p. 603)
de jure segregation (p. 604)
de facto segregation (p. 604)
affirmative action (p. 609)
quota (p. 610)
reverse discrimination (p. 610)
citizen (p. 613)
jus soli (p. 613)

jus sanguinis (p. 613)
naturalization (p. 614)
alien (p. 614)
expatriation (p. 614)
denaturalization (p. 615)
deportation (p. 617)

## Practicing the Vocabulary

**Matching** *Choose a term from the list above that best matches each description.*

**1.** A person who leaves his or her home in order to escape the dangers of war, political persecution, or other causes
**2.** The law of the soil; a means by which one acquires citizenship
**3.** Type of law that required separate facilities for African Americans and whites
**4.** An act by which one voluntarily forfeits citizenship
**5.** Segregation as a result of laws
**6.** Rule that sets a minimum or maximum number of promotions, hires, or acceptances for members of a specific group

**Word Recognition** *Replace the underlined definition with the correct term from the list above.*

**7.** Some immigrants and members of minority groups try to merge into and become part of the dominant culture of a country.
**8.** The Federal Government, States, and private companies have instituted policies that require them to take positive steps to remedy past discrimination.
**9.** A person who gains citizenship through fraud or deception can suffer the loss of citizenship through a court order.
**10.** *Brown* v. *Board of Education* brought an end to separation of one group from another in schools.
**11.** The United States can be described as including a mix of different people.

## Reviewing Main Ideas

### Section 1

**12.** Briefly describe the trends in the composition of the population over the course of American history.
**13.** Briefly describe the historical treatment of minority groups in the United States.
**14. (a)** List two ways that Latin American communities in the United States differ from one another. **(b)** Why do some people believe the category "Asian American" is too broad?
**15.** In what respect do women as a group resemble minority groups?

### Section 2

**16.** What kind of equality does the Constitution guarantee?
**17.** According to the Supreme Court, what standards must laws that discriminate between groups meet?
**18.** Briefly describe the history of racial segregation from the late 1800s to today.
**19.** On what grounds will the present-day Supreme Court uphold a law that treats women differently from men?

### Section 3

**20. (a)** Briefly describe the history of civil rights legislation between the 1870s and today. **(b)** Explain how you would divide the history of civil rights legislation into three periods, and why.
**21. (a)** What was the major piece of civil rights legislation enacted during the 1960s? **(b)** What are its major features?
**22.** Summarize the reasoning behind affirmative action programs. What is the main criticism of these programs?
**23.** Under what circumstances have affirmative action programs generally been allowed by the courts?

### Section 4

**24.** Describe the ways in which people can become citizens of the United States.
**25.** Describe the ways in which people can lose citizenship.
**26.** Briefly describe immigration in the United States today.
**27.** Identify two controversies surrounding undocumented aliens.

the present, affirmative action programs were adopted.
**21. (a)** The Civil Rights Act of 1964. **(b)** Prohibits discrimination at public accommodations; prohibits discrimination in any program receiving federal funds; and forbids discrimination by employers and unions in all job-related matters.
**22.** Affirmative action attempts to overcome the harmful effects of past discrimination. Programs

are criticized for causing reverse discrimination.
**23.** If race or sex is only one factor in the program and if the program seeks to overcome real imbalances resulting from past discrimination.

### Section 4

**24.** By birth, if born to a United States citizen or if born in the United States; by naturalization, if both parents are naturalized,

or through the courts.
**25.** Voluntarily, through expatriation, or through naturalization if it is shown that they acquired citizenship fraudulently.
**26.** The law limits the annual number to 675,000, has a family-preference policy, and says that only people who qualify for citizenship will be admitted.
**27.** Taking away jobs and putting stress on public services.

## Critical Thinking Skills

**28. *Applying the Chapter Skill*** Study the population data on page 595. Use appropriate mathematical skills to interpret social studies information by answering the following questions: **(a)** Based on the table, which ethnic group had the greatest increase in population in the 1990s? **(b)** Based on the bar graph, which had the greatest growth rate? **(c)** Why are your answers to the first two questions different? **(d)** Which group had the greatest growth rate in the 1980s? What was the rate? **(e)** Use the total Hispanic population (35,306) and percentage (12.5%) to determine the total U.S. population in 2000. Explain your reasoning.

**29. *Making Comparisons*** Recall what you read in Section 2 regarding the Supreme Court's attitude toward women. **(a)** How has this attitude changed from the late 1800s to today? **(b)** How has society's attitude changed?

**30. *Making Comparisons*** Analyze changes in American culture brought about by racial integration. Consider American culture when segregation was legal. How has integration changed the culture?

**31. *Making Decisions*** Consider the process by which aliens can become naturalized American citizens. **(a)** In your opinion, should this process be easier or more difficult? **(b)** What standards should be added or removed?

## Analyzing Political Cartoons

Using your knowledge of American government and this cartoon, answer the questions below.

**32. (a)** What form of discrimination is referenced by this cartoon? **(b)** How does this cartoon reverse the usual situation?

**33.** Why is "glass ceiling" an appropriate metaphor for this form of discrimination?

 **Take It to the Net**

Additional support materials and activities for Chapter 21 of *Magruder's American Government* can be found in the Social Studies area at the Prentice Hall School Web site. **www.phschool.com**

---

### ★ You Can Make a Difference

Are there any opportunities in your school or community to mentor students who need attention—for example, recent immigrants who speak little English or students from disadvantaged backgrounds? How could you and your class organize to help these fellow students? Consider forming a group of volunteer mentors to offer help in various areas, such as specific school subjects, community orientation, citizenship tests, or language practice.

## Participation Activities

**34. *Current Events Watch*** Find a recent news article dealing with affirmative action. Then construct two editorials, one in favor of affirmative action and one opposed to it. Begin each editorial with a reference to the news article and explain how this article relates to your argument. When you have finished both editorials, have a classmate read them and rate your thoroughness and objectivity.

**35. *Graphing Activity*** Find recent data on per capita income for African American and white men and women. Then draw a line graph that shows how per capita income has changed over time for all four categories. Write a paragraph describing your conclusions.

**36. *It's Your Turn*** Interview a relative or a family friend who moved to the United States from another country or who experienced the civil rights struggles of the 1950s and 1960s. Talk to them about their experiences. Do they have any personal stories that capture a sense of the time? Do they believe their experiences were typical? How do they feel about television and film portrayals of immigrants' lives or the civil rights struggle? What lessons would they like to convey to members of your generation? Use your interview to write a personal history written from the point of view of that person. **(Interviewing a Relative)**

 **Take It to the Net**

**Chapter 21 Self-Test** As a final review activity, take the Chapter 21 Self-Test in the Social Studies area at the Web site listed below, and receive immediate feedback on your answers.

**www.phschool.com**

## Point-of-Use Resources

 **Guide to the Essentials of American Government** Chapter 21 Test, page 116 provides multiple-choice questions to test students' knowledge of the chapter.

**Test Bank CD-ROM** Chapter 21 Test

**Chapter Test** Chapter Tests booklet

---

## Critical Thinking Skills

**28. (a)** Hispanic origin **(b)** Asian American **(c)** The Hispanic population is much larger than the Asian American population, so a greater population does not necessarily translate into a greater percentage increase. **(d)** Asian American; about 95% **(e)** Around 275 million—the total population can be found by taking the given population figure for a group and dividing by the given percentage. For white, the equation is $226,265,000 = (82.2 \div 100)$ x total population

**29. (a)** Students might suggest that, in the eyes of the Court, women today are nominally and in many respects legally equal to men. **(b)** Students might observe that there is evidence of continued discrimination against women, indicating that society's attitudes have changed more slowly.

**30.** Answers will vary, but should include examples of minority influences on the American cultural landscape.

**31. (a)** Answers will vary. **(b)** Make sure students can defend their answers based on a clear understanding of citizenship.

## Analyzing Political Cartoons

**32. (a)** Gender discrimination. **(b)** The character laments the fact that a male bee cannot obtain the highest position; usually, sex-based discrimination complaints are made by women.

**33.** It implies that customs often create invisible barriers to advancement, even if laws have changed.

## You Can Make a Difference

Before they form their group, encourage students to brainstorm a list of needs that recent immigrants might have.

## Participation Activities

**34.** Students' editorials should reveal an understanding of the pros and cons of affirmative action.

**35.** Students' graphs should show careful research of the data. Students should be able to draw clear comparisons between the per capita incomes of African American men and women and white men and women.

**36.** Students' interviews should be well organized and clearly written.

# UNIT 6

## Comparative Political and Economic Systems

### Introducing the Unit

Unit 6 introduces students to the political and economic systems of other countries. Chapter 22 analyzes the British Parliamentary system, the characteristics of Japan's constitutional monarchy, Mexico's system of government, the history, break-up, and future of the former Soviet Union, and the characteristics of China's constitution and Communist Party, as well as China's relationship with Taiwan. Chapter 23 explores the principles of a free market system, the nature of socialist political and economic thought, and the history and end of Soviet communism.

### Focus Activity

Concentrate students' attention on the political and economic systems of other countries by writing the following quotation on the board:

*"The history of the world is none other than the progress of the consciousness of freedom."*
—G.W. F. Hegel

Have students consider the following after they have read the quotation.

◆ How do government structures in other countries differ from the U.S. federal government?
◆ Do you agree with this statement? Why or why not?
◆ Use these questions as springboards to a general class discussion about students' views of the political and economic systems of other countries.

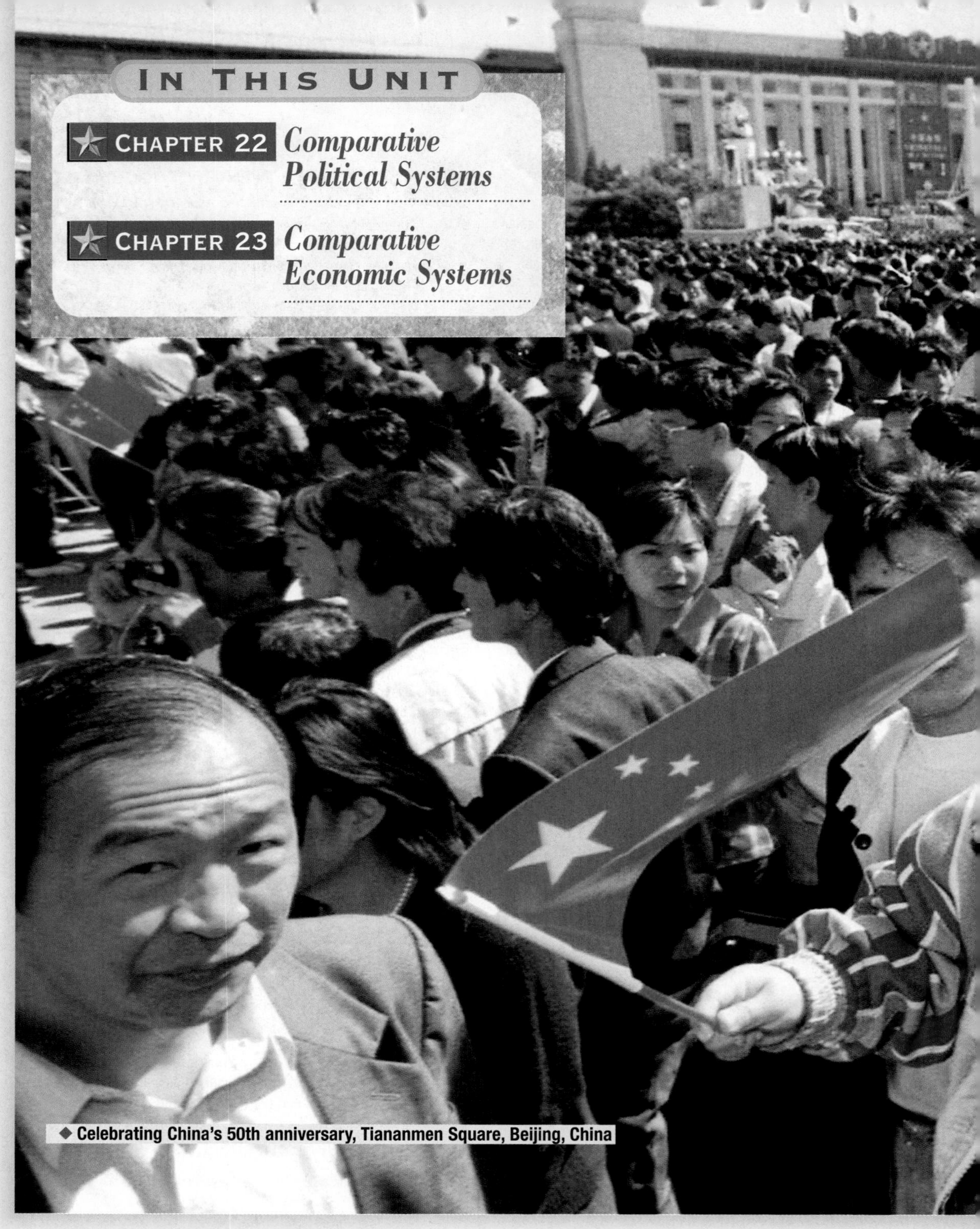

◆ **Celebrating China's 50th anniversary, Tiananmen Square, Beijing, China**

 **Corner**

The following Close Up features appear in this unit.
*Close Up on the Supreme Court* may be found on the following pages of this unit: 653, 677
*Close Up on Primary Sources* may be found on the following pages of this unit: 644, 671

To keep up-to-date on Close Up news and activities, visit Close Up Online at

**www.closeup.org**

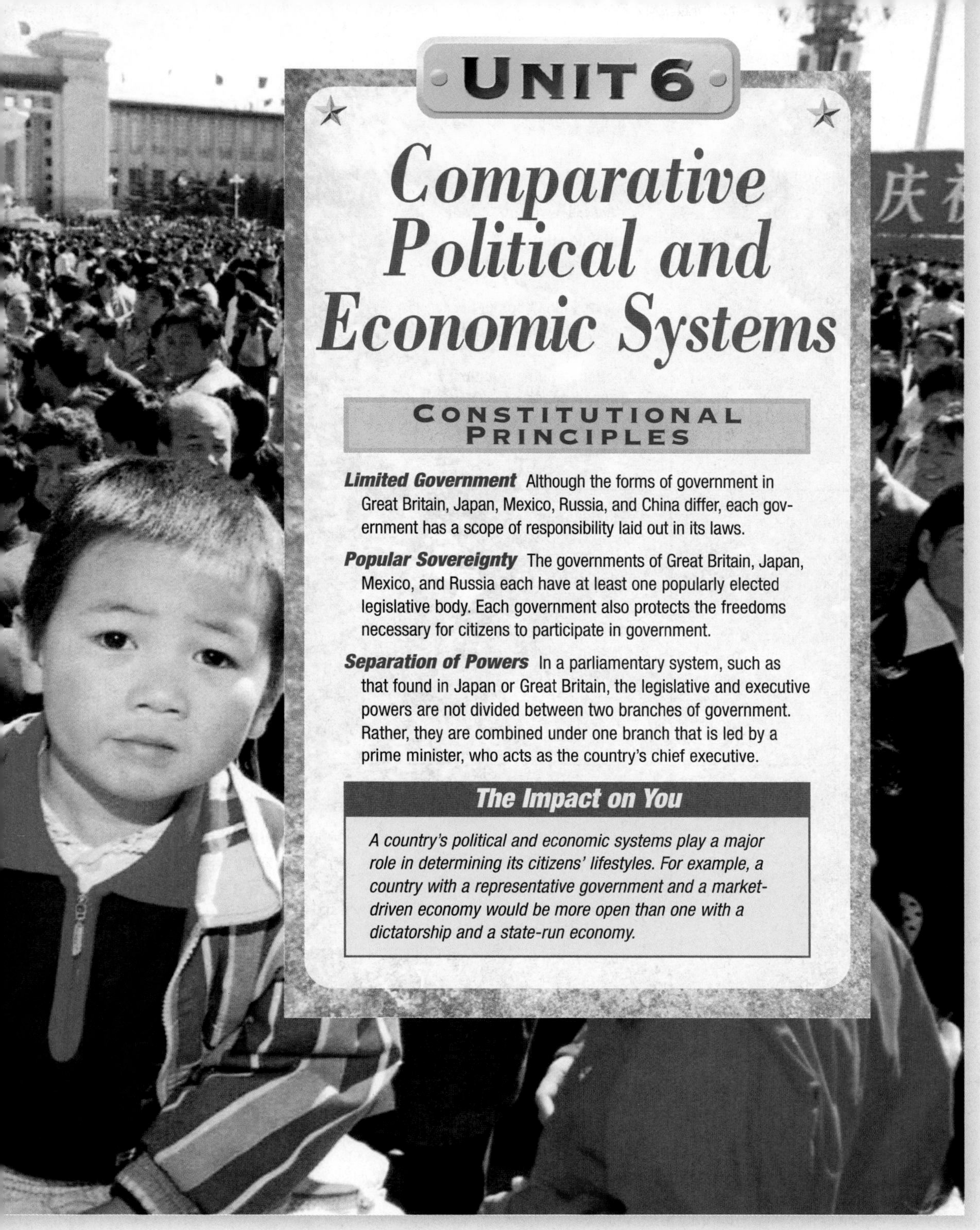

# UNIT 6

# Comparative Political and Economic Systems

## Constitutional Principles

***Limited Government*** Although the forms of government in Great Britain, Japan, Mexico, Russia, and China differ, each government has a scope of responsibility laid out in its laws.

***Popular Sovereignty*** The governments of Great Britain, Japan, Mexico, and Russia each have at least one popularly elected legislative body. Each government also protects the freedoms necessary for citizens to participate in government.

***Separation of Powers*** In a parliamentary system, such as that found in Japan or Great Britain, the legislative and executive powers are not divided between two branches of government. Rather, they are combined under one branch that is led by a prime minister, who acts as the country's chief executive.

### The Impact on You

*A country's political and economic systems play a major role in determining its citizens' lifestyles. For example, a country with a representative government and a market-driven economy would be more open than one with a dictatorship and a state-run economy.*

## Pressed for Time?

### Instruction Plus!

The resources you need to support your instruction of this chapter are conveniently located in a single box. This innovative package provides an instructional advantage in the classroom with its ready-to-use tools in a variety of formats.

- **Magruder's American Government Video Collection**
- **Keep It Current Web-based Activities Presentation Pro CD-ROM**
- **Section Support Transparencies**
- **Guide to the Essentials Current Issues**

## Spotlight on Technology

**Take it to the Net**
Offers student-appropriate Internet activities and links that extend core content. Visit us at the Social Studies area. **www.phschool.com**
Be sure to check out this month's **eTeach** online discussion with a Master Government Teacher.

**Keep It Current CD-ROM** Includes government-related projects by unit. Use it to link to the Prentice Hall School Web site where you will find daily updates.

**Magruder's American Government Video Collection**
Chapter-by-chapter video selections bring key government concepts to life.

**ABC News Civics and Government Videotape Library**
These high-interest stories from ABC News relate to core content.

**Simulations and Data Graphing CD-ROM** Provides interactive federal budget and stock market simulations, and skills practice with statistical data.

**Prentice Hall Presentation Pro CD-ROM** Provides multimedia lecture notes for each chapter.

**ExamView® Test Bank CD-ROM** Allows you to create, edit, and print out chapter level tests.

**Resource Pro® CD-ROM** Teaching Resources that offer lesson planning flexibility, test-generation capability, and resource manageability.

**Social Studies Skills Tutor CD-ROM** Provides interactive practice in geographic literacy, critical thinking and reading, visual analysis, and communications.

**Section Support Transparencies** Illustrates key government concepts through graphs, charts, photos, and cartoons.

**Basic Principles of the Constitution Transparencies**
Illustrates key principles of the Constitution.

**Section Reading Support Transparency System**
Delivers the main idea of each section in the student text through graphic organizers.

# Comparative Political Systems

| Section Objectives | Print and Technology Resources | |
|---|---|---|
| **1 Great Britain** (pp. 626–632) <br><br> 1. Examine the elements that make up Britain's unwritten constitution. <br> 2. Identify the role of the British monarchy. <br> 3. Explain the role of Parliament. <br> 4. Analyze changes that have occurred in regional and local government in Britain. <br> 5. Describe the British court system. <br><br> **TEKS 1A, 13A, 13B, 13C, 21A, 22A, 22B, 22C, 22D** | • **Unit 6 booklet** Guided Reading and Review, p. 2 Section 1 Quiz, p. 3 <br> • **Lesson Plans booklet** Section 1, p. 94 <br> • **Political Cartoons booklet** Section 1, p. 86 <br> • **Section Reading Support Transparencies** | • **Block Scheduling with Lesson Strategies booklet** p. 30 <br> • **Basic Principles of the Constitution Transparencies** 20 <br> • **Section Support Transparencies** 89, 188 <br> • **Presentation Pro CD-ROM** Section 1 <br> • **Social Studies Skills Tutor CD-ROM** |
| **2 Japan** (pp. 634–638) <br><br> 1. Examine early Japanese government and the Japanese constitution. <br> 2. Summarize the structure and functions of the National Diet. <br> 3. Explain how the prime minister and cabinet perform the nation's executive functions. <br> 4. Examine the Japanese bureaucracy, political parties, and courts. <br> 5. Understand regional and local government in Japan. <br><br> **TEKS 13A, 13B, 13C, 21A, 21E, 22A, 22B, 22D** | • **Unit 6 booklet** Guided Reading and Review, p. 4 Section 2 Quiz, p. 5 <br> • **Lesson Plans booklet** Section 2, p. 95 <br> • **Political Cartoons booklet** Section 2, p. 87 <br> • **Section Reading Support Transparencies** | • **Block Scheduling with Lesson Strategies booklet** p. 30 <br> • **Government Assessment Rubrics booklet** p. 24 <br> • **Section Support Transparencies** 90, 189 <br> • **Presentation Pro CD-ROM** Section 2 |
| **3 Mexico** (pp. 639–643) <br><br> 1. Summarize Mexico's early political history. <br> 2. Examine Mexico's three branches of government. <br> 3. Describe recent changes in Mexico's national politics. <br> 4. Explain how Mexico's regional and local government is structured. <br><br> **TEKS 13A, 13B, 13C, 21A, 21D, 21E, 22A, 22B, 22D** | • **Unit 6 booklet** Guided Reading and Review, p. 6 Section 3 Quiz, p. 7 <br> • **Lesson Plans booklet** Section 3, p. 96 <br> • **Political Cartoons booklet** Section 3, p. 88 <br> • **Close Up on Primary Sources booklet** The Canadian System of Government, p. 24 | • **The Living Constitution booklet** pp. 5, 19–20 <br> • **Basic Principles of the Constitution Transparencies** 6, 28 <br> • **Section Support Transparencies** 91, 190 <br> • **Presentation Pro CD-ROM** Section 3 <br> • **Section Reading Support Transparencies** |
| **4 Russia** (pp. 645–649) <br><br> 1. Summarize Russia's political history after the Bolshevik Revolution. <br> 2. Outline the structure of the Soviet government. <br> 3. Describe Mikhail Gorbachev's reforms. <br> 4. Identify events leading to the fall of the Soviet Union. <br> 5. Examine the structure of the Russian government today. <br><br> **TEKS 13A, 13B, 13C, 21A, 21D, 21E, 22A, 22B, 22D** | • **Unit 6 booklet** Guided Reading and Review, p. 8 Section 4 Quiz, p. 9 <br> • **Lesson Plans booklet** Section 4, p. 97 <br> • **Section Reading Support Transparencies** | • **Political Cartoons booklet** Section 4, p. 89 <br> • **Section Support Transparencies** 92, 191 <br> • **Presentation Pro CD-ROM** Section 4 |
| **5 China** (pp. 650–652) <br><br> 1. Examine China's political background. <br> 2. Describe China's government today. <br> 3. Analyze the political significance to the United States of the island of Taiwan. <br><br> **TEKS 4A, 13A, 13B, 13C, 17C, 21A, 21C, 21E, 22A, 22B, 22D** | • **Unit 6 booklet** Guided Reading and Review, p. 10 Section 5 Quiz, p. 11 Skills for Life Activity, p. 12 <br> • **Lesson Plans booklet** Section 5, p. 98 <br> • **Political Cartoons booklet** Section 5, p. 90 <br> • **Section Reading Support Transparencies** | • **Close Up on the Supreme Court booklet** *Reno* v. *ACLU*, p. 23 <br> • **The Basic Principles of the Constitution Posters** <br> • **Section Support Transparencies** 93, 192 <br> • **Presentation Pro CD-ROM** Section 5 |

# Block Scheduling Strategies

The *Magruder's American Government* program addresses block-scheduling strategies in a variety of ways. For easy reference, side-column activities that fit a block format are marked ▦ **Block Strategy.** Each section also contains a **Block Scheduling Strategies** box describing at least two block-format activities that address and extend core content from the section. The **Block Scheduling with Lesson Strategies booklet** found in the Teaching Resources contains additional block-scheduling activities for each chapter.

## Take It to the Net

Visit the Social Studies area at the Prentice Hall School Web site. Once there, you can find additional links, current events connections, and activities to enrich chapter content for *Magruder's American Government,* as well as a Self-Test for students. Be sure to check out this month's **eTeach** online discussion with a Master Teacher.

### www.phschool.com

## Pressed for Time?

If you are running short on time to cover this chapter, consider one of the following options:

- Use the **Presentation Pro CD-ROM** to create an outline for this chapter.
- Use one of the **Pressed for Time** activities found on p. 27.
- Use the Section Summaries for Chapter 2, from **Guide to the Essentials of American Government (English and Spanish).**

 ## Video Connections

Prentice Hall offers two video programs to reinforce and extend chapter content. Show students *The Blessings of Liberty* from the **ABC News Civics and Government Videotape Library** and *Prayer in Schools: A Nationwide Debate* from the **Magruder's American Government Video Collection.**

## Assessment Options

- Section Quizzes, **Unit 6 booklet,** pp. 3, 5, 7, 9, 11
- Chapter 22 Assessment, pp. 654–655
- **Guide to the Essentials of American Government,** Chapter 22 Test, p. 122

### Core Assessment

Chapter 22 Test, Chapter Tests booklet
ExamView® Test Bank CD-ROM Chapter 22
Government Assessment Rubrics

### Standardized Test Preparation

#### Diagnose and Prescribe

Diagnostic Tests for High School
Social Studies Skills

#### Review and Reteach

Review Book for Government

#### Practice and Assess

Test-Taking Strategies With
   Transparencies for High School
Test Prep Book for Government

# Chapter 22 Teacher's Edition Index

## Comparative Political Systems

### Introducing the Chapter

In this chapter, students will use the case studies of Great Britain, Japan, Mexico, Russia, and China to explore various systems of government around the world.

### Make It Relevant

**You Can Make a Difference**

The next best thing to meeting the people of another country is to correspond with them. Organize a group of students to conduct Internet or other research to identify international pen pal organizations. Have the group evaluate each organization, and make recommendations to the class. Then have the class organize a pen pal program for younger students in their school or community. The older students should guide their younger peers in developing their correspondence.

**Service Learning**

### Constitutional Principles

Emphasize the following basic principles as students read Chapter 22. Have the class respond to the questions, and then ask volunteers to explain which of the five countries discussed in this section most closely resembles the United States, and which the least.

**Popular Sovereignty** What events bolstered the concept of popular sovereignty in Russian history?

**Limited Government** Which of the five countries discussed in this chapter could be said to have the least commitment to limited government?

**Separation of Powers** How does separation of powers in Great Britain compare to that in the United States?

CHAPTER 22

# Comparative Political Systems

*"No one pretends that democracy is perfect or all-wise. Indeed, it has been said that democracy is the worst form of government except all those other forms that have been tried from time to time."*

—Winston Churchill (1947)

Although Americans would agree with Churchill that democracy is the best system available, democratic governments vary greatly. Differences include how power is divided and how leaders are chosen. Many nations, of course, are not democracies at all, but authoritarian systems.

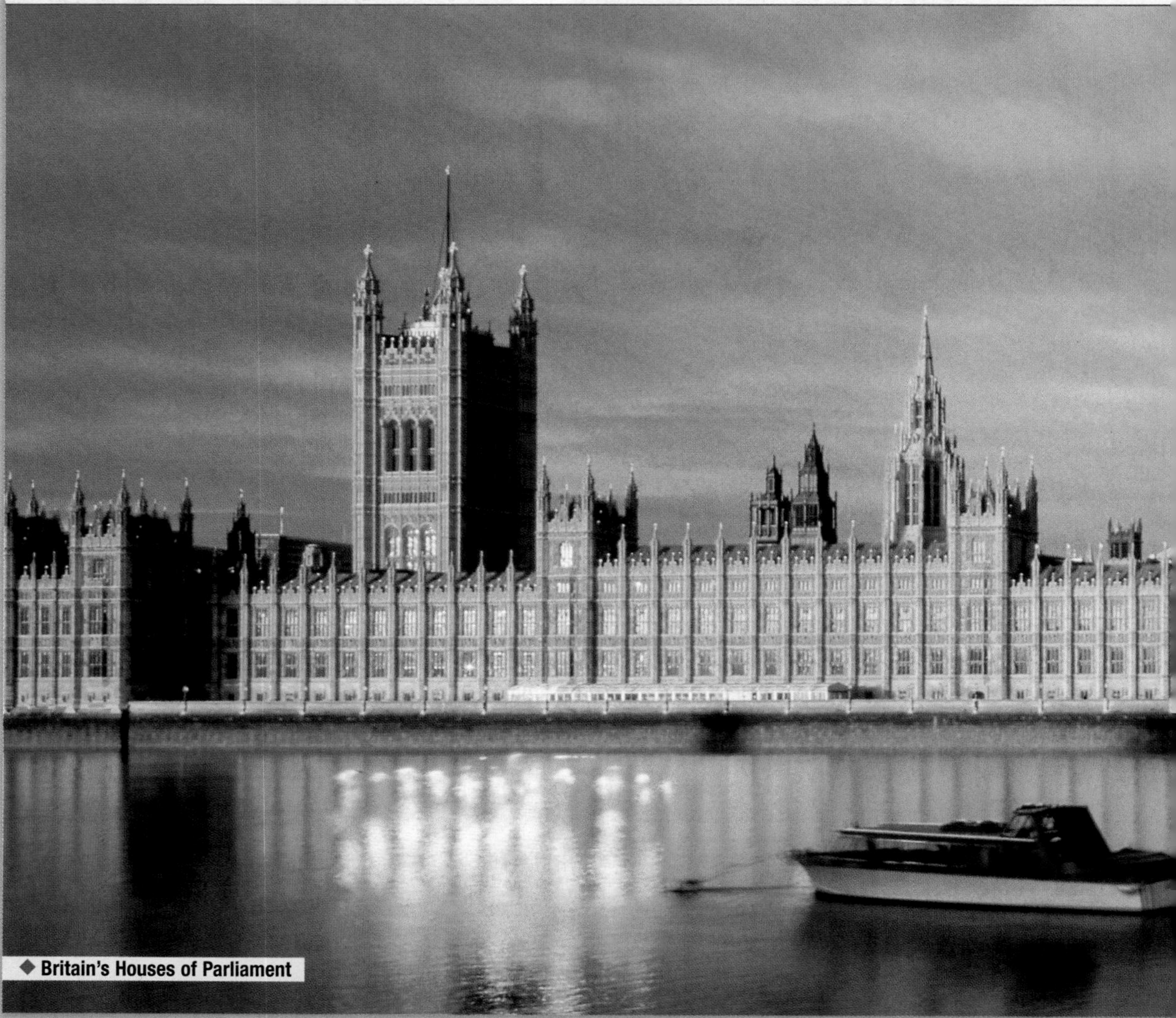

◆ Britain's Houses of Parliament

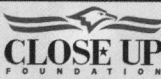

### CLOSE UP FOUNDATION Corner

The following resources are available only from the Close Up Foundation to support the concepts discussed in Chapter 22 "Comparative Political Systems":

- ◆ *International Relations: Understanding the Behavior of Nations*
- ◆ *The United Nations at Work*
- ◆ *The Breakup of the Soviet Union*

**CLOSE UP FOUNDATION Online**

To keep up-to-date on Close Up news and activities, visit Close Up Online at

**www.closeup.org**

Close Up Foundation
44 Canal Center Plaza
Alexandria, VA 22314-1592
800-765-3131

## ★ You Can Make a Difference

**A GOOD WAY** to understand another country is to meet its people. Mariko Asano, a university student in Kyoto, Japan, first got that chance in 1997 on a short-term project with Habitat for Humanity in the Philippines. Habitat builds homes for people who cannot otherwise afford them. Mariko liked her work so much that she returned to the Philippines the next year to lead a student work team. "I've learned that I can make a difference in the world by being connected with people who have a similar wish," Mariko said.

### Keep It Current

Items marked with this logo are periodically updated on the Internet. Keep up-to-date with what's in the news. To get current information on political systems in other countries, go to **www.phschool.com**

### SECTION 1

#### Great Britain (pp. 626–632)
★ Britain's unitary government is based on an unwritten constitution.
★ Britain's hereditary monarch reigns but does not rule.
★ Britain's bicameral Parliament holds judicial and executive power.
★ Britain recently began a process of devolution, or the delegation of authority to regional governments.

### SECTION 2

#### Japan (pp. 634–638)
★ Japan's constitution was written with American guidance after World War II; it contains a unique anti-military clause.
★ Japan's legislature, the National Diet, consists of the House of Councillors and the House of Representatives.
★ Japan's prime minister and cabinet are chosen by and are responsible to its House of Representatives.
★ Japan has an independent judicial system.
★ Although Japanese prefectures (districts) have many responsibilities, they have far less power than American States.

### SECTION 3

#### Mexico (pp. 639–643)
★ Mexican history demonstrates the importance of constitutional representative government.
★ Mexico's government includes an executive branch headed by the president, a bicameral legislature, and a national judiciary.
★ The 2000 presidential election resulted in the defeat of the Institutional Revolutionary Party (PRI), which had controlled Mexican government and politics for over 70 years.

### SECTION 4

#### Russia (pp. 645–649)
★ Russia was the dominant republic of the Soviet Union, which was ruled by the Communist Party for over 70 years.
★ In 1985, Mikhail Gorbachev instituted reforms aimed at restructuring economic and political life.
★ A wave of democratization led to the Soviet Union's fall in 1991.
★ The Russian government is struggling toward democracy and economic reform.

### SECTION 5

#### China (pp. 650–652)
★ In 1949, Communist leader Mao Zedong became head of the newly established People's Republic of China.
★ China's Communist Party dominates the country's government.
★ China's central government exerts direct control over local political subdivisions.
★ Both the People's Republic of China and the Republic of China (Taiwan) claim to be the lawful Chinese government.

## To Omit the Chapter

If you wish to skip Chapter 22, ask students to read the Chapter in Brief and assign the Guide to the Essentials before continuing to another chapter. You may also want to assign the Chapter 22 Test in the Chapter Test booklet. Then specific portions of Chapter 22 may be assigned to students needing reinforcement of key terms and concepts.

## To Preview the Chapter

To introduce students to key terms and concepts in each section, have them read the Chapter in Brief. You may also assign the Reading Strategy activities on pp. 627, 635, 640, 646, and 651 of this book.

## To Review the Chapter

When students have completed Chapter 22, you might want to assign the Guide to the Essentials or the Guided Reading and Review worksheets on pp. 2, 4, 6, 8, and 10 of the Unit 6 booklet.

## To Cover the Chapter Quickly

To cover the material in Chapter 22 quickly, use the following activity.

**Focus** Begin by listing on the board the various types of government. Under each type, volunteers should write the names of countries that they think have that type of government. If the five countries discussed in this section are not listed, add them.

**Instruct** Encourage students to fill in outlines for each country as you discuss it. Describe the types of government used in Great Britain, Japan, Mexico, Russia, and China. Add historical details that are relevant to understanding how government has evolved in each of these countries.

**Close/Reteach** Have students skim the text to find additional details to add to their outlines. Encourage students to use their outlines as a study guide for the chapter.

■ **Block Strategy (Average)**

### Keep It Current

## Internet Update

Use the Prentice Hall School Web site and the Keep It Current CD-ROM to find quick content updates.

Visit **www.phschool.com** for current events articles that are linked to Chapter 22. Critical thinking questions are included.

**Keep It Current CD-ROM** includes government-related projects by unit. Students complete each project using current information that they obtain by linking to the Prentice Hall School Web site from the CD-ROM.

**1** *Great Britain*

## Section Preview

### OBJECTIVES

1. **Examine** the elements that make up Britain's unwritten constitution.
2. **Identify** the role of the British monarchy.
3. **Explain** the role of Parliament.
4. **Analyze** recent changes in regional and local government in Britain.
5. **Describe** the British court system.

### WHY IT MATTERS

Unlike the United States, Great Britain has a unitary government that is based on an unwritten constitution. Britain's monarch is the head of state who reigns, but does not rule. Instead, Parliament holds legislative and executive power.

### POLITICAL DICTIONARY

★ monarchy
★ by-election
★ coalition
★ minister
★ shadow cabinet
★ devolution

L ike the United States, Great Britain[1] is a democracy. Indeed, the roots of American government are buried deep in English political and social history. Yet there are important differences between the two systems of government. Most of those differences grow out of this vital point: Unlike government in the United States, government in Great Britain is unitary and parliamentary in form and rests upon an unwritten constitution.

## Unwritten Constitution

Actually, it is not strictly true to say that the British constitution is entirely unwritten. Parts of the constitution can be found in books and charters. However, no single document serves as the British constitution.

The written part of the British constitution includes historic charters, acts of Parliament, and innumerable court decisions. The unwritten part derives from customs and usages—practices that have gained acceptance over time. The written parts are called the law of the constitution, and the unwritten parts are called the conventions of the constitution.

### The Law of the Constitution

Many historic documents figure in the written parts of Britain's constitution. Perhaps the best known is the Magna Carta of 1215. Others include the Petition of Right of 1628 and the Bill of Rights of 1689. Each of those documents was a landmark in the centuries-long struggle to limit the powers of the English monarch and advance the concept of due process of law.

Certain acts of Parliament also form a basic part of the British constitution. One example is the Representation of the People Act of 1969. That act lowered the voting age in all British elections from 21 to 18. In the United States, such a change required a formal amendment to the Constitution (the 26th Amendment).

Finally, centuries of court decisions have created a body of legal rules covering nearly every aspect of human conduct. Such decisions make up the common law. (See Chapter 24 for a discussion of the common law in the American legal system.)

◀ *The Magna Carta* This document, prepared on parchment and affixed with King John's seal, was a landmark in the struggle to limit the power of the British monarchy.

[1]The United Kingdom of Great Britain and Northern Ireland, often referred to as the UK or simply Britain, is located on a group of islands northwest of continental Europe. It contains four principal parts: England, Wales, Scotland, and Northern Ireland. The UK's population now exceeds 59 million.

## The Conventions of the Constitution

The truly unwritten part of the British constitution consists of the customs and practices of British politics. For example, no written rules give the lower house of Parliament the power to force the government to resign. This central feature of British government developed over the course of hundreds of years and is now a matter of custom.

With its open-ended constitution, the United Kingdom has a flexible set of rules that is always evolving and open to change. A majority vote in Parliament can easily remove an old provision of the constitution or add a new one. The flexibility of this system can be very useful. Without the delays and safeguards of a system such as that found in the United States, however, the danger of ill-considered and hasty action that might fundamentally alter the people's rights is ever present.

## The Monarchy

In contrast to republics such as the United States and France, Britain is a **monarchy,** with a hereditary ruler. While English monarchs once ruled with near-absolute power, their role has long since dwindled. They are now little more than figureheads.[2] Because her powers and duties are controlled by Britain's unwritten constitution, Elizabeth II, Britain's queen since 1952, is known as a constitutional monarch.

In formal terms, all acts of the British government are performed in the name of the queen. However, the prime minister and other high officials exercise the real power of government.[3] The queen appoints the prime minister (traditionally the leader of the majority party in the House of Commons), but her choice is subject to the approval of that house. She has no power to dismiss the prime minister or any other officer of the government. She has no veto over acts of Parliament. In short, today's monarch reigns but does not rule.[4]

## Parliament

Parliament is the central institution of British government. It holds both the legislative and the executive powers of the nation. In the United States, these powers are divided between separate and independent branches of government.

▲ *Pomp and Circumstance* The monarchy is a symbol of British history and traditions. Shown here are Queen Elizabeth II and her son Prince Charles opening a session of Parliament.

With its legislative power, Parliament passes Britain's laws. With its executive power, it chooses some of its members (the prime minister and the cabinet) to administer the departments of government and run the nation's affairs.

Parliament is bicameral. Its two houses are the House of Lords (the upper house) and the House of Commons (the lower house). Of the two, the House of Commons is by far the more powerful body.

### The House of Lords

Until recently, a majority of the members of the House of Lords were hereditary peers—persons who inherited noble titles from their ancestors. The other members, appointed for life by the queen on the advice of the prime minister, included bishops and archbishops, law lords (eminent jurists), and life peers. Life peers are

---

[2]Most present-day monarchs, especially in industrial democracies like Sweden, Norway, and Japan, are figureheads. In the developing world, however, the monarchs of such nations as Saudi Arabia and Morocco still wield considerable power.
[3]The individual who symbolizes a nation's sovereignty is called the head of state, and the individual who directs the government, the head of government. In the United States, the President is both head of state and head of government. In the United Kingdom, the queen is head of state, and the prime minister is head of government.
[4]Reformers make periodic calls for the abolition of the monarchy, proposing to turn over the role of head of state to someone with democratic credentials. The monarchy enjoys a high level of popularity with the public, however. Opinion polls conducted between 1993 and 2000 find that about 70 percent of those surveyed favor retaining the monarchy over becoming a republic.

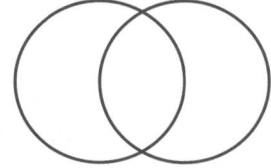

persons honored for their achievements in science, literature, the arts, politics, or business.

In 1999, the upper house underwent a dramatic change. Responding to long-standing criticism of the undemocratic nature of the House of Lords, Parliament passed legislation eliminating the 750 hereditary peers from the upper house.[5] As the reform process continues, future Lords likely will be selected through an independent appointments commission or some form of regional election.

The House of Lords holds only limited legislative power. The Lords can merely delay, not block, a House of Commons bill. If they reject a bill passed by the House of Commons, the Commons has only to approve the bill a second time, and it becomes law.

The upper chamber contributes to the legislative process mainly by improving the technical details of House of Commons bills. Some argue that the Lords fulfill an important role by at least delaying the passage of controversial bills, allowing tempers to cool, and giving the lower house more time to weigh the effects of its actions.

In addition to its legislative role, the House of Lords performs an important judicial function. Its law lords serve as the final court of appeals in both civil and criminal cases in the British court system.

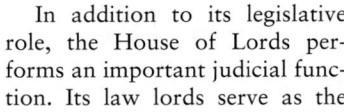

▲ *Law Lord* British law lords wear traditional dress. The House of Lords is the court of last resort in the British legal system.

### The House of Commons

The lower house, known familiarly as the Commons, has 659 members. They are regularly called MPs—members of Parliament. They are elected from single-member districts (constituencies) of roughly equal population. There are 529 constituencies in England, 72 in Scotland, 40 in Wales, and 18 in Northern Ireland.

A general election—one in which all seats in the Commons are at stake—takes place at least once every five years.[6] Election dates are not firmly fixed. If an MP dies or resigns, a special election called a **by-election** is held in that MP's constituency to choose a replacement.

The Commons meets in a small, rectangular chamber within the majestic Parliament building. The high-ceilinged House chamber was originally designed for just 350 members. It is, quite literally, a political arena. The members of rival parties sit on facing rows of benches, talking and sometimes hooting at one another. An open space occupies much of the center of the chamber, with a raised chair at one end for the presiding officer (known as the speaker).[7] Leading members of the major parties sit on the front rows of benches. Those who occupy the remaining rows are known as backbenchers.

The majority party largely controls the work of the Commons. While any MP can introduce a bill, the prime minister and the cabinet—who form what in parliamentary systems is called "the government"—offer most measures.

Up to ten standing committees consider bills and prepare them for final consideration by the full chamber. Committees in the Commons are generalists; that is, any committee may consider any bill. Their main task is to put measures in proper form for final floor consideration. All bills sent to committee must be reported to the floor, where a party-line vote generally follows the will of the government.

### The Prime Minister

The prime minister, although formally appointed by the queen, is in fact responsible to the House of Commons. When a single party holds a majority in the Commons, as usually happens, that party's leader becomes prime minister. If no single party holds a majority, a coalition must be formed. In this sense, a **coalition** is a temporary alliance of parties for the purpose of forming a government.

[5]Although the legislation abolished all hereditary peers in principle, 92 received a temporary reprieve and continue to sit in the House of Lords until the reform process is completed.

[6]In the most recent general election, held June 7, 2001, the Labour Party retained its majority in the House of Commons. Its candidates won 413 seats and garnered 40.3 percent of the popular vote. The Conservative Party won 166 seats and 31.7 percent of the vote, and the Liberal Democratic Party 52 seats and 18.2 percent. Seven minor parties took the other 28 seats and not quite 10 percent of the total vote. The next general election must be held no later than June 7, 2006.

[7]The speaker, elected by the Commons from among its members, acts as a neutral referee. By custom, a speaker runs unopposed in a general election and is regularly returned to office. Michael J. Martin was elected speaker in 2000; he is the 165th person to hold the post.

Two or more parties must agree on a common choice for prime minister and on a joint slate of cabinet members. Britain's last coalition government served during World War II, from 1940 to 1945.

## The Cabinet

The prime minister selects the members of the cabinet. Most cabinet members, or **ministers,** are members of the House of Commons. A few may sit in the House of Lords.

Collectively, the prime minister and the cabinet provide political leadership, both in making and carrying out public policy. Individually, cabinet ministers head the various executive departments. One minister serves as foreign secretary and is responsible for foreign affairs. Another serves as chancellor of the exchequer and is responsible for finance. All told there are about twenty ministers, each with his or her own department and functions. The size of the cabinet varies from time to time, depending on the wishes of the prime minister.

The opposition parties appoint their own teams of potential cabinet members. Each of these opposition MPs shadows, or watches, one particular member of the cabinet. If an opposition party should succeed in gaining a majority, its so-called **shadow cabinet** would then be ready to run the government.

## Calling Elections

In marked contrast to practice in this country, the British political system requires no fixed date for the holding of elections. Instead, British law requires only that a general election be held at least once every five years.

Normally, the prime minister decides when a general election will be held. As a rule, an election is called at a time when the prime minister and his advisors think the political climate favors the majority party candidates. If they have read the political tea leaves correctly, the prime minister's party very likely will strengthen its hold on the House of Commons (or at the least preserve its control). If they are wrong, however, the other major party will take over the government.

Occasionally, an election is triggered by quite different circumstances: when the government falls

▲ The House of Commons meets in a small chamber within the Parliament building. Members of rival parties sit facing each other. *Critical Thinking **How do the responsibilities of the House of Commons differ from those of the House of Lords?***

because it has lost the confidence (the support) of the House of Commons. A government with a sizable majority of seats in the Commons seldom has any trouble maintaining that support. The opposition can cut into the government's majority if it wins a series of by-elections, however. Or, more rarely, some majority MPs may become so upset with one or another of the government's policies that they join the opposition.

The government is judged to have lost the confidence of Parliament when and if it is defeated on some critical vote in the House of Commons. If the government loses a vote of confidence, the government falls. The prime minister must ask the queen to dissolve Parliament (end its sessions) and call a new general election.

This basic feature of British parliamentary government—the ability to change governments in this way—has great significance. It means that a prime minister who becomes either ineffective or generally unpopular can be removed from the office before his or her actions can cause serious damage to the political system.

Clearly, this feature avoids a difficult problem sometimes found in the American system of presidential government: continuing conflict, to the point of deadlock, between the executive and the legislative branches. However, the British arrangement does not allow for any system of checks and balances between the executive and the legislative branches as in the American system.

## Preparing for Standardized Tests

Have students read the passages under *The Cabinet* on this page and then answer the question below.

What is the *main* importance of the shadow cabinet?

**A** It acts as a "watchdog" on the party in power.

**B** It keeps the opposition party informed on important issues.

**C** It provides opposing points of view.

**D** It is ready to run the government should an opposition party gain power.

*Answer to . . .*

**Critical Thinking** Members of the Commons carry out all tasks needed to prepare bills; the Lords' only responsibility is that of delaying bills. However, the House of Lords also has a judicial function.

## Customize for

### Less Proficient Readers

Remind students that American government is rooted deeply in the social and political history of England. Ask them to create a chart or diagram that highlights the differences between the British unitary form of government and the federal form of government of the United States. Have students use the headings and subheadings in the section as clues for chart entries.

---

## Background Note

### Local Councils

In Wales, Scotland, and some areas of England and Northern Ireland, unitary local councils are responsible for all local government functions. In other areas, there are two tiers—county councils and district councils—which divide the responsibilities of local government between them. All local councils in the country are composed of elected councilors who serve four-year terms.

---

## Point-of-Use Resources

**ABC News Civics and Government Videotape Library**
*A Taxing Issue* (time: 3 minutes, 38 seconds)

**Great Britain**

0   75   150 Mile
0   75   150 Kilometer

Shetland Islands

Orkney Islands

Hebrides

North

SCOTLAND

Atlantic Ocean

North Sea

NORTHERN IRELAND

IRELAND   Irish Sea

ENGLAND

WALES   London ★

Celtic Sea

English Channel

FRANCE

**Type**
Constitutional Monarchy

**Constitution**
Unwritten: partly statutes, partly common law and practice

**Chief of state**
Queen Elizabeth II

**Head of government**
Prime Minister Tony Blair

**Executive branch**
Prime minister is head of majority party in House of Commons

**Legislative branch**
Bicameral Parliament consists of House of Lords and House of Commons

**Judicial branch**
Crown Court

Tony Blair

*Interpreting Maps* Britain's constitutional monarchy is based on a largely unwritten constitution. The prime minister is responsible to the House of Commons and is the real head of government. **Cite examples from the text to support this statement: The British monarch reigns but does not rule.**

### Political Parties

Political parties play a much greater role in the governing process in the United Kingdom than they do in the United States. You have just seen the principal demonstration of that fact: The party that wins a majority of the seats in the House of Commons forms the government. Indeed, it can be said that political parties are the cornerstone of the British system of government.

Two parties have dominated British politics in recent decades: the Conservative Party and the Labour Party. The Conservatives (the Tories) have long drawn support from middle- and upper-class Britons. They tend to favor private economic initiatives over government involvement in the nation's economic life, and they generally support the traditional British class system.

The Labour Party has regularly found most of its support in working-class voters. Labour tends to favor government involvement in the economic system and a more socially equal society. Historically, the Labour Party preached doctrinaire socialism, advocating the redistribution of wealth through the nationalization of basic industries and massive public welfare programs. Under the leadership of Prime Minister Tony Blair, however, the party has moderated its views and moved toward the center of the political spectrum.

Another group, the Liberal Democratic Party, also has a broad base in British politics. The Liberal Democrats are a centrist organization that emerged in 1988 out of a merger of two older parties: (1) the Liberal Party, one of the nation's two major parties until it was displaced by the Labour Party in the 1920s, and (2) the Social Democratic Party, a moderate splinter group that broke away from the Labour Party in 1981.

British parties are more highly organized and centrally directed than the major parties in American politics. High levels of party loyalty and party discipline characterize the British party system. Voter behavior clearly reflects that point. Voters regularly vote for candidates for the House of Commons on the basis of their party labels, not their individual qualifications.

## Regional and Local Government

Recall, Britain has a ministry government. There is no constitutional division of powers between the national government and regional or local governments in Britain, as in the American federal system. All power belongs to the central government.

### Answer to . . .

**Interpreting Maps** The monarch has no powers of veto or dismissal, and his or her power of appointment of the prime minister is subject to House of Commons approval.

The regional and local governments in the United Kingdom are creations of Parliament. To whatever extent these governments can deliver services or do anything else, it is only because the central government has created them, given them powers, and financed them. However, regional and local governments do play an important role in the country.

## Devolution

The UK is composed of four separate nations with different histories, cultures, and traditions. In order to provide for the distinctive governmental needs of the people of Scotland, Wales, and Northern Ireland, the UK has recently undergone a process of **devolution**—the delegation of authority from the central government to regional governments.

In 1998, the British Parliament passed three major acts of devolution. Those acts created a 129-member Scottish Parliament, a 60-member National Assembly for Wales, and a 108-member Northern Ireland Assembly. These bodies were to be democratically elected by the people of their respective regions.

These acts came in response to voter referenda in Scotland and Wales that endorsed the creation of Scottish and Welsh assemblies. The British Parliament was also honoring the 1998 "Good Friday" peace agreement in Northern Ireland. That agreement called for the establishment of an assembly in which unionists and nationalists (the two main opposing groups in Northern Ireland) could share the task of governing.

The British Parliament has given the devolved assemblies many important powers. Thus the Scottish Parliament has broad power to pass primary legislation on matters such as education, culture, health services, and housing. It also has the power, within limits, to vary the income tax, on the Scottish people.

The Northern Ireland Assembly has wide authority to legislate on matters previously dealt with by the Departments of Agriculture, Economic Development, Education, the Environment, Finance and Personnel, and Health and Social Services for Northern Ireland. The Welsh Assembly has less power to pass primary legislation, but is responsible for deciding how to implement most UK legislation in Wales. It also can decide how to spend funds allocated to Wales from the central government.

Although the British Parliament has assigned many responsibilities to the devolved bodies, it has reserved for itself the exclusive power to legislate on several matters that affect the whole of the United Kingdom. These include defense, foreign policy, and macroeconomic policy. The British Parliament also continues to legislate more broadly for England, which does not have a devolved assembly.

## Local Government

Local government bodies have been a feature of the British political landscape for much longer than have the recently established regional assemblies. Today, there are 467 local authorities of varying types in the United Kingdom.

Much as in the United States, local governments in the United Kingdom perform a broad range of functions, from running local schools and libraries to collecting trash and maintaining roads. Local councils fund these services largely through grants from the central government, which account for about half of all local government revenue. The several councils also raise revenue through taxes on domestic dwellings and local businesses.

▲ *A New Scottish Parliament* This computer model of the new Scottish Parliament shows an innovative, ultramodern complex. The buildings will be located in the historic Holyrood district of Edinburgh, Scotland's capital.

RESOURCE PRO

**Resource Pro® CD-ROM** contains an electronic version of each activity found in the Teaching Resources as well as additional resources such as Supreme Court cases. The Planning Express® feature allows you to customize and create daily lesson plans within minutes.

## Point-of-Use Resources

**Guide to the Essentials** Chapter 22, Section 1, p. 117 provides support for students who need additional review of section content. Spanish support is available in the Spanish edition of the Guide on p. 110.

**Quiz** Unit 6 booklet, p. 3 includes matching and multiple-choice questions to check students' understanding of Section 1 content.

**Presentation Pro CD-ROM** Quizzes and multiple-choice questions check students' understanding of Section 1 content.

## Answers to ...

### Section 1 Assessment

**1. (a)** There is no single document recording the British constitution. **(b)** The law of the constitution includes historic documents, acts of Parliament, and court decisions. The conventions consist of the customs and practices of British politics.
**2.** It is largely ceremonial; the monarch reigns, but does not make governmental decisions.
**3.** A coalition would need to be formed if no single party held the majority in the House of Commons.
**4.** Devolution is the delegating of authority from the central government to regional governments.
**5.** Parliament holds executive and legislative power while Congress holds only legislative power; members of the House of Lords are not popularly elected and perform judicial functions. The Prime Minister is appointed by the queen, not popularly elected; the Prime Minister has executive and legislative powers.

### Answer to ...

**Critical Thinking** Unlike the United States, the UK's courts and judges do not have judicial review, and courts may not overrule Parliament.

▲ The Old Bailey is England's most important Crown Court. Photographers are forbidden access when the court is in session, a rule that also applies to the U.S. Supreme Court. *Critical Thinking* **How do the United States and the United Kingdom differ on the question of judicial review?**

## The Courts

The UK has three separate court systems—one in England and Wales, one in Scotland, and one in Northern Ireland. In England and Wales, most civil cases are tried in county courts. Serious (indictable) criminal cases are tried in the Crown Court, and less serious criminal cases in the magistrates' courts.

Criminal cases in the Crown Court are tried by juries and judges, while the majority of civil cases and less serious criminal cases are heard by judges or magistrates alone. Both civil and criminal cases may be appealed through a hierarchy of appellate courts, with the House of Lords serving as the final court of appeal.[8] The court system in Northern Ireland closely parallels the system in England and Wales, with a similar hierarchical structure.

Because Scotland maintained a separate legal system after its union with England in 1707, Scotland's courts are completely different from those in the rest of the United Kingdom. The structure is simpler, with fewer hierarchical layers. Sheriffs' courts hear most civil and minor criminal cases. The Court of Session (the supreme civil court) and the High Court of Justiciary (the supreme criminal court) hear cases both originally and on appeal. Criminal cases from Scotland may not be appealed to the House of Lords.

Courts in the United Kingdom decide cases based primarily on parliamentary legislation and common law, or on the standards established by judicial precedent. They are not bound to uphold a constitution or bill of rights that stands higher than parliamentary law. Unlike the United States, the courts and judges in the UK, including the law lords, do not possess the power of judicial review. Even if they believe a law to be in violation of Britain's unwritten constitution, the courts may not overrule Parliament.

---

[8] If a case going through the British court system involves a point of European Union law, it may also be appealed beyond the House of Lords to the Court of Justice of the European Communities.

## Section 1 Assessment

**Key Terms and Main Ideas**

1. **(a)** In what sense does Britain have an unwritten constitution? **(b)** Describe the law of the constitution and the conventions of the constitution.
2. What is the role of the British **monarchy**?
3. Under what circumstances would a **coalition** government need to be formed in Britain?
4. Define **devolution** and explain its implications for local governments in Great Britain.

**Critical Thinking**

5. **Making Comparisons** What are the major differences between the British Parliament and the U.S. Congress? Between the prime minister and the President?

6. **Expressing Problems Clearly** You have read that a British government can fall if it loses the confidence of the House of Commons. What are the advantages and disadvantages of such a system?

**Take It to the Net**

7. The American system of government is rooted in the British system. Create a chart that shows at least five ways in which the British and United States governments are similar. Use the links provided in the Social Studies area at the following Web site for help in completing this activity. **www.phschool.com**

**6.** Possible answers: Advantages include avoiding deadlock between the executive and legislative branches; disadvantages include less emphasis on checks and balances.

**Take It to the Net**

7. Direct students to the Social Studies area at the Prentice Hall School Web site. The *Magruder's American Government* companion Web site includes the directions and links needed to complete the activity. It also provides a printable Internet activity worksheet with scoring rubrics for assessment. Charts should include at least five relevant similarities.

# SKILLS FOR LIFE

## Drawing Inferences

D rawing inferences means reading between the lines; that is, forming conclusions that are not stated directly but are suggested by other facts. For instance, the Queen of England appoints several officials of the Church of England. Knowing that in the United States, Congress and the President have no such powers, you can infer that British tradition does not separate the functions of church and state the way the United States Constitution requires.

Use the following steps to practice drawing inferences from what you read:

**1. Find the main idea in a sentence or passage.** To find information that is suggested but unstated in a passage, you have to understand the stated content of the passage. Reread the subsection entitled "The Monarchy," on page 627. You can state the main idea of the passage by answering these questions:
(a) In earlier times, what was the role of the monarchy in Britain?
(b) What is the role of the monarchy today?

**2. Apply other facts or prior knowledge.** You also read that opponents of the monarchy periodically try to have it abolished. You probably know that the monarchy has lasted for more than 1,000 years. This combination of facts should suggest to you certain inferences. What other facts do you know about the popularity of the monarchy that might help you draw inferences?

**3. Decide whether the information suggests an unstated fact or conclusion.** When you integrate, or combine, this series of facts, it's possible to infer that the majority of Britons still support the monarchy. What can you infer about the role of the monarchy in national unity and stability? Explain.

◀ At left, Britain's Queen Elizabeth II waves to crowds from her carriage during the celebration of her 60th birthday, in 1986. Below, the nation celebrates the Queen's Silver Anniversary, the 25th year of her reign, in 1977.

### Test for Success

If you were to read in the news that Britain's government had fallen, what might you be able to infer? Use the prior knowledge you gained by reading about British elections on page 629.

## Point-of-Use Resources

📁 **Skills for Life Activity** Unit 6 booklet, p. 12 provides an additional skill activity for this chapter.

💿 **Social Studies Skills Tutor CD-ROM**
Provides interactive practice in geographic literacy, critical thinking and reading, visual analysis, and communications.

### Test for Success

Possible answer: The prime minister's popularity diminished; he could no longer summon enough political support in Parliament.

---

## SKILLS FOR LIFE

### Drawing Inferences

**Focus** To prepare students to draw inferences from the text, first have them infer information from the photos on this page.

**Instruct** Direct students to study carefully the photos and caption at left. Prompt them to describe details, such as the gilt carriage, the embellished, historic-style uniforms, and the expressions on the faces of onlookers. Ask students to write a one-sentence statement that infers information about Britain's monarchy. Share responses with the class.

**Close/Reteach** After students complete Steps 1 through 3, have students compare what they inferred from the photo with what they inferred from the text.

### Answers . . .

**1. (a)** In earlier times, monarchs had absolute rule over their subjects. **(b)** Today the monarchy is largely ceremonial.
**2.** Possible answers: Britons in general revere their Queen. They spent a great deal of tax money to support royal pageantry. Support for the monarchy remains strong.
**3.** Possible answer: The monarchy has provided a focus for patriotic pride that has helped to unify the country for centuries.

## Section Preview

### OBJECTIVES

1. **Examine** early Japanese government and the Japanese constitution.
2. **Summarize** the structure and functions of the National Diet.
3. **Explain** how the prime minister and cabinet perform the nation's executive functions.
4. **Examine** the Japanese bureaucracy, political parties, and courts.
5. **Understand** regional and local government in Japan.

### WHY IT MATTERS

Like Great Britain, Japan is a parliamentary democracy. The emperor serves as a symbol of the state but has no power to govern. Instead, the bicameral parliament—the National Diet—is the highest institution of state power. The Diet's powerful House of Representatives chooses the country's prime minister and cabinet.

### POLITICAL DICTIONARY

★ consensus
★ dissolution
★ prefecture

Japan and the United States share in a lively exchange of ideas and goods. Each year, new technologies, music, television programs, and cuisine cross the boundary between these two very different cultures.

Japanese democracy reflects this flow of ideas. The roots of that democracy are embedded in the American occupation of Japan after World War II. After the war, Japan blended American principles with its own institutions to create a distinctive, homegrown form of democracy.

### Early Japanese Government

Japan, like Great Britain, is an island nation.[9] Also like the UK, Japan is a parliamentary democracy. The history of democratic government in Japan is quite brief, however. It spans only a little more than 50 years.

According to legend, the Japanese state was founded by the Emperor Jimmu in 660 B.C. The earliest written records indicate, however, that it began to emerge about 1,000 years later, in the 4th century A.D. The country evolved in almost complete isolation, untouched by forces and events in the outside world, over the next 1,500 years.

During that period of seclusion, a political system similar to that of medieval Europe developed. It was built around the *mikado*—an emperor who governed by divine right and who was, at least in theory, an absolute ruler. Real authority was exercised in his name by the *shogun* (a military dictator) and a number of noble families (*daimyo*) supported by their warrior servants (*samurai*).

Dutch and Portuguese traders had some contact with the Japanese in the 16th and 17th centuries. The country was not opened to any significant Western contacts until 1853, when a U.S. naval squadron made a polite but firm visit. Japan and the United States concluded a commercial treaty the following year. The Japanese then negotiated similar agreements with other Western powers.

Japan was soon committed to becoming a modern state. That drive eventually led to its attempt to conquer all of East Asia, and then to its crushing defeat in World War II.

The United States occupied Japan for nearly seven years following the war, from 1945

◄ This samurai suit of armor symbolizes Japan's feudal past.

[9]Japan includes more than 2,000 islands. Its four main islands—Honshu, Hokkaido, Kyushu, and Shikoku—hold 98 percent of its land area and most of its more than 127 million people.

to 1952. Far-reaching social, political, and economic reforms were put in place at the direction of the American occupation forces, commanded by General Douglas MacArthur. The nation's remarkable postwar economic recovery began during the occupation and so, too, did the development of its present political system. Today, Japan is the leading democracy and the leading economic power in the largely undemocratic non-Western world.

## The Constitution

Japan's present-day constitution, adopted in 1947, was written under the watchful eye of American authorities. The document explicitly rejects the earlier scheme of government, in which "sovereign power" was formally vested in the emperor. Today, the emperor serves as the symbol of the state and the unity of the people, but has no power to govern. That power belongs to the Japanese people, and they exercise it by secret ballot in elections held under universal adult suffrage.

The constitution contains a lengthy declaration of basic freedoms—in effect, a bill of rights. These include freedom of speech and press, freedom of religion, the right to a fair trial, equality of men and women, and the right "to maintain standards of wholesome and cultured living."

A unique anti-military clause is also part of the Japanese constitution. This clause says that the Japanese people "forever renounce war as a sovereign right of the nation." It adds: "Land, sea, and air forces, as well as other war potential, will never be maintained."

United States officials insisted on the clause because they feared a revival of Japanese militarism. Later, they began to see Japan as an ally in the cold war. With American encouragement, since 1954, Japanese leaders have given the clause a broad interpretation. They say that the clause rules out an army, a navy, and an air force, but not a so-called self-defense force. Thus, Japan has rebuilt its three arms of the military, calling them "ground, maritime, and air self-defense forces."

## The National Diet

Japan's parliament—the National Diet—is the highest organ of state power. The Diet contains an upper house, called the House of Councillors,

◄ His Majesty Akihito is the 125th emperor of Japan. He poses here with his wife, Empress Michiko. *Critical Thinking How is the role of the Japanese monarchy similar to that of the British monarchy?*

and a lower house, called the House of Representatives. As in Britain, the lower house wields the greater power. The prime minister and at least half of all cabinet ministers must be members of the Diet. The prime minister invariably comes from the lower house.

### House of Councillors

The House of Councillors has prestige but little power. Its 252 elected members sit for six years, in staggered terms. Because it has fewer responsibilities than the lower house, the House of Councillors tends to serve an essentially deliberative, advisory role. In short, its main function is to provide a forum for the country's leaders to discuss issues of concern to the nation.

### House of Representatives

The House of Representatives has many important powers. It can make, and also break, the Prime Minister. By a vote of no confidence, the House can force the Prime Minister either to resign or to dissolve the House of Representatives and call an early election. The lower house also has the power to make treaties, raise funds, and appropriate money. Both houses must pass bills on other matters. However, the lower house can override a negative vote in the upper house by passing a bill for a second time by a two-thirds majority.

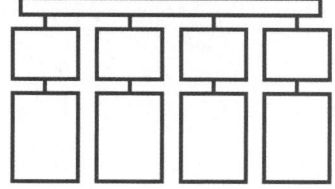

There are 480 seats in the lower house. The country is divided into 300 small single-member districts, and the voters in each of them choose one house member. The nation is also divided into 11 larger multi-seat districts. The voters in those constituencies fill the other 180 seats. Representatives serve for four years—or less if the house is dissolved and new elections are held.

### Consensus Politics

The atmosphere in both houses of the National Diet is sedate compared to that in the legislative bodies in Britain and the United States. Japanese society places great emphasis on avoiding confrontation. Therefore, politicians seek to reach **consensus**—broad agreement—on public questions. Political majorities try to avoid pushing through bills against strong opposition.

## Executive Functions

The prime minister and the cabinet perform the executive functions of government in the Japanese governmental system. The House of Representatives chooses the prime minister. This means that he is in fact picked by the political party with a majority of the seats (votes) in that body.

The prime minister appoints members of the cabinet, who serve as heads of major departments. Most cabinet ministers are members of the House of Representatives. Some are drawn

▲ *The Diet in Session* Members of the Diet practice consensus politics, seeking to avoid confrontation.

from the bureaucracy, an important element of Japanese government. Members of the cabinet have a collective responsibility for the actions of the government. A member who for some reason cannot support a program or decision usually resigns from office.

The prime minister has the power to dissolve (dismiss) the House of Representatives, but not the House of Councillors. This step, which can be taken at any time, is called **dissolution.** A dissolution triggers a general election at which the voters fill all 480 seats in the lower house.

## The Bureaucracy

The large Japanese bureaucracy, or civil service, enjoys unusual respect and power within Japanese society. Top members of the bureaucracy are technocrats—experts in technical and administrative affairs. They include many leading graduates of the nation's top universities, who compete to win civil service positions. Jobs in the bureaucracy do not pay as well as many private sector jobs do, and most of them demand long hours. Still, those jobs are highly prized by Japanese who want to serve the public and/or seek the prestige of civil service rank.

Japan's vast bureaucracy developed under the imperial oligarchy before World War II—in the economic as well as the administrative arenas. Today, it plays a key role in Japan's economy. The Ministry of Trade and Industry helps coordinate the strategies of many large Japanese firms.

## Political Parties

One party dominates the Japanese political system: the Liberal Democrats (the LDP). Despite the "liberal" in its title, the LDP generally follows conservative policies. It was born in 1955 out of a merger of several parties. That merger was prompted by American efforts to stabilize Japanese politics and thwart the aims of the Japan Socialist Party (the JSP), the Japan Communist Party (the JCP), and other left-wing groups.

For nearly 40 years, every Japanese prime minister came from the LDP. The party was wracked by scandals in the 1980s into the 1990s, however, and lost a vote of confidence in the lower house in 1993. In the ensuing election, many younger Liberal Democrats, who had pressed for reforms that the party's leaders rejected, left the LDP. They either formed new parties or joined other, established groups.

The LDP temporarily lost its hold on the government in the general election of 1993. A multi-party coalition, built by the Japan Socialist Party, and in which the LDP refused to participate, took power; but it collapsed in less than a year. The government was then run by an unusual alliance of archenemies: the JSP (now renamed the Japan Social Democratic Party) and the LDP. The LDP returned to power in 1996. It won less than a majority (only 239) of the seats in the House; but the party avoided the need to form a coalition government by striking a deal with two small parties. Those minor parties entered a most unusual arrangement in a parliamentary system: They pledged to support the government in the House but agreed to take no role in that government.

A new major party, the Democratic Party of Japan, arose out of the 1996 election. It was formed when dissenters in the other major parties joined forces to oppose the Liberal Democratic Party. Within a year, the Democratic Party had become the LDP's chief rival in Japanese politics.

The LDP weathered the most recent general election, in 2000—but just barely. It won only 233 seats in the House. The Democrats hold 127 seats and the other 120 belong to seven minor parties. The LDP retains its shaky control of the government, led by Prime Minister Junichiro Koizumi.

Koizumi, a party maverick, beat back the old guard in a party shake-up and became Prime Minister in 2001. To this point, he has proved quite popular with the Japanese people—a people beset by years of political scandal and economic pain.

## The Courts

Japan has an independent judicial system patterned on the American model, with trial courts at the local level, several intermediate appellate courts, and a Supreme Court. The courts hold the power of judicial review (the power to determine the constitutionality of governmental actions.)

The Supreme Court has seldom struck down an act of the Diet. It has three times found the apportionment of seats in the Diet to be unconstitutional, however. By the Court's reckoning, votes cast in many lightly populated rural districts were worth four to five times as much as votes cast in many densely populated urban districts. The Diet responded in 1994 by providing that 200 of the seats in its lower house were to be filled by proportional representation.

## Regional and Local Government

At the regional level, Japan is divided into 47 political subdivisions called **prefectures,** including three large metropolitan districts (for the cities of Tokyo, Osaka, and Kyoto), and a special district for the northern island of Hokkaido. Each of these districts has an elected governor

### *Spotlight* on Texas Government

**Texas in Wartime** Texans have traditionally been interested in foreign affairs, favoring interventionism over isolationism. Many have served proudly in the United States military.

Like most Americans, in 1940 Texans generally opposed direct involvement in the deepening European conflict, but favored President Roosevelt's efforts to provide aid for England. After the bombing of Pearl Harbor, and entrance of the United States into World War II, Texans made up 7 percent of the United States military even though the State had only 5 percent of the country's population. There were also more officers in the armed forces from Texas A&M University than from both United States military academies together.

A Texan, Lieutenant Audie L. Murphy, was the most highly decorated American of World War II. Another Texan, Commander Samuel D. Dealey, was the most highly decorated in the United States Navy. Texas was home to many military installations during World War II, and more prisoners of war were placed in Texas than in any other State.

More than half a million Texans served in the military during the Vietnam War, and over 2,100 Texans died in Vietnam. In all, 83 Texans have received the Medal of Honor for distinguished service at risk to themselves and above and beyond the call of duty.

**Analyzing Texas Government**

*What have been some of the contributions of Texans to the United States military?*

## Preparing for Standardized Tests

Have students read the passages under *Political Parties* on pp. 636–637 and then complete the sentence below.

Though Japan has a multiparty system, Japanese politics

Ⓐ are usually dominated by one party.

**B** are usually dominated by two parties.

**C** do not allow for splinter parties.

**D** restrict the activities of unpopular parties.

## Point-of-Use Resources

 **Guide to the Essentials** Chapter 22, Section 2, p. 118 provides support for students who need additional review of section content. Spanish support is available in the Spanish edition of the Guide on p. 111.

**Quiz** Unit 6 booklet, p. 5 includes matching and multiple-choice questions to check students' understanding of Section 2 content.

**Presentation Pro CD-ROM** Quizzes and multiple-choice questions check students' understanding of Section 2 content.

## Answers to . . .

### Section 2 Assessment

**1.** It contains a lengthy declaration of basic freedoms and an anti-military clause. Power belongs to the people.
**2.** The Diet is bicameral. The House of Councillors has an advisory role. The House of Representatives can pass a vote of no confidence, make treaties, raise funds, and make appropriations.
**3.** It creates an atmosphere in which confrontation is avoided and compromise is highly valued.
**4.** Although they are weaker than States, prefectures can lay some taxes; they also have control over high schools.
**5.** The war and its aftermath led to the democratization of government and marked the point at which Japan began the economic development that made it a leading economic power.
**6.** The National Diet and U.S. Congress are both bicameral; however, the House of Councillors is weaker than either house in Congress. Because the U.S. government is based on a balance of powers rather than a parliamentary system, Congress cannot

### Answer to . . .

**Interpreting Maps** As chief of state, the emperor symbolizes Japan's sovereignty. As head of government, the prime minister directs the government.

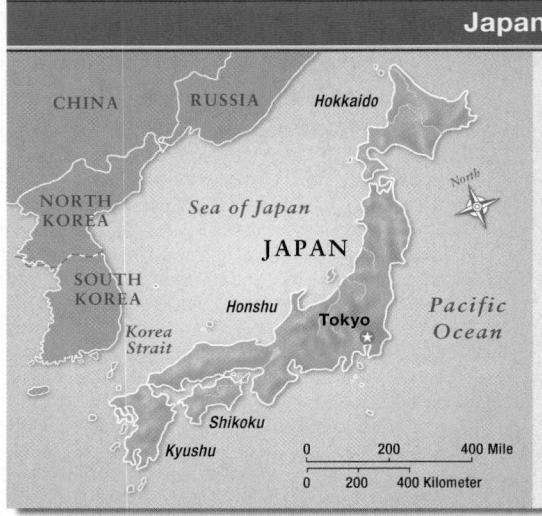

## Japan

| | |
|---|---|
| **Type** Constitutional Monarchy | **Judicial branch** Supreme court; chief justice appointed by monarch after designation by cabinet; all other justices appointed by cabinet |
| **Constitution** Adopted May 3, 1947 | |
| **Chief of state** Emperor Akihito | |
| **Head of government** Prime Minister Junichiro Koizumi | |
| **Executive branch** Prime minister designated by the National Diet | |
| **Legislative branch** Bicameral National Diet consists of House of Councillors and House of Representatives | **Junichiro Koizumi** |

 *Interpreting Maps* Japan's constitutional monarchy is based on a constitution written soon after World War II. The prime minister is responsible to the National Diet. *How do the roles of the emperor and prime minister differ?*

and legislature. The regional governments do such things as lay taxes to pay for roads, hospitals, and police protection. Unlike the United States, where high schools are usually a local responsibility, Japan gives the prefectures control over high schools.

Japan is a unitary state, and the prefectures are not comparable to the States in this country. Although the prefectures have many responsibilities, they must rely on the central government in Tokyo for the bulk of their funding.

Below the prefectures, more than 3,200 municipalities handle local issues. Municipalities range in size from villages of a few hundred to several cities with several million. Each municipality elects a mayor to a four-year term. Larger municipalities also vote for local assemblies, while small towns choose a council to govern with the mayor. As in the United States, local government deals with issues like fire protection, trash collection, local roads, water, and education up through the ninth year.

## Section 2 Assessment

**Key Terms and Main Ideas**
1. What are the main provisions of the Japanese constitution?
2. Outline the structure and basic responsibilities of the National Diet.
3. Why is **consensus** an important concept in Japanese government?
4. What is the role of **prefectures** in Japanese government?

**Critical Thinking**
5. **Determining Cause and Effect** In what ways is World War II the most significant event in modern Japanese political history?

6. **Making Comparisons** What are the major similarities and differences between the National Diet and the U.S. Congress? Between the court systems in Japan and the United States?

 **Take It to the Net**

7. Compare the preface of the Japanese constitution to the Preamble of the United States Constitution. Write a brief essay describing the similarities and differences between the two documents. Use the links provided in the Social Studies area at the following Web site for help in completing this activity. www.phschool.com

pass a vote of no confidence. The court systems in both countries are very similar.

**Take It to the Net**

7. Direct students to the Social Studies area at the Prentice Hall School Web site. The *Magruder's American Government* companion Web site includes the directions and links needed to complete the activity. It also provides a printable Internet activity worksheet with scoring rubrics for assessment. Essays should acknowledge that both documents place power in the hands of the people.

# ·3· Mexico

## Section Preview

### OBJECTIVES

1. **Summarize** Mexico's early political history.
2. **Examine** Mexico's three branches of government.
3. **Describe** recent changes in Mexico's national politics.
4. **Explain** how Mexico's regional and local government is structured.

### WHY IT MATTERS

In form, Mexico's political system is similar to that of the United States in that it has three independent branches of government. In operation, however, the Mexican political system is the product of Mexico's unique culture and history.

### POLITICAL DICTIONARY

★ **mestizo**
★ **nationalization**
★ **North American Free Trade Agreement (NAFTA)**

Mexico,[10] the United States' neighbor to the south, has a political system that is, in form, influenced by the American political system. In operation, however, it is the product of a unique combination of Mexico's history and the cultural makeup of its people. While Americans tend to think of Mexican history in terms of only a few specific historical events, its complex experience established the basis for the system that exists today.

## Early Political History

The first evidence of important civilization in Mexico dates back to about 1200 B.C. But Mexico is most commonly associated with the rich and complex Aztec civilization of the 15th and early 16th centuries A.D. That civilization gave way to Spanish colonialism in 1521, after Hernán Cortés defeated the Aztec emperor Cuauhtemoc in the battle of Tenochtitlán.

During the next three centuries, Spanish territorial claims expanded into North and South America. However, constant border disputes with England, France, and the newly independent United States seriously reduced Spain's area of domination by the early nineteenth century.

### Independence from Spain

Meanwhile, generations of Spaniards in Mexico intermixed with the native peoples, giving rise to a colonial elite with its own unique mestizo culture. A **mestizo** is a person with both Spanish or Portuguese and Native American ancestry. Because of the decline of the Spanish empire and conflicts over succession to the Spanish throne, the Mexicans were able to declare their independence from Spain in 1821. They then established a monarchy with an elected emperor.

The Mexican monarchy lasted only two years before General Antonio López de Santa Anna deposed the emperor and set up a democratic republic with a constitution (adopted in 1824). However, this republic was democratic only in the narrowest sense: most of the population, especially the Native Americans, could not participate.

Mexico's first constitution set the framework for dealing with several key issues and questions in the Mexican system: Should there be a centralized or a federal government? How much power should a single political leader have? How could Mexico remain independent from its powerful neighbor to the north and other major world powers?

Over the course of the next 100 years, these issues appeared, disappeared, and reappeared

▲ This stone carving dates from the era before Spanish colonialism in Mexico.

---

[10]Mexico is officially titled the United Mexican States. It has a population of just over 100 million people.

## ☐ Block Scheduling Strategies

Consider these suggestions to manage extended class time:

■ Have small groups of students prepare a fact sheet on Mexico, using details from the section. Tell students that the fact sheets are for people moving to Mexico who want to learn about the basic structure of Mexico's government and political system. Have each group compare its completed fact sheet to that of another group, and revise.

■ Have students review Section 2 of this chapter, and then create a comparison chart of Japan's Liberal Democratic Party and Mexico's PRI. Charts should include history, leadership, policies, years of dominance, and recent events. After they have finished, ask volunteers to summarize the influence of each of the two parties on their respective countries.

## Reading Strategy

### Drawing Inferences

Tell students that they will be reading about how Mexico's history has influenced its political system. Have students, as they read, note examples of this influence. Ask them to judge whether or not Mexico has profited from past experience.

### The *Living* Constitution

#### America's Place in the World

The Spanish-American War, the United States' first major overseas conflict, illustrates both America's isolationist and globalist tendencies. Some Americans supported the war on the grounds that it would spread democracy by liberating Cuba from Spain. Others supported the war as a means of expanding American economic and military power. Those who opposed the war either supported America's traditional isolationism or saw the war as an undemocratic attempt to secure economic and military power overseas.

#### Using the Time Line

Ask the class if the United States has become more or less isolationist over the course of the twentieth century. *(less)* Next, ask volunteers to categorize the time line items on the blackboard according to whether they primarily involve economic, military, or diplomatic affairs. You might want to have students prepare a pamphlet on the global challenges facing the United States in the coming years.

### Point-of-Use Resources

**Basic Principles of the Constitution Transparencies** Transparency 6, *The Living Constitution: Foreign Relations*

---

with regularity in Mexican politics. Mexico experienced dictatorships and reform movements, one of which led to a revised constitution in 1857. It also underwent periods of foreign invasion and interference as well as internal wars and revolution. Yet throughout this century of conflict, democratic reformers were able to gain political power at crucial times. These reformers reasserted the principles of Mexican independence and constitutional representative government.

### The Constitution of 1917

In the early 1900s, a reform movement called the Regeneration Group and a leader named Venustiano Carranza sparked a revolution. They removed the dictatorship of Porfirio Díaz and oversaw the writing of the Constitution of 1917.

The Mexican Constitution of 1917 was in many respects an updating of the documents of 1824 and 1857. It created, however, a system in which the government played a more active role in promoting the quality of Mexican social, economic, and cultural life. The rights of previously excluded portions of the population were also specified.

### Three Branches of Government

Like the Constitution of the United States, Mexico's fundamental law establishes a national government with three independent branches. The executive branch is headed by the president, the legislature is bicameral, and the judiciary is an independent entity.

### The President

The president of Mexico is popularly elected and serves a single six-year term. The term limit is intended to prevent a popular leader from becoming a dictator by winning several reelections.

The president selects the members of the council of ministers (the cabinet) and the other top civilian officers of the government. He also appoints the senior officers of the armed forces and all federal judges.

In addition to the powers usually held by a nation's chief executive, Mexico's president has the power to propose amendments to the constitution. These amendments must be ratified at both the national and state levels, by a two-thirds vote in each house of Congress and by a majority (at least 16) of the state legislatures.

# The *Living* Constitution

## America's Place in the World                                                    1900

During the first phase of its history, the United States tried to isolate itself from foreign conflicts. In the 1900s, however, the United States participated in two world wars, became a global superpower, and eventually became a major proponent of world trade. The time line lists critical developments concerning war, peace, and trade in the twentieth century.

**1898**
United States wins the Spanish-American War and acquires foreign territories.

**1917**
United States abandons neutrality to join the Allies in World War I.

## The General Congress

The national legislature, called the General Congress, is a bicameral body. It is composed of the Senate and the Chamber of Deputies.

There are 64 senators, two from each of the 31 Mexican states and two from the Federal District, which includes Mexico City. Senators are elected to six-year terms. Half are elected at the time of the presidential election and half at a mid-term election three years later.

The Chamber of Deputies has 500 members who are elected to three-year terms and cannot be reelected. Three hundred of the deputies are directly elected from districts of over 300,000 people. The rest of the seats are filled from the ranks of the various political parties, based on the percentage of the total vote each receives in the national election. Thus, the Chamber of Deputies is elected on a mixed system of direct and proportional representation.

The Congress meets from September 1 to December 31 each year. The combination of term limits and a short session work to give the General Congress a far less significant role than that played by the Congress in the United States.

## The Court System

Mexico's independent judicial system is very similar to that of the United States. Two systems of courts—state and federal—operate within the Mexican federal system. Each has its own jurisdiction.

The federal judiciary is built of district and circuit courts that function under the Supreme Court. These tribunals hear all cases that arise under federal law, including those that raise constitutional issues. The 31 separate state court systems are composed of trial and appellate courts. They hear civil and criminal cases in a structure headed by a state Supreme Court of Justice.

## National Politics

Mexico's national identity and the nation's freedom from foreign domination have been the leading themes of Mexico's national history. Those two themes remain fundamentally important in Mexican politics today.

### The PRI

Mexico has a multi-party system. However, like the Japanese system, it was dominated for decades by one powerful and successful

**1941**
United States declares war on the Axis Powers.

**1964**
Gulf of Tonkin Resolution approves U.S. military involvement in the Vietnam conflict.

**1993**
United States, Canada, and Mexico ratify the NAFTA free-trade agreement.

| 1925 | 1950 | 1975 | 2000 |
|------|------|------|------|

**1920**
Senate rejects Treaty of Versailles and American membership in the League of Nations.

**1945**
United States is a founding member of the United Nations.

**1995**
United States is a founding member of the World Trade Organization, formed to monitor and promote world trade.

**2001**
United States declares war on terrorism.

### Analyzing Time Lines

1. How do the entries for 1920 and 1945 show the different responses by the United States to the end of the two world wars?
2. What are some areas in which the United States has acted globally since World War II?

# CONSTITUTIONAL PRINCIPLES

### Separation of Powers

One of the most important players in Mexico's 2000 presidential election was the Federal Electoral Institute (IFE). Though the IFE has been in existence since 1989, it was not until 1996 that it was reformed to be independent of the executive branch. Headed by nine non-partisan counselors, the IFE for the first time succeeded in establishing measures to prevent election fraud—rampant for decades in Mexico—and give an

opposition party a real chance in the election. The IFE's work also renewed the Mexican people's faith in the electoral process.

### Activity

Have students write paragraphs in which they describe the dangers of an electoral commission headed by, or influenced by, the executive branch. Discuss students' paragraphs as a class.

**Customize for**

**English Language Learners**

## Customize for

### English Language Learners

Have students create a time line of important events in Mexico's history that have helped shape the nation's political climate. Encourage them to include the creation of national constitutions, the development of political parties, and the change brought about by legislation and elections. For each significant date, ask students to include a caption of the event. Ask for volunteers to present their time lines to the class.

---

## Background Note

### Economics

In Mexico, politics have long had an impact on economics. The Mexican presidency was controlled by the PRI for 71 years; rising inflation and monetary devaluation accompanied every presidential election since 1970. The worst example of this was in 1994; immediately following Ernesto Zedillo's election the peso became very devalued, sending the country into its worst recession since the 1930s. In 2000, by contrast, during the month following Vicente Fox's election to the presidency the value of the peso gained seven percent against the U.S. dollar, and the bolsa index—the Mexican equivalent of the Dow Jones—rose 16 points.

---

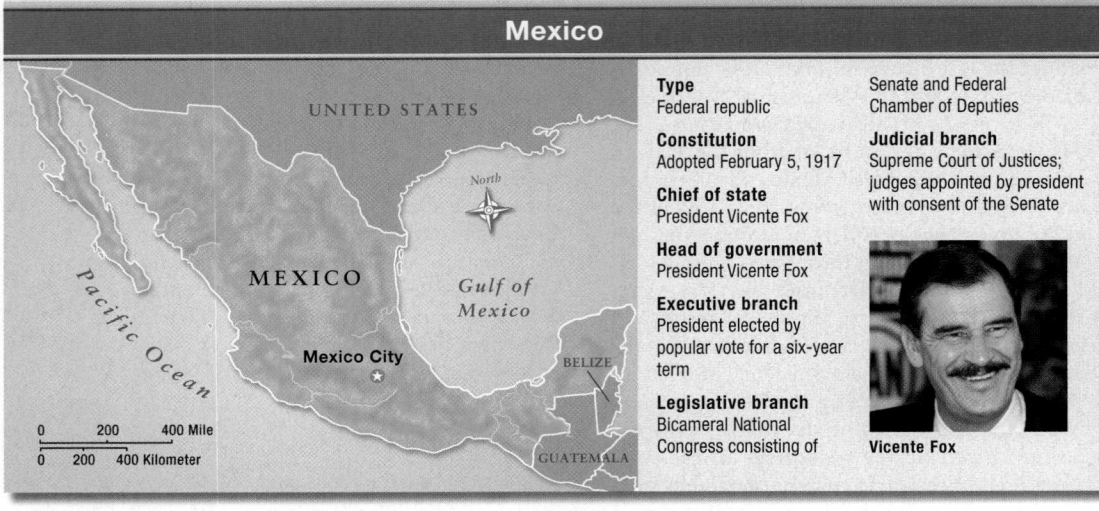

### Mexico

| | |
|---|---|
| **Type**<br>Federal republic | **Senate and Federal**<br>**Chamber of Deputies** |
| **Constitution**<br>Adopted February 5, 1917 | **Judicial branch**<br>Supreme Court of Justices; judges appointed by president with consent of the Senate |
| **Chief of state**<br>President Vicente Fox | |
| **Head of government**<br>President Vicente Fox | |
| **Executive branch**<br>President elected by popular vote for a six-year term | |
| **Legislative branch**<br>Bicameral National Congress consisting of | **Vicente Fox** |

*Interpreting Maps* In the federal republic of Mexico, the president is both chief of state and head of government. **What is the significance of the rise to power of Mexico's current president, Vicente Fox?**

force: the Institutional Revolutionary Party (PRI). The PRI controlled the government and politics of Mexico for more than 70 years. Its presidential candidates won every election from 1929, when the party was first organized, until the presidential election of 2000.

In 1928, General Alvaro Obregon was elected to succeed Plutarco Elias Calles as president. However, Obregon was assassinated before he could take office. The turmoil surrounding that event persuaded President Calles to remain in office, and in 1929, he and other leaders of the day formed the National Revolutionary Party (PRN). That group became the PRI in 1946.

The PRI began to take its long-term shape in the mid-1930s under the leadership of President Lazaro Cardenas del Rio. Cardenas presided over an extensive redistribution of land to the peasantry. In 1938, he restructured the party on the basis of four major groups in Mexican society: the peasants, organized labor, the military, and the popular sector (the middle class and professionals). In 1938 Cardenas also oversaw the **nationalization** of all United States oil companies in Mexico. (Nationalization is the governmental acquisition of private industry for public use.) He was thus ensured his place as a major hero of Mexican nationalism.

The PRI began to move away from its traditional labor base in the 1940s and 1950s. It became increasingly the party of business interests and sought to woo the people as a whole.

The PRI's dominant role was seriously threatened in the 1980s. The government had borrowed heavily from foreign lenders during the 1970s, expecting that oil prices would remain at their then-high levels. When oil prices declined sharply worldwide, the nation plunged into economic chaos. Debt problems led to severe cutbacks in government programs. Prices soared and investment capital fled the country.

The political consequences of that economic calamity were apparent in the elections of 1988. Although economic conditions had begun to improve, the PRI made its worst showing ever. Presidential candidate Carlos Salinas de Gortari won the election, and the party kept its solid hold on both houses of Congress. The PRI's electoral margins were narrow, however. Moreover, it is generally agreed that many of the claims of election fraud were valid.

President Salinas pursued broad-based economic, social, and electoral reforms during his six-year term. He also backed the **North American Free Trade Agreement (NAFTA).** This agreement, promoted by the United States, removed trade restrictions among the United

---

*Answer to . . .*

**Interpreting Maps** It was the first time since 1929 that the PRI did not win the presidency.

States, Canada, and Mexico, thus increasing cross-border trade.

In the 1994 national elections, the PRI's presidential candidate, Ernesto Zedillo Ponce de Leon, won 48.8 percent of the total vote, and the PRI kept control of the legislature. The 1997 off-year elections were a disaster for Zedillo and the PRI, however. The PRI's share of the Chamber of Deputies fell to 239 seats—less than a majority. The leftist Democratic Revolutionary Party (PRD) won 125 seats, while the conservative National Action Party (PAN) took 122 seats.

### The 2000 Election

By 2000 the PRI faced what only a few years earlier had seemed a complete impossibility: the loss of the presidency. Over recent years, PAN and PRD candidates had won increasing numbers of federal, state, and local offices. Now both parties took dead aim at the nation's highest office.

Public opinion—and world attention—forced the PRI to guarantee a fraud-free presidential contest in 2000. When all the votes had been counted, the PRI's Francisco Labastida had only one third of the total vote. The PRD's candidate, Cuauhtemoc Cardenas, won one fifth of all the ballots. The victor, with a plurality of 45 percent, was the PAN candidate, Vicente Fox.

President Fox was inaugurated on December 1, 2000. Since Fox and his party lack a majority in the General Congress, Mexico's new president must work with the PRD—and the PRI—

▲ *National Palace, Mexico City* Built on the site where the Aztec emperor Montezuma's palace once stood, the National Palace houses the presidential and other executive offices of the Mexican government.

as he builds the first non-PRI government in Mexico's modern political history.

## Regional and Local Government

Mexico is divided into 31 states and one Federal District. The Federal District includes Mexico City and is administered by a governor appointed by the president. Each of the 31 state constitutions provides for a governor, a unicameral legislature, and state courts. Each governor is elected to a single six-year term and its legislators to three-year terms. The governor appoints judges. The states have the power to legislate on local matters and to levy taxes, but most of their funding comes from the national level.

## Point-of-Use Resources

**Guide to the Essentials** Chapter 22, Section 3, p. 119 provides support for students who need additional review of section content. Spanish support is available in the Spanish edition of the Guide on p. 112.

**Quiz** Unit 6 booklet, p. 7 includes matching and multiple-choice questions to check students' understanding of Section 3 content.

**Presentation Pro CD-ROM** Quizzes and multiple-choice questions check students' understanding of Section 3 content.

### Answers to . . .

### Section 3 Assessment

**1.** The country experienced dictatorships and reform movements, foreign interference, and internal revolution.
**2.** The Mexican government consists of three independent branches—an executive branch led by a president, a judicial branch, and a bicameral legislature.
**3.** The government acquisition of private industry for public use.
**4.** NAFTA removed trade restrictions among the U.S., Mexico, and Canada, thus increasing trade across the borders of those countries.
**5.** Advantages: More time to accomplish goals; since there is no possibility of reelection, avoids conflicts of interest. Disadvantages: An unpopular president is in office for a longer period of time; since there is no possibility of reelection, presidents may not act according to the will of the people.
**6.** When the people lost faith in the PRI, they were able to elect a president from another party.

## Section 3 Assessment

### Key Terms and Main Ideas

**1.** Briefly summarize Mexico's history in the first century after gaining independence from Spain.
**2.** In what major ways are the three branches of Mexican government similar to those in the United States?
**3.** What is **nationalization**?
**4.** What is the significance of the **North American Free Trade Agreement (NAFTA)**?

### Critical Thinking

**5.** **Drawing Inferences** The president of Mexico serves for a single six-year term. What do you think are the advantages and disadvantages of a single six-year term compared to the four-year term with possible reelection that we have in the United States?
**6.** **Drawing Conclusions** How was the 2000 election a reflection of Mexican democracy?

 **Take It to the Net**

**7.** Choose an aspect of the Mexican government to compare to the U.S. government. Possible topics include the party system or the structure and functions of a branch of government. Present your findings in a 1–2 minute oral report. Use the links provided in the Social Studies area at the following Web site for help in completing this activity. **www.phschool.com**

### Take It to the Net

**7.** Direct students to the Social Studies area at the Prentice Hall School Web site. The *Magruder's American Government* companion Web site includes the directions and links needed to complete the activity. It also provides a printable Internet activity worksheet with scoring rubrics for assessment. Oral reports should show an understanding of the chosen aspect of both the Mexican and U.S. governments.

## Democratic Reform in Mexico

**Focus** Have students recount problems with elections in Mexico discussed in the text. Then have them read and respond to the selections from Vicente Fox's inaugural address.

**Instruct** Organize the class into several groups. Pair the groups to collaborate on a television news report about the election of Vicente Fox. Have one group in each pair prepare an historical overview of the PRI. Have the other group prepare an editorial piece entitled "Mexican Democracy and Reform: the 2000 Election."

**Close/Reteach** After the presentations, have students discuss the strengths and weaknesses of each presentation. Then have students consider the reforms that were mentioned in the presentations and prioritize them from most to least important.

**Keep It Current CD-ROM** includes government-related projects by unit. The CD-ROM links to the Prentice Hall School Web site and may be used for daily updates.

### Answers to . . .

**Analyzing Primary Sources**
**1.** Students' answers will vary but should mention Fox's intent to lead an open, honest, democratic government and the seven reforms he outlines here.
**2.** Responses will differ. Students should turn to the text to support their answers; for example, the student who identifies optimism and realism might point to the last paragraph and note the repeated use of the phrase "Let us" and the short, clear declarative sentences.
**3.** Economic and security problems at home and globally.

---

 CLOSE UP FOUNDATION *on Primary Sources*

# Democratic Reform in Mexico

*On July 2, 2000, Mexican voters ended 71 years of control by the Institutional Revolutionary Party (PRI) when they elected a new president, Vicente Fox of the National Action Party (PAN). In his Inaugural Address, Fox outlined reforms intended to lead to open, honest, democratic government.*

I cannot fail to mention that I am taking office as head of the Executive Branch under new circumstances. The sovereign decision of those who voted on July 2nd was unprecedented. No individual can claim all the credit for this achievement, but we cannot fail to recognize the contribution each has made. On that day, millions of Mexican men and women from every part of the country came to cast their vote. All of us participated in this civic celebration.

*Mexican President Vicente Fox*

For perhaps the first time in our history, no one arrived too late, nor were any left behind. Nothing hindered the free expression of our democratic will; no one died that day to make this possible. At the end of the day, the victory belonged to all of us. . . .

In order to guarantee both an effective democracy and democratic effectiveness, I am making the commitment to promote seven key reforms that I gathered during my presidential campaign and that represent the Mexican people's mandate for change.

- One reform will consolidate the democratic progress we have made so that all people may speak freely and be heard.
- One reform will create progress in the fight against poverty and for social equality, so that no mother lacks enough money to buy milk for her children.
- An educational reform that will assure the development of better human capital and that no young person in our country—no matter how poor he or she may be—fails to complete his or her education due to a lack of resources.
- A reform that will guarantee economic growth with stability, so that our young people will never again have to leave their homes and immigrate to another country.
- A reform that decentralizes Federal powers and resources, in order to give the states, municipalities, and communities greater vitality.
- A reform that assures transparency and accountability in the work of governing, in order to eliminate corruption and deception.
- A reform that combats our lack of safety and does away with impunity, so that every family may sleep peacefully. . . .

Let us put aside pessimism and apathy. Let us be optimists while still keeping our feet on the ground. Let us build the future with realism and joy, and day by day let us turn our present, ours and that of our families, into a better future for all men and women. It is in our hands and within our reach, with the efforts of all, we will all be better for it. Let us start today.

### Analyzing Primary Sources

1. Summarize Fox's goals for Mexico.
2. What word or phrase would you use to characterize Vicente Fox, based on this speech? Explain your answer.
3. What circumstances might make Fox's reforms difficult to achieve?

---

 CLOSE UP FOUNDATION *Corner*

📁 **Close Up on Primary Sources** The Canadian System of Government, p. 24, extends this feature with a primary source activity.

 CLOSE UP FOUNDATION **Online**

To keep up-to-date on Close Up news and activities, visit Close Up Online at

**www.closeup.org**

# ★4 *Russia*

## Section Preview

### OBJECTIVES

1. **Summarize** Russia's political history after the Bolshevik Revolution.
2. **Outline** the structure of the Soviet government.
3. **Describe** Mikhail Gorbachev's reforms.
4. **Identify** events leading to the fall of the Soviet Union.
5. **Examine** the structure of the Russian government today.

### WHY IT MATTERS

The Soviet dictatorship controlled Russia for more than 70 years. It began to undergo broad changes when Mikhail Gorbachev gained power in 1985. In 1991, the once-mighty Soviet Union dissolved. Today, the Russian people are still learning to organize and run democratic institutions.

### POLITICAL DICTIONARY

★ **purge**
★ **soviets**
★ *perestroika*
★ *glasnost*

---

**R**ussia[11] is a government in transition, moving—somewhat fitfully—toward democracy and a market economy. The country's recent history shows clearly that political change is rarely a straight, smooth, or easy path.

## Political History

The Soviet Union was the modern successor to the Russian empire, which began to emerge in the fifteenth century and was formally established by Peter the Great in 1721. A succession of tyrannical czars ruled the empire. Czarist rule began to collapse after heavy losses in the Russo-Japanese War (1904–1905) and World War I (1914–1917).

### The Bolshevik Revolution

The first period of Soviet government began in 1917 with the Bolshevik Revolution and the emergence of the Communist Party of the Soviet Union (CPSU). After a brief revolution in March 1917, Czar Nicholas abdicated. A short-lived democratic government arose headed by Alexander Kerensky.

A second coup, led by V. I. Lenin, overthrew that government on November 7, 1917, bringing the Communist Party to power. Lenin[12] was the architect of what became the Soviet Union. He began to transform an underdeveloped, tradition-bound country into the world's first communist state.

### Stalin

Lenin's death in 1924 prompted a fierce struggle for power, and Josef Stalin[13] emerged as the new Soviet leader. Stalin consolidated his power over the next several years in a series of **purges.** Technically, a "purge" is a purification. Stalin "purified" the government by having his rivals and millions of other dissidents jailed, exiled, or executed. Through an intensive and brutal program of industrialization and forced collectivization of agriculture, he built the Soviet Union into a major industrial and military power.

The Soviets suffered staggering losses in World War II. Nevertheless, at war's end they controlled all of Eastern Europe and emerged as one of the world's two superpowers. Rivalry with the United States and an aggressive foreign policy brought on the cold war that lasted from the late 1940s until the early 1990s.

▲ *V. I. Lenin*

---

[12]Lenin was born Vladimir Ilyich Ulyanov in Simbirsk in 1870. He took the name Lenin in 1901, probably adapting it from the great Lena River in Siberia, where he had been exiled in 1897.

[13]Stalin was born Iosif Vissarionovich Dzhugashvili in 1879. He served as one of Lenin's closest aides and adopted the name Stalin (man of steel) some time before the revolution.

---

[11]Russia is officially titled the Russian Federation. Its population, which is declining, is now some 145 million people.

---

## ★4 *Russia*

**Objectives** You may wish to call students' attention to the objectives in the Section Preview. The objectives are reflected in the main headings of the section.

**Bellringer** Ask students to describe the physical sensations of riding a roller coaster. Explain that in this section they will learn how the Russian people have been on a kind of roller coaster ride since the early 1900s, and that the ride may not yet be over.

**Vocabulary Builder** Ask students which term in the Political Dictionary can refer to mass imprisonment and executions. Have a volunteer read the dictionary definitions of *purge.* Then ask which two terms refer to reforms. (glasnost *and* perestroika)

### Pressed for Time?

#### Quick Lesson Plan

1. **Focus** Tell students that the Soviet Union began with a violent revolution and ended with a fairly peaceful revolution. Ask students to discuss what they know about these two revolutions.
2. **Instruct** Ask students what group ran the government of the Soviet Union. Discuss the Communist Party's overriding control of the country, how reforms set the stage for the fall of the Soviet Union, and who controls Russia today.
3. **Close/Reteach** Remind students that Russia was part of a communist state for more than 70 years. Ask students to create a chart comparing government structure in the Soviet Union with that in modern Russia.

---

### ▣ Block Scheduling Strategies

Consider these suggestions to manage extended class time:

■ Have students prepare a section of a textbook intended for middle school students. Sections should be titled "Russian Political History, 1721–1991," and should include brief descriptions of relevant events and people. Encourage students to include an annotated time line in their section.

■ Write on the board: "The Russian Federation is a democratic federal legally-based state with a republican form of government." Ask students if they agree with this description from the Federation's national referendum of 1993. If they agree, have them use information from the text to support it. If they disagree, have them rewrite the description in their own words.

**645**

## Reading Strategy

### Organizing Information/Outline

Ask students to copy down the main headings and subheadings in outline form, leaving space for details. Have them fill in the details as they read the section.

### Background Note

#### Recent Scholarship

Alena V. Ledeneva's book *Russia's Economy of Favours: Blat, Networking and Informal Exchange* is fascinating because it explores a culture vastly different from that of western societies. Ledeneva draws from a wide array of sources—cartoons, interviews, language, and literature—to describe the system of exchange that developed under Soviet rule and persists under the Federation. Blat is "the use of personal networks and informal contacts to obtain goods and services in short supply and to find a way around formal procedures." A response to failures in the political and economic systems, it has become a way of life, and is still in use today even when more conventional means are available.

### Point-of-Use Resources

📁 **Guided Reading and Review** Unit 6 booklet, p. 8 provides students with practice identifying the main ideas and key terms of this section.

📁 **Lesson Plans** For lesson planning suggestions, see p. 97 of the Lesson Plans booklet.

📁 **Political Cartoons** See p. 89 of the Political Cartoons booklet for a cartoon relevant to this section.

📖 **Section Support Transparencies** Transparency 92, *Visual Learning;* Transparency 191, *Political Cartoon*

▲ **Red Square** Moscow's Red Square has long been the scene of demonstrations, parades, and speeches. It is dominated by the towers of St. Basil's Cathedral (left) and the Kremlin (right), once the symbol of Russian communism.

## Soviet Government Structure

The Soviet Union—officially, the Union of Soviet Socialist Republics (USSR)—comprised 15 republics, each inhabited by a major nationality group, such as Georgians or Tajiks. The largest and most important of the republics was Russia. It included more than 70 percent of the land area of the Soviet Union and more than half its population.

The country's complex government consisted of several layers of elected **soviets** (councils) at the factory, farm, city, regional, and national levels. However, major policy decisions were made at the top by the Communist Party leadership.

### The Soviet Constitution

The structure and powers of the Soviet system were set out in the constitution of the Soviet Union. Unlike the constitutions of Western democracies, the Soviet constitution did not embody fundamental law, nor was it a charter intended to limit governmental power. In addition, although the constitution contained several civil rights provisions, it did not guarantee Soviet citizens such basic rights as free speech, press, and association. Rather, it declared that "[t]he exercise by citizens of rights and freedoms must not injure the interests of society and the state."

### The Legislature

Under communist control, the legislature, called the Supreme Soviet, was a kind of puppet theater. It assembled for a few days each year to rubber-stamp the decrees of the CPSU. Citizens could vote for members of the legislature, but in general only one candidate ran for each office. This candidate was either a Communist Party member or a vocal supporter of the party.

### The Communist Party

From the revolution of 1917 until 1990, the Communist Party was the only political party in the Soviet Union. The CPSU was an elite party, composed of some 19 million specially chosen people—only about nine percent of the adult population. It was organized like a pyramid. At the bottom were some 400,000 primary party organizations (once called cells), each headed by a party committee. At the top were the Central Committee, the Politburo, and the general secretary.

The Central Committee assembled once every six months. It elected the much smaller Politburo, which was the body that in fact ran the party. The Politburo (political bureau) was a full-time decision-making body, made up of experienced and powerful party leaders. Most of them also held key government posts.

The general secretary headed the Politburo and had broad powers. After the Stalin era, the general secretary usually also held the top post in government.

## Gorbachev's Reforms

A brief second stage of Soviet government began in 1985 when Mikhail Gorbachev became general secretary of the party. Gorbachev undertook a reform program that rested on the principles of *perestroika* and *glasnost*. **Perestroika** was the restructuring of political and economic life. **Glasnost** was the policy of openness under which the government increased its tolerance of dissent and freedom of expression.

Gorbachev concentrated his reform efforts in three areas: the legislature, the executive, and the Communist Party.

1. *The Legislature.* Under Gorbachev, the legislature was composed of the large Congress of People's Deputies and the smaller Supreme Soviet. Voters elected two thirds of the 2,250 members of

the Congress of People's Deputies. The election of those deputies in 1989 marked the first time that the Soviet Union had held competitive, multi-candidate elections. The Congress chose some of its members to form the Supreme Soviet.

The Supreme Soviet that met from 1989 to 1991 had the power to make laws, approve the national budget, confirm the appointments of top government officials, and declare war. Importantly, it also elected the president of the Soviet Union.

2. *The President.* Gorbachev also created a new office: president of the Soviet Union. As president, Gorbachev appointed the other top government officials, set the lawmaking agenda for the Supreme Soviet, headed the defense establishment, and conducted Soviet foreign policy.

3. *The CPSU.* Democratic reforms reduced the party's power. In 1990, it lost its exclusive position, and a number of smaller political parties emerged. Gorbachev, the most visible symbol of the Soviet political system, began to regularly present himself as head of state—the president of the Soviet Union—rather than as head of the party.

## Fall of the Soviet Union

In 1989, encouraged by Gorbachev's emphasis on *glasnost,* a wave of democratization rolled across Eastern Europe. Independence movements gained strength in the Baltic Soviet states of Lithuania, Latvia, and Estonia.

By the middle of 1990, the republics of Russia, Ukraine, and Byelorussia, as well as several smaller republics, had declared independence from the Soviet central authority. In elections in 1991, Russians named Boris Yeltsin president of the Russian Republic. Yeltsin further challenged the Soviet government by resigning from the Communist Party and having the laws of the Russian Republic declared sovereign over Russia's population and territory.

Events quickly moved beyond Gorbachev's control. In August 1991, Gorbachev and his wife were vacationing in the Crimea when a group of hard-line Communist Party leaders placed him under house arrest. They objected to the new democratic reforms and wanted a return to the policies of the old Soviet government.

When the Soviet public heard of the attempted coup, thousands of protesters took to the streets of Moscow, raising the white, blue, and red Russian (not Soviet) flag. Leading the protest was Russian President Boris Yeltsin. After several tense days, the conspirators surrendered. The coup had failed.

In the months that followed, extraordinary changes occurred. The three Baltic republics departed from the Union. Soon the remaining 12 republics left the Union as well.

### Background Note
#### Politics and Literature

The Communist government of the former Soviet Union had a great impact on the nation's literature. Aleksandr Solzhenitsyn, a Russian novelist, was interred in prisons and labor camps for eight years because of a letter he wrote criticizing Stalin. He based numerous books on these years. Solzhenitsyn was awarded the Nobel Prize for Literature in 1970, but refused it for four years fearing that the government would prohibit his re-entry into the U.S.S.R. In 1974, Solzhenitsyn was charged with treason and exiled from the Soviet Union because of the publication of the first book in his trilogy, "The Gulag Archipelago," which dealt with the treatment of prisoners in labor camps under Lenin and Stalin. Upon his exile, he was finally able to claim his Nobel Prize.

### Take It to the Net

For career-related links and activities, visit the *Magruder's American Government* companion Web site in the Social Studies area at the Prentice Hall School Web site.

**Russia**

0 200 400 Mile
0 200 400 Kilometer

Arctic Ocean

NORWAY
SWEDEN
FINLAND
BELARUS    **Moscow**
UKRAINE          **RUSSIA**
KAZAKHSTAN      MONGOLIA      CHINA
TURKMENISTAN      CHINA
USA

**Type**
Federation

**Constitution**
Adopted December 12, 1993

**Chief of state**
President Vladimir V. Putin

**Head of government**
Premier Mikhail Kasyanov

**Executive branch**
President elected for four-year term; premier appointed by president

**Legislative branch**
Bicameral Federal Assembly consists of the Federation Council and the State Duma

**Judicial branch**
Constitutional Court, Supreme Court, Superior Court of Arbitration; judges appointed for life by Federation Council on recommendation of the president

**Vladimir V. Putin**

 *Interpreting Maps* The Constitution of 1993 gives the president a central role in Russian government. The president, who is elected by direct popular vote, appoints the prime minister. ***How did Mikhail Gorbachev reform the Soviet government?***

## Make It Relevant

### Careers in Government—Area Specialist

Area specialists are experts on certain places. For example, an area specialist on Russia knows Russian geography, history, culture, government, politics, literature, and the Russian language. Area specialists must know the smallest details, and develop a "feel" for their area. Their knowledge and intuition is of tremendous value to U.S. policymakers in making informed foreign policy decisions. Many foreign policy blunders have been averted because of the insight of area specialists.

**Skills Activity** Have pairs of students make area booklets of chosen regions or countries that provide an overview of geography, economy, politics, and culture. Then have individual students write paragraphs explaining why they would or would not be interested in a career as an area specialist. **(Average)**

**Answer to . . .**
**Interpreting Maps** Gorbachev called for the first competitive, multi-candidate elections ever held in the Soviet Union; he created the office of president of the Soviet Union; he reduced the power of the Communist Party.

# *Voices* on Government

The career of **Vaclav Havel**—playwright, essayist, and politician—symbolizes the great changes in world politics in the second half of the twentieth century. When Czechoslovakia was under Soviet domination, Havel went to jail for his dissident views. Then the country peacefully overthrew the Communist regime, and he became the Czech president. On New Year's Day 1990, he spoke about the future:

❝ *We cannot blame the previous rulers for everything, not only because it would be untrue but also because it could blunt the duty that each of us faces today, namely the obligation to act independently, freely, reasonably, and quickly. Let us not be mistaken: the best government in the world, the best parliament and the best president, cannot achieve much on their own. . . . Freedom and democracy include participation and therefore responsibility from us all.* ❞

## Evaluating the Quotation

*(a) What do you think Havel means by "participation"? (b) Why might the transition to democracy be difficult for people after 40 years of totalitarian rule?*

Boris Yeltsin became the major proponent of a radical economic reform plan. As the elected leader of the dominant republic in the Soviet Union, Yeltsin's power overshadowed that of Gorbachev. Recognizing reality, Gorbachev resigned on December 25, 1991. By the end of the year, the Soviet Union was no more.

# Russian Government Today

Since 1991, the government of Russia has moved toward democracy and economic reform. Will it in fact reach that goal?

## The Constitution of 1993

A new constitution was approved in a national referendum in late 1993. It proclaims the Russian Federation to be "a democratic federal legally-based state with a republican form of government." It also sets out a new government structure and contains an extensive list of individual rights—including guarantees of freedom of speech, press, association, and religious belief. Furthermore, the constitution provides that every citizen has a right to freedom of movement within the federation, to housing, and to free medical care and education.

## Political Parties

Today, the one-party system of the Soviet era has been replaced by a multiparty system. More than 40 parties now operate in Russian politics. Besides the Communists, these include the right-wing, ultranationalist Liberal Democratic Party; Our Home Is Russia, which favors economic and social reform; and *Yabloko* ("apple"), a liberal reform party.

## The Executive Branch

The constitution of 1993 created a government built on a separation of powers between the executive and legislative branches. In theory, the branches are independent and equal. In reality, the constitution gives the president a central role. He defines the "basic directions of domestic and foreign policy" and represents Russia in the world community.

The president appoints a prime minister, as well as other ministers who head the executive departments of the government. The prime minister, who carries the administration's programs to the assembly, is second-in-command of the executive branch. The prime minister is also first in the line of succession.

The president is elected by direct popular vote for a term of four years, and may not serve more than two consecutive terms. He or she must be a Russian citizen, at least 35 years old, and a resident of Russia for 10 years.

Recall that Boris Yeltsin was elected president of the old Russian Republic in 1991. Yeltsin kept his office under the new constitution in 1993. In a historic election in June 1996, he faced challenges from nine other candidates (including Gorbachev).

A different outcome might have changed the direction of reform in Russia, but Yeltsin was reelected. He was, however, beset by health problems and by accusations of corruption in his inner circle. He often appeared to make erratic decisions, naming—and firing—several prime ministers.

In a surprise move, Yeltsin resigned at the end of December 1999, yielding the presidency to his latest prime minister, Vladimir Putin. Putin won election on his own in March 2000.

## The Legislature

Russia's legislature, the Federal Assembly, is a bicameral body. Its upper house, the Council of the Federation, is composed of 178 members, two members from each of Russia's 89 constituent regions. The lower house, the State Duma, has 450 members, called deputies. The members of both houses are popularly elected for four-year terms.

The Duma is the more powerful chamber. Any measure passed by the Duma but rejected by the Council may nonetheless become law if it is passed again by the Duma by at least a two-thirds majority. The Duma also must approve the president's choice of a prime minister.

Presidential vetoes can be overridden by a two-thirds vote in each house. The Duma can also be dissolved in much the same way as can the House of Commons in Great Britain.

## Constitutional Court

Under the 1993 constitution, a 19-member Constitutional Court can rule on the constitutionality of federal laws, actions of the president and assembly, and the laws of local governments. Its judges are elected to 12-year terms.

**Interpreting Political Cartoons** *(a) Who is most likely the speaker in this cartoon? (b) To what political situation does the cartoon refer?*

## Regional and Local Governments

Local governments in Russia are a patchwork of different organizational structures. The Russian Federation comprises 49 *oblasts* (provinces) and 6 large, thinly populated territories, all of which are headed by elected governors. The governors of these regions have traditionally exercised great power.

The federation also includes 21 republics, which are home to ethnic, non-Russian minorities, and 10 autonomous areas. Each republic elects a president. Independence is a burning issue in several republics. The Republic of Chechnya attempted to break away from the Russian Federation in 1994, and the Russian military has been engaged there ever since.

## Section 4 Assessment

### Key Terms and Main Ideas

1. (a) What were the roles of Lenin and Stalin in creating the communist state? (b) How did Stalin use **purges?**
2. What was Gorbachev's purpose in introducing *perestroika* and *glasnost?*
3. Briefly describe the events that led to the fall of the Soviet Union.
4. How did the Constitution of 1993 differ from the old Soviet constitution?

### Critical Thinking

5. **Drawing Inferences** Gorbachev hoped to create a democratic and open system of government while preserving the communist system. In what way were these goals incompatible?

6. **Identifying Assumptions** The Soviet constitution declared that "[t]he exercise by citizens of rights and freedoms must not injure the interests of society and the state." What assumption underlies this statement?

 **Take It to the Net**

7. Read about *glasnost* and *perestroika*. Write a short essay explaining how these two concepts were revolutionary in Russia at the time and how they led to a change of government. Use the links provided in the Social Studies area at the following Web site for help in completing this activity. **www.phschool.com**

 **Take It to the Net**

7. Direct students to the Social Studies area at the Prentice Hall School Web site. The *Magruder's American Government* companion Web site includes the directions and links needed to complete the activity. It also provides a printable Internet activity worksheet with scoring rubrics for assessment. Essays should show an understanding of how the concepts of reform and openness were revolutionary in Russia.

5. The communist system is based on a one-party state; the Communist Party has no opposition. A democratic system is based on a variety of opinions and opposing groups.
6. The needs of the state and society as a whole are more important than individual rights.

## Point-of-Use Resources

**Guide to the Essentials** Chapter 22, Section 4, p. 120 provides support for students who need additional review of section content. Spanish support is available in the Spanish edition of the Guide on p. 113.

**Quiz** Unit 6 booklet, p. 9 includes matching and multiple-choice questions to check students' understanding of Section 4 content.

**Presentation Pro CD-ROM** Quizzes and multiple-choice questions check students' understanding of Section 4 content.

## Answers to . . .

### Section 4 Assessment

**1. (a)** Lenin began the development of Russia into a communist state; Stalin built the Soviet Union into a major industrial and military power. **(b)** Stalin "purified" the government by having millions of dissidents jailed, exiled, or executed.
**2.** Gorbachev wanted to restructure economic and political life and to increase the government's tolerance of freedom of expression.
**3.** In 1985, Gorbachev undertook a reform program, initiating a series of independence movements throughout Eastern Europe. When Yeltsin became president of the new Russian Republic in 1991, he resigned from the Communist Party and declared Russia's laws sovereign. Fifteen republics then left the Union.
**4.** The Constitution of 1993 proclaims that the Russian Federation is a democratic state; it contains an extensive list of individual rights. The Soviet constitution did not limit government power or guarantee basic rights.

### Answer to . . .

**Interpreting Political Cartoons**
**(a)** Boris Yeltsin. **(b)** Before his resignation in December 1999, Yeltsin named and fired several prime ministers.

## Section Preview

### OBJECTIVES

1. **Examine** China's political background.
2. **Describe** China's government today.
3. **Analyze** the political significance to the United States of the island of Taiwan.

### WHY IT MATTERS

The People's Republic of China is controlled by the Chinese Communist Party, the largest political party in the world. Although the Chinese government is pursuing economic reform, it continues to repress political dissent.

### POLITICAL DICTIONARY

★ Cultural Revolution
★ autonomous

**Objectives** You may wish to call students' attention to the objectives in the Section Preview. The objectives are reflected in the main headings of the section.

**Bellringer** Ask students to suppose that they are taking a long bike trip with a group of people. Some riders disagree at first on the best route to take, but eventually everyone is headed in the same direction, on the same road—all except one rider, who insists on taking a completely different road. Explain that in this section they will read about a country that has decided to follow a different political road.

**Vocabulary Builder** Point out the terms in the Political Dictionary. Ask students whether they have heard the term *cultural revolution* applied to popular culture (a new type of music, for example). Then ask what they know about China's Cultural Revolution.

## Pressed for Time?

### Quick Lesson Plan

1. **Focus** Tell students that China's Communist Party is still firmly in control of the Chinese government. Ask them to discuss what they know about China's political history since 1949.

2. **Instruct** Ask students to show the structure of the Communist Party and the national government on the chalkboard. Have them describe the role of the National People's Congress in China's political system. *("rubber stamps" Communist Party policies)* Then discuss Mao's and Deng's effects on China as well as the issue of Taiwan.

3. **Close/Reteach** Remind students that the Chinese constitution reflects current governmental policies, not fundamental law. Ask pairs of students to create sets of questions about China's constitution, recent history, and national and local governments, and then quiz each other.

▲ This 1967 poster features Chairman Mao. Demonstrators are holding copies of the "Little Red Book," which contains the basic tenets of Chinese communism.

The governments you have looked at to this point have a number of features in common. The government of China, on the other hand, lives in a world unto itself.

## Political Background

Although the political history of what is today China can be traced back some 5,000 years, China's present-day government has existed for little more than 50 years.[14] The People's Republic of China was born in 1949 after decades of civil war. Those years of bitter strife pitted China's Nationalist government, led by Chiang Kai-shek, against rebel communists led by Mao Zedong.

The United States supported Chiang's Nationalist government during World War II and for a few years thereafter. But American aid was often misused by corrupt officials and by the ineffective commanders of the ill-trained Nationalist army.

At the same time, Mao, a committed communist, organized a patriotic movement that appealed to the Chinese peasantry, whom the Nationalist elite had long ignored. His Red Army vanquished the Nationalists in a series of battles in the immediate postwar years.

## China Under Mao

By 1949, Mao's forces had captured the Chinese capital, Beijing. Nationalist forces fled the mainland for the island of Taiwan. In October 1949, communist forces established the People's Republic of China, with Mao as its leader.

Mao was bent on increasing agricultural and industrial production. He turned to central planning and instituted a series of Five-Year Plans. Frequent and often drastic changes in policy produced chaos and regularly thwarted economic development.

By the mid-1960s, Mao was determined to purge China of what he called the "Four Olds" —old thoughts, old culture, old customs, and old habits. In the **Cultural Revolution,** begun in 1966, Mao's young, dedicated Red Guards attacked and bullied teachers, intellectuals, and anyone else who seemed to lack revolutionary fervor.

Artists and scholars were sent to farms to be "re-educated"; ancient books and art were destroyed. By 1968, however, the havoc created by the Cultural Revolution persuaded Mao to abandon that effort.

## Reform and Repression

Deng Xiaoping came to power after Mao's death in 1976. Deng's reforms loosened the government's strict controls on the economy and encouraged some forms of private enterprise.

---

[14]The population of the People's Republic of China now exceeds 1.3 billion; that figure does not include more than 7 million residents of Hong Kong.

## Block Scheduling Strategies

Consider these suggestions to manage extended class time:

■ Divide the class into two groups. Have each group skim the text for important terms or concepts and develop five clues for each term. Then have students take turns standing and asking the other group to identify the correct term or concept. The person asking the question should first identify the country to which the clue applies. This activity can be adjusted into a game format with assigned point values for correct answers, based on the number of clues needed before answering.

■ Have students hold a mock national press conference for world powers. Divide the class into six groups; five will represent the countries discussed in this chapter, while the sixth will represent the U.S. The U.S. group will develop a list of questions to ask each country about their social, economic, and political developments in their nation's history. Each of the other groups should have the same amount of time to respond.

## China

| | | |
|---|---|---|
| **Type**<br>Communist state | | **Legislative branch**<br>Unicameral National<br>People's Congress |
| **Constitution**<br>Adopted December 4, 1982 | | **Judicial branch**<br>Supreme People's Court,<br>judges appointed by National<br>People's Congress |
| **Chief of state**<br>President Jiang Zemin | | |
| **Head of government**<br>Premier Zhu Rongji | | |
| **Executive branch**<br>President elected by National<br>People's Congress for a<br>five-year term; premier<br>nominated by president,<br>confirmed by National People's<br>Congress | |
**Jiang Zemin** |

0    500    1000 Miles
0    500    1000 Kilometer

RUSSIA · KAZAKHSTAN · MONGOLIA · Beijing · CHINA · NEPAL · INDIA · MYANMAR · LAOS · VIETNAM · NORTH KOREA · SOUTH KOREA · Yellow Sea · Taiwan · Hong Kong · South China Sea

 *Interpreting Maps* The People's Republic of China is a communist state in which the top-ranking members of the Communist Party hold the highest positions in the government and the military. ***How does the size and location of Taiwan place it in danger from its communist neighbor?***

Although the Chinese government relaxed economic controls under Deng, it tolerated no political dissent. In May 1989, students and workers in many parts of the country held demonstrations calling for democracy. In early June, government soldiers with tanks attacked pro-democracy protesters in Tiananmen Square, in the heart of Beijing. Thousands of protestors were killed, outraging people around the world.

## China Today

Today, China's leaders continue to encourage economic reforms. At the same time, they also continue to impose harsh limits on human rights.

### The Constitution

When the communists gained power, the People's Political Consultative Conference adopted a provisional constitution. That document became the basis for a new constitution adopted by the first session of the National People's Congress in 1954.

Unlike the Constitution of the United States and those of most other nations, China's constitution is not intended to be fundamental law. Instead, it is supposed to reflect current governmental policies. China has had four constitutions since its founding—in 1954, 1975, 1978, and 1982.

### China's Communist Party

China's Communist Party (the CCP) has some 58 million members, and is, by far, the largest political party in the world. The top-ranking members of the party hold the highest positions in the government and the military. In short, the CCP *is* the government of China.

Recall the organization of the Communist Party in the former Soviet Union. The present-day Chinese Communist Party has a similar structure. Its main units are the National Party Congress, the Central Committee, the Politburo, and the Secretariat.

The National Party Congress has some 1,900 members who meet approximately every five years to elect a Central Committee of about 300 members. The Central Committee elects the much smaller Politburo. The Politburo makes party policy, while the Secretariat makes the party's day-to-day decisions.

### The National Government

The national government of China is composed of two main bodies, the National People's Congress and the State Council.

*1. National People's Congress.* The nearly 3,000 deputies of the National People's Congress are elected by local people's con-

## Point-of-Use Resources

 **Guide to the Essentials** Chapter 22, Section 5, p. 121 provides support for students who need additional review of section content. Spanish support is available in the Spanish edition of the Guide on p. 114.

**Quiz** Unit 6 booklet, p. 11 includes matching and multiple-choice questions to check students' understanding of Section 5 content.

**Presentation Pro CD-ROM** Quizzes and multiple-choice questions check students' understanding of Section 5 content.

## Answers to . . .

### Section 5 Assessment

**1. (a)** After years of strife, Mao Zedong's communist forces vanquished Chiang Kai-shek's Nationalists. Mao established the People's Republic of China; Chiang Kai-shek fled to Taiwan, which he proclaimed the Republic of China. **(b)** Mao's attempt to purge China of traditional culture.

**2.** On the basis of current government policies.

**3.** The relationship is strained; both governments claim to be the true rulers of China.

**4.** It is a special administrative region of China.

**5.** China and Russia are both attempting economic reform. China, however, especially in its policies regarding dissent, is not pursuing political reform.

**6.** Top-ranking members of the Communist Party hold the country's highest positions in the government and the military.

▲ The British returned the prosperous island of Hong Kong to Chinese control in 1997.

gresses throughout China. According to the Chinese constitution, the National People's Congress is the highest governmental authority. In reality, it has little power. It performs its major function when it passes the policy decisions of the State Council and the CCP on to lower levels of government.

*2. The State Council.* The State Council is the main body in the executive branch of Chinese government. It is headed by the premier, who is chosen by the Central Committee of the CCP. The premier, vice-premiers, state councilors, and secretary-general meet regularly as a standing committee. This Standing Committee of the State Council possesses major decision-making authority, and its decisions have the force of law.

### The Judicial System

A nationwide system of "people's courts" deals with both criminal and civil cases. Those courts are supervised by the Supreme People's Court—in effect, the nation's Supreme Court. Capital punishment may be the penalty for conviction of any of a long list of crimes: murder, treason, bribery, and many others. Most guarantees of fair trial are absent from Chinese law.

### Local Political Divisions

China has a unitary government, with the central government exerting direct control over local subdivisions. Local administrative regions include 22 provinces and 5 **autonomous** (independent) regions whose people are mostly ethnic minorities. Hong Kong, which the British returned to China's control in 1997, is a special administrative region of China with its own governor and provisional legislature.

### Taiwan

When Mao's forces took over the mainland in 1949, Chiang Kai-shek and the Nationalists fled to the island of Formosa (Taiwan), establishing the Republic of China. Today the People's Republic of China considers Taiwan one of its provinces. In turn, the Republic of China (Taiwan) takes the position that its National Assembly rules all of China. The United States supports Taiwan with military and other resources in an effort to keep the island from being swallowed politically and economically by its enormous communist neighbor.

## Section **5** Assessment

**Key Terms and Main Ideas**

1. **(a)** Summarize the events that led to the establishment of the People's Republic of China. **(b)** What was the **Cultural Revolution**?
2. On what basis does China change its constitution?
3. What is the relationship between the People's Republic of China and the Republic of China (Taiwan)?
4. What is Hong Kong's status today?

**Critical Thinking**

5. **Making Comparisons** Compare efforts at economic and political reform in China with those in Russia today.

6. **Checking Consistency** Give evidence from the section to support the following statement: *The Chinese Communist Party dominates the political life of China.*

 **Take It to the Net**

7. Read about the flooding of China's Yantze River valley in order to create hydroelectric power. Analyze and evaluate the consequences of this government policy on the physical and human characteristics of the region in a new article for a hypothetical Chinese newspaper. Use the links provided in the Social Studies area at the following Web site for help in completing this activity.
**www.phschool.com**

**Take It to the Net**

**7.** Direct students to the Social Studies area at the Prentice Hall School Web site. The *Magruder's American Government* companion Web site includes the directions and links needed to complete the activity. It also provides a printable Internet activity worksheet, with scoring rubrics for assessment. News articles should reveal careful research into the topic and an understanding of the interaction between government policy and human and physical geography.

# on the Supreme Court

## May the Government Regulate the Internet?

*Efforts to protect young people from inappropriate materials on the Internet run the risk of violating the First Amendment rights of adult Internet users. How far can the Federal Government go in regulating the transmission of such materials over the Internet?*

### Reno v. ACLU (1997)

Congress passed the Telecommunications Act of 1996 to reduce regulation and promote the rapid deployment of new telecommunications technologies. Most of the law deals with encouraging competition in local telephone, video, and over-the-air broadcasting. One portion of the law, called the Communications Decency Act of 1996, imposes restrictions on the content of information that may be communicated by electronic devices.

Two key sections of the Communications Decency Act are informally called the "indecent transmission" provision and the "patently offensive display" provision. They make it a crime to use any telecommunications device to make an indecent or obscene comment to a person known to be under 18 years old, or knowingly to send or display offensive messages in a way that makes them available to persons under 18. There is an exception for people who take "good faith, reasonable, effective and appropriate actions" to restrict access by minors, such as by requiring persons to provide proof of age.

A group of 47 organizations, including the American Civil Liberties Union, challenged the law as unconstitutional. A federal district court ordered the government not to enforce the law, which the court said was too vague and broad. On behalf of the Federal Government, Attorney General Janet Reno appealed to the Supreme Court.

### Arguments for Reno

1. The government historically has had broad rights to regulate the broadcast industry and to protect minors from offensive materials. It should be allowed the same powers regarding the Internet.

2. The law clearly explains which activities are not permitted.

3. The law's "good faith" exception will protect those who are not seeking to engage in unlawful conduct.

### Arguments for the ACLU

1. The Internet is fundamentally different from broadcast media. It has not historically been regulated by the Federal Government, and is not as "invasive" as radio or television.

2. The law is too vague, because it is often impossible to determine whether a particular communication will violate its provisions. Terms such as "indecent" are not defined in the law, and their meaning will vary from person to person.

3. The law is too broad, because efforts to comply with the law will have the effect of interfering with communication among adults. Often it is not possible to determine whether a person who participates in an Internet conversation or has access to Internet materials is under 18 years old.

### Decide for Yourself

1. Review the constitutional grounds on which each side based its arguments and the specific arguments each side presented.

2. Debate the opposing viewpoints presented in this case. Which viewpoint do you favor?

3. Predict the impact of the Court's decision on the growth of the Internet and on government efforts to protect minors from indecent materials. (To read a summary of the Court's decision, turn to the Supreme Court Glossary on page 799.)

 Corner

📁 **Close Up on the Supreme Court** *Reno v. ACLU,* p. 23 provides an activity to extend coverage of this case.

 Online

To keep up-to-date on Close Up news and activities, visit Close Up Online at

**www.closeup.org**

---

## May the Government Regulate the Internet?

**Focus** Explain that many people view the Internet as an ideal tool for spreading democracy because it provides an open forum for debating a wide variety of opinions. Then explain that others believe the government should pass a law restricting the ability of minors to gain access to sexually explicit materials on the Internet.

**Instruct** Discuss whether under the First Amendment the Federal Government has the power to regulate children's access to the Internet. Following class debate, have the class vote on how they would decide the case. Then have the class read the Supreme Court's decision to find out if their decision agrees with the Court's.

**Close/Reteach** Explain that some countries have tried to regulate or restrict access to the Internet for reasons other than protecting minors. For instance, China has attempted to restrict access and has jailed political dissidents for criticizing the government online.

💿 **Keep It Current CD-ROM** includes government-related projects by unit. The CD-ROM links to the Prentice Hall School Web site and may be used for daily updates.

### Answers to . . .
**Decide for Yourself**

1. Reno argued that the government has traditional rights concerning regulation of broadcasting. The ACLU argued that the Internet is a completely different medium, and, more importantly, that the law in question is too broad and vague to be useful.

2. Answers will vary, but should be supported with valid reasoning.

3. The Court ruled in favor of the ACLU, holding that both provisions of the Communications Decency Act violated the First Amendment.

**653**

## Practicing the Vocabulary

**1.** purge
**2.** Cultural Revolution
**3.** mestizo
**4.** prefecture
**5.** by-election
**6.** *Perestroika:* a plan for restructuring political and economic life. *Glasnost:* the policy of openness.
**7.** Nationalization: the government acquisition of private industry for public use. Devolution: the delegation of authority from the central government to regional governments.
**8.** Shadow cabinet: team of opposition party MPs who watch one particular member of the cabinet. Soviets: elected councils in the Soviet Union.
**9.** Monarchy: rule by a king or queen. Minister: a cabinet member in a parliamentary system.
**10.** Coalition: a temporary alliance of parties to form a government. Consensus: broad agreement.

## Reviewing Main Ideas
### Section 1

**11.** The British constitution consists of a written portion (the law) and an unwritten portion (the conventions).
**12. (a)** Parliament has two houses—the House of Lords and the House of Commons. **(b)** In 1999, Parliament passed legislation that eliminated the 750 peers from the House of Lords.
**13.** The prime minister is chosen from the majority party or a coalition of parties in Parliament. The prime minister then selects the cabinet from among the members of Parliament.

### Section 2

**14. (a)** It renounces war and forbids the nation from establishing a military. **(b)** The United States, which occupied Japan after World War II, insisted on the clause. **(c)** To allow a self-defense force.
**15. (a)** The Diet consists of an upper house, the House of Councillors, and a lower house, the House of Representatives. **(b)** The prime minister is selected from the majority party or coalition in the House of Representatives.
**16.** It is well-respected, powerful, and cooperates closely with industry.

### Section 3

**17.** Spain conquered Mexico in 1521,

## Political Dictionary

| | | |
|---|---|---|
| monarchy (p. 627) | dissolution (p. 636) | soviets (p. 646) |
| by-election (p. 628) | prefecture (p. 637) | *perestroika* (p. 646) |
| coalition (p. 628) | mestizo (p. 639) | *glasnost* (p. 646) |
| minister (p. 629) | nationalization (p. 642) | Cultural Revolution (p. 650) |
| shadow cabinet (p. 629) | North American Free Trade Agreement (NAFTA) (p. 642) | autonomous (p. 652) |
| devolution (p. 631) | | |
| consensus (p. 636) | purge (p. 645) | |

## Practicing the Vocabulary

**Matching**  *Choose a term from the list above that best matches each description.*

**1.** Stalin's elimination of rivals and other dissidents
**2.** Movement intended to cleanse China of the "Four Olds"
**3.** A person with both Spanish or Portuguese and Native American ancestry
**4.** Political subdivision in Japan
**5.** A special election held to fill a vacant seat in the House of Commons

**Word Relationships**  *Distinguish between the words in each pair.*

**6.** *perestroika/glasnost*
**7.** nationalization/devolution
**8.** shadow cabinet/soviets
**9.** monarchy/minister
**10.** coalition/consensus

## Reviewing Main Ideas

### Section 1

**11.** In what ways does Great Britain's constitution differ from the United States Constitution?
**12. (a)** Briefly describe the organization of Britain's Parliament. **(b)** What recent change has been made in the House of Lords?
**13.** How are Britain's prime minister and cabinet members chosen?

### Section 2

**14. (a)** What is the anti-military clause of Japan's constitution? **(b)** Why is it part of that constitution? **(c)** How have interpretations of the clause changed over time?
**15. (a)** Briefly describe the organization of the National Diet. **(b)** How are the prime minister and cabinet chosen?
**16.** List three characteristics of the Japanese bureaucracy.

### Section 3

**17.** Briefly describe Mexico's history up to 1821.
**18. (a)** Describe Mexico's three branches of government. **(b)** Compare Mexico's three branches of government with the three branches of the United States government.

**19. (a)** What was the role of the PRI in the Mexican political system before 2000? **(b)** Who won the presidency in 2000?

### Section 4

**20. (a)** Briefly describe the importance of Lenin and Stalin in Soviet history. **(b)** Describe the Soviet Union at the end of World War II.
**21. (a)** Outline Gorbachev's plans for reform. **(b)** How successful were they?
**22.** Briefly describe the government of Russia today.

### Section 5

**23.** Describe the government of China under Mao Zedong.
**24.** What is the role of the Communist Party in the People's Republic of China?
**25.** Why does Taiwan have a government separate from that of mainland China?

beginning a period of Spanish colonization that lasted until 1821, when Mexico declared its independence.
**18. (a)** Executive, legislative, and judicial. **(b)** The structure and functions of the three branches are very similar in both countries.
**19. (a)** The PRI dominated Mexican politics. **(b)** Vicente Fox; as a result, the PRI was no longer the dominant party.

### Section 4

**20. (a)** Lenin began and Stalin completed the development of Russia into a communist state and a major power. **(b)** The Soviet Union controlled all of Eastern Europe and had emerged as one of the world's two superpowers.
**21. (a)** To restructure economic and political life, to increase freedom of expression, to allow multi-candidate elections, to create the office of president,

and to reduce the Communist Party's power. **(b)** Very successful; they led to the fall of the Soviet Union. Russia is still struggling, however, toward a stable government and economy.
**22.** The Russian government is theoretically built on a separation of powers between the executive and legislative branches, but the president has a central role. The legislature is bicameral.

## Critical Thinking Skills

**26.** *Applying the Chapter Skill*  What can you infer about China's Communist Party from the fact that despite its enormous power, it includes only about 5 percent of the nation's population?

**27.** *Making Decisions*  Create a table to compare the U.S. system of government with other political systems. Show similarities and differences between the U.S. system and that of Britain, Japan, Mexico, Russia, and China.

**28.** *Making Comparisons*  You have read that the American government is deeply rooted in the British system. Explain briefly how the American and British constitutions are similar and different.

**29.** *Drawing Inferences*  As part of the consensus politics practiced in Japan, political majorities in the National Diet try to avoid pushing through a bill against strong opposition. **(a)** How does this practice differ from politics in the United States? **(b)** What are the advantages and disadvantages of the Japanese system?

## Analyzing Political Cartoons

Using your knowledge of comparative government and this cartoon, answer the questions below.

**30.** Dragons have figured prominently in Chinese culture for centuries. What is the significance of the dragon in this cartoon?

**31. (a)** To what political situation does the cartoon refer?
**(b)** What is the political significance of this situation to the United States?

## Participation Activities

**32.** *Current Events Watch*  Choose one of the countries covered in this chapter. Scan magazines and newspapers for articles about recent political events in that country. Then prepare an oral update on your chosen country's government and politics to present to your classmates. Use charts, graphs, or copies of photos to accompany your update if you choose.

**33.** *Time Line Activity*  Create a time line that traces the events in Russia and the former Soviet Union from 1985 to the present. Illustrate your time line with drawings and copies of newspaper and magazine photos.

**34.** *It's Your Turn*  Interview a recent immigrant from one of the countries covered in the chapter or from another country of your choice. Find out the ways (if any) that this person participated in politics and how he or she views the government of his or her country of origin. Why did he or she come to the United States? How does he or she view the United States government? Write up your interview to share with the class. **(Conducting an Interview)**

## Point–of–Use Resources

 **Guide to the Essentials of American Government** Chapter 22 Test, page 122 provides multiple-choice questions to test students' knowledge of the chapter.

**Test Bank CD-ROM** Chapter 22 Test

**Chapter Test** Chapter Tests booklet

## Section 5

**23.** Mao strictly controlled the country's centrally planned economy, and was responsible for the havoc created by the Cultural Revolution.
**24.** The Communist Party and the Chinese government are synonymous.
**25.** When the Red Army defeated the Nationalists in 1949, Nationalist forces fled to Taiwan. Mao Zedong established the People's Republic of China on the mainland.

## Critical Thinking Skills
**26.** The Communist Party is an elite and nonrepresentative body.
**27.** Tables should include each country listed, and columns (or rows) for similarities to and differences from the United States government.
**28.** Both limit the power of rulers and advance the concept of due process. The British constitution, however, is based on a flexible set of rules that is always evolving. The U.S. Constitution is based on rules that require a complex process to effect change.
**29. (a)** In the United States, disagreement is an expected part of politics. **(b)** Advantages: Compromises can be reached more quickly without legislation getting bogged down. Disadvantages: Legislation may be bland rather than bold. Minority opinions may not be heard.

## Analyzing Political Cartoons
**30.** The dragon represents the menacing strength of China.
**31. (a)** The People's Republic of China and the Republic of China (Taiwan) both claim to represent the true Chinese government. **(b)** The situation makes it difficult for the United States to maintain diplomatic ties with both countries.

## You Can Make a Difference
Encourage students to determine their own interests and skills before contacting a group, so that they can find volunteer work most suitable to them.

## Participation Activities
**32.** Oral updates should show an understanding of issues involving the chosen country's government.
**33.** Time lines should include significant events in Russia from the Gorbachev era to the present.
**34.** Interviews should reflect questions and answers that help students understand another country's government.

# Comparative Economic Systems

| Section Objectives | Print and Technology Resources | |
|---|---|---|
| **1 Capitalism** (pp. 658–664) | • **Unit 6 booklet** Guided Reading and Review, p. 13 Section 1 Quiz, p. 14 | • **Government Assessment Rubrics booklet** p. 20 |
| 1. Identify the factors of production. | • **Lesson Plans booklet** Section 1, p. 99 | • **Basic Principles of the Constitution Transparencies** 29 |
| 2. Describe the free enterprise system and laissez-faire theory. | • **Political Cartoons booklet** Section 1, p. 91 | • **Section Support Transparencies** 94, 193 |
| 3. Analyze government policies that influence the economy at the local, State, and national levels. | • **Block Scheduling with Lesson Strategies booklet** p. 30 | • **Presentation Pro CD-ROM** Section 1 |
| 4. Compare and contrast three types of business organizations. | • **Close Up on Primary Sources booklet** *The Wealth of Nations*, p. 30 | • **Section Reading Support Transparencies** |
| 5. Explain the role of profit and loss in a free enterprise system. | • **The Living Constitution booklet** p. 4 | • **Social Studies Skills Tutor CD-ROM** |
| **TEKS 6A, 6C, 8B, 8F, 9G, 17C, 21A, 21C, 21D, 21E, 22A, 22B** | | |
| **2 Socialism** (pp. 666–670) | • **Unit 6 booklet** Guided Reading and Review, p. 15 Section 2 Quiz, p. 16 | Working to Eliminate Child Labor, pp. 18–19 |
| 1. Define socialism and explain how it developed from the Industrial Revolution. | • **Lesson Plans booklet** Section 2, p. 100 | • **Section Support Transparencies** 95, 194 |
| 2. Identify important characteristics of socialist economies. | • **Political Cartoons booklet** Section 2, p. 92 | • **Presentation Pro CD-ROM** Section 2 |
| 3. Describe socialism in developing countries. | • **Close Up on Primary Sources booklet** New Labour in Great Britain, p. 25 | • **Simulations and Data Graphing CD-ROM** |
| 4. Evaluate the pros and cons of socialism. | • **Close Up on Participation booklet** | • **Section Reading Support Transparencies** |
| **TEKS 6C, 13A, 17C, 21A, 21C, 21D, 21E, 22A, 22B** | | |
| **3 Communism** (pp. 672–676) | • **Unit 6 booklet** Guided Reading and Review, p. 17 Section 3 Quiz, p. 18 Skills for Life Activity, p. 19 | • **Close Up on the Supreme Court booklet** *Shelley* v. *Kraemer*, p. 24 |
| 1. Summarize the theories of Karl Marx. | • **Lesson Plans booklet** Section 3, p. 101 | • **The Basic Principles of the Constitution Posters** |
| 2. Outline the characteristics of communist economics. | • **Political Cartoons booklet** Section 3, p. 93 | • **Section Support Transparencies** 96, 195 |
| 3. Describe communism in the Soviet Union, China, and other nations. | • **Section Reading Support Transparencies** | • **Presentation Pro CD-ROM** Section 3 |
| **TEKS 6C, 13A, 21A, 21C, 22A, 22B** | | |

# Block Scheduling Strategies

The *Magruder's American Government* program addresses block-scheduling strategies in a variety of ways. For easy reference, side-column activities that fit a block format are marked ▦ **Block Strategy.** Each section also contains a **Block Scheduling Strategies** box describing at least two block-format activities that address and extend core content from the section. The **Block Scheduling with Lesson Strategies booklet** found in the Teaching Resources contains additional block-scheduling activities for each chapter.

## Take It to the Net

Visit the Social Studies area at the Prentice Hall School Web site. Once there, you can find additional links, current events connections, and activities to enrich chapter content for *Magruder's American Government,* as well as a Self-Test for students. Be sure to check out this month's **eTeach** online discussion with a Master Teacher.

### www.phschool.com

## Pressed for Time?

If you are running short on time to cover this chapter, consider one of the following options:
- Use the **Presentation Pro CD-ROM** to create an outline for this chapter.
- Use one of the **Pressed for Time** activities found on p. 27.
- Use the Section Summaries for Chapter 2, from **Guide to the Essentials of American Government (English and Spanish).**

 ## Video Connections

Prentice Hall offers two video programs to reinforce and extend chapter content. Show students *The Blessings of Liberty* from the **ABC News Civics and Government Videotape Library** and *Prayer in Schools: A Nationwide Debate* from the **Magruder's American Government Video Collection.**

## Assessment Options
- Section Quizzes, **Unit 6 booklet,** pp. 14, 16, 18
- Chapter 23 Assessment, pp. 678–679
- **Guide to the Essentials of American Government,** Chapter 23 Test, p. 126

### Core Assessment
Chapter 23 Test, Chapter Tests booklet
ExamView® Test Bank CD-ROM Chapter 23
Government Assessment Rubrics

### Standardized Test Preparation
#### Diagnose and Prescribe
Diagnostic Tests for High School
Social Studies Skills

#### Review and Reteach
Review Book for Government

#### Practice and Assess
Test-Taking Strategies With
 Transparencies for High School
Test Prep Book for Government

## Chapter 23 Teacher's Edition Index

# Comparative Economic Systems

## Introducing the Chapter

In this chapter, students will learn about the three main types of economic systems—capitalism, socialism, and communism—and how they shape political systems and people's lives around the world.

### Make It Relevant

★ *You Can Make a Difference*

Direct a pair of students to contact appropriate child welfare offices in your community or State. Have them interview officials with the goal of determining what the public can do to help stop abuse of children. After the pair has reported to the class, develop a program that implements the welfare office's suggestion. Oversee students as they conceive, design, and implement the plan. Consider inviting a child welfare official to the class to assist students in the organization and implementation of their program.

**Service Learning**

## CONSTITUTIONAL PRINCIPLES

Emphasize the following basic principles as students read Chapter 23. Have the class respond to the questions, and then ask volunteers to choose one economic system and explain its impact on each principle.

**Popular Sovereignty** Why do free enterprise systems uphold popular sovereignty more than other economic systems?

**Limited Government** How have some socialist governments been moving toward more limited government?

**Separation of Powers** Which economic system requires no separation of powers?

# Comparative Economic Systems

*"You do not like communism. We do not like capitalism. There is only one way out—peaceful coexistence."*

—Nikita Khrushchev (1956)

Capitalism, socialism, and communism are the main types of economic systems, and they have often come into conflict. Which of those systems a nation follows has a major impact on its political system and many other aspects of people's lives. Many real-world economic systems include some elements of the other two types.

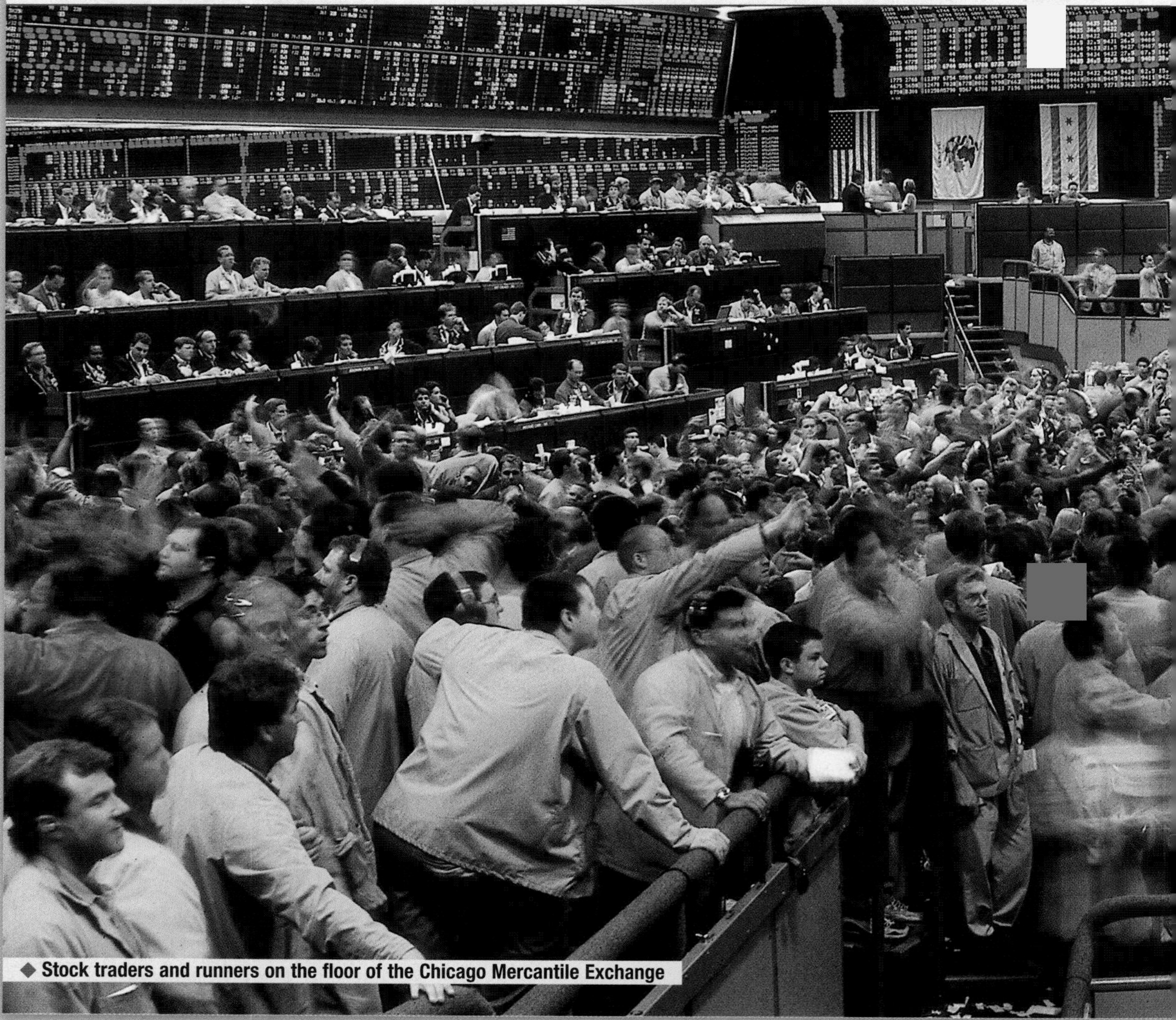

◆ Stock traders and runners on the floor of the Chicago Mercantile Exchange

*Corner*

The following resources are available only from the Close Up Foundation to support the concepts discussed in Chapter 23 "Comparative Economic Systems":

◆ *The American Economy: Government's Role, Citizen's Choice*
◆ *Trade is Everybody's Business*
◆ *The Breakup of the Soviet Union*

To keep up-to-date on Close Up news and activities, visit Close Up Online at

**www.closeup.org**

Close Up Foundation
44 Canal Center Plaza
Alexandria, VA 22314-1592
800-765-3131

## You Can Make a Difference

**ONE OF THE WORLD'S** best-known young activists, Craig Kielburger has crusaded against a sad feature of economic life in some countries—child labor. In 1995, when he was 12, Craig read about a Pakistani boy who had been killed for speaking out against child labor. Craig took up the fight and started "Free the Children" with his classmates in Toronto, Canada. In a few years, the organization had more than 10,000 members in 25 countries. Craig himself traveled to South Asia to talk to child workers in sweatshops. "Free the Children" worked for new laws and raised money to build schools for former child laborers. "We [kids] can be incredibly powerful if we join together," he said.

### Keep It Current

Items marked with this logo are periodically updated on the Internet. Keep up-to-date with what's in the news. To get current information on economic systems, go to **www.phschool.com**

### SECTION 1

#### Capitalism (pp. 658–664)

★ Capitalism is another name for the free enterprise system.
★ Entrepreneurs use land, labor, brain power, and capital to produce goods and services.
★ Private ownership, individual initiative, profit, and competition are the fundamental elements of capitalism.
★ A mixed economy is one in which the government intervenes to promote and regulate the economy.
★ Businesses may be organized as sole proprietorships, partnerships, or corporations.

### SECTION 2

#### Socialism (pp. 666–670)

★ In a socialist economy, the government strives for social and economic equality for all members of society.
★ Karl Marx (1818–1883) and his collaborator Frederick Engels (1820–1895) laid out the basic tenets of modern-day socialism.
★ The British Labour Party and other "Social Democratic Parties" in Europe believe that the ends of socialism can be gained by peaceful, democratic means.
★ Socialist economies feature government ownership of industry, high taxes, and generous public welfare programs.
★ Although socialism began in industrial countries, many developing nations were attracted to socialism by the promise of equality and economic growth.

### SECTION 3

#### Communism (pp. 672–676)

★ Karl Marx predicted that the final stage in human history would be a world of peaceful, democratic communes.
★ No country has ever created a political/economic system that even remotely resembles Marx's ideal.
★ Communist economies depend on a strong central government that owns all industry and farmland and plans all parts of the national economy.
★ In the Soviet Union, Lenin and Stalin created a communist dictatorship that controlled all aspects of life.
★ China, Cuba, North Korea, Vietnam, and other countries have also experimented with communism.

### To Omit the Chapter

If you wish to skip Chapter 23, ask students to read the Chapter in Brief and assign the Guide to the Essentials before continuing to another chapter. You may also want to assign the Chapter 23 Test in the Chapter Test booklet. Then specific portions of Chapter 23 may be assigned to students needing reinforcement of key terms and concepts.

### To Preview the Chapter

To introduce students to key terms and concepts in each section, have them read the Chapter in Brief. You may also assign the Reading Strategy activities on pp. 659, 667, and 673 of this book.

### To Review the Chapter

When students have completed Chapter 23, you might want to assign the Guide to the Essentials or the Guided Reading and Review worksheets on pp. 13, 15, and 17 of the Unit 6 booklet.

### To Cover the Chapter Quickly

To cover the material in Chapter 23 quickly, use the following activity.

**Focus** Ask students what is one of the major differences between the United States and China (or the former Soviet Union). Explain that communism, which is often associated closely with these countries' political organizations, is an *economic* system.

**Instruct** Define the three major economic systems. Explain that these systems were originally theories developed by various philosophers or political thinkers in response to historical conditions. Describe the ideas of Locke, Marx, and Lenin, and how these ideas were implemented in developed and developing nations around the world.

**Close/Reteach** As students read through the chapter, have them fill in a chart about capitalism, socialism, and communism. Charts should include the theorists, leaders, and historical events relevant to each, as well as examples of nations that use each system today.

■ **Block Strategy (Average)**

## Keep It Current

## Internet Update

Use the Prentice Hall School Web site and the Keep It Current CD-ROM to find quick content updates.

Visit **www.phschool.com** for current events articles that are linked to Chapter 23. Critical thinking questions are included.

**Keep It Current CD-ROM** includes government-related projects by unit. Students complete each project using current information that they obtain by linking to the Prentice Hall School Web site from the CD-ROM.

**Objectives** You may wish to call students' attention to the objectives in the Section Preview. The objectives are reflected in the main headings of the section.

**Bellringer** Tell students that people who start new businesses work very long hours, but most new businesses fail. Ask students why, considering these facts, they would ever want to start their own business. Explain that in this section, they will learn about what drives people in a capitalist system to start a business.

**Vocabulary Builder** Ask students to try to use three terms from the Political Dictionary in a single sentence. Have volunteers read their sentences and explain the meaning of each term they used. Encourage students to refine their understanding of these terms as they read the section.

---

## Pressed for Time?

### Quick Lesson Plan

**1. Focus** Tell students that the United States economy is a free enterprise system. Ask students to discuss what they know about the characteristics of a free enterprise system.

**2. Instruct** Be sure students realize that the factors of production apply to all economies. Ask them why it is said that the United States has a mixed economy. Discuss how our economy differs from a "pure" free enterprise system. Then have students explain the different types of American businesses and what drives them.

**3. Close/Reteach** Remind students that profit is a vital part of the free enterprise system. Have students write an explanation of the "profit motive" and other concepts in the section as if they were communicating with a student in the fifth grade.

---

## Point-of-Use Resources

📁 **Block Scheduling with Lesson Strategies** Activities for Chapter 23 are presented on p. 30.

---

# **1** *Capitalism*

## Section Preview

### OBJECTIVES

1. **Identify** the factors of production.
2. **Describe** the free enterprise system and laissez-faire theory.
3. **Analyze** government policies that influence the economy at the local, State, and national levels.
4. **Compare and contrast** three types of business organizations.
5. **Explain** the role of profit and loss in a free enterprise system.

### WHY IT MATTERS

Although the American free enterprise system is rooted in classic laissez-faire theory, government plays a major role in the nation's economic life—and so in the economic life of every person in this country.

### POLITICAL DICTIONARY

★ **factors of production**
★ **capital**
★ **capitalist**
★ **entrepreneur**
★ **free enterprise system**
★ **laws of supply and demand**
★ **monopoly**
★ **trust**
★ **laissez-faire theory**

---

**Y**ou have confronted these questions several times in this book: What are the functions a government ought to undertake? What should it have the power to do? What should it not be allowed to do? Certainly these questions can be asked of just about all areas of human activity, but they are raised very significantly in the realm of economic affairs.

Questions of politics and economics are inseparable. The most important economic questions faced by a nation are also political questions. For example: Who should decide what goods will be produced? How should goods and services be distributed and exchanged within a nation? What types of income or property ought to be taxed? What social services should a government provide?

Capitalism provides one response to all of these questions. Many aspects of capitalism will be familiar to you because the United States (along with countries such as Japan) follows this system.

## Factors of Production

Certain resources are necessary to any nation's economy, no matter what economic system it follows. Economists call these basic resources, which are used to make all goods and services, the **factors of production.**

### Land

One factor of production is land, which in economic terms includes all natural resources. Land has a variety of economic uses, such as agriculture, mining, and forestry. Along with farms and property, economists consider the water in rivers and lakes and the coal, iron, and petroleum found beneath the ground to be part of the land.

▲ In a capitalist system, prices are determined by decisions in the market.

---

## 🔲 Block Scheduling Strategies

Consider these suggestions to manage extended class time:

■ Have students make collages for each factor of production described in the text—land, labor, capital, and entrepreneurs. Have students draw or clip pictures from magazines that provide visual details about each factor.

■ Tell students that they are to pitch the idea of the free enterprise system to the leaders of a socialist country who are considering changing their economic system. Have small groups of students present one aspect of the free enterprise system—private ownership, individual initiative, profit, and competition; two other groups should present facts about mixed economies and business organizations. Have the class make its presentation as a whole.

## The Factors of Production

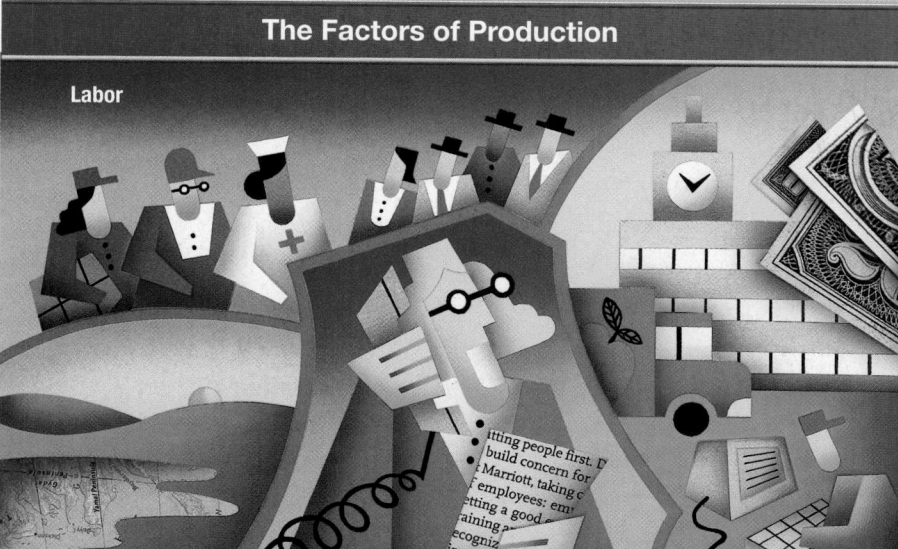

Labor

Land    Entrepreneur    Capital

*Interpreting Diagrams* Land, labor, and capital are the building blocks of the economy. An entrepreneur brings these three factors together to create goods and offer services. ***Give specific examples of land, labor, and capital involved in producing a jacket.***

### Labor

A second factor of production is a human resource—labor. Men and women who work in mines, factories, offices, hospitals, and other places all provide labor that is an essential part of a nation's economy. In a free market economy, individuals "own" their labor and can sell it to any employer.

### Capital

The third factor of production is **capital**—all the human-made resources that are used to produce goods and services. Physical capital (also called "capital goods") includes money, but it also describes the buildings, machines, and computers workers need to turn labor and land into goods and services. Human capital includes knowledge and skills that workers gain from their work experience—an investment in themselves. Note that capital is a product of the economy that is then put back, or reinvested, into the economy.

Someone who owns capital and puts it to productive use is called a **capitalist.** The term is most often applied to people who own large businesses

or factories, but can apply to smaller investors as well. The United States economy is called capitalistic because it depends on the energy and drive of thousands of individual capitalists.

### The Role of the Entrepreneur

To actually produce goods and services, someone must bring together and organize the factors of production. An **entrepreneur**—literally, an "enterpriser"—is an individual with the drive and ambition to combine land, labor, and capital resources to produce goods or offer services. Entrepreneurs start businesses and make them grow, driving the economic growth that contributes to the high standard of living of modern capitalistic societies.

## Free Enterprise System

Capitalism is often called a **free enterprise system.** This is an economic system characterized by private or corporate ownership of capital goods (physical capital) and investments that

## Organizing Information

To make sure students understand the main points of this section, you may wish to use the tree map graphic organizer to the right.

Tell students that a tree map can be used to record information about a main topic, its main ideas, and supporting details. Have students use a tree map to record information about the factors of production. Main ideas should include land, labor, capital, and role of the entrepreneur.

**Teaching Tip** A template for this graphic organizer can be found in the Section Support Transparencies, Transparency 3.

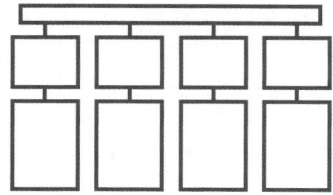

## Learning Styles

**Visual, Spatial** In their notebooks, have students create a web diagram with *free enterprise* in the center of it. Ask them to supply the four characteristics of a free enterprise system as extensions of the web, along with an example for each. Underneath the web on the same sheet of paper, ask students to list the factors of production for an economic system and how they apply to the concept of free enterprise. Ask for volunteers to share their diagrams with the class.
**(Average)**

---

## Make It Relevant

### Students Make a Difference

Eugene Echevarria is a budding businessman. He is the operations manager for CudaCom Printing & Publishing, a firm that makes and sells everything from business cards to banners. Its customers are students and staff at Coral Reef High School in south Miami, Florida, as well as local private businesses. CudaCom is run by the Academy of Business and Finance in the high school, and is staffed entirely by students. In addition to making a profit, its purpose is to teach students the ins and outs of running a business.

Eugene wants to go on to study business administration in college, but he already has a good start as an entrepreneur. His career as a DJ began at the age of 12; now his business, Miami DJs, earns $500 a weekend. Eugene plans to start several more businesses—and to become a millionaire by age 40. "I believe it could happen," he declares.

▲ **Renewal and Rebirth** In a free enterprise system, entrepreneurs try to put land, labor, and/or capital to the best possible (most profitable) use. Through this process, resources can be put to better use. These unused port buildings in New York City's South Street Seaport have reopened as shops.

are determined by private decision rather than by state control. This system operates in a free market.

A free enterprise system lets consumers, entrepreneurs, and workers enjoy freedom of choice. Consumers can choose from a variety of products and services. Entrepreneurs can switch from one business to another. Workers can quit their jobs and take new ones.

There are four fundamental factors in a free enterprise system: private ownership, individual initiative, profit, and competition.

### Private Ownership

One distinctive characteristic of capitalism is that private individuals and companies own most of the means of production—that is, the resources used to produce goods and services. They decide how this productive property will be used. For example, an individual may use capital to build a business, say, or invest in technology. What the property produces is theirs, as well. The owners of productive property are sometimes individuals, but often may be groups of people who share ownership of a company.

In a free enterprise system, individuals also own the right to their labor. Individuals sell their labor by taking a job, and the pay they receive represents the price of their work. In other economic systems, workers may have little choice about what kinds of work they will do and little opportunity to change jobs.

Along with private ownership, the protection of people's property rights is also important. The 5th and 14th amendments to the Constitution declare that no person may be deprived "of life, liberty, or property, without due process of law." The 5th amendment also says that "just compensation" be paid to owners when private property is taken for public use.

### Individual Initiative

In our economy, entrepreneurs are an essential factor in the production of goods and services. Under a free enterprise system, all individuals are free to start and run their own businesses (their own enterprises). They are also free to dissolve those businesses.

That is not necessarily true in other kinds of economic systems. In some places, government officials and public planners make economic decisions about what to produce and how to produce it. Centralized decision making, not individual initiative, controls the production and distribution of goods and services.

### Profit

Just as individuals are free to choose how they will spend or invest their capital, under a free enterprise system, they are also entitled to benefit from whatever their investment or enterprise earns or gains in value. The "profit motive" is the desire to gain from business dealings. It is one reason that entrepreneurs are willing to take risks.

### Competition

The freedom to enter or start a new business at any time leads to competition. Competition is a situation in which a number of companies offer the same product or service. They then must compete against one another for customers. In a free enterprise system, competition often helps to hold down prices and keep quality high. This is because customers are likely to buy from the company with the best product at the lowest price. Competition thus promotes efficiency; the producer has the incentive (more sales) to keep costs low.

Under competitive conditions, the laws of supply and demand determine prices. Supply is the quantity of goods or services for sale. Demand is the desire of potential buyers for those goods and services. According to the **laws of supply and demand,** when supplies become more plentiful, prices tend to drop. As supplies become scarcer, prices tend to rise. By the same token, if demand drops (that is, if there are few buyers), sellers will probably lower their prices in order to make a sale. If demand rises, sellers can raise prices.

Competition does not always work smoothly. Sometimes a single business becomes so successful that all of its rivals go out of business. A firm that is the only source of a product or service is called a **monopoly.** Monopolies can be very powerful in the marketplace. Practically speaking, they can charge as much as they want for a product. Since there is no other supplier of that good or service, the consumer must pay the monopoly price or do without.

Political leaders in the United States decided late in the nineteenth century that monopolies were dangerous. American leaders were especially concerned about a type of monopoly called a **trust.** A trust is a device by which several corporations in the same line of business combine to eliminate competition and regulate prices. In the nineteenth century, trusts controlled the markets for sugar and petroleum. Businesses and consumers had no choice but to buy these goods from the sugar and petroleum trusts.

In response, the Federal Government passed the Sherman Antitrust Act of 1890, which remains the basic law against monopolies today. It prohibits "every contract, combination in the form of a trust or otherwise, or conspiracy in restraint of trade or commerce among the several States, or with foreign nations."

The Antitrust Division in the Department of Justice watches business activities to determine whether competition within an industry is threatened. It can, for example, stop the sale or merger of a company if it might result in the elimination of competitive conditions in the marketplace. On rare occasions, the Department of Justice has broken up an existing monopoly to bring competition into a market. The Federal Government dissolved John D. Rockefeller's Standard Oil Trust in 1911, ending his monopoly over the petroleum industry. Similarly, the

Federal Government broke up American Telephone and Telegraph (AT&T) into several so-called "Baby Bells" to introduce competition into the market for telephone calls. However, the break-up process is time-consuming and not always successful.

In the mid-1990s, the Justice Department challenged Microsoft Corporation's efforts to control the market for its browser—the software that enables its users to access the World Wide Web. In 2000, a federal district judge held Microsoft to be an illegal monopoly that seeks to dominate its market and destroy its competition. He recommended that the computer giant be splintered into two or more competing companies. The Bush administration has not pushed for the break-up, however. Microsoft appealed the ruling, and the case will likely reach the Supreme Court in the near future.

## Laissez-Faire Theory

Early capitalist philosophers believed that, if only government did not interfere, the free enterprise system could work automatically. Adam Smith presented the classic expression of that view in his book, *The Wealth of Nations,* in 1776. Smith wrote that when all individuals are free to pursue their own private interests, an "invisible hand"

*Interpreting Political Cartoons* The Federal Government's Department of Justice sued Microsoft Corporation in the 1990s to restore competition to the software industry. *How does the absence of competition hurt consumers?*

## CONSTITUTIONAL PRINCIPLES

**Limited Government**
Adam Smith's book *The Wealth of Nations* introduced not only laissez-faire capitalism, but the idea of economics as a separate discipline. Smith advocated severe limits on government in the area of economics. He was specifically responding to the English government's practice at that time to form monopolies to grant exclusive trading rights to certain companies. But Smith's ideas also stemmed from his belief that people's capacity for reason regulated their

actions, and was ultimately more influential on economics than government could be.

**Activity**
Have students read the selection from *The Wealth of Nations* in the Close Up on Primary Sources booklet in the *Teaching Resources.* Ask them to summarize the selection in a paragraph, using their own words. Then ask them to find specific examples in the passages that refer to the idea of limited government.

## Voices on Government

**Sadako Ogata** of Japan heads the United Nations High Commission for Refugees (UNHCR). This agency works to help the thousands of people uprooted from their home countries by political and economic conflicts around the world. Ogata sees a direct link between the living conditions of the world's individual communities and the welfare of the global community as a whole.

*"It is essential that political leaders and the civil society in developed countries—including in the United States—be visionary enough to provide support to social and economic reconstruction and to the reconciliation between divided communities, even in countries and regions which are of less immediate strategic interest to them. Only by putting an end to the recurrence of conflicts, and of refugee flows everywhere, will global security be ensured."*

### Evaluating the Quotation

*How might the plight of refugees in some distant land be disruptive to the peace and security of powerful nations like the United States? Do you agree with Ogata that developed nations should help other countries in need? Why or why not?*

works to promote the general welfare. In short, Smith preached laissez-faire capitalism.[1]

**Laissez-faire theory** holds that government should play a very limited, hands-off role in society. Governmental activity should be confined to: (1) foreign relations and national defense, (2) the maintenance of police and courts to protect private property and the health, safety, and morals of the people, and (3) those few other functions that cannot be performed by private enterprise at a profit. The proper role of government in economic affairs should be restricted to functions intended to promote and protect the free play of competition and the operation of the laws of supply and demand.

Laissez-faire capitalism has never in fact operated in this country. Nevertheless, the concept

---

[1]The term *laissez-faire* comes from a French idiom meaning "to let alone."

had, and still has, a profound effect on the structure of the American economic system.

## Influence of Government Policies

Although the American economic system is essentially private in character, government has always played a large part in it. Economists usually describe an economy in which private enterprise and governmental participation coexist as a mixed economy.

Governments at every level regulate many aspects of American economic life. For example, the government prohibits trusts, protects the environment, and ensures the quality of food.

In addition, government policies promote many aspects of American economic life. For example, the government constructs public roads and highways, provides such services as the postal system, the census, and weather reports, and offers many kinds of subsidies and loan programs that help entrepreneurs and businesses to prosper.

The government also conducts some enterprises that might well be operated privately. Examples are found in every aspect of government, including public education, the postal system, various forms of transportation, and water and power systems. Some well-known examples are Amtrak, which provides passenger train service across the country, and the Tennessee Valley Authority, which generates and sells electricity in eight southern States.

Mixed economies are common in Europe and in former communist countries. In Britain, the government provides free medical care to all. The government of the People's Republic of China owns steel mills and factories. Germany's federal government requires large companies to give workers representation on managing boards and France forbids most companies from asking employees to work more than 35 hours a week. In each of these mixed economies, government intervention co-exists with independent companies and market forces.

## Types of Business Organizations

The United States economy contains a number of gigantic companies with thousands of employees and with factories or offices all over the world.

An American firm can organize as a sole proprietorship (left), a partnership (center), or a corporation (right). As a company grows and leaders take on new responsibilities, the company may change from one form to another. *Critical Thinking* **Why is a large manufacturer like Ford unlikely to succeed as a sole proprietorship?**

Still, most businesses in the United States are relatively small. Some 80 percent of businesses employ fewer than 20 people.

There are three basic types of business organizations: sole proprietorships, partnerships, and corporations. Each has advantages and disadvantages.

### Sole Proprietorships

Businesses owned by a single individual are sole proprietorships. Typical of businesses in this category might be a hair salon, a garage, or an ice cream shop. Three quarters of businesses in the United States are sole proprietorships. However, because most sole proprietorships are small, they produce only a small fraction of annual sales in the United States.

Sole proprietorships are the most flexible form of business organization. A major advantage of sole proprietorships is that the single owner can make decisions quickly. The owner enjoys full control of the company, and can draw a salary or close the business without needing the approval of others. A major disadvantage is that the owner is personally liable for debts the business might build up. Sole proprietorships

are also limited by the owner's ability to contribute resources and manage the business.

### Partnerships

Businesses owned by two or more individuals, called partners, are partnerships. Lawyers and architects are some professionals who often work in partnerships.

An advantage of a partnership is that it can draw on the resources of more than one person for capital to start or expand the business. Different people bring different strengths and perspectives to a business, and a partnership can provide the best framework for entrepreneurs to use their skills to create a small business. A disadvantage is that these differences can also lead to conflict among partners. In addition, partnerships may end if one partner leaves or dies.

### Corporations

Corporations include both small companies and large national firms that you encounter every day. Unlike many partnerships, corporations have many owners, called shareholders. A share is a fraction of ownership in the corporation. A corporation can continue indefinitely because a shareholder's

### Make It Relevant

## Careers in Government—Business Manager

The private sector and the government are two separate areas of the U.S. economy, but the distinction is blurring in many government offices. In recent years, government agencies across the country have adapted private business techniques—for example, "customer service" programs. In some States, government programs are expected to turn a profit on their own. Such changes in American government

have opened up many opportunities for individuals with business training to contribute to their country. **Skills Activity** Have students interview a government official who manages an agency in a businesslike way, and share their interviews with the class. Then have individual students write paragraphs explaining why they would or would not be interested in this career. **(Average)**

**663**

## Point-of-Use Resources

**Guide to the Essentials** Chapter 23, Section 1, p. 123 provides support for students who need additional review of section content. Spanish support is available in the Spanish edition of the Guide on p. 116.

**Quiz** Unit 6 booklet, p. 14 includes matching and multiple-choice questions to check students' understanding of Section 1 content.

**Presentation Pro CD-ROM** Quizzes and multiple-choice questions check students' understanding of Section 1 content.

## Answers to . . .

### Section 1 Assessment

**1.** Physical capital includes property and tools used by workers. Human capital includes intangible skills and education.
**2.** Entrepreneurs start new businesses and tap new markets, creating goods, services, and needed jobs.
**3.** One.
**4.** Government should deal primarily with national security and public order. Economic responsibilities can be handled in the free market.
**5.** Possible answer: Human capital, because skills and education are difficult to measure and value.
**6.** Government aid can help industry focus on research and development rather than on surviving economically, thus leading to scientific discoveries and innovations. Competition keeps companies working to develop better products than their competitors. Examples include the Sherman Antitrust Act, the breakup of Standard Oil, AT&T, and Microsoft.

▲ Financial gains and losses are an element of the free market system that entrepreneurs can always expect.

death does not affect the legal status of the corporation. In other words, the corporation exists as its own legal entity, independent from the existence of any stockholders. Under the Supreme Court's interpretation of the 14th Amendment, a corporation enjoys the same legal status as a person.

Corporations can draw their capital from hundreds and even thousands of investors. This enables them to finance such costly projects as putting an earth satellite in orbit or building an oil pipeline. Shareholders are responsible only for the amount of money they have invested. If the business fails, they can lose that amount, but no more. Shareholders have limited liability and are not held responsible for any debts the corporation might have.

One disadvantage of corporations is that their income is taxed twice. First, the corporation pays a tax on its profits. Then, individual shareholders pay a tax on the dividends they are paid.

## Profit and Loss

What drives the capitalist economy? The best answer, most often, is profit.

To understand what profit is, you must first understand the idea of investment. An investment is a sum of money, or capital, that is put into a business enterprise. For example, if you buy a car to start a business delivering groceries, what you pay for the car is an investment.

The profit will be the amount of money you earn from the business, after you have subtracted the costs associated with earning that money—in this case, the purchase of the car and the costs of operating it, plus whatever you pay yourself. If earnings are less than the costs, the business has not made a profit; instead, it has taken a loss.

Taking risks and making investments, therefore, are an essential part of the capitalist system. Every year, many businesses fail for lack of profit. Businesses that survive tend to be those that have learned to make the most efficient use of the factors of production.

## Section 1 Assessment

**Key Terms and Main Ideas**
1. What is the difference between physical and human **capital?**
2. Why are **entrepreneurs** important to a **free enterprise system?**
3. How many companies control a market in a **monopoly?**
4. What is the proper role of government according to **laissez-faire theory?**

**Critical Thinking**
5. **Making Comparisons** Of the factors of production, which do you believe is the most difficult to measure? Explain your answer.

6. **Recognizing Cause and Effect** How might U.S. government policies fostering competition and entrepreneurship result in scientific discoveries and technological innovations? Use examples to support your conclusions.

 **Take It to the Net**

7. Study the Index of Economic Freedom. A high degree of economic freedom indicates a free market system. Which countries exhibit the most economic freedom? What conclusions can you draw from this data? Use the links provided in the Social Studies area at the following Web site for help in completing this activity. **www.phschool.com**

 **Take It to the Net**

**7.** Direct students to the Social Studies area at the Prentice Hall School Web site. The *Magruder's American Government* companion Web site includes the directions and links needed to complete the activity. It also provides a printable Internet activity worksheet with scoring rubrics for assessment. Conclusions should accurately reflect data from the Index.

# SKILLS FOR LIFE

## Interpreting Line Graphs

Throughout the 1990s, the world's oil consumers enjoyed low petroleum prices. In fact, in the late 1990s, prices when adjusted for inflation plunged to their lowest levels in decades. Major oil producers in the Middle East and elsewhere suffered severely from the loss of revenues. In 1999, the producers were finally able to agree on large cuts in oil production. From what you know about supply and demand (page 661), use the steps below to interpret the information in Graph A.

**1. Identify the type of information presented on the graph.** The graph title and the labels on the x axis and y axis tell the meanings of the points and lines on the graph. Look at Graph A and answer these questions: (a) What do the numbers on the x axis (horizontal) and the y axis (vertical) represent? (b) What relationship does the line graph describe?

**2. Read the data on the graph.** Before studying overall patterns, look at specific elements of the graph.

For example: (a) What is the maximum cost per barrel of oil that can be shown on this graph? (b) How many years does the graph cover? (c) Why were these dates chosen?

**3. Study the data on the graph to draw conclusions.** You already know that U.S. oil supplies dropped sharply in the late 1990s. In the previous section, you learned what happens to prices when supplies of a product are reduced. Use this knowledge to draw a conclusion from Graph A. State your conclusion in a sentence or two.

### Test for Success

In our free-enterprise economy, wages are usually determined not by the government but by what the free market will pay for labor. Wages also follow the laws of supply and demand for labor. Use this knowledge to draw conclusions from Graph B.

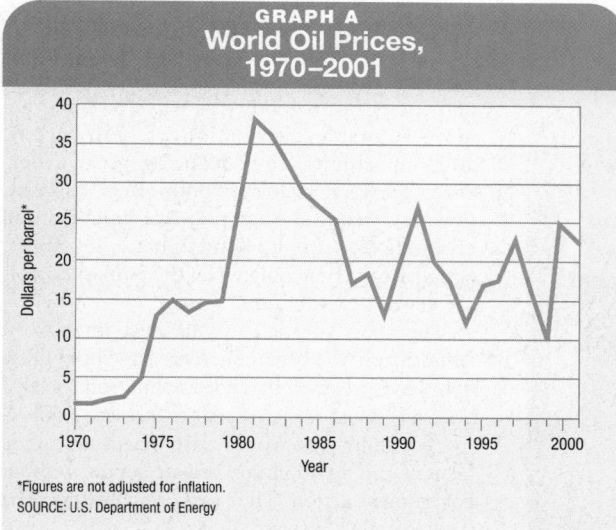

**GRAPH A**
**World Oil Prices, 1970–2001**

*Figures are not adjusted for inflation.
SOURCE: U.S. Department of Energy

**GRAPH B**
**Wage Rates, by Occupation, 1980–2000**

SOURCE: U.S. Bureau of Labor Statistics

## Point-of-Use Resources

📁 **Skills for Life Activity** Unit 6 booklet, p. 20 provides an additional skill activity for this chapter.

💿 **Social Studies Skills Tutor CD-ROM**
Provides interactive practice in geographic literacy, critical thinking and reading, visual analysis, and communications.

### Test for Success

Possible answers: From 1980 to 2000, average wages rose steadily. Workers in construction and manufacturing did better than average. Workers in service and retail jobs had increases as well, but remained below average, possibly because employers were not willing to pay high wages for these often low-skilled or unskilled jobs.

## SKILLS FOR LIFE

### Interpreting Line Graphs

**Focus** Graph information about classmates, then have them interpret the graphs.

**Instruct** Have students work in small groups. Each group should decide on three or four pieces of quantifiable data that they can collect by interviewing classmates. Guide them to choose questions that are not too personal, such as the number of hours spent viewing television each week. Students should interview members of other groups, then put their findings in the form of line graphs. Have them exchange graphs with another group, then use the steps on this page to interpret the meaning of the graphs.

**Close/Reteach** Have members of each group present their analyses to the class.

### Answers . . .

**1. (a)** The x axis gives the date span of the graph; the y axis gives the price per gallon of a barrel of oil, in non-inflation-adjusted dollars. **(b)** The graph shows how world oil prices rose and fell from 1970 to 2001.

**2. (a)** $40. **(b)** 31 years. **(c)** Because they show a wide range of prices over a long period of time.

**3.** Possible answer: World oil prices fluctuated greatly from 1970 to 2000. In the early 1980s, falling oil supplies caused prices to skyrocket.

## 2 Socialism

**Objectives** You may wish to call students' attention to the objectives in the Section Preview. The objectives are reflected in the main headings of the section.

**Bellringer** Ask students to raise their hands if they would favor giving a free college education and free medical and dental benefits to everyone. Then ask who would favor tripling taxes. Explain that in this section, they will learn some of the pros and cons of an economic system that combines public welfare with high taxes.

**Vocabulary Builder** Point out the term *bourgeoisie* in the Political Dictionary. Ask students whether this term has a positive or negative connotation. Link *bourgeoisie* (capitalists) with *proletariat* (workers) by telling students that for socialists, these terms distinguished two opposing social classes.

### Pressed for Time?

## Quick Lesson Plan

**1. Focus** Tell students that government plays a strong role in a socialist economy. Ask students to discuss what they know about the benefits of such an economy.

**2. Instruct** Ask students how socialism originated. Have them describe conditions during the Industrial Revolution and the radical changes socialists proposed. Then discuss the pros and cons of socialism.

**3. Close/Reteach** Remind students that socialism began as a reaction to the Industrial Revolution. Have them write two letters as workers concerned with their life and times. The first should be written in a capitalist society in the mid-1800s and the second in a socialist society today.

## Section Preview

### OBJECTIVES

1. **Define** socialism and explain how it developed from the Industrial Revolution.
2. **Identify** important characteristics of socialist economies.
3. **Describe** socialism in developing countries.
4. **Evaluate** the pros and cons of socialism.

### WHY IT MATTERS

Industrial countries in Western Europe and agricultural countries around the world have developed socialist economies. In these countries, the government plays a strong role in managing the economy and protecting the rights and benefits of individual workers.

### POLITICAL DICTIONARY

★ socialism
★ proletariat
★ bourgeoisie
★ welfare state
★ market economy
★ centrally planned economy

You know that in the United States all people are entitled to equal protection under the law. Political equality, of course, is not the same as economic equality. The capitalistic system of the United States enables some to achieve greater financial rewards than others.

One economic system, however, does seek to distribute wealth equitably throughout society. This section is about that system.

► Britain's Labour Party won control of the British government in 1997 elections. One of the world's most prominent socialist parties, the Labour Party created a universal health care system and took over key industries when it governed Britain in the late 1940s.

## What Is Socialism?

**Socialism** is an economic and political philosophy based on the idea that the benefits of economic activity—wealth—should be equitably distributed throughout a society. This fairness is achieved through the principle of collective (that is, public) ownership of the most important means by which goods and services are produced and distributed. Socialist nations can also be democracies, but still must have centralized planning to achieve these aims.

Socialists reject the strong emphasis on individualism and competition for profit that lie at the heart of capitalistic thought and practice. Instead, they emphasize cooperation and social responsibility as ways to achieve a more equitable distribution of both income and opportunity, thus reducing great differences between rich and poor. Real equality, they say, requires that political equality and economic equality go hand in hand. Economic equality can come only when the public controls the centers of economic power.

The roots of socialism lie deep in history. Almost from the beginning there have been those who have dreamed of a society built on socialist doctrine. Most earlier socialists foresaw a collective economy that would arise out of, and then be managed by, voluntary private action, without government action. Thus early socialist doctrine is often called "private socialism."

### Block Scheduling Strategies

Consider these suggestions to manage extended class time:

■ Have students make annotated time lines of the development of socialism. Time lines should begin with the Industrial Revolution and end with the 1997 Labour Party elections in Britain. Encourage students to find supplemental information in encylopedias or on the Internet.

■ After students have read about the pros and cons of capitalistic and socialistic economies, conduct a panel debate on the subject. Have small groups assign the roles of panelists, moderators, audience, and journalists to group members. Once the panel has finished its debate, call on journalists to report the results to the class.

# The Industrial Revolution

Much of present-day socialism was born in the 19th century. It developed out of the Industrial Revolution—the great social changes that swept western nations as they moved from an agricultural to an industrial economy.

The Industrial Revolution was well under way in Great Britain by the late eighteenth century and spread through Western Europe and to the United States in the nineteenth century. Cities expanded rapidly, and large factories replaced smaller, home-based industry.

Many observers of nineteeth-century British factories and cities were appalled by the conditions they found. Men and women often worked 14- to 16-hour days in filthy, noisy, and unsafe conditions for low pay. Small children regularly worked alongside their parents, for even less pay. Most factory workers and their families lived in dank, crowded, and unhealthful slums.

These conditions led many to seek social and economic reforms. Some argued for much more radical change.

## Karl Marx

Karl Marx (1818–1883), the father of modern-day socialism, was the most significant critic of capitalism to emerge in the nineteenth century. Much of his work and most of his extensive writings were done in collaboration with Friedrich Engels (1820–1895).

In 1848, Marx and Engels wrote *The Communist Manifesto,* "to do for history," Engels later said, "what Darwin's theory has done for biology." This political document condemned the misery caused by the Industrial Revolution. It called upon oppressed workers across Europe to free themselves from "capitalist enslavement."

Marx believed that capitalism was fatally flawed. The **proletariat**—the workers—were being so badly abused by the **bourgeoisie**—the capitalists—that they were certain to rise up and overthrow the capitalistic system. The pamphlet ended with this rallying cry:

> **PRIMARY Sources** *“The proletarians have nothing to lose but their chains. They have a world to win. Workingmen of all countries, unite!”*
>
> —Friedrich Engels and Karl Marx, *The Communist Manifesto*

▲ Thousands left the British countryside in the 1800s to live and work in dirty, overcrowded cities like Newcastle (above). Their experiences inspired Karl Marx (right) and Friedrich Engels to write of a new "working class." *Critical Thinking* **According to Marx, how would workers eventually react to their working conditions?**

## Socialists and Communists

A powerful socialist movement took shape among European workers and thinkers during the middle and late nineteenth century. Almost all socialists accepted Marx's criticism of capitalism. The movement was deeply split, however, by the question of how best to achieve socialism. Some argued that a socialist society could come only out of a "violent and bloody revolution." Over time, those who took that view came to be called communists.

Others argued that socialism could be attained by peaceful means through the democratic process. Today, the terms *socialism* and *socialist* are usually used to identify those evolutionary socialists.

The British Labour Party and the major "social democratic" parties in Europe are leading

RESOURCE PRO®

**Resource Pro® CD-ROM** contains an electronic version of each activity found in the Teaching Resources as well as additional resources such as Supreme Court cases. The Planning Express® feature allows you to customize and create daily lesson plans within minutes.

## Reading Strategy

### Drawing Inferences

Tell students that they will be reading about how socialism was designed to solve particular problems in society. Have students, as they read, infer for each feature of socialism a societal problem that feature was meant to address.

## Point-of-Use Resources

📁 **Guided Reading and Review** Unit 6 booklet, p. 15 provides students with practice identifying the main ideas and key terms of this section.

📁 **Lesson Plans** For lesson planning suggestions, see p. 100 of the Lesson Plans booklet.

📁 **Political Cartoons** See p. 92 of the Political Cartoons booklet for a cartoon relevant to this section.

📁 **Close Up on Participation** Working to Eliminate Child Labor, pp. 18–19 uses the topic of teenagers getting involved in child labor awareness to help students plan and carry out service learning projects.

📠 **Section Support Transparencies** Transparency 95, *Visual Learning;* Transparency 194, *Political Cartoon*

## Answer to . . .

**Critical Thinking** Marx predicted that workers would rebel and overthrow capitalism.

examples of that brand of socialism. At various times in recent history, those parties have controlled their governments and have instituted many socialist programs through democratic means. In the 1997 elections, however, Labour Party leaders deliberately chose to follow a "third way," moving away from socialism. Socialist parties in France and Germany have also reconsidered some of the socialist objectives that have become too expensive to maintain.

## Characteristics of Socialist Economies

Countries with a socialist government typically enact one or more of these public policies to achieve the aims of socialism: nationalization, broadening of public services, high taxation, and a centrally planned economy.

### Nationalization

Placing enterprises under governmental control, often by taking over privately owned industries, is called nationalization. In the last chapter you read about the nationalization of the oil industry in Mexico in the 1930s. In a democratic country such as Britain, a government may nationalize an enterprise and pay the former owners what it considers a fair price. Often, however, governments have nationalized industries without paying any compensation.

Nationalization under socialism rarely includes all businesses in a country. Socialist governments usually want to control certain sectors

▲ The French government owns most of that country's largest airline, Air France. *Critical Thinking* **As voters, what power do workers in nationalized companies have over their employer?**

with many workers and a few dominant firms, such as utilities, transportation, and steel. They allow many smaller companies to remain in private hands. Also, the government may want industries that are based on newly emerging technologies to remain private. This is because individual initiative and entrepreneurial risk-taking are so important during the early phases of a business.

A goal of many socialist governments is to give each company's workers a say in deciding how the company is run. Sweden's Social Democratic Party, for example, has a plan for gradually transferring ownership of private companies to their workers. Elected worker representatives now sit on many companies' boards of directors.

### Public Welfare

Socialists place great importance on assuring that everyone in a society is decently housed and fed. Stated another way, socialists aim to guarantee the public welfare by providing for the equal distribution of necessities and services—including retirement pensions, inexpensive health care, free university education, and housing for the poor.

Countries that provide extensive social services at little or no cost to the users are often called **welfare states.** In such countries, medical and dental services may be provided free or for a small charge. People who lose their jobs or who are physically unable to work receive government payments that are nearly as high as their former wages. All people above retirement age receive government pensions. Parents may receive government payments for each child until the child reaches the age of 18. Workers in Europe receive paid maternity leave and several weeks of paid vacation each year—benefits rarely matched in other countries.

### Taxation

All governments in capitalist and socialist states get their funds from taxation. Because social welfare services are quite expensive, however, taxes in socialist countries tend to be high. Taxes may take 50 or 60 percent of an individual's total income.

Socialists tend to place most of the burden on the upper and middle classes, consistent with

*Answer to . . .*

**Critical Thinking** Workers can vote against a government that does not defend their interests.

their philosophy of achieving a more equal distribution of wealth. Tax rates can amount to 90 percent of a wealthy person's income.

## Centrally Planned Economy

Economies can be divided into several categories, depending on how basic economic decisions are made. Under capitalism, key decisions are made by thousands of private individuals and companies through the give and take of the marketplace. For that reason, a capitalist economy is also called a **market economy.**

Under socialism, economic decision making is more centralized. In a **centrally planned economy,** government bureaucrats plan how an economy will develop over a period of years. They set targets for production and direct investment into specific industries. Because the government, to varying degrees, controls the economy, this is also called a "command economy."

A democratic socialist country may or may not have strict central planning. Market conditions and private businesses are likely to play a role as well as government planning. With a few exceptions, most modern economies are such mixed economies.

## Socialism in Developing Countries

Socialism has won a large following in developing countries. There, public ownership and centralized planning are common.

One reason for socialism's appeal is that most developing countries are starting from scratch at building industry. They have no tradition of locally controlled, large-scale industry. Large existing industries are often owned by foreign companies. By nationalizing a foreign-owned company and placing local people in charge, a political leader can win broad public support.

Socialism also appeals to leaders who want to mobilize an entire nation behind a program of industrial growth. Through central planning, leaders can channel investment into the parts of the economy they think are most essential.

Often, however, guided growth of this sort requires painful sacrifices by a nation's people. High taxes skim off a large part of people's income. The government may devote so much attention to one or two basic industries that the

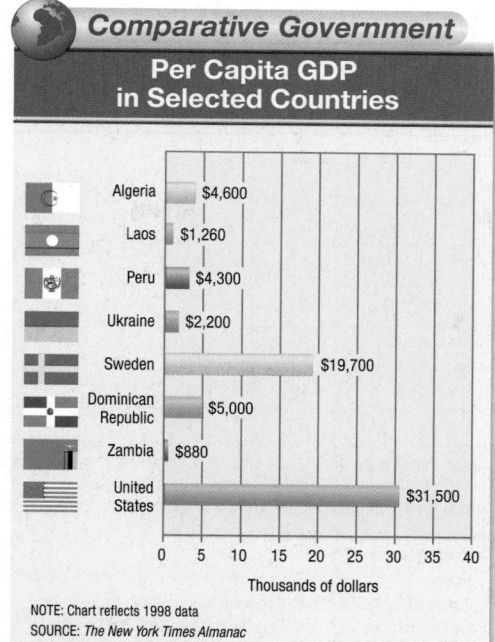

### Comparative Government

#### Per Capita GDP in Selected Countries

| Country | Per Capita GDP |
|---|---|
| Algeria | $4,600 |
| Laos | $1,260 |
| Peru | $4,300 |
| Ukraine | $2,200 |
| Sweden | $19,700 |
| Dominican Republic | $5,000 |
| Zambia | $880 |
| United States | $31,500 |

NOTE: Chart reflects 1998 data
SOURCE: *The New York Times Almanac*

**Interpreting Graphs** Researchers cannot easily compare per capita GDP to measure quality of life because the cost of food, housing, and other goods is different in each country. However, large differences stand out. *How does per capita GDP in the United States compare to per capita GDP in the other countries listed above?*

production of food or consumer goods may be neglected. Then public unrest may develop.

Political instability is a persistent problem in developing nations. In such nations, this instability is one reason that socialist and other governments often turn to authoritarian methods. Few developing nations have succeeded in establishing the democratic versions of socialism found in parts of the industrial world.

## Pros and Cons

Both capitalistic and socialistic economies have their strengths and weaknesses. For supporters of capitalism, it is easy to see weaknesses in the theory and practice of socialism. For supporters of socialism, on the other hand, capitalism seems filled with faults.

Critics say socialist countries have a tendency to develop too many layers of bureaucracy. They say this complicates decision making and has a

### Preparing for Standardized Tests

Have students read the passages under *Socialism in Developing Countries* on this page and then answer the question below.

Which of the following is *not* a reason that developing countries adopt socialism?

**(A)** It gives people more say in government.

**B** It allows leaders to win broad public support.

**C** It encourages the growth of key industries.

**D** It enables leaders to channel investments easily.

*Answer to . . .*

**Interpreting Graphs** Per capita GDP is much higher in the United States than in the other countries listed.

## Point-of-Use Resources

**Guide to the Essentials** Chapter 23, Section 2, p. 124 provides support for students who need additional review of section content. Spanish support is available in the Spanish edition of the Guide on p. 117.

**Quiz** Unit 6 booklet, p. 16 includes matching and multiple-choice questions to check students' understanding of Section 2 content.

**Presentation Pro CD-ROM** Quizzes and multiple-choice questions check students' understanding of Section 2 content.

## Answers to . . .

### Section 2 Assessment

**1.** Karl Marx.

**2.** The bourgeoisie controls the economy, and therefore has control over the lives of the proletariat, or the working people.

**3.** Answers will vary; students should mention the extensive social services that welfare states provide at little or no cost to citizens.

**4.** The government plays a strong role by setting quotas for industry and directing investment into certain parts of the economy.

**5.** A socialist might try to eliminate unemployment through government investment and aid to companies. A capitalist might argue that the best approach is to reduce government intervention and allow entrepreneurs the freedom to create new jobs.

**6.** Answers will vary; students should mention the pros and cons of capitalist and socialist systems as they relate to social services.

### Answer to . . .

**Interpreting Graphs** Unemployment rose and remained high in France and Italy, while it declined steadily in the United States.

---

### Comparative Government

**Unemployment in Selected Countries, 1990–2000**

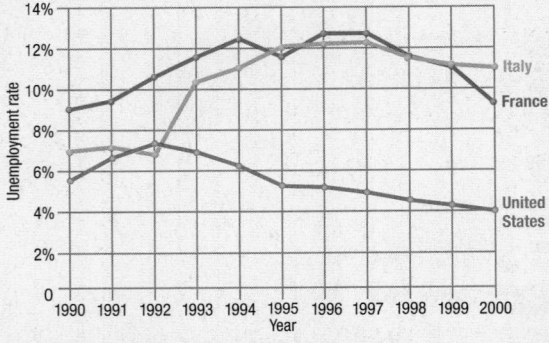

NOTE: Italy data for April 2000. Data for other countries are for July 2000.

SOURCE: Organization for Economic Co-operation and Development; *Handbook of International Economic Statistics*

**Interpreting Graphs** Compared to Americans, workers in France and Italy enjoy more vacation days, less expensive health care, and greater legal protection against losing their jobs. One unintended result is that companies hire fewer new workers to avoid paying the high cost of these benefits. *Although France, Italy, and the United States all enjoyed strong economic growth in the 1990s, how did unemployment rates respond differently in these three countries?*

deadening effect on individual initiative. As a result, critics say, socialist economies are slower to take advantage of new technologies.

In the eyes of socialism's critics, the smooth running of an economy is too complex to be directed by central planners. Too many unpredictable events are involved, and too many clashing interests are at stake. For all its faults, they argue, the invisible hand of the market economy works more efficiently than the visible hand of central planning.

Another criticism is that socialism deprives people of the freedom to decide for themselves how to use their income. Since workers get to keep only a part of their earnings after taxes, they have little incentive to work harder and earn more. Why work hard when your basic needs will be taken care of anyway?

In response, socialists reply that it is fairer to supply everyone with basic needs, such as medical care. They point to the inequalities of wealth and power that exist under capitalism. Socialists argue that socialism is morally superior to capitalism because it evens out inequalities. In their view, socialism makes political democracy work more smoothly by supplementing it with economic democracy.

Defenders of socialism also argue that it gives workers and ordinary citizens more control over their daily lives. Under capitalism, they say, a company's management can abruptly decide to close an unprofitable factory. The company has no obligation to ask its workers' opinions, even though such a decision can throw thousands out of work and disrupt an entire community. This could not happen under socialism, the argument goes. Workers and community leaders would sit on the company's board. They would help decide what was best for the entire work force and community—not just for the company's investors and shareholders.

### Section 2 Assessment

**Key Terms and Main Ideas**

1. Who is considered the father of **socialism**?
2. According to socialist theory, what is the relationship between the **proletariat** and the **bourgeoisie**?
3. Describe a **welfare state** in your own words.
4. What role does the government play in a **centrally planned economy**?

**Critical Thinking**

5. **Making Comparisons** How might a socialist and a capitalist government differ in treatment of the problem of unemployment?

6. **Making Decisions** Should the government have the responsibility of providing health care for every citizen? Why or why not?

 **Take It to the Net**

7. Read about the working conditions that children endured during the Industrial Revolution. Then, identify those problems that no longer affect young adults in the work force today. Use the links provided in the Social Studies area of the following Web site for help in completing this activity. **www.phschool.com**

 **Take It to the Net**

**7.** Direct students to the Social Studies area at the Prentice Hall School Web site. The *Magruder's American Government* companion Web site includes the directions and links needed to complete the activity. It also provides a printable Internet activity worksheet with scoring rubrics for assessment. Students should accurately identify problems that no longer exist because of new legislation.

# The Third Way

*After losing four consecutive elections to Britain's Conservative Party, the British Labour Party moved away from its socialist roots to embrace a "third way" between socialism and a free market economy. Party leader Tony Blair issued this statement of party beliefs before the 1997 election. The Labour Party went on to win a landslide victory and has been in power since that time.*

I want a country in which people get on, do well, make a success of their lives. I have no time for the politics of envy. We need more successful entrepreneurs, not fewer of them. But these life-chances should be for all the people. And I want a society in which ambition and compassion are seen as partners not opposites—where we value public service as well as material wealth.

New Labour believes in a society where we do not simply pursue our own individual aims but where we hold many aims in common and work together to achieve them. How

*Prime Minister Tony Blair*

we build the industry and employment opportunities of the future; how we tackle the division and inequality in our society; how we care for and enhance our environment and quality of life; how we develop modern education and health services; how we create communities that are safe, where mutual respect and tolerance are the order of the day. These are things we must achieve together as a country.

The vision is one of national renewal, a country with drive, purpose and energy. A Britain equipped to prosper in a global economy of technological change; with a modern welfare state; its politics more accountable; and confident of its place in the world.

. . . a new and distinctive approach has been mapped out, one that differs from the solutions of the old left and those of the Conservative right. This is why new Labour is new. . . .

The old left would have sought state control of industry. The Conservative right is content to leave all to the market. We reject both approaches. Government and industry must work together to achieve key objectives aimed at enhancing the dynamism of the market, not undermining it.

In industrial relations, we make it clear that there will be no return to [the aggressive labor tactics] of the 1970s. There will instead be basic minimum rights for the individual at the workplace, where our aim is partnership not conflict between employers and employees.

In economic management, we accept the global economy as a reality and reject the isolationism and "go-it-alone" policies of the extremes of right or left.

## Analyzing Primary Sources

1. Describe Tony Blair's vision for a new Britain in your own words.
2. How does Tony Blair try to distance the Labour Party from its past socialist policies? Why did he do so?
3. What is the Labour Party's view of the global economy and world trade?
4. Do you believe Blair's Third Way between socialism and free market capitalism is practical? Explain.

## CLOSE UP
FOUNDATION

### *Corner*

📁 **Close Up on Primary Sources** New Labour in Great Britain, p. 25, extends this feature with a primary source activity.

## CLOSE UP
FOUNDATION | Online

To keep up-to-date on Close Up news and activities, visit Close Up Online at

**www.closeup.org**

## The Third Way

**Focus** Ask students to define and discuss *capitalism, socialism,* and *communism.* Then have students read the article and identify elements of these systems that are associated with the "third way."

**Instruct** Ask students to identify movements away from state-regulated economies that have occurred since the end of the cold war. Then ask students to summarize why the Labour Party might want to distance itself from its socialist roots. Call on volunteers to present their reasons to the class.

**Close/Reteach** After the presentations are finished, ask students to discuss the pros and cons of a mixed economy versus a laissez-faire economy.

💿 **Keep It Current CD-ROM** includes government-related projects by unit. The CD-ROM links to the Prentice Hall School Web site and may be used for daily updates.

### *Answers to . . .*
**Analyzing Primary Sources**
1. Answers will vary, but should suggest that Blair's vision represents a compromise between capitalist and socialist economic goals.
2. By criticizing state control of industry, aggressive labor tactics, and isolationism; to emphasize economic partnership rather than conflict.
3. It supports the global economy.
4. Answers will vary. Those who argue it is practical could mention that it is a form of mixed economy. Those who argue that it is impractical could point out the difficulty of balancing the two approaches.

**Objectives** You may wish to call students' attention to the objectives in the Section Preview. The objectives are reflected in the main headings of the section.

**Bellringer** Have students suppose that they have a job that pays them the same wage no matter how well or poorly they perform. Would they work extra hard or take it easy? Explain that in this section, they will learn about an economic system in which workers face this same question.

**Vocabulary Builder** Begin by reviewing the prefixes *com-* and *col-*, which both mean "together, with, or jointly." Point out the words starting with *com-* or *col-* in the Political Dictionary. Have students look up their meanings to see how they are linked. Then write the appropriate definitions on the board.

---

## Pressed for Time?

### Quick Lesson Plan

**1. Focus** Tell students that communism arose in direct opposition to capitalism. Ask students to discuss what they know about Karl Marx and his theory of how communism would replace capitalism.

**2. Instruct** Ask students to explain the role of the Communist Party in a communist-run country. Review Karl Marx's theories, and discuss how they were put into practice in the real world by the Soviet Union, China, and other communist nations.

**3. Close/Reteach** Remind students that the effects of industrialization caused Marx and others to seek an economic system in which the interests of workers came first. Have students write a paragraph evaluating whether communism was the answer to Marx's quest.

---

## Section Preview

### OBJECTIVES

1. **Summarize** the theories of Karl Marx.
2. **Outline** the characteristics of communist economies.
3. **Describe** communism in the Soviet Union, China, and other nations.

### WHY IT MATTERS

Karl Marx once predicted that the workers of the world would overthrow capitalism and create an ideal communist society. Although communist governments emerged in Russia and China in the last century, the reality of communism rarely matched Marx's theory.

### POLITICAL DICTIONARY

- communism
- five-year plan
- collectivization
- Gosplan
- privatization
- Great Leap Forward
- commune

---

Modern communism is a political, economic, and social theory developed by Karl Marx in the mid-1800s.[2] Nearly one third of the world's people once lived under communism, but since the collapse of the Soviet Union, it is the guiding economic principle in only a handful of countries. Almost every one of those countries, in fact, is taking steps toward a free market system.

### Karl Marx's Theory

**Communism** is often called a collectivist ideology, which calls for the collective, or state, ownership of land and other productive property. Karl Marx

▲ **May Day Parade** On the first of May, people in the Soviet Union celebrated the workers of their country and the world. The banner depicts the revolutionary founder of the Soviet Union, V. I. Lenin (left), as well as Friedrich Engels (center) and Karl Marx (right).

and Friedrich Engels first set out its basic concepts in *The Communist Manifesto* (1848).

In another major work, *Das Kapital* (1867), Marx analyzed the workings of capitalism. He based the work on four closely related concepts: his theory of history, the labor theory of value, the nature of the state, and the dictatorship of the proletariat.

1. *Marx's View of History.* To Marx, all of history was a story of class struggle—of social classes competing for the control of labor and productive property. One class was the oppressors; the other, the oppressed. In the Middle Ages, the struggle was between the nobility and their serfs. In the modern world, the bourgeoisie oppressed the proletariat.

According to Marx, the class struggle in the modern era would become so intense that the masses would revolt and bring down the bourgeoisie. The communists' political role was to hasten the revolution, by violence if necessary.

2. *The Labor Theory of Value.* Marx rejected the free enterprise ideas of profit and competition. In his view, the value of a commodity was set by the amount of labor put into it. A pair of shoes or a rebuilt bicycle is worth a certain

---

[2]The word *communism* comes from the Latin *communis*, meaning "common, belonging to all." The idea of communal property dates back at least to the early Greeks. In the fourth century B.C., Plato proposed a system of communal property in *The Republic*.

---

## Block Scheduling Strategies

Consider this suggestion to manage extended class time:

■ Randomly assign small groups one of the three economic systems discussed in the chapter. Then ask the class to choose an industry that plays an important role in the economic well-being of most countries (i.e. agriculture, medicine, transportation, etc.). Have groups make

a presentation that describes how this industry would carry out its daily operations in relation to the government and the private and public sectors. Encourage students to consider issues such as what will be produced, who will produce it, and how the products will be distributed throughout the country.

amount because it takes that much labor to produce it. Therefore, communists say, the laborer should receive that value in full.

3. *The Nature of the State.* Marx saw the state and its government as the tools by which the capitalists maintained their power and privileges. Other social institutions also played a role in enforcing capitalist control over the masses. Marx described religion as "the opiate of the people"—a sort of drug that persuades workers to tolerate their harsh lot in this life in the hope that someday they will gain what Marx called a "fictional afterlife."

4. *The Dictatorship of the Proletariat.* Marx did not believe that revolution would bring the final form of communism—the classless society. First, he predicted a transitional phase during which an authoritarian state would represent and enforce the interests of the masses. This he called the "dictatorship of the proletariat." Once the goal of classlessness was realized, the state would "wither away."

Based on these four concepts, Marx envisioned a "free, classless society." Social classes would vanish and the people in common would own all property. Exploitation of labor and unemployment would disappear. Abundant goods would be available to all according to their needs.

Marx also expected that workers in different countries—for example, France and Germany—would share a bond far stronger than national loyalties. Thus, communism would also end nationalism, a major cause of European wars.

## Characteristics of Communist Economies

Marx believed that the revolution would come first in industrialized countries with large working-class populations—in particular, France, Germany, Great Britain, and then the United States. Ironically, the revolution occurred first in Russia, then a backward, mainly agricultural nation, in 1917, and later in largely agricultural nations in Asia.[3]

Marx's theories did not provide even a rough blueprint for the formation of a communist society. Communism has taken different forms in different places, but certain characteristics are common.

▲ When northern Vietnam became a communist state, most people lived in the countryside and worked on farms, as they still do today. *Critical Thinking How well did Vietnam fit Karl Marx's description of a country ready for communism?*

1. *Role of the Communist Party.* In any communist-run nation, the Communist Party holds the decision-making power in both the government and the economy. Party leaders also hold the top government positions. From top to bottom, the two institutions run parallel to each other. Inevitably, such centralized political and economic control means control over social, intellectual, and religious life as well.

2. *Central Planning.* Because government makes all the economic decisions, bureaucrats must plan and supervise production in factories, farms, and stores. Typically, a **five-year plan** plays a key role in this economy. The plan shows how leaders want the economy to develop over the next five years. It sets economic goals that dictate where to emphasize growth in industry or agriculture and what each individual factory and farm must produce. The plan also sets prices and decides how goods and services will be distributed.

---

[3]In his later years, Marx did recognize the possibility that his theories might first be tested in Russia. Lenin also took the Russia-first view, in the early 1900s. He thought that less advanced countries, with their comparatively small industrial populations, offered certain advantages to a revolutionary movement—notably, the effectiveness with which workers could be organized and controlled.

### ACTIVITY

## American Government, American Humor

Share the following joke with students:

*"A new manager of a collective farm finds two letters from his predecessor, with instructions to open the first when difficulties begin. When the farm fails to meet its quotas, the manager opens the first letter, which says: 'Blame me.' He does. It buys some time. But the farm fails again and he comes under fresh criticism, so he opens the second letter. It says: 'Prepare two letters.'"*

—quoted by George F. Will

**Discussion** Have students explain what *economic, political,* and *social* features of a communist economy the joke addresses. Ask: How does this joke explain in a nutshell both the failure of communism and the triumph of capitalism?

**(Challenging)**

## Answer to . . .

**Critical Thinking** Architect, baker, factory worker, and mother.

▲ Typical of Soviet art, *Builders of Communism* glorifies Soviet workers, including a farmer, a welder, a miner, and an architect. *Critical Thinking According to this picture, what were some roles of women in the Soviet Union?*

3. *Collectivization.* Collective or state ownership of the means of production is one pillar of communism. One major step in creating a communist economy is the merger of small private farms into large government-owned agricultural enterprises. This process of **collectivization** may be voluntary in theory, but in many countries peasant farmers have been coerced into giving up land. Millions died while resisting collectivization in the Soviet Union.

4. *State Ownership.* Industrial enterprises, transportation, and other parts of the economy are also state-owned. This part of the system varies greatly from country to country. In China, for example, provincial and municipal governments, not a central government ministry, own enterprises such as housing, banks, hospitals, and stores.

## The Soviet Union

Lenin and his followers took power in Russia in 1917 and began immediately to build a communist state. After a difficult transition, the Soviet Union became a one-party state, with communists in control of the country's social, political, and economic institutions by the time of Lenin's death in 1924. Lenin's successor, Josef Stalin, tightened that control into an authoritarian dictatorship.

### The Five-Year Plans

Stalin introduced centralized planning, run by a large agency, **Gosplan.** The First Five-Year Plan (1928–1933) demanded collectivization of agriculture and higher production of chemicals, petroleum, and steel. Later five-year plans also emphasized heavy industry, and the Soviet Union achieved rapid, if uneven, industrialization. Unfortunately, those advances came at the cost of scarce consumer goods, housing, and urban services. Housing, food, and goods were rationed, and sewers, water systems, and other needs lagged behind a dramatic growth in urban population.[4]

### Social Policies

The Soviet Union gave its citizens free education, medical care, and even youth summer camps. It was far from a classless society, however. To spur production, economic incentives, cars, and vacation homes went to party officials, bureaucrats, and factory managers. Artists, musicians, and athletes also were rewarded with special privileges. Thus, Stalin created an elite class that owed its privileged status to the Communist Party. He also corrupted the Marxian ideal of economic and social equality.

### Gorbachev's Reforms

When Mikhail Gorbachev became Soviet leader in 1985, he inherited an economic system that had changed little since the Stalin years. Economic growth and productivity had declined sharply.

Under *perestroika,* leaders gave more authority to local farm and factory managers, loosened price controls, linked salaries to performance, and allowed some profit incentives. *Perestroika* raised expectations, but it did not increase output. Bureaucrats resisted change, and poor harvests, strikes, and shortages of food and consumer goods made conditions worse. Gorbachev and the Communist Party gave up their leadership of the economy when the Soviet Union collapsed in 1991.

---

[4]The First Five-Year Plan, launched in 1928, was declared completed in 1932, nine months ahead of schedule. The second plan ran from 1932 to 1937 and the third from 1937 until it was interrupted by the German invasion of the Soviet Union in 1941. The Twelfth Five-Year Plan was in place when the Soviet Union collapsed in late 1991.

## Transition to a Free Market

Clearly, Russia's transition to a free market system and its moves toward democracy were closely linked. The economic plans that Russian President Boris Yeltsin put in place in 1991 and 1992 called for radical changes, including the lifting of price controls and the privatization of farms and factories. **Privatization** is returning nationalized enterprises to private ownership.

The transition to a market economy has not been easy. Thousands of enterprises were put into private hands, sometimes by giving shares or vouchers to workers, but many are still badly run.

A new elite class of entrepreneurs has made a fortune in today's Russian economy. At the same time, many ordinary Russians have suffered the effects of high inflation, a fall in the value of Russian currency, and the loss of their state pensions. Corruption is rampant, and most people have grown poorer. A complete transition to a market economy awaits strong leadership willing to enforce laws and thoroughly reform the system.

## China

Mao Zedong, the founder of the People's Republic of China, was a Marxist. Mao departed from Marx's theory that a workers' revolt would lead to communism. He believed the peasantry would be the key to a communist revolution in China.

After Mao took control of the country in 1949, China developed its own version of a planned economy. Despite its huge population, it lacked skilled workers. The government improved technical and scientific education and then assigned workers to jobs in the state sector. Government regulated the labor market, giving workers little choice about where they worked.

### The Great Leap Forward

The five-year plan for 1958, the **Great Leap Forward,** was a drastic attempt to modernize China quickly. All elements of free enterprise, such as rural markets, were eliminated. Collective farms were brought together into a larger unit, the **commune.**

Communes grew into self-sufficient bodies run by party officials. These officials oversaw farms, industries, and government in a region as well as managed social policy. Workers received the same rewards no matter how much they produced, so there were few incentives to work hard. The Great Leap Forward was a disastrous failure, followed by severe famine.

### Deng Xiaoping's Reforms

A new leader, Deng Xiaoping, came to power in 1977 and made great changes in the economy. Deng's program of the "Four Modernizations" aimed to improve agriculture, industry, science and technology, and defense. He wanted "socialism with Chinese characteristics."

Deng was more practical and far less ideological than Mao and his dedicated followers. He began to move China from central planning to a market economy and invited foreign investors into China.

Today, China's economic system is a maze of different levels of government bodies and economic units. The state-owned sector is shrinking, while collective enterprises owned and managed by the people of a workplace or residential unit are growing. Private enterprises—mostly small shops and businesses—are also flourishing, as is investment from other countries.

◄ President Jiang Zemin of China is now leading his country's difficult transition to a free market economy. Today, China invests less money in state-owned industries and works hard to encourage foreign investment in China and Chinese exports to the West. *Critical Thinking What would Karl Marx think of China's Communist Party?*

## Spotlight on Technology

**Magruder's American Government Video Collection**

The Magruder's Video Collection explores key issues and debates in American government. Each segment examines an issue central to chapter content through use of historical and contemporary footage. Commentary from civic leaders in academics, government, and the media follow each segment. Critical-thinking questions focus students' attention on key issues, and may be used to stimulate discussion.

Use the Chapter 23 video segment to compare Cuban and American economic opportunities. This segment focuses on the growing number of Cuban baseball players who are defecting to the United States in order to play on Major League teams.

## Point-of-Use Resources

**Guide to the Essentials** Chapter 23, Section 3, p. 125 provides support for students who need additional review of section content. Spanish support is available in the Spanish edition of the Guide on p. 118.

**Quiz** Unit 6 booklet, p. 18 includes matching and multiple-choice questions to check students' understanding of Section 3 content.

**Presentation Pro CD-ROM** Quizzes and multiple-choice questions check students' understanding of Section 3 content.

## Answers to . . .

### Section 3 Assessment

**1.** Answers will vary; students should allude to collective ownership of land and other productive property.
**2.** To plan the economy of the Soviet Union.
**3.** Small private farms are combined to create large collective farms controlled by the state.
**4.** The People's Republic of China.
**5.** Soviet communism did not achieve equality. Instead, the state created a new elite with access to privileges and hard-to-find goods.
**6.** Answers will vary, but should reflect an understanding of the features of communist systems.

▲ Fidel Castro watches a May Day parade in Havana, Cuba. Cuba remains the only communist country in the Americas. Castro has ruled Cuba as a personal dictatorship for over 40 years.

## Other Communist Nations

Several other countries, mainly in Asia, have centrally planned economies. Most, however, are bringing in some free market elements. Other communist economies have not lasted. Those in the Soviet satellites of Eastern Europe disappeared in the upheavals of 1989–1990.

In Cuba, Fidel Castro led a revolution that overthrew the corrupt rule of Fulgencio Batista in 1959. After Castro nationalized American holdings, the United States broke with him. The Soviet Union supported Castro, and in 1961, he declared himself a Marxist.

Cuba depended heavily on Soviet economic aid. As a result, the fall of the Soviet Union caused an economic crisis in Cuba. In response, the government relaxed economic controls, encouraging tourism and some small businesses.

Communism also took root in Southeast Asia. At the end of World War II, Ho Chi Minh, a communist who had studied in Moscow, fought for Vietnam's independence from French colonial rule. Two wars—one against the French, one against the United States—left the communists in control. Vietnam's government uses five-year plans to guide the economy, and like China, it has made market-oriented reforms.

Communist influence spilled over from Vietnam into neighboring Laos and Cambodia. Laos adopted communism in 1975, and Cambodia had a communist government under Vietnamese control from 1979 to 1993.

One of the last communist countries is North Korea. At the end of World War II, the Korean peninsula was divided between a Soviet-backed regime in the north and an American-backed government in the south. After the Korean War (1950–1953), the peninsula remained divided, and North Korea retreated into isolation.

North Korea's centrally planned economy has not achieved much growth. Agriculture was collectivized in the 1950s, although small private plots can grow food for rural markets. Severe food shortages plague the country today. North Korea lost foreign aid and trading partners when other communist governments fell, and has begun to reach out to its former enemy to the south.

## Section 3 Assessment

**Key Terms and Main Ideas**
1. Describe **communism** in your own words.
2. What was the purpose of **Gosplan**?
3. What happens during **collectivization**?
4. Which country experienced the **Great Leap Forward**?

**Critical Thinking**
5. **Drawing Inferences** How well did Soviet communism follow the communist ideal of economic and social equality?

6. **Drawing Conclusions** Is a dictatorship necessary to the existence of a communist society? Why or why not?

 **Take It to the Net**

7. Russia is one nation trying to make the transition from a centrally planned economy to a market economy. Describe two actions taken to reform the Russian economy. How well are these reforms working? Use the links provided in the Social Studies area at the following Web site for help in completing this activity. www.phschool.com

 **Take It to the Net**

**7.** Direct students to the Social Studies area at the Prentice Hall School Web site. The *Magruder's American Government* companion Web site includes the directions and links needed to complete the activity. It also provides a printable Internet activity worksheet with scoring rubrics for assessment. Descriptions should include careful analysis of two actions.

# on the Supreme Court

# May Courts Enforce Discriminatory Private Agreements?

*The Equal Protection Clause of the 14th Amendment bars States from discriminating against people based on their race or color. What happens if private individuals make an agreement that discriminates, and one of them later breaks that agreement? Should a court enforce the agreement?*

## Shelley v. Kraemer (1948)

In 1911, thirty property owners in St. Louis, Missouri, signed a restrictive covenant (an agreement limiting the ways in which a piece of property can be used). In this agreement, the property owners promised not to sell their property to non-whites during the next 50 years. The agreement did not restrict the use of the property in any other way.

In 1945, a black family, the Shelleys, bought one of the properties that was subject to the covenant. Kraemer and other property owners governed by the covenant brought suit in the circuit court, seeking to block the Shelleys from taking possession of the property and to reverse the sale. The trial court refused to do so. It concluded that the agreement was not intended to become effective until signed by all the property owners in the district, and that some owners had never signed.

The Missouri Supreme Court reversed the trial court opinion, ruling that the agreement was effective and that it did not violate the Shelleys' constitutional rights. The Shelleys then appealed to the United States Supreme Court.

## Arguments for Shelley

1. It would be unconstitutional for States to pass laws or ordinances restricting property ownership or occupancy based on race or color. Therefore, the courts should not enforce any agreement that imposes such restrictions.
2. Although the Equal Protection Clause of the 14th Amendment applies only to "State action" and does not restrict actions by private individuals, judicial enforcement of private

agreements is "State action" within the meaning of the 14th Amendment.
3. The purpose of the 14th Amendment was to establish equality of basic rights and to preserve those rights from discrimination by the States based on race and color. For the courts to enforce the restrictive covenant would not be consistent with that purpose.

## Arguments for Kraemer

1. This case does not involve action by State legislators or city councils. Private individuals entered into the agreement at issue.
2. The Equal Protection Clause of the 14th Amendment applies only to "State action" and does not restrict actions by private individuals. Judicial enforcement of private agreements does not amount to "State action" within the meaning of the 14th Amendment.
3. There is no discrimination because the Missouri courts would equally enforce covenants that exclude white people from property ownership.

### Decide for Yourself

1. Review the constitutional grounds on which each side based its arguments and the specific arguments each side presented.
2. Debate the opposing viewpoints presented in this case. Which viewpoint do you favor?
3. Predict the impact of the Court's decision on discrimination. (To read a summary of the Court's decision, turn to the Supreme Court Glossary on page 799.)

---

 *Corner*

📁 **Close Up on the Supreme Court** *Shelley* v. *Kraemer,* p. 24 provides an activity to extend coverage of this case.

 **Online**

To keep up-to-date on Close Up news and activities, visit Close Up Online at

**www.closeup.org**

---

## May Courts Enforce Discriminatory Private Agreements?

**Focus** Explain that World War II triggered a mass migration of African Americans into the nation's industrial cities. With workers in short supply, many migrants found jobs in the arms industry. When African Americans tried to use their earnings to purchase new homes, some white neighborhoods resisted by requiring white home purchasers to sign restrictive covenants, prohibiting the later sale of their homes to African Americans.

**Instruct** Discuss the arguments from the feature and identify the most convincing argument for each side. Then have the class vote on how they would decide the case. Finally, have the class read the Court's decision and discuss its reasoning.

**Close/Reteach** *Shelley* was a milestone in the civil rights movement. The National Association for the Advancement of Colored People provided a legal team for the case, headed by future Supreme Court justice Thurgood Marshall, which went on to represent African Americans in many landmark civil rights cases.

💿 **Keep It Current CD-ROM** includes government-related projects by unit. The CD-ROM links to the Prentice Hall School Web site and may be used for daily updates.

### Answers to . . .

**Decide for Yourself**
**1.** Shelley cited the 14th Amendment in arguing that States could not allow discrimination against them due to race. Kraemer cited the same Amendment, arguing that it applies only to "State action" and not private individuals, meaning that the property owners had the right to discriminate.
**2.** Answers will vary, but should be supported with valid reasoning.
**3.** The Court ruled in favor of the Shelleys, asserting that by enforcing the private covenant, the State violated their 14th Amendment rights.

## Practicing the Vocabulary

1. trust
2. bourgeoisie
3. free enterprise system
4. welfare state
5. Gosplan
6. proletariat
7. centrally planned economy
8. capital
9. collectivization
10. entrepreneur
11. laissez-faire theory

## Reviewing Main Ideas

### Section 1

12. **(a)** Land, labor, and capital. **(b)** Entrepreneurs use these factors to create goods and offer services.
13. Capital is owned by individuals and corporations. Private decisions determine how that capital is used.
14. **(a)** Competition keeps prices low and quality high. **(b)** A market may become a monopoly, which can lead to higher prices and less innovation.
15. Answers include: Carry out foreign relations and defend the country from attack; protect private property, public health, safety, and morals; carry out other tasks that private companies cannot carry out profitably.
16. **(a)** The owner enjoys full control and can make quick decisions. **(b)** A corporation can attract large investments of capital; a corporation is stable because it can endure even as individuals leave.

### Section 2

17. **(a)** To distribute wealth equitably throughout society. **(b)** Factory workers lived and worked in poor conditions while their employers usually prospered. Socialists wanted to redistribute some of the employers' wealth to improve the lives of workers.
18. **(a)** Under capitalism, the proletariat—workers—are oppressed by the bourgeoisie—those who own capital. **(b)** Socialists agree to work with the government to improve the lives of workers, while communists call for a revolution to overturn capitalism and the state.
19. Answers include: Nationalization of industries, a welfare state, high tax rates, and central planning.
20. **(a)** Socialism allows newly independent countries to take over foreign-owned industries, plan new

## Political Dictionary

factors of production (p. 658)
capital (p. 659)
capitalist (p. 659)
entrepreneur (p. 659)
free enterprise system (p. 659)
laws of supply and demand (p. 661)
monopoly (p. 661)
trust (p. 661)

laissez-faire theory (p. 662)
socialism (p. 666)
proletariat (p. 667)
bourgeoisie (p. 667)
welfare state (p. 668)
market economy (p. 669)
centrally planned economy (p. 669)
communism (p. 672)

five-year plan (p. 673)
collectivization (p. 674)
Gosplan (p. 674)
privatization (p. 675)
Great Leap Forward (p. 675)
commune (p. 675)

## Practicing the Vocabulary

**Matching** *Choose a term from the list above that best matches each description.*

1. An organization of several firms that controls the only source of a product or service
2. In Marxist terms, the capitalists
3. Economic system in which individuals are free to start and run their own businesses
4. A government that assumes the role of promoter of citizen welfare through programs that provide health care, education, and pensions
5. Central institution that planned the economy of the Soviet Union

**Fill in the Blank** *Choose a term from the list above that best completes the sentence.*

6. Marx believed the _____ would one day rise up and overthrow the capitalist system.
7. An economy in which the government directs factories and farms and decides what to produce and how much is a _____.
8. _____ consists of the wealth and tools used to produce goods and services.
9. During _____, many individual farms are combined to create one giant farm.
10. If existing companies do not see and meet demand, a(n) _____ may start a new business and do so.
11. _____ recommends that government play a very small role in the economy.

## Reviewing Main Ideas

### Section 1

12. **(a)** What are the factors of production? **(b)** What role do the factors of production play in an economy?
13. What are the hallmarks of a free enterprise economy?
14. **(a)** Why is competition important to a free enterprise economy? **(b)** What will happen to a market without competition?
15. According to laissez-faire theory, what are the three duties of government?
16. **(a)** What are the advantages of a sole proprietorship? **(b)** What are the advantages of a corporation?

### Section 2

17. **(a)** What is the purpose of socialism? **(b)** How did events in the 19th century contribute to socialism's popularity?
18. **(a)** Briefly describe Karl Marx's basic ideas about the capitalist system. **(b)** What is the difference between socialism and communism?

19. Describe three characteristics commonly found in socialist countries.
20. **(a)** Why has socialism been popular in developing countries? **(b)** How successful has socialism been in these countries?
21. What are the major criticisms of socialism?

### Section 3

22. Briefly describe Marx's view of history and the labor theory of value.
23. Describe four characteristics of communist countries.
24. In what ways did the Soviet Union fail to meet Marx's predictions?
25. Describe the problems facing the Soviet economy under Gorbachev and the Russian economy today.
26. **(a)** What changes did Mao make as leader of the People's Republic of China? **(b)** How did Deng Xiaoping differ from Mao?

industrial development from the ground up, and motivate people to support a political leader. **(b)** It has not succeeded in creating long-term economic growth.
21. Critics complain that socialism creates a big, unresponsive government that discourages individual initiative and freedom.

### Section 3

22. Marx wrote that history is the story of the struggle between economic classes, and people would advance through several stages of government until the proletariat won power and established a communist society. The labor theory of value states that a good's value is based solely on the amount of labor put into it.
23. A strong Communist Party, central planning, collective agriculture, and state ownership of industry and property.
24. The Soviet Union began as

an agricultural country, not an industrial country. The state grew stronger, rather than weaker, and new class divisions appeared.
25. Russia has not yet developed a functioning market economy. Some problems have been corruption, inflation, and poverty.
26. **(a)** Mao improved education and introduced collectivization and central planning. **(b)** Deng Xiaoping moved China toward a free market system.

## Critical Thinking Skills

**27.** *Applying the Chapter Skill* Review the line graph on page 670 and answer the following questions. **(a)** What does the horizontal axis measure? **(b)** When did unemployment in the United States reach its highest point during the 1990s? **(c)** Which of the three countries listed had the highest unemployment rate in 1997?

**28.** *Recognizing Propaganda* Mao Zedong renamed his country the "People's Republic of China" after the communist takeover in 1949. **(a)** How did this new name reflect the theories of Karl Marx? **(b)** Based on your reading in this chapter, is this an appropriate name for a communist state? Explain your answer.

**29.** *Drawing Inferences* Consider the common criticism of socialism on the grounds that it discourages individual initiative. **(a)** What assumption about initiative underlies this criticism? **(b)** Is this assumption valid? Why or why not? **(c)** How does a free enterprise system differ from socialism in its treatment of individuals?

## Analyzing Political Cartoons

Using your knowledge of economic systems and this cartoon, answer the questions below.

**30.** What does this cartoon imply about Russia's experiences since the end of communism?

**31.** How do "Russian communism" and "Russian capitalism" compare with ideal forms of communism and capitalism?

 **You Can Make a Difference**

Help educate your classmates about child-labor laws. Contact the U.S. Department of Labor or your State's department of labor to learn more about current U.S. child-labor laws. Then create a poster or display sheet that could be posted in the school guidance office, outlining the hours children are allowed to work and any types of jobs they are not allowed to perform. Your poster should also note whether the hours and types of jobs vary depending on the age of the child.

## Participation Activities

**32.** *Current Events Watch* Review newspapers and magazines from the past month and find articles that discuss businesses or the economy in China, Russia, and Germany. Are these countries described as communist, socialist, capitalist, or a combination? Based on your reading in this chapter, how would you categorize these three economies?

**33.** *Chart Activity* Create a chart or table in which you compare the role of government in the U.S. free enterprise system with the other economic systems you have read about in this chapter. Include the reasons why these systems developed and their advantages and disadvantages.

**34.** *It's Your Turn* It is 1932. The world is in the midst of the Great Depression, and you are a young politician running for office. You must convince people that you have the best solution for the country's economic problems. Write a speech in which you explain why you have chosen your particular party and describe the goals of your party. What legislation will you support? Why should people vote for your party instead of the alternatives? After you have written your speech, present it to your class. **(Writing a Speech)**

 **Take It to the Net**

*Chapter 23 Self-Test* As a final review activity, take the Chapter 23 Self-Test in the Social Studies area at the Web site listed below, and receive immediate feedback on your answers.

**www.phschool.com**

 **Take It to the Net**

Additional support materials and activities for Chapter 23 of *Magruder's American Government* can be found in the Social Studies area at the Prentice Hall School Web site.
**www.phschool.com**

## Critical Thinking Skills

**27. (a)** The year. **(b)** 1992. **(c)** France.
**28. (a)** Karl Marx believed that working people, rather than the bourgeoisie, would govern themselves in a communist state. **(b)** Answers will vary, but students should acknowledge that people in communist states have little or no say in government.
**29. (a)** Possible answer: It assumes that people are motivated by the prospect of their own personal success and wealth; thus, taking away that prospect destroys a person's initiative. **(b)** Answers will vary, but should be supported with valid reasoning. **(c)** Answers will vary, but might allude to social services, taxes, and the nature of business under each system.

## Analyzing Political Cartoons

**30.** Russians have fared poorly under communism and capitalism.
**31.** Neither system matches the ideals described in this chapter.

## You Can Make a Difference

Refer students to the "Working to Eliminate Child Labor" feature in the Close Up on Participation booklet in the *Teaching Resources* for ideas on planning and carrying out service learning projects related to this theme.

## Participation Activities

**32.** Answers will vary, but news stories should support the student's conclusions.
**33.** Charts should be clearly organized and should contain a comprehensive list of other economic systems discussed in the chapter. Data should be supported by chapter content.
**34.** Speeches should demonstrate an understanding of the party's beliefs.

## Point-of-Use Resources

**Guide to the Essentials of American Government** Chapter 23 Test, page 126 provides multiple-choice questions to test students' knowledge of the chapter.

**Test Bank CD-ROM** Chapter 23 Test

**Chapter Test** Chapter Tests booklet

## Participating in Texas State and Local Government

### Introducing the Unit

Unit 7 introduces students to government at the State and local levels. Chapter 24 examines the structure, organization, and powers of State legislatures, the office of governor, local governments, and the governments in American cities. Chapter 25 explores the many services provided by States for their citizens, major sources of State and local revenue, the overall organization of the State court systems and the different kinds of law applied there.

### Focus Activity

Concentrate students' attention on the government at the State and local levels by writing the following quotation on the board:

*"How can a people unaccustomed to freedom in small affairs learn to use it temperately in great affairs?"*
                    —Alexis de Tocqueville

Have students consider the following after they have read the quotation.

◆ What does de Tocqueville imply about government that deals "in small affairs"?
◆ Do you agree with de Tocqueville's reasoning? Why or why not?
◆ Use these questions as springboards to a general class discussion about students' views on State and local governments.

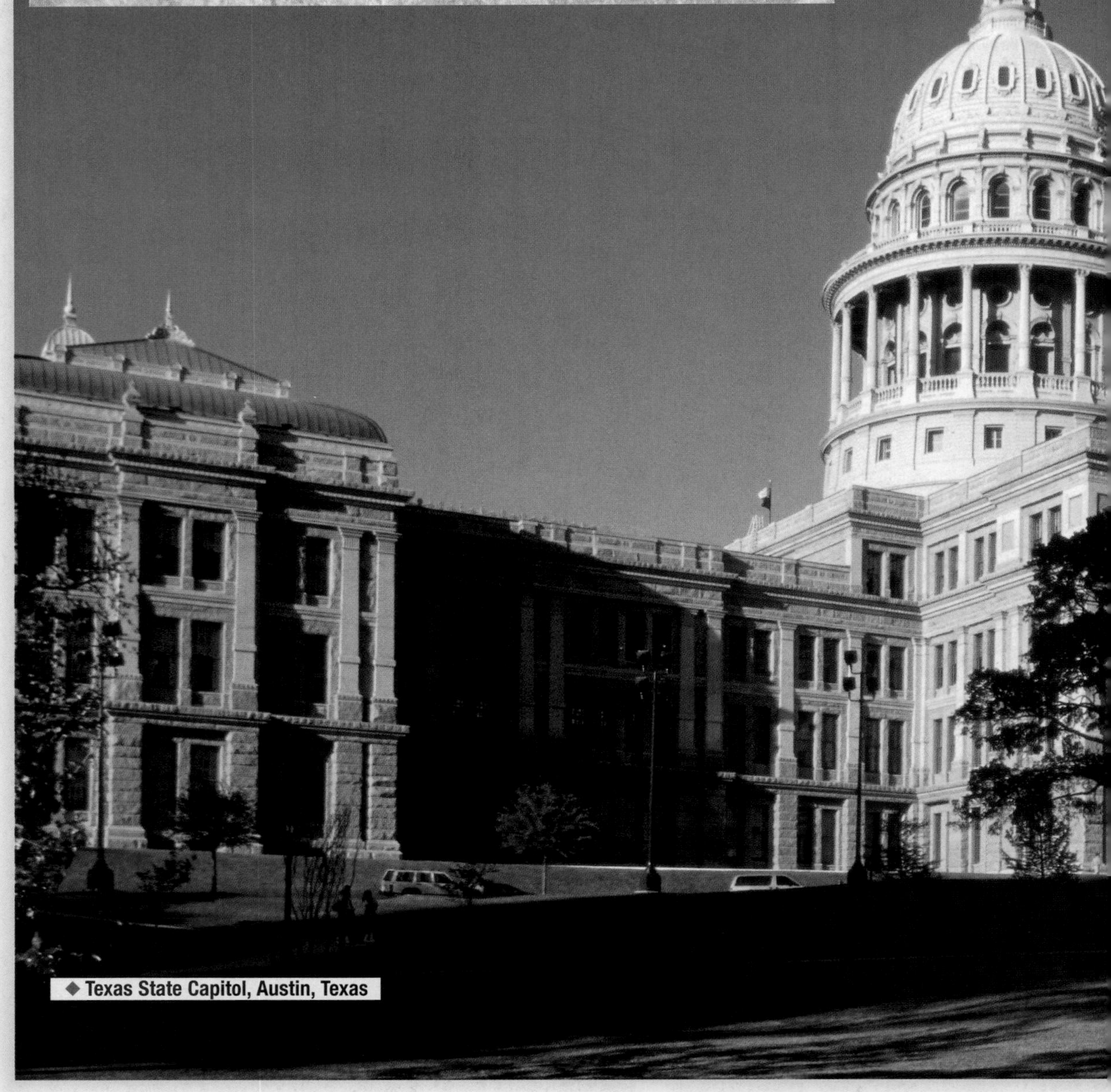

◆ **Texas State Capitol, Austin, Texas**

### Corner

The following Close Up features appear in this unit.
*Close Up on the Supreme Court* may be found on the following page of this unit: 713, 745
*Close Up on Primary Sources* may be found on the following pages of this unit: 701, 724

To keep up-to-date on Close Up news and activities, visit Close Up Online at

**www.closeup.org**

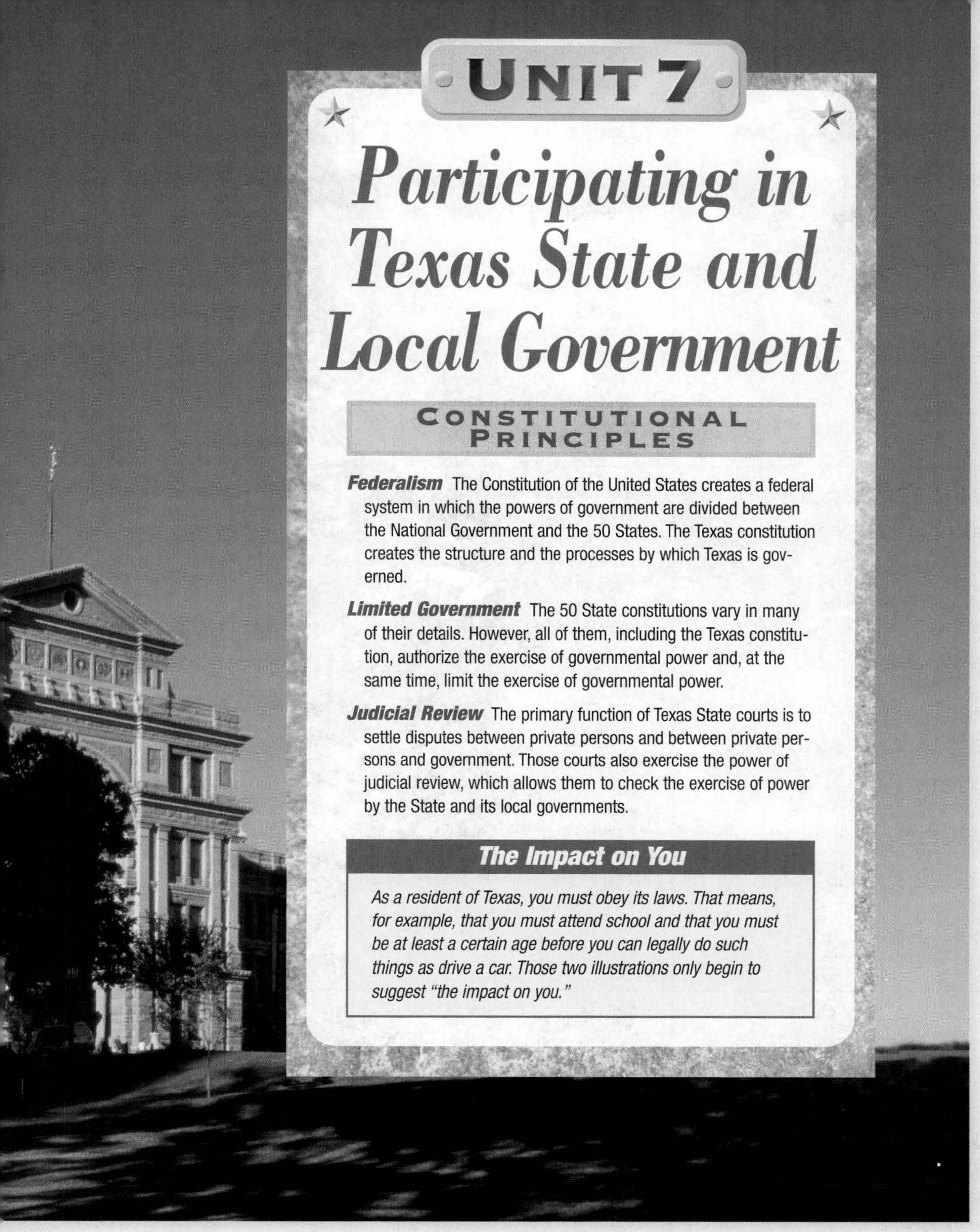

# UNIT 7

# Participating in Texas State and Local Government

## CONSTITUTIONAL PRINCIPLES

***Federalism*** The Constitution of the United States creates a federal system in which the powers of government are divided between the National Government and the 50 States. The Texas constitution creates the structure and the processes by which Texas is governed.

***Limited Government*** The 50 State constitutions vary in many of their details. However, all of them, including the Texas constitution, authorize the exercise of governmental power and, at the same time, limit the exercise of governmental power.

***Judicial Review*** The primary function of Texas State courts is to settle disputes between private persons and between private persons and government. Those courts also exercise the power of judicial review, which allows them to check the exercise of power by the State and its local governments.

### The Impact on You

*As a resident of Texas, you must obey its laws. That means, for example, that you must attend school and that you must be at least a certain age before you can legally do such things as drive a car. Those two illustrations only begin to suggest "the impact on you."*

## Pressed for Time?

### Instruction Plus!

The resources you need to support your instruction of this chapter are conveniently located in a single box. This innovative package provides an instructional advantage in the classroom with its ready-to-use tools in a variety of formats.

- **Magruder's American Government Video Collection**
- **Keep It Current Web-based Activities**
  **Presentation Pro CD-ROM**
- **Section Support Transparencies**
- **Guide to the Essentials**
  **Current Issues**

## Spotlight on Technology

**Take it to the Net**
Offers student-appropriate Internet activities and links that extend core content. Visit us at the Social Studies area. **www.phschool.com**
Be sure to check out this month's **eTeach** online discussion with a Master Government Teacher.

**Keep It Current CD-ROM**
Includes government-related projects by unit. Use it to link to the Prentice Hall School Web site where you will find daily updates.

**Magruder's American Government Video Collection**
Chapter-by-chapter video selections bring key government concepts to life.

**ABC News Civics and Government Videotape Library**
These high-interest stories from ABC News relate to core content.

**Simulations and Data Graphing CD-ROM** Provides interactive federal budget and stock market simulations, and skills practice with statistical data.

**Prentice Hall Presentation Pro CD-ROM** Provides multimedia lecture notes for each chapter.

**ExamView® Test Bank CD-ROM**
Allows you to create, edit, and print out chapter level tests.

**Resource Pro® CD-ROM**
Teaching Resources that offer lesson planning flexibility, test-generation capability, and resource manageability.

**Social Studies Skills Tutor CD-ROM** Provides interactive practice in geographic literacy, critical thinking and reading, visual analysis, and communications.

**Section Support Transparencies**
Illustrates key government concepts through graphs, charts, photos, and cartoons.

**Basic Principles of the Constitution Transparencies**
Illustrates key principles of the Constitution.

**Section Reading Support Transparency System**
Delivers the main idea of each section in the student text through graphic organizers.

# Governing the State of Texas

| Section Objectives | Print and Technology Resources |
|---|---|
| **1 The Texas State Constitution** (pp. 684–688)<br><br>1. Examine the history, contents, and importance of the first State constitutions.<br>2. Describe the history of the Texas constitution.<br>3. Examine the Texas constitution today.<br>4. Explain the process for constitutional change.<br>5. Discuss the reasons for constitutional change and revision.<br><br>**TEKS 8A, 8D, 9H, 21A, 21D, 21E, 22A, 22B, 22D** | • **Unit 7 booklet**<br>Guided Reading and Review, p. 2<br>Section 1 Quiz, p. 3<br>• **Lesson Plans booklet** Section 1, p. 102<br>• **Political Cartoons booklet** Section 1, p. 94<br>• **Block Scheduling with Lesson Strategies booklet** p. 31<br><br>• **Government Assessment Rubrics booklet** p. 14<br>• **Government Resources Handbook**<br>• **Section Support Transparencies** 97, 196<br>• **Presentation Pro CD-ROM** Section 1<br>• **Section Reading Support Transparencies** |
| **2 The Texas State Legislature** (pp. 689–693)<br><br>1. Compare the structure and functions of the Texas State government with those of the federal system.<br>2. Describe the election process, terms, and compensation of Texas State legislators.<br>3. Explain the powers and organization of the Texas State legislature.<br>4. Summarize the legislative process at the State level.<br><br>**TEKS 9H, 10D, 11A, 17C, 21A, 21B, 21C, 21E, 22A, 22B, 22D** | • **Unit 7 booklet**<br>Guided Reading and Review, p. 4<br>Section 2 Quiz, p. 5<br>• **Lesson Plans booklet** Section 2, p. 103<br>• **Political Cartoons booklet** Section 2, p. 95<br>• **Section Reading Support Transparencies**<br><br>• **The Living Constitution booklet** pp. 21–22<br>• **Basic Principles of the Constitution Transparencies** 49<br>• **Section Support Transparencies** 98, 197<br>• **Presentation Pro CD-ROM** Section 2 |
| **3 The Governor and State Administration** (pp. 694–700)<br><br>1. Describe the governorship of Texas.<br>2. Summarize the governor's many roles, including the powers, duties, and limitations of the office.<br>3. Examine the duties and powers of the lieutenant governor of Texas.<br>4. List and describe the other State executive offices and boards.<br><br>**TEKS 9H, 11A, 17C, 21A, 21C, 21E, 22A, 22B** | • **Unit 7 booklet**<br>Guided Reading and Review, p. 6<br>Section 3 Quiz, p. 7<br>• **Lesson Plans booklet** Section 3, p. 104<br>• **Political Cartoons booklet** Section 3, p. 96<br>• **Section Reading Support Transparencies**<br><br>• **Close Up on Primary Sources booklet** Term Limits Across the Country, p. 26<br>• **Section Support Transparencies** 99, 198<br>• **Presentation Pro CD-ROM** Section 3 |
| **4 In the Courtroom** (pp. 702–705)<br><br>1. Identify and define the kinds of law applied in Texas State courts.<br>2. Compare and contrast civil law and criminal law.<br>3. Describe the jury system in Texas.<br><br>**TEKS 9C, 9H, 17C, 21A, 21C, 22A, 22B, 22D** | • **Unit 7 booklet**<br>Guided Reading and Review, p. 8<br>Section 4 Quiz, p. 9<br>• **Lesson Plans booklet** Section 4, p. 105<br>• **Political Cartoons booklet** Section 4, p. 97<br><br>• **Section Support Transparencies** 100, 199<br>• **Presentation Pro CD-ROM** Section 4<br>• **Section Reading Support Transparencies**<br>• **Social Studies Skills Tutor CD-ROM** |
| **5 The Courts and Their Judges** (pp. 707–712)<br><br>1. Explain how Texas State courts are organized and describe the work of each kind of Texas State court.<br>2. Examine and evaluate the different ways that judges are selected.<br><br>**TEKS 9C, 9H, 11A, 17C, 21A, 21C, 21D, 21E, 22A, 22B, 22C, 22D** | • **Unit 7 booklet**<br>Guided Reading and Review, p. 10<br>Section 5 Quiz, p. 11<br>Skills for Life Activity, p. 12<br>• **Lesson Plans booklet** Section 5, p. 106<br>• **Political Cartoons booklet** Section 5, p. 98<br>• **Block Scheduling with Lesson Strategies booklet** p. 31<br>• **Close Up on the Supreme Court booklet** City of Philadelphia v. New Jersey, p. 25<br>• **Section Reading Support Transparencies**<br><br>• **Close Up on Participation booklet** Planting the Seeds of Change, pp. 16–17<br>• **The Living Constitution booklet** p. 7<br>• **The Basic Principles of the Constitution Posters**<br>• **Basic Principles of the Constitution Transparencies** 21<br>• **Section Support Transparencies** 101, 200<br>• **Presentation Pro CD-ROM** Section 5<br>• **Simulations and Data Graphing CD-ROM** |

The *Magruder's American Government* program addresses block-scheduling strategies in a variety of ways. For easy reference, side-column activities that fit a block format are marked ▪ **Block Strategy.** Each section also contains a **Block Scheduling Strategies** box describing at least two block-format activities that address and extend core content from the section. The **Block Scheduling with Lesson Strategies booklet** found in the Teaching Resources contains additional block-scheduling activities for each chapter.

## Take It to the Net

Visit the Social Studies area at the Prentice Hall School Web site. Once there, you can find additional links, current events connections, and activities to enrich chapter content for *Magruder's American Government,* as well as a Self-Test for students. Be sure to check out this month's **eTeach** online discussion with a Master Teacher.

### www.phschool.com

## Assessment Options

- Section Quizzes, **Unit 7 booklet,** pp. 3, 5, 7, 9, 11
- Chapter 24 Assessment, pp. 714–715
- **Guide to the Essentials of American Government,** Chapter 24 Test, p. 132

### Core Assessment
Chapter 24 Test, Chapter Tests booklet
ExamView® Test Bank CD-ROM Chapter 24
Government Assessment Rubrics

### Standardized Test Preparation
#### Diagnose and Prescribe
Diagnostic Tests for High School
Social Studies Skills

#### Review and Reteach
Review Book for Government

#### Practice and Assess
Test-Taking Strategies With
    Transparencies for High School
Test Prep Book for Government

## Pressed for Time?

If you are running short on time to cover this chapter, consider one of the following options:
- Use the **Presentation Pro CD-ROM** to create an outline for this chapter.
- Use one of the **Pressed for Time** activities found on p. 27.
- Use the Section Summaries for Chapter 2, from **Guide to the Essentials of American Government (English and Spanish).**

 ## Video Connections

Prentice Hall offers two video programs to reinforce and extend chapter content. Show students *The Blessings of Liberty* from the **ABC News Civics and Government Videotape Library** and *Prayer in Schools: A Nationwide Debate* from the **Magruder's American Government Video Collection.**

---

## Chapter 24 Teacher's Edition Index

### Introducing the Chapter

In this chapter, students will learn how the three branches of government are structured and how they function at the State level.

## CONSTITUTIONAL PRINCIPLES

Emphasize the following basic principles as students read Chapter 24. Have the class respond to the questions, and then ask volunteers to describe whether these principles work at the State level in the same way they do at the national level.

**Popular Sovereignty** How were early State governments structured around the idea of popular sovereignty?

**Judicial Review** In what way do State courts act as a check on the conduct of other State agencies?

*"Better public schools, greater economic opportunity, safer streets and communities, and a budget surplus—they are all clear signs of a Texas moving forward—of a State that is strong and vibrant."*
—Texas Governor Rick Perry (2001)

Texas is unique in its geography, size, and history; but it is quite similar to the other 50 States in the structure of its government. All States have written constitutions. Like the Federal Government, each has an executive, a legislative, and a judicial branch.

◆ **The Texas House of Representatives**

## Corner

The following resources are available only from the Close Up Foundation to support the concepts discussed in Chapter 24:

◆ *Perspectives: Readings on Contemporary American Government*
◆ *Active Citizenship Today Field Guide for Students*

 Online

To keep up-to-date on Close Up news and activities, visit Close Up Online at

**www.closeup.org**

Close Up Foundation
44 Canal Center Plaza
Alexandria, VA 22314-1592
800-765-3131

## You Can Make a Difference

**ALTHOUGH THE GOVERNOR,** legislature, and courts do the big work of governing the States, much of the day-to-day needs of communities would not be met without local activists and volunteers. In San Antonio, Texas, students at R.G. Cole High School formed an organization to ease the isolation suffered by special needs students on campus. The group, called IMPACT (Inspiring Miracles: Parents and Children Together) Partners, operates reading assistance, instrument lessons, Braille training, sports teams and more. Special events include sports events with the San Antonio Raiders and the San Antonio Spurs.

### Keep It Current

Items marked with this logo are periodically updated on the Internet. Keep up-to-date with what's in the news. To get current information on State government, go to **www.phschool.com**

### SECTION 1

#### The Texas State Constitution (pp. 684–688)

★ The first State constitutions were based on popular sovereignty and limited government, and they provided for a separation of powers, checks and balances, and protection of individual rights.
★ The Texas State constitution retains those basic principles; it also sets out the structure, powers, and processes of government, and details methods of constitutional change.

### SECTION 2

#### The Texas State Legislature (pp. 689–693)

★ As in the federal system, the legislature is the lawmaking branch of State government. It has the power to pass any law that does not conflict with the State constitution or with federal law.
★ State legislators are chosen by popular vote.
★ State legislatures are organized much like Congress, and the legislative process is also similar to that of Congress.

### SECTION 3

#### The Governor and State Administration (pp. 694–700)

★ The governor is the chief executive officer of the State.
★ In addition to executive powers, a governor has some legislative and judicial powers.
★ The lieutenant governor holds considerable power in Texas government.

### SECTION 4

#### In the Courtroom (pp. 702–705)

★ The law is the code of conduct by which society is governed. State courts apply constitutional, statutory, and administrative law as well as common law and equity.
★ The law can also be classified as either criminal or civil law.
★ There are two kinds of juries: the grand jury, which brings indictments; and the petit jury, which decides the facts in trials.

### SECTION 5

#### The Courts and Their Judges (707–712)

★ The Texas State judicial system consists of five tiers of courts.
★ Texas has two high courts, the State Supreme Court and the Court of Criminal Appeals.

## Pressed for Time?

### To Omit the Chapter

If you wish to skip Chapter 24, ask students to read the Chapter in Brief and assign the Guide to the Essentials before continuing to another chapter. You may also want to assign the Chapter 24 Test in the Chapter Test booklet. Then specific portions of Chapter 24 may be assigned to students needing reinforcement of key terms and concepts.

### To Preview the Chapter

To introduce students to key terms and concepts in each section, have them read the Chapter in Brief. You may also assign the Reading Strategy activities on pp. 685, 690, 695, 703 and 708 of this book.

### To Review the Chapter

When students have completed Chapter 24, you might want to assign the Guide to the Essentials or the Guided Reading and Review worksheets on pp. 2, 4, 6, 8, and 10 of the Unit 7 booklet.

### To Cover the Chapter Quickly

To cover the material in Chapter 24 quickly, use the following activity.

**Focus** Have students describe the basic function of the Federal Government (the three branches, the executive leader, the courts, etc.). As they do so, create an outline of this structure on the board.

**Instruct** As you point to each part of the structure you have outlined, describe how that structure applies to State governments. Explain the powers of each branch of State government, and include in the discussion the role of State constitutions and how they function today.

**Close/Reteach** Ask students to recreate the outline from the board in their notebooks, and fill in details about it as they read through the chapter.

🔲 **Block Strategy (Average)**

## Keep It Current

### Internet Update

Use the Prentice Hall School Web site and the Keep It Current CD-ROM to find quick content updates.

Visit **www.phschool.com** for current events articles that are linked to Chapter 24. Critical thinking questions are included.

**Keep It Current CD-ROM** includes government-related projects by unit. Students complete each project using current information that they obtain by linking to the Prentice Hall School Web site from the CD-ROM.

# 1 The Texas State Constitution

## Section Preview

### OBJECTIVES

1. **Examine** the history, contents, and importance of the first State constitutions.
2. **Describe** the history of the Texas constitution.
3. **Examine** the Texas constitution today.
4. **Explain** the process for constitutional change.
5. **Discuss** the reasons for constitutional change and revision.

### WHY IT MATTERS

The constitution of Texas is the supreme law of the State. It is based on popular sovereignty and limited government. It includes a bill of rights that guarantees basic human rights to Texans.

### POLITICAL DICTIONARY

★ popular sovereignty
★ limited government
★ initiative
★ fundamental law
★ statutory law

---

The Constitution of Texas is the supreme law of Texas, just as the United States Constitution is the supreme law of the country. It sets out the ways in which the government of Texas is organized, and it distributes power among the various branches of State government. It authorizes the government's exercise of sovereign power, but also places limits on the exercise of that power. As the supreme law of Texas, the State's constitution is superior to all State and local laws within Texas. Through their constitution, Texans can structure their State government the way they want.

Every State's constitution, however, is subordinate to the Constitution of the United States. (See Article VI, Section 2, the Supremacy Clause.) Because of this, no provision in the Texas constitution may contradict the provisions of the United States Constitution. In other words, the Texas constitution cannot take powers away from the Federal Government and cannot restrict rights granted to individuals by the federal Bill of Rights.

## The First State Constitutions

From the beginning, government in this country has been based on written constitutions. In fact, the United States has sometimes been described as "a land of constitutions." Each of the fifty States has a written constitution.

America's experience with these documents dates from 1606, when King James I granted a charter to the Virginia Company. That act led to the settlement at Jamestown in the following year and, with it, the first government in British North America. Later, each of the other English colonies was also established and governed on the basis of a written charter. Most of the colonial charters served as models for the first State constitutions. In Connecticut and Rhode Island the old charters seemed so well suited to the needs of the day that they were carried over as constitutions almost without change.[1]

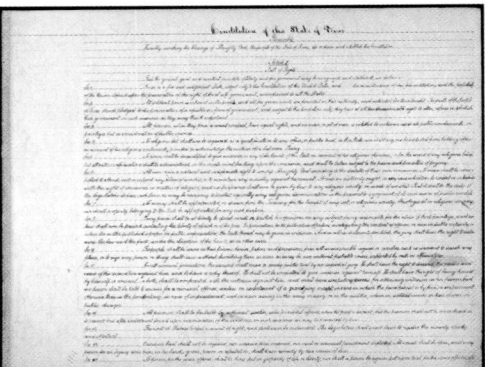
▲ The Texas State Constitution

---

[1] Connecticut did not write a new document until 1818, and Rhode Island not until 1842.

The first State constitutions were adopted by the legislatures without being submitted to the people for approval. In 1780, a popularly elected convention prepared a new constitution for Massachusetts.[2] The voters of that State then ratified the constitution. Most State constitutions in effect today were drafted by assemblies representing the people and were ratified by popular vote before becoming effective.

Because the first State constitutions came out of the Revolutionary period, they shared many of the same basic features. The doctrines of separation of powers and checks and balances were built into each of the new constitutions. Each also proclaimed the principles of **popular sovereignty** and **limited government**. That is, in each of them the people were recognized as the sole source of authority for government. And in each constitution, the powers given to the new government were closely limited. Seven constitutions began with a lengthy bill of rights. All of them made it clear that the sovereign people held "certain unalienable rights" that government must respect.

The early State constitutions also contained provisions (and had some important omissions) that by today's standards would seem quite undemocratic. No constitution provided for full religious freedom. Each constitution also set rigid qualifications for voting and for office-holding, and all gave property owners a highly favored standing.

## History of the Texas Constitution

The Constitution of the Republic of Texas was written in 1836 by a convention of fifty-nine delegates. The people of the Republic ratified the constitution soon afterwards.

Much of the document was patterned after the Constitution of the United States and those of several other States. This first Texas constitution separated governmental powers into the legislative, executive, and judicial branches, and it created checks and balances among the branches. It allowed slavery, extended citizenship to people other than "Africans, the descendents of Africans, and Indians," and did not allow women to vote.

The Texas constitution also drew on influences from Spanish and Mexican law. It adopted

"Now you try to get a fire started while I draft a constitution."

▲ *Interpreting Political Cartoons* **(a) How important does the cartoonist think a written constitution is? How do you know? (b) Do you agree? Explain.**

community property (shared ownership by married couples), gave homestead exemptions and protections, and granted special relief to debtors.

To amend the constitution, one session of the Texas legislature had to approve the amendment, then the following session had to reapprove it, and finally the people of Texas had to adopt it by popular vote. This process proved to be so difficult that this original constitution was never amended.

In 1845, a new constitution was written to provide government for Texas as a new State of the United States. The United States accepted it on December 29, 1845.

After Texas voted to secede from the Union, the State adopted the Constitution of 1861. This document reflected the move from the United States to the Confederate States of America. It had stronger provisions for States rights and slavery, but stopped short of legalizing the African slave trade.

The Constitutional Convention of 1866 completed a new Texas constitution following the Civil War. Another convention was convened two years later but broke up without agreeing on a final document. However, the work of the

[2]As noted in Chapter 2, with independence Massachusetts relied on the colonial charter in force prior to 1691 as its first State constitution. New Hampshire adopted its second and present constitution in 1784. It followed the Massachusetts pattern of popular convention and popular ratification.

## Reading Strategy
### Drawing Inferences
Tell students that most State constitutions are too long and too old. Encourage them to think, as they read, how this affects the functioning of State governments.

## Background Note
### Constitutional Issues
The Massachusetts constitution of 1780 and New Hampshire's constitution of 1784, both still in force, are the oldest State constitutions still in use. In fact, the constitutions of these two States are older than all other written constitutions in effect in the world today. At the other extreme, Louisiana has adopted new constitutions eleven times since statehood, most recently in 1974. Georgia adopted its tenth and current constitution in 1982.

## Point-of-Use Resources

**Guided Reading and Review** Unit 7 booklet, p. 2 provides students with practice identifying the main ideas and key terms of this section.

**Lesson Plans** For lesson planning suggestions, see p. 102 of the Lesson Plans booklet.

**Political Cartoons** See p. 94 of the Political Cartoons booklet for a cartoon relevant to this section.

**Section Support Transparencies** Transparency 97, *Visual Learning;* Transparency 196, *Political Cartoon*

## Organizing Information

To make sure students understand the main points of this section, you may wish to use the web graphic organizer to the right.

Tell students that a web can be used to record information about a topic. Have students use the web to record details about the six categories of principles on which State constitutions are based.

**Teaching Tip** A template for this graphic organizer can be found in the Section Support Transparencies, Transparency 1.

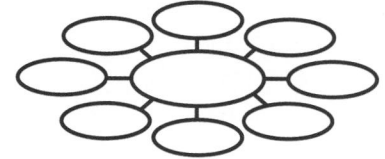

### Answers to . . .
**Interpreting Political Cartoons (a)** Very important. It is one of the first two things that these castaways need to do; it is as necessary to survival as building a fire. **(b)** Answers will vary, but should be reasoned.

▲ *A State Constitutional Convention* James Madison addresses the Virginia Constitutional Convention of 1829–1830.

1868–69 Convention was subsequently organized and published as the Constitution of 1869 and was adopted by the people.

In 1874, members of the Texas legislature attempted to draft a new constitution directly but could not get enough votes for it to be adopted. There was strong feeling in the State that the legislative role was not democratic and that a constitutional convention should be used instead, and one was convened in 1875. The voters approved the resulting constitution the following year. Where the 1874 constitution would have increased the power of government, the 1876 constitution sharply limited governmental powers.

## The Texas Constitution Today

The present-day Texas constitution is over a hundred years old, but it is also very new. Hundreds of amendments have been proposed since 1876, and many have been adopted. The vigor with which amendments are offered, debated, and then either approved or rejected shows how alive the constitution remains.

Like all State constitutions, the Constitution of Texas can be described in terms of six general categories: basic principles, civil rights, governmental structure, governmental powers, processes for change, and miscellaneous provisions.

1. *Basic Principles.* Every State's fundamental law is built on the principles of popular sovereignty and limited government. That is, each State constitution recognizes that government exists only with the consent of the people, and that it must operate within certain, often closely defined bounds. The constitution of Texas pledges the preservation of a republican form of government and recognizes Texans' right to alter, abolish, or reform their government.

2. *Protections of Civil Rights.* State constitutions typically include a bill of rights that lists the rights that individuals hold against the State and its officers and agencies. Often these rights are similar to those in the United States Constitution. Texas's bill of rights provides for equal rights and guarantees freedom of religion and freedom of speech. It protects against unreasonable searches and seizures and grants fundamental protections to people accused of a crime.

Citizens may also use their State constitution to restrict the State government or to enhance individual liberty in ways that go beyond the United States Constitution. Texas's constitution prohibits "outlawing" or transporting a convicted felon out of State for a crime committed in Texas, guarantees individual citizens the right to bear arms, and gives specific rights to the victims of crimes.

3. *Governmental Structure.* Every State constitution deals with the structure of government at both the State and the local levels. A few follow the national pattern, providing only a broad outline. Most, however, cover the subject of governmental organization at length, and often in great detail.

As in all other States, the constitution of Texas provides for the separation of governmental powers into three separate branches: executive, legislative, and judicial. Like all other States, Texas creates a system of checks and balances, prohibiting any branch from exercising powers that are attached to another branch.

4. *Governmental Powers and Processes.* All State constitutions list, in detail, the powers vested in the executive branch (the governor and other executive officers), the legislature, the courts, and the units of local government. The powers to tax, spend, borrow, and provide for education are very prominent. So, too, are such processes as elections, legislation, and intergovernmental (State-local) relations.

The Texas constitution creates a bicameral legislature: a senate with 31 members and a house with 150 members. Senators are elected for four years and representatives for two years. The constitution contains detailed provisions regarding legislative functioning.

The constitution also creates a State Ethics Commission, provides for creation of Rural Fire Prevention Districts and Emergency Services Districts, creates a Veterans Land Board and a Texas Water Development Board, and contains many other specific provisions relating to legislative functions.

The Executive Department established by the Texas constitution includes the Governor as Chief Executive Officer of the State, and a Lieutenant Governor, Secretary of State, Comptroller of Public Accounts, and Attorney General. The Judicial Department includes the Texas Supreme Court, the Court of Criminal Appeals, civil Courts of Appeals, District Courts, County Courts, Commissioners Courts, Courts of Justices of the Peace. The Legislature has the power to create other courts.

5. *Constitutional Change.* Like the national Constitution, the State constitutions have been altered over the years by both formal amendments and informal procedures. But State constitutions tend to be more detailed and specific, so there generally is much less room for informal procedures. As a result, constitutional development at the State level has come about primarily through formal changes rather than informal procedures.

6. *Miscellaneous Provisions.* Most State constitutions begin with a preamble, which has no legal force but does set out the purposes of those who drafted and adopted the document. The Texas constitution's preamble reads: "Humbly invoking the blessings of Almighty God, the people of the State of Texas, do ordain and establish this Constitution."

State constitutions typically also contain a number of "dead letter" provisions, items that have no current force and effect but still remain a part of the constitution because they have not been formally repealed. For example, until 1969 the Texas constitution included an entire constitutional section dealing with Spanish and Mexican land titles.

## Constitutional Change

Two kinds of formal changes have been used to amend State constitutions: (1) amendments, which usually deal with one or a few provisions in a constitution; and (2) revisions, which are

### How to Propose Changes to a State Constitution

**PROPOSAL BY A CONVENTION**
- Constitutional conventions are used most often to revise existing constitutions and to write new ones.
- Every State legislature can call a constitutional convention. That call is generally subject to voter approval.

**PROPOSAL BY A LEGISLATURE**
- Most constitutional amendments are proposed by the legislature.
- The process varies among the States. Where the process is simpler, more amendments are proposed and adopted.

**PROPOSAL BY INITIATIVE**
Voters can propose amendments in some States:
- A specified number of voters must sign a petition.
- The proposal goes on the ballot.
- The people approve or reject the amendment.

*Interpreting Charts* This chart shows only how changes to State constitutions are proposed; in most States, voters must ratify those changes. **Which method of proposing constitutional changes does Texas use today?**

large-scale changes that affect the constitution more broadly. Most of the formal changes in State constitutions have been made by amendment.

The Texas constitution sets out the means by which it may be replaced by a new constitution or amended. The process involves two basic steps: proposal and then ratification. The Texas legislature may propose constitutional amendments. If two thirds of the members of each house approve, the proposed amendment will be submitted to the voters. If a majority of votes cast favor the amendment, then it becomes part of the constitution.

Various States have differing procedures for constitutional amendment, as shown in the chart above. In many States, amendments can be proposed by conventions. However, because they are both costly and time consuming, conventions are most often used for the broader purpose of revision, and most amendments are proposed by the legislature.

As we have seen, Texas has used constitutional conventions to revise its constitutions in the past. The current State constitution, however, gives the legislature the exclusive authority to propose constitutional changes.

### Preparing for Standardized Tests

Have students read the passages under *Constitutional Change* on this page and then answer the question below.

Who has been responsible for writing and revising most State constitutions?

**A** the voters
**B** the legislature
**C** the governor
**D** conventions

## Point-of-Use Resources

**Guide to the Essentials** Chapter 24, Section 1, p. 127 provides support for students who need additional review of section content. Spanish support is available in the Spanish edition of the Guide on p. 120.

**Quiz** Unit 7 booklet, p. 3 includes matching and multiple-choice questions to check students' understanding of Section 1 content.

**Presentation Pro CD-ROM** Quizzes and multiple-choice questions check students' understanding of Section 1 content.

## Answers to . . .

### Section 1 Assessment

**1.** Popular sovereignty means that the people are the source of authority for government.
**2. (a)** By convention: The legislature calls a constitutional convention to write a new State constitution or revise an old one. By a legislature: The State legislature proposes amendments. By initiative: A specified number of voters sign a petition for a constitutional amendment; the proposal goes on the ballot and is either rejected or approved by the voters. **(b)** Texas legislature may propose amendments. If two thirds of the members of each house approve, proposed amendment goes to the voters. Amendment is ratified if approved by a majority of voters.
**3.** Fundamental law is of basic or lasting importance and is part of constitutions. Statutory law is law passed by the legislature, and is more easily changed than fundamental law.
**4.** Answers will vary. Students may suggest that the development of government may not have been as orderly or have resembled the English pattern so closely.
**5.** Possible answer: The process of constitutional change is lengthy and cumbersome; these changes are often not a high priority for either government officials or the public.

---

Ratification by popular vote is required in Texas, as it is in every State except Delaware.[3] Some States require approval by more than fifty percent of those voting. In 17 States the voters themselves can propose constitutional amendments through the **initiative**, a process in which a certain number of qualified voters sign petitions in favor of a proposal. The proposal then goes directly to the ballot, for approval or rejection by the people.

## The Need for Reform

Almost all State constitutions would benefit from some degree of revision and reform. The typical document is cluttered with unnecessary details, burdensome restrictions, and obsolete sections. It also carries much repetitious, even contradictory, material. Moreover, it fails to deal with many of the pressing problems that the States and their local governments currently face. Even the newest and most recently rewritten constitutions tend to carry over a great deal of material from earlier documents and suffer from these same faults.

---

[3]In Delaware, if an amendment is approved by a two-thirds vote in each house of the legislature at two successive sessions, it then becomes effective. In South Carolina, final ratification, after a favorable vote by the people, depends on a majority vote in both houses of the legislature. Both the Alabama and South Carolina constitutions provide that amendments only of local, as opposed to Statewide, application need be approved only by the voters in the affected locale.

---

Length was not a problem for the first State constitutions. They were quite short, ranging from New Jersey's 1776 constitution (2,500 words) to the 1780 Massachusetts constitution (12,000 words). These early State constitutions were meant simply to be statements of basic principle and organization. Purposely, they left to the legislature—as well as to time and practice—the task of filling in the details as they became necessary.

Through the years, however, State constitutions have grown and grown. Texas's constitution is one of the longest in the nation. It has 390 amendments, compared to 27 in the U. S. Constitution, and is about 2.5 times longer than the average State constitution.

Most State constitutions would be improved if the legislatures and the voters separated **fundamental law**, which should properly be in the constitution, from more routine **statutory law**, which can be passed by the legislature. The line separating fundamental and statutory law may be blurry in some cases. But many provisions clearly do not need to go in the State constitution. For example, California's constitution contains a ban on taxing fruit and nut trees planted within the past four years! Putting statutory provisions in the constitution makes the document unnecessarily long and complex and obscures the important points of fundamental law that the constitution should showcase. It also makes it harder to make routine changes in governing law when they are needed.

---

## Section **1** Assessment

### Key Terms and Main Ideas

1. Explain the concept of **popular sovereignty.**
2. **(a)** List and explain three ways changes to State constitutions can be proposed. **(b)** How may the Texas constitution be amended and ratified?
3. What is the difference between **fundamental law** and **statutory law?**

### Critical Thinking

4. **Predicting Consequences** Might the governments of the English colonies or the early States have developed differently if they had not had written charters or constitutions? Explain your answer.

5. **Drawing Inferences** Why might many State constitutions have been allowed to become so lengthy, repetitive, and full of outdated provisions?

 **Take It to the Net**

6. Read the Texas bill of rights, and then review the Federal Bill of Rights. Are there many similarities or are there more differences? Write a paragraph comparing and contrasting the two documents. Use the links provided in the Social Studies area of the following Web site for help in completing this activity. **www.phschool.com**

---

 **Take It to the Net**

**6.** Direct students to the Social Studies area at the Prentice Hall School Web site. The *Magruder's American Government* companion Web site includes the directions and links needed to complete the activity. It also provides a printable Internet activity worksheet with scoring rubrics for assessment. Paragraphs should include both similarities and differences, and should cover all the basic rights in both documents.

## 2 The Texas State Legislature

Each State constitution establishes a legislative body that is, in effect, the powerhouse of that State's government. The size of a legislature, the details of its organization and procedures, the frequency and length of its sessions, and even its official name vary among the States. However, State legislatures share a fundamental feature with one another: they are lawmaking bodies.

## The Legislature: Structure and Size

In all States the legislature is the lawmaking branch of State government. Its basic function goes to the heart of American democracy: The legislature is responsible for translating the public will into the State's public policy.

The Texas legislature carries out that responsibility as a bicameral body modeled after the Congress of the United States. Texas's upper house is called the Senate, and the lower house is called the House of Representatives. In fact, all State legislatures but one are bicameral. The exception is Nebraska, which calls its single chamber the Legislature.

Although there is no ideal size for a legislative body, two basic considerations are important. First, a legislature, and each of its houses, should not be so large as to hamper the orderly conduct of the people's business. Second, it should not be so small that the many views and interests within the State cannot be represented adequately. The Texas Senate has 31 members, representing 31 districts that are about equal in population. The Texas House of Representatives has 150 members, elected from 150 districts that are all about equal in population.

▲ The Texas State Seal

## The State Legislators

Today, there are 7,611 State legislators—5,532 representatives and 2,079 senators—among the 50 States. Nearly all of them are Republicans or Democrats; fewer than 40 belong to minor parties or are Independents. Only one in five of them are women.

### Qualifications

Every State's constitution sets out formal requirements of age, citizenship, and residence for legislators. In Texas, representatives must be at least 21 and senators must be at least 26. Each representative must have lived in the State for two years before his or her election and the last year thereof as a resident of his or her district. Each senator must have lived in the State for five years before election and the last year thereof as a resident of his or her district.

students' attention on key issues, and may be used to stimulate discussion.

In Texas and the rest of the States, the realities of politics place other qualifications on those

▲ *Law and Order* Members of the Texas House raise a point of order while considering a bill.

1. *Executive Powers.* Some of the nonlegislative powers are executive in nature. The Texas senate must approve the governor's appointment of most State officials, for example. In some States the legislature itself appoints certain executive officeholders.

2. *Judicial powers.* The legislature also has certain judicial powers; the chief illustration is the power of impeachment. The legislature can remove any State executive officer or judge through that process.

3. **Constituent power**. The legislature plays a role in constitution-making and the constitutional amendment process. Since this does not involve the making of statutes, this function—the constituent power—is a nonlegislative one.

## Organization of the Texas Legislature

The Texas State legislature is organized in much the same manner as Congress. It has presiding officers and a committee system.

### The Presiding Officers

Those who preside over the sessions of the State legislative chambers are usually powerful political figures, not only in the legislature itself but elsewhere in State politics.

The Texas house elects its own presiding officer, known as the speaker. The Texas constitution provides that the lieutenant governor—an elected member of the executive branch—serves as the president of the senate. The senate also

hope of separating State and local issues from national politics.

selects a president *pro tempore* to serve when the lieutenant governor is absent.

The chief duties of those presiding officers center on the conduct of the legislature's floor business. These duties are also a major source of their power. The presiding officers refer bills to committee, recognize members who seek the floor, and interpret and apply the rules of their chamber to its proceedings.

Unlike the Speaker of the House in Congress, the speaker in the Texas house appoints the chairperson and most members of each house committee. The lieutenant governor has the same power in the senate.

### The Committee System

The committee system in the Texas legislature works much as it does in Congress. Committee members do much of the work of the legislature when they determine which bills will reach the floor and inform the full chamber on measures they have handled. The 77th Texas legislature, which convened in January 2001, had 12 standing committees in the senate and 36 in the house.

The standing committees in each chamber are generally set up by subject matter, such as committees on highways, education, and so on. A bill may be amended or even very largely rewritten in committee. Often, it is simply not acted on. Conference committees—usually ad hoc. groups made up of members of both houses—are also widely used in the Texas legislature. These committees resolve house and senate versions of the same bill.

The "pigeonholing" of bills is as well known in Texas as it is in Congress. (See page 336.) In Texas such a bill is usually assigned to a "Siberia" subcommittee—a committee where it is known that the bill has little chance of "escaping."

## The Legislative Process in Texas

The major steps in the legislative process in the Texas legislature are much like those in Congress. You can review the process in Congress by studying the diagram on page 345.

### Sources of Bills

Legally, only a member may introduce a bill in either chamber in any State legislature. So, in the strictest sense, legislators themselves are the source of all measures introduced. In broader terms, however, the lawmakers are the authors of only a handful of bills.

A large number of bills come from officers and agencies of State and local government. Every governor has a legislative program, and often an extensive and ambitious one.

Bills also come from a wide range of private sources. In fact, the largest single source for proposed legislation in Texas appears to be interest groups. Those groups and their lobbyists have one overriding purpose: to influence public policy to benefit their own special interests. Of course, some bills do originate with private individuals—business people, farmers, labor union members, and other citizens—who, for one reason or another, think that "there ought to be a law. . . ."

## Direct Legislation

Several States allow voters to take a direct part in lawmaking. The main vehicles for this participation are the initiative and the referendum.

1. *The Initiative.* Through the initiative process, voters in 17 States can propose constitutional amendments. In 27 States, voters can also use the initiative to propose ordinary statutes. The initiative can take two quite different forms: the more common direct initiative and the little-used indirect initiative.

In both kinds of initiative, a certain number of qualified voters (which varies from State to State) must sign initiative petitions to propose a law. Where the direct initiative is used, the measure goes directly to the ballot, usually at the next general election. If the voters approve the measure, it becomes law. If not, it dies.

In the indirect initiative, the proposal goes first to the legislature. That body may pass it, making it a law. If the legislature does not pass it, the measure then goes to the voters.

2. *The Referendum.* A **referendum** is a process by which a legislative measure is referred to the State's voters for approval. Three forms of the referendum are used among the States: mandatory, optional, and popular.

A mandatory referendum requires that the legislature refer a measure to the voters. Thus, in every State except Delaware, proposed constitutional amendments must be submitted to the electorate. In several States other measures, such as those approving the borrowing of funds, must also go to the voters.

An optional referendum measure is one that the legislature refers to the voters voluntarily. Such measures are usually "hot potatoes"—issues lawmakers would rather not take direct responsibility for deciding themselves.

Under the popular referendum, the people may demand via a petition that a measure passed by the legislature be referred to them for final action. Usually, however, the petitioners cannot gather the required number of signatures to force a popular vote on the matter.

In Texas the initiative is not used at all at the State level. The referendum is used only to approve constitutional amendments. Texas cities of more than 5,000 may use the initiative and the referendum, and they often do so.

## Section 2 Assessment

### Key Terms and Main Ideas
1. What kinds of laws illustrate the **police power?**
2. What three kinds of nonlegislative powers does the Texas legislature have?
3. What are the three usual sources of bills?
4. In what limited ways are the intiative and **referendum** used in Texas?

### Critical Thinking
5. **Making Comparisons** Consider what you know about Congress and the Texas legislature. (a) In what areas are they most alike? (b) In what areas are they most different?
6. **Analyzing Information** Suppose you are a member of an

interest group that wants to get State funding to clean up a river or to build a new highway. What steps would you follow to get a funding bill introduced and passed in your State legislature?

 **Take It to the Net**

7. Browse the State legislature pages for several States. Select a State other than Texas, and write a report about its legislative process. Include how this process compares and contrasts with the legislative process in Congress. Use the links provided in the Social Studies area of the following Web site for help in completing this activity. **www.phschool.com**

**Take It to the Net**

7. Direct students to the Social Studies area at the Prentice Hall School Web site. The *Magruder's American Government* companion Web site includes the directions and links needed to complete the activity. It also provides a printable Internet activity worksheet with scoring rubrics for assessment. Reports should include both similarities and differences, and cover all important processes.

## Point-of-Use Resources

**Guide to the Essentials** Chapter 24, Section 2, p. 128 provides support for students who need additional review of section content. Spanish support is available in the Spanish edition of the Guide on p. 121.

**Quiz** Unit 7 booklet, p. 5 includes matching and multiple-choice questions to check students' understanding of Section 2 content.

**Presentation Pro CD-ROM** Quizzes and multiple-choice questions check students' understanding of Section 2 content.

## Answers to . . .

### Section 2 Assessment

1. Laws that protect and promote the public health, safety, morals, and welfare.
2. Executive powers such as approval of governor's appointments; judicial powers such as the power of impeachment; and constituent power such as revising and amending the constitution.
3. Bills can be introduced only by legislators, but some originate with the governor or agencies of governments; others come from private sources, such as lobbyists or individuals.
4. The initiative is not used at all at the State level, but both it and the referendum are used by Texas cities of more than 5,000. The referendum is used only to approve constitutional amendments at the State level.
5. **(a)** Similarities include: basic function, bicameral structure, powers, organization, legislative process. **(b)** Differences include: representation in both houses in Texas is based on population, term length, biennial session.
6. Possible answer: Lobby a sympathetic member of the legislature to introduce a bill; lobby other legislators, including appropriate committee members and chairpersons; try to gain the support of the governor to put more pressure on the legislature and to prevent a veto; create a public-awareness campaign to rally public support.

## 3 The Governor and State Administration

## Section Preview

### OBJECTIVES

1. **Describe** the governorship of Texas.
2. **Summarize** the governor's many roles, including the powers, duties, and limitations of the office.
3. **Examine** the duties and powers of the lieutenant governor of Texas.
4. **List and describe** the other State executive offices and boards.

### WHY IT MATTERS

The governor is the chief executive of Texas. Although his or her executive powers are limited in several important ways, the people of the State look to the governor for leadership in State affairs. Other important State executive officers often are elected directly by the people.

### POLITICAL DICTIONARY

★ item veto
★ clemency
★ pardon
★ commutation
★ reprieve
★ parole

The governor is the principal executive officer in Texas. He or she is always a central figure in State politics, and is often a well-known national personality as well. The governor of Texas, like all governors today, holds an office that is the direct descendant of the earliest public office in American politics, the colonial governorship, established in Virginia in 1607.

### The Governorship

In colonial America, the actions of the royal governors inspired much of the resentment that fueled the Revolution. That attitude was carried over into the first State constitutions. Most government powers were given to the legislatures; the new State governors, for the most part, had little real authority. In every State except Massachusetts and New York, the governor was chosen by the legislature, and in most of them only for a one-year term.

That original separation of powers soon proved unsatisfactory. Many of the State legislatures abused their powers. Several fell prey to special interests, and the governors were unable to respond. So, as States wrote new constitutions and revised the older ones, they curbed the powers of the legislatures and increased the powers of the governors.

▲ James Pinckney Henderson, the first governor of Texas

Through the early 1800s, the power to choose the governor was taken from the legislature and given to the people. The veto power was vested in the governor, and the gubernatorial powers of appointment and removal were increased.

Beginning with Illinois in 1917, most States have reorganized and strengthened the executive branch to make the governor the State's chief executive in more than name. To a greater or lesser degree, governors are much more powerful figures today than in decades past.

### Qualifications

Anyone who wants to become the governor of a State must be able to satisfy a set of formal qualifications. In Texas, he or she must be an American citizen, be at least 30 years of age, and have lived in the State for at least five years.

Clearly, these formal qualifications are not very difficult to meet. It is the informal qualifications that have real meaning. To become a governor, a person must have those characteristics that will first attract a party's nomination and then attract the voters in the general election.

Those characteristics vary from election to election. Race, gender, religion, name recognition, personality, party identification, experience, ideology, the ability to use television effectively—these and several other factors are all part of the mix.

Over time, more than 2,400 persons have served as governors of the various States. To this point (2002), only 18 have been women—and five of those 18 hold office today: Jeanne Shaheen of New Hampshire, first elected in 1996; Jane Dee Hull of Arizona, who as secretary of state succeeded to the office in 1997 and who then won it in her own right in 1998; Ruth Ann Minner of Delaware and Judy Martz of Montana, both elected in 2000; and Jane Swift of Massachusetts, who succeeded to the office from the lieutenant-governorship in 2001.[4] Texas has had a woman governor three times: Miriam Ferguson (1925–1927 and 1933–1935), and Ann Richards (1991–1995).

## Selection

The governor is chosen by popular vote in every State. In Texas, gubernatorial candidates are picked in a direct primary. Nearly half the States now provide for the joint election of the governor and the lieutenant governor, although Texas voters elect them independently.

## Term

In Texas, the governor is elected to a four-year term with no limitation on re-election. In fact, governors are elected to four-year terms nearly everywhere today.[5] Only New Hampshire and Vermont still provide for two-year terms. More than half the States limit the number of terms a governor may serve, usually to two terms. Only Virginia has a single-term limit.

## Succession

Governors are mortal. Occasionally, one of them dies in office. Many of them are also politically ambitious. Every so often, one resigns in midterm—perhaps to become a United States senator or to accept a presidential appointment.

When a vacancy does occur, it sets off a game of political musical chairs in the State. The political plans and timetables of a number of public personalities are affected by the event. However,

▲ Texas Governor Rick Perry is shown outside the State Capitol.
*Critical Thinking Lawmakers must cope with big demands on available money. What should their priorities be?*

no matter what causes a vacancy, every State's constitution provides for a successor. The Texas State constitution provides that the lieutenant governor is first in the line of succession.

## Removal

In Texas, the governor may be removed from office by impeachment and conviction. Only one Texas governor, Jim Ferguson, has ever been ousted by impeachment. Ferguson was impeached in 1917 after being indicted for misappropriation of funds and embezzlement in the wake of a controversy over his veto of an appropriations measure for the University of Texas.

## Compensation

Gubernatorial salaries now average over $100,000 a year. In Texas, the governor makes about $115,000 a year. He or she is provided with an official residence and a fairly generous expense account.

To a governor's salary and other material compensation must be added the intangibles of honor and prestige that go along with the office. It is this factor, along with a sense of public duty, that often brings many of our better citizens to seek the office. Several Presidents were governors

---

[4]Twelve other women have been elected to a governorship: Nellie Ross (Wyoming, 1925–1927), Miriam Ferguson (Texas, 1925–1927, 1933–1935), Lurleen Wallace (Alabama, 1967–1968), Ella Grasso (Connecticut, 1975–1980), Dixie Lee Ray (Washington, 1977–1981), Martha Layne Collins (Kentucky, 1983–1987), Madeleine Kunin (Vermont, 1985–1991), Kay Orr (Nebraska, 1987–1991), Joan Finney (Kansas, 1991–1995), Ann Richards (Texas, 1991–1995), Barbara Roberts (Oregon, 1991–1995), and Christine Todd Whitman (New Jersey, 1994–2001). Also, Rose Mofford (who had been secretary of state) succeeded to the governorship in Arizona in 1988, and she served until 1991.

[5]The all-time record for both gubernatorial service and electoral success belongs to George Clinton of New York. He sought and won seven three-year terms as governor and held the office from 1777 to 1795 and again from 1801 to 1804. Clinton was later Vice President of the United States, from 1805 to 1812.

**RESOURCE◉PRO®**

**Resource Pro® CD-ROM** contains an electronic version of each activity found in the Teaching Resources as well as additional resources such as Supreme Court cases. The Planning Express® feature allows you to customize and create daily lesson plans within minutes.

## Customize for
### More Advanced Students

Ask students to find a recent important message delivered by the governor (for example, a State of the State address). Have them prepare a report or presentation in which they discuss what the message revealed about the governor's political agenda and the powers of the office. Students should include in their report ways in which the governor might use the executive, legislative, and judicial powers to accomplish the proclaimed goals. Allow time in class for students to give their presentations.

### Background Note
#### Mom and Pop Governors

Miriam Ferguson ran for governor after her husband, James "Pa" Ferguson was impeached and removed by the Texas legislature in 1917. Ma's ire over her husband's treatment was expressed by her pardoning of over 3,700 convicted felons and her refusal of all extradition requests from other States. In her 1924 campaign, supporters of Ma Ferguson chanted campaign slogans such as, "Me for Ma, and I ain't got a durn thing against Pa," "A bonnet and not a hood," and "Two governors for the price of one." Opponents rebutted with, "Not Ma for me. Too much Pa."

▲ **From Governor to President** Standing under a portrait of Stephen F. Austin in the Senate Chambers of the State Capitol, then President-elect George W. Bush resigned as Governor of Texas, December 21, 2000.

before entering the White House, including, since 1900, William McKinley, Theodore Roosevelt, Woodrow Wilson, Calvin Coolidge, Franklin Roosevelt, Jimmy Carter, Ronald Reagan, Bill Clinton, and George W. Bush.

## The Governor's Many Roles

The governor of Texas is the best known elected official in the State. However, he or she is not the most powerful officeholder in Texas. That distinction belongs to the lieutenant governor, whose office is discussed later in this section. While making the governor the chief executive,

[6]These States are Alaska, Arizona, California, Colorado, Georgia, Idaho, Kansas, Louisiana, Michigan, Minnesota, Montana, Nevada, New Jersey, North Dakota, Oregon, Rhode Island, Washington, and Wisconsin.

the Texas constitution places significant limits on his or her authority. In fact, compared with most other States, Texas has a weak governor.

Texas history helps explain the State's distrust of a strong chief executive. When Texas was under Spanish and then Mexican rule, the governor was merely an agent of the central government. Texas became a State during a time of strong antigovernment sentiment, and the State's first constitution, drawn up in 1845, reflected this attitude in the limits it placed on the chief executive. The constitution of 1876, Texas's fifth constitution and still in force today, was drawn up by Texans who felt that the governor held too much power in the State. Legislation since that time has done little to increase the governor's authority.

### Executive Powers

The presidency and the governorships are similar in several ways, but the comparison can be pushed too far. Remember, the Constitution of the United States makes the President the executive in the National Government. State constitutions, on the other hand, regularly describe the governor as the chief executive in the State's government. The distinction here, between the executive and the chief executive, is a critical one. The executive authority is fragmented in most States, but it is not at the national level.

In Texas and 18 other States,[6] the executive authority is shared by a number of "executive officers"—a lieutenant governor, a secretary of state, an attorney general, and so on. Most of these executive officers are popularly elected, and for that reason, they are very largely beyond the governor's direct control.

In short, most State constitutions so divide the executive authority that the governor can best be described as a "first among equals." In addition, the Texas governor has less power than the governors of many other States. Yet, whatever the realities of the distribution of power in Texas, the people look to the governor for leadership in State affairs. It is also the governor whom they hold responsible for the conduct of those affairs and for the overall condition of the State.

The governor's basic legal responsibility is regularly found in a constitutional provision that directs the chief executive "to take care that the laws be faithfully executed." Though the executive power may be divided, the governor is given a number of specific powers with which to accomplish that task.

1. *Appointment and Removal.* The governor can best execute—enforce and administer—the law with subordinates of his or her own choosing. Hence, the powers of appointment and removal are, or should be, among the most important in the governor's arsenal.

A leading test of any administrator is his or her ability to select loyal and able assistants. Two major factors work against the governor's effectiveness here, however. First is the existence of those other elected executives; the people choose them and the governor cannot remove them. In Texas, for example, the governor has the power to appoint only one constitutionally mandated member of the executive branch, the secretary of state. Texas voters elect the other members of the executive branch—the lieutenant governor, the attorney general, the comptroller of public accounts, the commissioner of the general land office, and the commissioner of agriculture. (These positions are described on page 699–700.)

Second, the State's constitution and statutes place restrictions on the governor's power to hire and fire. In Texas, the constitution requires that the governor's appointees be confirmed by a two-thirds vote of the senate. Despite these restrictions, the Texas governor has the authority to fill many important posts on State boards, agencies, and commissions. How a governor exercises this power is a key to his or her success.

2. *Supervisory Powers.* The governor of Texas does not have the authority to give orders to other elected members of the executive branch. He or she does have the power to supervise the work of thousands of men and women who staff the State's executive branch, however. Here again, the constitution and statutes of the State have limited the governor's authority. Many State agencies are subject to the governor's direct control, but many are not. The governor's powers of persuasion and ability to operate through informal channels (such as party leadership and appeals to the public) can therefore make a significant difference in his or her ability to supervise the executive branch.

3. *Budget-Making Power.* In Texas, the governor prepares a biennial budget that goes to the

▲ Texas National Guard troops were called into action during severe flooding in the Houston area in 2001. *Critical Thinking* *When does the National Guard perform military functions?*

legislature. The governor's budget, however, is usually overshadowed by the budget drawn up by the Legislative Budget Board. Many Texans see the Legislative Budget Board as the single most important arm of the Texas legislature. The Board is co-chaired by the lieutenant governor and the house speaker. Its ten members, all legislators, appoint the State's budget director.

4. *Military Powers.* The Texas constitution makes the governor the commander in chief of the State militia—in effect, of the Texas units of the National Guard. The National Guard is the organized part of the State militia. In a national emergency, the National Guard may be ordered into federal service by the President.

## Legislative Powers

Every State's principal executive officer has important formal legislative powers. These powers, together with the governor's own political clout, often make the governor, in effect, the State's chief legislator.

1. *The Message Power.* This is really the power to recommend legislation, and a strong governor can do a lot with it.

Much of what the legislature does centers on the governor's program for legislative action. That program is given to the lawmakers in a yearly State of the State address as well as in special sessions.

## Preparing for Standardized Tests

Have students read the information under *Budget-Making Power* on this page and then answer the question below.

What does this passage seem to be saying about the governor's budget-making power?

**A** It is all-important.

**B** It is useless.

**C** It is non-existent.

**D** It is shared.

## American Government, American Humor

Share the following quotation with students:

*"I know of no method to secure the repeal of bad or obnoxious laws so effective as their stringent execution."*

—Ulysses S. Grant

**Discussion** Have students explain what Grant meant by his remark. Ask: What implications might his belief hold for the way a governor acts?

**(Challenging)**

## Customize for

### English Language Learners

Have students create a pamphlet entitled *About the Governor*. Ask them to use a question-and-answer format to identify the qualifications, selection, term, succession, compensation, powers, and functions of the office. Encourage students to use section headings, and bolded and italicized words to get them started. Have students share their pamphlet with a partner to compare information.

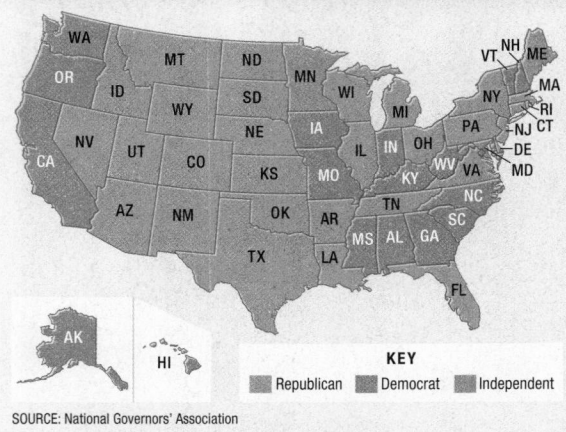

**Party Control of Governorships, 2001**

KEY
Republican  Democrat  Independent

SOURCE: National Governors' Association

*Interpreting Maps* **(a) In what region(s) of the country do the Democrats control the most governorships? (b) Where is Republican strength the greatest?**

2. *Special Sessions.* The governor has the power to call the legislature into special sessions. In addition, the only items to be considered in a special session are those submitted by the governor. The basic purpose of this power is to permit the State to meet extraordinary situations. Note, however, that the power can also be an important part of the governor's legislative arsenal. On occasion, a governor has persuaded reluctant legislators to pass a bill by threatening to call them back in a special session if they adjourn the regular session without having passed the bill.

3. *The Veto Power.* The governor has the power to veto measures passed by the legislature. This power—as well as the threat to use it—is often the most potent power the governor has in influencing the work of the legislature.

Unlike the President, the governor of Texas does not have the pocket veto.[7] That is, those bills the governor neither signs nor vetoes after the legislature adjourns become law without his or her signature.

In Texas, however, the governor's veto power does include the **item veto**. That is, the governor may veto one or more items in a bill without rejecting the entire measure. The item veto is restricted to items in appropriations bills. It is regularly used to cancel what the governor deems inappropriate or unaffordable legislative appropriations.

The vote needed to override a governor's veto is two thirds of the full membership in each house. In actual practice, the governor rejects few measures passed by the legislature. However, when the veto power is used, it is quite effective. Few vetoes are overridden.

### Judicial Powers

In every State the governor has several judicial powers. Most of them are powers of executive **clemency**, or powers of mercy that may be shown toward those convicted of a crime.[8] They include the powers of pardon, commutation, reprieve, and parole.

By the power to **pardon**, a governor may release a person from the legal consequences of a crime. In most States, a pardon may be full or conditional, and it can be granted only after conviction. By the power of **commutation**, a governor may reduce the sentence imposed by a court. Thus a death sentence may be commuted to life imprisonment. The power to **reprieve** postpones the execution of a sentence. The power to **parole** allows the release of a prisoner short of the complete term of the original sentence. (It is worth noting, however, that the governor of Texas cannot set aside a death sentence. He or she can only delay the sentence for 30 days at most.)

In Texas, these judicial powers are shared with a Board of Pardons and Paroles, whose members are appointed by the governor. The board recommends reprieves, commutations, and pardons, and the governor either approves or denies the recommendations. The board, not the governor, has the power to grant paroles.

### Miscellaneous Duties

Every governor must perform many other, often time-consuming duties. To list a few: The governor receives official visitors and welcomes other distinguished persons to the State, dedicates new buildings and parks, opens the State fair, and addresses many organizations and public

---

[7]The governor has the pocket veto in only 14 States: Alabama, Delaware, Hawaii, Massachusetts, Michigan, Minnesota, New Hampshire, New Mexico, New York, North Carolina, Oklahoma, Vermont, Virginia, Wisconsin.

[8]An extradition request from another State also puts the governor in a judicial role.

## Answer to . . .

**Interpreting Maps (a)** The Southeast and West Coast. **(b)** The Plains States of the Midwest and the Southwest.

gatherings. In addition, the governor is often called on to help settle labor disputes, to travel elsewhere in the country and sometimes abroad to promote the State and its trade interests, and to endorse worthy causes. The list is endless.

## The Lieutenant Governor

The lieutenant governor of Texas, as president of the senate, is a powerful figure in the legislature. [9] Considering the limited executive authority of the governor, many experts consider the power of the lieutenant governor to rival—or surpass—that of the governor.

The lieutenant governor of Texas is unique in that he or she is part of both the executive and legislative branches. As in most States, the lieutenant governor in Texas assumes the powers and duties of the governor when the governor is unable to serve or is absent from the State. In Texas, however, the lieutenant governor is elected separately from the governor, and each can be members of different political parties.

The Texas constitution names the lieutenant governor the president of the senate. That's where the lieutenant governor derives most of his or her power. Senate rules give the lieutenant governor a great deal of influence in shaping State policy and influencing laws that may eventually be passed by the senate.

In his or her leadership role in the senate, the lieutenant governor has the right to debate and vote on all issues when the senate sits as a committee of the whole. He or she also has the right to cast the deciding vote in a senate tie and is required to sign all bills and resolutions. He or she is also one of five members of the Legislative Redistricting Board, which apportions the State into senatorial and representative districts in the event the legislature is unable to do so.

The lieutenant governor is also a member of several legislative boards and committees, including the powerful Legislative Budget Board. As you have read, the Legislative Budget Board provides the legislature with a recommended budget at the beginning of every session. In many other States, this is done only in the executive branch. The Legislative Budget Board exerts a significant influence on State spending. Thus by his or her chairship and power to make appointments to

▲ Texas Lieutenant Governor Bob Bullock (served 1991–1999) was one of the State's most popular elected officials. The Texas State History Museum is dedicated to Bullock.

this Board, the lieutenant governor exerts a powerful influence on public policy.

## Other Executive Officers

The governor of Texas must also share the control of his or her administration with five other officers of the executive department. In Texas, all but one of these offices are filled by popular election. The individuals who fill them must have a variety of different qualifications for these jobs.

### The Secretary of State

The secretary of state is the State's chief clerk and record keeper. He or she controls a great variety of public documents, records the official acts of the governor and the legislature, and administers the election laws. This is the only executive office filled by appointment by the

[9]In Tennessee, the presiding officer of the Senate (the speaker) is also, by statute, the lieutenant governor. The office does not exist in Arizona, Maine, New Hampshire, New Jersey, Oregon, West Virginia, and Wyoming.

## Make It Relevant

### Careers in Government—Archaeologist

State archaeologists are charged with identifying, analyzing, and preserving their State's archaeological treasures. They often work ahead of builders, to ensure that invaluable sites are protected, or at least mapped and cataloged before they are built over. State archaeologists also learn about the early inhabitants of their State, from prehistoric peoples to the residents of just a few decades ago.

**Skills Activity** Have a pair of students conduct Internet or other research to learn about their State's archaeological offices. They should summarize what they find for their classmates, and alert them of any volunteer opportunities. Then have individual students write paragraphs explaining why they would or would not be interested in this career. **(Average)**

 **Take It to the Net**

For career-related links and activities, visit the *Magruder's American Government* companion Web site in the Social Studies area at the Prentice Hall School Web site. **www.phschool.com**

## Point-of-Use Resources

 **Guide to the Essentials** Chapter 24, Section 3, p. 129 provides support for students who need additional review of section content. Spanish support is available in the Spanish edition of the Guide on p. 122.

**Quiz** Unit 7 booklet, p. 7 includes matching and multiple-choice questions to check students' understanding of Section 3 content.

**Presentation Pro CD-ROM** Quizzes and multiple-choice questions check students' understanding of Section 3 content.

## Answers to . . .
## Section 3 Assessment

**1.** Formal qualifications: American citizen at least 30 years of age and must have lived in the State for at least 5 years. Selection: direct primary. Term: 4 years.

**2.** Appointment and removal, supervising the executive branch, budget-making, and being commander in chief of the National Guard.

**3.** President of the senate, with right to cast the deciding vote in a senate tie. Required to sign all bills and resolutions. A member of the Legislative Redistricting Board and several legislative boards and committees.

**4.** Clemency is mercy shown to a person convicted of a crime. Pardon is releasing a person from the legal consequences of a crime. Commutation is reducing a sentence imposed by a court. Reprieve is postponing the execution of a sentence. Parole is allowing the release of a prisoner short of the complete term of the original sentence.

**5.** This is true because the lieutenant governor, as president of the senate, holds a great deal of influence in shaping State policy and influencing laws that might be passed by the senate.

**6.** Possible answer: The President would have less power, and would be only the *chief* executive rather than *the* executive. Government would be less efficient.

---

governor. As with most of the elected executives, the secretary of state has little real discretionary power or authority.

### The Comptroller

The comptroller is the chief financial officer of Texas, charged with collecting taxes and making payments out of the State treasury. Most of those payments go to meet the many agency payrolls of the State and to pay the bills for the various goods or services supplied to the State. The comptroller also certifies the availability of funds budgeted by the legislature.

### The Attorney General

The attorney general is the State's lawyer. He or she acts as the legal advisor to State officers and agencies as they perform their official functions, represents Texas in court, and oversees the work of local prosecutors as they try cases on behalf of the State.

Much of the power of the office centers on the attorney general's formal written interpretations of constitutional and statutory law. These interpretations, called opinions, are issued to answer questions raised by the governor, other executive officers, legislators, and local officials regarding the lawfulness of their actions or proposed actions. In Texas these opinions have the force of law unless successfully challenged in court.

### Commissioner of the General Land Office

The duties of the commissioner of the general land office are to manage and collect rentals and leases for State-owned lands, award mineral leases on State lands, and award mineral leases in the State's riverbeds and tidelands.

### Commissioner of Agriculture

The commissioner of agriculture is responsible for the administration of all Texas laws that relate to agriculture. A strong possibility of conflict of interest exists within the department, however, since it has the responsibility to (1) administer the laws so that consumers and labor are protected and (2) promote the agribusiness industry.

## Elected Executive Boards

In addition to these executive officers, Texas State government includes a number of important boards and commissions filled by popular election.

### The Railroad Commission

One of the most important regulatory boards in the State is the Railroad Commission of Texas. A three-member board elected for six-year overlapping terms, the Railroad Commission has the responsibility to regulate commercial trucks, buses, oil and gas pipelines, oil and gas drilling and pumping activities, gas utilities, and intrastate railroads. It also oversees waste disposal of oil and gas.

### State Board of Education

This board is a 15-member body elected for four-year overlapping terms from single-member districts. The State Board of Education implements education laws, establishes policy, and oversees the Texas Education Agency.

---

## Section 3 Assessment

**Key Terms and Main Ideas**

1. What are the formal qualifications for office, selection, and term of the governor of Texas?
2. List the executive powers of the Texas governor.
3. What are the duties of the lieutenant governor of Texas?
4. Briefly explain these judicial powers of a governor: **clemency, pardon, commutation, reprieve,** and **parole.**

**Critical Thinking**

5. **Identifying Central Issues** You have read that the governor of Texas, although he or she is the State's principal executive officer, has limited authority. Explain how this is so.

6. **Predicting Consequences** What effect on the National Government do you think there would be if the President's cabinet—like the State executive officers—were directly elected by the people?

### Take It to the Net

7. Learn more about the governor of Texas. Follow the links to the Texas governor's Web site. After reading the information on the site, list five new facts that you learned about your governor and why these facts are important. Use the links provided in the Social Studies area of the following Web site for help in completing this activity. **www.phschool.com**

---

### Take It to the Net

7. Direct students to the Social Studies area at the Prentice Hall School Web site. The *Magruder's American Government* companion Web site includes the directions and links needed to complete the activity. It also provides a printable Internet activity worksheet with scoring rubrics for assessment. Lists should include good reasons for the importance of the facts selected.

# on Primary Sources

## The Promise of America

*The ceremony that officially made Wallace B. Jefferson a member of the Texas Supreme Court took place in the Texas Senate on May 10, 2001. During the ceremony, the new justice told this story about a "coincidence of history."*

Sometime in the mid 1850s a district judge from McLennan County, Texas, ruled that a free man, even a free black man, could not be bound by contract to sell himself into slavery. . . .

The same judge who ruled that the slave contract was void was a slave owner himself. His slave, named Shedrick Willis, was my great, great, great grandfather. Much has been written about the exquisite irony that now almost 140 years later Willis's [descendant] will occupy a seat on the highest civil court in the State of Texas. But for me this coincidence of history is much more than ironic. These two men, Shedrick Willis and Judge Nicolas William Battle, mark not only the intersection in this country between slavery and freedom, but between the rule of law and anarchy.

You see, Judge Battle before the war was a fervent state's rights democrat. Indeed, he left the bench during the Civil War to fight for his beliefs. While history has shown that the period immediately following the Civil War was marred by violence in those jurisdictions where public officials disregarded the law and tolerated oppression of former slaves, Judge Battle would have none of that.

Newly appointed again to the District Court . . . Judge Battle fought against any combinations that would disregard the law. It was written about Judge Battle during this time that "he had come to accept the Constitution as it is and its expositions by the Supreme Court of the United States as authoritative and final. . . ." So Judge Battle respected the law and enforced it regardless of any public sentiment to the contrary.

Wallace B. Jefferson

And then there was Shedrick Willis, a newly freed slave living in a county where some were openly advocating his oppression. Yet, somehow this man, a blacksmith by trade, rose above his previous state of absolute servitude to become a leader in the community. He served on the Waco City Council for two terms after the Civil War. Now in these two men do we not have perfect examples of the promise of America—that we be judged by those willing to strictly abide by the law even if it conflicts with public opinion or personal predilection, and that we each, no matter what our prior circumstance, have the opportunity in this great land to excel in business or to become leaders in the community.

Adherence to the law, even in the face of "combinations that would outrage the law," is a conviction I will take with me as Judge Battle did to the bench. [With] a will to overcome the most dire circumstances imaginable, I will lean on Shedrick Willis's example in that regard when confronted with seemingly hopeless situations. The lives and lessons of these two long dead men should inspire us all.

### Analyzing Primary Sources

1. What was the "coincidence of history" that Jefferson spoke about?
2. Do you think that Judge Battle's decisions concerning former slaves were courageous? Why or why not?
3. How could you apply the lessons of Jefferson's story to your own life?

---

 **Close Up on Primary Sources** Term Limits Across the Country, p. 26, extends this feature with a primary source activity.

To keep up-to-date on Close Up news and activities, visit Close Up Online at
**www.closeup.org**

---

## The Promise of America

**Focus** Discuss with students how the lives of African Americans have changed since the days before the Civil War. Point out that Wallace Jefferson's story is replayed, in different situations and to varying degrees, all across the United States. Ask students to consider the idea that a public official must enforce even those laws with which they disagree. Ask them to give ways in which any citizen may properly protest what they consider to be an unjust law.

**Instruct** Explain to students that after his initial appointment to the Supreme Court, Wallace Jefferson will have to be elected by the voters to retain his post. How does that fact make Jefferson's promise to adhere to the law despite public sentiment to the contrary an even more lofty goal?

**Close/Reteach** Have students write a children's book telling the story of Shedrick Willis and Judge Nicolas William Battle. Stories should use simple sentences and a minimum of text on each page. Students may illustrate their stories if they wish.

**Keep It Current CD-ROM** includes government-related projects by unit. The CD-ROM links to the Prentice Hall School Web site and may be used for daily updates.

### Answers to . . .
**Analyzing Primary Sources**
1. That the descendant of a former slave was appointed to the highest civil court in the State of Texas in 2001.
2. Students should recognize that, in the South following the Civil War, the view that former slaves should be treated fairly was probably unpopular.
3. Answers will vary, but should demonstrate an understanding of Jefferson's story and its implications.

**Objectives** You may wish to call students' attention to the objectives in the Section Preview. The objectives are reflected in the main headings of the section.

**Bellringer** Ask students what happens if a basketball player breaks a rule during a game. Focus the answers on who decides whether the player is "guilty" of an infraction and what the penalty might be. Explain that in this section, students will learn about different kinds of courts and how they handle disputes.

**Vocabulary Builder** Point out the terms in the Political Dictionary. Tell students that the following pairs of terms have related but distinctly different meanings: *criminal law, civil law; felony, misdemeanor; jury, information.* Ask them to brainstorm the differences.

## Section Preview

### OBJECTIVES

1. **Identify** and define the kinds of law applied in Texas State courts.
2. **Compare** and contrast civil law and criminal law.
3. **Describe** the jury system in Texas.

### WHY IT MATTERS

Five forms of law make up the code of conduct by which Texas and the rest of the nation are governed. One of the most important of these is common law, which developed through precedent. Law can also be classified as either criminal or civil. Grand juries are sometimes used to indict in criminal cases; a simpler process known as the information is also used. Petit juries decide cases in trials.

### POLITICAL DICTIONARY

★ common law
★ precedent
★ criminal law
★ felony
★ misdemeanor
★ civil law
★ jury
★ information

The principal function of the Texas State courts, as for all the State courts, is to decide disputes between private persons and between private persons and government. In addition, because nearly all of these courts can exercise the power of judicial review, they act as potent checks on the conduct of all of the other agencies of both State and local government.

## Kinds of Law Applied in Texas State Courts

The role of all courts in the United States is to resolve conflicts and interpret the law.[10] The law is the code of conduct by which society is governed. It is made up of several different forms, including constitutional law, statutory law, administrative law, common law, and equity.

1. *Constitutional Law.* The highest form of law in this country is based on the provisions of the United States Constitution and the fifty State constitutions and on judicial interpretations of these documents.

2. *Statutory Law.* This form of law consists of the statutes (laws) enacted by legislative bodies, including the United States Congress, the Texas legislature, the people (through the initiative or referendum), and city councils and other local legislative bodies.

3. *Administrative Law.* This form of law is composed of the rules, orders, and regulations that are issued by federal, State, or local executive officers, acting under proper constitutional or statutory authority.

4. *Common Law.* The common law makes up a large part of the law of each State except Louisiana.[11] **Common law** is unwritten, judge-made law that has developed over centuries from those generally accepted ideas of right and wrong that have gained judicial recognition. It covers nearly all aspects of human conduct. State courts apply common law except when it is in conflict with written law.

◄ Colonial courts, like this one, followed British legal tradition.

---

[10] In its overall sense, the term *law* may be defined as the whole body of "rules and principles of conduct which the governing power in a community recognizes as those which it will enforce or sanction, and according to which it will regulate, limit, or protect the conduct of its members"; *Bouvier's Law Dictionary,* 3rd revision, Vol. II.

[11] Because of an early French influence, Louisiana's legal system is largely based on French legal concepts, derived from Roman law. Nevertheless, the common law has worked its way into Louisiana law.

### Pressed for Time?

#### Quick Lesson Plan

1. **Focus** Tell students that the law is the code of conduct by which society is governed. Ask students to discuss what they know about common law.
2. **Instruct** Ask students which form of law overrides the other: statutory law or common law. *(statutory)* Discuss these and the other forms of law with students, including the difference between criminal and civil law. Then examine the jury system.
3. **Close/Reteach** Remind students that most court disputes involve arguments over how, or whether, precedents apply to a case. Ask students to write a report explaining precedents, common law, and other elements of the legal system to a person who is applying for American citizenship.

## ☐ Block Scheduling Strategies

Consider these suggestions to manage extended class time:
■ Divide the class into small groups of students. Assign each one of the forms of law used by Texas State courts (constitutional, statutory, administrative, common, equity). Have each group write short descriptions or details from its assigned form on strips of paper. Collect all strips of paper in a container, and have students draw one and read it aloud. The class can then determine which form is being described.

■ Have students create a jury simulation. Each group should prepare a list of evidence related to a a crime committed by a theoretical suspect. After each team has completed its list, have teams exchange lists. Each team will then act as a jury to reach a verdict in another team's case. Ask each jury to then discuss its verdict with the team that created the evidence.

The common law originated in England. It grew out of the decisions made by the king's judges on the basis of local customs. It developed as judges, coming upon situations similar to those found in earlier cases, applied and reapplied the rulings from those earlier cases. Thus, little by little, the law of these cases became common throughout England and, in time, throughout the English-speaking world. That is, the common law developed as judges followed earlier decisions and applied the rule of *stare decisis,* "let the decision stand."

American courts generally follow that same rule. A decision, once made, becomes a **precedent**, or a guide to be followed in all later, similar cases, unless compelling reasons call for its abandonment and the setting of a new precedent.

The common law is not a rigidly fixed body of rules controlled in every case by a clear line of precedents that can be easily found and applied. Judges are regularly called on to interpret and reinterpret the existing rules in the light of changing times and circumstances.

In other words, most legal disputes in American courts are fought out largely over the application of precedents. The opposing lawyers try to persuade the court that the precedents support their side of the case or that the general line of precedents should not, for some reason, be followed.

The importance of the common law in the American legal system cannot be overstated. Statutory law does override common law, but many statutes are based on the common law. Those statutes are, in effect, common law translated into written law.

*5. Equity.* This branch of the law supplements common law. It developed in England to provide equity—"fairness, justice, and right"—when remedies under the common law fell short of that goal.

Over the years, English common law became somewhat rigid. Remedies were available only through various writs, or orders, issued by the courts. If no writ was issued to the relief sought in a case, the courts could not act.

Those who were thus barred from the courts—for whom there was no adequate remedy at common law—appealed to the king for justice. These appeals were usually referred to the chancellor, a member of the king's council. By the

▲ Some people feel that trial juries should be abolished. *Critical Thinking Do you agree, or do you feel that juries are an important part of our legal system? After reading this section, explain your answer.*

middle of the fourteenth century, a special court of chancery, or equity, was set up. Over time, a system of rules developed in the chancery court, and equity assumed a permanent place in the English legal system.

Today, the most important difference between common law and equity is this: The common law is mostly remedial, while equity is preventative. Thus, the common law applies to or provides a remedy for matters after they have happened; equity seeks to stop wrongs before they occur.

To illustrate this point, suppose your neighbors plan to add a room to their house. You think that a part of the planned addition will be on your land and will destroy your rose garden. You can prevent the construction by getting an injunction, which is a court order prohibiting a specified action by the party named in the order.

A court is likely to grant the injunction for two reasons: (1) the threat to your property is immediate, and (2) the law can offer no fully satisfactory remedy once your garden has been destroyed. It is true that money damages might be assessed under common law, but no amount of money can give back the pride or the pleasure your roses now give you.

The early colonists brought both equity and the common law to America. At first, different courts administered the two forms of law. In time, though, most States provided for the administration of both forms by the same courts, and the procedural differences between the two are disappearing.

## Reading Strategy

### Organizing Information/Outline

Ask students to copy down the main headings and subheadings in outline form, leaving space for details. Have them fill in the details as they read the section.

## Point-of-Use Resources

📁 **Guided Reading and Review** Unit 7 booklet, p. 8 provides students with practice identifying the main ideas and key terms of this section.

📁 **Lesson Plans** For lesson planning suggestions, see p. 105 of the Lesson Plans booklet.

📁 **Political Cartoons** See p. 97 of the Political Cartoons booklet for a cartoon relevant to this section.

📊 **Section Support Transparencies** Transparency 100, *Visual Learning;* Transparency 199, *Political Cartoon*

## Organizing Information

To make sure students understand the main points of this section, you may wish to use the flowchart graphic organizer to the right.

Tell students that a flowchart can be used to record a sequence of events. Have students use a flowchart to show the processes that take place in grand jury or petit jury trials.

**Teaching Tip** A template for this graphic organizer can be found in the Section Support Transparencies, Transparency 4.

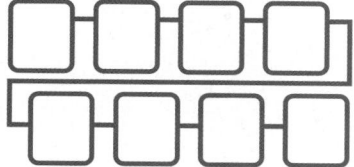

### Answer to . . .

**Critical Thinking** Answers will vary. Students supporting the jury system may cite the independence and common sense of juries; students opposed may cite the time and expense of using juries, and question their competence.

*Interpreting Political Cartoons* **According to this cartoon, what kinds of decisions do juries make? Is that an accurate interpretation of the jury system?**

*"He's big, all right, and he's definitely a wolf, but it'll be up to a jury to decide whether or not he's bad."*

## Criminal and Civil Law

You have probably heard reference to criminal law and civil law. The law is generally split into these two categories.

The area of the law that defines public wrongs—offenses against the public order—and provides for their punishment is the **criminal law**. A criminal case is brought by the State against a person accused of committing a crime. The State, as the prosecution, is always a party in a criminal case.

Crimes are of two kinds: A **felony** is the greater crime and may be punished by a heavy fine or imprisonment or even death. A **misdemeanor** is the lesser offense, punishable by a small fine and/or a short jail term.

The **civil law** relates to human conduct, to disputes between private parties, and to disputes between private parties and government that are not covered by criminal law. Civil cases are usually referred to as suits, or lawsuits, and often lead to the award of money or a fine. Civil law can involve a wide range of issues, including divorce and custody disputes, torts (private wrongs against a person or property), and contracts.

## The Jury System

A **jury** is a body of persons selected according to law who hear evidence and decide questions of fact in a court case. There are two basic types of juries in the American legal system: (1) the grand jury and (2) the petit jury.

The major function of the grand jury is to determine whether the evidence against a person charged with a crime is sufficient to justify a trial. The grand jury is used almost exclusively in criminal proceedings. The petit jury is the trial jury, and it is used regularly in both civil and criminal cases.

### The Grand Jury

Grand juries vary greatly in size from State to State. In Texas, the grand jury consists of 12 people. At least nine of those jurors must agree that an accused person is probably guilty before a formal accusation is made.

The Texas constitution states that no person may be tried for a major (felony) crime without being indicted by a grand jury. Grand juries may inquire into a minor (misdemeanor) crime; however, the county attorney or the district attorney usually files misdemeanor indictments.

When a grand jury is impaneled, or selected, the judge instructs the jurors to find a true bill of indictment against any and all persons whom the prosecuting attorney brings to their attention and identifies as probably guilty. The judge also instructs them to bring a presentment, or accusation, against any persons who they, of their own knowledge, believe have violated the State's criminal laws.

The grand jury generally meets in secret. To preside over its sessions, the jurors select one of their number to be foreperson. The prosecuting attorney (who in Texas may be a private party serving as a *pro tempore* prosecutor) or citizen with a complaint presents witnesses and evidence against the accused. The jurors may question those witnesses and may summon others to testify against a suspect.

After receiving the evidence and hearing witnesses, the grand jury deliberates alone and in secret. The jurors then move to the courtroom, where their report, including any indictments they may have returned, is read in their presence.

The grand jury has several disadvantages: It is expensive, cumbersome, and time-consuming. Therefore, most States, including Texas, depend more heavily on a much simpler process of accusation: the information.

### The Information

An **information** is a formal charge filed by the prosecutor, without the action of a grand jury. It is now used in Texas for most minor offenses.

The information has much to recommend it. It is far less costly and time-consuming than a grand jury. Also, since grand juries most often follow the prosecutor's recommendations, many argue that a grand jury is really unnecessary.

The chief objection to abandoning the grand jury appears to be the fear that some prosecutors may abuse their powers and be overzealous at the expense of both defendants and justice.

### The Petit Jury

Anyone who is indicted on a criminal charge is entitled to trial by a jury. The defendant in a civil case is also entitled to a jury. If a defendant in either type of case chooses to waive a jury trial, the decision will be left in the hands of the judge. In either criminal or civil cases, a jury trial is heard by a petit jury, which reviews the evidence and decides the disputed facts.

The number of trial jurors may vary. As it developed in England, the jury consisted of "twelve men good and true." In Texas at the county level, the petit jury consists of six persons; in the State district court, it numbers twelve.

In a criminal case in Texas, the jury's verdict must be unaminous in order to convict. Otherwise, it must report a verdict of guilty or guilt not proved (beyond a reasonable doubt). In a civil case in county court, five of the six jurors must agree on a verdict. Civil cases heard at the district level require ten of the twelve jurors to reach a decision. If the jurors cannot agree on a verdict (a so-called hung jury), usually a new jury is impaneled and the case tried again.

### Selection of Jurors

Petit jurors in Texas are chosen mainly from lists of registered voters and licensed drivers. All jurors in Texas must meet the same qualifications. They must be at least 18 years old, they must be qualified to vote in the county in which they are to serve as a juror, they must be able to read and write English, and they must not have been convicted of or be under indictment for a felony. Legal exemptions are minimal: anyone over age 70, anyone with legal custody of a child under 10 (usually the mother), and students. However, the judge routinely dismisses others, and the attorneys involved frequently eliminate still more potential jurors.

As with the grand jury, the States are moving away from the use of the trial jury. Leading reasons are the greater time and cost of jury trials. The competence of the average jury and the impulses that may lead it to a verdict are often questioned, as well. Much criticism of the jury system is directed not so much at the system itself as at its operation.

Several things should be said in favor of the jury system, however. It has a long and honorable place in the development of Anglo-American law. Its high purpose is to promote a fair trial, by providing an impartial body to hear the charges. A jury tends to bring the common sense of the community to bear on the law and its application. The jury system gives citizens a chance to take part in the administration of justice, and it fosters a greater confidence in the judicial system.

## Section 4 Assessment

**Key Terms and Main Ideas**

1. Define **common law, criminal law,** and **civil law.**
2. What is the difference between a **felony** and a **misdemeanor?**
3. Name two kinds of **juries,** and tell what they do.
4. What does it mean when a judge follows a legal **precedent?**

**Critical Thinking**

5. **Checking Consistency** Most processes of government in this country must be open to public scrutiny, but a grand jury works in secret. **(a)** Why might this be so? **(b)** Do you think this secrecy is a good idea? Explain your answer.
6. **Identifying Alternatives** Describe a situation in which someone might seek an injunction. Then write a brief

argument in favor of granting the injunction and a brief argument against granting this remedy.

 **Take It to the Net**

7. Read about grand juries and how they operate in the American judicial system. Create an outline of the most important facts about grand juries. Then tell which fact you found most surprising and why. Use the links provided in the Social Studies area of the following Web site for help in completing this activity. **www.phschool.com**

 **Take It to the Net**

7. Direct students to the Social Studies area at the Prentice Hall School Web site. The *Magruder's American Government* companion Web site includes the directions and links needed to complete the activity. It also provides a printable Internet activity worksheet with scoring rubrics for assessment. Outlines should cover the most important facts.

## Point-of-Use Resources

Guide to the Essentials Chapter 24, Section 4, p. 130 provides support for students who need additional review of section content. Spanish support is available in the Spanish edition of the Guide on p. 123.

Quiz Unit 7 booklet, p. 9 includes matching and multiple-choice questions to check students' understanding of Section 4 content.

Presentation Pro CD-ROM Quizzes and multiple-choice questions check students' understanding of Section 4 content.

### Answers to . . .

### Section 4 Assessment

**1.** Common law is unwritten judge-made law that has developed over centuries. Criminal law defines offenses against the public order and provides for their punishment. Civil law relates to disputes between private parties or private parties and the government.
**2.** A felony is a more serious crime than a misdemeanor; it is punishable by a heavy fine and imprisonment or death while a misdemeanor is punishable by a small fine and short jail term.
**3.** The grand jury determines whether evidence against a person charged with a crime is sufficient to justify a trial. A petit jury is a trial jury; it hears evidence and decides disputed facts.
**4.** The judge is using decisions in previous cases as a guide for deciding the present case.
**5. (a)** Answers will vary. Students may suggest that the jury hears much unsubstantiated evidence which is not challenged by counsel; if that evidence is false or misleading, it could ruin a person's reputation even without that person being indicted or convicted. Secrecy also protects the jurors from outside influences. **(b)** Answers will vary, but should reflect sound reasoning.
**6.** Answers will vary, but should reflect an understanding of injunctive relief—the need for immediate relief and the fact that the law will not be able to offer satisfactory remedy once the act has been done.

## SKILLS FOR LIFE

### CITIZENSHIP

### Serving on a Jury

**Focus** To explore the responsibilities of serving on a jury, hold a mock trial on a topic of students' choosing.

**Instruct** Have a group of student "prosecutors" scan the media for accounts of interesting trials in the news. Find a trial for which details are available, and conduct a trial on that case. Choose a judge, a defendant, a defense team, and a jury. Have both sides explain what type of juror would be most advantageous to their side. During the trial, the judge should caution jurors to follow Steps 1–5 on this page.

**Close/Reteach** After the verdict is read, jurors should respond to questions from the class about how the deliberations were conducted and what challenges arose during the discussions.

### Answers . . .

**1.** Possible answer: By analyzing your views to see what assumptions they are based on.

**2.** Students might consider specific situations. For example: Would they vote to convict a lawbreaker who was nonviolently protesting if they believed in the lawbreaker's cause?

**3.** Answers should suggest that absolute certainty is rarely possible, but that no real doubt should remain.

**4.** Evidence and testimony that are presented in court are deemed acceptable by the court. If jurors are influenced by other ideas, their opinions might be biased.

**5.** Media coverage or the opinions of fellow jurors might be biased; they could sway a juror away from his or her true opinions.

---

## Serving on a Jury

Someday you may receive a notice ordering you to appear for jury duty. This is a rare opportunity to observe the U.S. justice system at work. That system relies on the participation of ordinary citizens in the judicial process.

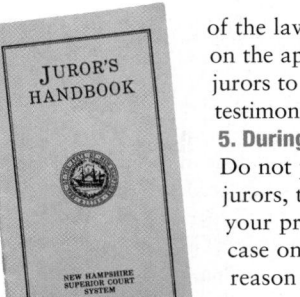

JUROR'S HANDBOOK

NEW HAMPSHIRE SUPERIOR COURT SYSTEM

Potential jurors are selected from voting and driver registration lists, and summoned to appear in court. How long they must serve varies from place to place. People with certain hardships, such as health, language, or job problems, may be excused from jury duty.

When you arrive at the courthouse, you might be dismissed without having served at all. Or you might be chosen to appear for jury selection. In this phase, lawyers for both sides question potential jurors and select those they think will be favorable to their side. Many people still are rejected at this stage.

If you are chosen for a jury, you and the other jurors will receive instructions prior to the start of trial. The following steps are adapted from those instructions:

**1. Do not be influenced by bias.** Your decision should not be affected by any sympathies or dislikes you might have for either side in the case. How might you avoid biased thinking?

**2. Follow the law as it is explained to you.** Your job is to determine whether or not someone broke the law, regardless of whether you approve of the law. Would you find this requirement difficult? Explain.

**3. Remember that the defendant is presumed innocent.** The government has the burden of proving a defendant guilty beyond a "reasonable doubt." If it fails to do so, then the verdict must be "not guilty." What does "reasonable doubt" mean to you?

**4. Keep an open mind.** Do not form or state any opinion about the case until you have heard all the evidence, the closing arguments

of the lawyers, and the judge's instructions on the applicable law. Why is it important for jurors to base their opinions on evidence and testimony alone?

**5. During the trial, do not discuss the case.** Do not permit anyone, including fellow jurors, to talk about the case with you or in your presence. Avoid media coverage of the case once the trial has begun. What is the reason for this rule?

### Test for Success

Under "three strikes" laws in several States, a person who commits a third felony can be jailed for 25 years to life. Such laws are aimed to keep violent, habitual criminals behind bars. But the laws are also being applied to nonviolent crimes, such as stealing a bicycle. Some juries have resisted convicting people they know are guilty because the possible penalties are so harsh. If you were a juror on such a case, would you vote to convict? Consider the instructions to jurors given on this page.

### Test for Success

Students should refer to Steps 1 through 5 in their explanations.

### Point–of–Use Resources

📁 **Skills for Life Activity** Unit 7 booklet, p. 12 provides an additional skill activity for this chapter.

💿 **Social Studies Skills Tutor CD-ROM** Provides interactive practice in geographic literacy, critical thinking and reading, visual analysis, and communications.

# 5 *The Courts and Their Judges*

## Section Preview

### OBJECTIVES

1. **Explain** how Texas State courts are organized and describe the work of each kind of Texas State court.
2. **Examine** and evaluate the different ways that judges are selected.

### WHY IT MATTERS

The Texas State courts hear thousands of cases each year—criminal and civil. Many of those cases involve only minor offenses or routine disputes. Others involve horrific crimes or quarrels involving millions of dollars.

### POLITICAL DICTIONARY

★ justice of the peace
★ warrant
★ preliminary hearing
★ appellate jurisdiction

---

They deal with everything from traffic tickets to murder, from disputes over a few dollars to settlements involving millions. They are the State courts and the judges who sit in them. In this section, you will read about the way the Texas courts are organized.

## Organization of the Texas Court System

The Texas State judicial system consists of five tiers of courts, with local trial courts making up the bottom tier and the two highest appellate courts as the top tier. Taken together, the tiers include some 3,000 courts spread throughout the State.

### Local Trial Courts

At the bottom of the judicial system, in the first tier of courts, are justice of the peace courts and municipal courts that act as local trial courts.

1. *Justice of the Peace Courts.* **Justices of the peace**—JPs—are popularly elected. For the most part, JPs try misdemeanors, cases involving such

petty offenses as traffic violations, disturbing the peace, public drunkenness, and the like. They settle civil disputes involving less than $5,000. They also issue certain kinds of warrants, hold preliminary hearings, and often perform marriages.

A **warrant** is a court order authorizing, or making legal, some official action. Search warrants and arrest warrants are the most common. A **preliminary hearing** is generally the first step in a major criminal prosecution. There, the judge decides if the evidence is, in fact, enough to hold that person—bind that person over—for action by the grand jury or the prosecutor.

Another function of a justice court is to handle small claims cases. Many people cannot afford the costs of suing for the collection of a small debt. Small claims courts are designed for

▶ Judge Roy Bean (seated at table, at left) tries an accused horse thief in Langtry, Texas, in 1900. In the West of that time, JP's often *were* "the law" in their communities. *Critical Thinking How much confidence would you have had in the justice dispensed in this "courtroom"? Why?*

---

---

# Reading Strategy

## Finding Evidence

Tell students that the Texas State court system is organized to provide justice in an efficient manner. Have them read the section to find evidence that this statement is or is not accurate.

## Point-of-Use Resources

**Guided Reading and Review** Unit 7 booklet, p. 10 provides students with practice identifying the main ideas and key terms of this section.

**Lesson Plans** For lesson planning suggestions, see p. 106 of the Lesson Plans booklet.

**Political Cartoons** See p. 98 of the Political Cartoons booklet for a cartoon relevant to this section.

**Close Up on Participation** Planting the Seeds of Change, pp. 16–17 uses the topic of teenagers getting involved in community revitalization to help students plan and carry out service learning projects.

**Section Support Transparencies** Transparency 101, *Visual Learning*; Transparency 200, *Political Cartoon*

**ABC News Civics and Government Videotape Library** *Peer Mentoring* (time: about four minutes)

**Simulations and Data Graphing CD-ROM** offers data graphing tools that give students practice with creating and interpreting graphs.

*Answer to . . .*
Interpreting Graphs 1975–1985.

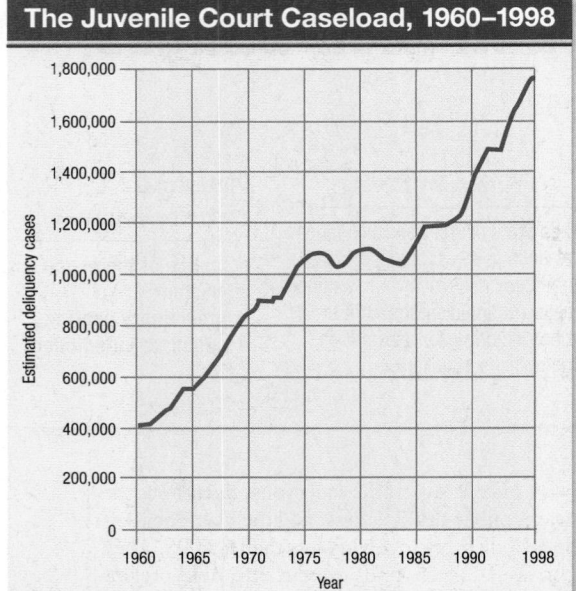

**The Juvenile Court Caseload, 1960–1998**

SOURCE: *Office of Juvenile Justice and Delinquency Prevention Statistical Briefing Book, 2001*

**Interpreting Graphs** This graph shows the estimated number of juvenile court cases nationwide. ***During which 10 years did the increase in juvenile court cases level off?***

just such situations. In them, a person can bring a claim for little or no cost. The proceedings are usually informal, and the judge often handles the matter without attorneys for either side.

2. *Municipal Courts.* Municipal courts are found in the State's larger cities and many of its middle-sized and small ones. The jurisdiction of municipal courts is citywide. They hear criminal cases in which the fines are under $2,000. Traffic violations make up the vast majority of their workload. The city council or other governing body appoints most municipal judges, but voters elect them in some cities.

## County-Level Courts

County-level courts make up the second tier of courts in Texas. They include constitutional county courts, one for each Texas county, and county courts at law. The constitutional county courts are so named because the Texas constitution establishes them as courts of record.

County courts at law are established by the State legislature to help out in larger counties whose single constitutional county court cannot handle the caseload. County-level courts handle minor criminal cases as well as civil matters such as probate.[12] Probate cases involve proving the validity of wills and otherwise settling estates. County-level courts also hear appeals from the local trial courts.

## General Trial Courts

Most of the more important civil and criminal cases heard in Texas are heard in the State's general trial courts. Texas is divided into about 400 judicial districts, each ordinarily covering one or more counties. Each district has at least one general trial court known as the district court, and the most populous districts have many district courts. Most legal actions brought under State law begin in these courts.

These general trial courts are courts of "first instance." That is, they exercise original jurisdiction over most of the cases they hear. When cases do come to them on appeal from a lower court, a trial *de novo* (a new trial, as though the case had not been heard before) is usually held.

The trial court is seldom limited as to the kinds of cases it may hear. Although its decision on the facts in a case is usually final, disputes over questions of law may be carried to a higher court.

In the more heavily populated districts of Texas, district courts may specialize in areas such as family law or juvenile justice. Family law includes cases involving adoptions, divorce, and child welfare. Juvenile justice involves minors who are arrested for some offense or otherwise come to the attention of the police or other authorities.

Individuals under 18 years of age generally are not subject to the justice of the courts in which adults are tried. Instead they are tried in juvenile courts. The juvenile justice system is designed to address the special needs and problems of young people. This system generally emphasizes rehabilitation more than punishment. However, under certain circumstances juvenile courts do refer certain offenders to an adult criminal court for trial.

---

[12]The chief executive officer of a Texas county is called the county judge. Despite the title, he or she is equivalent to a mayor of a city or a governor of a State, and holds little, if any, judicial power. In most States the county judge would be called the "county executive." In small counties, however, the county judge handles probate cases.

## Preparing for Standardized Tests

Have students read the passages under *General Trial Courts* on this page and then answer the question below.

Texas general trial courts hear all but which of the following?

**A** overflow cases from the supreme court's docket

**B** criminal cases

**C** cases appealed from lower courts

**D** adoption cases

Outside of the more populous districts, the existing courts take care of family-law as well as juvenile-justice cases. General trial courts, as well as county-level courts, handle these matters as part of their regular caseload.

## Intermediate Appellate Courts

Texas has 14 courts of appeals that stand between the trial courts and the State's highest courts. These intermediate appellate courts serve to ease the burden of the high courts. Most of their work involves the review of cases decided in the general trial courts and the county-level courts. In other words, these appeals courts exercise mostly **appellate jurisdiction**. Their original jurisdiction, where it exists, is limited to a few specific kinds of cases—election disputes, for example.

In exercising their appellate jurisdiction, these courts do not hold trials. Rather, they hear oral arguments from attorneys, study the briefs (written arguments) that attorneys submit, and review the record of the case in the lower court.

Ordinarily, an appellate court does not concern itself with the facts in a case. Rather, its decision turns on whether the law was correctly interpreted and applied in the court below. Its decision may be reviewed by the State's high court, but its disposition of a case is usually final.

## The State's Highest Courts

Texas is one of only two States that have two high courts. (The other State is our neighbor to the north, Oklahoma.) The State Supreme Court is the highest appellate court in civil cases. The Court of Criminal Appeals is the court of last resort in criminal cases. Their major function is to review the decisions of lower courts in those cases that are appealed to them.[13]

The size of each court is fixed by the Texas constitution. Nine justices, including a chief justice, serve on the Supreme Court. The Court of Criminal Appeals consists of nine judges, including a presiding judge.

Members of the Supreme Court and the Court of Criminal Appeals are elected in a Statewide vote to six-year terms. In the 1994 elections, Sharon Keller of Dallas became the first woman to serve on the Court of Criminal Appeals, and she was elected the court's presiding judge in 2000. As of 2001, three other

*Interpreting Political Cartoons* (a) What does the cartoon suggest about the use of the appeals process in this country? (b) Should those convicted of a crime be able to appeal their convictions as many times as they wish? Explain your answer.

women served with her, and three women also served on the Supreme Court. In May 2001 Wallace Jefferson of San Antonio became the first African American on the Texas Supreme Court when the governor appointed him to fill a vacant seat.

The State's highest courts are the courts of last resort in the Texas judicial system. They have the final say in all matters of State law. Remember, however, that many cases also raise questions of federal law. So, the United States Supreme Court may review some Texas decisions. But not very many State decisions actually go to the federal Supreme Court.[14] Recall that an appeal from a State's high court will be heard in the federal Supreme Court only if (1) a "federal question," meaning some matter of federal law, is involved in the case and (2) the Supreme Court agrees to hear that appeal.

In short, most of the Texas highest court decisions are final. The oft-heard claim, "I'll fight this case all the way to the United States Supreme Court," is almost always just so much

---

[13]The State's highest court is known as the Supreme Court in 45 States. But in Maine and Massachusetts it is called the Supreme Judicial Court; in Maryland and New York, the Court of Appeals; and in West Virginia, the Supreme Court of Appeals. Two States actually have two high courts.

[14]Many of the cases that have reached the Supreme Court involved the 14th Amendment's Due Process and Equal Protection clauses.

ACTIVITY

## Extended Class Periods

**Time** 90 minutes.
**Purpose** Conduct an interview with a juror.
**Grouping** 3 to 4 students.
**Activity** Each group will develop a list of interview questions they would like to ask a justice of the peace, magistrate, or judge. (Questions might touch on the person's background, their duties, specific experiences they have had, etc.) After groups have agreed upon their final list of questions, they should elect a member to conduct the interview.
**Roles** Discussion leader, recorder, interviewer, interviewee, spokesperson.
**Close** After groups have conducted the interview, a spokesperson should report the results of the interview.

■ **Block Strategy**
**(Basic)**

## Point-of-Use Resources

🗔 **Block Scheduling with Lesson Strategies** Activities for Chapter 24 appear on p. 31.

## Comparative Government

### Crime Rates of Selected Countries

| Country | Offenses Reported to the Police per 100,000 People | | | | |
|---|---|---|---|---|---|
| | Total* | Personal | | Property | |
| | | Murder | Assault | Burglary | Automobile Theft |
| Bangladesh | 64 | 1.9 | 3.6 | 4.6 | 0.6 |
| Finland | 14,799 | 0.6 | 40.0 | 1,934.9 | 53.2 |
| Hungary | 3,789 | 4.3 | 79.3 | 767.4 | 51.1 |
| Kenya | 484 | 6.4 | 54.1 | 76.9 | 9.7 |
| Jordan | 751 | 2.0 | 19.1 | 43.4 | 28.5 |
| Kuwait | 1,171 | 1.7 | 46.5 | 75.9 | 18.2 |
| Japan | 1,490 | 1.0 | 14.4 | 198.1 | 27.8 |
| Peru | 1,178 | 9.3 | 104.3 | 87.0 | 22.7 |
| Canada | 10,351 | 5.2 | 769.1 | 1,326.2 | 545.9 |
| Thailand | 351 | 7.7 | 25.4 | 9.9 | 3.3 |
| United States | 5,374 | 9.0 | 430.2 | 1,041.8 | 591.2 |

*Figure for total offenses reported includes crimes other than those listed in the table.
SOURCE: *Encyclopaedia Britannica, Book of the Year,* 1999

**Interpreting Tables** This table shows only the crimes reported to the police, and then breaks out only certain kinds of crimes. **(a) Which country has the highest number of reported crimes per 100,000 people? (b) What kinds of crimes are committed most often there? (c) Which kinds are rare?**

hot air—or misinformation about the State judicial system.[15]

### Unified Court Systems

The typical State court system, including that of Texas, is organized geographically rather than by types of cases. Thus, the general trial courts are most often set up so that each hears those cases arising within its own district, circuit, or county, no matter what the subject matter may be.

In these map-based systems, a judge must hear cases in nearly all areas of the law. A backlog of cases can and often does build up in some courts, while judges sit with little to do in others. Moreover, uneven interpretations and applications of the law may and sometimes do occur from one part of the State to another.

To overcome these difficulties, a number of States recently have begun to abandon geographical organization. They have turned, instead, to a unified court system, one that is organized on a functional, or case-type, basis.

In a completely unified court system, there is technically only one court for the entire State. It is presided over (administered) by a chief judge or judicial council. The single court has within it a number of levels, or sections, such as supreme, intermediate appellate, and general trial. Within each section, divisions are established to hear cases in certain specialized or heavy caseload areas of the law—criminal, juvenile, family, and other areas that need special attention.

In such an arrangement, a judge can be assigned to that section or division to which his or her talents and interests seem best suited. To relieve overcrowded dockets, judges may be moved from one section or division to another. In short, the unified court system is a modern response to the old common law adage: "Justice delayed is justice denied."

## Selection of Judges

More than 3,000 judges sit in the Texas State and local courts today. They are chosen in one of three ways: (1) popular election, (2) appointment by the governor, or (3) appointment by the local executive (the county Commissioners Court or city council).

Popular election is the most widely used method for selecting Texas judges. When a judge's term comes to an end, usually the position will be filled through a partisan—and often expensive and fiercely competitive—election. Many vacancies, however, occur before the end of an elective term. When that happens, the vacancy is filled by appointment until the next election.

Popular election is also the most widely used method of picking judges in the rest of the country. The voters choose about three fourths of all judges sitting in American courts today. The governor appoints nearly a fourth of all State

---

[15]State law regularly gives its lower courts final jurisdiction over many types of minor cases. In those cases, the lower court is the State's court of last resort. If any review is to be had, it can be only in the U.S. Supreme Court. Such reviews are extremely rare.

*Answer to . . .*

**Interpreting Tables (a)** Finland.
**(b)** Burglary. **(c)** Murder and assault.

judges today. In three States—Delaware, Massachusetts, and New Hampshire—the governor names all judges. In several other States, the governor has the power to appoint all or many judges, but under a special arrangement known as the Missouri Plan, explained later in this section. Selection by the legislature is used least often. The legislature now chooses all or at least most judges in only three States: Connecticut, South Carolina, and Virginia.

## How Should Judges Be Selected?

Most people believe that judges should be independent—in other words, that they should "stay out of politics." Whatever method of selection is used should be designed with that goal in mind.

Nearly all authorities agree that selection by the legislature is the most political of all the methods of choosing judges. Few favor it. So, the question really is: Which is better, popular election of judges or appointment by the governor?

Those who favor popular election generally make the democratic argument. Because judges "say the law," interpret and apply it, they should be chosen by and answer directly to the people. Some also argue that the concept of separation of powers is undercut if the executive (the governor) has the power to name the members of the judicial branch.

Those who favor appointment by the governor argue that only those who are well qualified should carry out the judicial function. The fact that a person has the support of a political party or is a good vote-getter does not mean that person has the capacity to be a good judge. Proponents of executive appointment insist that it is the best way to ensure that those persons who preside in courts will have the qualities most needed in that role: absolute honesty and integrity, fairness, and the necessary training and ability in the law.

At best, deciding between these two positions is difficult. The people have often made excellent choices, and governors have not always made wise and nonpolitical ones. Still, most authorities come down on the side of gubernatorial appointment, largely because those characteristics that make a good judge and those that make a good candidate are not often found in the same person.

Popular election is both widely used and widely supported. Party organizations and interest groups have strongly opposed moves to abandon it. So, most attempts to revise the method of judicial selection have kept at least some element of voter choice.

## The Missouri Plan

For more than 75 years now, the American Bar Association (ABA) has sponsored an approach

## Customize for

### Less Proficient Readers

Have students create an advertisement in which they promote a unified court system and the Missouri Plan for selecting judges. In their advertisements, ask students to explain these two plans and how they promise to offer improvements over conventional plans for organizing courts and selecting judges. Allow students various options for their ads, including posters, billboards, or brochures. Ask for volunteers to share their work.

## Point-of-Use Resources

The Living Constitution Judicial Review, p. 7

Basic Principles of the Constitution Transparencies Transparencies 37-43, *Judicial Review*

▲ Many Texas judges are elected and campaign along with others running for office (left). State District Judge Molly Francis instructs the jury after closing arguments (right). *Critical Thinking* **(a) What are the pros and cons of electing judges? (b) What kinds of cases are heard in State district courts?**

## CONSTITUTIONAL PRINCIPLES

### Judicial Review
State court systems mirror the national court system, and State supreme courts have a role similar to that of the national Supreme Court in providing final decisions. Because only cases involving points of federal law will be referred to the national Supreme Court, the importance of State supreme courts in deciding cases that involve the basic issues of people's lives cannot be overemphasized.

### Activity
Refer students to the Web site of the Texas supreme court; or, assign a different State supreme court to each student. (links can be found at **www.phschool.com**) Have students give short oral reports on their State that describe the composition of the court and recent important decisions.

*Answer to . . .*

**Critical Thinking (a)** Popular election is most democratic, but it can make judges subject to political pressures. **(b)** District courts may specialize in areas such as family law or juvenile justice.

## Point-of-Use Resources

**Guide to the Essentials** Chapter 24, Section 5, p. 131 provides support for students who need additional review of section content. Spanish support is available in the Spanish edition of the Guide on p. 124.

**Quiz** Unit 7 booklet, p. 11 includes matching and multiple-choice questions to check students' understanding of Section 5 content.

**Presentation Pro CD-ROM** Quizzes and multiple-choice questions check students' understanding of Section 5 content.

### Answer to . . .

**Evaluating the Quotation** To show that they are qualified to make judgments with fairness and impartiality; answers will vary.

### Answers to . . .

## Section 5 Assessment

**1.** JPs preside in rural areas over the lowest courts in the State judicial system and try minor offenses, issue certain kinds of warrants, hold preliminary hearings, and perform marriages.

**2. (a)** Review of cases decided in lower, or trial, courts. **(b)** Intermediate appellate courts and State supreme courts.

**3.** General trial courts exercise original jurisdiction, and hear both criminal and civil cases.

**4.** A warrant is a court order authorizing an official action. The need to obtain a warrant—such as a search warrant—means that government must show a legitimate reason for infringing on a person's rights; therefore warrants are protections of those rights against government abuse.

**5.** Answers will vary, but should be logically argued and supported by facts.

**6.** Answers will vary, but might include knowledge of the law and judicial processes, good judgment, honesty and integrity, and fairness.

# Voices on Government

**Chief Justice Richard Barajas** was the first Hispanic ever elected to the El Paso, Texas, Court of Appeals. In 1994, he was appointed Chief Justice and has been elected since then without opposition. Chief Justice Barajas is a nationally recognized lecturer and has written articulately about the role of the judiciary.

*" The jurist must be held to the highest standards of integrity and ethical conduct, much more so than the standards to which members of the executive and legislative branches are held accountable. Consequently, the ultimate standard for judicial conduct must be more than effortless obedience to the law, but rather, must be conduct which constantly reaffirms one's fitness for the high responsibilities of judicial office and which continuously maintains, if not furthers, the belief that an independent judiciary exists to protect the citizen from both government overreaching and individual self-help. "*

## Evaluating the Quotation

*Why does Chief Justice Barajas believe that judges must be held to a higher standard of conduct than members of the other branches of government? Do you agree with his point of view?*

that combines the election and appointment processes. Because its adoption in Missouri in 1940 involved much political drama and attracted wide attention, the method is often called the Missouri Plan. Some form of the Missouri Plan is now in place in just over half of the States.

Missouri's version is still more or less representative of how the plan is implemented in the other States that use it. The governor appoints the seven justices of the State's supreme court, the 32 judges of the court of appeals, and all judges who sit in certain of the State's trial courts. The governor must make each appointment from a panel, or list, of three candidates recommended by a judicial nominating commission. The commission is made up of a sitting judge, several members of the bar, and private citizens.

Each judge named by the governor serves until the first general election after he or she has been in office for at least a year. The judge's name then appears on the ballot—without opposition. The voters decide whether or not that judge should be kept in office.

If the vote is favorable, the judge then serves a regular term: six years for a trial court judge and 12 years for one who sits on a higher court in Missouri. Thereafter, the judge may seek further terms in future retain-reject elections. Should the voters reject a sitting judge, the process begins again.

## Section 5 Assessment

### Key Terms and Main Ideas
1. What are the duties of a **justice of the peace?**
2. **(a)** What is **appellate jurisdiction? (b)** Which State courts have this jurisdiction?
3. Describe the work of the general trial courts.
4. What is a **warrant?** Why are warrants important?

### Critical Thinking
5. **Demonstrating Reasoned Judgment** How do you think judges should be selected? Choose one of the methods described in this section, and "make a case for it" by creating a strong, well-supported argument in its favor.

6. **Drawing Inferences** What qualities make a good judge? Write job descriptions or "want ads" for a general court judge and an appellate judge.

 **Take It to the Net**

7. Find out what cases are currently being heard in the Texas State Supreme Court and the Texas Court of Criminal Appeals. Choose one case and describe the issues involved in an oral report to the class. Use the links provided in the Social Studies area of the following Website for help in completing this activity. **www.phschool.com**

 **Take It to the Net**

**7.** Direct students to the Social Studies area at the Prentice Hall School Web site. The *Magruder's American Government* companion Web site includes the directions and links needed to complete the activity. It also provides a printable Internet activity worksheet with scoring rubrics for assessment. Oral reports should show an understanding of the facts involved in the case.

# on the Supreme Court

## Can States Restrict Undesirable Imports?

*The Commerce Clause (Article 1, Section 8, Clause 3) gives Congress the power to regulate interstate trade. Thus States generally cannot restrict the flow of goods and services from other States. Does this mean that a State cannot prevent the importing of certain items that it believes will be harmful to its residents' quality of life?*

### City of Philadelphia v. New Jersey (1978)

In the early 1970s, the amount of solid and liquid waste in New Jersey was increasing rapidly, and waste disposal sites in the State were beginning to fill up. The State legislature decided that "the public health, safety and welfare require that the treatment and disposal within this State of all wastes generated outside of the State be prohibited." In 1973 it passed a law banning any person from bringing into New Jersey any solid or liquid waste from outside the State, except garbage to be fed to pigs. The State Commissioner of Environmental Protection had authority to make specific exceptions to the ban. The Commissioner issued rules excepting four narrow categories of waste.

The law affected not only the operators of private landfills in New Jersey, but also the cities in other States that had contracts with those landfills. Several cities and landfill operators sued New Jersey and its Department of Environmental Protection in State court, where the judge declared the law unconstitutional because it violated the Commerce Clause. On appeal, the State supreme court reversed the ruling of the lower court. The court declared that the law was constitutional because it had significant health and environmental objectives and did not discriminate against or place an excessive burden on interstate commerce. The plaintiffs then appealed to the United States Supreme Court.

### Arguments for City of Philadelphia

1. Restricting the importation of waste products is a form of regulation of interstate trade. This is a power that the Constitution gives to Congress, not the States.

2. The law discriminates against out-of-state waste simply because of its origin. States may not constitutionally discriminate against articles of commerce produced outside the State.

3. The law makes out-of-state businesses bear the full burden of conserving New Jersey's remaining landfill space. States may not try to isolate themselves from a problem that is common to many States by creating a barrier to interstate trade.

### Arguments for New Jersey

1. The movement of waste is not "commerce" as that term is used in the Constitution, because waste, unlike legitimate articles of commerce, cannot be put to effective use.

2. States should have great flexibility in deciding to ban harmful or potentially harmful articles from their territory.

3. The restriction on waste significantly benefits the State's environment and affects interstate commerce only minimally, at most.

### Decide for Yourself

1. Review the constitutional grounds on which each side based its arguments and the specific arguments each side presented.

2. Debate the opposing viewpoints presented in this case. Which viewpoint do you favor?

3. Predict the impact of the Court's decision on efforts by the individual States and by the Federal Government to improve the environment. (To read a summary of the Court's decision, turn to the Supreme Court Glossary on page 799.)

 *Corner*

📁 **Close Up on the Supreme Court** *City of Philadelphia* v. *New Jersey,* p. 25 provides an activity to extend coverage of this case.

To keep up-to-date on Close Up news and activities, visit Close Up Online at

**www.closeup.org**

---

## Can States Restrict Undesirable Imports?

**Focus** In 1786, delegates from several States met to discuss ways of regulating economic competition between the States. Many States had passed laws unfairly favoring their economy at the expense of other States. After discussing the problem, a second convention was set to amend the Articles of Confederation in order to allow for national trade regulations. That convention went on to draft the Constitution.

**Instruct** Ask the class how the Constitution dealt with the problem of interstate economic competition. *(The Commerce Clause)* Then discuss how the delegates to the Constitutional Convention might have answered the title question.

**Close/Reteach** Discuss whether a law intended to protect a State's rivers from pollution by banning the importation of garbage by boat violates the Commerce Clause. Have students prepare a pamphlet expressing their opinion as to that law's constitutionality.

💿 **Keep It Current CD-ROM** includes government-related projects by unit. The CD-ROM links to the Prentice Hall School Web site and may be used for daily updates.

### Answers to . . .
**Decide for Yourself**

**1.** Philadelphia argued that by restricting the importation of waste products, New Jersey was interfering with interstate trade as protected by the Commerce Clause. New Jersey argued that waste cannot be considered "commerce," and moreover the State had the authority to disallow harmful articles.
**2.** Answers will vary, but should be supported with valid reasoning.
**3.** The Court ruled in favor of Philadelphia, saying that New Jersey's statute violated the Commerce Clause.

**CHAPTER 24** Assessment

## Practicing the Vocabulary

**1.–10.** Sentences should accurately reflect the meaning of each term in the context of chapter content.
**11.** clemency
**12.** statutory law
**13.** felony
**14.** precedent
**15.** initiative
**16.** common law

## Reviewing Main Ideas

### Section 1

**17.** Popular sovereignty and limited government.
**18.** In 1845, a constitution was written for the new State of Texas. When Texas seceded from the Union, it adopted the constitution of 1861. After the Civil War, a new constitution was adopted in 1869. The constitution in use today was written in 1876 and has been amended hundreds of times.
**19.** Proposal, by a constitutional convention, a legislature, or by initiative; and ratification, usually by the vote of the people.
**20.** Length and age.

### Section 2

**21.** The power to pass laws that do not conflict with federal law or the State constitution; executive powers (approval of governor's appointments); judicial powers (impeachment); constituent power, or constitution-making and amending.
**22.** Nominated at party primaries and elected by popular vote.
**23. (a)** Bills are introduced by a legislator, considered by a committee which reports to its house of the legislature, and then voted on by each house.
**(b)** Initiative allows qualified voters to use petition to secure ballot proposals, which may then be voted on.

### Section 3

**24.** Appointment and removal of other State executives, supervision of the State's executive branch, preparing the budget, commanding the National Guard, the message power, calling special sessions of the legislature, the veto, and executive clemency.
**25.** President of the senate, member of the Legislative Redistricting Board and the Legislative Budget Board.

## Political Dictionary

popular sovereignty **(p. 685)**
limited government **(p. 685)**
initiative **(p. 688)**
fundamental law **(p. 688)**
statutory law **(p. 688)**
police power **(p. 691)**
constituent power **(p. 692)**
referendum **(p. 693)**
item veto **(p. 698)**
clemency **(p. 698)**

pardon **(p. 698)**
commutation **(p. 698)**
reprieve **(p. 698)**
parole **(p. 698)**
common law **(p. 702)**
precedent **(p. 703)**
criminal law **(p. 704)**
felony **(p. 704)**
misdemeanor **(p. 704)**
civil law **(p. 704)**

jury **(p. 704)**
information **(p. 704)**
justice of the peace **(p. 707)**
warrant **(p. 707)**
preliminary hearing **(p. 707)**
appellate jurisdiction **(p. 709)**

## Practicing the Vocabulary

***Using Words in Context*** *For each of the terms below, write a sentence that shows how it relates to this chapter.*

1. popular sovereignty
2. reprieve
3. referendum
4. item veto
5. police power
6. civil law
7. limited government
8. justice of the peace
9. appellate jurisdiction
10. warrant

***Fill in the Blank*** *Choose a term from the list above that best completes each sentence.*

**11.** The power of executive _____ includes the power to pardon or parole a convicted criminal.
**12.** Laws passed by the legislature are called _____.
**13.** A _____ is more serious than a misdemeanor.
**14.** A _____ is a guide to be followed in later cases.
**15.** The _____ is a process by which voters can petition to propose constitutional amendments and legislation.
**16.** The basis of much American law is the unwritten, judge-made law called _____ that developed in England.

## Reviewing Main Ideas

### Section 1

**17.** What are the two basic principles on which all State constitutions are based?
**18.** Briefly trace the history of the Texas constitution.
**19.** Describe the two basic steps of constitutional change.
**20.** Name at least two reasons that many State constitutions are in need of reform.

### Section 2

**21.** What powers does the Texas State legislature have?
**22.** How are Texas State legislators chosen?
**23. (a)** What are the usual steps in the legislative process? **(b)** Describe the initiative and referendum processes that some States allow.

### Section 3

**24.** List the powers of the governor of Texas.
**25.** What is the role of the lieutenant governor of Texas?

**26.** Name three other executive officers in State government and describe what they do.

### Section 4

**27.** Name and describe the four kinds of law applied in Texas State courts.
**28.** What is the importance of common law to the judicial system?
**29. (a)** What are the two kinds of juries? **(b)** Describe what each kind of jury does.

### Section 5

**30.** What are the functions of local trial courts, county-level courts, general trial courts, intermediate appellate courts, and Texas high courts?
**31. (a)** What are the three ways that judges are selected? **(b)** Which are the most widely used methods?

**26.** Three of the following: The lieutenant governor succeeds the governor and, in Texas, holds considerable powers. The secretary of state is the State's chief clerk and record keeper. The treasurer is the custodian of State funds, the chief tax collector, and paymaster. The attorney general interprets the law for and is the legal advisor to State officials and agencies.

### Section 4

**27.** Constitutional law, statutory law, administrative law, and common law.
**28.** It is the basis for most statutory law and represents generally accepted ideas of right and wrong that are judicially recognized.
**29. (a)** Grand jury and petit jury. **(b)** The grand jury determines whether evidence against a person charged with a crime is suf-

ficient to justify a trial. A petit jury hears evidence and decides disputed facts.

### Section 5

**30.** Local trial courts handle minor civil disputes, misdemeanors, and small claims cases, and, in cities, minor criminal cases and traffic violations. County-level courts handle minor criminal cases, civil matters, and appeals

## Critical Thinking

**32. Applying the Chapter Skill**  Contact the office of the jury commissioner or similar official in your district, and find out the kinds of juries on which you are eligible to serve (or will be, when you turn 18). For example, are you eligible to serve on a grand jury or just a petit, or trial, jury? Can you serve in both civil and criminal matters? Make a list of the courts, the kinds of cases, and the locations where you would be eligible to serve.

**33. Identifying Central Issues**  Describe how the system of checks and balances works in State government. What limits does each branch of government place on the other two? Then compare these checks and balances with those in the federal system.

**34. Recognizing Ideologies**  There is a long history in this country of relying on "a jury of one's peers" to decide court cases. **(a)** What does that reveal about traditional American beliefs concerning ordinary citizens and government officials? **(b)** What does the recent trend away from the jury system reveal about current American attitudes?

**35. Expressing Problems Clearly**  In your opinion, what should be the characteristics required of all judges in the Texas judicial system? Explain your answer.

## Analyzing Political Cartoons

Using your knowledge of American government and this cartoon, answer the questions below.

"Look, the american people don't want to be bossed around by federal bureaucrats. They want to be bossed around by state bureaucrats."

**36.** What does the cartoon suggest about the speakers' perception of the difference between State and federal governments?

**37.** What can State and local government provide for Texans that the federal government cannot?

 **Take It to the Net**

Additional support materials and activities for Chapter 24 of *Magruder's American Government* can be found in the Social Studies area at the Prentice Hall School Web site. **www.phschool.com**

### ★ You Can Make a Difference

If you were talking with visitors about the history of Texas, what could you tell them? What native peoples lived where you live now? Do you know who the first European and Asian settlers of your area were? Why did they choose to live here? Use resources from your local historical society and from the State historical society to prepare a display and map of the early history of Texas. If possible, use copies of drawings or photographs of the native peoples and of the settlers and their settlements.

## Participation Activities

**38. Current Events Watch**  Find out more about the governor and lieutenant governor of Texas. Research their political biographies, including qualifications for the job and campaign positions in the most recent election. Also find out how they use the powers of the office and the powers of persuasion and influence. Sum up your findings in a short essay. You may wish to include the research you did for the Take It to the Net Activity on page 700.

**39. Diagraming Activity**  Using the information in this chapter and additional research, make a diagram of the major steps in the process of changing a State constitution. Be sure to include both the rewriting or revising of a constitution and the amendment process.

**40. It's Your Turn**  Suppose Texas were considering the Missouri Plan for selecting judges. Take a position for or against the plan, and write a speech to deliver at a hearing on the subject. State your position clearly, and support it with reasons and facts. Remember, your audience will be listening to—not reading—your speech. If you are against the plan, be sure to present and propose an alternative. **(Writing a Speech)**

 **Take It to the Net**

**Chapter 24 Self-Test**  As a final review activity, take the Chapter 24 Self-Test in the Social Studies area at the Web site listed below, and receive immediate feedback on your answers.

**www.phschool.com**

## Point-of-Use Resources

 **Guide to the Essentials of American Government** Chapter 24 Test, page 132 provides multiple-choice questions to test students' knowledge of the chapter.

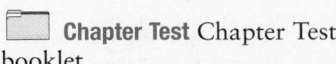 **Test Bank CD-ROM** Chapter 24 Test

**Chapter Test** Chapter Tests booklet

---

from local trial courts. General trial courts hear the more important civil and criminal cases. Intermediate appellate courts review cases decided in general trial courts and the county-level courts. Texas high courts hear appeals from lower courts.

**31. (a)** Popular election, appointment by the governor, and appointment by the legislature. **(b)** Election and appointment by the governor.

### Critical Thinking Skills

**32.** Lists should be complete and detailed.

**33.** The executive branch can limit the legislature through the veto; the legislative branch can limit the executive through appropriations, overriding a veto, and impeachment; it can also impeach judges. The judicial branch can limit the other branches through judicial review of laws passed by the legislature and official orders of executive officials and departments. This is similar to the federal system.

**34. (a)** Possible answer: Faith in the common people and a suspicion of government. **(b)** Possible answer: A desire for fast, inexpensive results; less confidence in the motivation and competence of jurors (common people).

**35.** Answers will vary, but should demonstrate an understanding of the duties of a Texas judge.

### Analyzing Political Cartoons

**36.** That State governments are more connected with the people and their concerns.

**37.** An understanding of the unique concerns and issues facing Texans.

### You Can Make a Difference

Displays and maps should be accurate and clearly indicate the native peoples of the area and the first European or Asian settlers and their reasons for coming to the area.

### Participation Activities

**38.** Essays should include both the pertinent facts and a well-supported evaluation of the governor and lieutenant governor.

**39.** Diagrams should reflect the steps for both processes of constitutional change—rewriting or revising and amending—in a clear, illustrative way.

**40.** Speeches should state a position clearly, and support it with logical argument and specific examples, using appropriate persuasive language.

# Texas Local Government and Finance

| Section Objectives | Print and Technology Resources |
|---|---|

## 1 Texas Counties and Special Districts
*(pp. 718–723)*

1. Identify the major elements of the nation's counties.
2. Analyze the structure and functions of county governments in Texas.
3. Explain the reasons behind the creation of special districts.
4. Describe the functions of Texas school districts.
5. Identify two forms of local government used outside Texas.

**TEKS 9I, 21A, 21D, 21E, 22A, 22B, 22C, 22D**

- **Unit 7 booklet**
  Guided Reading and Review, p. 13
  Section 1 Quiz, p. 14
- **Lesson Plans booklet** Section 1, p. 107
- **Political Cartoons booklet** Section 1, p. 99
- **Block Scheduling with Lesson Strategies booklet** p. 31
- **Close Up on Primary Sources booklet** New Ideas for Metropolitan Regions, p. 27
- **The Living Constitution booklet** p. 3
- **Government Assessment Rubrics booklet** p. 22
- **Simulations and Debates booklet** pp. 34–38
- **Section Support Transparencies** 102, 201
- **Presentation Pro CD-ROM** Section 1
- **Section Reading Support Transparencies**

## 2 Cities and Metropolitan Areas in Texas and the Nation
*(pp. 725–732)*

1. Examine reasons for America's shift from a rural to an urban society.
2. Compare and contrast the major forms of city government.
3. Evaluate the need for city planning and list some municipal functions.
4. Outline the challenges that face suburbs and metropolitan areas.
5. Describe efforts toward cooperation among local governments.

**TEKS 9I, 21A, 21C, 21D, 21E, 22A, 22B, 22C, 22D**

- **Unit 7 booklet**
  Guided Reading and Review, p. 15
  Section 2 Quiz, p. 16
- **Lesson Plans booklet** Section 2, p. 108
- **Political Cartoons booklet** Section 2, p. 100
- **Block Scheduling with Lesson Strategies booklet** p. 31
- **Government Assessment Rubrics** booklet p. 26
- **Basic Principles of the Constitution Transparencies** 50
- **Section Support Transparencies** 103, 202
- **Presentation Pro CD-ROM** Section 2
- **Section Reading Support Transparencies**

## 3 Providing Important Services
*(pp. 733–737)*

1. Analyze the structure and functions of State government.
2. Identify the types of services that Texas State and local governments provide.

**TEKS 9H, 9I, 21A, 21E, 22A, 22B, 22C, 22D, 23A**

- **Unit 7 booklet**
  Guided Reading and Review, p. 17
  Section 3 Quiz, p. 18
- **Lesson Plans booklet** Section 3, p. 109
- **Political Cartoons booklet** Section 3, p. 101
- **Section Reading Support Transparencies**
- **Social Studies Skills Tutor CD-ROM**
- **Close Up on Primary Sources booklet** Gerald B. H. Solomon, Arguments for Passing Welfare Reform Bill, p. 69
- **Section Support Transparencies** 104, 203
- **Presentation Pro CD-ROM** Section 3
- **Simulations and Data Graphing CD-ROM**

## 4 Financing State and Local Government
*(pp. 739–744)*

1. Describe the major Federal and State limits on raising revenue.
2. List the four principles of sound taxation.
3. Identify major tax and nontax sources of Texas State and local revenue.
4. Explain the State budget process.

**TEKS 6A, 6B, 9H, 9I, 10D, 17C, 21A, 21C, 22A, 22B, 22C, 22D**

- **Unit 7 booklet**
  Guided Reading and Review, p. 19
  Section 4 Quiz, p. 20
  Skills for Life Activity, p. 21
- **Lesson Plans booklet** Section 4, p. 110
- **Political Cartoons booklet** Section 4, p. 102
- **Section Reading Support Transparencies**
- **Close Up on the Supreme Court booklet** *Board of Estimate of New York v. Morris*, p. 26
- **The Living Constitution booklet** p. 4
- **The Basic Principles of the Constitution Posters**
- **Section Support Transparencies** 105, 204
- **Presentation Pro CD-ROM** Section 4

# Block Scheduling Strategies

The *Magruder's American Government* program addresses block-scheduling strategies in a variety of ways. For easy reference, side-column activities that fit a block format are marked  **Block Strategy.** Each section also contains a **Block Scheduling Strategies** box describing at least two block-format activities that address and extend core content from the section. The **Block Scheduling with Lesson Strategies booklet** found in the Teaching Resources contains additional block-scheduling activities for each chapter.

## Take It to the Net

Visit the Social Studies area at the Prentice Hall School Web site. Once there, you can find additional links, current events connections, and activities to enrich chapter content for *Magruder's American Government,* as well as a Self-Test for students. Be sure to check out this month's **eTeach** online discussion with a Master Teacher.

### www.phschool.com

## Pressed for Time?

If you are running short on time to cover this chapter, consider one of the following options:
- Use the **Presentation Pro CD-ROM** to create an outline for this chapter.
- Use one of the **Pressed for Time** activities found on p. 27.
- Use the Section Summaries for Chapter 2, from **Guide to the Essentials of American Government (English and Spanish).**

##  Video Connections

Prentice Hall offers two video programs to reinforce and extend chapter content. Show students *The Blessings of Liberty* from the **ABC News Civics and Government Videotape Library** and *Prayer in Schools: A Nationwide Debate* from the **Magruder's American Government Video Collection.**

## Assessment Options

- Section Quizzes, **Unit 7 booklet,** pp. 14, 16, 18, 20
- Chapter 25 Assessment, pp. 746–747
- **Guide to the Essentials of American Government,** Chapter 25 Test, p. 137

### Core Assessment

Chapter 25 Test, Chapter Tests booklet
ExamView® Test Bank CD-ROM Chapter 25
Government Assessment Rubrics

### Standardized Test Preparation

#### Diagnose and Prescribe

Diagnostic Tests for High School
Social Studies Skills

#### Review and Reteach

Review Book for Government

#### Practice and Assess

Test-Taking Strategies With
    Transparencies for High School
Test Prep Book for Government

---

# Chapter 25 Teacher's Edition Index

# Texas Local Government and Finance

# Texas Local Government and Finance

## Introducing the Chapter

In this chapter, students will learn about the various units of local government, how they are financed, and what services they provide.

### Make It Relevant

⭐ *You Can Make a Difference*

Review with students the service learning project(s) with which they have been involved. Elicit from them their honest appraisals of the nature, effectiveness, and value of their work. Then have individual students write journal entries in which they explore ways they can continue to be of service to their communities. In their journal entries (or, as a class), have students make a pledge to themselves or to others that they will continue to search for and take advantage of opportunities to serve their community.

**Service Learning**

## CONSTITUTIONAL PRINCIPLES

Emphasize the following basic principles as students read Chapter 25. Have the class respond to the questions, and then ask volunteers to describe the importance of local government, in terms of the functioning of American democracy.

**Limited Government** In what ways do units of local government limit the power of the Federal Government?

**Separation of Powers** How does separation of powers work at the level of local government?

**Popular Sovereignty** How do New England towns particularly uphold popular sovereignty?

"*I've had the chance to represent Dallas all around the world. These travels have reinforced my belief that no matter our skin color, our religion, our size or shape—people are essentially the same.*"
—Dallas Mayor Ron Kirk, (1999)

People everywhere have the same needs, many of which are fulfilled by local governments. Indeed, it is to local government that most people look for help and services.

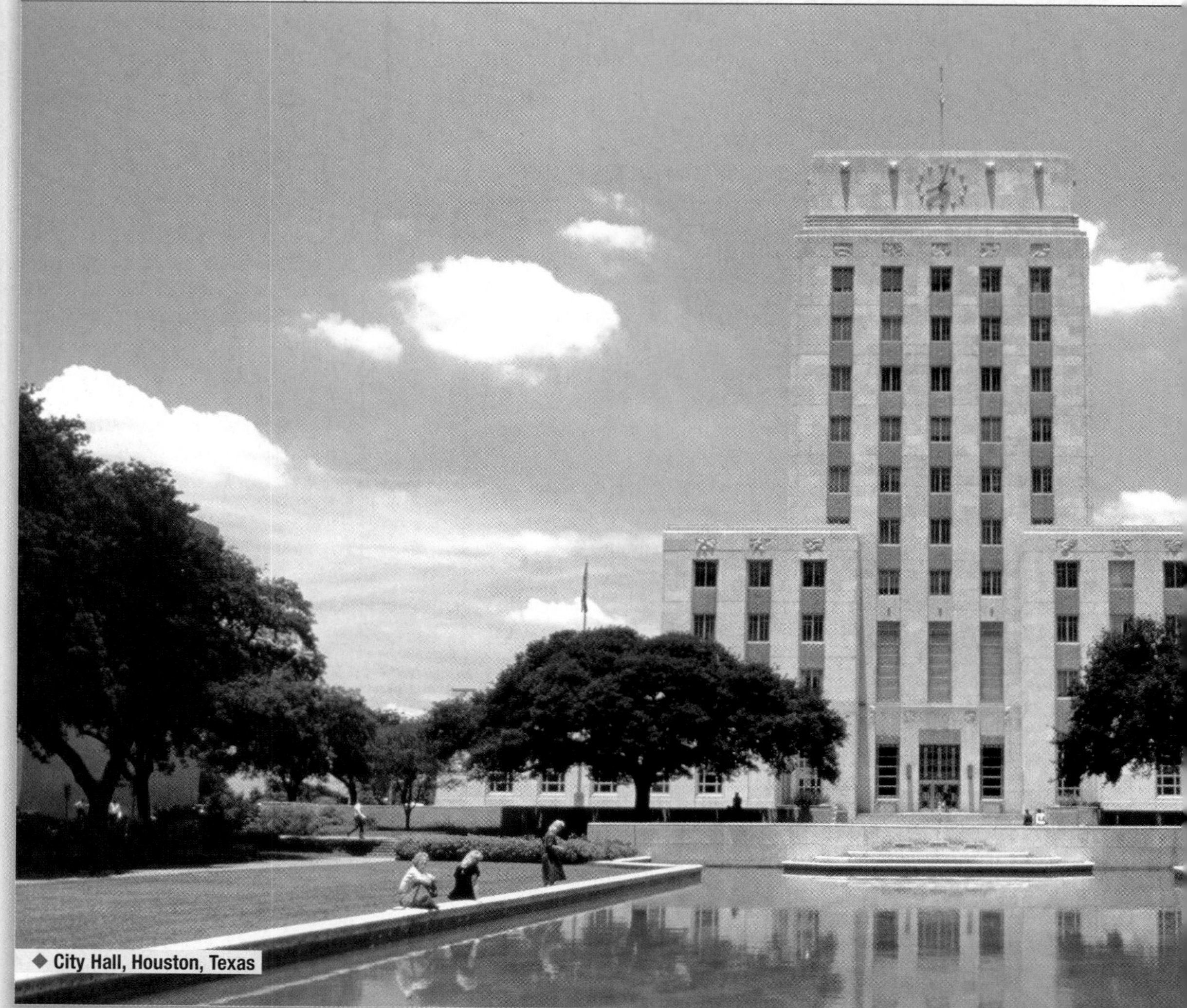

◆ **City Hall, Houston, Texas**

## Corner

The following resources are available only from the Close Up Foundation to support the concepts discussed in Chapter 25 "Local Government and Finance":

◆ *Perspectives: Readings on Contemporary American Government*
◆ *Active Citizenship Today Field Guide for Students*

To keep up-to-date on Close Up news and activities, visit Close Up Online at

**www.closeup.org**

Close Up Foundation
44 Canal Center Plaza
Alexandria, VA 22314-1592
800-765-3131

## You Can Make a Difference

**NO MATTER HOW** many services a city provides, communities need volunteers of all ages. In Washington, D.C., a diverse group of young people work with DC-YAR, part of the organization Youth As Resources, to bridge cultural and racial differences and to support grass-roots projects for other urban youth. Bsrat Mezghebe and N'erin Brown, both high school juniors, served on the DC-YAR board. There they reviewed project proposals from other young people, such as a community spring cleanup and a book of children's stories about different cultures. N'erin was impressed that "so many youth were into helping the community. They're helping to regenerate our generation."

### Keep It Current

Items marked with this logo are periodically updated on the Internet. Keep up-to-date with what's in the news. To get current information on Texas local government and finance, go to **www.phschool.com**

### SECTION 1

## Texas Counties and Special Districts
*(pp. 718–723)*

★ Counties or their equivalents exist in all but two States. Their functions vary depending on region.
★ County government affects the daily lives of all Texans.
★ Special districts provide a wide variety of services, including water and sewage, police and fire, and airport and park services.
★ Towns and townships are forms of local government that exist in certain parts of the country.

### SECTION 2

## Cities and Metropolitan Areas in Texas and the Nation *(pp. 725–732)*

★ Most Americans live in urban areas.
★ City governments take one of three forms: mayor-council, commission, or council-manager.
★ Population shifts from cities to suburbs have left cities in Texas and throughout the nation with fewer resources. One response has been the creation of metropolitan districts.

### SECTION 3

## Providing Important Services *(pp. 733–737)*

★ Under the federal system, States and their local governments have many powers and provide many important services.
★ Texas State and local governments provide education, help ensure public welfare and safety, and build and maintain highways.

### SECTION 4

## Financing State and Local Government
*(pp. 739–744)*

★ The federal Constitution, the 14th Amendment, and the Texas State constitution restrict State and local taxing powers.
★ Most tax experts agree with Scottish economist Adam Smith that there are four principles of sound taxation.
★ Texas State and local governments rely on a variety of tax and nontax sources of revenue.
★ The State budget is the means by which Texas plans the control and use of public money.

## Pressed for Time?

### To Omit the Chapter
If you wish to skip Chapter 25, ask students to read the Chapter in Brief and assign the Guide to the Essentials before continuing to another chapter. You may also want to assign the Chapter 25 Test in the Chapter Test booklet. Then specific portions of Chapter 25 may be assigned to students needing reinforcement of key terms and concepts.

### To Preview the Chapter
To introduce students to key terms and concepts in each section, have them read the Chapter in Brief. You may also assign the Reading Strategy activities on pp. 719, 726, 734, and 740 of this book.

### To Review the Chapter
When students have completed Chapter 25, you might want to assign the Guide to the Essentials or the Guided Reading and Review worksheets on pp. 13, 15, 17, and 19 of the Unit 7 booklet.

### To Cover the Chapter Quickly
To cover the material in Chapter 25 quickly, use the following activity.

**Focus** Begin by asking the class what kind of local government governs their area. Then ask what other units of local government they are familiar with. Write each kind on the board, and have volunteers provide characteristics of each.

**Instruct** Define and describe the structure of counties, towns, townships, cities, and metropolitan districts. Explain the services that each unit of government provides, and how each type of local government is financed.

**Close/Reteach** Emphasize the importance of local government in the United States. After students have read the chapter, ask: Would it be possible for a nation as large as the United States to function efficiently without local governments? Have them provide examples in support or opposition.

■ **Block Strategy (Average)**

## Keep It Current

### Internet Update

Use the Prentice Hall School Web site and the Keep It Current CD-ROM to find quick content updates.

Visit **www.phschool.com** for current events articles that are linked to Chapter 25. Critical thinking questions are included.

**Keep It Current CD-ROM** includes government-related projects by unit. Students complete each project using current information that they obtain by linking to the Prentice Hall School Web site from the CD-ROM.

# ·1· Texas Counties and Special Districts

**Objectives** You may wish to call students' attention to the objectives in the Section Preview. The objectives are reflected in the main headings of the section.

**Bellringer** Have students suppose that they want a fishing license. Ask them where they would go to get one. Explain that in this section they will learn about various units of local government and how they serve the people—including the issuing of fishing licenses.

**Vocabulary Builder** Ask students to study the terms in the Political Dictionary. Have them suggest which of these local units of government often takes on tasks that the others cannot or will not do. Encourage them to explain their reasoning.

## Pressed for Time?

### Quick Lesson Plan

**1. Focus** Tell students that most Americans live in areas with county governments. Ask students to discuss what they know about the various functions of county governments.

**2. Instruct** Ask students to name the governing body of a Texas county. *(the Commissioners Court)* Discuss the structure of county government and why it needs reform. Then examine the functions of this and other units of local government.

**3. Close/Reteach** Remind students that some New England towns still practice direct democracy. Ask students to create a chart listing the forms of local government discussed in this section, where they are found, their structure, and their functions.

## Point-of-Use Resources

📁 **Block Scheduling with Lesson Strategies** Activities for Chapter 25 are presented on p. 31.

---

## Section Preview

### OBJECTIVES

1. **Identify** the major elements of the nation's counties.
2. **Analyze** the structure and functions of county governments in Texas.
3. **Explain** the reasons behind the creation of special districts.
4. **Describe** the functions of Texas school districts.
5. **Identify** two forms of local government used outside Texas.

### WHY IT MATTERS

What county do you live in? What school district? Do you live in a special district? Your life is affected everyday by the decisions of these local governments.

### POLITICAL DICTIONARY

★ county
★ township
★ special district

---

The nation has the magnificent Capitol in Washington, D.C., and Texas has its own impressive capitol in Austin. These structures serve as centers for Federal and State governments. In most communities, however, local government has no grand dome. Government in these places is visible mainly in the form of the day-to-day services that keep communities going.

In spite of its humble appearance, local government is vital to the lives of every American. As one measure of this fact, recall that of the 87,504 units of government across the nation, 87,453 of these are local. In this section, you will read about two major forms of local government in Texas—

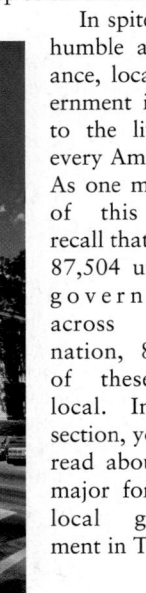

▲ Georgetown, Texas, is just one of the nation's 87,453 units of local government.

the county and the special district. In order to get a sense of the complicated pattern of local government across the country, you also will read about two forms of local government that are used outside Texas.

## The Nation's Counties

A **county** is a major unit of local government in most States. Like all local governments, it is created by the State.[1] There are 3,043 counties in the United States. No close relationship exists between the size of a State and the number of counties it has. The number of counties in a given State runs from none in Connecticut and Rhode Island to as many as 254 in Texas.

In Louisiana, units of government known elsewhere as counties are called parishes. In Alaska, they are known as boroughs. In addition to Connecticut and Rhode Island, several other places across the country have no organized county government. Almost 10 percent of the nation's population lives in those areas today.

The function of county government varies widely from region to region. Counties serve almost solely as judicial districts in the New England States. There, towns carry out most of

---

[1] Recall that whether they are providing services, regulating activities, collecting taxes, or doing anything else, local governments can only act because the State has established them and has given them power to do so.

---

## 🔲 Block Scheduling Strategies

Consider these suggestions to manage extended class time:

■ After students have read the section, have them decide which unit of local government they think is most useful, most effective, and most in keeping with American democracy. Ask them to write short paragraphs about their choice, including specific examples. Encourage students to read their paragraphs to the class.

■ Write topics pertaining to local government on a series of flashcards (for example, governing body, functions, area, who is in charge, etc.). Divide the class into three groups, assigning each *county, township,* or *special district*. Have students study their assigned unit of government. Then have students randomly draw a card, and describe the attributes of their assigned unit of government that relate to the topic.

the functions undertaken by counties elsewhere. In many Mid-Atlantic and Midwestern States, counties are divided into subdivisions called **townships**. In these States, counties and townships share the functions of rural local government. In rural areas of the South and the West, counties are the major units of government.

San Bernardino County in southern California is the largest county in the United States in terms of area, covering 20,064 square miles. Kalawao County in Hawaii is the smallest, covering only 13 square miles. Counties within each State can vary widely in area.

Counties also differ greatly in terms of population. More than 9 million people now live in Los Angeles County, California. Census takers could find only 67 residents of Loving County in West Texas in 2000. Most counties—in fact nearly three fourths of them—have populations of fewer than 50,000.

## County Governments in Texas

Texas has more counties—254—than any other State in the country. In terms of population, the smallest Texas county is Loving, mentioned above, and the largest is Harris County, with a population of 3.4 million.

County government is almost ignored by the average city resident. That individual would be surprised to realize in how many ways county government affects the lives of Texas citizens. Almost any time a citizen is required to conduct business with the State, he or she does it with the county. Whether you live in rural West Texas or in the Dallas-Fort Worth metroplex, when you register to vote, apply for your car registration, file birth certificates, or get a marriage license, you will do so at the county courthouse.

### The Commissioners Court

The governing body of a Texas county is the Commissioners Court. This is not a court in the judicial sense, as the commissioners do not consider legal cases. Instead, the Commissioners

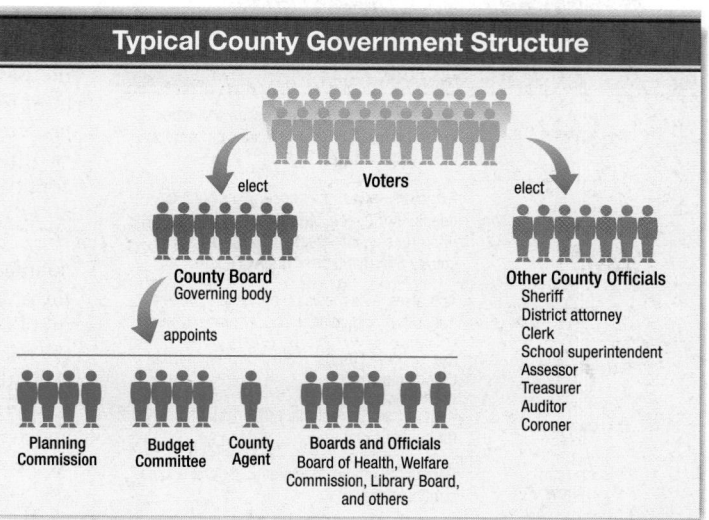

**Typical County Government Structure**

elect  Voters  elect

County Board
Governing body

appoints

Other County Officials
Sheriff
District attorney
Clerk
School superintendent
Assessor
Treasurer
Auditor
Coroner

Planning Commission  Budget Committee  County Agent  Boards and Officials
Board of Health, Welfare Commission, Library Board, and others

*Interpreting Diagrams* A typical county government has a governing body, a number of boards or commissions, appointed bureaucrats, and elected officials. ***Why might the fact that the county governing body shares its powers with other elected officials lead to confusion?***

Court sets policy and directs the administration of the county. Among its most important duties are establishing a county budget and setting tax rates.

The Commissioners Court consists of four commissioners and a county judge. Each county is divided into four commissioners precincts, each of which elects a commissioner to the court. The county judge is elected in a countywide vote, and he or she is an important political figure in most Texas counties. The commissioners and the county judge serve four-year, overlapping terms. Thus, there are always some experienced members in office. The county judge acts as presiding officer of the Commissioners Court and as the chief administrative officer of the county. The county judge also presides over the county court.

### Other County Officials

Most Texas counties elect five other county officers, each to a four-year term. These officers, and their principal duties, include:

1. The sheriff, who keeps the jail, furnishes police protection in rural areas, carries out the orders of the local courts, and often acts as the tax collector.

2. The county clerk, who registers and records such documents as deeds, mortgages, birth and marriage certificates, and divorce decrees.

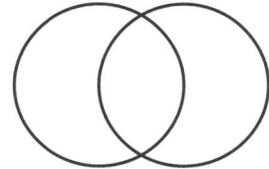

A C T I V I T Y

## Extended Class Periods

**Time** 90 minutes.
**Purpose** Make a chart of Texas State government.
**Grouping** Four to six students.
**Activity** Each group should create a chart of Texas State government that provides information such as the size and characteristics of the legislature, the names of key State officials, the number and names of counties and large cities, and other important information. (Provide groups with resources that contain the information they need or have them consult the Government Resources Handbook in the *Teaching Resources* for possible sources of information.)
**Roles** Manager, researchers, artists.
**Close** Groups may refer to their charts as the class discusses the function and services of each unit of government.

■ **Block Strategy**
**(Basic)**

## Point-of-Use Resources

☐ **Government Assessment Rubrics** Cooperative Learning Project: Product, p. 22

☐ **Block Scheduling with Lesson Strategies** Additional activities for Chapter 25 appear on p. 31.

## Typical Elected County Officials and Their Duties

| | |
|---|---|
| **SHERIFF** | Runs county jail; provides police protection in rural areas; carries out local court orders; often collects taxes |
| **CLERK** | Registers and records documents such as deeds, mortgages, birth/death certificates; often runs county elections; is secretary to county board and clerk of local courts |
| **ASSESSOR** | Appraises (sets the value of) taxable property in the county and collects county property taxes |
| **TREASURER** | Keeps county funds; makes payments from these funds |
| **AUDITOR** | Keeps financial records; authorizes payments for county expenses |
| **DISTRICT ATTORNEY** | Conducts criminal investigations; prosecutes criminal cases |
| **SCHOOL SUPERINTENDENT** | Administers public elementary and secondary schools in the county |
| **CORONER** | Investigates violent deaths; certifies causes of deaths not attended by a physician |

*Interpreting Tables* Elected county officials include people with a wide range of responsibilities that affect local communities. For example, surveyors like the woman pictured here help map local property accurately. *Which of these officials might affect your own daily life?*

3. The assessor and collector of taxes, who appraises (sets the value of) all of the taxable property in the county and collects the county property taxes.

4. The county treasurer, who keeps county funds and makes authorized payments from these funds.

5. The district attorney, who acts as the prosecuting attorney, carries out criminal investigations, and prosecutes those who break the law.

## Evaluation of County Government

As valuable as county government has been in the past and as viable as it continues to be in most rural counties, it does present some serious problems in urban areas of the State. There are two major obstacles confronting the urban county in trying to deal with its problems.

1. The State constitution establishes the same basic organization and structure for all 254 counties, regardless of population. So, although the challenges facing a large, urban county are more complex than those facing a rural county, the method for dealing with them remains essentially the same.

2. Texas counties have no authority to pass laws and have very limited regulatory authority. That means that when they are confronted by a new problem, or the reappearance of an old one, they often have to go to the legislature to request passage of a law giving them the authority to handle that specific issue. There is growing support to pass State legislation giving counties, particularly urban ones, some type of limited ordinance-making power. Interest groups have succeeded in blocking such proposals in the past, however.

## Special Districts

There are more than 2,000 **special districts** in the State of Texas. A special district is an independent unit created to perform one or more related governmental functions at the local level. These districts are found in almost mind-boggling variety and in every State.

Mosquito control districts, port authorities, airport authorities, and water districts are among the most common. Special districts are particularly useful when they fill a need that existing governmental units do not provide because they do not have the legal authority or financial base to do so. Such districts are relatively easy to set up, and they can focus their efforts on a specific problem.

The Greater Harris County 9-1-1 Emergency Network provides one example of how special districts develop. In the early 1980s, Harris County, which includes the city of Houston, had more than 150 seven-digit emergency telephone numbers connecting to fire departments, police stations, and other government agencies. To get help in an emergency, a citizen had to find and dial the number of the agency that served their area. At times, confusion over which number to call led to unnecessary loss of life and property.

No single local government had the authority or the financial base to coordinate emergency efforts. In 1983, however, Harris County voters approved the creation of a special district designed to handle emergencies. Within the special district, any emergency can be reported by dialing 9-1-1, toll-free. When this enhanced emergency number is dialed, the caller's telephone number and address are automatically communicated to the medical, police, and fire authorities responsible for that address. Today this special district serves some 4.2 million citizens and answers more than a million calls each year. The success of this special district led to the creation of additional 9-1-1 districts throughout the State.

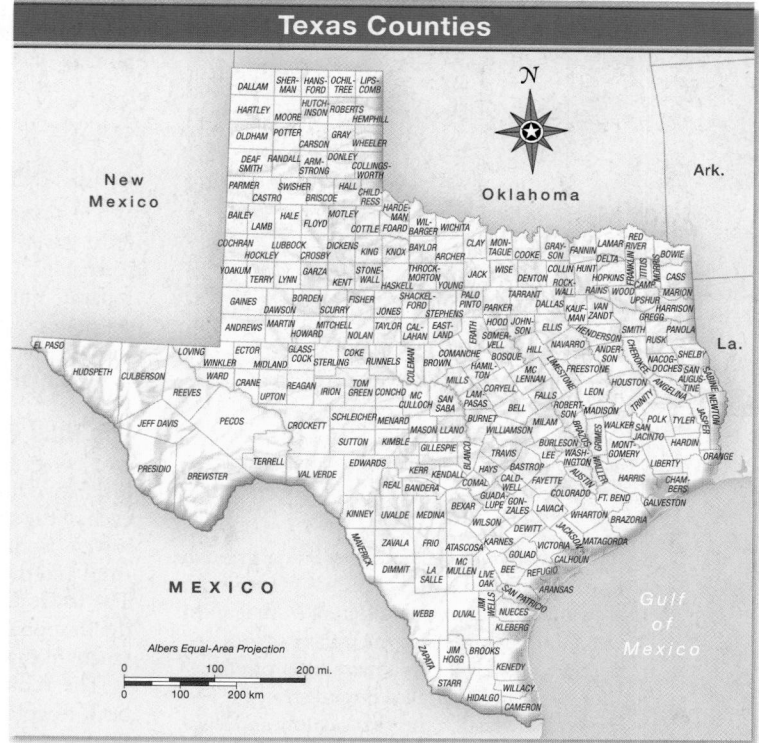

**Texas Counties**

Interpreting Maps Texas is divided into 254 counties. *Which counties would you expect to be the most densely populated? Explain your answer.*

## School Districts

Texas has more than 1,000 school districts. Virtually all of them are independent school districts (ISDs). The term "independent" refers to independence from county government. The Texas public school system was originally organized at the county level with a county school superintendent in charge of the program. Over time, however, the schools came to be administered and funded as entirely separate governmental units independent of county government. Each ISD is governed by an elected board of trustees that deals directly with the Texas Education Agency, a State agency that administers the public school system.

School districts that are not independent are classified as common school districts. By 2000, the number of common school districts had dropped to six. Common school districts are administered at the county level.

Most ISD boards have seven members. These elected officials are responsible for a host of details. The school board can hire and fire teachers, construct new schools, buy school supplies, and set district school tax rates. (In some cases, however, tax rate increases must be approved by voters.) The district board also selects a superintendent of schools to oversee the daily administration of policy.

Elections for district school boards are often among the most hotly contested local races. School board elections can play a major part in determining the books that students will use and the kinds of things they will be taught. These are critical issues for many parents, and voter turnout for school board elections can be heavy.

As noted above, local school boards can set tax rates. Tax revenue is a major part of a local district's budget, with federal funds adding a

## CONSTITUTIONAL PRINCIPLES

**Popular Sovereignty**
The town meeting has long been a vehicle of local government in New England. Praised as an ideal form of direct democracy, the idea of the town meeting has been appropriated by people and organizations in different contexts. The U.S. Department of State, for example, holds informational "Town Meetings" in which citizens may meet with and question State Department policymakers. In 1992, presidential candidate Ross Perot suggested "electronic town halls," by

which the President could "meet with" American citizens regularly and learn their opinions.
**Activity**
Have students discuss the usefulness of an idea like Perot's "electronic hall meeting." Students should consider such factors as: How could such an idea be carried out? How could participation be wide enough to include all people? Are there groups of people who might be automatically excluded? Have them list pros and cons for the idea, and share them with the class.

▲ The tradition of the town meeting is still alive in many small New England towns. *Critical Thinking* **How does the town meeting reflect the ideal of direct democracy?**

significant smaller amount. The State, through various regulations and funds, attempts to smooth out the financial differences that exist between the wealthier and the poorer school districts and to ensure an adequate level of education for all students in all school districts.

For several decades, the Texas courts and legislature have addressed differences in the property tax base of poor school districts and rich school districts. Poor school districts have low property assessments, typically because there is little industry in these areas and housing values are low. Other districts have high property assessment, either because they are home to industry or because property values are high.

Texas courts, in a case brough by low-income parents in San Antonio, have held that the Texas school finance system violated the Texas constitution. During the 1990s, the legislature passed

---

[2] The term *town* is used in some States as the legal designation for smaller urban places; it is also sometimes used as another word for township. Township is also a federal public lands survey term, used to identify geographic units (often called congressional townships), each having exactly 36 square miles (36 sections).

[3] When a clan in England or in Northern Europe settled in a particular place, it usually built a wall around it. In Old English, the word for wall was *tun.* In time, the space within the wall became known as the tun, and then the town. As the New England towns grew in number and in population, it became necessary to survey their boundaries. The small and irregular shapes that resulted were called "townships" (town shapes). The suffix *ship* comes from the Old English word *scip,* meaning "shape."

several laws (often referred to as "Robin Hood plans") that required richer districts to share a portion of their taxes with poorer districts.

## Towns and Townships: Local Government Outside Texas

While Texas uses the county as a major unit of local government, other States use the town or township. The town or township is found as a separate unit of local government in nearly half the States. Although little known in the South or the West, it is found through the region stretching from New England to the Midwest.[2]

### The New England Town

In New England, the town is a major unit of local government. Except for a few major cities, each of the six States in the region is divided into towns. Each town generally includes all of the rural and the urban areas within its boundaries. The town delivers most of the services that are the responsibility of cities and counties elsewhere in the country.

The roots of the New England town reach back to colonial times.[3] The Pilgrims landed at Plymouth Rock in 1620 as an organized congregation. They quickly set up a close-knit community in which their church and their government were almost one. Other Puritan congregations followed the Pilgrims' pattern.

The desire to be near the church, the real or perceived threat from Native Americans, the severe climate, and the fact that the land was not suited to large farms or plantations led the settlers to form tight little communities. Their settlements were soon known as towns, as in England.

At least in form, much of town government today is little changed from colonial times. The main feature is the town meeting, long praised as the ideal vehicle of direct democracy. The town meeting is an assembly open to all the town's eligible voters. It meets yearly, and sometimes more often, to levy taxes, make spending and other policy decisions, and elect officers.

Between town meetings, the board of selectmen/selectwomen chosen at the annual meeting manages the town's business. Typically, the board is a three-member body responsible for such things as roads, schools, care of the poor, and sanitation. Other officers regularly selected at the annual meeting include the town clerk, a tax assessor, a tax collector, a constable, road commissioners, and school board members.

The ideal of direct democracy is still alive in many smaller New England towns. It has given way, however, to the pressures of time, population, and the complexities of public problems in many larger towns. There, representative government has largely replaced it. Town officers are often elected before the yearly gathering. Many of the decisions once made by the assembled voters are now made by the selectmen and selectwomen. In recent years, several towns have gone to a town manager system for the day-to-day administration of local affairs.

## Townships

Townships are found as units of local government from New York and New Jersey west to the Dakotas, Nebraska, and Kansas. Nowhere do townships blanket the State, however.

In New York, New Jersey, and Pennsylvania, townships were formed as areas were settled and the people needed the services of local government. Consequently, the township maps of those States often resemble crazy-quilts. From Ohio westward, however, township lines are more regular. They mostly follow the lines drawn in federal public land surveys. Many are perfect squares.

About half of these States provide for annual township meetings, like those held in New England towns. Otherwise, the governing body is a three- or five-member board, generally called the board of trustees or board of supervisors. Its members are elected for two-year or four-year terms, or they serve because they hold other elected township offices. Township officers often include a supervisor, a clerk, a treasurer, an assessor, a constable, a justice of the peace, and a number of road commissioners.

A municipality (urban political unit) within a township—especially if it is large—usually exists as a separate governmental entity. Thus, township functions tend to be rural. They involve such matters as roads, cemeteries, drainage, and minor law enforcement.

Many people believe that townships have outlived their usefulness. More than half the States get along without them, suggesting that they are not indispensable. Many rural townships have been abolished in the past few decades. They have fallen victim to declining populations, improvements in transportation, and a host of other factors.

Some of the more densely populated townships appear to have brighter futures than their country cousins, however. This seems especially true in the suburban areas around some larger cities. Some States, such as Pennsylvania, now allow townships to exercise many of the powers and furnish many of the services once reserved to cities.

## Section 1 Assessment

### Key Terms and Main Ideas
1. What is a **county**?
2. How does a **township** differ from a **special district**?
3. **(a)** What is the governing body of a county in Texas? **(b)** List three elected officials commonly found in county government.
4. What is an independent school district?

### Critical Thinking
5. **Drawing Conclusions** Why do you think the Texas constitution established the same basic organization and structure for all counties in Texas?

6. **Drawing Inferences** Review the functions of county government and special districts. List and describe at least three examples of how one of these governing bodies affects the day-to-day lives of people in your community.

### Take It to the Net

7. Learn about the population, economics, and government of your own county. Summarize your findings in a table or series of graphs. Use the links provided in the Social Studies area at the following Web site for help in completing this activity. **www.phschool.com**

### Take It to the Net

7. Direct students to the Social Studies area at the Prentice Hall School Web site. The *Magruder's American Government* companion Web site includes the directions and links needed to complete the activity. It also provides a printable Internet activity worksheet with scoring rubrics for assessment. Students' tables or graphs should include appropriate information about their counties.

## Point-of-Use Resources

**Guide to the Essentials** Chapter 25, Section 1, p. 133 provides support for students who need additional review of section content. Spanish support is available in the Spanish edition of the Guide on p. 126.

**Quiz** Unit 7 booklet, p. 14 includes matching and multiple-choice questions to check students' understanding of Section 1 content.

**Presentation Pro CD-ROM** Quizzes and multiple-choice questions check students' understanding of Section 1 content.

## Answers to . . .

### Section 1 Assessment

1. A major unit of local government.
2. A township is a unit of local government in Mid-Atlantic and Midwestern States. A special district is an independent unit of local government created to perform one or more governmental functions.
3. **(a)** The Commissioners Court. **(b)** Examples include: sheriff, clerk, assessor, treasurer, auditor, district attorney, school superintendent, coroner.
4. A school district administered and funded separately from county government.
5. To provide more consistent and efficient government at the local level.
6. Examples include: Counties build and maintain roads; special districts govern water use or airports.

 **on Primary Sources**

# Seeing the Regional Future

*Urban planner William Fulton is a senior research fellow at Claremont Graduate University Research Institute. In this selection, he argues that the future of economic development lies in the growth of large regions, not individual cities and towns.*

The Dallas-Ft. Worth Metroplex is a regional economy.

Not long ago, I sat down to lunch with all of the planning directors and economic development specialists in Redding, California. . . . The Redding area has suffered from sluggish economic growth in recent years, and for close to two hours these local officials took turns telling me about the troubles their community faced and the "assets" they had to work with in confronting them. . . . "And, of course, we have a state university with a good reputation," one of the planning directors said. "That's a great help." All the others nodded in agreement.

. . . I had spent the better part of two days touring Redding, and I had seen no educational institution more substantial than a community college. "Where?" I asked. "What university?" And then they explained. The school they were referring to was the California State University campus in Chico . . . 75 miles away.

It had never occurred to me before that a college in one city might be part of the economic foundation of another city. But in fact, it makes perfect sense. As a smaller town located in a rural area, Redding will probably never have all the big-ticket items a city needs if it is going to compete effectively in the modern economy. But it's not really Redding that's competing. It's the whole northern part of the Sacramento Valley: Redding, Chico and a whole string of other towns that are interrelated economically. We live in the age of the region, not the age of the city. . . . If regions are the new building blocks of the world economy—if it is the region that matters,

not the nation or the city or the state—then it is the region that should also be the locus of economic development policy. . . .

You have to swallow a lot of pride in order to think this way and understand what role your community might really play in creating a strong regional economy. After all, this nation is filled with Chicos that don't want to associate with Redding, and Seattles that want nothing to do with Boise. And going against that territorial instinct can sound like political suicide to a lot of local officials. But any successful business owner will tell you that if you want to get rich, you can't be too haughty [overly proud] about what your product is or the customers you sell it to. The future belongs to the politicians who understand that Chico is a part of Redding and Seattle is a part of Boise—and all these combinations are part of regional economies that will be rich at home only to the extent that they can sell successfully to the rest of the world.

### Analyzing Primary Sources

1. What did Fulton realize during his meeting with Redding city officials, and how did he arrive at this point of view?
2. What does Fulton mean when he says, "Chico is a part of Redding and Seattle is a part of Boise"?
3. Why might political leaders have trouble accepting the approach to economic development that Fulton suggests?

 *Corner*

**Close Up on Primary Sources** New Ideas for Metropolitan Regions, p. 27, extends this feature with a primary source activity.

## Section Preview

### OBJECTIVES

1. **Examine** reasons for America's shift from a rural to an urban society.
2. **Compare and contrast** the major forms of city government.
3. **Evaluate** the need for city planning and list some municipal functions.
4. **Outline** the challenges that face suburbs and metropolitan areas.
5. **Describe** efforts toward cooperation among local governments.

### WHY IT MATTERS

Most Texans live in cities. The larger the urban population, the more extensive the need for services, efficient and responsive government, and creative solutions to problems.

### POLITICAL DICTIONARY

★ charter
★ mayor-council government
★ strong-mayor government
★ weak-mayor government
★ commission government
★ council-manager government
★ zoning
★ metropolitan area

**Objectives** You may wish to call students' attention to the objectives in the Section Preview. The objectives are reflected in the main headings of the section.

**Bellringer** Ask students to brainstorm a list of ideas that they associate with the word *city*. Write these ideas on the board. Ask students to discuss why they have these associations. Explain that in this section, they will learn about the rise of the city and about how cities are governed.

**Vocabulary Builder** Point out the terms in the Political Dictionary. Ask students which form of government they think is the oldest and most widely used: mayor-council, commission, or council-manager. Have them suggest how the strong-mayor and weak-mayor forms differ. Then discuss how the other terms might relate to cities.

We are a nation of city dwellers. Where once our population was small, mostly rural, and agricultural, it is now large, mostly urban, and dominated by technology, manufacturing, and service industries. In 1790, a mere 5 percent of the population lived in the nation's few cities. Today, 75 percent of Americans live in cities and other urban areas.[4]

## America's Rural-Urban Shift

Nine years before the first census, James Watt had patented his double-acting steam engine, making large-scale manufacturing possible. Robert Fulton patented his steamboat in 1809, and George Stephenson his locomotive in 1829. These inventions made possible the transportation of raw materials to factories and, in turn, the wide distribution of manufactured goods.

Almost overnight, home manufacturing gave way to industrial factories, and populations began to concentrate in the new industrial and transportation centers. Cities began to grow rapidly.

At the same time, the invention of several mechanical farm implements reduced the labor needed on farms. Fewer people grew more food, and the surplus farm population began to move to the cities. By 1860, the nation's population had increased more than sevenfold. The urban population had multiplied thirty times. By 1900, nearly two fifths of Americans lived in urban areas. By 1920, more than half of the population were urban dwellers.

Today, some 225 million people—75 percent of the population—live in the nation's cities and their surrounding suburbs. The figure is slightly higher than average in Texas, where 80 percent of the population is urban. For local governments in Texas, as in every State, America's rural-urban shift has had dramatic consequences.

When large numbers of people live close to one another, there is much more strain on local governments. They must provide water, police

▲ The Riverwalk in San Antonio, Texas, is an excellent example of urban renewal and city planning.

---

[4]Depending on local custom and State law, municipalities may be known as cities, towns, boroughs, or villages. The use and meaning of these terms vary among the States. The larger municipalities are known everywhere as cities, and the usual practice is to use that title only for those communities with a significant population.

### Pressed for Time?

#### Quick Lesson Plan

**1. Focus** Tell students that the governments of growing cities must be able to handle the increasing needs of their people. Ask students to discuss what they know about the services that cities provide.

**2. Instruct** Ask students who creates city governments and why. *(the State, to meet residents' need for services)* Discuss with students the forms and functions of city government. Then explore how city planning has helped cities and how cities and their suburbs interact.

**3. Close/Reteach** Remind students that the three major forms of city government all have a mayor, but the mayor's role varies in each. Ask students to make a chart showing the advantages and disadvantages of each form.

---

### 📖 Block Scheduling Strategies

Consider these suggestions to manage extended class time:

■ Divide the class into small groups, assigning each one of the three basic forms of local government (mayor-council, commission, and council-manager). Have each group develop a presentation on its form that describes its structure, who holds power and how he or they are elected. Presentations should also include a list of pros and cons for that type of government.

■ Have small groups of students plan a theoretical city. Groups should develop plans for zoning, transportation, and city services. In addition to a written plan, have each group create a map of their city with a key of services and zoning laws. When they are finished, groups should present their plans to the class and compare them.

## Reading Strategy

### Self-Questioning

Ask students to look at every heading and subheading in the section and turn it into a question that begins with *Who, What, How,* or *Why.* Have them read the section to answer their questions.

## Point-of-Use Resources

📁 **Guided Reading and Review** Unit 7 booklet, p. 15 provides students with practice identifying the main ideas and key terms of this section.

📁 **Lesson Plans** For lesson planning suggestions, see p. 108 of the Lesson Plans booklet.

📁 **Political Cartoons** See p. 100 of the Political Cartoons booklet for a cartoon relevant to this section.

📖 **Section Support Transparencies** Transparency 103, *Visual Learning;* Transparency 202, *Political Cartoon*

## Background Note

### Behind the Scenes

How are the two largest cities in Texas run? In Houston, a popularly elected mayor serves as the chief executive of a mayor-council form of government. The mayor and the 14 members of the Houston city council are elected to two-year terms, and the mayor appoints the heads of nearly all city departments. Dallas has a council-manager form of government. Voters elect a mayor and 10 council members to two-year terms. The mayor and the council then hire a city manager who performs much of the managerial work of the city government.

**Answer to . . .**
**Critical Thinking** Local government must provide more services; local budgets are strained.

▲ If you compare this early 1900s photo (top) with the recent photo (bottom) of Austin, Texas, you can clearly see the city's growth. *Critical Thinking* **What is the impact of the growth of the nation's cities on local governments?**

and fire protection, sewers, waste removal, traffic regulation, public health facilities, schools, and recreation. The larger the population, the more extensive—and expensive—these services become. How—and how well—an urban area meets the demand for services may depend on the form of its government.

## Forms of City Government

Unlike the Texas county, the Texas city can exercise a large degree of independence from the State. The State legislature, in trying to maximize local control for its citizens while not losing control of local government, allows the cities to operate under one of two broad guidelines.

Cities with populations under 5,000 operate under rules set by the State legislature. These cities are known as general-law cities. Cities with populations of more than 5,000 may operate as general-law cities or they may draw up their own charters and become home-rule cities. A city **charter** is like a constitution. If the proposed charter does not violate the State constitution, and a majority of voters approve, the city then operates as a home-rule city. Home-rule cities have considerable discretion in how they conduct their municipal affairs. Some 300 cities—more than 90 percent of the cities that qualify—have chosen the home-rule charter.

Although variations can and do exist, each city in Texas, as well as in the rest of the country, has one of three basic forms of government. These are (1) a mayor-council, (2) a commission, or (3) a council-manager form of government.

### The Mayor-Council Form

Nationally, the **mayor-council government** is the oldest and still the most widely used type of city government. In Texas most general-law cities, but less than 15 percent of home-rule cities, have chosen the mayor-council form. This form features an elected mayor as the chief executive and an elected council as its legislative body.

*The council.* The members of the council are popularly elected. They serve either two- or four-year terms. Council members are now most often elected from single-member districts, although many Texas cities also elect some council members from the city at large.

*The mayor.* Generally, the voters elect the mayor. In some places, however, the council chooses one of its members to serve as mayor. The mayor presides at council meetings, usually may vote only to break a tie, and may recommend ordinances.

Mayor-council governments are often described as either the strong-mayor type or the weak-mayor type, depending on the powers given to the mayor. Most mayor-council cities operate under the weak-mayor rather than the strong-mayor plan. The strong-mayor form is generally found in larger cities, such as Houston.

In a **strong-mayor government** the mayor heads the city's administration. Houston's mayor, for example, presides over the city council and has the power to hire department heads, sign

## Mayor-Council Form of Government

**Strong Mayor Model**

Voters

elect → **Mayor** Chief Executive

elect → **Council** Legislative body

appoints → **Department Heads** Administrators of agencies such as public safety, public works, finance, education

**Weak Mayor Model**

Voters

elect → **Mayor** Chief Executive

elect → **Council** Legislative body

appoints → **Department Heads** Administrators of agencies such as public safety, public works, finance, education

*Interpreting Diagrams* This diagram compares and contrasts the two basic forms of mayor-council governments. *(a) What are the major differences between the two forms of city government? (b) Which is the better system for a large city? Explain your answer.*

ordinances passed by the council, and prepare the budget. Typically, a strong mayor is able to exercise vigorous leadership in making city policy and running the city's affairs.

In a **weak-mayor government**, the mayor has much less formal power. Executive duties are shared with other elected officials, such as the clerk, treasurer, city engineer, police chief, and council members. Powers of appointment, removal, and budget are shared with the council or exercised by that body alone.

Still, the mayor-council form has the following three large defects: (1) It depends heavily on the capacities of the mayor. (2) A major dispute between the mayor and the council can stall the workings of city government. (3) It is quite complicated and so is often little understood by the average citizen.

### The Commission Form

The **commission government** is simple in structure. Three to nine, but usually five, commissioners are popularly elected. Together, they form the city council, pass ordinances, and control the purse strings. Individually, they head the different departments of city government: police, fire, public works, finance, parks, and so

on. Thus, both legislative and executive powers are centered in one body.

The commission form of government was first used in Galveston, Texas, in 1901. A tidal surge had swept the island city the year before, killing some 6,000 people and laying much of the city of Galveston to waste. The old mayor-council regime was unable to cope with the emergency. The Texas legislature thus gave Galveston a new charter, providing for five commissioners to make and enforce the law in the stricken city. Intended to be temporary, the arrangement proved so effective that it soon spread to other Texas cities and then elsewhere in the country. By 1920, some 500 cities nationwide, including 75 in Texas, had adopted the commission form.

Depending on the city, either the voters or the commissioners themselves choose a commissioner to serve as the mayor. Like the other commissioners, the mayor heads one of the city's departments. He or she also presides at council meetings and represents the city at ceremonies. The mayor generally has no more authority than the other commissioners, however.

The simplicity of the commission form won the support of municipal reformers in the early

## Preparing for Standardized Tests

Have students read the passages under *The Mayor-Council Form* on pp. 726–727 and then answer the question below.

Which of the following is NOT a criticism of mayor-council government?

**A** It relies on the capacities of the mayor.

**B** Mayor-council disputes can stall government.

**C** The mayor has strong leadership in running city affairs.

**D** It is complicated and hard to understand.

*Answer to . . .*

**Interpreting Diagrams (a)** In the strong mayor model, the mayor appoints department heads and holds a number of responsibilities. In the weak mayor model, the council appoints department heads; the mayor and the council share responsibilities. **(b)** The strong-mayor form, because it offers clear leadership.

## Extended Class Periods

**Time** 90 minutes.

**Purpose** Hold a class debate over the different forms of city government.

**Grouping** Four groups, one for each of the three types of city government and one that will act as a jury to decide the winner of the debate.

**Activity** Each group will present arguments that support their form of city government over the other alternatives. In addition to listing advantages to their specific type of government, encourage groups to cite examples where this government has been successful.

**Roles** Discussion leader, recorder, spokesperson.

**Close** Hold a debate in which each group is allotted the same amount of time for speeches and rebuttals. Have a group of jurors determine the winner of the debate.

■ **Block Strategy (Average)**

## Point-of-Use Resources

🗀 **Government Assessment Rubrics** Class Discussion, p. 26

🗀 **Block Scheduling with Lesson Strategies** Additional activities for Chapter 25 appear on p. 31.

*Answer to . . .*

**Interpreting Diagrams** No; the legislative and executive functions are contained within the same governmental body, the commissioners.

### Commission Form of Government

Voters

elect

Board of Commissioners
forms the city council

Mayor   Public Works   Finance   Public Safety   Education

Commissioners individually serve as department heads or as mayor.

*Interpreting Diagrams* The commission form of government is one of the most uncomplicated systems for a city. ***Does a system of checks and balances exist in this form of government?***

1900s. However, experience pointed up serious flaws, and its popularity fell off rapidly.

The commission form has three chief defects:

1. The lack of a single chief executive (or, the presence of several chiefs among equals) makes it difficult to assign responsibility. This can also mean that the city has no effective political leadership.

2. A built-in tendency toward "empire building" often surfaces. Each commissioner tries to draw as much of the city's money and influence as possible to his or her own department.

3. A lack of coordination plagues the topmost levels of policymaking and administration. Each commissioner is likely to equate the citywide public good with the particular interests and functions of his or her department.

### The Council-Manager Form

Under the United States political system, it takes a certain type of skill to get elected to public office. It takes a different set of skills, however, to administer a fairly large city. Rarely are both sets of skills found in the same individual. As a result, the voters in many cities have adopted the council-manager form of government.

The **council-manager government** is a modification of the mayor-council form. Its main features are (1) a strong council of usually five or seven members elected at-large on a nonpartisan ballot; (2) a weak mayor chosen by the voters;

and (3) a manager, the city's chief administrative officer, named by the council.

The form first appeared in Ukiah, California. In 1904, that city's council appointed an "executive officer" to direct the work of city government. In 1908, a similar step in Staunton, Virginia, attracted the attention of municipal reformers, who then pushed for the adoption of council-manager government throughout the country. The first charter expressly providing for the council-manager form was granted to the city of Sumter, South Carolina, in 1912.

The council is the city's policymaking body. The manager carries out the policies that the council makes. He or she is directly responsible to that body for the efficient administration of the city. The manager serves at the council's pleasure and may be dismissed at any time and for any reason.

Today, most city managers are professionally trained career administrators. As chief administrator, the manager directs the work of all city departments and has the power to hire and fire all city employees. The manager also prepares the budget for council consideration and controls the spending of the funds the council appropriates.

The council-manager plan has the backing of nearly every expert on municipal affairs, and its use has spread widely. It is now found in more than 8,000 communities across the nation, including most cities with populations between 25,000 and 250,000. In Texas 251 of 290 home-rule cities use the council-manager form. They include such major cities as Austin, Corpus Christi, Dallas, Fort Worth, Galveston, Lubbock, and San Antonio.

The council-manager plan has three major advantages over other forms of city government:

(1) It is simple in form. (2) It is clear who has the responsibility for policy, on the one hand, and for its application, on the other. (3) It relies on highly trained experts who are skilled in budgeting, planning, and other administrative techniques.

In theory, the nonpolitical manager carries out the policies enacted by the council. Yet in practice the sharp distinction between making policy and applying policy seldom exists. The manager is very often the chief source for new ideas and fresh approaches to the city's problems. On the other hand, the city council often finds it politically useful to share the responsibility with the city manager.

Some critics of council-manager government hold that it is undemocratic, because the chief executive is not elected. Others say that it does not offer strong political leadership. This is a shortcoming, they argue, particularly in larger cities, where the population is often quite diverse and has competing interests. Support for this view can be seen in the fact that only a handful of cities with over half a million residents have a council-manager form of government nationwide. Those include Dallas, Fort Worth, and San Antonio, Texas.

## City Planning

Most cities developed haphazardly, without a plan. The results of this lack of planning can be seen in what is often called the core area or the inner city. These are the older and usually overcrowded central sections of larger cities.

Industrial plants were placed anywhere their owners chose to build them. Rail lines were run through the heart of the community. Towering buildings shut out the sunlight from the narrow streets below. Main roads were laid out too close together and sometimes too far apart. Examples are endless.

### Planning Growth

Many cities today have seen the need to create order out of their random growth. Most have established some sort of planning agency. This agency usually consists of a planning commission, supported by a trained professional staff.

A number of factors have prompted this step. The need to correct past mistakes has often been a compelling reason, of course. Then, too, many cities have recognized both the advantages that can result, and the pitfalls that can be avoided, through well-planned and orderly development. The Federal Government has spurred cities on. Most federal grant and loan programs require that cities that seek aid must first have a master plan as a guide to future growth.

### City Zoning

The practice of dividing a city into a number of districts, or zones, and regulating the uses to

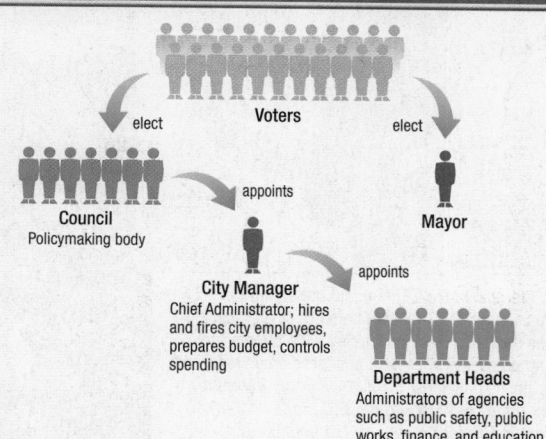

**Council-Manager Form of Government**

*Interpreting Diagrams* In the council-manager form of government, a professional manager sees that necessary services are performed for city residents. *What are the advantages of the council-manager system over the other forms of city government?*

which property in each of them may be put is called **zoning**. Generally, a zoning ordinance places each parcel of land in the city into one of three zones: residential, commercial, or industrial.

Each of these zones is then divided into subzones. For example, each of several residential zones may be broken down into several areas. One may be just for single-family residences. Another may allow both one-family and two-family dwellings. In another, apartment houses and other multifamily units may be allowed.[5]

Most zoning ordinances also prescribe limits on the height and area of buildings, determine how much of a lot may be occupied by a structure, and set out several other such restrictions on land use. They often have "setback" requirements, which state that structures must be placed at least a certain distance from the street and from other property lines.

Zoning is really a phase of city planning, and an important means for ensuring orderly growth. Zoning still meets opposition from

---

[5]Nonconforming uses in existence before a zoning ordinance is passed are almost always allowed to continue. Most ordinances give the city council the right to grant exceptions, called variances, in cases where property owners might suffer undue hardships.

## Spotlight on Technology

**Magruder's American Government Video Collection**

The Magruder's Video Collection explores key issues and debates in American government. Each segment examines an issue central to chapter content through use of historical and contemporary footage. Commentary from civic leaders in academics, government, and the media follow each segment. Critical-thinking questions focus students' attention on key issues, and may be used to stimulate discussion.

Use the Chapter 25 video segment to explore how city planning and zoning affect a city's income. (time: about five minutes) This segment focuses on Providence, Rhode Island, where the mayor is developing areas of urban blight to increase the city's tax base.

▲ Pierre-Charles L'Enfant laid out a plan for Washington, D.C., (above) before a single building was erected. His plan included wide streets running parallel east to west and large areas reserved for public buildings. *Critical Thinking Examine the photo of Washington, D.C., today (right). How is L'Enfant's plan still in evidence?*

many who object to this interference with their right to use their property as they choose. Even so, nearly every city of any size in the United States is zoned today. The city of Houston remains the largest city in the nation without an official zoning ordinance. The city council has tried three times in the past 50 years to zone the city, but Houston voters have rejected such an ordinance each time. The latest rejection came in a referendum in 1993.

Zoning ordinances must, of course, be reasonable. Remember that the 14th Amendment prohibits any State, and thus its cities, from depriving any person of life, liberty, or property without due process of law. Each of the 50 State constitutions contains a similar provision.

Clearly, zoning does deprive a person of the right to use his or her property for certain purposes. Thus, if an area is zoned only for single-family dwellings, you cannot build an apartment house or a service station on your property in that zone. Zoning can also reduce the value of a particular piece of property. A choice corner lot, for example, may be much more valuable with a drive-in restaurant on the property than a house.

While zoning may at times deprive a person of liberty or property, the key question always is this: Does it do so without due process? That is, does it do so unreasonably?

The question of reasonableness is one for the courts to decide. The Supreme Court first upheld zoning as a proper use of police power in *Euclid* v. *Amber Realty Co.*, 1926, a case involving an ordinance enacted by the city council of Euclid, Ohio.

## Municipal Functions

The services a city provides are so extensive that it is almost impossible to catalog them. Most larger cities, and many smaller ones, issue annual reports on the city's condition. These are often book-length publications.

Cities provide police and fire protection. They build and maintain streets, sidewalks, bridges, street lights, parks and playgrounds, swimming pools, golf courses, libraries, hospitals, schools, correctional institutions, day-care centers, airports, public markets, parking facilities, auditoriums, and sports arenas. They furnish public health and sanitation services, such as sewers and wastewater treatment, garbage collection and disposal, and disease prevention and eradication programs.

In addition, cities operate water, gas, light, and public transportation systems. They regulate traffic, building codes, pollution, and public utilities. Many cities also build and manage public housing projects, provide summer youth camps, build and operate docks and other harbor facilities, and maintain tourist attractions.

*Answer to . . .*

**Critical Thinking** There are still side streets running parallel and large open areas partially occupied by public buildings.

# Suburbs and Metropolitan Areas

The growth of urban areas has raised many problems for city dwellers. Urban growth also affects residents of nearby suburbs.

### The Suburban Boom

About half of all Americans live in suburbs today. The nation's suburbs began to grow rapidly in the years immediately after World War II, and then on through the 1950s and 1960s.

Mass construction techniques spurred new growth in the housing industry. In addition, the Serviceman's Readjustment Act of 1944, known as the G.I. Bill of Rights, or G.I. Bill, provided veterans with housing loans, education subsidies, and other benefits. Created to handle the post World War II problem of millions of veterans pouring back into the U.S. economy, the G.I. Bill has been widely recognized as one of the most important acts of Congress. Millions who would have flooded the labor market opted for education benefits instead. Millions also took advantage of the G.I. Bill's loans to purchase new homes in the nation's rapidly growing suburbs.

The suburban growth rate slowed somewhat in the 1970s, but it rebounded in the 1980s and 1990s, especially around the Sunbelt cities of the South and West. Suburban growth in Texas followed the nationwide pattern. Aided in the early years by the G.I. Bill, this dramatic population shift stemmed from Americans' desire for more room, cheaper land, greater privacy, and less smoke, dirt, noise, and congestion. People also sought less crime, newer and better schools, safer streets, lower taxes, and higher social status. The car and the freeway turned millions of rooted city dwellers into mobile suburbanites.

Businesses followed customers to the suburbs, often clustering in shopping centers or malls. Many industries moved from the central city in search of cheaper land, lower taxes, and a more stable labor supply. Industries also sought an escape from city

▲ Fire protection is one of the most essential city services. *Critical Thinking* **Why are such services as police and fire protection the function of local rather than National Government?**

building codes, health inspectors, and other regulations. These developments stimulated suburban growth.

This "suburbanitis," as some call it, has added to city-dwellers' woes. As high-income families have moved out, they have taken their civic, financial, and social resources with them. They have left behind center cities with high percentages of older people, low-income families, and minorities. Inevitably, both the need for and the stress on city services have multiplied.

### Metropolitan Areas

Both suburbanites and city dwellers alike face their share of problems including the need for water supplies, sewage disposal, police and fire protection, transportation, and traffic control.

Attempts to meet the needs of **metropolitan areas**—cities and the areas around them—have taken several forms. Over the years, annexation has been the standard means. Outlying areas have simply been brought within a city's boundaries. Many suburbanites resist annexation, however. Cities, as well, have often been hesitant to take on the burdens involved.

Another approach has been to create special districts designed to meet the problems of heavily populated urban areas. Their boundaries frequently cut across county and city lines to include an entire metropolitan area. They often are called metropolitan districts.

These metropolitan districts are generally set up for a single purpose—for example, parks, as in the Cleveland Metropolitan Park Development District. In some cases, however, these districts can also handle a number of functions.

In Oregon, a regional agency known as Metro is responsible for land-use and transportation planning, solid-waste disposal programs, and the operation of the Oregon Convention Center, the Oregon Zoo, Portland's Center for the Performing Arts, and other public facilities.

Yet another approach to the challenges facing metropolitan areas is increasing the authority of

 ***Take It to the Net***

For career-related links and activities, visit the *Magruder's American Government* companion Web site in the Social Studies area at the Prentice Hall School Web site.

---

## Make It Relevant

### Careers in Government—City Park Worker

Americans love their parks. Most urban areas in the U.S. have several small parks and one or more large ones. Local governments spend about $4 billion a year on their parks, including the money to pay the nation's 300,000-plus city park workers. These men and women work at a wide variety of jobs, from designing gardens to entertaining park visitors to accounting park finances. They enjoy the advantages of a government job—and what has to be an unbeatable work environment. **Skills Activity** Have students visit a local park, and try to list jobs that must be fulfilled to run it. Then have students consider which of these jobs they might enjoy doing, and write paragraphs explaining why they would or would not be interested in a career as a city park worker. **(Basic)**

*Answer to . . .*

**Critical Thinking** Local officials are better equipped to know what and where services are needed.

## Point–of–Use Resources

**Guide to the Essentials** Chapter 25, Section 2, p. 134 provides support for students who need additional review of section content. Spanish support is available in the Spanish edition of the Guide on p. 127.

**Quiz** Unit 7 booklet, p. 16 includes matching and multiple-choice questions to check students' understanding of Section 2 content.

**Presentation Pro CD-ROM** Quizzes and multiple-choice questions check students' understanding of Section 2 content.

## Answers to . . .

### Section 2 Assessment

**1.** The mayor-council, commission, and council-manager forms.
**2.** The official name of the city, boundaries, a declaration that the city is a municipal corporation, outline of city form.
**3.** Whether the mayor or the council appoints department heads; whether power is shared with the council or exercised by the mayor alone.
**4.** Examples: Police and fire protection; build and maintain streets, bridges, and libraries; furnish public health and sanitation facilities; operate water, gas, light, and transportation systems.
**5.** Advantages: **(a)** It can provide strong leadership. **(b)** Simplicity; short ballot. **(c)** Simplicity; responsibilities clear; relies on trained experts. Disadvantages: **(a)** Depends heavily on mayor's capabilities; disputes between the mayor and the council can stall government; complicated. **(b)** Lacks a single chief executive; tends toward "empire-building"; lacks coordination among commissioners. **(c)** Seen as undemocratic; does not offer strong leadership.

### Answer to . . .

**Interpreting Political Cartoons**
**(a)** Tourists are stopping at a scenic lookout **(b)** Urban sprawl has replaced natural vistas.

*Interpreting Political Cartoons* **(a)** What is happening in this cartoon? **(b)** What does the cartoon suggest about urban sprawl?

counties. Among local governments around the country, counties are generally the largest in area and are most likely to include those places demanding new and increased services.

## Cooperation Among Local Governments

Like other areas of the country, Texas recognizes the need for coordination and cooperation among local governments. The State has attempted to meet this need through the creation of councils of governments (COGs). The first council of governments was organized in 1966 with the creation of the North Central Texas Council of Governments. Since then, 23 other COGs have been created.

Councils of governments, which are also known as regional councils, consist of representatives of various local governments within a specified group of counties. For example, the East Texas Council of Governments serves 139 local governments, including 14 counties, 72 cities, 40 school districts, and 13 other special districts.

Membership is voluntary and based on a vote of the local government's officials. For example, if a Texas county joins a council of government, it does so by a vote of the Commissioners Court.

Councils of governments work to assist local governments in a variety of ways. A primary function is to coordinate planning and development of local services, such as public transportation. COGs may also be called on by the State and Federal governments to help evaluate local requests for State or federal funds.

## Section 2 Assessment

### Key Terms and Main Ideas
1. What are three major forms of city government?
2. What kinds of provisions might you find in a city **charter?**
3. What are the key differences between a **strong-mayor government** and a **weak-mayor government?**
4. List at least five functions of municipal governments.

### Critical Thinking
5. **Making Comparisons** Create a chart comparing the advantages and disadvantages of these types of city government: **(a)** the mayor-council form; **(b)** the commission form; **(c)** the council-manager form.
6. **Determining Cause and Effect** Trace the history of American population shifts, first to the cities and then to the suburbs. Include economic and social reasons for the trends.

7. **Drawing Conclusions** How did the G.I. Bill help bring about change in American culture?

 **Take It to the Net**

8. Read about the effect of urbanization on water supply and quality. Then create a flowchart that shows (1) why urbanization affects water supply and quality, (2) how urbanization affects water supply and quality, and (3) how communities can meet these challenges. Use the links provided in the Social Studies area at the following Web site for help in completing this activity. **www.phschool.com**

**6.** Possible answer: In 1790, only 5 percent of the nation's population lived in cities. Today 75 percent live in cities and suburbs. This shift occurred as population began to concentrate in industrial and transportation centers at the same time that fewer people were needed on farms.
**7.** More people could afford to buy houses in the suburbs, thus contributing to suburban growth.

 **Take It to the Net**

8. Direct students to the Social Studies area at the Prentice Hall School Web site. The *Magruder's American Government* companion Web site includes the directions and links needed to complete the activity. It also provides a printable Internet activity worksheet with scoring rubrics for assessment. Students' flowcharts should indicate an understanding of the impact of urbanization on water supply and quality.

## Section Preview

### OBJECTIVES

1. **Analyze** the structure and functions of State government.
2. **Identify** the types of services that Texas State and local governments provide.

### WHY IT MATTERS

People are often unaware of the vast array of services provided by State and local governments. The cost of these services has become a huge burden to many States, including Texas, which struggle to keep up with the expenses of growing populations.

### POLITICAL DICTIONARY

★ **Medicaid**
★ **welfare**
★ **entitlement**

Texas State government, you may by now have noticed, is quite similar in form to the Federal Government. Each has three branches of government, a bicameral legislature, its own constitution, and so on. Given these similarities, it is easy to overlook the many unique features and functions of Texas State government, and the many services it provides to its citizens.

## What State Governments Do

Over the course of this book, you have read many times about the key role of the States in the American federal system. Recall that the Framers feared a strong central government. As a result, they created a system in which the States held many important powers. The Constitution reserves to the States all those powers not expressly delegated to Congress and not specifically denied to the States. These reserved powers are broad—in fact, they are too numerous to list here. In addition, the exercise of these powers varies greatly from one State to the next. Again, that fact reflects the conscious aim of the Framers and the federal system they created.

Along with the powers reserved to the States come some important responsibilities. Like the Federal Government, State governments aim to fulfill the purposes set forward in the Preamble to the Constitution; that is, they seek to "establish Justice, insure domestic Tranquility, provide for the common defence, promote the general Welfare, and secure the Blessings of Liberty. . . . "

## Services That Texas Provides

Texas provides services to its citizens in two ways: (1) directly, through State agencies and programs, and (2) indirectly, through the local governments they establish. The services that Texas and its local units provide fall into a number of broad categories.

### Education

The education of Texas residents is one of the most important responsibilities that the State has assumed. It is also the most expensive entry in the State budget. At more than $19 billion,

◀ *Students at the University of Texas, Austin.* The State of Texas plays a major role in funding the University of Texas system.

**733**

## Reading Strategy

### Organizing Information

Tell students that they will be reading about the many services that the Texas State government provides. As they read, have them create a web diagram to organize the information in the section. (They might write *State Services* in the center circle and the general categories in the surrounding circles.)

## Point-of-Use Resources

**Guided Reading and Review** Unit 7 booklet, p. 17 provides students with practice identifying the main ideas and key terms of this section.

**Lesson Plans** For lesson planning suggestions, see p. 109 of the Lesson Plans booklet.

**Political Cartoons** See p. 101 of the Political Cartoons booklet for a cartoon relevant to this section.

**Section Support Transparencies** Transparency 104, *Visual Learning;* Transparency 203, *Political Cartoon*

**Simulations and Data Graphing CD-ROM** offers data graphing tools that give students practice with creating and interpreting graphs.

---

### Background Note

#### Behind the Scenes

With nearly 4 million students in Texas public schools today, the Texas Education Agency takes its responsibilities seriously. In its "Compact with Texans," the agency names the following principles to which it aspires: trustworthiness, responsibility, respect, caring, citizenship, and fairness. The TEA is striving to boost the percentages of students passing State tests and graduating from high school.

---

### *Answer to ...*

**Interpreting Graphs** Possible answer: Their role is significant. The impact of much of the spending shown on the graph can be seen daily as people attend school, drive on State and local highways, or visit State and local parks.

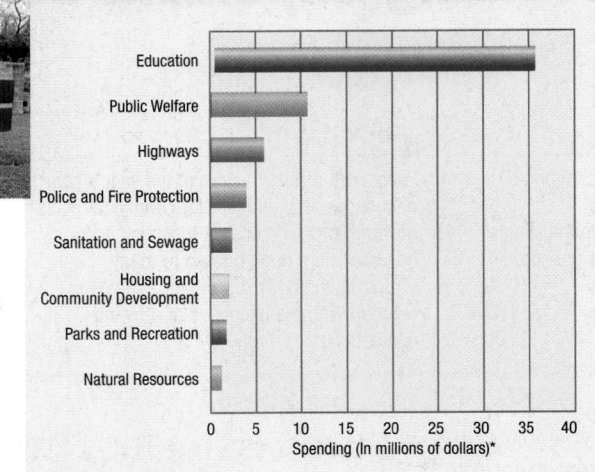

**Selected Texas State and Local Spending***

*Interpreting Graphs* This graph shows major categories of Texas State and local spending, including State parks, as shown above. **What do these categories suggest about the role of State and local spending in Texans' daily lives?**

SOURCE: U. S. Census Bureau

education represents nearly 40 percent of all State expenditures.

The cost of providing for public education rises each year, and at the same time, voters demand better schools. As a result, State and local governments have continually increased their educational funding, especially for students in the primary and secondary grades.

Primary and secondary public education is largely the responsibility of local governments. Local taxes, especially property taxes, provide more than half of the funding for schools. The State provides somewhat less than half, and the rest comes from the Federal Government. The total spent on students in Texas public primary and secondary schools topped $25 billion for the school year ending in 2000. That worked out to an average expenditure of more than $6,300 per student.

Where does the money provided by the State of Texas come from? The Texas constitution of 1876 provided a Permanent School Fund from which the legislature provides funds to school districts. The Permanent School Fund is an endowment overseen by the State Board of Education and consisting of revenues from State lands, including their oil and gas revenues. (An endowment is a gift of money or property that provides income for a person or institution.) The interest from this endowment must be used to support public schools. The State also appropriates money from its annual taxes to school districts.

In addition, the State sets guidelines in order to maintain high quality in the schools. For example, State laws establish teacher qualifications, curricula, quality standards for educational materials, and the length of the school year.

At the college and university levels, the State likewise plays a major role. The State understands that for businesses to succeed in Texas, a ready supply of highly trained college graduates is key. Such a labor pool is also necessary to attract new businesses.

Every State has a public higher education system, and in Texas that system is extensive. It includes 35 public universities, 50 community colleges, 7 medical schools and other health-related institutions, 7 multi-institution teaching centers, 4 technical colleges, and 3 state colleges.

Education at State universities and colleges is generally much less expensive than at private institutions. In fact, tuition costs for State residents enrolled at Texas colleges and universities are among the lowest in the country. Nevertheless, several Texas universities, such as the University of Texas (Austin) and Texas A & M, are among the ranks of the nation's finest institutions.

### Public Health and Welfare

Texas takes an active role in promoting the health and welfare of its citizens. The State pursues this goal by a variety of means and through the functions of such State agencies as the Department of Human Services and the Department of Mental Health and Mental Retardation. Health and human services ranks as the second largest service expenditure in the State, after education, and makes up about one third of the State budget.

1. *Public health.* Texas funds ambitious public health programs. The State operates public hospitals and offers direct care to millions of citizens. It immunizes children against dangerous childhood diseases, such as measles and mumps. With the Federal Government, Texas also administers **Medicaid,** which provides medical insurance to low-income families.

Soaring costs in the health-care industry have placed a great strain on many States' budgets, however. Many governors, State legislators, mayors, and other public officials, including those in Texas, are among the leading advocates of reform of the nation's health-care system.

2. *Cash assistance.* Another major area in which States contribute to the well-being of their citizens is cash assistance to the poor, commonly called **welfare.** The States, Texas among them, are now taking a leading role in this area.

Between 1936 and 1996, the Federal Government provided cash assistance to needy families through the Aid to Families with Dependent Children (AFDC) program.[6] AFDC was an **entitlement** program, which means that anyone who met the eligibility requirements was entitled to receive benefits.

The Federal Government and the States shared the costs of providing AFDC benefits. These costs rose dramatically as the number of AFDC recipients skyrocketed from 1.7 percent of the nation's population in 1960 to 4.1 percent in 1970, 4.7 percent in 1980, and an all-time high of 5.5 percent in 1993 and 1994.

Critics of AFDC pointed to its soaring costs and expanding caseloads as signs of serious problems with the program. They also saw the lack of a limit on the number of months a person could receive AFDC benefits as a serious omission. As a result, these critics argued, the program encouraged people to depend on government assistance rather than to become self-supporting.

In 1996, Congress responded to these concerns by passing the Personal Responsibility and Work Opportunity Reconciliation Act. This act replaced AFDC with a new and strikingly different program, Temporary Assistance for Needy Families (TANF).

---

[6]AFDC was authorized by Title IV of the Social Security Act of 1935. Until 1962, the program was named Aid to Dependent Children, as the 1935 act was aimed simply at needy dependent children.

Unlike AFDC, TANF is a block grant: The Federal Government gives States a fixed amount of money each year, regardless of whether the number of TANF recipients rises or falls. States are free to use the federal grant, plus the State funds that they are obliged to contribute, to design and implement their own welfare programs.

TANF limits recipients to a total of five years of assistance during the course of their lifetime. (Some States have imposed even shorter time limits.) It also requires recipients to work or participate in some form of vocational training or community service.

Texas serves its TANF recipients through an employment and training program called Choices. The program supports participants in

## Spotlight on Texas Government

**Texas Universities** Texas is justifiably proud of its State university system. The faculty includes eight Nobel laureates, one Pulitzer Prize winner, and many members of prestigious academic societies. Over $1 billion in research is conducted within the system every year.

There are currently over 150,000 students enrolled in the University of Texas system. Slightly over half the enrolled students are minorities, and just over half are women. Four of the five American undergraduate schools with the greatest number of Hispanics graduating are within the Texas system.

The Texas Constitution of 1876 instructed the legislature to set up "a university of the first class" and authorized the voters to decide where it should be located. The legislature created the University of Texas in 1881. By vote of the people, the main university was located in Austin and the medical branch in Galveston. Since that time the legislature has expanded the University to its current 15 institutions, including 9 academic and 6 health organizations.

Texas A&M University, the first public institution of higher education in Texas, was opened in 1876 as the Agricultural and Mechanical College of Texas. It owes its origin to the Morrill Act of 1862, which established the nation's land-grant college system. Today the curriculum includes not only agriculture and engineering, but architecture, business, education, liberal arts, medicine, and the sciences. The University's College of Architecture provides direct assistance to rural residents along the Mexican border, and the George Bush School of Government and Public Service prepares leaders in the private, public, and non-profit sectors of society.

**Analyzing Texas Government**

*How does the State as a whole benefit from having strong universities?*

---

**RESOURCE PRO®**

Resource Pro® CD-ROM contains an electronic version of each activity found in the Teaching Resources as well as additional resources such as Supreme Court cases. The Planning Express® feature allows you to customize and create daily lesson plans within minutes.

# SKILLS FOR LIFE

## Filing a Consumer Complaint

One of the functions of American government is to protect consumers. If you believe you're the victim of a money scam, an unsafe product, shoddy repair work, false advertising, or a warranty that was not honored, you can file a consumer complaint. The box below lists federal and private sources of consumer help. For State help, try the attorney general's office. To file a complaint, follow these steps:

**1. Keep all records of transactions.** Get estimates in writing. If a company representative gives you promises over the telephone, ask for them in writing. Get the name of the representative you're speaking with, the time of the call, and take notes from the conversation. What kinds of paper work should you save?

**2. If you do not get satisfaction, file a complaint.** Many disagreements can be worked out between you and the individual or company involved. But if that doesn't work, determine what government

agency handles your type of problem and file your complaint in writing. Using these letter-writing tips, write a sample first sentence of a complaint letter:

• Include specific facts, such as the date and place of your purchase and a serial or model number. If you are complaining about a service you received, describe the service and who performed it.
• Include <u>copies</u> of all relevant documents.
• Your tone should be firm, but polite—not angry, sarcastic, or threatening. The person reading your letter probably was not responsible for your problem, but may be helpful in fixing it.

**3. File the complaint promptly.** Some complaints must be made within a certain amount of time, so don't delay. What should you do if you get no response?

### Help for Consumers

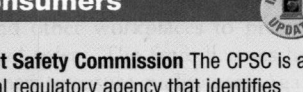

**Consumer Product Safety Commission** The CPSC is an independent federal regulatory agency that identifies unsafe consumer products and has the authority to ban the sale of them. CPSC responds to consumer complaints.
http://www.cpsc.gov

**Consumer Information Center** The CIC, based in Pueblo, Colorado, is perhaps the best-known source of federal consumer information. The CIC publishes a free catalog of more than 200 free and low-cost publications.
http://www.pueblo.gsa.gov/backgrnd.htm

**ConsumerWorld** This is a nonprofit Web site with links to federal, State, local, and private consumer resources. Read about the latest money scams, file a complaint, learn about your consumer rights, find the wholesale price of a car, or look up product reviews.
http://www.consumerworld.org

### Test for Success

Write a fictional letter to a State consumer protection agency to complain about a defective product you bought. Briefly describe problems you had in getting the manufacturer to fix or replace the product.

# Financing State and Local Government

## Section Preview

### OBJECTIVES

1. **Describe** the major Federal and State limits on raising revenue.
2. **List** the four principles of sound taxation.
3. **Identify** major tax and nontax sources of Texas State and local revenue.
4. **Explain** the State budget process.

### WHY IT MATTERS

You pay State and local taxes—indeed, you cannot avoid them. Like most of us, you probably find them to be at least inconvenient, but they are also quite necessary for financing State and local government.

### POLITICAL DICTIONARY

★ sales tax
★ regressive tax
★ income tax
★ progressive tax
★ property tax
★ assessment
★ inheritance tax
★ estate tax
★ State budget

You know by now that government is an expensive proposition, and it is becoming more so from year to year. Altogether, the 50 States and their thousands of local governments now take in and spend well over $1 trillion a year. How does Texas government get all the money it needs, and how do its officials decide what to spend it on?

## Limits on Raising Revenue

This year the State of Texas will take in nearly $50 billion in revenue. About half of it will come from taxes, and the rest will come from a number of nontax and federal sources. Recall that taxes are charges made to raise money for public purposes.

The power to tax is one of the major powers States share with the National Government. In a strictly legal sense, then, the Texas government's taxing power is limited only by the restrictions imposed by the federal Constitution and those imposed by Texas law.[7]

Local governments collect taxes too, of course. However, all of them acquire their taxing power from the State. Thus, Texas constitutional and statutory provisions, as well as the restrictions set out in the United States Constitution, limit the taxing powers of local governments in Texas.

### Federal Limitations

The Federal Constitution does place some restrictions on the power to tax at the State and local levels. Although few in number, those limits have a major impact on the States and their local governments.

1. *Interstate and Foreign Commerce.* The Constitution denies the States the power to "lay any Imposts or Duties on Imports or Exports"

---

[7]Remember, a State's power to tax is also limited by any number of practical considerations, such as economic and political factors.

▲ Property taxes, including those on houses such as these, are a major source of local revenue.

---

**739**

## Reading Strategy

### Drawing Inferences

Tell students that they will be reading about the financing of State and local government. Have them suppose that the State of Texas needs to increase revenues significantly to meet its spending needs. Have them note, as they read, all the possible ways to solve this problem. They should also note solutions that are forbidden by federal or State law.

## Point-of-Use Resources

📁 **Guided Reading and Review** Unit 7 booklet, p. 19 provides students with practice identifying the main ideas and key terms of this section.

📁 **Lesson Plans** For lesson planning suggestions, see p. 110 of the Lesson Plans booklet.

📁 **Political Cartoons** See p. 102 of the Political Cartoons booklet for a cartoon relevant to this section.

📁 **Section Support Transparencies** Transparency 105, *Visual Learning*; Transparency 204, *Political Cartoon*

---

and "any Duty of Tonnage."[8] In effect, the States are prohibited from taxing interstate and foreign commerce. The Supreme Court has often held that because the Constitution gives Congress the power to regulate that trade, the States are generally forbidden to do so.

2. *The Federal Government and Its Agencies.* The Supreme Court's decision in *McCulloch* v. *Maryland,* 1819, bars States from taxing the Federal Government or any of its agencies or functions. They are forbidden to do so because, as Chief Justice Marshall put it in *McCulloch*: "The power to tax involves the power to destroy." (See page 95.)

3. *14th Amendment Limitations.* The Due Process and Equal Protection clauses place limits on the power to tax at the State and local levels. The Due Process Clause requires that taxes (1) be imposed and administered fairly, (2) be not so heavy as to actually confiscate property, and (3) be imposed only for public purposes. The Equal Protection Clause forbids making unreasonable classifications for the purpose of taxation. The clause thus forbids tax classifications made on the basis of race, religion, nationality, political party membership, or any other factors that are deemed to be unreasonable.

Most tax laws involve some form of classification, however. An income tax is applied only to the class of persons who have income. Likewise, a cigarette tax is collected only from those who buy cigarettes, a property tax only from those who own property, and so on. The Equal Protection Clause does not prevent these and similar classifications, because they are reasonable ones.

### State Limitations

Each State's constitution limits the taxing powers of that State. State constitutions also limit the taxing powers of their local governments. As local units have no independent powers, the only taxes they can impose are those the State allows them to levy. For example, the Texas constitution provides that taxes be levied only for public purposes and that they be applied uniformly. It also provides that taxes be collected only within the geographic limits of the governmental units that levy them and that no arbitrary or unreasonable classifications be made for tax purposes. As in most of the States, the Texas constitution and statutes exempt the properties of churches, private schools, museums, cemeteries, and the like from taxation.

## The Principles of Sound Taxation

Any tax, if taken by itself, can be shown to be unfair. If a government's total revenues were to come from one tax—say, a sales, an income, or a property tax—its tax system would be inequitable. Some people would bear a much greater burden than others, and some would bear little or none. Each tax should thus be defensible as part of a tax system.

In his classic 1776 book *The Wealth of Nations,* Scottish economist Adam Smith laid out four principles of a sound tax system, which most tax experts still cite today:

▲ **Petroleum Revenues** Texas levies a tax on the production of oil and natural gas, generating a significant source of revenue for the State.

**PRIMARY Sources** "1. *The subjects of every state ought to contribute towards the support of the government as nearly as possible, in proportion to their respective abilities; that is, in proportion to the revenue which they respectively enjoy under the protection of the state.* 2. *The tax which each individual is bound to pay ought to be certain, and not arbitrary.*

---

[8]Article I, Section 10, Clauses 2 and 3.

---

## Organizing Information

To make sure students understand the main points of this section, you may wish to use the web graphic organizer to the right.

Tell students that a web provides an outline of a main idea and its supporting details. Have students use the web to record information about how the State of Texas raises money. *Sources of Revenue* should appear in the center circle of the web.

**Teaching Tip** A template for this graphic organizer can be found in the Section Support Transparencies, Transparency 1.

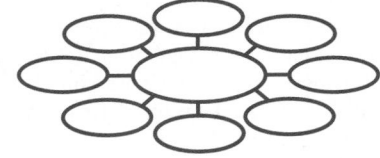

*3. Every tax ought to be levied at the time, or in the manner, in which it is most likely to be convenient for the contributor to pay it.*
*4. Every tax ought to be so contrived as to take out and to keep out of the pockets of the people as little as possible over and above what it brings into the public treasury. . . .* "

Shaping a tax system that meets these standards of equality, certainty, convenience, and economy is just about impossible. Still, that goal should be pursued.

## Sources of Texas State Revenue

Article 3, Section 49, of the Texas constitution says in part "No debt shall be created by or on behalf of the state. . . ." This simple statement has a considerable impact on the Texas budgetary process. Unlike the Federal Government, Texas cannot use deficit financing, which is borrowing with the intent of paying back the debt sometime in the future. The State constitution requires that Texas operate on a "pay as you go" basis.

As in most States, the Texas government's largest source of revenue is State taxes, which comprise approximately 51 percent of the State's income. Federal funds provide an additional 30 percent or so. The remaining 19 percent comes from miscellaneous nontax sources, such as court fines, the sale and leasing of public lands, and interest from loans, investments, and late tax payments.

### The Sales Tax

The sales tax accounts for more than half of all tax monies the State of Texas collects each year. It provides nearly 30 percent of all State revenue.

A **sales tax** is a tax placed on the sale of various commodities; the purchaser pays it. It may be either general or selective in form. A general sales tax is one applied to the sale of most commodities. A selective sales tax is one placed only on the sale of certain commodities, such as cigarettes, liquor, or gasoline.

Texas levies a general sales tax of 6.25 percent, compared with a low of 3 percent in Colorado and a high of 7 percent in Mississippi and Rhode Island. The State exempts certain items from the tax, such as food items, drugs,

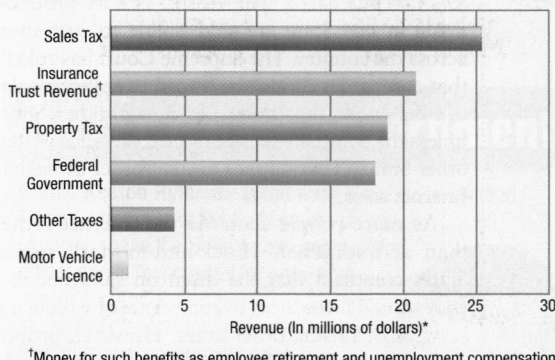

### Selected Texas State and Local Revenue*

Sales Tax
Insurance Trust Revenue[†]
Property Tax
Federal Government
Other Taxes
Motor Vehicle Licence

Revenue (In millions of dollars)*

[†]Money for such benefits as employee retirement and unemployment compensation that is held in interest-paying trust funds

SOURCE: U. S. Census Bureau

*Interpreting Graphs* This graph shows the major sources of State and local revenue in Texas. ***Are the types of taxes shown on the graph the fairest ways for Texas and its local governments to pay for services? Explain your answer.***

and newspapers. In addition to Texas, 44 other States levy a general sales tax.

All States now levy a selective sales tax on gasoline, alcoholic beverages, insurance policies, and cigarettes. Most States also impose additional selective sales taxes.[9] For example, Texas levies a selective sales tax on hotel and motel accommodations and automobile purchases.

Sales taxes are widely used for two major reasons: (1) They are easy to collect, and (2) they are dependable revenue producers. Yet a sales tax is a **regressive tax**—that is, it is not levied according to a person's ability to pay. Everyone in Texas who buys, say, a hammer has to pay the same amount of sales tax on it. Therefore, to a poor person who buys the hammer the tax is a heavier burden than it is to a wealthy person who buys it. Critics of regressive taxes say that States should not raise so much of their revenue from citizens least able to pay.

### Sales Taxes and the Internet

The latest controversy over sales taxes involves the Internet. The last few years have seen explosive

---

[9]Alaska, Delaware, Montana, New Hampshire, and Oregon have no general sales tax, but each imposes selective sales taxes.

A C T I V I T Y

**American Government, American Humor**
Share the following quotation with students:

*"The thing generally raised on city land is taxes."*
—Charles Dudley Warner

**Discussion** Have students explain Warner's pun. Ask: What does it say about the way local governments are financed? What does it say about citizens' attitude toward that financing?
**(Basic)**

## Customize for

### Less Proficient Readers

Using the words from the Political Dictionary in this section, ask students to create a crossword puzzle, word search, or other type of word game. Have them include with their game clues or definitions for each of the terms. After the word activities have been created, ask students to exchange with a partner. Students can return completed activities to the original creator for grading.

## Point–of–Use Resources

📁 **The Living Constitution** Limited Government, p. 4

📖 **Basic Principles of the Constitution Transparencies** Transparency 16-22, *Limited Government*

*Answer to . . .*

**Interpreting Graphs** Students' answers should show an understanding of the difference between regressive and progressive taxes and their relative fairness.

---

## CONSTITUTIONAL PRINCIPLES

**Limited Government**
State legislatures have the power to decide what taxes a State will levy, and at what rates. However, the people of a State have often affected the levying of State taxes through use of ballot initiatives or referenda. In the 2000 general election, ballot initiatives concerning State taxes were raised in about a third of the States.

**Activity**
Have students research tax-related ballot initiatives and referenda in the 2000 election. Assign groups several States, and have them describe any tax-related initiatives and whether they passed or failed. Use the links provided at the Magruder's companion Web site.
**www.phschool.com**

**741**

## Point-of-Use Resources

**Guide to the Essentials** Chapter 25, Section 4, p. 136 provides support for students who need additional review of section content. Spanish support is available in the Spanish edition of the Guide on p. 129.

**Quiz** Unit 7 booklet, p. 20 includes matching and multiple-choice questions to check students' understanding of Section 4 content.

**Presentation Pro CD-ROM** Quizzes and multiple-choice questions check students' understanding of Section 4 content.

## Answers to . . .

### Section 4 Assessment

**1. (a)** Regressive, because it is not levied according to a person's ability to pay. When a poor person and a wealthy person buy the same item, the tax is a heavier burden on the poor person. **(b)** Progressive, because it is levied according to a person's ability to pay. The higher a person's income, the more tax he or she pays.
**2.** States cannot tax interstate and foreign commerce, or the Federal Government or any of its agencies or functions. Taxes must be fair and may be imposed only for public purposes.
**3.** Through sales taxes, income taxes, property taxes, inheritance and estate taxes, amusement taxes, and license fees.
**4.** Corporate income; franchise license; oil and natural gas production.
**5. (a)** (1) Citizens should contribute to the government in proportion to their income. (2) The tax amount should be clear. (3) Paying taxes should be convenient. (4) The tax amount should not exceed what is necessary to run the government and its programs.
**(b)** It is important that (1) taxes are levied fairly; (2) taxpayers know exactly how much they are paying in taxes; (3) taxpayers be able to fulfill their tax obligations easily; (4) people do not have to pay excessive amounts in taxes.
**6. (a)** Lotteries can increase a State's income, but the people who partici-

growth in sales made over the Web. Yet States are prohibited from collecting sales taxes on most Internet purchases. The reason is that products

The States and many of their local governments also make money from a number of publicly operated business enterprises. Toll bridges and toll roads are popular in the East. Several States, notably Washington, are in the ferry business. North Dakota markets a flour sold under the brand name Dakota-Maid and is in the commercial banking business. California operates a short railway line in San Francisco.

Many cities throughout the country own and operate their water, electric power, and bus transportation systems. Some cities operate farmers' markets; rent space in their office buildings, warehouses, and housing projects; and operate dams and wharves. Receipts from such businesses support the local governments that own them.

Texas and many other States have relaxed their once-strict antigambling laws, hoping to attract dollars, jobs, and tourists. State-run lotteries now bring in some $12 billion a year for 38 States and the District of Columbia, including $1.3 billion in revenue from the Texas Lottery.

### Borrowing

Texas and its local governments often must borrow money for unusually large undertakings, such as the construction of public buildings, bridges, and highways, that cannot be paid for out of current income. That borrowing is often done by issuing bonds, much as the Federal

The individual income tax is usually a **progressive tax**—that is, the higher your income, the more tax you pay. Income tax rates

Government does. Texas State and local bonds are easy to market because the interest from them is not taxed by the Federal Government or by the State of Texas.

In the past, many State and local governments have defaulted on their debts. Thus, most State constitutions now place detailed limits on the power to borrow. States' debts now exceed $450 billion, and local governments owe more than $700 billion. In Texas the State government debt is nearly $15 billion, and local governments owe more than $75 billion.

## The Texas State Budget

A **State budget** is a financial plan for the use of public money, personnel, and property. In its budget, the State sets its priorities and decides who gets what and how much.

Forty-seven States have adopted the executive budget, by which the governor has the power to prepare the State budget and the authority to administer the funds that the legislature has appropriated. In Texas, Mississippi, and South Carolina, however, the governor and the legislature share responsibility for the preparation of the budget. The Texas governor does have the power to administer the appropriated funds, but otherwise the budget process in Texas is another reflection of how the governor's power is limited.

## Section 4 Assessment

### Key Terms and Main Ideas

1. Explain whether the following taxes are either **regressive** or **progressive**: **(a)** sales tax; **(b)** income tax.
2. What limits does the Federal Government put on States' ability to tax?
3. In what ways do States tax individuals?
4. In what ways do States tax businesses?

### Critical Thinking

5. **Determining Relevance (a)** Restate in your own words Adam Smith's four principles of sound taxation. **(b)** What do you think makes each of them important?

6. **Identifying Alternatives (a)** What might be the advantages and disadvantages of raising revenue through a State-run lottery? **(b)** a State-run business? **(c)** property taxes?

### Take It to the Net

7. Find out how other States get revenue. Then create a table that compares Texas State revenue sources with those from at least one other State in a different region of the country. How do revenue sources differ among States? What might be the reasons for these differences? Use the links provided in the Social Studies area at the following Web site for help in completing this activity.
**www.phschool.com**

pate are often those least able to afford to do so. **(b)** State-run businesses can increase a State's income, but can give government an unfair advantage over private businesses.
**(c)** Property taxes can be equitable because the people with the most-highly valued property pay the most taxes. However, property taxes can become so high that people can no longer afford to own their property.

### Take It to the Net

7. Direct students to the Social Studies area at the Prentice Hall School Web site. The *Magruder's American Government* companion Web site includes the directions and links needed to complete the activity. It also provides a printable Internet activity worksheet with scoring rubrics for assessment. Students should show how Texas State revenue compares with the revenue of a State in another region and draw appropriate conclusions.

# on the Supreme Court

## Must Local Government Follow the "One Person, One Vote" Rule?

*As the Supreme Court ruled in **Baker v. Carr** (1962), State legislatures must be apportioned according to population so that each person's vote has roughly equal weight. Should this principle apply to local government as well?*

### Board of Estimate of City of New York v. Morris (1989)

New York City's Board of Estimate manages all city property, sets salaries of city employees, grants all city contracts, and shares authority with the City Council over the city budget. The Board has eight members: the mayor, comptroller, and president of the city council (chosen by citywide election), and the presidents of New York's five boroughs (chosen by borough election). The three citywide members each have two votes on the Board, while the borough representatives have one.

Morris and others who lived and voted in Brooklyn, the most populous borough, filed suit in 1981. They argued that the vote of each person in the less-populous boroughs counted more than each vote in Brooklyn, because all boroughs had equal representation on the Board despite great differences in population.

A federal district court dismissed the case, concluding that the Board was a "nonelective, nonlegislative body." Therefore, past Supreme Court decisions regarding apportionment did not apply to the Board. A court of appeals reversed that decision. It concluded that the Board really is an elective body, and ordered the district court to decide whether the Board's selection process met the "one person, one vote" standard. The district court ruled that it did not meet this standard, the court of appeals agreed with that ruling, and the City appealed to the Supreme Court.

### Arguments for the Board of Estimate

1. The Board is a unique political body with non-legislative powers. Thus it should not have to meet the "one person, one vote" standard that legislatures must meet.
2. The Board has proven itself effective in the past and should not be disturbed. It is essential to the governing of New York City.
3. The fact that boroughs of unequal population have equal representation on the Board is not critical, because the three citywide members have double votes and can outvote the five borough members. Thus citywide interests predominate on the Board.

### Arguments for Morris

1. In order for all citizens to have fair and effective representation in government, all votes must carry approximately equal weight. The Board's structure is inconsistent with this principle.
2. The principle of "one person, one vote" applies to local governments as well as to State legislatures. The Board is sufficiently legislative in its powers and must follow this principle.
3. The at-large members do not always vote together, so their majority is only theoretical.

---

### Decide for Yourself

1. Review the constitutional grounds on which each side based its arguments and the specific arguments each side presented.
2. Debate the opposing viewpoints presented in this case. Which viewpoint do you favor?
3. Predict the impact of the Court's decision on local elections and local politics. (To read a summary of the Court's decision, turn to the Supreme Court Glossary on page 799.)

---

## Corner

 **Online**

📁 **Close Up on the Supreme Court** *Board of Estimate of City of New York v. Morris,* p. 26 provides an activity to extend coverage of this case.

To keep up-to-date on Close Up news and activities, visit Close Up Online at

**www.closeup.org**

---

## Must Local Government Follow the "One Person, "One Vote" Rule?

**Focus** Before reading the feature, have students review *Baker v. Carr,* discussed in the Chapter 1 *Close Up on the Supreme Court* feature. Then call on a volunteer to explain the "one person, one vote" rule. *(In a representative democracy, all persons' votes should be roughly equal in weight)* Finally, elicit students' responses to the question posed in the title.

**Instruct** Have the class read the feature, choose the side that they agree with, and draw a poster that represents their point of view. Call on volunteers to present their poster to the class. Finally, have the class read and then discuss the Court's decision.

**Close/Reteach** Explain that the Court's decision was in part based on the argument that the Board possessed sufficient legislative powers to require the application of the "one person, one vote" rule. Have students brainstorm a list of the Board's functions that are legislative in character. *(manages city property; sets salaries; grants city contracts; shares authority over the city budget)*

💿 **Keep It Current CD-ROM** includes government-related projects by unit. The CD-ROM links to the Prentice Hall School Web site and may be used for daily updates.

### Answers to . . .
**Decide for Yourself**
**1.** The Board argued that it is a unique body with non-legislative powers, and thus does not have to meet the same standards that legislative bodies do. Morris argued that the "one person, one vote" principle applies to local governments.
**2.** Answers will vary, but should be supported with valid reasoning.
**3.** The Court ruled in favor of Morris, asserting that the Board violated the Equal Protection Clause, because each borough had equal representation despite nonequal populations.

**745**

## Practicing the Vocabulary

**1.** county
**2.** commission government
**3.** strong-mayor government
**4.** income tax
**5.** progressive tax
**6.–12.** Sentences should reflect the meaning of each term in the context of chapter content.

## Reviewing Main Ideas
### Section 1

**13.** Counties and special districts.
**14.** Counties are the main units of local government in Texas.
**15.** An independent unit of government created to form one or more special governmental functions.
**16.** To include all of the town's eligible voters in making decisions that affect the town.

### Section 2

**17. (a)** Mayor-council, commission, and council-manager. **(b)** Council-manager.
**18.** Haphazardly, with little or no consideration of how their growth would lead to problems in the future.
**19.** Suburbanitis depletes many cities of residents and businesses, leaving behind cities that are disproportionately poor and in need of costly services.
**20.** COGs consist of local government representatives from a number of counties. They work to assist local government.

### Section 3

**21.** Examples include education, health and welfare, public safety, highways, regulation of business.
**22.** To reduce costs and to discourage people from becoming dependent on government assistance.
**23.** State police and law-enforcement services; State corrections systems.
**24.** Booming prison populations, insufficient funds.

### Section 4

**25.** States cannot tax interstate commerce, any agency of the Federal Government, or in such a way as to violate due process and

## Political Dictionary

| | | |
|---|---|---|
| county (p. 718) | zoning (p. 730) | property tax (p. 742) |
| township (p. 718) | metropolitan area (p. 731) | assessment (p. 742) |
| special district (p. 720) | Medicaid (p. 735) | inheritance tax (p. 742) |
| charter (p. 726) | welfare (p. 735) | estate tax (p. 742) |
| mayor-council government (p. 726) | entitlement (p. 735) | State budget (p. 744) |
| strong-mayor government (p. 726) | sales tax (p. 741) | |
| weak-mayor government (p. 727) | regressive tax (p. 741) | |
| commission government (p. 727) | income tax (p. 742) | |
| council-manager government (p. 728) | progressive tax (p. 742) | |

## Practicing the Vocabulary

**Matching**  *Choose a term from the list above that best matches each description.*

1. The major unit of local government in most States except Rhode Island and Connecticut
2. A form of city government consisting of three to nine popularly elected commissioners who form a city council
3. A form of city government in which the mayor heads the city administration, prepares the budget, and generally exercises strong leadership
4. A tax on individual and corporate income
5. A tax that is based on a person's ability to pay

**Using Words in Context**  *For each of the terms below, write a sentence that shows how it relates to this chapter.*

6. county
7. charter
8. entitlement
9. special district
10. estate tax
11. metropolitan area
12. zoning

## Reviewing Main Ideas

**Section 1** .........................................................
13. What are the major forms of local government in Texas?
14. Describe the function of counties in Texas.
15. What is a special district?
16. What is the purpose of the New England town meeting?

**Section 2** .........................................................
17. **(a)** What are the basic forms of city government? **(b)** What form is used by most home-rule cities in Texas?
18. Briefly describe how most cities in the United States developed.
19. Describe the impact of "suburbanitis."
20. How are the councils of governments an example of regional cooperation in Texas?

**Section 3** .........................................................
21. Briefly describe the major categories of services that Texas provides to its citizens.

22. Why was Aid to Families with Dependent Children replaced by the Temporary Assistance to Needy Families program?
23. In what ways do States try to ensure the public safety of their citizens?
24. What challenges do States face in ensuring public safety?

**Section 4** .........................................................
25. What are the general limits on the power of State and local governments to tax?
26. List the major categories of taxes that exist at the State and local level.
27. What are the four principles of a sound tax system, according to Adam Smith?
28. What accounts for the largest source of State revenue in Texas?

equal protection. States often also have their own constitutional limits; there are political limits as well.
**26.** Sales, income, property, inheritance and estate, and various business taxes.
**27.** Citizens support the government based on the ability to pay (equality); taxes to be certain, not arbitrary (certainty); taxes to be levied in a manner most convenient to the taxpayer (convenience); taxes to be kept as low as possible (economy).
**28.** State taxes.

## Critical Thinking Skills

**29. *Applying the Chapter Skill*** A local jewelry store insists on charging you for fixing your watch, although it is still under warranty. Write a brief consumer complaint letter to a State agency. Describe the documents you have copied and attached to support your claim.

**30. *Predicting Consequences*** Different regions of the country rely on different forms of local government. Explain how differences from region to region might affect the selection of a form of government.

**31. *Understanding Point of View*** Some school districts face an uphill battle for funding in communities with a large elderly population. Why? Explain the points of view that might be involved in such a situation.

**32. *Formulating Questions*** Create a list of questions that you would ask your city or town's mayor or other local official to find out more about local government in your community.

## Analyzing Political Cartoons

Using your knowledge of American government and this cartoon, answer the questions below.

*"As for me, I believe in no taxation, with or without representation."*

**33.** Describe the situation depicted in the cartoon.
**34.** What would be the impact on government and the services it provides if there were no taxes?

 **Take It to the Net**

Additional support materials and activities for Chapter 25 of *Magruder's American Government* can be found in the Social Studies area at the Prentice Hall School Web site. **www.phschool.com**

 **You Can Make a Difference**

What volunteer opportunities does your community have for high school-age youth? Use the telephone book or the Internet to check on organizations or events such as Youth As Resources, City Year, local food banks, National Youth Service Day, or Students Against Destructive Decisions. With your classmates, assemble a directory of volunteer opportunities and make it available in local high schools.

## Participation Activities

**35. *Current Events Watch*** Find a news report on a proposal to improve the amount or type of funding for schools. Analyze the proposal: What impact would it have on State and local governments and on school administrators? Would you support or oppose the proposal?

**36. *Chart Activity*** Research the type and organization of your local government. What are the key positions in the government, and what are their functions? Who has the most power, or is it shared? Summarize your findings in a chart or diagram like the ones in Section 2.

**37. *It's Your Turn*** You have just become a budget analyst for your State or local government. Review the graphs on pages 734 and 741. They reflect both the expense of various services and the services people think are most valuable. Choose one of the charts, and write a speech explaining how you would seek to change the percentage of funds allocated to certain categories to reflect your or your community's values. **(Writing a Speech)**

 **Take It to the Net**

**Chapter 25 Self-Test** As a final review activity, take the Chapter 25 Self-Test in the Social Studies area at the Web site listed below, and receive immediate feedback on your answers.

**www.phschool.com**

## Critical Thinking Skills

**29.** Students' letters should follow the steps described on page 738.
**30.** The choice of a type of local government might be based on factors such as population concentration or the region's history.
**31.** The elderly might reason that since they do not use the schools, they should not have to pay for them. Families with school-age children might reason that everyone is responsible for educating a community's children and that good schools help insure high property values, thus benefiting everyone.
**32.** Possible questions: Which model of city government does our community most resemble? What are the most important services that our local government provides?

## Analyzing Political Cartoons

**33.** Revolutionary soldiers are commenting on the Patriots' protest against taxation without representation in the British Parliament.
**34.** There would be no money to run the government or provide services.

## You Can Make a Difference

You might refer students to the Close Up on Participation booklet in the *Teaching Resources* for ideas on planning and carrying out service-learning projects.

## Participation Activities

**35.** Students' analyses should show an understanding of the funding proposal they have located and should clearly explain why they support or oppose it.
**36.** Students' charts should indicate an understanding of the structure of their local government.
**37.** Students' speeches should reflect an understanding of the way in which budget allocations can reflect a community's values.

## Point-of-Use Resources

**Guide to the Essentials of American Government** Chapter 25 Test, page 137 provides multiple-choice questions to test students' knowledge of the chapter.

**Test Bank CD-ROM** Chapter 25 Test

**Chapter Test** Chapter Tests booklet

# Reference Section

Supreme Court Glossary

Glossary

Spanish Glossary

Index

Acknowledgments

Stop the Presses

Databank

Outline of the Constitution

United States Constitution

Historical Documents

# Databank

## The United States: A Statistical Profile

| State | Capital | Population (in thousands) | | | Land Area in Sq. Mi. | % Land Federally Owned | Population per Sq. Mi. |
|---|---|---|---|---|---|---|---|
| | | 2000 | 1990 | % Change | | | |
| **United States** | **Washington, D.C.** | **281,422** | **248,710** | **13.2** | **3,536,278** | **28.8** | **79.6** |
| Alabama | Montgomery | 4,447 | 4,041 | 10.1 | 50,750 | 3.4 | 87.6 |
| Alaska | Juneau | 627 | 550 | 14.0 | 570,374 | 67.9 | 1.1 |
| Arizona | Phoenix | 5,131 | 3,665 | 40.0 | 113,642 | 45.6 | 45.2 |
| Arkansas | Little Rock | 2,673 | 2,351 | 13.7 | 52,075 | 10.2 | 51.3 |
| California | Sacramento | 33,872 | 29,760 | 13.8 | 155,973 | 44.9 | 217.2 |
| Colorado | Denver | 4,301 | 3,294 | 30.6 | 103,729 | 36.4 | 41.5 |
| Connecticut | Hartford | 3,406 | 3,287 | 3.6 | 4,845 | 0.5 | 703.0 |
| Delaware | Dover | 784 | 666 | 17.6 | 1,955 | 2.1 | 401.0 |
| Florida | Tallahassee | 15,982 | 12,938 | 23.5 | 53,937 | 8.3 | 296.3 |
| Georgia | Atlanta | 8,186 | 6,478 | 26.4 | 57,919 | 5.6 | 141.3 |
| Hawaii | Honolulu | 1,212 | 1,108 | 9.3 | 6,423 | 14.7 | 188.7 |
| Idaho | Boise | 1,294 | 1,007 | 28.5 | 82,751 | 62.5 | 15.6 |
| Illinois | Springfield | 12,419 | 11,431 | 8.6 | 55,593 | 1.8 | 223.4 |
| Indiana | Indianapolis | 6,080 | 5,544 | 9.7 | 35,870 | 2.2 | 169.5 |
| Iowa | Des Moines | 2,926 | 2,777 | 5.4 | 55,875 | 0.7 | 52.4 |
| Kansas | Topeka | 2,688 | 2,478 | 8.5 | 81,823 | 1.3 | 32.9 |
| Kentucky | Frankfort | 4,042 | 3,685 | 9.7 | 39,732 | 4.8 | 101.7 |
| Louisiana | Baton Rouge | 4,469 | 4,220 | 5.9 | 43,566 | 4.5 | 102.6 |
| Maine | Augusta | 1,275 | 1,228 | 3.8 | 30,865 | 1.0 | 41.3 |
| Maryland | Annapolis | 5,296 | 4,781 | 10.8 | 9,775 | 3.2 | 541.8 |
| Massachusetts | Boston | 6,349 | 6,016 | 5.5 | 7,838 | 1.6 | 810.0 |
| Michigan | Lansing | 9,938 | 9,295 | 6.9 | 56,809 | 11.2 | 174.9 |
| Minnesota | St. Paul | 4,919 | 4,375 | 12.4 | 79,617 | 8.7 | 61.8 |
| Mississippi | Jackson | 2,845 | 2,573 | 10.5 | 46,914 | 5.9 | 60.6 |
| Missouri | Jefferson City | 5,595 | 5,117 | 9.3 | 68,898 | 4.8 | 81.2 |
| Montana | Helena | 902 | 799 | 12.9 | 145,556 | 28.0 | 6.2 |
| Nebraska | Lincoln | 1,711 | 1,578 | 8.4 | 76,878 | 1.5 | 22.3 |
| Nevada | Carson City | 1,998 | 1,202 | 66.3 | 109,806 | 83.1 | 18.2 |
| New Hampshire | Concord | 1,236 | 1,109 | 11.4 | 8,969 | 13.2 | 137.8 |
| New Jersey | Trenton | 8,414 | 7,730 | 8.9 | 7,419 | 3.4 | 1,134.1 |
| New Mexico | Santa Fe | 1,819 | 1,515 | 20.1 | 121,364 | 34.2 | 15.0 |
| New York | Albany | 18,976 | 17,990 | 5.5 | 47,224 | 0.4 | 401.8 |
| North Carolina | Raleigh | 8,049 | 6,629 | 21.4 | 48,718 | 8.0 | 165.2 |
| North Dakota | Bismarck | 642 | 639 | 0.5 | 68,994 | 4.2 | 9.3 |
| Ohio | Columbus | 11,353 | 10,847 | 4.7 | 40,953 | 1.5 | 277.2 |
| Oklahoma | Oklahoma City | 3,451 | 3,146 | 9.7 | 68,679 | 2.9 | 50.2 |
| Oregon | Salem | 3,421 | 2,842 | 20.4 | 96,002 | 52.6 | 35.6 |
| Pennsylvania | Harrisburg | 12,281 | 11,882 | 3.4 | 44,820 | 2.4 | 274.0 |
| Rhode Island | Providence | 1,048 | 1,003 | 4.5 | 1,045 | 0.6 | 1,002.9 |
| South Carolina | Columbia | 4,012 | 3,487 | 15.1 | 30,111 | 6.1 | 133.2 |
| South Dakota | Pierre | 755 | 696 | 8.5 | 75,896 | 5.6 | 9.9 |
| Tennessee | Nashville | 5,689 | 4,877 | 16.7 | 41,219 | 6.1 | 138.0 |
| Texas | Austin | 20,852 | 16,987 | 22.8 | 261,914 | 1.7 | 79.6 |
| Utah | Salt Lake City | 2,233 | 1,723 | 29.6 | 82,168 | 64.5 | 27.2 |
| Vermont | Montpelier | 609 | 563 | 8.2 | 9,249 | 6.3 | 65.8 |
| Virginia | Richmond | 7,079 | 6,187 | 14.4 | 39,598 | 9.0 | 178.8 |
| Washington | Olympia | 5,894 | 4,867 | 21.1 | 66,581 | 28.5 | 88.5 |
| West Virgina | Charleston | 1,808 | 1,793 | 0.8 | 24,087 | 7.6 | 75.1 |
| Wisconsin | Madison | 5,364 | 4,892 | 9.6 | 54,314 | 5.6 | 98.8 |
| Wyoming | Cheyenne | 494 | 454 | 8.9 | 97,105 | 49.9 | 5.1 |
| Washington, D.C. | | 572 | 607 | -5.7 | 61 | 23.4 | 9,377.0 |

Sources: Bureau of the Census, Federal Election Commission, Federal Elections 2000 (June 2001, p. 12)

| State | Population (in thousands) | | | | Popular Vote, 2000 Presidential Election | | | | | |
|---|---|---|---|---|---|---|---|---|---|---|
| | % Urban | African American | Hispanic† Origin | % Foreign Born | George W. Bush (Republican) | % | Al Gore (Democrat) | % | All Others | % |
| **United States** | **80.1** | **34,862** | **31,337** | **7.9** | **50,455,156** | **47.87** | **50,992,335** | **48.38** | **3,949,150** | **3.75** |
| Alabama | 70.1 | 1,139 | 45 | 1.1 | 941,173 | 56 | 692,611 | 48 | 32,488 | 2 |
| Alaska | 41.5 | 24 | 25 | 4.5 | 167,398 | 59 | 79,004 | 28 | 39,158 | 14 |
| Arizona | 87.8 | 176 | 1,084 | 7.6 | 781,652 | 51 | 685,341 | 45 | 65,023 | 4 |
| Arkansas | 48.6 | 411 | 54 | 1.1 | 472, 940 | 51 | 422,768 | 46 | 26,073 | 3 |
| California | 96.7 | 2,487 | 10,460 | 21.7 | 4,567,429 | 42 | 5,861,203 | 53 | 537,224 | 5 |
| Colorado | 84.0 | 176 | 604 | 4.3 | 883,748 | 51 | 738,227 | 42 | 119,393 | 7 |
| Connecticut | 95.6 | 309 | 279 | 8.5 | 561,094 | 38 | 816,015 | 56 | 82,416 | 6 |
| Delaware | 81.6 | 149 | 28 | 3.3 | 137,288 | 42 | 180,068 | 55 | 10,266 | 3 |
| Florida | 93.0 | 2,333 | 2,334 | 12.9 | 2,912,790 | 49 | 2,912,253 | 49 | 138,067 | 2 |
| Georgia | 68.9 | 2,236 | 240 | 2.7 | 1,419,720 | 55 | 1,116,230 | 43 | 60,854 | 2 |
| Hawaii | 73.1 | 34 | 95 | 14.7 | 137,845 | 37 | 205,286 | 56 | 24,820 | 7 |
| Idaho | 38.3 | 8 | 93 | 2.9 | 336,937 | 67 | 138,637 | 28 | 26,047 | 5 |
| Illinois | 84.5 | 1,854 | 1,276 | 8.3 | 2,019,421 | 43 | 2,589,026 | 55 | 133,676 | 3 |
| Indiana | 71.7 | 498 | 154 | 1.7 | 1,245,836 | 57 | 901,980 | 41 | 51,486 | 2 |
| Iowa | 44.6 | 58 | 62 | 1.6 | 634,373 | 48 | 638,517 | 48 | 42,673 | 3 |
| Kansas | 56.4 | 157 | 148 | 2.5 | 622,332 | 58 | 399,276 | 37 | 50,610 | 5 |
| Kentucky | 48.3 | 288 | 35 | 0.9 | 872,492 | 56 | 638,898 | 41 | 32,797 | 2 |
| Louisiana | 75.2 | 1,415 | 119 | 2.1 | 927,871 | 53 | 792,344 | 45 | 45,441 | 3 |
| Maine | 35.8 | 6 | 9 | 3.0 | 286,616 | 44 | 319,951 | 49 | 45,250 | 7 |
| Maryland | 92.7 | 1,454 | 199 | 6.6 | 813,797 | 40 | 1,140,782 | 56 | 65,901 | 3 |
| Massachusetts | 96.1 | 405 | 391 | 9.5 | 878,502 | 32 | 1,616,487 | 60 | 207,995 | 8 |
| Michigan | 82.6 | 1,415 | 276 | 3.8 | 1,953,139 | 46 | 2,170,418 | 51 | 108,944 | 3 |
| Minnesota | 70.1 | 149 | 93 | 2.6 | 1,109,659 | 45 | 1,168,266 | 48 | 160,760 | 7 |
| Mississippi | 35.9 | 1,010 | 24 | 0.8 | 572,844 | 58 | 404,614 | 41 | 16,726 | 2 |
| Missouri | 68.0 | 617 | 91 | 1.6 | 1,189,924 | 50 | 1,111,138 | 47 | 58,830 | 2 |
| Montana | 33.4 | 3 | 16 | 1.7 | 240,178 | 58 | 137,126 | 33 | 33,693 | 8 |
| Nebraska | 51.8 | 68 | 77 | 1.8 | 433,862 | 62 | 231,780 | 33 | 31,377 | 4 |
| Nevada | 86.1 | 140 | 304 | 8.7 | 301,575 | 49 | 279,978 | 46 | 27,417 | 4 |
| New Hampshire | 60.2 | 9 | 20 | 3.7 | 273,559 | 48 | 266,348 | 47 | 29,174 | 5 |
| New Jersey | 100.0 | 1,197 | 1,027 | 12.5 | 1,284,173 | 40 | 1,788,850 | 56 | 114,203 | 4 |
| New Mexico | 57.0 | 46 | 708 | 5.3 | 286,417 | 48 | 286,783 | 48 | 25,405 | 4 |
| New York | 91.9 | 3,222 | 2,661 | 15.9 | 2,403,374 | 35 | 4,107,697 | 60 | 310,928 | 5 |
| North Carolina | 67.1 | 1,686 | 176 | 1.7 | 1,631,163 | 56 | 1,257,692 | 43 | 22,407 | 1 |
| North Dakota | 43.1 | 4 | 7 | 1.5 | 174,852 | 61 | 95,284 | 33 | 18,120 | 6 |
| Ohio | 81.0 | 1,304 | 185 | 2.4 | 2,350,363 | 50 | 2,183,628 | 46 | 168,007 | 4 |
| Oklahoma | 60.5 | 262 | 137 | 2.1 | 744,337 | 60 | 474,276 | 38 | 15,616 | 1 |
| Oregon | 72.7 | 62 | 213 | 4.9 | 713,577 | 46 | 720,342 | 47 | 100,049 | 6 |
| Pennsylvania | 84.5 | 1,170 | 326 | 3.1 | 2,281,127 | 46 | 2,485,967 | 51 | 146,025 | 3 |
| Rhode Island | 93.8 | 50 | 69 | 9.5 | 130,555 | 32 | 249,508 | 61 | 29,049 | 7 |
| South Carolina | 70.0 | 1,157 | 54 | 1.4 | 785,937 | 57 | 565,561 | 41 | 31,219 | 2 |
| South Dakota | 34.0 | 5 | 9 | 1.1 | 190,700 | 60 | 118,804 | 38 | 6,765 | 2 |
| Tennessee | 67.8 | 913 | 67 | 1.2 | 1,061,949 | 51 | 981,720 | 47 | 32,512 | 2 |
| Texas | 84.5 | 2,470 | 6,045 | 9.0 | 3,799,639 | 59 | 2,433,746 | 38 | 174,252 | 3 |
| Utah | 76.7 | 19 | 151 | 3.4 | 515,096 | 67 | 203,053 | 26 | 52,605 | 7 |
| Vermont | 27.9 | 3 | 5 | 3.1 | 119,775 | 41 | 149,022 | 51 | 25,511 | 9 |
| Virginia | 78.1 | 1,385 | 266 | 5.0 | 1,437,490 | 52 | 1,217,290 | 44 | 84,667 | 3 |
| Washington | 82.9 | 204 | 377 | 6.6 | 1,108,864 | 45 | 1,247,652 | 50 | 130,917 | 5 |
| West Virgina | 41.9 | 56 | 10 | 0.9 | 336,475 | 52 | 295,497 | 46 | 16,152 | 2 |
| Wisconsin | 67.8 | 293 | 140 | 2.5 | 1,237,279 | 48 | 1,242,987 | 48 | 118,341 | 4 |
| Wyoming | 29.6 | 4 | 29 | 1.7 | 147,947 | 68 | 60,481 | 28 | 9,923 | 4 |
| Washington, D.C. | 100.0 | 319 | 38 | 9.7 | 18,073 | 9 | 171,923 | 85 | 11,898 | 6 |

† Persons of Hispanic origin may be of any race.

# Political Map of the United States

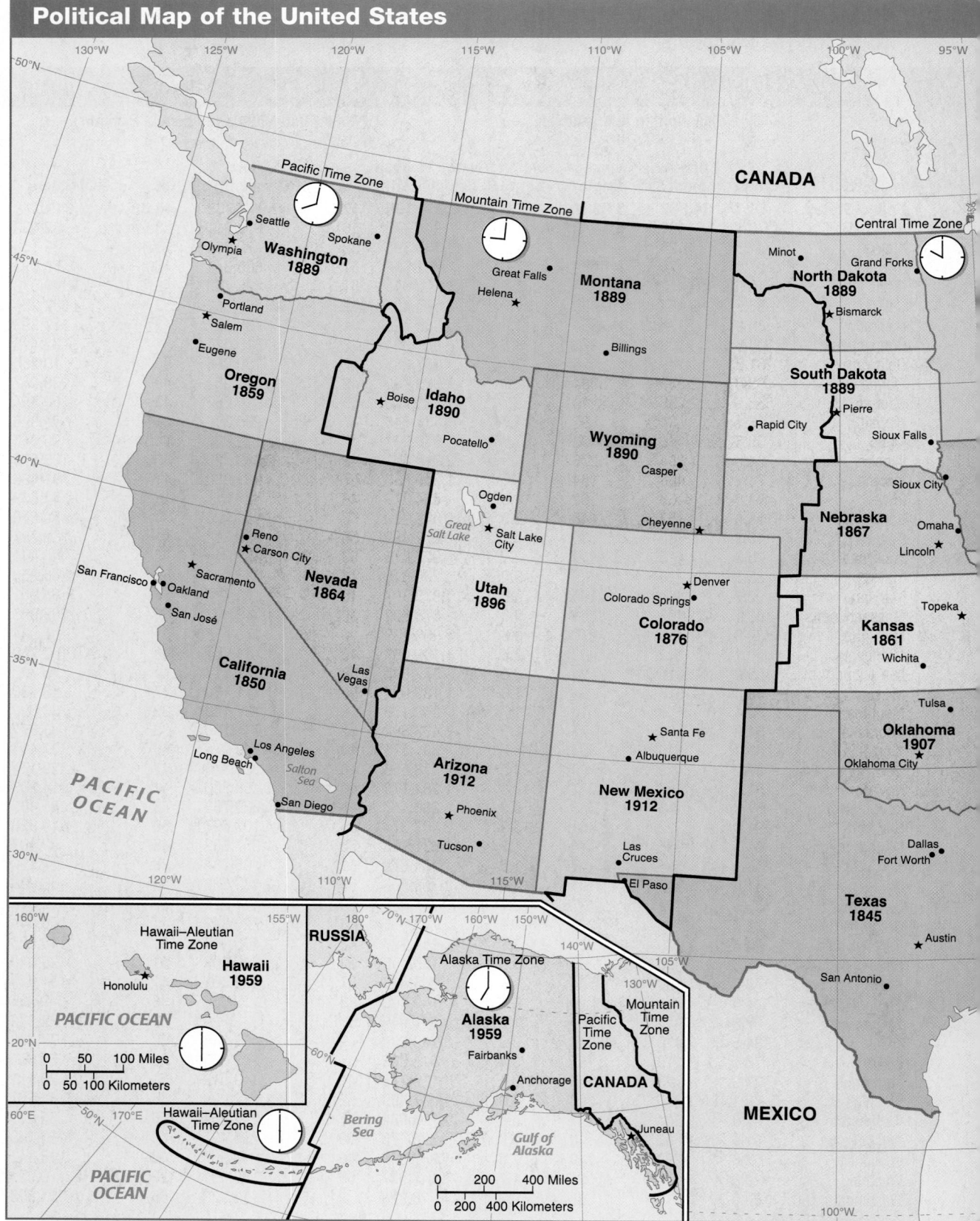

CANADA

Atlantic Time Zone

**Maine
1820**
• Bangor

Eastern Time Zone

**Vermont
1791**
• Burlington
Augusta ★
• Montpelier
• Lewiston
• Portland

**New Hampshire
1788**

Concord ★
Manchester ★
**Massachusetts
1788**

**Minnesota
1858**
• Duluth

Lake Superior

**Wisconsin
1848**
• St. Paul
• Minneapolis
• Green Bay

Lake Huron

**Michigan
1837**
• Grand Rapids
★ Lansing
• Detroit

Lake Ontario

Albany ★
• Rochester
**New York
1788**
• Buffalo
Hartford ★
★ Providence
**Rhode Island 1790**
Boston ★
**Connecticut
1788**

**Iowa
1846**
• Des Moines

• Milwaukee
• Madison

Lake Erie

Toledo
Cleveland
Akron
**Ohio
1803**

**Pennsylvania
1787**
• Pittsburgh
Harrisburg ★
• Philadelphia
Newark •
New York •
Jersey City •
• Trenton
**New Jersey
1787**

**Illinois
1818**
• Peoria
• Springfield ★
• Chicago
Gary •
Fort Wayne •

**Indiana
1816**
• Indianapolis
★ Columbus
• Cincinnati

**West Virginia
1863**
• Charleston
• Huntington
Frankfort ★
Wilmington •
Baltimore •
• Dover
**Delaware
1787**
☆ Washington, DC
Annapolis •
**Maryland
1788**

**Missouri
1821**
• Kansas City
• St. Louis
Jefferson City ★

• Louisville
• Lexington

**Kentucky
1792**

Richmond ★
**Virginia
1788**
• Norfolk

ATLANTIC
OCEAN

• Springfield

**Arkansas
1836**
• Fort Smith

Nashville ★
• Knoxville
**Tennessee
1796**
• Memphis

Winston-Salem •
• Greensboro
★ Raleigh
• Charlotte
**North Carolina
1789**

• Little Rock ★

**Mississippi
1817**
★ Jackson

• Atlanta
• Macon

**South Carolina
1788**
★ Columbia

• Charleston

Birmingham •
**Alabama
1819**
Montgomery ★
• Columbus
**Georgia
1788**
• Savannah

**Louisiana
1812**
• Shreveport

• Mobile
• Pensacola
★ Tallahassee
• Jacksonville

Baton Rouge ★
Lake Pontchartrain
• New Orleans

**Florida
1845**
• Tampa
Lake Okeechobee

• Houston

Gulf of Mexico

• Miami

Tropic of Cancer

N
W E
S

⊛ National capital

★ State capital

• Other city

**1787** Year of admission to the Union

━━ Boundaries of time zones

0        150        300 Miles
0      150      300 Kilometers

90°W   85°W   80°W   75°W   70°W   65°W   60°W
95°W   90°W   85°W   80°W   75°W

50°N   45°N   40°N   35°N   30°N   25°N   20°N

## Presidents of the United States

| NAME | PARTY | STATE[a] | ENTERED OFFICE |
|---|---|---|---|
| George Washington (1732–1799) | Federalist | Virginia | 1789 |
| John Adams (1735–1826) | Federalist | Massachusetts | 1797 |
| Thomas Jefferson (1743–1826) | Dem-Rep [b] | Virginia | 1801 |
| James Madison (1751–1836) | Dem-Rep | Virginia | 1809 |
| James Monroe (1758–1831) | Dem-Rep | Virginia | 1817 |
| John Q. Adams (1767–1848) | Dem-Rep | Massachusetts | 1825 |
| Andrew Jackson (1767–1845) | Democrat | Tennessee (SC) | 1829 |
| Martin Van Buren (1782–1862) | Democrat | New York | 1837 |
| William H. Harrison (1773–1841) | Whig | Ohio (VA) | 1841 |
| John Tyler (1790–1862) | Democrat | Virginia | 1841 |
| James K. Polk (1795–1849) | Democrat | Tennessee (NC) | 1845 |
| Zachary Taylor (1784–1850) | Whig | Louisiana (VA) | 1849 |
| Millard Fillmore (1800–1874) | Whig | New York | 1850 |
| Franklin Pierce (1804–1869) | Democrat | New Hampshire | 1853 |
| James Buchanan (1791–1868) | Democrat | Pennsylvania | 1857 |
| Abraham Lincoln (1809–1865) | Republican | Illinois (KY) | 1861 |
| Andrew Johnson (1808–1875) | Democrat [c] | Tennessee (NC) | 1865 |
| Ulysses S. Grant (1822–1885) | Republican | Illinois (OH) | 1869 |
| Rutherford B. Hayes (1822–1893) | Republican | Ohio | 1877 |
| James A. Garfield (1831–1881) | Republican | Ohio | 1881 |
| Chester A. Arthur (1829–1896) | Republican | New York (VT) | 1881 |
| Grover Cleveland (1837–1908) | Democrat | New York (NJ) | 1885 |
| Benjamin Harrison (1833–1901) | Republican | Indiana (OH) | 1889 |
| Grover Cleveland (1837–1908) | Democrat | New York (NJ) | 1893 |
| William McKinley (1843–1901) | Republican | Ohio | 1897 |
| Theodore Roosevelt (1858–1919) | Republican | New York | 1901 |
| William H. Taft (1857–1930) | Republican | Ohio | 1909 |
| Woodrow Wilson (1856–1924) | Democrat | New Jersey (VA) | 1913 |
| Warren G. Harding (1865–1923) | Republican | Ohio | 1921 |
| Calvin Coolidge (1872–1933) | Republican | Massachusetts (VT) | 1923 |
| Herbert Hoover (1874–1964) | Republican | California (IA) | 1929 |
| Franklin Roosevelt (1882–1945) | Democrat | New York | 1933 |
| Harry S Truman (1884–1972) | Democrat | Missouri | 1945 |
| Dwight D. Eisenhower (1890–1969) | Republican | New York (TX) | 1953 |
| John F. Kennedy (1917–1963) | Democrat | Massachusetts | 1961 |
| Lyndon B. Johnson (1908–1973) | Democrat | Texas | 1963 |
| Richard M. Nixon (1913–1994) | Republican | New York (CA) | 1969 |
| Gerald R. Ford (1913– ) | Republican | Michigan (NE) | 1974 |
| James E. Carter (1924– ) | Democrat | Georgia | 1977 |
| Ronald W. Reagan (1911– ) | Republican | California (IL) | 1981 |
| George H.W. Bush (1924– ) | Republican | Texas (MA) | 1989 |
| William J. Clinton (1946– ) | Democrat | Arkansas | 1993 |
| George W. Bush (1946– ) | Republican | Texas | 2001 |

George Washington

Abraham Lincoln

Theodore Roosevelt

[a] State of residence when elected; if born in another State, that State in parentheses.
[b] Democratic-Republican
[c] Johnson, a War Democrat, was elected Vice-President on the coalition Union Party ticket.
[d] Resigned October 10, 1973.
[e] Nominated by Nixon, confirmed by Congress on December 6, 1973.
[f] Nominated by Ford, confirmed by Congress on December 19, 1974.

| Age On Taking Office | Religion | Ancestry | Vice President(s) |
|---|---|---|---|
| 57 | Episcopalian | English | John Adams |
| 61 | Unitarian | English | Thomas Jefferson |
| 57 | ———— | Welsh | Aaron Burr/George Clinton |
| 57 | Episcopalian | English | George Clinton/Elbridge Gerry |
| 58 | Episcopalian | Scottish | Daniel D. Tompkins |
| 57 | Unitarian | English | John C. Calhoun |
| 61 | Presbyterian | Scots-Irish | John C. Calhoun/Martin Van Buren |
| 54 | Dutch Reformed | Dutch | Richard M. Johnson |
| 68 | Episcopalian | English | John Tyler |
| 51 | Episcopalian | English | none |
| 49 | Presbyterian | Scots-Irish | George M. Dallas |
| 64 | Episcopalian | English | Millard Fillmore |
| 50 | Unitarian | English | none |
| 48 | Episcopalian | English | William R. King |
| 65 | Presbyterian | Scots-Irish | John C. Breckinridge |
| 52 | ———— | English | Hannibal Hamlin/Andrew Johnson |
| 56 | ———— | English | none |
| 46 | Methodist | English-Scottish | Schuyler Colfax/Henry Wilson |
| 54 | Methodist | Scottish | William A. Wheeler |
| 49 | Disciples of Christ | English | Chester A. Arthur |
| 51 | Episcopalian | Scots-Irish | none |
| 47 | Presbyterian | English-Irish | Thomas A. Hendricks |
| 55 | Presbyterian | English | Levi P. Morton |
| 55 | Presbyterian | English-Irish | Adlai E. Stevenson |
| 54 | Methodist | Scots-Irish | Garret A. Hobart/Theodore Roosevelt |
| 42 | Dutch Reformed | Dutch | Charles W. Fairbanks |
| 51 | Unitarian | English | James S. Sherman |
| 56 | Presbyterian | Scots-Irish | Thomas R. Marshall |
| 55 | Baptist | English-Scottish-Irish | Calvin Coolidge |
| 51 | Congregationalist | English | Charles G. Dawes |
| 54 | Quaker | Swiss-German | Charles Curtis |
| 51 | Episcopalian | Dutch | John N. Garner/Henry A. Wallace/Harry S Truman |
| 60 | Baptist | English-Scottish-Irish | Alben W. Barkley |
| 62 | Presbyterian | Swiss-German | Richard M. Nixon |
| 43 | Roman Catholic | Irish | Lyndon B. Johnson |
| 55 | Disciples of Christ | English | Hubert H. Humphrey |
| 56 | Quaker | Scots-Irish | Spiro T. Agnew [d]/Gerald R. Ford [e] |
| 61 | Episcopalian | English | Nelson A. Rockefeller [f] |
| 52 | Baptist | English-Scottish-Irish | Walter F. Mondale |
| 69 | Episcopalian | English-Scottish-Irish | George H. W. Bush |
| 64 | Episcopalian | English | J. Danforth Quayle |
| 46 | Baptist | English | Albert Gore, Jr. |
| 54 | Episcopalian | English | Richard B. Cheney |

Woodrow Wilson

Franklin Roosevelt

Ronald Reagan

## Political Map of the World

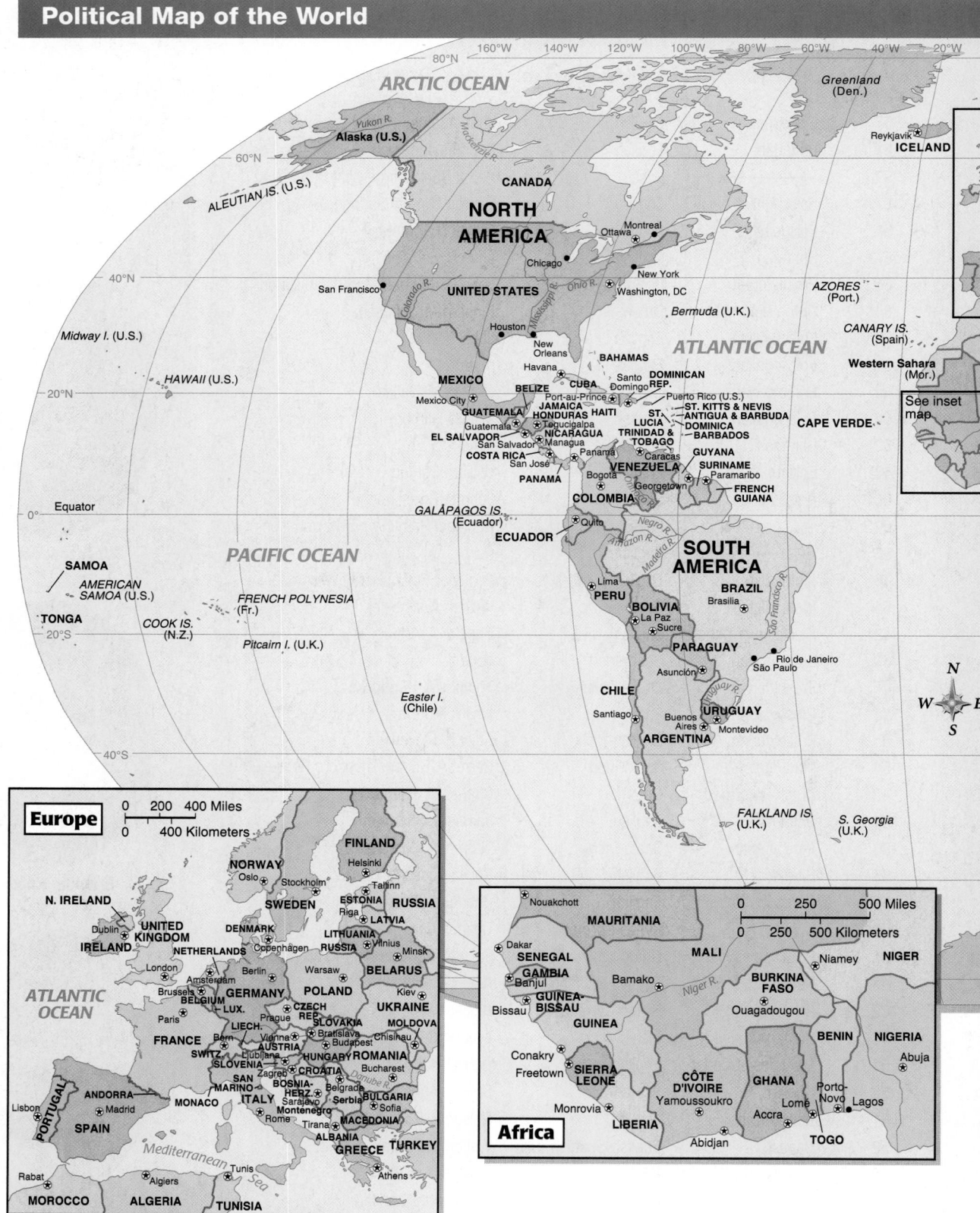

ARCTIC OCEAN

*Greenland*
(Den.)

Alaska (U.S.)

Reykjavik ✪
**ICELAND**

*ALEUTIAN IS. (U.S.)*

**CANADA**

**NORTH
AMERICA**

Montreal
Ottawa ✪ ✪

Chicago ✪

New York

San Francisco ✪
**UNITED STATES**

Washington, DC

*AZORES*
(Port.)

*Bermuda (U.K.)*

**ATLANTIC OCEAN**

*Midway I. (U.S.)*

Houston ✪

New
Orleans

Havana

**BAHAMAS**

*CANARY IS.*
(Spain)

**Western Sahara**
(Mor.)

*HAWAII (U.S.)*

**MEXICO**

Mexico City ✪

**BELIZE**
**GUATEMALA**

Santo
Domingo

**DOMINICAN
REP.**

**CUBA**

**CAPE VERDE**

See inset
map

Port-au-Prince
Guatemala ✪
**JAMAICA**
**HONDURAS** **HAITI**
Tegucigalpa ✪
**EL SALVADOR**
San Salvador ✪
**NICARAGUA**
Managua ✪

**ST.
LUCIA**

Puerto Rico (U.S.)
**ST. KITTS & NEVIS**
**ANTIGUA & BARBUDA**
**DOMINICA**
**BARBADOS**

**COSTA RICA**
San José ✪

Panamá ✪

**TRINIDAD &
TOBAGO**

**PANAMA**

**GUYANA**
**SURINAME**

Caracas
**VENEZUELA**

Paramaribo
**FRENCH
GUIANA**

Bogotá ✪

Georgetown

**COLOMBIA**

Equator

*GALÁPAGOS IS.*
(Ecuador)

Quito ✪

**ECUADOR**

**PACIFIC OCEAN**

**SOUTH
AMERICA**

**SAMOA**

*AMERICAN
SAMOA (U.S.)*

Lima ✪
**PERU**

**BRAZIL**

Brasília ✪

*FRENCH POLYNESIA*
(Fr.)

**BOLIVIA**
La Paz ✪
Sucre ✪

**TONGA**

*COOK IS.*
(N.Z.)

*Pitcairn I. (U.K.)*

**PARAGUAY**

Rio de Janeiro
São Paulo

Asunción ✪

*Easter I.*
(Chile)

**CHILE**

**URUGUAY**

N

W ✦ E

Santiago ✪

Buenos
Aires ✪

Montevideo

S

**ARGENTINA**

*FALKLAND IS.*
(U.K.)

*S. Georgia*
(U.K.)

### Europe

0   200   400 Miles

0         400 Kilometers

**FINLAND**

Helsinki ✪

**NORWAY**

Oslo ✪

Tallinn

Stockholm ✪

**N. IRELAND**

**SWEDEN**

**ESTONIA**

Riga

**RUSSIA**

Dublin ✪
**UNITED
KINGDOM**

**DENMARK**

**LATVIA**

**LITHUANIA**

**IRELAND**

**NETHERLANDS**

Copenhagen ✪

Vilnius ✪

**RUSSIA**

Minsk ✪

London ✪

Amsterdam ✪

Berlin ✪

Warsaw ✪

**BELARUS**

**ATLANTIC
OCEAN**

Brussels ✪
**BELGIUM**

**GERMANY**
**LUX.**

**POLAND**

Kiev ✪

Paris ✪

**CZECH
REP.**
Prague ✪

**UKRAINE**

**LIECH.**

**SLOVAKIA**

Bratislava
Vienna ✪

**MOLDOVA**
Chisinau ✪

**FRANCE**

Bern ✪
**SWITZ.**

**AUSTRIA**
Budapest ✪

**SLOVENIA**
Ljubljana ✪
**CROATIA**
Zagreb ✪

**HUNGARY** **ROMANIA**

Bucharest ✪

**SAN
MARINO**
**BOSNIA-
HERZ.**

Belgrade ✪
Sarajevo ✪

**Danube R.**

**ANDORRA**

**MONACO**

**ITALY**
**Montenegro**

**Serbia**
**BULGARIA**
Sofia ✪

Lisbon ✪

Madrid ✪

Rome ✪
Tirana ✪

**MACEDONIA**

**PORTUGAL**

**SPAIN**

**ALBANIA**

**GREECE**

**TURKEY**

*Mediterranean
Sea*

Tunis ✪

Athens ✪

Rabat ✪

Algiers ✪

**MOROCCO**

**ALGERIA**

**TUNISIA**

### Africa

Nouakchott ✪

**MAURITANIA**

0      250      500 Miles

0     250     500 Kilometers

Dakar ✪
**SENEGAL**

**MALI**

Niamey ✪

**NIGER**

**GAMBIA**
Banjul ✪

Bamako ✪

**BURKINA
FASO**

**GUINEA-
BISSAU**

*Niger R.*

Bissau ✪

**GUINEA**

Ouagadougou ✪

Conakry ✪

Freetown ✪

**SIERRA
LEONE**

**CÔTE
D'IVOIRE**

Yamoussoukro ✪

**GHANA**

**BENIN**

Porto-
Novo ✪

**NIGERIA**

Abuja ✪

Lagos ●

Monrovia ✪

**LIBERIA**

Abidjan ✪

Lomé ✪

Accra ✪

**TOGO**

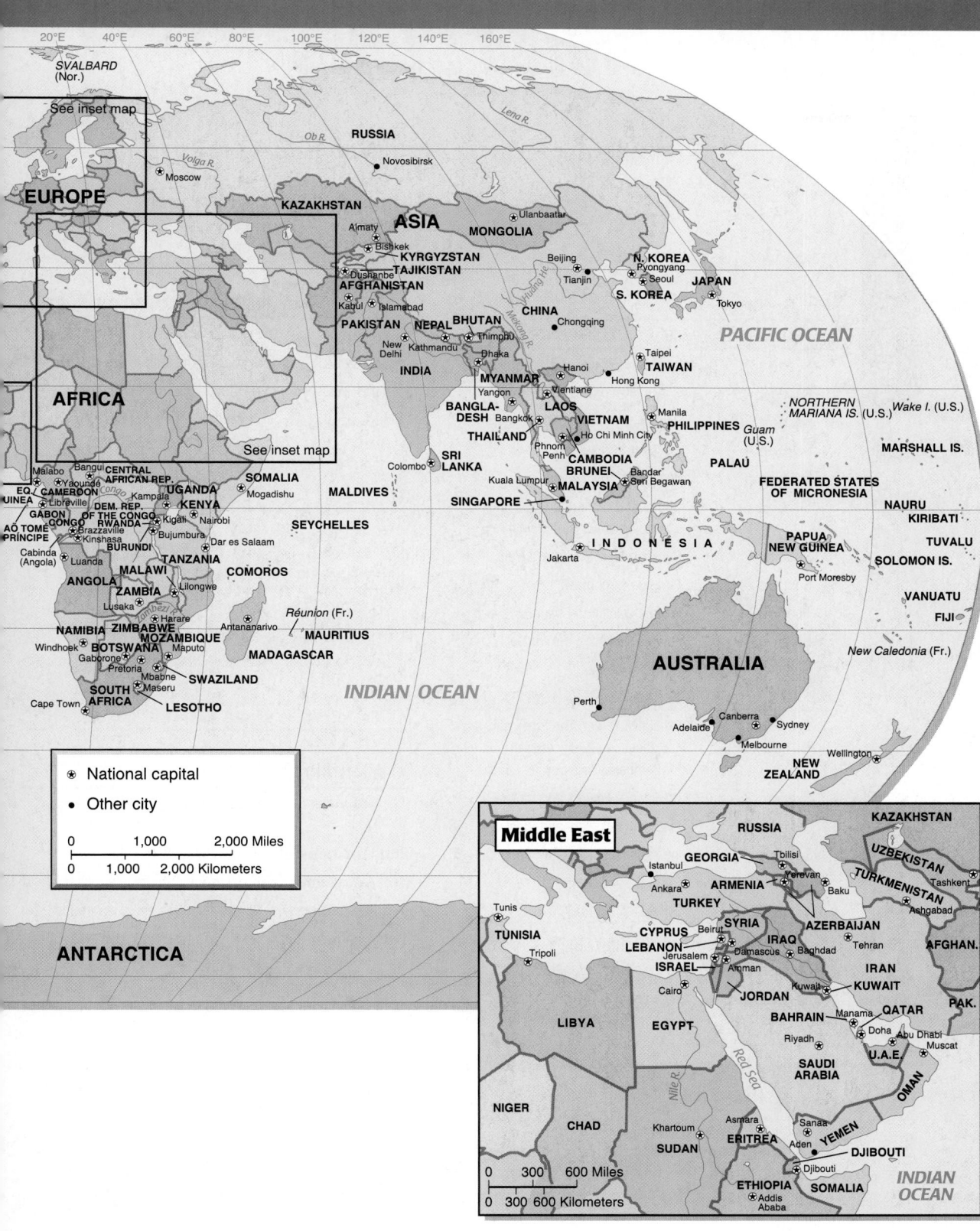

20°E  40°E  60°E  80°E  100°E  120°E  140°E  160°E

SVALBARD (Nor.)

See inset map

**EUROPE**

RUSSIA

*Ob R.*

Novosibirsk

*Volga R.*

Moscow

*Lena R.*

KAZAKHSTAN

**ASIA**

Almaty

Ulanbaatar

MONGOLIA

Bishkek

KYRGYZSTAN

TAJIKISTAN

Dushanbe

AFGHANISTAN

Beijing

*Huang He*

N. KOREA

Pyongyang

Tianjin

Seoul

S. KOREA

**JAPAN**

Tokyo

Kabul

Islamabad

CHINA

Chongqing

PACIFIC OCEAN

PAKISTAN

NEPAL

BHUTAN

Thimphu

*Mekong R.*

New Delhi

Kathmandu

Dhaka

INDIA

Hanoi

Taipei

TAIWAN

MYANMAR

Yangon

Hong Kong

BANGLA-DESH

Bangkok

LAOS

Vientiane

VIETNAM

Manila

PHILIPPINES

Guam (U.S.)

NORTHERN MARIANA IS. (U.S.)

Wake I. (U.S.)

THAILAND

Ho Chi Minh City

Phnom Penh

CAMBODIA

BRUNEI

Bandar Seri Begawan

PALAU

MARSHALL IS.

Colombo

SRI LANKA

**AFRICA**

See inset map

MALDIVES

Kuala Lumpur

SINGAPORE

MALAYSIA

FEDERATED STATES OF MICRONESIA

NAURU

Malabo

Bangui

CENTRAL AFRICAN REP.

UGANDA

SOMALIA

Mogadishu

SEYCHELLES

I N D O N E S I A

KIRIBATI

Yaounde

EQ. GUINEA

CAMEROON

*Congo*

Kampala

KENYA

Nairobi

Jakarta

PAPUA NEW GUINEA

TUVALU

SOLOMON IS.

GABON

Libreville

DEM. REP. OF THE CONGO

RWANDA

Kigali

BURUNDI

Bujumbura

Dar es Salaam

Port Moresby

AO TOME PRINCIPE

Brazzaville

Kinshasa

TANZANIA

VANUATU

Cabinda (Angola)

Luanda

MALAWI

COMOROS

Réunion (Fr.)

FIJI

ANGOLA

ZAMBIA

*Zambezi*

Lilongwe

MAURITIUS

Lusaka

Harare

Antananarivo

NAMIBIA

ZIMBABWE

MOZAMBIQUE

MADAGASCAR

INDIAN OCEAN

**AUSTRALIA**

Windhoek

BOTSWANA

Maputo

Gaborone

Pretoria

Mbabne

SWAZILAND

Perth

SOUTH AFRICA

Maseru

LESOTHO

Adelaide

Canberra

Sydney

Cape Town

Melbourne

Wellington

NEW ZEALAND

⊛  National capital

•  Other city

0      1,000      2,000 Miles

0    1,000   2,000 Kilometers

**ANTARCTICA**

### Middle East

RUSSIA

KAZAKHSTAN

Istanbul

GEORGIA

Tbilisi

UZBEKISTAN

TURKMENISTAN

Tashkent

Ankara

ARMENIA

Yerevan

Baku

Ashgabad

TURKEY

AZERBAIJAN

AFGHAN.

Tunis

CYPRUS

Beirut

SYRIA

IRAQ

TUNISIA

LEBANON

Jerusalem

Damascus

Baghdad

Tehran

IRAN

Tripoli

ISRAEL

Amman

PAK.

Cairo

JORDAN

Kuwait

KUWAIT

LIBYA

EGYPT

BAHRAIN

Manama

QATAR

Riyadh

Doha

Abu Dhabi

Muscat

*Nile R.*

*Red Sea*

SAUDI ARABIA

U.A.E.

OMAN

NIGER

CHAD

Khartoum

Asmara

Sanaa

YEMEN

DJIBOUTI

SUDAN

ERITREA

Aden

Djibouti

INDIAN OCEAN

ETHIOPIA

Addis Ababa

SOMALIA

0   300   600 Miles

0   300  600 Kilometers

Outline of the Constitution

# An Outline of the Constitution of the United States

**Focus** Ask students to describe their student government. Is there a constitution? If so, what is its purpose? What is the procedure for making changes? If there is no constitution, would student government benefit from one? Why or why not? Explain that student governments and other organizations often use the Constitution of the United States as their model.

**Instruct** Review the issues that divided Federalists and Anti-Federalists. Discuss how the Constitution preserves popular sovereignty and limits the powers of government while avoiding the weaknesses of the Articles of Confederation. Write the Six Basic Principles of the Constitution on the chalkboard. Ask students to explain each one in their own words. Then ask them to find examples of each principle within the Constitution.

Discuss how the Bill of Rights protects Americans' basic rights. Ask students to make a list of examples of the rights that are protected in their own lives.

**Close/Reteach** The Constitution provides a broad explanation of the limits of government, based on six basic principles. It has protected the rights of Americans for over 200 years.

> "The American Constitution is the most wonderful Work ever struck off at a given time by the brain and purpose of man."
>
> —William E. Gladstone

**Preamble**

| ARTICLE I | LEGISLATIVE DEPARTMENT |
|---|---|
| Section 1. | Legislative Power, the Congress |
| Section 2. | House of Representatives |
| Section 3. | Senate |
| Section 4. | Elections and Meetings |
| Section 5. | Legislative Proceedings |
| Section 6. | Compensation, Immunities, and Disabilities of Members |
| Section 7. | Revenue Bills; President's Veto |
| Section 8. | Powers of Congress |
| Section 9. | Powers Denied to Congress |
| Section 10. | Powers Denied to the States |

| ARTICLE II | EXECUTIVE DEPARTMENT |
|---|---|
| Section 1. | Executive Power; The President; Term; Election; Qualifications; Compensation; Oath of Office |
| Section 2. | President's Powers and Duties |
| Section 3. | President's Powers and Duties |
| Section 4. | Impeachment |

| ARTICLE III | JUDICIAL DEPARTMENT |
|---|---|
| Section 1. | Judicial Power; Courts; Terms of Office |
| Section 2. | Jurisdiction |
| Section 3. | Treason |

| ARTICLE IV | RELATIONS AMONG THE STATES |
|---|---|
| Section 1. | Full Faith and Credit |
| Section 2. | Privileges and Immunities of Citizens |
| Section 3. | New States, Territories |
| Section 4. | Protection Afforded to States by the Nation |

| ARTICLE V | PROVISIONS FOR AMENDMENT |
|---|---|

| ARTICLE VI | PUBLIC DEBTS; SUPREMACY OF NATIONAL LAW; OATH |
|---|---|
| Section 1. | Validity of Debts |
| Section 2. | Supremacy of National Law |
| Section 3. | Oaths of Office |

| ARTICLE VII | RATIFICATION OF CONSTITUTION |
|---|---|

| AMENDMENTS | |
|---|---|
| 1st Amendment | Freedom of Religion, Speech, Press, Assembly, and Petition |
| 2nd Amendment | Right to Keep, Bear Arms |
| 3rd Amendment | Lodging Troops in Private Homes |
| 4th Amendment | Search, Seizures, Proper Warrants |
| 5th Amendment | Criminal Proceedings, Due Process, Eminent Domain |

## Point-of-Use Resources

**The Constitution Study Guide** provides an in-depth study of the Constitution, from its roots in English law and customs to how it has been redefined by the Supreme Court. The Guide also provides section and chapter reviews, Supreme Court case studies, and a Road to Ratification time line.

**The Constitution Study Guide Teacher's Manual** provides section-by-section lesson plans, graphic organizer masters, and a complete testing program.

## Customize for

### English Language Learners

Ask a volunteer to read the Preamble to the Constitution aloud. Then have students paraphrase the Preamble in their own words, first in their native language, then in English.

## Customize for

### Less Proficient Readers

Help students begin reading the Constitution by having volunteers read the first several sections and clauses aloud, then read the appropriate paraphrase in the Commentary. Point out that students can look to the Commentary to help them understand the reading.

## Customize for

### More Advanced Students

Have students research one amendment to the Constitution and give a report to the class on the importance of the amendment and its impact on American society.

## Point-of-Use Resources

**The Living Constitution** See pp. 6–13 for an overview of the Six Basic Principles of the Constitution.

**Six Basic Principles of the Constitution Posters** These double-sided posters present an illustrated overview of each of the Six Basic Principles of the Constitution.

Note: The original Constitution did not have a title, nor were the sections or clauses numbered. These later editorial changes were added for convenience.

The Preamble states the broad purposes the Constitution is intended to serve—to establish a government that provides for greater cooperation among the States, ensures justice and peace, provides for defense against foreign enemies, promotes the general well-being of the people, and secures liberty now and in the future. The phrase *We the People* emphasizes the twin concepts of popular sovereignty and of representative government.

## LEGISLATIVE DEPARTMENT

### Section 1. Legislative power; Congress

Congress, the nation's lawmaking body, is bicameral in form; that is, it is composed of two houses: the Senate and the House of Representatives. The Framers of the Constitution purposely separated the lawmaking power from the power to enforce the laws (Article II, the Executive Branch) and the power to interpret them (Article III, the Judicial Branch). This system of separation of powers is supplemented by a system of checks and balances; that is, in several provisions the Constitution gives to each of the three branches various powers with which it may restrain the actions of the other two branches.

### Section 2. House of Representatives

**Clause 1. Election** Electors means voters. Members of the House of Representatives are elected every two years. Each State must permit the same persons to vote for United States representatives as it permits to vote for the members of the larger house of its own legislature. The 17th Amendment (1913) extends this requirement to the qualification of voters for United States senators.

**Clause 2. Qualifications** A member of the House of Representatives must be at least 25 years old, an American citizen for seven years, and a resident of the State he or she represents. In addition, political custom, not law, requires that a representative also reside in the district from which he or she is elected.

**Clause 3. Apportionment** The number of representatives each State is entitled to is based on its population, which is counted every 10 years in the census. Congress reapportions the seats among the States after each census. In the Reapportionment Act of 1929, Congress fixed the permanent size of the House at 435 members with each State having at least one representative. Today there is one House seat for approximately every 650,000 persons in the population.

The words "three-fifths of all other persons" referred to slaves and reflected the Three-Fifths Compromise reached by the Framers at Philadelphia in 1787; the phrase was made obsolete, was in effect repealed, by the 13th Amendment in 1865.

**Clause 4. Vacancies** The executive authority refers to the governor of a State. If a member leaves office or dies before the expiration of his or her term, the governor is to call a special election to fill the vacancy.

## PREAMBLE

We the People of the United States, in Order to form a more perfect Union, establish Justice, insure domestic Tranquility, provide for the common defence, promote the general Welfare, and secure the Blessings of Liberty to ourselves and our Posterity, do ordain and establish this Constitution for the United States of America.

### Article I.

### Section 1.

All legislative Powers herein granted shall be vested in a Congress of the United States, which shall consist of a Senate and House of Representatives.

### Section 2.

1. The House of Representatives shall be composed of Members chosen every second Year by the People of the several States, and the Electors in each State shall have the Qualifications requisite for Electors of the most numerous Branch of the State Legislature.

2. No Person shall be a Representative who shall not have attained to the age of twenty-five Years, and been seven Years a Citizen of the United States, and who shall not, when elected, be an Inhabitant of that State in which he shall be chosen.

3. Representatives ~~and direct Taxes~~* shall be apportioned among the several States which may be included within this Union, according to their respective Numbers, ~~which shall be determined by adding to the whole Number of free Persons, including those bound to Service for a Term of Years and excluding Indians not taxed, three fifths of all other Persons.~~ The actual Enumeration shall be made within three Years after the first Meeting of the Congress of the United States, and within every subsequent term of ten Years, in such Manner as they shall by Law direct. The Number of Representatives shall not exceed one for every thirty Thousand, but each State shall have at Least one Representative; and, until such enumeration shall be made, the State of New Hampshire shall be entitled to choose three, Massachusetts eight, Rhode Island and Providence Plantations one, Connecticut five, New York six, New Jersey four, Pennsylvania eight, Delaware one, Maryland six, Virginia ten, North Carolina five, South Carolina five, and Georgia three.

4. When vacancies happen in the Representation from any State, the Executive Authority thereof shall issue Writs of Election to fill such Vacancies.

*The black lines indicate portions of the Constitution altered by subsequent amendments to the document.

**5.** The House of Representatives shall choose their Speaker and other Officers; and shall have the sole Power of Impeachment.

## Section 3.

**1.** The Senate of the United States shall be composed of two Senators from each State ~~chosen by the Legislature thereof~~ for six Years; and each Senator shall have one Vote.

**2.** Immediately after they shall be assembled in Consequences of the first Election, they shall be divided, as equally as may be, into three Classes. The Seats of the Senators of the first Class shall be vacated at the Expiration of the second Year; of the second Class, at the Expiration of the fourth Year; and of the third Class, at the Expiration of the sixth Year; so that one-third may be chosen every second Year; ~~and if Vacancies happen by Resignation, or otherwise, during the Recess of the Legislature of any State, the Executive thereof may make temporary Appointments until the next Meeting of the Legislature, which shall then fill such Vacancies.~~

**3.** No Person shall be a Senator who shall not have attained to the Age of thirty Years, and been nine Years a Citizen of the United States, and who shall not, when elected, be an Inhabitant of that State for which he shall be chosen.

**4.** The Vice President of the United States shall be President of the Senate but shall have no Vote, unless they be equally divided.

**5.** The Senate shall choose their other Officers, and also a President pro tempore, in the Absence of the Vice President, or when he shall exercise the Office of President of the United States.

**6.** The Senate shall have the sole Power to try all Impeachments. When sitting for that Purpose, they shall be on Oath or Affirmation. When the President of the United States is tried, the Chief Justice shall preside: And no Person shall be convicted without the Concurrence of two thirds of the Members present.

**7.** Judgment in Cases of Impeachment shall not extend further than to removal from Office, and disqualification to hold and enjoy any Office of honor, Trust, or Profit under the United States: but the Party convicted shall nevertheless be liable and subject to Indictment, Trial, Judgment and Punishment, according to Law.

**Clause 5. Officers; impeachment** The House elects a Speaker, customarily chosen from the majority party in the House. Impeachment means accusation. The House has the exclusive power to impeach, or accuse, civil officers; the Senate (Article I, Section 3, Clause 6) has the exclusive power to try those impeached by the House.

## Section 3. Senate

**Clause 1. Composition, election, term** Each State has two senators. Each serves for six years and has one vote. Originally, senators were not elected directly by the people, but by each State's legislature. The 17th Amendment, added in 1913, provides for the popular election of senators.

**Clause 2. Classification** The senators elected in 1788 were divided into three groups so that the Senate could become a "continuing body." One-third of the Senate's seats are up for election every two years.

The 17th Amendment provides that a Senate vacancy is to be filled at a special election called by the governor; State law may also permit the governor to appoint a successor to serve until that election is held.

**Clause 3. Qualifications** A senator must be at least 30 years old, a citizen for at least nine years, and must live in the State from which elected.

**Clause 4. Presiding officer** The Vice President presides over the Senate, but may vote only to break a tie.

**Clause 5. Other officers** The Senate chooses its own officers, including a president pro tempore to preside when the Vice President is not there.

**Clause 6. Impeachment trials** The Senate conducts the trials of those officials impeached by the House. The Vice President presides unless the President is on trial, in which case the Chief Justice of the United States does so. A conviction requires the votes of two-thirds of the senators present.

No President has ever been convicted. In 1868 the House voted eleven articles of impeachment against President Andrew Johnson, but the Senate fell one vote short of convicting him. In 1974 President Richard M. Nixon resigned the presidency in the face of almost certain impeachment by the House. The House brought two articles of impeachment against President Bill Clinton in late 1998. Neither charge was supported by even a simple majority vote in the Senate, on February 12, 1999.

**Clause 7. Penalty on conviction** The punishment of an official convicted in an impeachment case has always been removal from office. The Senate can also bar a convicted person from ever holding any federal office, but it is not required to do so. A convicted person can also be tried and punished in a regular court for any crime involved in the impeachment case.

United States Constitution

### Section 4. Elections and Meetings

**Clause 1. Election** In 1842 Congress required that representatives be elected from districts within each State with more than one seat in the House. The districts in each State are drawn by that State's legislature. Seven States now have only one seat in the House: Alaska, Delaware, Montana, North Dakota, South Dakota, Vermont, and Wyoming. The 1842 law also directed that representatives be elected in each State on the same day: the Tuesday after the first Monday in November of every even-numbered year. In 1914 Congress also set that same date for the election of senators.

**Clause 2. Sessions** Congress must meet at least once a year. The 20th Amendment (1933) changed the opening date to January 3.

### Section 5. Legislative Proceedings

**Clause 1. Admission of members; quorum** In 1969 the Supreme Court held that the House cannot exclude any member-elect who satisfies the qualifications set out in Article I, Section 2, Clause 2.

A majority in the House (218 members) or Senate (51) constitutes a quorum. In practice, both houses often proceed with less than a quorum present. However, any member may raise a point of order (demand a "quorum call"). If a roll call then reveals less than a majority of the members present, that chamber must either adjourn or the sergeant at arms must be ordered to round up absent members.

**Clause 2. Rules** Each house has adopted detailed rules to guide its proceedings. Each house may discipline members for unacceptable conduct; expulsion requires a two-thirds vote.

**Clause 3. Record** Each house must keep and publish a record of its meetings. The *Congressional Record* is published for every day that either house of Congress is in session, and provides a written record of all that is said and done on the floor of each house each session.

**Clause 4. Adjournment** Once in session, neither house may suspend (recess) its work for more than three days without the approval of the other house. Both houses must always meet in the same location.

### Section 6. Compensation, Immunities, and Disabilities of Members

**Clause 1. Salaries; immunities** Each house sets its members' salaries, paid by the United States; the 27th Amendment (1992) modified this pay-setting power. This provision establishes "legislative immunity." The purpose of this immunity is to allow members to speak and debate freely in Congress itself. Treason is strictly defined in Article III, Section 3. A felony is any serious crime. A breach of the peace is any indictable offense less than treason or a felony; this exemption from arrest is of little real importance today.

**Clause 2. Restrictions on office holding** No sitting member of either house may be appointed to an office in the executive or in the judicial branch if that position was created or its salary was increased during that member's current elected term. The second

### Section 4.

1. The Times, Places and Manner of holding Elections for Senators and Representatives, shall be prescribed in each State by the Legislature thereof; but the Congress may at any time by law make or alter such Regulations, except as to the Places of choosing Senators.

2. The Congress shall assemble at least once in every Year, and such Meeting shall be on the first Monday in December, unless they shall by Law appoint a different Day.

### Section 5.

1. Each House shall be the Judge of the Elections, Returns and Qualifications of its own Members, and a Majority of each shall constitute a Quorum to do Business; but a smaller Number may adjourn from day to day, and may be authorized to compel the Attendance of absent Members, in such Manner, and under such Penalties, as each House may provide.

2. Each House may determine the Rules of its Proceedings, punish its Members for disorderly Behavior, and, with the Concurrence of two thirds, expel a Member.

3. Each House shall keep a Journal of its Proceedings, and from time to time publish the same, excepting such Parts as may in their Judgment require Secrecy; and the Yeas and Nays of the Members of either House on any question shall, at the Desire of one fifth of those Present, be entered on the Journal.

4. Neither House, during the Session of Congress, shall, without the Consent of the other, adjourn for more than three days, nor to any other Place than that in which the two Houses shall be sitting.

### Section 6.

1. The Senators and Representatives shall receive a Compensation for their Services, to be ascertained by Law, and paid out of the Treasury of the United States. They shall in all Cases, except Treason, Felony, and Breach of the Peace, be privileged from Arrest during their Attendance at the Session of their respective Houses, and in going to and returning from the same; and for any Speech or Debate in either House, they shall not be questioned in any other Place.

2. No Senator or Representative shall, during the Time for which he was elected, be appointed to any civil Office under the Authority of the United States, which shall have been created, or the Emoluments whereof shall have

been increased during such time; and no Person holding any Office under the United States, shall be a Member of either House during his Continuance in Office.

## Section 7.

1. All Bills for raising Revenue shall originate in the House of Representatives; but the Senate may propose or concur with amendments as on other Bills.

2. Every Bill which shall have passed the House of Representatives and the Senate, shall, before it become a law, be presented to the President of the United States: If he approve, he shall sign it, but if not he shall return it, with his Objections to that House in which it shall have originated, who shall enter the Objections at large on their Journal, and proceed to reconsider it. If after such Reconsideration two thirds of the House shall agree to pass the Bill, it shall be sent, together with the Objections, to the other House, by which it shall likewise be reconsidered, and if approved by two thirds of that House, it shall become a Law. But in all such Cases the Votes of both Houses shall be determined by Yeas and Nays, and the Names of the Persons voting for and against the Bill shall be entered on the Journal of each House respectively. If any Bill shall not be returned by the President within ten Days (Sunday excepted) after it shall have been presented to him, the Same shall be a law, in like Manner as if he had signed it, unless the Congress by their Adjournment, prevent its Return, in which Case it shall not be a Law.

3. Every Order, Resolution, or Vote to which the Concurrence of the Senate and House of Representatives may be necessary (except on a question of adjournment) shall be presented to the President of the United States; and before the Same shall take Effect, shall be approved by him, or, being disapproved by him, shall be repassed by two thirds of the Senate and House of Representatives, according to the Rules and Limitations prescribed in the Case of a Bill.

## Section 8.

The Congress shall have Power

1. To lay and collect Taxes, Duties, Imposts and Excises to pay the Debts and provide for the common Defence and general Welfare of the United States; but all Duties, Imposts and Excises, shall be uniform throughout the United States;

2. To borrow Money on the credit of the United States;

3. To regulate Commerce with foreign Nations, and among the several States, and with the Indian Tribes;

part of this clause—forbidding any person serving in either the executive or the judicial branch from also serving in Congress—reinforces the principle of separation of powers.

## Section 7. Revenue Bills, President's Veto

**Clause 1. Revenue bills** All bills that raise money must originate in the House. However, the Senate has the power to amend any revenue bill sent to it from the lower house.

**Clause 2. Enactment of laws; veto** Once both houses have passed a bill, it must be sent to the President. The President may (1) sign the bill, thus making it law; (2) veto the bill, whereupon it must be returned to the house in which it originated; or (3) allow the bill to become law without signature, by not acting upon it within 10 days of its receipt from Congress, not counting Sundays. The President has a fourth option at the end of a congressional session: If he does not act on a measure within 10 days, and Congress adjourns during that period, the bill dies; the "pocket veto" has been applied to it. A presidential veto may be overridden by a two-thirds vote in each house.

**Clause 3. Other measures** This clause refers to joint resolutions, measures Congress often passes to deal with unusual, temporary, or ceremonial matters. A joint resolution passed by Congress and signed by the President has the force of law, just as a bill does. As a matter of custom, a joint resolution proposing an amendment to the Constitution is not submitted to the President for signature or veto. Concurrent and simple resolutions do not have the force of law and, therefore, are not submitted to the President.

## Section 8. Powers of Congress

**Clause 1.** The 18 separate clauses in this section set out 27 of the many expressed powers the Constitution grants to Congress. In this clause Congress is given the power to levy and provide for the collection of various kinds of taxes, in order to finance the operations of the government. All federal taxes must be levied at the same rates throughout the country.

**Clause 2.** Congress has power to borrow money to help finance the government. Federal borrowing is most often done through the sale of bonds on which interest is paid. The Constitution does not limit the amount the government may borrow.

**Clause 3.** This clause, the Commerce Clause, gives Congress the power to regulate both foreign and interstate trade. Much of what Congress does, it does on the basis of its commerce power.

**Clause 4.** Congress has the exclusive power to determine how aliens may become citizens of the United States. Congress may also pass laws relating to bankruptcy.

**Clause 5.** Congress has the power to establish and require the use of uniform gauges of time, distance, weight, volume, area, and the like.

**Clause 6.** Congress has the power to make it a federal crime to falsify the coins, paper money, bonds, stamps, and the like of the United States.

**Clause 7.** Congress has the power to provide for and regulate the transportation and delivery of mail; "post offices" are those buildings and other places where mail is deposited for dispatch; "post roads" include all routes over or upon which mail is carried.

**Clause 8.** Congress has the power to provide for copyrights and patents. A copyright gives an author or composer the exclusive right to control the reproduction, publication, and sale of literary, musical, or other creative work. A patent gives a person the exclusive right to control the manufacture or sale of his or her invention.

**Clause 9.** Congress has the power to create the lower federal courts, all of the several federal courts that function beneath the Supreme Court.

**Clause 10.** Congress has the power to prohibit, as a federal crime: (1) certain acts committed outside the territorial jurisdiction of the United States, and (2) the commission within the United States of any wrong against any nation with which we are at peace.

**Clause 11.** Only Congress can declare war. However, the President, as commander in chief of the armed forces (Article II, Section 2, Clause 1), can make war without such a formal declaration. Letters of marque and reprisal are commissions authorizing private persons to outfit vessels (privateers) to capture and destroy enemy ships in time of war; they were forbidden in international law by the Declaration of Paris of 1856, and the United States has honored the ban since the Civil War.

**Clauses 12 and 13.** Congress has the power to provide for and maintain the nation's armed forces. It established the air force as an independent element of the armed forces in 1947, an exercise of its inherent powers in foreign relations and national defense. The two-year limit on spending for the army insures civilian control of the military.

**Clause 14.** Today these rules are set out in a lengthy, oft-amended law, the Uniform Code of Military Justice, passed by Congress in 1950.

**Clauses 15 and 16.** In the National Defense Act of 1916, Congress made each State's militia (volunteer army) a part of the National Guard. Today, Congress and the States cooperate in its maintenance. Ordinarily, each State's National Guard is under the command of that State's governor; but Congress has given the President the power to call any or all of those units into federal service when necessary.

**Clause 17.** In 1791 Congress accepted land grants from Maryland and Virginia and established the District of Columbia for the nation's capital. Assuming Virginia's grant would never be needed, Congress returned it in 1846. Today, the elected government of the District's 69 square miles operates under

**4.** To establish an uniform Rule of Naturalization, and uniform Laws on the subject of Bankruptcies throughout the United States;

**5.** To coin Money, regulate the Value thereof, and of foreign Coin, and fix the Standard of Weights and Measures;

**6.** To provide for the Punishment of counterfeiting the Securities and current Coin of the United States;

**7.** To establish Post Offices and post Roads;

**8.** To promote the Progress of Science and useful Arts, by securing, for limited Times to Authors and Inventors the exclusive Right to their respective Writings and Discoveries;

**9.** To constitute Tribunals inferior to the supreme Court;

**10.** To define and punish Piracies and Felonies committed on the high Seas, and Offences against the Law of nations;

**11.** To declare War, grant Letters of Marque and Reprisal, and make Rules concerning Captures on Land and Water;

**12.** To raise and support Armies; but no Appropriation of Money to that Use shall be for a longer Term than two Years;

**13.** To provide and maintain a Navy;

**14.** To make Rules for the Government and Regulation of the land and naval Forces;

**15.** To provide for calling forth the Militia to execute the Laws of the Union, suppress Insurrections and repel Invasions;

**16.** To provide for organizing, arming, and disciplining the Militia, and for governing such Part of them as may be employed in the Service of the United States, reserving to the States respectively the Appointment of the Officers, and the Authority of training the Militia according to the discipline prescribed by Congress;

**17.** To exercise exclusive Legislation in all Cases whatsoever, over such District (not exceeding ten Miles square) as may, by Cession of Particular States, and the Acceptance of Congress, become the Seat of the Government of the United States, and to exercise like

Authority over all Places purchased by the Consent of the Legislature of the State in which the Same shall be, for the Erection of Forts, Magazines, Arsenals, Dockyards and other needful Buildings;—And

**18.** To make all Laws which shall be necessary and proper for carrying into Execution the foregoing Powers and all other Powers vested by this Constitution in the Government of the United States, or in any Department or Officer thereof.

## Section 9.

**1.** The Migration or Importation of such Persons as any of the States now existing shall think proper to admit, shall not be prohibited by the Congress prior to the Year one thousand eight hundred and eight, but a Tax or duty may be imposed on such Importation, not exceeding ten dollars for each Person.

**2.** The Privilege of the Writ of Habeas Corpus shall not be suspended, unless when in Cases of Rebellion or Invasion the public safety may require it.

**3.** No Bill of Attainder or ex post facto Law shall be passed.

**4.** No Capitation, or other direct, Tax shall be laid, unless in Proportion to the Census of Enumeration hereinbefore directed to be taken.

**5.** No Tax or Duty shall be laid on Articles exported from any State.

**6.** No Preference shall be given by any Regulation of Commerce or Revenue to the Ports of one State over those of another: nor shall Vessels bound to, or from, one State, be obliged to enter, clear or pay Duties in another.

**7.** No Money shall be drawn from the Treasury, but in Consequence of Appropriations made by Law; and a regular Statement and Account of the Receipts and Expenditures of all public Money shall be published from time to time.

**8.** No Title of Nobility shall be granted by the United States: And no Person holding any Office of Profit or Trust under them, shall, without the Consent of the Congress, accept of any present, Emolument, Office, or Title, of any kind whatever, from any King, Prince, or foreign State.

## Section 10.

**1.** No State shall enter into any Treaty, Alliance, or Confederation; grant Letters of Marque and Reprisal; coin Money; emit Bills of Credit; make any Thing but

the authority of Congress. Congress also has the power to acquire other lands from the States for various federal purposes.

**Clause 18.** This is the Necessary and Proper Clause, also often called the Elastic Clause. It is the constitutional basis for the many and far-reaching implied powers of the Federal Government.

## Section 9. Powers Denied to Congress

**Clause 1.** The phrase "such persons" referred to slaves. This provision was part of the Commerce Compromise, one of the bargains struck in the writing of the Constitution. Congress outlawed the slave trade in 1808.

**Clause 2.** A writ of habeas corpus, the "great writ of liberty," is a court order directing a sheriff, warden, or other public officer, or a private person, who is detaining another to "produce the body" of the one being held in order that the legality of the detention may be determined by the court.

**Clause 3.** A bill of attainder is a legislative act that inflicts punishment without a judicial trial. See Article I, Section 10, and Article III, Section 3, Clause 2. An *ex post facto* law is any criminal law that operates retroactively to the disadvantage of the accused. See Article I, Section 10.

**Clause 4.** A capitation tax is literally a "head tax," a tax levied on each person in the population. A direct tax is one paid directly to the government by the taxpayer—for example, an income or a property tax; an indirect tax is one paid to another private party who then pays it to the government—for example, a sales tax. This provision was modified by the 16th Amendment (1913), giving Congress the power to levy "taxes on incomes, from whatever source derived."

**Clause 5.** This provision was a part of the Commerce Compromise made by the Framers in 1787. Congress has the power to tax imported goods, however.

**Clause 6.** All ports within the United States must be treated alike by Congress as it exercises its taxing and commerce powers. Congress cannot tax goods sent by water from one State to another, nor may it give the ports of one State any legal advantage over those of another.

**Clause 7.** This clause gives Congress its vastly important "power of the purse," a major check on presidential power. Federal money can be spent only in those amounts and for those purposes expressly authorized by an act of Congress. All federal income and spending must be accounted for, regularly and publicly.

**Clause 8.** This provision, preventing the establishment of a nobility, reflects the principle that "all men are created equal." It was also intended to discourage foreign attempts to bribe or otherwise corrupt officers of the government.

## Section 10. Powers Denied to the States

**Clause 1.** The States are not sovereign governments and so cannot make agreements or otherwise negotiate with foreign states; the power to conduct foreign relations is an exclusive power of the National Government. The power to coin money is also an exclusive power of the National Government. Several powers forbidden to the National Government are here also forbidden to the States.

**Clause 2.** This provision relates to foreign, not interstate, commerce. Only Congress, not the States, can tax imports; and the States are, like Congress, forbidden the power to tax exports.

**Clause 3.** A duty of tonnage is a tax laid on ships according to their cargo capacity. Each State has a constitutional right to provide for and maintain a militia; but no State may keep a standing army or navy. The several restrictions here prevent the States from assuming powers that the Constitution elsewhere grants to the National Government.

## EXECUTIVE DEPARTMENT

### Section 1.  President and Vice President

**Clause 1. Executive power, term** This clause gives to the President the very broad "executive power," the power to enforce the laws and otherwise administer the public policies of the United States. It also sets the length of the presidential (and vice-presidential) term of office; see the 22nd Amendment (1951), which places a limit on presidential (but not vice-presidential) tenure.

**Clause 2. Electoral college** This clause establishes the "electoral college," although the Constitution does not use that term. It is a body of presidential electors chosen in each State, and it selects the President and Vice President every four years. The number of electors chosen in each State equals the number of senators and representatives that State has in Congress.

**Clause 3. Election of President and Vice President** This clause was replaced by the 12th Amendment in 1804.

---

gold and silver Coin a Tender in Payment of Debts; pass any Bill of Attainder, ex post facto Law, or Law impairing the Obligation of Contracts, or grant any Title of Nobility.

**2.** No State shall, without the Consent of the Congress, lay any Imposts or Duties on Imports or Exports, except what may be absolutely necessary for executing its inspection Laws; and the net Produce of all Duties and Imposts, laid by any State on Imports or Exports, shall be for the Use of the Treasury of the United States; and all such Laws shall be subject to the Revision and Control of the Congress.

**3.** No State shall, without the Consent of Congress, lay any Duty of Tonnage, keep Troops, or Ships of War in time of Peace, enter into any Agreement or Compact with another State, or with a foreign Power, or engage in War, unless actually invaded, or in such imminent Danger as will not admit of delay.

## Article II

### Section 1.

**1.** The executive Power shall be vested in a President of the United States of America. He shall hold his Office during the Term of four Years, and, together with the Vice President, chosen for the same Term, be elected as follows:

**2.** Each State shall appoint, in such Manner as the Legislature thereof may direct, a Number of Electors, equal to the whole Number of Senators and Representatives to which the State may be entitled in the Congress: but no Senator or Representative, or Person holding an Office of Trust or Profit, under the United States, shall be appointed an Elector.

**3.** ~~The Electors shall meet in their respective States, and vote by Ballot for two Persons, of whom one at least shall not be an Inhabitant of the same State with themselves. And they shall make a List of all the Persons voted for, and of the Number of Votes for each; which List they shall sign and certify, and transmit sealed to the Seat of the Government of the United States, directed to the President of the Senate. The President of the Senate shall, in the Presence of the Senate and House of Representatives, open all the Certificates, and the Votes shall then be counted. The Person having the greatest Number of Votes shall be the President, if such Number be a majority of the whole Number of Electors appointed; and if there be more than one who have such Majority, and have an equal Number of Votes, then, the House of Representatives shall immediately choose by Ballot one of them for President; and if no Person have a Majority, then from the five highest on the List the said House shall in like Manner choose the President. But in choosing the President, the Votes shall be taken by States, the Representatives from each State having one Vote; a quorum for this Purpose shall consist of a Member or Members from two thirds of the States, and a Majority of~~

all the States shall be necessary to a Choice. In every
Case, after the Choice of the President, the Person having
the greatest Number of Votes of the Electors shall be the
Vice President. But if there should remain two or more
who have equal Votes, the Senate shall choose from them
by Ballot the Vice President.

**4.** The Congress may determine the Time of choosing the
Electors, and the Day on which they shall give their
Votes; which Day shall be the same throughout the
United States.

**5.** No Person except a natural born Citizen, or a Citizen of
the United States, at the time of the Adoption of this
Constitution, shall be eligible to the Office of President; neither shall any person be eligible to that Office who shall not
have attained to the Age of thirty-five Years, and been fourteen Years a Resident within the United States.

**6.** In Case of the Removal of the President from Office,
or of his Death, Resignation, or Inability to discharge the
Powers and Duties of the said Office, the Same shall
devolve on the Vice President, and the Congress may by
Law provide for the Case of Removal, Death,
Resignation or Inability, both of the President and Vice
President, declaring what Officer shall then act as
President, and such Officer shall act accordingly, until the
Disability be removed, or a President shall be elected.

**7.** The President shall, at stated Times, receive for his
Services, a Compensation, which shall neither be
increased nor diminished during the Period for which he
shall have been elected, and he shall not receive within
that Period any other Emolument from the United States,
or any of them.

**8.** Before he enter on the Execution of his Office, he shall
take the following Oath or Affirmation:
"I do solemnly swear (or affirm) that I will faithfully execute the Office of President of the United States, and will
to the best of my Ability, preserve, protect and defend the
Constitution of the United States."

## Section 2.
**1.** The President shall be Commander in Chief of the
Army and Navy of the United States, and of the Militia
of the several States, when called into the actual Service
of the United States; he may require the Opinion, in writing, of the principal Officer in each of the executive
Departments, upon any Subject relating to the Duties of
their respective Offices, and he shall have Power to Grant
Reprieves and Pardons for Offences against the United
States, except in Cases of Impeachment.

**2.** He shall have Power, by and with the Advice and
Consent of the Senate, to make Treaties, provided two
thirds of the Senators present concur; and he shall nominate, and by and with the Advice and Consent of the
Senate, shall appoint Ambassadors, other public Ministers

**Clause 4. Date** Congress has set the date for the choosing of
electors as the Tuesday after the first Monday in November
every fourth year, and for the casting of electoral votes as the
Monday after the second Wednesday in December of that year.

**Clause 5. Qualifications** The President must have been born a
citizen of the United States, be at least 35 years old, and have
been a resident of the United States for at least 14 years.

**Clause 6. Vacancy** This clause was modified by the 25th
Amendment (1967), which provides expressly for the succes-
sion of the Vice President, for the filling of a vacancy in the Vice
Presidency, and for the determination of presidential inability.

**Clause 7. Compensation** The President now receives a salary
of $400,000 and a taxable expense account of $50,000 a
year. Those amounts cannot be changed during a presidential
term; thus, Congress cannot use the President's compensation
as a bargaining tool to influence executive decisions. The
phrase "any other emolument" means, in effect, any valuable
gift; it does not mean that the President cannot be provided
with such benefits of office as the White House, extensive staff
assistance, and much else.

**Clause 8. Oath of office** The chief justice of the United States
regularly administers this oath or affirmation, but any judicial
officer may do so. Thus, Calvin Coolidge was sworn into office
in 1923 by his father, a justice of the peace in Vermont.

## Section 2. President's Powers and Duties
**Clause 1. Military, civil powers** The President, a civilian,
heads the nation's armed forces, a key element in the
Constitution's insistence on civilian control of the military. The
President's power to "require the opinion, in writing" provides
the constitutional basis for the cabinet. The President's power
to grant reprieves and pardons, the power of clemency, extends
only to federal cases.

**Clause 2. Treaties, appointments** The President has the sole
power to make treaties; to become effective, a treaty must be
approved by a two-thirds vote in the Senate. In practice, the
President can also make executive agreements with foreign
governments; these pacts, which are frequently made and

usually deal with routine matters, do not require Senate consent. The President appoints the principal officers of the executive branch and all federal judges; the "inferior officers" are those who hold lesser posts.

**Clause 3. Recess appointments** When the Senate is not in session, appointments that require Senate consent can be made by the President on a temporary basis, as "recess appointments."

## Section 3. President's Powers and Duties

The President delivers a State of the Union Message to Congress soon after that body convenes each year. That message is delivered to the nation's lawmakers and, importantly, to the American people, as well. It is shortly followed by the proposed federal budget and an economic report; and the President may send special messages to Congress at any time. In all of these communications, Congress is urged to take those actions the Chief Executive finds to be in the national interest. The President also has the power: to call special sessions of Congress; to adjourn Congress if its two houses cannot agree for that purpose; to receive the diplomatic representatives of other governments; to insure the proper execution of all federal laws; and to empower federal officers to hold their posts and perform their duties.

## Section 4. Impeachment

The Constitution outlines the impeachment process in Article I, Section 2, Clause 5 and in Section 3, Clauses 6 and 7.

## JUDICIAL DEPARTMENT
### Section 1. Courts, Terms of Office

The judicial power conferred here is the power of federal courts to hear and decide cases, disputes between the government and individuals and between private persons (parties). The Constitution creates only the Supreme Court of the United States; it gives to Congress the power to establish other, lower federal courts (Article I, Section 8, Clause 9) and to fix the size of the Supreme Court. The words "during good behavior" mean, in effect, for life.

## Section 2. Jurisdiction

**Clause 1. Cases to be heard** This clause sets out the jurisdiction of the federal courts; that is, it identifies those cases that may be tried in those courts. The federal courts can hear and decide—have jurisdiction over—a case depending on either the subject matter or the parties involved in that case. The jurisdiction of the federal courts in cases involving States was substantially restricted by the 11th Amendment in 1795.

and Consuls, Judges of the supreme Court, and all other Officers of the United States, whose Appointments are not herein otherwise provided for, and which shall be established by Law: but the Congress may by Law vest the Appointment of such inferior Officers, as they think proper, in the President alone, in the Courts of Law, or in the Heads of Departments.

3. The President shall have Power to fill up all Vacancies that may happen during the Recess of the Senate, by granting Commissions which shall expire at the End of their next Session.

### Section 3.

He shall from time to time give to the Congress Information of the State of the Union, and recommend to their Consideration such Measures as he shall judge necessary and expedient; he may, on extraordinary Occasions, convene both Houses, or either of them, and in Case of Disagreement between them, with Respect to the Time of Adjournment, he may adjourn them to such Time as he shall think proper; he shall receive Ambassadors and other public Ministers; he shall take Care that the Laws be faithfully executed, and shall Commission all the Officers of the United States.

### Section 4.

The President, Vice President and all Civil Officers of the United States, shall be removed from Office on Impeachment for and Conviction of, Treason, Bribery, or other high Crimes and Misdemeanors.

## Article III
### Section 1.

The judicial Power of the United States, shall be vested in one supreme Court, and in such inferior Courts as the Congress may from time to time ordain and establish. The Judges, both of the supreme and inferior Courts, shall hold their Offices during good Behavior, and shall, at stated Times, receive for their Services, a Compensation, which shall not be diminished during their Continuance in Office.

### Section 2.

1. The judicial Power shall extend to all Cases, in Law and Equity, arising under this Constitution, the Laws of the United States, and Treaties made, or which shall be made, under their Authority;— to all Cases affecting Ambassadors, other public ministers, and Consuls;— to all Cases of Admiralty and maritime Jurisdiction;— to Controversies to which the United States shall be a Party;— to Controversies between two or more States;— between a State and Citizens of another State;— between Citizens of different States;— between Citizens of the same State claiming Lands under Grants of different States, and between a State, or the Citizens thereof, and foreign States, Citizens, or Subjects.

**2.** In all Cases affecting Ambassadors, other public Ministers and Consuls, and those in which a State shall be a Party, the supreme Court shall have original Jurisdiction. In all the other Cases before mentioned, the supreme Court shall have appellate Jurisdiction, both as to Law and Fact, with such Exceptions, and under such Regulations as the Congress shall make.

**3.** The trial of all Crimes, except in Cases of Impeachment, shall be by Jury; and such Trial shall be held in the State where the said Crimes shall have been committed; but when not committed within any State, the Trial shall be at such Place or Places as the Congress may by Law have directed.

## Section 3.

**1.** Treason against the United States shall consist only in levying War against them, or in adhering to their Enemies, giving them Aid and Comfort. No Person shall be convicted of Treason unless on the Testimony of two Witnesses to the same overt Act, or on Confession in open Court.

**2.** The Congress shall have Power to declare the Punishment of Treason, but no Attainder of Treason shall work Corruption of Blood, or Forfeiture except during the Life of the Person attainted.

## *Article IV*

### Section 1.

Full Faith and Credit shall be given in each State to the public Acts, Records, and judicial Proceedings of every other State. And the Congress may by general Laws prescribe the Manner in which such Acts, Records and Proceedings shall be proved, and the Effect thereof.

### Section 2.

**1.** The Citizens of each State shall be entitled to all Privileges and Immunities of Citizens in the several States.

**2.** A Person charged in any State with Treason, Felony, or other Crime, who shall flee from justice, and be found in another State, shall on Demand of the executive Authority of the State from which he fled, be delivered up, to be removed to the State having Jurisdiction of the Crime.

**3.** ~~No Person held to Service or Labor in one State, under the Laws thereof, escaping into another, shall, in Consequence of any Law or Regulation therein, be discharged from Service or Labor, but shall be delivered up on Claim of the Party to whom such Service or Labor may be due.~~

**Clause 2. Supreme Court jurisdiction** Original jurisdiction refers to the power of a court to hear a case in the first instance, not on appeal from a lower court. Appellate jurisdiction refers to a court's power to hear a case on appeal from a lower court, from the court in which the case was originally tried. This clause gives the Supreme Court both original and appellate jurisdiction. However, nearly all of the cases the High Court hears are brought to it on appeal from the lower federal courts and the highest State courts.

**Clause 3. Jury trial in criminal cases** A person accused of a federal crime is guaranteed the right to trial by jury in a federal court in the State where the crime was committed; see the 5th and 6th amendments. The right to trial by jury in serious criminal cases in the State courts is guaranteed by the 6th and 14th amendments.

## Section 3. Treason

**Clause 1. Definition** Treason is the only crime defined in the Constitution. The Framers intended the very specific definition here to prevent the loose use of the charge of treason—for example, against persons who criticize the government. Treason can be committed only in time of war and only by a citizen or a resident alien. Two witnesses must testify to the same act.

**Clause 2. Punishment** Congress has provided that the punishment that a federal court may impose on a convicted traitor may range from a minimum of five years in prison and/or a $10,000 fine to a maximum of death; no person convicted of treason has ever been executed by the United States. No legal punishment can be imposed on the family or descendants of a convicted traitor. Congress has also made it a crime for any person (in either peace or wartime) to commit espionage or sabotage, to attempt to overthrow the government by force, or to conspire to do any of these things.

## *RELATIONS AMONG STATES*

### Section 1. Full Faith and Credit

Each State must recognize the validity of the laws, public records, and court decisions of every other State.

### Section 2. Privileges and Immunities of Citizens

**Clause 1. Residents of other States** In effect, this clause means that no State may discriminate against the residents of other States; that is, a State's laws cannot draw unreasonable distinctions between its own residents and those of any of the other States. See Section 1 of the 14th Amendment.

**Clause 2. Extradition** The process of returning a fugitive to another State is known as "interstate rendition" or, more commonly, "extradition." Usually, that process works routinely; some extradition requests are contested however—especially in cases with racial or political overtones. A governor may refuse to extradite a fugitive; but the federal courts can compel an unwilling governor to obey this constitutional command.

**Clause 3. Fugitive slaves** This clause effectively nullified the 13th Amendment, which abolished slavery in 1865.

### Section 3. New States; Territories

**Clause 1. New States** Only Congress can admit new States to the Union. A new State may not be created by taking territory from an existing State without the consent of that State's legislature. Congress has admitted 37 States since the original 13 formed the Union. Five States—Vermont, Kentucky, Tennessee, Maine, and West Virginia—were created from parts of existing States. Texas was an independent republic before admission. California was admitted after being ceded to the United States by Mexico. Each of the other 30 States entered the Union only after a period of time as an organized territory of the United States.

**Clause 2. Territory, property** Congress has the power to make laws concerning the territories, other public lands, and all other property of the United States.

### Section 4. Protection Afforded to States by the Nation

The Constitution does not define "a republican form of government," but the phrase is generally understood to mean a representative government. The Federal Government must also defend each State against attacks from outside its border and, at the request of a State's legislature or its governor, aid its efforts to put down internal disorders.

## PROVISIONS FOR AMENDMENT

This section provides for the methods by which formal changes can be made in the Constitution. An amendment may be proposed in one of two ways: by a two-thirds vote in each house of Congress, or by a national convention called by Congress at the request of two-thirds of the State legislatures. A proposed amendment may be ratified in one of two ways: by three-fourths of the State legislatures, or by three-fourths of the States in conventions called for that purpose. Congress has the power to determine the method by which a proposed amendment may be ratified. The amendment process cannot be used to deny any State its equal representation in the United States Senate. To this point, 27 amendments have been adopted. To date, all of the amendments except the 21st Amendment were proposed by Congress and ratified by the State legislatures. Only the 21st Amendment was ratified by the convention method.

## NATIONAL DEBTS, SUPREMACY OF NATIONAL LAW, OATH

### Section 1. Validity of Debts

Congress had borrowed large sums of money during the Revolution and later during the Critical Period of the 1780s. This provision, a pledge that the new government would honor those debts, did much to create confidence in that government.

### Section 2. Supremacy of National Law

This section sets out the Supremacy Clause, a specific declaration of the supremacy of federal law over any and all forms of State law. No State, including its local governments, may make or enforce any law that conflicts with any provision in the Constitution, an act of Congress, a treaty, or an order, rule, or regulation properly issued by the President or his subordinates in the executive branch.

### Section 3.

1. New States may be admitted by the Congress into this Union; but no new State shall be formed or erected within the Jurisdiction of any other State; nor any State be formed by the Junction of two or more States, or Parts of States, without the Consent of the Legislatures of the States concerned as well as of the Congress.

2. The Congress shall have Power to dispose of and make all needful Rules and Regulations respecting the Territory or other Property belonging to the United States; and nothing in this Constitution shall be so construed as to Prejudice any Claims of the United States, or of any particular State.

### Section 4.

The United States shall guarantee to every State in this Union a Republican Form of Government, and shall protect each of them against Invasion; and on Application of the Legislature, or of the Executive (when the Legislature cannot be convened) against domestic Violence.

## Article V

The Congress, whenever two thirds of both Houses shall deem it necessary, shall propose Amendments to this Constitution, or, on the Application of the Legislatures of two thirds of the several States, shall call a Convention for proposing Amendments, which, in either Case, shall be valid to all Intents and Purposes, as Part of this Constitution, when ratified by the Legislatures of three fourths of the several States, or by Conventions in three fourths thereof, as the one or the other Mode of Ratification may be proposed by the Congress; Provided that no Amendment which may be made prior to the Year One thousand eight hundred and eight shall in any Manner affect the first and fourth Clauses in the Ninth section of the first Article; and that no State, without its Consent, shall be deprived of its equal Suffrage in the Senate.

## Article VI

### Section 1.

All Debts contracted and Engagements entered into, before the Adoption of this Constitution, shall be as valid against the United States under this Constitution, as under the Confederation.

### Section 2.

This Constitution, and the Laws of the United States which shall be made in Pursuance thereof; and all Treaties made, or which shall be made, under the Authority of the United States, shall be the supreme Law of the Land; and the Judges in every State shall be bound thereby, anything in the constitution or Laws of any State to the Contrary notwithstanding.

## Section 3.

The Senators and Representatives before mentioned, and the Members of the several State legislatures, and all executive and judicial Officers, both of the United States and of the several States, shall be bound by Oath or Affirmation, to support this Constitution; but no religious Test shall ever be required as a Qualification to any Office or public Trust under the United States.

## Article VII

The ratification of the Conventions of nine States, shall be sufficient for the Establishment of this Constitution between the States so ratifying the same.

Done in Convention by the Unanimous Consent of the States present the Seventeenth Day of September in the Year of our Lord one thousand seven hundred and Eighty-seven and of the Independence of the United States of America the twelfth. In witness whereof We have hereunto subscribed our Names.

| | |
|---|---|
| Attest: William Jackson, SECRETARY | **NEW YORK** Alexander Hamilton |
| George Washington, PRESIDENT AND DEPUTY FROM VIRGINIA | **NEW JERSEY** William Livingston David Brearley William Paterson Jonathan Dayton |
| **NEW HAMPSHIRE** John Langdon Nicholas Gilman | **PENNSYLVANIA** Benjamin Franklin Thomas Mifflin Robert Morris |
| **MASSACHUSETTS** Nathaniel Gorham Rufus King | George Clymer Thomas Fitzsimons Jared Ingersoll James Wilson Gouverneur Morris |
| **CONNECTICUT** William Samuel Johnson Roger Sherman | |

| | |
|---|---|
| **DELAWARE** George Read Gunning Bedford, Jr. John Dickinson Richard Bassett Jacob Broom | **NORTH CAROLINA** William Blount Richard Dobbs Spaight Hugh Williamson |
| **MARYLAND** James McHenry Dan of St. Thomas Jennifer Daniel Carroll | **SOUTH CAROLINA** John Rutledge Charles Cotesworth Pinckney Charles Pinckney Pierce Butler |
| **VIRGINIA** John Blair James Madison, Jr. | **GEORGIA** William Few Abraham Baldwin |

# AMENDMENTS

## 1st Amendment.

Congress shall make no law respecting an establishment of religion, or prohibiting the free exercise thereof, or abridging the freedom of speech, or of the press; or the right of the people peaceably to assemble, and to petition the Government for a redress of grievances.

### Section 3. Oaths of Office

This provision reinforces the Supremacy Clause; all public officers, at every level in the United States, owe their first allegiance to the Constitution of the United States. No religious qualification can be imposed as a condition for holding any public office.

### RATIFICATION OF CONSTITUTION

The proposed Constitution was signed by George Washington and 37 of his fellow Framers on September 17, 1787. (George Read of Delaware signed for himself and also for his absent colleague, John Dickinson.)

The first 10 amendments, the Bill of Rights, were each proposed by Congress on September 25, 1789, and ratified by the necessary three-fourths of the States on December 15, 1791. These amendments were originally intended to restrict the National Government—not the States. However, the Supreme Court has several times held that most of their provisions also apply to the States, through the 14th Amendment's Due Process Clause.

### 1st Amendment. Freedom of Religion, Speech, Press, Assembly, and Petition

The 1st Amendment sets out five basic liberties: The guarantee of freedom of religion is both a protection of religious thought and practice and a provision against a state religion. The guarantees of freedom of speech and press assure to all persons a right to speak, publish, and otherwise express their views. The guarantees of the rights of assembly and petition protect the right to join with others in public meetings, political parties, interest groups, and other associations to discuss public affairs and influence public policy. None of these rights is guaranteed in absolute terms, however; like all other civil rights guarantees, each of them may be exercised only with regard to the rights of all other persons.

### 2nd Amendment. Bearing Arms

The right of the people to keep and bear arms was insured by the 2nd Amendment.

### 3rd Amendment. Quartering of Troops

This amendment was intended to prevent what had been common British practice in the colonial period.

### 4th Amendment. Searches and Seizures

The basic rule laid down by the 4th Amendment is this: Police officers have no general right to search for or seize evidence or seize (arrest) persons. Except in particular circumstances, a proper warrant (a court order) must be obtained with probable cause (on reasonable grounds) before evidence is seized or a suspect is arrested. This guarantee is reinforced by the exclusionary rule, developed by the Supreme Court: Evidence gained as the result of an unlawful search or seizure cannot be used at the court trial of the person from whom it was seized.

### 5th Amendment. Criminal Proceedings; Due Process; Eminent Domain

A person can be tried for a serious federal crime only if he or she has been indicted (charged, accused of that crime) by a grand jury. No one may be subjected to double jeopardy—that is, tried twice for the same crime. All persons are protected against self-incrimination; no person can be legally compelled to answer any question in any governmental proceeding if that answer could lead to that person's prosecution. The 5th Amendment's Due Process Clause prohibits unfair, arbitrary actions by the Federal Government; a like prohibition is set out against the States in the 14th Amendment. Government may take private property for a legitimate public purpose; but when it exercises that power of eminent domain, it must pay a fair price for the property seized.

### 6th Amendment. Criminal Proceedings

A person accused of crime has the right to be tried in court without undue delay and by an impartial jury. The defendant must be informed of the charge upon which he or she is to be tried, has the right to cross-examine hostile witnesses, and has the right to require the testimony of favorable witnesses. The defendant also has the right to be represented by an attorney at every stage in the criminal process.

### 7th Amendment. Civil Trials

This amendment applies only to civil cases heard in federal courts. A civil case does not involve criminal matters; it is a dispute between private parties or between the government and a private party. The right to trial by jury is guaranteed in any civil case in a federal court if the amount of money involved in that case exceeds $20 (most cases today involve a much larger sum); that right may be waived (relinquished, put aside) if both parties agree to a bench trial (a trial by a judge, without a jury).

### 8th Amendment. Punishment for Crimes

Bail is the sum of money that a person accused of crime may be required to post (deposit with the court) as a guarantee that he or she will appear in court at the proper time. The amount of bail required and/or a fine imposed as punishment must

### 2nd Amendment.

A well-regulated Militia being necessary to the security of a free State, the right of the people to keep and bear Arms, shall not be infringed.

### 3rd Amendment.

No Soldier shall, in time of peace be quartered in any house, without the consent of the Owner, nor, in time of war, but in a manner to be prescribed by law.

### 4th Amendment.

The right of the people to be secure in their persons, houses, papers, and effects, against unreasonable searches and seizures, shall not be violated, and no Warrants shall issue, but upon probable cause, supported by Oath or affirmation, and particularly describing the place to be searched, and the persons or things to be seized.

### 5th Amendment.

No person shall be held to answer for a capital, or otherwise infamous crime, unless on a presentment or indictment of a Grand Jury, except in cases arising in the land or naval forces, or in the Militia, when in actual service in time of War, or public danger; nor shall any person be subject for the same offence to be twice put in jeopardy of life or limb; nor shall be compelled in any criminal case to be a witness against himself, nor be deprived of life, liberty, or property, without due process of law; nor shall private property be taken for public use, without just compensation.

### 6th Amendment.

In all criminal prosecutions, the accused shall enjoy the right to a speedy and public trial, by an impartial jury of the State and district wherein the crime shall have been committed, which district shall have been previously ascertained by law, and to be informed of the nature and cause of the accusation; to be confronted with the witnesses against him; to have compulsory process for obtaining witnesses in his favor, and to have the Assistance of Counsel for his defence.

### 7th Amendment.

In Suits at common law, where the value in controversy shall exceed twenty dollars, the right of trial by jury shall be preserved, and no fact tried by a jury, shall be otherwise re-examined in any Court of the United States, than according to the rules of the common law.

### 8th Amendment.

Excessive bail shall not be required, nor excessive fines imposed, nor cruel and unusual punishment inflicted.

bear a reasonable relationship to the seriousness of the crime involved in the case. The prohibition of cruel and unusual punishment forbids any punishment judged to be too harsh, too severe for the crime for which it is imposed.

## 9th Amendment.

The enumeration in the Constitution, of certain rights, shall not be construed to deny or disparage others retained by the people.

### 9th Amendment. Unenumerated Rights
The fact that the Constitution sets out many civil rights guarantees, expressly provides for many protections against government, does not mean that there are not other rights also held by the people.

## 10th Amendment.

The powers not delegated to the United States by the Constitution, nor prohibited by it to the States, are reserved to the States respectively, or to the people.

### 10th Amendment. Powers Reserved to the States
All of those powers the Constitution does not grant to the National Government, and at the same time does not forbid to the States, belong to each of the States, or to the people of each State.

## 11th Amendment.

The Judicial power of the United States shall not be construed to extend to any suit in law or equity, commenced or prosecuted against one of the United States by Citizens of another State, or by Citizens or Subjects of any Foreign State.

### 11th Amendment. Suits Against States
Proposed by Congress March 4, 1794; ratified February 7, 1795, but official announcement of the ratification was delayed until January 8, 1798. This amendment repealed part of Article III, Section 2, Clause 1. No State may be sued in a federal court by a resident of another State or of a foreign country; the Supreme Court has long held that this provision also means that a State cannot be sued in a federal court by a foreign country or, more importantly, even by one of its own residents.

## 12th Amendment.

The Electors shall meet in their respective States and vote by ballot for President and Vice President, one of whom, at least, shall not be an inhabitant of the same State with themselves; they shall name in their ballots the person voted for as President, and in distinct ballots the person voted for as Vice President, and they shall make distinct lists of all persons voted for as President, and of all persons voted for as Vice President, and of the number of votes for each, which lists they shall sign and certify, and transmit sealed to the seat of the government of the United States, directed to the President of the Senate;— The President of the Senate shall, in the presence of the Senate and the House of Representatives, open all the certificates and the votes shall then be counted;— the person having the greatest Number of votes for President shall be the President, if such number be a majority of the whole number of Electors appointed; and if no person have such a majority, then, from the persons having the highest numbers not exceeding three on the list of those voted for as President, the House of Representatives shall choose immediately, by ballot, the President. But in choosing the President, the votes shall be taken by States, the representation from each State having one vote; a quorum for this purpose shall consist of a member or members from two thirds of the States, and a majority of all the States shall be necessary to a choice. And if the House of Representatives shall not choose a President whenever the right of choice shall devolve upon them, before the fourth day of March next following, then the Vice President shall act as President, as in case of death or other constitutional disability of the President. The person having the greatest number of votes as Vice President, shall be the

### 12th Amendment. Election of President and Vice President
Proposed by Congress December 9, 1803; ratified June 15, 1804. This amendment replaced Article II, Section 1, Clause 3. Originally, each elector cast two ballots, each for a different person for President. The person with the largest number of electoral votes, provided that number was a majority of the electors, was to become President; the person with the second highest number was to become Vice President. This arrangement produced an electoral vote tie between Thomas Jefferson and Aaron Burr in 1800; the House finally chose Jefferson as President in 1801. The 12th Amendment separated the balloting for President and Vice President; each elector now casts one ballot for someone as President and a second ballot for another person as Vice President. Note that the 20th Amendment changed the date set here (March 4) to January 20, and that the 23rd Amendment (1961) provides for electors from the District of Columbia. This amendment also provides that the Vice President must meet the same qualifications as those set out for the President in Article II, Section 1, Clause 5.

Vice President, if such number be a majority of the whole number of Electors appointed, and if no person have a majority, then from the two highest numbers on the list, the Senate shall choose the Vice President; a quorum for the purpose shall consist of two thirds of the whole number of Senators, a majority of the whole number shall be necessary to a choice. But no person constitutionally ineligible to the office of President shall be eligible to that of Vice-President of the United States.

## 13th Amendment. Slavery and Involuntary Servitude

Proposed by Congress January 31, 1865; ratified December 6, 1865. This amendment forbids slavery in the United States and in any area under its control. It also forbids other forms of forced labor, except punishments for crime; but some forms of compulsory service are not prohibited—for example, service on juries or in the armed forces. Section 2 gives to Congress the power to carry out the provisions of Section 1 of this amendment.

## 13th Amendment.

**Section 1.** Neither slavery nor involuntary servitude, except as a punishment for crime whereof the party shall have been duly convicted, shall exist within the United States, or any place subject to their jurisdiction.

**Section 2.** Congress shall have power to enforce this article by appropriate legislation.

## 14th Amendment. Rights of Citizens

Proposed by Congress June 13, 1866; ratified July 9, 1868. Section 1 defines citizenship. It provides for the acquisition of United States citizenship by birth or by naturalization. Citizenship at birth is determined according to the principle of *jus soli*— "the law of the soil," where born; naturalization is the legal process by which one acquires a new citizenship at some time after birth. Under certain circumstances, citizenship can also be gained at birth abroad, according to the principle of *jus sanguinis*—"the law of the blood," to whom born. This section also contains two major civil rights provisions: the Due Process Clause forbids a State (and its local governments) to act in any unfair or arbitrary way; the Equal Protection Clause forbids a State (and its local governments) to discriminate against, draw unreasonable distinctions between, persons.

Most of the rights set out against the National Government in the first eight amendments have been extended against the States (and their local governments) through Supreme Court decisions involving the 14th Amendment's Due Process Clause.

The first sentence here replaced Article I, Section 2, Clause 3, the Three-Fifths Compromise provision. Essentially, all persons in the United States are counted in each decennial census, the basis for the distribution of House seats. The balance of this section has never been enforced and is generally thought to be obsolete.

## 14th Amendment.

**Section 1.** All persons born or naturalized in the United States and subject to the jurisdiction thereof, are citizens of the United States and of the State wherein they reside. No State shall make or enforce any law which shall abridge the privileges or immunities of citizens of the United States; nor shall any State deprive any person of life, liberty, or property, without due process of law; nor deny to any person within its jurisdiction the equal protection of the laws.

**Section 2.** Representatives shall be apportioned among the several States according to their respective numbers, counting the whole number of persons in each State, excluding Indians not taxed. But when the right to vote at any election for the choice of electors for President and Vice President of the United States, Representatives in Congress, the Executive and Judicial officers of a State, or the members of the Legislature thereof, is denied to any of the male inhabitants of such State, being twenty-one years of age and citizens of the United States, or in any way abridged, except for participation in rebellion, or other crime, the basis of representation therein shall be reduced in the proportion which the number of such male citizens shall bear to the whole number of male citizens twenty-one years of age in such State.

**Section 3.** No person shall be a Senator or Representative in Congress, or elector of President and Vice President, or hold any office, civil or military, under the United States, or under any State, who, having previously taken an oath, as a member of Congress, or as an officer of the United States, or as a member of any State legislature, or as an executive or judicial officer of any State, to support the Constitution of the United States, shall have engaged in insurrection or rebellion against the same, or given aid or comfort to the enemies thereof. But Congress may, by a vote of two thirds of each House, remove such disability.

This section limited the President's power to pardon those persons who had led the Confederacy during the Civil War. Congress finally removed this disability in 1898.

**Section 4.** The validity of the public debt of the United States, authorized by law, including debts incurred for payment of pensions and bounties for services in suppressing insurrection or rebellion, shall not be questioned. But neither the United States nor any State shall assume or pay any debt or obligation incurred in aid of insurrection or rebellion against the United States, or any claim for the loss or emancipation of any slave; but all such debts, obligations and claims shall be held illegal and void.

Section 4 also dealt with matters directly related to the Civil War. It reaffirmed the public debt of the United States; but it invalidated, prohibited payment of, any debt contracted by the Confederate States and also prohibited any compensation of former slave owners.

**Section 5.** The Congress shall have power to enforce, by appropriate legislation, the provisions of this article.

## 15th Amendment.

**Section 1.** The right of citizens of the United States to vote shall not be denied or abridged by the United States or by any State on account of race, color, or previous condition of servitude.

**Section 2.** The Congress shall have power to enforce this article by appropriate legislation.

### 15th Amendment. Right to Vote— Race, Color, Servitude

Proposed by Congress February 26, 1869; ratified February 3, 1870. The phrase "previous condition of servitude" refers to slavery. Note that this amendment does not guarantee the right to vote to African Americans, or to anyone else. Instead, it forbids the States from discriminating against any person on the grounds of his "race, color, or previous condition of servitude" in the setting of suffrage qualifications.

## 16th Amendment.

The Congress shall have power to lay and collect taxes on incomes, from whatever source derived, without apportionment among the several States, and without regard to any census or enumeration.

### 16th Amendment. Income Tax

Proposed by Congress July 12, 1909; ratified February 3, 1913. This amendment modified two provisions in Article I, Section 2, Clause 3, and Section 9, Clause 4. It gives to Congress the power to levy an income tax, a direct tax, without regard to the populations of any of the States.

## 17th Amendment.

The Senate of the United States shall be composed of two Senators from each State, elected by the people thereof, for six years; and each Senator shall have one vote. The electors in each State shall have the qualifications requisite for electors of the most numerous branch of the State legislatures.

When vacancies happen in the representation of any State in the Senate, the executive authority of such State shall issue writs of election to fill such vacancies: *Provided,* That the legislature of any State may empower the executive thereof to make temporary appointments until the people fill the vacancies by election as the legislature may direct.

This amendment shall not be so construed as to affect the election or term of any Senator chosen before it becomes valid as part of the Constitution.

### 17th Amendment. Popular Election of Senators

Proposed by Congress May 13, 1912; ratified April 8, 1913. This amendment repealed those portions of Article I, Section 3, Clauses 1 and 2 relating to the election of senators. Senators are now elected by the voters in each State. If a vacancy occurs, the governor of the State involved must call an election to fill the seat; the governor may appoint a senator to serve until the next election, if the State's legislature has authorized that step.

United States Constitution

## 18th Amendment. Prohibition of Intoxicating Liquors

Proposed by Congress December 18, 1917; ratified January 16, 1919. This amendment outlawed the making, selling, transporting, importing, or exporting of alcoholic beverages in the United States. It was repealed in its entirety by the 21st Amendment in 1933.

## 19th Amendment. Equal Suffrage—Sex

Proposed by Congress June 4, 1919; ratified August 18, 1920. No person can be denied the right to vote in any election in the United States on account of his or her sex.

## 20th Amendment. Commencement of Terms; Sessions of Congress; Death or Disqualification of President-Elect

Proposed by Congress March 2, 1932; ratified January 23, 1933. The provisions of Sections 1 and 2 relating to Congress modified Article I, Section 4, Clause 2, and those provisions relating to the President, the 12th Amendment. The date on which the President and Vice President now take office was moved from March 4 to January 20. Similarly, the members of Congress now begin their terms on January 3. The 20th Amendment is sometimes called the "Lame Duck Amendment" because it shortened the period of time a member of Congress who was defeated for reelection (a "lame duck") remains in office.

This section deals with certain possibilities that were not covered by the presidential selection provisions of either Article II or the 12th Amendment. To this point, none of these situations has occurred. Note that there is neither a President-elect nor a Vice President-elect until the electoral votes have been counted by Congress, or, if the electoral college cannot decide the matter, the House has chosen a President or the Senate has chosen a Vice President.

Congress has not in fact ever passed such a law. See Section 2 of the 25th Amendment, regarding a vacancy in the vice presidency; that provision could some day have an impact here.

# United States Constitution

## 18th Amendment.

Section 1. After one year from the ratification of this article the manufacture, sale, or transportation of intoxicating liquors within, the importation thereof into, or the exportation thereof from the United States and all territory subject to the jurisdiction thereof for beverage purposes is hereby prohibited.

Section 2. The Congress and the several States shall have concurrent power to enforce this article by appropriate legislation.

Section 3. This article shall be inoperative unless it shall have been ratified as an amendment to the Constitution by the legislatures of the several States, as provided in the Constitution, within seven years of the date of the submission hereof to the States by Congress.

## 19th Amendment.

The right of citizens of the United States to vote shall not be denied or abridged by the United States or by any State on account of sex.

Congress shall have power to enforce this article by appropriate legislation.

## 20th Amendment.

Section 1. The terms of the President and Vice President shall end at noon on the 20th day of January, and the terms of Senators and Representatives at noon on the 3d day of January, of the years in which such terms would have ended if this article had not been ratified; and the terms of their successors shall then begin.

Section 2. The Congress shall assemble at least once in every year, and such meeting shall begin at noon on the 3d day of January, unless they shall by law appoint a different day.

Section 3. If, at the time fixed for the beginning of the term of the President, the President elect shall have died, the Vice President elect shall become President. If a President shall not have been chosen before the time fixed for the beginning of his term, or if the President-elect shall have failed to qualify, then the Vice President elect shall act as President until a President shall have qualified; and the Congress may by law provide for the case wherein neither a President elect nor a Vice President elect shall have qualified, declaring who shall then act as President, or the manner in which one who is to act shall be selected, and such person shall act accordingly until a President or Vice President shall have qualified.

Section 4. The Congress may by law provide for the case of the death of any of the persons from whom the House of Representatives may choose a President whenever the right of choice shall have devolved upon them, and for the case of the death of any of the persons from whom the Senate may choose a Vice President whenever the right of choice shall have devolved upon them.

**Section 5.** Sections 1 and 2 shall take effect on the 15th day of October following the ratification of this article.

**Section 6.** This article shall be inoperative unless it shall have been ratified as an amendment to the Constitution by the legislatures of three fourths of the several States within seven years from the date of its submission.

Section 5 set the date on which this amendment came into force.

Section 6 placed a time limit on the ratification process; note that a similar provision was written into the 18th, 21st, and 22nd amendments.

## 21st Amendment.

**Section 1.** The eighteenth article of amendment to the Constitution of the United States is hereby repealed.

**Section 2.** The transportation or importation into any State, Territory, or possession of the United States for delivery or use therein of intoxicating liquors, in violation of the laws thereof, is hereby prohibited.

**Section 3.** This article shall be inoperative unless it shall have been ratified as an amendment to the Constitution by conventions in the several States, as provided in the Constitution, within seven years from the date of the submission hereof to the States by the Congress.

### 21st Amendment. Repeal of 18th Amendment

Proposed by Congress February 20, 1933; ratified December 5, 1933. This amendment repealed all of the 18th Amendment. Section 2 modifies the scope of the Federal Government's commerce power set out in Article I, Section 8, Clause 3; it gives to each State the power to regulate the transportation or importation and the distribution or use of intoxicating liquors in ways that would be unconstitutional in the case of any other commodity. The 21st Amendment is the only amendment Congress has thus far submitted to the States for ratification by conventions.

## 22nd Amendment.

**Section 1.** No person shall be elected to the office of the President more than twice, and no person who has held the office of President, or acted as President, for more than two years of a term to which some other person was elected President shall be elected to the office of the President more than once. But this Article shall not apply to any person holding the office of President, when this Article was proposed by the Congress, and shall not prevent any person who may be holding the office of President, or acting as President, during the term within which this Article becomes operative from holding the office of President or acting as President during the remainder of such term.

**Section 2.** This article shall be inoperative unless it shall have been ratified as an amendment to the Constitution by the legislatures of three fourths of the several states within seven years from the date of its submission to the States by the Congress.

### 22nd Amendment. Presidential Tenure

Proposed by Congress March 24, 1947; ratified February 27, 1951. This amendment modified Article II, Section I, Clause 1. It stipulates that no President may serve more than two elected terms. But a President who has succeeded to the office beyond the midpoint in a term to which another President was originally elected may serve for more than eight years. In any case, however, a President may not serve more than 10 years. Prior to Franklin Roosevelt, who was elected to four terms, no President had served more than two full terms in office.

## 23rd Amendment.

**Section 1.** The District constituting the seat of Government of the United States shall appoint in such manner as the Congress may direct:

A number of electors of President and Vice President equal to the whole number of Senators and Representatives in Congress to which the District would be entitled if it were a State, but in no event more than the least populous State; they shall be in addition to those appointed by the States, they shall be considered, for the purposes of

### 23rd Amendment. Presidential Electors for the District of Columbia

Proposed by Congress June 16, 1960; ratified March 29, 1961. This amendment modified Article II, Section I, Clause 2 and the 12th Amendment. It included the voters of the District of Columbia in the presidential electorate; and provides that the District is to have the same number of electors as the least populous State—three electors—but no more than that number.

the election of President and Vice President, to be electors appointed by a State; and they shall meet in the District and perform such duties as provided by the twelfth article of amendment.

**Section 2.** The Congress shall have power to enforce this article by appropriate legislation.

## 24th Amendment. Right to Vote in Federal Elections—Tax Payment

Proposed by Congress September 14, 1962; ratified January 23, 1964. This amendment outlawed the payment of any tax as a condition for taking part in the nomination or election of any federal officeholder.

## 24th Amendment.

**Section 1.** The right of citizens of the United States to vote in any primary or other election for President or Vice President, for electors for President or Vice President, or for Senator or Representative in Congress, shall not be denied or abridged by the United States or any State by reason of failure to pay any poll tax or other tax.

**Section 2.** The Congress shall have power to enforce this article by appropriate legislation.

## 25th Amendment. Presidential Succession, Vice Presidential Vacancy, Presidential Inability

Proposed by Congress July 6, 1965; ratified February 10, 1967. Section 1 revised the imprecise provision on presidential succession in Article II, Section 1, Clause 6. It wrote into the Constitution the precedent set by Vice President John Tyler, who became President on the death of William Henry Harrison in 1841.

Section 2 provides for the filling of a vacancy in the office of Vice President. Prior to its adoption, the office had been vacant on 16 occasions and had remained unfilled for the remainder of each term involved. When Spiro Agnew resigned the office in 1973, President Nixon selected Gerald Ford in accord with this provision; and, when President Nixon resigned in 1974, Gerald Ford became President and then chose Nelson Rockefeller as Vice President.

This section created a procedure for determining if a President is so incapacitated that he cannot perform the powers and duties of his office.

## 25th Amendment.

**Section 1.** In case of the removal of the President from office or of his death or resignation, the Vice President shall become President.

**Section 2.** Whenever there is a vacancy in the office of the Vice President, the President shall nominate a Vice President who shall take office upon confirmation by a majority vote of both Houses of Congress.

**Section 3.** Whenever the President transmits to the President *pro tempore* of the Senate and the Speaker of the House of Representatives his written declaration that he is unable to discharge the powers and duties of his office, and until he transmits to them a written declaration to the contrary, such powers and duties shall be discharged by the Vice President as Acting President.

**Section 4.** Whenever the Vice President and a majority of either the principal officers of the executive departments or of such other body as Congress may by law provide, transmit to the President *pro tempore* of the Senate and the Speaker of the House of Representatives their written declaration that the President is unable to discharge the powers and duties of his office, the Vice President shall immediately assume the powers and duties of the office as Acting President.

Thereafter, when the President transmits to the President *pro tempore* of the Senate and the Speaker of the House of Representatives his written declaration that no inability exists, he shall resume the powers and duties of his office unless the Vice President and a majority of either the principal officers of the executive department or of such other body as Congress may by law provide, transmit within four days to the President *pro tempore* of the Senate and the Speaker of the House of Representatives their written declaration that the President is unable to discharge the powers and duties of his office. Thereupon Congress shall decide the issue, assembling within forty-eight hours for that purpose if not in session. If the Congress, within twenty-one days after receipt of the latter written declaration, or, if Congress is not in session, within twenty-one days after Congress is required to assemble, determines by two-thirds vote of both Houses that the President is unable to discharge the powers and duties of his office, the Vice President shall continue to discharge the same as Acting President; otherwise, the President shall resume the powers and duties of his office.

Section 4 deals with the circumstance in which a President will not be able to determine the fact of incapacity. To this point, Congress has not established the "such other body" referred to here. This section contains the only typographical error in the Constitution; in its second paragraph, the word "department" should in fact read "departments."

## 26th Amendment.

**Section 1.** The right of citizens of the United States, who are eighteen years of age or older, to vote shall not be denied or abridged by the United States or by any State on account of age.

**Section 2.** The Congress shall have the power to enforce this article by appropriate legislation.

### 26th Amendment. Right to Vote—Age

Proposed by Congress March 23, 1971; ratified July 1, 1971. This amendment provides that the minimum age for voting in any election in the United States cannot be more than 18 years. (A State may set a minimum voting age of less than 18, however.)

## 27th Amendment.

No law varying the compensation for the services of the Senators and Representatives, shall take effect, until an election of Representatives shall have intervened.

### 27th Amendment. Congressional Pay

Proposed by Congress September 25, 1789; ratified May 7, 1992. This amendment modified Article I, Section 6, Clause 1. It limits Congress's power to fix the salaries of its members—by delaying the effectiveness of any increase in that pay until after the next regular congressional election.

# Historical Documents

## The Code of Hammurabi

*The* Code of Hammurabi, *believed to date before 1750 B.C., is a series of laws decreed by Hammurabi, the ruler of the city of Babylon when that ancient city was at the peak of its power. Inscribed on stone columns over seven feet high, these laws were intended to inform the people of what they could and could not do. They were written down and codified so that judges and administrators would have a uniform set of rules to follow in deciding disputes and imposing penalties for crimes. The* Code *consists of 280 sections that deal with such matters as land tenure, property rights, trade and commerce, family relations, and the administration of justice. Selected sections of the* Code *are excerpted below:*

If a man practice (robbery) and be captured, that man shall be put to death. . . .

If a man has come forward in a lawsuit for the witnessing of false things, and has not proved the thing that he said, if that lawsuit is a capital case, that man shall be put to death. If he came forward for witnessing about corn or silver, he shall bear the penalty (which applies to) that case.

If a man has concealed in his house a lost slave or slave-girl belonging to the Palace or to a subject, and has not brought him (or her) out at the proclamation of the Crier, the owner of the house shall be put to death.

If a fire has broken out in a man's house, and a man who has gone to extinguish it has cast his eye on the property of the owner of the house and has taken the property of the owner of the house, that man shall be thrown into the fire.

If a man is subject to a debt bearing interest, and Adad (the Weather-god) has saturated his field or a high flood has carried (its crop) away, or because of lack of water he has not produced corn in that field, in that year he shall not return any corn to (his) creditor. He shall . . . not pay interest for that year.

If a man has donated field, orchard or house to his favourite heir and has written a sealed document for him (confirming this), after the father has gone to his doom, when the brothers share he (the favorite heir) shall take the gift that his father gave him, and apart from that they shall share equally in the property of the paternal estate.

If an artisan has taken a child for bringing up, and has taught him his manual skill, (the child) shall not be (re)claimed. If he has not taught him his manual skill, that pupil may return to his father's house.

If a man aid a male or female slave . . . to escape from the city gates, he shall be put to death. . . .

If a man be in debt and sell his wife, son, or daughter, or bind them over to service, for three years they shall work in the house of the purchaser or master; in the fourth year they shall be given their freedom. . . .

If a builder has made a house for a man but has not made his work strong, so that the house he made falls down and causes the death of the owner of the house, that builder shall be put to death. If it causes the death of the son of the owner of the house, they shall kill the son of the builder.

If a man would put away [divorce] his wife who has not borne him children, he shall give her money to the amount of her marriage settlement and he shall make good to her the dowry which she brought from her father's house and then he may put her away.

If a son has struck his father, they shall cut off his hand.

If a man has destroyed the eye of a man of the "gentleman" class, they shall destroy his eye. If he has broken a gentleman's bone, they shall break his bone. If he has destroyed the eye of a commoner or broken a bone of a commoner, he shall pay one mina (about $300) of silver. If he has destroyed the eye of a gentleman's slave, he shall pay half the slave's price.

If a gentleman's slave strikes the cheek of a man of the "gentleman" class, they shall cut off (the slave's) ear.

If a gentleman strikes a gentleman in a free fight and inflicts an injury on him, that man shall swear "I did not strike him deliberately," and he shall pay the surgeon.

# Madison's *Notes:* Debate of June 6 on the Virginia Plan

*James Madison's* Notes *enable readers today to gain a glimpse of the debates that took place behind closed doors at the Constitutional Convention held in Philadelphia in the summer of 1787. Excerpted here are portions of Madison's* Notes *on the debate of June 6 on the Virginia Plan's call for a bicameral (two house) legislature.*

MR. PINCKNEY [S.C.], according to previous notice and rule obtained, moved "that the first branch of the national legislature be elected by the state legislatures, and not by the people," contending that the people were less fit judges in such a case, and that the legislatures would be less likely to promote the adoption of the new government if they were to be excluded from all share in it.

MR. RUTLEDGE [S.C.] seconded the motion.

MR. GERRY [MASS.]: Much depends on the mode of election. In England the people will probably lose their liberty from the smallness of the proportion having a right of suffrage. Our danger arises from the opposite extreme; hence in Massachusetts the worst men get into the legislature. Several members of that body had lately been convicted of infamous crimes. Men of indigence, ignorance, and baseness spare no pains, however dirty, to carry their point against men who are superior to the artifices practised. He was not disposed to run into extremes. He was as much principled as ever against aristocracy and monarchy. It was necessary, on the one hand, that the people should appoint one branch of the government in order to inspire them with the necessary confidence. . . . His idea was that the people should nominate certain persons in certain districts, out of whom the state legislatures should make the appointment.

MR. WILSON [PA.]: He wished for vigor in the government, but he wished that vigorous authority to flow immediately from the legitimate source of all authority. The government ought to possess not only, first, the *force* but, second, the *mind or sense* of the people at large. The legislature ought to be the most exact transcript of the whole society. Representation is made necessary only because it is impossible for the people to act collectively. . . .

MR. SHERMAN [CONN.]: If it were in view to abolish the state governments, the elections ought to be by the people. If the state governments are to be continued, it is necessary, in order to preserve harmony between the national and state governments, that the elections to the former should be made by the latter. The right of participating in the national government would be sufficiently secured to the people by their election of the state legislatures. The objects of the Union, he thought, were few: (1) defense against foreign danger; (2) against internal disputes and a resort to force; (3) treaties with foreign nations; (4) regulating foreign commerce and drawing revenue from it. These, and perhaps a few lesser objects, alone rendered a confederation of the states necessary. All other matters, civil and criminal, would be much better in the hands of the states. . . .

COLONEL MASON [VA.]: Under the existing Confederacy, Congress represent the *states,* not the *people* of the states; their acts operate on the *states,* not on the individuals. The case will be changed in the new plan of government. The people will be represented; they ought therefore to choose the representatives. The requisites in actual representation are that the representatives should sympathize with their constituents, should think as they think and feel as they feel, and that, for these purposes, [they] should even be residents among them. Much, he said, had been alleged against democratic elections. He admitted that much might be said; but it was to be considered that no government was free from imperfections and evils and that improper elections, in many instances, were inseparable from republican governments. . . .

MR. MADISON [VA.] considered an election of one branch, at least, of the legislature by the people immediately as a clear principle of free government, and that this mode, under proper regulations, had the additional advantage of securing better representatives as well as of avoiding too great an agency of the state governments in the general one. He differed from the member from Connecticut (Mr. Sherman) in thinking the objects mentioned to be all the principal ones that required a national government. Those were certainly important and necessary objects; but he combined with them the necessity of providing more effectually for the security of private rights and the steady dispensation of justice.

Interferences with these were evils which had more, perhaps, than anything else produced this Convention. Was it to be supposed that republican liberty could long exist under the abuses of it practised in some of the states? . . .

All civilized societies would be divided into different sects, factions, and interests, as they happened to consist of rich and poor, debtors and creditors, the landed, the manufacturing, the commercial interests, the inhabitants of this district or that district, the followers of this political leader or that political leader, the disciples of this religious sect or that religious sect. In all cases where a majority are united by a common interest or passion, the rights of the minority are in danger. What motives are to restrain them? . . .

Conscience, the only remaining tie, is known to be inadequate in individuals; in large numbers, little is to be expected from it. . . .

What has been the source of those unjust laws complained of among ourselves? Has it not been the real or supposed interest of the major number? Debtors have defrauded their creditors. The landed interest has borne hard on the mercantile interest. The holders of one species of property have thrown a disproportion of taxes on the holders of another species.

The lesson we are to draw from the whole is that where a majority are united by a common sentiment, and have an opportunity, the rights of the minor party become insecure. In a republican government the majority, if united, have always an opportunity. . . .

MR. DICKINSON [DEL.] considered it as essential that one branch of the legislature should be drawn immediately from the people and as expedient that the other should be chosen by the legislatures of the states. This combination of the state governments with the national government was as politic as it was unavoidable. In the formation of the Senate, we ought to carry it through such a refining process as will assimilate it as near as may be to the House of Lords in England. He repeated his warm eulogiums on the British constitution. He was for a strong national government but for leaving the states a considerable agency in the system. The objection against making the former dependent on the latter might be obviated by giving to the Senate an authority permanent and irrevocable for three, five, or seven years. Being thus independent, they will speak and decide with becoming freedom.

MR. READ [DEL.]: Too much attachment is betrayed to the state governments. We must look beyond their continuance. A national government must soon of necessity swallow all of them up. They will soon be reduced to the mere office of electing the national Senate. He was against patching up the old federal system; he hoped the idea would be dismissed. It would be like putting new cloth on an old garment. The Confederation was founded on temporary principles. It cannot last; it cannot be amended. If we do not establish a good government on new principles, we must either go to ruin or have the work to do over again. . . .

MR. PIERCE [GA.] was for an election by the people as to the first branch and by the states as to the second branch, by which means the citizens of the states would be represented both *individually* and *collectively*.

GENERAL PINCKNEY wished to have a good national government and at the same time to leave a considerable share of power in the states. An election of either branch by the people, scattered as they are in many states, particularly in South Carolina, was totally impracticable. He differed from gentlemen who thought that a choice by the people would be a better guard against bad measures than by the legislatures. . . .

The state legislatures also, he said, would be more jealous and more ready to thwart the national government if excluded from a participation in it. The idea of abolishing these legislatures would never go down.

MR. WILSON would not have spoken again but for what had fallen from Mr. Read; namely, that the idea of preserving the state governments ought to be abandoned. He saw no incompatibility between the national and state governments, provided the latter were restrained to certain local purposes; nor any probability of their being devoured by the former. . . .

On the question for electing the first branch by the state legislatures as moved by Mr. Pinckney, it was negatived.

# Pledge of Allegiance

## By FRANCIS BELLAMY

*The Pledge of Allegiance first appeared in 1892 in a magazine called* The Youth's Companion. *The original Pledge, attributed to Francis Bellamy, stated: "I pledge allegiance to my Flag and the Republic for which it stands; one Nation indivisible with liberty and justice for all." In 1924, "my Flag" was changed to "the Flag of the United States of America." Congress officially recognized the Pledge in 1942 and added the words "under God" in 1954.*

I pledge allegiance to the Flag of the United States of America, and to the Republic for which it stands, one nation under God, indivisible, with liberty and justice for all.

# *The Federalist* No. 10 (James Madison)

*One of the 29 essays believed to have been written by James Madison, the tenth of*
The Federalist *papers presents Madison's observations on dealing with the "mischiefs of faction" and the advantages of a republican (representative) form of government over that of a pure democracy. This essay was first published on November 23, 1787.*

Among the numerous advantages promised by a well-constructed Union, none deserves to be more accurately developed than its tendency to break and control the violence of faction. The friend of popular governments never finds himself so much alarmed for their character and fate as when he contemplates their propensity to this dangerous vice. He will not fail, therefore, to set a due value on any plan which, without violating the principles to which he is attached, provides a proper cure for it. The instability, injustice, and confusion introduced into the public councils have, in truth, been the mortal diseases under which popular governments have everywhere perished; as they continue to be the favorite and fruitful topics from which the adversaries to liberty derive their most specious declamations.

The valuable improvements made by the American constitutions on the popular models, both ancient and modern, cannot certainly be too much admired; but it would be an unwarrantable partiality to contend that they have as effectually obviated the danger on this side, as was wished and expected. Complaints are everywhere heard from our most considerate and virtuous citizens, equally the friends of public and private faith, and of public and personal liberty, that our governments are too unstable, that the public good is disregarded in the conflicts of rival parties, and that measures are too often decided, not according to the rules of justice and the rights of the minor party, but by the superior force of an interested and overbearing majority. However anxiously we may wish that these complaints had no foundation, the evidence of known facts will not permit us to deny that they are in some degree true.

It will be found, indeed, on a candid review of our situation, that some of the distresses under which we labor have been erroneously charged on the operation of our governments; but it will be found, at the same time, that other causes will not alone account for many of our heaviest misfortunes; and, particularly, for that prevailing and increasing distrust of public engagements, and alarm for private rights, which are echoed from one end of the continent to the other. These must be chiefly, if not wholly, effects of the unsteadiness and injustice with which a factious spirit has tainted our public administrations.

By a faction, I understand a number of citizens, whether amounting to a majority or minority of the whole, who are united and actuated by some common impulse of passion, or of interest, adversed to the rights of other citizens, or to the permanent and aggregate interests of the community.

There are two methods of curing the mischiefs of faction: the one, by removing its causes; the other, by controlling its effects.

There are again two methods of removing the causes of faction: the one, by destroying the liberty which is essential to its existence; the other, by giving to every citizen the same opinions, the same passions, and the same interests.

It could never be more truly said than of the first remedy that it was worse than the disease. Liberty is to faction what air is to fire, an ailment without which it instantly expires. But it could not be less folly to abolish liberty, which is essential to political life, because it nourishes faction, than it would be to wish the annihilation of air, which is essential to animal life, because it imparts to fire its destructive agency.

The second expedient is as impracticable as the first would be unwise. As long as the reason of man continues fallible, and he is at liberty to exercise it, different opinions will be formed. As long as the connection subsists between his reason and his self-love, his opinions and his passions will have a reciprocal influence on each other; and the former will be objects to which the latter will attach themselves. The diversity in the faculties of men, from which the rights of property originate, is not less an insuperable obstacle to a uniformity of interests. The protection of these faculties is the first object of government. From the protection of different and unequal faculties of acquiring property, the possession of different degrees and kinds of property immediately results; and from the influence of these on the sentiments and views of the respective proprietors ensues a division of the society into different interests and parties.

The latent causes of faction are thus sown in the nature of man; and we see them everywhere brought into different degrees of activity, according to the different circumstances of civil society. A zeal for different opinions concerning religion, concerning government, and many other points, as well of speculation as of practice; an attachment of different leaders ambitiously contending for preeminence and power; or to persons of other descriptions whose fortunes have been interesting to the human passions, have, in turn, divided mankind into parties, inflamed them with mutual animosity, and rendered them much more disposed to vex and oppress each other than to cooperate for their common good. So strong is this propensity of mankind to fall into mutual animosities that, where no substantial occasion presents itself, the most frivolous and fanciful distinctions have been sufficient to kindle their unfriendly passions and excite their most violent conflicts. But the most common and durable source of factions has been the various and unequal distribution of property.

Those who hold and those who are without property have ever formed distinct interests in society. Those who are creditors and those who are debtors fall under a like discrimination. A landed interest, a manufacturing interest, a mercantile interest, a moneyed interest, with many lesser interests, grow up of necessity in civilized nations and divide them into different classes, actuated by different sentiments and views. The regulation of these various and interfering interests forms the principal task of modern legislation and involves the spirit of party and faction in the necessary and ordinary operations of the government.

No man is allowed to be a judge in his own cause, because his interest would certainly bias his judgment and, not improbably, corrupt his integrity. With equal, nay, with greater reason, a body of men are unfit to be both judges and parties at the same time; yet what are many of the most important acts of legislation but so many judicial determinations, not indeed concerning the rights of single persons, but concerning the rights of large bodies of citizens? And what are the different classes of legislators but advocates and parties to the causes which they determine? Is a law proposed concerning private debts? It is a question to which the creditors are parties on one side and the debtors on the other. Justice ought to hold the balance between them. Yet the parties are, and must be, themselves the judges; and the most numerous party or, in other words, the most powerful faction must be expected to prevail.

Shall domestic manufactures be encouraged, and in what degree, by restrictions on foreign manufactures? [These] are questions which would be differently decided by the landed and the manufacturing classes, and probably by neither with a sole regard to justice and the public good. The apportionment of taxes on the various descriptions of property is an act which seems to require the most exact impartiality; yet there is, perhaps, no legislative act in which greater opportunity and temptation are given to a predominant party to trample on the rules of justice. Every shilling with which they overburden the inferior number is a shilling saved to their own pockets.

It is in vain to say that enlightened statesmen will be able to adjust these clashing interests and render them all subservient to the public good. Enlightened statesmen will not always be at the helm. Nor, in many cases, can such an adjustment be made at all without taking into view indirect and remote considerations, which will rarely prevail over the immediate interest which one party may find in disregarding the rights of another or the good of the whole. The inference to which we are brought is that the *causes* of faction cannot be removed and that relief is only to be sought in the means of controlling its *effects*.

If a faction consists of less than a majority, relief is supplied by the republican principle, which enables the majority to defeat its sinister views by regular vote. It may clog the administration, it may convulse the society; but it will be unable to execute and mask its violence under the forms of the Constitution. When a majority is included in a faction, the form of popular government, on the other hand, enables it to sacrifice to its ruling passion or interest both the public good and the rights of other citizens. To secure the public good and private rights against the danger of such a faction, and at the same time to preserve the spirit and the form of popular government, is then the great object to which our inquiries are directed. Let me add that it is the great desideratum by which this form of government can be rescued from the opprobrium under which it has so long labored and be recommended to the esteem and adoption of mankind.

By what means is this object attainable? Evidently by one of two only. Either the existence of the same passion or interest in a majority at the same time must be prevented, or the majority, having such coexistent passion or interest, must be rendered, by their number and local situation, unable to concert and carry into effect schemes of oppression. If the impulse and the opportunity be suffered to coincide, we well know that neither moral nor religious motives can be relied on as an adequate control. They are not found to be such on the injustice and violence of individuals and lose their efficacy in proportion to the number combined together, that is, in proportion as their efficacy becomes needful.

From this view of the subject it may be concluded that a pure democracy, by which I mean a society consisting of a small number of citizens who assemble and administer the government in person, can admit of no cure for the mischiefs of faction. A common passion or interest will, in almost every case, be felt by a majority of the whole; a communication and concert result from the form of government itself; and there is nothing to check the inducements to sacrifice the weaker party or an obnoxious individual. Hence it is that such democracies have ever been spectacles of turbulence and contention; have ever been found incompatible with personal security or the rights of property; and have in general been as short in their lives as they have been violent in their deaths. Theoretic politicians, who have patronized this species of government, have erroneously supposed that by reducing mankind to a perfect equality in their political rights, they would, at the same time, be perfectly equalized and assimilated in their possessions, their opinions, and their passions.

A republic, by which I mean a government in which the scheme of representation takes place, opens a different prospect and promises the cure for which we are seeking. Let us examine the points in which it varies from pure democracy, and we shall comprehend both the nature of the cure and the efficacy which it must derive from the Union.

The two great points of difference between a democracy and a republic are: first, the delegation of the government, in the latter, to a small number of citizens elected by the rest; secondly, the greater number of citizens, and greater sphere of country, over which the latter may be extended.

The effect of the first difference is, on the one hand, to refine and enlarge the public views by passing them through the medium of a chosen body of citizens, whose wisdom may best discern the true interest of their country, and whose patriotism and love of justice will be least likely to sacrifice it to temporary or partial considerations. Under such a regulation, it may well happen that the public voice, pronounced by the representatives of the people, will be more consonant to the public good than if pronounced by the people themselves, convened for the purpose. On the other hand, the effect may be inverted. Men of factious tempers, of local prejudices, or of sinister designs may, by intrigue, by corruption, or by other means, first obtain the suffrages, and then betray the interests of the people. The question resulting is, whether small or extensive republics are more favorable to the election of proper guardians of the public weal; and it is clearly decided in favor of the latter by two obvious considerations:

In the first place, it is to be remarked that, however small the republic may be, the representatives must be raised to a certain number, in order to guard against the cabals of a few; and that, however large it may be, they must be limited to a certain number, in order to guard against the confusion of a multitude. Hence, the number of representatives in the two cases not being in proportion to that of the two constituents, and being proportionally greater in the small republic, it follows that, if the proportion of fit characters be not less in the large than in the small republic, the former will present a greater option, and consequently a greater probability of a fit choice.

In the next place, as each representative will be chosen by a greater number of citizens in the large than in the small republic, it will be more difficult for unworthy candidates to practice with success the vicious arts by which elections are too often carried; and the suffrages of the people being more free, will be more likely to center in men who possess the most attractive merit and the most diffusive and established character.

It must be confessed that in this, as in most other cases, there is a mean, on both sides of which inconveniences will be found to lie. By enlarging too much the number of electors, you render the representative too little acquainted with all their local circumstances and lesser interests; as by reducing it too much, you render him unduly attached to these and too little fit to comprehend and pursue great and national objects. The federal Constitution forms a happy combination in this respect: the great and aggregate interests being referred to the national, the local and particular to the state legislatures.

The other point of difference is the greater number of citizens and extent of territory which may be brought within the compass of republican than of democratic government; and it is this circumstance principally which renders factious combinations less to be dreaded in the former than in the latter. The smaller the society, the fewer probably will be the distinct parties and interests composing it; the fewer the distinct parties and interests, the more frequently will a majority be found of the same party; and the smaller the number of individuals composing a majority, and the smaller the compass within which they are placed, the more easily will they concert and execute their plans of oppression. Extend the sphere and you take in a greater variety of parties and interests; you make it less probable that a majority of the whole will have a common motive to invade the rights of other citizens; or if such a common motive exists, it will be more difficult for all who feel it to discover their own strength and to act in unison with each other. Besides other impediments, it may be remarked that, where there is a consciousness of unjust or dishonorable purposes, communication is always checked by distrust in proportion to the number whose concurrence is necessary.

Hence, it clearly appears that the same advantage which a republic has over a democracy, in controlling the effects of factions, is enjoyed by a large over a small republic—is enjoyed by the Union over the States composing it. Does the advantage consist in the substitution of representatives whose enlightened views and virtuous sentiments render them superior to local prejudices and to schemes of injustice? It will not be denied that the representation of the Union will be most likely to possess these requisite endowments. Does it consist in the greater security afforded by a greater variety of parties, against the event of any one party being able to outnumber and oppress the rest? In an equal degree does the increased variety of parties comprised within the Union increase this security? Does it, in fine, consist in the greater obstacles opposed to the concert and accomplishment of the secret wishes of an unjust and interested majority? Here, again, the extent of the Union gives it the most palpable advantage.

The influence of factious leaders may kindle a flame within their particular States but will be unable to spread a general conflagration through the other States. A religious sect may degenerate into a political faction in a part of the Confederacy; but the variety of sects dispersed over the entire face of it must secure the national councils against any danger from that source. A rage for paper money, for an abolition of debts, for an equal division of property, or for any other improper or wicked project will be less apt to pervade the whole body of the Union than a particular member of it; in the same proportion as such a malady is more likely to taint a particular county or district than an entire State.

In the extent, and proper structure of the Union, therefore, we behold a republican remedy for the diseases most incident to republican government. And according to the degree of pleasure and pride we feel in being republicans, ought to be our zeal in cherishing the spirit and supporting the character of Federalists.

# *The Federalist* No. 51 (James Madison)

To what expedient, then, shall we finally resort, for maintaining in practice the necessary partition of power among the several departments as laid down in the Constitution? The only answer that can be given is that as all these exterior provisions are found to be inadequate the defect must be supplied, by so contriving the interior structure of the government as that its several constituent parts may, by their mutual relations, be the means of keeping each other in their proper places. Without presuming to undertake a full development of this important idea, I will hazard a few general observations which may perhaps place it in a clearer light, and enable us to form a more correct judgment of the principles and structure of the government planned by the convention.

In order to lay a due foundation for that separate and distinct exercise of the different powers of government, which to a certain extent is admitted on all hands to be essential to the preservation of liberty, it is evident that each department should have a will of its own; and consequently should be so constituted that the members of each should have as little agency as possible in the appointment of the members of the others. Were this principle rigorously adhered to, it would require that all the appointments for the supreme executive, legislative, and judiciary magistracies should be drawn from the same fountain of authority, the people, through channels having no communication whatever with one another. Perhaps such a plan of constructing the several departments would be less difficult in practice than it may in contemplation appear. Some difficulties, however, and some additional expense would attend the execution of it. Some deviations, therefore, from the principle must be admitted. In the constitution of the judiciary department in particular, it might be inexpedient to insist rigorously on the principle; first, because peculiar qualifications being essential in the members, the primary consideration ought to be to select that mode of choice which best secures these qualifications; secondly, because the permanent tenure by which the appointments are held in that department must soon destroy all sense of dependence on the authority conferring them.

It is equally evident that the members of each department should be as little dependent as possible on those of the others for the emoluments annexed to their offices. Were the executive magistrate, or the judges, not independent of the legislature in this particular, their independence in every other would be merely nominal.

But the great security against a gradual concentration of the several powers in the same department consists in giving to those who administer each department the necessary constitutional means and personal motives to resist encroachments of the others. The provision for defense must in this, as in all other cases, be made commensurate to the danger of attack. Ambition must be made to counteract ambition. The interest of the man must be connected with the constitutional rights of the place. It may be a reflection on human nature that such devices should be necessary to control the abuses of government. But what is government itself but the greatest of all reflections on human nature? If men were angels, no government would be necessary. If angels were to govern men, neither external nor internal controls on government would be necessary. In framing a government which is to be administered by men over men, the great difficulty lies in this: You must first enable the government to control the governed; and in the next place, oblige it to control itself. A dependence on the people is, no doubt, the primary control on the government; but experience has taught mankind the necessity of auxiliary precautions.

This policy of supplying, by opposite and rival interests, the defect of better motives might be traced through the whole system of human affairs, private as well as public. We see it particularly displayed in all the subordinate distributions of power; where the constant aim is to divide and arrange the several offices in such a manner as that each may be a check on the other—that the private interest of every individual may be a sentinel over the public rights. These inventions of prudence cannot be less requisite in the distribution of the supreme powers of the State.

But it is not possible to give to each department an equal power of self-defense. In republican government, the legislative authority necessarily predominates. The remedy for this inconveniency is to divide the legislature into different branches; and to render them, by different modes of election, and different principles of action, as little connected with each other as the nature of their common functions and their common dependence on the society will admit. It may even be necessary to guard against dangerous encroachments by still further precautions. As the weight of the legislative authority requires that it should be thus divided, the weakness of the executive may require, on the other hand, that it should be fortified. An absolute negative on the legislature appears, at first view, to be the natural defense with which the executive magistrate should be armed. But perhaps it would be neither altogether safe nor alone sufficient. On ordinary occasions it might not be exerted with the requisite firmness, and on extraordinary occasions it might be perfidiously abused. May not this defect of an absolute negative be supplied by some qualified connection between this weaker department and the weaker branch of the stronger department, by which

the latter may be led to support the constitutional rights of the former, without being too much detached from the rights of its own department?

If the principles on which these observations are founded be just, as I persuade myself they are, and they be applied as a criterion to the several State constitutions, and to the federal Constitution, it will be found that if the latter does not perfectly correspond with them, the former are infinitely less able to bear such a test.

There are, moreover, two considerations particularly applicable to the federal system of America, which place that system in a very interesting point of view.

*First.* In a single republic, all the power surrendered by the people is submitted to the administration of a single government; and the usurpations are guarded against by a division of the government into distinct and separate departments. In the compound republic of America, the power surrendered by the people is first divided between two distinct governments, and then the portion allotted to each subdivided among distinct and separate departments. Hence a double security arises to the rights of the people. The different governments will control each other, at the same time that each will be controlled by itself.

*Second.* It is of great importance in a republic not only to guard the society against the oppression of its rulers, but to guard one part of the society against the injustice of the other part. Different interests necessarily exist in different classes of citizens. If a majority be united by a common interest, the rights of the minority will be insecure. There are but two methods of providing against this evil: The one by creating a will in the community independent of the majority—that is, of the society itself; the other, by comprehending in the society so many separate descriptions of citizens as will render an unjust combination of a majority of the whole very improbable, if not impracticable. The first method prevails in all governments possessing an hereditary or self appointed authority. This, at best, is but a precarious security; because a power independent of the society may as well espouse the unjust views of the major as the rightful interests of the minor party, and may possibly be turned against both parties. The second method will be exemplified in the federal republic of the United States. Whilst all authority in it will be derived from and dependent on the society, the society itself will be broken into so many parts, interests, and classes of citizens, that the rights of individuals, or of the minority, will be in little danger from interested combinations of the majority. In a free government the security for civil rights must be the same as that for religious rights. It consists in the one case in the multiplicity of interests, and in the other in the multiplicity of sects. The degree of security in both cases will depend on the number of interests and sects; and this may be presumed to depend on the extent of country and number of people comprehended under the same government. This view of the subject must particularly recommend a proper federal system to all the sincere and considerate friends of republican government, since it shows that in exact proportion as the territory of the Union may be formed into more circumscribed Confederacies, or States, oppressive combinations of a majority will be facilitated: the best security, under the republican forms, for the rights of every class of citizens, will be diminished; and consequently, the stability and independence of some member of the government, the only other security, must be proportionally increased. Justice is the end of government.

It is the end of civil society. It ever has been and ever will be pursued until it be obtained, or until liberty be lost in the pursuit. In a society under the forms of which the stronger faction can readily unite and oppress the weaker, anarchy may as truly be said to reign as in a state of nature, where the weaker individual is not secured against the violence of the stronger: And as, in the latter state, even the stronger individuals are prompted by the uncertainty of their condition to submit to a government which may protect the weak as well as themselves. So, in the former state, will the more powerful factions or parties be gradually induced, by a like motive, to wish for a government which will protect all parties, the weaker as well as the more powerful. It can be little doubted that if the State of Rhode Island was separated from the Confederacy and left to itself, the insecurity of rights under the popular form of government within such narrow limits would be displayed by such reiterated oppressions of factious majorities that some power altogether independent of the people would soon be called for by the voice of the very factions whose misrule had proved the necessity of it. In the extended republic of the United States, and among the great variety of interests, parties, and sects which it embraces, a coalition of a majority of the whole society could seldom take place on any other principles than those of justice and the general good; whilst there being thus less danger to a minor from the will of the major party, there must be less pretext, also, to provide for the security of the former, by introducing into the government a will not dependent on the latter; or, in other words, a will independent of the society itself. It is no less certain that it is important, notwithstanding the contrary opinions which have been entertained, that the larger the society, provided it lie within a practicable sphere, the more duly capable it will be of self-government. And happily for the *republican cause*, the practicable sphere may be carried to a very great extent by a judicious modification and mixture of the *federal principle*.

# *The Federalist* No. 78 (Alexander Hamilton)

We proceed now to an examination of the judiciary department of the proposed government. In unfolding the defects of the existing Confederation, the utility and necessity of a federal judicature have been clearly pointed out. It is the less necessary to recapitulate the considerations there urged as the propriety of the institution in the abstract is not disputed; the only questions which have been raised being relative to the manner of constituting it, and to its extent. To these points, therefore, our observations shall be confined.

The manner of constituting it seems to embrace these several objects: 1st. The mode of appointing the judges. 2nd. The tenure by which they are to hold their places. 3rd. The partition of the judiciary authority between different courts and their relations to each other.

*First.* As to the mode of appointing the judges: this is the same with that of appointing the officers of the Union in general and has been so fully discussed in the two last numbers that nothing can be said here which would not be useless repetition.

*Second.* As to the tenure by which the judges are to hold their places: this chiefly concerns their duration in office, the provisions for their support, the precautions for their responsibility.

According to the plan of the convention, all judges who may be appointed by the United States are to hold their offices *during good behavior*; which is conformable to the most approved of the State constitutions, and among the rest, to that of this State. Its propriety having been drawn into question by the adversaries of that plan is no light symptom of the rage for objection which disorders their imaginations and judgments. The standard of good behavior for the continuance in office of the judicial magistracy is certainly one of the most valuable of the modern improvements in the practice of government. In a monarchy it is an excellent barrier to the despotism of the prince; in a republic it is a no less excellent barrier to the encroachments and oppressions of the representative body. And it is the best expedient which can be devised in any government to secure a steady, upright, and impartial administration of the laws.

Whoever attentively considers the different departments of power must perceive that, in a government in which they are separated from each other, the judiciary, from the nature of its functions, will always be the least dangerous to the political rights of the Constitution; because it will be least in a capacity to annoy or injure them. The executive not only dispenses the honors but holds the sword of the community. The legislature not only commands the purse but prescribes the rules by which the duties and rights of every citizen are to be regulated. The judiciary, on the contrary, has no influence over either the sword or the purse; no direction either of the strength or of the wealth of the society, and can take no active resolution whatever. It may truly be said to have neither FORCE nor WILL but merely judgment; and must ultimately depend upon the aid of the executive arm even for the efficacy of its judgments.

This simple view of the matter suggests several important consequences. It proves incontestably that the judiciary is beyond comparison the weakest of the three departments of power; that it can never attack with success either of the other two; and that all possible care is requisite to enable it to defend itself against their attacks. It equally proves that though individual oppression may now and then proceed from the courts of justice, the general liberty of the people can never be endangered from that quarter; I mean so long as the judiciary remains truly distinct from both the legislature and the executive. For I agree that "there is no liberty if the power of judging be not separated from the legislative and executive powers." And it proves, in the last place, that as liberty can have nothing to fear from the judiciary alone, but would have everything to fear from its union with either of the other departments; that as all the effects of such a union must ensue from a dependence of the former on the latter, notwithstanding a nominal and apparent separation; that as, from the natural feebleness of the judiciary, it is in continual jeopardy of being overpowered, awed, or influenced by its coordinate branches; and that as nothing can contribute so much to its firmness and independence as permanency in office, this quality may therefore be justly regarded as an indispensable ingredient in its constitution, and, in a great measure, as the citadel of the public justice and the public security.

The complete independence of the courts of justice is peculiarly essential in a limited Constitution. By a limited Constitution, I understand one which contains certain specified exceptions to the legislative authority; such, for instance, as that it shall pass no bills of attainder, no *ex post facto* laws, and the like. Limitations of this kind can be preserved in practice no other way than through the medium of courts of justice, whose duty it must be to declare all acts contrary to the manifest tenor of the Constitution void. Without this, all the reservations of particular rights or privileges would amount to nothing.

Some perplexity respecting the rights of the courts to pronounce legislative acts void, because contrary to the Constitution, has arisen from an imagination that the doctrine would imply a superiority of the judiciary to the legislative power. It is urged that the authority which can declare the acts of another void must necessarily be superior to the one whose acts may be declared void. As this doctrine is of great importance in all the American constitutions, a brief discussion of the grounds on which it rests cannot be unacceptable.

There is no position which depends on clearer principles than that every act of a delegated authority, contrary to the tenor of the commission under which it is exercised, is void. No legislative act, therefore, contrary to the Constitution, can be valid. To deny this would be to affirm that the deputy is greater than his principal; that the servant is above his master; that the representatives of the people are superior to the people themselves; that men acting by virtue of powers may do not only what their powers do not authorize, but what they forbid.

If it be said that the legislative body are themselves the constitutional judges of their own powers and that the construction they put upon them is conclusive upon the other departments, it may be answered that this cannot be the natural presumption where it is not to be collected from any particular provisions in the Constitution. It is not otherwise to be supposed that the Constitution could intend to enable the representatives of the people to substitute their *will* to that of their constituents. It is far more rational to suppose that the courts were designed to be an intermediate body between the people and the legislature in order, among other things, to keep the latter within the limits assigned to their authority. The interpretation of the laws is the proper and peculiar province of the courts. A constitution is, in fact, and must be regarded by the judges as, a fundamental law. It therefore belongs to them to ascertain its meaning as well as the meaning of any particular act proceeding from the legislative body. If there should happen to be an irreconcilable variance between the two, that which has the superior obligation and validity ought, of course, to be preferred; or, in other words, the Constitution ought to be preferred to the statute, the intention of the people to the intention of their agents.

Nor does this conclusion by any means suppose a superiority of the judicial to the legislative power. It only supposes that the power of the people is superior to both, and that where the will of the legislature, declared in its statutes, stands in opposition to that of the people, declared in the Constitution, the judges ought to be governed by the latter rather than the former. They ought to regulate their decisions by the fundamental laws rather than by those which are not fundamental.

This exercise of judicial discretion in determining between two contradictory laws is exemplified in a familiar instance. It not uncommonly happens that there are two statutes existing at one time, clashing in whole or in part with each other and neither of them containing any repealing clause or expression. In such a case, it is the province of the courts to liquidate and fix their meaning and operation. So far as they can, by any fair construction, be reconciled to each other, reason and law conspire to dictate that this should be done; where this is impracticable, it becomes a matter of necessity to give effect to one in exclusion of the other. The rule which has obtained in the courts for determining their relative validity is that the last in order of time shall be preferred to the first. But this is a mere rule of construction, not derived from any positive law but from the nature and reason of the thing. It is a rule not enjoined upon the courts by legislative provision but adopted by themselves, as consonant to truth and propriety, for the direction of their conduct as interpreters of the law. They thought it reasonable that between the interfering acts of an *equal* authority that which was the last indication of its will should have the preference.

But in regard to the interfering acts of a superior and subordinate authority of an original and derivative power, the nature and reason of the thing indicate the converse of that rule as proper to be followed. They teach us that the prior act of a superior ought to be preferred to the subsequent act of an inferior and subordinate authority; and that accordingly, whenever a particular statute contravenes the Constitution, it will be the duty of the judicial tribunals to adhere to the latter and disregard the former.

It can be of no weight to say that the courts, on the pretense of a repugnancy, may substitute their own pleasure to the constitutional intentions of the legislature. This might as well happen in the case of two contradictory statutes; or it might as well happen in every adjudication upon any single statute. The courts must declare the sense of the law; and if they should be disposed to exercise *will* instead of *judgment,* the consequence would equally be the substitution of their pleasure to that of the legislative body. The observation, if it prove anything, would prove that there ought to be no judges distinct from that body.

If, then, the courts of justice are to be considered as the bulwarks of a limited Constitution against legislative encroachments, this consideration will afford a strong argument for the permanent tenure of judicial offices, since nothing will contribute so much as this to that independent spirit in the judges which must be essential to the faithful performance of so arduous a duty.

This independence of the judges is equally requisite to guard the Constitution and the rights of individuals from the effects of those ill humors which the arts of designing men, or the influence of particular conjunctures, sometimes disseminate among the people themselves, and which, though they speedily give place to better information, and more deliberate reflection, have a tendency, in the meantime, to occasion dangerous innovations in the government, and serious oppressions of the minor party in the community. Though I trust the friends of the proposed Constitution will never concur with its enemies in questioning that fundamental principle of Republican government which admits the right of the people to alter or abolish the established Constitution whenever they find it inconsistent with their happiness; yet it is not to be inferred from this principle that the representatives of the people, whenever a momentary inclination happens to lay hold of a majority of their constituents incompatible with the provisions in the existing Constitution would, on that account, be justifiable in a violation of those provisions; or that the courts would be under a greater obligation to connive at infractions in this shape than when they had proceeded wholly from the cabals of the representative body. Until the people have, by some solemn and authoritative act, annulled or changed the established form, it is binding upon themselves collectively, as well as individually; and no presumption, or even knowledge of their sentiments, can warrant their representatives in a departure from it prior to such an act. But it is easy to see that it would require an uncommon portion of fortitude in the judges to do their duty as faithful guardians of the Constitution, where legislative invasions of it had been instigated by the major voice of the community.

But it is not with a view to infractions of the Constitution only that the independence of the judges may be an essential safeguard against the effects of occasional ill humors in the society. These sometimes extend no farther than to the injury of the private rights of particular classes of citizens, by unjust and partial laws. Here also the firmness of the judicial magistracy is of vast importance in mitigating the severity and confining the operation of such laws. It not only serves to moderate the immediate mischiefs of those which may have been passed but it operates as a check upon the legislative body in passing them; who, perceiving that obstacles to the success of iniquitous intention are to be expected from the scruples of the courts, are in a manner compelled, by the very motives of the injustice they mediate, to qualify their attempts. This is a circumstance calculated to have more influence upon the character of our governments than but few may be aware of. The benefits of the integrity and moderation of the judiciary have already been felt in more States than one; and though they may have displeased those whose sinister expectations they may have disappointed, they must have commanded the esteem and applause of all the virtuous and disinterested. Considerate men of every description ought to prize whatever will tend to beget or fortify that temper in the courts; as no man can be sure that he may not be tomorrow the victim of a spirit of injustice, by which he may be a gainer today. And every man must now feel that the inevitable tendency of such a spirit is to sap the foundations of public and private confidence and to introduce in its stead universal distrust and distress.

That inflexible and uniform adherence to the rights of the Constitution, and of individuals, which we perceive to be indispensable in the courts of justice, can certainly not be expected from judges who hold their offices by a temporary commission. Periodical appointments, however regulated, or by whomsoever made, would, in some way or other, be fatal to their necessary independence. If the power of making them was committed either to the executive or legislature there would be danger of an improper complaisance to the branch which possessed it; if to both, there would be an unwillingness to hazard the displeasure of either; if to the people, or to persons chosen by them for the special purpose, there would be too great a disposition to consult popularity to justify a reliance that nothing would be consulted but the Constitution and the laws.

There is yet a further and a weighty reason for the permanency of the judicial offices which is deducible from the nature of the qualifications they require. It has been frequently remarked with great propriety that a voluminous code of laws is one of the inconveniences necessarily connected with the advantages of a free government. To avoid an arbitrary discretion in the courts, it is indispensable that they should be bound down by strict rules and precedents which serve to define and point out their duty in every particular case that comes before them; and it will readily be conceived from the variety of controversies which grow out of the folly and wickedness of mankind that the records of those precedents must unavoidably swell to a very considerable bulk and must demand long and laborious study to acquire a competent knowledge of them. Hence it is that there can be but few men in the society who will have sufficient skill in the laws to qualify them for the stations of judges. And making the proper deductions for the ordinary depravity of human nature, the number must be still smaller of those who unite the requisite integrity with the requisite knowledge. These considerations apprise us that the government can have no great option between fit characters; and that a temporary duration in office which would naturally discourage such characters from quitting a lucrative line of practice to accept a seat on the bench would have a tendency to throw the administration of justice into hands less able and less well qualified to conduct it with utility and dignity. In the present circumstances of this country and in those in which it is likely to be for a long time to come, the disadvantages on this score would be greater than they may at first sight appear; but it must be confessed that they are far inferior to those which present themselves under the other aspects of the subject.

Upon the whole, there can be no room to doubt that the convention acted wisely in copying from the models of those constitutions which have established *good behavior* as the tenure of their judicial offices, in point of duration; and that so far from being blamable on this account, their plan would have been inexcusably defective if it had wanted this important feature of good government. The experience of Great Britain affords an illustrious comment on the excellence of the institution.

# *Anti-Federalist Responses*
## Arguments Against the Adoption of the Constitution

*When the Constitutional Convention of 1787 produced the new Constitution, many thoughtful, patriotic people from all over the country opposed its adoption. These Anti-Federalists, as they were known, had a number of objections to the Constitution. Five of their most significant objections were these: (1) The new Constitution was a document written by and for the primary benefit of a wealthy and powerful aristocracy. (2) The Constitution lacked a bill of rights. (3) The Constitutional Convention was not authorized to do anything but amend the Articles of Confederation; therefore, the Constitution was an illegal document. (4) States would be wholly subordinate to the new National Government and lose their sovereignty. (5) The powers given to the new United States Government were so extensive as to lead inevitably to tyranny and despotism. The following documents provide a sampling of Anti-Federalist arguments.*

### Richard Henry Lee

*Lee from Virginia wrote the best-known Anti-Federalist essays of the time, "Letters from the Federal Farmer to the Republican." These excerpts are from these letters written in October 1787.*

The present moment discovers a new face in our affairs. Our object has been all along to reform our federal system and to strengthen our governments—to establish peace, order, and justice in the community—but a new object now presents. The plan of government now proposed is evidently calculated totally to change, in time, our condition as a people. Instead of being thirteen republics under a federal head, it is clearly designed to make us one consolidated government. . . . This consolidation of the states has been the object of several men in this country for some time past. Whether such a change can ever be effected, in any manner; whether it can be effected without convulsions and civil wars; whether such a change will not totally destroy the liberties of this country, time only can determine. . . .

The Confederation was formed when great confidence was placed in the voluntary exertions of individuals and of the respective states; and the framers of it, to guard against usurpation, so limited and checked the powers that, in many respects, they are inadequate to the exigencies of the Union. We find, therefore, members of Congress urging alterations in the federal system almost as soon as it was adopted. . . .

We expected too much from the return of peace, and, of course, we have been disappointed. Our governments have been new and unsettled; and several legislature, [by their actions] . . . have given just cause of uneasiness. . . .

The conduct of several legislatures touching paper-money and tender laws has prepared many honest men for changes in government, which otherwise they would not have thought of—when by the evils, on the one hand, and by the secret instigations of artful men, on the other, the minds of men were become sufficiently uneasy, a bold step was taken, which is usually followed by a revolution or a civil war. A general convention for mere commercial purposes was moved for—the authors of this measure saw that the people's attention was turned solely to the amendment of the federal system; and that, had the idea of a total change been started, probably no state would have appointed members to the Convention. The idea of destroying, ultimately, the state government and forming one consolidated system could not have been admitted. A convention, therefore, merely for vesting in Congress power to regulate trade was proposed. . . .

The plan proposed appears to be partly federal, but principally, however, calculated ultimately to make the states one consolidated government.

The first interesting question therefore suggested is how far the states can be consolidated into one entire government on free principles. In considering this question, extensive objects are to be taken into view, and important changes in the forms of government to be carefully attended to in all their consequences. The happiness of the people at large must be the great object with every honest statesman, and he will direct every movement to this point. If we are so situated as a people as not to be able to enjoy equal happiness and advantages under one government, the consolidation of the states cannot be admitted.

\* \* \*

There are certain unalienable and fundamental rights, which in forming the social compact ought to be explicitly ascertained and fixed. A free and enlightened people, in forming this compact, will not resign all their rights to those who govern, and they will fix limits [a bill of rights] to their legislators and rulers, which will soon be plainly seen by those who are governed, as well as by those who govern; and the latter will know they cannot be passed unperceived by the former and without giving a general alarm. These rights should be made the basis of every constitution; and if a people be so situated, or have such different opinions, that they cannot agree in ascertaining and fixing them, it is a very strong argument against their attempting to form one entire society, to live under one system of laws only.

\* \* \*

It may also be worthy our examination how far the provision for amending this plan, when it shall be adopted, is of any importance. No measures can be taken toward amendments unless two-thirds of the Congress, or two-thirds of the legislature of the several states, shall agree. While power is in the hands of the people, or democratic part of the community, more especially as at present, it is easy, according to the general course of human affairs, for the few influential men in the community to obtain conventions, alterations in government, and to persuade the common people that they may change for the better, and to get from them a part of the power. But when power is once transferred from the many to the few, all changes become extremely difficult; the government in this case being beneficial to the few, they will be exceedingly artful and adroit in preventing any measures which may lead to a change; and nothing will produce it but great exertions and severe struggles on the part of the common people. Every man of reflection must see that the change now proposed is a transfer of power from the many to the few, and the probability is the artful and ever active aristocracy will prevent all peaceful measures for changes, unless when they shall discover some favorable moment to increase their own influence.

\* \* \*

It is true there may be danger in delay; but there is danger in adopting the system in its present form. And I see the danger in either case will arise principally from the conduct and views of two very unprincipled parties in the United States—two fires, between which the honest and substantial people have long found themselves situated. One party is composed of little insurgents, men in debt, who want no law and who want a share of the property of others—these are called levelers, Shayites, etc. The other party is composed of a few but more dangerous men, with their servile dependents; these avariciously grasp at all power and property. You may discover in all the actions of these men an evident dislike to free and equal government, and they will go systematically to work to change, essentially, the forms of government in this country—these are called aristocrats. . . .

. . . The fact is, these aristocrats support and hasten the adoption of the proposed Constitution merely because they think it is a stepping-stone to their favorite object. I think I am well-founded in this idea; I think the general politics of these men support it, as well as the common observation among them that the proffered plan is the best that can be got at present; it will do for a few years, and lead to something better. . . .

## Luther Martin

*Martin, the leading Anti-Federalist from Maryland, attended the Constitutional Convention as a delegate. In this excerpt from a speech before the Maryland State legislature on November 29, 1787, he defends his decision to leave the Convention before its work was finished.*

It was the states as states, by their representatives in Congress, that formed the Articles of Confederation; it was the states as states, by their legislatures, who ratified those Articles; and it was there established and provided that the states as states (that is, by their legislatures) should agree to any alterations that should hereafter be proposed in the federal government, before they should be binding; and any alterations agreed to in any other manner cannot release the states from the obligation they are under to each other by virtue of the original Articles of Confederation. The people of the different states never made any objection to the manner in which the Articles of Confederation were formed or ratified, or to the mode by which alterations were to be made in that government—with the rights of their respective states they wished not to interfere. Nor do I believe the people, in their individual capacity, would ever have expected or desired to have been appealed to on the present occasion, in violation of the rights of their respective states, if the favorers of the proposed Constitution, imagining they had a better chance of forcing it to be adopted by a hasty appeal to the people at large (who could not be so good judges of the dangerous consequence), had not insisted upon this mode . . . .

It was also my opinion that, upon principles of sound policy, the agreement or disagreement to the proposed system ought to have been by the state legislatures; in which case, let the event have been what it would, there would have been but little prospect of the public peace being disturbed thereby; whereas the attempt to force down this system, although Congress and the respective state legislatures should disapprove, by appealing to the people and to procure its establishment in a manner totally unconstitutional, has a tendency to set the state governments and their subjects at variance with each other, to lessen the obligations of government, to weaken the bands of society, to introduce anarchy and confusion, and to light the torch of discord and civil war throughout this continent. All these considerations weighed with me most forcibly against giving my assent to the mode by which it is resolved that this system is to be ratified, and were urged by me in opposition to the measure.

. . . [A] great portion of that time which ought to have been devoted calmly and impartially to consider what alterations in our federal government would be most likely to procure and preserve the happiness of the Union was employed in a violent struggle on the one side to obtain all power and dominion in their own hands, and on the other to prevent it; and that the aggrandizement of particular states, and particular individuals, appears to have been much more the subject sought after than the welfare of our country . . . .

When I took my seat in the Convention, I found them attempting to bring forward a system which, I was sure, never had entered into the contemplation of those I had the honor to represent, and which, upon the fullest consideration, I considered not only injurious to the interest and rights of this state but also incompatible with the political happiness and freedom of the states in general. From that time until my business compelled me to leave the Convention, I gave it every possible opposition, in every stage of its progression. I opposed the system there with the same explicit frankness with which I have here given you a history of our proceedings, an account of my own conduct, which in a particular manner I consider you as having a right to know. While there, I endeavored to act as became a freeman and the delegate of a free state. Should my conduct obtain the approbation of those who appointed me, I will not deny it would afford me satisfaction; but to me that approbation was at most no more than a secondary consideration—my first was to deserve it. Left to myself to act according to the best of my discretion, my conduct should have been the same had I been even sure your censure would have been my only reward, since I hold it sacredly my duty to dash the cup of poison, if possible, from the hand of a state or an individual, however anxious the one or the other might be to swallow it . . . .

### William Findley, Robert Whitehill, and John Smilie

*Findley, Whitehill, and Smilie—who were delegates to the Pennsylvania State convention—believed that they and other opponents of the Constitution were prevented from expressing their views because of the political maneuverings of the Federalists. This excerpt is from "The Address and Reasons of Dissent of the Minority of the Convention of the State of Pennsylvania to their Constituents,"* which the three men published in the *Pennsylvania Packet and Daily Advertiser* on December 18, 1787.

The Continental Convention met in the city of Philadelphia at the time appointed. It was composed of some men of excellent character; of others who were more remarkable for their ambition and cunning than their patriotism; and of some who had been opponents to the independence of the United States. The delegates from Pennsylvania were, six of them, uniform and decided opponents to the constitution of the commonwealth [the Articles of Confederation]. The convention sat upward of four months. The doors were kept shut, and the members brought under the most solemn engagements of secrecy. Some of those who opposed their going so far beyond their powers, retired, hopeless, from the convention; others had the firmness to refuse signing the plan altogether; and many who did sign it, did it not as a system they wholly approved but as the best that could be then obtained; and notwithstanding the

time spent on this subject, it is agreed on all hands to be a work of haste and accommodation. . . .

Our objections are comprised under three general heads of dissent, viz.:

We dissent, first, because it is the opinion of the most celebrated writers on government, and confirmed by uniform experience, that a very extensive territory cannot be governed on the principles of freedom otherwise than by a confederation of republics, possessing all the powers of internal government but united in the management of their general and foreign concerns. . . .

We dissent, secondly, because the powers vested in Congress by this Constitution must necessarily annihilate and absorb the legislative, executive, and judicial powers of the several states, and produce from their ruins one consolidated government, which from the nature of things will be *an iron-handed despotism*, as nothing short of the supremacy of despotic sway could connect and govern these United States under one government.

As the truth of this position is of such decisive importance, it ought to be fully investigated, and if it is founded, to be clearly ascertained; for, should it be demonstrated that the powers vested by this Constitution in Congress will have such an effect as necessarily to produce one consolidated government, the question then will be reduced to this short issue, viz.: whether satiated with the blessings of liberty, whether repenting of the folly of so recently asserting their unalienable rights against foreign despots at the expense of so much blood and treasure, and such painful and arduous struggles, the people of America are now willing to resign every privilege of freemen, and submit to the dominion of an absolute government that will embrace all America in one chain of despotism; or whether they will, with virtuous indignation, spurn at the shackles prepared for them, and confirm their liberties by a conduct becoming freemen. . . .

We dissent, thirdly, because if it were practicable to govern so extensive a territory as these United States include, on the plan of a consolidated government, consistent with the principles of liberty and the happiness of the people, yet the construction of this Constitution is not calculated to attain the object; for independent of the nature of the case, it would of itself necessarily produce a despotism, and that not by the usual gradations but with the celerity that has hitherto only attended revolutions effected by the sword.

To establish the truth of this position, a cursory investigation of the principles and form of this Constitution will suffice.

The first consideration that this review suggests is the omission of a Bill of Rights ascertaining and fundamentally establishing those unalienable and personal rights of men, without the full, free, and secure enjoyment of which there can be no liberty, and over which it is not necessary for a good government to have the control—the principal of which are the rights of conscience, personal liberty by the clear and unequivocal establishment of the writ of habeas corpus, jury trial in criminal and civil cases, by an impartial jury of the vicinage or county, with the common law proceedings for the safety of the accused in criminal prosecutions; and the liberty of the press, that scourge of tyrants, and the grand bulwark of every other liberty and privilege. The stipulations heretofore made in favor of them in the state constitutions are entirely superseded by this Constitution. . . .

# Articles of Confederation

*In force from March 1, 1781 to March 4, 1789*

To all to whom these Presents shall come, we the undersigned Delegates of the States affixed to our Names send greeting. Whereas the Delegates of the United States of America in Congress assembled did on the fifteenth day of November in the Year of our Lord One Thousand Seven Hundred and Seventy seven, and in the Second Year of the Independence of America agree to certain articles of Confederation and perpetual Union between the States of New Hampshire, Massachusetts Bay, Rhode Island and Providence Plantations, Connecticut, New York, New Jersey, Pennsylvania, Delaware, Maryland, Virginia, North Carolina, South Carolina and Georgia in the Words following, viz. "Articles of Confederation and perpetual Union between the states of New Hampshire, Massachusetts Bay, Rhode Island and Providence Plantations, Connecticut, New York, New Jersey, Pennsylvania, Delaware, Maryland, Virginia, North Carolina, South Carolina and Georgia.

[ART. I.] The Stile of this confederacy shall be "The United States of America."

[ART. II.] Each state retains its sovereignty, freedom and independence, and every Power, Jurisdiction and right, which is not by this confederation expressly delegated to the United States, in Congress assembled.

[ART. III.] The said states hereby severally enter into a firm league of friendship with each other, for their common defence, the security of their Liberties, and their mutual and general welfare, binding themselves to assist each other, against all force offered to, or attacks made upon them, or any of them, on account of religion, sovereignty, trade, or any other pretence whatever.

[ART. IV.] The better to secure and perpetuate mutual friendship and intercourse among the people of the different states in this union, the free inhabitants of each of these states, paupers, vagabonds and fugitives from Justice excepted, shall be entitled to all privileges and immunities of free citizens in the several states; and the people of each state shall have free ingress and regress to and from any other state, and shall enjoy therein all the privileges of trade and commerce, subject to the same duties, impositions and restrictions as the inhabitants thereof respectively, provided that such restriction shall not extend so far as to prevent the removal of property imported into any state, to any other state of which the Owner is an inhabitant; provided also that no imposition, duties or restriction shall be laid by any state, on the property of the united states, or either of them.

If any Person guilty of, or charged with treason, felony, or other high misdemeanor in any state, shall flee from Justice, and be found in any of the united states, he shall upon demand of the Governor or executive power, of the state from which he fled, be delivered up and removed to the state having jurisdiction of his offence.

Full faith and credit shall be given in each of these states to the records, acts and judicial proceedings of the courts and magistrates of every other state.

[ART. V.] For the more convenient management of the general interests of the united states, delegates shall be annually appointed in such manner as the legislature of each state shall direct, to meet in Congress on the first Monday in November, in every year, with a power reserved to each state, to recall its delegates, or any of them, at any time within the year, and to send others in their stead, for the remainder of the Year.

No state shall be represented in Congress by less than two, nor by more than seven Members; and no person shall be capable of being a delegate for more than three years in any term of six years; nor shall any person, being a delegate, be capable of holding any office under the united states, for which he, or another for his benefit receives any salary, fees or emolument of any kind.

Each state shall maintain its own delegates in a meeting of the states, and while they act as members of the committee of the states.

In determining questions in the united states, in Congress assembled, each state shall have one vote.

Freedom of speech and debate in Congress shall not be impeached or questioned in any Court, or place out of Congress, and the members of congress shall be protected in their persons from arrests and imprisonments, during the time of their going to and from, and attendance on congress, except for treason, felony, or breach of the peace.

[ART. VI.] No state without the Consent of the united states in congress assembled, shall send any embassy to, or receive any embassy from, or enter into any conference, agreement, or alliance or treaty with any King, prince or state; nor shall any person holding any office of profit or trust under the united states, or any of them, accept of any present, emolument, office or title of any kind whatever from any king, prince or foreign state; nor shall the united states in congress assembled, or any of them, grant any title of nobility.

No two or more states shall enter into any treaty, confederation or alliance whatever between them, without the consent of the united states in congress assembled, specifying accurately the purposes for which the same is to be entered into, and how long it shall continue.

No state shall lay any imposts or duties, which may interfere with any stipulations in treaties, entered into by the united states in congress assembled, with any king, prince or state, in pursuance of any treaties already proposed by congress, to the courts of France and Spain.

No vessels of war shall be kept up in time of peace by any state, except such number only, as shall be deemed necessary by the united states in congress assembled, for the defence of such state, or its trade; nor shall any body of forces be kept up by any state, in time of peace, except such number only, as in the judgment of the united states, in congress assembled, shall be deemed requisite to garrison the forts necessary for the defence of such state; but every state shall always keep up a well regulated and disciplined militia, sufficiently armed and accounted, and shall provide and constantly have ready for use, in public stores, a due number of field pieces and tents, and a proper quantity of arms, ammunition and camp equipage.

No state shall engage in any war without the consent of the united states in congress assembled, unless such state be actually invaded by enemies, or shall have received certain advice of a resolution being formed by some nation of Indians to invade such state and the danger is so imminent as not to admit of a delay, till the united states in congress assembled can be consulted: nor shall any state grant commissions to any ships or vessels of war, nor letters of marque or reprisal, except it be after a declaration of war by the united states in congress assembled, and then only against the kingdom or state and the subjects thereof, against which war has been so declared, and under such regulations as shall be established by the united states in congress assembled, unless such state be infested by pirates, in which case vessels of war may be fitted out for that occasion, and kept so long as the danger shall continue, or until the united states in congress assembled shall determine otherwise.

[ART. VII.] When land-forces are raised by any state for the common defence, all officers of or under the rank of colonel, shall be appointed by the legislature of each state respectively by whom such forces shall be raised, or in such manner as such state shall direct, and all vacancies shall be filled up by the state which first made the appointment.

[ART. VIII.] All charges of war, and all other expences that shall be incurred for the common defence or general welfare, and allowed by the united states in congress assembled, shall be defrayed out of a common treasury, which shall be supplied by the several states, in proportion to the value of all land within each state, granted to or surveyed for any Person, as such land and the buildings and improvements thereon shall be estimated according to such mode as the united states in congress assembled, shall from time to time direct and appoint. The taxes for paying that proportion shall be laid and levied by the authority and direction of the legislatures of the several states within the time agreed upon by the united states in congress assembled.

[ART. IX.] The united states in congress assembled, shall have the sole and exclusive right and power of determining on peace and war, except in the cases mentioned in the sixth article—of sending and receiving ambassadors—entering into treaties and alliances, provided that no treaty of commerce shall be made whereby the legislative power of the respective states shall be restrained from imposing such imposts and duties on foreigners, as their own people are subjected to, or from prohibiting the exportation or importation of any

species of goods or commodities whatsoever—of establishing rules for deciding in all cases, what captures on land or water shall be legal, and in what manner prizes taken by land or naval forces in the service of the united states shall be divided or appropriated—of granting letters of marque and reprisal in times of peace—appointing courts for the trial of piracies and felonies committed on the high seas and establishing courts for receiving and determining finally appeals in all cases of captures, provided that no member of congress shall be appointed a judge of any of the said courts.

The united states in congress assembled shall also be the last resort on appeal in all disputes and differences now subsisting or that hereafter may arise between two or more states concerning boundary, jurisdiction or any other cause whatever; which authority shall always be exercised in the manner following. Whenever the legislative or executive authority or lawful agent [of any] state in controversy with another shall present a petition to congress stating the matter in question and praying for a hearing, notice thereof shall be given by order of congress to the legislative or executive authority of the other state in controversy, and a day assigned for the appearance of the parties by their lawful agents, who shall then be directed to appoint by joint consent, commissioners or judges to constitute a court for hearing and determining the matter in question; but if they cannot agree, congress shall name three persons out of each of the united states, and from the list of such persons each party shall alternately strike out one, the petitioners beginning, until the number shall be reduced to thirteen; and from that number not less than seven, nor more than nine names as congress shall direct, shall in the presence of congress be drawn out by lot, and the persons whose names shall be so drawn or any five of them, shall be commissioners or judges, to hear and finally determine the controversy, so always as a major part of the judges who shall hear the cause shall agree in the determination: and if either party shall neglect to attend at the day appointed, without shewing reasons, which congress shall judge sufficient, or being present shall refuse to strike, the congress shall proceed to nominate three persons out of each state, and the secretary of congress shall strike in behalf of such party absent or refusing; and the judgment and sentence of the court to be appointed, in the manner before prescribed, shall be final and conclusive; and if any of the parties shall refuse to submit to the authority of such court, or to appear to defend their claim or cause, the court shall nevertheless proceed to pronounce sentence, or judgment, which shall in like manner be final and decisive, the judgment or sentence and other proceedings being in either case transmitted to congress, and lodged among the acts of congress for the security of the parties concerned: provided that every commissioner, before he sits in judgment, shall take an oath to be administered by one of the judges of the supreme or superior court of the state, where the cause shall be tried, "well and truly to hear and determine the matter in question, according to the best of his judgment, without favour, affection or hope of reward;" provided also that no state shall be deprived of territory for the benefit of the united states.

All controversies concerning the private right of soil claimed under different grants of two or more states, whose jurisdictions as they may respect such lands, and the states which passed such grants are adjusted, the said grants or either of them being at the same time claimed to have originated antecedent to such settlement of jurisdiction, shall on the petition of either party to the congress of the united states, be finally determined as near as may be in the same manner as is before prescribed for deciding disputes respecting territorial jurisdiction between different states.

The united states in congress assembled shall also have the sole and exclusive right and power of regulating the alloy and value of coin struck by their own authority, or by that of the respective states—fixing the standard of weights and measures throughout the united states—regulating the trade and managing all affairs with the Indians, not members of any of the states, provided that the legislative right of any state within its own limits be not infringed or violated—establishing and regulating post-offices from one state to another, throughout all the united states, and exacting such postage on the papers passing thro' the same as may be requisite to defray the expences of the said office—appointing all officers of the land forces, in the service of the united states, excepting regimental officers—appointing all the officers of the naval forces, and commissioning all officers whatever in the service of the united states—making rules for the government and regulation of the said land and naval forces, and directing their operations.

The united states in congress assembled shall have authority to appoint a committee, to sit in the recess of congress, to be denominated "A Committee of the States," and to consist of one delegate from each state; and to appoint such other committees and civil officers as may be necessary for managing the general affairs of the united states under their direction—to appoint one of their number to preside, provided that no person be allowed to serve in the office of president more than one year in any term of three years; to ascertain the necessary sums of Money to be raised for the service of the united states, and to appropriate and apply the same for defraying the public expences—to borrow money, or emit bills on the credit of the united states, transmitting every half year to the respective states an account of the sums of money so borrowed or emitted—to build and equip a navy—to agree upon the number of land forces, and to make requisitions from each state for its quota, in proportion to the number of white inhabitants in such state; which requisition shall be binding, and thereupon the legislature of each state shall appoint the regimental officers, raise the men and clothe, arm and equip them in a soldier like manner, at the expence of the united states, and the officers and men so clothed, armed and equipped shall march to the place appointed, and within the time agreed on by the united states in congress assembled. But if the united states in congress assembled shall, on consideration of circumstances judge proper that any state should not raise men, or should raise a smaller number than its quota, and that any other state should raise a greater number of men than the quota thereof, such extra number shall be raised, officered, clothed, armed and equipped in the same manner as the quota of such state, unless the legislature of such state shall judge that such extra number cannot be safely spared out of the same, in which case they shall raise, officer, clothe, arm and equip as many of such extra number as they judge can be safely spared. And the officers and men so clothed, armed and equipped, shall march to the place appointed, and within the time agreed on by the united states in congress assembled.

The united states in congress assembled shall never engage in a war, nor grant letters of marque and reprisal in time of peace, nor enter into any treaties or alliances, nor coin money, nor regulate the value thereof, nor ascertain the sums and expences necessary for the defence and welfare of the united states, or any of them, nor emit bills, nor borrow money on the credit of the united states, nor appropriate money, nor agree upon the number of vessels of war, to be built or purchased, or the number of land or sea forces to be raised, nor appoint a commander in chief of the army or navy, unless nine states assent to the same: nor shall a question on any other point, except for adjourning from day to day be determined, unless by the votes of a majority of the united states in congress assembled.

The congress of the united states shall have power to adjourn to any time within the year, and to any place within the united states, so that no period of adjournment be for a longer duration than the space of six Months, and shall publish the Journal of their proceedings monthly, except such parts thereof relating to treaties, alliances or military operations as in their judgment require secrecy; and the yeas and nays of the delegates of each state on any question shall be entered on the Journal, when it is desired by any delegate; and the delegates of a state, or any of them, at his or their request shall be furnished with a transcript of the said Journal, except such parts as are above excepted, to lay before the legislatures of the several states.

[ART. X.] The committee of the states, or any nine of them, shall be authorised to execute, in the recess of congress, such of the powers of congress as the united states in congress assembled, by the consent of nine states, shall from time to time think expedient to vest them with; provided that no power be delegated to the said committee, for the exercise of which, by the articles of confederation, the voice of nine states in the congress of the united states assembled is requisite.

[ART. XI.] Canada acceding to this confederation, and joining in the measures of the united states, shall be admitted into, and entitled to all the advantages of this union: but no other colony shall be admitted into the same, unless such admission be agreed to by nine states.

[ART. XII.] All bills of credit emitted, monies borrowed and debts contracted by, or under the authority of congress, before the assembling of the united states, in pursuance of the present confederation, shall be deemed and considered as a charge against the united states, for payment and satisfaction whereof the said united states, and the public faith are hereby solemnly pledged.

[ART. XIII.] Every state shall abide by the determinations of the united states in congress assembled, on all questions which by this confederation are submitted to them. And the Articles of this confederation shall be inviolably observed by every state, and the union shall be perpetual; nor shall any alteration at any time hereafter be made in any of them; unless such alteration be agreed to in a congress of the united states, and be afterwards confirmed by the legislatures of every state.

And whereas it hath pleased the Great Governor of the World to incline the hearts of the legislatures we respectively represent in congress, to approve of, and to authorize us to ratify the said articles of confederation and perpetual union. Know ye that we the undersigned delegates, by virtue of the power and authority to us given for that purpose, do by these presents, in the name and in behalf of our respective constituents, fully and entirely ratify and confirm each and every of the said articles of confederation and perpetual union, and all and singular the matters and things therein contained: And we do further solemnly plight and engage the faith of our respective constituents, that they shall abide by the determinations of the united states in congress assembled, on all questions, which by the said confederation are submitted to them. And that the articles thereof shall be inviolably observed by the states we respectively represent, and that the union shall be perpetual. In Witness whereof we have hereunto set our hands in Congress. Done at Philadelphia in the state of Pennsylvania the ninth Day of July in the Year of our Lord one Thousand seven Hundred and Seventy-eight, and in the third year of the independence of America.

JOSIAH BARTLETT
JOHN WENTWORTH Jun$^r$
August 8$^{th}$ 1778
On the part & behalf of
the State of New Hampshire

JOHN HANCOCK
SAMUEL ADAMS
ELBRIDGE GERRY
FRANCIS DANA
JAMES LOVELL
SAMUEL HOLTEN
On the part and behalf of
the State of Massachusetts Bay

WILLIAM ELLERY
HENRY MARCHANT
JOHN COLLINS
On the part and behalf
of the State of Rhode Island
and Providence Plantations

ROGER SHERMAN
SAMUEL HUNTINGTON
OLIVER WOLCOTT
TITUS HOSMER
ANDREW ADAMS
On the part and behalf of
the State of Connecticut

JA$^S$ DUANE
FRA$^S$ LEWIS
W$^M$ DUER.
GOUV MORRIS

On the Part and Behalf of
the State of New York

JNO WITHERSPOON
NATH$^L$ SCUDDER
On the Part and in Behalf of
the State of New Jersey.
Nov$^r$ 26, 1778.—

ROB$^T$ MORRIS
DANIEL ROBERDEAU
JON$^A$ BAYARD SMITH.
WILLIAM CLINGAN
JOSEPH REED
22$^d$ July 1778
On the part and behalf of
the State of Pennsylvania

THO M:KEAN
Feby 12 1779
JOHN DICKINSON
May 5$^{th}$ 1779
NICHOLAS VAN DYKE,
On the part & behalf of
the State of Delaware

JOHN HANSON
March 1 1781
DANIEL CARROLL d$^o$
On the part and behalf
of the State of Maryland

RICHARD HENRY LEE
JOHN BANISTER
THOMAS ADAMS

JN$^O$ HARVIE
FRANCIS LIGHTFOOT LEE
On the Part and Behalf of
the State of Virginia

JOHN PENN
July 21$^{st}$ 1778
CORN$^S$ HARNETT
JN$^O$ WILLIAMS
On the part and Behalf
of the State of N$^O$ Carolina

HENRY LAURENS
WILLIAM HENRY DRAYTON
JN$^O$ MATHEWS
RICH$^D$ HUTSON.
THO$^S$ HEYWARD Jun$^r$
On the part & behalf of
the State of South Carolina

JN$^O$ WALTON
24th July 1778
EDW$^D$ TELFAIR.
EDW$^D$ LANGWORTHY
On the part and behalf of
the State of Georgia

# Gettysburg Address

*Abraham Lincoln delivered the following address on November 19, 1863, at the dedication of the National Cemetery in Gettysburg, Pennsylvania, site of a major Civil War battle. The eloquent speech, which took only two minutes to deliver, soon became one of the world's most-quoted orations.*

Four score and seven years ago our fathers brought forth on this continent, a new nation, conceived in Liberty, and dedicated to the proposition that all men are created equal.

Now we are engaged in a great civil war, testing whether that nation, or any nation so conceived and so dedicated, can long endure. We are met on a great battle-field of that war. We have come to dedicate a portion of that field, as a final resting place for those who here gave their lives that that nation might live. It is altogether fitting and proper that we should do this.

But, in a larger sense, we can not dedicate—we can not consecrate—we can not hallow—this ground. The brave men, living and dead, who struggled here, have consecrated it, far above our poor power to add or detract. The world will little note, nor long remember what we say here, but it can never forget what they did here. It is for us the living, rather, to be dedicated here to the unfinished work which they who fought here have thus far so nobly advanced. It is rather for us to be here dedicated to the great task remaining before us—that from these honored dead we take increased devotion to that cause for which they gave the last full measure of devotion—that we here highly resolve that these dead shall not have died in vain—that this nation, under God, shall have a new birth of freedom—and that government of the people, by the people, for the people, shall not perish from the earth.

# The Emancipation Proclamation
## Issued by President Abraham Lincoln on January 1, 1863

Whereas on the 22d day of September, A.D. 1862, a proclamation was issued by the President of the United States, containing, among other things, the following, to wit:

"That on the 1st day of January, A.D. 1863, all persons held as slaves within any State or designated part of a State the people whereof shall then be in rebellion against the United States shall be then, thenceforward, and forever free; and the Executive Government of the United States, including the military and naval authority thereof, will recognize and maintain the freedom of such persons and will do no act or acts to repress such persons, or any of them, in any efforts they may make for their actual freedom.

"That the executive will on the 1st day of January aforesaid, by proclamation, designate the States and parts of States, if any, in which the people thereof, respectively, shall then be in rebellion against the United States; and the fact that any State or the people thereof shall on that day be in good faith represented in the Congress of the United States by members chosen thereto at elections wherein a majority of the qualified voters of such States shall have participated shall, in the absence of strong countervailing testimony, be deemed conclusive evidence that such State and the people thereof are not then in rebellion against the United States."

Now, therefore, I, Abraham Lincoln, President of the United States, by virtue of the power in me vested as Commander-in-Chief of the Army and Navy of the United States in time of actual armed rebellion against the authority and government of the United States, and as a fit and necessary war measure for suppressing said rebellion, do, on this 1st day of January, A.D. 1863, and in accordance with my purpose so to do, publicly proclaimed for the full period of one hundred days from the first day above mentioned, order and designate as the States and parts of States wherein the people thereof, respectively, are this day in rebellion against the United States the following, to wit:

Arkansas, Texas, Louisiana (except the parishes of St. Bernard, Plaquemines, Jefferson, St. John, St. Charles, St. James, Ascension, Assumption, Terrebonne, Lafourche, St. Mary, St. Martin, and Orleans, including the city of New Orleans), Mississippi, Alabama, Florida, Georgia, South Carolina, North Carolina, and Virginia (except the forty-eight counties designated as West Virginia, and also the counties of Berkeley, Accomac, Northhampton, Elizabeth City, York, Princess Anne, and Norfolk, including the cities of Norfolk and Portsmouth), and which excepted parts are for the present left precisely as if this proclamation were not issued.

And by virtue of the power and for the purpose aforesaid, I do order and declare that all persons held as slaves within said designated States and parts of States are, and henceforward shall be, free; and that the Executive Government of the United States, including the military and naval authorities thereof, will recognize and maintain the freedom of said persons.

And I hereby enjoin upon the people so declared to be free to abstain from all violence, unless in necessary self-defense; and I recommend to them that, in all cases when allowed, they labor faithfully for reasonable wages.

And I further declare and make known that such persons of suitable condition will be received into the armed service of the United States to garrison forts, positions, stations, and other places, and to man vessels of all sorts in said service.

And upon this act, sincerely believed to be an act of justice, warranted by the Constitution upon military necessity, I invoke the considerate judgment of mankind and the gracious favor of Almighty God.

Over the course of the Civil War, nearly 180,000 African Americans wore the Union uniform.

# Supreme Court Glossary

### Agostini v. Felton (1997)

Decision: The Court decided that it was appropriate to reconsider *Aguilar* v. *Felton* as subsequent cases had undermined several of the assumptions, for example that public employees placed at parochial schools would "inevitably inculcate religion," upon which the decision was based. The Court then found that New York City's Title I Program did not violate any of the criteria used "to evaluate whether government aid has the effect of advancing religion: it does not result in governmental indoctrination; define its recipients by reference to religion; or create an excessive entanglement." As a result, the Court concluded that "a federally funded program providing supplemental, remedial instruction to disadvantaged children on a neutral basis is not invalid under the Establishment Clause when such instruction is given on the premises of sectarian schools by government employees pursuant to a program containing safeguards" against excessive entanglement between government and religion.

### Baker v. Carr (1962)

Decision: The Supreme Court held that the federal courts do have jurisdiction and authority to review the constitutionality of a State's electoral apportionment. The voters are entitled to a trial on their allegation that the Tennessee apportionment violated the United States Constitution by diluting their votes and denying them equal protection of the law. The federal courts may impose remedies if the voters can show that their votes do not count for substantially the same amount as votes of others in the State.

### Bethel School District #403 v. Fraser (1986)

(1st Amendment, freedom of speech) A high school student gave a sexually suggestive political speech at a high school assembly to elect student officers. The school administration strongly disciplined the student, Fraser, who argued that school rules unfairly limited his freedom of political speech. Fraser's view was upheld in State court. Washington appealed to the Supreme Court, which found that "it does not follow. . . that simply because the use of an offensive form of expression may not be prohibited to adults making what the speaker considers a political point, the same latitude must be permitted to children in a public school."

### Board of Estimate of City of New York v. Morris (1989)

Decision: The reapportionment requirement of "one-person, one-vote" applies to the Board of Estimate. The Board has sufficient legislative functions that its composition must fairly represent city voters on an approximately equal basis. The fact that some members are elected citywide is one factor to be considered in evaluating the fairness of the electoral structure, but it is not determinative. The City's expressed interests—that the Board be effective and that it accommodate natural and political boundaries as well as local interests—does not justify the size of the deviation from the "one-person, one-vote" ideal. The City could structure the Board in other ways that would

further these interests while minimizing the discrimination in voting power.

### Bob Jones University v. United States (1983)

(14th Amendment in conflict with 1st Amendment) Bob Jones University, a private school, denied admission to applicants in an interracial marriage or who "espouse" interracial marriage or dating. The Internal Revenue Service then denied tax exempt status to the school because of racial discrimination. The university appealed, claiming their policy was based on the Bible. The Court upheld the IRS ruling, stating that ". . . Government has a fundamental overriding interest in eradicating racial discrimination in education."

### Brown v. Board of Education of Topeka (1954)

(14th Amendment, Equal Protection Clause) Probably no twentieth century Supreme Court decision so deeply stirred and changed life in the United States as Brown. A 10-year-old Topeka girl, Linda Brown, was not permitted to attend her neighborhood school because she was an African American. The Court heard arguments about whether segregation itself was a violation of the Equal Protection Clause and found that it was, commenting that "in the field of public education the doctrine of 'separate but equal' has no place. . . . Segregation is a denial of the equal protection of the laws." The decision overturned *Plessy* v. *Ferguson,* 1896.

### City of Philadelphia v. New Jersey (1978)

Decision: The Court decided that New Jersey may not restrict the importation of solid or liquid waste that originated outside the State. The Commerce Clause protects all objects of interstate trade, including waste. A State may not discriminate against items that are identical except for their origin, and thus may not prohibit out-of-state waste that is no different from domestically produced waste. Although waste disposal is a problem in many locations, States may not constitutionally deal with the problem by erecting a barrier against the movement of interstate trade.

### The Civil Rights Cases (1883)

(14th Amendment, Equal Protection Clause) The Civil Rights Act of 1875 included punishments of businesses that practiced discrimination. The Court ruled on a number of cases involving the Acts in 1883, finding that the Constitution, "while prohibiting discrimination by governments, made no provisions . . . for acts of racial discrimination by private individuals." The decision limited the impact of the Equal Protection Clause, giving tacit approval for segregation in the private sector.

### Communist Party of Indiana v. Whitcomb (1974)

Decision: The Supreme Court ruled that the required oath was unconstitutional. Although the Court agreed that the

Constitution entrusted control of the electoral process to the States, it held that the States may not infringe upon basic constitutional rights in exercising that control. People have a right to organize themselves into political parties according to their beliefs, to run for elected office, and to vote for candidates based on those beliefs. A political party may hold an abstract belief in violent political change without necessarily advocating unlawful violent action. The States may forbid advocacy of the use of force only when that advocacy is directed to inciting or producing imminent lawless action and is likely to incite such action.

### Cruzan v. Missouri (1990)

(14th Amendment, Due Process Clause) After Nancy Beth Cruzan was left in a "persistent vegetative state" by a car accident, Missouri officials refused to comply with her parents' request that the hospital terminate life-support. The Court upheld the State policy under which officials refused to withdraw treatment, rejecting the argument that the Due Process Clause of the 14th Amendment gave the parents the right to refuse treatment on their daughter's behalf. Although individuals have the right to refuse medical treatment, "incompetent" persons are not able to exercise this right; without "clear and convincing" evidence that Cruzan desired the withdrawal of treatment, the State could legally act to preserve her life.

### Dennis v. United States (1951)

(1st Amendment, freedom of speech) The Smith Act of 1940 made it a crime for any person to work for the violent overthrow of the United States in peacetime or war. Eleven Communist party leaders, including Dennis, had been convicted of violating the Smith Act, and they appealed. The Court upheld the Act.

### Dred Scott v. Sandford (1857)

(5th Amendment, individual rights) This decision upheld property rights over human rights by saying that Dred Scott, a slave, could not become a free man just because he had traveled in "free soil" States with his master. A badly divided nation was further fragmented by the decision. "Free soil" federal laws and the Missouri Compromise line of 1820 were held unconstitutional because they deprived a slave owner of the right to his "property" without just compensation. This narrow reading of the Constitution, a landmark case of the Court, was most clearly stated by Chief Justice Roger B. Taney, a States' rights advocate.

### Engel v. Vitale (1962)

(1st Amendment, Establishment Clause) The State Board of Regents of New York required the recitation of a 22-word nonsectarian prayer at the beginning of each school day. A group of parents filed suit against the required prayer, claiming it violated their 1st Amendment rights. The Court found New York's action to be unconstitutional, observing, "There can be no doubt that. . . religious beliefs [are] embodied in the Regent's prayer."

### Edwards v. South Carolina (1963)

(1st Amendment, freedom of speech and assembly) A group of mostly African American civil rights activists held a rally at the South Carolina State Capitol, protesting segregation. A hostile crowd gathered and the rally leaders were arrested and convicted for "breach of the peace." The Court overturned the convictions, saying, "The Fourteenth Amendment does not permit a State to make criminal the peaceful expression of unpopular views."

### Escobedo v. Illinois (1964)

(6th Amendment, right to counsel) In a case involving a murder confession by a person known to Chicago-area police who was not afforded counsel while under interrogation, the Court extended the "exclusionary rule" to illegal confessions in State court proceedings. Carefully defining an "Escobedo Rule," the Court said, "where. . . the investigation is no longer a general inquiry . . . but has begun to focus on a particular suspect . . . (and where) the suspect has been taken into custody . . . the suspect has requested . . . his lawyer, and the police have not . . . warned him of his right to remain silent, the accused has been denied . . . counsel in violation of the Sixth Amendment."

### Ex parte Milligan (1866)

(Article II, executive powers) An Indiana man was arrested, treated as a prisoner of war, and imprisoned by a military court during the Civil War under presidential order. He claimed that his rights to a fair trial were interfered with and that military courts had no authority outside of "conquered territory." He was released because, "the Constitution . . . is a law for rulers and people, equally in war and peace, and covers . . . all . . . men, at all times, and under all circumstances." The Court held that presidential powers to suspend the writ of *habeas corpus* in time of war did not extend to creating another court system run by the military.

### Flast v. Cohen (1968)

Decision: The Supreme Court concluded that the rule announced in *Frothingham* v. *Mellon* expressed a practical policy of judicial self-restraint rather than an absolute constitutional limitation on the power of federal courts to hear taxpayer suits. While mere status as a federal taxpayer ordinarily will not give sufficient "standing" to allow a person to challenge the constitutionality of a federal law, there may be times when taxpayers are appropriate plaintiffs. *Flast* v. *Cohen,* in which plaintiffs argued that the First Amendment specifically prohibited taxing them in order to support religious activities, was one in which their role as taxpayers was well suited to the challenge they sought to assert. The Court ruled that they had standing to sue, and allowed them to proceed with their case.

### Furman v. Georgia (1972)

(8th Amendment, capital punishment) Three different death penalty cases, including *Furman,* raised the question of racial imbalances in the use of death sentences by State courts. Furman had been convicted and sentenced to death in Georgia. In deciding to overturn existing State death-penalty laws, the Court noted that there was an "apparent arbitrariness of the use of the sentence. . . ." Many States rewrote their death-penalty statutes and these were generally upheld in *Gregg* v. *Georgia,*1976.

### Gibbons v. Ogden (1824)

(Supremacy Clause) This decision involved a careful examination of the power of Congress to "regulate interstate commerce." Aaron Ogden's exclusive New York ferry license gave him the right to operate steamboats to and from New York. He said that Thomas Gibbons's federal "coasting license" did not include "landing rights" in New York City. The Court invalidated the New York licensing regulations, holding that federal regulations should take precedence under the Supremacy Clause. The decision strengthened the power of the United States to regulate any interstate business relationship. Federal regulation of the broadcasting industry, oil pipelines, and banking are all based on *Gibbons*.

## Gideon v. Wainwright (1963)

(6th Amendment, right to counsel) In 1961 a Florida court found Clarence Earl Gideon guilty of breaking and entering and sentenced him to five years in prison. Gideon appealed his case to the Supreme Court on the basis that he had been unconstitutionally denied counsel during his trial due to Florida's policy of only providing appointed counsel in capital cases. The Court granted Gideon a new trial, and he was found not guilty with the help of a court-appointed attorney. The "Gideon Rule" upheld the 6th Amendment's guarantee of counsel of all poor persons facing a felony charge, a further incorporation of Bill of Rights guarantees into State constitutions.

## Gitlow v. New York (1925)

(1st Amendment, freedom of speech) A New York socialist, Gitlow, was convicted under a State law on "criminal anarchy" for distributing copies of a "left-wing manifesto." For the first time, the Court considered whether the 1st Amendment applied to State laws. The case helped to establish what came to be known as the "incorporation" doctrine, under which, it was argued, the provisions of the 1st Amendment were "incorporated" by the 14th Amendment, thus applying to State as well as federal laws. Although New York law was not overruled in this case, the decision clearly indicated that the Supreme Court could make such a ruling. Another important incorporation case is *Powell* v. *Alabama,* 1932.

## Goldberg v. Kelly (1970)

Decision: The Court ruled that public aid recipients are entitled to a pre-termination hearing at which he or she (directly or through an attorney) may offer arguments, present evidence, and cross-examine witnesses. In its decision, the Court held that welfare benefits are a matter of statutory entitlement for persons who are eligible to receive them. Before terminating benefits, the government must therefore comply with the requirements of procedural due process.

## Goss v. Lopez (1975)

(14th Amendment, Due Process Clause) Ten Ohio students were suspended from their schools without hearings. The students challenged the suspensions, claiming that the absence of a preliminary hearing violated their 14th Amendment right to due process. The Court agreed with the students, holding that "having chosen to extend the right to an education. . . Ohio may not withdraw that right on grounds of misconduct, absent fundamentally fair procedures to determine whether the misconduct has occurred, and must recognize a student's legitimate entitlement to a public education as a property interest that is protected by the Due Process Clause."

## Gregg v. Georgia (1976)

(8th Amendment, cruel and unusual punishment) A Georgia jury sentenced Troy Gregg to death after finding him guilty on two counts each of murder and armed robbery. Gregg appealed the sentence, claiming that it violated the "cruel and unusual punishment" clause of the 8th Amendment and citing *Furman* v. *Georgia,* 1972, in which the court held that Georgia's application of the death penalty was unfair and arbitrary. However, the Court upheld Gregg's sentence, stating for the first time that "punishment of death does not invariably violate the Constitution."

## Griswold v. Connecticut (1965)

(14th Amendment, Due Process Clause) A Connecticut law forbade the use of "any drug, medicinal article, or instrument for the purpose of preventing conception." Griswold, director of Planned Parenthood in New Haven, was arrested for counseling married persons and, after conviction, appealed. The Court overturned the Connecticut law, saying that "various guarantees (of the Constitution) create zones of privacy. . ." and questioning, ". . .would we allow the police to search the sacred precincts of marital bedrooms. . . ?" The decision is significant for raising for more careful inspection the concept of "unenumerated rights" in the 9th Amendment, later central to *Roe* v. *Wade,* 1973.

## Hazelwood School District v. Kuhlmeier (1988)

(1st Amendment, freedom of speech) In 1983, the principal of Hazelwood East High School in Missouri removed two articles from the upcoming issue of the student newspaper, deeming their content "inappropriate, personal, sensitive, and unsuitable for student readers." Several students sued the school district, claiming that their 1st Amendment right to freedom of expression had been violated. The Court upheld the principal's action, stating that "a school need not tolerate student speech that is inconsistent with its basic educational mission, even though the government could not censor similar speech outside the school." School officials had full control over school-sponsored activities "so long as their actions are reasonably related to legitimate pedagogical concerns. . . ."

## Heart of Atlanta Motel, Inc. v. United States (1964)

Decision: The Court ruled that Congress could outlaw racial segregation of private facilities that are engaged in interstate commerce. The Court's decision stated, "If it is interstate commerce that feels the pinch, it does not matter how 'local' the operation which applies the squeeze. . . . The power of Congress to promote interstate commerce also includes the power to regulate the local incidents thereof, including local activities. . . which have a substantial and harmful effect upon that commerce."

## Hutchinson v. Proxmire (1979)

Decision: The Court held that the Speech or Debate Clause gives members of Congress immunity from suit for defamatory statements made within the legislative chambers, but the privilege does not extend to comments made in other locations, even if they merely repeat what was said in Congress. The newsletters and press release were not within the deliberative process nor were they essential to the deliberation of the Senate. They also were not part of the "informing function" of members of Congress, since they were not a part of legislative function or of the deliberations that make up the legislative process. The comments were merely designed to convey information on the Senator's individual positions and beliefs. Finally, although Hutchinson had received extensive attention in the media as a result of his receipt of the Golden Fleece Award, he was not a public figure prior to that controversy and thus is entitled to the greater protection against defamation that is extended to non-public figures. The fact that the public may have an interest in governmental expenditures does not make Hutchinson himself a public figure.

### Illinois v. Wardlow (2000)

Decision: The Supreme Court refused to say that flight from the police will always justify a stop or that it will never do so. Instead, the Court ruled that flight can be an important factor in determining whether police have "reasonable suspicion" to stop a suspect. The trial court will have to determine in each case whether the information available to the police officers, including the fact of a suspect's flight, was sufficient to support the stop.

### In Re Gault (1966)

(14th Amendment, Due Process Clause) Prior to the Gault case, proceedings against juvenile offenders were generally handled as "family law," not "criminal law" and provided few due process guarantees. Gerald Gault was assigned to six years in a State juvenile detention facility for an alleged obscene phone call. He was not provided counsel and not permitted to confront or cross-examine the principal witness. The Court overturned the juvenile proceedings and required that States provide juveniles "some of the due process guarantees of adults," including a right to a phone call, to counsel, to cross-examine, to confront their accuser, and to be advised of their right to silence.

### Ingraham v. Wright (1977)

Decision: A majority of the Supreme Court concluded that the 8th Amendment historically protected people convicted of crimes, and does not apply to public school students. If authorized by local law or custom, public schools have the right to administer reasonable discipline, and students do not have a due process right to notice or a hearing before punishment administered in accordance with law or custom.

### Johnson v. Santa Clara Transportation Agency (1987)

(Discrimination) Under their affirmative action plan, the Transportation Agency in Santa Clara, California, was authorized to "consider as one factor the sex of a qualified applicant" in an effort to combat the significant underrepresentation of women in certain job classifications. When the Agency promoted Diane Joyce, a qualified woman, over Paul Johnson, a qualified man, for the job of road dispatcher, Johnson sued, claiming that the Agency's consideration of the sex of the applicants violated Title VII of the Civil Rights Act of 1964. The Court upheld the Agency's promotion policy, arguing that the affirmative action plan created no "absolute bar" to the advancement of men but rather represented "a moderate, flexible, case-by-case approach to effecting a gradual improvement in the representation of minorities and women . . . in the Agency's work force, and [was] fully consistent with Title VII."

### Korematsu v. United States (1944)

Decision: The Court upheld the military order in light of the circumstances presented by World War II. "Pressing public necessity may sometimes justify the existence of restrictions which curtail the civil rights of a single racial group." The Court noted, however, that racial antagonism itself could never form a legitimate basis for the restrictions.

### Lemon v. Kurtzman (1971)

(1st Amendment, Establishment Clause) In overturning State laws regarding aid to church-supported schools in this and a similar Rhode Island case, the Court created the *Lemon* test limiting ". . . excessive government entanglement with religion." The Court noted that any State law about aid to religion must meet three criteria: (1) purpose of the aid must be clearly secular, (2) its primary effect must neither advance nor inhibit religion, and (3) it must avoid "excessive entanglement of government with religion."

### Mapp v. Ohio (1962)

(4th and 14th Amendments, illegal evidence and Due Process Clause) Admitting evidence gained by illegal searches was permitted by some State constitutions before *Mapp*. Cleveland police raided Dollree Mapp's home without a warrant and found obscene materials. She appealed her conviction, saying that the 4th and 14th Amendments protected her against improper police behavior. The Court agreed, extending "exclusionary rule" protections to citizens in State courts, saying that the prohibition against unreasonable searches would be "meaningless" unless evidence gained in such searches was "excluded." This case further developed the concept of "incorporation" begun in *Gitlow v. New York*, 1925.

### Marbury v. Madison (1803)

(Article III, judicial powers) After defeat in the 1800 election, President Adams appointed many Federalists to the federal courts, but James Madison, the new secretary of state, refused to deliver the commissions. William Marbury, one of the appointees, asked the Supreme Court to enforce the delivery of his commission based on a provision of the Judiciary Act of 1789 that allowed the Court to hear such cases on original jurisdiction. The Court refused Marbury's request, finding that the relevant portion of the Judiciary Act was in conflict with the Constitution. This decision, written by Chief Justice Marshall, established the evaluation of federal laws' constitutionality, or "judicial review," as a power of the Supreme Court.

### McCulloch v. Maryland (1819)

(Article I, Section 8, Necessary and Proper Clause) Called the "Bank of the United States" case. A Maryland law required federally chartered banks to use only a special paper to print paper money, which amounted to a tax. James McCulloch, the cashier of the Baltimore branch of the bank, refused to use the paper, claiming that States could not tax the Federal Government. The Court declared the Maryland law unconstitutional, commenting ". . . the power to tax implies the power to destroy."

## Miami Herald Publishing Co. v. Tornillo (1974)

Decision: The Supreme Court found that the right of reply statute violated freedom of the press as guaranteed by the First Amendment. The statute improperly intrudes into the editorial function of newspapers by deciding what must be published. The command to publish something is as great an intrusion as a command not to publish something would be. In addition, the statute penalizes newspapers by requiring them to commit production costs and newspaper space to articles that they may not wish to publish.

## Miranda v. Arizona (1966)

(5th, 6th, and 14th Amendments, rights of the accused) Arrested for kidnapping and sexual assault, Ernesto Miranda signed a confession including a statement that he had "full knowledge of [his] legal rights. . . ." After conviction, he appealed, claiming that without counsel and without warnings, the confession was illegally gained. The Court agreed with Miranda that "he must be warned prior to any questioning that he has the right to remain silent, that anything he says can be used against him in a court of law, that he has the right to. . . an attorney and that if he cannot afford an attorney one will be appointed for him. . . ." Although later modified by *Nix v. Williams,* 1984, and other cases, *Miranda* firmly upheld citizen rights to fair trials in State courts.

## New Jersey v. T.L.O. (1985)

(4th and 14th Amendments) After T.L.O., a New Jersey high school student, denied an accusation that she had been smoking in the school lavatory, a vice-principal searched her purse and found cigarettes, marijuana, and evidence that T.L.O. had been involved in marijuana dealing at the school. T.L.O. was then sentenced to probation by a juvenile court, but appealed on the grounds that the evidence against her had been obtained by an "unreasonable" search. The Court rejected T.L.O.'s arguments, stating that the school had a "legitimate need to maintain an environment in which learning can take place," and that to do this "requires some easing of the restrictions to which searches by public authorities are ordinarily subject. . ." The Court thus created a "reasonable suspicion" rule for school searches, a change from the "probable cause" requirement in the wider society.

## New York Times v. United States (1971)

(1st Amendment, freedom of the press) In 1971 *The New York Times* obtained copies of classified Defense Department documents, later known as the "Pentagon Papers," which revealed instances in which the Johnson Administration had deceived Congress and the American people regarding United States policies during the Vietnam War. A United States district court issued an injunction against the publication of the documents, claiming that it might endanger national security. On appeal, the Supreme Court cited the 1st Amendment guarantee of a free press and refused to uphold the injunction against publication, observing that it is the obligation of the government to prove that actual harm to the nation's security would be caused by the publication. The decision limited "prior restraint" of the press.

## Nixon v. Fitzgerald (1982)

Decision: The Court ruled that a President or former President is entitled to absolute immunity from liability based on his official acts. The President must be able to act forcefully and independently, without fear of liability. Diverting the President's energies with concerns about private lawsuits could impair the effective functioning of government. The President's absolute immunity extends to all acts within the "outer perimeter" of his duties of office, since otherwise he would be required to litigate over the nature of the acts and the scope of his duties in each case. The remedy of impeachment, the vigilant scrutiny of the press, the Congress, and the public, and presidential desire to earn reelection and concern with historical legacy all protect against presidential wrongdoing.

## Nixon v. Shrink Missouri Government PAC (2000)

Decision: In *Buckley* v. *Valeo,* 1976, the Supreme Court had upheld a $1000 limit on contributions by individuals to candidates for federal office. In *Nixon* v. *Shrink Missouri Government PAC,* the Court concluded that large contributions will sometimes create actual corruption, and that voters will inevitably be suspicious of the fairness of a political process that allows wealthy donors to contribute large amounts. The Court concluded that the Missouri contribution limits were appropriate to correct this problem and did not impair the ability of candidates to communicate their messages to the voters and to mount an effective campaign.

## Olmstead v. United States (1928)

(4th Amendment, electronic surveillance) Olmstead was engaged in the illegal sale of alcohol. Much of the evidence against him was gained through a wiretap made without a warrant. Olmstead argued that he had "a reasonable expectation of privacy," and that the *Weeks* v. *United States* decision of 1914 should be applied to exclude the evidence gained by the wiretap. The Court disagreed, saying that Olmstead intended "to project his voice to those quite outside . . . and that . . . nothing tangible was taken." Reversed by subsequent decisions, this case contains the first usage of the concept of "reasonable expectation of privacy" that would mark later 4th Amendment decisions.

## Oregon v. Mitchell (1970)

Decision: The Supreme Court was unable to issue a single opinion of the Court supported by a majority of the justices. However, in a series of separate opinions, differing majority groups agreed that (1) the 18-year-old minimum-age requirement of the Voting Rights Act Amendments is valid for national elections but not for State and local elections; (2) the literacy test provision is valid in order to remedy discrimination against minorities; and (3) the residency and absentee balloting provisions are a valid Congressional regulation of presidential elections.

## Plessy v. Ferguson (1896)

(14th Amendment, Equal Protection Clause) A Louisiana law required separate seating for white and African American citizens on public railroads, a form of segregation. Herman Plessy argued that his right to "equal protection of the laws" was violated. The Court held that segregation was permitted if facilities were equal. The Court interpreted the 14th Amendment as "not intended to give Negroes social equality but only political and civil equality. . . ." The Louisiana law was seen as a "reasonable exercise of (State) police power. . ." Segregated public facilities were permitted until *Plessy* was overturned by the *Brown* v. *Board of Education* case of 1954.

### Powell v. Alabama (1932)

(6th Amendment, right to counsel) The case involved the "Scottsboro boys," seven African American men accused of sexual assault. This case was a landmark in the development of a "fundamentals of fairness" doctrine of the Court over the next 40 years. The Scottsboro boys were quickly prosecuted without the benefit of counsel and sentenced to death. The Court overturned the decision, stating that poor people facing the death penalty in State courts must be provided counsel, and commenting, ". . . there are certain principles of Justice which adhere to the very idea of free government, which no [State] may disregard." The case was another step toward incorporation of the Bill of Rights into State constitutions.

### Printz v. United States (1997)

Decision: The Court ruled that the Brady Act's interim provision requiring certain State or local law enforcement agents to perform background checks on prospective handgun purchasers was unconstitutional. Although no provision of the Constitution deals explicitly with federal authority to compel State officials to execute federal law, a review of the Constitution's structure and of prior Supreme Court decisions leads to the conclusion that Congress does not have this power.

### Regents of the University of California v. Bakke (1978)

Decision: The Supreme Court issued a narrow ruling that invalidated the medical school's special admission program and directed the regents to admit Bakke but that did not overturn all affirmative action programs. Although the University of California's policy was unacceptable, "the goal of achieving a diverse student body is sufficiently compelling to justify consideration of race in admissions decisions under some circumstances." The Court indicated that it would consider discrimination and affirmative action questions on a case-by-case basis.

### Reno v. ACLU (1997)

Decision: The Supreme Court ruled that the "indecent transmission" provision and the "patently offensive display" provision of the Communications Decency Act violated the 1st Amendment's freedom of speech. The Internet does not have the special features (such as historical governmental oversight, limited frequencies, and "invasiveness") that have justified allowing greater regulation of content in radio and television. The Federal Government failed to show that the good faith defenses in the statute were technologically or commercially viable ways of effectively reducing the impermissible burden on protected speech. Because the Act is overbroad in violation of the 1st Amendment, the Court did not consider whether it was also overly vague in violation of the 5th Amendment.

### Reno v. Condon (2000)

Decision: The Court upheld the federal law that forbids States from selling addresses, telephone numbers, and other information that drivers put on license applications. They agreed with the Federal Government that information, including motor vehicle license information, is an "article of commerce" in the interstate stream of business and therefore is subject to regulation by Congress. The Court emphasized that the statute did not impose on the States any obligation to pass particular laws or policies and thus did not interfere with the States' sovereign functions.

### Roe v. Wade (1973)

(9th Amendment, right to privacy) A Texas woman challenged a State law forbidding the artificial termination of a pregnancy, saying that she "had a fundamental right to privacy." The Court upheld a woman's right to choose in this case, noting that the State's "important and legitimate interest in protecting the potentiality of human life" became "compelling" at the end of the first trimester, and that before then, ". . . the attending physician, in consultation with his patient, is free to determine, without regulation by the State, that . . . the patient's pregnancy should be terminated." The decision struck down the State regulation of abortion in the first three months of pregnancy and was modified by *Planned Parenthood of Southeastern PA v. Casey,* 1992.

### Rostker v. Goldberg (1981)

Decision: The Court ruled that women did not have to be included in the draft registration. The purpose of having draft registration was to prepare for the actual draft of combat troops if they should be needed. Since Congress and the President had both consistently decided not to use women in combat positions, it was not necessary for women to register either. The Court also noted that the role of women in the armed services had been debated extensively in the Congress, and concluded that the legislature had reached a thoughtful, reasoned conclusion on this issue.

### Roth v. United States (1951)

(1st Amendment, freedom of the press) A New York man named Roth operated a business that used the mail to invite people to buy materials considered obscene by postal inspectors. The Court, in its first consideration of censorship of obscenity, created the "prevailing community standards" rule, which required a consideration of the work as a whole. In its decision, the Court defined as obscene that which offended "the average person, applying contemporary community standards." In a case decided the same day, the Court applied the same "test" to State obscenity laws.

### Schenck v. United States (1919)

(1st Amendment, freedom of speech) Charles Schenck was an officer of an antiwar political group who was arrested for alleged violations of the Espionage Act of 1917, which made active opposition to the war a crime. He had urged thousands of young men called to service by the draft act to resist and to avoid induction. The Court limited free speech in time of war, stating that Schenck's words, under the circumstances, presented a "clear and present danger. . . ." Although later decisions modified the decision, the Schenck case created a precedent that 1st Amendment guarantees were not absolute.

## School District of Abington Township, Pennsylvania v. Schempp (1963)

(1st Amendment, Establishment Clause) A Pennsylvania State law required reading from the Bible each day at school as an all-school activity. Some parents objected and sought legal remedy. When the case reached the Court, it agreed with the parents, saying that the Establishment Clause and Free Exercise Clause both forbade States from engaging in religious activity. The Court created a rule holding that if the purpose and effect of a law "is the advancement or inhibition of religion," it "exceeds the scope of legal power."

## Shelley v. Kraemer (1948)

Decision: The Court ruled that "in granting judicial enforcement of the restrictive agreements . . . the States have denied petitioners the equal protection of the laws. . . ." No individual has the right under the Constitution to demand that a State take action that would result in the denial of equal protection to other individuals. The Court rejected the respondents' argument that, since state courts would also enforce restrictive covenants against white owners, enforcement of covenants against black owners did not constitute a denial of equal protection. "Equal protection of the laws is not achieved through indiscriminate imposition of inequalities."

## Sheppard v. Maxwell (1966)

(14th Amendment, Due Process Clause) Dr. Samuel Sheppard was convicted of murdering his wife in a trial widely covered by national news media. Sheppard appealed his conviction, claiming that the pretrial publicity had made it impossible to get a fair trial. The Court rejected the arguments about "press freedom," overturned his conviction, and ordered a new trial. As a result of the Sheppard decision, some judges have issued "gag" orders limiting pretrial publicity.

## Tennessee Valley Authority v. Hill (1978)

(Article I, Section 8, Necessary and Proper Clause) In 1975 the secretary of the interior found that the Tennessee Valley Authority's work on the Tellico Dam would destroy the endangered snail darter's habitat in violation of the Endangered Species Act of 1975. When the TVA refused to stop work on the project, local residents sued and won an injunction against completion of the dam from the federal court of appeals. The TVA appealed, arguing that the project should be completed since it had already been underway when the Endangered Species Act had passed and, with full knowledge of the circumstances of the endangered fish, Congress had continued to appropriate money for the dam in every year since the Act's passage. However, the Supreme Court found the injunction against the TVA's completion of the dam to be proper, stating "examination of the language, history, and structure of the legislation. . . indicates beyond doubt that Congress intended endangered species to be afforded the highest priorities."

## Tinker v. Des Moines School District (1969)

Decision: The Court upheld the students' First Amendment rights. Because students do not "shed their constitutional rights to freedom of speech or expression at the schoolhouse gate," schools must show a possibility of "substantial disruption" before free speech can be limited at school. Students may express personal opinions as long as they do not materially disrupt classwork, create substantial disorder, or interfere with the rights of others. In this case, the wearing of black armbands was a "silent, passive expression of opinion" without these side effects and thus constitutionally could not be prohibited by the school.

## United States v. Amistad (1841)

In 1839 two Spaniards purchased a group of kidnapped Africans and put them aboard the schooner *Amistad* for a journey from Cuba to Principe. The Africans overpowered the ship's crew, killing two men, and ordered the Spaniards to steer towards Africa. The crew steered instead toward the United States coast, where the U.S. brig *Washington* seized the ship, freeing the Spaniards and imprisoning the Africans. A series of petitions to the courts ensued, in which the Spaniards claimed the Africans as their property, and the Americans who had seized the ship claimed a share of the cargo, including the Africans, as their lawful salvage. The Court, however, declared that the Africans were not property and issued a decree that the unlawfully kidnapped Africans "be and are hereby declared to be free."

## United States v. Eichman (1990)

Decision: The Court agreed with the trial courts' rulings that the Flag Protection Act violated the 1st Amendment. Flag-burning constitutes expressive conduct, and thus is entitled to constitutional protection. The Act prevents protesters from using the flag to express their opposition to governmental policies and activities. Although the protesters' ideas may be offensive or disagreeable to many people, the government may not prohibit them from expressing those ideas.

## United States v. General Dynamics Corp. (1974)

A deep-mining coal producer, General Dynamics Corp., acquired control of a strip-mining coal producer, United Electric Coal Companies. The Government filed suit against the company, claiming that the acquisition violated the Clayton Act by limiting competition in coal sales and production through increasing the concentration of ownership among a small group of producers. The Court rejected the Government's argument, finding that, although the acquisition may have increased concentration of ownership, it did not threaten to substantially lessen competition and was therefore not in violation of the Clayton Act.

## United States v. Leon (1984)

(4th Amendment, exclusionary rule) Police in Burbank, California, gathered evidence in a drug-trafficking investigation using a search warrant issued by a state court judge. Later a District Court found that the warrant had been improperly issued and granted a motion to suppress the evidence gathered under the warrant. The Government appealed the decision, claiming that the exclusionary rule should not apply in cases where law enforcement officers acted in good faith, believing the warrant to be valid. The Court agreed and established the "good-faith exception" to the exclusionary rule, finding that the rule should not be applied to bar evidence "obtained by officers acting in reasonable reliance on a search warrant issued by a detached and neutral magistrate but ultimately found to be invalid."

## United States v. Lopez (1990)

(Article I, Section 8, Commerce Clause) Alfonzo Lopez, a Texas high school student, was convicted of carrying a weapon in a school zone under the Gun-Free School Zones Act of 1990. He appealed his conviction on the basis that the Act, which forbids "any individual knowingly to possess a firearm at a place that [he] knows. . . is a school zone," exceeded Congress's legislative power under the Commerce Clause. The Court agreed that the Act was unconstitutional, stating that to uphold the legislation would "bid fair to convert congressional Commerce Clause authority to a general police power of the sort held only by the States."

## United States v. Nixon (1974)

(Separation of powers) During the investigation of the Watergate scandal, in which members of President Nixon's administration were accused of participating in various illegal activities, a special prosecutor subpoenaed tapes of conversations between Nixon and his advisors. Nixon refused to release the tapes but was overruled by the Court, which ordered him to surrender the tapes, rejecting his arguments that they were protected by "executive privilege." The President's "generalized interest in confidentiality" was subordinate to "the fundamental demands of due process of law in the fair administration of criminal justice."

## Wallace v. Jaffree (1985)

(1st Amendment, Establishment Clause) An Alabama law authorized a one-minute period of silence in all public schools "for meditation or voluntary prayer." A group of parents, including Jaffree, challenged the constitutionality of the statute, claiming it violated the Establishment Clause of the 1st Amendment. The Court agreed with Jaffree and struck down the Alabama law, determining that "the State's endorsement. . . of prayer activities at the beginning of each schoolday is not consistent with the established principle that the government must pursue a course of complete neutrality toward religion."

## Walz v. Tax Commission of the City of New York (1970)

(1st Amendment, Establishment Clause) State and local governments routinely exempt church property from taxes. Walz claimed that such exemptions were a "support of religion," a subsidy by government. The Court disagreed, noting that such exemptions were just an example of a "benevolent neutrality" between government and churches, not a support of religion. Governments must avoid taxing churches because taxation would give government a "control" over religion, prohibited by the "wall of separation of church and state" noted in *Everson* v. *Board of Education*, 1947.

## Watkins v. United States (1957)

Decision: The Court held that Watkins was not given a fair opportunity to determine whether he was within his rights in refusing to answer the Committee's questions. Congress has no authority to expose the private affairs of individuals unless justified by a specific function of Congress. Congress's investigative powers are broad but not unlimited, and must not infringe on 1st Amendment rights of speech, political belief, or association. When witnesses are forced by subpoena to testify, the subject of Congressional inquiry must be articulated in the Committee's charter or explained at the time of testimony if 1st Amendment rights are in jeopardy.

## West Virginia Board of Education v. Barnette (1943)

(1st Amendment, freedom of religion) During World War II the West Virginia Board of Education required all students to take part in a daily flag saluting ceremony or else face expulsion. Jehovah's Witnesses objected to the compulsory salute, which they felt would force them to break their religion's doctrine against the worship of any "graven image." The Court struck down the rule, agreeing that a compulsory flag salute violated the 1st Amendment's exercise of religion clause and stating "no official, high or petty, can prescribe what shall be orthodox in politics, nationalism, religion, or other matters of opinion. . . ."

## Board of Education of Westside Community Schools v. Mergens (1990)

(1st Amendment, Establishment Clause) A request by Bridget Mergens to form a student Christian religious group at school was denied by an Omaha high school principal. Mergens took legal action, claiming that a 1984 federal law required "equal access" for student religious groups. The Court ordered the school to permit the club, stating, "a high school does not have to permit any extracurricular activities, but when it does, the school is bound by the . . . [Equal Access] Act of 1984. Allowing students to meet on campus and discuss religion is constitutional because it does not amount to 'State sponsorship of a religion.'"

## Wisconsin v. Yoder (1972)

(1st Amendment, Free Exercise Clause) Members of the Amish religious sect in Wisconsin objected to sending their children to public schools after the eighth grade, claiming that such exposure of the children to another culture would endanger the group's self-sufficient agrarian lifestyle essential to their religious faith. The Court agreed with the Amish, while noting that the Court must move carefully to weigh the State's "legitimate social concern when faced with religious claim for exemption from generally applicable educational requirements."

# Glossary

Number(s) after each definition refer to page(s) where the term is defined.

**Absentee voting** Provisions made for those unable to get to their regular polling places on election day. p. 189

**Acquit** Find not guilty of a charge. p. 311

**Act of admission** A congressional act admitting a new State to the Union. p. 100

**Adjourn** Suspend, as in a session of Congress. p. 264

**Administration** The officials in the executive branch of a government and their policies and principles. p. 416

**Affirmative action** A policy that requires most employers take positive steps to remedy the effects of past discriminations. p. 609

**Albany Plan of Union** Plan proposed by Benjamin Franklin in 1754 that aimed to unite the 13 colonies for trade, military, and other purposes; the plan was turned down by the colonies and the Crown. pp. 35–36

**Alien** Foreign-born resident, or noncitizen. pp. 534, 614

**Ambassador** An official representative of the United States appointed by the President to represent the nation in matters of diplomacy. p. 471

**Amendment** A change in, or addition to, a constitution or law. p. 72

**Amnesty** A blanket pardon offered to a group of law violators. p. 408

**Anti-Federalists** Those persons who opposed the ratification of the Constitution in 1787–1788. p. 56

**Appellate jurisdiction** The authority of a court to review decisions of inferior (lower) courts; *see* original jurisdiction. pp. 509, 709

**Apportion** Distribute, as in seats in a legislative body. p. 267

**Appropriate** Assign to a particular use. p. 305

**Articles** Numbered sections of a document. The unamended Constitution is divided into seven articles. p. 65

**Articles of Confederation** Plan of government adopted by the Continental Congress after the American Revolution; established "a firm league of friendship" among the States, but allowed few important powers to the central government. p. 44

**Assemble** To gather with one another in order to express views on public matters. p. 555

**Assessment** The process of determining the value of property to be taxed. p. 742

**Assimilation** The process by which people of one culture merge into, and become part of, another culture. p. 597

**At-large election** Election of an officeholder by the voters of an entire governmental unit (e.g. a State or country) rather than by the voters of a district or subdivision. p. 270

**Attorney General** The head of the Department of Justice. p. 424

**Authoritarian** A form of government in which those in power hold absolute and unchallengeable authority over the people. All dictatorships are authoritarian. p. 13

**Autocracy** A form of government in which a single person holds unlimited political power. p. 13

**Autonomous** Independent. p. 652

**Bail** A sum of money that the accused may be required to post (deposit with the court) as a guarantee that he or she will appear in court at the proper time. p. 585

**Balance the ticket** When a presidential candidate chooses a running mate who can strengthen his chance of being elected by virtue of certain ideological, geographic, racial, ethnic, gender, or other characteristics. p. 362

**Ballot** The device voters use to register a choice in an election. p. 190

**Bankruptcy** The legal proceeding by which a bankrupt person's assets are distributed among those to whom he or she owes debts. p. 300

**Bench trial** A trial in which the judge alone hears the case. pp. 580, 705

**Bicameral** An adjective describing a legislative body composed of two chambers. p. 31

**Bill** A proposed law presented to a legislative body for consideration. p. 334

**Bill of Attainder** A legislative act that inflicts punishment without a court trial. p. 577

**Bill of Rights** The first ten amendments to the Constitution. pp. 76, 532

**Bipartisan** Supported by two parties. pp. 120, 440

**Blanket primary** A voting process in which voters receive a long ballot containing the names of all contenders, regardless of party, and can vote however they choose. p. 183

**Block grant** One type of federal grants-in-aid for some particular but broadly defined area of public policy; *see* grants-in-aid. p. 103

**Bourgeoisie** The social class between the aristocracy and the proletariat class; the middle class. p. 667

**Boycott** Refusal to buy or sell certain products or services. p. 36

**Budget** A financial plan for the use of money, personnel, and property. p. 744

**Bureaucracy** A large, complex administrative structure that handles the everyday business of an organization. p. 414

**Bureaucrat** A person who works for a bureaucratic organization; *see* bureaucracy. p. 415

**By-election** A special election held to choose a replacement for a member of parliament, in the event of a death. p. 628

**Cabinet** Presidential advisory body, traditionally made up of the heads of the executive departments and other officers. p. 81

**Capital** All the human-made resources that are used to produce goods and services. p. 659

**Capitalist** Someone who owns capital and puts it to productive use; often applied to people who own large businesses. p. 659

**Capital punishment** The death penalty. p. 587

**Categorical grant** One type of federal grants-in-aid; made for some specific, closely defined, purpose; *see* grants-in-aid. p. 102

**Caucus** As a nominating device, a group of like-minded people who meet to select the candidates they will support in an upcoming election. p. 180

**Censure** Issue a formal condemnation. p. 312

**Centrally planned economy** A system in which government bureaucrats plan how an economy will develop over a period of years. p. 669

**Certificate** A method of putting a case before the Supreme Court; used when a lower court is not clear about the procedure or rule of law that should apply in a case and asks the Supreme Court to certify the answer to a specific question. p. 521

**Charter** A city's basic law, its constitution; a written grant of authority from the king. pp. 31, 726

**Checks and balances** System of overlapping the powers of the legislative, executive, and judicial branches to permit each branch to check the actions of the others; *see* separation of powers. p. 67

**Chief administrator** Term for the President as head of the administration of the Federal Government. p. 355

**Chief citizen** Term for the President as the representative of the people, working for the public interest. p. 355

**Chief diplomat** Term for the President as the main architect of foreign policy and spokesperson to other countries. p. 355

**Chief executive** Term for the President as vested with the executive power of the United States. p. 354

**Chief legislator** Term for the President as architect of public policy and the one who sets the agenda for Congress. p. 355

**Chief of party** Term for the President as the leader of his or her political party. p. 355

**Chief of state** Term for the President as the ceremonial head of the United States, the symbol of all the people of the nation. p. 354

**Citizen** A member of a state or nation who owes allegiance to it by birth or naturalization and is entitled to full civil rights. p. 613

**Civil case** A case involving a noncriminal matter such as a contract dispute or a claim of patent infringement. p. 513

**Civil law** The portion of the law relating to human conduct, to disputes between private parties, and to disputes between private parties and government not covered by criminal law. p. 704

**Civil liberties** The guarantees of the safety of persons, opinions, and property from the arbitrary acts of government, including freedom of speech and freedom of religion. p. 533

**Civil rights** A term used for those positive acts of government that seek to make constitutional guarantees a reality for all people, e.g., prohibitions of discrimination. p. 533

**Civil service** Those civilian employees who perform the administrative work of government. p. 437

**Civilian tribunal** A court operating as part of the judicial branch, entirely separate from the military establishment. p. 525

**Clemency** Mercy or leniency granted to an offender by a chief executive; *see* pardon and reprieve. pp. 407, 699

**Closed primary** A party nominating election in which only declared party members can vote. p. 182

**Cloture** Procedure that may be used to limit or end floor debate in a legislative body. p. 344

**Coalition** A temporary alliance of several groups who come together to form a working majority and so to control a government. pp. 122, 628

**Coattail effect** The effect of a strong candidate running for an office at the top of a ballot helping to attract voters to other candidates on the party's ticket. p. 190

**Cold war** A period of more than 40 years during which relations between the two superpowers were at least tense, and often hostile. A time of threats and military build up. p. 485

**colleague** A co-worker. p. 277

**Collective security** The keeping of international peace and order. p. 485

**Collectivization** Collective or state ownership of the means of production. p. 674

**Commander in chief** Term for the President as commander of the nation's armed forces. p. 355

**Commerce and Slave Trade Compromise** An agreement during the Constitutional Convention protecting slave holders; denied Congress the power to tax the export of goods from any State, and, for 20 years, the power to act on the slave trade. p. 53

**Commerce power** Exclusive power of Congress to regulate interstate and foreign trade. p. 297

**Commission government** A government formed by commissioners, heads of different departments of city government, who are popularly elected to form the city council and thus center both legislative and executive powers in one body. p. 728

**Committee chairman** Member who heads a standing committee in a legislative body. p. 325

**Committee of the Whole** A committee that consists of an entire legislative body; used for a procedure in which a legislative body expedites its business by resolving itself into a committee of itself. p. 339

**Common law** An unwritten law made by a judge that has developed over centuries from those generally accepted ideas of right and wrong that have gained judicial recognition. p. 702

**Commune** A large grouping of several collective farms. p. 675

**Communism** An ideology which calls for the collective, or state, ownership of land and other productive property. p. 672

**Commutation** The power to reduce (commute) the length of a sentence or fine for a crime. pp. 408, 699

**Compromise** An adjustment of opposing principles or systems by modifying some aspect of each. p. 20

**Concurrent jurisdiction** Power shared by federal and State courts to hear certain cases. p. 508

**Concurrent powers** Those powers that both the National Government and the States possess and exercise. p. 93

**Concurrent resolution** A statement of position on an issue used by the House and Senate acting jointly; does not have the force of law and does not require the President's signature. p. 335

**Concurring opinion** Written explanation of the views of one or more judges who support a decision reached by a majority of the court, but wish to add or emphasize a point that was not made in the majority decision. p. 522

**Confederation** A joining of several groups for a common purpose. pp. 15, 35

**Conference committee** Temporary joint committee created to reconcile any differences between the two houses' versions of a bill. p. 333

**Connecticut Compromise** Agreement during the Constitutional Convention that Congress should be composed of a Senate, in which States would be represented equally, and a House, in which representation would be based on a State's population. p. 52

**Consensus** General agreement among various groups on fundamental matters; broad agreement on public questions. pp. 121, 292, 636

**Constituency** The people and interests that an elected official represents. p. 277

**Constituent power** The non-legislative power of Constitution-making and the constitutional amendment process. p. 692

**Constitution** The body of fundamental laws setting out the principles, structures, and processes of a government. p. 4

**Constitutionalism** Basic principle that government and those who govern must obey the law; the rule of law; *see* limited government. p. 65

**Containment** A policy based in the belief that if communism could be kept within its existing boundaries, it would collapse under the weight of its internal weaknesses. p. 486

**Content neutral** The government may not regulate assemblies on the basis on what might be said. p. 556

**Continuing resolution** A measure which allows agencies to continue working based on the previous year's appropriations. p. 462

**Continuous body** Governing unit (e.g. the United States Senate) whose seats are never all up for election at the same time. p. 277

**Controllable spending** An amount decided upon by Congress and the President to determine how much will be spent each year on many individual government expenditures, including environment protection programs, aid to education, and so on. p. 459

**Copyright** The exclusive, legal right of a person to reproduce, publish, and sell his or her own literary, musical, or artistic creations. p. 302

**Council-manager government** A modification of the mayor-council government, it consists of a strong council of members elected on a non-partisan ballot, a weak mayor, elected by the people, and a manager, named by the council; *see* mayor-council government; *see* also weak mayor government. p. 728

**County** A major unit of local government in most States. p. 718

**Court-martial** A court composed of military personnel, for the trial of those accused of violating military law. p. 525

**Criminal case** A case in which a defendant is tried for committing a crime as defined by the law. p. 513

**Criminal law** The portion of the law that defines public wrongs and provides for their punishment. p. 704

**Cultural Revolution** Begun in 1966, Mao Tse Tung's Red Guards attacked, bullied, and "reeducated" teachers, intellectuals, and anyone else who seemed to lack revolutionary fervor. p. 650

**Custom duty** A tax laid on goods brought into the United States from abroad, also known as tariffs, import duties, or imposts. p. 451

**De facto segregation** Segregation even if no law requires it, e.g., housing patterns. p. 604

**De jure segregation** Segregation by law, with legal sanction. p. 604

**Defendant** In a civil suit, the person against whom a court action is brought by the plaintiff; in a criminal case, the person charged with the crime. p. 509

**Deficit** The yearly shortfall between revenue and spending. p. 455

**Deficit financing** Practice of funding government by borrowing to make up the difference between government spending and revenue. p. 296

**Delegated powers** Those powers, expressed, implied, or inherent, granted to the National Government by the Constitution. p. 89

**Democracy** A form of government in which the supreme authority rests with the people. p. 5

**Denaturalization** The process through which naturalized citizens may involuntarily lose their citizenship. p. 615

**Deportation** A legal process in which aliens are legally required to leave the United States. p. 617

**Détente** A relaxation of tensions. p. 488

**Deterrence** The policy of making America and its allies so militarily strong that their very strength will discourage, or prevent, any attack. p. 485

**Devolution** The delegation of authority from the central government to regional governments. p. 631

**Dictatorship** A form of government in which the leader has absolute power and authority. p. 5

**Diplomatic immunity** When an ambassador is not subject to the laws of the state to which they are accredited. p. 471

**Direct popular election** Proposal to do away with the electoral college and allow the people to vote directly for President and Vice President. p. 383

**Direct primary** An election held within a party to pick that party's candidates for the general election. p. 182

**Direct tax** A tax that must be paid by the person on whom it is levied; *see* indirect tax. p. 296

**Discharge petition** A procedure enabling members to force a bill that has been pigeonholed in committee onto the floor for consideration. p. 336

**Discrimination** Bias, unfairness. p. 570

**Dissenting opinion** Written explanation of the views of one or more judges who disagree with (dissent from) a decision reached by a majority of the court; *see* majority opinion. p. 522

**Dissolution** The power of the Prime Minister to dissolve the House of Representatives. p. 636

**District plan** Proposal for choosing presidential electors by which two electors would be selected in each State according to the Statewide popular vote and the other electors would be selected separately in each of the State's congressional districts. p. 382

**Division of powers** Basic principle of federalism; the constitutional provisions by which governmental powers are divided on a geographic basis (in the United States, between the National Government and the States). pp. 14, 89

**Docket** A court's list of cases to be heard. p. 513

**Doctrine** Principle or fundamental policy. p. 308

**Domestic affairs** All matters not directly connected to the realm of foreign affairs. pp. 422, 468

**Double jeopardy** Part of the 5th Amendment which says that no person can be put in jeopardy of life or limb twice. Once a person has been tried for a crime, he or she cannot be tried again for the same crime. p. 578

**Draft** Conscription, or compulsory military service. p. 480

**Due process** The government must act fairly and in accord with established rules in all that it does. p. 564

**Due Process Clause** Part of the 14th Amendment which guarantees that no state deny basic rights to its people. p. 535

**Economic protest parties** Parties rooted in poor economic times, lacking a clear ideological base, dissatisfied with current conditions and demanding better times. p. 133

**Electoral college** Group of persons chosen in each State and the District of Columbia every four years who make a formal selection of the President and Vice President. pp. 81, 366

**Electoral votes** Votes cast by electors in the electoral college. p. 365

**Electorate** All of the people entitled to vote in a given election. pp. 129, 148, 383

**Eminent domain** Power of a government to take private property for public use. p. 304

**Enabling act** A congressional act directing the people of a United States territory to frame a proposed State constitution as a step towards admission to the Union. p. 99

**English Bill of Rights** Document written by Parliament and agreed on by William and Mary of England in 1689, designed to prevent abuse of power by English monarchs; forms the basis for much in American government and politics today. p. 30

**Engross** To print a bill in its final form. p. 340

**Entitlement** A benefit that federal law says must be paid to all those who meet the eligibility requirements, e.g., Medicare, food stamps, and veterans' pension. pp. 458, 735

**Entrepreneur** An individual with the drive and ambition to combine land, labor, and capital resources to produce goods or offer services. p. 659

**Espionage** Spying. p. 477

**Establishment Clause** Separates church and state. p. 537

**Estate tax** A levy imposed on the assets of one who dies. pp. 451, 742

**Ex post facto law** A law applied to an act committed before its passage. p. 577

**Excise tax** A tax laid on the manufacture, sale, or consumption of goods and/or the performance of services. p. 451

**Exclusionary rule** Evidence gained as the result of an illegal act by police cannot be used against the person from whom it was seized. p. 573

**Exclusive jurisdiction** Power of the federal courts alone to hear certain cases. p. 508

**Exclusive powers** Those powers that can be exercised by the National Government alone. p. 93

**Executive agreement** A pact made by the President directly with the head of a foreign state; a binding international agreement with the force of law but which (unlike a treaty) does not require Senate consent. pp. 80, 400

**Executive Article** Article II of the Constitution. Establishes the presidency and gives the executive power of the Federal Government to the President. p. 390

**Executive departments** Often called the Cabinet departments, they are the traditional units of federal administration. p. 424

**Executive Office of the President** An organization of several agencies staffed by the President's closest advisors. p. 419

**Executive order** Directive, rule, or regulation issued by a chief executive or subordinates, based upon constitutional or statutory authority and having the force of law. p. 394

**Executive power** The power to execute, enforce, and administer law. p. 4

**Expatriation** The legal process by which a loss of citizenship occurs. p. 614

**Expressed powers** Those delegated powers of the National Government that are spelled out, expressly, in the Constitution; also called the "enumerated powers." pp. 89, 290

**Extradition** The legal process by which a fugitive from justice in one State is returned to that State. p. 107

**Faction** A conflicting group. p. 127

**Factors of production** Basic resources which are used to make all goods and services. p. 658

**Federal budget** A detailed financial document containing estimates of federal income and spending during the coming fiscal year. p. 421

**Federal government** A form of government in which powers are divided between a central government and several local governments. p. 14

**Federalism** A system of government in which a written constitution divides power between a central, or national, government and several regional governments. pp. 70, 88

**Federalists** Those persons who supported the ratification of the Constitution in 1787–1788. p. 56

**Felony** A serious crime which may be punished by a heavy fine and/or imprisonment or even death. p. 704

**Filibuster** Various tactics (usually long speeches) aimed at defeating a bill in a legislative body by preventing a final vote; associated with the U.S. Senate; *see* cloture. p. 343

**Fiscal year** The 12-month period used by a government and the business world for its record-keeping, budgeting, revenue-collecting, and other financial management purposes. p. 421

**Five-year plan** A plan which projects economic development over the next five years. p. 673

**Floor leaders** Members of the House and Senate picked by their parties to carry out party decisions and steer legislative action to meet party goals. p. 324

**Foreign affairs** A nation's relationships with other countries. p. 468

**Foreign aid** Economic and military aid to other countries. p. 491

**Foreign policy** A group of policies made up of all the stands and actions that a nation takes in every aspect of its relationships with other countries; everything a nation's government says and does in world affairs. p. 469

**Formal amendment** Change or addition that becomes part of the written language of the Constitution itself through one of four methods set forth in the Constitution. p. 73

**Framers** Group of delegates who drafted the United States Constitution at the Philadelphia Convention in 1787. p. 48

**Franchise** The right to vote. p. 148

**Franking privilege** Benefit allowing members of Congress to mail letters and other materials postage-free. p. 283

**Free enterprise system** An economic system characterized by private or corporate ownership of capital goods; investments that are determined by private decision rather than by state control, and determined in a free market. pp. 20, 659

**Free Exercise Clause** The second part of the constitutional guarantee of religious freedom, which guarantees to each person the right to believe whatever he or she chooses to believe in matters of religion. p. 542

**Full Faith and Credit Clause** Constitution's requirement that each State accept the public acts, records, and judicial proceedings of every other State. p. 106

**Fundamental law** Laws of basic and lasting importance which may not easily be changed. p. 686

**Gender gap** Measurable differences between the partisan choices of men and women today. p. 169

**General election** The regularly scheduled election at which voters make a final selection of officeholders. p. 179

**Gerrymandering** The drawing of electoral district lines to the advantage of a party or group. pp. 159, 271

**Gift tax** A tax on a gift by a living person. p. 451

**Glasnost** The Soviet policy of openness under which tolerance of dissent and freedom of expression increased. p. 646

**Gosplan** A large agency in the Soviet Union, introduced by Stalin, to run centralized planning. p. 674

**Government** The institution through which a society makes and enforces its public policies. p. 4

**Government corporation** Corporations within the executive branch subject to the President's direction and control, set up by Congress to carry out certain business-like activities. p. 434

**Grand jury** The formal device by which a person can be accused of a serious crime. p. 577

**Grants-in-aid program** Grants of federal money or other resources to States, cities, counties, and other local units. p. 101

**Grass roots** Of or from the people, the average voters. p. 253

**Great Leap Forward** The five-year plan for 1958 which was an attempt to quickly modernize China. p. 675

**Hard money** Campaign money that is subject to regulations by the FEC. p. 202

**Heterogeneous** Of another or different race, family or kind; composed of a mix of elements. p. 594

**Ideological parties** Parties based on a particular set of beliefs, a comprehensive view of social, economic, and political matters. p. 132

**Immigrant** Those people legally admitted as permanent residents of a country. p. 594

**Impeach** To bring formal charges against a public official; the House of Representatives has the sole power to impeach civil officers of the United States. p. 311

**Imperial presidency** Term used to describe a President as an "emperor" who acts without consulting Congress or acts in secrecy to evade or deceive Congress; often used in reference to Richard Nixon's presidency. p. 392

**Implied powers** Those delegated powers of the National Government that are suggested by the expressed powers; those "necessary and proper" to carry out the expressed powers; *see* delegated powers, expressed powers. pp. 90, 290

**Income tax** A tax levied on the income of individuals and/or corporations. p. 741

**Incorporation** The process by which a State establishes a city as a legal body. p. 726

**Incumbent** The current officeholder. p. 127

**Independent agencies** Additional agencies created by Congress located outside the Cabinet departments. p. 430

**Independent executive agencies** Agencies headed by a single administrator with regional subunits, but lacking Cabinet status. p. 431

**Independent regulatory commissions** Independent agencies designed to regulate important aspects of the nation's economy, largely beyond the reach of presidential control. p. 431

**Independents** A term used to describe people who have no party affiliation. p. 171

**Indictment** A formal complaint before a grand jury which charges the accused with one or more crimes. p. 578

**Indirect tax** A tax levied on one party but passed on to another for payment. p. 296

**Inferior courts** The lower federal courts, beneath the Supreme Court. p. 507

**Information** A formal charge filed by a prosecutor without the action of a grand jury. p. 704

**Inherent powers** Powers delegated to the National Government because it is the government of a sovereign state within the world community. pp. 91, 290

**Inheritance tax** A tax levied on the beneficiary's share of an estate. p. 742

**Initiative** A process in which a certain number of qualified voters sign petitions in favor of a proposal, which then goes directly to the ballot. p. 687

**Injunction** A court order that forces or limits the performance of some act by a private individual or by a public official. p. 161

**Integration** The process of bringing a group into equal membership in society. p. 603

**Interest** A charge for borrowed money, generally a percentage of the amount borrowed. p. 454

**Interest group** Private organizations whose members share certain views and work to shape public policy. p. 216

**Interstate compact** Formal agreement entered into with the consent of Congress, between or among States, or between a State and a foreign state. p. 105

**Involuntary servitude** Forced labor. p. 569

**Isolationism** A purposeful refusal to become generally involved in the affairs of the rest of the world. p. 468

**Item veto** A governor may veto one or more items in a bill without rejecting the entire measure. p. 699

**Jim Crow law** A law that separates people on the basis of race, aimed primarily at African Americans. p. 602

**Joint committee** Legislative committee composed of members of both houses. p. 333

**Joint resolution** A proposal for action that has the force of law when passed; usually deals with special circumstances or temporary matters. p. 335

**Judicial power** The power to interpret laws, to determine their meaning, and to settle disputes within the society. p. 4

**Judicial review** The power of a court to determine the constitutionality of a governmental action. p. 69

**Jurisdiction** The authority of a court to hear a case. p. 508

**Jury** A body of persons selected according to law who hear evidence and decide questions of fact in a court case. p. 704

**Jus sanguinis** The law of blood, which determines citizenship based on one's parents' citizenship. p. 613

**Jus soli** The law of soil, which determines citizenship based on where a person is born. p. 613

**Justice of the Peace** A judge who stands on the lowest level of the State judicial system and presides over justice courts. p. 707

**Keynote address** Speech given at a party convention to set the tone for the convention and the campaign to come. p. 373

**Labor union** An organization of workers who share the same type of job, or who work in the same industry, and press for government policies that will benefit their members. p. 244

**Laissez-faire theory** A theory which suggests that government should play a very limited role in society. p. 662

**Law of supply and demand** A law which states that when supplies of goods and services become plentiful, prices tend to drop. When supplies become scarcer, prices tend to rise. pp. 21, 661

**Legal tender** Any kind of money that a creditor must, by law, accept in payment for debts. p. 299

**Legislative power** The power to make a law and to frame public policies. p. 4

**Libel** False and malicious use of printed words. p. 546

**Liberal constructionist** One who argues a broad interpretation of the provisions of the Constitution, particularly those granting powers to the Federal Government. p. 291

**Limited government** Basic principle of American government which states that government is restricted in what it may do, and each individual has rights that government cannot take away; *see* constitutionalism, popular sovereignty. pp. 29, 685

**Line agency** An agency which performs the tasks for which the organization exists. p. 418

**Line-item veto** A President's cancellation of specific dollar amounts (line items) from a congressional spending bill; instituted by a 1996 congressional act, but struck down by a 1998 Supreme Court decision. p. 406

**Literacy** A person's ability to read or write. p. 156

**Lobbying** Activities by which group pressures are brought to bear on legislators, the legislative process, and all aspects of the public-policy-making process. p. 251

**Magistrate** A justice who handles minor civil complaints and misdemeanor cases that arise in an urban setting. p. 708

**Magna Carta** Great Charter forced upon King John of England by his barons in 1215; established that the power of the monarchy was not absolute and guaranteed trial by jury and due process of law to the nobility. p. 29

**Major parties** In American politics, the Republican and the Democratic parties. p. 116

**Majority opinion** Officially called the Opinion of the Court; announces the Court's decision in a case and sets out the reasoning upon which it is based. p. 522

**Mandate** The instructions or commands a constituency gives to its elected officials. p. 216

**Market economy** Economic system in which decisions on production and consumption of goods and services are based on voluntary exchange of markets. p. 669

**Mass media** Those means of communication that reach large audiences, especially television, radio, printed publications, and the Internet. pp. 211, 391

**Mayor-council government** The oldest and most widely used type of city government—an elected mayor as the chief execu-

tive and an elected council as its legislative body. p. 726

**Medicaid** A program administered by the State to provide medical insurance to low-income families. p. 735

**Medium** A means of communication; something which transmits information. p. 223

**Mestizo** A person with both Spanish or Portuguese and Native American ancestry. p. 639

**Metropolitan area** A city and the area around it. p. 731

**Minister** Cabinet members, most commonly of the House of Commons. p. 629

**Minor party** One of the political parties not widely supported. p. 119

**Miranda Rule** The constitutional rights which police must read to a suspect before questioning can occur. p. 582

**Misdemeanor** A lesser offense, punishable by a small fine and/or a short jail term. p. 704

**Mixed economy** An economy in which private enterprise exists in combination with a considerable amount of government regulation and promotion. p. 21

**Monarchy** A government lead by a hereditary ruler. p. 627

**Monopoly** A firm that is the only source of a product or service. p. 661

**Multiparty** A system in which several major and many lesser parties exist, seriously compete for, and actually win, public offices. p. 122

**National bonus plan** Proposal for electing a President by which the winner of the popular vote would receive a bonus of 102 electoral votes in addition to his or her State-based electoral college votes. If no one received at least 321 electoral votes, a run-off election would be held. p. 384

**National convention** Meeting at which a party's delegates vote to pick their presidential and vice-presidential candidates. p. 372

**Nationalization** The governmental acquisition of private industry for public use. p. 642

**Naturalization** The legal process by which citizens of one country become citizens of another. pp. 302, 614

**Necessary and Proper Clause** Constitutional clause that gives Congress the power to make all laws "necessary and proper" for executing its powers; *see* implied powers. p. 305

**New Jersey Plan** Plan presented as an alternative to the Virginia Plan at the Constitutional Convention; called for a unicameral legislature in which each State would be equally represented. p. 51

**Nomination** The process of candidate selection in a democracy. p. 178

**Nonpartisan election** Elections in which candidates are not identified by party labels. p. 184

**North American Free Trade Agreement** An agreement which removed trade restrictions among the United States, Canada, and Mexico, thus increasing cross-border trade. p. 642

**Oath of office** Oath taken by the President on the day he takes office, pledging to "faithfully execute" the office and "preserve, protect, and defend" the Constitution. p. 393

**Off-year election** Congressional election that occurs between presidential election years. pp. 164, 269

**Oligarchy** A form of government in which the power to rule is held by a small, usually self-appointed elite. p. 13

**One-party system** A political system in which only one party exists. p. 123

**Open primary** A party-nominating election in which any qualified voter can take part. p. 183

**Opinion leader** Any person who, for any reason, has an unusually strong influence on the views of others. p. 212

**Ordinance power** Power of the President to issue executive orders; originates from the Constitution and acts of Congress. p. 394

**Original jurisdiction** The power of a court to hear a case first, before any other court. p. 509

**Oversight function** Review by legislative committees of the policies and programs of the executive branch. p. 281

**Pardon** Release from the punishment or legal consequences of a crime, by the President (in a federal case) or a governor (in a State case). pp. 407, 699

**Parliamentary government** A form of government in which the executive branch is made up of the prime minister, or premier, and that official's cabinet. p. 16

**Parochial** Church-related, as in a parochial school. p. 538

**Parole** The release of a prisoner short of the complete term of the original sentence. p. 699

**Partisan** Lawmaker who owes his/her first allegiance to his/her political party and votes according to the party line. p. 281

**Partisanship** Government action based on firm allegiance to a political party. p. 117

**Party caucus** A closed meeting of a party's House or Senate members; also called a party conference. p. 324

**Party identification** Loyalty of people to a political party. p. 171

**Party in power** In American politics, the party in power is the party that controls the executive branch of government—i.e., the presidency at the national level, or the governorship at the State level. p. 118

**Patent** A license issued to an inventor granting the exclusive right to manufacture, use, or sell his or her invention for a limited period of time. p. 303

**Patronage** The practice of giving jobs to supporters and friends. p. 438

**Payroll tax** A tax imposed on nearly all employers and their employees, and on self-employed persons—the amounts owed by employees withheld from their paychecks. p. 450

**Peer group** People with whom one regularly associates, including friends, classmates, neighbors, and co-workers. p. 212

**Perestroika** The restructuring of political and economic life under the rule of Mikhail Gorbachev. p. 646

**Perjury** The act of lying under oath. p. 311

**Persona non grata** An unwelcome person; used to describe recalled diplomatic officials. p. 401

**Petition of Right** Document prepared by Parliament and signed by King Charles I of England in 1628; challenged the idea of the divine right of kings and declared that even the monarch was subject to the laws of the land. p. 30

**Picketing** Patrolling of a business site by workers who are on strike. p. 551

**Plaintiff** In civil law, the party who brings a suit or some other legal action against another (the defendant) in court. p. 509

**Platform** A political party's formal statement of basic principles, stands on major issues, and objectives. p. 373

**Pluralistic society** A society which consists of several distinct cultures and groups. p. 121

**Plurality** In an election, the number of votes that the leading candidate obtains over the next highest candidate. p. 120

**Pocket veto** Type of veto a chief executive may use after a legislature has adjourned; when the chief executive does not sign or reject a bill within the time allowed to do so; see veto. p. 346

**Police power** The authority of each State to act to protect and promote the public health, safety, morals, and general welfare of its people. pp. 566, 691

**Political Action Committee** The political extension of special-interest groups which have a major stake in public policy. p. 197

**Political efficacy** One's own influence or effectiveness on politics. p. 166

**Political party** A group of persons who seek to control government through the winning of elections and the holding of public office. p. 116

**Political socialization** The process by which people gain their political attitudes and opinions. p. 168

**Politico** Lawmaker who attempts to balance the basic elements of the trustee, delegate, and partisan roles; see trustee, delegate, partisan. p. 281

**Poll book** List of all registered voters in each precinct. p. 155

**Poll tax** A special tax, demanded by States, as a condition of voting. p. 157

**Polling place** The place where the voters who live in a certain precinct go to vote. p. 190

**Popular sovereignty** Basic principle of the American system of government which asserts that the people are the source of any and all governmental power, and government can exist only with the consent of the governed. pp. 39, 685

**Preamble** Introduction. p. 65

**Precedent** Court decision that stands as an example to be followed in future, similar cases. pp. 522, 703

**Precinct** The smallest unit of election administration; a voting district. pp. 140, 190

**Preclearance** Mandated by the Voting Rights Act of 1965, the prior approval by the Justice Department of changes to or new election laws by certain States. p. 162

**Prefecture** The 47 political subdivisions into which Japan is divided. p. 637

**Preliminary hearing** The first step in a major criminal prosecution where the judge decides if the evidence is enough to hold the person for action by the grand jury or the prosecutor. p. 708

**President of the Senate** The presiding officer of a senate; in Congress, the Vice President of the United States; in a State's legislature, either the lieutenant governor or a senator. p. 323

**President pro tempore** The member of the United States Senate, or of the upper house of a State's legislature, chosen to preside in the absence of the president of the Senate. p. 323

**Presidential elector** A person elected by the voters to represent them in making a formal selection of the Vice President and President. p. 365

**Presidential government** A form of government in which the executive and legislative branches of the government are separate, independent, and coequal. p. 15

**Presidential primary** An election in which a party's voters (1) choose State party organization's delegates to their party's national convention, and/or (2) express a preference for their party's presidential nomination. p. 369

**Presidential succession** Scheme by which a presidential vacancy is filled. p. 359

**Presidential Succession Act of 1947** Law specifying the order of presidential succession following the Vice President. p. 360

**Presiding officer** Chair. p. 45

**Preventive detention** A law which allows federal judges to order that an accused felon be held, without bail, when there is good reason to believe that he or she will commit yet another serious crime before trial. p. 586

**Prior restraint** The government cannot curb ideas before they are expressed. p. 549

**Privatization** The process of returning national enterprises to private ownership. p. 675

**Privileges and Immunities Clause** Constitution's stipulation (Article IV, Section 2) that all citizens are entitled to certain "privileges and immunities," regardless of their State of residence; no State can draw unreasonable distinctions between its own residents and those persons who happen to live in other States. p. 107

**Probable Cause** Reasonable grounds, a reasonable suspicion of crime. p. 571

**Procedural due process** The government must employ fair procedures and methods. p. 565

**Process of incorporation** The process of incorporating, or including, most of the guarantees in the Bill of Rights into the 14th Amendment's Due Process Clause. p. 535

**Progressive tax** A type of tax proportionate to income. pp. 449, 742

**Project grant** One type of federal grants-in-aid; made for specific projects to States, localities, and private agencies who apply for them. p. 103

**Proletariat** The working class. p. 667

**Propaganda** A technique of persuasion aimed at influencing individual or group behaviors to create a particular belief, regardless of its validity. p. 249

**Property tax** A tax levied on real and personal property. p. 742

**Proportional plan** Proposal by which each presidential candidate would receive the same share of a State's electoral vote as he or she received in the State's popular vote. p. 382

**Proportional representation rule** Rule applied in Democratic primaries whereby any candidate who wins at least 15 percent of the votes gets the number of State Democratic convention delegates based on his or her share of that primary vote. p. 371

**Proprietary** Organized by a proprietor (a person to whom the king had made a grant of land). p. 32

**Prorogue** Adjourn, as in a legislative session. p. 265

**Public affairs** Those events and issues that concern the people at large, e.g., politics, public issues, and the making of public policies. pp. 208, 239

**Public agenda** The public issues on which the people's attention is focused. p. 228

**Public debt** All of the money borrowed by the government and not yet repaid, plus the accrued interest on that money; also called the national debt or federal debt. pp. 296, 455

**Public-interest group** An interest group that seeks to institute certain public policies of benefit to all or most people in this country, whether or not they belong to or support that organization. p. 247

**Public opinion** The complex collection of the opinions of many different people; the sum of all their views. p. 209

**Public opinion poll** Devices that attempt to collect information by asking people questions. p. 217

**Public policy** All of the goals a government sets and the various courses of action it pursues as it attempts to realize these goals. pp. 4, 236

**Purge** The process of reviewing lists of registered voters and removing the names of those no longer eligible to vote; a purification. pp. 155, 645

**Quasi-judicial** Having to do with powers that are to some extent judicial. p. 433

**Quasi-legislative** Having to do with powers that are to some extent legislative. p. 433

**Quorum** Least number of members who must be present for a legislative body to conduct business; majority. pp. 58, 339

**Quota** A rule requiring certain numbers of jobs or promotions for members of certain groups. p. 610

**Quota sample** A sample deliberately constructed to reflect several of the major characteristics of a given population. p. 219

**Random sample** A certain number of randomly selected people who live in a certain number of randomly selected places. p. 218

**Ratification** Formal approval, final consent to the effectiveness of a constitution, constitutional amendment, or treaty. p. 44

**Reapportion** Redistribute, as in seats in a legislative body. p. 267

**Recall** A petition procedure by which voters may remove an elected official from office before the completion of his or her regular term. p. 696

**Recognition** The exclusive power of a President to recognize (establish formal diplomatic relations with) foreign states. p. 400

**Redress** Satisfaction of a claim payment. p. 524

**Referendum** A process by which a legislative measure is referred to the State's voters for final approval or rejection. p. 693

**Refugee** One who leaves his or her home to seek protection from war, persecution, or some other danger. p. 597

**Regional security alliances** Treaties in which the U.S. and other countries involved have agreed to take collective action to meet aggression in a particular part of the world. p. 492

**Register** A record or list of names, often kept by an official appointed to do so. p. 439

**Registration** A procedure of voter identification intended to prevent fraudulent voting. p. 154

**Regressive tax** A tax levied at a flat rate, without regard to the level of a taxpayer's income or ability to pay them. pp. 451, 741

**Repeal** Recall. p. 37

**Representative government** System of government in which public policies are made by officials selected by the voters and held accountable in periodic elections; see democracy. p. 29

**Reprieve** An official postponement of the execution of a sentence; see pardon. pp. 407, 699

**Reservation** Public land set aside by a government for use by Native American tribes. p. 596

**Reserved powers** Those powers that the Constitution does not grant to the National Government and does not, at the same time, deny to the States. p. 92

**Resolution** A measure relating to the business of either house, or expressing an opinion; does not have the force of law and does not require the President's signature. p. 335

**Revenue sharing** Form of federal monetary aid under which Congress gave a share of federal tax revenue, with virtually no restrictions, to the States, cities, counties, and townships. p. 102

**Reverse discrimination** Discrimination against the majority group. p. 610

**Right of association** The right to associate with others to promote political, economic, and other social causes. p. 558

**Right of legation** The right to send and receive diplomatic representatives. p. 470

**Rider** Unpopular provision added to an important bill certain to pass so that it will "ride" through the legislative process. p. 335

**Rule of law** Concept that holds that government and its officers are always subject to the law. p. 66

**Runoff primary** A primary in which the top two vote-getters in the first direct primary face one another. p. 184

**Sales tax** A tax placed on the sale of various commodities, paid by the purchaser. p. 741

**Sample** A representative slice of the public. p. 218

**Search warrant** A court order authorizing a search. p. 566

**Secretary** An official in charge of a department of government. p. 424

**Sectionalism** A narrow-minded concern for, or devotion to, the interests of one section of a country. p. 129

**Sedition** The crime of attempting to overthrow the government by force, or to disrupt its lawful activities by violent acts. p. 547

**Seditious speech** The advocating, or urging, of an attempt to overthrow the government by force, or to disrupt its lawful activities with violence. p. 547

**Segregation** The separation of one group from another. p. 602

**Select committee** Legislative committee created for a limited time and for some specific purpose; also known as a special committee. p. 331

**Senatorial courtesy** Custom that the Senate will not approve a presidential appointment opposed by a majority party senator from the State in which the appointee would serve. p. 81

**Seniority rule** Unwritten rule in both houses of Congress reserving the top posts in each chamber, particularly committee chairmanships, for members with the longest records of service. p. 326

**Separate-but-equal doctrine** A constitutional basis for laws that separate one group from another on the basis of race. (Jim Crow Laws.) p. 602

**Separation of powers** Basic principle of American system of government, that the executive, legislative, and judicial powers are divided among three independent and coequal branches of government; see checks and balances. p. 66

**Session** Period of time during which, each year, Congress assembles and conducts business. p. 264

**Shadow cabinet** Members of opposition parties who watch, or shadow, particular Cabinet members, and would be ready to run the government. p. 629

**Shield law** A law which gives reporters some protection against having to disclose their sources or reveal other confidential information in legal proceedings. p. 550

**Single-interest group** Political action committees that concentrate their efforts exclusively on one issue. p. 251

**Single-issue parties** Parties that concentrate on only one public policy matter. p. 132

**Single-member district** Electoral district from which one person is chosen by the voters for each elected office. pp. 120, 270

**Slander** False and malicious use of spoken words. p. 547

**Socialism** A philosophy based on the idea that the benefits of economic activity should be fairly distributed. p. 666

**Soft money** Money given to State and local party organizations for voting-related activities. p. 201

**Sound bite** Short, sharply focused reports that can be aired in 30 or 45 seconds. p. 229

**Sovereign** Having supreme power within its own territory; neither subordinate nor responsible to any other authority. p. 6

**Soviets** A government council, elected by and representing the people. p. 646

**Speaker of the House** The presiding officer of the House of Representatives, chosen by and from the majority party in the House. p. 322

**Special district** An independent unit created to perform one or more related governmental functions at the local level. p. 722

**Special session** An extraordinary session of a legislative body, called to deal with an emergency situation. p. 265

**Splinter parties** Parties that have split away from one of the major parties. p. 133

**Split-ticket voting** Voting for candidates of different parties for different offices at the same election. pp. 141, 171

**Spoils system** The practice of giving offices and other favors of government to political supporters and friends. p. 438

**Staff agency** An agency which supports the chief executive and other administrators by offering advice and other assistance in the management of the organization. p. 418

**Standing committee** Permanent committee in a legislative body to which bills in a specified subject-matter area are referred; *see* select committee. p. 329

**State** A body of people living in a defined territory who have a government with the power to make and enforce law without the consent of any higher authority. p. 5

**Statutory law** A law passed by the legislature. p. 688

**Straight-ticket voting** The practice of voting for candidates of only one party in an election. p. 171

**Straw vote** Polls that seek to read the public's mind simply by asking the same question of a large number of people. p. 217

**Strict constructionist** One who argues a narrow interpretation of the Constitution's provisions, in particular those granting powers to the Federal Government. p. 291

**Strong-mayor government** A type of government in which the mayor heads the city's administration. p. 727

**Subcommittee** Division of existing committee that is formed to address specific issues. p. 336

**Subpoena** An order for a person to appear and to produce documents or other requested materials. p. 313

**Subsidy** A grant of money, usually from a government. p. 197

**Substantive due process** The government must create fair policies and laws. p. 565

**Successor** A person who inherits a title or office. p. 311

**Suffrage** The right to vote. p. 148

**Surplus** More income than spending. p. 455

**Symbolic speech** Expression by conduct; communicating ideas through facial expressions, body language, or by carrying a sign or wearing an arm band. p. 551

**Tax** A charge levied by government on persons or property to meet public needs. p. 295

**Tax return** A declaration of taxable income and of the exemptions and deductions claimed. p. 449

**Term** The two-year period of time during which Congress meets. p. 264

**Terrorism** The use of violence to intimidate a government or society. p. 478

**Three-Fifths Compromise** An agreement at the Constitutional Convention to count a slave as three-fifths of a person when determining the population of a State. p. 52

**Township** A subdivision of a county. p. 718

**Trade association** Interest groups within the business community. p. 244

**Transient** Person living in a State for only a short time, without legal residence. p. 153

**Treason** Betrayal of one's country; in the Constitution, by levying war against the United States or offering comfort or aid to its enemies. p. 588

**Treaty** A formal agreement between two or more sovereign states. pp. 80, 399

**Trust** A device by which several corporations in the same business work to eliminate competition and regulate prices. p. 661

**Trustee** Lawmaker who votes based on his or her conscience and judgment, not the views of his or her constituents. p. 281

**Two-party system** A political system dominated by two major parties. p. 119

**UN Security Council** A 15-member panel which bears the UN's major responsibility for keeping international peace. p. 496

**Unconstitutional** Contrary to constitutional provision and so illegal, null and void, of no force and effect. p. 69

**Uncontrollable spending** Spending that Congress and the President have no power to change directly. p. 459

**Unicameral** An adjective describing a legislative body with one chamber; *see* bicameral. p. 32

**Unitary government** A centralized government in which all government powers belong to a single, central agency. p. 14

**Urbanization** The percentage of the population of a State living in cities of more than 250,000 people or in suburbs of cities with more than 50,000. p. 737

**Veto** Chief executive's power to reject a bill passed by a legislature; literally (Latin) "I forbid"; *see* pocket veto. pp. 67, 346

**Virginia Plan** Plan presented by delegates from Virginia at the Constitutional Convention; called for a three-branch government with a bicameral legislature in which each State's membership would be determined by its population or its financial support for the central government. p. 51

**Ward** A unit into which cities are often divided for the election of city council members. p. 140

**Warrant** A court order authorizing, or making legal, some official action, such as a search warrant or an arrest warrant. p. 708

**Weak-mayor government** A type of government in which the mayor shares his or her executive duties with other elected officials. p. 727

**Welfare** Cash assistance to the poor. p. 735

**Welfare state** Countries that provide extensive social services at little or no cost to the users. p. 668

**Whips** Assistants to the floor leaders in the House and Senate, responsible for monitoring and marshalling votes. p. 325

**Winner-take-all** An almost obsolete system whereby a presidential aspirant who won the preference vote in a primary automatically won all the delegates chosen in the primary. p. 371

**Writ of assistance** Blanket search warrant with which British custom officials had invaded private homes to search for smuggled goods. p. 571

**Writ of certiorari** An order by a higher court directing a lower court to send up the record in a given case for review; from the Latin meaning "to be more certain." p. 520

**Writ of habeas corpus** A court order which prevents unjust arrests and imprisonments. p. 576

**Zoning** The practice of dividing a city into a number of districts and regulating the uses to which property in each of them may be put. p. 730

# Spanish Glossary

**Absentee voting/Voto en Ausencia** Medidas para que voten, en el día de la elección, aquellas personas que no puedan hacerlo en su lugar habitual de votación. Pág. 189

**Acquit/Absolver** Determinar que no se es culpable de un delito. Pág. 311

**Act of admission/Decreto de Admisión** Una ley del Congreso mediante la cual se admite a un nuevo estado dentro de la Unión. Pág. 100

**Adjourn/Aplazamiento** Suspender, por ejemplo, una sesión del Congreso. Pág. 264

**Administration/Administración** Los funcionarios de la rama ejecutiva de un gobierno, así como sus políticas y sus directores. Pág. 416

**Affirmative action/Acción afirmativa** Una política que exige que la mayoría de los empleados lleve a cabo ciertas acciones para remediar los efectos de discriminaciones pasadas. Pág. 609

**Albany Plan of Union/Plan de Unión Albany** Proyecto propuesto por Benjamín Franklin en 1754 cuyo objetivo era unir a las 13 colonias respecto a asuntos comerciales, militares, así como para otros propósitos; las colonias y la Corona rechazaron el plan. Págs. 35–36

**Alien/Extranjero residente** Nacido en otro país, o persona que no es ciudadano. Págs. 534, 614

**Ambassador/Embajador** Delegado oficial designado por el Presidente para que represente a la nación en asuntos diplomáticos. Pág. 471

**Amendment/Enmienda** Cambio o adición a la Constitución o a las leyes. Pág. 72

**Amnesty/Amnistía** Perdón general que se brinda a un grupo de violadores de la ley. Pág. 408

**Anti-Federalists/Anti-federalistas** Aquellas personas que se opusieron a la ratificación de la Constitución en 1787–1788. Pág. 56

**Appellate jurisdiction/Tribunal de apelación** Autoridad de una corte para revisar decisiones de cortes inferiores; *ver* original jurisdiction/jurisdicción original. Págs. 509, 709

**Apportion/Prorrateo** Distribuir, como los escaños de un cuerpo legislativo. Pág. 267

**Appropriate/Asignar** Destinar a un uso particular. Pág. 305

**Articles/Artículos** Secciones numeradas de un documento. La Constitución, sin enmiendas, está dividida en siete artículos. Pág. 65

**Articles of Confederation/Artículos de la Confederación** Plan de gobierno adoptado por el Congreso Continental, después de la Independencia de los Estados Unidos; se enunciaron como "un vínculo firme de amistad" entre los estados; no obstante, delegaron unos cuantos poderes importantes al gobierno central. Pág. 44

**Assemble/Congregar** Reunirse con otras personas para expresar puntos de vista sobre asuntos públicos. Pág. 555

**Assessment/Valuación** Proceso para determinar el valor de una propiedad que será gravada. Pág. 742

**Assimilation/Asimilación** Proceso mediante el cual las personas de una cultura se fusionan con otra y se convierten en parte de ella. Pág. 597

**At-large election/Elección general** Elección de un funcionario público por los votantes de una unidad gubernamental completa (por ejemplo, un estado o país), en vez de por los votantes de un distrito o subdivisión. Pág. 270

**Attorney General/Procurador general** El titular del Departamento de Justicia. Pág. 424

**Authoritarian/Autoritario** Forma de gobierno en donde aquellos que ejercen el poder imponen un poder absoluto e inapelable sobre el pueblo. Todas las dictaduras son autoritarias. Pág. 13

**Autocracy/Autocracia** Forma de gobierno en la que una sola persona ejerce un poder político ilimitado. Pág. 13

**Autonomous/Autónomo** Independiente. Pág. 652

**Bail/Fianza** Suma de dinero que se exige que el acusado desembolse (es decir, que deposite en la corte) como garantía de que se presentará en dicha corte en el momento apropiado. Pág. 585

**Balance the ticket/Designar al compañero de fórmula** Cuando un candidato presidencial elige al candidato a la vicepresidencia que reforzará sus oportunidades de ser triunfador, gracias a las características ideológicas, geográficas, raciales, étnicas, de género, o debido a otras virtudes. Pág. 362

**Ballot/Papeleta electoral** Medio que los votantes utilizan para señalar su preferencia en una elección. Pág. 190

**Bankruptcy/Bancarrota** Procedimiento mediante el cual los bienes de una persona declarada en bancarrota se distribuyen entre las personas con las que tiene deudas. Pág. 300

**Bench trial/Juicio ante judicatura** Proceso en donde sólo el juez escucha el caso. Págs. 580, 705

**Bicameral/Bicameral** Adjetivo que describe un cuerpo legislativo compuesto por dos cámaras. Pág. 31

**Bill/Proyecto de ley** Ley propuesta que se presenta a un cuerpo legislativo para su consideración. Pág. 334

**Bill of Attainder/Escrito de proscripción y confiscación** Acto legislativo que inflige un castigo sin que haya un juicio ante jurado de por medio. Pág. 577

**Bill of Rights/Declaración de derechos** Las primeras diez enmiendas a la Constitución. Págs. 76, 532

**Bipartisan/Bipartidista** Apoyado por dos partidos. Págs. 120, 440

**Blanket primary/Elecciones primarias generales** Proceso de elección en el que los votantes reciben una papeleta electoral grande que contiene los nombres de todos los contendientes, sin importar el partido, y en el cual pueden elegir como lo deseen. Pág. 183

**Block grant/Subsidio en conjunto** Tipo de subsidio público federal; proporcionado para alguna área particular pero ampliamente definida; *ver* grants-in-aid program/programa de subvención de fondos públicos. Pág. 103

**Bourgeoisie/Burguesía** Clase social ubicada entre la aristocracia y la clase media; la clase trabajadora. Pág. 667

**Boycott/Boicot** Rechazo a vender o a comprar determinados productos o servicios. Pág. 36

**Budget/Presupuesto** Plan financiero para la utilización del dinero, el personal y la propiedad. Pág. 744

**Bureaucracy/Burocracia** Estructura administrativa grande y compleja que gobierna los negocios cotidianos de una organización. Pág. 414

**Bureaucrat/Burócrata** Persona que trabaja en una organización burocrática; *ver* bureaucracy/burocracia. Pág. 415

**By-election/Elección suplementaria** Elección especial llevada a cabo para sustituir a un miembro del Parlamento, en caso de muerte. Pág. 628

**Cabinet/Gabinete** Cuerpo consultivo del Presidente que tradicionalmente está compuesto por los titulares de los departamentos ejecutivos y otros funcionarios. Pág. 81

**Capital/Capital** Todos los recursos hechos por el hombre que se utilizan para producir bienes y servicios. Pág. 659

**Capitalist/Capitalista** Persona que posee capital y le da un uso productivo; término que en la mayor parte de los casos se aplica a las personas que poseen grandes negocios o fábricas. Pág. 659

**Capital punishment/Pena capital** La pena de muerte. Pág. 587

**Categorical grant/Subsidio categórico** Tipo de subsidio público; proporcionado para algún propósito específico y rigurosamente definido; *ver* grants-in-aid program/programa de subvención de fondos públicos. Pág. 102

**Caucus/Junta de dirigentes** En función de instrumento nominativo, grupo de personas con ideología similar que se reúne para seleccionar a los candidatos que apoyarán en una elección venidera. Pág. 180

**Censure/Censurar** Emitir una condena formal. Pág. 312

**Centrally planned economy/Economía centralmente planificada** Sistema en el que burócratas gubernamentales planean la forma en que la economía se desarrollará durante determinados años. Pág. 669

**Certificate/Certificación** Método de remitir un caso a la Corte Suprema; se utiliza cuando una corte inferior no está segura de qué procedimiento o regla deberá aplicar en un caso y consulta a la Corte Suprema para que certifique una respuesta a una pregunta específica. Pág. 521

**Charter/Carta constitucional** Ley básica de una ciudad, su constitución; concesión escrita de autoridad por parte del rey. Págs. 31, 726

**Checks and balances/Sistema de pesos y contrapesos** Mecanismo en el que se traslapan los poderes de las ramas legislativas, ejecutivas y judiciales para permitir que cada rama verifique las acciones de las otras dos; *ver* separation of powers/separación de poderes. Pág. 67

**Chief administrator/Administrador en jefe** Nombre que se da al Presidente en cuanto a que es el jefe de la administración del gobierno federal. Pág. 355

**Chief citizen/Primer ciudadano** Nombre que se da al Presidente, en cuanto a que es representante del pueblo y trabaja para el interés público. Pág. 355

**Chief diplomat/Diplomático titular** Nombre que se da al Presidente en cuanto a que es el arquitecto principal de la política exterior y el vocero ante otros países. Pág. 355

**Chief executive/Primer mandatario** Nombre que se da al Presidente, en cuanto a que está investido con el poder ejecutivo de los Estados Unidos. Pág. 354

**Chief legislator/Legislador en jefe** Nombre que se da al Presidente en cuanto a que es arquitecto de la política pública y uno de los que determina la agenda del Congreso. Pág. 355

**Chief of party/Jefe del partido** Nombre que se da al Presidente en cuanto a que es líder de su partido político. Pág. 355

**Chief of state/Jefe de estado** Nombre que se da al Presidente en cuanto a que es titular ceremonial de los Estados Unidos, el símbolo de toda la gente de la nación. Pág. 354

**Citizen/Ciudadano** Miembro de un estado o nación a la cual le debe lealtad por nacimiento o naturalización y al que se le acreditan todos los derechos civiles. Pág. 613

**Civil case/Caso civil** Caso que involucra un asunto no criminal, como un litigio por contrato, o una demanda por violación de patentes. Pág. 513

**Civil law/Ley civil** Área de la ley que se relaciona con la conducta humana, con litigios entre partes privadas, así como entre partes privadas y el gobierno, la cual no abarca la ley penal. Pág. 704

**Civil liberties/Libertades civiles** Garantías concernientes a la seguridad, opiniones y propiedad de las personas en contra de actos arbitrarios del gobierno; también incluyen la libertad de expresión y de religión. Pág. 533

**Civil rights/Derechos civiles** Término utilizado para aquellos actos positivos del gobierno que pretenden hacer realidad las garantías constitucionales para todo el pueblo, por ejemplo la prohibición de la discriminación. Pág. 533

**Civil service/Servicio Civil** Grupo de empleados públicos desempeñan el trabajo administrativo del gobierno. Pág. 437

**Civilian tribunal/Tribunal civil** Corte que funciona como parte de la rama judicial, el cual está separado por completo de la institución militar. Pág. 525

**Clemency/Indulgencia** Misericordia o piedad que dispensa el Presidente a un delincuente; *ver* pardon/perdón y reprieve/suspensión de la ejecución. Págs. 407, 699

**Closed primary/Elección primaria cerrada** Elección para una nominación partidista en la que sólo los miembros declarados del partido pueden votar. Pág. 182

**Cloture/Limitación del debate** Procedimiento que puede utilizarse para restringir o terminar un debate verbal de un cuerpo legislativo. Pág. 344

**Coalition/Coalición** Una alianza temporal de varios grupos que se agrupan para alcanzar el poder mayoritario y controlar el gobierno. Págs. 122, 628

**Coattail effect/Efecto de refilón** Efecto que produce un fuerte candidato a un puesto de elección, situado en primer sitio, mediante el cual ayuda a atraer votantes hacia otros candidatos de su mismo partido. Pág. 190

**Cold war/Guerra Fría** Periodo de más de 40 años de duración en el que las relaciones entre las dos superpotencias fueron por lo menos tensas, y a menudo hostiles. Época de amenazas y de desarrollo militar. Pág. 485

**colleague/colega** Compañero de trabajo. Pág. 277

**Collective security/Seguridad colectiva** Conservación de la paz y el orden internacionales. Pág. 485

**Collectivization/Colectivización** Hacer colectivos o propiedad del estado los medios de producción. Pág. 674

**Commander in chief/Comandante en jefe** Nombre que se da al Presidente en cuanto a que es el comandante de las fuerzas armadas de la nación. Pág. 355

**Commerce and Slave Trade Compromise/Avenencia de comercio y trata de esclavos** Acuerdo durante la Convención Constitucional que protegió los intereses de los dueños de esclavos, al negarle al Congreso el poder de gravar la exportación de bienes desde cualquier estado, así como el poder de actuar, durante 20 años, en contra de la trata de esclavos. Pág. 53

**Commerce power/Poder mercantil** Poder exclusivo del Congreso para regular el comercio interestatal e internacional. Pág. 297

**Commission government/Junta municipal** Gobierno formado por comisionados, titulares de distintos departamentos del gobierno de la ciudad, que se eligen por voto popular para formar el Consejo de la ciudad y, por consiguiente, reúnen los poderes legislativos y ejecutivos en un solo cuerpo. Pág. 728

**Committee chairman/Presidente de comisión** Miembro que encabeza una comisión permanente en un cuerpo legislativo. Pág. 325

**Committee of the Whole/Comité Plenario** Comité que consiste en la totalidad de un cuerpo legislativo; utilizado para un procedimiento mediante el cual un cuerpo legislativo da curso a sus asuntos transformándose en un comité en sí. Pág. 339

**Common law/Derecho consuetudinario** Ley no escrita sancionada por un juez y que se ha desarrollado a lo largo de los siglos con base a aquellas ideas generalmente aceptadas de lo bueno y lo malo que se han ganado un reconocimiento judicial. Pág. 702

**Commune/Comuna** Un grupo grande de diversas granjas colectivas. Pág. 675

**Communism/Comunismo** Ideología que exige la propiedad colectiva, o estatal, de la tierra y de otros medios de producción. Pág. 672

**Commutation/Conmutación** El poder de reducir (conmutar) la duración de una sentencia o el monto de la multa de un crimen.

Págs. 408, 699

**Compromise/Compromiso** Avenencia entre principios o sistemas opuestos, mediante la modificación de algún aspecto de cada uno de ellos. Pág. 20

**Concurrent jurisdiction/Jurisdicción coincidente** Poder compartido por cortes federales y estatales para atender ciertos casos. Pág. 508

**Concurrent powers/Poderes concurrentes** Aquellos poderes que el gobierno nacional y los estados poseen y ejercen. Pág. 93

**Concurrent resolution/Resolución conjunta** Enunciado de una posición sobre un asunto utilizado por la Cámara de Representantes y el Senado al actuar conjuntamente; no tiene la fuerza de la ley y no requiere la firma del Presidente. Pág. 335

**Concurring opinión/Opinion coincidente** Explicación escrita de los puntos de vista de uno o más jueces que apoyan una decisión alcanzada por una mayoría de la corte, pero en la que se desea añadir o recalcar un punto que no se remarcó en la decisión mayoritaria. Pág. 522

**Confederation/Confederación** Unión de diversos grupos para un propósito común. Págs. 15, 35

**Conference committee/Comité de Consulta** Comité conjunto temporal creado para reconciliar cualquier diferencia entre las versiones de las dos cámaras legislativas sobre una propuesta de ley. Pág. 333

**Connecticut Compromise/Acuerdo de Connecticut** Acuerdo alcanzado durante la Convención Constitucional respecto a que el Congreso debería estar integrado por un Senado en donde cada estado estuviera representado de manera igualitaria, y una Cámara de Representantes en la que la representación estuviera basada en la población de cada estado. Pág. 52

**Consensus/Consenso** Acuerdo general entre diversos grupos respecto a temas fundamentales; amplio acuerdo sobre temas varios. Págs. 121, 292, 636

**Constituency/Distrito electoral** Las personas e intereses que un funcionario elegido representa. Pág. 277

**Constituent power/Poder constituyente** Poder no legislativo de la elaboración de la Constitución y del proceso de enmiendas constitucionales. Pág. 692

**Constitution/Constitución** Cuerpo de leyes fundamentales que delinean los principios, las estructuras y los procesos de gobierno. Pág. 4

**Constitutionalism/Constitucionalismo** Principio básico que establece que el gobierno y los gobernantes deben obedecer la ley; el gobierno de la ley; *ver* limited government/gobierno limitado. Pág. 65

**Containment/Contención** Política basada en la creencia de que si el comunismo se pudiera limitar dentro de sus fronteras existentes, se derrumbaría bajo el peso de sus debilidades internas. Pág. 486

**Content neutral/Voto neutral** El gobierno no regulará a las asambleas en lo concerniente a lo que se expresará en ellas. Pág. 556

**Continuing resolution/Resolución ininterrumpida** Medida que permite que las agencies continuen funcionando sobre la base de las asignaciones del año anterior. Pág. 462

**Continuous body/Cuerpo legislativo ininterrumpido** Unidad gubernamental (por ejemplo, el Senado de Estados Unidos) cuya totalidad de escaños nunca se elige al mismo tiempo. Pág. 277

**Controllable spending/Gasto controlable** Cantidad de dinero decidida entre el Congreso y el Presidente y que señala el monto anual de muchos gastos gubernamentales individuales, como programas para protección del ambiente, ayuda a la educación, etcétera. Pág. 459

**Copyright/Derechos de autor** Derechos legales y exclusivos de una persona para reproducir, publicar y vender su trabajo creativo literario, artístico, o musical. Pág. 302

**Council-manager government/Gobierno de consejo-superintendente** Una modificación del gobierno de consejo-alcalde, que consiste en un vigoroso consejo de miembros elegido mediante un sufragio no partidista; un alcalde débil, elegido por el pueblo y un superintendente nombrado por el consejo; *ver* mayor-council government/gobierno de consejo-alcalde; *ver también* weak-mayor government/gobierno de alcalde débil. Pág. 728

**County/Condado** Una unidad importante de gobierno local en la gran parte de los estados. Pág. 718

**Court-martial/Corte marcial** Corte compuesta por personal militar para juzgar a los que están acusados de violar la ley militar. Pág. 525

**Criminal case/Caso criminal** Caso en el que se juzga al acusado por cometer un crimen, tal y como éste se define en la ley. Pág. 513

**Criminal law/Derecho penal** Área de la ley que define los agravios públicos y que establece su castigo. Pág. 704

**Cultural Revolution/Revolución cultural** Al comenzarse en 1966, los guardias rojos de Mao Tse Tung atacaron e intimidaron a los maestros, intelectuales y a cualquier otra persona que fuera sospechosa de carecer de fervor revolucionario e iniciaron un proceso para "reeducarlos". Pág. 650

**Customs Duty/Derecho de aduana** Impuesto gravado sobre los bienes traídos a los Estados Unidos desde el exterior, también se conoce como arancel, impuesto sobre importaciones o tasa sobre importaciones. Pág. 451

**De facto segregation/Discriminación de facto o de hecho** Segregación, incluso si la ley no lo exige, por ejemplo en la asignación de vivienda. Pág. 604

**De jure segregation/Discriminación de jure o de ley** Segregación con base en la ley, que implica una sanción legal. Pág. 604

**Defendant/Acusado** En un juicio civil, es la persona en contra de quien el demandante pide ejecutar una acción judicial; en un caso criminal, es la persona acusada de un crimen. Pág. 509

**Deficit/Déficit** La diferencia anual entre los ingresos y los egresos. Pág. 455

**Deficit financing/Déficit financiero** Práctica de subvencionar al gobierno mediante préstamos, a fin de compensar la diferencia entre los gastos y los ingresos gubernamentales. Pág. 296

**Delegated powers/Poderes delegados** Poderes explícitos, implícitos o inherentes que la Constitución transfiere al gobierno nacional. Pág. 89

**Democracy/Democracia** Forma de gobierno en donde la autoridad suprema reside en el pueblo. Pág. 5

**Denaturalization/Desnaturalización** Proceso en el que los ciudadanos naturalizados pueden perder su ciudadanía de manera involuntaria. Pág. 615

**Deportation/Deportación** Proceso legal mediante el que se les exige a los extranjeros que abandonen los Estados Unidos. Pág. 617

**Détente/Relajamiento** Disminución de las tensiones. Pág. 488

**Deterrence/Disuasión** Política de convertir a los Estados Unidos y sus aliados en una fuerza militar tan poderosa que su fortaleza desaliente, o prevenga, cualquier ataque. Pág. 485

**Devolution/Delegación** Transferencia de la autoridad del gobierno central a los gobiernos regionales. Pág. 631

**Dictatorship/Dictadura** Forma de gobierno en la que el líder ejerce poder y autoridad absolutos. Pág. 5

**Diplomatic immunity/Inmunidad diplomática** Cuando un embajador no está sujeto a las leyes del estado en el que se le acredita como tal. Pág. 471

**Direct popular election/Elección popular directa** Propuesta para abolir el colegio electoral y permitir que la gente elija de manera directa al Presidente y al Vicepresidente. Pág. 383

**Direct primary/Elección primaria directa** Elección realizada dentro de un partido para escoger a los candidatos del partido para una elección general. Pág. 182

**Direct tax/Impuesto directo** Gravamen que debe pagar la persona a la que se le impone; *ver* indirect tax/impuesto indirecto. Pág. 296

**Discharge petition/Petición de exoneración** Procedimiento que permite a los miembros autorizar una propuesta de ley que se ha estancado en una comisión de debate para su consideración. Pág. 336

**Discrimination/Discriminación** Prejuicio, injusticia. Pág. 570

**Dissenting opinión/Opinión disidente** Explicación escrita de los puntos de vista de uno o más jueces, que está(n) en desacuerdo con una decisión tomada por la mayoría de la corte; *ver* majority opinion/opinión mayoritaria. Pág. 522

**Dissolution/Disolución** Poder del Primer Ministro para disolver la Cámara de Representantes. Pág. 636

**District Plan/Plan de Distrito** Propuesta para elegir a los electores presidenciales, mediante la cual se seleccionarían dos electores en cada estado, de acuerdo con el voto popular de todo ese estado, y los otros electores se elegirían de manera separada en cada uno de los distritos del Congreso de ese estado. Pág. 382

**Division of powers/División de poderes** Principio básico del federalismo; las estipulaciones constitucionales que establecen que los poderes gubernamentales están separados de acuerdo con bases geográficas (en los Estados Unidos, se dividen entre el gobierno nacional y los estados). Págs. 15, 89

**Docket/Agenda** Lista de casos de una corte por atender. Pág. 513

**Doctrine/Doctrina** Principio de política fundamental. Pág. 308

**Domestic affairs/Asuntos internos** Todas cuestiones no conectadas al campo de los asuntos exteriores. Págs. 422, 468

**Double jeopardy/Doble juicio** Parte de la 5ª enmienda que establece que no se puede poner en riesgo la vida de una persona o su integridad física dos veces. Una vez que se ha juzgado por un crimen a una persona, no puede volvérsele a juzgar por el mismo delito. Pág. 578

**Draft/Reclutamiento** Conscripción o servicio militar obligatorio. Pág. 480

**Due process/Proceso legal establecido** El gobierno debe actuar con justicia y de acuerdo con las reglas establecidas en todo lo que hace. Pág. 564

**Due Process Clause/Cláusula del proceso legal establecido** Parte de la 14ª enmienda que garantiza que ningún estado negará los derechos básicos a su pueblo. Pág. 535

**Economic protest parties/Partidos de protesta económica** Partidos surgidos en tiempos de descontento económico, los cuales carecen de una base ideológica bien definida, están insatisfechos por las condiciones presentes y exigen mejores épocas. Pág. 133

**Electoral college/Colegio electoral** Grupo de personas (electores presidenciales) elegidos cada cuatro años en todos los estados y en el Distrito de Columbia a fin de hacer una elección formal del Presidente y Vicepresidente. Págs. 81, 366

**Electoral votes/Votos electorales** Votos emitidos por los electores en el Colegio electoral. Pág. 365

**Electorate/Electorado** Todas las personas que tienen derecho a votar en una elección determinada. Págs. 129, 148, 383

**Eminent domain/Dominio supremo** Poder de un gobierno de expropiar la propiedad privada para uso público. Pág. 304

**Enabling act/Ley de habilitación** Una ley del Congreso que orienta al pueblo de un territorio de los Estados Unidos para que redacte una constitución propuesta para el estado, como un paso hacia la admisión de dicho estado dentro de la Unión. Pág. 99

**English Bill of Rights/Declaración inglesa de los derechos** Documento redactado por el Parlamento y aceptado por William y Mary de Inglaterra en 1689, elaborado para evitar el abuso del poder por parte de los monarcas ingleses; constituye la base de muchas cosas del gobierno y la política estadounidenses actuales. Pág. 30

**Engross/Transcribir** Imprimir un proyecto de ley en su forma final. Pág. 340

**Entitlement/Derecho** Beneficio que la ley federal establece que se debe pagar a todos los que cumplan los requisitos para ser elegibles, por ejemplo: el seguro médico, bonos de comida y pensión para los veteranos. Pág. 458, 735

**Entrepreneur/Empresario** Individuo con el impulso y la ambición de combinar los recursos de la tierra, la mano de obra y el capital para producir bienes u ofrecer servicios. Pág. 659

**Espionage/Espionaje** Acto de espiar. Pág. 477

**Establishment Clause/Cláusula del establecimiento** Separa a la iglesia del estado. Pág. 537

**Estate tax/Impuesto testamentario** Gravamen sobre los bienes de una persona que muere. Págs. 451, 742

**Ex post facto law/Ley ex post facto** Ley que se aplica a un acto cometido con anterioridad a la aprobación de la ley. Pág. 577

**Excise tax/Impuesto al consumo** Gravamen sobre la manufactura, venta o consumo de bienes y/o al suministro de servicios. Pág. 451

**Exclusionary rule/Regla de exclusión** Evidencia obtenida como resultado de una acción ilegal de la policía y que no puede utilizarse contra la persona arrestada. Pág. 573

**Exclusive jurisdiction/Jurisdicción exclusiva** Poder exclusivo de las cortes federales para atender ciertos casos. Pág. 508

**Exclusive powers/Poderes exclusivos** Poderes que pueden ejercerse sólo por el gobierno nacional. Pág. 93

**Executive agreement/Acuerdo ejecutivo** Pacto hecho de manera directa por el Presidente con otro jefe de un estado extranjero; un pacto internacional obligatorio con la fuerza de la ley pero que no requiere (a diferencia de un tratado) de la aprobación del Senado. Págs. 80, 400

**Executive Article/Artículo del ejecutivo** El segundo artículo de la Constitución. Define la presidencia y le otorga el poder ejecutivo del gobierno federal al Presidente. Pág. 390

**Executive departments/Oficinas del poder ejecutivo** A menudo llamadas oficinas del gabinete; son las unidades tradicionales de la administración federal. Pág. 424

**Executive Office of the President/Oficina ejecutiva del Presidente** Una organización compleja, que abarca diversas oficinas separadas, cuyo personal está compuesto por los consejeros y asistentes más cercanos al Presidente. Pág. 419

**Executive order/Orden ejecutiva** Directiva, regla o reglamento expedida por un primer mandatario o por sus subordinados, con base en su autoridad estatutaria o constitucional y la cual tiene fuerza de ley. Pág. 394

**Executive power/Poder ejecutivo** Poder para ejecutar, administrar y obligar al cumplimiento de la ley. Pág. 4

**Expatriation/Expatriación** Proceso legal mediante el cual ocurre la pérdida de ciudadanía. Pág. 614

**Expressed powers/Poderes explícitos** Aquellos poderes delegados del gobierno nacional que se señalan explícitamente en la Constitución; también se conocen como los "poderes ennumerados." Págs. 89, 290

**Extradition/Extradición** Proceso legal a través del cual un fugitivo de la justicia en un estado se envía a ese estado. Pág. 107

**Faction/Facción** Un grupo disidente. Pág. 127

**Factors of production/Factores de producción** Recursos básicos que se utilizan para elaborar todos los bienes y servicios. Pág. 658

**Federal budget/Presupuesto federal** Documento financiero detallado que contienen las estimaciones de las recaudaciones y gastos que anticipan los ingresos y egresos federales durante el año fiscal venidero. Pág. 421

**Federal government/Gobierno federal** Forma de gobierno en la que los poderes están divididos entre un gobierno central y diversos gobiernos locales. Pág. 14

**Federalism/Federalismo** Sistema de gobierno en el que una constitución escrita divide los poderes del gobierno, sobre una base territorial, entre un gobierno central (o nacional) y diversos gobiernos regionales. Págs. 70, 88

**Federalists/Federalistas** Personas que apoyaron la ratificación de la Constitución en 1787–1788. Pág. 56

**Felony/Felonía** Un crimen grave que puede castigarse con una gran multa, la prisión o incluso la muerte. Pág. 704

**Filibuster/Obstrucción** Diversas tácticas (por lo general, prolongar el debate verbal) dirigidas a derrotar una propuesta de ley en un cuerpo legislativo, evitando así que se tenga un voto final; a menudo se asocia con el Senado de los Estados Unidos; *ver* cloture/limitación del debate. Pág. 343

**Fiscal year/Año fiscal** Periodo de 12 meses utilizado por el gobierno y el mundo de los negocios para su contabilidad, presupuesto, recaudación de ingresos y otros propósitos financieros. Pág. 421

**Five-year plan/Plan quinquenal** Plan que hace proyecciones sobre el desarrollo económico durante los siguientes cinco años. Pág. 673

**Floor leaders/Líderes de fracciones partidistas** Miembros de la Cámara de Representantes y del Senado elegidos por sus partidos con el objeto de llevar a cabo las decisiones partidistas e impulsar la acción legislativa a fin de que cumplan con los propósitos partidistas. Pág. 324

**Foreign Affairs/Asuntos exteriores** Relaciones de una nación con otros países. Pág. 468

**Foreign aid/Ayuda extranjera** Auxilio militar y económico a otros países. Pág. 491

**Foreign policy/Política exterior** Conjunto de políticas conformado por todas las posturas y acciones que una nación asume en cada uno de los aspectos de sus relaciones con otros países; todo lo que el gobierno de una nación expresa y hace respecto a los asuntos mundiales. Pág. 469

**Formal amendment/Enmienda formal** Cambio o adición que se convierte en parte del lenguaje escrito de la Constitución misma, mediante uno de los cuatro métodos enunciados de la Constitución. Pág. 73

**Framers/Redactores** Grupo de delegados que esbozaron la Constitución de los Estados Unidos en la Convención de Filadelfia en 1787. Pág. 48

**Franchise/Sufragio** Derecho a votar. Pág. 148

**Franking privilege/Exención de franquicia** Beneficio otorgado a los miembros del Congreso que les permite enviar por correo cartas y otros materiales sin pagar los derechos del correo. Pág. 283

**Free enterprise system/Sistema de libre empresa** Sistema económico caracterizado por la propiedad privada o corporativa de los bienes de capital; inversiones que están determinadas por una decisión privada, en vez del control estatal, y están sujetas a un mercado libre. Págs. 20, 659

**Free Exercise Clause/Cláusula de la libertad de cultos** Segunda parte de la garantía constitucional de libertad religiosa, que garantiza a todo mundo el derecho de creer en lo que ella escoja en materia de religión. Pág. 542

**Full Faith and Credit Clause/Cláusula de fe y crédito cabal** Requisito constitucional (Artículo IV, Sección 1) según el cual cada estado acepta (da "fe y crédito cabal") los actos públicos, documentos y procedimientos judiciales de cualquier otro estado. Pág. 106

**Fundamental law/Ley fundamental** Leyes de importancia primordial y duradera que no se cambiarán con facilidad. Pág. 686

**Gender gap/Brecha de género** Diferencias medibles entre las elecciones partidistas actuales de hombres y mujeres. Pág. 169

**General election/Elección general** Elección programada regularmente en la que los votantes hacen una selección final de los funcionarios públicos. Pág. 179

**Gerrymandering/Demarcación arbitraria** Establecimiento de los límites de los distritos electorales de modo que den ventaja a un partido. Págs. 159, 271

**Gift tax/Impuesto a los regalos** Gravamen sobre los regalos dados por una persona viva. Pág. 451

**Glasnost/Glásnost** Política de apertura bajo la cual el gobierno ruso incrementó su tolerancia a la disensión y a la libertad de expresión. Pág. 646

**Gosplan/Gosplán** Importante oficina de la Unión Soviética, creada por Stalin, para llevar a cabo la planificación centralizada. Pág. 674

**Government/Gobierno** Institución mediante la cual una sociedad lleva a cabo y hace cumplir sus políticas públicas. Está compuesto por aquellas personas que ejercen sus poderes, aquellos que tienen autoridad y control sobre el pueblo. Pág. 4

**Government corporation/Corporación gubernamental** Instituciones dentro de la rama ejecutiva que están sujetas a la dirección y control del Presidente, formadas por el Congreso para que realicen determinadas actividades de tipo empresarial. Pág. 434

**Grand jury/Gran Jurado** El dispositivo formal a través del cual puede acusarse a una persona de un crimen serio. Pág. 577

**Grants-in-aid program/Programa de subvención de fondos públicos** Subvenciones de dinero federal o de otros recursos para los estados y/o sus ciudades, condados y otras unidades locales. Pág. 101

**Grass roots/Fundamentos** De extracción popular, los votantes promedio. Pág. 253

**Great Leap Forward/Gran salto hacia adelante** Plan quinquenal de 1958 que fue un intento de modernizar rápidamente a China. Pág. 675

**Hard money/Fondos fiscalizados** Dinero de campaña que está sujeto a las regulaciones de la FEC. Pág. 202

**Heterogeneous/Hetereogéneo** De diferente raza, familia o especie; compuesto por una mezcla de elementos. Pág. 594

**Ideological parties/Partidos ideológicos** Partidos basados en un conjunto determinado de creencias, un punto de vista comprehensivo sobre asuntos sociales, económicos y políticos. Pág. 132

**Immigrant/Inmigrante** Persona que es admitida legalmente en calidad de residente permanente de un país. Pág. 594

**Impeach/Impugnar** Fincar cargos formales en contra de un funcionario público; la Cámara de Representantes tienen el exclusivo poder de impugnar a los funcionarios públicos de los Estados Unidos. Pág. 311

**Imperial presidency/Presidencia imperial** Término utilizado para describir a un Presidente como "emperador", quien actúa sin consultar al Congreso o de manera secreta para evadir o engañarlo. Pág. 392

**Implied powers/Poderes implícitos** Aquellos poderes delegados del gobierno nacional que se sugieren o están implícitos por los poderes explícitos; aquellos que son "necesarios y apropiados" para realizar los poderes explícitos; *ver* delegated powers/poderes delegados, expressed powers/poderes explícitos. Págs. 90, 290

**Income tax/Impuesto sobre el ingreso** Gravamen sobre el ingreso de los individuos y/o corporaciones. Pág. 741

**Incorporation/Incorporación** Proceso mediante el cual un estado establece a una ciudad como un cuerpo legal. Pág. 726

**Incumbent/Titular** El funcionario público actual. Pág. 127

**Independent agencies/Oficinas independientes** Agencias adicionales creadas por el Congreso y que se ubican fuera de los departamentos del gabinete. Pág. 430

**Independent executive agencies/Oficinas ejecutivas independientes** Agencias que incluyen a la mayor parte de las agencias independientes, que están organizadas de una forma muy similar a los departamentos del gabinete y cuyo titular es un administrador que tiene subunidades operativas regionales pero que carece del estatus del gabinete. Pág. 431

**Independent regulatory commissions/Comisiones regulatorias independientes** Agencias independientes cuya función es regular aspectos importantes de la economía de la nación, en su mayoría fuera del control y dirección del Presidente. Pág. 431

**Independents/Independientes** Término usado para describir a las personas que carecen de filiación partidista. Pág. 171

**Indictment/Denuncia** Queja formal que el fiscal expone ante un gran jurado, que incluye cargos al acusado por uno o más crímenes. Pág. 578

**Indirect tax/Impuesto indirecto** Gravamen a una parte pero transferido a otra para su pago. Pág. 296

**Inferior courts/Cortes inferiores** Las cortes federales menores, que están por debajo de la Corte Suprema. Pág. 507

**Informal amendment/Enmienda informal** Cambio en la Constitución que no se hace mediante una enmienda escrita, sino por la experiencia del gobierno bajo la Constitución; los métodos incluyen: (1) aprobación de la legislación básica por parte del Congreso; (2) acciones llevadas a cabo por el Presidente; (3) decisiones clave de la Corte Suprema; (4) actividades de los partidos políticos; y (5) costumbre. Pág. 79

**Information/Información** Acusación oficial presentada por un acusador sin acción de parte del jurado. Pág. 704

**Inherent powers/Poderes inherentes** Aquellos poderes delegados del gobierno nacional que le pertenecen de manera inherente, debido a que es el gobierno de un estado soberano de la comunidad mundial. Págs. 91, 290

**Inheritance tax/Impuesto sobre la herencia** Gravamen sobre la parte de la herencia del beneficiario. Pág. 742

**Initiative/Iniciativa** Proceso en el que determinado número de votantes calificados firman peticiones a favor de una propuesta, la cual se pasa después directamente a la cédula de votación. Pág. 687

**Injunction/Mandato** Orden judicial que fuerza o limita el desempeño de determinado acto, mediante la intervención de un individuo privado o un funcionario público. Pág. 161

**Integration/Integración** El proceso de ofrecer a un grupo una pertenencia igualitaria dentro de la sociedad. Pág. 603

**Interest/Interés** Cargo que se hace por el dinero prestado, por lo general es un porcentaje de la cantidad prestada. Pág. 454

**Interest group/Grupo de interés** Organizaciones privadas cuyos miembros comparten determinados puntos de vista y trabajan para dar forma a las políticas públicas. Pág. 216

**Interstate compact/Pacto interestatal** Acuerdo formal suscrito con el consentimiento del Congreso, entre dos estados o entre un estado y un estado extranjero, el cual está autorizado por la Constitución. (Artículo I, Sección 10). Pág. 105

**Involuntary servitude/Servidumbre involuntaria** Trabajo forzado. Pág. 569

**Isolationism/Aislacionismo** Rechazo voluntario a verse involucrado, de manera general, en los asuntos del resto del mundo. Pág. 468

**Item veto/Veto de artículo** Un gobernador puede vetar uno o más artículos de una propuesta de ley, sin que rechace toda la medida. Pág. 699

**Jim Crow law/Ley Jim Crow** Tipo de ley que separa a un grupo de personas del resto de la gente, con base en la raza, dirigido principalmente a los afroamericanos. Pág. 602

**Joint committee/Comité conjunto** Comité legislativo compuesto por miembros de ambas cámaras. Pág. 333

**Joint resolution/Resolución conjunta** Propuesta de acción que tiene la fuerza de ley cuando se aprueba; a menudo tiene que ver con circunstancias especiales o asuntos temporales. Pág. 335

**Judicial power/Poder judicial** Poder para interpretar las leyes, determinar su significado y resolver las disputas que surgen dentro de la sociedad. Pág. 4

**Judicial review/Revisión judicial** Poder de una corte para determinar la constitucionalidad de una acción gubernamental. Pág. 69

**Jurisdiction/Jurisdicción** Autoridad de una corte para atender (juzgar y decidir) un caso. Pág 508

**Jury/Jurado** Conjunto de personas seleccionadas de acuerdo con la ley para que escuchan la evidencia y deciden cuestiones de hechos en un caso de la corte. Pág. 704

**Jus sanguinis/*Jus sanguinis*** Ley de la sangre que define la ciudadanía con base en la ciudadanía de los padres. Pág. 613

**Jus soli/*Jus soli*** Ley del territorio que determina la ciudadanía con base en el lugar de nacimiento de la persona. Pág. 613

**Justice of the Peace/Juez de paz** Juez que está en el nivel inferior del sistema judicial estatal y preside las cortes de justicia. Pág. 707

**Keynote address/Discurso de apertura** Alocución dada en una convención de partido para establecer el tono de la convención y de la futura campaña. Pág. 373

**Labor union/Sindicato laboral** Organización de trabajadores que comparten el mismo tipo de trabajo, o que laboran en la misma industria y que presiona por lograr políticas gubernamentales que beneficien a sus miembros. Pág. 244

**Laissez-faire theory/Teoría del dejar hacer** Teoría que sugiere que el gobierno debería desempeñar un papel limitado dentro de la sociedad. Pág. 662

**Law of supply and demand/Ley de la oferta y la demanda** Ley que establece que cuando los suministros de bienes y servicios son abundantes, entonces los precios tienden a bajar. Cuando los suministros escasean, entonces los precios tienden a subir. Págs. 21, 661

**Legal tender/Moneda de curso legal** Cualquier moneda que un acreedor debe aceptar, por ley, como pago de deudas. Pág. 299

**Legislative power/Poder legislativo** Poder para hacer una ley y redactar políticas públicas. Pág. 4

**Libel/Libelo** Utilización falsa y maliciosa de las palabras impresas. Pág. 546

**Liberal constructionist/Construccionista liberal** Aquel que argumenta una amplia interpretación de las estipulaciones de la Constitución, en particular las que otorgan poderes al gobierno federal. Pág. 291

**Limited government/Gobierno limitado** Principio básico del sistema estadounidense de gobierno que establece que el gobierno está restringido en cuanto a lo que puede hacer, y en donde el individuo tiene ciertos derechos que el gobierno no puede enajenar; *ver* constitutionalism/constitucionalismo, popular sovereignty/soberanía popular. Págs. 29, 685

**Line agency/Agencia del ramo** Oficina que desempeña las tareas para las que la organización existe. Pág. 418

**Line-item veto/Veto de partida** Cancelación presidencial de ciertas cantidades de dólares (partidas) de una cuenta de gastos del Congreso; este veto se instituyó en 1996 mediante una ley del Congreso, pero la Suprema Corte lo derogó en 1998. Pág. 406

**Literacy/Alfabetismo** Capacidad de una persona para leer o escribir. Pág. 156

**Lobbying/Cabildeo** Actividades mediante las que las presiones de un grupo se aplican a los legisladores y al proceso legislativo, incluyendo todos los métodos utilizados por el grupo para dirigir las presiones hacia todos los aspectos del proceso de creación de políticas públicas. Pág. 251

**Magistrate/Magistrado** Juez que atiende a demandas civiles menores y casos de faltas leves que surgen en un contexto urbano. Pág. 708

**Magna Carta/Carta Magna** Constitución que los barones impusieron al rey John de Inglaterra en 1215; estableció el principio de que el poder del monarca no era absoluto y garantizó los derechos fundamentales, como el de un juicio con jurado y procesos establecidos legales para la nobleza. Pág. 29

**Major parties/Partidos principales** En la política estadounidense, los partidos Demócrata y Republicano. Pág. 116

**Majority opinion/Opinión mayoritaria** Llamada oficialmente Opinión de la Corte; anuncia la decisión de la Corte sobre el caso y describe el razonamiento sobre el que ésta se basa. Pág. 522

**Mandate/Mandato** Las intrucciones u órdenes que un grupo de votantnes da a sus funcionarios electos. Pág. 216

**Market economy/Economía de mercado** Un sistema económico en el que se basa las decisiones de la producción y el consumo de bienes en el intercambio voluntario de mercados. Pág. 669

**Mass media/Medios masivos de comunicación** Aquellos medios de comunicación que llegan a grandes audiencias, sobre todo la radio, televisión, publicaciones impresas e Internet. Págs. 211, 391

**Mayor-council government/Gobierno de consejo-alcalde** El más antiguo y más utilizado tipo de gobierno municipal: un alcalde electo como Presidente y un consejo electo como su cuerpo legislativo. Pág. 726

**Medicaid/Medicaid** Programa administrado por el Senado para proporcionar seguro médico a las familias de bajos ingresos. Pág. 735

**Medium/Medio** Un medio de comunicación; algo que transmite información. Pág. 223

**Mestizo/Mestizo** Persona que tiene ancestros portugueses o españoles e indios americanos. Pág. 639

**Metropolitan area/Área metropolitana** La ciudad y el área que le circunda. Pág. 731

**Minister/Ministro** Miembro del gabinete, y más frecuentemente de la Cámara de los Comunes. Pág. 629

**Minor party/Partido minoritario** Partido político que no cuenta con gran apoyo. Pág. 119

**Miranda Rule/Regla Miranda** Derechos constitucionales que la policía debe especificar a un sospechoso antes de que pueda hacérsele una interrogación. Pág. 582

**Misdemeanor/Falta leve** Delito menor que se castiga mediante una pequeña multa o un breve período de encarcelamiento. Pág. 704

**Mixed economy/Economía mixta** Sistema económico en donde la iniciativa privada existe en combinación con una considerable regulación y promoción gubernamental. Pág. 21

**Monarchy/Monarquía** Gobierno encabezado por un gobernante hereditario. Pág. 627

**Monopoly/Monopolio** Empresa que es la única fuente de un producto o servicio. Pág. 661

**Multiparty/Multipartidista** Sistema en el que varios partidos importantes y muchos secundarios existen, compiten seriamente y en realidad ganan puestos de elección popular. Pág. 122

**National Bonus Plan/Plan de bono nacional** Propuesta para elegir al Presidente y Vicepresidente, mediante el cual se le otorgaría una suma nacional de 102 votos electorales al ganador del voto popular, además de los votos del colegio electoral de su estado. Si ningún candidato recibe al menos 321 votos electorales, se llevaría a cabo una elección complementaria. Pág. 384

**National convention/Convención nacional** Reunión en la que los delegados de un partido votan para elegir a sus candidatos a la presidencia y vicepresidencia. Pág. 372

**Nationalization/Nacionalización** Adquisición gubernamental de la industria privada para uso público. Pág. 642

**Naturalization/Naturalización** Proceso legal mediante el cual los ciudadanos de un país se convierten en ciudadanos de otro. Págs. 302, 614

**Necessary and Proper Clause/Cláusula de necesidad y conveniencia** Cláusula constitucional que otorga al Congreso el poder de expedir leyes "necesarias y convenientes" para el ejercicio de sus poderes; *ver* implied powers/poderes implícitos. Pág. 305

**New Jersey Plan/Plan Nueva Jersey** Plan presentado en la Convención Constitucional como una alternativa al Plan Virginia; proponía una legislatura unicameral en la que cada estado estuviera representado de forma equitativa. Pág. 51

**Nomination/Nominación** Proceso de selección de candidatos en una democracia. Pág. 178

**Nonpartisan election/Elección no partidista** Elección en la que los candidatos no están identificados por membretes de partidos. Pág. 184

**North American Free Trade Agreement/Tratado de Libre Comercio de Norteamérica** Acuerdo que elimina las restricciones comerciales entre los Estados Unidos, Canadá y México, con lo cual se incrementa el comercio transfronterizo. Pág. 642

**Oath of office/Juramento al asumir un cargo** Juramento que hace el Presidente el día que asume la presidencia, jurando "cumplir fielmente" con sus responsabilidades, así como "preservar, proteger y defender" la Constitución. Pág. 393

**Off-year election/Elección intermedia** Elección del Congreso que ocurre entre las elecciones presidenciales. Págs. 164, 269

**Oligarchy/Oligarquía** Forma de gobierno en la que el poder de gobernar lo ejerce una elite pequeña y por lo general autonombrada. Pág. 13

**One-party system/Sistema unipartidista** Sistema político en el que sólo existe un partido. Pág. 123

**Open primary/Elección primaria abierta** Elección partidista de nominación en la que cualquier votante calificado puede tomar parte. Pág. 183

**Opinion leader/Líder de opinión** Cualquier persona que por alguna razón tiene una poderosa influencia en los puntos de vista de otras. Pág. 212

**Ordinance power/Poder de decreto** Poder del Presidente de emitir órdenes ejecutivas; se fundamenta en la Constitución y en los actos del Congreso. Pág. 394

**Original jurisdiction/Jurisdicción original** Poder de una corte de atender un caso antes que otra corte. Pág. 509

**Oversight function/Función de vigilancia** Revisión de las políticas y los programas de la rama ejecutiva por parte de los comités legislativos. Pág. 281

**Pardon/Perdón** Exoneración del castigo o de las consecuencias legales de un crimen que lleva a cabo el Presidente (en el caso federal) o el gobernador (en el caso estatal). Págs. 407, 699

**Parliamentary government/Gobierno parlamentario** Forma de gobierno en la que la rama ejecutiva está conformada por el primer ministro, o premier, y el gabinete oficial. Pág. 16

**Parochial/Parroquial** Relacionado con la iglesia, como las escuelas parroquiales. Pág. 538

**Parole/Liberación bajo palabra** Libertad condicional de un prisionero poco antes de que termine el lapso de su sentencia original. Pág. 699

**Partisan/Partidista** Legislador que le debe fidelidad, en primer lugar, a su partido político, por lo que vota de acuerdo con la línea del partido. Pág. 281

**Partisanship/Partidarismo** Acción gubernamental basada en la vigorosa fidelidad a un partido político. Pág. 117

**Party caucus/Junta de dirigentes de partido** Reunión cerrada de los miembros de la Cámara de Representantes o del Senado; también se conoce como Conferencia de partido. Pág. 324

**Party identification/Identificación con el partido** Lealtad de la gente hacia un partido político. Pág. 171

**Party in power/Partido en el poder** En la política estadounidense, el partido en el poder es aquel que controla la rama ejecutiva; es decir la presidencia, a nivel nacional, o la gubernatura, a nivel estatal. Pág. 118

**Patent/Patente** Licencia expedida a un inventor para garantizar el derecho exclusivo de manufactura, uso o venta de su invento, durante un tiempo limitado. Pág. 303

**Patronage/Patrocinio** Práctica de dar trabajo a los simpatizantes y amigos. Pág. 438

**Payroll tax/Impuesto sobre la nómina** Gravamen tasado a casi todos los empleadores y sus empleados, así como a las personas autoempleadas; cantidad debida por los empleados que se les descuenta de su salario. Pág. 450

**Peer group/Grupo de camaradas** Gente con la que uno se asocia regularmente y que incluye a socios, amigos, compañeros de clase, vecinos y compañeros de trabajo. Pág. 212

*Perestroika*/**Perestroika** Reestructuración de la vida política y económica durante el gobierno de Mijail Gorbachov. Pág. 646

**Perjury/Perjurio** El hecho de mentir bajo juramento. Pág. 311

**Persona non grata/Persona *non grata*** Una persona que no es bienvenida; se utiliza para describir a los funcionarios diplomáticos destituidos. Pag. 401

**Petition of Right/Solicitud de Derecho** Documento preparado por el Parlamento y firmado por el rey Charles I de Inglaterra en 1628; cuestionó la idea del derecho divino de los reyes y declaró que incluso el monarca está sujeto a las leyes de la tierra. Pág. 30

**Picketing/Vigilancia** Manifestación de los trabajadores en el sitio donde están en huelga. Pág. 551

**Plaintiff/Demandante** En el derecho civil, la parte que entabla un juicio u otra acción legal contra otra (el demandado) en una corte. Pág. 509

**Platform/Plataforma** Un enunciado formal por parte de un partido político respecto a sus principios básicos, opiniones sobre cuestiones políticas importantes y objetivos. Pág. 373

**Pluralistic society/Sociedad pluralista** Sociedad que está formada por distintos grupos y culturas. Pág. 121

**Plurality/Mayoría** En una elección, el número de votos que el candidato que va a la punta tiene de ventaja sobre su competidor más cercano. Pág. 120

**Pocket veto/Veto indirecto** Tipo de veto que el Presidente puede utilizar después de que una legislatura se suspende; se aplica cuando un Presidente no firma formalmente o rechaza una propuesta de ley, dentro del tiempo comprendido para eso; *ver* Veto. Pág. 346

**Police power/Facultad policial** Autoridad de cada estado para proteger y promover la salud pública, la seguridad, la moral y el bienestar general de su pueblo. Págs. 566, 691

**Political Action Committee/Comité de acción política** Extensión política de grupos de interés especiales, los cuales tienen un gran interés en la política pública. Pág. 197

**Political efficacy/Eficacia política** La influencia o eficacia individual en la política. Pág. 166

**Political party/Partido político** Grupo de personas que buscan controlar el gobierno mediante el triunfo en las elecciones y la conservación de los puestos públicos. Pág. 116

**Political socialization/Socialización política** Proceso mediante el que la gente obtiene sus actitudes y opiniones políticas. Pág. 168

**Politico/Político** Legislador que intenta equilibrar los elementos básicos de los miembros del directorio, los delegados y los roles partidistas; *ver* trustee/independiente, delegate/delegado, partisan/partidista. Pág. 281

**Poll book/Padrón electoral** Lista de todos los votantes registrados en cada distrito. Pág. 155

**Poll tax/Impuesto sobre el padrón electoral** Gravamen especial, exigido por los estados como una condición para votar. Pág. 157

**Polling place/Casilla electoral** Lugar donde los votantes que viven en cierto distrito acuden a votar. Pág. 190

**Popular sovereignty/Soberanía popular** Principio básico del sistema estadounidense de gobierno que establece que el pueblo es la fuente de todos los poderes gubernamentales, y que el gobierno sólo puede existir con el consentimiento de los gobernados. Págs. 39, 685

**Preamble/Preámbulo** Introducción. Pág. 65

**Precedent/Precedente** Decisión judicial que se toma como un ejemplo a seguir en el futuro para casos similares. Págs. 522, 703

**Precinct/Distrito** Unidad mínima de la administración electoral; distrito de votación. Págs. 140, 190

**Preclearance/Preautorización** Ordenada por la Ley de Derechos de Votos de 1965, respecto a la aprobación anterior, por parte del Departamento de Justicia, de los cambios en las leyes electorales existentes o nuevas en ciertos estados. Pág. 162

**Prefecture/Prefectura** Las 47 subdivisiones en las que se divide Japón. Pág. 637

**Preliminary hearing/Audiencia preliminar** El primer paso del procesamiento de un crimen mayor, en el que el juez decide si la evidencia basta para que la persona comparezca ante el gran jurado o ante el fiscal para ser sujeto de una acción. Pág. 708

**President of the Senate/Presidente del Senado** Funcionario que preside un Senado; en el Congreso es el Vicepresidente de los Estados Unidos; en la legislatura estatal, cualquier vicegobernador o un senador. Pág. 323

**President *pro tempore*/Presidente *pro tempore*** Miembro del Senado de Estados Unidos, o de la cámara superior de la legislatura estatal, elegido para ser Presidente, en caso de ausencia del Presidente del Senado. Pág. 323

**Presidential elector/Elector presidencial** Persona elegida por los votantes para representarlos en la selección formal del Presidente y Vicepresidente. Pág. 365

**Presidential government/Gobierno presidencial** Forma de gobierno en la que las ramas ejecutivas y legislativas del gobierno están separadas, son independientes y están en la misma jerarquía. Pág. 15

**Presidential primary/Elección presidencial primaria** Elección en la que los votantes de un partido: (1) eligen a varios o a todos los delegados de la organización partidista estatal para la convención nacional de su partido, y/o (2) expresan una preferencia por alguno de los distintos contendientes para la nominación presidencial de su partido. Pág. 369

**Presidential succession/Sucesión presidencial** Plan mediante el cual se resuelve la vacante presidencial. Pág. 359

**Presidential Succession Act of 1947/Ley para la sucesión presidencial de 1947** Ley que especifica el orden para la sucesión presidencial, después del Vicepresidente. Pág. 360

**Presiding officer/Primer funcionario** Presidente. Pág. 45

**Preventive detention/Arresto preventivo** Ley que permite a los jueces federales ordenar que un acusado de felonía sea arrestado, sin derecho a fianza, cuando existen buenas razones para creer que cometerá otro crimen grave antes del juicio. Pág. 586

**Prior restraint/Prohibición anticipada** El gobierno no puede reprimir las ideas antes de que se expresen. Pág. 549

**Privatization/Privatización** Regresar las empresas nacionales a la iniciativa privada. Pág. 675

**Privileges and Immunities Clause/Cláusula de privilegios e inmunidades** Estipulación constitucional (Artículo IV, Sección 2), en que se conceden ciertos "privilegios e inmunidades" a los ciudadanos, sin importar su estado de residencia; ningún estado puede hacer distinciones no razonables entre sus propios residentes y aquellas personas que vivan en otros estados. Pág. 107

**Probable Cause/Causa probable** Fundamentos razonables, sospecha razonable de un crimen. Pág. 571

**Procedural due process/Procesos legales establecidos** El gobierno debe emplear procedimientos y métodos justos. Pág. 565

**Process of incorporation/Proceso de incorporación** Proceso de integrar, o incluir, la mayor parte de las garantías de la Declaración de los derechos en la Cláusula de proceso legal establecido de la 14a enmienda. Pág. 535

**Progressive tax/Impuesto progresivo** Tipo de impuesto que es proporcional con el ingreso. Págs. 449, 742

**Project grant/Subvención de proyecto** Tipo de subvención de fondos públicos; proporcionada para proyectos específicos de los estados, las localidades y las oficinas privadas que la solicitan. Pág. 103

**Proletariat/Proletariado** La clase trabajadora. Pág. 667

**Propaganda/Propaganda** Una técnica inmoral de persuasión orientada a influir en los comportamientos individuales o colectivos con el objeto de originar una creencia particular, independientemente de su validez. Pág. 249

**Property tax/Impuesto a la propiedad** Gravamen sobre los bienes raíces y la propiedad personal. Pág. 742

**Proportional plan/Plan proporcional** Propuesta para seleccionar electores presidenciales, mediante la cual cada candidato recibiría la misma cantidad de votos electorales de un estado que recibió durante la votación popular del estado. Pág. 382

**Proportional representation rule/Regla de la representación proporcional** Procedimiento aplicado en las elecciones primarias del partido Demócrata, en el cual cualquier candidato que gane al menos el 15% de los votos emitidos en una elección primaria, obtienen el número de delegados a la convención estatal demócrata, que le corresponda a esa proporción de las primarias. Pág. 371

**Proprietary/Propiedad** Organizada por un dueño (persona a quien el rey le ha otorgado tierras). Pág. 32

**Prorogue/Prórroga** Aplazamiento, como en la sesión legislativa. Pág. 265

**Public affairs/Asuntos públicos** Aquellos acontecimientos y asuntos que importan al público en general, por ejemplo: la política, los temas públicos y la determinación de las políticas públicas. Págs. 208, 239

**Public agenda/Agenda pública** Asuntos públicos sobre los cuales está enfocada la atención de las personas. Pág. 228

**Public debt/Deuda pública** Todo el dinero que ha pedido prestado el gobierno a lo largo de los años y que todavía no paga, además del interés acumulado sobre ese capital; también se conoce como deuda nacional o deuda federal. Págs. 296, 455

**Public-interest group/Grupo de interés público** Grupo de interés que busca instituir determinadas políticas públicas de beneficio para la mayoría de las personas de su país, sin importar si pertenecen o apoyan a la organización. Pág. 247

**Public opinion/Opinión pública** Colección compleja de opiniones de diversas personas; la suma de todos sus puntos de vista. Pág. 209

**Public opinion poll/Encuestas de opinión pública** Dispositivos que intentan recolectar información al hacerle preguntas a las personas. Pág. 217

**Public policy/Políticas públicas** Todas las metas que un gobierno se fija, así como los distintos cursos de acción que toma en sus intentos por llevar a cabo esos objetivos. Págs. 4, 236

**Purge/Purga** Proceso de revisión de las listas de los votantes registrados y de la eliminación de los nombres que ya no son elegibles para votar; una depuración. Págs. 155, 645

**Quasi-judicial/Cuasi-judicial** Que tiene que ver con los poderes que en alguna forma son judiciales. Pág. 433

**Quasi-legislative/Cuasi-legislativo** Que tiene que ver con poderes que son legislativos en cierta medida. Pág. 433

**Quorum/Quórum** Mínimo número de miembros que debe estar presente para que un cuerpo legislativo funcione; mayoría. Págs. 58, 339

**Quota/Cuota** Regla que requiere que determinado número de trabajos o ascensos se den en miembros de ciertos grupos. Pág. 610

**Quota sample/Muestra de cuota** Muestra deliberadamente hecha para reflejar ciertas características importantes de una determinada población. Pág. 219

**Random sample/Muestra aleatoria** Determinado número de gente seleccionada al azar y que vive en ciertos lugares seleccionados de manera aleatoria. Pág. 218

**Ratification/Ratificación** Aprobación formal, consentimiento definitivo de la eficacia de una constitución, de una enmienda constitucional o de un tratado. Pág. 44

**Reapportion/Reasignación** Redistribución, como los escaños en un cuerpo legislativo. Pág. 267

**Recall/Retirada inesperada** Procedimiento de petición por el que los votantes puedan destituir a un funcionario oficial antes de terminar su mandato. Pág. 696

**Recognition/Reconocimiento** El poder exclusivo de un Presidente para reconocer (establecer relaciones diplomáticas) a estados extranjeros. Pág. 400

**Redress/Resarcir** Satisfacer una queja, por lo general mediante un pago. Pág. 524

**Referendum/Referendo** Proceso mediante el cual una medida legislativa se consulta con los votantes de los estados para su aprobación o rechazo final. Pág. 693

**Refugee/Refugiado** Persona que abandona su hogar para buscar protección contra la guerra, la persecución o algún otro peligro. Pág. 597

**Regional security alliances/Alianzas regionales de seguridad** Tratados mediante los cuales los Estados Unidos y otros países han acordado actuar colectivamente para enfrentar una agresión en una determinada parte del mundo. Pág. 492

**Register/Padrón** Registro o lista de nombres, a menudo bajo el cuidado de un funcionario asignado para esa labor. Pág. 439

**Registration/Registro** Procedimiento de identificación del voto pensado para evitar votaciones fraudulentas. Pág. 154

**Regressive tax/Impuesto regresivo** Gravamen con una tasa semejante, sin considerar el nivel de ingreso de los contribuyentes o su capacidad para pagarlo. Págs. 451, 741

**Repeal/Revocación** Derogación. Pág. 37

**Representative government/Gobierno representativo** Sistema de gobierno en el que las políticas públicas están elaboradas por funcionarios elegidos por los votantes y que rinden cuentas en elecciones periódicas; *ver* democracy/democracia. Pág. 29

**Reprieve/Suspensión** Un aplazamiento oficial de la ejecución de una sentencia; *ver* pardon/perdón. Págs. 407, 699

**Reservation/Reservación** Terrenos públicos que un gobierno reserva para el uso de las tribus nativas estadounidenses. Pág. 596

**Reserved powers/Poderes reservados** Aquellos poderes que la Constitución no otorga al gobierno nacional, pero que tampoco niega, al mismo tiempo a los estados. Pág. 92

**Resolution/Resolución** Medida relativa al funcionamiento de cualquier Cámara, o una expresión de opinión sobre un asunto; no tiene la fuerza de una ley y no requiere la firma del Presidente. Pág. 335

**Revenue sharing/Participación en los ingresos** Forma de ayuda monetaria federal, vigente de 1972 a 1987, bajo la cual el Congreso daba una participación anual de los ingresos tributarios, sin que virtualmente hubiera ninguna restricción en su uso, a los estados y sus ciudades, condados y villas. Pág. 102

**Reverse discrimination/Discriminación inversa** Segregación en contra del grupo mayoritario. Pág. 610

**Right of association/Derecho de asociación** Derecho de asociarse con otros para promover causas políticas, sociales, económicas y de otra índole. Pág. 558

**Right of legation/Derecho de legación** Derecho a enviar y recibir representantes diplomáticos. Pág. 470

**Rider/Cláusula adicional** Provisión poco probable de ser aprobada por méritos propios, que se agrega a un proyecto de ley importante que se tiene la seguridad que será aprobado, así que dicha cláusula "cabalga" por todo ese proceso legislativo. Pág. 335

**Rule of law/Gobierno de la ley** *ver* constitutionalism/constitucionalismo. Pág. 66.

**Runoff primary/Elección primaria complementaria** Elección primaria en la que los dos candidatos con más votos en la elección primaria directa se enfrentan; el ganador de esa votación se convierte en el nominado. Pág. 184

**Sales tax/Impuesto a las ventas** Gravamen sobre las ventas de distintos bienes, el cual paga el comprador. Pág. 741

**Sample/Muestra** Una porción representativa del público. Pág. 218

**Search warrant/Orden de allanamiento** Autorización judicial para hacer registros. Pág. 566

**Secretary/Secretario** Funcionario a cargo de un departamento de gobierno. Pág. 424

**Sectionalism/Regionalismo** Preocupación estrecha, o devoción por los intereses de una región del país. Pág. 129

**Sedition/Sedición** Crimen de intentar derrocar al gobierno mediante la fuerza, o de interrumpir las actividades legales por medio de actos violentos. Pág. 547

**Seditious speech/Discurso sedicioso** El llamado o el apoyo a un intento de derrocar al gobierno mediante la fuerza, o a la interrupción de actividades legales por medio de la violencia. Pág. 547

**Segregation/Segregación** Separación de un grupo respecto a otro. Pág. 602

**Select committee/Comité selecto** Comité legislativo creado por un tiempo limitado y para algún propósito específico; también se conoce como comité especial. Pág. 331

**Senatorial courtesy/Cortesía senatorial** Costumbre de que el Senado no aprobará una nominación presidencial, si esa designación no es aprobada por el senador del partido mayoritario de ese estado, en donde la persona designada habría de servir. Pág. 81

**Seniority rule/Regla de antigüedad** Regla no escrita de ambas Cámaras del Congreso, de acuerdo con la cual, los puestos más altos de cada una de ellas los ocuparán aquellos miembros que tengan un historial de servicio más antiguo; se aplica de forma más estricta a las presidencias de los comités. Pág. 326

**Separate-but-equal doctrine/Doctrina de iguales pero separados** Base constitucional para leyes que segregan a un grupo respecto a otro, con base en la raza. (Leyes Jim Crow.) Pág. 602.

**Separation of powers/Separación de poderes** Principio básico del sistema de gobierno estadounidense, según el cual los poderes ejecutivo, legislativo y judicial están divididos en tres ramas independientes e iguales; *ver* checks and balances/pesos y contrapesos. Pág. 66

**Session/Sesión** Período regular durante el cual reune el Congreso para atender a asuntos oficiales. Pág. 264

**Shadow cabinet/Gabinete alterno** Miembros de los partidos de oposición que vigilan, o supervisan, a un miembro particular del gabinete, y que estarían listos para ejercer el gobierno. Pág. 629

**Shield law/Ley Escudo** Ley que ofrece a los reporteros cierta protección contra la revelación de sus fuentes o la publicación de otra información confidencial durante los procedimientos legales. Pág. 550

**Single-interest group/Grupos de un único interés** Comités de acción política que concentran sus esfuerzos exclusivamente en un solo asunto. Pág. 251

**Single-issue parties/Partidos de un único asunto** Partidos que se concentran en un solo aspecto de la política pública. Pág. 132

**Single-member district/Distrito de un solo miembro** Distrito electoral en donde los votantes eligen, en la papeleta electoral, una sola persona para cada cargo. Págs. 120, 270

**Slander/Calumnia** Utilización falsa y maliciosa del discurso hablado. Pág. 547

**Socialism/Socialismo** Filosofía económica y política basada en la idea de que los beneficios de la actividad económica deberían distribuirse de manera equitativa a toda la sociedad. Pág. 666

**Soft money/Fondos no fiscalizados** Fondos otorgados al estado y a organizaciones partidistas locales para actividades relacionadas con el voto, por ejemplo: registro de votantes, envío de propaganda por correo, anuncios. Pág. 201

**Sound bite/Informe sucinto** Informaciones breves y concisas que pueden despacharse en 30 ó 45 segundos. Pág. 229

**Sovereign/Soberano** Tener poder supremo y absoluto dentro de su propio territorio; no estar subordinado ni ser responsable ante ninguna otra autoridad. Pág. 6

**Soviets/Soviets** Consejo de gobierno elegido por el pueblo y que lo representa. Pág. 646

**Speaker of the House/Vocero de la Cámara** Funcionario que preside la Cámara de Representantes y que es electo por el partido mayoritario en la Cámara, al cual pertenece. Pág. 322

**Special district/Distrito especial** Unidad independiente creada para llevar a cabo una o más funciones gubernamentales relacionadas a nivel local. Pág. 722

**Special session/Sesión especial** Sesión extraordinaria de un cuerpo legislativo, convocada para tratar una situación de emergencia. Pág. 265

**Splinter parties/Partidos de escisión** Partidos formados por la fractura de uno de los principales partidos; la mayor parte de los partidos pequeños importantes en el ámbito político estadounidense son partidos de escisión. Pág. 133

**Split-ticket voting/Voto diferenciado** Votar, en la misma elección, por candidatos de distintos partidos para puestos diferentes. Págs. 141, 171

**Spoils system/Sistema de prebendas** Práctica de ofrecer cargos y otros favores gubernamentales a los simpatizantes y amigos políticos. Pág. 438

**Staff agency/Oficina de apoyo** Tipo de agencia cuya función es dar respaldo al Presidente y a otros administradores, ofreciendo consejos y otro tipo de asistencia en la administración de la organización. Pág. 418

**Standing committee/Comisión permanente** Comité permanente de un cuerpo legislativo a quien se presentan las propuestas de ley sobre una materia específica; *ver* comité selecto. Pág. 329

**State/Estado** Conjunto de personas que viven en un territorio definido y que tienen un gobierno con el poder de legislar y de hacer cumplir la ley, sin tener el consentimiento de una autoridad superior. Pág. 5

**Statutory law/Ley estatuida** Ley aprobada por los legisladores. Pág. 688

**Straight-ticket voting/Voto duro** Práctica de votar en una elección por los candidatos de un solo partido. Pág. 171

**Straw vote/Encuesta pre-electoral** Encuestas que pretenden conocer la opinión de la gente haciendo simplemente la misma pregunta a una gran cantidad de personas. Pág. 217

**Strict constructionist/Construccionista estricto** Persona que defiende una interpretación estrecha de las estipulaciones de la Constitución, en particular las referentes al otorgamiento de poderes al gobierno federal. Pág. 291

**Strong-mayor government/Gobierno de alcalde vigoroso** Tipo de gobierno en el que el alcalde encabeza la administración de la ciudad. Pág. 727

**Subcommittee/Subcomité** División de un comité existente que se forma para atender asuntos específicos. Pág. 336

**Subpoena/Citación** Orden para que se presente una persona o para que se elaboren documentos u otros materiales solicitados. Pág. 313

**Subsidy/Subsidio** Una subvención de dinero, por lo general por un gobierno. Pág. 197

**Substantive due process/Proceso legal duradero** El gobierno debe crear políticas y leyes justas. Pág. 565

**Successor/Sucesor** Persona que hereda un título o un cargo. Pág. 311

**Suffrage/Sufragio** El derecho de votar. Pág. 148

**Surplus/Superávit** Cuando hay más ingresos que gastos. Pág. 455

**Symbolic speech/Discurso simbólico** Expresión mediante la conducta; comunicación de ideas a través de expresiones faciales, lenguaje corporal o mediante el uso de un signo o portando una banda en el brazo. Pág. 551

**Tax/Impuesto** Cargo gravado por el gobierno a las personas o propiedades, con el objeto de satisfacer las necesidades públicas. Pág. 295

**Tax return/Declaración de impuestos** Declaración del ingreso gravable y de las exenciones y deducciones exigidas. Pág. 449

**Term/Término** Lapso especificado durante el cual se desempeñará en el cargo un funcionario elegido. Pág. 264

**Terrorism/Terrorismo** El uso de violencia para intimidar a un gobierno o sociedad. Pág. 478

**Three-Fifths Compromise/Avenencia de las tres quintas partes** Acuerdo logrado en la Convención Constitucional respecto a que un esclavo debería contarse como tres quintas partes de una persona, para propósitos de determinar la población de un estado. Pág. 52

**Totalitarian/Totalitario** Gobierno que ejerce un poder (autoridad) dictatorial en casi todos los aspectos de los asuntos humanos. Pág. 14

**Township/Municipio** División de un condado. Pág. 718

**Trade association/Asociación comercial** Grupos de interés dentro de la comunidad de los negocios. Pág. 244

**Transient/Transeúnte** Persona que vive en un estado sólo por un breve tiempo, sin residencia legal. Pág. 153

**Treason/Alta traición** Deslealtad hacia el país propio; en la Constitución, librar una guerra en contra de los Estados Unidos, proporcionar aliento u ofrecer ayuda a sus enemigos. Pág. 588

**Treaty/Tratado** Acuerdo formal entre dos o más estados soberanos. Págs. 80, 399

**Trust/Cartel** Mecanismo mediante el cual diversas corporaciones de la misma línea de negocios se ponen de acuerdo para eliminar a la competencia y regular los precios. Pág. 661

**Trustee/Independiente** Legislador que vota en cada asunto de acuerdo con su conciencia y su juicio independiente, sin considerar las opiniones de sus electores o de otros grupos. Pág. 281

**Two-party system/Sistema bipartidista** Sistema político dominado por dos partidos importantes. Pág. 119

**UN Security Council/Consejo de Seguridad de la ONU** Panel de 15 miembros que tiene la máxima responsabilidad de la ONU para la conservación de la paz internacional. Pág. 496

**Unconstitutional/Inconstitucional** Contrario a las estipulaciones constitucionales y, por lo tanto, ilegal, nulo e inválido, que no tiene fuerza ni efecto. Pág. 69

**Uncontrollable spending/Gasto incontrolable** Gastos que ni el Congreso ni el Presidente tienen el poder de cambiar de manera directa, incluyendo los intereses de la deuda. Pág. 459

**Unicameral/Unicameral** Adjetivo que describe un cuerpo legislativo con una sola Cámara; *ver* bicameral. Pág. 32

**Unitary government/Gobierno unitario** Gobierno centralizado en el que los poderes ejercidos por el gobierno pertenecen a una única oficina central. Pág. 14

**Urbanization/Urbanización** Porcentaje de la población de un estado que vive en ciudades de más de 250,000 personas, o en los suburbios de las ciudades que tienen más de 50,000 habitantes. Pág. 737

**Veto/Veto** Poder del Presidente para rechazar un proyecto de ley aprobado por una legislatura; literalmente (latín) "Prohíbo"; *ver* pocket veto/veto indirecto. Págs. 67, 346

**Virginia Plan/Plan Virginia** Proyecto presentado por los delegados de Virginia en la Convención Constitucional; proponía un gobierno con tres poderes y una legislatura bicameral en la que la representación de cada estado estuviera determinada por su población o por su apoyo financiero al gobierno central. Pág. 51

**Ward/Distrito** Unidad en la que suelen dividirse las ciudades para la elección de los miembros del consejo municipal. Pág. 140

**Warrant/Mandamiento** Orden judicial que autoriza o hace legal alguna acción oficial, como la orden de allanamiento o la orden de arresto. Pág. 708

**Weak-mayor government/Gobierno de alcalde débil** Tipo de gobierno en el que el alcalde comparte las obligaciones ejecutivas con otros funcionarios electos. Pág. 727

**Welfare/Beneficencia** Ayuda en efectivo a los pobres. Pág. 735

**Welfare state/Estado benefactor** Países que ofrecen una amplia gama de servicios sociales a un bajo costo o de manera gratuita para los usuarios. Pág. 668

**Whips/Whips** Auxiliares de los líderes de las fracciones partidistas en la Cámara de Representantes y el Senado que son responsables de vigilar y ordenar los votos. Pág. 325

**Winner-take-all/El ganador se lleva todo** Sistema casi obsoleto en donde un aspirante presidencial que ganaba la preferencia del voto en las elecciones primarias, automáticamente obtenía el apoyo de todos los delegados elegidos en dichas elecciones. Pág. 371

**Writ of assistance/Auto de ayuda** Orden general de allanamiento con la que los funcionarios aduanales británicos invadían los hogares privados en busca de bienes de contrabando. Pág. 571

**Writ of certiorari/Auto de avocación *o certiorari*** Orden emitida por una corte superior dirigida a una corte inferior para que remita el expediente de un determinado caso para su revisión; el significado en latín de la expresión es "tener mayor certeza". Pág. 520

**Writ of habeas corpus/Auto de *habeas corpus*** Orden judicial que evita arrestos y encarcelamientos injustos. Pág. 576

**Zoning/Zonificación** Práctica de dividir a una ciudad en determinado número de distritos y de regular los usos que se dará a la propiedad en cada uno de ellos. Pág. 730

# SE/TE Index

**Note:** Entries with a page number followed by an *(c)* denote reference to a chart on that page; those followed by a *(p)* denote a photo; those followed by a *(m)* denote a map; those followed by a *(g)* denote a graph. Entries in blue can be found in the Teacher's Edition wrap.

SE/TE Index

# Acknowledgments

**Team Credits** The people who made up the **Magruder's American Government** team—representing editorial, editorial services, design services, market research, on-line services/multimedia development, product marketing, production services, and publishing processes—are listed below. Bold type denotes core team members.

**Joyce Barisano, Roger Calado,** Todd Christy, Bob Craton, Deborah Dukeshire, **Paul Gagnon, Mary Hanisco, Lance Hatch,** Kerri Hoar, Katharine Ingram, Marcia Lord, Chris Maniatis, **Dotti Marshall, Grace Massey,** Judi Pinkham, Dorothy Preston, Lynn Robbins, **Luess Sampson-Lizotte,** Emily Soltanoff, Mark Staloff, Susan Swan, Merce Wilczek

## Cover Design
Sweetlight Creative Partners; Paul Gagnon

## Cover Image
The White House: Peter Gridley/FTG International

## Illustration
**Tables and graphs:** Accurate Art, Inc., Outlook/ANCO, and Matt Mayerchak **Creative Art:** Steve Artley **20, 145, 185, 201, 240, 349, 383, 558, 579, 585, 621;** Annie Bissett **133;** Jim Bliss **134;** Kathy W. Boake **738;** Doug Bowles **453;** James Bozzini **517;** Ken Condon **344;** Richard Ewing **291, 518;** Leighton & Co./Lisa Manning **6, 659;** MapQuest.com, Inc **72;** Karen Minot **16, 31, 57, 73, 101, 128–129,140, 151, 180, 183, 184, 191, 193, 199, 209, 219, 266, 276, 280, 295, 304, 308, 322, 333, 367, 369, 380, 395, 400, 417, 439, 461, 509, 510, 513, 523, 541, 565, 578, 587, 595, 614, 615, 687, 697, 719, 727, 728, 729;** Brucie Rosch **155, 575;** Neil Stewart **68, 330, 345, 420, 426, 472, 507, 514, 520;** Baker Vail **100, 263, 268, 270, 271, 487, 492, 630, 638, 642, 647, 651, 724**

## Picture Research
Paula Wehde

## Photography
**Front Matter Page i,** ©2000 Tom Wachs/Washington Stock Photo, Inc.

**Table of Contents Page iv tl,** National Portrait Gallery, Smithsonian Institution/Art Resource, NY; **iv m,** H. Armstrong Roberts; **iv bl, bm,** The Granger Collection, New York; **iv br,** AP Photo/Dennis Cook; **v bl,** Russ Lappa; **v tr,** Corbis-Bettman; **v m,** P.F. Gyro/Corbis Sygma; **v br,** Daemmrich/Corbis Sygma; **vi tl,** Jeffery S. Underwood, Ph.D.,United States Air Force Museum Historian; **vi bl,** Collection of Ralph J. Brunke; **vi br,** UPI/Corbis-Bettmann; **vi inset,** Collection of Bette Lane. Photograph ©Rob Huntley/Lightstream; **vii t,** Corbis; **vii tm,** White House Historical Association; **vii bm,** Dennis Brack/Black Star; **vii b,** D. Hudson/Corbis Sygma; **viii tl,** Corbis; **viii bl,** Sandra Baker/Liaison Agency; **viii bm,** Corbis-Bettmann; **viii br,** SuperStock; **ix t,** Corbis-Bettmann; **ix m,** AP/Wide World Photos; **ix b,** Paula Lerner/Woodfin Camp & Associates; **x,** White House Historical Association; **xi,** Richard Bloom/ SABA Press Photos; **xii l,** The Granger Collection, New York; **xii r,** Corbis; **xiii,** The Granger Collection, New York; **xvi t,** Tony Freeman/PhotoEdit; **xvi b,** Art Resource, New York; **xvii tl,** D. Lada/H. Armstrong Roberts; **xvii tm,** H. Armstrong Roberts; **xvii tr,** A.Tovy/H. Armstrong Roberts; **xvii ml, mr,** Supreme Court Historical Society; **xvii bl,** Joe Sohm/Visions of America.

**UNIT 1 Page xx–1,** Smithsonian Institution; **2–3,** Corbis-Bettman; **4 all,** Visions of America; **5,** Thomas E. Franklin/Bergen Record/Corbis SABA; **7 tl,** The Granger Collection, New York; **7 bl,** Brenda Carter/ National Geographic Society; **7 m,** Erich Lessing/Art Resource; **7 r,** Corbis-Bettmann; **8,** By permission of Johnny Hart and Creators Syndicate, Inc.; **9,** AP Photo/Tim Sharp; **11,** The Granger Collection, New York; **13,** Deb Hebib/Concord Monitor/Impact Visuals; **14 l,** Memorial De Caen/Sygma; **14 r,** Tom Wurl/Stock Boston; **17,** Pictures Now; **18,** The Granger Collection, New York; **19,** ChromoSohm/Sohm; **21,** Dick Blume/The Image Works; **25,** ©The New Yorker Collection 1983 Ed Fisher from cartoonbank.com. All Rights Reserved.; **26–27,** A. Kord/H. Armstrong Roberts; **28,** ©Christie's Images, Ltd. 1999; **29, 33,** The Granger Collection, New York; **34,** Colonial Williamsburg Foundation; **35,** National Portrait Gallery, Smithsonian Institution/Art Resource, New York; **36, 37,** The Granger Collection, New York; **40,** Independence National Historic Park Collection; **41,** SuperStock; **41–42,** Corbis-Bettmann; **42 t,** ©1997 North Wind Pictures; **42 b,** SuperStock; **43,** Corbis; **44, 46,** The Granger Collection, New York; **47,** G. Ahrens/H. Armstrong Roberts; **48,** The Granger Collection, New York; **50,** Art Resource, New York; **52,** Museum of American Textile History, Grant Heilman Photography; **54,** Independence National Historic Park Collection; **56,** American Antiquarian Society; **58 l,** Corbis-Bettmann; **58 m,** The Library Company of Philadelphia; **58 r, 61,** The Granger Collection, New York; **62–63,** Art Resource, New York; **64, 64–65,** The Granger Collection, New York; **65,** AP Photo/Dennis Cook; **66,** Hulton Getty; **67,** J.B. Handelsman/cartoonbank.com; **68 l,** D. Lada/H. Armstrong Roberts; **68 m,** H. Armstrong Roberts; **68 r,** A.Tovy/H. Armstrong Roberts; **69,** SuperStock; **69,** Dennis Brack/Black Star; **70,** Kevin Flaming/Corbis; **71,** Paul Scott/Corbis Sygma; **74,** The Granger Collection, New York; **75 t, 75 bl,** UPI/Corbis-Bettmann; **75 br,** H. Armstrong Roberts; **77,** Dave Schaefer/The Picture Cube; **78,** The Granger Collection, New York; **79,** Russ Lappa; **80 t,** Wernher Krutein/Liaison Agency; **80 b,** Peter Turnley/Black Star; **81,** The Granger Collection, New York; **82 l,** Russ Lappa; **82 r,** Archive Photos; **85,** Ed Fisher/cartoonbank.com; **86–87,** Joe Sohm/Visions of America; **88,** Tony Freeman/PhotoEdit; **89 t,** Les Stone/Sygma; **89 b,** David R. Frazier Photolibrary/ Photo Researchers; **90 l,** Mark C. Burnett/Stock Boston; **90 m,** Jeff Greenberg/Stock Boston; **90 r,** AP Photo; **91,** Amy Toensing/Corbis Sygma; **92,** Dave Lawrence/The Stock Market; **94 ,** Index Stock Imagery; **96,** Stock Boston; **97,** The Granger Collection, New York; **98,** NOAA/Science Photo Library/Photo Researchers; **99,** Lazaro Fresquet; **101,** Michael Dwyer/Stock Boston; **102,** Bob Daemmrich/Stock Boston; **104,** Skjold Photographs; **105,** David N. Davis/Photo Researchers; **106,** Russ Lappa; **107,** Bob Daemmrich/Stock Boston; **108,** David Sailors/The Stock Market; **111,** Frank Cotham/cartoonbank.com.

**UNIT 2 Page 112–113,** Sipa Press; **114–115,** Richard Ellis/Corbis Sygma; **116 both,** Ian Wagreich/Illustrative Images; **117,** Daemmrich/Corbis Sygma; **118 l,r,** Ian Wagreich /Illustrative Images; **118 m,** Najlah Feanny/SABA Press Photos; **119,** Russ Lappa; **120,** Michael Smith/Liaison Agency; **121 t,** "Dunagin's People" by Ralph Dunagin, Reprinted with special permission of N.A.S., Inc.; **121 b,** Larry Downing/Corbis Sygma; **122,** Regis Bossu/Corbis Sygma; **123,** National Portrait Gallery, Smithsonian Institution, Art Resource, New York; **125,** The Granger Collection, New York; **126,** Museum of American Political Life, University of Hartford, West Hartford, CT; **127 both,** The Granger Collection, New York; **128,** Museum of American Political Life, University of Hartford, West Hartford, CT; **131,** Donald Reilly; **132 t,** Museum of American Political Life; **132 bl, br,** Russ Lappa; **134 r,** Corbis; **134 the rest,** The Granger Collection, New York; **136,** AP Photo/Rich Pedronelli; **137,** Joe Sohm/The Image Works; **139 l,** Laimute Druskis/Stock Boston; **139 r,** AP Photo/File; **141 t,** AP Photo/Rick Wilking; **141 bl,** Dunagin; **141 br,** Steve Sack; **146–147,** The Piedmont Library/Art Resource, New York; **148 l,** Joe Griffin/Archive Photos; **148 r,** The Granger Collection, New York; **149 t,** Bob Daemmrich Photography; **149 l,** The Granger Collection, New York; **149 r,** Library of Congress; **151,** Prentice Hall; **152,** Joseph Sohm/ChromoSohm; **153,** ©1870 Harper's Weekly; **154,**"Taylor"/*Albuquerque Tribune,* N.M./Rothco; **155,** Mauldin/© 1952 *St. Louis Post-Dispatch;* **157,** © 1978 Matt Herron/Take Stock; **158,** ©2000 Mick Stevens from cartoonbank.com. All rights reserved.; **159,** Eve Arnold/Magnum Photos; **160,** The Granger Collection, New York; **161 both,** Corbis-Bettmann; **162,** Charles Moore/Black Star; **163,** Corbis-Bettmann; **165,** "ROB ROGERS" Reprinted by permission of UFS, Inc.; **166,** KAL/*The Baltimore Sun;* **169 t,** Gordon Hodge/Corbis Sygma; **169 inset,** A. Ramey/Stock Boston; **171,** Tom Vano; **175,** © 1986 *The Philadelphia Inquirer.* Reprinted with permission of Universal Press Syndicate. All rights reserved.; **176–177,** Michael Newman/PhotoEdit; **178,** Spencer Grant/PhotoEdit; **179 l,** ©1968 Burt Glinn/Magnum Photos, Inc.; **179 ml,** Owen Franken/ Stock Boston; **179 mr,** Arthur Grace/Corbis Sygma; **179 r,** ©1992 Matthew McVay/SABA Press Photos; **181 both,** The Museum of American Political Life, University of Hartford, West Hartford, CT; **182,** "Dunagin's People" by Ralph Dunagin. Reprinted with special permission of N.A.S., Inc.; **186,** J. Patrick Forden/Corbis Sygma; **187,** UPI/Corbis-Bettman; **188,** Haviv/SABA Press Photos; **189,** Rick Friedman/Black Star; **192,** The Museum of American Political Life, University of Hartford, West Hartford, CT; **194,** Russ Lappa; **195 t,** Bob Daemmrich/Stock Boston; **195 b,** Tony Freeman/PhotoEdit; **196,** Federal Election Commission; **198 l,** Russ Lappa; **198 m,** Paul Conklin/PhotoEdit; **198 r,** Peter Blakely/SABA Press Photos; **202,** ©The New Yorker Collection, 1997 Mick Stevens from cartoonbank.com. All Rights Reserved.; **205,** Steve Sack; **206–207,** NCSA, University of Illinois/Science Photo Library/Photo Researchers, Inc.; **209,** Booth/cartoonbank.com; **210 l,** Gabe Kirchheimer/Black Star; **210 m,** Bob Daemmrich Photography; **210 r,** Tony Freeman/PhotoEdit; **213,** Detroit News; **214,** AP Photo/Harry Cabluck; **215,** R. Ellis/Corbis Sygma; **216,** Najlah Feanny/SABA Press Photos; **217 t,** Harris Interactive; **217 b,** Prentice Hall; **218,** Reprinted by permission of United Features Syndicate; **220,** Corbis; **221,** By permission of Mike Luckovich and Creators Syndicate; **222 l,** Dana White/ PhotoEdit; **222 r,** Concept by Tassos Gioia at Avote.com; **223, 224 l,** Corbis; **224 r,** Bob Daemmrich Photo, Inc.; **226,** Sam Saregent/Liaison Agency; **228,** Patrick Forestier/ Corbis Sygma; **229,** Courtesy of Joseph Turow; **230,** Russ Lappa; **233,** MacNelly/MacNelly.com/*Chicago Tribune*; **234–235,** ©1999 Thomas Dodge/AGStockUSA; **236,** Russ Lappa; **237 l,** Families USA; **237 m,** P.F. Gyro/Corbis Sygma; **237 r,** Bob Daemmrich/Stock Boston; **238, 239,** David Maung/Impact Visuals; **242,** Bob Daemmrich/The Image Works; **243** both, Courtesy of Lake Norman Chamber of Commerce; **244,** Antoine Serra/Corbis Sygma; **245 l,** Porterfield-Chickering/ Photo Researchers, Inc.; **245 r,** Lianne Enkelis/Stock Boston; **246,** Martin Simon/SABA Press Photos; **248,** AP Photo/Ron Edmonds; **249,** Austin Arc ; **250 t,** Paul Conklin/PhotoEdit; **250 b,** Ira Wyman/Corbis Sygma; **251,** Mike Keefe/Courtesy *Denver Post;* **252 t,** © 1993 Washington Stock Photo; **252 b,** David Young-Wolff/ PhotoEdit; **253 l,** American Conservative Union; **253 r,** ACLU; **257,** Schwadron/Rothco.

**UNIT 3 Page 258–259,** R. Krubner/H. Armstrong Roberts; **260–261,** Ian Wagreich /Illustrative Images; **262,** Ken Lambert/*Washington Times* via Newsmakers/Liaison Agency; **265,** AP/Wide World Photos; **266,** Corbis; **271,** Corbis-Bettmann; **273,** Troy Glasgow/Black Star; **274,** Kevin Siers, *The Charlotte Observer,* King Features Syndicate; **275,** The Granger Collection, New York; **278,** ©1890 Puck; **279,** AP Photo/Linda Spillers; **281,** Richard Ellis/Getty Images; **282 l and m,** Courtesy of Rep. Ileana Ros-Lehtinen; **282 r,** Ian Wagreich/Illustrative Images; **283,** Joseph Farris/cartoonbank.com; **287,** © 1999 by Herblock in *The Washington Post;* **288–289,** Markel/Liaison Agency; **290,** Library of Congress; **291 t,** Courtesy, Office of Secretary of Education; **292,** Bob Artley, Courtesy *Washington* (Minn) *Daily Globe;* **293,** Jeff Greenberg/New England Stock Photography; **294,** Najlah Feanny/Stock Boston; **297,** The Granger Collection, New York; **298 l,** Jim Leynse/SABA Press Photos; **298 r,** Erica Langner/Black Star; **298 inset,** PhotoDisc, Inc.; **299 b,** Courtesy Cybercoin; **299 the rest,** Courtesy of the Federal Reserve Bank of San Francisco; **300,** Andrew Sacks/AGStockUSA; **303 all,** Russ Lappa; **305,** "The Federal Procession in N.Y., 1788" from Lamb's History of the City of N.Y. American Antiquarian Society. Hand-colored by Sandi Rygiel/Picture Research Consultants; **306 l,** Library of Congress; **306 r,** Collection of Ralph J. Brunke; **307 t,** Jeffery S. Underwood, Ph.D.,United States Air Force Museum Historian; **307 b,** Harry Edelman/Black Star; **309,** R. Ellis/Corbis Sygma; **310,** UPI/Corbis-Bettmann; **310 inset,** Collection of Bette Lane. Photograph©Rob Huntley/Lightstream; **311 tl,** SuperStock; **311 bl,** Collection of Bill McClenaghan; **311 tr,** Corbis; **311 br,** Terry Ashe/Liaison Agency; **313,** RolandFreeman/Magnum Photos; **314,** Corbis; **317,** © 2000 by Herblock in the *Washington Post;* **318–319,** Ian Wagreich /Illustrative Images; **320,** United States Congress; **321,** Brad Markel/Liaison Agency; **322,** Tribune Media

Services; **323,** AP Photo/Ron Edmonds; **327,** AP Photo/Joe Marquette; **328,** Brad Markel/Liaison Agency; **329,** AP Photos/U.S. Mint; **330,** A.Tovy/H. Armstrong Roberts; **334,** United States House of Representatives; **336, 337,** Corbis; **338,** Tomaschoff, Rheinische Post, Dusseldorf Germany/ Creators & Writers Syndicate; **339,** Courtesy of Rivers for Congress; **341 both,** The Granger Collection, New York; **342,** United States Senate; **343,** AP/Wide World Photos; **346,** Kevin Lamarque/Getty Images.

**UNIT 4 Page 350–351,** Peter Gridley/FPG International; **352–353,** Jim Verchio/USAF/Getty Images; **354,** White House Historical Society; **355,** Markel/Liaison Agency; **356 t,** Corbis; **356 b,** The Granger Collection, New York; **357 t,** Allan Tannenbaum/Corbis Sygma; **357 b,** Benainous-Hires-Rey/Liaison Agency; **358,** Dennis Brack/Black Star; **359,** AP Photo/White House, Cecil Stoughton; **360,** Martha Bates/Stock Boston; **361 l,** Russ Lappa; **361 r,** Fred Ward/Black Star; **362,** Frank Cotham from cartoonbank.com; **363,** Reuters News Media/Corbis; **364,** Michael Philippot/Corbis Sygma; **365,** Sally Andersen-Bruce/Museum of American Political Life; **365 buttons,** Museum of American Political Life; **366 l,** The Granger Collection, New York; **366 m and r, 370 t,** Corbis; **370 b,** Courtesy George W. Bush Campaign Website; **371,** Corbis; **372,** Ohman/Tribune Media Services; **373,** David Young-Wolff/PhotoEdit; **374 t,** Ian Wagreich/ Illustrative Images; **374 b,** AP Photo/Dan Loh; **378 tl** and **tr,** Ian Wagreich/Illustrative Images; **378 b,** Bob Daemmrich/ Corbis Sygma; **379 l,** ©1993 Joseph Sohm/ChromoSohm/Photo Researchers, Inc.; **379 r,** White House; **387,** The New Yorker Collection 1987, Charles Barsotti from cartoonbank.com; **388–389,** AP Photo/Kenneth Lambert; **390,** J.L. Atlan/Corbis Sygma; **391** Adams, Garfield, McKinley, Taft, Art Resource, New York; **391 the rest,** White House Historical Association; **393,** St. John's Masonic Lodge of New York; **394 tr,** Richard Strauss/Smithsonian Institution; **394 top insets,** Jeff Tinsley/Smithsonian Institution; **394 bl,** AP Photo/Steve Helber; **395,** Rob Crandall/Stock Boston; **396,** AP/Wide World Photos; **397,** Courtesy *News & Observer* (N.C.) Distributed by L.A. Times Syndicate; **398 l,** Dennis Brack/Black Star; **398 r,** J.P. Laffont/Corbis Sygma; **399,** Bettmann/Corbis; **400,** AP Photo/Thomas Van Houtryve; **401 t,** The Granger Collection, New York; **401 tm, m,** Corbis; **401 bm,** D. Hudson/Corbis Sygma; **401b,** AP Photo/Eric Draper; **402,** AFP Corbis; **404, 405,** Corbis; **406,** Special Collections Bowdoin Library; **407,** Chicago Historical Society; **408,** AP/Wide World Photos; **411,** ©1999 Herblock/*The Washington Post;* **412–413,** AP Photo/Doug Mills; **414,** Russ Lappa; **415,** Corbis Sygma; **416 l,** U.S. Securities and Exchange Commision; **416 m,** Federal Bureau of Investigation; **416 r,** Farm Credit Administration Agency; **417 l,** A.Tovy/H. Armstrong Roberts; **417 m,** H. Armstrong Roberts; **417 r,** D. Lada/H. Armstrong Roberts; **419,** Dirck Halstead/Liaison Agency; **421 l,** Corbis; **421 m,** U.S. Department of Health and Human Services; **421 r,** A. Ramey/PhotoEdit; **423,** The Granger Collection, New York; **424,** The Granger Collection, New York; **425 l,** Paul Conclin/PhotoEdit; **425 m,** Cary Wolinsky/Stock Boston; **425 r,** Rob Crandall/Stock Boston; **428,** AFP Corbis; **429,** Drew Shenemen/Courtesy of *Newark Star Ledger;* **430,** Russ Lappa; **431,** Larry Downing/Corbis Sygma; **433,** Russ Lappa; **434,** Milepost 92 1/2 /Corbis; **436,** Central Intelligence Agency; **437,** Corbis; **438,** Library of Congress; **443,** Reprinted by permission, Tribune Media Services; **444–445,** AP Photo/Dan Loh; **446,** Jim Berry/NEA, Inc.; **447 l,** Dagmar Ehling/Photo Researchers, Inc.; **447 m,** Sam Saregent/Liaison Agency; **447 r,** Frank Siteman/Photri; **450,** Michael A. Dwyer/Stock Boston; **451,** Prentice Hall; **454,** Russ Lappa; **455,** Brad Markel/Liaison Agency; **457,** Steve Lindstrom/*Duluth News-Tribune;* **458,** Corbis; **459 l,** Tom McCarthy/Photri; **459 r,** Eric Horan/Liaison Agency; **459 inset,** Russ Lappa; **462,** Bruce Beattie/©98 *Daytona Beach News-Journal;* **465,** Draper Hill/Courtesy *Detroit News;* **465–467,** Carol Barneon/Black Star; **468,** The Granger Collection, New York; **469,** AFP Corbis; **470,** Alex Wong/Getty Images; **471,** Corbis; **474,** From THE BRASS RING, © 1971 by William Mauldin; **475,** Les Stone/Corbis Sygma; **476,** Corbis-Bettmann; **477 both,** US Coast Guard; **478,** AP Photo/Chris O'Meara; **479,** Stone; **481,** Sandra Baker/Liaison Agency; **483,** Library of Congress; **484,** National Archives; **487,** Corbis; **488,** Christopher Morris/Black Star; **491,** AP Photo/CARE; **494,** AP Photo/Misha Japardice; **495,** Doug Armand/Stone; **496,** Reuters NewMedia, Inc./Corbis; **497,** Russ Lappa; **501,** ©The New Yorker Collection 1985, James Stevensen from cartoonbank.com. All Rights Reserved.

**UNIT 5 Page 502–503,** P.Costas/Washington Stock Photo; **504–505,** Dennis Breck/Black Star; **508 t,** Sam C. Pierson, Jr. 1990/Photo Researchers, Inc.; **508 b,** Ian Wagreich/ Illustrative Images; **510,** Dennis Brack/Black Star; **512,** John Lennon/Corbis Sygma; **513,** Federal Court of Appeals for the 5th Circuit; **515,** Corbis Bettmann; **516,** Corbis Sygma; **519,** US Supreme Court; **520,** Dorothy Littell Greco/Stock Boston; **522,** Supreme Court Historical Society; **524 t,** US Claims Court; **524 b,** ©2000 John R. Welch, White Mountain Apache Tribe Historic Preservation Officer; **525 l,** Courtesy Judge Eugene R. Sullivan; **525 r,** U.S. Court of Appeals; **529,** Corbis-Bettmann; **530,** Camerique/H. Armstrong Roberts; **533,** UPI/Corbis-Bettmann; **534,** Corbis Sygma; **535,** Tony Freeman/PhotoEdit; **537,** The Granger Collection, New York; **538,** Bob Daemmrich/Stock Boston; **539,** Corbis; **541,** George Olsen/Woodfin Camp & Associates; **542,** Eunice Harris/Photo Researchers, Inc.; **543,** From the private collection of Rabbi Albert I. Slomovitz, Ph.D.; **545,** A. Ramey/Stock Boston; **546,** AP Photo/George Bridges; **547,** National Archives; **548,** Yates-Brickman/King Features Syndicate; **549,** Fred Ward/Black Star; **550,** International Stock; **552,** Michael Abramson/ Black Star; **554,** AP/Wide World Photos; **555,** Bob Daemmrich, Inc.; **557,** Laura Kleinhenz/SABA Press Photos; **561,** © The New Yorker Collection 1991, Mischa Richter from cartoonbank.com. All Rights Reserved.; **562–563,** Stone; **564,** Hulton GettyPicture Library; **566,** ©The New Yorker Collection 1970, J.B. Handelsman from cartoonbank.com. All Rights Reserved.; **569,** Michelle Agins/NYT Pictures; **570,** Marc Asnin/SABA Press Photos; **572,** Markel/Liaison Agency; **576,** Library of Congress; **580 l,** AP Photo/John Giles; **580 r,** Lauren Greenfield/Corbis Sygma; **581,** Wayne Stayskal/Courtesy *Tampa Tribune;* **583,** Corbis-Bettmann; **584,** Flip Schulke/Black Star; **586 l,** Andrew Lichenstein/Corbis Sygma; **586 r,** Kevin Maloney/Liaison Agency; **591,** ©The New Yorker Collection 1999, Jack Ziegler from cartoonbank.com. All Rights Reserved.; **592–593,** Corbis-Bettmann; **594,** Bob Daemmrich/Stock Boston; **596,** Fabian Falcon/Stock Boston; **597,** Matthew McVay/SABA Press Photos; **599,** Hulton Getty; **600,** Russ Lappa; **601,** Sandra Baker/Liaison Agency; **602,** Corbis; **603,** The Newark Art Museum/Art Resource, New York; **604,** Library of Congress; **605 l,** Corbis-Bettmann; **605 r,** Stock Boston; **607,** Corbis-Bettmann; **608,** SuperStock; **610,** AP Laser Photo; **611,** David Young-Wolff/PhotoEdit; **612,** Rod Rolle/Liaison Agency; **617,** Bill Aron/PhotoEdit; **618,** ©Don Wright, *The Palm Beach Post.*

**UNIT 6 Page 622–623,** AP Photo/Greg Baker; **624–625,** Ed Pritchard/Stone; **626,** National Archives; **627,** AP Photo/Max Nash/POOL; **628, 629,** Universal Pictorial Press Agency; **630,** Corbis; **631,** The Scottish Parliament; **632,** Universal Pictorial Press Agency; **633 t,** T. Graham/ Corbis Sygma; **633 b,** James Andanson/Corbis Sygma; **634,** The Granger Collection, New York; **635,** Krug/Action Press/SABA Press Photos; **636,** AP Photo/Itsuolnouye; **638,** Mayama/Liaison/Getty Images; **639,** J.P. Laffont/Corbis Sygma; **640,** Museum of Flight/Corbis; **641 l,** Woodfin Camp & Associates; **641 tr,** The Image Works; **641 br,** Lester Lefkowitz/The Stock Market; **642,** Corbis; **643,** Richard During/Stone; **644,** AP Photo/Marco Ugarte; **645,** Corbis; **646,** The Stock Market; **647,** Sergei Guneyev/SABA Press Photos; **648,** Jeffrey Mrkowitz/Corbis Sygma; **649,** James McCloskey/Courtesy *Staunton Daily News Leader;* **650,** The Granger Collection, New York; **651,** Porter Gifford/ Liaison Agency; **652,** Hugh Sitton/Stone; **655,** Gary Brookins/Courtesy *Richmond Times-Dispatch;* **656–657,** Joseph Sohm/Stock Boston; **658,** Myrleen Ferguson/ PhotoEdit; **660,** Jeff Greenberg/PhotoEdit; **661,** Steve Sack; **662,** Reiss/Action Press/SABA Press Photos; **663 l,** David Young-Wolff/PhotoEdit; **663 m,** Gary Conner/PhotoEdit; **663 r,** Michael L. Abramson/Woodfin Camp & Associates; **664,** Russ Lappa; **665,** Mathieu Polak/Corbis Sygma; **667 t,** Hulton Corbis; **667 inset,** Corbis; **668,** AP/Wide World Photos; **671,** Corbis Sygma; **672,** Sovfoto/Eastfoto; **673,** Owen Franken/Stock Boston; **674,** Sovfoto/Eastfoto; **675,** R. Ellis/Corbis Sygma; **675,** AP/Wide World Photos; **679,** Danziger.

**UNIT 7 Page 680–681,** Larry Lee/Corbis; **682-683,** Daemmrich/The Image Works; **684,** Texas State Library & Archives Commission; **685,** From The Rotarian, June, 1972. By permission of the publisher; **686,** Virginia Historical Society; **689,** Bob Daemmrich/Stock Boston; **690,** The Granger Collection, New York; **691 l,** Corbis; **691 r,** Najlan Feanny/SABA Press Photos; **692,** Bob Daemmrich/Stock Photo; **694,** Texas State Library & Archives Commission; **695,** AP Photo/Harry Cabluck; **696,** AP Photo/Eric Gay; **697,** Master Sgt. Anna M. Wagner, 100th Mobile Public Affairs Detachment Texas National Guard; **699 inset,** Bob Daemmrich Photo; **699,** Bob Daemmrich Photo; **701,** AP Photo/Deborah Cannon; **702,** North Wind Picture Archives; **703,** Bob Daemmrich/Pictor; **704,** ©The New Yorker Collection 1999, Michael Maslin from cartoonbank.com. All Rights Reserved; **706 t,** Russ Lappa; **706 b,** Bob Daemmrich/Stock Boston; **707,** National Archives; **709,** ©The New Yorker Collection 1999, Michael Maslin from cartoonbank.com. All Rights Reserved; **711 l,** Bob Daemmrich Photo; **711 r,** AP Photo/Richard Michael; **712,** Courtesy of the Office of Chief Justice Richard Barajas; **715,** Robert Mankoff/cartoonbank.com. All Rights Reserved; **716–717,** Bob Rowan/Corbis; **718,** Bob Daemmrich Photo; **720,** Bob Daemmrich/Stock Boston; **722,** Paula Learner/Woodfin Camp & Associates; **725,** Wolfgang Kaehler/Liaison Agency; **726 t,** Bob Daemmrich Photo; **726 b,** Bob Daemmrich Photo; **730 l,** The Granger Collection; **730 r,** R. Foulds/Washington Stock Photo; **731,** The Image Works; **732,** ©2001 The New Yorker Collection from cartoonbank.com. All Rights Reserved; **733,** Bob Daemmrich Photo; **734,** Bob Daemmrich Photo; **736 1,** David Buton/SABA Press Photos; **736 m,** Kevin Horan/Stock Boston; **736 r,** Wernher/Liaison Agency; **739,** Catherine Karnow/Woodfin Camp & Associates; **740,** Joe Raedle/Getty Images; **742,** Reprinted with permission from the Minneapolis Star and Tribune; **743,** Courtesy, Office of Carol Keeton Rylander; **747,** ©The New Yorker Collection 1955, Ed Fisher from cartoonbank.com. All Rights Reserved

**End Matter Page 748 background,** P. Costas/Washington Stock; **748 tl, tr,** The Granger Collection, New York; **748 mr,** Rob Crandall/Stock Boston; **748 bl,** UPI/Corbis-Bettmann; **748 br,** AP Photo/Stephan Savoia; **749,** The Granger Collection, New York; **754 all,** Art Resource, New York; **755 t,** White House; **755 the rest,** White House Historical Association; **797,** Library of Congress; **798,** Chicago Historical Society.

## Text Acknowledgments

**Page 78,** "Letters of Liberty" adapted, with permission from the publisher, from THE BILL OF RIGHTS: A USER'S GUIDE, © 2000. Close Up Foundation, Alexandria, Virginia; **96,** "The New Federalism: Two Views" adapted, with permission from the publisher, from PERSPECTIVES: READINGS ON CONTEMPORARY AMERICAN GOVERNMENT, © 1989. Close Up Foundation, Alexandria, Virginia; **158,** "The Dangers of Voter Apathy" reprinted, with permission from the publisher, from PERSPECTIVES: READINGS ON CONTEMPORARY AMERICAN GOVERNMENT, © 1997. Close Up Foundation, Alexandria, Virginia; **214,** From "Demographics Drive the Latino Media Story" by Kim Campbell, staff writer for the Christian Science Monitor, Thursday, June 21, 2001; **246,** From "Message to America" GENERAL POWELL'S CORNER by General Colin Powell; **248,** From "Destination: The American Dream" Keynote Address, 89th Annual National Urban League, Houston, Texas, August 9, 1999; **328,** From "24 Years of House Work…and the Place Is Still a Mess" © 1998 by Pat Schroeder. Reprinted with permission of Andrews McMeel Publishing. All rights reserved; **364,** "Vice Presidency" from THE READER'S COMPANION TO AMERICAN HISTORY, edited by Eric Foner and John A Garraty. Copyright © 1991 by Houghton Mifflin Company. Reprinted by permission of Houghton Mifflin Company. All rights reserved; **516,** From "The Constitutional Litmus Test" Nadine Strossen, The American Prospect No. 14, Summer 1993; **545,** From "State of the First Amendment" from FREEDOM FORUM. Used by permission of the First Amendment Center; **584,** From GIDEON'S TRUMPET by Anthony Lewis. Copyright © 1954 & renewed 1992 by Anthony Lewis. Reprinted by permission from Random House, Inc.; **607,** "Perspectives on the Constitution" adapted, with permission from the publisher, from PERSPECTIVES: READINGS ON CONTEMPORARY AMERICAN GOVERNMENT, © 1989. Close Up Foundation, Alexandria, Virginia; **671,** Tony Blair's speech from the Labour Party Annual Conference 2000. Reprinted by permission of the Labour Party U.K.; **724,** Republished with permission of Congressional Quarterly Inc., from "Seeing the Regional Future" by William Fulton from GOVERNING, APRIL 1999; permission conveyed through Copyright Clearance Center, Inc.

**NOTE: Every effort has been made to locate the copyright owner of material reprinted in this book. Omissions brought to our attention will be corrected in subsequent editions.**

# Stop the Presses

*Bury me on my face; for in a little while everything will be turned upside down.*

—Diogenes

On this and the following page you will find a number of last-minute items which, for reasons of timing, could not be included in the main body of the text.

 See also the companion Web site for *Magruder's American Government* at www.phschool.com

## War on Terrorism

Clearly, the war on terrorism has affected the lives of everyone in this country in many different ways. And it will continue to do so for many years to come.

The compelling need to combat both the reality and the threat of bioterrorism, the disappearance of the federal budget surplus, and the hefty increases in military spending and the funding for other components of national security are fairly obvious illustrations of the ways in which this new and different kind of war has and will impact all of us. Tightened security at airports and in the skies and widespread job losses also make the point. So, too, do concerns about the mails, television and other segments of the nation's communications systems, about the health care system and our food supply, and about the nation's infrastructure—power plants, dams, water systems, railroads, pipelines, and so on.

Recall in Chapter 8 we made the point that historic events can have a major impact on public attitudes as, for example, did the Great Depression of the 1930s, World War II, the Civil Rights Movement of the 1960s, and the War in Vietnam. The terrorist attacks on September 11, 2001, and all that has occurred since then appear to have done just that.

In Chapter 8 we described that dramatic shift in the public's attitude toward government over the past 40 years. The American people emerged from World War II and the prosperous 1950s with a generally favorable view of government and the Federal Government in particular. All that changed in the 1960s and 1970s, however. For a generation now, the American people have been very often critical of their government and have mistrusted it.

The situation has changed remarkably. Consider the poll results below. They typify the relevant public opinion polls taken from the late 1950s to date.

Is this change in attitude toward government only a temporary phenomenon—or will it prove to be a long-lasting one? And if, in fact, there has been sustained shift here, what effect will that have on the political socialization of today's youth?

## Supreme Court Cases

Among the cases the Supreme Court will hear and likely decide in its current term, three stand out. Two involve freedom of religion, and the other, affirmative action.

—*Watchtower Bible and Tract Society* v. *Stratton, Ohio,* was brought by Jehovah's Witnesses—the sect whose victories in several cases in the 1930s and 1940s helped to define the present-day shape of the 1st Amendment. In this case, the sect challenged a door-to-door canvassing ordinance enacted by the village of Stratton, Ohio. That law says that any person or group that wants to go door-to-door for the "purposes of advocating, promoting, selling, and/or explaining any product, service, organization, or cause" must first obtain a permit from the mayor's

| Question: How much of the time do you think you can trust the government in Washington to do the right things? | | 1958 | 2000 | 2001 |
|---|---|---|---|---|
| | Just about always | 16% | 4% | 13% |
| | Most of the time | 57% | 38% | 51% |
| | Some of the time | 23% | 56% | 35% |
| | Never | 0% | 2% | 1% |

SOURCES: University of Michigan National Election Study, 1958 data; Gallup Poll, 2000 data; ABC News-*Washington Post* poll, September 25–27; *USA Today*, October 1, 2001

Stop the Presses

office. And, this is key to the case: The permit must identify the person or organization to whom it is issued.

The village and the sect have a history of strained relations. In its original form, later changed, the ordinance gave village residents an opportunity to indicate that they did not wish to be visited by Jehovah's Witnesses.

In their door-to-door ministry, the sect regularly distributes religious pamphlets, and tries to get people to discuss the Bible. But this case goes beyond religious speech. In *McIntyre* v. *Ohio*, 1995, the Court struck down an Ohio law that prohibited the distribution of any "political communication" that did not include the sponsor's name and address. The Witnesses argue that that ruling should be extended to include religious speech—and, in effect, *all* speech. To that end, they quoted this from the majority opinion by Justice John Paul Stevens in the earlier case: "Anonymity is a shield from the tyranny of the majority." See pages 542–544, 546, 555.

—*Zellman* v. *Simmon-Harris* is a "school-choice" case—and one of the most important church-state cases to reach the Court in years. It presents this question: Does the Constitution permit the use of taxpayer-financed vouchers (checks) that parents can use toward the payment of parochial school tuition?

The case was brought by the State of Ohio and supporters of a school-choice program in effect in Cleveland since 1996. Of the nearly 4,000 children enrolled in the Cleveland program, 96 percent attend parochial schools. The United States Court of Appeals for the 6th Circuit struck down the program in 2000; it found that the program had "the impermissible effect of promoting sectarian schools."

Lawmakers, educators, and several religious and civil rights groups have fought over voucher programs for a decade. Supporters say the programs are permissible because parents, not government, decide whether and how to spend the money. They also argue that school-choice gives students, mainly those from low-income families, an alternative to troubled public schools. Their opponents say that vouchers amount to an unconstitutional diversion of public money to religious institutions. They say that vouchers are simply a creative way to channel public funds to religious coffers. See pages 538–542.

—*Adarand Constructors* v. *Mineta* is the first significant affirmative action case to reach the Court in the past six years. It presents an opportunity for the nine justices to set out their views on this highly divisive, politically charged issue.

The case is, in fact, a continuation of the Court's last major affirmative action case, *Adarand Constructors* v. *Pena*, 1995 (see pages 611–612). There, the Court voided a Federal Highway Administration program that gave bonuses to contractors if 10 percent or more of their highway work was subcontracted to businesses owned by Hispanics, African Americans, or other minorities. That decision made it much more difficult for the Federal Government to use affirmative action programs—because the Court held that such programs can be put in place *only* when they are "narrowly tailored" to overcome specific, clearly provable instances of discrimination.

In the present case, Adarand Constructors is back before the Court to challenge a ruling by the Court of Appeals for the 10th Circuit. That court found that a watered-down affirmative action program for highway grants meets the strict standard set in the 1995 case and is therefore constitutional. See pages 609–612.

Among the other cases on the High Court's docket:
—*Atkins* v. *Virginia*. Does the execution of a mentally disabled man convicted of murder violate the constitutional prohibition of cruel and unusual punishment? See pages 587–588.

—*Ashcroft* v. *Free Speech Coalition*. Does that part of the Child Pornography Prevention Act of 1998 that makes it a federal crime to distribute, receive, or possess an image that appears to be of a minor engaged in "sexually explicit conduct" violate the 1st Amendment's Free Speech Clause? See pages 548–549.

—*Ashcroft* v. *American Civil Liberties Union*. Does that part of the Child Online Protection Act of 1998 that makes it a federal crime to transmit over the Internet, for commercial purposes, material that is "harmful to minors" violate the 1st Amendment's Free Speech Clause? See pages 548–549.

—*HUD* v. *Rucker*. Does a federal policy that provides for the eviction of an entire family from a public housing complex because of the drug activity of one family member violate the 5th Amendment's Due Process Clause? See pages 564–565.

—*Owasso Independent School District* v. *Falvo*. Does the federal law that requires the privacy of educational records prevent teachers from allowing students to grade each other's papers, and to call out the results? See pages 536, 567.

**Stop the Presses**